LIFESPAN DEVELOPMENT

FIFTH EDITION

LIFESPAN DEVELOPMENT

FIFTH EDITION

Jeffrey S. Turner   Donald B. Helms

MITCHELL COLLEGE

HARCOURT BRACE COLLEGE PUBLISHERS

Fort Worth   Philadelphia   San Diego   New York   Orlando   Austin   San Antonio
Toronto   Montreal   London   Sydney   Tokyo

Publisher • *Ted Buchholz*
Acquisitions Editor • *Tina Oldham*
Senior Developmental Editor • *Meera Dash*
Project Editor • *Angela Williams*
Production Manager • *Debra Jenkin*
Senior Art Director • *Diana Jean Parks*
Picture Editor • *Sandra Lord*
Literary Permissions Editor • *Julia Stewart*
Cover/Marginal Illustrations • *Ruby Aranguiz*

Requests for permission to make copies of any part of the work should be mailed to: Harcourt Brace & Company, Permissions Department, 6277 Sea Harbor Drive, Orlando, FL 32887-6777.

Address for Editorial Correspondence
Harcourt Brace College Publishers, 301 Commerce Street, Suite 3700, Fort Worth, TX 76102

Address for Orders
Harcourt Brace and Company, 6277 Sea Harbor Drive, Orlando, FL 32887
1-800-782-4479, or 1-800-433-0001 (in Florida)

Text and photo acknowledgments begin on page 435.

ISBN: 0-15-500996-6

Library of Congress Catalogue Number: 93-80877

Printed in the United States of America

4 5 6 7 8 9 0 1 2 3 048 9 8 7 6 5 4 3 2 1

Preface

The development of a human being over the course of the lifespan is a remarkable and dramatic saga. From before birth, through childhood, and as the individual matures into an adolescent and then an adult, development is characterized by ever-changing proportions, capacities, and circumstances. Over the course of seven or eight decades, a person acquires a vast array of skills and capacities, from learning how to walk and speaking a language, to developing a distinctive personality and understanding the culture into which one is born. As the lifespan unfolds, a person develops the capacity to think and learn in complex ways, relate to others in meaningful ways, and adjust to the challenges that characterize each life stage.

Investigating such milestones, including how growth and development are shaped and reshaped in one form or another every day, is the goal of this textbook. From the very beginnings of its own life to its eventual culmination, we designed this book to uncover the sequences and patterns of growth that influence the course of human development. We hope that our narrative of the life journey provides you not only with an understanding of human development but also with insights into your own lifespan. By studying how individuals develop and mature, it is likely that you'll be able to unravel the factors that contribute to similarities and differences among people of all ages.

Developmental psychology occupies a central place in psychology and represents an active field of study in the 1990s. Indeed, new and exciting research findings have emerged since the previous edition of this textbook. Developmental psychologists have added new dimensions to our understanding. On the part of the general public, fascination with the dynamics of human development continues to grow, and all indications are that such research activity and general interest will only increase in years to come.

FEATURES OF THE BOOK

The fifth edition of *Lifespan Development* reflects significant updating and rewriting. In making such changes, we wanted to build upon the success of earlier editions and develop a superior pedagogical tool. Ultimately, our goal was to provide readers with a comprehensive yet understandable view of contemporary lifespan development. Some of the overarching benefits of *Lifespan Development,* fifth edition, follow.

Themes of the Lifespan

Seven salient issues, or themes, focus on the nature and course of lifespan development and reappear throughout all stages of the life cycle. These key themes, of vital importance to a solid conceptual understanding of development, are the interrelatedness of aging processes, theoretical perspectives on lifespan development, the interaction of heredity and environment, epigenetics, continuity and discontinuity, active and reactive models of development, and gender issues. Chapter 1 introduces the themes. New to the fifth edition, questions in the margin highlight these compelling issues. It is our hope that students will discover the importance of these issues to the discipline of lifespan development, as well as their relevance and application to their own development.

Readability and Applicability

An easy-to-understand writing style remains one of the critically acclaimed features of the book. Rather than providing an encyclopedic account of developmental psychology, we try to convey the essence of this discipline in an interesting way. We have attempted to address the interests and needs of students and to offer practical applications of theoretical material. Many sections were rewritten to enhance readability. The result of these efforts is a succinct presentation of the discipline of lifespan development, one that does not overwhelm readers with detail.

Balanced Coverage of the Entire Life Cycle

Lifespan Development devotes full attention to all stages of human development, including the adult years. Chapters relating to adulthood are not simply added at the end of the book. Instead, they are an integral part of the main theme of this textbook—the total development of the person from conception to death. Such integrated treatment enables students to see the continuum of the life cycle and to understand how early growth stages influence later life.

Flexible Table of Contents

The convenient 12-chapter format makes *Lifespan Development* a highly teachable textbook. The structural framework allows readers to study human development in a chronological or a topical fashion. This feature provides instructors with course flexibility. The introductory chapters covering such topics as research methodology, theories, and genetics remain essential to both approaches. Should a chronological approach to the course be chosen, the instructor can then follow the sequential, chronological divisions, or "developmental" chapters: prenatal through neonatal development, infancy and toddlerhood, early childhood, middle childhood, adolescence, young adulthood, middle adulthood, late adulthood, and death and bereavement.

Should a topical approach be preferred, the instructor can make use of the fact that each of these chronological divisions is broken into relatively small, compact units. Because these units are used consistently, a topic such as "personality and social development" can be studied from a chronological, topical, or combined approach. Thus, "personality and social development" can be dealt with as a subject in itself (with appropriate readings from each developmental chapter) or within the chronological framework of each developmental chapter as the term progresses. To facilitate such planning, the book includes a topical table of contents, in addition to the brief and detailed tables of contents.

Up-to-Date Research

Throughout the fifth edition of *Lifespan Development,* new material has been added, and existing sections have been rewritten and expanded to give readers the most up-to-date information possible. As a result, the book is soundly based in research and offers the reader the most current information available. *The text now contains over 2,500 reference citations, and over 1,500 of these are new to this edition. Virtually all of the 1,500 new research citations are from the 1990s.* Of the text's total references, over 90% are after 1990. Of course, classic studies in the field have been retained and their relevancy explained.

Innovative Pedagogy

Lifespan Development features a variety of innovative pedagogical aids designed to promote the comprehension and retention of textual material. These aids encourage active involvement with the text, particularly the nurturance of critical thinking skills. The new, colorful design for this edition supports the pedagogy and includes a generous but selective use of figures, graphs, charts, and photos. Each chapter begins with an outline, which includes the major contents of the chapter. The book also contains a complete bibliography and page-referenced glossary. More specialized pedagogical aids include the following:

What Do You Think?

Each chapter begins with a section designed to stimulate thinking and arouse curiosity before the chapter is read. By the time each chapter is concluded, the issues raised will have been addressed.

Lifespan Development in Action Boxes

Special action boxes clearly identified throughout the book offer applications to the material in the chapter. They are designed to bridge the gap between theory and the daily experiences of students. The scope of such boxes cuts across the entire lifespan, from "Suggestions for a Healthy Pregnancy" and "How to Help Children Become Better Thinkers," to "Narrowing Down the Field of Career Possibilities" and "Easing the Burden of Caregiving."

Focus on Diversity Boxes (NEW!)

Boxes that highlight cultural diversity, also clearly identified throughout the book, explore important topics in the field of human development. One of the best ways to understand human development is with a knowledge of other cultural practices and behaviors. The fifth edition contains a number of new boxes emphasizing multicultural and ethnicity issues and topics, as well as an assortment of international and cross-cultural themes. A wide range of topics is featured, such as "Beyond Conservation: The Many Sides to Bilingualism," "The Family Life of Puerto Rican Children," "College-Bound Minority Adolescents," and "The Ties That Bind: Intergenerational Relations of African Americans."

Margin Thinking Questions (NEW!)

New to the fifth edition and found within the margins of the entire text are thinking questions. These questions prod students' thinking about the seven important life-span themes and enable readers to see the importance and relevance of these issues throughout the entire life cycle. Each question focuses on one of the seven themes, which are easily identified by the text design.

Unit Reviews

At the end of each unit of each developmental chapter is a brief summary. These summaries help students to crystallize the material being read, by identifying and integrating the major points.

Chapter Reviews

Each chapter concludes with a detailed summary, focusing on the major points covered. This pedagogical aid is designed to help students recall important concepts and to assist in overall rates of retention. In the developmental chapters, these summaries are divided into the appropriate units.

Terms You Should Know

Following each chapter review is a list of key terms. Definitions of the key terms can be found in the chapter or in the glossary near the end of the book. Key terms are printed in bold and defined throughout the text.

End of Chapter "Thinking in Action" Questions (NEW!)

Each chapter now has a set of conclusory questions requiring students to consider issues covered in the chapter and to apply their knowledge to real-life situations. Some of these questions suggest practical exercises for students alone or in groups.

Recommended Readings

We conclude each chapter with an annotated list of five readings. All of these recommended publications are new to the fifth edition. They represent some of the most recent and important contributions to the field of human development.

WHAT ELSE IS NEW TO THE FIFTH EDITION

In addition to the general revisions and new features, considerable updating and development of topics characterize the fifth edition. The following captures some of the more specific changes:

Chapter One: Introduction to Lifespan Development

- A reorganized section on what developmental psychology is, including new information on contextual influences, developmental dynamics, and critical periods.
- A new section on developmental issues and themes. This section introduces the seven life-span issues that are emphasized throughout the entire textbook.
- A new section on the importance of scientific methodology in developmental psychology, as well as revised and expanded discussions of research techniques.

Chapter Two: Theories of Lifespan Development

- Major reorganization and expansion of the chapter so that the student is introduced to *psychological, sociological,* and *biological* theories of lifespan development.
- New material related to psychological theories, including information-processing theory, neo-ethology and sensitive periods, and the theoretical viewpoints of Jane Loevinger, Carl Rogers, and Urie Bronfenbrenner.
- New coverage of sociological theories, including symbolic interactionism, social exchange, family development, and conflict theory.
- New coverage of biological theories, including the wear-and-tear, cellular, and immunity viewpoints.
- Revised and expanded critiques of each theory, which expose the student to the theory's strengths and weaknesses, and a concluding discussion designed to put all lifespan theories into perspective.

Chapter Three: Genetics, Heredity, and Environment

- Rewritten and expanded sections on fundamental genetic mechanisms and processes.
- New material on the detection and treatment of fetal problems and defects, including chorionic villus sampling and intrauterine fetal surgery.
- A new section on the future of genetic research.

Chapter Four: Prenatal Development, Birth, and Neonatal Adjustments

- New material on conception and implantation, prenatal sexual differentiation, fetal brain development, and the impact of drugs on prenatal development.
- New material on the human immunodeficiency virus (HIV) and the acquired immune deficiency syndrome (AIDS) among newborns.
- Revised and expanded coverage of labor and delivery, including new material on neonatal adjustments and adaptations.
- New section on infertility, including reproductive technologies such as in-vitro fertilization, artificial insemination, surrogate motherhood, and embryo transfer, as well as the controversial issues raised by such interventions.

Chapter Five: Infancy and Toddlerhood

- A new section on memory storage systems and the development of memory during childhood.
- A new section on gender-role development, including conceptualizations of sex and gender as well as theoretical perspectives.
- Updated coverage of mental and language development, attachment, and emotional development.

Chapter Six: Early Childhood

- New material on nutritional influences on child development, bilingualism, imagination, and play.
- A new section on child maltreatment, including physical abuse, incest, and child sexual abuse.
- Expanded and updated coverage of gender-role development, sibling relations, school influences, peer group interaction, and prosocial development.

Chapter Seven: Middle Childhood

- A new section on how children develop an understanding of death.
- A new section on learning disabilities.
- Updated research on concept development, problem-solving abilities, language development, emotional development, moral development, family and school influences, children's friendships, and the impact of play on growth and development.

Chapter Eight: Adolescence

- New material on adolescent cognitive development, including adolescent egocentrism and post-formal operations.
- A new section on gender differences in adolescent friendships.
- An updated and expanded section on adolescent sexual behavior, including implications of adolescent sexual activity, discussions of unsafe sex practices, and the impact of sexual values on adolescent sexual behavior.

Chapter Nine: Young Adulthood

- Updated and expanded information on exercise, nutrition, and physical well-being.
- New material on dating, love, and the impact of gender roles on dating behaviors.
- Revised and updated sections on fertility patterns, parenting adjustments and adaptations, and lifestyle choices and options.

Chapter Ten: Middle Adulthood

- An updated and expanded section on health disorders of middle age, gender differences in the midlife transition, post-parental adjustments, and careers at midlife.
- A new section on personality change and stability at midlife.
- A revised and updated section on caring for aging parents, including patterns of intergenerational care and assistance.

Chapter Eleven: Late Adulthood

- Updated and expanded sections on external and internal aging, physical well-being, personality continuity and discontinuity, and institutional care.
- New sections on the life review and reminiscence, psychological maladjustment, and adjusting to retirement.
- Important new research findings on Alzheimer's disease and other types of dementia.

Chapter Twelve: Death and Bereavement

- Revised and updated sections on hospices, definitions and components of death, and bereavement.
- New material on the right to die, including important Supreme Court rulings as well as the medical and moral issues raised by the euthanasia movement.
- An expanded section on grief, including patterns of functional coping and adjustment during widowhood.

COMPLETE TEACHING PACKAGE

The ancillary package for *Lifespan Development* was significantly revised and expanded for the fifth edition. The result is a strongly integrated multimedia package, which offers a variety of learning and teaching aids.

Study Guide

Prepared by Joyce Bishop of Golden West College, the study guide is completely rewritten and expanded with illustrations and presentation that emphasize accuracy and promote active learning. Each chapter has learning objectives, an outline that allows students to take notes in class and while reading the chapter, creative vocabulary exercises, an additional glossary for English as a second language, illustrations and activities, practice tests, and explanations of the correct answers to these tests.

Instructor's Resource Guide

Written by Ellen Pastorino of Gainesville College, the Instructor's Resource Guide is significantly expanded. It begins with a course planner, including general teaching suggestions, a sample syllabus, class projects that help students integrate the life stages, and ways to use the other items of the teaching package. Then, each chapter contains a chapter overview, chapter objectives, and an extensive lecture outline featuring activities, discussion ideas, Thinking in Action applications, written assignments, additional readings, suggested films and videos, and handouts that can be used in class or as assignments. The format of the outline allows instructors to easily locate films, readings, and activities for a specific topic. The middle section includes an extensive video and laser disc guide. The end of the manual consists of transparency masters designed to reinforce material from the text.

Test Bank

Prepared by Rickard Sebby of Southeast Missouri State University, the test bank now contains approximately 80 to 100 multiple-choice items per chapter. Several new items ask the student to apply material and are labelled accordingly. The test bank classifies each item as factual, applied, or conceptual cognitive type and indicates which items test understanding of material in the book's boxed features. The test bank is coordinated with the teaching objectives from the Instructor's Resource Guide and is available in printed as well as computerized formats. New to this edition, the computerized software ExaMaster is available in IBM 3½ and 5¼ and Macintosh versions and is available with Gradebook Software.

Overhead Transparencies: Developmental Series

Instructors using *Lifespan Development,* fifth edition, have access to a set of 100 full-color overhead transparency acetates designed to facilitate understanding of key concepts. These transparencies are meant to supplement (not duplicate) coverage from the textbook.

Harcourt Brace Video Library

Harcourt Brace offers a large and varied choice of video programs, which complement one another in their various approaches to lifespan development. An instructor's manual is available for each of these programs. Use of the videos is based on the Harcourt Brace video policy.

"Seasons of Life" Video Programs

A study of lifespan psychology, "Seasons of Life" includes five one-hour programs—each covering a chronological phase of the lifespan—that examine the drama of human development. David Hartman is the host with John Kotre, professor of psychology at the University of Michigan–Dearborn.

"Childhood" Video Programs

In seven topical one-hour programs, "Childhood" presents an insightful and richly textured examination of the various influences that shape people as individuals and members of families and societies. It offers a strong cross-cultural perspective on child development. "Childhood" is a production of thirteen/WNET and the Childhood Project, Inc., part of the Ambrose Video Collection.

"Time to Grow" Video Programs

The "Time to Grow" series offers an introductory course in child development consisting of 26 half-hour television programs and coordinated print materials. The series follows a chronological approach, including the most recent theoretical and applied perspectives about effective ways of caring for and working with children.

"Discovering Psychology" Teaching Modules

The "Discovering Psychology" video series condenses the most salient information from the television course of the same name. Clips of experiments are interwoven with interviews of prominent researchers, featuring Jean Piaget, Renee Baillargeon, Judy DeLoache, Michael Meany, Eleanor Maccoby, Daniel Levinson, and others. Each module is divided into segments lasting less than five minutes. The two developmental modules, #10 on Physical and Cognitive Development, and #11 on Social and Personality Development, have been made available to users of this textbook.

Harcourt Brace Human Development Videodisk

A new human development videodisk will be available to instructors who use *Lifespan Development,* fifth edition. Quantity of videos and videodisks is based on the Harcourt Brace per-adoption policy.

These textbook features give both students and instructors a well-rounded and comprehensive learning and teaching package. Above all, we hope that you will find the fifth edition of *Lifespan Development* enlightening and enjoyable. We are eager to share with you the excitement of studying the development of the most complex of all life forms—human beings. Welcome to the field of lifespan development.

ACKNOWLEDGEMENTS

Although the authors bear the responsibility for the textbook's contents, many individuals contributed to its development, preparation, and ultimate publication. We extend our appreciation to those psychologists who played a role in the success of the first four editions, as well as the following individuals who reviewed the manuscript and contributed to the improvement of the fifth edition:

- Joyce Bishop, Golden West College
- Ronald C. Blue, Lehigh County Community College
- Carol Lynn Davis, University of Southern Maine
- Clifford A. Gray, Pueblo Community College
- Kevin Keating, Broward Community College, North Campus
- Ellen Pastorino, Gainesville College
- Dorothy L. Renn, St. Cloud State University
- Rickard A. Sebby, Southeast Missouri State University
- Vincent Sullivan, Pensacola Junior College
- Frank Vitro, Texas Women's University
- Dorothy K. Wood, Essex Community College
- Peggy Wroten, Northeast Mississippi Community College

We also wish to thank the people at Harcourt Brace who brought their expertise to this project.

We extend our appreciation to Tina Oldham, Acquisitions Editor, for seeing the ongoing importance of this project. Meera Dash, Senior Developmental Editor, brought enthusiasm and creativity to the fifth edition and improved the quality of the text in a myriad of ways. Thanks are also directed to Angela Williams, Project Editor; Diana Jean Parks, Senior Art Director; Debra Jenkin, Production Manager; Sandra Lord, Picture Editor; and Julia Stewart, Literary Permissions Editor.

A number of our teaching colleagues and professional associates have our gratitude for stimulating our thinking and offering useful suggestions: Thomas Blank, David Brailey, David Corsini, Velma Murry, James O'Neil, Karl Rexer, Ronald Sabatelli, Nancy Sheehan, and Catherine Wright. And, finally, to our wives and children go our heartfelt appreciation. Writing always requires its share of personal and family sacrifices, but the patient understanding of our loved ones enabled us to devote the long hours necessary to the completion of this successful project. Their empathy, support, and love were sources of continual inspiration from the beginning of our efforts to produce this book. Because of them, the fifth edition of *Lifespan Development* has become a reality.

Jeffrey S. Turner
Donald B. Helms

About the Authors

Jeffrey S. Turner is a professor of psychology at Mitchell College in New London, Connecticut. He has taught at the college level for over 20 years, and, with co-author Donald B. Helms, has written textbooks in the areas of developmental psychology, marriage and family development, and human sexuality. Among their titles are *Exploring Child Behavior,* Third Edition (Brooks/Cole, 1986), *Contemporary Adulthood,* Fifth Edition (Harcourt Brace, 1994), and *Marriage and Family: Traditions and Transitions* (Harcourt Brace, 1988). Turner holds a doctoral degree from the University of Connecticut, specializing in human development and family relationships. His current areas of interest include Piagetian reasoning processes, child and adolescent development, and sexuality education. He is married and has three children, including twin boys.

Donald B. Helms is also a professor of psychology at Mitchell College. His background includes training in counseling, psychometrics, and industrial and physiological psychology. For four years, he was stationed at the School of Aerospace Medicine in San Antonio, Texas, as a neurophysiological research psychologist with the Air Force. There he was a member of a research team that participated in basic and applied investigations for the Air Force's vestibular laboratory, often under contract to NASA, and was involved in the screening process for the astronaut program. Since that time, he has taught a wide variety of psychology courses at several colleges. His current areas of interest are moral and cognitive development, including abstract and creative thought processes. He is married and has three children.

Contents in Brief

Detailed Table of Contents

Topical Table of Contents

Introduction to Lifespan Development

What Do You Think?

INTRODUCTION

AN OVERVIEW OF DEVELOPMENTAL PSYCHOLOGY

DEVELOPMENTAL ISSUES AND THEMES

THE STUDY OF LIFESPAN DEVELOPMENT: RESEARCH METHODS

Chapter Review • Terms You Should Know • Thinking in Action • Recommended Readings

WHAT
DO
YOU
THINK?

• How long do you expect to live? If you haven't thought much about it, this chapter will provide you with some things to consider, including life expectancy. For example, whereas at the turn of the century, life expectancy at birth was about 47 years, today it hovers near 75 years. What factors account for this increase in life expectancy, and what have researchers learned about aging processes in general?

• "As the twig is bent, so grows the child." Undoubtedly you've heard that expression many times, but we'd like to give it a new twist in this chapter. As you launch into this material, consider the importance of the early years to the life cycle. Are later life developments connected to early developments by a thread of continuity or is change more evident? We would like you to consider other related issues as well. For example, some researchers feel that locked within an infant's mind and body are the genetic blueprints that will dictate the course of all future growth and development. Others maintain it is the environment that brings out a person's unique characteristics and qualities. Still others say it is a mixture of these two forces. What do you think? This chapter will help you in your search for answers to these and other important issues in lifespan development.

• Although developmental psychology is one of psychology's youngest subfields, our knowledge of the life cycle has grown rapidly. Today, developmental psychologists are able to explain many facets of aging processes, be it during the beginning or waning years of life. How do they set out to explore growth and development and design the research they undertake? What problems, if any, do they encounter in their quest for scientific explanations of lifespan development?

INTRODUCTION

Sandra M. enjoyed limited popularity and sustained a low B average through her public schooling. She dated and fell in love with her boyfriend Bill while in high school and, although tempted, they held back from having sexual intercourse. About a year after high school, Sandy and Bill were married, and in the next 7 years added two girls and a boy to their family. Sandy was a respected and able civic leader, but, although busy, she always refrained from taking on too many tasks so she could spend time with her family. All who knew them were aware of how happy Sandy and Bill were. A week after Sandy's 29th birthday, she left a note on the mantel telling Bill she had to "find herself" and would never again return to him or the kids.

George G. is a happy but often lonely octogenarian. The youngest of seven children, George helped around the house as a youngster and worked in a general store when he was 12. He held similar part-time jobs until he was 15 and announced to his family (all of whom were either living at home or had homes minutes away) that he was "off to see the world." He left home with a suitcase of clothes, about $9 in his pocket, and two letters of recommendation, one from his priest and the other from the owner of the store where he had worked. George had many adventures while he traveled and had the opportunity to learn a great deal about himself and others. By the age of 26, George had settled down, married, and started his own family. All of his children are now grown and have families of their own. Today, George still takes special delight in recalling his exciting adventures to the other residents of the Oakdale Home for the Aged.

As a child, Marsha J. was a classic underachiever. She possessed much potential but never took full advantage of it. Although she was promoted in the school system each year, teachers regularly commented on her lack of both motivation and academic desire. It was not until Marsha left high school and enrolled in a college business course that things began to change. For the first time in her life, she really enjoyed the course content, so much so that she enrolled in several other classes the following semester. The next year, she went to college full time and, after completing her degree work, graduated at the top of her class. Today, Marsha is in charge of an extremely successful accounting firm with office centers in 10 cities. Regarding her life accomplishments, she likes to call herself a late bloomer.

For years, David L. had been a dedicated company man. He worked hard at his job, seldom took time off, and often put in overtime. Moreover, he never complained about his work, which is why it came as a surprise one day when he announced he was tired of his job and its repetitious routines. He left the company a few weeks later, saying he had found a job in a totally different and more challenging line of work.

What causes people to behave the way they do? What might have influenced the behavior of Sandra M.? Why would she suddenly run away from a seemingly rewarding family life? Her friends (some of whom married right after high school and are still happily married) were unable to see any inner torment before she ran off. What motivated George G. to leave the "nest" and embark on his own to see the world? These are but some of the questions and problems that developmental psychologists seek to explore. Could any of these behaviors have been predicted? How do developmental psychologists go about studying people's behavior? What effects do childhood experiences have on adult behavior? Investigating such issues lies at the heart of this textbook.

AN OVERVIEW OF DEVELOPMENTAL PSYCHOLOGY

These introductory examples indicate that people do not remain constant—nor does their behavior. Throughout our lifespan, we change from year to year, month to month, and even day to day. To live is to change. **Developmental psychology,** which explores these lifelong changes, is one approach to the study of behavior. More specifically, developmental psychology is the scientific study of the growth, development, and behavioral changes of humans, from conception to death. Developmental psychology is also referred to as lifespan development or human development.

The comprehensive study of the life cycle has only recently emerged as a pursuit of scientific research, particularly in comparison to the investigation of childhood and adolescence, which has been the focus of most scientific literature. A number of reasons account for this lag: First, life expectancy was relatively short in the past, so the study of the all-too-brief adult years was, apparently, of little interest to researchers. Second, it was (and to some extent, still is) assumed that adults are best understood in terms of their childhood experiences; thus an adult was perceived as an end product rather than as a continuously developing person. Third, infancy, childhood, and adolescence

Human development researchers explore the entire life cycle, from the beginning of life to its eventual culmination. As shown in these photos, the same person at different stages of the life cycle captures the many facets of aging processes. This man grows from a toddler to an adult on these two pages.

present the researcher with obvious and observable changes—especially physical, mental, and personality differences—to study. Although such changes, in fact, occur throughout the life cycle, they are not as readily detectable later in life, with the possible exception of old age. Thus, in the past few decades, considerable time, money, and research have been directed toward the preadult stages of the life cycle. This is a paradox because many psychologists believe adulthood represents the longest and perhaps most significant stage of the life cycle.

The rapid increase of the adult population has stimulated research interest. A glance at demographics reveals there are more individuals in the life stage of adulthood than in any other stage. Approximately 61% of the population is between the ages of 18 and 64 and the median age is 30.6 years. Another 11.6% is 65 years and older. This latter group represents one of the fastest growing population segments in the country (U.S. Bureau of the Census, 1992). Figure 1-1 displays the aged population as a percentage of the total U.S. population.

Today, developmental psychologists recognize adulthood as a critical phase of the life cycle and view the later stages of life as important periods for studying a diversity of scientific issues. By studying the events of adulthood, such as occupational status, marriage, or parenthood, the life cycle is placed in a more balanced perspective. Coupled with the accumulated research on the years preceding adulthood, aging processes, consequently, may be viewed as lifelong processes.

What are the major factors that help transform a child into an adolescent and, later, into an adult? Is an adult solely the sum of past experiences, or does an adult outgrow childhood experiences and start behaving according to social factors and stimuli from adult society? These types of questions are difficult to answer, for uncovering the trends of lifespan development is not an easy task. Indeed, psychology might be called the obstinate science, for it is most difficult

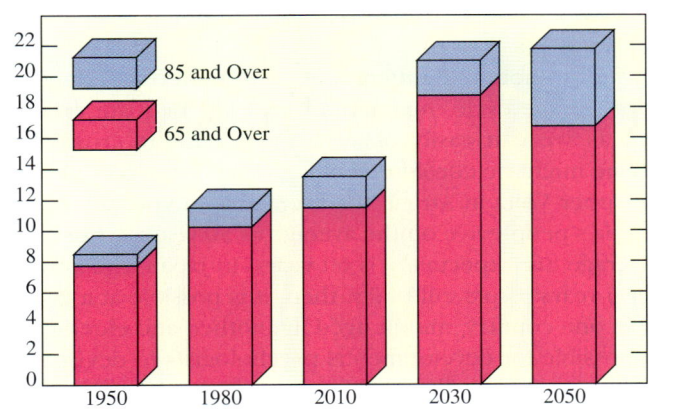

FIGURE 1-1

Percentage Distribution of U.S. Elderly Population, with Projections to 2050.

The elderly population is expected to continue to grow. The most rapid increase is anticipated between the years 2010 and 2030 when the baby boom generation reaches age 65. By the year 2010, persons aged 65 years and older are expected to represent about 13% of the population, and this percentage will likely climb to almost 22% by 2030.

SOURCE: U.S. Bureau of the Census, 1992.

to discover any *laws* of behavior. But we must begin somewhere. We must take that first step, open that first door, and peer down the corridor in the hope of finding the pathway that leads to knowledge of human behavior, for it is knowledge that allows us to reach our potentials and lead fuller, richer lives. When the study of psychology started, that door was opened, but it was dark on the other side; we did not understand behavior. But one candle was lit and then another. Maybe we have reached only the anteroom, but we have even more candles, and their brilliance illuminates further recesses—more paths for us to pursue. Today, we are still following those paths in the hope of discovering more principles of behavior so we can learn how and why people develop and behave as they do.

To answer the questions regarding lifespan development, we must examine and investigate seemingly diverse areas: physiology, education, religion, family, home, community, culture, socioeconomic status, genetic inheritance, psychosocial history, and countless other areas. To evaluate all these variables is a massive undertaking, but also a tremendously exciting task, particularly because the discipline of developmental psychology itself is in a state of infancy: As one of psychology's newest subfields, its scientific lifespan lies ahead. Welcome to developmental psychology.

Conceptualizations of the Life Cycle

When does life begin? Does adolescence begin at age 13 or at puberty? When does young adulthood end and middle adulthood begin? When does one reach late adulthood? To investigate lifespan development, it is helpful to have systems of age classification (see Figure 1-2). These systems, which lifespan development researchers have arranged and rearranged, are constructed primarily to help clarify and organize data. Some researchers propose the stages of the human life cycle may be interpreted in various ways. For instance, the same person might be classified as mature, old, or developing, depending on whether physiological, social, psychological, or anatomical criteria are being used. It should be recognized, however, that there is continuity in the life cycle of the human being. Only for scientific convenience do we identify stages of development. Life does not start or stop at the beginning or end of stages or age classification systems.

It is important to note that differences of opinion exist concerning conceptualizations of the life cycle. Age alone is not an adequate criterion for stage classification, as we can easily observe by examining cross-cultural life expectancies: One might be considered old in one culture but not in another. For example, in Upper Volta in Africa, the average life expectancy hovers near 40 years. Indonesia's people live on the average of 50 years, whereas in the Philippines, the average life expectancy is 60 years. In Japan, the average individual lives almost 80 years. Cross culturally, then, it is possible at a given age to be a young adult in one country, middle-aged in another, and elderly in yet another. Thus it is impossible for developmental psychologists to devise a universal age classification system.

In past historical eras, children were often viewed as miniature adults. Certain aspects of this perception still hold true today, particularly the emulation of adult attire and fashions.

The reasons for such differences in cross-cultural life expectancy are difficult to pinpoint. The greater life expectancy in developed nations, compared to underdeveloped countries, has been attributed to such factors as improved medical care, control of infectious diseases, technological advances, better working conditions, and nutritious diets. Such illustrations of the nature of aging processes underscore the need to carefully examine both the individual and the generalizations made in age classification systems.

This discussion also implies that life expectancy at various historical periods must be taken into consideration. More specifically, we would have difficulty in attempting to adapt present-day life expectancies to those of past eras. For example, at the turn of the century in the United States the life expectancy was 47.3 years. Today this figure has risen to about 75.2 years, an increase of almost 28 years. Furthermore, the chance of surviving to older ages has also increased in our society. U.S. citizens who reach their 65th birthday today can expect to

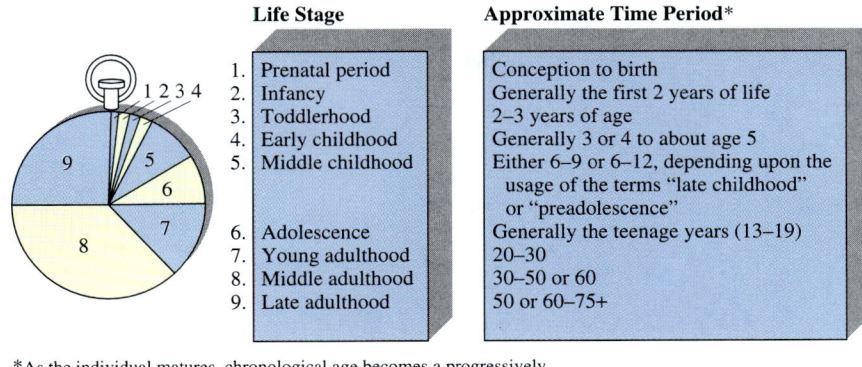

	Life Stage	Approximate Time Period*
1.	Prenatal period	Conception to birth
2.	Infancy	Generally the first 2 years of life
3.	Toddlerhood	2–3 years of age
4.	Early childhood	Generally 3 or 4 to about age 5
5.	Middle childhood	Either 6–9 or 6–12, depending upon the usage of the terms "late childhood" or "preadolescence"
6.	Adolescence	Generally the teenage years (13–19)
7.	Young adulthood	20–30
8.	Middle adulthood	30–50 or 60
9.	Late adulthood	50 or 60–75+

*As the individual matures, chronological age becomes a progressively poorer criterion to use.

FIGURE 1-2

A Timetable of Life-span Development.

The identification of stages in the lifespan helps researchers organize data. Such conceptualizations of the lifespan are sequential and directly related to ages. However, it must be recognized that aging processes are life-long and do not start or stop at the beginning or end of stages.

live another 16.8 years, compared to 12 years at the turn of the century (National Center for Health Statistics, 1992b; U.S. Bureau of the Census, 1992).

Compare today's figures in the United States to a life expectancy of about 25 years in Rome at A.D. 100 or 35 years in England during the 1200s! Moreover, consider the problems we face when attempting to understand the developmental period known as *childhood* as it existed in past centuries. In many cultures, right up through the medieval period, there was not one word to capture this critical developmental stage, largely because childhood, as we know it today, simply did not exist. In most cases, *infancy* was the term applied to the first 6 years of life. During this period, children were kept at home and attended to by their mothers to learn the folkways and mores of their culture.

Between the ages of 6 and 9, children, for all intents and purposes, entered *adulthood*. They either were sent directly into the workaday world or were given an apprenticeship to train for a particular vocation. Remarkably, the developmental period classified today as middle childhood was nonexistent, and most, if not all, of adolescence was omitted because the child began assuming adult responsibilities early in life.

Furthermore, the term *youth* generally signified *the prime of one's life.* Youth, during the Middle Ages, was followed immediately by the stage referred to as *old age!* Moreover, at 20, an age when most young adults in modern society are still preparing for a career, William the Conqueror had already been victorious in the struggle for control of Normandy. Charlemagne had recorded numerous victories in battle before he was crowned king of the Franks at age 26. There are young adults today who make significant and sometimes truly great contributions to society, but few, if any, are capable of shaping history as these individuals did. In contemporary Western societies, it is far more likely that such feats are accomplished by "older" adults.

As civilizations changed and technology progressed, the lives of humans changed also. With the advent of more complex divisions of labor, additional training and education were needed for job preparation, a factor that extended the developmental periods. As the lifespan lengthened, the periods of early, middle, and late adulthood emerged, lengthened in time, and began to assume

Aging experiences, while universal, reflect unique cultural, ethnic, and class differences.

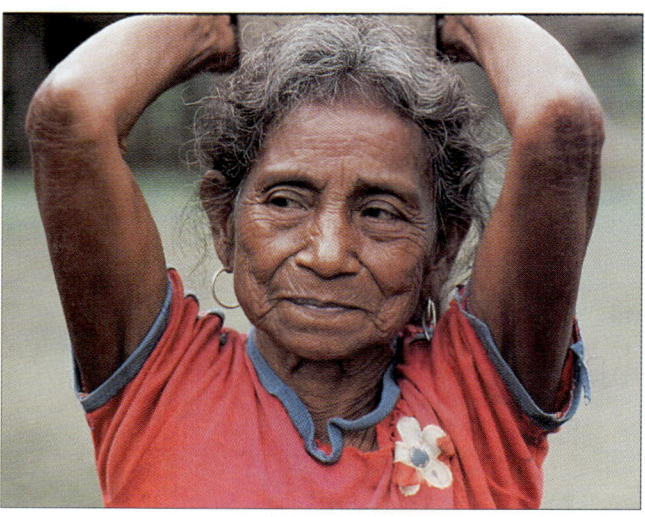

their own unique identities within the life cycle. Compared with past centuries, our view of various life stages has changed considerably. Furthermore, it is expected that age classification systems will continue to change in years to come.

Contextual Influences on Lifespan Development

The foregoing discussion suggests that any effort to explore developmental issues must take into account contextual influences. **Contextual influences** are those arising from the interrelationship between the changing person and the changing world. As such, contextual influences embrace such factors as culture, history, and life events. Paul Baltes (1979, 1987) writes that a wide array of contextual influences interact in complex ways, in the process affecting the life pattern of the individual. Baltes and colleagues (Baltes, Cornelius, & Nesselroade, 1979) believe there are three major sets of factors that influence individual development: normative age-graded, normative history-graded, and nonnormative life events.

Normative age-graded influences are those normal or typical determinants that are closely related to one's age and therefore rather predictable because they are similar for most of us. Some of these are biological, such as the onset of menarche and menopause. Other normative age-graded influences involve socialization and cultural customs, such as marriage or retirement. These are sometimes referred to as developmental influences because their occurrence correlates highly with chronological age.

Normative history-graded influences are events that are widely experienced in a culture at a particular time. Such events can be biological (e.g., epidemics, malnutrition) or environmental (e.g., economic depression, war). However, biological and environmental events are often mutually influential. Normative history-graded influences often give a particular generation its unique identity, such as the Vietnam War or Great Depression generations.

As an illustration of normative history-graded influences, consider the longitudinal research of Glen Elder (1991). He studied women who grew up in the

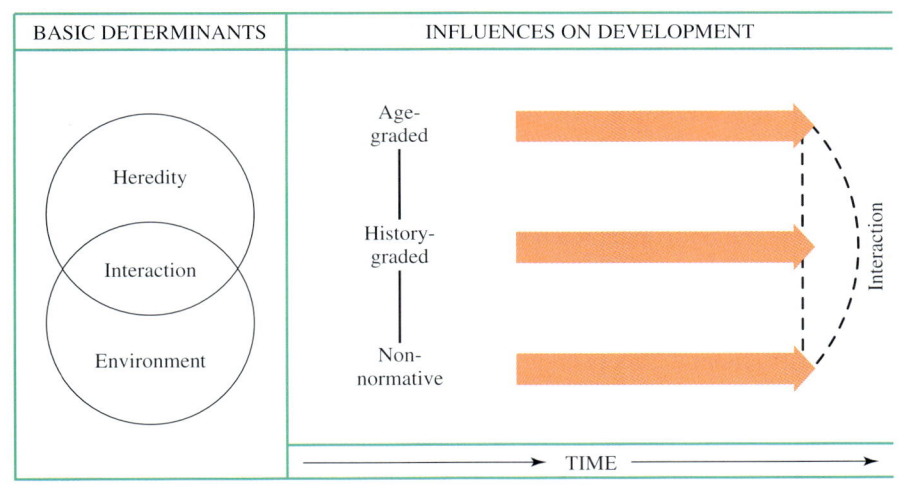

BASIC DETERMINANTS	INFLUENCES ON DEVELOPMENT

FIGURE 1-3

Three Systems of Influence over Lifespan Development.

The interaction of three systems of influences regulates the nature of life-span development: onto-genetic (age-graded), evolutionary (history-graded), and nonnorma-tive. Further explanation of the figure is contained in Baltes, Cornelius, and Nesselroade (1979) and Baltes and Willis (1978).

SOURCE: Adapted from Baltes, P. B., Cornelius, S. W., & Nessel-roade, J. R. (1979). Cohort effects in developmental psychology. In J. R. Nesselroade & P .B. Baltes (Eds.), *Longitudinal research in the behavioral sciences: Design and analysis.* New York: Academic Press.

Depression, experienced the mobilization of World War II, and matured in the period of affluence following the war. Many of the subjects succeeded in rising above their childhood disadvantage and achieving fulfilling lives into late adulthood. Indeed, it was discovered that economic hardship of earlier times enhanced the emotional resilience and health among elderly women from the middle socioeconomic classes. However, such experiences created negative health outcomes among women from the working classes.

Nonnormative influences refer to environmental and biological determinants that, although significant, do not occur in everyone; nor, when they do occur, do they happen at a particular age. Thus nonnormative influences are unpredictable. Examples would include unemployment, winning a lottery, a birth defect, the onset of disease, or the unexpected death of a loved one.

These three sets of contextual influences interact with each other and appear to wax and wane at different times in an individual's life (Baltes & Reese, 1984). Age-graded influences appear to dominate development from conception through childhood and puberty but then are on the wane until they reemerge in late adulthood. History-graded and nonnormative influences become more common and powerful determinants during early and middle adulthood. For lifespan development researchers, particularly those exploring adult life, history-graded and nonnormative influences are especially important forces to examine. Figure 1–3 depicts the three systems of contextual influence.

Developmental Dynamics: Growth, Maturation, and Learning

Thus far, we have looked at ways researchers have sought to conceptualize the life cycle as well as the forces that shape individual variations in aging. Researchers have also devised ways to categorize the manner in which the organism exhibits developmental change throughout life. To fully understand conceptualizations of the life cycle, as well as the ongoing nature of development within age classification systems, you must learn to differentiate between growth, maturation, and learning.

Growth refers to an actual biological or quantitative increase in size, such as the enlargement of the body or any of its component parts by an increase in the number of cells. An infant who is 20 inches long at birth and later measures 30 inches has *grown* 10 inches. Increases in head size, heart size, arm and leg length, weight, and so on, are generally referred to as results of the growth process (as distinguished from maturation or learning). In some instances, certain parts of the body exhibit a reduction in growth due to aging processes. For instance, a shrinkage of disks in the spinal column during late adulthood contributes to a slight loss of physical stature (see Chapter 11).

One major difference between growth and maturation is the greater possibility of environmental effects on growth; for example, if you eat more, you may gain more weight. Maturation, like growth, is also most easily understood as a biological change. But, whereas growth refers to an increase in the number of cells, **maturation** refers to the development of the cells to the point that they can be fully utilized by the organism. Maturation involves genetically controlled alterations that bring the cell to a point of ripeness, or *readiness*. In later chapters we explore the concept of readiness as it relates to such important developmental areas as locomotion (walking) and language acquisition.

To demonstrate the relationship between maturation and learning, a definition of learning is needed. **Learning** is generally defined as a relatively permanent change in behavior as the result of experience (learning does not include behavioral changes from injury, drugs, fatigue, or maturation). Learning is dependent on maturation, for learning cannot take place until appropriate maturation has occurred. For example, the ability to learn abstract concepts cannot occur until both the growth and maturation of the cortical cells in the brain that are used for abstract thinking have reached a state of readiness; until that happens, we cannot learn certain concepts of mathematics, operate at higher levels of morality, or understand metaphors.

Development and Critical Periods

Finally, researchers acknowledge the influence of critical periods on developmental dynamics. A **critical period** is a specific period of time when an environmental event exerts its greatest impact on the developing organism. *Ethologists,* researchers who explore human and animal behavior in natural settings (see Chapter 2), are particularly interested in exploring the dynamics of critical periods. They not only feel organisms are especially sensitive to certain external stimuli, but also maintain that some minimal sensory stimulation is needed during a specific time period if the organism is to develop normally.

As we discover in the next chapter, some researchers maintain a *sensitive period* exists in humans, a highly significant time frame early in life that affects the course of certain developmental dynamics. To illustrate, in humans there seems to be a sensitive period between 6 and 16 months, when the infant will usually attach itself to the primary caretaker. Prior to 6 months, babies may be handled by one and all, but it is during the critical period that attachment appears to develop. Those infants who, for one reason or another, are not left long in the care of one person may have difficulties in experiencing and expressing warm human relations. And research shows that institutionalized children deprived of stimulation tend to show maladaptive emotional and social behavior later in life (Rutter, 1990). In later chapters, we investigate whether or not sensitive periods exist in other developmental arenas, such as language acquisition, cognitive development, and gender-role development.

At this juncture, let's summarize the key points of this discussion. Developmental psychology is a relatively recent subfield of psychology that explores human development from its very beginnings to its eventual culmination. Numerous conceptualizations of the life cycle have emerged over the years, and such classifications are useful in organizing data. However, it is recognized that continuity characterizes the life cycle, and that life does not start or stop at the beginning or end of stages. Moreover, contextual forces such as culture, history, and life events are influential in shaping whatever conceptualizations of the life cycle are used. Finally, the dynamics of development within specific stages or against the broader backdrop of lifespan conceptualizations must take into account growth, maturation, learning, and critical periods.

DEVELOPMENTAL ISSUES AND THEMES

It is important to recognize that a number of important issues and themes exist regarding the nature and course of lifespan development. As you will discover, these issues and themes are multifaceted and weave themselves throughout all stages of the life cycle. As shown in Figure 1-4 (see p. 12), these key issues and themes are the interrelatedness of aging processes, theoretical perspectives on lifespan development, the interaction of heredity and environment, epigenetics, continuity and discontinuity, active and reactive models of development, and gender issues.

These issues and themes have served to spark considerable intellectual curiosity. Moreover, they have helped lifespan development researchers to categorize an ever-increasing amount of knowledge, in the process illustrating how concepts compare and contrast with one another. We find these issues and themes so compelling that a series of margin questions has been designed to highlight them as they appear throughout the text. (See the corresponding icons, as introduced on the following pages.) In so doing, it is our hope you will discover the importance of these issues and themes to the discipline of lifespan development, as well as their relevance and application to your own development.

The Interrelatedness of Aging Processes

Aging consists of lifelong experiences. However, it must be clearly understood that aging represents an interaction of processes and does not exist as a singular event. In this regard, lifespan development researchers recognize the interrelatedness of three major aging processes: psychological, social, and biological.

Psychological aging is the individual's own perception of aging processes and consists of such elements as cognition, self-esteem, motivation, and feelings. In this regard psychological aging can be defined as behavioral reactions that accompany the experience of growing old. A comment such as "I feel as old as the hills today" may serve as an example of a psychological reaction to a bodily state or change. Interestingly a biologically young person may feel psychologically old and the reverse is also true.

INTERRELATEDNESS OF AGING PROCESSES

EPIGENETICS

GENDER
ISSUES

ACTIVE AND
REACTIVE MODELS
OF DEVELOPMENT

INTERRELATEDNESS
OF AGING
PROCESSES

CONTINUITY
AND DISCONTINUITY

INTERACTION
OF HEREDITY
AND
ENVIRONMENT

THEORETICAL
PERSPECTIVES
ON LIFESPAN
DEVELOPMENT

FIGURE 1-4

Major Themes and Issues in Lifespan Development.

These issues and themes are multifaceted and recurrent, regardless of the developmental process or life stage being studied.

Social aging refers to the manner in which one's society intertwines with aging experiences. Age-graded expectations are important to consider when examining social aging, including those attached to roles, status, styles of dress, and verbal and nonverbal language. Some societies, for example, encourage youthful behavior and downplay the role of the elderly, whereas others regard maturity as a virtue. To go one step further, we generally expect an older couple at a rock music concert to react differently from adolescents attending the same event. Some of us frown on older adults when they wear clothing characteristic of their younger counterparts (and vice versa). And many expect such events as marriage and child rearing to take place at certain ages.

Biological aging refers to the manner in which the body functions over time. As we grow older, the body experiences changes in skeletal composition, sensory capacities, heart rate, and tissue structure, to name but a few areas. In general, the aging process in a biological sense causes the body to slowly degenerate and deteriorate.

It is important to stress that no one process of aging exists alone. Thus a 14-year-old adolescent female in the throes of puberty (biological aging) may believe that mentally she is a mature woman in the full sense of the word (psychological aging), but her parents may believe she is too young to begin dating

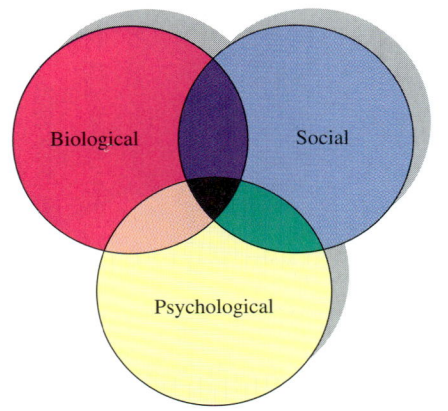

FIGURE 1-5
Three Processes of Aging.

Aging is a multifaceted experience. Developmental psychologists maintain that the three main processes of aging are biological, social, and psychological.

and thus place restrictions on her social life (social aging). As another illustration a 75-year-old man (biological aging) may be very pleased with his past life experiences and not regard advancing age as an obstacle to future success (psychological aging). He totally enjoys the retirement community in which he resides because it encourages an active lifestyle and places no age restrictions on activities or entertainment (social aging). These two examples illustrate the manner in which aging exists as a multifaceted experience (see Figure 1-5). As you read on, you'll discover how theoretical perspectives of lifespan development can be conceptualized according to psychological, social, and biological frameworks.

Theoretical Perspectives of Lifespan Development

How do we best view the dynamics of lifespan development? How should the existing literature be interpreted? What types of theories can be used as a framework for lifespan development research? As you'll discover in the next chapter, it is important for lifespan development researchers to develop some type of theoretical base, a conceptual framework that provides a foundation as well as a guide for the particular topic being investigated. A theory organizes and gives meanings to facts, and it serves as a springboard for further research. A theoretical framework also helps guide researchers with questions related to research settings and designs. As we noted, lifespan development theories can be grouped on the basis of psychological, social, and aging parameters. In the specially designed margin questions that appear throughout the text, we will prod your thinking about the various theoretical frameworks that exist in lifespan development and how they can be applied to the topic at hand.

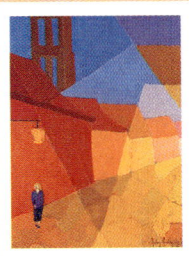

THEORETICAL ISSUES

The Interaction of Heredity and Environment

Fundamental to most topics in the field of lifespan development is the nature-nurture issue. From a definitive point of view, the **nature-nurture issue** is the relative role of one's genetic or inherited endowment in respect to the relative importance of the nurturing environment (Bouchard, 1984; Plomin, 1988, 1989). Related to the study of lifespan development, the nature-nurture issue

INTERACTION OF HEREDITY AND ENVIRONMENT

The manner in which heredity and environment converge to shape the course of human development has sparked considerable debate.

poses a number of thought-provoking questions: What impact does heredity or environment have on growth and development? Is heredity responsible for the developmental changes we see throughout life, or are they more the product of one's environment? Or is there a middle ground on this issue, perhaps suggesting that development is the product of an involved interplay between biological and environmental forces? Questions such as these can be directed toward a number of behavioral phenomena that unfold across the lifespan, such as intelligence, alcoholism, or sexual orientation, to name but a few.

Positing questions such as these have plagued lifespan development researchers for years, with many disagreements developing in the process (Hay, 1985; Henderson, 1982; Loehlin, Willerman, & Horn, 1988; Plomin & Thompson, 1988). Currently, researchers who are **nativists** (or hereditarians) believe much behavior is dependent on genetic endowment. The opposite group, the **environmentalists,** asserts that environment is the major contributor to an individual's behavior. Because there are few definitive answers, the question of how much heredity and environment contribute to development is probably a futile one. To most, the critical issue is how these two forces *interact* with one another to affect development; those adopting this stance are sometimes referred to as **interactionists** (Fox, 1984; Plomin, 1986, 1988; Plomin, DeFries, & McClearn, 1989; Scarr & Kidd, 1983).

■ Epigenetics

EPIGENETIC PRINCIPLE

Hereditarians also recognize what is referred to as the **epigenetic principle;** epigenesis is a theory that states everything develops because of genetic programming. Thus they believe a significant amount of human development is controlled by our inherited genetic structure, a set of blueprints or directions

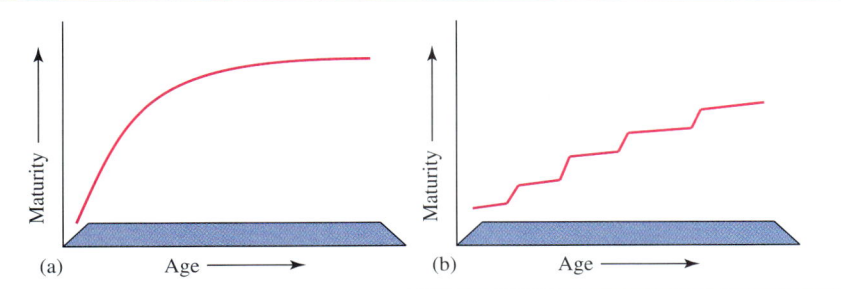

(a) Maturity / Age

(b) Maturity / Age

FIGURE 1-6
Models of Development.

Graph *a* illustrates the *continuous model of development.* Here we see a gradual increase in maturity during childhood and adolescence. Graph *b* represents the *discontinuous model of development* (such as proposed by Freud and Piaget). Here we can see how "stages" of maturation exist at certain age levels.

that all humans possess. However, we must not play down the role of experience, for epigenetics recognizes the constant interplay of genetic and environmental factors as contributors to development. As we point out next, epigenesis is closely related to discontinuity, which embodies the notion that as we reach higher levels of development, new characteristics emerge. Erik Erikson's formulation of personality development is a good example of a theory based on the epigenetic principle.

Continuity and Discontinuity

Another critical theme in lifespan development is the **continuity-discontinuity issue** (Bornstein & Krasnegor, 1989; Storandt & VandenBos, 1989). Those emphasizing continuity see growth as being quantitatively acquired through interaction with the environment. The analogy of a seed being placed in the ground, sprouting, and gradually growing to maturity illustrates the concept of continuity. Similarly, those who see the life cycle marked more by stability than change see slow methodical change or gradation, with less relationship to the individual's age. A **continuous model of development,** then, emphasizes a subtle flow of maturation throughout the life cycle rather than distinct change. Within the field of lifespan development, this is referred to as a one-stage model of growth. A glance at the literature shows that many researchers in the field of lifespan development have supplied thoughts on the nature of continuity (Caspi, 1987; Caspi, Bem, & Elder, 1989; Conley, 1984, 1985a, 1985b; Costa & McCrae 1988, 1989; Finn, 1986; Haan, Millsap, & Hartka, 1986; Helson & Moane, 1987; Kogan, 1990; McCrae & Costa, 1987; Rodin, 1987; Stevens & Truss, 1985; Sugarman, 1986).

CONTINUOUS AND DISCONTINUOUS HUMAN DEVELOPMENT

Discontinuity is characterized by distinct spurts in growth and development (see Figure 1-6 for a depiction of both discontinuous and continuous models of development). Researchers emphasizing discontinuous development tend to stress the role of heredity (nature) and maturation in the growth sequence. The analogy of a frog's life beginning as an egg, hatching into a tadpole, and then experiencing distinct amphibious stages illustrates the concept of discontinuity. Thus a **discontinuous model of development** emphasizes qualitative changes that make individuals fundamentally different from what they were like before. For those perceiving the life cycle more as a time of constant change, significant and fundamental transformations would thus be stressed. Discontinuous development emphasizes stages of development, the assumption being that before one stage can occur, the person must have emerged from a previous stage. Stages of development are relatively sequential, with a definite order that allows no stage to be skipped, and are directly related to ages. Examples of discontinuous (or *age-stage*) theories emphasizing change during adulthood are those proposed by Erik Erikson (1950, 1958, 1959, 1963, 1968a, 1968b, 1969, 1978, 1982); Jane Loevinger (1966, 1976, 1979; Loevinger, Wessler, & Redmore, 1970a, 1970b; Loevinger et al., 1985); Daniel Levinson (1977, 1980, 1981, 1984, 1986, 1990, in press; Levinson & Gooden, 1985; Levinson et al., 1978); and Robert Peck (1968).

Related to the continuity-discontinuity issue is whether lifespan development reflects *stability* or *change.* The issue here is whether later developments in life are connected to earlier developments, or whether they represent distinct changes. As we'll discover, researchers in the field of lifespan development have long been drawn to why some people's behaviors remain consistent over time, why other people change, and why the behavior of still others reflects a mixture of both endurance and alteration. Many questions swirl around the issue of stability and change in lifespan development: If behavior does remain stable, does it reflect a long developmental plateau? Or, if change is apparent, is it the result of a series of abrupt age-related modifications? If both stability and change characterize the life cycle, is there an equal blending of the two forces? Do environmental forces or do processes occurring within the person determine stability and change? These are not easy questions to answer, and we will wrestle with them as they surface throughout the textbook.

Active and Reactive Models of Development

Theories of lifespan development often view people as either active or reactive in relationship to their environment. Environmentalists, for example, believe environmental forces shape human behavior much as the rocks, sand, water, wind, and waves shape a piece of driftwood. Driftwood exposed to a harsh and rugged environment has a splintered and jagged appearance; driftwood softly molded and shaped over time by sands and calm oceans has a much smoother surface. Like driftwood, humans are passive, but have the ability to react to environmental stimuli.

ACTIVE AND REACTIVE MODELS OF DEVELOPMENT

An **active model of development** suggests that individuals are not passive beings, but are capable of actively governing and regulating their own development. Certain behavioral programming through our genetic inheritance gives these theories a biological basis. Rather than picturing a piece of driftwood afloat, visualize the wood as having a sail or even a motor. Under these conditions, the organism can chart its own path in a self-directed way. The latter theory stresses our intellectual ability to seek from the environment what arouses our interest. We select the environments suitable to meet our rational needs. A good example of an active model of development is cognitive-developmental theory (see Chapter 2).

A **reactive model of development,** on the other hand, emphasizes the importance of the environment and considers our surroundings to be a critical determinant in the overall development of the individual. Theories such as behaviorism (see Chapter 2) maintain we are conditioned by forces (e.g., reinforcement) from the environment. The driftwood relentlessly subjected to the elements each day and its eventual appearance might be symbolic of this position.

Gender Issues

Lifespan development researchers expend considerable energy exploring gender issues, including such topics as the dynamics of gender-role development, and gender similarities and differences. Engaging you, the reader, to explore your attitudes, beliefs, and feelings about gender issues and helping you to see their impact over the course of the life cycle represents one of our primary writing ambitions.

Our concept of masculinity and femininity represents an important component of growth and development. Beginning early in the life cycle, various sources transmit attitudes and behaviors appropriate to our gender, and gradually "gender-appropriate" activities, preferences, and personality attributes emerge. As we see throughout this book, gender-role development has numerous implications for a diversity of lifespan topics, including peer interactions, school experiences, family life, dynamics within intimate relationships, occupational choices, and perceptions of aging processes, to name but a handful.

GENDER SIMILARITIES AND DIFFERENCES

Within the field of lifespan development, early studies on gender comparisons were scant, and most of the research was conducted by men. In the 1990s, however, we are starting to see more extensive investigations of gender issues, most notably women and aging (Harrison, 1991; O'Grady-LeShane, 1990; Rosenthal, 1990; Thane, 1992). There are many topics regarding gender issues that need to be explored, such as personality development, satisfaction over the life cycle, role adaptations, and achievement motivations. With more women in the labor force for longer periods of time, we are also in need of research examining how their career lives compare and contrast with those of men, including retirement experiences (Day, 1991; Dietz, 1991; Rayman & Allshouse, 1990; Wingrove & Slevin, 1991).

THE STUDY OF LIFESPAN DEVELOPMENT: RESEARCH METHODS

As we stated in the beginning of this chapter, developmental psychology is generally defined as the scientific study of the growth, development, and behavioral changes of humans from conception to death. Science has many definitions. It refers to the techniques and methods used in gathering facts or data and may also be used in reference to an organized and systematic body of knowledge. The field of developmental psychology qualifies on both counts. It is important to mention, too, that the research gathered by developmental psychologists reflects common scientific goals and principles (Miller, 1986). Paramount among these are the principles of description, explanation, prediction, and control.

- *Description.* Description, the most common denominator of science, is the systematic collection of available information about a phenomenon or event. Description is a largely empirical process that often relies on counting, frequencies, percentages, and descriptive statistics. Suppose we wanted to explore the topic of mate selection during young adulthood. Description might entail asking people to list all the factors that entered into their choice of a mate and then analyzing all the responses to see which factors appear to be most important, which least important, and so on.

- *Explanation.* An explanation attempts to provide reasons for why something happens or is the way it is. Lifespan development researchers seek to identify antecedents and consequences of the behaviors of interest. Explaining mate selection might involve forming hypotheses as to what underlies the factors found to be most significant. For example, we might need to look at such things as similarities in personal goals and in the ways people conceptualize male and female roles in our society.

- *Prediction.* A prediction tells in advance that something is going to occur. Prediction rests on the same empirical and theoretical underpinning as explanation. That is, the same ideas and relationships must be grasped in order to explain what has occurred and to predict what is likely to happen. We might want to test our ideas about mate selection in another study in order to discover if what we've hypothesized is valid.

- *Control.* When we understand a phenomenon and can explain and predict it, we may be able to control it. That is, we can try to promote it, if we judge it good, useful, and worthwhile. Or we may be able to prevent it or to intervene and change it if we judge it useless or harmful. For example, we might want to promote such useful activities as dating long enough to get to know a prospective partner well and meeting members of his or her family. We might also want to develop ways of intervening in troubled partnerships, or of helping people to resolve problems they didn't see or anticipate.

The Scientific Method

When developmental psychologists are curious about some phenomenon, they must begin their scientific investigation with a plan or structure. Broadly defined, the **scientific method** is an organized series of steps designed to promote maximum objectivity and consistency in gathering and interpreting observable evidence. It is the use of the scientific method and related activities that qualifies lifespan development as a science. The scientific method often begins and ends with researchable questions, because new hypotheses are often generated by a particular research study. Related to our earlier discussion, most of these steps come under the scientific principles of description and explanation. The degree to which each of the four scientific principles we've discussed is involved in the steps we describe next will vary according to the purpose of the study, its size, and whether the researcher is primarily interested in describing, explaining, predicting, or testing. Also, action taken in one stage has a direct influence on other stages, providing a special need for understanding the entire process. Let's look now at the stages in the research process:

- *Selection of the problem.* During this initial phase, the investigator decides on an area of interest. In selecting a problem, the researcher might draw on what has been learned from earlier studies or from literature read in connection with other studies. For example, a researcher might be interested in exploring what factors affect the decision to exercise during middle adulthood.

- *Formulating the hypothesis.* A tentative explanation that will predict the results of the study is developed. The hypothesis is tentative at this point because it may be revised (or even abandoned) after a formal review of the literature has been conducted. As an example, the researcher might hypothesize that more middle-aged men than women choose to exercise during later life.

- *Reviewing the literature.* Now the researcher reviews the relevant literature in order to define the problem more clearly and to state the appropriate hypotheses. It is important at this point to discover if the specific study in mind has been done and if so, what its parameters were. For example, was it definitive enough that it's not worth replicating at this point? Did it leave any unanswered questions? Were there specific research flaws that can be remedied?

- *Listing the measures.* The investigator now identifies all available measures to help gather the data. These might include questionnaires, observations, and case studies. The research instruments best suited for assessing patterns of exercise among middle-aged men and women must be studied.

- *Describing the subjects.* Now the researcher very carefully describes the subjects to be included in the study. An important goal of this step is to balance subjects so a representative sample of the population under investigation is obtained. For example, age, gender, and socioeconomic level are factors that can often influence research findings unless evenly distributed among subjects. In studying patterns of exercise among middle-aged men and women, then, we might want to equate subjects on the basis of socioeconomic class, something that might well influence their attitudes and behaviors with respect to exercising.

- *Constructing a research design and measurement devices.* At this step, the investigator completely explains the procedures for carrying out the study so the hypothesis can be tested. The variable being investigated will be measured by the appropriate research instruments. For example, a researcher might use an existing survey to discover patterns of exercise among middle-aged men and women, or a new measurement device might have to be constructed.

- *Analyzing the data.* When measurements have been completed, the researcher must analyze the collected data. For example, a researcher might compare two group scores on a questionnaire scale measuring rates of exercise.

- *Generating conclusions.* The researcher then has to carefully study the gathered data and his or her analyses, and relate the results to the original hypotheses. Sometimes the results will confirm the hypotheses and sometimes they will not. Results that refute a hypothesis may send us back to the beginning of the research process.

- *Writing the research report.* In this last step, a description of the entire study is written and disseminated to interested people. Successful research investigations often enable investigators to turn their attention to the issue of control. That is, when a phenomenon is understood and we can explain and predict it, we may be able to exert some control over it. If it was found, for example, that most middle-aged men and women do not exercise on a regular basis, we might try to devise an exercise intervention plan that would seek to enhance the physical well-being of this population segment. In this way, we would forge a link between data, theory, and the practical application of knowledge. (Rubinson & Neutens, 1987)

■■ Observation—The Key to Knowledge

The collection of data begins when some type of observation is made, whether by somewhat unsophisticated means (watching children at play) or by very technical processes (recording brain waves on an electroencephalograph). Regardless of the techniques employed to gather data, these methods fall under the general classification of *observation*. Theories or, possibly, laws may be formulated from observations, provided, of course, that the data are supportive.

In surveying past literature, we find that some ideas about adult behavior were developed without the support of empirical evidence. The difficulty with such theoretical preconceptions is the assumption that one's point of view is correct because it makes a sensible story. This is the primary problem of myth versus science. Even some highly developed theories of lifespan development require more data than what is provided. A theory may make a good narrative about how things evolved to where they are now, but if the theory contains little empirical evidence, it cannot offer a plausible basis for action.

Although it is true that ideas may emerge following the observation of a solitary incident, we must recognize the danger of generalizing from a limited number of situations. Consequently, while a study of one subject may be of assistance toward studying that individual, it does not necessarily mean other subjects will exhibit identical behavior or, if they do, that it will be for the same reasons.

Seeing the dangers in single-subject research methods (while still acknowledging their significant role in psychology), researchers have striven to test their suppositions on larger segments of the population. Many graduate schools, for example, now have working agreements with nearby hospitals that enable researchers to study newborns, with the parents' permission, within hours after birth. New techniques of study and evaluation, especially in such areas as electroencephalography (study of brain waves) and visual abilities (seeing objects, tracking moving objects, visual preferences, and so on), have been discovered and put to use.

Types of Observation   Several different types of observation are employed in lifespan development. **Naturalistic observation** is the examination of behavior under *unstructured* (natural) conditions. **Structured observation** represents a slight extension of naturalistic observation, enabling the researcher to administer simple tests. **Participant observation** involves the researcher as a participant in the interaction being studied. When this is done, the researcher's direct involvement with the subjects provides observational data. These forms of observation differ markedly from **controlled experiments,** which employ situations that require subjects to be placed in contrived and perhaps unnatural environments.

Sometimes, the results obtained from certain controlled experiments are of little value because they have a tendency to create unnatural behavior. However, it is felt by some researchers that the same could hold true for observational techniques in general. This is especially true when researchers impose themselves on others without invitation. The more obtrusive the observer, the greater the chance of subjects behaving in artificial or guarded ways.

The foregoing suggests that research designs must be carefully executed. Naturalistic and structured observations, as well as controlled experiments, can

Observation is an important research methodology for lifespan development researchers. Here, the observation of children is enhanced with the use of a one-way window, a pane of glass which allows viewing in one direction only.

be extremely valuable in gathering significant information. However, the fact remains that the naturalistic method, at least partially, reduces the individual's awareness of being observed.

Historical Antecedents of Human Observation: The Baby Biography

Historically, the earliest recorded forms of human observation were termed **baby biographies,** day-by-day accounts of the development of an infant or young child. One of the earliest baby biographers, Johann Pestalozzi (1740–1827), a leading educator of his day, recorded his son's activities (age 2½) for 3 weeks and later published the account. Included in his many observations were comments on the role of the mother, whom he believed to be the most important educator in the child's life. Pestalozzi stated that behavioral patterns are first learned through the child's *observation and imitation* of the mother's actions.

Wilhelm T. Preyer (1841–1897), a physiologist, was interested in overall mental development. This interest was manifested in an account (later published as three separate books) of his son's development during the first 4 years of life, a baby biography that many psychologists consider collectively a classic. Preyer, like Pestalozzi, observed several behavioral patterns, including socialization processes and the child's tendency to imitate others.

Charles Darwin (1809–1882) impressed many people with his interest in children, particularly in 1877 when he published a baby biography on the development of his firstborn son. The following quotation shows his observational skills:

> During the first seven days various reflex actions, namely sneezing, hiccuping, yawning, stretching, and of course sucking and screaming, were well performed by my infant. On the seventh day I touched the naked sole of his foot with a bit of paper, and he jerked it away, curling at the same time his toes, like a much older child when tickled. The perfection of these reflex movements shows that

Charles Darwin (1809–1882) was born in Shrewsbury, England, and became a pioneer in the development of the baby biography.

the extreme imperfection of the voluntary ones is not due to the state of the muscles or of the coordinating centres, but to that of the seat of the will. . . . With respect to vision—his eyes were fixed on a candle as early as the 9th day, and up to the 45th day nothing else seemed thus to fix them; but on the 49th day his attention was attracted by a bright-coloured tassel, as was shown by his eyes becoming fixed and the movements of his arms ceasing. It was surprising how slowly he acquired the power of following with his eyes an object if swinging at all rapidly; for he could not do this well when seven and a half months old. (Kessen, 1965, pp. 118-119)

Most baby biographies were a progressive step forward from the armchair philosophies and philosophical presuppositions that had dominated the past. The resulting interest in these accounts during the 18th and 19th centuries helped, in turn, to give impetus to all subfields of developmental psychology, not just to the study of the early years of life. One of the more notable baby biographies of the 1900s was undertaken by Jean Piaget (see Chapter 2), who observed and recorded the early cognitive development of his three children. As more and more observations were made, simple techniques and testing devices were initiated, giving rise to a number of highly sophisticated observation and measuring devices. Thus the myths and preconceptions that were present in earlier historical periods were replaced by more systematic and precise accounts of the nature of lifespan development.

Techniques of Naturalistic Observation   Frequently, developmental psychologists are required to observe human behavior, especially that of children, in a number of different situations, such as during school, at play, or even in a grocery or department store. Whether observers are stationed behind one-way windows or simply attempt to keep unobtrusively out of sight, certain points

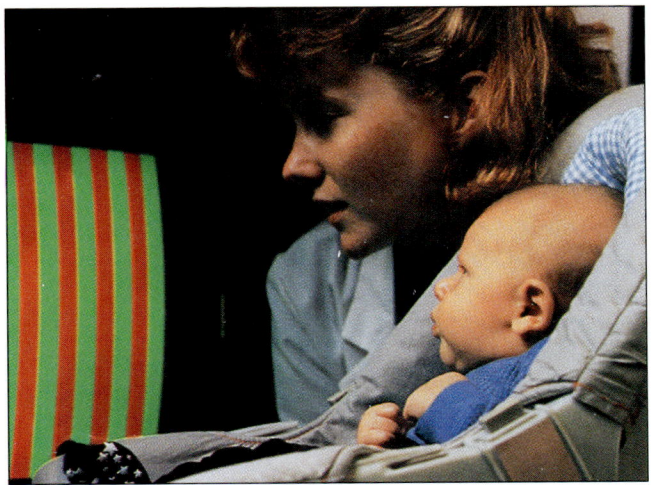

Compared with earlier methods of observation and assessment, the scientific apparatus of today's researchers is highly refined and sophisticated. This eight-week-old infant is being tested for color vision.

regarding effective observation skills should be kept in mind. The following may serve as general guidelines for observing people of all ages, although it must be noted that observation techniques are used on children more than adults.

1. Remain out of the way as much as possible. When individuals discover they are being observed, especially children, they sometimes change natural behavior or act in atypical ways.

2. With paper and pencil, tape recorder, or video camera, record such things as the physical setting and the activities the people are engaging in (e.g., eating a snack, reading, shopping, talking). You might also want to focus on the physical appearances of those being observed, or gestures and mannerisms.

3. Following your recording of the physical setting and activities, pay attention to the behavior of at least one person. Focus on such behaviors as group entry skills, prosocial behaviors, social withdrawal, and the like.

4. Make an effort to now reexamine the larger group. What kinds of interactions take place on a larger scale? For instance, if you are observing children's competitive sports, what kinds of coaching interactions or parenting behaviors occur? If you are observing adolescents in a social situation, what is unique about their modes of interaction?

5. Once you are done with your observations, write a report that objectively describes what you've seen and heard. This needs to be done immediately so you can accurately recall all observational details.

Whether subjected to simple or complex methods of observation, it is important people feel at ease so the observation or measurement will not affect their spontaneity and natural behavior. Thus, if testing is to be effective, it must take place in a friendly, nonthreatening atmosphere. If feasible, the researcher should spend several sessions with the subject(s) (beware of allowing positive or negative emotions to interfere with scoring—i.e., an extra point because the child is "cute" or the adult has a friendly smile) to avoid any unnecessary apprehensions or other behavior that might interfere with the situation.

Rapport is especially important if accurate responses are to be elicited. It would be unwise, for example, to tell people who fear failure that they will be tested to see how well they compare with associates. Failure of the test may occur not because of limited capabilities, but because the experimenter has raised their anxiety level to a point that interferes with an otherwise natural response. This may be avoided if rapport and understanding are established initially. For techniques on how to develop rapport, as well as other observational strategies, see Bentzen (1993) and Hessler (1992).

As noted earlier, ethologists study animal behavior in natural settings. As such, they represent another group of scientists using naturalistic observation. Some ethologists attempt to gain insights into human behavior by comparing animal behavior with human behavior. Konrad Lorenz and Niko Tinbergen, two Nobel Prize-winning ethologists, believed that humans, like many other animals, will band together to protect a territory—one of the primary reasons for human aggression.

Case Study

The **case study** focuses on a single person rather than a group of people. Its purpose is to accumulate developmental information. Studying a single subject over an extended time period yields a great deal of information on that one person. Usually, interviews are the primary source of data, and information is often gathered about significant life events, such as those pertaining to family, education, and vocation. Although this method is excellent in such areas as clinical treatment of maladjusted individuals, we can never be certain this knowledge will help us in understanding others. And because the case study typically involves a single researcher and only a few cases, its reliability must be supported by testing the hypotheses generated by means of more systematic research techniques, such as a survey or an experimental study.

Survey

A survey is valuable in lifespan development research endeavors. A **survey** is a technique for gathering information from people and usually takes the form of a questionnaire or an interview. A survey is directed toward a *sample,* a group of people representative of a larger population.

If taking a questionnaire, those within the sample mark their own answers. Background information is often gathered (e.g., age, education of the respondent), but respondents remain anonymous. The latter is particularly important because subjects often do not want to be identified with their answers on sensitive topics. Researchers are drawn to surveys because they are easy to administer and inexpensive. Results are immediately available and the procedure does not involve the training of interviewers.

However, researchers must take care in the wording of instructions as well as the actual items appearing on questionnaires. Wording must be concise so respondents do not get frustrated or confused. Frustrated or confused respondents often give inaccurate information or, in some instances, give up completely. Surveys can supply researchers with valuable data on how people think and act, but only if this assessment device is properly designed and worded.

Interviews, on the other hand, require a face-to-face encounter. In the standard procedure, a trained interviewer asks questions and then records the responses. Although the interview technique is more expensive than questionnaires, it is generally more flexible and yields more accurate data. When used properly, the interview has the following advantages over the questionnaire:

- Interviewers can explain the purpose of the investigation, establish rapport, discuss the interview, and respond to questions at any time. Such factors tend to enhance the cooperation rate.

- A primary strength of the interview is its participation rate. Conversely, a limitation of the mailed questionnaire is its low return rate.

- Interviewers can listen to the responses as well as observe the respondent. Facial expressions, mood, and body language are often valuable in fathoming the totality of information provided by the interview.

- Related to the previous point, skilled interviewers can "read" respondents. That is, a respondent's moods can be assessed and information can be sought accordingly. It is likely the same data can be gathered in a different way at a later time in the same interview, thus enabling the interviewer to determine the truthfulness of the gathered responses and look for developmental trends.

- Face-to-face interaction can be important in building needed rapport, which, in turn, often leads to a higher level of respondent motivation. When this happens, the quality of data is likely to be superior to that gathered when respondents are participating out of pressure or obligation.

- The interview is especially valuable for collecting data that is sensitive or personal. Once trust has been established by skilled researchers, respondents tend to disclose such information.

- It is generally recognized that people enjoy talking. Employing the proper skills, interviewers can channel conversation so that a more thorough understanding of the topic can result. (Adams & Schvaneveldt, 1985)

It is important to recognize, though, that interviews have their drawbacks. For example, although items on questionnaires are uniform and consistent, a staff of interviewers can ask the same question in different ways. Such a mixture of interviewing styles can contaminate a research design. Additionally, interviewers may not record clear and concise responses. For that matter, some interviewers may be uncertain about which responses to record, and as we pointed out earlier, the interview technique is more expensive to operate than the questionnaire format. Finally, a drawback for both surveys and interviews is the "words versus deeds" issue. By this, a gap might exist between what respondents *say* and what they in fact *do*. Thus respondents might give answers they think are compatible with the expectations of the researcher or consistent with peer standards.

The Correlational Method

Sometimes lifespan development researchers want to see if a relationship exists between variables. As examples, we might want to discover if there is a relationship between alcohol consumption during a woman's pregnancy and a newborn's intelligence, or if sexuality education programming promotes greater contraceptive use among adolescents. To explore the relationship between variables such as these, a technique called the **correlational method**

Establishing rapport with subjects and creating a nonthreatening atmosphere are important research considerations.

might be employed. Although the statistics involved can sometimes get complicated, the idea behind the correlational method is simple: Two variables are correlated when changes in one variable are associated with changes in the other variable. A *positive* or *direct* correlation exists when one variable tends to increase as the other increases. If one variable tends to decrease while the other increases, a *negative* or *inverse* correlation is said to exist. If there is no relationship between the variables, we say they are *uncorrelated.* The correlational method can be used to assess data obtained from many different types of research techniques, including questionnaires, surveys, and experiments.

It is important to understand that correlational data do not establish cause-and-effect relationships. When interpreting correlations in lifespan development or any other discipline, remember that a high correlation does not necessarily indicate a causal relationship exists between two variables. For example, a high positive correlation between attendance in sexuality education programs and contraceptive usage among adolescents does not prove sexuality education classes will cause better use of contraceptives. The correlation might be due to other factors—perhaps intelligence, motivation, or a person's ability to see another's point of view. Even when correlations are very strong, they do not provide sufficient information to infer causality.

The Experimental Method

The **experimental method** in psychology is a series of steps by which the researcher tries to determine relationships between differing phenomena, either to discover principles underlying behavior or to find cause-and-effect relationships. The experimental method is employed in lifespan development just as it is in other scientific fields.

Each experimental investigation must follow a procedure that is relevant to the phenomenon being investigated. Therefore, the scientific method used for one experiment may differ completely from the method used for an investigation of a completely different nature. For example, studying how school-age children relate to authoritarian teachers would involve methods totally different from those employed for investigating the behavioral reactions of the middle-aged adult to stress. However, the basic principles of experimental methods remain the same. Regardless of specific experimental differences, certain common terms, definitions, and formats are universal to those using the experimental method.

The experimental method typically begins with a **hypothesis,** an educated guess made by researchers regarding what they think the results will be. Let us suppose our hypothesis is that students will know more about the discipline of developmental psychology after a semester is over than they did before they enrolled. Before testing our hypothesis on a large group of people, say 1,000 undergraduate students, we would perform a **pilot study,** a small-scale research investigation designed to discover problems, errors, or other obstacles that might develop when the large-scale study is undertaken. Discovering procedural problems while testing 10 or 20 subjects will save much time, effort, and many headaches before we begin testing 1,000 subjects.

In some types of research, two groups of subjects are chosen to prove or disprove the hypothesis. One group is called the **experimental group,** which is subjected to special conditions and is carefully observed by the experimenter. The special treatment given to the experimental group is called the **independent variable.** Concerning our hypothesis, the experimental group would comprise students enrolled in and receiving formal instruction (the independent variable) in developmental psychology. The behavior affected by the independent variable, that is, the degree of knowledge acquired in class from the professor, is termed the **dependent variable.**

Our other group of subjects, called the **control group,** is used primarily for comparison purposes. The control group would not receive the independent variable, the formal instruction in developmental psychology, given to the experimental group.

To determine whether a hypothesis is correct, *pre-* and *posttests* are usually administered to both experimental and control groups. In our case, the pre- and posttests would seek to measure the students' knowledge of developmental psychology. Thus pre- and posttests are administrations of the dependent variable. Changes (if any) would appear in the experimental group, especially when contrasted with the control group. Figure 1-7 displays the experimental method.

Some research designs do not use a control group. Let us assume we want to discover what types of configurations (shapes, forms, etc.) appeal to newborn infants. In this experiment, we might electronically connect a pacifier to a video monitor. If an infant sucks on the pacifier, the configuration remains on the monitor; if the infant fails to suck, the image disappears. Studies have shown that infants prefer complex patterns over simple ones. In an experiment such as this, there is no need for the control group. The configuration is the independent variable, and the time spent sucking is the dependent variable (behavior).

Finally, we need to point out that when conducting experimental research, especially lifespan development, researchers must seek to control whatever extraneous variables they can. By seeking to control factors possibly affecting the

FIGURE 1-7

A Hypothetical Experimental Design.

Experimental research is designed to facilitate the determination of relationships between differing phenomena. Here, we can see the steps in discovering if taking a course in developmental psychology will improve one's knowledge about the discipline.

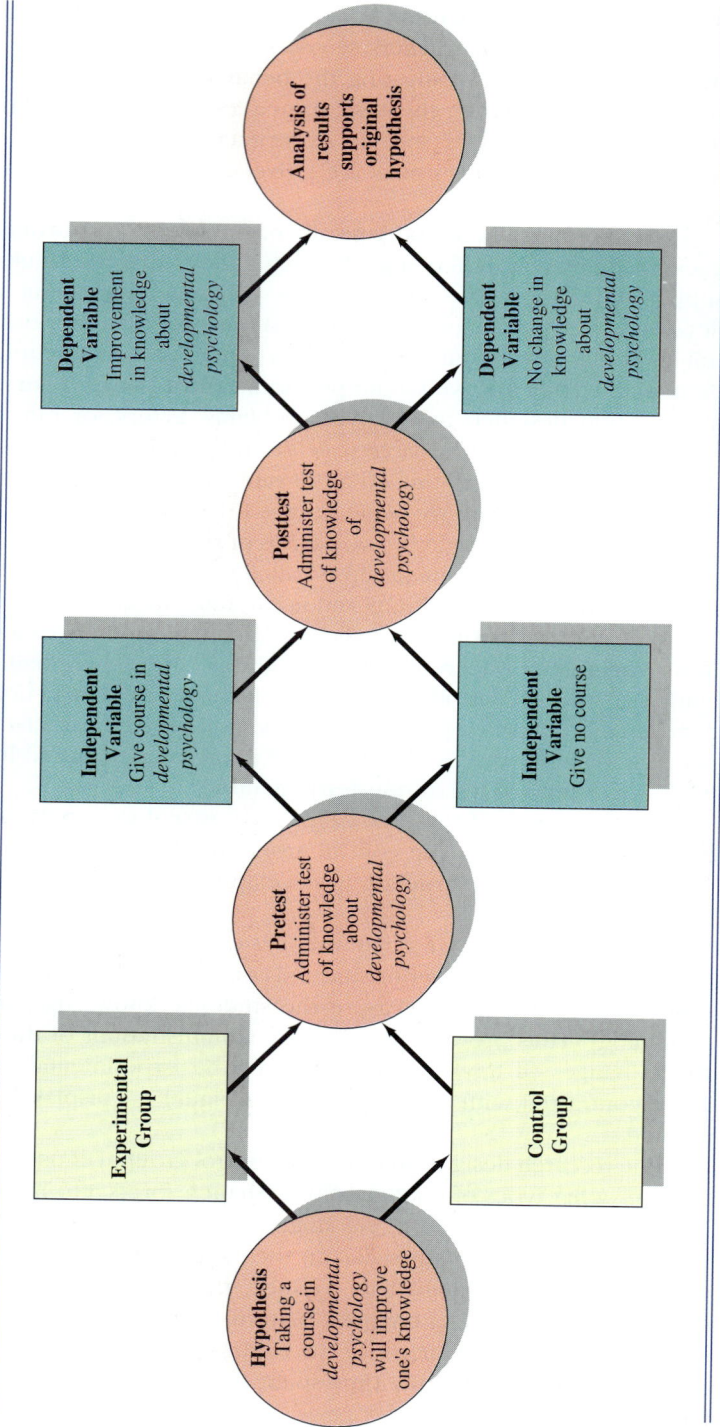

outcome of experimental research, a researcher has greater confidence in making cause-and-effect statements. This is particularly important when we consider the enormous number of variables that developmental psychologists must take into account when seeking to pinpoint causal factors in development.

Longitudinal and Cross-Sectional Research Designs

Two popular strategies for gathering data are the longitudinal and cross-sectional research designs. In lifespan development we are looking for the processes that cause the changes which occur as we age. The simplest way to do this is to find people of different ages, ask them questions, test them, or make measurements and see if people of different ages are the same for any given characteristic. Any differences are termed age differences. This approach to gathering data is the cross-sectional design. In a **cross-sectional design,** researchers obtain comparative data from different groups of subjects more or less simultaneously. In studying adult development, then, the analyst would select a number of groups of subjects aged (for example) 20, 30, 40, and 60 and record the differences among the various age groups. The differences would then be analyzed.

A second technique of gathering information is the longitudinal design. In a **longitudinal design,** the analyst collects data on the same group of individuals at intervals over a considerable period (years and sometimes even decades). Let us suppose someone wanted to collect data concerning various facets of early adult development. The researcher employing the longitudinal design might begin by studying a particular group at age 20. Follow-up studies would be made at fairly regular intervals until the subjects reached age 40. At each follow-up session, relevant data would be recorded to be applied to the final research analysis. Differences found between people at different ages are called *age changes.*

Each design has its own advantages and disadvantages (see Table 1-1 on the following page). For example, the cross-sectional approach is relatively inexpensive, easier to execute, and not overly time consuming, but it sometimes overlooks individual changes and it might be contaminated with generational differences. The longitudinal method probably provides a fairly accurate picture of developmental changes within an individual, but this approach is time consuming, generally expensive, and frequently suffers from subject attrition (S. Menard, 1991). Whichever design is used, the data will be only as good as the measurement techniques used to obtain them and the conception behind their collection. These factors operate in any methodological design.

Age and Cohort Factors

To fully comprehend the differences between the longitudinal and cross-sectional designs, you must understand such factors as age and cohorts. In either design *age* is always a variable. A second variable is **cohort,** a reference to those people born at approximately the same time (the same year or within a few years of each other). Because they are born about the same time, cohorts have experienced situations and events unique to their particular age group.

Not only do cohorts grow old together, they travel through the lifespan together. They experience similar historical events together that can influence

TABLE 1-1

Comparison Between Longitudinal and Cross-Sectional Designs

Factor	Longitudinal	Cross-Sectional
Method of procedure	Examines and reexamines same group repeatedly over the years	Examines several groups (from different levels of development) simultaneously over a short time period
Cost	Research is generally expensive	Research is relatively inexpensive
Time involved	Several years to several decades; frequent loss of contact with subjects	Relatively little time—months, weeks, or even days
Collection and use of data	Collection of data is as long as the experiment. Because many data are collected, much time is needed for interpretation	Quick collection with rapid interpretation of results
Personnel needed	Many people under capable researcher	Relatively few (may need only one researcher)
Major advantages	Allows many data showing individual growth and developmental changes	Large amounts of data can be gathered within a short period of time
Major disadvantages	Requires much time and finance; loss of subject by moving, death, and the like	Loses sight of individual changes; provides only a representative group of various ages, controls, and the like

their thinking, their values and attitudes, and their very lives. Utilizing information covered earlier in this chapter, such experiences provide a good illustration of normative history-graded contextual influences. To illustrate cohort factors, being a 20-year-old in 1930 was different from being a 20-year-old in 1994. Thus the age factor distinguishes people by their chronological age, and the cohort factor places that age within a historical time frame.

Furthermore, historical events affect different age groups in different ways. A war has a different effect on 18-year-olds than it does on 6-year-olds. It also may affect the parents of the 18-year-olds in different ways from the parents of 6-year-olds. Of course, war has its greatest effect on those who are actually called to do the fighting. Here we can see that different age groupings of cohorts are affected differently by the same historical event.

With age and cohort factors in mind, let us reexamine the nature of cross-sectional and longitudinal studies. All of the subjects in a longitudinal study are members of the same cohort. If a study was started in 1950 with 20-year-olds, and these subjects were tested every 5 years, we would be gathering information about *age changes*. In a cross-sectional design we would be studying subjects who were perhaps 25, 30, 35, and 40 years of age. Here we would be gathering information about *age differences*. In a cross-sectional study the results may be affected by age or cohort differences.

A number of contextual forces shape the course of lifespan development, including historical events. Historical events such as the Great Depression often give a particular generation its unique identity.

Cohort analysis is an effort among researchers to explore the experiences common to a particular age group. Whenever a research design is put into operation and data are collected, we must go a step further and examine cohort differences. This is especially true in cross-sectional studies because we are dealing with subjects of varying ages at the same time. For example, suppose 20-year-olds score extremely well on intelligence tests compared to 70-year-olds. Is it because of intellectual superiority or because the former group had the advantage of more schooling as they were growing up? To cite another instance, let us say we discover in our data that 60-year-olds are more financially cautious than 25-year-olds. Could that have been influenced by the 60-year-olds living through the stock market crash and the Great Depression? Or is it because the 25-year-olds were reared in a world of charge cards, layaways, and instant credit? Or might it be both?

When two or more factors such as age and cohort cannot be assessed separately, the data is said to be *confounded.* Cross-sectional designs for the most part are inexpensive and can be quickly executed, but they always contain **confounded data,** in that the facts may be attributed to either age or cohort differences.

Longitudinal studies can also give us confounded data. More specifically, longitudinal studies have a tendency to confound a person's age with time-of-measurement changes. As a result, we cannot really tell whether changes in a person are the result of developmental processes or of environmental influences.

One other weakness of the longitudinal design is that of repeated measurement. Here the subject is repeatedly given the same tests over time. The gathered results may therefore be due not to improvement, but rather to familiarity with the test itself. All of this discussion illustrates the many ways scientists are confronted with confounded data.

Sequential Designs

Sequential designs are various combinations of the longitudinal and cross-sectional designs. These combinations are attempts to eliminate or at least reduce the weaknesses and improve on the strengths of the two classic designs. The four sequential designs that we look at are the time-lag design, the time sequence design, the cohort design, and the cross-sequential design.

A **time-lag design** is the simplest of the sequential research designs. Subjects are tested who are the same age, but not in the same cohort group. In other words, you are comparing people of the same age but at different times. Suppose someone had studied the morals of 20-year-old college students back in 1960, and you wanted to compare them with today's 20-year-old college students. To do this, you would replicate the 1960 study, and because age has been held constant, it is not a variable that would confound your results. This design allows us to examine cohort effect without any confounding of age, and, as we just mentioned, is the least complex of the sequential designs.

A **time sequential design** involves two or more sequential cross-sectional studies. Suppose the study on morality in 20-year-olds was more than a one-shot deal. Let's assume the researcher had examined 20-, 30-, 40-, and 50-year-olds. This, of course, is a cross-sectional study. Now, however, let's assume this experiment was repeated in 1970, 1980, and 1990. This is now a time sequential design. In other words, when you replicate a cross-sectional study at a new time, you have the time sequential design. Age and cohort are confounded, but we assume it does not seriously affect our results.

Cohort sequential designs involve two or more sequential longitudinal studies. Each must cover the same range of ages. To continue with the example we've been using, we would examine the morality of one group of cohorts when they are age 20 in 1960 and then when they become age 30, 40, and 50. Meanwhile we start examining a second group of cohorts who become 20-year-olds in 1970, and maybe a third group of cohorts that reach age 20 in 1980. We now have three parallel longitudinal studies. This design allows us to look at individuals as they change over time and see whether this same change occurs in different cohort groups. Unfortunately, the cohort sequential design is extremely time consuming.

Finally, we come to the **cross-sequential design,** which is, more or less, a combination of the longitudinal and the cross-sectional design. Here, we examine two or more cohorts of different age ranges at two or more times of testing. This then is a longitudinal study that has cross-sectional applications. It allows us to separate cohort and history factors from each other, but it does not provide clear information on age-related changes.

Research Problems in Lifespan Development

Numerous difficulties confront researchers studying lifespan development. Researchers must never manipulate the subjects and their environments to a degree that will endanger their physical, mental, or emotional well-being, or it will interfere with normal developmental processes. Ethical standards, therefore, must be foremost in the researchers' minds. For example, some researchers believe children are more vulnerable than adults to stressful situations; consequently, more care must be taken when planning a study or experiment in which children are involved. Here are examples of other considerations: Is it ethical to subject individuals to situations where they are bound to fail? Is it ethical to issue to the subject misinformation to see how it affects behavior? Is it ethical to mistreat a child or an adult? Is it ethical to observe people when they are not aware they are being observed? The answer to some of these questions is obvious: No. In practice, many questions of ethics are not so easily answered. In the next section, we supply ethical guidelines for conducting lifespan development research.

A second research problem, particularly when a study involves older adults, is that there are relatively few research instruments available to measure the various characteristics of aging processes. Those in use tend to be questionable not only in terms of validity and reliability but also in regard to distortion of actual findings. Even the observation of adults poses difficulties for the researcher, especially when adult behavior is compared to that of children or adolescents. Once they know they are being observed or questioned for a purpose, adults are not as spontaneous and are much more suspicious than their younger counterparts. The longitudinal research technique has also been especially vulnerable to criticism. Although it can be a reliable design, adults represent a highly mobile segment of the population and are unlikely to remain in the same location for repeated testing. Other problems relative to the longitudinal study are its rather expensive operating costs and its time-consuming nature—subjects may die before the study is completed.

Another area of concern, pointed out earlier in this chapter, is that not enough research efforts have been directed toward women and their aging experience. Relatedly, there is limited information available on aging among racial and ethnic groups. Although interest and data on African Americans have been growing, there is still a void in the literature available on Hispanics, Orientals, and Native Americans, to name but a few groups. All people do not have the same needs or experience the same conditions of aging. Rather the circumstances of one's existence and background to a large extent shape one's development across the life cycle (Gunter, 1991; Jackson, Chatters, & Taylor, 1992; Kunitz & Levy, 1991; Maddox, 1992; Milligan, 1990; Pang, 1991; Secundy, 1992; Stanford, Lockery, & Schoenrock, 1990; Wray, 1991). Similarly, we need to better understand the impact of neighborhoods and communities on aging experiences, including rural and urban differences (Buckwalter, 1991a, 1991b; Gerritsen, Wolffensperger, & Van Den Heuve, 1990; Johnson, 1991; McCulloch, 1991).

▬ Ethical Issues in Lifespan Development Research

All scientists face questions of ethics, especially those whose research involves humans. As we indicated, lifespan development researchers must be especially concerned with ethical standards, and the American Psychological Association (APA) has studied, developed, and revised ethical guidelines over the years (1979, 1981, 1990, 1992). These guidelines, which are reviewed annually, state that the researchers' ultimate responsibility is to assess their research to determine if any ethical problems exist and discuss such problems with collaborators, assistants, students, and employees. In other words, a full ethical evaluation by the entire research team, as well as fellow psychologists, should be undertaken before research commences. Some other important considerations are as follows:

Ethical practice requires the investigator to inform the participant of all features of the research that reasonably might be expected to influence willingness to participate and to explain all other aspects of the research about which the participant inquires.

Ethical research practice requires the investigator to respect the individual's freedom to decline to participate in research or to discontinue participation at any time.

Ethically acceptable research begins with the establishment of a clear and fair agreement between the investigator and the research participant that clarifies the responsibilities of each. The investigator has the obligation to honor all promises and commitments included in that agreement.

The ethical investigator protects participants from physical and mental discomfort, harm, and danger. If the risk of such consequences exists, the investigator is required to inform the participant of that fact, secure consent before proceeding, and take all possible measures to minimize distress. A research procedure may not be used if it is likely to cause serious and lasting harm to participants.

Where research procedures may result in undesirable consequences for the participant, the investigator has the responsibility to detect and remove or correct these consequences, including, where relevant, long-term aftereffects.

Information obtained about the research participants during the course of an investigation is confidential.

Because children may be more susceptible to stress, extreme care must be taken when a researcher is planning to involve them in a study. Because of this, the Division of Developmental Psychology of the APA has added additional ethical standards, including the following:

No matter how young the child, he or she has rights that supersede the rights of the investigator.

The investigator uses no research operations that may harm the child either physically or psychologically. Psychological harm, to be sure, is difficult to define; nevertheless, its definition remains a responsibility of the investigator.

The informed consent of parents or of those legally designated to act *in loco parentis* is obtained, preferably in writing. Informed consent requires that the parent be given accurate information . . . on the purpose and operations of the research, albeit in layperson's terms. The consent of parents is not solicited by any claims of benefit to the child. Not only is the right of parents to refuse consent respected, but parents must be given the opportunity to refuse.

Teachers of courses related to children should present the ethical standards of conducting research on human beings to their students.

CHAPTER REVIEW

Behavior, never constant, ever changing, is the subject matter of the field of developmental psychology. More precisely, developmental psychology encompasses the growth, maturation, and learning of the organism from conception to death. Conceptualizations of the life cycle are useful in clarifying and organizing research; however, lifespan development researchers recognize that life does not start or stop at the beginning or end of stages. It is also understood that contextual influences such as culture, history, and life events impact on whatever life cycle classifications are used. Developmental dynamics must also take into account the nature of growth, maturation, learning, and critical periods.

A number of important issues and themes exist regarding the nature and course of lifespan development. These key issues and themes are the interrelatedness of aging processes, theoretical perspectives on lifespan development, the interaction of heredity and environment, epigenetics, continuity and discontinuity, active and reactive models of development, and gender issues. These issues and themes weave themselves throughout all stages of the life cycle, and over the years have succeeded in sparking considerable intellectual curiosity.

Developmental psychology is considered a science, and the research gathered reflects the principles of description, explanation, prediction, and control. When investigating phenomena, developmental psychologists utilize the scientific method, an organized series of steps designed to promote maximum objectivity in gathering and interpreting observable evidence. Today's scientific investigations, undoubtedly, are more precise than the single baby biographies of the past, and we explored the various research methodologies that exist. Observation, which many consider to be the key to knowledge, consists of three types: naturalistic, structured, and participant. The case study focuses on a single person rather than a group of people. A survey is a technique for gathering information from people and consists of a questionnaire or an interview. The correlational method involves statistics, and the results indicate if a relationship between two variables are correlated. However, a correlation does not prove one variable actually is the cause of the other.

The experimental method is a systematic means by which the experimenter seeks to determine relationships between differing phenomena. It is employed either to discover principles underlying behavior or to find cause-and-effect relationships. The experimental method includes independent and dependent variables, the former referring to the stimulus or special treatment given the subjects and the latter referring to the behavior subjects exhibit after they have received the independent variable.

With the longitudinal design, the developmental processes of the same group of subjects are studied over a period of years. The cross-sectional design is quicker and easier to use than the longitudinal design because data can be collected from many age groups simultaneously. On the other hand, subtle changes, perceptible in the longitudinal design, are often missed in the cross-sectional approach.

Researchers must also take into account cohort differences as data are evaluated. Cohort differences refer to the fact that subjects born at about the same historical time experience situations and events unique to that age group. Sequential designs are various combinations of the longitudinal and cross-sectional designs and consist of four variations: time-lag, time sequence, cohort design, and cross-sequential design.

Studying lifespan development poses numerous issues and challenges to contemporary researchers. For example, researchers must adhere to rigorous ethical standards when conducting their investigations. Discovering suitable research instruments may also prove to be troublesome, particularly when older adults are studied. Another area of concern is that not enough research efforts have been directed toward aging experiences among women, racial, and ethnic groups. Researchers also need to better understand the impact of neighborhoods and communities on lifespan development, including rural and urban differences.

TERMS YOU SHOULD KNOW

active model of development
baby biography
biological aging
case study
cohort
cohort analysis
cohort sequential design
confounded data
contextual influences
continuity-discontinuity issue
continuous model of
   development
control group
controlled experiments
correlational method
critical period
cross-sectional design
cross-sequential design
dependent variable
developmental psychology
discontinuous model of
   development
environmentalist
epigenetic principle
experimental group
experimental method

growth
hypothesis
independent variable
interactionist
learning
longitudinal design
maturation
nativist
naturalistic observation
nature-nurture issue
nonnormative influences
normative age-graded influences
normative history-graded
   influences
participant observation
pilot study
psychological aging
reactive model of development
scientific method
sequential designs
social aging
structured observation
survey
time-lag design
time sequential design

THINKING IN ACTION

• The nature-nurture controversy intrigues all educated people, and your local public TV station has asked you to participate as the moderator/devil's advocate in their upcoming special, *The Nature and Nurture of Human Existence.* Prepare an overview of the nature-nurture issue and then develop a series of controversial statements/questions that will provoke heated debate from both sides of the aisle.

• As you learned in this chapter, three interrelated processes of aging are psychological, social, and biological. List as many characteristics as you can in each of these three categories to describe your own aging processes. Now do the same for a friend your own age. How do your lists compare? Do certain aging processes seem more prevalent than others?

• You have been wondering about the effects of television violence on children. Is there as much violence as authorities are now saying? How would you use observational techniques to determine the amount of violence? What different categories of violence would you use? Would you distinguish real-life violence from cartoon violence? Do children? Design a series of experiments you think would help us understand the ramifications of TV violence on children's behavior.

• Hi-Tech Pharmaceuticals has asked for your assistance in evaluating a new drug they believe will reduce hyperactivity in children. Using appropriate research methods, design an experiment that might shed light on the usefulness of this medication. As you undertake this endeavor, be sure to use the appropriate research terminology you acquired in this chapter.

RECOMMENDED READINGS

1. Bornstein, M. H., & Lamb, M. E. (Eds.). (1992). *Developmental psychology: An advanced textbook (3rd ed.).* Hillsdale, NJ: Erlbaum.

    A higher-level but excellent account of a variety of theories and methods covering cognitive, perceptual, language, moral, social, and emotional development, among others. This book is for the student who enjoys exploring philosophical ideas.

2. Day, A. T. (1991). *Remarkable survivors: Insights into successful aging among women.* Washington, DC: Urban Institute Press.

    An interesting and thought-provoking look at the female aging experience, including the strategies used by women to negotiate later life's developmental transitions.

3. Jackson, J. S., Chatters, L. M., & Taylor, R. J. (Eds.). (1992). *Aging in black America.* Newbury Park, CA: Sage.

    This reader contains many interesting topics, including health, social functioning, psychological well-being, and retirement.

4. Lonergan, E. T. (Ed.). (1991). *Extending life, enhancing life: A national research agenda on aging.* Washington, DC: National Academy Press.

    Among other themes is how social structures and social changes affect aging experiences.

5. Miller, D. C. (1991). *Handbook of research design and social measurement (3rd ed.).* Newbury Park, CA: Sage.

    One of the most comprehensive collections of social research methods available.

CHAPTER 2

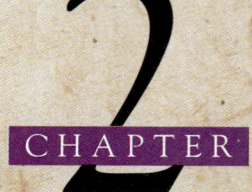

Theories of Lifespan Development

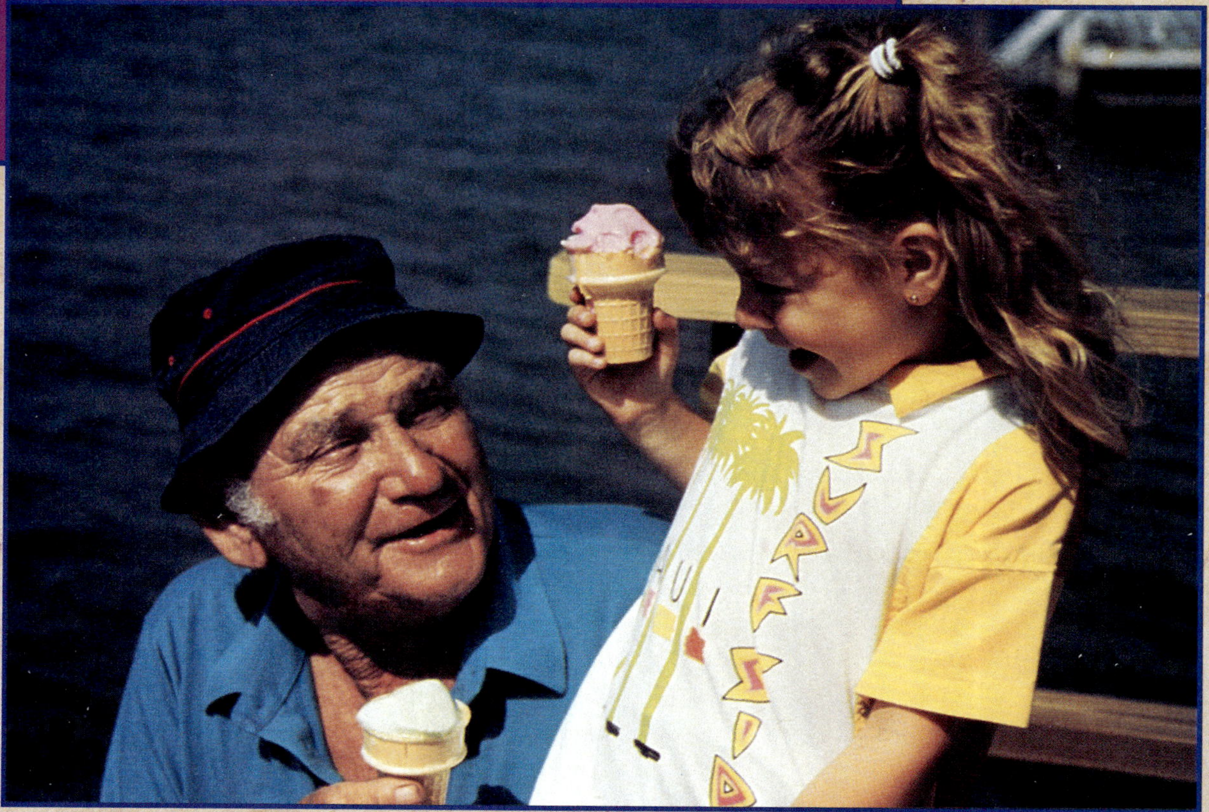

What Do You Think?

INTRODUCTION

WHAT MAKES A GOOD LIFESPAN DEVELOPMENT THEORY?

PSYCHOLOGICAL THEORIES OF LIFESPAN DEVELOPMENT

Psychodynamic Theories
Psychoanalytic Theories
Freud's Theory of Personality
Erikson's Psychosocial Theory
Other Psychodynamic Theories
A Critique of Psychodynamic Theories
Cognitive Theories
Piaget's Cognitive-Developmental Theory
Information Processing Theory
A Critique of Cognitive Theories
Learning Theories
Behaviorism
Social Learning Theory

A Critique of Learning Theories
Ethological Theory
Ethology and the Study of Critical Periods
A Critique of Ethological Theory
Humanistic Theory
Maslow's Theory of Self-Actualization
Rogers's Self-Concept Theory
A Critique of Humanistic Theory
Ecological Theory
Bronfenbrenner's Ecological Theory
A Critique of Ecological Theory
**Noteworthy Adult Psychological
  Theories**

SOCIOLOGICAL THEORIES OF LIFESPAN DEVELOPMENT

Symbolic Interactionism
Social Exchange Theory
Family Development Theory

Conflict Theory
A Critique of Sociological Theories

BIOLOGICAL THEORIES OF LIFESPAN DEVELOPMENT

Wear-and-Tear Theory
Cellular Theory

Immunity Theory
A Critique of Biological Theories

PUTTING LIFESPAN DEVELOPMENT THEORIES INTO PERSPECTIVE

Chapter Review • Terms You Should Know • Thinking in Action • Recommended Readings

• Carl Jorgensen and his brother Phil are in their 60s and have always been close. Their birthdays are 2 years apart, but Carl looks 10 years younger than Phil. Phil has always been the more even-tempered and quieter of the two; Carl has long been more temperamental and talkative. And, although people remark that Phil has always been somewhat of a loner, Carl is remembered as always being a joiner. How might such developmental dynamics be explained? What factors account for the differences that exist between Carl and Phil? In this chapter, we discover how theories seek to explain such phenomena, including the constancies and changes that exist in lifespan development.

• Lifespan development researchers study people of all ages in a wide range of situations, from the gender-typed play behaviors of children to the adjustments faced by elderly people. To guide researchers who study the course and processes of development, various theories have been formulated. As we discover in this chapter, such theories are grouped according to psychological, sociological, and biological properties. What distinguishes these different types of theories? How does each type seek to focus on different aspects of development? How might these categories shape our thinking about growth and development?

• Erikson . . . Piaget . . . Watson . . . Maslow. Theorists such as these are considered influential in the field of lifespan development, and their contributions have enabled us to better understand the many dynamics attached to aging. Thanks to their efforts, we have a better idea of the developmental similarities and differences that exist over the life cycle, including how such dynamics unfold. Do some lifespan development theorists have broader appeal than others, and if so, what criteria are used to make such judgments? Do some theorists provide a better conceptual base for grounding research or sparking additional levels of scientific inquiry? In this chapter we address such questions as we explore the major theories of lifespan development.

INTRODUCTION

In lifespan development, we assume changes in behavior are not random or accidental. We believe all behavior change can be understood in terms of developmental dynamics. Although humans develop in similar ways over the course of the lifespan, it must be understood that everyone also develops in individual ways. We need to understand what principles are involved that produce similarity as well as the forces that produce individuality. As we learned in the last chapter, we must also take into account important themes and issues that shape the life course, such as nature and nurture, gender similarities and differences, and continuity and discontinuity. Such complex and multifaceted issues herald the need for theoretical perspectives of lifespan development.

WHAT MAKES A GOOD LIFESPAN DEVELOPMENT THEORY?

How do we make the study of lifespan development more scientific and accurate? How can researchers more precisely interpret events occurring over the course of the lifespan? Obviously, we must do more than collect facts, for facts are like a pile of bricks, useless without a structure. The structure that we build to explain lifespan development is called a **theory.** A theory is really a perspective, one of several ways we can view development. A developmental theory not only attempts to describe and explain changes in behavior as we age but attempts to show individual differences in these changes, for example, differences between males and females, African Americans and Hispanics, urban and rural dwellers, and so on. In other words, an effective theory should be able to describe and explain the course of development generally as well as specifically, such as with the variations just listed. A good theory will also explain why your best friend is changing but in a different way than you are.

There are a wide variety of theories, many of them no more than speculative. The most speculative or weakest theories need considerably more research to support them. They are sometimes based on preconceptions. That a theoretical preconception sounds right or makes sense is no guarantee it is correct. In the field of lifespan development, as well as in other disciplines, reliable data are needed. This is as true for research undertaken in the laboratory as it is for general theories related to life.

The better theories are generally those that have stood up to additional research and empirical (scientific) evidence. Let us acknowledge, too, that theories do not always remain constant any more than we do. At best, they offer research potential, with the understanding that more methodological refinement and improvement is always needed.

The best theories in lifespan development as well as any other discipline are those that evolve and in the process become more logically and empirically sound. Such theories are also internally consistent, with no statements that contradict each other. Moreover, good theories always come to serve a heuristic purpose: a conceptual framework to guide other perspectives and generate new observations and insight.

Theories are constructed with whatever knowledge is available at any given time. They are never complete and thus are always open to challenge. They must be dynamic, open to ever-increasing data being discovered by our research scientists. Presumably, our theories or perspectives are more theoretical than empirical. Whenever a theory is judged to be incomplete or not fully consistent, it is often referred to as a **prototheory.** Most theories in lifespan development are really prototheories. Prototheories are initial assumptions that provide an orientation and research direction. They are initially formed more as guidelines than as firmly held assumptions and are frequently modified when new empirical evidence so dictates. When they cannot be modified, they are discarded (Miller, 1993; Thomas, 1992).

In the pages that follow, we explore a number of different theories that can be applied to the study of lifespan. These theories are grouped according to psychological, sociological, and biological conceptual properties. We remind you that such a classification reflects the three processes of aging presented in the last chapter. Table 2-1 displays such a division.

PSYCHOLOGICAL THEORIES OF LIFESPAN DEVELOPMENT

Psychological theories of lifespan development emphasize behavioral characteristics and include such elements as personality, cognition, self-esteem, motivation, and feelings. Among the psychological theories of most importance for our purposes are the psychodynamic, cognitive-developmental, behavioristic, social learning, humanistic, and ecological perspectives.

TABLE 2-1
Lifespan Development Theories

Psychological Theories	Sociological Theories	Biological Theories
Psychoanalysis	Symbolic Interactionism	Wear-and-Tear Theory
Cognitive-Developmental Theory	Social Exchange Theory	Cellular Theory
Behaviorism	Family Development Theory	Immunity Theory
Social Learning Theory	Conflict Theory	
Ethological Theory		
Humanism		
Ecological Theory		

Psychodynamic Theories

Psychodynamic theories are those psychological theories that emphasize the dynamics of the unconscious mind and one's past experiences as being the major determinants of future behavior. The original psychodynamic theory was the psychoanalytic school of thought, devised by Sigmund Freud. More recent additions to psychodynamic theories include those of Erik Erikson, Robert Peck, and Jane Loevinger, all of whom are included in this chapter.

Psychoanalytic Theories The original **psychoanalytic theory** was founded by Sigmund Freud. Freud, like so many others of his day, came to psychology via other routes. While practicing medicine in clinics, he became interested in neurophysiology, especially the functions of the brain. He spent considerable time seeking to understand abnormal brain functions and mental disorders, a pursuit that would eventually lead him to the field of psychology.

Although many of his views are controversial, quite a few psychologists have been influenced by at least one of his ideas on lifespan development. He devised a theory of personality (with the underlying dynamics of the id, ego, and superego) that has applications to the behavior of both child and adult. He also proposed the theory of **psychosexual stages of development,** an explanation of behavior that places great importance on the development and maturation of body parts and on early life experiences. One's past, he felt, plays an important role in determining one's present behavior. Furthermore, Freud's analysis of defense mechanisms has helped explain how defensive behavior originates.

Freud perceived human beings' essential psychological nature as based on *desire* rather than on *reason.* His focus in psychoanalysis was primarily on human passions or emotions and only secondarily on rational abilities or intellect. According to Freud, the child is born with basic animal instincts that operate at the unconscious level of thought. These instincts, or irrational needs, require immediate gratification. Development, therefore, is partially dependent on the transformation of the so-called animal desires into socially acceptable, rational behavior.

Freud's influence can be seen in the research of other psychologists, including that of his daughter Anna Freud, who was one of the early investigators of

Sigmund Freud (1856–1939) was born in Frieberg, Moravia (in what later became part of Czechoslovakia), and founded the original psychoanalytic theory.

child's play. He also stimulated the works of a number of neo-Freudians, particularly Erik Erikson, who devised a theory of personality that stresses psychosocial stages of development. We look at Erikson's theory later in this chapter.

Sigmund Freud developed a theory of how neuroses develop. This theory, in conjunction with his explanation of personality, describes the psychosexual stages through which a child must pass prior to reaching adulthood and normal maturity. His developmental explanation originated not from his direct study of children but from the extraction of information from adult neurotics, initially through hypnosis and later through the cathartic process termed **free association.** The only child Freud ever saw as a patient was Little Hans, and he was seen only once (the remainder of his analysis was conducted via correspondence with Hans's father). Freud's method of study raises serious questions about how much faith to place in the childhood events postulated in his theory. Patients may be unable to recollect events that took place years ago, and, even if they can, their experiences may have no correlation with the experiences of more normal children. Nonetheless, his work stands as an important hallmark in the development of personality.

Freud's Theory of Personality

LEVELS OF FREUDIAN CONSCIOUSNESS One of Freud's major beliefs was that individuals are generally not aware of the underlying reasons for their behavior. He assumed that mental activity must occur at three levels of consciousness. He called the first level the **conscious** level of awareness. Freud used this term to refer to what a person is thinking or experiencing at any given moment. Immediate awareness of one's surroundings are very fleeting: Our conscious thoughts flow as water in a stream; hence this phenomenon is sometimes called our *stream of consciousness.*

INTERACTION OF HEREDITY AND ENVIRONMENT

Given the emphasis that Freud placed on instinctual drives, how would you view his theory in relation to the nature-nurture issue? Relatedly, how does the epigenetic principle help explain his developmental theory?

The second level is called the **preconscious** and refers to all of a person's stored knowledge and memories that are capable of being brought up to the conscious level. For example, if we ask you what your home telephone number is, you are capable of retrieving it from your preconscious even though you were probably not thinking of your telephone number as you were reading this sentence.

The third and largest level of consciousness is the **unconscious,** a vast area of irrational wishes, shameful urges, socially unacceptable sexual desires, fears, and aggressive feelings, as well as anxiety-producing thoughts that have been *repressed* (pushed down to the unconscious to be forgotten). Because these feelings are very threatening to us, we keep them locked in the unconscious mind. When we dream, these feelings and urges are sometimes released, but generally in a distorted way so we will not recognize them. However, these beliefs, urges, desires, and so forth, are all motivators of behavior and influence us in some unconscious way.

PERSONALITY COMPONENTS: ID, EGO, AND SUPEREGO Freud proposed that the **id** is the original inherited system, the instinctive aspect of the personality triumvirate. The id contains the basic motivational drives for our physiological needs such as food, water, sex, and warmth. All emotions are housed within the id and add a further dimension to what Freud described as "unconscious motivational forces."

The id contains the driving life force of an organism. One such dynamic force is the **libido,** which supplies *libidinal energy.* (*Libido* means lust or desire in Latin.) When this energy builds up, there is an increase in *tension* and unhappiness, which must be released by the organism. When the *tension level* is lowered, feelings of contentment and pleasure arise. The id also operates on the **hedonistic principle** (pleasure principle), which is, in many respects, an extension of homeostasis (the tendency of the body to maintain internal equilibrium). This hedonistic drive pushes the organism to seek what produces a pleasurable state and to avoid what causes any discomfiture. The id's forces, operating at the unconscious level, drive the organism toward instant gratification of its primary or biological needs. Freud also writes of a tension level. Without tension we have no motivation, but as a biological need arises, it increases the tension level, and the higher this level, the greater our motivation to satisfy this emerging need.

Freud believed an infant operates solely at the id level for the first 8 months of life until the ego commences its slow and gradual development. Until this time, the id is in total control of the child's behavior. Thus when the internal tension level increases because of hunger pangs, soiled or wet diapers, gas bubbles, or other tension-producing stimuli, the infant will cry until the tension level is changed to an acceptable or pleasurable state.

The **ego** is the organism's contact with the external environment. Its purpose is to satisfy the desires or demands of the id and, later, the superego. As the ego develops, it learns to operate on the **reality principle;** that is, it learns to choose attainable goals before discharging tension or energy, which makes for a more efficient ego. However, Freud viewed the ego as a servant of the id, not as a separate or sovereign entity. According to Freud, the ego exists to further the aims of the id. Over a long time, socially acceptable behavior may prove to be more beneficial to the organism than behavior that produces instant gratification. However, until the former type of behavior is learned, infants, toddlers, or preschoolers operate at a "gimme, gimme, gimme" level, wanting everything for themselves immediately and exhibiting little tolerance for more acceptable behavior. Ego maturity is, in part, the process of restraining the id's demands until they can be met according to the mores, folkways, and values of one's culture.

The third component of the Freudian personality system is the **superego,** which appears when the child is approximately 5 years old. It operates on what might be called the perfection principle. The superego consists of the internalization of the morals taught by one's religion, society, and family. The superego is similar to the id, in that it makes largely unconscious demands on the ego. However, the superego also resembles the ego by virtue of its intent to exercise control over the id's urges. The child who steals without compunction because it is allowable according to his or her principles will suffer no emotional consequences for such an act or, at best, might intellectualize the possibilities of getting caught. The child whose values say theft is improper behavior and whose superego is sufficiently developed to operate on such a principle will be bothered by the conscience and will most likely experience emotions such as guilt or remorse. The opposite set of emotions originates from the ego ideal, the portion of the superego that makes one feel good for having behaved according to one's internalized principles.

Behavior, then, can be defined as the result of the *interaction* of these three personality components and their relationship to the outer world, each one seeking to attain a form of psychological satisfaction by directly influencing behavior (see Figure 2-1). Thus, when the id signals the ego that the body is in need of fluids, the ego, evaluating reality, attempts to choose an appropriate form of behavior to satisfy the id. This would be accomplished by conforming to acceptable social behaviors (such as not drinking from a puddle) and by adhering to standards within the superego (not stealing soda water).

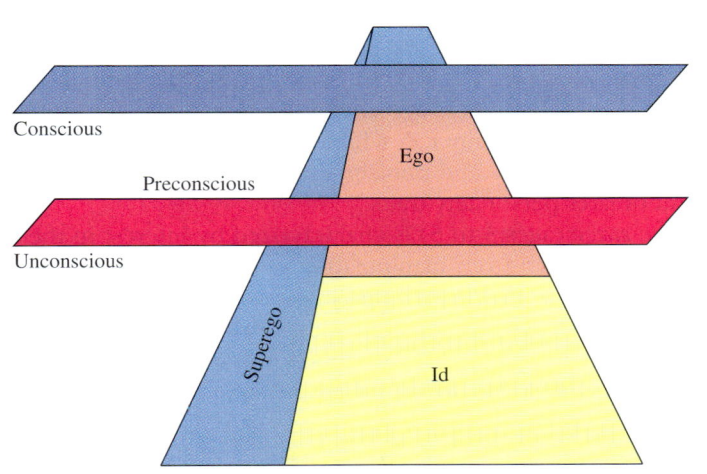

FIGURE 2-1
The Relationship of the Id, Ego, and Superego to Levels of Consciousness.

According to Freud, most personality processes are beneath a conscious level of awareness. They take place at either the preconscious or the unconscious level; thus the ego and superego are only partly conscious, and the id is wholly unconscious.

EGO DEFENSE MECHANISMS Freud believed that sex and aggression are two basic instinctive drives of the id. These drives cause no conflict in most of the animal kingdom, but in humans, they are often diametrically opposed to cultural values. The satisfaction of these basic drives leads to a struggle between the id, ego, and superego as to what behavior should be adopted. In the course of this struggle, the individual often becomes highly anxious, which produces an increase in the person's tension level. The ego must alleviate this tension; if it cannot be accomplished by consciously coping (that is, finding a satisfactory solution), unconscious ego forces take over. These protective devices are called **defense** (or coping) **mechanisms**—the unconscious means used by the ego to reduce conflict and tension. Many people believe the explanation of ego defense mechanisms to be among Freud's major contributions to psychology.

Probably the foremost defense mechanism described by Freud is **repression.** Here, tension- or anxiety-producing thoughts and experiences are forced to the unconscious level. Mild repression, such as conveniently forgetting your dental appointment, may help lower your anxiety level for a while. However, when anxiety-producing thoughts and experiences are repressed, but continue to operate at the unconscious level, more serious behavior disorders may develop. Other defense mechanisms such as rationalization, projection, and regression are discussed in Chapter 7.

FREUD'S PSYCHOSEXUAL DEVELOPMENTAL THEORY In utilizing an *epigenetic* and *discontinuous* framework, Freud identified five stages of psychosexual development (complete coverage of these stages can be found throughout the textbook). During the *oral stage* (ages 0 to 1½), the mouth is the primary source of pleasure. Enjoyment is derived from being fed or from sucking on a pacifier or one's thumb. Freud maintained that either the overgratification or undergratification of this need—and of others to follow—may lead to what he labeled a **fixation.** A fixation is a preoccupation with one particular aspect of psychosexual development (e.g., thumb sucking) that may interfere with or manifest itself in subsequent psychosexual stages. Thus the child fixated at the oral stage, perhaps deprived of thumb sucking, may seek to fulfill this need later in life. Such behaviors as smoking, gum chewing, or nail biting may be the individual's way of gratifying the previously deprived oral need.

During the *anal stage* (ages 1½ to 3), the anus and the buttocks become the source of sensual pleasure. Satisfaction is derived from expelling or withholding feces, but external conflicts are encountered when toilet training begins. Freud maintains that the manner in which parents conduct toilet training, particularly the use of rewards and punishments, may have consequences for the development of later personality traits.

The *phallic stage* (ages 3 to 5) is characterized by interest in the genital organs. Pleasure is derived from manipulating one's genitals, and curiosity is directed toward the anatomical differences between the sexes. Children also have a tendency to develop romantic feelings toward parents of the opposite sex. The attraction of boys to their mothers is called the *Oedipus complex* and the romantic feelings of girls toward their fathers is labeled the *Electra complex.*

The *latency period* (ages 6 to 11) represents a rather tranquil period compared to the psychosexual turbulence of previous stages. However, there is an increased awareness of personal identity, surroundings, and the importance of social interaction. The latency period is also a time of ego refinement, for the child seeks to develop those character traits deemed socially acceptable. Coping or defense mechanisms begin to develop as children attempt to avoid failure or rejection in the face of life's growing expectations and demands.

Freud's final psychosexual period is called the *genital stage* (the adolescent years). This stage chronicles the simultaneous reemergence of the first three stages, as puberty introduces a time of biological upheaval. During this time, adolescents become interested in members of the opposite sex. Individuals may encounter their first experience with romantic love, although immature emotional interactions permeate the early phases of this stage. In time, however, people realize they are capable of giving and receiving mature love. See Table 2-2 for a summary of Freud's psychosexual stages.

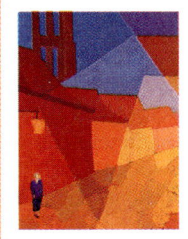

THEORETICAL ISSUES

How applicable do you think psychoanalytic theory is? Do you feel as though it represents the real world of children and adolescents? Why or why not?

Erikson's Psychosocial Theory   Erik H. Erikson (1950, 1958, 1959, 1963, 1968a, 1968b, 1969, 1978, 1982) was one of the world's foremost psychoanalytic scholars. His fascinating early life included crafting large woodcuts, especially of children, and teaching art in Vienna, where he received a Montessori teaching certificate. He also studied with Anna Freud. Finally, he combined these interests and published articles on the application of psychoanalytic theory to educational issues. He later studied children's play and child-rearing practices and observed growth and developmental processes of the ego.

Of his many books, *Childhood and Society* (1963) is probably the best known, for in it Erikson first presented and summed up his major theory. Erikson contends that the process of socializing the child into a given culture occurs as the person passes through eight innately determined, sequential stages

TABLE 2-2
Freud's Psychosexual Stages of Development

Stage	Age	Psychosexual Developments
Oral	0–1½	Pleasure such as eating, sucking, and vocalizing derived from oral cavity.
Anal	1½–3	Pleasure derived from anal area, including retention and expulsion of feces. External conflicts may result when toilet training begins.
Phallic	3–5	Pleasure derived from manipulation of genital organs. Curiosity directed toward sexuality of self and others. Emergence of Oedipus and Electra complexes for males and females, respectively.
Latency period	6–11	Tranquil period of time between stages. Refinement of self-concept and increased peer group interaction. Emergence of coping or defense mechanisms.
Genital	Adolescence	Onset of puberty and discovery of new sexual feelings. Development of heterosexual attraction. Beginning of romantic love.

Erik Erikson (1902–1994) was born in Frankfurt, Germany, and developed eight stages of personality development—each characterized by a psychosocial crisis that must be successfully resolved.

he calls **psychosocial stages of development.** Thus, like Freud, Erikson posited an epigenetic developmental scheme. Also similar to Freud, Erikson was concerned with ego development. However, although recognizing the individual's instinctual drives and interest in different parts of the body in a pre-scribed sequence, Erikson emphasizes the child's interactions with the environment. Thus he views the ego, not the id, as the major driving force of behavior. Erikson also differs in that he studied healthy personalities (rather than neurotic people, such as Freud analyzed) to arrive at his theory.

Erikson also disagrees with Freud's emphasis on infantile sexuality. Owing to his anthropological training, Erikson perceives the child's behavior as resulting from societal influences. His comprehensive theory of development encompasses the years from infancy through old age. For Erikson, the course of development is reversible, meaning the events of later childhood can undo—for better or worse—personality foundations built earlier in life. For Freud, basic personality structure is essentially fixed by age 5. However, for both theorists, stages are related to ages in the sense that age leads to movement to a new stage, regardless of experience and regardless of reorganizations at previous stages.

Essential to Erikson's theory is the development of the ego and the ego's ability to deal with a series of crises or potential crises throughout the individual's life-span. Each stage of life has a crisis that is related in some way to an element in society. The development of personality begins with ego strengths that commence at birth; as the years pass, ego strength is accrued, one quality at a time. Each quality undergoes rapid growth at a critical period of development. Thus, like Freud, Erikson developed a *discontinuous* theory of lifespan development.

The first of Erikson's eight psychosocial crises (see Table 2-3) is called *basic trust versus basic mistrust* (ages 0 to 1). During this stage, the nature of parental interactions with the infant is critical. If infants are recipients of

TABLE 2-3
Erikson's Stages/Crises of Psychosocial Development

Stage/Crisis	Age	Human Relationships Involved	Desired Outcome of Crisis
Trust vs. mistrust	0–1	Parents/caretaker	Hope
Autonomy vs. shame and doubt	1–3	Parents/caretaker	Will
Initiative vs. guilt	3–5	Family	Purpose
Industry vs. inferiority	6–11	Neighborhood/school	Competence
Identity vs. role confusion	Adolescence	Peer groups	Fidelity
Intimacy vs. isolation	Young adulthood	Friends/spouse	Love
Generativity vs. self-absorption	Middle adulthood	Family interactions/job acquaintances	Care
Integrity vs. despair	Old age	All people	Wisdom

proper care, love, and affection, they develop a sense of trust. If these basic needs are not met, they become suspicious, fearful, and mistrusting of their surroundings.

During *autonomy versus doubt* (ages 1 to 3), developing motor and mental abilities gives the child the opportunity to experience independence. If this growing urge to explore the world is encouraged, children grow more confident in themselves and more autonomous in general. However, if their developing independence is met with parental disapproval or discouragement, children may question their own abilities and harbor doubts about their own adequacy.

During the third stage, children experience the psychosocial crisis known as *initiative versus guilt* (ages 3 to 5). Increasingly refined developmental capacities prompt the child to self-initiate environmental exploration and discovery. Parental reinforcement will encourage such initiative and promote purpose- and goal-directiveness. Parental restrictiveness, on the other hand, is likely to promote guilt whenever children seek to discover the world on their own.

Industry versus inferiority (ages 6 to 11) is characterized by the child's desire to manipulate objects and learn how things work. Such an industrious attitude typically leads to a sense of order, a system of rules, and an important understanding about the nature of one's surroundings. Inferiority may result, however, if adults perceive such behavior as silly, mischievous, or troublesome.

The fifth psychosocial crisis, perhaps Erikson's most famous concept, is *identity versus role confusion* (adolescence). The task is to develop an integrated sense of self, one that is personally acceptable and, it is hoped, distinct from others. Failure to nurture an accurate sense of personal identity may lead to the dilemma of role confusion. This frequently leads to feelings of inadequacy, isolation, and indecisiveness.

The task of *intimacy versus isolation* (young adulthood), stage six, is to develop close and meaningful relationships with others. Having attained a sense of personal identity in the previous stage, individuals are now able to share themselves with others on a moral, emotional, and sexual level. For many, intimacy means marriage; for others, it implies the establishment of warm and nurturant friendships (not that the former cannot encompass the latter). Those

EPIGENETIC PRINCIPLE

How would you compare and contrast the epigenetic schemes proposed by Erikson and Freud? Do you agree or disagree with each proposed set of stages? Why or why not?

unable or unwilling to share themselves with others suffer a sense of loneliness or isolation.

Erikson's seventh stage is called *generativity versus self-absorption* (middle adulthood). The positive pole of this stage, generativity, means that adults are willing to look beyond themselves and to express concern about the future of the world in general. A caring attitude, for example, is directed toward the betterment of society and future generations. The self-absorbed person tends to be preoccupied with personal well-being and material gain.

The final stage is *integrity versus despair* (late adulthood). Those persons nurturing a sense of integrity have typically resolved previous psychosocial crises and are able to look back at their lives with dignity, satisfaction, and personal fulfillment. The unsuccessful resolution of previous crises is likely to produce a sense of despair. For these individuals, past lives are usually viewed as a series of disappointments, failures, and misfortunes.

Other Psychodynamic Theories

ROBERT PECK'S THEORY Another discontinuous theory of personality development has been developed by Robert Peck (1968). Peck provides an extension to the personality development theory proposed by Erikson. He chooses to elaborate on psychological adjustments characterizing middle and late adulthood. Similar to Erikson's theory, Peck proposes a series of crises needing to be addressed by the aging adult. The following is a summary of these adjustments (we present full coverage within appropriate chapters of the text):

PSYCHOLOGICAL ADJUSTMENTS OF MIDDLE ADULTHOOD

• *Valuing Wisdom Versus Valuing Physical Powers.* Individuals who age most successfully are those who "invert" their previous hierarchy of values, giving mental ability a higher position than physical prowess, both as their standard for self-evaluation and as their primary means of problem solving.

• *Socializing Versus Sexualizing in Human Relationships.* Aging may motivate men and women to value one another as individual personalities rather than primarily as sex objects. The sexual element may become decreasingly significant as interpersonal living takes on new dimensions of empathy, understanding, and emotional compassion.

• *Cathectic Flexibility Versus Cathectic Impoverishment.* Cathectic flexibility, the ability to be emotionally flexible, is crucial in middle age because of such psychologically critical developments as loss of parents or the departure of children from the home. Adapting positively to such changes by finding new objects of emotional focus is important at this time.

• *Mental Flexibility Versus Mental Rigidity.* The key challenge here is remaining flexible in one's opinions and actions, as well as being receptive to new ideas. The flexible adult will strive to master life's experiences, to achieve some degree of detached perspective on them, and to use them as provisional guides to the solution of new problems.

PSYCHOLOGICAL ADJUSTMENTS OF LATE ADULTHOOD

• *Ego Differentiation Versus Work-Role Preoccupation.* Personal worth must be reappraised and redefined after retirement so the adult can take satisfaction in activities that extend beyond the work role. Establishing a variety of valued self-attributes so any one of several alternatives can be pursued with satisfaction is an important challenge.

- *Body Transcendence Versus Body Preoccupation.* The retirement years tend to bring a decline in resistance to illness and recuperative powers, along with an increase in bodily aches and pains. Learning to adjust to these physical changes while maintaining life satisfaction and fulfillment are important concerns.

- *Ego Transcendence Versus Ego Preoccupation.* Accepting the inevitability of one's death is a crucial adjustment of later life. Such a task requires a deep, active effort to make life more meaningful and satisfying, including for those who will go on living after one dies. In so doing, individuals are experiencing a vital, gratifying absorption in the future, and they are doing all they can to make it a good world for those around them.

JANE LOEVINGER'S THEORY Stimulated by the work of Freud and Erikson, Jane Loevinger (1966, 1976, 1979; Loevinger, Wessler, & Redmore, 1970a, 1970b; Loevinger et al., 1985) provides a unique discontinuous theory. The thrust of her theory is on the developing ego and how it integrates and balances the various personality components. Loevinger feels the process by which individuals come to recognize themselves as unique beings and to sustain a stable self-concept is a fairly long one. Ego development is apparent throughout seven stages, each of which reveals a qualitatively different level of functioning. The following is a brief overview of these stages:

- *Presocial* (infancy). During this early stage of ego development, infants have no concept of the needs and desires of those around them. They are interested in their own ego fulfillment and gratification.

- *Impulsive* (early childhood). This stage represents a continuation of the presocial phase. Although infants and toddlers are becoming more aware of the needs of others, they are most concerned with their own basic motivations and drives.

- *Self-protective* (early school years). Here, children seek to gain control and dominance over others. Rules are obeyed to avoid distress, and the individual begins to use coping mechanisms in an effort to reduce frustration and failure.

- *Conformist* (late childhood and early adolescence). The sense of self is judged by external characteristics, such as physical appearance, possessions, and reputations. As the stage title implies, similarity between oneself and others becomes important at this time.

- *Conscientious* (late adolescence). Here, individuals discover the personal relevancy of societal standards of behavior. Emerging ideals also become evident at this age, largely as the result of a developing sense of inner self. This subjective inner ego state is also the basis for self-criticism.

- *Autonomy* (adulthood). The ego is autonomous when it can tolerate, rather than condemn, opposing opinions and viewpoints. During this stage, respect is accorded to others who hold differing convictions and principles.

- *Integration* (adulthood). This stage also encompasses the adult years and represents a full acceptance of who one is in terms of ego development. This includes one's

GENDER SIMILARITIES AND DIFFERENCES

Utilizing the theories contained in this chapter, can you think of ways that gender similarities and differences might influence the course of psychological development? Do you think certain theories account for gender similarities or differences better than others? Why or why not?

strengths as well as weaknesses, and one's successes as well as failures. Conflicting internal demands and the demands of others are now reconciled and tolerated. Integration in this sense implies peace with oneself, recognition of one's total being, and an appreciation of the individuality of others.

A Critique of Psychodynamic Theories   From this brief account of psychodynamic theories, we can see that both Freud and Erikson are interactionists. First, they describe basic biological (heredity) drives. As indicated, both theories have an epigenetic basis; they believe development is predetermined by genetic principles and proceeds along a discontinuous or age-stage pathway. They both recognize the importance of the environment. For example, Freud states that psychosexual fixations occur when the biological needs are not met through interaction with the environment. (How does Mom or Dad toilet train the child?) Erikson expresses environmental importance when he discusses the organism's transition through a psychosocial crisis. (Does the infant receive enough care and trust from the environment?)

American psychology has placed heavy emphasis on empirical evidence to support a theory. Unfortunately, psychoanalytic theory does not lend itself to such experimentation and thus is not as popular as it once was. Objective data is rarely found; therefore, much support of this theory is subjective. Although it is practically impossible to test and measure the unconscious forces that Freud describes, many still recognize their presence. Freud is also criticized for overemphasizing childhood sexuality and the correct way to interpret dreams.

On the positive side, his theory has influenced thinking and research in developmental psychology. For example, his concepts of identification and sex typing (discussed in more detail later) have produced much research activity.

Erikson's theory has increased the credibility of psychoanalysis. By extending the psychosexual with the psychosocial and adding the cultural to the biological, as well as ego strengths and identities to ego defense systems, he has broadened the psychoanalytic framework. His ideas appear to be much more acceptable than those of many of his cohorts who also wrote in the psychoanalytic tradition. Although Erikson's writings are interesting, he has been criticized for his loose connections of case studies and conclusions. His theory, like Freud's, is difficult to support with empirical evidence. Similar criticism can also be leveled toward the theories of Peck and Loevinger. Consequently, such theories make it difficult to accrue supportive empirical evidence.

▬ Cognitive Theories

Cognitive theories of lifespan development represent another category of psychological theories. These theories emphasize a wide range of thought processes and embrace such elements as perceiving, thinking, and understanding. Some, such as Piaget's cognitive-developmental theory, explore the progressive changes that take place in thinking abilities over time. Others, such as information processing theory, seek to understand the mental dynamics used to acquire, store, and retrieve information.

Piaget's Cognitive-Developmental Theory   Our understanding of the cognitive developments in childhood has been considerably enhanced through the efforts of Swiss psychologist Jean Piaget. His theory of conceptual development

Jean Piaget (1896–1980) was born in Neuchâtel, Switzerland, and became a leading force in the field of cognitive development.

is unique and one of the most comprehensive to date. Although his work was not widely recognized by the psychology community in the United States until the 1950s, Piaget has been regarded as a leading authority in the field of **cognitive-developmental theory** (Piaget, 1926, 1928, 1929, 1932, 1952, 1954, 1962, 1965, 1969, 1972).

Although often referred to as a child psychologist, Piaget characterized himself as a *genetic epistemologist* (*genetic* means beginning; *epistemology* is the study of knowledge). Piaget asked how knowledge develops in the human organism. To answer this question, he studied children and their mental processes. To Piaget, the term *cognition* was synonymous with intelligence, and he considered cognition to be a biological process, just as biologists consider digestion to be a biological process. We might say that Piaget studied the "biology of thinking."

For example, Piaget had observed that different age levels yield different levels of comprehension and reasoning. A 3-year-old, for example, has rudimentary reasoning skills but can solve problems that escaped him or her at 2. Similarly, a 4-year-old may be able to deal with some concepts unsolved a year before yet be unable to keep pace with the thinking of a 7-year-old. All of this led Piaget to believe intellectual development proceeds in an orderly sequence characterized by specific growth stages. He postulated that these growth stages enable the child to develop certain concepts necessary for intellectual maturity. Consequently, Piaget believed conceptual development to be a building process, a series of qualitative intellectual advancements that can transport the child from a world of fantasy into a world of reality.

His explanation of this systematic process, the most important theme in all his writings, has provided fields such as psychology and education with a detailed and methodical analysis of cognitive development. In it, people, especially children, are viewed as developing organisms acquiring conceptual awareness as they pass through five orderly and progressive stages. At the base of these stages is an explanation of how people interpret and store the vast amounts of stimuli to which they are exposed. These concepts now require our examination.

ELEMENTS OF COGNITIVE ACTIVITY The Piagetian design for mental growth hinges on two important principles: organization and adaptation. *Organization* is the ability to order and classify in the mind new experiences, termed **schemata;** it is a fundamental and innate process in all children. As the infant is exposed to new stimuli, the mind is able to construct a mental organization that is capable of categorizing and integrating these schematic elements into regular systems. Sensory stimuli—objects and events—are just two examples of schematic organization. *Adaptation* cannot take place unless there is a schema. Successful adaptation will give the individual a meaningful understanding of the surrounding environment. Adaptation depends on the mental processes of *assimilation* and a*ccommodation.*

Assimilation is the more primitive of the two mental processes. Through assimilation, the child will perceive and interpret new information in terms of existing knowledge and understanding. Put another way, children attempt to explain new phenomena by referring to their current frame of reference. Assimilation is conservative in that its primary function is to make the unfamiliar, familiar, to reduce the new to the old. A child who has been exposed only to cars, for example, may call a truck or a bus a car, simply because this is the only vehicle name stored in the child's existing mental organization. Along the same lines, a young child, after learning what a horse is, may see a cow and also call it a horse. In learning theory, this is called *stimulus generalization:* responding to similar stimuli as though they were the same.

Accommodation, on the other hand, is the more advanced form of adaptation. Accommodation refers to the restructuring of mental organization in order that new information may be included. Whereas the process of assimilation molds the object or event to fit within the person's existing frame of reference, accommodation changes the mental structure so new experiences may be added. Thus if an incident takes place that does not correspond with an existing mental framework, individuals may revise their way of thinking in order to interpret that event. The child who effectively used accommodation skills in the previous example will develop a new mental structure to categorize a truck after it is realized that trucks cannot be put in the category of cars, or that cows belong in a category separate from horses. In learning theory, this is called *stimulus discrimination,* defined as the ability to distinguish between different but similar stimuli.

The development of thinking, therefore, relies on changes made in the mental structure of the child. The balance between assimilation and accommodation, called **equilibration,** is the key; the ability to change old ways of thinking in order to solve new problems is the true yardstick for measuring intellectual growth.

TABLE 2-4
Piaget's Stages of Cognitive Development

Stage	Age	Significant Cognitive Developments
Sensorimotor development	0–2	Engagement in primitive reflex activity. Gradual increase in sensory and motor awareness. Little distinction made between the self and the environment, although meaningful interactions with surroundings and the establishment of object permanence characterize later phases of this stage.
Preoperational thought	2–7	Increase in language and concept development. Child is largely egocentric. Animism is prevalent in thinking. Employment of mental images to represent the world is increasingly evident by the end of this stage; increased perceptual sensitivity, although discrimination is based on obvious physical appearances. Failure to understand the law of conservation. In general, thinking is intuitive in nature and frequently impulsive.
Concrete operations	7–11	Can understand the law of conservation and reverse mental operations. Objects can be classified and ordered in a series along a dimension (such as size), and relational concepts (*A* is larger than *B*) are understood. Abstract problems remain elusive.
Formal operations	11–15	Abstract thought and scientific reasoning emerge. Problems are approached with advanced logic and reason. Individuals follow logical propositions and reason by hypothesis.

STAGES OF COGNITIVE DEVELOPMENT Piaget has proposed four stages of cognitive development (see Table 2-4). The first stage is labeled *sensorimotor development* (ages 0 to 2). During this early phase of development, the infant exercises rudimentary sensory and motor awareness and functions almost exclusively by means of reflexive responses. In the beginning, limited cognitive activity takes place and little distinction is made between the self and the environment. By the end of the first year, however, meaningful interactions with one's surroundings have begun. For example, by the end of this period the infant may shake or strike a crib mobile if its movement proves to be interesting; and when objects disappear from sight, the infant knows that, instead of disappearing totally "out of sight, out of mind," they remain permanent in reality.

During *preoperational thought* (ages 2 to 7), the child demonstrates an increase in language abilities, and concepts become more elaborate. Children are largely *egocentric* (self-centered) and view the world from their own perspective. Thinking tends to be impulsive, and the discrimination of objects tends to be on the basis of obvious physical appearances. By the end of this stage, the world is increasingly represented by the use of mental images.

By the time *concrete operations* (ages 7 to 11) is reached, individuals grasp the concept of conservation. They now understand that an object can conserve its amount, weight, or mass when it is poured into a different-sized container, placed into a different position, or molded into a different shape. The ability to consider viewpoints of others, classify objects and order them in a series along a dimension (such as size), and understand relational concepts (*A* is larger than *B*) is evident. However, a significant limitation of this stage is the child's inability to solve problems of an abstract nature.

Formal operations (ages 11 to 15), sometimes called *formal thought*, is the final stage of Piaget's theory. Abstract thinking is now possible and scientific

ACTIVE AND REACTIVE MODELS OF DEVELOPMENT

Why do you think Piaget's theory reflects an active model of development? How many examples can you think of that capture an individual's active involvement with the environment?

TABLE 2-5
Major Epigenetic Theories: A Summarization Through Adolescence

Freud Psychosexual	*Erikson* Psychosocial	*Piaget* Cognitive-developmental
Oral Stage (0–1½) The oral zone is the first erogenous zone to reach neural maturation. Thus the infant's primary environmental interaction is around the mouth.	**Oral-Sensory Stage (0–1)** Oral and sensory maturation interact with environment. Crisis of trust vs. mistrust.	**Sensorimotor Stage (0–2)** Maturation of sense organs and the sensory and motor areas of the brain precede cognitive functioning.
Anal Stage (1½–3) Anal zone neural maturation precedes awareness of these body functions (bowel and bladder training).	**Muscular-Anal (1–3)** Neurologic maturation precedes environmental interaction and resolution of autonomy vs. doubt crisis.	**Preoperational Stage (2–7)** Areas of the brain (e.g., hearing and speech centers) must mature prior to basic thought processes involving vocabulary, mental imagery, intuitive thought, etc.
Phallic Stage (3–5) Neural maturation surrounding sex organs brings awareness of sex identity. Curiosity about self and others.	**Locomotor-Genital (3–5)** Maturation of neurons surrounding sex organs and continued neuromuscular development interact with environment when initiative vs. guilt crisis must be resolved.	
Latency Period (6–11) No major biological changes occurring. Sensorimotor development continues bringing pleasure from knowledge, skills, interpersonal relationships.	**Latency Stage (6–11)** Essentially the same as Freud's description of the latency period with addition of industry vs. inferiority crisis.	**Concrete Operations (7–11)** Continued maturation of cerebral cortex brings cognitive skills to new level. Also allows awareness of other people's viewpoints and improvements in interpersonal relations.
Genital Stage (Adolescence) Biological upheaval (hormonal and neurological) incorporates first three stages. Pleasure from heterosexual relations.	**Puberty & Adolescence** Biological maturation processes unfolding while psychological crisis of identity vs. role confusion peaks and needs to be resolved.	**Formal Operations (11–15)** Brain maturity allows for scientific reasoning, logic, abstract thinking.

problem-solving strategies emerge. When a problem is approached, a hypothesis is drawn and the individual develops several potential solutions. Advanced logic and reason accompany formal operations. Such thinking abilities herald the relinquishment of childhood mental operations and the emergence of mature adult thought.

In summation, we can see that Piaget, like Freud, has a biological background that shows up in his explanation of cognitive development. He places heavy emphasis on genetics with his age-stage theory based on epigenesis (see Table 2-5 for a comparison of Piaget's, Freud's, and Erikson's epigenetic theories). He is an interactionist, however, in that he accents how the environment provides the food for thought. And his theory places humans in an active (versus passive) role of learning.

Information Processing Theory   Another explanation of cognition is **information processing theory,** which explains how people acquire, store, and retrieve information. In many respects, parallels can be drawn to information processing theory and how a computer stores, analyzes, and produces data. Of course, the human mind is more complex than a computer, especially within thinking processes such as creative and reflective thought. However, many feel (e.g., Klahr, 1989; Kuhn, 1989; Kuhn, Amsel, & O'Loughlin, 1988) that a greater understanding of certain mental processes can be gained by analyzing cognition along computer model lines.

Information processing theory explains cognition by proposing a step-by-step sequence of events. First, we must acknowledge that a wide array of stimuli bombard the sense organs. However, we are selective in what information we process, as well as what information we filter out. Indeed, perceptual processes may interfere with reality (for example, several eye witnesses may "see" the same incident, but each may interpret it differently). This information remains in the sense organ (sensory register) for a fraction of a second prior to its being forwarded to the brain for further processing.

On reaching the brain, there appear to be at least two additional types of memory. The first is referred to as short-term or working memory. It has a lifespan of about 20 seconds unless the information is renewed through rehearsal. Material that is not rehearsed is generally forgotten, but rehearsed material is forwarded to our long-term memory storage system from where it can be retrieved pretty much at will. (For more information on memory dynamics, see Chapters 5, 10, and 11.) It is through this sequence that information processing theory exposes the mental operations necessary to receive, perceive, remember, and utilize information.

A Critique of Cognitive Theories   Piaget spent his lifetime modifying and expanding his theory, which was instrumental in changing how psychologists view lifespan development. Once exposed to Piaget's ideas, no one can view cognitive development in quite the same way. Whereas Freud emphasized emotional development, Piaget gave cognition the central role in development and gave developmental psychology a whole new perspective.

Piaget's theory integrates many facts, some of which might first appear unrelated. However, it is generally acknowledged (e.g., Thomas, 1992) that the cognitive-developmental model is internally consistent, coherent, and tightly interrelated. It also has stimulated and continues to stimulate a vast amount of research that has generally been supportive of his ideas (Beilin, 1989). Piaget's ideas have also stimulated research in other areas, most notably the moral development theory of Lawrence Kohlberg (see Chapter 7). All this empirical evidence has made his theory more viable, especially because it addresses greater areas of behavior (e.g., learning, education, moral and social development) than probably any other discontinuous theory. Another strength of his theory is that it is open to alternatives, a fact evidenced by a substantial amount of neo-Piagetian literature (Case, 1991a).

As far as criticisms are concerned, much of Piaget's research was done on a very small sample of the population—sometimes only on his own three children. For this he has been criticized extensively, even though replication studies have supported his ideas on the concepts but not always on the ages when children reach a given stage. Also, he has been criticized for his conception of stages as rather invariant structures, along with his limited explanations of deviations from these stages. His theory has also been criticized because he never attempted to show its applicability to everyday life. He has also been faulted for the technique he used when asking questions, an interviewing style that is difficult to duplicate with each and every subject due to individual differences of examiner and examinee (Gelman, 1991; Spelke, 1991).

Information processing theory has its proponents and critics as well. Regarding the former, some feel it is useful in describing mental processes and represents a viable alternative to the discontinuous model of cognition offered by Piaget. Moreover, it has succeeded in stimulating considerable research to date. Critics argue that a computer model of human cognition just doesn't provide the depth or detail necessary to explain how a knowledge base is acquired. Along these lines, it is felt the information processing model makes little attempt to align itself with what is known about the physiology of the brain or perceptual mechanisms. Information processing theory also does not take culture or any other contextual influences into account.

■ Learning Theories

Learning theories of lifespan development emphasize that behavior is shaped by the interaction of the organism with the environment. Probably more attention has been paid to learning theory than to any other psychological theory. Psychologists run rats through mazes, put pigeons and rats in Skinner boxes, and devise numerous experiments to measure human learning. Although we have learned many facts as a result, there are still many unanswered questions about what actually constitutes learning.

Some psychologists, especially learning theorists, feel very uncomfortable with theories of behavior that propose such abstract concepts as mental elements (e.g., ego, conscience, and soul), or mental functions (e.g., assimilation, repression, and cognition). Piaget, Freud, Erikson, and others who study mental life often present a somewhat untestable theory. Learning theorists often have misgivings over such mentalistic theory and have attempted to be more objective and scientifically oriented. Stated bluntly, their credo is, "If you can't measure it, it doesn't exist." As we discover next, the first theorist to proclaim this position was John Broadus Watson.

Behaviorism   The school of thought known as **behaviorism** was launched by John Broadus Watson. This theory maintains that environmental interaction is responsible for various types of behaviors: how to get along with others, pass tests, or cope with a variety of everyday situations, to name a few. The behavioristic school of thought was advanced in the 1950s by B. F. Skinner, who concentrated on exploring the nature of *reinforcement* and reinforcing stimuli. Skinner devised elaborate problem boxes for his experimental animals, popularly known today as Skinner boxes. The boxes were designed in such a way that a reward (food pellet) would be dispensed if a lever or button was correctly manipulated by the subject. Skinner found that through trial-and-error responses, animals could indeed learn to operate the proper mechanisms in the box to receive a reward. His theory, explaining the nature of this type of learning, has come to be known by several titles, including operant conditioning, instrumental learning, and Skinnerian conditioning (Skinner, 1951, 1953, 1957, 1961).

B. F. Skinner (1904–1990) was born in Susquehanna, Pennsylvania, and brought great advances to the theory of behaviorism.

The emphasis in operant conditioning is on **positive reinforcement:** A response followed by a reward is more likely to be repeated whenever the organism finds itself in a situation similar to the one in which reinforcement occurred. Skinner reasoned that organisms are not normally under continuously paired stimuli from the environment. He postulated that although an organism learns to some degree through trial-and-error responses, true learning depends primarily on which behaviors are accompanied by reinforcement. Skinner stated that most behaviors are responses emitted by an organism when it has a choice of various responses. His view is that most responses are not associated with any stimuli; they simply occur. These instrumentally conditioned responses are called **operants** because they operate on the environment. Skinner believed the nature of these consequences to be critical, as they determined the future behavior of the organism. Furthermore, Skinner's definition of learning is strictly operational; if the behavior cannot be measured, then no learning is assumed to have taken place. Furthermore, no assumptions can be made regarding internal cognitive states because they are considered immeasurable.

REINFORCEMENT IN OPERANT CONDITIONING Although Skinner differentiates reinforcement into various types, remember his contention that learning is measured by overt muscular responses to a stimulus or stimulus situation. Skinner's concern is not with the growth and development of an individual nor with inherited potential; it is strictly with types of reinforcers and their effects on behavior.

Let's examine Skinner's concept of positive and negative reinforcement. As indicated, positive reinforcement is a stimulus that, when presented to a subject, strengthens and increases the likelihood of a desired response. For example, a gold star attached to the homework paper of a young child may increase

THEORETICAL ISSUES

In what ways have your past or present teachers used positive or negative reinforcement? How did such techniques affect your behavior? Were some more effective than others? Why?

the probability of acceptable schoolwork in the future. In this example, the gold star is a type of stimulus a child might seek or approach. In another example, a worker is awarded a new title or given a meritorious pay raise that may increase the probability of continued excellence in the workplace. In this example, the title or money is a stimulus the adult might seek out or approach. (On the other hand there are stimuli or situations we try to avoid or escape from, such as pain, being yelled at, or being hurt in some way. These stimuli are called aversive or noxious.)

Negative reinforcement occurs when we behave in a way that reduces or eliminates an aversive stimulus. For example, it is 10 a.m. and the teacher announces to her third-grade students that it is time for arithmetic. As the students get out their books, Johnny, who hates arithmetic, begins to misbehave. The teacher tells him to stand in the corner; Johnny is now pleased because he got out of doing math. Note that the teacher believes she is punishing Johnny but, in actuality, she has negatively reinforced his behavior, thus increasing the chance he will misbehave again in order to avoid arithmetic. In another example, a supervisor announces there will be a training session for all employees. Joe makes some sarcastic remark and the boss tells him he is no longer welcome to attend. Joe is pleased because he has found these meetings to be a waste of time. Again, note that the supervisor believes she is punishing Joe, but, in actuality, she has negatively reinforced his behavior, thus increasing the chances he will be sarcastic again in order to avoid attending future training sessions.

Negative reinforcement is not the same as punishment. Punishment usually follows an unacceptable response in a desire to eliminate its future probability: reprimanding a worker for unacceptable job performance, for example. Punishment may decrease the probability of a behavior reoccurring. Negative reinforcement seeks to increase the probability of a desired response by removing annoying, aversive, or noxious stimuli. Thus the Skinnerian approach defines a **reinforcer** as anything that strengthens the probability of a response. The definition of a reinforcement depends entirely on its effects on future behavior. There is no assumption of need reduction.

Primary and secondary reinforcers are two additional types of reinforcement. **Primary reinforcement** represents a satisfying stimulus related to primary unlearned drives (food and drink are primary reinforcers related to the hunger and thirst drives). **Secondary reinforcement** is a stimulus that was previously neutral but, when paired frequently over successive trials with a primary reinforcer, gains reinforcing qualities of its own. For example, if a light flashes on in a Skinner box every time the bar is pressed, the light soon acquires reinforcement properties because it is paired with the resulting reward. Eventually, the organism will press the bar simply to see the light turn on. For adults, praise, approval, attention, or money all represent secondary reinforcement.

PRACTICAL APPLICATIONS OF REINFORCEMENT Positive reinforcement, negative reinforcement, and punishment are naturally occurring events in the lives of all of us and, as such, play vital roles in determining behavioral patterns. In fact, some behaviorists believe they are the sole determinants of whether a stimulus-response (S-R) unit will become part of a person's repertoire of behavior. S-R learning refers to any solitary behavioral unit in which a stimulus is followed by one response. Most behaviors, however, are composed of a series of complex actions or a string of S-Rs. A number of S-Rs placed in a series is called a **chain.** Chains may consist of a series of nonverbal behaviors, such as getting in a car, closing the door, fastening the seat belt, putting the key in the ignition, and placing the foot on the accelerator. Chains may also consist of verbal associations, such as reciting the Pledge of Allegiance or remembering the lyrics to your alma mater song, or recalling a fraternity or sorority pledge. Each link in a chain is learned from external cues and then placed in an appropriate position to produce the desired behavior. Chains represent a natural extension of S-R conditioning.

Shaping behavior, an outgrowth of operant conditioning, is the establishment of desirable chains by molding or developing a series of S-R situations into a desired behavioral pattern. A shaping technique called *successive approximations* refers to the step-by-step series of reinforcements that eventually produce a desired S-R behavior. Suppose we wish to develop a previously nonexistent behavior. Obviously, if the desired behavior is not present, it cannot be reinforced. Therefore, we reinforce behaviors that approximate the desired behavior until it becomes more frequent. Thus shaping and successive approximations represent the dispensing of reinforcement in order to refine a response gradually and to produce a chain or behavioral pattern similar to the one desired.

Punishment, as we learned earlier, is incorrectly and frequently used interchangeably with such terms as *discipline, negative reinforcement,* and *nonreward* situations. Punishment or aversive conditioning does not imply negative reinforcement, and the two can be distinguished by their effect on behavior. As we noted earlier, both positive and negative reinforcement increase the probability of a given response being repeated. However, it is highly questionable whether punishment can completely extinguish an organism's response. It appears more likely that punishment brings about temporary suppression of a given behavioral response. When the threat of punishment is removed, the suppressed behavior may reappear. In fact, punishment may produce increased resistance to extinction; instead of eliminating a response, punishment may lead to its greater persistence. As an attempt to extinguish behavior, punishment is used either by applying an unpleasant stimulus (verbal abuse) or by withholding a pleasant stimulus (not offering overtime work) (see Figure 2-2).

For obvious ethical reasons, little experimental research is available on punishment and its effects, but it is generally recognized that punishment may have deleterious effects on the organism especially in the realm of emotional development. Upon being punished by parents, bosses, or society, people may exhibit an increase in arousal level usually in the form of aggression. They often become less aware of environmental happenings as they withdraw from the threatening situation. This response limits the person's ability to attend to and process information. Moreover, negative emotions may become generalized and be extended from one situation to others.

Behaviorism is a continuous theory of development as opposed to the age-stage or discontinuous theories proposed by Freud, Erikson, and Piaget. Developmental changes do not depend on biological maturation but on reinforcement

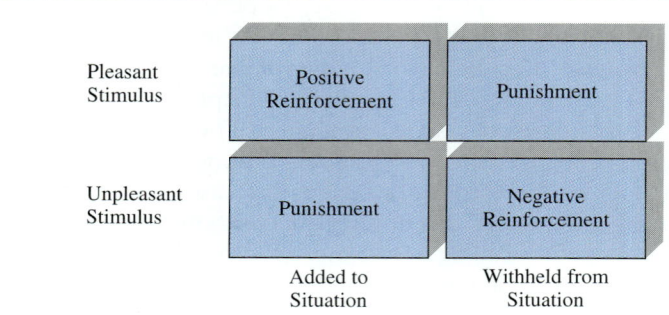

FIGURE 2-2
Punishment and Reinforcement Variables.

Shown are conditions that produce categories of operant conditioning. For example, a pleasant stimulus added to a situation results in positive reinforcement. A pleasant stimulus removed from a situation is considered punishment.

from the environment. As such it emphasizes the environmental position not the hereditary stance. However, we could still describe behaviorism as an interactionist position because the biological organism does interact with the environment. Epigenesis has no role in this theory, and behaviorism reflects a passive, rather than an active model of development.

Social Learning Theory   **Social learning theory** suggests that behavior is influenced by observing and copying others. Proponents of this theory maintain that most learning theories are based on structured laboratory situations, which often have few similarities to real-world learning. Much of human behavior involves the simultaneous interaction of people and multiple stimuli. Experiments involving puzzle boxes, mazes, and operant chambers may offer learning principles, but they hardly explain a child's table manners or why one child shares toys with another. In short, most laboratory experiments do not explain many aspects of social behavior.

Social learning researchers devote their time not to laboratory research but to direct observation of children's behavior in both structured and unstructured situations. Albert Bandura (1962, 1977, 1986, 1989, 1991), one such researcher, casts serious doubts on Skinner's theories of successive approximations as a means of explaining all behavior. Bandura does not dispute that shaping can occur, but he asserts this is only a partial explanation of behavior and that other aspects of learning are probably more important, for example, learning by imitating the cues emitted by others.

OBSERVATIONAL LEARNING Bandura states that verbal cues generally accompany other techniques of shaping and can serve as symbolic models that can be imitated. He believes that *imitation, modeling,* and **observational learning** account for many of a child's behavioral patterns. It has been questioned, however, whether imitation is truly a different form of learning. Some theorists (e.g., Miller & Dollard, 1941; Skinner, 1953) have maintained that reinforcement of specific imitative responses leads to a generalized tendency toward imitation. In this fashion, they believe, many behaviors can be imitated without being reinforced. According to this view, imitation is a special case of instrumental conditioning. Bandura, on the other hand, argues that imitation is a separate and distinct form of learning, requiring unique principles.

Albert Bandura (1925–   ) was born in Mundare, Canada, and defined the theory of social learning (also called social cognitive theory).

In an interesting series of studies, Bandura and associates have shown how and under what conditions observational learning occurs. In one study, 5-year-old children were brought individually into a room in which an adult *model* was playing with Tinker Toys. Suddenly, the model turned to a large inflated Bobo doll and began to assault it in novel ways. The doll was knocked over, sat on, and punched in the nose. The adult model then let the Bobo doll up, only to smash it repeatedly on the head with a wooden mallet. Finally, the doll was thrown in the air and kicked by the adult, who all the while muttered, "Sock him in the nose, hit him down, throw him in the air, kick him, pow!"

Shortly after being exposed to this situation, the children were deliberately made angry by having attractive toys withheld from them. This part of the experiment was intended to enhance the possibility of an aggressive behavioral display. A second group of children was angered in the same fashion but was not exposed to the model.

When the experimenter left the room, toys were provided for each child to play with alone. Meanwhile, a group of hidden "judges" rated the resulting behavior. It was found that the children who had observed the model's behavior became aggressive, exhibiting behavior almost identical to that displayed by the model. They too punched the doll in the nose and walloped it with a mallet and yelled "Kick him, pow!" and other phrases used by the model. This experiment emphasizes that children not only learn certain behavioral patterns through observation but also learn them *without any external reinforcement*. In another phase of this experiment, under the same experimental conditions, the children saw similar acts of aggression committed in an animated cartoon film. The results were very similar (Bandura & Walters, 1963).

Having established that learning can occur without reinforcement, Bandura designed a similar experiment to determine the exact roles of reward and punishment in influencing behavior. In this study, three groups of children viewed three different films of a model yelling at and punching the Bobo doll. However, one movie showed the model being punished for the aggressive behavior, the

THEORETICAL ISSUES

Utilize the principles of social learning theory and think of at least two role models in your own life. What kinds of behaviors did you choose to imitate and why? Can you offer other examples of observational learning from your own personal experiences?

second film ended with the model being praised, and the third film ended with neither praise nor punishment being given to the model.

After the films were viewed, each child was left alone in a room. Children from the group seeing the model being praised for aggressive behavior were more apt to behave aggressively than either of the other groups. The least aggressive group was the one that saw the model being punished. However, in a later phase of the experiment, the children were told they would be *rewarded* if they did everything the model had done in the film. Differences between groups immediately vanished. Thus reinforcements administered to a model influence the performance, but not the acquisition, of initiative responses. However, Bandura's frequently contrived procedures make it difficult to determine the extent to which observational learning applies to the everyday lives of children (Bandura, 1962).

OTHER DIMENSIONS OF SOCIAL LEARNING THEORY Although Bandura and others have criticized behaviorism, Skinner did not modify his position. This has forced some dissatisfied behaviorists to move toward the social learning theory position, and they have been joined by some cognitive psychologists who wish to study dimensions of behavior other than cognition. Thus a revised social learning theory school of thought, or what some are calling **cognitive social learning theory,** has emerged.

This new school of thought emphasizes a number of general themes:

1. Human beings and environment continuously interact. In other words, we influence our environment as much as it influences us.
2. We can learn through observation without any immediate external reinforcement.
3. Learning and acquiring knowledge must be distinguished from performance. Reinforcement may not be essential in acquiring behavior; it is important in guiding and influencing our daily behaviors.
4. Our cognitive expectations and perceptions affect what we do, and our awareness of the consequences of a given behavior influences our choice of behavior.
5. We are active processors of information, not, as behaviorists might have us believe, mechanical persons. Because of our cognitive processes, we engage in self-regulation, evaluating and controlling our behavior.

As these themes illustrate, cognitive social learning theory encompasses not only the original school of thought but also cognitive theory, behaviorism, and ideas from humanistic theory (Mischel,1987; Mischel & Mischel, 1977).

Of the theories presented in this chapter, social learning theory is undergoing the most rapid changes. Initially it was a social personality theory (e.g., Miller & Dollard, 1941); then came observational learning (e.g., Bandura, 1962). These two forces gradually merged and expanded to become social learning theory. Today the movement is expanding even more as theorists recognize that behaviorism and cognitive development are valid and not mutually exclusive.

Originally, then, social learning theory was interactionist and, on the nature-nurture continuum, environmentalist. As the theory continues to develop and assimilate cognitive theory, we see the inclusion of epigenesis and some accompanying age-stage factors that have more of a hereditarian viewpoint.

A Critique of Learning Theories   For decades behaviorism was the dominant theory in the United States until Piaget's cognitive developmental framework gave us a new perspective on developmental change. Social learning theory also made inroads into the thinking of some behaviorists.

Behaviorism under the early guidance of Watson and the subsequent tutelage of Skinner has been experimentally vigorous. However, some researchers still have misperceptions about Skinner's theory (DeBell & Harless, 1992). No theory also has as much empirical support as behaviorism. Behaviorism has been inadequate from the viewpoint of many theoreticians because it reduces behavior to simple robotlike S-R units, which has led some to label this the mechanical man theory. Behaviorism has also been criticized for inadequately explaining the role of cognition.

Social learning theory focuses on the interplay of internal cognitive states and social behavior, which behaviorism does not. By itself (without incorporating cognitive theory), however, it does not adequately explain cognition. The observational learning dimension of social learning theory has some empirical support but lacks the experimental data and precise definitions that support behaviorism. Yet it is more scientific than either cognitive theory or psychoanalysis.

Social learning theory adds a significant dimension to behaviorism. First, by recognizing the role of cognition in learning and that learning can occur without reinforcement, Bandura's work has helped explain the more complex behaviors that puzzled critics of behaviorism.

Critics have said that social learning theory is no more than observational learning which, in turn, is no more than mimicking behavior. Bandura, however, believes people can symbolically construct complex new behaviors by watching or listening to others.

■■■ Ethological Theory

Ethological theory is the study of human and animal behavior in natural settings. Initially influenced by the writings of Charles Darwin, this school of thought seeks to understand behavior in an evolutionary context and places considerable emphasis on the role of instinct in development. Notable contributors to ethology, besides Darwin, include Konrad Lorenz, John Bowlby, and Robert Hinde.

Observing an organism in its natural setting enables ethologists to learn how a species adapts to its environment. Ethologists maintain that we cannot understand why birds build nests unless we see how this behavior protects them from natural predators. Similarly, we cannot hope to understand the development of children's social groups or status hierarchies unless we observe free-play situations and appreciate how and why such socialization behavior emerges. Psychologists who restrict themselves to the laboratory study of animals and humans may miss critical aspects of behavior. Thus ethologists engage in *naturalistic observation* (Crain, 1985).

Ethologists regard instincts as important aspects of behavior to study. Instincts have several dimensions. First, instincts are activated by a specific *external stimulus*. The rescuing behavior of a hen when her chicks are in danger is a reaction to the chicks' distress calls. Similarly, a young pheasant will rush for cover when it hears its parents' warning call, and a young jackdaw will follow its parents in the air only when they take off at a certain angle and speed. Such protective parental behaviors toward offspring, although differing in content, are not so different for the human species (Crain, 1985; Miller, 1989; Thomas, 1992).

Ethology and the Study of Critical Periods   Ethologists maintain that in some species possessing instincts, there is a *critical period*. As we learned in the last chapter, a critical period is a specific time in which an environmental event will have its greatest impact on the developing organism. According to Austrian zoologist Konrad Lorenz and others, strong bonds of attachment develop between the caretaker and the young during the critical period. Lorenz also suggests that imprinting is important for some species. **Imprinting** is an organism's rapid attachment to an object, usually its caretaker, and takes place shortly after birth. This type of behavior is readily observed among fowl, which attach themselves to and follow their mother just hours after birth.

Lorenz wanted to know if imprinting would occur if another stimulus were introduced during the critical period. To find out, he divided a number of Graylag goose eggs into two groups. One group was hatched by the mother; the other group was placed in an incubator. After the goslings in the first group were hatched, Lorenz observed that they immediately followed the mother wherever she went. However, the goslings hatched in the incubator never saw their mother and attached themselves to the first moving object they encountered, which happened to be Lorenz. Subsequently, the goslings followed Lorenz about each day; later in life, they even preferred his company to the company of other geese (Lorenz, 1965).

Other imprinting studies have revealed more dramatic findings. For example, mallard ducklings exposed to a wooden decoy (equipped with a concealed tape recorder emitting duck sounds) hours after birth followed it rather than their mother. Other objects, including footballs and tin cans, have been successfully implemented during the critical period.

Several factors are related to the critical period and imprinting. Of paramount importance is the fact that the critical period varies among species, and imprinting can occur only during this short period. For example, the critical period for rhesus monkeys seems to span the first 6 months of life, whereas in fowl, as we observed earlier, it is much shorter.

Another important dimension of imprinting is the amount of time spent in contact with the mother object. Longer periods of contact with the object during the critical period (and the earlier in the critical period the better) are more effective than shorter periods. Furthermore, such attributes as movement, color, and size seem to capture the attention of the organism more than objects without distinguishing characteristics.

It is difficult to assess if a critical period exists in humans, and no conclusive answers have been furnished. Humans are far more complex than other species and exhibit unique attachment behaviors. The issue is also complicated because human infants do not possess the necessary locomotor skills to physically follow their caretakers.

However, this does not mean the work of Lorenz and others has no application to the study of lifespan development. Neo-ethologists such as Robert Hinde (1983, 1989) envision a less rigid concept of the critical period, called a sensitive period, being applied to the study of lifespan development. A **sensitive**

THEORETICAL ISSUES

Do you agree there are sensitive periods in the lives of humans? If so, what kinds of developmental dynamics do you think would be affected during infancy, childhood, or even adolescence?

Konrad Lorenz (1903–   ) was born in Vienna, Austria, and made notable contributions to ethological theory with his interesting research with Grayleg goslings.

period is a highly significant time frame early in life that affects the course of developmental dynamics. The sensitive period is a broader and more flexible time frame for behavior to emerge, often over a period of months or even years. Children may have sensitive periods for such behaviors as attachment, language, and gender-role development, to name but a few areas (Bornstein, 1987; Bowlby, 1989; Rutter, 1990). Indeed, some neo-ethologists are now suggesting that personality and social relationships have an ethological base; that is, they have an evolutionary/genetic heritage (Hinde, 1989).

A Critique of Ethological Theory   Ethology places a heavy emphasis on the biology of behavior. As such, hereditary mechanisms, epigenetic schemes, and species-specific behavior are considered important within this theoretical scheme. As evolutionists, ethologists recognize that the organism's survival mechanisms are tied to the environment; ethology is also an interactionist theory because it recognizes the role of the environment.

In the past, ethology has limited itself to describing the behavior of birds, mammals, fish, and the like; only recently has it included the behavior of humans. Therefore, as a relatively newcomer to the field of lifespan development, it has not yet become a strong force. However, it has succeeded in showing that animal and human behavior are not as unrelated as we might initially expect.

As with any scientific endeavor, the description of the phenomena being studied comes before the explanation of the phenomena. Thus a weakness of ethology is its lack of an explanation for *why* certain behaviors occur. Perhaps, in time, neo-ethology will have a greater impact on the field. Meanwhile, neo-ethology broadens our perspective, gives us new ideas, and, as a theory should, raises more questions about the course of lifespan development.

▬ Humanistic Theory

Humanistic theory emphasizes the individual's uniqueness, personal potential, and inner drives. A person's self-concept and the maximization of human potential are paramount concerns of this school of thought. Humanistic psychology is often referred to as the *third force* in psychology because it challenges environmental learning theories and psychoanalytic stances. Humanists contend that individuals are not controlled exclusively by their external environment, nor is their behavior dominated by the irrational forces of the unconscious. Rather, people are free and creative and capable of growth and self-actualization.

Maslow's Theory of Self-Actualization   Like the other schools of thought we have discussed, humanistic psychology has been shaped by numerous contributors. Most notable are Abraham Maslow and Carl Rogers. Maslow developed a theory of motivation stating that individuals not only have the more obvious biological and psychological needs, but also are driven to attain uniqueness and the full development of their potentialities, capacities, and talents. This uniqueness and pinnacle of success is referred to by Maslow as **self-actualization.** To reach this pinnacle of self-fulfillment, the basic needs must first be satisfied (Maslow, 1968, 1970).

At the heart of Maslow's theory is the assumption that human needs (and consequently motivations) exist in a hierarchy, from the most basic to the most advanced. The further one progresses up this motivational pyramid, the more distinctly human one becomes. Higher motives will develop only when the more basic ones have been satisfied.

As Figure 2-3 shows, the first set of needs in the hierarchy are *physiological* in nature, embracing adequate nourishment, rest, and the like. At the second

Abraham Maslow (1908–1970) was born in Brooklyn, New York, and developed humanistic theory.

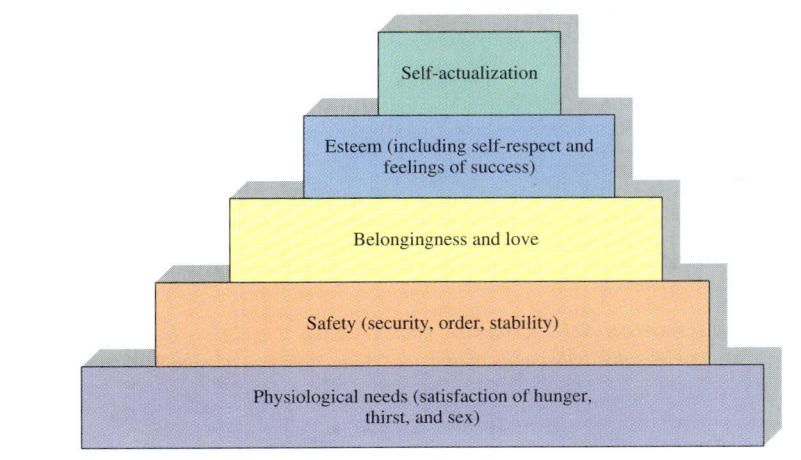

FIGURE 2-3
Maslow's Hierarchy of Needs.

According to Maslow, human needs and motivations exist in a hierarchical fashion, with self-actualization representing the peak or zenith. Self-actualization represents the harmonious integration of the personality and enables individuals to make full use of their potential.

level are *safety* needs, which motivate the person to achieve a sense of security. Next is the need for *belongingness and love*. Belongingness may be defined as the need to be part of a group and to experience sharing. *Esteem* is the fourth level of the hierarchic pyramid. By esteem, Maslow means that individuals must receive feedback from others (in the form of respect and assurance) in order to realize they are worthwhile and competent. The fifth need, *self-actualization,* means fulfilling one's individual nature in all its aspects. To reach the fulfillment of one's potential, all previous needs have to be met adequately. An essential component of self-actualization is freedom from cultural and self-imposed restraints.

The quest for self-actualization begins early in life. According to Maslow's hierarchy of needs, neither children nor adults can strive toward creativity unless fundamental needs have been met. The attainment of self-actualization also requires considerable ego strength, acceptance from peers, and self-respect. Self-actualization may not be attained until the middle years of adulthood. In the years prior to middle age, energy is frequently dissipated in diverse directions, including sexual relationships, educational advancement, career, marriage, and parenthood. The need to achieve financial stability during the young adult years consumes considerable psychic energy. By middle age, however, many people have managed to fulfill most of these needs and can spare the energy to strive toward ego maturity. In Chapter 10, we supply detailed coverage of characteristics and behaviors associated with self-actualizing persons.

Rogers's Self-Concept Theory   As we indicated, Carl Rogers (1961, 1974, 1980) is another important contributor to humanistic theory. Rogers is recognized as the founding figure of client-centered therapy, later renamed *person-centered therapy.* This kind of therapy utilizes humanism as a conceptual foundation and maintains that people can become *fully functioning* human beings only when they are given the freedom and emotional support that enables them to grow psychologically.

THEORETICAL ISSUES

If self-actualization means, in part, discovering and developing our potentials, what would you suggest we do to help both young and old find these hidden potentials?

Rogers states that each of us has a *real self,* which consists of our self-perceptions, and an *ideal self,* which represents the self we would like to become. When these two selves are congruent, we are probably living without conflict and likely in the process of developing into fully functioning people. However, when these two selves are incongruent, we likely suffer from such conditions as lack of self-esteem, rigidity, feelings of inferiority, guilt, and other negative emotions, all of which serve to stifle positive self-development. Rogers thus envisions healthy growth and development embracing congruency and movement toward such important personality dimensions as flexibility, autonomy, and self-acceptance.

A Critique of Humanistic Theory Humanists have reacted negatively to dry "mechanical person" theories because they believe there is a dignity and richness in human life, which is not included in the other types of developmental theories. Unfortunately, humanistic theory has less empirical evidence to support it than does any other theory mentioned in this text. There simply are no methodologies that allow us to measure self-actualization, fulfillment of potential, happiness, and so forth.

Although the ideas of Maslow and Rogers have been mostly directed to adult development, humanistic theory has application to children and adolescents. It has become increasingly recognized that emphasizing a person's uniqueness and potentials is important throughout the life cycle, but especially so during the formative years. Both Maslow and Rogers stress the notion of helping both young and old to accept their total being and the strivings that characterize the process of "becoming." Thus the application of humanistic theory to early as well as later development, including how we can promote activities that create fulfillment and individuality, has important application to the field of lifespan development.

Ecological Theory

Ecological theory is another relatively recent addition to the study of lifespan development, but it has proven influential in recent years. Essentially, this perspective centers on the importance of culture or context in shaping the course of development. To best understand behavior as it unfolds throughout the life cycle, we must pay close attention to the environmental context in which the person lives, including the other people involved.

Bronfenbrenner's Ecological Theory Urie Bronfenbrenner (1979, 1986, 1989) has proposed a sociocultural view of development that enables us to better understand how ecological issues can be explored. His theory consists of four overlapping environmental systems that interact with the person and influence overall development. These four environmental systems are the microsystem, mesosystem, exosystem, and macrosystem. Let's briefly examine each.

The *microsystem* is the system closest to the individual and consists of the family, neighborhood, school, playground, place of work, and so forth. Because the microsystem represents firsthand experiences, of special importance are the behaviors of the people in these contexts. The microsystem changes as the child becomes an adolescent and the adolescent becomes an adult.

The *mesosystem* reflects how microsystems influence each other. For example, a parent's relationship with the child's friends or teachers as well as

Urie Bronfenbrenner (1917–) was born in Moscow and founded ecological theory, a sociocultural view of development.

how a church might affect child-rearing styles reflect the influence of the mesosystem.

The *exosystem* refers to the wider context in which the individual might not participate directly, but is still nonetheless affected. Examples of the exosystem might be legal or welfare systems, school boards, or local governments.

The *macrosystem* represents the culture and subculture in which we live. The macrosystem is important because it shapes our values, beliefs, social roles, and lifestyle. It is best thought of as a societal blueprint, the totality of all other systems passed on from generation to generation.

These four environmental systems constantly interact with one another and mold our behavior. Researchers utilizing this approach carefully explore the ways in which these components directly or indirectly interact with one another. In so doing, an appreciation is gained of the numerous and diverse sociocultural influences that impact on a person's life. Related to the latter, the person is regarded as an active participant in initiating and responding to developmental processes.

A Critique of Ecological Theory   Ecological theory is a welcome addition to developmental psychology. It is one of the few perspectives offering insight into how the developing person is shaped by contextual influences, and such a conceptual framework is useful in studying lifespan development. People of all ages are affected by the systems proposed by Bronfenbrenner; consequently, his theory has the potential of shedding new light on aging experiences. One of the limitations of ecological theory, though, is that it downplays the importance of biological and cognitive forces. Other criticisms are leveled at the difficulty in pinpointing where one microsystem leaves off and another begins, and the difficulty in assessing the strength of the various system components (Thomas, 1992).

▬ Noteworthy Adult Psychological Theories

As we draw our discussion of psychological theories to a close, we provide a brief overview of some noteworthy adult psychological theories. Our purpose

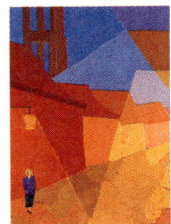

THEORETICAL ISSUES

Can you chart the impact of ecological forces on your own life? What people, events, and other contextual influences constitute your microsystem, mesosystem, exosystem, and macrosystem? How have they changed over time?

in doing this is twofold. First, we recognize that the study of adult psychological dynamics has long been foreshadowed by theories focusing on childhood and adolescence. A true lifespan perspective needs to acknowledge research exploring adult psychological development. Second, the theories that follow appear in detail throughout the text. A brief look now at their operating principles will prepare you for the discussions that follow.

DANIEL LEVINSON'S THEORY Daniel Levinson (1977, 1980, 1981, 1984, 1986, 1990, in press; Levinson et al., 1978; Levinson & Gooden, 1985) provides another example of a discontinuous personality emphasizing change. In his research, Levinson chose to study 40 males ranging in age between 35 and 45 (although he excluded females in his original research, Levinson is soon to publish a book about women's personality development). Levinson describes what he calls a "life structure," which refers to the underlying pattern of a person's behavior at a given time in life. There are three aspects to a person's life structure: sociocultural world (e.g., ethnicity, occupation, class, status, religion); self-aspects (complex patterns of wishes, anxieties, conflicts, moral values, talents and skills, fantasies, and modes of feeling, thought, and action); and participation in the world (how a person uses and is used by the world).

ROGER GOULD'S THEORY Roger Gould (1978, 1980) also explored stages of adult personality development with a discontinuous design. His research is similar to Levinson's, although Gould used a more extensive population sample. His research suggests that adulthood is not a plateau but rather a time for the continuous unfolding of the self. Gould's primary emphasis is on the importance of striving toward adult levels of consciousness and discarding irrational childhood notions about oneself and the world in general.

ROBERT HAVIGHURST'S THEORY Robert Havighurst (1972, 1980, 1987) stresses the importance of mastering developmental tasks appropriate to a given life stage. He used Erikson's concepts of the interaction between the individual and society and noted that most societies appear to have a timetable for the accomplishment of various tasks. He has identified what he terms *developmental tasks*. These developmental tasks may originate from physical maturation, from the pressure of the surrounding society on the person, and from the desires, aspirations, and values of the emerging personality. For example, infants and young children must learn to walk and talk, to distinguish right from wrong, and so forth. Adults, too, have developmental tasks appropriate to various stages of their personal and social growth. Successful achievement of these tasks constitutes the building blocks to success, with future tasks all leading toward happiness. Failure to satisfactorily complete these tasks can lead to unhappiness, difficulty with accomplishing future tasks, and disapproval by society. Havighurst suggests six developmental periods throughout the life cycle that require the mastery of developmental tasks. The following are the three groups of tasks for adults. Note that they do not have to be accomplished in the order presented.

EARLY ADULTHOOD (ROUGHLY AGES 18–30)

1. Getting started in an occupation.
2. Selecting a mate.
3. Learning to live with a marriage partner.

4. Starting a family.

5. Rearing children.

6. Managing a home.

7. Taking on civic responsibilities.

8. Finding a congenial social group.

MIDDLE ADULTHOOD (ROUGHLY 30–60)

1. Assisting teenage children to become responsible and happy adults.

2. Achieving adult social and civic responsibility.

3. Reaching and maintaining satisfactory performance in one's occupational career.

4. Developing adult leisure-time activities.

5. Relating to one's spouse as a person.

6. Accepting and adjusting to the physiological changes of middle age.

7. Adjusting to aging parents.

LATER ADULTHOOD (ROUGHLY 60–END OF LIFE)

1. Adjusting to decreasing physical strength and health.

2. Adjusting to retirement and reduced income.

3. Adjusting to death of one's spouse.

4. Establishing an explicit affiliation with one's age group.

5. Adopting and adapting social roles in a flexible way (such as expansion in family, community, or hobbies, or a slowdown in all activities).

6. Establishing satisfactory physical living arrangements.

CONTINUOUS AND DISCONTINUOUS HUMAN DEVELOPMENT

After reviewing all of the psychological theories, how do you think each addresses the issue of continuity and change? Which theories recognize that psychological development is a gradual but continuous process? Which see development as abrupt changes that occur from one phase to another?

SOCIOLOGICAL THEORIES OF LIFESPAN DEVELOPMENT

The second major category of lifespan development theories includes **sociological theories of lifespan development,** which emphasize how growth and development occur against the backdrop of society. Such theories focus on a wide assortment of issues, such as roles, relationship interactions, and family dynamics, and can be applied to any number of topics related to the lifespan: peer dynamics, school experiences, intimate friendships, interactions with neighbors, marriage, parenthood, grandparenthood, caring for aging family members, social support systems, and vocational involvement. Examples of sociological frameworks that can be applied to the study of lifespan development are symbolic interactionism, social exchange, family development, and conflict theories.

■ Symbolic Interactionism

Symbolic interactionism emphasizes the association between symbols (i.e., shared meanings) and interactions (i.e., verbal and nonverbal actions and communications). Essentially, this approach seeks to understand how humans, in concert with one another, create symbolic worlds and how these worlds, in turn, shape human behavior. Within the field of lifespan development, symbolic interactionists are particularly interested in how persons nurture both a concept of self and their identities through social interaction, thus enabling them to independently assign and assess value to their lives (LaRossa & Reitzes, in press; Passuth & Bengston, 1992).

Symbolic interactionism, then, carefully analyzes the actions of individuals because covert activity is deemed crucial in understanding the impact of society on development. Thus the dynamics of lifespan development are best understood when they are examined in the context of the social setting in which they take place. Relatedly, patterns of interaction, such as those taking place during peer group or sibling interactions, parent-child relations, or caring for an aging family member, are best understood when their shared meanings are fathomed.

This theory is especially useful in analyzing how individuals adjust to various roles as they develop. As an example, consider the retirement role. Symbolic interactionists would view the retirement role as a process rather than a set of rigidly defined expectations or rules. Individuals develop their roles through cooperative patterns of interaction, processes that usually involve role-taking (learning about the retirement role, including its expectations). For married couples, one adjusts and modifies the retirement role based on what he or she perceives the other is going to do. Symbolic interactionists are particularly interested in the active role of couples as they negotiate and modify their way throughout the retirement experience. Satisfaction with the retirement role hinges on congruent expectations between wife and husband. Given this logic, symbolic interactionists would probably argue that incongruent expectations account for any stress, tension, and conflict experienced during this time.

Social Exchange Theory

Social exchange theory proposes that our interactions are largely governed by self-interest. Individuals desire the maximum positive outcomes or rewards in relationships along with the least amount of costs or trade-offs. Within the exchange context, a type of bargaining situation exists; that is, individuals weigh the rewards gained against the costs incurred. This bartering of rewards and costs determines the flow of our relationships with others. At the heart of exchange theory is the notion that individuals will involve themselves in rewarding relationships and avoid those that are too costly.

Social exchange theory would emphasize how constraints interact with satisfactions and impact on persons of all ages. Thus this theory might prove useful in analyzing the perceived costs and rewards of such topics as children's friendships, prosocial behavior, adolescent dating behaviors, or caring for an aging parent. Consider as another example how social exchange theorists would approach the topic of parenthood. It might be argued that most couples enter into parenthood with the hope it will be a mutually gratifying endeavor, and that children are desired because of the perceived rewards and gratifications they offer (Goetting, 1986; Goldberg, Michaels, & Lamb, 1986; Harriman, 1986). However, many couples experience a system of deficient reward exchange; that is, the costs and sacrifices of parenthood may outweigh the benefits (Fawcett, 1988; Ruble et al., 1988; Sussman, 1988; Ventura, 1987). Social exchange theorists would emphasize the concepts of equity and fairness when examining the scope of parenthood; thus tension and stress often develop when reciprocity between parents is lacking. The key to establishing and maintaining parental satisfaction is the negotiation of expectation.

Social exchange theory is quite useful when examining the pileup of demands facing new parents, particularly mothers. In addition to caring for their children, mothers usually have to extend themselves and handle many of the father's needs (Cowan et al., 1985; Hoffman, L. W., 1989; Kamo, 1988; McHale & Huston, 1985; Spitze, 1988). Besides managing the bulk of the domestic chores, most women today also work outside of the home. From a social exchange perspective, it is plausible that the pileup of demands facing mothers is due, at least in part, to a power difference between husband and wife. Exchange theorists would point out that the balance of power in relationships is on the side of the partner contributing the greatest resources to the marriage. The relatively greater power of husbands in marriages may thus be due to the fact that they exert greater control over such valued resources as income and occupational status. This power appears to intensify when a child is brought into the relationship. Indeed, as evidenced by her increased domestic workload and child-care responsibilities, it is conceivable that many wives sacrifice power and resources when they become mothers (Sabatelli & Shehan, in press).

Social exchange theory is also useful in analyzing the decrease in marital satisfaction that often takes place among families with young children. This diminishment in satisfaction may be partly due to a rise in expectations at this point in the family life cycle. The family with young children stage follows a family life cycle stage usually high in marital satisfaction (the early years of marriage), and it is accompanied by escalating investments and demands. This increase in marital expectations requires that outcomes be expanded so satisfaction levels can be maintained. In this fashion, overall satisfaction may decline at this time because outcomes are not increased proportionately to the rise in expectations, and couples are often unable to discuss their changing expectations (Sabatelli, 1988; Sabatelli & Shehan, in press).

Family Development Theory

To understand how **family development theory** relates to lifespan development, we must keep in mind that family life represents a series of stages, orderly transitions that present members with an assortment of life course events and challenges (Aldous, 1977; Elder, 1977; Hill, 1964; McGoldrick & Carter, 1982; Rowe, 1981). Stages are usually characterized by the addition or subtraction of family members (through birth, death, or a family member leaving home), the developmental stages children experience, or the family's connection with other social systems, such as a family member's retirement from the labor force (Mattesich & Hill, 1987). In this fashion, a predictable chronology of family life stages can be charted: the unattached young adult; the newly married couple; the family with young children; the family with adolescents; the launching of grown children; and the family in later life (McGoldrick & Carter, 1982).

Because the family life cycle is viewed as an orderly sequence of events, the challenges inherent in each stage need to be adequately addressed before the next stage is encountered. To illustrate this theory, let's consider the aging couple being cared for by adult children. Such a unique family life stage poses an assortment of challenges for both generations and offers contrast to the demands posed at other points in the family life cycle. Generally, it is recognized that intergenerational caregiving brings the potential to initiate stress and requires the adaptive behavior of both adult children and aging parents. In this sense, a period of disorganization and emotional upheaval occurs during which adult children make various attempts to adapt to the needs of aging parents, and vice versa. The eventual outcome of this stage is frequently governed by the way in

Sociological theories of lifespan development shed light on a number of important issues and themes, including relationship dynamics and patterns of family interaction.

which all concerned perceive the event and how resourceful they are during the adjustment period.

Conflict Theory

Conflict theory seeks to expose how disequilibrium, disharmony, and conflict are inevitable features of aging experiences. Because of its inevitability, conflict is not viewed as an evil force; rather, it is an expected feature of social systems. Indeed, with age persons face the perpetual problem of coming to terms with themselves and the conflicting interests of those around them. Important concepts within this conceptual framework are power, competition, resources, negotiating, and bargaining (Lips, 1991; Sprey, 1975, 1979).

Related to the study of lifespan development, conflict theorists might emphasize the constant interplay of negotiation, problem solving, and conflict management. To use our example of retirement again, think of the potential for conflict, particularly when there is discontent or disagreement about household routines or responsibilities. The issue of power often weaves itself through such issues; that is, tension and conflict around domestic responsibilities are often fueled by the underlying issues of inequality or control. Or, as we discover in Chapter 10, the potential for intergenerational friction is quite possible when adult children provide care for aging parents, particularly when the latter are sick or disabled. For many, conflict often originates from such factors as conflicting interests or dwindling resources when coping with the multiple demands of caregiving.

A Critique of Sociological Theories

Sociological theories of lifespan development are useful because they focus on what happens to individuals socially as they develop. Such theories also illuminate the relationship between a society's social system and its younger and older members. As with the psychological theories we explored, these sociological theories are worthwhile for organizing research on lifespan development and relating concepts to one another. Over the years, these conceptual frameworks have become more sophisticated and made commendable efforts to link observations and logic. Symbolic interactionism and social exchange, in particular, appear to offer a useful set of concepts for developing hypotheses.

However, all of the presented conceptual frameworks have their share of drawbacks. For example, critics of symbolic interactionism point out that this perspective lacks methodological rigor in its research and is not particularly applicable to the study of large-scale social structures. Social exchange theory has been accused of being too individualistic and abstract. Critics of family development theory claim it is difficult to establish agreement on when particular stages are reached. Moreover, variations of family life, such as those created by divorce or multigenerational living, tend to elude this theoretical explanation. Finally, conflict theory has not been extensively tested by researchers, and its conceptual properties, as well as specific predictive ability, needs to be developed.

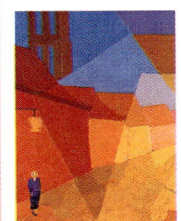

THEORETICAL ISSUES

How do you think sociological theories of lifespan development compare to those of a psychological nature? Are they as scientifically rigorous? How would you rate their application?

BIOLOGICAL THEORIES OF LIFESPAN DEVELOPMENT

Biological theories of lifespan development focus on the complex physiological processes that occur over the course of the life cycle. Biological theories are geared more toward the study of later life aging processes but are important to recognize throughout the entire life span. As we discover in the chapters ahead, the growth and aging of cells is lifelong, from the moment of conception to the final years of late adulthood. Moreover, biological forces converge with psychological and sociological dynamics and affect the life course of the whole person. Although the nature of biological changes is not precisely understood, this grouping of theories sheds light on what we do know. Among the more prominent biological theories are the wear-and-tear, cellular, and immunity perspectives.

■ Wear-and-Tear Theory

The **wear-and-tear theory** asserts that the organism simply wears out, much like a machine, over the course of the life cycle. Over time, the body has accumulated steady increases of damage due to external sources. These sources may be direct (lethal agents) or indirect (the organism is weakened and is consequently more susceptible to such influences as malnutrition, addictions, and stress). By the time late adulthood is reached, the body is exhausted and vulnerable to some extraneous factor that eventually destroys the organism (Bowles, 1981).

■ Cellular Theory

Cellular theory pays close attention to the role that errors in cell division play in aging processes. An error could produce two faulty cells, which would then divide, creating four faulty cells, divide again producing eight, and so on. Whatever function that particular group of cells had would thus be impaired.

INTERRELATEDNESS OF AGING PROCESSES

What signs of biological aging do you see in the mirror? Have these physical changes affected any aspects of your personality or social life? What biological changes do you think you'll see 20 years from now?

Cellular theory also pays attention to what are called *free radicals* and the concept of *cross-linkage*. A free radical is a highly reactive molecule that has become separated during a chemical reaction. Free radicals will try to unite with almost any other molecule they come in contact with, particularly those of fibrous protein. When this happens, they become cross-linked, or bound at the middle. Should this cross-linkage become extensive, the normal functions of these proteins are affected and they become less resilient and tougher.

These latter changes associated with the body's fibrous protein represent the focal point of the closely allied *collagen theory*. Collagen is the basic structural component of connective tissue. It consists of large fibrous, elastic molecules, and it is found in all body organs. For example, it is found in its pure form in tendons; it is also found in bones, between cells, in muscle fibers, and in the walls of blood vessels. Collagen is flexible, and it also offers great resistance to pulling forces. In its flexibility and strength, collagen is analogous to a cable that ties a ship to a wharf. Although it is sufficiently pliable to be coiled when not in use, the cable will not allow movement of the ship while at anchor. In much the same manner, fibrous collagen allows skin, tendons, or blood vessels to transmit tension and compression without becoming deformed. These fibers are exceedingly strong, capable of being stretched and then returning to their natural length. If, however, they are stretched for a long enough period of time, the stretched length gradually becomes their basic length, a process known as "creeping" (Eyre, 1980; Guyton, 1981). The accompanying Lifespan Development in Action box provides an exercise to examine your own skin elasticity and collagen.

As collagen loses its elastic properties due to the earlier described cross-linkage process, organs become less resilient. For example, the bones of the elderly are fragile because of a change in bone mineralization, which makes them more porous and brittle. Decrease in the quality of collagen also allows calcium salts to be deposited in this now-degenerating tissue. Calcium salts, which are normally inhibited from accumulating in tissue other than bone, are deposited in arterial walls, causing arteries to become bonelike tubes, a condition known as arteriosclerosis.

Immunity Theory

Finally, the **immunity theory** proposes that change in the body's immune system results in physical degeneration. More specifically, as the body ages, its immune system becomes less efficient, resulting in the survival of harmful cells that can cause damage. Thus the body loses its ability to protect itself from disease and malfunctioning cells. Related to immunity theory is *autoimmunity theory*. This theory suggests that with age there are more mutations and changes in the body's cell division. The body itself, however, reacts differently to these changes. The cell mutations or other changes may lead to protein that the body does not recognize as part of its system. The body perceives this as foreign matter and responds by producing antibodies—the autoimmune response. The end result is that the body is launching an attack on itself.

A Critique of Biological Theories

Biological theories are useful because they help us to better understand the impact aging has on the performance of the total organism. However, because

Lifespan Development in Action

SKIN ELASTICITY AND COLLAGEN: A SIMPLE TEST

It is fairly easy to observe the effects of collagen change and cross-linkage in the skin. Place your wrist and hand palm down on a flat surface, with the fingers stretched as widely as possible. Take a pinch of skin on the back of the hand between the thumb and forefinger and pull it up as far as you comfortably can (see Figure 2-4). Hold this pinched skin for 5 seconds, then quickly release it. Count the seconds that it takes for the skin to smooth itself.

The skin usually snaps back very rapidly in healthy teenagers. Between the teenage years and age 45, 2 or 3 seconds are usually required. After this, though, the time increases rapidly. For a 65-year-old, about 20 seconds are required. In an 80-year-old, the pinched skin may still form a visible ridge 5 minutes later. This is because of the cross-linkage damage to collagen that accompanies the aging process. The skin becomes far less resilient and flexible over time. (Pearson & Shaw, 1982; Walford, 1983)

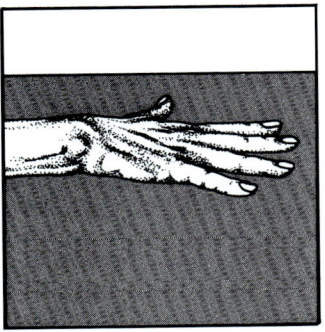 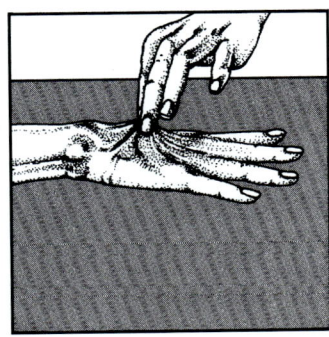

FIGURE 2-4
A Test for Skin Elasticity.

By pinching the skin on the back of the hand (right), you can see how the effects of collagen change over time. The skin snaps back quickly in teenagers and young adults. It takes longer in older adults because of reduced skin flexibility.

aging is a multifaceted experience, no one biological theory adequately explains the total complexities of growing old (Briggs, 1990; Brock, 1991). More research is definitely needed in the sphere of biological theories, including efforts to test the relative merits of the wear-and-tear, cellular, and immunity perspectives.

PUTTING LIFESPAN DEVELOPMENT THEORIES INTO PERSPECTIVE

Psychological, sociological, and biological theories have helped us to better understand the complex nature of lifespan development. They not only represent conceptual frameworks that organize and give meaning to facts, but also serve as foundations for further research. These theoretical frameworks also help to guide researchers with questions related to research settings and designs. For example, they help to address such issues as what aspects of behavior to measure, how observations should be conducted, and where such observations should take place.

Whether exploring such topics as gender-role development, emotional behavior, mate selection, or retirement adjustments, developmental psychologists must seek to establish a solid conceptual foundation and a unifying framework in their research endeavors. They must avoid focusing on one or two isolated constructs while ignoring the impact of factors found to be significant in other investigations. By utilizing a solid theoretical foundation, we can build on our knowledge of lifespan development and discover how factors are related to each other. Thus an important feature of lifespan development is the link forged between research and theory.

Recognize, too, that even though facts are the building blocks of a science, they cannot "prove" theories. Theories are not either "true" or "false," with disconfirming evidence indicating the lack of general validity. Instead, a theory is a guide that may be supported by additional data or not supported because of conflicting data. Theories are characterized by their tentative nature and are always being tested and refined. As new facts emerge, theories are questioned, challenged, revised, and even rejected.

The student of lifespan development must also realize that theories do not have to be examined or weighed in an either/or perspective. They are not necessarily mutually exclusive or independent of one another, and several of these approaches or forces may be operating at different times or under different conditions. For example, the fact that a child may be at a specific stage according to Piaget's cognitive-developmental theory does not mean principles of reinforcement are not operating at the same time, nor does it mean that one's acquisition of knowledge is not being shaped by observational learning, all within a contextual setting. Relatedly, an older adult can experience the convergence of theoretical forces by encountering the Eriksonian psychosocial crisis of integrity versus despair, a new social exchange network brought on by retirement, and biological changes that are best explained by the wear-and-tear theory. Although psychological, sociological, and biological theories represent efforts to explain various aspects of lifespan development, it is not uncommon for one or all theories to be applied simultaneously.

Given such theoretical convergence, we suggest you become eclectic in your analysis of lifespan development, picking and choosing those bits of viewpoints that you can accept. Then you can develop your own ideas and possibly theories of lifespan development. Think of your ideas as a lens and the various theories as filters. The views you select will filter out some facts and impose a pattern on those you admit. It might be interesting to see how your own theoretical perspective of lifespan development changes as you read this book and attend class. By the end of the semester, the chances are that you'll have a clearer understanding of your own viewpoints as well as a unified portrait of the field of lifespan development.

A final word about theories. Ideally, theoretical frameworks guide behavior and sharpen observational skills. We hope these theoretical perspectives can clarify your own thoughts and viewpoints on lifespan development through your own personal experiences. As you acquaint yourself with the research investigations discussed in later chapters, knowledge of theoretical perspectives will help you see which conceptual frameworks guided a particular researcher. As we indicated in the last chapter, we will help you focus on theoretical perspectives with a specially designed set of margin thinking questions. As you address these questions, you may want to refer back to this chapter to review what you've learned.

CHAPTER REVIEW

Theories are perspectives or explanations of how we develop, both as a species and as individuals. A good theory is supported by empirical evidence, and over the course of time it becomes more logically and empirically sound. Effective theories are also internally consistent, with no statements that contradict each other. When theories are judged to be incomplete or inconsistent they are often called prototheories. Most theories in lifespan development are considered prototheories.

Theories of lifespan development can be conceptualized according to psychological, social, and biological frameworks. Psychological theories emphasize behavioral characteristics and include such elements as personality, cognition, self-esteem, motivation, and feelings. Among the psychological theories we discussed were the psychodynamic, cognitive, learning, ethological, humanistic, and ecological perspectives.

Psychodynamic theories are those psychological theories that emphasize the dynamics of the unconscious mind and one's past experiences as being the major determinants of future behavior. The psychodynamic perspective is reflected in the psychosexual perspective taken by Freud and the psychosocial orientation emphasized by Erikson. Cognitive theories emphasize a wide range of thought processes and embrace such elements as perceiving, thinking, and understanding. Piaget's cognitive-developmental theory and information processing theory are examples of this category. Learning theories, such as behaviorism and social learning theory, emphasize that behavior is shaped by the interaction of the organism with the environment.

Ethology, the study of human and animal behavior in natural settings, seeks to understand behavior in an evolutionary context and places considerable emphasis on the role of instinct in development. Maslow and Rogers are linked with humanistic theory, a perspective that emphasizes the individual's uniqueness, personal potential, and inner drives. Ecological theory, most notably the work of Bronfenbrenner, places emphasis on the importance of culture or context in shaping the course of development. We concluded this section of our discussion with some noteworthy adult psychological theories, namely the works of Levinson, Gould, and Havighurst.

The second major category of lifespan development theories comprises those of a sociological nature. Sociological theories of lifespan development emphasize how growth and development occur against the backdrop of society, and include symbolic interactionism, social exchange, family development, and conflict theories. Symbolic interactionism seeks to understand how humans, in concert with one another, create symbolic worlds and how these worlds, in turn, shape human behavior. Social exchange theory proposes that the negotiation of rewards and costs determines the flow of our relationships with others. Family development theory holds that family life progresses in a series of stages and that the challenges inherent in each stage must be addressed before the family can adequately cope with those of the next stage. Finally, conflict theory seeks to expose how disequilibrium, disharmony, and conflict are inevitable features of aging experiences.

The third and final category of theories is biological in scope. Such theories focus on the complex physiological processes that occur over the course of the life cycle and include the wear-and-tear, cellular, and immunity perspectives. The wear-and-tear theory asserts that the organism simply wears out, much like a machine, over the course of the life cycle. Cellular theory examines the role that errors in cell division play in aging processes. Lastly, the immunity theory proposes that change in the body's immune system results in physical degeneration. As the body ages, its immune system becomes less efficient, resulting in the survival of harmful cells that can cause damage.

TERMS YOU SHOULD KNOW

accommodation
assimilation
behaviorism
biological theories of lifespan
   development
cellular theory
chain
cognitive-developmental theory
cognitive social learning theory
cognitive theories
conflict theory
conscious
defense mechanism
ecological theory
ego
equilibration
ethological theory
family development theory
fixation
free association
hedonistic principle
humanistic theory
id
immunity theory
imprinting
information processing theory
learning theories
libido
negative reinforcement
observational learning

operants
positive reinforcement
preconscious
primary reinforcement
prototheory
psychoanalytic theory
psychodynamic theories
psychological theories of
   lifespan development
psychosexual stages of
   development
psychosocial stages of
   development
reality principle
reinforcer
repression
schemata
secondary reinforcement
self-actualization
sensitive period
shaping behavior
social exchange theory
social learning theory
sociological theories of lifespan
   development
superego
symbolic interactionism
theory
unconscious
wear-and-tear theory

THINKING IN ACTION

• We grouped theories of lifespan development into psychological, sociological, and biological categories. In analyzing the relative contributions of each category, do you believe one grouping has more influence than the rest? If you were a researcher studying lifespan development, how might your selected category of theories filter your perceptions of growth and development?

• This chapter exposed you to the major theories applicable to the study of lifespan development. Which theory best supports your view of the life cycle? Why does it have more merit than the others? To illustrate its usefulness, select several lifespan development topics (e.g., peer group interaction, school experiences, marriage, vocational choice, retirement) and show how your theory offers valuable insights and explanations.

• At the end of this chapter, we stressed the importance of becoming eclectic in your analysis of theories so you can nurture your own ideas about lifespan development. Using some mental gymnastics, combine two or more theories that were presented in this chapter, and form your own eclectic theory.

RECOMMENDED READINGS

1. Alexander, C. N., & Langer, E. J. (Eds.). (1990). *Higher stages of human development.* New York: Oxford University Press.

   Among the topics are cognitive, moral, and personality development.

2. Beilin, H. (1992). Piaget's enduring contribution to developmental psychology. *Developmental Psychology, 28* (2), 191–204.

   A look at how Piaget shaped the field of lifespan development, including the developmental mechanisms he proposed.

3. Birren, J. E., & Bengston, V. L. (Eds.). (1992). *Emergent theories of aging* (2nd ed.). New York: Springer.

   Social theories of lifespan development are given good coverage in this book of readings.

4. Horowitz, F. D. (1992). John B. Watson's legacy: Learning and the environment. *Developmental Psychology, 28* (3), 360–367.

   Watson's contributions are discussed in relation to his own time, with respect to his historical influence and in light of current issues in developmental psychology.

5. Thomas, R. M. (1992). *Comparing theories of child development.* Belmont, CA: Wadsworth.

   The author provides balanced coverage of major developmental theories, including an excellent analysis and critique of each.

Genetics, Heredity, and Environment

What Do You Think?

INTRODUCTION

THE GENETICS OF LIFE

BIOCHEMICAL GENETICS: BASIC CONCEPTS

Basic Cell Structure
Fundamental Genetic Principles
Determination of Gender
Sex- or X-Linked Characteristics

DNA: The Blueprint of Life
Genetic Individuality
Simple Types of Gene Action

BEHAVIORAL GENETICS

Polygenes and Behavior
Intelligence and Behavior
Twin Studies: Methodology

Inheritability of Behavioral Traits

GENETIC ABERRATIONS AND MUTATIONS

Down Syndrome
Klinefelter's Syndrome (XXY)
Turner's Syndrome (XO)

Cri-du-Chat Syndrome
Triple X Syndrome (XXX)
XYY Syndrome

GENETIC COUNSELING

Stages of Genetic Counseling
Detecting and Treating Fetal Problems
    and Defects
Amniocentesis

Chorionic Villus Sampling (CVS)
Ultrasonography
Fetoscopy
Intrauterine Fetal Surgery

FUTURE DIRECTIONS IN GENETIC RESEARCH

Chapter Review • Terms You Should Know • Thinking in Action • Recommended Readings

• Bill and Jim are in the third grade. They are fraternal twins, yet Bill's reading level is 2 years ahead of his chronological age, whereas Jim is barely able to keep up with his classwork. How can we account for the difference in their reading abilities?

• Through chromosomal aberrations, that is, too many or too few chromosomes or genes, normal growth and development are disrupted. For example, a male can develop such female physical characteristics as enlarged breasts, or a female may never enter puberty and consequently remain sterile for her entire life. Other genetic aberrations create webbed fingers and toes, heads with distorted shapes, and other deformed body parts. How do chromosomes and genes cause such abnormalities? Read on to discover the answers that genetic researchers have supplied.

• Two brown-eyed parents with dark wavy hair have three children who are spitting images of them. But their fourth child is tall and has straight blond hair and blue eyes. How can these latter differences be explained? How can two brown-eyed parents have a blue-eyed child? Why do some children born of the same parents have such similarities, whereas others bear no resemblance to anyone in the family? We unravel some of the genetic mysteries about generational similarities and variations.

INTRODUCTION

Conception occurs, and 9 months later Ann is born. Her physical appearance is determined primarily by genetic inheritance, which endows her with a blueprint for her biological growth and development. If her parents are Ugandans, her genetic code will contain a program for her to look, grow, and develop along the lines of other Ugandans. If they are Eskimo, Navajo, Siberian, or Swedish, for example, she would inherit a different genetic code that would express itself in different ways.

The genetic blueprint also bestows certain behavioral predispositions. Ann may have inherited a biochemical or neuromuscular makeup that will give her the potential to become an outstanding athlete, a musical virtuoso, a math whiz, a vocalist, or an intellectual. She may have inherited a tendency to be hyperactive, very passive, alcoholic, or even schizophrenic.

There is more to behavior than genetic inheritance, however. Ann was born into a family within a specific culture. She will learn which behaviors are acceptable in the family, the neighborhood, and society. She will also develop her own interests and motivations. Her environment may be restrictive or supportive, and she may have few or many opportunities to develop the skills that match her inherited aptitudes. Environment and heredity are strong forces that will help determine not only how she will behave but how long she will live. How do environment and heredity interact? What is their role in influencing behavior? This chapter investigates and tries to answer these questions.

THE GENETICS OF LIFE

What governs the process whereby a fertilized egg develops into a fully functioning infant, complete with arms, legs, nose, eyes, ears, internal organs, and an individuality all its own? The key to this magnificent story is a special code

Genetic inheritance is responsible for a wide range of traits and predispositions.

contained in the nucleus of each cell. This code, unique to and different for every individual, is gradually being understood by scientists.

Each cell contains a set of genetic blueprints that directs the cell to multiply itself and become a fully developed organism. It is true for all animal species: Each cell contains a full set of directions locked inside its nucleus. This is what makes a mouse different from a bird, a flower different from a tree, and siblings different from each other.

Frequently, the terms *genetics* and *heredity* are used interchangeably. They are not synonymous, however. The word **genetic** (genesis) refers to the origin, or beginning. When we speak of genetics, we refer to the beginning life cell and its progressive development according to the principles of genetics. Because this cell has received developmental instructions from both parents, the organism will inherit characteristics from both of them; this is known as heredity. Genetics is the scientific study of how inheritance operates.

Heredity refers to the parents' transmission of certain characteristics to their offspring. Put another way, it is the tendency of offspring to resemble their parents. When offspring, whether plant or animal, differ from their parents, these differences are referred to as **variations.** Generally, fewer variations among closely related species are expected than from more divergent or less closely related animals. For example, the children of two brown-eyed, dark-haired, and olive-skinned people or two blue-eyed blonds will look more like their parents than will the children of a father of Irish-Scottish-Norwegian background and a mother of Italian-Mexican-Eskimo genetic background. The offspring of this latter mating would have more variation.

Although genetics did not become a science until recently, trial-and-error methods of manipulating inherited characteristics of plants and animals from one generation to the next have been used for centuries. Even without a working scientific knowledge of genetics, we have, over thousands of years, developed hundreds of species to serve specific functions. For example, observing

Genes control inheritable characteristics, from freckled skin to eye and hair color.

that a large bull tends to produce similar offspring, farmers bred species of cattle solely to increase the quantity of beef. Cows have been bred that can produce many gallons of milk. Others, although producing fewer gallons, yield milk high in butterfat, especially usable for butter, cream, and similar dairy products. In other instances, some species of horses have been bred for pure strength to pull plows and heavy loads, whereas others are bred primarily for their racing ability.

Dogs and dog breeding stand out in the field of heredity; the American Kennel Club currently recognizes over 130 breeds of dogs in the United States. Although virtually all of today's dogs originated from either one or two common ancestors, natural selection and artificial breeding have produced well over 150 species. Dogs can be categorized into groups according to certain behavioral characteristics, enabling breeders to capitalize on inherited genetic predispositions. For example, because terriers have an inherited predisposition to dig in the ground, they are used to help rid the land of small vermin. Collies and sheepdogs have a natural herding instinct, and sporting dogs such as setters and pointers may have either unusually good sight or a good sense of smell that enables them to aid hunters. The resultant behavior of each breed is partially determined by inherited characteristics, but it is the environment (training) that helps develop these inborn traits. Observant trainers will note a dog's natural tendencies and train the animal accordingly. For example, it is easier to train a collie than a bulldog to herd sheep. Heredity and environment go hand in hand.

What is true of other species is also true of humans. If two pygmies mate, you get a pygmy; if two very tall blond people mate, they will most likely have tall blond offspring; if two schizophrenics mate, there is a strong likelihood their children will become schizophrenic themselves. That is the nature of inheritance.

Although scientists have long observed "hereditary tendencies," no meaningful explanations for the phenomena were put forward until the mid-1800s when Gregor Mendel, a monk, discovered some fundamental laws of genetics while experimenting with peas. Since that initial breakthrough, the science of genetics has been active and there have been many dramatic discoveries. However, before we can understand some of these genetic revelations, we must first understand cells and cellular behavior.

BIOCHEMICAL GENETICS: BASIC CONCEPTS

Biology, genetics, and lifespan development are, at first glance, three different and separate disciplines; yet upon inspection, they are closely related. Earlier, we mentioned that genetics is the science of heredity. More specifically, it is the science that studies chromosomes and genes and how they control a cell's activity and govern life processes. The geneticist is interested in the chemical analysis of the chromosomes. Behavior genetics attempts to understand how these chemical processes produce physical and behavioral characteristics.

Although the field of psychology is mainly interested in the processes by which genetics *affects* behavior, psychologists need not understand all of the

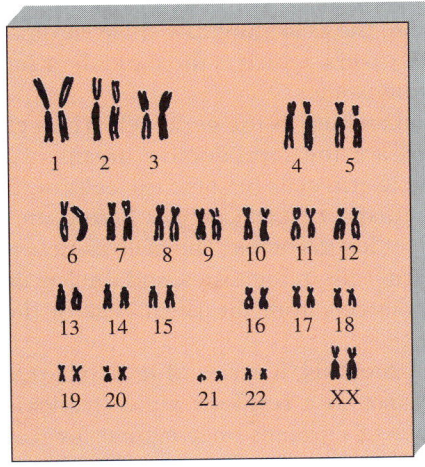 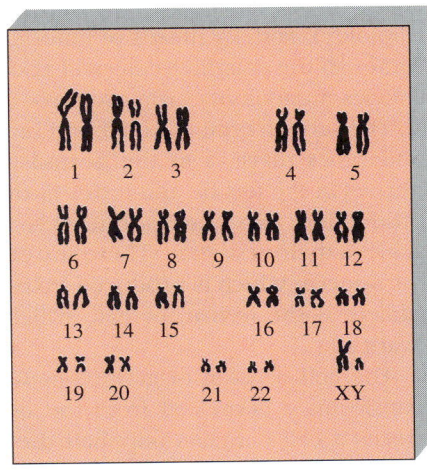

FIGURE 3-1
Human Chromosomes Grouped into 23 Pairs.

Female chromosomes are shown in the box on the left and male chromosomes on the right.

biochemical processes that occur in the cell. They should, however, be familiar with the fundamental principles of genetic and hereditary processes.

Basic Cell Structure

A **cell** is a living unit of organized material that contains a nucleus and is enclosed in a membrane. The entire living substance that constitutes a cell is known as **protoplasm,** which can be subdivided into two general types: **cytoplasm,** the protoplasm found inside the cell but outside the nucleus; and **nucleoplasm,** the protoplasm found inside the nuclear membrane. The cell also contains **ribosomes,** small particles in the cytoplasm that manufacture essential products for the cell.

The **nucleus,** located in or near the center of the cell, is the control center of the cell's activity. Inside the nucleus are **chromosomes,** thin rodlike structures that contain the directions for the cell's activity. Chromosomes occur in pairs and the number varies according to the species. Humans have 23 pairs of chromosomes per cell, or 46 chromosomes altogether (see Figure 3-1).

Organisms have only two types of cells: **somatic cells** and **germ cells.** The term *soma* means body; thus most of the approximately 1 trillion cells found in the human body are somatic cells. In order for growth to take place, somatic cells undergo a process of division called **mitosis.** In mitosis, the chromosomes inside the nucleus pair up along its center; then, after duplicating themselves, they move to opposite poles. The original cell (and nucleus), called the **parent cell,** begins to pull apart, and two new nuclei are formed that contain the new sets of chromosomes. Each of these new cells is called a **daughter cell.** The key fact to remember about mitosis is that the two new daughter cells are identical to the original parent cell and maintain the same number of chromosomes. Figure 3-2 illustrates the process of mitosis.

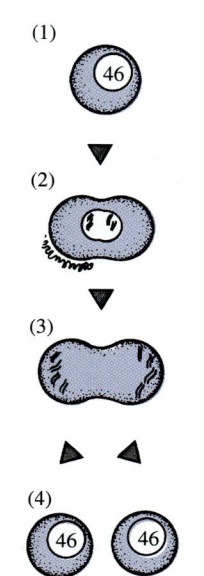

(1)

(2)

(3)

(4)

FIGURE 3-2
Mitosis.

Mitosis is the process whereby a parent cell divides to become two daughter cells, each containing the original number of chromosomes. The diagram illustrates (1) the body cell with the original 46 chromosomes; (2) before cell division, the chromosomes duplicate themselves; (3) the chromosomes migrate to opposite sides of the dividing cell; and (4) the two new cells each contain 46 chromosomes.

When a cell has its full quota of chromosomes, it is said to be in the **diploid state.** In humans, the parent cell always has 23 pairs of chromosomes (diploidy), and, by means of mitotic division, the cells duplicate their chromosomes so the daughter cells will also have 23 pairs, which is the diploid, or full species number, of chromosomes—46 chromosomes.

The second type of cell found in the human body is the germ cell. This cell undergoes division in the **gonads,** which are the reproductive organs: the ovaries in the female and testes in the male. Germ cells become the cells of reproduction, or sex cells, but must first undergo certain changes before they achieve their new state. These sex cells are called **gametes.** The male gamete is the **sperm,** which is produced from the germ cells in the testes, and the female gamete is the **ovum,** or *egg,* which is produced from the germ cells of the ovaries.

The cell division of germ cells is called **meiosis,** a series of divisions that transforms a germ cell from the diploid state to a **haploid state** (haploidy means a cell contains only half the number of chromosomes natural for that species). Meiotic division, therefore, pertains to a parent germ cell splitting into two daughter cells, the same process as mitosis *except* the chromosomes do not duplicate themselves. This leaves each daughter cell in the haploid state. Thus meiosis in the male organism produces a sperm sex cell that contains 23 chromosomes and in the female, an ovum with 23 chromosomes. Conception occurs when the sperm fertilizes the ovum and creates a single cell in the diploid state. This enables a cell to receive its full component of chromosomes, complete with coded instructions. Figure 3-3 shows the process of meiosis.

Fundamental Genetic Principles

In addition to the terminology covered thus far, as a student of lifespan development you need to be aware of certain other fundamental genetic principles. Among the more important are the following:

CHROMOSOMES AND GENES As indicated, chromosomes are located inside the cell's nucleus. A chromosome (colored body) is a thin rodlike structure that contains small genetic units called genes, the true units of heredity.

DOMINANT GENE A **dominant gene** is any gene that, when present, always expresses its hereditary characteristic. An uppercase letter is used to represent the dominant condition (e.g., B for brown eyes).

RECESSIVE GENE A **recessive gene** is one whose hereditary characteristics are present only when paired with another recessive gene. Its hereditary characteristics are not observable when paired with a dominant gene. It is designated by the lowercase letter that is used for the dominant gene (e.g., b for blue, gray, hazel, or green eyes—all recessive to brown).

HOMOZYGOUS (SAMENESS OF GENES) **Homozygous** describes a condition in which both genes of a gene pair are identical for a given trait—both dominant or both recessive (e.g., BB or bb).

ALLELE An **allele** is any member of alternate sets in the same gene pair. The alleles for eye color might be B from the father and b from the mother.

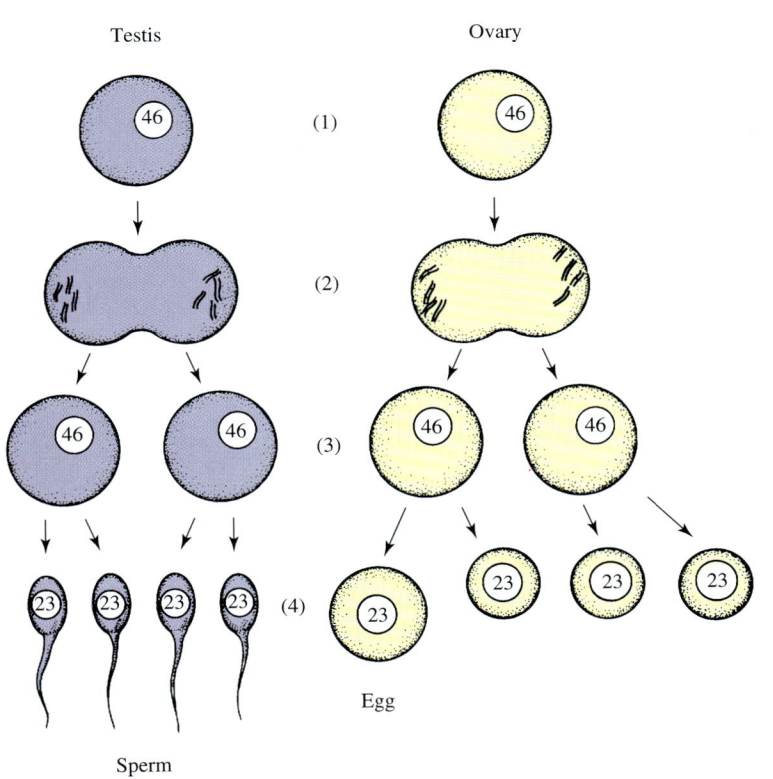

Testis

Ovary

(1)

(2)

(3)

(4)

Egg

Sperm

FIGURE 3-3
Meiosis.

Meiosis is the cell division in which sperm and ova are created. Compared to mitosis, there is a reduction in chromosomes when the sex cells divide. The diagram shows (1) the sperm and egg cell, each containing 46 chromosomes; (2) each chromosome duplicates itself before cell division takes place; (3) cell division creates two new cells, each with 46 chromosomes; and (4) another cell division occurs, resulting in four new cells, each having 23 single chromosomes.

HETEROZYGOUS (MIXED OR TWO TYPES OF GENES) **Heterozygous** describes a condition in which each gene of a gene pair differs for a given trait—one dominant, one recessive gene (e.g., Bb).

PHENOTYPE A **phenotype** is the visible or easily measurable appearance of an organism. A brown-eyed person is said to have a brown phenotype for eye color; a blue-eyed person has a phenotype for blue eyes.

GENOTYPE A **genotype** refers to the actual genetic makeup (gene pair) of an organism. If the blue-eyed person has a bb gene pair, its genotype is blue for both genes. When an organism exhibits a dominant phenotype, we can only guess at the genotype. Is a brown-eyed person genotypically BB or Bb? He or she could be either.

■ Determination of Gender

If we were to line up the 46 chromosomes of the human female somatic or germ cell in two columns, each containing 23 chromosomes, we would see that all 23 are in pairs; they are identical in appearance, and they have the same function (e.g., to determine eye color). The 23rd set of chromosomes are usually referred to as the sex chromosomes, for they determine the sex of the child

FIGURE 3-4

The Mating of Sex Chromosomes and the Resultant Sex of the Offspring.

When a man and woman conceive a child together, the union of their germ cells produces either a girl (XX) or a boy (XY), depending on whether the sperm that succeeds in fertilizing the ovum carries an X or a Y chromosome.

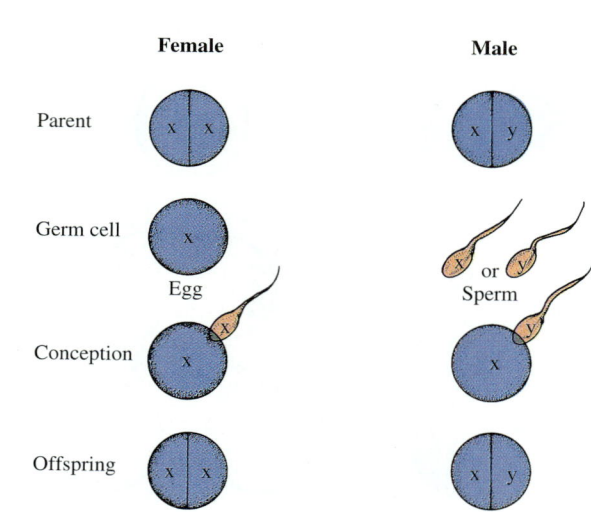

(Figure 3-1). In the female's cells, the 23rd pair ordinarily consists of two X chromosomes. However, when we look at the chromosomes in a male, we see the first 22 are pairs, but in position 23, we can easily see it is not a pair at all— it is a mismatch. One chromosome is shaped like an X, the other like a Y.

Throughout history, many a queen has lost her throne (or even her life) for not giving birth to a male heir. But it is not the female who determines the sex of the child, but the male. Remember that during meiosis the chromosomes in the gamete divide in half and that one half becomes the egg. For the female, no matter which half becomes fertilized, the egg always—and only—contains an X. The male, however, can contribute a sperm cell that has either an X or a Y chromosome. If the X-carrying sperm penetrates the egg, the offspring will be a girl; if the Y does, it will be a boy (see Figure 3-4).

Recent evidence indicates that one gene (a small segment of a chromosome that controls or influences an inheritable characteristic), ordinarily found on the Y chromosome, determines a person's sex. The **testis-determining factor,** or *TDF,* is associated with that gene. Researchers believe this gene launches a sequence of events that leads to male sexual development. If the gene containing the TDF is absent, the individual will be female (Page et al., 1987).

Sex- or X-Linked Inheritance

The chromosome in the 23rd position determines not only the sex of one's offspring but the **sex-linked characteristics** as well. Because the X chromosome is approximately three times as large as the Y chromosome, a female has approximately three times as many genes on her 23rd chromosome as a male does. The difference in gene numbers on the sex chromosomes is the key to understanding sex-linkage. From the 22 pairs of **autosomes** (any chromosome

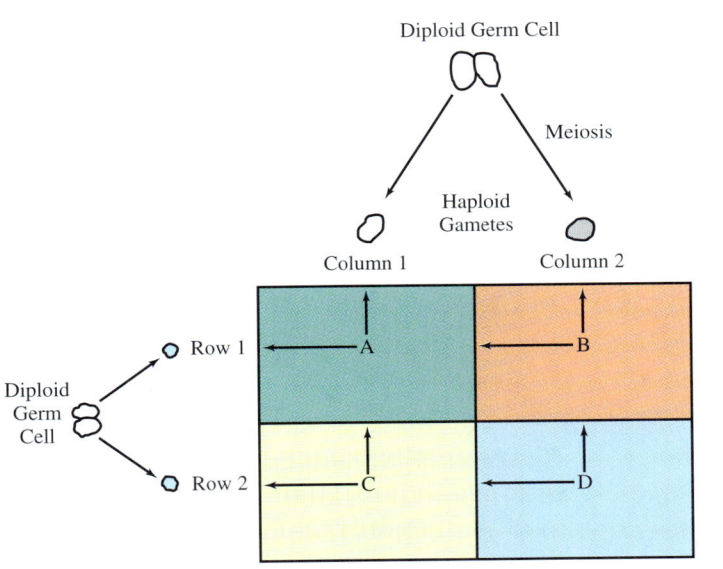

Diploid Germ Cell

Meiosis

Haploid
Gametes

Column 1   Column 2

Row 1 — A — B

Diploid
Germ
Cell

Row 2 — C — D

FIGURE 3-5

A Punnett Square for Sex-Linked Characteristics.

The columns represent the two possible female gametes; the rows, the two possible male gametes. The four squares A, B, C, and D represent every possible genotype available for that one characteristic. For example, square A represents the fertilization of the egg type represented in column 1 by the male gamete in row 1. Square D represents the female type of gamete 2 as fertilized by the male gamete from row 2.

other than the sex-determining pair), an individual might inherit a recessive gene for some undesirable trait, but if inheritance has also given that individual a normal dominant gene, the undesirable trait will not be expressed. However, on the sex-determining chromosomes, there is frequently no such balancing tendency because the Y chromosome lacks corresponding genes.

The best way to illustrate the possible inheritance from parents to offspring, including sex-linked characteristics, is to utilize the Punnett square (named after an English geneticist), a diagrammatic way to compute the possible geno-types and phenotypes for any given characteristic (Figure 3-5). Because chromosomes and their component genes occur in pairs but separate during mitosis, there are two gametes left for any one sex. Although there is no way of knowing exactly which male gamete will fertilize which female gamete, one can calculate, in advance, the statistical probabilities of certain characteristics.

One of the better known sex-linked characteristics is color blindness. The retina of the eye contains cones, specialized nerve cells that respond to color stimuli. There are three kinds of cones, each of which is sensitive to one of three basic colors: red, green, and blue. The most common form of color blind-ness is the *deutan,* or green, insensitive type, where the weakness of color per-ception makes the color green appear red.

The gene for determining color vision is located on the X chromosome. If a male has this recessive faulty gene on his X chromosome, he will be color-blind because there is no corresponding gene on the Y chromosome to counteract this condition. Affected fathers will have no affected offspring unless the mother is a carrier. Because all of his sons receive Y chromosomes from him and X chromosomes from their mother, they will in no way be affected. How-ever, all of his daughters will be carriers and the chances are 50% of their male offspring will be color-blind (see Figure 3-6).

FIGURE 3-6
Transmission of Sex-Linked Characteristics.

Some examples of sex-linked characteristics are color blindness and hemophilia. The lowercase *a* represents the recessive characteristics.

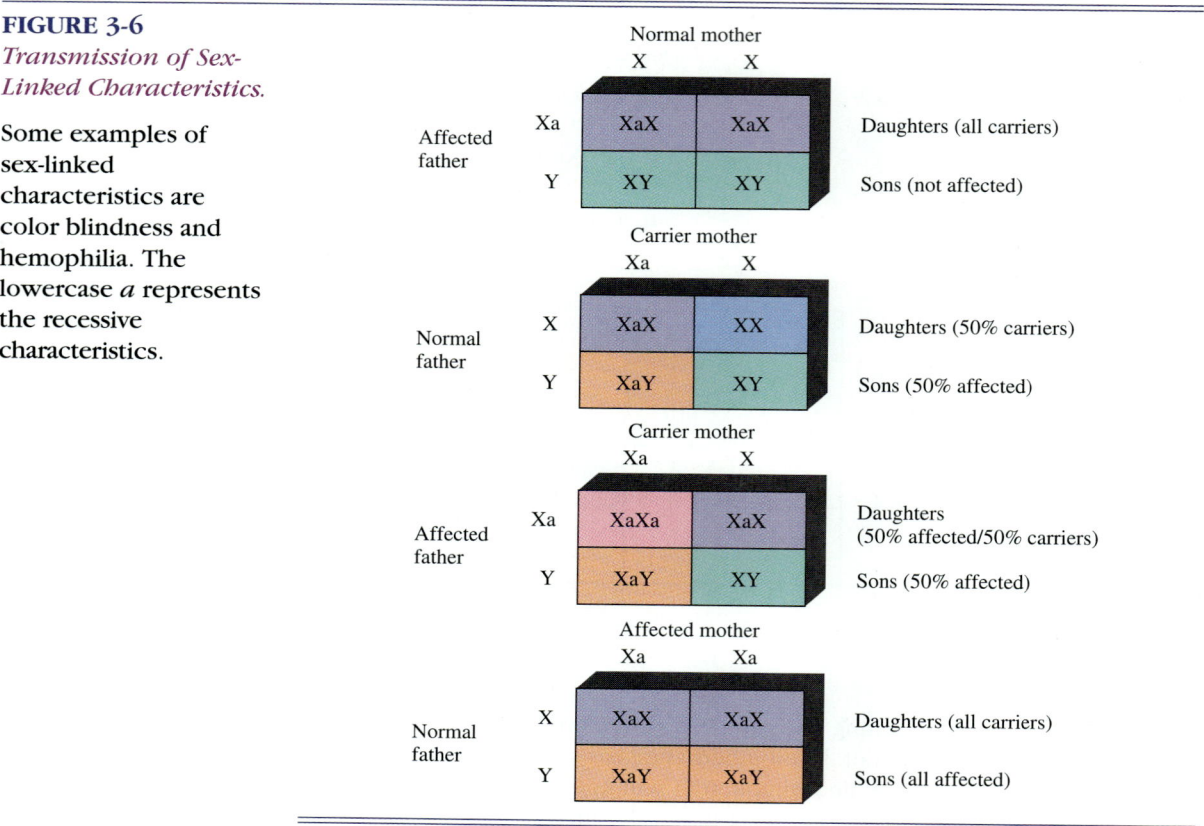

Another well known sex-linked characteristic is hemophilia, or bleeders disease. This condition is caused by a recessive X-linked gene that fails to produce the plasma protein *antihemophilic globulin* (AHG), which is necessary for normal blood clotting. Persons with this disease bleed excessively from minor injuries and are more likely than the average person to bleed to death from serious injury. The same inheritance pattern that color blindness follows is in operation with the inheritance of hemophilia. Males with the faulty X chromosome become hemophilic because they have no alternate gene on the Y chromosome to counteract this condition (see Figure 3-6).

We have considered only sex-linked characteristics that are carried on the X chromosome, but there is also evidence of Y-linked sex characteristics. Unlike X-linked, the Y-linked are passed on only from father to son. For example, *Hairy pinna,* long hair growing on the ears, appears to be Y-linked. To date, there is much uncertainty as to what other Y-linked characteristics exist.

Finally, we should mention **sex-limited genes.** These genes are normally expressed in only one sex, although they are carried by both sexes. Unlike X-linked genes, sex-limited characteristics include primary sex traits (related only to the organs of reproduction) and secondary sex characteristics (differences in skeletal and muscular growth, breasts, beard, etc.). *Pattern baldness,* a trait common to males, is also considered sex-limited.

▬ DNA: The Blueprint of Life

Now let us peer inside the nucleus of a cell to discover just what the genetic code entails. Under a microscope, the chromosome looks like a thin, colored, rodlike thread. A gene is simply a very small portion of a chromosome, and it has a specific function. Chemically, the structure of a chromosome (or gene) is called **deoxyribonucleic acid,** or more simply **DNA.** The genes are the part of the DNA structure that carry hereditary instructions for the development of the organism.

The study of DNA offers researchers many puzzles. Slowly, though, we are increasing our knowledge of its role in genetic functioning. In future years, we hope to learn how DNA interacts with other cellular components to express the information it encodes (Felsenfeld, 1985).

DNA looks like a long spiral staircase or twisting ladder. It has rungs, or steps, that are attached to and supported by an external framework. This framework consists of alternating molecules of sugar and phosphate. The steps are composed of only four chemicals—*adenine* (A), *thymine* (T), *guanine* (G), and *cytosine* (C). Each step consists of two chemicals joined together (Figure 3-7). The chemical adenine will bond (link up) only with the chemical thymine, and guanine and cytosine will bond only with each other.

A **gene** is a segment of a chromosome that controls or influences inheritable characteristics. A gene comprises several hundred or even several thousand rungs of the DNA ladder. When activated, each rung will lead to the production of specific proteins or enzymes. Some genes may be several hundred steps

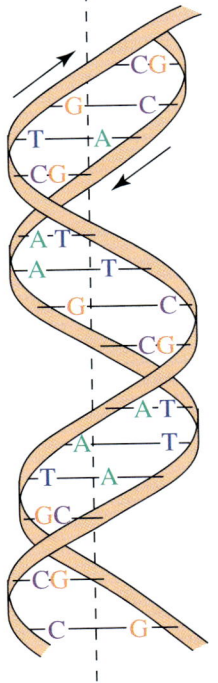

FIGURE 3-7

A Section of the DNA Molecule as Described by Watson and Crick.

Each rung on the helix is composed either of adenine (A) and thymine (T) or guanine (G) and cytosine (C).

INTERACTION OF HEREDITY AND ENVIRONMENT

Make up a list of all the genetically inherited characteristics you recognize in yourself. Label each one either dominant or recessive, and indicate whether this characteristic is from your mother's, father's, or both sides of the family. Modify this list as you proceed through the chapter.

long, others several thousand. Although it is not known exactly how many genes are on a chromosome, a frequent estimate has been 20,000, which would give human beings approximately 460,000 gene pairs. Some theories even double this number, bringing the total closer to 1 million.

A gene is DNA material arranged in a specific fashion so an accompanying specific protein can be synthesized (manufactured). To make a long and complex story short and simple, this dormant genetic blueprint becomes active at an appropriate time. The activated gene duplicates itself, but with minor chemical alterations (uracil replaces thymine, for example). Instead of being DNA, it now becomes **ribonucleic acid, or RNA.** More specifically, it is called **messenger RNA** because its purpose is to carry a genetic message (the genetic code) outside the nucleus to a ribosome, a cellular body that synthesizes protein.

To understand the process of protein synthesis, you should know that your body consists of protein from the top of your scalp to the tip of your toes. Your eye color, your bones, your heart, your spleen, and everything else is protein. It is in the ribosomes that protein is manufactured. Remarkably, ribosomes can synthesize almost a million different types of proteins by mixing together various amino acids. **Amino acids,** which exist in only 20 to 30 different varieties (no one knows for sure), are the true building blocks in life. All protein in all life originates from amino acids.

We might compare the ribosome to a pharmacist, who follows the directions on a prescription (the chemically coded message that messenger RNA delivers). The directions might read "Mix one part amino acid 2 with two parts amino acid 18, add one part amino acid 12," and so on. This combination of amino acids would produce one protein. If the genetic code was calling for heart muscle protein, many messenger RNAs would be sent to all the ribosomes in the cytoplasm. The RNAs would deliver their directions to the ribosome, which would then mix the appropriate amino acids according to the genetic instruction.

Soon the cell would be swollen with heart protein, and mitosis would take place. Now two cells would manufacture heart protein, divide, and then there would be four. In 9 months' time, in a similar way for every body part, a total of approximately 7 pounds of protein is produced. In this complex fashion, a single cell becomes a human infant.

For any given characteristic, an organism may receive one dominant gene from *each* parent (homozygous genotype and dominant phenotype), or one recessive gene from each parent (homozygous genotype, recessive phenotypic characteristic), or a dominant gene from one parent and a recessive from the other (heterozygous genotype, phenotype of the dominant characteristic).

Genetic Individuality

To understand physical and psychological inheritance, you must understand that during the process of meiosis, chromosomes line up opposite each other and then meiotically split into daughter cells. But remember that most of the genes on one chromosome differ from the genes on the opposite chromosome. Although chromosomes line up, there is no factor requiring that they line up on the right or the left side. They may do either (Figure 3-8).

This means the number of genetically different sex cells an individual can produce is 2^{23} or 8,388,608. In other words, the male can produce over 8

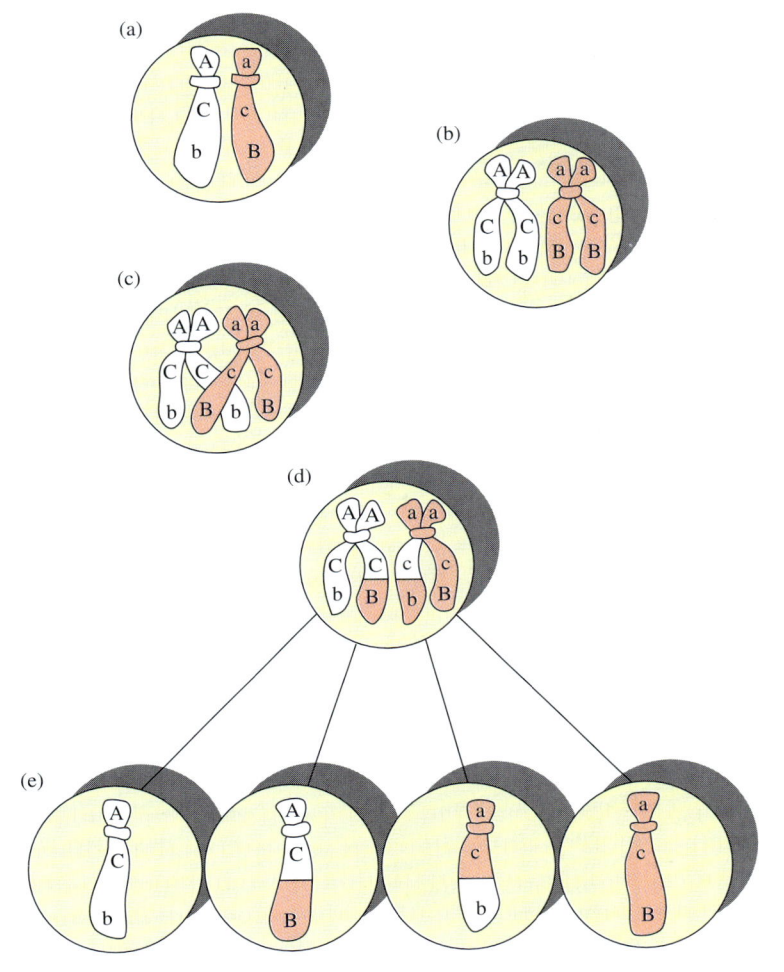

FIGURE 3-8
Gene Crossover.

This diagram illustrates crossing over—the exchange of genes from one chromosome to another. Moving from steps (a) through (e) we start by showing one chromosome pair in the male gamete; the chromosome on the left is from his mother, the one on the right from his father. As the process of meiosis begins, we can see the duplication of chromosomes (b), the exchange or crossing over of some genetic material (c and d), and finally the formation of four sperm, showing different combinations of genetic material from his parents that will be passed on to his offspring.

SOURCE: Adapted from McClearn, G. E. (1963). The inheritance of behavior. In L. J. Postman (Ed.), *Psychology in the making.* New York: Knopf, p. 163.

million *genetically different* sperm and the female can produce the same number of different eggs. By calculating the various combinations of sperm penetrations of the egg, we find that one man and woman together can produce approximately 64 billion genetically different offspring without ever having two that are identical (identical twins being the exception).

Among other things, this means that in organisms as genetically complex as humans, heredity represents not only the passing on of certain characteristics (Table 3-1) but also the transmission of individual differences. Consider a family in which the children have physical characteristics that are as different as night and day. Yet there are other parents who produce offspring whose appearances are almost mirror images of each other. How is this possible? The answer is that when both parents carry homozygous genes for a certain characteristic, the children will all be homozygous for that same characteristic. If both parents have paired homozygous genes for blue eyes, black hair, and a "Roman" nose,

TABLE 3-1
Dominant and Recessive Characteristics

Characteristics in the left-hand column (the phenotype) dominate characteristics in the right-hand column.

	Dominant Traits	*Recessive Characteristics*
Eye coloring	Brown eyes Gray, green, hazel Blue	Gray, green, hazel, blue eyes Blue Albino (pink)
Vision	Farsightedness Normal vision Normal sight Normal color vision	Normal vision Nearsightedness Night vision Color blindness*
Hair	Dark hair Nonred hair (blond, brunette) Curly hair Full head of hair Widow's peak hairline	Blond hair, light hair (red hair) Red hair Straight hair Baldness* Normal hairline
Facial features	Dimples in cheek Unattached earlobes "Roman" nose Broad lips	No dimples Attached earlobes Straight nose Thin lips
Appendages	Extra digits Fused digits Short digits Fingers lacking one joint Limb dwarfing Clubbed thumb Double-jointedness	Normal number Normal Normal Normal length Normal proportion Normal thumb Normal joints
Other	Immunity to poison ivy Normal coloring (pigmented skin) Normal blood clotting Normal hearing Normal hearing Normal intelligence Normal enzyme production	Susceptibility to poison ivy Albinism Hemophilia* Congenital deafness Deaf mutism Amaurotic idiocy Phenylketonuria

*Sex-linked characteristics.

all children will have these characteristics. Those parents who are heterozygous for various traits may have offspring without recognizable similarities. Therefore, heredity means familial similarities as well as individual differences. We shall soon see that as early as the second month after conception, some inherited physical characteristics begin to develop.

■ Simple Types of Gene Action

The statement that brown eyes dominate blue eyes does not account for the various *shades* of brown and blue, as well as hazel, green, and gray eyes. It is because of such complexities that *dominant* and *recessive* are inadequate terms for the more complex features of biochemical activity. In fact, strictly speaking, both terms are partial misnomers. A dominant gene does not actually dominate a recessive gene. The terms *active* and *passive* serve much better to describe a gene's activity (sometimes referred to as *biochemically active* or *passive*).

The recessive, or passive, gene manufactures very few messenger RNAs and, consequently, very little protein. The dominant gene is more active, manufacturing more RNA and, consequently, more protein. To illustrate this point, let us examine eye coloring, a prime example of a gene's *activity level*. The iris (colored part) of all eyes is made up of practically the same protein (called *melanin*). The so-called color of the eyes is, in essence, an optical illusion, dependent on the amount of melanin produced. Babies, whether kittens, puppies, or humans, are usually born with blue eyes, regardless of the eventual eye color. Does this mean the iris first produces blue melanin then brown melanin? The answer is no. It means that melanin, in small amounts, appears blue. The more active a gene is, the more melanin (pigment) will be produced and the darker the iris appears (see Figures 3-9 and 3-10).

An absence of melanin indicates the gene is neither biochemically active nor biochemically passive. Rather, the gene is inactive. Without the production of melanin, the eye has no coloration and appears to be pink because, without

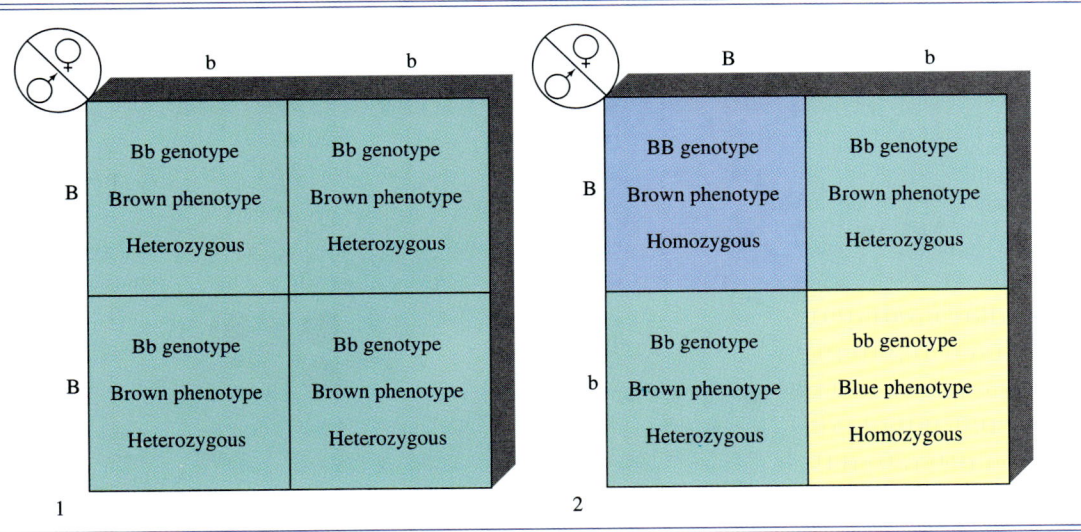

FIGURE 3-9
A Punnett Square for Eye Color.

Each numbered square represents a couple: (1) All children born to this couple, regardless of how many, will have brown eyes but will be "carriers" (have recessive genes) for blue eyes. (2) Two parents with brown eyes (their phenotype) may have a heterozygous genotype—Bb. If the recessive gene is present in an egg that is fertilized by a sperm carrying the recessive gene for blueness, they can have a blue-eyed child. In theory, one quarter of their children would have blue eyes.

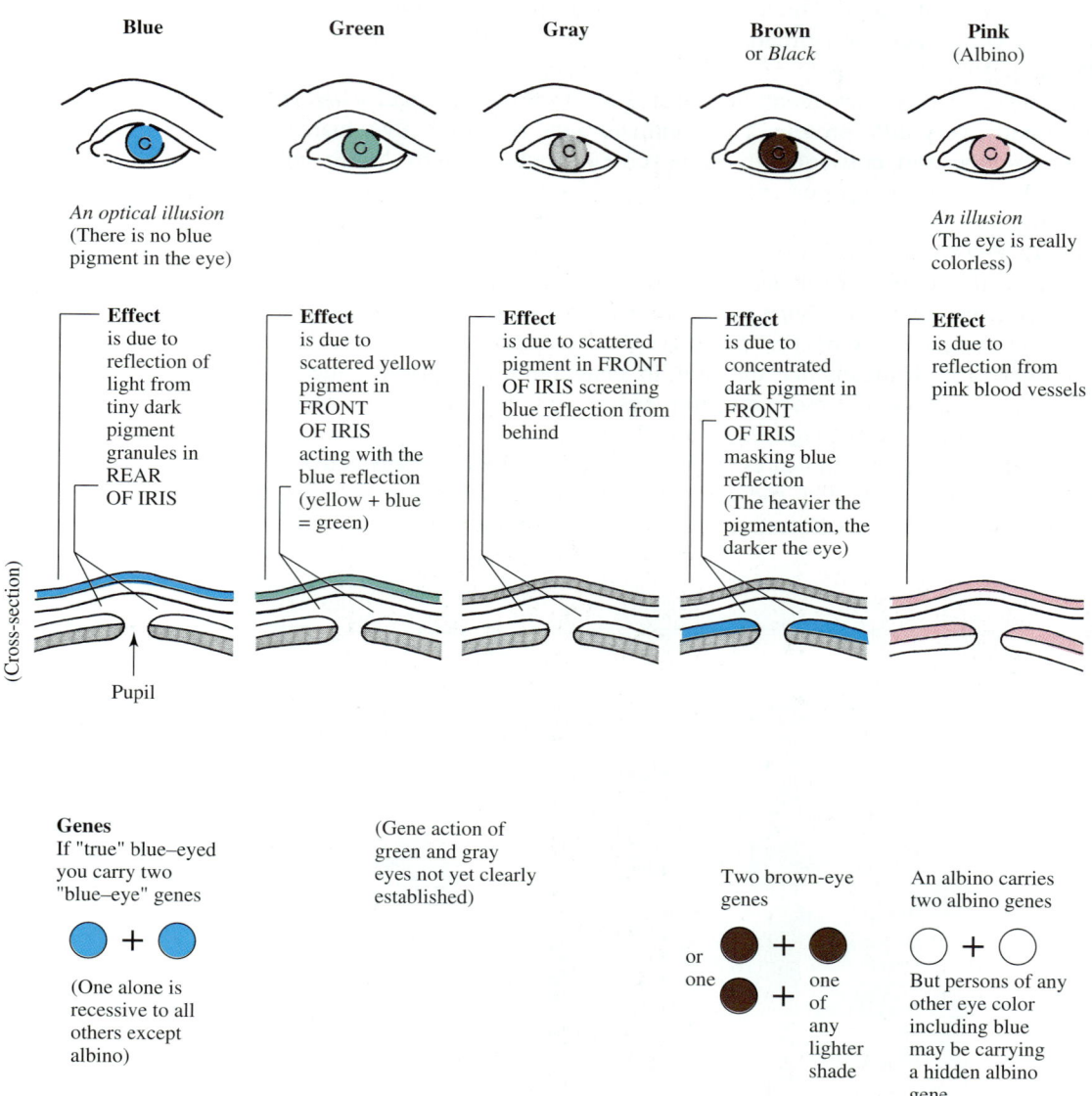

FIGURE 3-10

What Makes Your Eye Color?

Although eye color appears different, this is not because of the presence of different pigments. Rather, differences in eye color are due to the mass or density of the pigmentation itself. The more dense the pigment, the darker the iris appears.

SOURCE: Adapted from Scheinfeld, A. (1950). *The new you and heredity.* Philadelphia: Lippincott.

Albino individuals have deficient pigmentation, including translucent or milky skin, white or colorless hair, and a pink coloration within the pupils of the eyes.

pigmentation, the small blood vessels at the rear of the iris are visible. A person unable to produce any melanin is called an *albino*.

A person's eye color is an "effect." That is, blue eyes appear "bluer" under a clear blue sky or when a person wears blue clothing. Likewise, complementary brown clothing will make brown eyes appear darker or lighter.

Hair color is determined by the same principle; very little melanin produces naturally white hair (found primarily in Scandinavian peoples); small amounts of pigment produce blonds; larger melanin deposits produce brown hair; and the largest deposits of pigment granules produce black hair. As with eye coloring, it is the same melanin but in different quantities. Hair color, like eye color, is affected by other factors, such as the thickness, dryness, or oiliness of the hair or the lightness or darkness of a room or other environmental surroundings. Red hair seems to be caused by a supplementary gene, one that appears only if no other dominant gene is present (see Figure 3-11).

Genes, then, have *degrees of activity* whose rates may change during the course of development. It is somewhat uncommon, but not unusual, for a person's hair color to change (genetically, not artificially) throughout his or her life. For example, it is possible for a person born with platinum hair color to become blond at age 5; "strawberry blond" at age 20; red-headed at age 23; blond, again, at age 25; and so on. Scalp hair is frequently a different color from facial, pubic, or other body hairs, whose characteristics are evidently governed by separate genes.

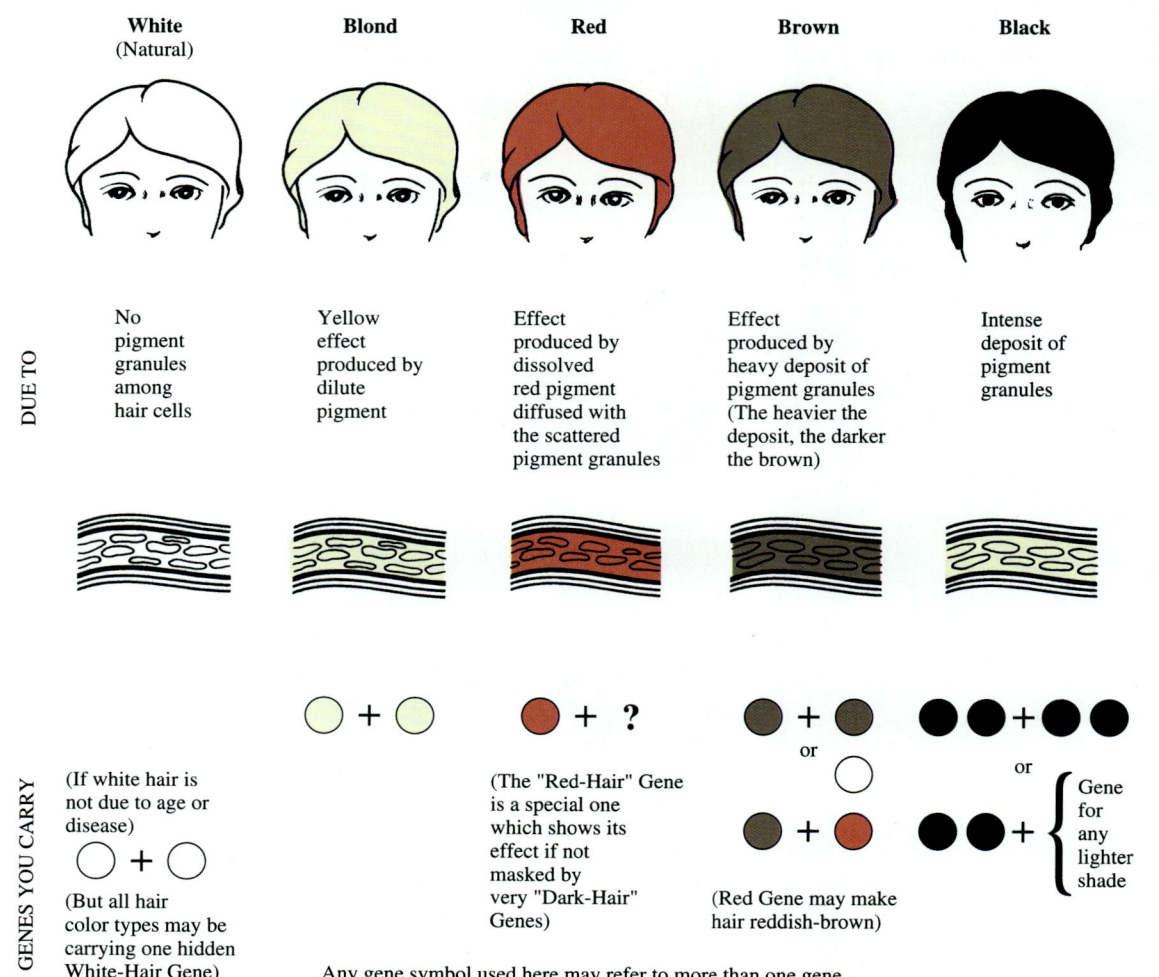

FIGURE 3-11

What Makes Your Hair Color?

Similar to Figure 3–10, hair color is not due to the presence of different pigments. Instead, it is the density of pigment that creates hair color. The more dense the pigment, the darker the hair color.

SOURCE: Adapted from Scheinfeld, A. (1950). *The new you and heredity.* Philadelphia: Lippincott.

Blood typing provides another illustration of why *dominant* and *recessive* are inadequate terms that should be replaced by the terms *active* and *passive.* Although there are over 100 different chemicals in the blood, most people are familiar with only the four main blood types: A, B, AB, and O. Figure 3-12 shows two homozygous blood types; the female has type A, and the male has type B.

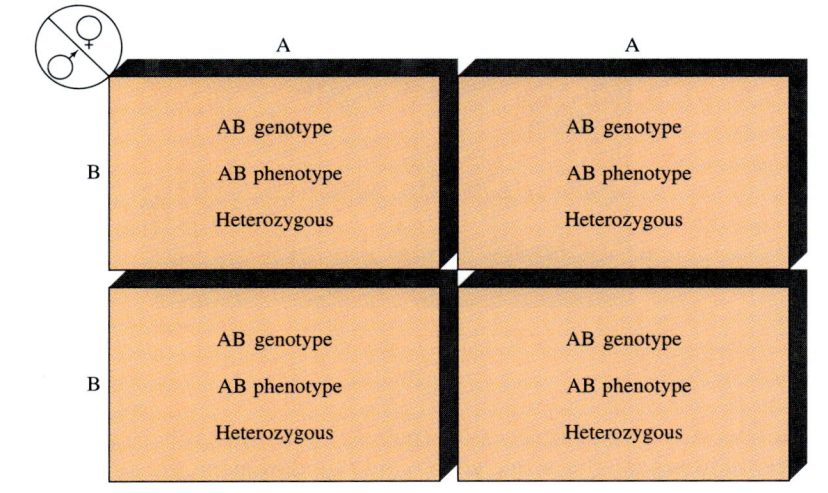

FIGURE 3-12

A Punnett Square for Blood Type.

All children born to this couple will have type AB blood. One gene does not dominate the other.

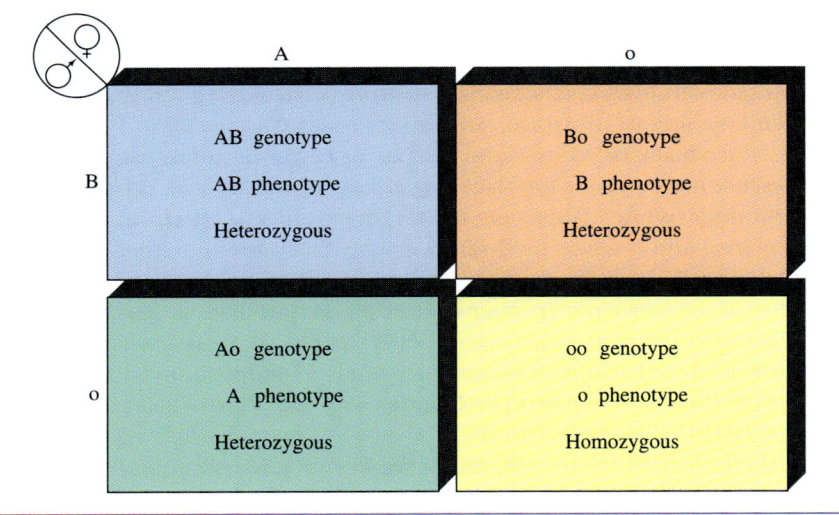

FIGURE 3-13

A Punnett Square for Blood Type O.

Blood type O, like other recessive characteristics, does not express itself unless a dominant gene is absent.

All of their offspring will be type AB, with neither A nor B dominating the other. Each child receives an active gene for the production of the chemical labeled A, as well as an active gene for the protein chemical called B. Therefore, both proteins (chemicals) are found in the bloodstream. The genetic action is mutually exclusive, not additive as in eye or hair coloration. The so-called recessive gene in blood typing is type O, a blood type that produces so little protein, it is barely measurable.

In Figure 3-13 we can see that a type A or B person knows his or her phenotype, but not genotype, whereas type AB or O knows both phenotype and

FIGURE 3-14

A Punnett Square for Mating White and Black Andalusian Fowl.

When an all-black Andalusian fowl mates with an all-white one, all young are BW genotype and iridescent blue phenotype.

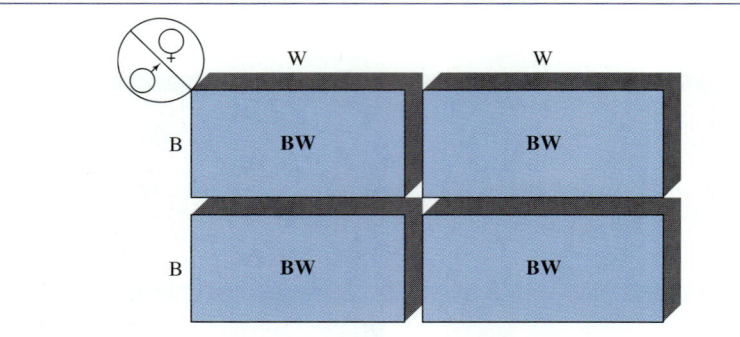

genotype. Because type O is recessive (passive), one must inherit an "O" from each parent, otherwise the active gene would be dominant. Persons with phenotype A or B may not know their genotype (it could be AA or AO; BB or BO), unless, of course, one parent is type O, in which case they would know they had a passive O in addition to their "dominant" A or B.

Genetic **blending action** is the last type of biochemical activity we discuss in this chapter. It refers to the process whereby a person inherits two different genes, but rather than one dominating the other or both acting independently of each other (e.g., blood type), they blend together.

The Andalusian fowl, a chickenlike creature, provides a good example of genetic blending action. In nature, Andalusian fowls occur only in two strains—they are either black or white—and they live geographically separated; thus all black fowl are homozygous for black and always produce black offspring; white always produce white. However, if the geographical separation is removed (e.g., in a zoo) and a white fowl mates with a black fowl, neither color dominates. Rather, all the offspring are iridescent blue! Here, the proteins have blended, evidently forming another chemical reaction that causes this beautiful new color. To answer the question students usually ask next—what happens if two iridescent blues mate?—Figures 3-14 and 3-15 help to unveil the mystery. As you can see, the resulting possibilities are one fourth black, one fourth white, and one half iridescent blue.

We have offered relatively simple examples of physical characteristics. Behavioral traits, however, are more difficult to explain. They are more complex, therefore more difficult to study. Thus we know more about the inheritance of superficial traits, such as pigmentation, than we do about the inheritance of more complicated characteristics, such as intelligence.

BEHAVIORAL GENETICS

A little boy, hugging a violin, walks out onto the stage at New York's Carnegie Hall. There is a flutter of applause from the thousands of persons filling the auditorium. The little boy tucks his violin under his chin and begins to play. The audience, skeptical, watches, listens. A tiny hand sweeps the bow back and forth, tiny fingers fly over the strings, streams of melody, now shrill, now full-throated,

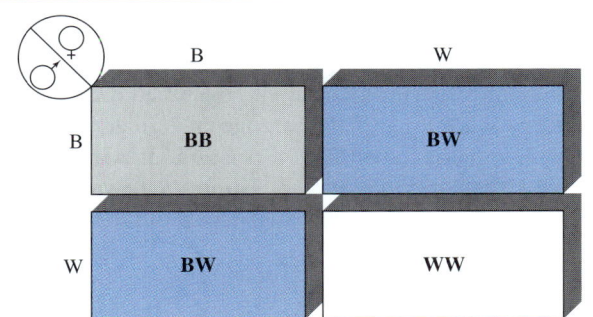

FIGURE 3-15

A Punnett Square for Mating Iridescent Blue Andalusian Fowl.

The mating of two iridescent Andalusian fowl results in 50% of their offspring being iridescent blue, 25% black, and 25% white.

cascade forth. Already, in those first minutes, many mature musicians out front know that in all their years of study and work they have not been able to achieve such mastery. Soon they, and the others, quite forget that this is a little boy who is playing. As if drawn by invisible bonds, they are carried out of the hall, into the night, higher and higher. Then suddenly there is a burst of notes like a rocket's shower of golden stars . . . the music stops . . . and they are all back again in Carnegie Hall, incredulously storming with their bravos a little boy—a little boy who in a few hours may be crying because he isn't allowed to stay up and play with his toys. (Scheinfeld, 1950, p. 234)

In his study of musical inheritance Scheinfeld noted that such situations have occurred periodically, although infrequently, through the centuries. He also pointed out that true virtuosity in playing an instrument appears extremely early in life, the average age being just 4¾ years. For those who believe environmental factors, rather than genetic, are the major influence of musical talent, Scheinfeld cites case histories. Artur Rubinstein, for example, was brought up in a poor family in which no musical instruments were available. However, Rubinstein spontaneously created and sang his own songs. Scheinfeld also tells of a number of children exhibiting musical greatness in their second and third years of life; the more familiar names include Chopin, Mozart, Heifetz, Rachmaninoff, Ormandy, and Toscanini.

Scheinfeld's evidence suggests that truly great musical ability depends heavily on genetics. In all probability, several genes are involved in producing such virtuosos. This, however, does not eliminate the role of environment; rather, a favorable environment must exist if the talent is to be allowed full expression. Yet the most conducive environment in the world for the development of musical ability will be of limited value if the inherited potential is not present. Consider, for example, the sheer number of children who have suffered through years of music or voice lessons, simply because their parents may have believed that "practice makes perfect."

The study of the relationship between genetic variations and behavioral variations (such as that of musicality) is known as **behavioral genetics,** a fairly recent and complex field of exploration. Behavioral genetics studies behavior that is directly or indirectly under genetic control. Behavior is seldom controlled by one protein, which is the case with certain physical traits. Rather, most behavior is influenced by the multiple production of proteins (genetic traits), the individual's past interactions with the environment, current environmental factors, and the organism's current biochemical state (Plomin, 1990).

The complexities of these interacting variables make their scientific investigation difficult. Consequently, our knowledge of human inherited behavior is extremely limited, forcing us to use such terms as **behavioral predisposition.** Such a term implies that one may have a *tendency* toward certain behavioral characteristics, given certain unspecified environmental conditions.

Polygenes and Behavior

It has been implied that each gene has a definite and singular task, yet this is seldom the case. Instead, most physical and behavioral characteristics are under the direction of **polygenes,** genes that work together with additive and/or complementary effects. Obviously, the more genes that work together on a single task, the more difficult the research becomes. Polygenes increase the number of individual differences found in the anatomical and physiological structure of persons. In fact, no two people are biochemically identical. Therefore, they will react differently to similar biochemical environments (not only medicines but all foods, which, in the final analysis, are chemical compositions). This partially explains why some people can eat or drink foods that may upset the systems of others.

To understand polygenes, we must be aware of an individual's *constitution,* a reference to the physical and mental makeup of a person. *Makeup* is a rather vague term that refers to the general biochemical state created by polygenes. When we speak of a person having a strong physical constitution, we are referring to his or her strength or health. When a person is said to have a "weak stomach," the inference is to a constitutional weakness established by polygenes. One's biochemical makeup seems to contain varying degrees of immunity or susceptibility to irritations, allergies, tuberculosis, poison ivy, diabetes, and hundreds of other biological disorders.

All diseases interact to some degree with the environment. People who are susceptible to tuberculosis, for example, may never develop it if they live in a healthy clean-air environment. A person who is susceptible to poison ivy may seldom contract it if he or she has no contact with the plant. By the same token, a person basically immune to poison ivy may be exposed to it many times without contracting a rash. If, however, this person were to lie down in a poison ivy patch, there probably would not be enough "immunity" to keep him or her from contracting a good case of it.

Another example is *diabetes mellitus,* a condition that—the evidence suggests—begins as a constitutional tendency (possibly two or more recessive genes, i.e., biochemically inactive). These inactive genes can produce only limited amounts of insulin; therefore, when a person gains too much weight or eats too many carbohydrates, insulin production becomes insufficient, forcing the person to add insulin to the system. In this instance, environmental interaction is the amount and type (protein, carbohydrates, etc.) of food intake, the consequent body weight, and the quantity of insulin produced (a genetically determined factor).

INTERACTION OF HEREDITY AND ENVIRONMENT

Develop a list of your strengths and your weaknesses, for example, in math, sports, music, reading, and so on. To what extent do you believe each to be influenced by heredity? Environment? Interactionism? Why?

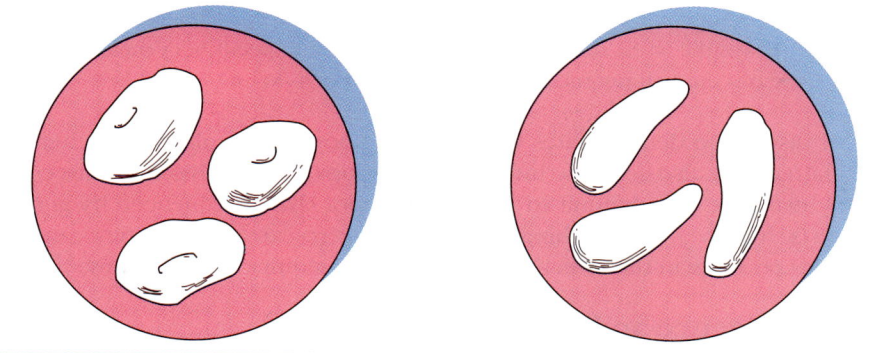

FIGURE 3-16
Sickle-Cell Anemia.

Erythrocytes (red blood cells) on the left are capable of carrying the "normal" amount of oxygen; the sickle-shaped cells, on the right, are incapable of carrying sufficient oxygen.

Adapted from Goldsby, R.A. (1971). *Race and Races*. New York: Macmillan.

Sickle-cell anemia, a disease of the red blood cells, is a relatively common disorder (1 in 400) among blacks of African background (Whaley & Wong, 1989). Normally, a red blood cell is shaped like a disk, but a minor genetic mutation changes the shape of the red blood cell to a hook-shaped "sickle" (Figure 3-16). These cells die very quickly (causing anemia and, possibly, death) because of their inability to carry oxygen. Because it is a recessive trait, individuals who inherit this recessive homozygous condition may eventually die from it. Blacks may have SS (normal red blood cells), Ss (a tendency toward anemia), or ss (sickle-cell anemia). It is interesting to note that in this country, an Ss constitution can weaken a person's health, but the recessive "s" gene plays a dual role: It produces a protein (chemical) makeup that immunizes the individual from malaria. Therefore, blacks who live in Africa and have the heterozygous Ss possess a biological advantage over those carrying homozygous SS genes!

In summary, genes and polygenes produce a biochemical state that may be referred to, currently, only as one's constitution or predisposition. Because these predispositions are heritable, it can be advantageous to a physician to know a patient's family medical history, which is why we spend a considerable amount of time in doctors' offices and hospitals listing the diseases and illnesses of our parents and other relatives. Diabetes, sickle-cell anemia, heart and kidney conditions, cataracts, and even mental disorders often are familial.

The following case clearly shows how a familial disorder may be diagnosed by genetic means even when symptoms might indicate conditions other than those that actually exist:

This child had a very dry skin, sparse hair, poorly developed teeth, and a tendency to become feverish upon the slightest exertion. Hypothyroidism (undersecretion of the thyroid gland) results in such symptoms, and the child's condition was thus diagnosed and he was put on thyroid medication. But the treatment seemed to aggravate the condition, and another doctor was called in. Fortunately, this man had had training in genetics, and made a study of the child's family history. He found that one of the parents and a number of the relatives showed similar, but less severe, symptoms, and he diagnosed the condition as an inherited disease, ectodermal dysplasia. Among the symptoms of this disease is an absence of normal sweat glands. In a normal person the body is cooled

INTERACTION OF HEREDITY AND ENVIRONMENT

Some people do genealogical research to help them understand familial predispositions toward certain diseases such as cancer, diabetes, heart ailments, kidney problems, and so forth. What would your research reveal?

through the evaporation of perspiration from the skin, but in persons without normal perspiration, the body is easily overheated. Hence, the administration of thyroxine was the worst sort of treatment, for thyroxine speeds body metabolism and increases the heat output. (Winchester, 1975, pp. 4–5)

Our discussion demonstrates that genes are not just simple units of hereditary matter; they also combine into working groups called polygenes. This complexity makes it very difficult to identify behavior that is influenced by genes. Scientists, however, are reaching a point in their research where they can see signposts pointing in the direction their scientific inquiry should follow.

Intelligence and Behavior

Psychologists most often disagree among themselves about the nature and origin of mental disorders, personality traits, and, especially, intelligence. Intelligence is a broad term that encompasses an individual's proficiency in a wide variety of intellectual (cognitive) areas, including problem-solving, number abilities, vocabulary, and so on. Regarding the development of intelligence, some favor the explanations offered by the environmental camp, others adhere to the inheritability of intelligence, and still others take a middle course.

Concerning the controversy over intelligence, the evidence indicates that people are born with differing genetic makeups, and it is also more or less obvious (depending on your outlook) that people inherit differing potentials, abilities, and intelligences.

Twin Studies: Methodology   In theory, the only way to determine which effects are genetic and which are environmental is to hold one of these variables constant while manipulating the other. In other words, if we could totally control the environmental conditions of persons from the moment of conception onward, any resulting difference could therefore be considered as genetic. This method, of course, is impossible. The alternative is to manipulate the environment of two persons who have an identical genetic makeup. Through the phenomenon of identical twins, this is possible.

To design an experiment that will yield practical data, three groupings of twins are required. Group 1 should consist of identical twins (genetically identical) who have been reared together, thus providing *similar* environments. Group 2 should consist of identical twins reared apart, preferably in *dissimilar* environments. Group 3 should comprise fraternal twins (genetically dissimilar) reared together and preferably of the same sex—opposite sexes have a greater variance in their environment because they tend to socialize more with members of their own sex (Smith, 1965). See Table 3-2 to see how this trigroup methodology is executed.

Comparing the results of such studies (see Table 3-3) demonstrates that identical twins reared together are much closer in intelligence than are fraternal twins reared together, both having similar environments. In other words, similar environments are not sufficient to equalize intelligence. In support of this thesis, the results also indicate that the intelligence scores of identical twins reared apart are more similar than are the scores of fraternal twins reared in the same environment. But this does not rule out varying degrees of environmental effects. It has been found (Smith, 1965) that identical twins are more likely to

TABLE 3-2
Trigroup Method of Studying Genetic Versus Environmental Influences on Behavior: Examples for Intelligence

	Twin Type	Environmental Factor	Interpretation of Results
Group 1	Identical twins (genetically identical)	Reared together (similar environment)	Assuming IQs are similar, these results could be due to either genetic or environmental factors.
Group 2	Identical twins (genetically identical)	Reared apart (dissimilar environment)	If IQs are markedly different, the assumption will be that environment plays a major role. If IQs are similar, a genetic influence will be assumed.
Group 3	Fraternal twins (preferably of the same sex) (genetically different)	Reared together (similar environment)	If environment is the significant factor, correlations will be about the same as for identical twins reared together.

TABLE 3-3
Statistical Correlations of Intelligence Among Family Relations

Relationship	Correlation
Monozygotic twins	
Reared together	.86
Reared apart	.79
Dizygotic twins	
Reared together	.60
Siblings	
Reared together	.47
Reared apart	.24
Parent/child	.40
Foster parent/child	.31
Cousins	.15

These correlations are composited from 111 different studies from all parts of the world. In general, the closer the genetic relationship of two people, the higher the correlation between their IQs.

Adapted from Bouchard, T. J. Jr. (1981). Familial studies of intelligence: A review. *Science, 212* (4498), 1055–1059.

have mutual friendships and share experiences than are fraternal twins, possibly accounting somewhat for the higher correlation in their IQs. Because fraternal twins are more likely to share similar environments than other siblings are, there should be a closer correlation for fraternal twins than for other siblings, which indeed is the case. Environment, therefore, though evidently not the major force shaping intelligence, does have an influence.

Another method of demonstrating the degree of inheritability of intelligence is to compare children brought up with their biological parents with children reared by foster parents (Table 3-3). Theoretically, if environment was the major determining factor, children's IQs would be approximately the same as those of the other people in the household environment in which they were reared. Normally, we find the relationship between genetic parents and children to be 0.50. Therefore, the similarities in children adopted by foster parents would point to the greater importance of environment, whereas the differences would suggest the hereditary role. Some researchers have found that adopted children have IQs closer to those of their genetic parents than to those of their foster parents.

While the controversy about the major influences on intelligence continues, we can only await the development of new research techniques to supply us with the answers to our questions. Meanwhile, we must also explore the nature of both intelligence and intellectual potential. If society (parents, educators, psychologists, etc.) can provide appropriate vehicles for the enhancement of each individual's potential, the questions now being asked regarding the nature-nurture issue may become moot.

Inheritability of Behavioral Traits   The same general methodology for determining inheritability of intelligence can be used to discover to what degree, if any, various other behavior patterns are influenced by the laws of genetics. Behavior that is unique, different, or even bizarre is more noticeable and measurable than is so-called normal behavior. This is because distinct abnormal behavior is more readily measured by a statistical analysis than is the range of more normal behaviors.

There are studies revealing at least minimal evidence that certain basic behaviors are inherited (Plomin, McClearn, Pederson, & Nesselroade, 1988; Tellegen, Lykken, Bouchard, & Wilcox, 1988). However, it is a very unclear area and one where it is wise to tread lightly until experimental results offer more substantial evidence. It is speculated, however, that certain personality traits (e.g., aggressiveness, smiling responses, fear, shyness, moodiness), as well as certain psychological disorders (such as depression and schizophrenia) may be inherited (Gottesman & Shields, 1982; Horowitz & Dudek, 1983). The activity level evident in a newborn seems to persist through at least the first few years of life, indicating again a genetic predisposition. Children assessed at 21 months of age as being inhibited or uninhibited in social situations continued to exhibit these traits at ages 5½ and, at least to a certain extent, 7½ (Kagan, Reznick, Snidman, & Gibbons, 1988).

Schizophrenia is a psychotic disorder characterized by thought disturbances and is often accompanied by delusions, hallucinations, and other maladaptive behaviors. There are strong arguments to support both genetic and environmental causes of schizophrenia. The question is whether schizophrenia develops from traumatic early childhood experiences or from genetically produced chemical imbalances—or from a combination of both.

Again, studies of identical twins reared in the same environment, identical twins reared in separate environments, and fraternal twins reared in the same environment are the preferred methods for studying the genetics of schizophrenia. The compilation of studies shown in Table 3-4 shows that the statistical evidence points directly to an inheritable genetic predisposition toward acquiring schizophrenia. There are several significant studies, however, that indicate zero concordance (degree of similarity between twins) rate.

INTERACTION OF HEREDITY AND ENVIRONMENT

Do you believe there are any inherited behavioral characteristics such as math ability, musicality, hyperactivity, or artistic talent in your family? Can you think of a family that has some behavior that suggests inheritability?

Some researchers believe that certain personality traits, such as aggression, may be inherited.

TABLE 3-4

Concordance Rates for Schizophrenia in Newer Twin Studies.
The concordance rate is the percentage of pairs in which both twins are diagnosed schizophrenic.

	MZ Pairs		DZ Pairs	
	Total Pairs	*Rate (%)*	*Total Pairs*	*Rate (%)*
Finland, 1963/1971	17	35	20	13
Norway, 1967	55	45	90	15
Denmark, 1973	21	56	41	27
United Kingdom, 1966/1987	22	58	33	15
Norway, 1991	31	48	28	4
United States, 1969/1983	164	31	268	6
Pooled Concordance				
Median	310	46	480	14
Weighted Mean		39		10

Adapted from Gottesman, I. I. (1991). *Schizophrenia Genesis.* New York: WH Freeman.

In one study, researchers discovered a significantly higher concordance for schizophrenia between members of identical twin pairs than between members of fraternal twin pairs (Gottesman & Shields, 1982). They found that of 28 pairs of identical twins, there was a 42% concordance for schizophrenia. Their procedure was to identify members of twin pairs from among a population of schizophrenic patients and then to determine how many of these individuals had a twin who was also schizophrenic (of all members of the twin pairs who were schizophrenic, 42% had a schizophrenic twin). The concordance between the members of fraternal twin pairs was only 9%, from a sample of 34 pairs.

An environmental argument is that although one may inherit the predisposition to schizophrenia (or any other behavioral trait), it does not necessarily follow that an individual will actually become schizophrenic (if that were the case, our correlations for identical twins would be a perfect 1.00). Organisms interact with their environment; therefore, a person who is predisposed toward schizophrenia may never develop it if he or she is in an appropriate, positive environment. As in the example of immunity or susceptibility to poison ivy, persons may be highly predisposed to schizophrenia, but if they never are in an environment capable of triggering it, they will never contract it.

It is by now evident that the influence of polygenes and an organism's genetic interaction with the environment are difficult areas to explore. Although it is true that animal research has yielded significant results, human behaviors are generally investigated with fewer controls. However, even though general personality traits and characteristics remain difficult to discern, chromosomal changes can be detected through modern techniques. Gross changes in chromosomes allow insights into the tiny world of the gene. In the next section, we discuss the more obvious and common genetic problems.

GENETIC ABERRATIONS AND MUTATIONS

The activity of a cell, including the chromosomes' activities, is governed by biological principles. Biological principles reveal a somewhat high frequency of errors in the chemical behavior of the genetic code. One such "error," or dysfunction, is termed **mutation,** which refers to any sudden change that occurs in the genetic material of an organism. The word *mutant,* in any of the forms, does not imply *negative* change, although we generally conjure up ideas of some horrible change or deformity. Mutations may be positive, negative, or neutral. They also signal that a change in the genetic code (sex cells) has taken place, whereby a new gene can be passed on to the next generation.

In this textbook, the causes of mutations are divided into two groups: chromosomal abnormalities and mutagenic, or teratogenic, agents. Chromosomal abnormalities are occurrences that affect either the number of genes and/or chromosomes for a given species or the arrangement of genes on a chromosome. During normal meiosis, the 23 pairs of chromosomes line up, divide, and go to their new sex cell. Suppose, however, that one pair of chomosomes does not separate, so that both migrate to the same sex cell. In the case of a woman, one egg would now have an extra chromosome (23 + 1 = 24) and one egg would have lost a chromosome (23 − 1 = 22). If one of these eggs became fertilized, the absence or excess of 20,000 to 40,000 genes would obviously cause some change in the offspring. Chromosomal abnormalities increase as age increases (Hook, 1981).

When one chromosome of a pair is missing, the condition is called *monosomy.* Another abnormality is having an extra chromosome, called *trisomy* (tri = 3, somy = bodies), which can occur on any chromosome position. If, for example, there are three chromosomes on chromosome position number 21, it is referred to as trisomy 21; if three chromosomes are located in the 17th position, it is termed trisomy 17. Trisomy may also occur if one chromosome duplicates itself after meiosis has taken place. Some of the names of the more common and severe mutations are recognized, at least in name, by many laypersons, whereas others are less well known. The following discussion briefly describes some chromosomal abnormalities. Chromosomes are classified according to number and letters.

Down Syndrome

Down syndrome (also called **trisomy 21**), named after its discoverer, results when there is an extra chromosome on the 21st position. Individuals with this condition generally have an epicantric eye fold (resembling that of Asians) and round heads. They are usually mentally retarded and, until recently, died young because of respiratory problems, heart weaknesses, and high susceptibility to leukemia. Antibiotics have extended the lifespan of many who suffer from this disorder. Statistics show that women over age 40 are more likely to give birth to Down syndrome babies than are younger women. More specifically, mothers at age 20 have an incidence of 1 birth in 1,667; by maternal age 35, 1 in 378; and by age 45, a staggering 1 birth in every 30 (Masters, Johnson, & Kolodny, 1992). Although numerous theories attempt to explain this phenomenon, none have done so satisfactorily.

A person with Down syndrome (Trisomy 21) has an extra chromosome in the twenty-first position.

Klinefelter's Syndrome (XXY)

Males with **Klinefelter's syndrome** have two normal X chromosomes plus the Y chromosome (although they may have more than two X chromosomes— e.g., XXXXY; see Sheridan & Radlinski, 1988). They have small external male sex organs but the general body contour of a female, including enlarged breasts. Those affected are sterile and often below average in intelligence. As with trisomy 21, older women more frequently give birth to males having this condition than do younger women.

Turner's Syndrome (XO)

Turner's syndrome is a monosomy condition (only one sex chromosome) that affects approximately 1 female of every 2,000 births (Sutton, 1980). The afflicted female may look somewhat normal at birth because clinical signs do not appear until puberty. The physical characteristics include a webbed neck, short fingers (polydactylism), and short stature. No secondary sex characteristics appear at the time of puberty and those afflicted with this syndrome are sterile. Although they are normally not mentally retarded, they often have learning problems (Kalat, 1992).

Cri-du-Chat Syndrome

Cri-du-chat syndrome is caused by a partial loss of chromosome 5 and produces many disorders, including severe mental retardation, microcephaly (very small brain), growth retardation, low birth weight, and divergent strabismus (little eye control). In French, *cri-du-chat* means cry of the cat, a reference to the mutated vocal cords that only allow the afflicted youngster to make mewing sounds. These children generally die shortly after birth.

Triple X Syndrome (XXX)

The **triple X syndrome** affects females, many of whom are virtually physically normal except for menstrual irregularities and premature menopause. However, mild mental retardation is common. Females possessing three, four, and five Xs have also been found. Usually the more sex chromosomes, the greater the level of retardation (Rovet & Netley, 1983).

XYY Syndrome

The XYY syndrome is a genetic disorder in which males have an extra Y chromosome. In the 1960s, when Richard Speck brutally murdered eight women in Chicago, the news media brought the XYY syndrome to the attention of the general public. Physicians and others associated with the case revealed that Speck had this syndrome, and it was speculated that the extra Y chromosome added an aggressive, violent streak to a person's nature. However, subsequent research (e.g., Witkin et al., 1976) has found that XYY males are no more likely to commit crimes than are XY males. However, those with this syndrome tend to be taller than average (over 6 feet) and below average in intelligence. As youngsters, some tend to be unmanageable and fearless.

We have discussed but a sample of chromosomal abnormalities in this section. Others include trisomy 17, 18 (Kupke & Muller, 1989), 22, and partial trisomy; the Philadelphia chromosome (monosomy 21, which causes leukemia in later life); E trisomy syndrome; D syndrome; and many more (Schinzel, 1984). As genetic advances take place, so will our knowledge of these and other forms of human behavior. With such knowledge, our understanding of growth and development for all stages of the life cycle will escalate.

GENETIC COUNSELING

Although some genetic defects occur randomly, more often there is a pattern to their occurrence. As geneticists have learned more about the way one generation transmits a defect to another, they have been able to counsel parents about the potential risks to their unborn children. Today, there is a network of genetic counseling centers across the country. They are staffed by physicians or specially trained "genetic associates" and equipped with computerized information retrieval systems that provide immediate access to available facts and statistics about certain problems (Black & Weiss, 1989; Mack & Berman, 1988).

Most expectant parents are at a low risk for having a baby with genetic problems and need never see a genetic counselor. In many cases, an obstetrician will talk to a couple about the most common problems, referring to a genetic counselor those with a need for more expertise:

- Couples whose blood tests show them both to be carriers of a genetic disorder.
- Prospective parents who belong to certain racial groups who are at high risk for certain genetic disorders. For example, blacks of African background are vulnerable to sickle-cell anemia.
- Prospective parents who have already borne one or more children with genetic birth defects.
- Couples who know of hereditary defects in their families.
- Women who have had three or more miscarriages.
- Couples who are closely related, because the risk of inherited disease in the offspring is greatest when parents are related (for example, one in eight for first cousins).
- Women who are over 35. (Eisenberg et al., 1991)

■ Stages of Genetic Counseling

There are three stages of the genetic counseling process (Lauersen, 1983; Lauersen & Bouchez, 1991). The first stage is assembling a complete family history, which can provide information about the genetic basis of any disorder that might be present. Once this information has been gathered, the genetic counselor often recommends special blood tests or a complete chromosome count for the wife and/or the husband.

The second stage is the genetic counselor's interpretation of the evidence. Each case is different, and any number of conclusions are possible. Establishing or excluding a genetic or chromosomal condition is often a complex undertaking, as birth defects are not always the result of genetic factors. A birth defect can be caused by a random or inherited chromosomal abnormality; it can be transmitted by a single gene from one parent or a matching gene from both parents; it can be caused by environmental factors; or it can result from what is called multifactorial inheritance—a combination of environmental and/or several genetic causes. After the counselor has assembled the available evidence, he or she will try to diagnose the disease and then calculate the chances of an occurrence or recurrence within a couple's immediate family, by consulting statistics from other, similar cases.

The final stage occurs after the genetic counselor has outlined the probable or possible risks and presents the available options to the prospective parents. Here, the couple makes its own decision. Some prospective parents with a heritable genetic disorder may choose artificial insemination or try to adopt a child rather than to risk an affected pregnancy. Others may take a calculated risk and the woman becomes pregnant, or they may choose to continue an existing pregnancy, hoping the child will not be seriously disabled.

▬ Detecting and Treating Fetal Problems and Defects

Today, the risk of bearing a child with a disease incompatible with normal life has been considerably reduced by new prenatal testing methods and other forms of medical intervention. Among these methods are amniocentesis, ultrasonography, fetoscopy, and intrauterine fetal surgery. Let's examine each more closely.

Amniocentesis   **Amniocentesis** allows the detection of chromosomal abnormalities in the fetus. The amniotic fluid is sampled by inserting a hollow needle through the mother's abdominal wall and into the amniotic sac. A syringe is then attached, and the amniotic fluid is withdrawn. This fluid contains discarded fetal cells, which can be observed, measured, and analyzed for size, shape, and number (see Figure 3-17).

Amniocentesis is an important medical advancement, but it does not always provide clear-cut answers. If an extra chromosome is found at chromosome position 21, for example, we know the child will inherit Down syndrome and will be mentally retarded. However, other test results offer only statistical data. Hemophilia, the inability of the blood to clot, is a good illustration. If two XXs are found, the fetus is female and will probably not have hemophilia. If the test reveals the fetus is male, there is a 50% chance he will be a hemophiliac. Which X chromosome he inherited from the mother cannot, as yet, be determined.

Another example is the *Lesch-Nyhan syndrome,* a severe neurological disease that occurs in males and is characterized by mental retardation, involuntary writhing motions, and compulsive self-mutilation of the lips and fingertips by biting. In amniocentesis, the fetal cells are removed, cultured, and submitted to X-ray film. Whereas normal cells absorb the radiation, the Lesch-Nyhan cells remain free of radioactivity.

Another rare condition, found mostly among Jews of eastern European origin, is *Tay-Sachs disease,* which causes blindness, mental retardation, and early childhood death. This disease is caused by an enzyme deficiency that can be detected in fetal amniotic cells.

In addition to these conditions, other forms of information related to prenatal life can be gathered by amniocentesis, including the following:

Sex of the fetus   Skin cells sloughed off by the fetus accumulate in the amniotic fluid. Under the microscope all male cells are different from all female cells.

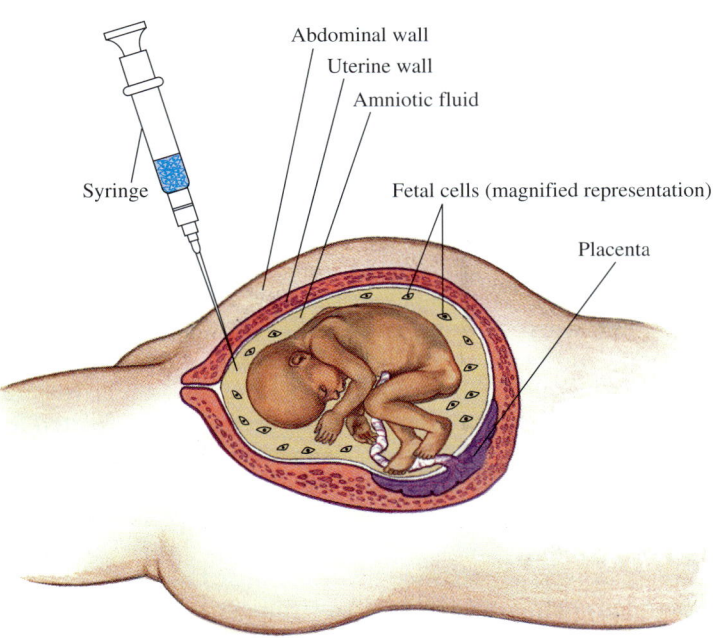

Abdominal wall
Uterine wall
Amniotic fluid
Syringe
Fetal cells (magnified representation)
Placenta

FIGURE 3-17
The Technique of Amniocentesis.

Amniotic fluid is withdrawn so the fetal cells can be analyzed for chromosomal abnormalities

Age of the fetus   Measuring discarded cells in the fluid also tells the maturity of the lungs, which is itself an indication of fetal age.

Metabolic disorders   Amniotic fluid reveals metabolic disorders caused by missing or defective enzymes.

Oxygen flow to the fetus   Gases dissolved in the amniotic fluid reveal the amount of oxygen that the fetus is receiving and whether it is at risk. Acidity of the amniotic fluid, often caused by an inadequate flow of oxygen, is another indication of fetal distress. (Hotchner, 1990)

For women wishing to undergo amniocentesis, the 14th to the 16th week of pregnancy seems optimal. There are sufficient fetal cells in the amniotic sac, which itself is large enough to lessen the likelihood of the needle injuring the fetus. This also allows time for a safe abortion, if desired. For an interesting cross-cultural comparison of amniocentesis use, see the accompanying Focus on Diversity box.

Chorionic Villus Sampling (CVS)   A more recent diagnostic procedure for birth defects is called **chorionic villus sampling** (CVS). The test includes insertion of a thin catheter through the vagina or abdomen into the uterus where some of the chorionic villi (threadlike protrusions on the membrane surrounding the placenta) are removed and analyzed. This procedure can detect many of the genetic disorders found by amniocentesis, but it is not considered as precise with more subtle abnormalities. The advantage of CVS over amniocentesis is that it can be accomplished as early as the 7th week rather than the 14th and

Focus on Diversity

AMNIOCENTESIS USE IN INDIA

In addition to its ability to detect chromosomal abnormalities, amniocentesis also is capable of revealing the sex of the fetus. Although this is not the purpose of amniocentesis, there has been some concern that people would use it to select the sex of their children, aborting a child if it was not of the desired sex. In fact, this is just what happened in India in the 1980s, providing an interesting cross-cultural example of how values affect genetics and medical technology.

Beginning in the early 1980s, pregnant women in India began using amniocentesis in large numbers and aborting their unborn children if they were female. In India, male children have long been preferred. This tradition dates back centuries, especially in remote areas where sons help in the fields, add to the family income, and offer parents security in old age.

Amniocentesis is chiefly used elsewhere in the world to determine the health of the fetus, but its use in India solely to determine the sex of the fetus set off a raging controversy between women's groups and doctors who administered the test. Women's groups contended that when amniocentesis test results led to abortion, it was an outrage against morality and against females in general. Many doctors maintained, though, that it was an alternative in overcrowded India to the practice of women having six or seven unwanted daughters to gain a son.

Amniocentesis was first introduced in India as a technique for sex determination in 1982, in the northern state of Punjab. Bombay then became the center for the practice. Over 20 clinics specializing in amniocentesis testing are scattered throughout the city, along with many more individual physicians offering it. Most of the clinics are capable of more than 1,000 procedures a year, and many also perform abortions. No official figures are available on the sex of aborted fetuses in India, but speculation is that almost all are female. The cost of amniocentesis in 1992 dollar figures ran from $10 to $25. The procedure is advertised on trains and buses, often with unabashed praise for male children.

Despite government policies that foster family planning, India's population of about 780 million is expected to grow to 1 billion shortly after the year 2000. Abortion is not officially part of the country's family planning policy, but it is legal and easily attainable. Whereas a son is a prize for an Indian family, a daughter is viewed as a deficit, and female infanticide is still a problem in some tribal areas. Daughters usually don't earn money and must be provided with hefty dowries for their marriages. (Chhaya, 1987; Turner & Rubinson, 1993)

---

yields results faster. However, one of the risks of CVS is spontaneous abortion after it is performed. One study (Hogge, Schonberg, & Golbus, 1986) revealed a 3.8% rate of spontaneous abortion after CVS was conducted.

Ultrasonography **Ultrasonography** (also called ultrasound) is used for such purposes as estimating fetal age, detecting the position of the fetus, identifying multiple pregnancies, and detecting physical defects. In the ultrasonography procedure, ultrasonic waves are transmitted to and from the mother's abdomen through a cluster of quartz crystals placed inside a small hand-held

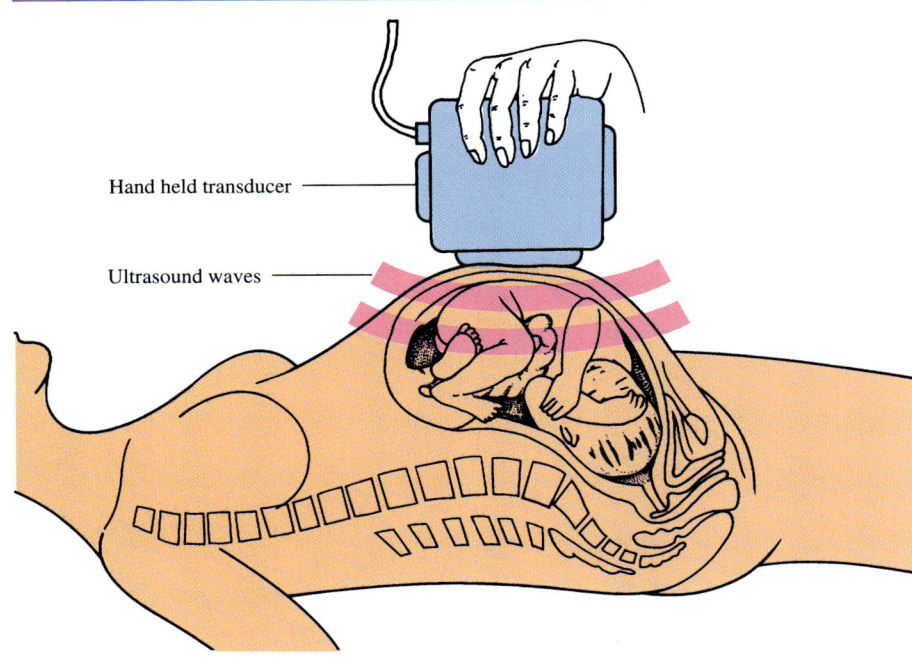

Hand held transducer

Ultrasound waves

FIGURE 3-18
An Ultrasound Examination with a Hand-Held Transducer.

Ultrasound waves will be transmitted to and from the mother's abdomen, creating an image of the fetus on a special monitor (not shown).

transducer. When the transducer is moved over the surface of the skin, the ultrasound waves are directed against the placenta and the amniotic sac containing the baby. Once the waves hit a permanent organ they will be deflected outward and can be picked up through a special receptor, which, in turn, feeds the transmitted impulses of sound into a scanning machine that prints them out onto the ultrasound screen. A clear picture of the various fetal organs can be put together by moving the transducer over different areas of the abdomen. The size, location, and contour of various organs can then be measured and analyzed (Lauersen, 1983). Figure 3-18 depicts the technique of ultrasonography.

Fetoscopy **Fetoscopy** enables the physician to view the fetus directly and take blood and skin samples for chromosomal and biochemical studies. Fetoscopy is particularly useful in diagnosing hemoglobin disorders, including sickle-cell anemia, hemophilia, and disorders of the white blood cells. It involves a fetoscope, a viewing instrument with a diameter slightly greater than a large needle. It is placed through the abdominal wall and into the amniotic cavity in much the same manner as in performing amniocentesis (see Figure 3-19). The fetoscope contains a high-powered fiber-optic light source that allows a view of the fetal and placental surfaces, but due to the small diameter of the fetoscope, the area observed at any one moment is quite limited. The fetoscope is equipped with biopsy forceps that are used to obtain samples of tissues from the fetus. The prenatal diagnosis of a variety of congenital skin diseases is also possible with this technique. By inserting a tiny needle into the placenta and

FIGURE 3-19
The Fetoscopy Procedure.

A telescopic instrument called a fetoscope enables physicians to diagnose a number of fetal problems, including hemoglobin disorders and congenital skin diseases.

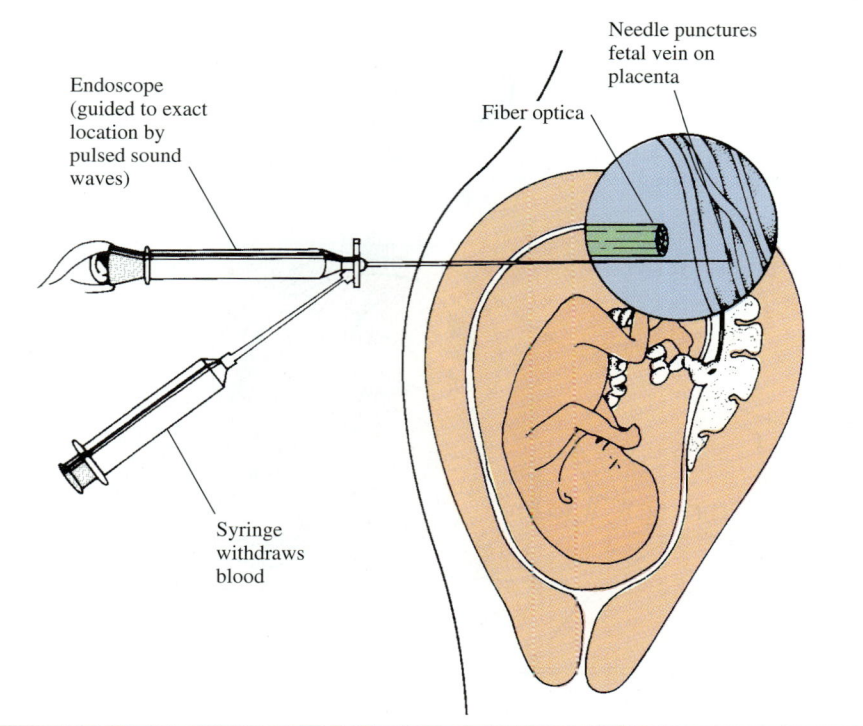

Endoscope (guided to exact location by pulsed sound waves)

Fiber optica

Needle punctures fetal vein on placenta

Syringe withdraws blood

umbilical cord, doctors have been able to obtain samples of fetal blood for analysis (Lauersen, 1983; Shapiro, 1983).

Intrauterine Fetal Surgery   **Intrauterine fetal surgery** involves micro-surgery on the unborn child to correct problems diagnosed during the mother's pregnancy. Such delicate surgical operations, aimed at improving an infant's chance of survival and preventing permanent damage, might be performed to correct defects such as *hydrocephalus* (excessive fluid within the skull) or obstruction of the fetal bladder. In addition, if the fetal blood supply is inefficient or the baby's health is in jeopardy, blood transfusions can be injected into the umbilical cord. Or medicines, nutrients, and vitamins can be injected into the amniotic fluid, which in turn can be absorbed by the fetus.

In 1991, a fetus-to-fetus tissue transplant operation added a new dimension to intrauterine fetal surgery (Hilts, 1991). Blood cells from the liver tissue of a fetus aborted in an ectopic pregnancy were injected into the chest cavity of a fetus diagnosed with *Hurler's syndrome* (a genetic disorder characterized by the inability of cells to produce an enzyme capable of breaking down sugar in some cells). The transplanted cells settled in the fetus's liver and from there traveled to bone marrow, where they manufactured cells that traveled to other parts of the body and created the needed enzyme. Because the transplant was done in the womb, the immature immune system of the fetus did not reject the foreign cells. Although intrauterine fetal surgery such as this is still experimental, it offers hope for genetic disorders as well as other impairments before delivery. Further research and follow-up studies are needed to fully assess such innovative prenatal surgery.

FUTURE DIRECTIONS IN GENETIC RESEARCH

This chapter introduced the field of genetics and explained how this discipline applies to the study of lifespan development. It explored fundamental genetic concepts, the importance of behavioral genetics, problems such as genetic aberrations and mutations, and genetic counseling. This chapter emphasized what we know about genetics, heredity, and environment, as well as some of the areas needing further scientific inquiry.

What does the future hold for genetic research? Obviously, the growing sophistication of this discipline has enabled scientists to view the mechanisms of genetics in new ways. Advanced equipment has permitted detailed analyses of genetic transmission and upgraded our knowledge of cellular anatomy and physiology, including genetic malfunctioning. Such innovative techniques have led to a number of important scientific advancements and breakthroughs.

The U.S. government-sponsored *Human Genome Project,* as well as a number of private research laboratories, provides evidence of the kinds of research taking place. In 1990, the National Institutes of Health established the $3 billion, 15-year Human Genome Project to map out every single human gene, rung by rung, or about 3.5 billion base pairs. The work was divided among nine different genetic research laboratories, which are expected to pool their eventual findings. It is hoped such research may provide clues or even cures for such diseases as immunodeficiency disorders, Huntington's disease, and even cancers. Private industries involved in genetic research, sometimes referred to as *bio-tech companies,* are also in the race to unravel genetic secrets. Both private industry and the individual scientists contracted by the Human Genome Project are allowed to patent their discoveries. In other words, they can own the patent to your genes!

Researchers have also demonstrated that it is possible to change a person's genetic structure, a procedure known as *genetic engineering.* For example, genetic engineering can identify a specific gene, remove it from one organism, and place it in another. As we shall presently see, such forms of genetic manipulation have the potential of paying dividends with inherited diseases. However, for many the potential for altering the genetic characteristics of humans is worrisome. Opponents cite the possibility of humans creating or genetically altering life-forms, or using selective breeding techniques such as the Nazis attempted during World War II. At the very least, genetic engineering poses a number of moral, religious, medical, and legal issues that must be addressed.

To illustrate an important breakthrough in genetic engineering, in 1993 scientists demonstrated they could use a form of genetic engineering to correct the underlying genetic defect that causes cystic fibrosis, a fatal inherited disease. Cystic fibrosis results from a mutation in a gene that produces a specialized protein. The protein is designed to control the flow of chloride in and out of the cells that line a person's airways. When the protein is missing, thick

INTERACTION OF HEREDITY AND ENVIRONMENT

How do you view the future of genetic research? Do you think the prospect of identifying and possibly controlling certain genes sheds new light on the nature-nurture issue? Why or why not?

mucus accumulates in the lungs, causing lung damage and eventual death, often by age 30.

In a series of experimental studies, genetic researchers inserted a healthy copy of the gene into an adenovirus, a common cold virus. They then put the genetically altered virus into the nasal passages of subjects with cystic fibrosis. Once inserted, the virus infected the cells that lined the nasal passage and were carried in the gene. In time, the gene made its protein and corrected the chloride flow defect.

Moving beyond genetic engineering, scientists in the 1990s have explored the potential impact of genetics in other important areas, such as the origins of sexual orientation. Sexual orientation (see Chapter 9) is generally viewed as the result of biological, psychological, and interactionist forces, although a precise and conclusive explanation of the origins of sexual orientation has yet to emerge. However, in 1991 a resurgence of interest in the potential role that genetics plays in sexual orientation took place. Bailey and Pillard (1991) studied concordance rates of homosexuality in 56 identical twins, 54 fraternal twins, and 57 adopted brothers of gay men. They discovered that 52% of the identical twin brothers of gay men were also gay, compared with 22% of the fraternal twins and 11% of the genetically unrelated brothers. The researchers estimated that the degree of the genetic contribution to homosexuality could range from 30% to 70%, depending on varying estimates of the prevalence of homosexuality in the United States and how representative the sample is to twins in the general population. In addition to a genetic link, the researchers also acknowledged environmental forces in shaping sexual orientation.

Another important study conducted in 1991 by neurobiologist Simon LeVay also shows that sexual orientation may have genetic origins. In this investigation, autopsied brain tissue from a portion of the hypothalamus in 19 gay men, 16 heterosexual men, and 6 heterosexual women was examined. It was discovered that in gay men, a small segment of the anterior hypothalamus was only one quarter to one half the size of this area in heterosexual men and closer to the size of the area in heterosexual women. This segment was almost undetectable in gay men, but about the size of a large grain of sand in heterosexual men.

It was speculated that the hypothalamic variation arises during fetal development, but whether it is the result of genetics or hormonal interactions during pregnancy that affect fetal brain development is unclear. LeVay also did not rule out the possibility that sexual orientation could somehow influence neural pathways later in life.

These kinds of research activities and studies illustrate the importance of genetic research, including new directions for the future. As we go to press, researchers have been successful in pinpointing the location of a variety of disease-causing genes, including the ones indicating *Huntington's chorea* (a neurological disease), *Menkes syndrome* (a type of mental disorder), *amyotrophic lateral sclerosis* (Lou Gehrig's disease or ALS), and *Fragile X* (a form of mental retardation). Given the spark created by such interests and activities, additional interest and discoveries are likely to mushroom in years to come. The field of genetics has occupied an influential place in the lifespan development literature, but now with an eye toward the future, it has the potential of having even more impact and becoming more riveting.

CHAPTER REVIEW

Human genetics is the study of the origin of life. Geneticists study chromosomes and genes to determine what inheritable characteristics they contain. Heredity refers to what and how characteristics are transmitted from parent to offspring. Offspring can be genetically similar to their parents or exhibit genetic variation.

Within the nucleus of a cell are chromosomes that are made up of genes. The chemical makeup of a chromosome is called deoxyribonucleic acid, or DNA, sometimes referred to as the blueprint of life. Its structure is like a spiraling staircase, each step or rung consisting of two bases that bond together: adenine bonds with thymine, and cytosine bonds with guanine. A gene is made up of hundreds to thousands of these rungs having a common function such as eye or skin color. When a gene is activated, it makes a copy of itself, although some chemical changes also take place. This copy is named messenger RNA (ribonucleic acid), which carries a genetic code to the ribosomes that lie outside the nucleus. The ribosome mixes amino acids to produce protein (all body cells are made of protein).

Humans have 23 pairs of chromosomes, or a total of 46, both parents each contributing 23 chromosomes. The cell division of the body or somatic cells is termed mitosis. During mitosis, the parent cell with its diploid or full species number of chromosomes produces two daughter cells, each of which also contains the diploid number of chromosomes (46). In the sex cells (sperm and egg), the parent gamete, which has 46 chromosomes, undergoes meiosis, a type of cell division in which each new sperm or egg is given half the number of chromosomes (23). This is called a haploid state. When a sperm penetrates the egg, the fertilized egg or zygote has the full quota of chromosomes for a new life to begin.

A child's sex is determined by the chromosomes that appear in the 23rd position. If the offspring receives an X from both parents, the child will be female (XX). If the child receives an X from the mother and a Y from the father, the child will be a boy (XY). In this chapter we also discussed how genes located in the 23rd position transmit sex-linked characteristics.

Genes are generally considered to be dominant or recessive; that is, the dominant genes express themselves in an observable way. This is called a person's phenotype. Genotype refers to a person's actual gene makeup. Blending occurs when two proteins produced by two genes mix and create a totally different phenotype.

Behavioral genetics is the field that studies the inheritance of predispositions, such as aptitude, intelligence, behavior disorders, aggressiveness, and passivity. Because it is so difficult to separate environmental influences from genetic influences, few data have yet been collected. However, by studying identical twins reared apart (identical genetic makeup, dissimilar environments), there is fairly strong evidence that many characteristics have a high degree of inheritability. There is also evidence that environmental forces are important to the development of these behaviors.

Genetic aberrations are the inheritance of mutated genes, genes that are mutated because of teratogenic agents or the inheritance of too many or too few chromosomes. One of the more common problems is Down syndrome, a condition in which an infant receives an extra chromosome in the 21st position, which leads to such physical characteristics as epicanthic eye folds and almost always to mental retardation. Other genetic aberrations include Klinefelter's syndrome (XXY), a condition in which a male with an extra X chromosome has underdeveloped sex organs and enlarged breasts, and Turner's syndrome (XO), a condition in which a female missing one sex chromosome has such physical defects as short fingers and stature, no secondary sex characteristics, and therefore no functional sex organs.

This chapter also examined the field of genetic counseling, including what it entails and who would benefit most from it. Also explored were the modern medical technologies used by genetic researchers and obstetricians, including amniocentesis, ultrasonography, fetoscopy, and intrauterine fetal surgery. We concluded this chapter with a brief look at the future of genetic research.

TERMS YOU SHOULD KNOW

allele
amino acid
amniocentesis
autosomes
behavioral genetics
behavioral predisposition
blending action
cell
chorionic villus sampling
chromosomes
cri-du-chat syndrome
cytoplasm
daughter cell
deoxyribonucleic acid (DNA)
diploid state
dominant gene
Down syndrome
fetoscopy
gamete
genes
genetics
genotype
germ cells
gonads
haploid state
heredity
heterozygous
homozygous
intrauterine fetal surgery
Klinefelter's syndrome
meiosis

messenger RNA
mitosis
mutation
nucleoplasm
nucleus
ovum
parent cell
phenotype
polygenes
protoplasm
recessive gene
ribonucleic acid (RNA)
ribosomes
sex-limited genes
sex-linked characteristics
sickle-cell anemia
somatic cells
sperm
testis-determining factor
triple X syndrome
trisomy 21
Turner's syndrome
ultrasonography
variations
XYY syndrome

THINKING IN ACTION

- It is the year 2020 and you have been assigned the task of designing a gene-dispensing machine for your employer, GENSEX. In addition to the slots for the XX and XY gender-determining chromosomes, develop a list of 10 other genetic choices you believe would motivate prospective parents to become GENSEX consumers.

- In a class action suit, you have been asked to prosecute an upstart company named GENSEX that is mass distributing genetic material. Meanwhile, GENSEX has asked you to be the defense attorney. Which side would you take, and what would be your opening arguments? Now take the opposite side and offer its opening arguments.

- Using knowledge you gained from Chapter 1, design a longitudinal study to determine, as best as you can, the relative roles of genetic inheritance versus the environment on mathematical ability. Include a hypothesis as part of your research design.

- Other than overt physical characteristics such as hair or eye color, list what you consider to be the most obvious inheritable behaviors. Also list the behaviors or personality characteristics that you consider are developed almost solely through the environment.

RECOMMENDED READINGS

1. Plomin, R., DeFries, J. C., & McClearn, G. E. (1989). *Behavioral genetics: A primer* (2nd ed.). New York: Freeman.

   The authors include a good discussion of twin studies and chromosomal abnormalities, among other interesting topics. One of the best books in the field of genetics.

2. Plomin, R., & Rende, R. (1991). Human behavioral genetics. *Annual Review of Psychology, 42,* 161–190.

   A thorough review of behavioral genetics and the relationship to personality, disabilities, and psychopathology.

3. Scheinfeld, A. (1972). *Heredity in humans* (2nd ed.). Philadelphia: Lippincott.

   A wonderfully informative book about the real-life meanings of genetic inheritance.

4. Stebbins, L. (1982). *Darwin to DNA, molecules to humanity.* San Francisco: Freeman.

   This book focuses on how genetics provide the blueprint for growth and development and shape the course of evolution.

5. Tsuang, M. T., & Vandermey, R. (1980). *Genes and the mind: The inheritance of mental illness.* New York: Oxford University Press.

   This text explores the possible biological and genetic origins of many serious mental disorders.

Prenatal Development, Birth, and Neonatal Adjustments

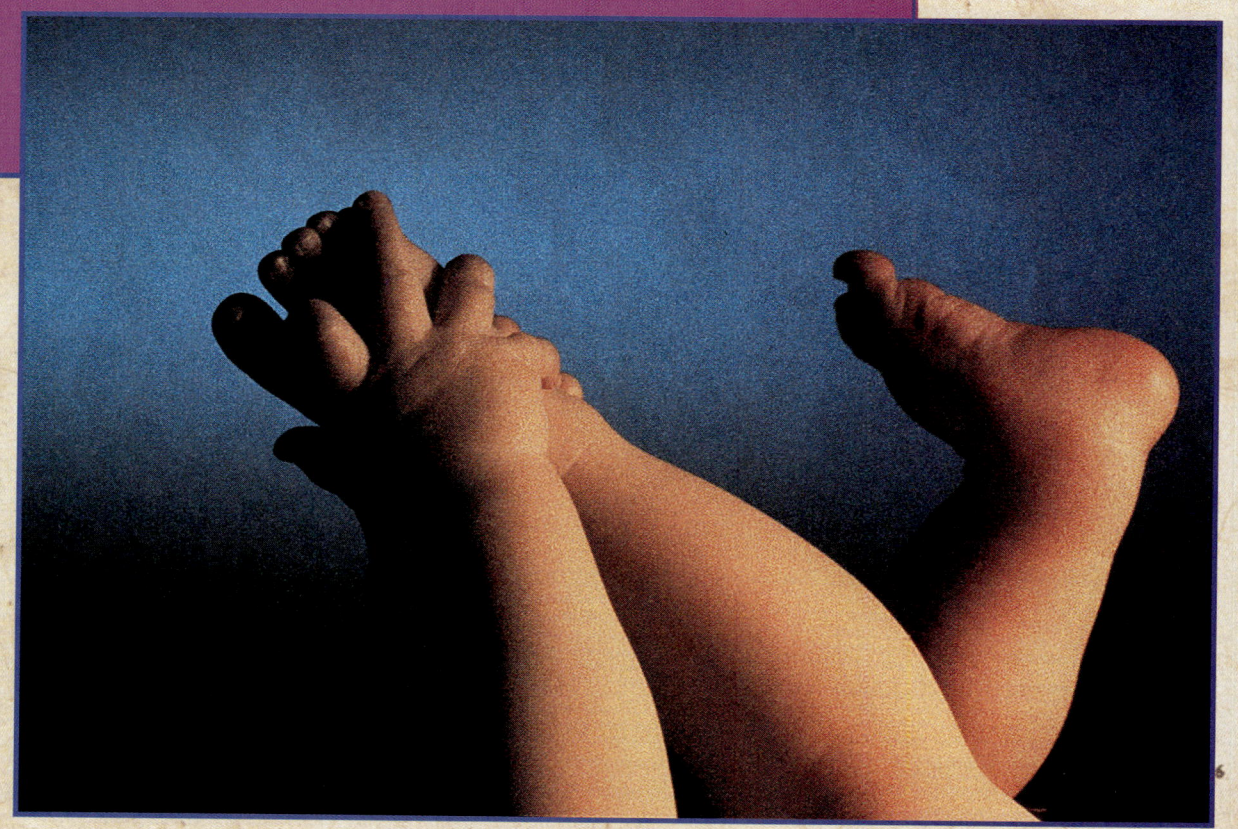

What Do You Think?

AT THE MOMENT OF CONCEPTION

Multiple Conception

PRENATAL DEVELOPMENT

First Trimester
First Month
Second Month
Third Month
Second Trimester
Fourth Month
Fifth Month

Sixth Month
Third Trimester
Seventh, Eighth, and Ninth Months
Gender Differences in Fetal Brain
   Development
Prematurity

THE PRENATAL ENVIRONMENT

Maternal Nutrition
Drugs

Maternal Emotions
Teratogenic Agents

PROBLEM PREGNANCIES

Toxemia
Rh Factor

Ectopic Pregnancy
Miscarriage

THE BIRTH PROCESS

Stages of Labor and Delivery
First Stage
Second Stage
Third Stage
Childbirth Techniques
Lamaze Method

Leboyer Method
Home Birth
Rooming-In and Birthing Room Facilities
Cesarean Delivery

NEONATAL ADJUSTMENTS AND ADAPTATIONS

Tests and Preventive Measures

Circumcision

INFERTILITY

Interventions for Infertility
In-Vitro Fertilization (IVF)
Artificial Insemination
Surrogate Motherhood

Embryo Transfer
Issues Related to Reproductive
   Technologies

Chapter Review • Terms You Should Know • Thinking in Action • Recommended Readings

WHAT DO YOU THINK?

• At the moment of conception, it's a single cell containing a genetic message from the mother and father. Approximately 9 months later, this microscopic fleck of tissue has been transformed into a fully developed fetus, weighing, on the average, 6 to 7 pounds and measuring between 18 and 21 inches, head to toe. The processes and events responsible for this development are one of nature's truly astounding miracles. Join us as we examine the earliest beginnings of lifespan development.

• Within the mother's womb, the fetus experiences secure and safe surroundings. However, women who smoke, drink alcohol or take other drugs, or eat poorly threaten the health of the unborn. What specific effects do such negative influences bear? What steps can pregnant women take to ensure the health of both mother and baby? This chapter supplies answers to these questions as we explore the importance of a healthy prenatal environment.

• "How do you plan to have your baby?" This is a question unasked in bygone eras because virtually all babies entered the world in a traditional birthing fashion. Today, though, a growing number of couples are choosing from a wide range of childbirth techniques, such as the Lamaze and Leboyer methods and home births. How do these techniques differ? What are their advantages and disadvantages? In this chapter, we provide answers to these questions.

• David and Judy Sullivan have always wanted to have children, but can't because of infertility. The problem, according to doctors, is that Judy has a defective fallopian tube, the result of scarring from a past infection. Undaunted, the Sullivans are now considering several sophisticated medical technologies to help them conceive a child: gamete intrafallopian transfer and zygote intrafallopian transfer. What are these reproductive technologies? How successful are they? Read on and learn more about high-tech pregnancies in the 1990s.

AT THE MOMENT OF CONCEPTION

Each month, approximately halfway through the 28-day menstrual cycle, one of a woman's ovaries releases a mature egg, or **ovum.** Gently pushed by cilia, the fine hairlike projectiles that line the fallopian tube, this egg begins about a week's journey to the uterus. The uterine walls have been accumulating a large supply of blood vessels to nourish the egg if it is fertilized in the fallopian tube. If the egg remains unfertilized, it disintegrates and is discharged from the body along with the built-up uterine lining as the menstrual flow.

Because sperm only have an effective life of about 72 hours and the egg an even shorter life, conception must occur within 24 to 36 hours of ovulation. Once ejaculation has taken place, sperm do not move well in the vagina's acidic environment, and many are killed by the hostile fluid. A number of sperm also die because of defects in their structure—for example, many lack the proper tail structure and never demonstrate the needed motility to reach a fallopian tube. Some travel along the wrong fallopian tube and degenerate without ever reaching their proper destination. Surviving sperm will travel a little less than half an inch every 5 minutes. About 300 from the original millions that started the journey will travel along the correct fallopian tube and reach the female ovum. Usually, this happens between 45 and 90 minutes after ejaculation. Once one sperm has penetrated the ovum, the ovum becomes impervious to other sperm.

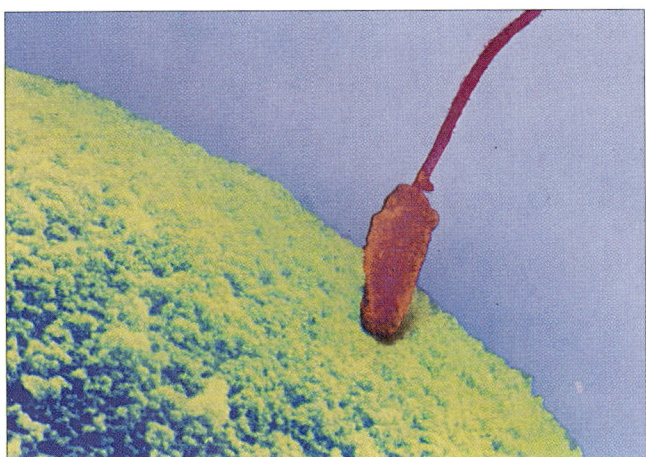

Conception occurs when the sperm and ovum unite. The fertilized egg is called the zygote.

The fertilized egg, containing its own 23 chromosomes plus the 23 chromosomes from the sperm, is called a **zygote.** The zygote goes through unique stages of development as it drifts down the 4-inch fallopian tube toward the uterus. During its journey, it begins to divide and multiply to form new cells. By the time the zygote reaches the uterus, which takes about 3 days, the original cell has become a tiny sphere called a **blastocyst.** The blastocyst, which now contains about 60 cells, is filled with fluid and covered by an outer layer of cells called the **trophoblast.** The trophoblast helps the blastocyst implant itself in the uterine wall and eventually gives rise to the placenta. The process of implantation takes between 7 and 10 days.

Multiple Conception

Conception usually occurs when a single sperm cell penetrates the female ovum to create a zygote. As a result, a single child is conceived. However, more than one child can be created at one time, a phenomenon known as multiple conception.

Multiple conceptions are far rarer than single ones. Approximately 30,000 sets of twins are born in the United States each year. Twins occur approximately once in every 90 births; triplets about once in 9,300 births; quadruplets once in 490,000; and quintuplets once in every 55 millon births. African Americans give birth to the most twins, and Asians give birth to the fewest. These figures indicate that although the conception of twins is relatively infrequent, they are the most common of multiple births.

There are two common categories of twins. **Identical twins** (or *monozygotic* twins) result when a single fertilized egg splits after conception. Identical twins are genetically alike, with the same physical characteristics such as sex, blood type, and eye color. **Fraternal twins** (or *dizygotic* twins) result when two female eggs are fertilized by two separate sperm cells. It is estimated that 70% percent of all twin births are fraternal. Fraternal twins are no more alike than are any two single children born to the same parents. They may or may not be of the same sex, and each possesses individual characteristics. To determine

Fraternal twins develop from two separate ova, and most have separate placentas. Identical twins typically share the same placenta.

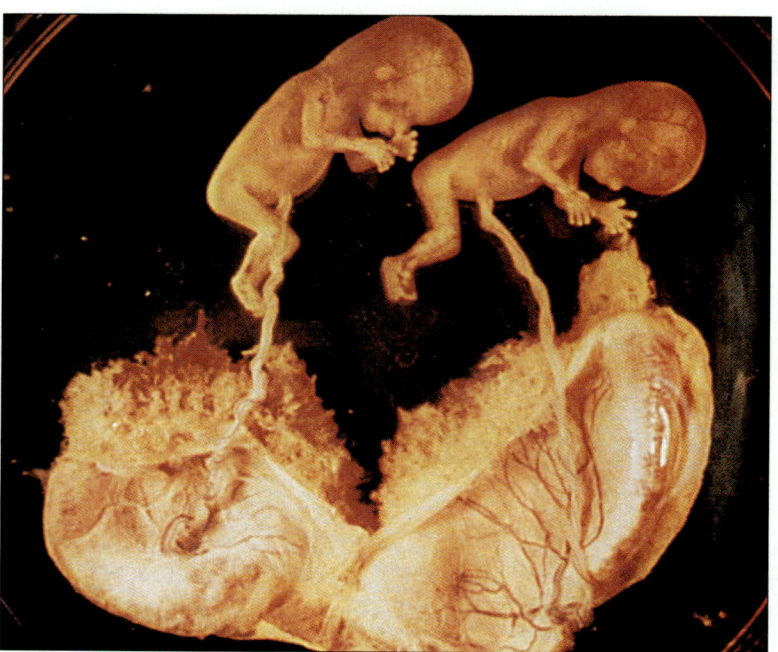

whether twins are fraternal or identical, certain tests, such as fingerprinting or blood typing, are made (the results should be the same for identical twins).

As indicated, identical twins result when a single fertilized egg splits after conception. If the separation is not complete, **conjoined twins** (Siamese) can result. Conjoined twins are rare, and often share a portion of the liver and perhaps other internal organs. When the fusion is minor, the twins can often be surgically separated; however, those with more extensive fusions usually fail to survive the operation. The ratio of conjoined twins to normal twin births is approximately 1 in 1,000. Conjoined twins are always identical and usually female.

On the average, twins have a gestation period that is approximately 25 days shorter than normal. Almost half of all twin births are premature. When they are delivered, the first twin is usually born head first; the second is often a breech (buttocks first) delivery.

PRENATAL DEVELOPMENT

The average full-term human pregnancy lasts about 270 days, from conception to full term, although some are as long as 300 days and others are as short as 240 days. Lifespan development researchers prefer to divide pregnancy into three equal segments called **trimesters** (a trimester is a period of about 3 months). Although the organism is both growing and developing throughout all phases of pregnancy, trimester division is somewhat simplified by the following classification system: The first trimester is primarily characterized by differential development of basic structures; the second trimester is characterized by both further development and growth; and the third trimester is characterized predominantly by growth. Table 4-1 displays the trimesters of prenatal development.

TABLE 4-1
The Three Trimesters of Prenatal Development

Trimester	Major Characterization
First (0–3 months)	Begins development of all internal organs, appendages, sense organs.
Second (4–6 months)	Continuation of development plus growth of organism from 3″ to 1′ in length and from 1 oz. to 1½ lbs. in weight.
Third (7–9 months)	Grows about 8″ in length, gains about 6 lbs.

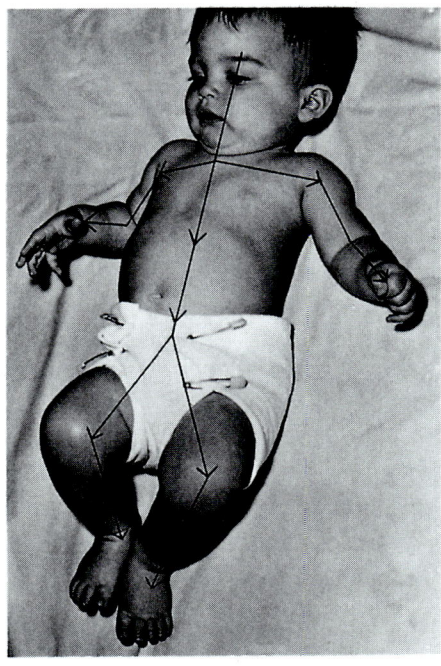

FIGURE 4-1
Cephalocaudal and Proximodistal Development.

Development and muscular control proceeds from head to tail (cephalocaudal) and from the center to the periphery (proximodistal).

In addition to the division of pregnancy into trimesters, we need to acknowledge two important principles of growth and development of the organism during prenatal development: cephalocaudal and proximodistal (see Figure 4-1). **Cephalocaudal development** means a head-to-tail, or downward, progression of bodily and motor skill growth. If we compare the physical rates of development of the head, trunk, and legs, we find the head grows the fastest. The trunk is next in overall rate of growth, followed by the legs. (This is true from conception through the full attainment of growth and development in

INTERACTION OF HEREDITY AND ENVIRONMENT

Because cephalocaudal and proximodistal patterns of growth emerge in a fairly predictable sequence at fairly predictable times, does this suggest to you a rather fixed genetic blueprint of development? How might the environment interact to shape the course of these physical growth sequences? How can you apply the nature-nurture issue to this topic?

young adulthood.) During the embryonic stage, the head and upper trunk develop before the abdominal area and the arms develop before the legs. (Those motor skills involving the use of the upper body will develop before those using the lower body.) This process continues to be true after the baby is born. For example, infants are capable of lifting their heads before they can lift their trunks and can sit upright before they can walk.

Proximodistal development refers to the physical and motor skill growth that progresses from the center of the body outward. For example, in the embryo and fetus, the trunk develops earlier than the shoulders or arms, whereas the fingers and toes develop at a much slower rate. Also, infants, young children, and even adolescents are capable of mastering motor skills involving the central parts of the body before those requiring the use of peripheral parts. Because of this, we typically develop the use of the shoulders and arms before we can master the use of the hands and fingers.

▬ First Trimester

First Month When the blastocyst becomes implanted in the uterine wall, the **embryonic period** begins. During this time, the cells begin to exhibit marked differentiation. The organism is called an **embryo** from the beginning of cell specialization until the end of the second month of pregnancy (approximately 2 to 8 weeks after fertilization).

On approximately the 18th day after conception, the embryo's heart structure begins to appear, and by about 3 weeks the heart has begun to undergo muscle contractions, although it is not under neural control. The heart beats and blood pulsates through a small enclosed bloodstream that is separate from the mother's. By the end of the first month, the central nervous system (brain and spinal cord) begins to develop. Specialized cells form a tubelike structure that eventually develops into the spinal column.

Such internal organs as the lungs, liver, kidneys, and endocrine glands are starting to develop, and the digestive system has begun to form. Small "buds" that will eventually become arms and legs start developing by the end of the first month. Throughout the course of prenatal life, leg development lags behind that of the arms. Four weeks after conception, the embryo measures only 0.2 inch in length but is 10,000 times larger than the zygote.

Second Month As the embryo enters its second month, rapid cell division and specialization continue. By the end of 8 weeks, the embryo is just over an inch long and weighs less than an ounce. A brain with two recognizable lobes has become apparent at the end of the spinal column. The limbs are also elongating, showing distinct division of knee and elbow, although they are less than ¼ inch long. More specifically, the shoulders, arms, hands, and fingers rapidly develop during the second month. Underneath the tissue of the arms and legs the bones continue to form and are becoming padded with muscles.

The internal organs also continue to develop quite rapidly, not only in form and structure, but also in functional properties. For example, the kidneys are capable of moving uric acid from the bloodstream, and the stomach can manufacture primitive digestive juices. By the sixth week, the ears appear, and by the end of the second month, the embryo's facial features look human. The nose, jaw, and eyebrows become recognizable.

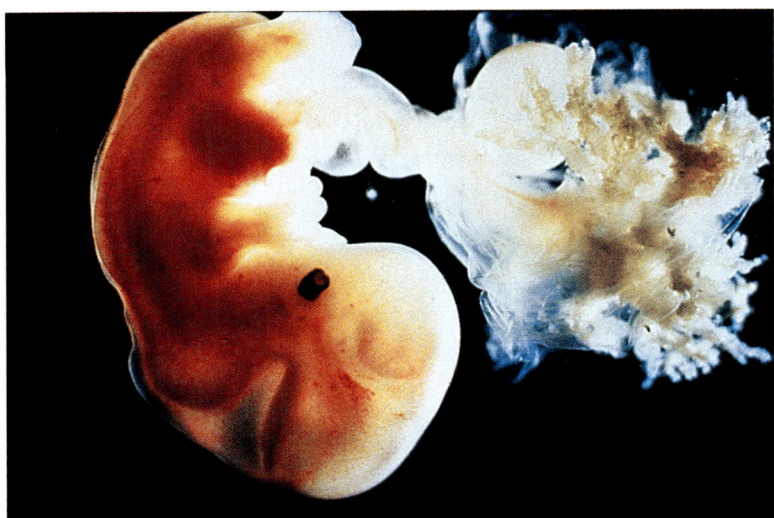

An embryo at one month.

The external genitalia of the embryo are evident by the end of the second month of prenatal life. Although there are genetic differences between males and females from the moment of conception, there is no way to tell males and females apart for the first 6 weeks or so. This is because the testes and ovaries have not yet developed. At this time, though, tissues begin forming that will differentiate the two sexes. The embryo's undifferentiated sex glands will develop into testes, if the embryo's 23rd chromosomal pair is an XY, or ovaries, if the pair is an XX (see Chapter 3). Once the sex glands develop, they begin to secrete hormones that direct both external and internal sexual differentiation.

However, it's a bit more complex than this. More specifically, at the end of the second month of prenatal life, two paired internal duct systems begin forming in both male and female embryos: the *Mullerian ducts,* the potential female structures of the fallopian tubes, uterus, and inner parts of the vagina; and the *Wolffian ducts,* the potential male structures of the epididymis, vas deferens, and seminal vesicles. In the case of male embryos, the testes begin secreting testosterone as well as a Mullerian-inhibiting hormone (MIH), a chemical that inhibits the further development of the Mullerian ducts. When this occurs, the Wolffian ducts begin developing into the epididymus, vas deferens, and seminal ducts while the Mullerian ducts shrink and eventually degenerate. Thus it takes the presence and action of two hormones—testosterone and MIH—to begin the course of male development.

For females, a different scenario takes place. Hormones do not play a role in their sexual differentiation. The absence of testicular hormones causes the Wolffian ducts to degenerate, and the Mullerian ducts begin developing into the fallopian tubes, uterus, and inner parts of the vagina.

Third Month   The end of the eighth week and the start of the ninth week mark the end of the embryonic period and the start of the **fetal period** (or the third through the ninth month of prenatal life). From now on, the developing organism is referred to as a **fetus.** During this time, the brain and spinal cord continue to mature. Brain cell development is especially rapid, and the brain's

A fetus at three months.

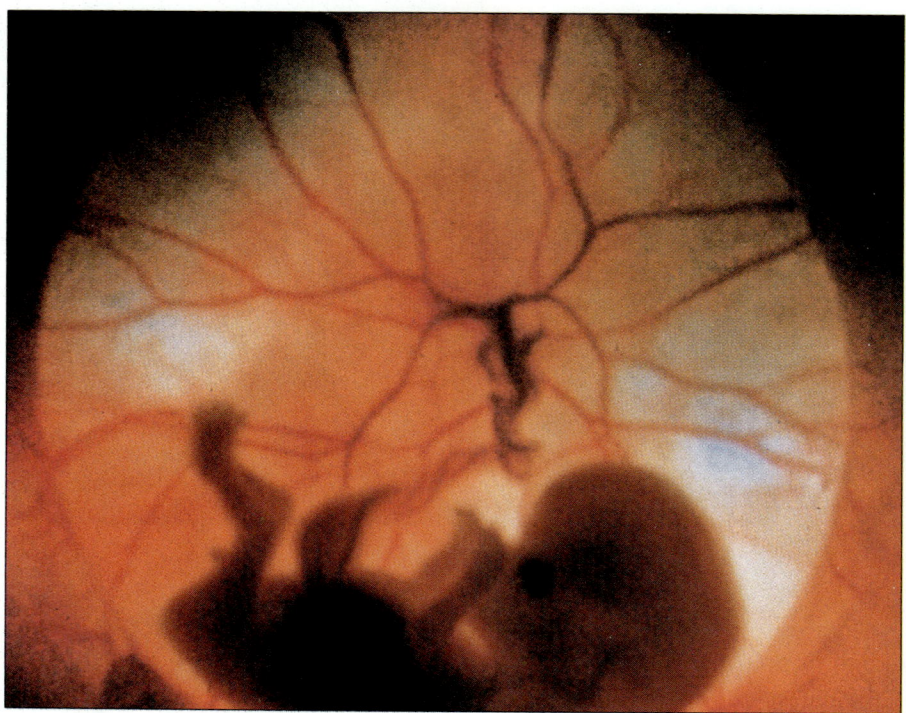

major structures begin to take shape. Also, the progressive maturation of both nerves and muscles, which leads to generalized movements in response to external stimulation, now occurs. The fetus will also turn as early as the ninth or tenth week (although the mother will be unaware of all this activity).

By the end of 12 weeks, the fetus can kick, curl the toes and fingers, move the thumb, and even squint in response to external stimulation. The fetus is now just over 3 inches long and weighs 1.6 ounces. Arms, hands, fingers, legs, feet, and toes are now fully formed. Even nails are developing on the fingers and toes. Tiny tooth sockets, complete with the "buds" of future teeth, are present in the jawbone. The eyes, almost fully developed, have lids that remain fused.

By the end of the trimester, a very tiny but highly complex organism is in utero. Other developments reveal how complex the organism has become. For example, the nerves and muscles have tripled in number. The heart can now be heard by use of special instruments, the kidneys are operable, and sexual development has reached the stage where sex can be ascertained. Meanwhile, the soft cartilaginous substance of the ribs and vertebrae have turned to bone.

INTRAUTERINE STRUCTURES AND MECHANISMS Within the mother's womb, fetal life is sustained by a vital support system consisting of an amniotic sac, placenta, and umbilical cord. Enveloping the fetus is a transparent membrane called the **amniotic sac.** Contained within the sac is **amniotic fluid,** which holds the fetus in suspension and protects it not only from being jarred but also from any pressures exerted by the mother's internal organs. It also serves to provide an even temperature for the fetus.

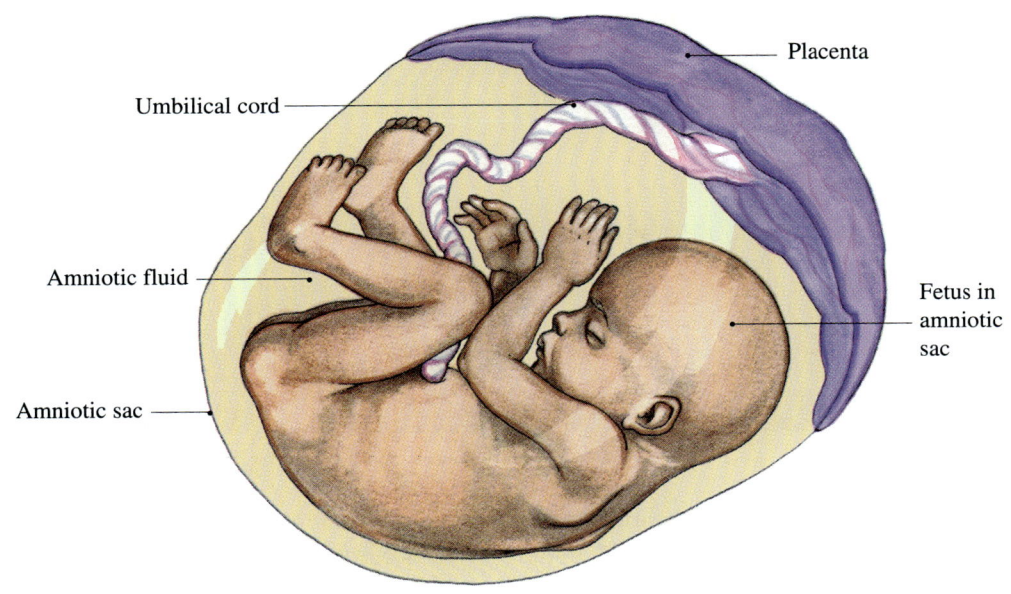

FIGURE 4-2
The Intrauterine
Environment of the Fetus.

The amniotic sac is filled with amniotic fluid and envelops the developing organism.
The placenta, attached to the uterine wall, is connected to the organism by the
umbilical cord.

products to be channeled from embryo to mother. It should be noted here that
there is no direct connection of blood vessels between mother and embryo.
Substances are transmitted to and from the mother's and embryo's blood vessels via the placenta. As we see shortly, the placenta is not a barrier, and many
substances—for example, drugs like aspirin—cross it. Sole source of food, oxygen, and water for the unborn, the placenta must grow in relation to the organism's needs. Originally microscopic in size, at birth the placenta is about 6 to 8
inches in diameter, a little over an inch in thickness, and weighs about 14 to 21
ounces.

Connecting the placenta to the fetus is the **umbilical cord.** The umbilical
cord contains three blood vessels: one a vein carrying oxygenated blood from
the placenta to the fetus, and two arteries that carry blood and waste products
from the fetus to the placenta. Because the umbilical cord is without nerves,
clamping and cutting the "belly button" at delivery is a painless matter. At birth,
the umbilical cord averages ⁹⁄₁₀ of an inch in diameter and is about 21 inches in
length. Figure 4-2 displays these intrauterine features.

▬ Second Trimester

Fourth Month   The second trimester is characterized not only by a continuation of the developmental processes but also by a rapid increase in growth as
well. The fetus now approaches over 5 inches in length and weighs approximately 5 ounces. The head is disproportionately large in comparison to the rest

A fetus at five months.

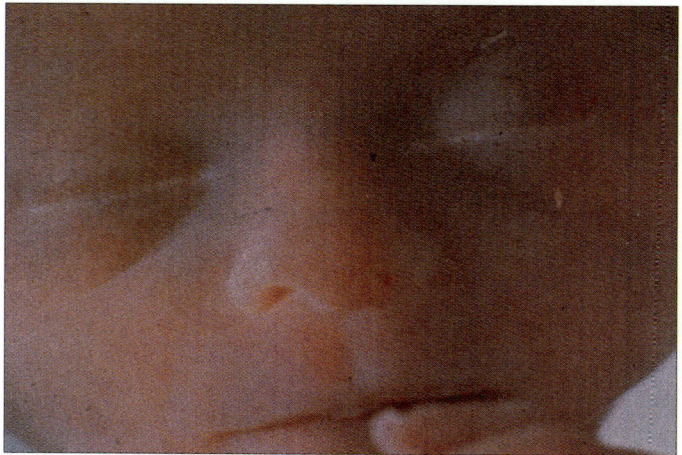

of the body, and the brain's major structures resemble those of an adult. A strong heartbeat is present, along with a fairly well developed digestive system. The eyebrows and genital organs are quite noticeable. Because the fetus is now quite active (its mouth can open and close), there is an increase in the intake of food, oxygen, and water. The placenta has increased from 3 to 4 inches in diameter, allowing for a more rapid exchange of nutrients and waste products between mother and fetus. In appearance, the fetal skin is translucent because of the blood flowing through the circulatory vessels and the lack of pigmentation in the skin.

Fifth Month   By the end of 20 weeks, a rapid increase in body size has occurred. The fetus is now 8 inches long and weighs just over 1 pound, a considerable gain from the 4 ounces of 16 weeks earlier. The eyelids are still fused shut and a fine downy growth of hair termed **lanugo** appears on the entire body. The skin is also usually covered with a waxylike substance called the **vernix caseosa.** Its purpose is to protect the fetus from constant exposure to the amniotic fluid. The internal organs are rapidly maturing with the exception of the lungs, which lag behind in development.

At between 16 and 18 weeks the first fetal movements are usually felt by the mother. This is known technically as **quickening.** As time progresses, the mother will become very much aware of the ripplings and flutterings inside her. The fetus now has both sleeping and waking moments. During wakefulness the fetus cries, sucks its thumb, hiccups, and performs somersaults!

Sixth Month   Just about a foot in length, the 6-month-old fetus has started accumulating subcutaneous fat and now weighs up to 1 pound 10 ounces. The skin becomes coarser and develops more pigmentation, and hair grows on the head. The eyelids have separated and tiny eyelashes can now be observed. The fingernails extend to the end of the fingers, and the fetus can now make a fist. A hardening of the bones has also begun. Despite all these signs of maturity, the fetus has only a slim chance of survival if it is born at this point in the pregnancy. The primary reason for death in premature infants is immaturity of the lungs and kidneys.

Third Trimester

Seventh, Eighth, and Ninth Months   The third trimester, consisting of the seventh, eighth, and ninth months of pregnancy, is marked primarily by rapid gains in size and weight. We choose to explore the developments taking place at this time as a whole, rather than following the previously used monthly chronology. We do so because development now is characterized by growth not nearly as clearly defined as it was during the first and second trimesters.

The fetus grows in length by 50% and gains nearly 6 pounds in the last 3 months. During the last 2 months the fetus gains an average of a half pound a week. The brain's cortical areas for motor and sensory behaviors continue to mature, and there is rapid development of the reflexes that will be seen at birth. The cortex also exhibits pronounced growth during these final months. During the eighth month, a male fetus's testes begin their descent toward the scrotum. As growth increases (much of the weight gain is subcutaneous fat) and the uterus becomes cramped, fetal movements are curtailed.

Gender Differences in Fetal Brain Development   At one time it was believed there were no structural or functional differences between the brains of males and females. Little was known about the effects of hormones on brain development until research with lower animal species provided some fascinating insights into the matter (Nottebohm & Arnold, 1976; Young, 1961). For example, it appears that during prenatal development, when the male gonads of many mammals begin to manufacture testosterone, they secrete it directly into the blood so it reaches the brain. Certain target cells in the brains of many animals are able to distinguish this hormone and to absorb it into their nuclei, where it regulates genetic mechanisms (Bloom & Lazerson, 1988).

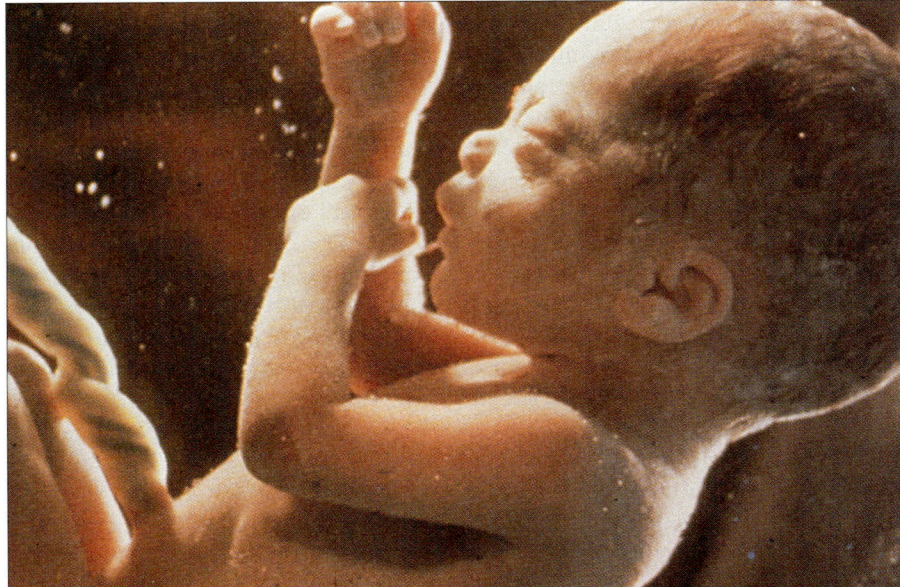

A fetus at six to nine months.

GENDER SIMILARITIES AND DIFFERENCES

As we discover in later chapters, females and males are more alike than different in such areas as verbal ability or logical reasoning. Given the fact that gender differences in brain structure and function appear to exist, do such findings surprise you? How do you see heredity and environment interacting to shape the course of development in cognitive spheres such as these?

We have also learned that the number and location of nerve synapses (connections) in the hypothalamuses of human male and female brains are influenced by the presence or absence of circulating testosterone during fetal life. (The hypothalamus is a small structure in the limbic system that serves a number of important purposes, including the regulation of sex hormones released by the pituitary gland.) The presence of testosterone in males during prenatal development appears to affect cells of the hypothalamus and to create, among other changes, an insensitivity to estrogen in the bloodstream. In females the absence of testosterone during fetal life promotes estrogen sensitivity. Eventually, female differentiation in the hypothalamus will enable sex hormones to coordinate the menstrual cycle, whereas male differentiation will orchestrate the manufacture of cyclic sex hormones (Cowan, 1986; Kalat, 1992; Kolb & Wishaw, 1988; Levinthal, 1990).

Other differences due to the presence or absence of circulating testosterone have been found in the left and right cerebral hemispheres of female and male brains (Rubin, Reinisch, & Haskett, 1981). The brain is divided into left and right hemispheres that look very much alike but differ greatly in function. Researchers have identified the left hemisphere as the site of language ability, writing, and logical thought (as used in mathematics and science), among other specializations. The right hemisphere appears to control primarily nonverbal functions, such as imagination, the expression of emotion, and artistic and musical endeavors.

Are there actual differences in human male and female brains? One study (Geschwind & Bahan, 1982) suggests that testosterone retards the growth of the left hemisphere in males but not in females. As a result, the researchers suggest, the right hemisphere is more developed in males. There is some support for this notion in the fact that left-handedness, which is associated with right-brain dominance, is much more common among males.

According to another study of male and female brains, a difference in the corpus callosum appears as early as the 26th week of prenatal life (Lacoste-Utamsing & Holloway, 1982). In women, these investigators claim, a portion of this band of nerve fibers is much wider and larger. Some writers have speculated that this greater size permits more interhemispheric communication in women (Bloom & Lazerson, 1988).

To sum up, there seems to be a fair amount of evidence that during fetal development circulatory hormones create gender differences in certain parts of the brain. However, we don't know what the impact of such differences may be on later behavior. As yet, we have no clear evidence of a correlation between gender differences in the brain and differences in the ways men and women behave. Probably biological factors *and* psychosocial forces combine to create gender differences in behavior. Thus, utilizing a major lifespan development theme covered in Chapter 1, gender differences are shaped by a convergence of biological, psychological, and social forces.

Prematurity   Because it is rare that a mother can pinpoint the exact day of conception, prematurity cannot effectively be defined in terms of days or months of gestation. Therefore, most medical doctors define **prematurity** (also called a *preterm infant*) as a condition in which an infant weighs less than 2,500 grams (5½ pounds) and has developed in utero for less than 36 weeks.

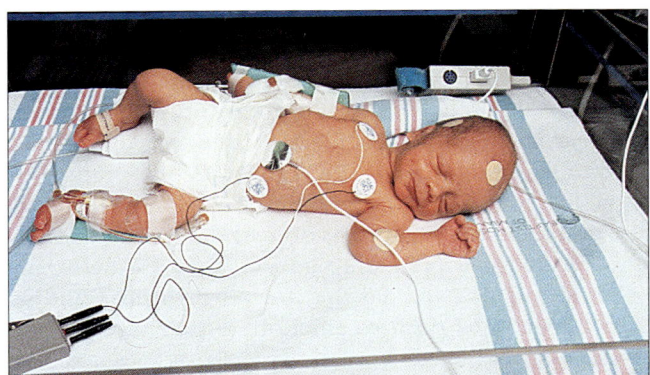

Premature infants have special needs and require various kinds of medical intervention.

Any neonate (newborn) weighing less than this will probably have at least some difficulty surviving, for a baby this tiny will not have reached a stage of sufficient development to survive outside of its mother. Premature infants often are incapable of breathing without aid or of regulating their body temperature. They also may lack the protective subcutaneous layer of fat.

Due to the efforts of contemporary researchers (e.g., Garcia-Coll et al., 1992; Myers et al.,1992), the field of lifespan development is obtaining a clearer picture of the many sides of prematurity. For example, we know a number of important factors can possibly contribute to its occurrence. Premature infants are most often born to women who are nonwhite, come from poor neighborhoods, suffer from malnutrition, or are diabetic. It has also been discovered that premature infants are not always just underweight. Relationships have been established between prematurity and cerebral palsy, epilepsy, hearing difficulties, and mental retardation. Some research (e.g., Gorga et al., 1991; Mazer, Piper, & Ramsay, 1988) indicates that when compared to full-term infants, premature infants exhibit impaired neuromotor behavior, such as in the areas of locomotion and eye-hand coordination.

Due to their low birth weight and small size, premature infants typically encounter difficulties during the first few years of life. However, we need to stress that most premature infants will eventually overcome these difficulties. Advancements in medical care, such as intravenous fluid therapy, artificial ventilation, and other forms of newborn support systems, have helped reduce the serious health consequences posed by prematurity. Supplemental stimulation to preterm infants, such as stroking and holding, has also shown to be beneficial to their development (Goldsmith, 1990; Landry et al., 1990; Levy-Shiff et al., 1990; Lyons-Ruth et al., 1990).

Some representative research will serve to illustrate the kinds of developmental lags apparent between premature and full-term infants. For example, one study (Rose, 1983) discovered that full-term and premature infants show differential rates of visual information processing. In her investigation 80 6- and 12-month-old full-term and premature infants were given a shape to view for short intervals of time. Using a paired comparison technique, they were then tested for visual recognition memory. Although the older subjects showed evidence of recognition memory after less familiarization time than the younger ones had, at both ages the premature infants required considerably longer familiarization than did the full-term babies. This pattern of performance was evident at the 6th as well as the 12th month of life. This suggests there are persistent differences between premature and full-term infants, at least in the first year, in this important facet of cognitive functioning.

Another study (Crnic, 1983) suggests that prematurity may also affect later social interaction. In this investigation, the psychosocial functioning of premature and full-term infants was observed during their first year of life. In general, it was found that premature infants were less active and less responsive than full-term infants. Nor did the preemies vocalize and smile as frequently, and they showed less positive emotion in their vocalizations. The pattern was apparent not only at age 4 months but also at ages 8 and 12 months.

Finally, an investigation by Judy Ungerer and Marian Sigman (1983) explored the developmental lags in premature babies for the first 3 years of life. The researchers assessed the play, sensorimotor, language, and general developmental skills of 20 preterm and 20 full-term infants in five sessions during the second and third years of life. The effects of biological maturity on play and sensorimotor skills were observed at 13.5 months, and less pervasive effects remained at 22 months. The premature infants were significantly delayed in sensorimotor, personal-social, and gross motor abilities at 13.5 months and in language abilities at 22 months beyond that predicted by biological maturity alone. Although these deficits had mostly been overcome by 3 years of age, the preterm infants performed somewhat more poorly on visual information processing tasks.

THE PRENATAL ENVIRONMENT

In 9 months' time the fetus must develop from a single cell to a highly complex being of approximately 7 pounds. As this development takes place, the fetus is influenced by its external and internal environment. The external fetal environment is the amniotic fluid. The internal environment consists not only of the proteins and enzymes manufactured within the organism but also of a continuous inflow of nutrients, hormones, oxygen, chemicals, and other substances from the mother's bloodstream.

We noted earlier that there is no direct connection between the blood vessels of mother and fetus. A mixing of blood in the placental region never occurs. Rather, molecules of many substances are released by the maternal bloodstream and pass through the placenta. If small enough, these substances are assimilated by the blood vessels within the umbilical cord, making the placenta an area of exchange. The placenta is not a filtration system. What passes through the placenta has an environmental impact on the fetus. Thus it is crucial that a pregnant woman eat right and stay healthy. In addition, she should be regularly seeing a physician, usually a specialist in obstetrics and gynecology, who is qualified to offer prenatal care (Coustan, 1990; Feinbloom, 1993; Hales, 1989; Henry & Feldhausen, 1989; Olds, London, & Ladewig, 1992).

Some studies indicate what constitutes a good environment. The age of the mother is one variable that must be considered. Data show that the best childbearing years are between ages 20 and 35. Before or after these years there is a greater risk of miscarriages and retardation. For example, recall how maternal age impacts on the chances of giving birth to a Down syndrome child. Women who are 20 have 1 chance in 1,667. Women aged 40, however, have 1 chance in 106 of giving birth to a child with Down syndrome (Masters, Johnson, & Kolodny, 1992). For women younger than 20, there are also increased risks, including premature births, delivery difficulties, and stillbirths. This is especially true for the growing number of mothers ages 15 and younger (Franklin, 1988; Giblin et al., 1989; Hotchner, 1990; Simkins, 1984).

Maternal Nutrition

The ability of the fetus to develop normally depends on nourishment supplied by the mother. Poor maternal nutrition may affect the fetus either directly, by not meeting its nutritional needs, or indirectly, by increasing the mother's susceptibility to disease. Malnutrition can cause not only poor health, rickets, scurvy, physical weakness, miscarriage, and stillbirth (a stillbirth is the birth of a fetus that has died), but possibly mental retardation as well. A seriously malnourished fetus can have as many as 20% fewer brain cells than the normal fetus (Chez & Chervenak, 1990).

The most serious damage (physical and mental abnormalities) occurs during **organogenesis** (the period marking the beginning of organ development, from the third week of pregnancy through the second or third month). After the period of the ovum, the embryonic cells proliferate rapidly and are unusually sensitive to environmental changes. The developing nervous system is vulnerable for at least the first 3, or possibly 6, months after conception, but it is especially sensitive from days 15 to 25. The heart is particularly susceptible from the 20th through the 40th day.

All of this points to the importance of eating balanced, sensible meals during pregnancy. Such meals must supply enough energy and nutrients to satisfy the mother's needs as well as those of her unborn child. Pregnancy is not a time for weight reduction, but neither is it a time for massive weight gain beyond what is necessary for the appropriate growth of fetal and maternal tissues. Although every woman should work out with her physician a pregnancy diet that is tailored to her particular needs, here are some general guidelines that are often considered in planning such a diet:

- Eat 2½ to 3½ ounces of protein daily.
- Consume 500 calories over your normal diet—that is, a total of about 2,600 per day. Caloric needs will be greater if the mother is underweight, under severe emotional stress, has had a previous miscarriage or stillbirth, or is having another baby within one year of giving birth—and especially if any combination of these factors exists.
- Use salt to season foods during cooking, but avoid adding extra salt at the table. It's also a good idea to avoid high-sodium foods like potato chips, ham, and sausage.
- Toward the end of the pregnancy, eat five or six small meals a day instead of three large ones—for your own comfort and easier digestion.
- Take daily vitamin supplements containing 30 to 60 mg of elemental iron and 0.2 to 0.4 mg (400 to 800 micrograms) of folacin.
- Remember that the nearer foods are to their natural state, the higher their food value: Fresh is best, frozen next, canned foods last (Hotchner, 1990).

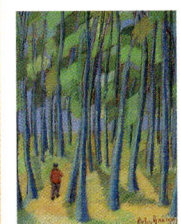

INTERACTION OF HEREDITY AND ENVIRONMENT

The manner in which the developing fetus, under genetic direction, is influenced by the prenatal environment provides us with an early variation of the nature-nurture issue. How do you see these two forces interacting and shaping the course of fetal development? Using information contained in this section, how might adverse aspects of the maternal environment cause structural damage or organ malfunction to the fetus?

In the accompanying Lifespan Development in Action box, we supply guidelines beyond nutritional considerations for a healthy pregnancy.

Drugs

All drugs pose potential problems for the embryo and fetus. The specific effects of drugs vary, depending not only on which drug is involved, but also on the quantity used and the time during pregnancy when it is taken. The following discussion highlights some of what we know about certain types of drugs.

NICOTINE How much nicotine is needed to produce which prenatal effects is not precisely known. Researchers who have weighed and measured the newborns of smokers and nonsmokers have found that the average baby born of a mother who smokes weighs less than the baby born of a nonsmoking woman. Although it is not known how or why this phenomenon occurs, an educated guess is that the fetus of a nonsmoker receives its full quota of oxygen; that of a smoking mother receives various gases, tars, and nicotine through the placenta, possibly at the expense of oxygen and/or of other nutrients (Behrman & Vaughn, 1987; Hillard & Panter, 1985).

Nicotine apparently has other bad effects. Just as adult heavy smokers have an increased heart rate, it has been suggested that the fetuses of women who smoke experience increased heart rates. Smoking may also lead to fetal hyperactivity. In addition, women who are heavy smokers are more apt than nonsmokers to give birth to premature babies. Finally, women who are heavy smokers are more likely to give birth to infants with life threatening complications such as respiratory infections and diseases (Khourg, Gomez-Farias, & Mulinare, 1989; Moore, 1988; Olds, London, & Ladewig, 1992; Vorhees & Mollnow, 1987).

During pregnancy, women need to maintain good health and follow proper nutritional guidelines.

Lifespan Development in Action

SUGGESTIONS FOR A HEALTHY PREGNANCY

During the course of a normal pregnancy, most women feel as well as at any other time in their lives. In fact, many feel even better while pregnant than ever before. However, even a low-risk pregnancy is put at high risk if prenatal care is absent or poor. Seeing a qualified practitioner regularly, beginning as soon as pregnancy is suspected, is vital for all expectant mothers. You should consult an obstetrician experienced with your particular condition if you are in a high-risk category. But being a good patient is just as important as having a good doctor. Be an active participant in your medical care—ask questions, report symptoms—but don't try to be your own doctor. In addition, pay attention to the following important areas:

Maintain a balanced diet. A good diet gives every pregnant woman the best odds of having a successful pregnancy and a healthy baby. It may also help to prevent gestational diabetes and hypertension.

Stop smoking. Quitting smoking as early in pregnancy as possible reduces many risks to mother and baby, including prematurity and low birth weight. Stopping smoking means both partners, too. If only one partner gives it up, he or she will continue to smoke passively by inhaling the smoke exhaled by the smoker.

Abstain from alcohol. Drinking very rarely or not at all will reduce the risk of birth defects, particularly of fetal alcohol syndrome, the result of high alcohol intake.

Avoid drugs. So little is known about the effects of drugs on fetal development that it is best to avoid taking any during pregnancy unless they are absolutely essential and prescribed by your doctor. This includes caffeine as well as over-the-counter drugs.

Strive for a sensible weight gain. A gradual, moderate weight gain may help prevent a variety of complications, including diabetes, hypertension, varicose veins, hemorrhoids, low birth weight, or difficult delivery due to an overly large fetus.

Seek to prevent infections. All infections—from common flu to urinary tract and vaginal infections to venereal diseases—should be prevented whenever possible. If contracted, however, infection should be treated promptly by a physician who knows you are pregnant.

Stay fit. It's best to begin pregnancy with a well-toned, exercised body, but it's never too late to start deriving the benefits of fitness. Regular exercise under a doctor's orders prevents constipation and improves respiration, circulation, muscle tone, and skin elasticity, all of which contribute to a more comfortable pregnancy and an easier, safer delivery.

Get adequate rest. Getting enough rest during pregnancy is far more important than getting everything done, especially in high-risk pregnancies. Don't wait until your body starts pleading for relief before you slow down. If your doctor recommends you begin your maternity leave earlier than you'd planned, take the advice. (Adapted from Eisenberg, Murkoff, & Hathaway, 1991)

ALCOHOL Heavy intake of alcohol can lead to **fetal alcohol syndrome,** a condition in which infants are often born undersized, mentally deficient, and with several physical deformities, such as abnormal limb development, facial abnormalities, and heart defects. Some children of alcoholic mothers develop complications later in life, including poor attention skills and slow reaction times (Abel, 1990; Brendt & Beckman, 1990; Streissguth et al., 1989; von Knorring, 1991).

One study (Streissguth, Barr, & Martin, 1983) examined the effects of maternal alcohol use during midpregnancy on infant habituation. Habituation refers to the tendency to get used to and eventually ignore stimuli that are experienced repeatedly. For example, a baby may first pay attention to a novel figure or pattern, but then, over time, pay less attention to it. Habituation is an important aspect of learning because it shows that memory is developing; that is, the baby remembers the stimuli he or she has been exposed to.

In this study mothers reported the amount of alcohol they consumed during the fifth month of pregnancy, and newborns were evaluated by means of a specialized infancy assessment test. It was found that maternal alcohol consumption was significantly related to poorer habituation and low arousal in newborns, even after the researchers adjusted for smoking by mothers, maternal age, nutrition during pregnancy, sex and age of the infant, and obstetric medication.

HEROIN, COCAINE, AND OTHER DRUGS Addictive drugs, such as heroin and cocaine, pass through the placenta readily, causing mothers who are addicts to give birth to babies who are also addicted (i.e., have developed a physiological dependence on the drug). An addicted newborn experiences all the symptoms (tremors, fever, convulsions, and breathing difficulties) that adults do when they go through withdrawal from the drug. These babies are generally smaller than average (heroin babies seldom weigh more than 5½ pounds) and exhibit disturbed sleep patterns as well, as impaired motor control (Hans, 1989).

Numerous researchers (e.g., Lester et al., 1991; Lipsitt, 1989; Lynch & McKeon, 1990; Neuspiel & Hamel, 1991) have found that cocaine and its derivatives (such as crack) used by the mother during the second half of pregnancy tend to cause fetal distress, irritability, hypertension, premature labor, and even death. And marijuana use during a woman's pregnancy has been linked to irritability and increased tremors during infancy as well as deficits in cognitive functioning later in childhood.

▬ Maternal Emotions

There are many misconceptions regarding the pregnant woman's environment and how it will affect the fetus. For example, if a woman had been frightened, the child would be born with a birthmark shaped like the object that had upset the mother. Another belief was that happy mothers would give birth to happy babies and worried mothers would have unhappy children. Although there is no truth to these old superstitions, there are some closely associated biological factors that must be considered. It is not the mother's emotions per se but the physiological changes that accompany her emotional state that may affect the behavior of her offspring (Chalmers, 1982).

Emotions (happiness, sadness, worry) do not directly influence the developing organism, but there is growing evidence that the hormones released while a mother is under great stress (anxiety) do affect the unborn. In fact, the mother's emotional state may affect both fetal and subsequent behavior. For example, willing pregnant women can be given a test to determine the degree of their anxiety. They are then classified as having high or low anxiety. The infants of these two groups of mothers are later observed and tested. By comparing the test results of the two groups, it was discovered that women subjected to severe or prolonged emotional stress during pregnancy are more prone to give birth to infants who are hyperactive, have low birth weights, are irritable, and have feeding problems and digestive disturbances. Furthermore, highly anxious women appear to have more spontaneous abortions and a higher percentage of premature infants, and they spend an average of 5 more hours in labor. They also tend to have more complicated and abnormal deliveries (Bloomberg, 1980).

■■ Teratogenic Agents

A **teratogenic agent** is any environmental substance that causes a change in the genetic code, which in turn produces any abnormality, anomaly, or malformation. It is important to distinguish between teratogenic agents and inherited teratogenes (inborn errors of metabolism—genes from one or both parents that will produce a mutant child).

Teratogenic agents affect genes and protein production in several ways. For example, they may damage genes and make them inoperable. Some agents are also chemically capable of substituting themselves in the genetic code, bonding themselves to a gene (or genes). In this way, a mutant enzyme is produced. At other times enzymes may be blocked or totally destroyed. More technically, teratogenic agents may act by means of any of the following: **agenesis** (genes cease their protein production so development halts); **incomplete development** (the failure of genes to complete the development or growth already commenced); or **developmental excess** (overgrowth of the whole organism or any of its parts).

A teratogenic agent is especially dangerous during the development of an organ (organogenesis). For example, thalidomide, which affects those genes that control the development of the appendages, can do its damage only when the genes for arms and legs are activated. It is during this time that the gene is vulnerable, as it is in an unbonded state. The gene is considered vulnerable because free-floating teratogenic agents such as thalidomide can attach themselves to its unbonded structure, resulting in agenesis. German measles (rubella), on the other hand, evidently enters into the genetic developmental code, producing mutant brain protein. The most dangerous time for the developing organism is the first 2 or 3 months after conception, for this is the major developmental period (Brendt & Beckman, 1990; Moore, 1988). However, deformations can occur at any time during development. Table 4-2 lists some suspected teratogenic agents.

ACQUIRED IMMUNE DEFICIENCY SYNDROME The **acquired immune deficiency syndrome (AIDS)** is an illness in which the human immunodeficiency virus destroys the ability of the body to fight off invaders, rendering a person vulnerable to a host of diseases. Although the incidence of childhood AIDS is low—approximately 2 to 3% of all AIDS cases—it is growing swiftly (Centers for Disease Control, 1992a; 1993). AIDS results from a virus called the *human*

INTERRELATEDNESS OF AGING PROCESSES

The experience of pregnancy is an important event in a woman's life and shows how developmental forces intertwine. Although the most obvious changes involve the biological domain, how do you think a woman's pregnancy affects her psychologically? From a social standpoint, how are her relationships with others affected, such as with her spouse? How can an understanding of these interrelated areas be used to provide prospective mothers with support and reassurance?

TABLE 4-2
Possible Teratogenic Agents

Category	Causative Agent	Effect
Physical agent	Irradiation (X rays)	Malformation of any organ, the organ involved depending on organism's state of development
Infectious agent	Rubella (German measles)	Brain damage (mental retardation), sensory and cranial nerve damage (especially vision and hearing)
	Quinine (?)	Possible deafness and congenital malformations, but not totally substantiated (*Note:* quinine water lacks sufficient quinine to be included in this group)
	Cortisone	Possibly contributes to formation of cleft palate
	Paint fumes (?)	Suspected by some of causing mental retardation (pregnant women would probably have to be in unventilated paint area for a substantial length of time to be affected)
Chemical agent	Thalidomide	If taken 21 to 22 days after conception, may cause absence of external ears, cranial nerve paralysis; 24 to 27 days, agenesis of arms; 28 to 29 days, agenesis of legs
	Vitamin A	Large doses taken throughout pregnancy may cause cleft palate, eye damage, congenital abnormalities
	Vitamin D	Large doses taken throughout pregnancy may cause mental retardation
	Alcohol	Heavy intake of alcohol can lead to *fetal alcohol syndrome,* which can produce subnormal IQs, physical deformities (e.g., facial abnormalities), and impaired cognitive functioning (e.g., poor attention skills).

immunodeficiency virus, and can be transmitted from an infected mother to her fetus or infant before, during, or shortly after birth (called *perinatal* transmission). (It should be noted, too, that children who receive transfusions of infected blood or blood products may also become infected.) As far as prenatal development is concerned, an infected mother may transmit HIV through the placenta to her unborn child. More rarely, infants have acquired the virus through ingestion of breast milk (HIV has been shown to be present in the breast milk of infected mothers) (Centers for Disease Control, 1992a, 1993; Cox, 1992; Surgeon General's Report on HIV Infection and AIDS, 1993).

Not all babies born to infected mothers will develop AIDS. For those who do, the prognosis is not favorable. Symptoms usually appear about 4 or 5 months after birth, and most succumb to infections that attack their weakened immune system before they are 3 years old. It is rare for these children to live as long as 6 years. To date, there is no cure for AIDS, although some drugs have been found to slow the progressive deterioration of the immune system

(Cohen, Sande, & Volberding, 1990; Goldsmith, 1992; Lederman, 1992; Mann, 1992; Samuels et al., 1992; Stine, 1993).

Infants born with AIDS have certain distinguishing characteristics. Most have a small head, a prominent forehead, protruding lips, a flattened nose bridge, and wide-set eyes. Many also have a bluish tinge to the whites of their eyes. Some infants do not seem sick at birth, but most will develop symptoms within 8 or 9 months. Infected infants often exhibit retarded motor and language growth and other developmental delays, cognitive deficits, and chronic diarrhea. Many have enlarged lymph nodes, liver, and spleen. And like adult victims of the disease, many children with AIDS are susceptible to bacterial infections such as pneumonia (Phair & Chadwick, 1992; Stine, 1993; Turner & Rubinson, 1993).

The spread of AIDS to children has given rise to a number of controversial issues (Grossman, 1988). One of these is whether all women who are planning pregnancies should consider HIV antibody testing. Many people believe that at least women who engage in high-risk sexual behaviors and those who use intravenous drugs should be tested when they become pregnant, and that those who test positive should be informed of the harmful effects of pregnancy on their own immunological status as well as on that of the fetus. For example, one study (Landers & Sweet, 1990) discloses that the progress of clinical symptoms in HIV-positive asymptomatic women may be accelerated by pregnancy, perhaps because of the immune alterations that naturally occur during any pregnancy. Many authorities (e.g., Olds, London, & Ladewig, 1992) stress that HIV-positive women should be straightforwardly counseled about the implications for themselves and the fetus and they should be offered therapeutic abortion.

Other concerns focus on the actual delivery of an infant from an HIV-infected mother. The pediatrician and delivery room attendants need to be informed ahead of time that the mother is infected because her body fluids and the placenta will contain HIV and therefore infection-control precautions must be taken.

Although many HIV-infected mothers care for their infected children, many others do not because of their medical and social problems. Who, then, is to care for these children? In recent years shelter and foster care programs have been reluctant to accept HIV-infected infants, and putting these children up for adoption isn't a practical answer either, for few people want to adopt an infected baby. Many communities have had to resort to some form of institutional care for these infants—a sad alternative that is far less likely to meet their developmental and emotional needs than an individual home would (Grossman, 1988; Prothrow-Stith, 1989). The Focus on Diversity box presents a special case of AIDS infection in the very young and examines the treatment and care provided for these children.

PROBLEM PREGNANCIES

Most pregnancies follow a normal course of development. Occasionally, however, development goes awry and serious problems result. Such conditions as toxemia, Rh factor incompatibility, ectopic pregnancy, and miscarriage require medical intervention.

Focus on Diversity

THE LITTLEST VICTIMS: CHILDREN WITH AIDS

The children are cared for on the third floor of the drab, gray Victor Babes Hospital, the only AIDS clinic in Bucharest, Romania. Amid the moans and wails of the children, nurses scurry about carrying syringes, vials, and wet cloths. They often have trouble keeping up with the children's assortment of medical needs.

Romania has an unusual epidemic of AIDS among children, concentrated in crowded orphanages and clinics and spread by the peculiar practice of giving blood transfusions to newborns (World Health Organization, 1991). For many years, in the hope of stimulating early growth in babies, Romanian doctors injected blood into the umbilical cord of newborns. Because each baby was given only a small amount of blood, one pint of HIV-contaminated blood could infect many, many babies.

Of the 2,000 Romanian children tested in 1990 in targeted clinics and orphanages, 250 had AIDS and another 200 tested positive for HIV. AIDS among babies is not unique to Romania, of course, but the authorities' willful neglect of the disease allowed it to spread rapidly. The problem was compounded by poverty, poor medical practices, and the large number of children abandoned to institutional care. The epidemic is one of the grim legacies of Nicolae Ceausescu, the former ruler of Romania, who was overthrown (and executed) in a revolution in 1989.

Almost two thirds of the AIDS babies in the clinic were brought there from orphanages. The orphanages, overcrowded, ill-equipped, and underheated, are another Ceausescu legacy, the product of harsh policies against birth control that resulted in thousands of unwanted children. Prior to the overthrow of Ceausescu, there was no official acknowledgment that AIDS existed in Romania. Thus it is only recently that data about the spread of the disease have become available. (Bohlen, 1990; Turner & Robinson, 1993)

Toxemia

Toxemia is a general term referring to the presence of a toxic substance in the blood. Toxemia takes two distinct forms: preeclampsia and eclampsia. In *preeclampsia* the mother's retention of salt and water leads to an increase in weight, swelling, and raised blood pressure. In severe cases, there may also be headaches, vomiting, visual disturbances, and urinary complications. Preeclampsia is potentially dangerous because it may cause the body's blood vessels to become constricted, reducing the flow of blood to the womb by as much as 50% and inevitably affecting the placenta and fetus.

Preeclampsia is treated with drugs that reduce blood pressure, bed rest, and, if needed, mild sedatives. Rest tends to stimulate the flow of blood to the kidneys and womb, as well as to increase the amount of urine produced. When left untreated, preeclampsia can lead to eclampsia, the more serious toxemia. *Eclampsia* is a rare disorder, affecting only 1 in 1,000 mothers. It typically begins with muscle spasms and rapid reflex movements, and eventually the woman goes into convulsions and seizures. In its most serious stages, eclampsia can threaten the lives of both fetus and mother. Usually, treatment for eclampsia calls for anticonvulsant drugs, blood pressure medication, and the prompt delivery of the baby (Iams & Zuspan, 1990; Speroff, Glass, & Kase, 1989).

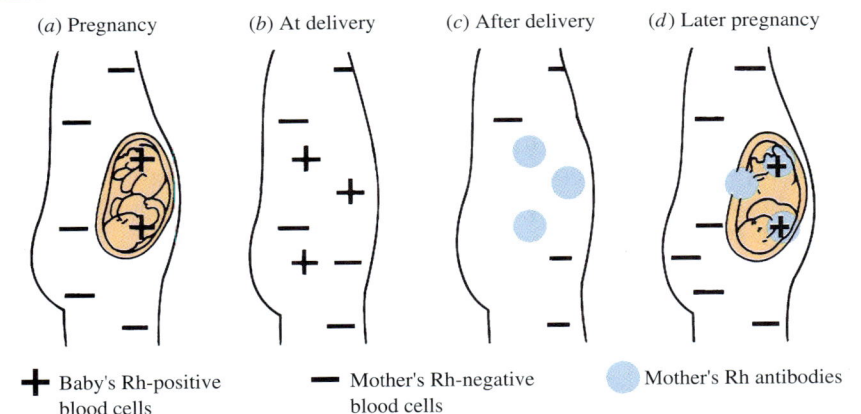

(a) Pregnancy   (b) At delivery   (c) After delivery   (d) Later pregnancy

✚ Baby's Rh-positive blood cells

▬ Mother's Rh-negative blood cells

● Mother's Rh antibodies

FIGURE 4-3
The Rh Factor.

While an Rh− mother is carrying an Rh+ baby *(a),* some of the baby's Rh+ blood enters the mother's body *(b).* Her body produces antibodies against this factor *(c).* When she carries a subsequent Rh+ baby, the antibodies cross the placenta and attack the baby's red blood cells *(d).* If after birth, abortion, or miscarriage, it is determined the baby's blood is Rh+, RhoGam, an anti-Rh antibody, is given to the Rh− mother within 72 hours. This suppresses the formation of anti-Rh antibodies and thus protects a future baby. The anti-Rh antibody cannot be given during pregnancy because it would pass through the placenta and damage the fetus's red blood cells.

▬ Rh Factor

The **Rh factor** refers to a substance found in red blood cells. Although a cure has been found, fetuses and newborns continue to die because their blood is Rh positive (Rh+) and their mother's is Rh negative (Rh−). Rh+ is a genetically dominant trait; thus the child of two Rh− parents or an Rh− father and Rh+ mother is not affected. The Rh factor comes into focus only when the father is Rh+ and the mother Rh−.

Positive and negative blood types are incompatible. It is common during the birth process for fetal blood to enter the maternal bloodstream during hemorrhaging. When the child is Rh+, this foreign substance to the Rh− mother is combatted by the production of antibodies. During the first birth there are few if any antibodies present, so the Rh factor is unimportant. When the female again becomes pregnant, however, these antibodies pass through the placenta and cause *erythroblastosis,* a condition where the antibodies attack the fetal blood cells, generally causing death.

Today, Rh immune globulin can be administered to the mother after the birth of each child, thus preventing the formation of antibodies and allowing an Rh incompatible couple to produce other healthy children. Figure 4-3 illustrates the Rh Factor.

▬ Ectopic Pregnancy

It is possible that in its journey to the uterus, the fertilized egg can become lodged in the wall of the fallopian tube. Called an **ectopic pregnancy** (or tubal pregnancy), this happens once in about 200 pregnancies and it produces an untenable situation. The tubes were not designed to harbor pregnancies. If a fertilized egg does become lodged in the tube it will continue to grow normally for a while; however, sooner or later the tube (as opposed to the flexible muscular uterus) will be unable to expand its delicate wall any further and burst. This invariably happens sometime during the first 3 months. It will produce bleeding directly into the abdominal cavity, which must be stopped by an abdominal operation to remove the tube.

Miscarriage

A **miscarriage** (or spontaneous abortion) is the termination of a pregnancy before the embryo or fetus has the opportunity to fully develop. About 1 out of 10 known pregnancies results in a miscarriage. It is estimated that 90% of all miscarriages occur during the first 3 months of pregnancy. Probably many more are unknown because some women abort without being aware they are pregnant during the early weeks of gestation (Abbott, 1989; Olds, London, & Ladewig, 1992).

In many miscarriages, the cause is a genetic abnormality. This creates a defective embryo that is unable to develop normally. Early miscarriage is viewed by some (e.g., Hales & Creasy, 1982) as a natural selection process in which the defective organism is rejected before it has a chance to fully develop.

Certain factors are believed to increase the risk of miscarriages. For example, miscarriages occur more often in women who smoke, consume large amounts of alcohol, or who are over the age of 35 or under the age of 15 (Korones, 1986; Simpson, 1990). Other factors suspected of triggering a miscarriage include rubella, X rays, or severe infections such as pneumonia. These latter factors are regarded as onetime events, though, and usually do not affect future pregnancies (Anderson, 1989; Eisenberg, Murkoff, & Hathaway, 1991).

THE BIRTH PROCESS

The fetus's physical development is complete by the end of the third trimester of pregnancy (see Figure 4-4). **Labor,** the climax of pregnancy, encompasses the processes involved in giving birth: uterine contractions, delivery of the baby, and expulsion of the placenta. The precise physiological mechanisms that trigger labor are unknown, although it is speculated the fetus's adrenal glands manufacture hormones that cause the placenta and the uterus to increase the secretion of *prostaglandins* (human hormones). Prostaglandins, in turn, stimulate the muscles of the uterus to contract. These uterine contractions, which are gradual at first and then increase in both regularity and intensity, are the first sign of labor for most women.

Before the onset of labor, most pregnant women experience a phenomenon known as lightening. **Lightening** means the fetus is beginning to settle into the pelvis, causing a downward movement of the uterus. Lightening can occur at any time during the last month of pregnancy, but usually it happens about 10 days before delivery.

Lightening enables the woman to breathe easier because the fetus is no longer pressing on her diaphragm. She may experience an increased need to urinate, though, since the fetal descent creates greater pressure on her bladder. Many women also report leg pain because of pressure on the sciatic nerve.

Many women experience "false labor," or *Braxton Hicks contractions,* before the onset of actual labor. Braxton Hicks contractions are irregular and painful contractions in the abdomen and groin area that do not affect the cervix. As we see shortly, true labor contractions create both size and structural changes in the cervix, and are usually also felt in the lower back and extend to the front of the abdomen.

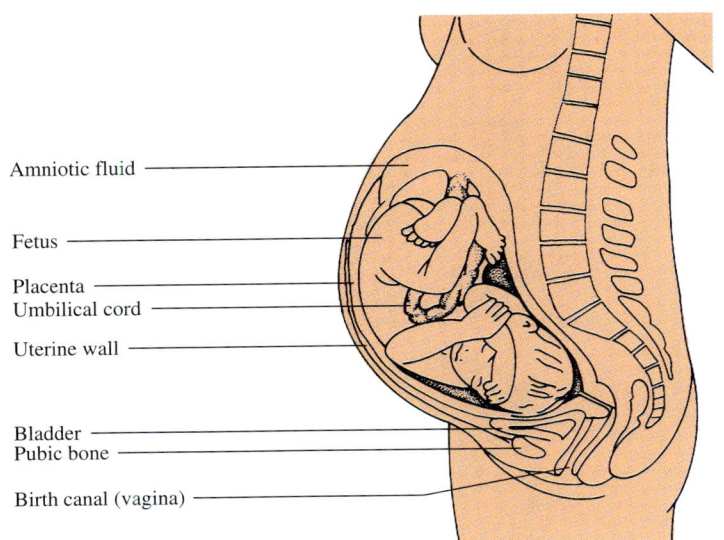

Amniotic fluid

Fetus

Placenta
Umbilical cord

Uterine wall

Bladder
Pubic bone

Birth canal (vagina)

FIGURE 4-4
A Full-Term Fetus.

The fetus is shown here in its safe and protective prenatal environment. The support system for the developing organism consists of three major parts: the placenta, the umbilical cord, and the fluid-filled amniotic sac.

Another sign of impending labor is a pinkish discharge from the vagina referred to as "pink" or "bloody show." However, some women do not experience this until the first stage of labor begins. The pink show is caused by the release of the mucus plug from inside the neck of the cervix. As the fetus descends, minute capillaries in the mucous membrane of the cervix tend to rupture. Usually, this creates a small quantity of blood, similar in amount to the blood loss at the beginning of a menstrual period, mixed with mucus. Sometimes there is an initial discharge of clear watery material instead of the show, which indicates the imminent rupture of the fetal membranes.

Beyond these classic early warnings, women report other signs of impending labor. Some experience a sudden burst of energy (commonly called "nesting behavior"). Others report increased backache and vaginal secretions. Still other women have a fluid loss in the final weeks of pregnancy. Finally, diarrhea or loose bowel movements are often reported.

Stages of Labor and Delivery

Labor is broken down into three stages. The first stage begins with the onset of true labor contractions and ends with the complete dilation of the cervix. The second stage consists of the delivery of the baby. The final stage is the expulsion of the placenta (Figure 4-5 depicts these three stages).

The duration of labor varies from woman to woman, although the average for first labors tends to be about 14 hours. This breaks down to about 12½ hours in the first stage, 1 hour and 20 minutes in the second stage, and 10 minutes in the third stage. Later labors tend to be about 6 hours shorter than first labors. This breaks down to an average of 7½ hours in the first stage, a half hour in the second stage, and 10 minutes in the final stage.

FIGURE 4-5
Three Stages of Birth.

The birth process consists of three stages. The first is rhythmic contractions of the uterus, a phase that enables the cervix to open. During the second stage, the uterus contracts and the baby is pushed into the birth canal and out of the mother's body. The third stage is the expulsion of the placenta.

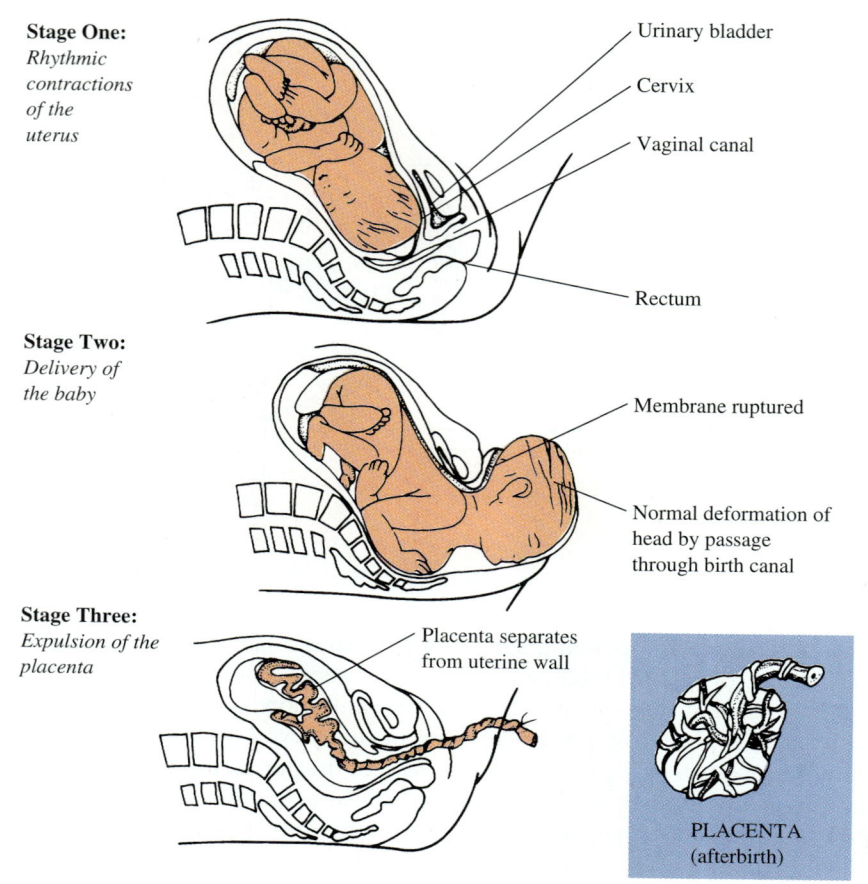

Stage One: *Rhythmic contractions of the uterus*

Urinary bladder
Cervix
Vaginal canal
Rectum

Stage Two: *Delivery of the baby*

Membrane ruptured
Normal deformation of head by passage through birth canal

Stage Three: *Expulsion of the placenta*

Placenta separates from uterine wall

PLACENTA (afterbirth)

First Stage   During the early parts of the first stage, uterine contractions are short and about 10 to 15 minutes apart. They produce a feeling of discomfort in the lower back, and gradually spread to the front of the abdomen. Rupture of the amniotic sac often occurs, causing the amniotic fluid to be released (this is commonly referred to as "breaking of the waters"), although this may happen a few days before labor begins. The amniotic fluid can release itself in a sudden gush or in a trickle. Sometimes the amniotic sac does not break on its own, even after labor is under way. In such cases, the obstetrician will rupture it deliberately.

As labor progresses, uterine contractions become more frequent and more painful. At their peak, contractions occur about every 2 to 3 minutes and last approximately 45 to 60 seconds. One sign of possible problems in the delivery of a child is the absence of such strong contractions.

Uterine contractions may be accompanied by labored breathing, abdominal and leg cramps, excessive perspiration, and nausea. Contractions also increase the amount of pink show because they tend to rupture capillary vessels in the cervix and lower uterine area.

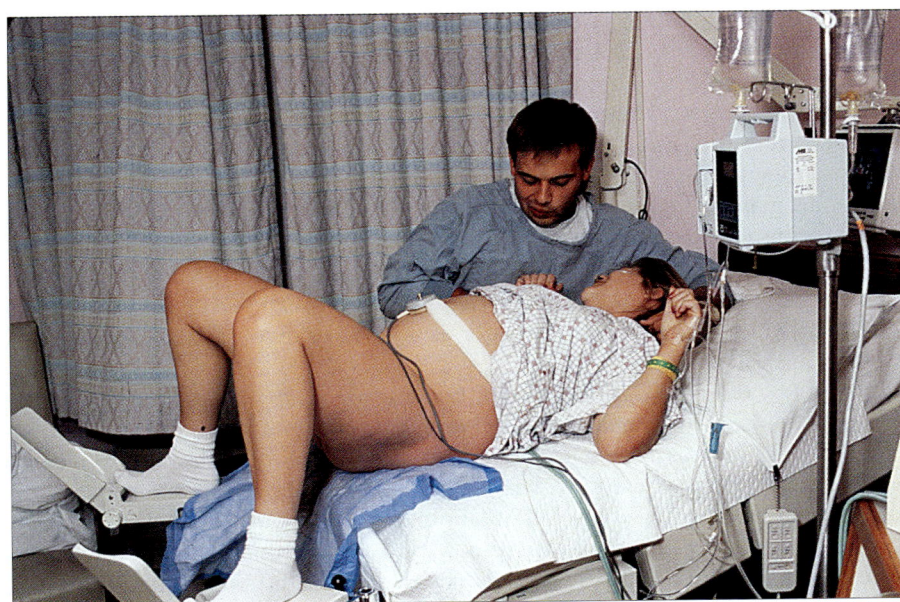

Going into labor is the culmination of months of anticipation and waiting.

Uterine contractions create effacement and dilation of the cervix. *Efface-ment* is the shortening and thinning of the cervical canal. As effacement oc-curs, the cervix changes from a long, thick structure to a structure that is paper thin. *Dilation* is the enlargement of the cervix so the fetus can successfully pass through it. From an opening of about 4 centimeters (about 1½ inches) during the first stage of labor, the cervix reaches full dilation with a diameter of 10 cen-timeters (about 4 inches). This is a temporary change. Immediately after child-birth, the cervix begins to contract, and by a week postpartum, it has returned to its normal size.

Second Stage   During the second stage of labor, contractions continue to be long and severe. The fetus begins to descend down the vagina, soon revealing its scalp through the vulva (the external female genitalia). Gradually, the vulva is stretched and eventually encircles the diameter of the baby's head (the head is normally the widest part of the fetus). **Crowning** is the encirclement of the largest diameter of the baby's head by the vulva. As the vulvar opening be-comes dilated and distended by the head, the woman's perineal area (the tissue located between the genital area and the anal canal) and anus stretch and pro-trude.

When crowning occurs, the baby is usually ready to be expelled. Delivery generally takes place between contractions and as slowly as possible. This is to help prevent lacerations during extreme vaginal stretching. An incision called an *episiotomy* may be made in the woman's perineum to protect it, the sphinc-ter, and the rectum from laceration and to shorten the second stage of labor (Cunningham, MacDonald, & Gant, 1989; Rockner, Wahlberg, & Olund, 1989).

Research indicates that an episiotomy is one of the most common proce-dures in childbirth (e.g., see Rockner, Wahlberg, & Olund, 1989). It is estimated that the rate of episiotomies in all births is over 60%. However, there has been some opposition to routine episiotomies in recent years (Thorp & Bowes, 1989). Critics maintain this procedure is an unnecessary surgical intrusion that is performed more for the convenience of the doctor than for the sake of the woman. They argue the vaginal opening can stretch on its own without tearing, and that an episiotomy causes pain and perineal discomfort when healing during the postpartum period. Additional complications associated with episiotomies may be infection and blood loss (Borgotta, Piening, & Cohen, 1989; Olds, London, & Ladewig, 1992).

It also may be necessary to use forceps, an obstetrical instrument designed to assist delivery. *Forceps* consist of two steel parts that cross each other like a pair of salad tongs and lock at the intersection. They may be used to gently pull or turn the baby, or both.

A forceps delivery may be chosen because the mother is unable to deliver even after complete dilation of the cervix. Or forceps may be necessary to assist the birth because the woman has heart disease and pushing is dangerous for her. Heart disease weakens the heart, making it more difficult for it to accommodate the higher workload of labor (Cruikshank, 1990; Olds, London, & Ladewig, 1992). In rare cases, there may be a danger that the uterus will rupture or the placenta will prematurely separate from the uterus. A doctor may also decide to use forceps when labor has been overlong and the mother is exhausted. Finally, a condition known as **fetal distress** may call for the use of forceps. This condition is defined by unusual changes in fetal activity, such as a slow, irregular heartbeat, indicating the fetus is in jeopardy (Cunningham, MacDonald, & Gant, 1989; Parer, 1989; Parer & Livingston, 1991). The use of forceps may pose some risks to the fetus, the most common being small areas of bruising or swelling along the sides of the face or in the scalp region, or temporary facial paralysis.

Delivery of the baby represents the second stage of labor.

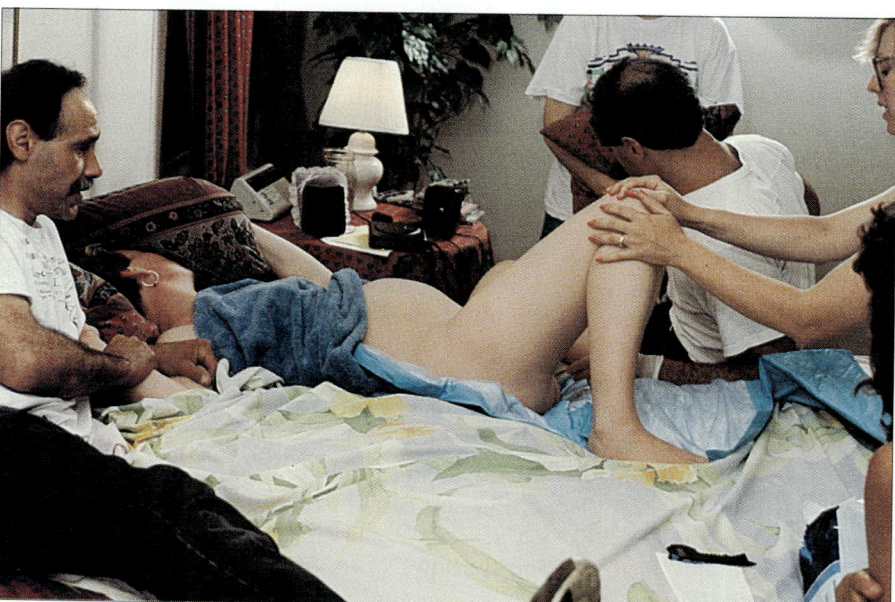

The umbilical cord is quite long (15 to 30 inches) to allow free movement of the baby during delivery. Sometimes, however, it becomes looped one or more times around the neck, arm, leg, or other parts of the body. Usually, this does not present a problem, for the cord can be slipped back over the baby's body or brought over its head. If the cord's specific position causes it to be compressed so the flow of oxygen to the baby is reduced, however, steps must be taken to relieve the compression. Should this prove impossible, an emergency cesarean section may have to be performed.

Most babies present in a head-downward position for delivery. Birth is facilitated by positional changes in the baby, including a rotating movement. This movement tends to accommodate the irregular shape of the pelvic canal by providing the smallest possible diameters of the presenting part. Thus the baby encounters as little resistance as possible. Once the head and shoulders are delivered, the baby's body is quickly expelled because of its smaller size.

After the birth, the umbilical cord still connects the baby to the placenta. However, pulsations in the cord soon diminish, indicating a reduced flow of blood to the baby. The cord is then clamped and cut with a pair of sterile surgical scissors about ½ to 1 inch from the abdomen. The clamp is removed in the newborn nursery about 24 hours after the cord has dried. The cord itself typically shrinks and falls off within a few days after birth (Iams & Zuspan, 1990; Olds, London, & Ladewig, 1992).

Not all babies are born in a head-downward position. Rather, about 5% engage themselves in what is called a **breech presentation.** A breech presentation means the lower part of the fetus appears first during delivery. In the *complete breech* the knees of the fetus are flexed and a sitting position appears to have been assumed. In a *frank breech* the legs of the fetus are bent straight up at the hips, with the knees straight. In a *footling breech* one or both feet or knees lie below the buttocks of the fetus. This can be either a single footling or a double footling, depending on whether one or both feet are coming first. Finally, a *kneeling breech* occurs when the legs are bent at the knees and the knees themselves are presented first. Breech presentations may prolong labor because the lower part of the fetus does not exert as much pressure on the cervix as the fetal head. Complicating matters is that the largest part of the fetus (the head) emerges last, which may increase the risks of trauma to the head, malformation, interference with respiration, and maternal infection (Cruikshank, 1990; Cunningham, MacDonald, & Gant, 1989; Olds, London, & Ladewig, 1992). Because of such risks, most obstetricians elect to deliver babies in the breech position by cesarean section, which we discuss shortly.

Third Stage The third and last stage of labor is the expulsion of the placenta. Once the baby has been delivered, the uterus begins to relax and contract, which reduces the area of placental attachment. This causes the placenta to detach itself and move toward the lower uterus. The actual expulsion of the placenta can generally be accomplished by the bearing-down efforts of the mother. If this is not possible, the clinician applies gentle traction to the cord while exerting pressure on the fundus (the upper, rounded portion of the uterus). This should be done only when the uterus is hard and there is no bleeding.

Many couples today are
sharing the childbirth
experience.

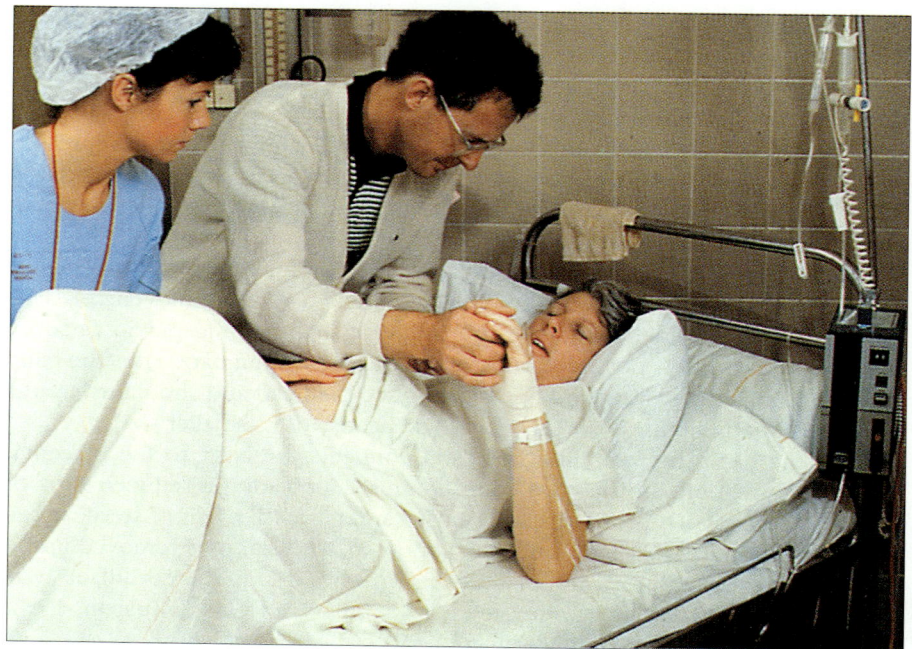

▬ Childbirth Techniques

Although large percentages of mothers continue to deliver their babies in traditional medical and hospital settings, growing numbers are pursuing alternatives to hospital labor and delivery. Most are doing so because they object to the use of anesthesia during delivery and to other medical intrusions on the mother and the baby. Some also object to the deemphasized role of the father in the delivery of the baby (Danziger & Wertz, 1989; Marshall, 1992; Wertz & Wertz, 1989). The following discussion highlights some of the childbirth techniques available to couples today. At the end of this section in one of our Lifespan Development in Action boxes, we provide some suggestions on how you can plan the delivery of your baby.

Lamaze Method   The **Lamaze method** (named after Fernand Lamaze, a French obstetrician) is one of the most popular alternative approaches. It represents an attempt to avoid the use of anesthesia and to allow both prospective father and mother to play an active role in the delivery of their baby. Expectant couples attend classes that stress special breathing exercises and relaxation responses. It is reasoned that fears during delivery cause women to tense their muscles, which delays the birth process and increases the mother's pain. Proponents of this approach feel that if women know what to expect and learn how to relax, their discomfort can be significantly reduced.

Leboyer Method   The **Leboyer method** emphasizes the importance of a gentle delivery and minimal trauma for the newborn. Developed by French obstetrician Frederick Leboyer and detailed in his book *Birth Without Violence* (1975), this delivery method offers a marked contrast to hospital childbirth procedures. The baby is born into a dimly lit delivery room that is kept relatively silent. Immediately after birth the infant is placed on the mother's stomach to be gently massaged, so that tactile stimulation and contact soothe the baby and promote bonding. The infant is then further soothed by a warm bath. Only after this is the baby given a routine medical examination.

Leboyer suggests that such steps are transitions that minimize the trauma of birth and the abrupt departure of the infant from the womb. Leboyer's ideas have not gained universal acceptance. Critics maintain it is dangerous to postpone the examination of the neonate after birth, especially when dim lighting may prevent the detection of vital life signs. Moreover, researchers (Maziade et al., 1986; Nelson et al., 1980) have not been able to find any long-range benefits among infants delivered by the Leboyer method.

Home Birth   More couples today opt for a **home birth.** Such births are likely to increase because many parents are rebelling against increased hospital costs and impersonal neonatal and postpartum care. Home births are especially popular among women who have some college education (Gilgoff, 1988; Pearse, 1987) and, as you'll discover in the Focus on Diversity box, home births are popular in other nations.

Home births are often conducted by certified **nurse-midwives,** trained delivery specialists who provide qualified medical care to expectant mothers. Usually the midwife has earned a bachelor's degree in nurse-midwifery and works on a medical team consisting of a gynecologist and an obstetrician. The nurse-midwife spends considerably more time with the mother before, during, and after the delivery and offers close, personal attention in a relaxed and comfortable setting. Some nurse-midwives have a private practice (depending on state licensure requirements); others work in physicians' offices, birthing clinics, hospitals, or in homes. There are also lay midwives who are trained by other midwives and not certified. Poor people often seek the services of lay midwives because the latter charge less than certified nurse-midwives.

For low-risk women, research indicates (Clark & Bennetts, 1982; Cohen, 1982; Gilgoff, 1988; Sullivan & Weitz, 1988) that home births are as safe as hospital births. Sandra Danziger and Dorothy Wertz (1989) add that women who give birth in familiar surroundings, at their own speed, without medication, often feel a sense of accomplishment and uninhibited family closeness that is difficult to experience in a hospital setting. However, home births often receive criticism. For example, medical personnel point to the security that hospitals offer against unforeseen complications, and, as indicated, midwives sometimes lack formal training (Pearse, 1987; Wolfson, 1986).

Rooming-In and Birthing Room Facilities   Rooming-in and birthing room hospital facilities are also increasing in popularity. A **rooming-in hospital facility** allows the mother to care for the newborn in her own room. The infant is usually brought to the mother's room within the first few hours after birth and remains there (rather than in the nursery) during the duration of hospitalization. A **birthing room** offers a homelike and relaxed atmosphere within the hospital delivery unit. The mother goes through labor and delivery in this room rather than being rushed to the delivery room prior to birth. Many couples today combine the birthing room with natural childbirth approaches to labor and delivery.

GENDER SIMILARITIES AND DIFFERENCES

What do you think about the greater participation of male partners in prepared childbirth? Do you think their participation creates a better childbirth experience for women? What kinds of assistance and support can fathers provide that you think are important for mothers-to-be?

Focus on Diversity

ALTERNATIVES TO THE HOSPITAL: HOME BIRTHS IN THE NETHERLANDS

At the turn of the century in the United States all but 5% of babies were born at home. Because there were fewer hospitals and physicians, a midwife was typically summoned to deliver the baby. But because of infant mortality and the availability of hospitals to handle difficult deliveries, home deliveries became less common. Today about 95% of all births take place in a hospital.

A unique comparison to the United States lies in the Netherlands where about 35% of all Dutch women give birth at home. Even though the Netherlands has a highly sophisticated health-care system, it leads the industrialized world in the proportion of women having babies at home. Midwives perform virtually all home and hospital births.

Interestingly, statistics show that the rate of infant mortality within a week of birth is higher in hospitals than at home. However, this is because virtually all problem births are detected in advance and take place in a hospital. In the Netherlands national health insurance policies cover most deliveries and regard home births as so safe that they will not pay for a hospital birth unless it is medically advised.

The popularity of home births is in large part due to the importance of the home in Dutch social life. The small geographical size of the Netherlands and its above-average roads enable expectant couples from any location to be at a hospital within half an hour, if need be. Should delivery take place in a hospital a short-stay policy adds further testimony to the importance placed on the home. Most mothers and their newborns are back in their homes within 5 hours after delivery.

Many hospitals today also offer a *birthing chair,* which elevates a woman's body so it is in a near-vertical position during delivery. Variations of birthing chairs have been around for centuries. The modern version of it usually has a molded seat that is set on a pedestal. A motor allows it to be tilted, elevated, or lowered.

■ Cesarean Delivery

In **cesarean delivery** (or C-section), the baby is delivered through a surgical incision made in the mother's abdominal and uterine walls. The word *cesarean* comes from the Latin *caedere,* meaning "to cut." Possible reasons for a cesarean section, besides breech presentation, are the mother's failure to progress normally through labor, a disproportion between the size of the fetus and that of the birth canal, fetal distress, abnormalities in the labor process, and a previous cesarean section in the mother. Related to the latter, though, it should be recognized that women with a previous cesarean section do not necessarily have to have one for later deliveries.

Cesarean delivery is not a recent innovation. An early Roman law known as *lex regia* required that a baby be removed from the uterus of any woman dying in late pregnancy. This law persisted under Roman rulers, eventually acquiring

Lifespan Development in Action

CHOOSING A BIRTHING STYLE THAT IS RIGHT FOR YOU

The birth of a child should be as comfortable and wonderful an experience as humanly possible. The expectant parents need to decide how and where the mother will deliver the baby and who will be at the event. Compatibility with the chosen practitioner is the most important consideration for the mother. She must feel secure that the practitioner and she have the same values, goals, and motives in the delivery process.

In choosing a practitioner, one way to determine the person for you is to ask women who have recently delivered their babies about their experiences. You can also visit all types of practices in your area, and even perhaps attend a birth to gain insight into the procedure. As you gather information, you might keep in mind the following:

QUESTIONS ABOUT LABOR AND DELIVERY

- Most births, perhaps as many as 90%, are normal and occur without complications, but birth does entail risks, no matter where it occurs. Where would you feel most comfortable in the event of a complication? Who would you want to be there?
- Birth attendants' philosophies vary. How much control do you want over the events during labor? How do you want to divide responsibility for what happens?
- What role do you want technological equipment to play in your labor and birth?
- The medical establishment considers home births unsafe and often disdains midwifery as a profession. How would you feel about going against conventional medical advice?
- The most thought-out plans may have to be altered if labor does not proceed as expected. How flexible are your plans? How would you feel about changing birth environments in midlabor?

QUESTIONS FOR DOCTORS

- What are their experiences with and attitudes toward the practices you have chosen for labor and delivery? How do they feel about labor-inducing drugs, electronic fetal monitoring, episiotomy, and anything else you would like to include or exclude?
- What have been their cesarean section rates? The national average is in the 20% range, but this is considered excessive by some health workers.
- Who are their backup doctors and do they share your attitudes toward your birth choices?

Continued . . .

CHOOSING A BIRTHING STYLE THAT IS RIGHT FOR YOU, Continued . . .

QUESTIONS FOR MIDWIVES

- How broad is the training and experience they have had?
- How have they handled emergencies?
- What kind(s) of backup do they have? Some midwives have a doctor who will assist or take over if a complication arises. Others have informal relations with the staff of a local hospital.
- How would they handle a transfer to a hospital, if it became necessary? Would they stay with you? (Adapted from Levinson, A.,1984)

the name *lex Caesarea* under the rule of the Caesars. Contrary to popular belief, the cesarean procedure is not named after Julius Caesar, nor was he delivered this way. The fact that Caesar's mother lived many years after his birth makes it very unlikely he was "untimely ripped" from her womb; the mortality rates for abdominal operations in ancient Rome were very high.

Although cesarean deliveries have recently begun a slow decline, they reached a high point in the late 1980s, when some 30% of births in U.S. hospitals were performed by this method (Danziger & Wertz, 1989; Freeman, 1990). Among the reasons for the great increase in the number of cesarean sections performed, from only about 4% in the 1950s, were the increasing numbers of older women and teenagers giving birth (both groups tend to have more difficulties in childbirth). Some writers (e.g., Freeman, 1990) argue, however, that obstetricians have often performed unnecessary cesareans because they can charge higher fees for this procedure.

Without question, cesarean sections have helped to reduce infant deaths. In the recent past, however, critics of the upsurge in cesarean births believe that many of the sections being done today are potentially harmful to both mother and child, posing such risks as postoperative infection (Dunn, 1990). Recovery from a cesarean may also make postpartum adjustment and new-baby care more difficult (Cohen & Estner, 1983; Davis & Rosen, 1986; Feinbloom & Forman, 1987).

NEONATAL ADJUSTMENTS AND ADAPTATIONS

The **neonate** is the technical name given to the newborn. As the neonate is adjusting to extrauterine life and parents are admiring their new arrival, delivery attendants are busy ensuring its survival. Respiration and heartbeat are the first concerns. Measures are taken to assure that respiration occurs as soon as the neonate is fully outside of its mother. Mucus and fluids are removed from the nose and mouth to assure normal respiration. After the delivery is completed, the neonate is held in a head-downward position, which prevents mucus and other matter (amniotic fluid, blood, etc.) from entering the respiratory passage. Gauze or a small suction bulb is generally used to clean out this matter, especially when a neonate has more than the normal amount of liquid present in its respiratory passage.

The birth cry does not always occur simultaneously with birth. Rather, the neonate gasps or cries shortly after the mucus has been removed and respiration commences. All that is required to stimulate crying is a gentle rubbing of the neonate's back, which also promotes the drainage of liquids from the respiratory passage. The traditional (now obsolete) slap on the buttocks is more than an unnecessary irritation; it can actually be dangerous.

Tests and Preventive Measures

Approximately 1 minute after birth and again 5 minutes later, a score is given to the neonate based on a systems check designed to evaluate critical life signs. The **Apgar test** is a relatively quick, simple, and safe procedure to evaluate the neonate's overall condition.

The Apgar test is based on five life signs: heart rate, respiration, muscle tone, reflex irritability, and color. A score of 0, 1, or 2 is given for each sign according to the degree of "life" present. By taking all of the vital life signs into account, the neonate can be given an Apgar score in a surprisingly short time. A total score of 7 to 10 indicates the neonate is in generally good condition. A score from 4 to 6 is considered fair, in which case further clearing of the air passage and immediate administration of oxygen are likely to be done. A score of 0 to 3 indicates the neonate is in critical condition and requires immediate emergency procedures.

Next the neonate's footprints are taken, as well as a fingerprint of the mother. This is required by law and essential for identification purposes in the rare event of a mixup in the hospital nursery. Weight in pounds and ounces (and in grams), head-to-heel length in inches, and the diameter of the largest

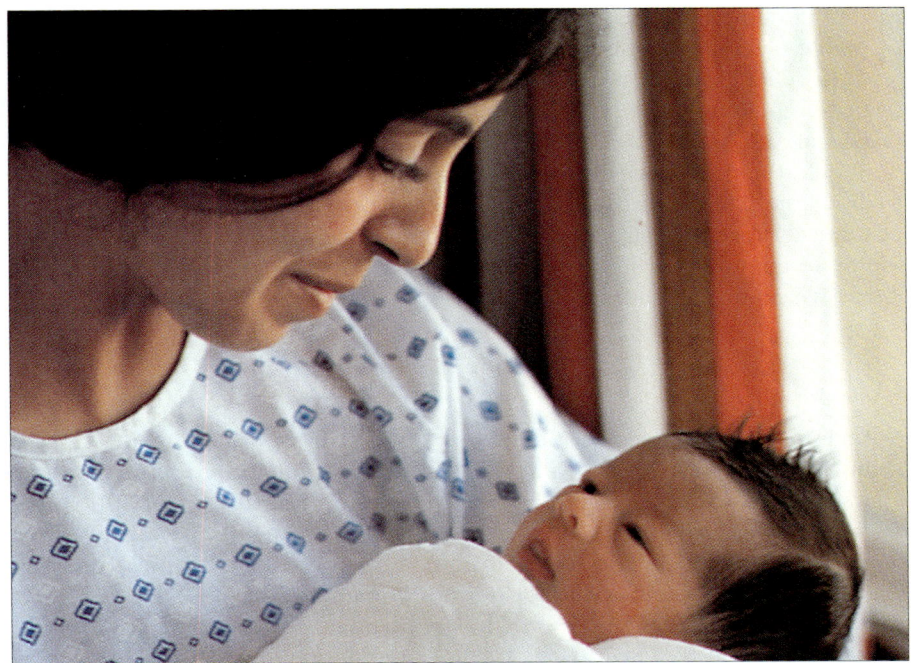

A nine-month journey ends, and a new chapter of the lifespan begins.

part of the neonate's head and chest are recorded. The neonate's temperature is also taken with a rectal thermometer.

Certain preventive measures are also taken. For example, the neonate is given an injection of vitamin K_1 to prevent hemorrhaging. In addition, all states require that because the eyes are especially vulnerable to gonococci in the birth canal, eye drops of silver nitrate or, more commonly today, ophthalmic erythromycin, be given to prevent the neonate from contracting gonorrhea. This treatment also wards off pneumococcal and chlamydial infections.

Circumcision

For many male neonates, **circumcision** is another adjustment to extrauterine life. Circumcision is the surgical removal of all or part of the prepuce, or foreskin, of the penis. Such a procedure thus permits exposure of the glans. About 90% of all babies in the United States were circumcised in the 1950s and 1960s, but this figure has dropped to about 70% today.

One of the major reasons for circumcision is the easier retraction of the foreskin for cleansing purposes. However, there are other reasons beyond cleanliness for circumcising a neonate: the desire to conform to a dominant cultural practice or religious rite of passage into manhood, the wish that the child resemble his father, and cosmetic appearance (King, Caddy, & Cohen, 1989; Lund, 1990; Scharli, 1989). Further motivating many parents is the fact that rates of cancer of the penis seem to be lower in circumcised males, although there is conflicting evidence on this (American Academy of Pediatrics, 1989; Lund, 1990). Additionally, the incidence of cervical cancer appears to be lower in females married to circumcised males.

Opponents of routine circumcision of male babies maintain that such surgery represents an unnecessary trauma in the life of the neonate. For that matter, circumcision may pose certain surgical risks, such as the development of penile ulcerations, adhesions, damage to the urethra, discomfort, and restlessness (Olds, London, & Ladewig, 1992). Opponents also feel that with good hygiene, uncircumcised males can be just as clean and comfortable as circumcised males.

Should the procedure be chosen, surgery is usually scheduled the day prior to discharge. This is to ensure the neonate has become well stabilized. A variety of surgical procedures are possible, and all produce minimal bleeding. In one of the more common techniques, the prepuce is pulled back and then clamped. Excessive prepuce is then cut off, and the prepuce is sutured in place.

INFERTILITY

Not all couples can become biological parents. **Infertility,** defined as the inability to achieve a pregnancy after at least a year of regular, unprotected intercourse, poses a special set of problems. It is estimated that about 15% of the population—approximately one in seven couples—is infertile at any given time. However, patience is sometimes the answer for many of these couples. Pregnancy statistics tell us that for normal women who aren't using birth control and are sexually active, 25% will be pregnant in the first month, 63% will be in 6 months, and 80% will be in 1 year. An additional 5 to 10% will become

Many couples have problems conceiving and bearing a child, but today a number of medical interventions exist.

pregnant the following year (Conkling, 1991; Greil, 1991; Hotchner, 1990; Muasher, 1987).

About 40% of infertility problems can be traced to the male, 40% to the female, and 20% of the time couples share the problem of infertility and the reasons often go unknown (Batterman, 1985; Frank, 1984; Hatcher et al., 1990; Olds, London, & Ladewig, 1992). Among the more common causes of male infertility are poor sperm quality, low sperm count, and poor sperm motility, or movement. One of the causes of decreased sperm number and motility is varicocele, a condition that causes dilation of veins near the testicles. Other causes of decreased sperm number might include chronic fatigue and illness; poor nutrition; excessive use of caffeine, tobacco, or marijuana; too frequent intercourse; hot spas or saunas; nervous stress; fear of impotence; hormone abnormalities; birth defects; certain medications and treatments such as radiation to the testes; and possibly tight underwear and pants. In addition, an undescended testicle or underdeveloped testes will fail to produce adequate numbers of sperm (Mahlstedt, 1987).

The most common causes of female infertility are the blockage of fallopian tubes and the failure to ovulate. A number of causes may account for blockage, including tubal scarring from pelvic infections. Growing numbers of women develop pelvic inflammatory disease when sexually transmitted diseases such as chlamydia spread into the uterus and fallopian tubes, in the process affecting a woman's ability to conceive. *Endometriosis,* a condition in which endometrial cells that normally line the uterus detach themselves and grow elsewhere in the pelvic cavity, may also cause infertility. Ovulatory defects include the inability of an ovary to develop or to release an egg or of the hypothalamus, pituitary, or ovaries to manufacture their hormones in proper amounts or sequence. Another cause of infertility is the failure of the cervix at midcycle to secrete cervical mucus, a necessity for sperm survival. Or the cervix may produce abnormal amounts of mucus, which impedes the movement of sperm (Lauersen & Bouchez, 1991; Mahlstedt, 1987; Muasher, 1987).

THEORETICAL ISSUES

How might symbolic interactionism focus on the role conflicts that infertile parents face and the expectations that have to be adjusted? If a couple is grappling with the choice of a reproductive technology, how might exchange theory be used to analyze the drawbacks and rewards of the decision-making process? Can you think of other applicable theoretical frameworks?

Infertility can be related to aging processes. Women under age 25 have about a 7% chance of being infertile, but by the age of 40, one out of every three females is unable to have a child. A woman in her 30s does not have many fertile years left. Male infertility is also partly determined by age; a man of 50 generally has a lower sperm count than a man of 20, although the natural decrease in his sperm count may not prevent him from having children if enough of his remaining sperm are healthy (Greil, 1991; Lauersen & Bouchez, 1991).

Other causes of infertility include sexual dysfunction, inappropriate timing of intercourse, and immunological factors. The mind/body connection can also not be overlooked. Stressful lifestyles, personal problems, vocational pressures, and general mental health may have physical effects on both male and female. And environmental conditions such as exposure to pesticides or work hazards are other considerations (Greenfeld et al., 1986; Mahlstedt, 1987).

Infertility brings considerable pressure and distress into the lives of couples. Patricia Mahlstedt (1987) writes that the process of diagnosing and treating infertility has a pervasive impact on those who encounter it, creating friction in the most stable marriage or intensifying existing problems between the partners. Even though this impact is usually greater when the treatment process is prolonged and/or unsuccessful, psychological pressures begin to develop when a couple realizes they are not conceiving as planned. Most begin to have doubts, worry, become frustrated, and wonder why they can't do something as natural as conceiving (Chandra, 1991; Pepe & Byrne, 1991).

Barbara Higgins (1990) believes infertile couples may face other consequences. Physical effects, including loss of sexual pleasure, related to the "task" orientation that procreation entails or discomfort from painful procedures and surgery are frequently reported by infertile couples. Grief, anger, and guilt reactions are common reactions from infertile spouses. Social changes may also occur, as infertile couples may alter their network interactions in attempts to avoid painful reminders of their childlessness.

The support of family and friends can be very beneficial to the infertile couple. In addition, other couples who have experienced infertility can provide beneficial support. One such self-help group is *RESOLVE*, a national organization offering counseling, referral, and support services to infertile couples. Through this group, infertile couples are able to meet and discuss their concerns with others who share their experience, including the traumatic physical, psychological, social, and relational effects of infertility. An added dimension to this peer support is the interaction between couples who have achieved resolution of the situation and those who are in the process of working it through. The first group of couples, who may have resolved their problem by achieving pregnancy or by adopting a child or even, ultimately, by viewing childlessness as an acceptable lifestyle, can provide a valuable model to the latter group (Higgins, 1990; Seibel, 1990).

Interventions for Infertility

The initial intervention for infertility usually includes a history and physical examination of both partners. The woman is often asked to chart her basal body temperature so the physician can assess the regularity of her menstrual cycle, when she is ovulating, and the optimum time for the couple to have intercourse.

The man may also be instructed to abstain from sexual activity for several days before the woman's fertile period is expected, in the hope his sperm count will rise. Sometimes the drug *Clomid* (clomiphene citrate) is administered to the woman to induce ovulation. Clomid works by stimulating the pituitary gland to secrete the luteinizing hormone and the follicle stimulating hormone, two hormones that help orchestrate the menstrual cycle. In one study (Archer, 1989) Clomid induced ovulation in 80% of a group of women studied, and 40% of these women became pregnant.

For men, fertility is tested with a semen analysis, which assesses the number, quality, and motility of sperm. Should infertility be traced to the male, surgery might be in order to repair blockage in the testicles, such as varicocele or blocked sperm ducts. Other forms of intervention might include the medical management of hormonal abnormalities or infections. Hormone therapy for men has not consistently demonstrated an increase in sperm production and is still considered largely experimental.

For women, blood and urine tests are given to determine estrogen, gonadotrophin, and progesterone levels, and cervical mucus tests are used to assess whether sperm can penetrate and survive within the cervix. A physician might use a laparoscope to assess the reproductive system and any disease or blockage. Microsurgery is sometimes employed to correct blocked fallopian tubes, and laser surgery has recently been used to treat endometriosis.

In about 75% of infertility cases, the aforementioned procedures prove successful. Should such measures be unsuccessful, hope lies in several sophisticated reproductive technologies: in-vitro fertilization, artificial insemination, surrogate motherhood, and embryo transfer. These technologies represent important medical breakthroughs, but they have also engendered serious legal and moral controversies. Let's examine each more closely.

In-Vitro Fertilization (IVF)   In **in-vitro fertilization** (IVF), sometimes referred to as test-tube fertilization, one or more ova are surgically removed from the mother, combined with the father's sperm, and placed into the uterus. The procedure is usually employed when the woman's fallopian tubes are blocked or diseased. Women with normal menstrual cycles and men with normal sperm counts are considered good candidates for IVF, which is one of the most common forms of reproductive technology. By 1993, an estimated 17,000 children were conceived this way in the world, and more than 200 IVF clinics were opened in the United States.

Although the pioneer successes with in-vitro fertilization used the woman's natural menstrual cycle for the procedure, clinics today experience higher success rates by hormonally stimulating ovulation with fertility drugs and "harvesting" three to five eggs, rather than just one naturally produced egg. To assess the exact time of ovulation, the physician examines the woman's abdomen by ultrasound. When the eggs are mature, they are removed from her body by a surgical technique called laparoscopy. In this technique, under general anesthesia, a small incision is made adjacent to the navel and a small tubelike scope is inserted, enabling the physician to see inside. The eggs are retrieved with a hollow needle and placed in a petri dish where they are allowed to mature for several hours before they are fertilized with the father's sperm. The fertilized eggs are then placed in an incubator. About 48 hours later, when each egg has gone through the cell divisions necessary to produce a blastocyst, several are implanted in the woman's uterus (Issacs & Holt, 1987; Speroff, Glass, & Kase, 1989).

The success rate of in-vitro fertilization varies depending on the clinic consulted. However, one study (Soules, 1985) revealed a 10% success rate per single embryo transfer, 15% per two embryos transferred, and 19% per three embryos transferred. Obviously, this means a woman's chances for conception improve when two or three embryos are replaced into her uterus. However, when more than three embryos are transferred, the risks of multiple pregnancies and miscarriage are thought to outweigh any benefit. The fate of the unused embryos has aroused a great deal of debate. The embryos may be discarded, or they may be used for research in order to improve IVF and enhance our understanding of embryo development. Or, in a more recent option, they can be "cryopreserved" (frozen) and then later thawed and implanted again, perhaps as a donation to another woman.

Variations of in-vitro fertilization have been developed in recent years. For example, in *gamete intrafallopian transfer* (GIFT), ova are gathered in much the same way just described and mixed with the father's sperm. Then, both ova and sperm are placed into one or both fallopian tubes, the normal site of fertilization. Should fertilization occur, the zygote then travels to the uterus, where prenatal development proceeds. Another technique is *zygote intrafallopian transfer* (ZIFT). Here, ova are retrieved and mixed with the father's sperm similar to in-vitro fertilization. However, the zygote is transferred back to the woman's body at a much earlier stage of cell division and, as in GIFT, is placed in the fallopian tube and not the uterus (Devroey, 1989; Olds, London, & Ladewig, 1992).

Artificial Insemination   **Artificial insemination** involves artificially injecting sperm (fresh or frozen) into a woman's vagina, either on or near the cervix, at the time of ovulation. There are three types of artificial insemination. One type uses sperm from the husband (called artificial insemination, homologous, or AIH), often when his sperm count is low or the wife has one of the earlier mentioned cervical mucus problems. Sometimes a physician injects several of the husband's ejaculations (which are preserved by refrigeration) in an effort to increase sperm count and motility. When the husband's sperm count is too low, artificial insemination by donor (artificial insemination, donor, AID) is practiced, which utilizes sperm from an unrelated, usually anonymous donor (Lasker & Borg, 1987). A third type combines a mixture of sperm from a man who has a low sperm count and sperm from an unrelated donor (artificial insemination, combined, AIC). In this case there can be some hope the resulting child may be the husband's (Issacs & Holt, 1987). Artificial insemination has an overall success rate of between 70 and 80%, usually by the third attempt.

Should a sperm donor be used, he is screened and matched as closely to the husband as possible for such characteristics as ethnic background, stature, complexion, and blood type. Special screening is also given to prevent genetic defects, sexually transmitted diseases, and other potential problems. Donor sperm is considered quite controversial (Dunn, Ryan, & O'Brien, 1988; Moghissi, 1989), and raises a number of issues. For example, many view artificial insemination by donor unnatural on the basis of moral and religious grounds, and concern has often been expressed over the criteria for the selection and screening of donors.

Surrogate Motherhood   **Surrogate motherhood** occurs when the father is fertile but the mother is unable to carry the child to term. In the technique, which is a variation of artificial insemination, a chosen surrogate mother is artificially inseminated with the husband's sperm. The surrogate mother carries and bears the child, which is then given back to the couple. About 500 babies have been born via surrogate motherhood. Costs for such a service, usually sponsored by a clinic or center, were approximately $20,000 in 1992. This usually includes about a $10,000 fee outright to the surrogate mother, the remainder going to the center's expenses. The surrogacy center handles the screening of candidates, arranges medical, legal, and psychological services, and offers a standard contract to govern the transaction.

Embryo Transfer   Somewhat related to surrogate motherhood is **embryo transfer,** although it is much more experimental. Infertile women are usually the candidates for this technique, which involves impregnating another woman with the father's sperm. After several days, the fertilized ovum is removed from her uterus and placed within the wife's uterus, which has been hormonally prepared to accept it. This is done when the menstrual cycle of the wife indicates she is prepared to accept a pregnancy. In some instances, the embryo is frozen and implanted at a later time.

Issues Related to Reproductive Technologies   Without question, technologies such as in-vitro fertilization, artificial insemination by donor, surrogate motherhood, and embryo transfer represent important medical breakthroughs. However, along with critical acclaim has come considerable controversy, particularly with respect to surrogacy. For example, the Catholic church and other groups oppose these scientific advances for religious reasons. As an illustration, the Vatican in 1987 issued an instruction that condemned artificial insemination even when the sperm is that of a husband (AIH), because the act involves masturbation and because "in seeking a procreation which is not the fruit of a specific act of conjugal union (AIH) objectively effects an analogous separation between the [goals] and the meanings of marriage." Other controversy originates from the legal front. For instance, although very few problems have arisen with AID offspring, only 25 states recognize their legitimacy. Also, no clear-cut or comprehensive laws cover the surrogate motherhood arrangement, perhaps the most complex controversy of all.

To illustrate the controversies posed by surrogate motherhood, consider the 1986 case of Baby M. The drama of Baby M played out over a 3-month period in the family law court in Hackensack, New Jersey. Mary Beth Whitehead, the surrogate mother who bore the child fathered through artificial insemination by William Stern, changed her mind and refused to accept the $10,000 for which she had contracted. Whitehead, the genetic mother, sued to gain custody of the child rather than give the baby to Stern and his wife. The court upheld the surrogacy contract as legal in New Jersey and awarded custody to the Sterns. However, it granted Whitehead visitation rights.

Four years later, in California, a surrogate mother who was genetically unrelated to the child she bore attempted to gain custody of the child from its

INTERRELATEDNESS OF AGING PROCESSES

Think of as many advantages and disadvantages posed by reproductive technologies, particularly those within biological, psychological, and social parameters. From your perspective, do the advantages outweigh the disadvantages, or vice versa?

genetic parents. Orange County Superior Court Judge Richard Parslow ruled that a test-tube baby boy belonged with his genetic parents rather than with the surrogate mother who carried him. Parslow rejected surrogate mother Anna Johnson's effort to be recognized as a third parent of the 5-week-old boy. Prior to this ruling, a genetically unrelated surrogate had never sought custody. In making the decision, Parslow said he did not want to split the child emotionally between "a three-parent, two natural-mom situation." He added that a surrogate carrying a genetic child for a couple does not acquire parental rights.

Perhaps the stormiest scenario for surrogate motherhood took place in 1983. Judy Stiver, a surrogate mother, entered into a contract with a married man, Alexander Malahoff. She delivered a child with microcephaly, a disorder indicating possible mental retardation. When the diagnosis was made, neither Stiver nor Malahoff wanted the child. Eventually a blood test for paternity was performed and the baby was determined to be that of Mrs. Stiver and her husband. The Stivers had been instructed to abstain from sexual intercourse before insemination took place.

These are not isolated and remote situations, and many more are likely to surface in years to come. In the last decade, there have been over 2,000 births through traditional surrogacy (in which a woman's ovum is fertilized with the sperm of a man whose wife cannot conceive) and as of 1992, almost 100 births through gestational surrogacy. Obviously, such arrangements pose difficult questions of law, ethics, and cultural mores. For example, what are the legal implications for a surrogate mother who changes her mind, or if the natural father changes his? What if the surrogate mother starts to drink, smoke, or take drugs during pregnancy? What happens if the natural father dies before birth, or if amniocentesis reveals a genetic disease? Should surrogate motherhood be banned as unnatural and immoral, a form of baby selling, so to speak? Or should it continue to be permitted as perhaps the only way some infertile couples will be able to have a child genetically related to at least one of them?

Such complex issues are also not restricted to surrogate motherhood. To illustrate, in 1989 a woman fought for control of seven frozen embryos in a divorce proceeding, the first case of its kind in the United States. Tennessee's Blount County Circuit Judge W. Dale Young had to decide whether the embryos should go to a husband who didn't want children at the time or to a wife who couldn't conceive naturally. As the case wore on, the seven embryos, no bigger than grains of sand, lay frozen in liquid nitrogen at a fertility center in eastern Tennessee.

Judge Young initially ruled in favor of Mary Sue Davis, awarding her temporary custody of the embryos. In making his decision, Young grappled with the issue of whether the embryos deserved consideration as potential children (if they did, he would have to decide who would best serve these children's interests), or if the embryos were considered property (if they were, the matter could be handled like any property dispute). Young ruled the embryos were children, not property, and that life began at conception. He added it was Mrs. Davis's right to carry the embryos to term.

However, Junior Lewis Davis, the estranged husband, immediately appealed the decision to the Tennessee Court of Appeals. In 1990, that court granted joint custody of the seven frozen embryos to the couple. Davis had asked during the initial trial that Mrs. Davis be barred from ever using any of the seven fertilized eggs without his consent. Davis also argued he had a right to control his own reproduction. He claimed that awarding the embryos to his wife would force him to become a father against his wishes.

The Tennessee Court of Appeals, in effect, agreed with Davis. It overturned the 1989 landmark decision, ruling that both biological parents shared an interest in the seven fertilized eggs. Judge Herschel P. Franks said it would be repugnant and offensive to constitutional principles to order Davis to bear the psychological, if not the legal, consequences of paternity against his will. Franks added that it would be equally repugnant to order Mrs. Davis to implant these fertilized eggs against her will.

After they married in 1980, Mrs. Davis had five tubal pregnancies, resulting in the rupture of one fallopian tube and the tying of the other. Hearing about the potential of reproductive technology, the couple entered a Tennessee in-vitro fertilization program in 1988. However, repeated efforts at retrieving an ovum from Mrs. Davis's ovaries, fertilizing it in a petri dish, and then implanting it in her uterus failed. During the last in-vitro fertilization attempt, doctors froze what are technically known as pre-embryos because they are composed of undifferentiated cells, and stored seven for future use. The Davises were never offered a consent form specifying, for example, what might become of their embryos in the event of death or divorce—an omission that helped pave the way for the conflict.

The Davis case, touching on the status of embryos and the rights of their parents, brings into sharp focus the legal and ethical problems raised by reproductive technologies. While medical knowledge races forward, the legal and ethical implications of such techniques spark intense debate. The Davis case illustrates that the rights—or at least the potential rights—of the embryos deserve consideration. The fact that the initial Davis decision recognized an embryo as a human being represents a landmark ruling, one that has implications for abortion policies as well as reproductive technologies. Such complexities illustrate that our ethics and societal norms have been unable to keep up with the rapid developments in this scientific area. Thus when disagreement occurs, the guidelines are few (Klein, 1989).

In a sense, advances in reproductive technologies have created a gap between science and public policy. Stephen Issacs and Renee Holt (1987) suggest that to narrow this gap we need to formulate some guiding principles for this new field and to find answers to the questions these principles raise. These investigators suggest five main principles: protection of children, respect for the right of privacy, assurance of informed consent, honoring individuals' intentions, and determining access to reproductive technology.

- **Protection of children.** How can the rights of artificially conceived children be protected? They need legitimacy. They need names and identities. They need access to their medical records when necessary. They need people willing to nurture and support them. And they need legal rights.

- **Respect for the right of privacy.** How can we guarantee people their constitutional right to make decisions about personal matters such as having a baby and keep governmental regulations as narrowly drawn and as unintrusive as possible?

- **Informed consent.** How can society ensure that informed consent governs all reproductive technology, so that participants are aware of risks, benefits, and costs, both monetary and emotional? This will involve counseling for anyone who needs it.

- **Honoring the parties' intentions.** Can reproductive technologies be provided in a manner that honors the intentions of the participants to accept or deny the responsibilities of parenthood, regardless of genetics, unless there are compelling reasons not to do so?

• **Access to reproductive technologies.** How can society establish uniform standards of screening for genetic and sexually transmitted diseases for anyone who is conceiving a child? Is it possible to redefine the concept of "family" in terms more accurately reflecting social reality? Can society define "capacity to parent" in ways that do not deny parenthood to people simply because they choose an alternative lifestyle?

As of 1991, 10 states had passed laws governing surrogacy contracts like the one under which Whitehead gave birth to the Sterns' child. However, many issues related to reproductive technology must still be studied and the problems they present be resolved. In the meantime, couples who want a child must research their options on their own—and think very carefully about the issues involved in their eventual choice (Issacs, 1986).

At a minimum, reproductive technologies radically circumvent the traditional transition to parenthood. They create a wide range of options in fertility and reproduction that beg to be studied. For example, it is now technically possible for a child to have three mothers: a genetic mother, who provides the egg; a bearing mother, who carries the fetus and bears the child; and a rearing mother. How can we weigh genetic contributions, the experience of childbearing, and the years of child rearing? Is motherhood on the verge of being redefined? Obviously, we will not find the answers to such questions overnight. However, the complex issues raised must nonetheless be addressed (Danziger & Wertz, 1989).

CHAPTER REVIEW

The average full-term human pregnancy lasts about 270 days, from conception to full term, although some are as long as 300 days and others are as short as 240 days. The moment of conception occurs when the male sperm penetrates the female egg to create a zygote. In the case of multiple conception, identical twins result when a single fertilized egg splits after conception, and fraternal twins result when two female eggs are fertilized by two separate sperm cells.

As the zygote travels along the fallopian tube, it begins to divide and multiply to form new cells, eventually forming a tiny sphere called a blastocyst. Upon reaching the uterus, the blastocyst attaches itself to the wall of the uterus. Here, prenatal development continues for 9 months, divided into three equal segments called trimesters. Each trimester of about 3 months encompasses a distinct phase of prenatal growth and development.

The intrauterine mechanisms of the amniotic sac, amniotic fluid, placenta, and umbilical cord provide the fetus with an ideal environment for growth and development to transpire. By the end of the ninth month, the average fetus weighs 6 to 7 pounds and measures between 18 and 21 inches head to toe. Internal systems and bodily processes are set to make the necessary extrauterine life adjustments.

During pregnancy, a mother must take steps to safeguard the prenatal environment and her own well-being. Among other health considerations are those related to nutrition, nicotine, drugs, and teratogens. Seeking a qualified practitioner and recognizing the danger signs of problem pregnancy are especially important. Complications and problems can accompany pregnancy and interfere with labor and delivery. Among them are toxemia, Rh factor incompatibility, ectopic pregnancy, and miscarriage.

Labor, the climax of the entire pregnancy cycle, represents the processes involved in giving birth: uterine contractions, delivery of the baby, and expulsion of the placenta. Although large percentages of mothers continue to deliver their babies in conventional medical settings, growing numbers are pursuing alternative birthing styles. Most are doing so because they object to the use of anesthesia during delivery and to other medical intrusions on the mother and the baby. Among the alternatives to traditional delivery are the Lamaze method, the Leboyer method, home births, and rooming-in and birthing room hospital facilities.

Infertility is defined as the inability to achieve a pregnancy after at least one year of regular, unprotected intercourse. Approximately 40% of infertility problems can be traced to the male, 40% to the female, and 20% of the time couples share the problem and the reasons often go unknown. In about 75% of infertility cases, medication and/or microsurgery proves successful. Should such measures prove unsuccessful, hope might lie in such reproductive technologies as in-vitro fertilization, artificial insemination, surrogate motherhood, and embryo transfer. We concluded this chapter with some of the complex issues that reproductive technologies pose.

TERMS YOU SHOULD KNOW

acquired immune deficiency
   syndrome (AIDS)
agenesis
amniotic fluid
amniotic sac
Apgar test
artificial insemination
birthing room
blastocyst
breech presentation
cephalocaudal development
cesarean delivery
circumcision
conjoined twins
crowning
developmental excess
ectopic pregnancy
embryo
embryonic period
embryo transfer

fetal alcohol syndrome
fetal distress
fetal period
fetus
fraternal twins
home birth
identical twins
incomplete development
infertility
in-vitro fertilization
labor
Lamaze method
lanugo
Leboyer method
lightening
miscarriage
neonate
nurse-midwife
organogenesis
ovum

placenta
prematurity
proximodistal development
quickening
Rh factor
rooming-in hospital facility
surrogate motherhood

teratogenic agent
toxemia
trimester
trophoblast
umbilical cord
vernix caseosa
zygote

THINKING IN ACTION

• You and your partner have just discovered you've conceived a child. In an effort to create the healthiest pregnancy possible, you've both decided to outline a prenatal plan encompassing nutritional considerations, activity and rest guidelines, and medical care. After reading this chapter, what kinds of specific considerations would you include? What risk factors would you identify? What would be the father's role in your plan?

• Drugs pose numerous problems to the unborn child. Think about how you would develop an awareness program for the students on your campus that will eventually benefit their children. What kinds of information would you include in your campaign? Are there certain drugs you feel need special attention?

• As you've learned, giving birth in a conventional hospital setting is not the only way to deliver a baby safely. Think about the options available today. If you were going to have a baby or were the partner of a woman about to give birth, which of the alternatives we've discussed would you choose? Why?

• You and your partner are unable to conceive a child naturally and are thinking about some of the reproductive technologies presented in this chapter. Develop a list of these measures, including the advantages and disadvantages of each. Do these reproductive technologies pose any religious, legal, or moral issues for you and your partner? Do certain technologies seem easier to consider than others? Why or why not?

RECOMMENDED READINGS

1. Eden, R. D., Boehm, F. H., & Haire, M. (Eds.). (1990). *Assessment and care of the fetus: Physiological, clinical and medicolegal principles.* Norwalk, CT: Appleton and Lange.

   A comprehensive and informative look at prenatal development, including medical intervention.

2. Eisenberg, A., Murkoff, H. E., & Hathaway, S. E. (1991). *What to expect when you're expecting* (rev. ed.). New York: Workman.

   One of the better pregnancy guides for mothers- and fathers-to-be. Loaded with practical suggestions and supportive guidance.

3. Feinbloom, R. I. (1993). *Pregnancy, birth, and the early months* (2nd ed.). Reading, MA: Addison-Wesley.

    See Chapter 3 for a thorough account of neonatal tests and preventive measures.

4. Lauersen, N., & Bouchez, C. (1991). *Getting pregnant: What couples need to know right now.* New York: Fawcett.

    A good overview of infertility and what couples can do to overcome it.

5. Marshall, C. (1992). *The expectant father.* Rockland, CA: Prima.

    The emphasis is on the supportive role fathers can play in a woman's pregnancy and childbirth.

Infancy and Toddlerhood

What Do You Think?

UNIT ONE: PHYSICAL DEVELOPMENT

Development of the Nervous System
Myelination and Brain Maturation
The Readiness Principle
Locomotion

Prehension
Prehension and the Development of
    Children's Art

UNIT TWO: MENTAL DEVELOPMENT

Jean Piaget's Sensorimotor Stage
Reflex Activities (0–1 month)
Primary Circular Reactions (1–4 months)
Secondary Circular Reactions (4–8 months)
Coordination of Secondary Schemes (8–12
    months)
Tertiary Circular Reactions (12–18 months)
Invention of New Means Through Mental
    Combinations (18–24 months)
Concept Development
Shape and Size Concepts
Spatial Concepts
Class Concepts
Time Concepts

Cognition and Memory
Types of Memory Storage Systems
Memory Development During Childhood
Sense-Organ Development
Vision
Depth Perception
Audition
Taste and Smell
Touch
Language Development
Language and the Brain
Theoretical Perspectives of Language
    Development
Developmental Stages of Language

UNIT THREE: PERSONALITY AND SOCIAL DEVELOPMENT

Attachment
Theoretical Perspectives of Attachment
Indicators of Attachment
Individual Variations in Attachment
Attachment and Contact/Comfort
Gender-Role Development
Sex and Gender: Some Definitions and
    Guidelines
Theoretical Perspectives of Gender-Role
    Development
Early Gender-Role Development

Emotional Development
Crying
Laughter and Humor
Fear and Anxiety
Anger and Aggression
Play Influences on the Developing Child
Exploratory and Manipulative Play
Destructive Play
Theories of Personality Development
Sigmund Freud's Psychosexual Theory
Erik Erikson's Psychosocial Theory

Chapter Review • Terms You Should Know • Thinking in Action • Recommended Readings

WHAT
DO
YOU
THINK?

• In the United States, children begin walking sometime between 13 and 15 months of age. In other nations, though, this timetable varies. For example, in Uganda, Africa, walking commences at about 9 months, and in Stockholm, Sweden, it begins at approximately 12 months. What factors account for such international differences? Can genetic factors or environmental factors explain such differences? We try to supply the answers later in this chapter.

• Out of the mouths of babes. Although infants present their parents with many diverse and exciting accomplishments, perhaps none overshadows the emergence of the first spoken word. This developmental milestone, which has something magical attached to it, is eagerly anticipated by parents. What cognitive and linguistic forces produce these early words? What stages of language precede and follow the first-word stage? We explore these and other issues in our discussion of language development during infancy and toddlerhood.

• Linus of *Peanuts* fame never leaves home without his security blanket. Chances are you had something similar when you were a child, although you were probably not as dramatic about it as this cartoon strip character is. You might have owned a security blanket, huggable doll, or a threadbare stuffed animal. These transitional objects are usually the recipients of childhood attachment behaviors: They are clung to in times of peace as well as turmoil; they are stroked and hugged; and they usually end up each night cradled in the arms of the sleeping child. What is it about soft and comforting transitional objects that promotes a sense of security? How does such behavior relate to attachment? This chapter gives you some answers that may make you pause and reflect on your own childhood guardian keepers.

• They have been called the children of the dream, the children of the Israeli kibbutz. Children on these collective farm settlements are separated from their parents shortly after birth and through their teenage years are reared in group settings. Among other goals, such child-rearing practices were implemented to eliminate Israel's patriarchal family structure, social classes, and gender-role stereotyping. Have these goals been attained? What is it like to spend one's childhood and adolescence in a kibbutz? Read on to learn more about this unique style of upbringing.

UNIT ONE: PHYSICAL DEVELOPMENT

Unlike the virtually helpless, generalized movement of the neonate, the infant's movement consists of a complex hierarchy of specific muscular behaviors. Control over voluntary movement is evident in numerous forms of physical expression, including walking and prehensile abilities, which develop in a sequential fashion. Although there are individual differences among infants in rates of body growth and motor achievement, growth and maturation for the most part proceed in a definite order.

This sequence of development is, to a great extent, due to the gradual maturation of cells in the brain. Even though the neonate is born with 10 to 14 billion cells in the cortex, most of these cells are immature and not yet able to function. As the cranial bones enlarge, the brain cells grow, mature, and become more chemically active. Until a cell reaches this physical and chemical level of maturity, learning cannot take place.

The foregoing is a simplified explanation of the brain's role in physical movement development. In order to comprehend its impact, we need to understand how the nervous system develops and how its primary parts function. Such an understanding will help explain many of the developments that occur over the course of the life cycle, including those changes accompanying aging processes.

Development of the Nervous System

The nervous system consists of two parts: the central and peripheral systems. The brain and the spinal cord constitute the **central nervous system;** the **peripheral nervous system** is a network of neural tissue that connects the brain and spinal cord with other parts of the body. Together, the central and peripheral nervous systems connect the body into a unified system under direct control of the brain (Levinthal, 1990).

The central nervous system grows rapidly during the early years. At birth, the human brain weighs about 350 grams. Certain areas of the forebrain are immature for the first few weeks, as indicated by their low levels of glucose use. However, development is rapid, and areas of the brain that were almost silent at birth approach adult patterns of activity within 7 to 8 months. At the end of the first year, the brain weighs 1,000 grams, not much less than the adult weight of 1,200 to 1,400 grams (Kalat, 1992).

Brain function is a complex activity involving the interaction of its parts. Let us say at the outset, though, that the parts of the brain do not develop evenly. Rather, its parts develop at different rates and follow unique timetables. Some parts of the brain, such as the cerebral cortex, experience both rapid and slow phases of development. We spend more time on this topic shortly.

The brain can be divided into three major parts: the forebrain, midbrain, and hindbrain (Figure 5-1). The **forebrain** is the frontal and upper part of the brain and represents the largest of the three divisions. It contains the brain center responsible for conscious thought and higher-order behavior. It is the forebrain

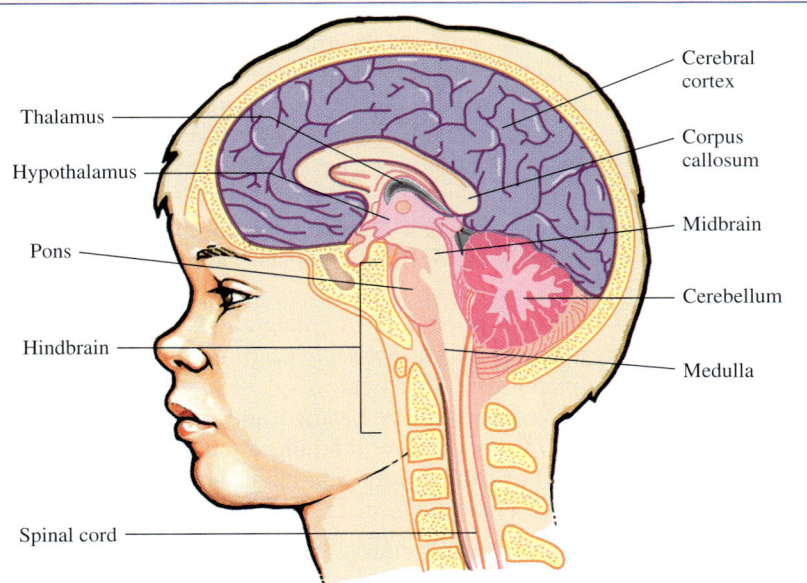

FIGURE 5-1
Major Structures of the Brain.

The entire nervous system grows in size and complexity during the early years. Brain structure becomes more differentiated, and myelination among nerve cells enables the central nervous system to perform increasingly complex functions.

that enables humans to surpass lower animal species in such areas as reasoning, speech, and complex patterns of muscle coordination.

The *cerebrum* is the largest portion of the forebrain and consists of a left and a right cerebral hemisphere connected by a bundle of nerve fibers called the *corpus callosum.* It is the corpus callosum that enables one hemisphere to know what the other is doing.

Although the two cerebral hemispheres look very much alike, they differ greatly in function. The left hemisphere controls movement on the right side of the body, and the right controls movement on the left. For example, if you scratch your head with your right hand, the left hemisphere of the brain is responsible for your movements. In addition, the left and right cerebral hemispheres control different functions. This type of hemispheric specialization is known as **lateralization** and emerges gradually during development. The left hemisphere is the site of language ability, systematic and logical thought (math, science, and so on), and writing, among other specializations. The right hemisphere controls primarily nonverbal functions, such as artistic or musical abilities, imagination, and the expression of emotion.

The two cerebral hemispheres are covered by the *cerebral cortex,* which is grayish and wrinkled in appearance. The cerebral cortex has a number of important functions, including memory, concentration, problem solving, and muscle coordination. It is the last part of the brain to develop, continuing its growth beyond adolescence into adulthood.

The cerebral cortex is divided into four lobes, or areas. The *occipital lobe,* located at the back of each hemisphere, enables the brain to interpret sensory information transmitted by the eyes. The *parietal lobe,* found at the top of each hemisphere, controls the sense of touch and transmits essential spatial information. The *temporal lobe,* located at the side of each hemisphere, is responsible for hearing and storage of permanent memories. The *frontal lobe,* located behind the forehead and at the front of each hemisphere, is involved in reasoning and thinking as well as body movement and control.

Two other parts of the forebrain are the thalamus and hypothalamus. The *thalamus,* located at the base of the cerebrum, relays nerve impulses from sensory pathways to the cerebral cortex. The *hypothalamus,* located beneath the thalamus, has a variety of functions, including the regulation of hunger, thirst, sexual functions, and body temperature. The hypothalamus is also a control center for pleasure and pain.

The **midbrain** is a connecting link between the forebrain and hindbrain. The midbrain controls movements of the eye muscles and relays visual and auditory information to higher brain centers.

The **hindbrain** is the lower portion of the brain and is responsible for bodily functions necessary for survival. The *medulla oblongata* connects the brain and spinal cord and helps regulate heartbeat, respiration, digestion, and blood pressure. The *cerebellum* controls body balance and coordination. It grows rapidly during the first two years of life and attains almost full size by the fifth year. The *pons* is located above the medulla and acts as a bridge between the two lobes of the cerebellum. The *reticular activating system* runs through the hindbrain into the midbrain and part of the forebrain. It is involved in arousal, attention, and the sleep cycle.

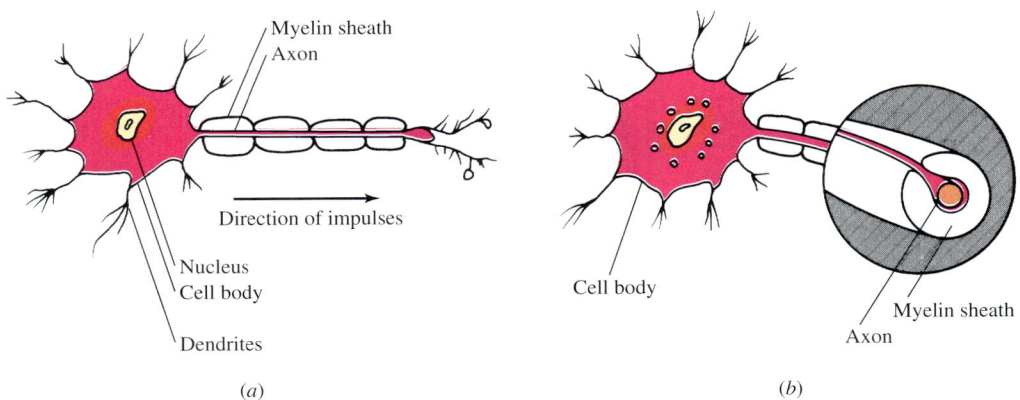

(a)   (b)

FIGURE 5-2
A Neuron and Myelination.

At left *(a)*, a diagram of a peripheral nervous system neuron. At right *(b)*, the manner in which the myelin sheath envelops the axon and insulates the nerve cell.

Myelination and Brain Maturation   The maturity of neurons in the brain is determined by the size of the cell, the length of the dendrites and axons, and the degree of myelination. **Myelination** is the process by which the neuron develops an outside coating, called **myelin.** This coating, or sheath, insulates the nerve cell and allows for the rapid transmission of chemoelectrical messages. Before myelination, signals may be dissipated in the surrounding body fluids instead of proceeding along the neural pathway. As the child grows older, though, neurons become increasingly myelinated. The significance of myelination can be observed in a number of developmental areas, such as increased efficiency in tying one's shoes or the ability to play in more refined sports than kickball as one gets older. Figure 5-2 shows the different parts of the neuron, including the myelin sheath.

We mentioned earlier that different parts of the brain develop at different times. During the first half year of life, those cells develop whose functions pertain to primary bodily movements. These cells are found in the motor (output-muscular) and the sensory-motor (input-muscular) areas of the brain, which control the development of various physical skills. Areas that mature later direct the development of various thinking processes. Figure 5-3, a diagram of an infant's brain, indicates the progression of development in the cortex.

The Readiness Principle   A child's ability to perform a physical task depends not only on the maturation of the neurons in the brain, but also on the maturation of the muscle and skeletal systems. Such a state of maturation is known as the **readiness principle.** Until children reach a state of readiness, they will be unable to perform a task, even with training or practice.

Consider the accomplishment of walking. A child will walk only when all systems are developed; if any of the systems are immature, the youngster will be unable to walk, despite all the coaxing in the world. In fact, too much pressure may result in frustration and anxiety. This does not mean an enriched or stimulating environment is not beneficial; just the opposite is true. Once the organism has reached a sufficient level of maturity, environmental enrichment can increase the learning of physical skills. Moreover, after the

FIGURE 5-3
Development of the Cortex.

The cortex develops at different rates. Darker shadings indicate the areas that mature earlier, and the numbers indicate the sequence of development.

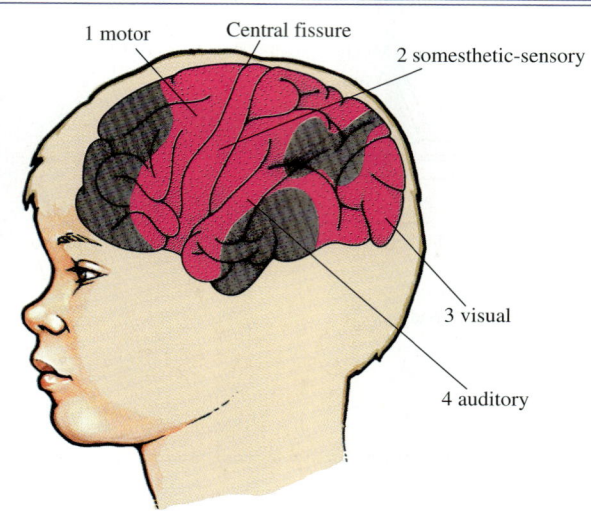

early years of physical development, motor skills are heavily influenced by the environment.

Locomotion

Locomotion is the ability to move from one location to another. The onset of locomotion occurs at about 2.5 months, the time when infants can raise their chest by means of arm support. By 5 months, infants can sit erect when supported.

Locomotion accelerates when infants acquire skill in using their arms and hands. This can be seen at the fifth month, the time when infants can roll over if placed on their back or stomach. Some forward mobility is evident by 6 months, and crawling begins by 8 months. Over the next several months, crawling acquires greater coordination as the legs develop and have an opportunity to exercise.

The first step is taken sometime between 13 and 15 months. Although this marks a time when body weight can be consistently supported, infants indeed look fragile and unsteady. Their legs are bowed because their weight is on the inner part of their feet, and their stomach is thrust forward, all of which gives them a rounded appearance. To maintain balance, their arms extend outward from their body.

During their early efforts, children try all types of steps imaginable. Early walking often includes staggering, lurching, sidestepping, and even stepping backward. Falling is very common during this stage, but infants always get up and continue with boundless energy.

It is important to mention that growing physical capacities blend with other developmental forces, including the cognitive prowess to master motor skills and the motivation to explore the environment (Newell, 1991). Walking does present dangers, though, and parents must realize the child is now able to

Greater coordination in the legs helps to perfect locomotion.

explore and investigate areas that were previously inaccessible. It is a challenge to keep a constant eye on the busy explorer. Because it is common for children to reach and examine lamps, cords, bottles, and other potentially dangerous objects, such items should be kept out of the child's reach. Without curtailing the toddler's developing initiative, we want to safeguard the environment. For cross-cultural variations on locomotion, see the accompanying Focus on Diversity box.

▬ Prehension

Being able to grasp objects between the fingers and opposable thumb, known as **prehension,** is a difficult area to study because the neonate is born with a grasp reflex, a subcortical response that will enable the hand to close if an object is placed in the palm. But the grasp reflex is not the same as the cortically controlled individual movements of fingers and thumbs that represent true prehension. At approximately 4 months, the grasp reflex subsides, and then prehension does not occur until about 5 to 6 months.

Prehension, like locomotion, follows a sequential pattern of development. At 20 weeks, the beginning of eye-hand coordination results in fewer misdirected attempts to reach objects. Although they have considerable difficulty in maintaining their grasp on an object, infants can direct their arm movements with greater efficiency. A study by George Butterworth and Brian Hopkins (1988) shows how infant reflexes and overall coordination become more refined during the early months. The two researchers filmed the spontaneous motor activity of newborns and analyzed arm and hand movements in slow motion. Their observations revealed that newborns move their hands to their mouths fairly regularly. It is particularly interesting that the mouth was eventually

THEORETICAL ISSUES

Beyond the mental faculties needed to perfect locomotor skills, how might psychosocial dynamics influence a child's first step? From an Eriksonian perspective, how do you think learning to walk reflects the toddler's quest for autonomy and initiative?

Focus on Diversity

ARE SOME TODDLERS A STEP AHEAD OF OTHERS?

The first step. It's a developmental achievement that invariably earns the excitement and pride of parents, relatives, and interested onlookers. Many record the event by videocamera while others make sure a snapshot is taken or that it's included in the baby's record book. However it's remembered, the development of walking symbolizes an important achievement in the life of the youngster: the transformation from infant to toddler.

As we've indicated, the first step is taken usually between the ages of 13 and 15 months, but this is just an average. Averages can be very misleading, and we emphasize that walking can begin before or after this time. Similar to all facets of growth and development, individual differences must be taken into account. Furthermore, many of the developmental timetables established for motor skills are based on the maturity of children in Western cultures. Children from other cultures do not necessarily follow these prescribed norms.

The motor skill development of Ugandan infants in Africa illustrates this latter point. Ugandan infants, on the average, sit without support as early as 4 months of age and walk by about 9 months. These achievements obviously come sooner than do those demonstrated by American

INTERACTION OF HEREDITY AND ENVIRONMENT

How can you apply the nature-nurture issue to the rather predictable sequences of prehensile and locomotion development? Do you see these timetables reflecting a genetic influence? What role does the environment play in encouraging the child to express these physical skills?

opened in anticipation of the arrival of the hand and that the movement did not require visual guidance. Research such as this shows how motor behaviors are characterized by growing levels of efficiency and refinement.

Researchers once thought the sequence of reaching, and prehension in general, was the result of maturational processes. Today, though, there are other ideas. For example, some feel eye-hand coordination involves a cognitive mapping of visual and motor schemes. This means infants acquire reaching and retrieval behavior by observing their hands within their visual field. One investigation (Mathew & Cook, 1990) sought to explore the nature of reaching movements by studying infants between the ages of 4 to 7 months. At all ages, the researchers found the initial direction of the reaching movement was correlated with target direction, providing evidence that the hand was cognitively aimed toward the target. Moreover, changes in movement direction made after the commencement of the movement tended to curve the hand path toward the target, providing evidence of error correction.

The ability to reach for (and grasp) objects continues to be refined. Between 5 and 6 months of age, the infant begins to use both hands simultaneously and becomes considerably more efficient in picking up objects. This advancement not only increases further hand-eye coordination but also gives the infant a greater variety of objects to manipulate.

Between 8 and 10 months, infants use their thumb and fingers together fairly consistently and discover many new uses for their hands and arms. For instance, infants of this age are able to support their weight on one arm while reaching for objects. They can also consistently pick up both large and small objects with a better coordinated movement. Figure 5-4 displays the development of prehension and how it compares to milestones in locomotion.

infants (Ainsworth, 1967; Konner, 1976; Super, 1981). Certain prehension abilities, muscle tone, and head control are also superior in Ugandan babies, although all of these advancements over Caucasian infants are greatest during the first year and then taper off (Geber & Dean, 1957).

There are several explanations for these cross-cultural variations in motor skill development. One explanation is that it is a genetic variation, as black American babies appear to be more advanced than white American infants in various phases of motor development during the first year. However, this is a controversial explanation. A more widely accepted theory is that African mothers encourage early head support and other types of muscle control. The infant is often carried on the mother's back (with no means of head support), and the infant spends considerable time on the floor, which provides an environment for exploration and muscular exercise. There is also considerable social stimulation and conversation from mother to child, factors that may also enhance motor precocity.

Interestingly, the age at which walking occurs also varies among European nations (Hindley et al., 1966). Children from Stockholm and Brussels take their first step at about 12.5 months, whereas youngsters from Zurich, London, and Paris do not do the same until about 13.5 months. Explanations here are even more difficult to formulate, although genetics, environmental stimulation, and the quality of health care have been offered. The lack of precise answers notwithstanding, this discussion shows how motor skill timetables may vary. Moreover, it illustrates how the nature-nurture issue expresses itself in many ways throughout the course of human development (Plomin, 1990).

At this point, we discuss handedness and its role in prehensile development. **Handedness** is the preference for and subsequent predominant use of one hand. Handedness shows few signs of developing during the first year. Most infants are ambidextrous and show no real preference for either hand. At approximately 19 months, though, hand preference makes its appearance, and an active and a passive hand emerge. By 2 years of age most children exhibit a definite preference, which is generally firmly established by the time they enter school. For about 95% of people, this preference is for the right hand.

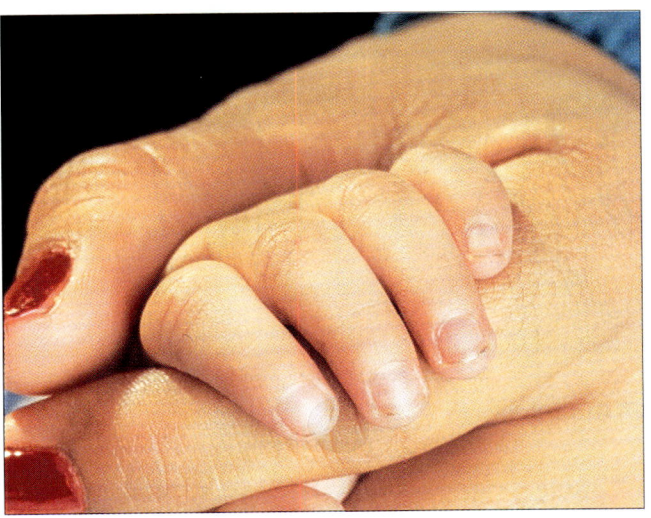

Similar to other motor skills, prehension unfolds in a sequential fashion.

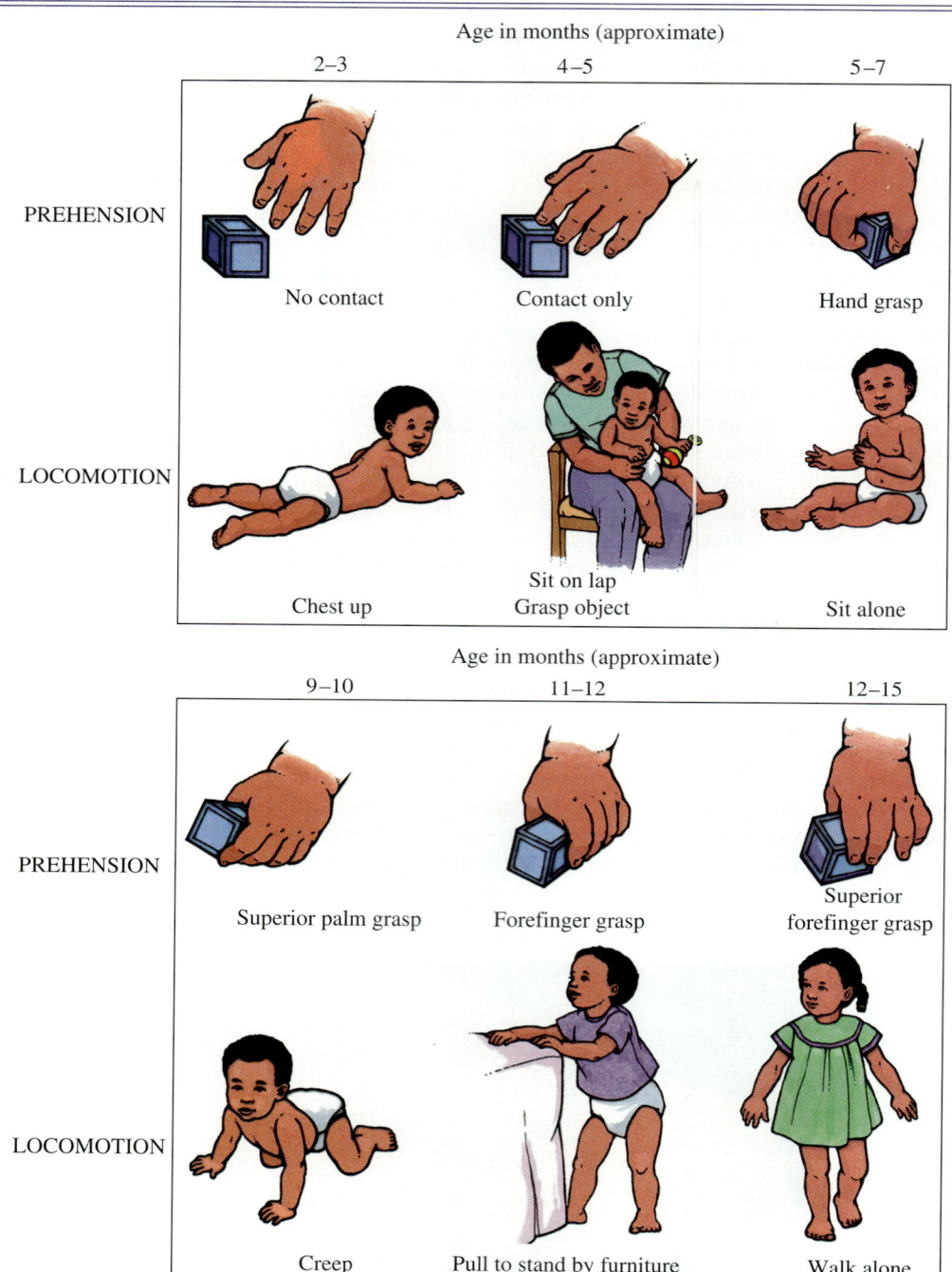

FIGURE 5-4

Milestones in Motor Skill Development.

Advancements in prehension and locomotion are pronounced during the years of infancy and toddlerhood and typically follow a sequence of accomplishments.

It is difficult to determine what factors create handedness. It could be caused by either environmental or genetic factors, but there is not a logically sound argument for one or the other. For example, when both parents are right-handed, there is a 92% chance their offspring will be right-handed. Should one parent be left-handed, there is an 80% chance their offspring will be right-handed. If both parents are left-handed, the figure for right-handedness diminishes to 50%. Such percentages might indicate a hereditary predisposition toward handedness. However, we should also consider environmental influences. For example, left-handed parents could be left-handed models the child may imitate.

Right-handers have advantages not available to left-handers. Left-handers gradually discover they must adjust to a predominantly right-handed world. For example, learning to write is one of the biggest obstacles, as the left hand often smears the letters that have just been written. Other disadvantages for the left-hander continue even after childhood. Sports equipment, games, tools, door-knobs, and even the handles on drinking fountains all are designed with the right-hander in mind.

Left-handers can overcome such hurdles, though, and they have no more adjustment difficulties throughout life than right-handers do. Research indicates no noticeable differences between the two in such areas as school achievement, motivation, and intelligence. Findings such as this indicate that left-handers are perfectly capable of overcoming whatever obstacles confront them in our predominantly right-handed world.

Prehension and the Development of Children's Art   One of the several observable indicators of children's developing prehensile abilities is artwork. Contemporary lifespan development researchers (e.g., Mortensen, 1991; Nichollas & Kennedy, 1992) regard children's artwork as an important activity, a form of expression that mirrors many facets of the youngster's growth and development.

The scribbling stage represents the foundation for children's artwork. Manipulating an artistic instrument requires considerable fine motor skill dexterity, and the progression of children's artwork reveals increasing refinement in this area. It is shortly after the first year that most infants become capable of making their initial attempts at scribbling, the first stage of artistic development. Before and even at this age, infants will attempt to eat or taste the drawing instrument rather than use it on paper. (For this reason, drawing instruments should be given to infants only under supervision.) However, once the purpose of the pencil or crayon has been demonstrated, most infants will immediately begin scribbling with delight and enthusiasm.

Unfortunately, scribbles are neglected by many adults, who insist the marks are nothing more than meaningless lines. On the contrary, scribbling is important to growing infants, not only because it enhances prehensile development and is one of their first visual accomplishments, but also because it gives them a sense of personal achievement and satisfaction.

Furthermore, scribbling becomes an activity with a purpose. Once they have made these marks, children will want to repeat the activity because of the pleasure it offers. Many find the task pleasurable, and others seem intent on varying their mark. Whatever the motivation, scribbles are a delightful creation during this early stage of development.

FIGURE 5-5
Children's Scribbles.

The development of scribbles requires neuro-muscular control and hand-eye coordination. In time, children will master the movements necessary to produce a wide range of scribbles, such as those illustrated here.

At first, infants are severely hampered in their attempts to produce marks on paper, the limits caused primarily by insufficient neuromuscular development and eye-hand coordination. Fine motor skills such as these typically lag behind large, or gross motor skills. Frequently, children drop the pencil or crayon or do not hold it at the proper angle. At other times, they miss the paper completely. But eventually, their arm-banging actions develop into more coordinated arm and hand movements. One of the more interesting qualities of scribbles is that they follow a fairly predictable pattern of development. The scribble first is a continuous to-and-fro movement represented graphically by a zigzag of pre-dominantly horizontal strokes; later, as circular movements of the hand become possible, "round" scribbling emerges.

Between the ages of 16 and 20 months, children acquire considerable flexibility and fluidity. Whereas their earlier attempts were characterized by jagged and abrupt markings, there is now a freer flow of artistic expression. Toward the end of the second year, there is increased refinement in children's scribbles, as evidenced by their ability to keep their marks within the boundaries of the page. This phase of development is sometimes referred to as controlled scribbling. In addition, they may experiment with a wider range of complex scribblings, as well as vary the amount of pressure they exert on the crayon. Figure 5-5 displays the different varieties of scribbles.

UNIT REVIEW—

↗ The maturation of brain cells is largely responsible for rates of body growth and development during infancy and toddlerhood. The ability to perform motor skills depends on both neural maturation and readiness.

continued . . .

> ↗ Locomotion is the ability to move from location to location, and it progresses in a developmental fashion. Cross-cultural variations exist in motor skill accomplishments.
>
> ↗ Prehension is grasping objects between the fingers and opposable thumb. It, too, proceeds in a developmental fashion. Handedness is the preference for, and the subsequent predominant use of, one hand.
>
> ↗ Prehensile development is enhanced through artwork, as it encourages fine motor skill dexterity and eye-hand coordination.

UNIT TWO: MENTAL DEVELOPMENT

Lifespan development researchers have long been interested in the higher-order mental processes that pertain to thinking, perceiving, and understanding. Technically, this field of study is known as **cognition.** Researchers in this area study the mental facilities that process, interpret, and categorize stimulus information.

The development of logical thinking is a highly complex process. Because of children's undeveloped reasoning capacities, their interpretation of their surrounding environment is frequently illogical and unrealistic. Loose concepts and explanations are formed and oriented into their existing frame of reference. Over time, though, children develop an accurate understanding of objects, people, and events in their surroundings, and they abandon illogical ideas in favor of logic and reason.

How these cognitive developments unfold is one of the central themes of this text. Before we begin our examination, though, we want to emphasize that mental gains throughout life take place against the backdrop of other development areas, particularly social relationships. Children's mental growth depends as much on adult stimulation and interaction patterns as it does on their intrinsic cognitive abilities. Symbolic representation, thought, and language cannot develop without interaction between adults and children.

With this understanding in mind, we first turn to the sensorimotor stage of cognitive development proposed by Jean Piaget. Then, we examine early concept formation, the interplay between cognition and memory, sense-organ development, and, finally, language development during the first 3 years of life.

■ Jean Piaget's Sensorimotor Stage

The first period of cognitive development, known in Piagetian terms as the **sensorimotor stage,** occurs during approximately the first 2 years of life. This stage is so named because most of the infant's learning abilities are directed toward the coordination of simple sensorimotor skills, which include such activities as grasping objects and the basic reflexes. The concepts covered in this stage may be of particular concern to parents of newborns or anyone observing children of this age level. Six substages comprise the sensorimotor period, each of which facilitates overall mental development. We remind you, though, that although Piaget's stages provide a useful timetable for the progression of cognitive development, replication studies have not always supported the ages when children reach a given stage.

Reflex Activities (0–1 month)   During their first month, infants are limited to only primitive **reflex activities,** such as crying or sucking. This is primarily because their cerebral cortex has not yet developed. However, as the cranial bones enlarge, the brain cells develop and become more chemically active. As a result, the infants' reflexes are modified and become more efficient. For example, whereas the sucking reflex is first directed toward all objects, the infant can later discriminate between objects that can be sucked, such as a breast or a bottle, and objects that cannot.

Primary Circular Reactions (1–4 months)   Should an infant discover a pleasurable behavior pattern, the chances are it will be repeated for its own sake. This is a **primary circular reaction.** For example, if sucking the thumb brings enjoyment, active efforts will be made to reproduce that action. Infants also begin to display signs of coordinating one action with another. This can be seen in the coordination of the hand and arm, which may permit greater coordination of thumb sucking. Infants may also try to look at whatever is grasped and reach for whatever happens to be seen. This is also a period when infants take a great deal of interest in themselves. They frequently are preoccupied with their own arms, hands, legs, feet, and the investigation of simple movements of their bodies.

Secondary Circular Reactions (4–8 months)   During the fourth to the eighth months, infants attempt to reproduce interesting events in the external environment that might have been first caused by accident. This is a **secondary circular reaction.** For example, infants may find the sides of the crib make an interesting noise if they are struck with the foot. Along these lines, if a rattle is shaken properly, it will create an interesting sound. Infants gradually become aware of the changes they can make, especially if a created event is different, amusing, or interesting. Another cognitive development during this stage is the *anticipatory* or *power of association* effect. This advancement will become an important aid to understanding cause-and-effect relationships because infants learn that certain events may be associated. Piaget observed that his son Laurent, especially during feeding time, associated a cradling position with being fed. As soon as he was in this position to eat, he wanted contact only with his mother's breast. An obvious association bond had been forged.

Coordination of Secondary Schemes (8–12 months)   During previous substages, infants had trouble understanding the concept of **object permanence,** the realization that objects exist even when they cannot be seen. If any object is hidden, say, behind a pillow, infants lacking object permanence will not search for it. An "out of sight, out of mind" principle is operating. But after 8 months, about the time object permanence is acquired, infants will search under and behind obstructions to recover desired objects. We might point out that some researchers are proposing new ideas about object permanence (Baillargeon & DeVos, 1991; Baillargeon & Graber, 1988). Some challenge the limitations of an 8-month-old's memory ability and suggest the ability to locate hidden objects is better developed than prior research suggests. If you want to

ACTIVE AND REACTIVE MODELS OF DEVELOPMENT

In each of these Piagetian substages, can you see how the infant's behavior reflects *active* involvement with the environment? How might such behaviors contrast with reactive involvements? Can you envision ways that reactive involvement might shape the course of infant cognitive development?

When concepts such as object permanence are understood, the environment acquires new meaning.

test a child's understanding of object permanence, we provide guidelines in the accompanying Lifespan Development in Action box.

Tertiary Circular Reactions (12–18 months) Infants' heightened interest in creating changes in their environment fuels primitive reasoning skills. By the end of the first year, the beginnings of simple trial-and-error behavior emerge. Also at this time are further gains in the understanding of object permanence. More specifically, infants no longer will look for an object in the place where they first found it if they see its position being changed. This is the **tertiary circular reaction,** which fooled them in the previous substage. However, if the change is not visible, they will continue to look for it in the first location. Infants still lack the ability to take into account displacements outside their immediate perceptions.

Invention of New Means Through Mental Combinations (18–24 months)
Before their second birthday, toddlers start creating mental images that enable

Lifespan Development in Action

A TEST OF OBJECT PERMANENCE: OUT OF SIGHT, OUT OF MIND?

One of the more important developments during the sensorimotor stage of cognitive development is the establishment of object permanence. A simple demonstration can be performed with infants 6 to 12 months of age to discover if an understanding of it has been achieved.

Select a small shiny object that is likely to capture the infant's attention, such as a coin, key, or ring. In plain view of the infant, place the object in the palm of your left hand. Then close both hands into a fist, making sure the fingers of your left hand hide the object from the infant's view. (During the initial trial, open both hands for several seconds in order to ensure the infant knows in which hand the object lies.) When given the opportunity to search for the missing object, the infant will undoubtedly seek to open your closed left hand. Repeat the process several times, each time hiding the object in the same hand.

Now, again in plain view, place the object in your right palm and, as in the initial trials, place both fists in front of the infant. Because the object is still conceived of as being in a special location, that is, in the place in which it was hidden and found, your now empty fist is often searched by the younger infant, who may ignore the right hand. Successful understanding of object permanence has yet to be developed.

them to devise new ways of dealing with the environment. This is the **invention of new means through mental combinations.** Now simple problems may be "thought out" before they are undertaken and "inner experimentation" allowed in order for new mental combinations to be formed. Toddlers can now locate an unseen object, even when they have not observed it being moved, because they can infer its possible movements. Such reasoning abilities herald the beginning of true conceptual thought. At the end of the sensorimotor stage, other noteworthy advances include the acquisition and refinement of basic sensory skills and motor responses, the establishment of anticipatory reactions, and the beginnings of mental flexibility. As we see in later chapters, all of these cognitive advancements form the foundation for more advanced levels of thinking and reasoning.

Concept Development

Developing cognitive skills relies considerably on the establishment and refinement of concepts. Broadly defined, a **concept** is a mental image that represents an object or event. As they become more complex, concepts connect groups of objects and events sharing common properties. Because concepts sort out and categorize daily experiences, they are regarded as underpinnings for cognition as a whole (Banks & Krajicek, 1991; Matlin, 1989; Reed, 1992).

The refinement of concepts is slow and often difficult for children. As youngsters are saturated with new information every day, they must either establish new concepts to represent this material or relate it to existing concepts. The difficulty of this becomes apparent when we consider, for example, how the concept "ball" must be refined. Once they have learned the proper verbal designation, children must learn that balls come in many different sizes, weights, and colors. Some bounce higher than others do, and some, such as snowballs, don't bounce at all. Some are used in sports activities and can be pitched, dribbled, or rolled. Children must also learn the word *ball* has other meanings, such as "have a ball," ballroom dancing, or "the whole ball of wax." From this one simple concept, you can see how difficult concept refinement is. Now let us examine concept development during the early years.

Shape and Size Concepts   Before children can develop accurate concepts, an object's properties must be correctly distinguished. Such properties include shape and size. The perception of shape and size begins early in life. Newborns, for example, are especially attracted to novel patterns, including depictions of the human face. When they look at faces, infants are especially attracted to contrasting areas of lightness and darkness, such as between the hairline and the eyes. As their scanning abilities become more refined, infants, by the sixth month, can also understand facial composition and recognize whether facial elements presented in drawings are scrambled or correctly arranged (Kaplan et al., 1988; Rose, 1988).

Accurate shape and size concepts rely considerably on **perceptual constancy,** the tendency of objects to appear the same under different viewing conditions. Because the retinal image changes when objects are examined from different standpoints, children may become confused when attempting to gauge their actual size or shape. For instance, when youngsters understand the concept of size constancy, a figure walking away or a boat disappearing into the horizon are not perceived as being miniature versions of the actual objects. Likewise, when shape constancy is understood, the various angles of a perceived object do not distort the object's actual shape. Thus, although dinner plates on the table appear elliptical when viewed at a certain angle and distance, shape constancy enables us to perceive them as circular. Surprisingly, infants seem to recognize size and shape constancy early in life. And with age, more accurate discriminations develop (Rose & Orlian, 1991; Skouteris, McKenzie, & Day, 1992; Slater et al., 1991).

Perceptual constancy is important throughout the entire life cycle. As Hans Wallach (1985) notes, the world continues to shift around observers as they move through it. As objects are approached, they expand and turn with respect to one's changing position. A turn or nod of the head alters the orientation of the surroundings; eye movements shift the image of the environmental motions caused by one's activity. With perceptual constancy, however, we perceive our surroundings as stable because we have compensated for such displacements.

Over time, youngsters will properly identify shapes and forms in their surroundings. Simple shapes, such as circles and squares, are learned first, and more complicated shapes, such as triangles and diamonds, are acquired later. Young children, however, cannot detect all shapes. Shapes having ambiguous or hidden dimensions are especially difficult to perceive (Ruffman, Olson, & Astington, 1991).

Another feature of objects that has to be learned is size. At first, the concept of size is difficult for children to grasp. Think of the trouble toddlers have in understanding, for example, how hollow cubes of varying sizes fit into one another. Initially, children may only handle the blocks or stack them upon one another. By age 2 or 3, though, children understand that the "little" blocks can be placed inside the "big" ones. As they become acquainted with objects in their surroundings, children gradually add a variety of "size" words to their vocabularies (Ebeling & Gelman, 1988; Hobbs & Bacharach, 1990; Sena & Smith, 1990).

Spatial Concepts   Spatial concepts are also difficult for youngsters to grasp. Because of their inexperience as observers, youngsters often do not realize that an object can take on different spatial appearances. In this respect, a child may have difficulty telling whether a standard figure has been placed to the left or right or in front of or behind other objects. Likewise, deciding whether an object is right-side up or upside down frequently produces confusion.

Children's difficulty in understanding spatial concepts is, in part, caused by their not knowing the terminology for describing the objects' different appearances (Stockman & Vaughn-Cooke, 1992). Information processing skills and attention also need to be taken into consideration, not only for spatial concepts but other perceptual challenges as well (Butterworth & Jarrett, 1991; Colombo et al., 1991; Jacobson et al., 1992). Young children's egocentric view of the environment also restricts development. In time, though, youngsters learn the correct terminology and transcend such egocentrism. In so doing, they can discriminate among spatial orientations and become aware of environmental change.

Class Concepts   Mental images representing object categories are known as class concepts. Confusion is apparent when young children are presented with object-class problems. For example, suppose youngsters are given a variety of blocks of different colors and shapes (see Figure 5-6). When asked to group these objects together, children of this age would most likely categorize them by **serialization** (also called *chaining*). This is the process whereby objects are grouped on a perceptual basis, in this case by color rather than shape. Although this is one kind of grouping organization, young children tend to rely on this one dimension. Older youngsters, however, are capable of classifying by shape, as well as color, if need be. One source (Freund, Baker, & Sonnenschein, 1990) indicates that children most successful in handling classification challenges are those skilled in such areas as strategic planning, flexibility, and modification.

Understanding the relationship between subclasses and classes also poses problems. To illustrate, suppose a youngster was given four red checkers and two black checkers and was asked if there were more black or more red checkers. This would not be difficult for the child. But if he or she were asked whether there were more red or more black *plastic* checkers, confusion would result. This is because parts and wholes cannot be comprehended simultaneously. This cognitive advancement, as we shall see, develops later in childhood.

Further, an investigation of the ability of preschoolers and second graders to understand classes and subclasses indicates that age, indeed, makes subjects more sensitive to differences (Gelman & O'Reilly, 1988). Some researchers

INTERRELATEDNESS OF AGING PROCESSES

Utilizing the theme of interrelated developmental forces, how do you think a young child's success or failure in the cognitive arena affects feelings of esteem or self-worth? How might a youngster's intellectual curiosity be shaped by different motivational states or psychosocial forces?

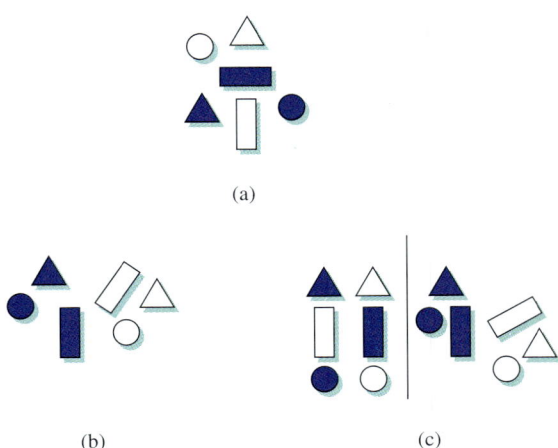

(a)

(b)   (c)

(Mervis & Mervis, 1988) believe the best way to help children learn to classify objects is through demonstration. Children aged 9 months were followed up to 30 months of age to determine their ability to classify objects. Although they could classify, efforts were characterized by earlier mentioned generalizations; unless guided by an adult (supplying the correct label, correction of the child's errors, and demonstration), demonstration was found to be the most important factor. Studies such as this reinforce the notion that adults are instrumental in shaping the child's early conceptual learning. For more detailed information on class inclusion, see Reyna (1991) and Howe and Rabinowitz (1991).

Time Concepts   Young children have a limited concept of time. Often, their understanding of it revolves around their daily activities, such as when dinner is served or when a parent comes home from work. Children also use, almost exclusively, the present tense when they converse. But by about age 3, they begin to understand words related to the past and the future.

Cognition and Memory

The ability to retain information from the past and apply it to present and future situations is an important aspect of mental functioning. It is through memory that past experiences influence our present thoughts and actions. Without memory, intellectual functioning would be virtually nonexistent, including the cognitive dynamics attached to concept development, perceptual awareness, and language acquisition and use (Martindale, 1991; Zechmeister & Johnson, 1992).

Types of Memory Storage Systems   Because we can't actually see inside our "memory machine," we have to assemble our current knowledge and make

FIGURE 5-6
The Development of Classification Skills.

When asked to group blocks of different shapes and colors (a), younger children typically restrict themselves to one dimension, such as color (b). Older children, though, can group according to other dimensions, in this case, both shape and color (c).

an educated guess at the processes involved in our memory system. One explanation is called the *information processing model*. It states there are three types of memory: sensory memory, short-term memory, and long-term memory.

Sensory memory refers to the information stored in a sense organ. Information in sensory storage lasts for a fraction of a second. Almost as soon as a sense organ is stimulated, the stimulus changes. Sensory stimulation amounts to a continuous, ever-changing bombardment on each sense organ. Using the visual sense as an example, information stimulates the visual receptors (rods and cones) on the retina of the eye, and this information is shot back to the visual cells at the back of the brain. The eye has done its job of relaying information from the environment; as long as there is light, there is visual stimulation, and this sense organ will continue to transmit all information to the brain.

The memory cells of the brain that process this incoming information are limited in ability. In fact, the average adult can hold only, on the average, seven bits of information and that generally, for only up to 20 seconds. This is called **short-term memory (STM),** for obvious reasons. First of all, much of what the sense organ delivers to short-term memory is lost almost immediately. For example, if we placed 25 typical everyday items on a table for a few seconds and then covered them, the average person when asked to list what they saw could name seven. Even though their list may include only seven correct responses (plus a few items that were not part of the display!) they would know there were many additional items they can't remember. In other words, the short-term memory system is a temporary storehouse for very small amounts of information. A typical example of short-term memory is finding a telephone number and remembering it just long enough to place the call.

Now one of two things will happen to these seven pieces of information in temporary storage: If not used, they will be forgotten, but if we continue to pay attention to them, that is, think about them, we can extend our memory. Thinking about information in our STM is called *rehearsal*. If you rehearse something once, you may be able to keep it in STM another 20 seconds; enough rehearsal will send it on its way to long-term memory.

Special types of rehearsal, sometimes called *encoding*, are usually required, a process of compacting information or organizing it into chunks so it can be placed into appropriate long-term memory categories. At other times, information may pass directly from the short-term to the long-term memory, presumably the result of its meaningfulness to or impact on the individual.

Long-term memory (LTM) refers to the storage of information for relatively long periods of time, even a lifetime. Once stored, memory can be retrieved, either through *recall* or *recognition*. Recall refers to the retrieval of a memory without cue. For example, an essay question asks you to recall information without giving you many cues. Recognition memory can be demonstrated by using a multiple-choice question. You may not remember something through recall, but you recognize it when you see it.

Short-term memory is also called *working memory*, or what Freud called the conscious mind (and William James, the father of American psychology, called the "stream of conscious"). Working memory (short-term memory) receives information not only from the sense organs, but from the long-term memory system as well. In fact the LTM can be equated to what Freud called the preconscious mind, that is, the memory bank. So the working memory is being bombarded with stimuli that are coming and going, and must decide what information should remain for conscious thought, what to rehearse for transfer to LTM, and what to ignore and thus forget.

Memory Development During Childhood   The development of memory throughout childhood reveals several interesting trends. At first, children are capable of holding only a few words or ideas in their minds. They frequently have difficulty remembering events that happened weeks, days, or even only hours before. This problem points to the small amount of information in their long-term memory store. However, it is generally recognized that, with age, children's memory significantly improves (Boller et al., 1990; Henry & Millar, 1991; Miller et al., 1991; Price & Goodman, 1990; Schneider & Sodian, 1991). Certain factors account for this improvement. First, children are able to increase their overall memory span (the number of items that can be held in the short-term bank) as they grow older. Whereas the average 3-year-old can store only three items in his or her memory span, the typical 8- to 12-year-old can hold six (Case, Kurland, & Goldberg, 1982; Wilkinson, 1981).

Another factor leading to improved memory abilities, as well as cognition as a whole, are two allied mental capacities: metacognition and metamemory abilities. **Metacognition** refers to one's awareness of how a cognitive process can be applied to a given mental task, for example, the rehearsal of events so they can be remembered. **Metamemory** refers to how one's own memory abilities can be used to prevent forgetting. As we see in later chapters, metacognition and metamemory skills have the potential of enhancing memory skills and problem solving throughout the lifespan.

Children will discover that metacognition and metamemory skills are valuable mental faculties. For example, youngsters will discover that paying close attention to objects and events and ignoring any distractions assists memory. So too does employing more efficient information processing and organization abilities and higher levels of motivation. Children's comprehension of these and other metacognitive processes steadily increases with age. The result is more refined and elaborate strategies for perceiving, storing, and retrieving environmental information (Cowan et al., 1991; Geary, Klosterman, & Adrales, 1990; Hashimoto, 1991; Miller et al., 1991).

THEORETICAL ISSUES

What theoretical perspectives might be applied to the development of memory skills during childhood? For example, might principles of behaviorism such as reinforcement be used to explain why certain events are remembered or forgotten? Do any cognitive-developmental or social learning dynamics seem applicable?

▬ Sense-Organ Development

With age, sense-organ efficiency improves because of the growing physical maturation of the sense organs as well as the increasing amounts of perceptual information that can be processed (Cuneo & Welsh, 1992; Levine & Shefner, 1991). The youngster's developing cognitive awareness of objects and events in the world also assists the maturation process. All of these developments enable toddlers to make remarkably fine discriminations of sights, sounds, and other sensory stimulations.

Vision   The visual system develops rapidly. By 4 months of age, infants' visual accommodation and focusing abilities are close to those of mature adults. Also developing rapidly is brightness sensitivity, which matures by approximately 3 months. The ability to see small objects with increasing clarity is also evident during the early months of infancy. Additionally, infants are able to follow and track remote objects with increasing efficiency (Daniel & Lee, 1990). Color perception is also evident at an early age. By approximately 4 months, the visual spectrum of the primary color categories of red, yellow, and blue can be perceived (Adams, 1989; Adams, Maurer, & Davis, 1986).

Depth Perception   **Depth perception** is an important visual ability that allows a person to distinguish downward slopes, descending steps, or edges of precipices. As we can imagine, the lack of depth perception for children may retard the development of their creeping, crawling, and walking abilities. However, it is known that infants perceive depth as early as the crawling stage.

We can measure depth perception by means of a **visual cliff** apparatus. This device is a split-level table designed with a "shallow" and a "deep" end. Half the table is on a normal plane and ends abruptly, although a glass plate extends over the entire table. The other half of the visual cliff drops several feet below the "edge." (Both sides of the table are covered with a checkerboard design to show the drop.) Thus infants are able to see the differences in depth, even though the surface is safe to crawl on.

Research has revealed that infants will not cross over to the deep end. Most crawling infants will peer through the glass, sometimes pat it, or even rest their faces on it. However, they will not venture over to the deep end. Even when mothers stood at the deep end and tried to coax their babies across, most refused to move forward. Findings such as this indicate the presence of depth perception at the crawling stage. Interestingly, depth perception is evident early in the life of not only humans, but in other land animals as well. Young chicks, rats, kittens, and goats all refuse to cross over the deep sides of a visual cliff. However, nonland animals such as turtles and ducks have a different reaction to a visual cliff. In fact, they show little, if any, hesitancy about crossing over to the deep side. It is conceivable the deep side of the visual cliff more closely resembles their natural surroundings.

Other investigations in depth perception show that infants as young as 2 or 3 months show differences in heart rate at the shallow and deep sides of the table. More specifically, the infants' heartbeat *decreases* when they are placed on the deep side, a common reaction of humans when they pause to orient themselves to new situations. At 8 months, however, the infants' heartbeat *increases,* an emotional reaction that typically accompanies fear. It has been surmised that older infants, having had more experiences in crawling—and falling—are able to perceive the potential danger associated with the deep side (Campos et al., 1978; Campos, Bertenthal, & Caplovitz, 1982).

Finally, research has been directed at the role of emotional signaling from caregivers on infants' visual cliff behavior. Of significance was a study headed by James Sorce (1985) that examined the effect of mothers' facial expressions of emotion on the visual cliff behavior of their infants. In this study, which consisted of four parts, 108 12-month-old infants were observed.

In the first part of the study, 19 infants viewed a facial expression of joy, and 17 infants viewed one of fear. In the second part, 15 infants viewed interest, and 18 infants viewed anger. In the third part, 19 infants viewed sadness. In the last phase, 23 infants were used to determine whether the expressions influenced the infants' evaluation of an ambiguous situation or whether they were effective in controlling behavior merely because of their discrepancy or unexpectedness.

Research utilizing visual cliff apparatus reveals that depth perception is present in infants at early ages.

The researchers found the infants watched facial expressions to clarify situations, a phenomenon known as **social referencing.** For example, if the mother looked joyful or interested and the infants used this as a social reference, they would cross over to the deep side. On the other hand, if the mother showed fear or anger, few infants would cross. In the absence of any depth whatsoever, few infants looked at the mother, but those who did, when the mother looked fearful, hesitated but crossed nonetheless. All of this prompted the researchers to conclude that facial expressions regulate behavior most clearly in uncertain situations. Other studies have found that social referencing is apparent when infants and toddlers encounter other types of novel situations (Camras & Sachs, 1991; Hirshberg, 1990; Hirshberg & Svejda, 1990; Rosen, Adamson, & Bakeman, 1992).

Audition   The auditory system also matures rapidly as children learn the associative value of sounds. At about 4 months, infants are aware of the sound of a familiar voice, crying, or novel sounds and will turn their heads in the direction of the sound. One study (Walker-Andrews & Lennon, 1991) indicates that 5-month-olds can discriminate vocal expressions of emotion when those expressions are presented in conjunction with a face. At approximately 6 to 8 months, infants can distinguish different sound frequencies (Spetner & Olsho, 1990) and make progressively finer auditory discriminations, such as with approaching and receding sounds (Clifton, Perris, & Bullinger, 1991; Morrongiello, Hewitt, & Gotowiec, 1991; Morrongiello & Rocca, 1990; Trehub et al., 1991).

Taste and Smell   Taste and smell both are remarkably well developed at birth. Through direct contact with many tastes and odors, children can differentiate and recognize these sensory stimuli. By the early years, children seem able to detect the same pleasant and unpleasant odors that adults can. However, it must be recognized there is a wide range of individual differences in taste and smell sensitivity (Blass, 1990; Rosenstein & Oster, 1988). During the first few months of life, infants are able to discriminate between sweet, sour,

INTERRELATEDNESS OF AGING PROCESSES

Does social referencing reflect the interrelatedness of developmental processes? How do you see an infant's cognitive faculties converging with social and emotional awareness to assist growing levels of environmental mastery?

bitter, and salty tastes (Bernstein, 1990; Harris, Thomas, & Booth, 1990; Rosenstein & Oster, 1988; Sullivan & Birch, 1990).

Touch   The infant is very sensitive to being touched, cuddled, and held (Olds, London, & Ladewig, 1992). The sense of touch is exercised considerably during the first year as infants explore objects not only with their fingers but with their tongue and lips as well. Skin contact and warmth provides stimulation for infants, and as we discover shortly, contact with familiar objects has implications for psychological and social development. Thus being able to tactually distinguish safe and secure objects contributes to attachment behaviors and the contact/comfort motive.

During toddlerhood, touch is one of the most pleasurable of the child's sensations. Furthermore, the sense of touch adds a great deal to cognitive awareness during these years, especially when exploration of the sensations of hardness and softness, roughness and smoothness, and warmth and cold are at their peak. Learning environments for infants and toddlers should thus provide as many experiences as possible to elevate touch sensitivity as well as the other major senses.

Language Development

One of lifespan development's most fascinating areas of study is how children learn to talk. The study of this developmental area, known as **psycholinguistics,** traces how children pass from the early stages of crying and babbling to spoken words and meaningful sentences. Psycholinguistics embraces the closely related areas of mental imagery, cognitive development, symbolization, and speech (Gleason, 1993; Hulit & Howard, 1993; Owens, 1992).

At the outset, you should realize that speech and language are related to, though also different from, each other. **Speech** is the concrete physical act of forming and sequencing the sounds of oral language. **Language** is the system of grammatical rules and semantics that makes speech meaningful.

Language and the Brain   The part of the brain most directly associated with language and its subsequent development is the left cerebral hemisphere. Rarely does damage to the right hemisphere produce any language disorders. Researchers have identified three areas in particular that serve specific biological functions. One of these parts is **Broca's area,** located adjacent to the region of the motor cortex that controls the movements of the lips, jaw, tongue, soft palate, and vocal cords. Its function apparently is to incorporate programs to coordinate these muscles in speech. Damage to Broca's area produces *motor aphasia* and causes speech to be slow and labored. However, comprehension of language is still possible.

A second region, located in the temporal lobe, is referred to as **Wernicke's area.** Wernicke's area is believed to be related to the comprehension of speech. When this part of the brain is damaged, speech is fluent but has little meaningful content, and comprehension is usually lost. Such a condition is called *sensory aphasia.*

The third area, a nerve bundle that connects the Broca's and Wernicke's areas, is called the **arcuate fasciculus.** When damage occurs here, speech remains fluent but it is abnormal. Such afflicted individuals utter meaningless

Perceptual sensitivity, combined with attention and attending skills, allows infants to become more aware of their surroundings.

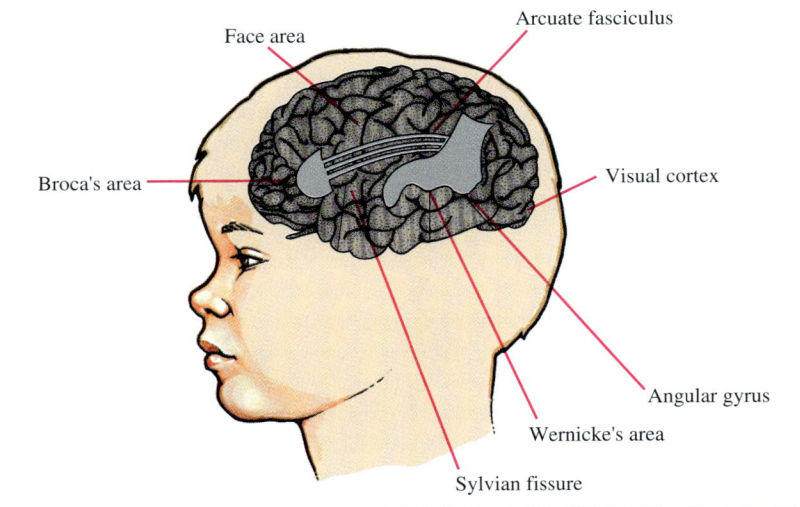

Face area

Arcuate fasciculus

Broca's area

Visual cortex

Angular gyrus

Wernicke's area

Sylvian fissure

FIGURE 5-7

Areas of the Brain Associated with Speech.

The left cerebral hemisphere is largely responsible for language production and comprehension. Broca's area, Wernicke's area, and the arcuate fasciculus are areas of particular importance.

phrases, and although they are able to comprehend spoken or written words, they cannot repeat them. Figure 5-7 depicts the brain's language centers.

Theoretical Perspectives of Language Development   Thus far, we have explained what language is and which parts of the brain control its expression. What we haven't explored is how a child learns a language. In other words, what factors account for an infant's babbling, the emergence of a child's first word, and the eventual fabrication of sentences? To answer such questions, three major theories of language development have been proposed: the behavioral, social learning, and innate perspectives.

BEHAVIORAL THEORY Behavioral theory states that language acquisition is a form of operant behavior in which children add new words to their vocabulary. New words are acquired because they fulfill the child's needs. The parents' use of positive reinforcement when their child uses the appropriate words or correct grammar may also increase his or her vocabulary (Skinner, 1957).

To date, behavioral theory of language acquisition has not gained much support. One of the main criticisms is that many parents usually pay more attention to whether their child's speech patterns are factually correct than to whether the grammar is correct. Consider the following: Suppose a child sees you reading this book and asks, "That a book?" A normal and seemingly natural inclination is to respond, "Yes, it is." If you do that, though, you are responding to the truth of the proposition, not to the fact that the child's question was ungrammatical. Put another way, you paid more attention to the facts of the remark than to the (incorrect) grammar.

SOCIAL LEARNING THEORY Social learning theorists maintain that children are able to acquire language by observing and imitating the adults in their surroundings. In this sense, parents may serve as models, not only offering remarks that the child may imitate, but also expanding on the child's utterances themselves. Thus imitation should play an important role in language development, especially because children want to be like adults, and fluent speech is an obvious characteristic of grown-ups. In this sense, an adult may say, "This is the baby's high chair," to be followed by the child's response of "baby high chair."

However, much like reinforcement theory, the social learning approach has fallen victim to criticism. Its critics maintain that although imitation does occur, it is not the pivotal feature of language acquisition. Even when children do imitate adult speech, they reformulate the sentence by using their own grammar. Acquiring new grammatical features through imitation, when it is exactly these

The manner in which children acquire a spoken language has different theoretical possibilities.

new features that are omitted, hardly explains the nature of acquisition. Yet the most dramatic evidence refuting imitation as an explanation of language acquisition is the language patterns of those children who cannot speak, yet can hear normally. The case of a young boy who fit into this category and never had the opportunity to imitate adult speech is an excellent example. He did, however, learn to comprehend a language. Results such as these support the conclusion that the theory of social learning leaves many questions about language development still unanswered (Lenneberg, 1962).

INNATE THEORY Finally, we come to the innate theory, proposed by Noam Chomsky (1968, 1980). Chomsky suggested that the human brain is programmed to enable individuals to create and understand language. This system of programming is called the **language acquisition device (LAD),** which depends on mature cells in the cerebral cortex. Because the cortex is not totally functional at birth, it must mature during the first year if the child is to develop an understanding of words. This innate device allows the brain to perform cognitive operations on the sounds received, enabling infants to produce grammar and to invent totally new sentences. Innate theory, then, views language development as a genetic phenomenon. Chomsky also asserted that sentences are generated by a system of rules, which enable children to listen to language and eventually fabricate sentences.

Also important to Chomsky's theory is the ability to analyze sentences, rather than just how sounds and words combine to form sentences. Sentences are analyzed by examining their two parts, the **surface structure** and the **deep structure.**

The rules of grammar dictate a sentence's surface structure. The deep structure is what a particular sentence means to the individual, or the conceptual framework of a language. Several examples should clarify the distinction between the two types. Consider the following:

The student attended the lifespan development class.
The lifespan development class was attended by the student.

The two surface structures are obviously different, but both sentences have the same meaning. That is, both share the same deep structure. Now, consider the following set of sentences:

They are eating apples.
They are eating apples.

Now the surface structures are identical, but the two sentences may have different deep structures. The sentence could mean that "People are in the process of eating some apples" or "The apples are the type people like to eat." These examples show that sentences may have the same surface structures but different deep structures.

Understanding the relationship between the deep and the surface structure of a sentence is referred to as a **transformation.** Transformations include the realization that statements not only can be interpreted differently but also can be expressed in different tenses. Although our example, "The student attended the lifespan development class," used the past tense, it could also have been expressed in other ways, such as "The student attends the lifespan development class" or "The student will attend the lifespan development class."

THEORETICAL ISSUES

How do you view these three theoretical perspectives of language development? Do you favor one more than the others? Do you lean toward eclecticism, choosing to select bits and pieces from each perspective?

Chomsky stated that certain facets of the deep structure are innate and universal among all natural languages. But the surface structures are specific to each language. He also maintained that children may learn to make correct transformations by first forming **kernel words,** words that can be strung together to make a statement that is usually declarative. From these basic words, transformations are learned and sentences are produced.

Chomsky's theory is an important and influential contribution to the field of psycholinguistics. Moreover, research tends to support his ideas. For example, children do follow the same universal patterns of speech sounds, such as cooing and babbling, before uttering their first word. A number of researchers have also observed that the early sentences of children of different nationalities are grammatically similar. Although individual languages (surface structures) vary from country to country, the underlying deep structures are remarkably uniform. From 1.5 to 2 years, children everywhere learn their native language and use similar grammatical systems (Brown, 1973; Slobin, 1970).

The innate theory of language development also is supported by the fact that speech is possible only when youngsters have attained a certain stage of physical maturation. Language is thus seen as developing in children as a product of biological development, rather than as being initiated by external influences. In support of this, it has been found that certain phases of language development correlate consistently with specific motor skill accomplishments (Lenneberg, 1967).

Developmental Stages of Language   Understanding the developmental stages of language requires an awareness of **phonology,** the speech sounds relevant to a language. More specifically, we need to examine the nature of phonemes, morphemes, vowels, and consonants.

A **phoneme** is a language's most fundamental element. English has more than 40 such basic sounds, and when combined, phonemes form words. A **morpheme,** on the other hand, is the smallest meaningful unit of a language. Some words contain one morpheme, and others have several. For example, the word *boys* has two morphemes: *boy* and *s*. A **vowel,** the most prominent sound in a syllable, is produced when air flows freely through the mouth cavity as it passes over the vocal cords. A **consonant** is a speech sound characterized by constriction or closure at one or more points in the breath channel. Now that we have identified these speech sounds, let us turn to the early stages of language development.

CRYING Crying represents infants' earliest vocalizations. There are many different varieties of cries, from the whimpering to the fussy to the more piercing colicky cry (Gustafson & Green, 1991; St. James-Roberts & Halil, 1991). Each type of cry usually has meaning, and parents usually learn to distinguish among the many varieties (Bisping et al., 1990; Zeskind et al., 1992). Although crying is not a language, it represents a type of communication, as it is the means by which infants convey their basic needs. Usually variations of the cry are the only vocalizations that take place during the first 6 to 8 weeks of life.

How do adults learn to recognize the various types of infant cries? Abraham Sagi's (1981) research underscored the importance of experience. Sagi designed an experiment that required 36 mothers and 32 nonmothers to identify infants' hunger, pain, and pleasure cries. The nonmothers were pregnant

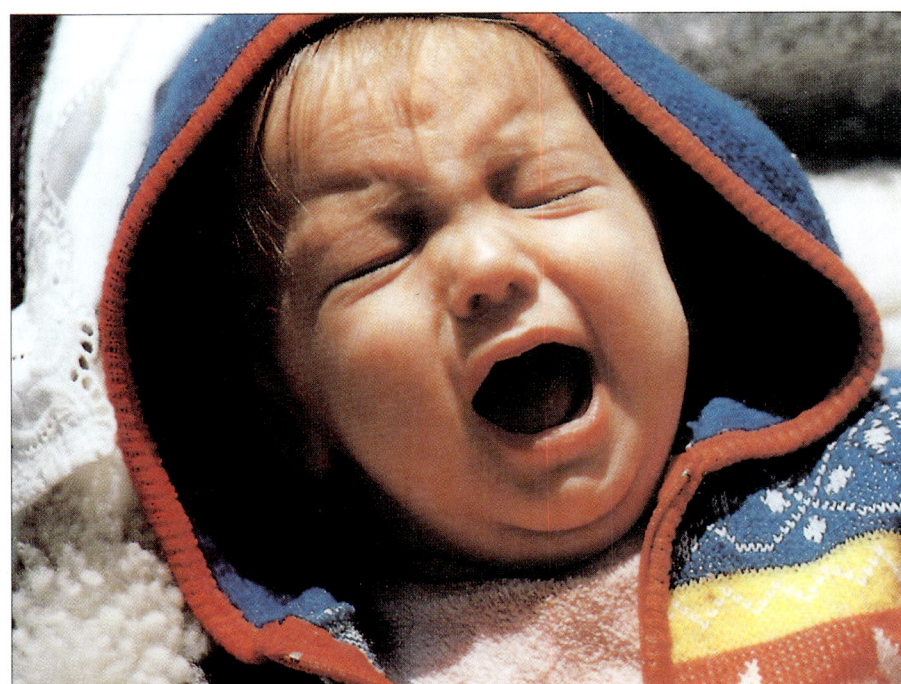

Crying represents an early form of communication.

women, 14 experienced in child care and 18 inexperienced. Among the mothers, 17 had one infant and 29 had one infant and an older child. The mothers responded more accurately than the nonmothers did, and in comparison with both the experienced and the inexperienced nonmothers, they were more skillful in identifying the infants' cries.

COOING AND BABBLING Between the second and third month, a type of vocalization called **cooing** emerges. Cooing includes such sounds as gurgling and mewing and generally indicates the infant is pleased, happy, or even excited. Though still not considered language, cooing, like crying, is a form of communication. It follows no grammatical rules and is an innate response. Also, it is expressed after a certain degree of maturation has been attained. More specifically, cooing requires muscular movements of the tongue that were not possible at birth. Cooing is a behavior that occurs not only in normal children but also in deaf youngsters. At approximately 8 months of age, it diminishes in all children.

At about 6 months, **babbling** emerges. Whereas cooing consists of vowel sounds, babbling includes both vowels and consonants. Infants from a variety of linguistic backgrounds babble in a similar fashion. This was shown in one study (Oller & Eilers, 1982) in which Spanish- and English-learning babies were compared. Syllable and vowel production was perceived as remarkably alike. In fact, for even the most sophisticated listeners, differences in the babbling of the two groups were hard to discern (Roug, Landberg, & Lundberg, 1989).

Babbling is important because it allows infants the opportunity to exercise their vocal apparatus, and it enables them to hear the range of sounds they are

INTERACTION OF HEREDITY AND ENVIRONMENT

Do you think an infant's state of biological maturation and readiness influences the effects of adult verbal stimulation? What kinds of brain cell maturation as well as control over the muscles of the throat, mouth, and tongue do infants need to respond to adult interaction? Can you see how such developments illustrate the constant interplay between biological and environmental influences?

capable of making. Babbling is also important because it is the first vocalization that bears any real resemblance to speech. Early phases in this developmental stage are often accompanied by excitation and motor movement. Infants seem to make sounds that arouse their interest. They often lie quietly while listening to sounds; at other times they babble in response to the verbal stimulation around them (Sachs, 1993). Whatever the context, babbling leads to increased control of sound (Blake & Boysson-Bardies, 1992; Levitt & Utman, 1992; Tiegerman, 1993).

During these early stages of development, children need the benefit of adult language stimulation. Such stimulation is regarded as critical to children's overall language development. Children need to hear speech around them in order to realize their linguistic potential (L. B. Adamson, 1992; Hoff-Ginsberg, 1991; Masataka, 1992; Valdez-Menchaca & Whitehurst, 1992). Adults who offer language stimulation to infants encourage more sound production than adults who offer no stimulation at all. Furthermore, such early stimulation appears to have long-lasting linguistic and cognitive benefits (Hulit & Howard, 1993; Obler, 1993; Owens, 1992).

An interesting cross-cultural investigation (Sigman et al., 1988) illustrates the positive benefits of language stimulation for the child. In this study, the social interactions experienced by Embu children between 15 and 30 months of age growing up in a rural Kenyan community were observed bimonthly. Children who were talked to frequently, whose vocalizations were responded to, and who engaged in sustained social interactions were rated higher on motor and mental achievement scales and showed more positive effect than children who were involved in limited forms of linguistic and social interaction.

THE HOLOPHRASE STAGE Few verbal accomplishments are more exciting to witness than the emergence of the first word, known technically as the **holophrase** stage. After cries, gurgles, cooing, and babbling, there is something magical about an infant's first word. On the average, this milestone occurs between the ages of 12 and 18 months. Although there are variations in the types of words acquired (Owens, 1992; Rice, 1989; Tiegerman, 1993), young children appear first to learn words that relate to important people, food, toys, body parts, and animals. These early words are primarily concrete nouns and verbs. However, we must recognize that the child may not understand all words spoken. That is, some words are acquired through imitation, so the youngster may not know what they actually represent.

This one-word stage becomes surprisingly complex over time. In fact, a one-word utterance may represent a complete sentence with its own sentence structure. As an illustration, the word *toy* may mean "I want my toy," "My toy is in the corner," or "My toy makes funny sounds." Holophrases thus come to mean the designated objects as well as the roles these objects play in the child's environment. Understanding the various meanings of one-word expressions is a difficult task for adults, who frequently have to pay close attention to voice intonations, gestures, and facial expressions in order to understand what is being said (Hulit & Howard, 1993; Maxim, 1993; Owens, 1992).

We might add, too, that before and during the holophrase stage, there is frequently a gap between the words to which children can mentally respond and those they can express verbally. Typically, infants can understand words before they can speak them. Known as the *receptive versus the expressive lag,* this linguistic phenomenon means that even though children cannot articulate words, they can nevertheless demonstrate their understanding of them or of directions spoken by adults. Thus an infant of 11 months may be able to follow the directive "Get the ball," yet may lack the linguistic ability to speak that same sentence or even parts of it. In time, however, the discrepancy between reception and expression lessens. Alert adults realize a child's inability to express words does not automatically mean he or she does not understand the situation at hand. On the contrary, children know much more than their linguistic ability allows them to express.

EARLY SENTENCES By approximately 18 months, children start using two-word expressions. Usually these utterances consist of single words that exist as separate entities. When spoken, there are separate intonations and pauses between the words. But eventually, they are connected and used in succession. The child's growing awareness of relations among words is considered influential in the development of early sentences as well as in other facets of cognitive activity (Hulit & Howard, 1993; Tager-Flusberg, 1993; Waxman & Senghas, 1992).

Sentence arrangement during toddlerhood consists of pivot and open class words. **Pivot words** are usually shorter and slower in developing than open class words. For instance the word *go* may be acquired and later become a pivot word used in such combinations as "Toy go," "Mommy go," or "Me go." The pivot word is usually, but not always, used as the second word in these sentences. Compared with open class words, pivot words rarely exist as single-word expressions. **Open class words,** conversely, consist of any of a large number of words that are not considered pivot words. Early vocabulary growth usually is of the open class variety.

Following the development of two-word expressions come telegraphic sentences. **Telegraphic sentences** are short and simple and consist mainly of nouns and verbs. They are labeled telegraphic because the sentences lack some words, as well as tense endings on verbs, plural endings on nouns, prepositions, and conjunctions. Despite such grammatical omissions, the words necessary to give the sentence meaning are included. As an illustration, suppose we wanted to put the following sentence into telegraphic form: "The soup I'm eating is hot." The telegraphic version is "Soup hot" or "This soup is hot." Note that the telegraphic sentence resembles a telegram.

Besides the developments made in sentence structure, there are other important linguistic gains. For example, the average vocabulary of a 3-year-old hovers near 900 words. Children's knowledge of **syntax,** or knowledge of grammatical rules, **semantics,** understanding word meanings, and **pragmatics,** the use of language in social situations, increases daily as they use language more and more as a vehicle to express their thoughts (Pease, Gleason, & Pan, 1993; Warren & McCloskey, 1993). Gains in speech perception and production during infancy and toddlerhood, as well as advancements in verbal comprehension, are widely noted in the literature (Hall, 1991; Jones, Smith, & Landau, 1991; Lieven et al., 1992; Marean et al., 1992; Reznick & Goldfield, 1992).

By their third year, youngsters are capable of becoming effective participants in conversations, even when the conversation involves more than two people (Dunn & Shatz, 1989). They are also becoming more skilled at adapting their verbalizations, such as requests, to the responses given by those around them (Marcos & Kornhaberle, 1992). And research (e.g., Morford & Goldin-Meadow,

1992) shows that toddlers are able to understand the use of gestures when they are used in combination with speech. Indeed, toddlers in this study were also able to understand gestures when they substituted for speech.

Toddlers are also adept at using a variety of word elements. For example, they are able to make plural nouns by adding an "s" and are able to put verbs in the past tense by adding "ed." Although such general rules permit inflections of regular words, irregular words pose difficulties. Consequently, the logical rules for making nouns plural and putting verbs into the past tense are indiscriminately applied to irregular words. Thus "foots" or "feets" may be the result of incorrect pluralization, and the "ed" ending may produce such incorrect inflections as "goed" for "went" or "doed" for "did."

Although such word endings may be amusing, pause for a moment and consider the child's logic for using them. If you look beyond the obvious incorrect inflection, the child has in fact mastered an important principle of the English language. That is, to form the past tense, one must add "ed." This the child has correctly done but has been tricked by the inconsistency of the English language.

Such a mistake is called an **overregularization** and is evidence that a language is not exclusively acquired through reinforcement or imitation. Youngsters could not have learned such words as "goed" or "doed" from adults because grownups do not use such overregularizations. Rather, children fabricate these words on the basis of overgeneralizing the principles they have learned. For a good review of the literature on overregularization, see Marcus and colleagues (1992).

UNIT REVIEW—

↗ Cognition consists of those mental processes pertaining to thinking, perceiving, and understanding.

↗ Piaget's sensorimotor stage encompasses the first 2 years of life and has six substages.

↗ Key concept refinement occurs in the areas of shape and size, space, class, and time.

↗ Cognition is greatly enhanced by developing memory abilities. Three types of memory storage systems are sensory memory, short-term memory, and long-term memory. Metacognition and metamemory skills have the potential of improving memory abilities throughout the lifespan.

↗ Children are also more alert to their environment because of improvements in vision, depth perception, audition, taste, smell, and touch.

↗ The brain contains language centers. There are several theories regarding how children learn a language, the most popular being the innate theory. Language follows a developmental progression: crying, cooing and babbling, the holophrase stage, and early sentences.

UNIT THREE: PERSONALITY AND SOCIAL DEVELOPMENT

Humans are social animals, and learning to make social adjustments is one of life's most important and complex developmental challenges. This task begins early in childhood and continues throughout life. In the beginning, socialization experiences are limited, but in time, youngsters become able to participate in new and challenging situations with others. The family, peer groups, and the school—to name but a few socialization agents—each influences the child in a unique way. The child will succeed in some social experiences, and these will generate positive self-regard. But other occurrences will be anxiety producing and ego threatening for the child. How each social situation is handled as time progresses will become a vital component of the child's developing personality.

Early social experiences enable children to understand themselves and their surroundings better. Indeed, their developing mental abilities fuse with early personality and social forces and enable them to create a sense of self, the realization that they are separate and unique individuals (Case, 1991b; Emde et al., 1991; Kagan, 1991; Lewis, 1991; Neisser, 1991). This developing awareness of how individuals perceive themselves and others, including other people's thoughts and feelings, is known as **social cognition.** Social cognition, requiring the use of developing mental strategies to understand oneself and the general fabric of social relations, clearly shows how developmental processes blend together.

Attachment

A child's parents and the emotional atmosphere of the home greatly influence the kind of person the youngster will become. During the early years, especially, parental attitudes toward the infant are critical. The infant may receive feelings that will foster a sense of love and security or those that will promote anxiety and mistrust.

Early personality and social development in particular is shaped by the infant's contact with someone who is familiar, trusted, and expected. **Attachment,** or the affectionate bond between infant and caregiver, is a vital component of healthy functioning (Bowlby, 1989; Egeland, 1989; Fox et al., 1989; Johnson & Fein, 1991; L. E. Schneider, 1991). Attachment serves as the first close relationship with another person and teaches the infant that others can be trusted. One's general tendency to be outgoing and friendly, as well as one's degree of social independence, temperament, and emotional investments in others, may be traced to the outcome of early attachment experiences (Cox et al., 1992; Vaughn et al., 1992). In this sense, infant attachments help determine the type of social animal we become, including the degree of comfort we feel in the presence of others.

Children develop strong attachments to both parents. However, the security of attachment to one parent is usually dependent on the security to the other parent (Fox, Kimmerly, & Schafer, 1991). In time, attachments will come to refer to those special relationships that make some people very important to a person and not readily replaceable by others. As they get older, children become attached to "best friends." Adolescents and adults in love become attached to their loved ones. Most individuals also become attached to groups, ideals, and even abstract ideas of great importance. Indeed, people seem to

CONTINUOUS AND DISCONTINUOUS HUMAN DEVELOPMENT

As you read this chapter's analysis of infancy and toddlerhood, do you see developments reflecting continuity and discontinuity? If you lean toward the continuity perspective, what kinds of developments do you see being added at a relatively gradual, uniform pace? From a discontinuous perspective, do you instead see certain developments occurring at different rates, fluctuating between periods of little change and times of abrupt change? Or do you see a mixture of the two positions?

develop their sense of self and identity out of their attachments as much as any other single factor (Bowlby, 1989; Hartup, 1989; Pederson et al., 1989; L. E. Schneider, 1991).

Utilizing a lifespan development perspective, Bem Allen (1990) observes that the dynamics of adult intimate relationships correspond to childhood attachments, and proposes some analogies between how people related to their parents and how they react to their intimate partners. For instance, the bond between parents and young children hinges in part on the responsivity and sensitivity of the parents. Whether youngsters in the first few years of life feel joy or distress depends on parents' sensitivity to their needs and willingness to fulfill their needs. Similarly, the mood of an individual depends considerably on whether one's partner is responding to his or her needs for affection and for reassurance that the relationship will continue.

According to Allen, youngsters whose parents come when beckoned by a cry or gesture and repeatedly demonstrate their love have a number of positive qualities. For instance, they tend to be happier than other children, whose parents are less attentive, less likely to be distressed, more willing to explore their surroundings, and more eager to interact with strangers. Individuals who are secure in the notion that their partners will be there for them when needed tend to be more relaxed, less defensive and worried, as well as more spontaneous and creative.

Also, behaviors that promote parent-child attachments include holding, touching, smiling, and making eye contact. Obviously, these are much the same behaviors that promote attachment between intimate partners. In addition, when separation occurs between children and parents as well as between intimate partners, common reactions are distress and sadness. Finally, those who are securely attached share an intense desire to share their accomplishments and discoveries. This is as true for children and parents as it is for partners within intimate relationships.

Theoretical Perspectives of Attachment   How and why does attachment occur? What determines the strength of the attachment bonds? Does attachment follow a developmental progression? Answering such questions has been an active field of investigation in the field of lifespan development, and from this research, four theoretical perspectives have emerged. These interpretations reflect the major schools of thought discussed in Chapter 2.

BEHAVIORAL THEORY Behavioral theory stresses that attachment is a learned, rather than an innate, process. This viewpoint suggests that attachment is a series of stimulus-response mechanisms, much as many other childhood behaviors are. It is reasoned that the mother, or other caregiver, who is initially a neutral stimulus, acquires secondary reinforcing properties over time. Infants learn the mother is the agent responsible for their primary reinforcers, such as tactile stimulation, milk, or warmth. Because she is continually associated with the dispensing of these primary reinforcers and with the satisfaction of the infant's basic needs, her continual physical presence becomes important to the infant.

COGNITIVE-DEVELOPMENTAL THEORY Cognitive-developmental theory views the attachment process as a reflection of the infant's developing mental abilities.

Bonds of attachment are formed early in life.

Attachment and proximity-seeking behavior ensue because the infant is cognitively aware of the perceptual differences between the mother and others in the environment. Attachment is further strengthened when the infant understands *person permanence,* the realization that the caregiver can exist even though she may not be physically present in the same room. The child's ability to construct a mental image of the mother's distinguishing characteristics will result in more proximity-seeking behavior.

ETHOLOGY THEORY Ethology theory proposes that an infant's social responsiveness develops largely through innate tendencies. A critical or sensitive period during the early months of life is said to make the infant especially receptive to the caregiver. During infancy, these innate systems are activated by the environment, and their expression elicits specific responses from the caregiver. Infant behaviors such as clinging and sucking promote close contact with the mother. Crying and distress capture the caregiver's attention, as do smiling and cooing. Later, infants call their mothers and follow them, further strengthening the bond between the two. Combined, these behaviors result in physical nearness and attachment to the caregiver. And as history reveals, infants who can maintain this closeness have the best hope for survival.

PSYCHOANALYTIC THEORY Finally, the psychoanalytic view, similar to the ethological approach, emphasizes instincts. Attachment is regarded as an emotional relationship shaped by the Freudian concept of instinctive psychic energy. During the child's psychosexual stages of development, this energy is directed toward the mother because she is perceived as a source of pleasure and satisfaction. As the child's primitive needs are met during the oral and anal stages, bonds of attachment strengthen, and the mother is recognized as a "love" object.

Indicators of Attachment   Besides the infant's desire to maintain contact with the caregiver, there are several visible clues to the developing attachment behaviors. One of these is the infant's smiling responses. During the first

INTERRELATEDNESS OF AGING PROCESSES

Utilizing your knowledge of the Piagetian developments occurring during the sensorimotor stage, do you see any connection between the concept of *person permanence* and *object permanence*? How do the two concepts compare and contrast? What other Piagetian principles you're familiar with might be applied to the study of attachment behavior?

month, the infant may form a *reflex smile*. This smile is primarily physiological and may be the infant's response to a number of different stimuli, including internal stimulation (a bubble of gas in the stomach), being fed, or being stroked on the cheek. Reflexive smiles are not socially oriented.

The *social smile* appears between the second or third month of life. This is true smiling as we know it and can be evoked by the appearance of a caregiver, a voice, movement, or certain noises. Many infants smile, open their eyes wide, and make cooing noises at the same time, called a "greeting response." As we see later on in this chapter, the caregiver's returning the greeting response often prompts the infant to continue this behavior.

The *selective social smile* occurs approximately between 5 and 6 months. Instead of smiling in an undifferentiated way, as in the social smile, the smile is now directed only to familiar social stimuli, such as the mother or other familiar caregivers. Unfamiliar faces are readily detected at this age and cause the infant's withdrawal behavior.

The selective social smile is linked to another clue of developing attachment behavior called **stranger anxiety.** During the first 6 months of life, infants do not express distress toward unfamiliar faces. At this point, though, anxiety and wariness are apparent when strangers are introduced. The infant is evidently able to detect a noticeable difference in the stranger's face, as compared with the mental image of the caregiver's features stored in his or her developing mind. Growing levels of cognitive awareness are thus connected to stranger anxiety as well as to the development of the social smile. As one might expect, the infant's overall distress levels are reduced when the primary caregiver is present, when the stranger approaches the infant with no sudden moves and shows positive affect, and when the stranger behaves naturally (Mangelsdorf, 1992; Smith, Eaton, & Hindmarch, 1982).

Remarkably, neonates just a few days old show some signs of distinguishing their mother's face from that of a stranger. This was apparent in a study undertaken by Gail Walton and colleagues (1992). Neonates between the ages of 12 and 36 hours produced significantly more sucking responses in order to see an image of their mother's face as opposed to the image of a stranger's face (Bushnell, Sai, & Mullin, 1989).

Another indication of attachment is **separation anxiety,** which occurs by approximately the 12th month. Separation from the caregiver is likely to result in the infants' considerable protest and distress. However, the infants' degree of protest and distress is affected by the situation in which they are left. For example, both their familiarity with the environment, including objects as well as people, as well as for some the possession of a transitional object (e.g., huggable doll or stuffed animal) tend to reduce anxious feelings and protest levels.

Individual Variations in Attachment   Attachment does not follow a universal pattern. Rather, there are individual variations in attachment behavior. For example, the strength of the attachment bond and its quality and security may differ from child to child. Also, there are psychological and emotional determinants of the attachment bond, such as the mother's expressive behaviors and personality stability (Izard et al., 1991; Van Ijzendoorn et al., 1992).

Lifespan development researchers have devised a number of ways to classify attachment behaviors. Three types of attachment, in particular, tend to be widely referred to in the literature: *securely attached, anxious-resistant,* and *anxious-avoidant.* Behaviors unique to each category can be observed when infants are placed in strange and unfamiliar surroundings, such as a room they've never seen before.

When placed in such a situation, *securely attached* infants typically turn to their mothers for comfort when it is needed, but they also attempt to explore the environment. They also exhibit little anxiety when their mothers are away for short periods of time. Upon the mother's return, however, these infants are happy and desire close contact with her.

Anxious-resistant infants do not explore the environment when they are placed in unfamiliar situations with their mothers. They are likely to be anxious and distressed when the mother is temporarily away and are ambivalent toward her when she returns. Upon her return, infants may cling to her at one point and then push her away.

Anxious-avoidant infants are relatively unattached to their mothers and exhibit little anxiety or distress when left alone. Furthermore, they demonstrate little response when their mothers reappear. Often, many will ignore their mother when she returns.

These three types of attachments are the result of different parenting styles. The mothers of securely attached infants usually are responsive and sensitive to their infants' needs. These mothers have succeeded in fostering a sense of trust and security in their children. Additionally, secure attachment reaps other benefits. For example, research shows (e.g., Pipp et al., 1992) that compared to insecurely attached infants, securely attached infants exhibit more complex knowledge about themselves and their mothers. Moreover, they interact more readily with others beyond the home, such as with child-care workers (Howes & Hamilton, 1992). Also, mother-toddler interaction during problem-solving tasks, particularly the quality of assistance and support given, is more evident among securely attached dyads. More specifically, positive attachment and involvement at home tends to predict effective, unconflicted problem-solving behaviors (Frankel & Bates, 1990).

The mothers of anxious-resistant infants tend to be insensitive and unresponsive to their children's needs. The latter holds true for mothers of anxious-avoidant infants, although they also tend to be more rejecting, particularly when their children desire close physical contact (Smith & Pederson, 1988; Thompson, Connell, & Bridges, 1988). Research also shows (e.g., Achermann, Dinneen, & Stevenson-Hinde, 1991) that compared to securely attached children, anxious-avoidant youngsters tend to ignore their mother's requests (e.g., during cleanup times after play activities), and exhibit greater amounts of babyish behavior. Other research (Fagot & Kavanaugh, 1990; Turner, 1991) shows that insecurely attached female children are more difficult to deal with and have more difficulty with peers than girls who are securely attached. Insecurely attached boys, on the other hand, tend to display greater levels of aggression and attention-seeking behaviors.

There are also other aspects of these attachment categories to consider. For example, mothers of securely attached infants often perceive greater support from their husbands than do the mothers of anxious-resistant and anxious-avoidant infants. It is proposed that mothers who do not perceive support from their husbands may experience higher levels of stress than those who do receive support. Consequently, they may be less psychologically available to their infants (Durrett et al., 1984).

THEORETICAL ISSUES

What role do you think the Eriksonian element of basic trust plays in the attachment relationship? Do you think its presence contributes to secure attachment? On the other hand, does mistrust plant the seeds for insecure attachment?

Evidence also exists (Jacobson & Frye, 1991) that social support from beyond the family assists mothers in forging bonds of attachment with their infants. In this investigation, low-income mothers between the ages of 17 and 32 were the recipients of maternal support and information from trained childcare specialists. The mothers received this support prenatally as well as during the first year postpartum. A control group of similarly matched mothers did not benefit from the intervention. At 14 months, infants from the experimental group scored higher than the control group on an attachment ratings scale.

In a related study, Alicia Lieberman and associates (1991) examined how psychotherapy can improve the quality of attachment and social-emotional functioning of mothers and infants. In the study, anxiously attached mothers and their children were assigned either to an experimental group, which received psychotherapeutic intervention over the course of one year, or a control group. During follow-up investigations, the intervention toddlers were significantly lower in avoidance, resistance, and anger, and significantly higher in partnership with their mothers than those in the control group. Additionally, intervention mothers had higher scores than those in the control group in empathy and interactiveness with their children. Studies such as these indicate that the presence of a supportive spouse, as well as the availability of outside social support groups and psychotherapeutic intervention, are influential in helping mothers create secure bonds of attachment to their children. For a unique cross-cultural contrast of attachment and child-rearing practices, see the accompanying Focus on Diversity box.

Attachment and Contact/Comfort   Researchers have long sought to find out why youngsters are drawn to **transitional objects,** soft objects that offer comfort to children, such as a security blanket, a cuddly stuffed animal, or a huggable doll. Moreover, the study of transitional objects helps to shed light on attachment behaviors because infants usually cling to the mother's clothing when feeding, or when seeking comfort or security.

A number of research investigations conducted by Harry Harlow (1958, 1962, 1971; Harlow & Zimmerman, 1959; Suomi & Harlow, 1971) have helped explain why such behaviors exist. Harlow's research focused on the behavior of rhesus monkeys in laboratory situations. In this study, two surrogate (substitute) mothers were built and placed in a cage; one was constructed of wire meshing and the other of the same material covered with a terry cloth wrapping. Each "mother" was equipped with a nursing bottle (the nipple of which protruded through the "chest") and a light bulb behind the body, which provided heat for the infant.

The infant monkeys were then divided into two groups; group A could receive nourishment only from the nursing bottle placed in the wire mother, whereas group B could receive milk from the bottle of the cloth-covered mother. The monkeys in group A fed from the wire mother, but they gradually spent less time with her. Eventually, these monkeys took nourishment and then spent the intervening time with the more comforting cloth mother. Several infants even clung to the cloth mother while reaching over to feed from the wire mother. On the other hand, the infants in group B spent considerable time clinging to the soft covering of their cloth mother and almost never ventured over to the other wire figure.

The cloth mother also played a central role in reducing the infant's fear and anxiety. This was apparent when a strange object (a mechanical teddy bear) was introduced into the cage with the infant, the cloth mother, and the wire mother. The infant invariably ran to the cloth mother and clung to her for security. After its fear was reduced by this form of contact and comfort, the infant would venture short distances from the mother and eventually attempt to explore the new object.

Harlow also studied the later behavior of those monkeys not benefiting from a real mother. It was learned that the mother's absence had severely hampered the monkeys' normal development, particularly in social and emotional maturation. Whereas the monkeys reared with cloth mothers overtly showed no problems in infancy, some were retarded later in life when compared with monkeys brought up by real mothers. More specifically, the experimental monkeys became socially maladjusted, ignoring others, and frequently passing time by biting and hugging themselves. Later, some of the females in the study group proved to be poor mothers, neglecting and abusing their young. However, when placed in the company of normal monkeys, the socially isolated monkeys began to recover from the effects of their experimental environment. This was largely because the normal monkeys encouraged social interaction and play behavior and discouraged solitary behavior. More recent research supports these studies and also suggests that formerly isolated monkeys adopted by a female within a social group become less maladjusted over time (Reite, Kaemingk, & Boccia, 1989).

THEORETICAL ISSUES

Can you think of ways the personality theories of Freud or Erikson can be applied to the study of why children use transitional objects? What other lifespan development theories might prove applicable?

The need for comfort and security is expressed in many ways.

Focus on Diversity

CHILDREN OF THE DREAM

In Israel, a unique type of child rearing contrasts sharply with the American style of upbringing and offers a unique cross-cultural view of attachment. The Israeli *kibbutz* is a collective settlement in which work is shared and everyone works toward common goals. In the kibbutz, children are reared in group settings, from the nursery to high school. The group of children into which one is born remains the same, and as a result, close bonds of attachment usually develop. During infancy, a *metapalet* (a child-care worker of the kibbutz) tends to the baby's basic needs. Parents visit the infant daily, and the mother returns as often as necessary to feed the child. When the infant is weaned from the mother, the metapalet assumes full responsibility for feeding the youngster.

As the children grow older, they move to other living arrangements and come into contact with other metapalets and teachers. During adolescence, teenagers are part of the "youth movement" that exposes them to the kibbutz and communal sphere. They are encouraged to make group decisions and to develop such capacities as cooperation and sensitivity toward others. At the end of adolescence, members of the kibbutz work with the adults and contribute to the economy.

Initially, it was hoped the kibbutz arrangement would revolutionize Jewish society and remove the division of social classes. In so doing, kibbutz youngsters represent the "children of the dream." The elimination of gender-role stereotyping and the patriarchal family structure was also envisioned. However, these goals have not yet been attained. For example, one source (Eshleman, 1991) notes that even though the kibbutz was founded on gender-egalitarian terms, most of the men are in agricultural and industrial roles and most of the women are in service or educational roles.

Research does show, however, that the children of the kibbutz grow up to be competent, emotionally stable, and well adjusted. For example, research (Levy-Shiff, 1983) shows that compared to Israeli family-reared youngsters, kibbutz children were more autonomous and self-reliant when faced with routine and daily tasks. Another study (Shapiro, 1982) revealed that kibbutz youngsters exhibit more effective stress-coping strategies, which may be related to the many attachments and adaptation abilities formed during the early years in the kibbutz. Other investigations (e.g., Nisan, 1984) tell us kibbutz children are better at sharing and cooperating than are

Harlow maintained that the maladjusted behaviors were probably caused by the real mothers gradually curtailing the clinging activities and promoting the infants' autonomy. The contact in infancy that real mothers provide also promotes the formation and differentiation of facial and bodily postural expressions, a factor that may make later social interactions easier.

All of Harlow's research has given us more insight into our knowledge of transitional objects as well as attachment behaviors. His research indicates that satisfaction of the hunger drive does not by itself promote and nurture the infant's attachment to the mother, a belief held for years by many. Rather, the attachment to the mother is encouraged by the need to establish contact with something that can offer comfort, softness, and warmth. Moreover, this need often manifests itself in the young child's selection of a cuddly or huggable transitional object. The use of a transitional object is considered a normal phase

nonkibbutz youngsters, and that their moral reasoning is more directed to the humanness of needy others (Eisenberg, Hertz-Lazarowitz, & Fuchs, 1990). However, other researchers (Bar-Tal, Raviv, & Shavit,1981) do not support the claim the kibbutz children are more altruistic than the nonkibbutz children.

Miriam Rosenthal (1991) compared the daily experiences of Israeli toddlers from kibbutz settings, family day care, and other out-of-home centers. From the perspective of the overall educational environment, the kibbutz was found to have the highest "structural" indicators of quality: small groups, small adult-to-child ratios, educational programming, training and experience of caregivers, and physical environment. And although no differences were found between the behaviors of caregivers from these three settings, kibbutz children engaged more often in both positive learning experiences and social behavior.

Moving beyond the realm of child development, it is interesting to see how kibbutz experiences impact on other facets of life. One study (Kaffman, 1989) examined how the living circumstances in the kibbutz affect the quality and intensity of postdivorce conflict. On the one hand, it can be reasoned that some of the friction attached to child custody and marital issues is minimized by the kibbutz framework of communal living. Conversely, it is possible that postdivorce tension intensifies due to the inevitable daily contact between the ex-spouses in the small, enmeshed social unit of the kibbutz. To find out which of the two scenarios was more likely, the researcher queried 100 divorced parents. Results showed that two thirds of the respondents had reached a satisfactory emotional and functioning level of adjustment with a high degree of cooperation between the ex-spouses by the second postseparation year.

Finally, the impact of the kibbutz on adult perceptions of occupations has been analyzed (Snarey & Lydens, 1990). As we discover in Chapter 9, adults' occupational status proves influential in shaping the course of moral and ego development. To discover the relative impact of employment on these developmental areas, kibbutz workers were compared with workers from an Israeli city and North American employees. Interestingly, results showed that kibbutz workers' moral and ego development was not significantly associated with educational, occupational, or social class standing. Such trends were likely due to the economic equality and collective ownership of property in the kibbutz. However, the other workers' moral and ego development was significantly associated with all measures of social status. Furthermore, work complexity was significantly associated with both moral and ego development only for kibbutz workers, suggesting they engage in jobs that are appropriate to their psychological development without creating social inequality.

of child development, particularly when youngsters encounter novel, irritating, or threatening situations (Lookabaugh & Fu, 1992). Transitional objects are typically outgrown as immature and dependent behavior is replaced with more independence and a more secure sense of self.

Gender-Role Development

There are many questions we can ask about gender differences in behavior, not only during the years of infancy and toddlerhood but throughout the lifespan. For example, are boys more physically active and aggressive than girls? Are women more nurturant and emotionally sensitive than men? Are there gender differences in the ways males and females engage in problem solving or other facets of cognitive processing?

Beneath such questions are more basic issues. If women and men do differ in such ways, what are the factors that create these differences? Are they biological or environmental? Or do gender differences result from the interaction of these two forces?

Searching for the answers to such questions is a persistent theme throughout this textbook. Although most of us are born clearly male or female, just knowing what sex we are doesn't necessarily establish how "feminine" or "masculine" we feel we are or how we conceptualize the roles we will play in society. The culture into which we're born teaches us what attitudes and behaviors are appropriate to our gender, and gradually we develop an identity, a sense of self, that incorporates these teachings or, sometimes, rebels against them. As we'll see, this development of the way we see ourselves functioning as men or women in society has important implications not only for our individual development but for the way we interact with others throughout the life cycle.

In the first part of this discussion, we introduce some important terminology designed to enhance your understanding of the material on gender-role development that appears throughout the textbook. We then spend some time examining some important theoretical perspectives on gender-role development. Finally, we explore how gender-role development begins during the years of infancy and toddlerhood.

Sex and Gender: Some Definitions and Guidelines   Students of lifespan development must understand that rather specific terminology is employed when describing how humans develop into men and women. At the most fundamental level, **sex** refers to a person's biological status of being a male or female. This biological status can be further broken down into **genetic sex,** which is determined by our chromosomal makeup, and **anatomical sex,** the physical characteristics and features that distinguish females from males. **Gender,** on the other hand, refers to the social meanings attached to being a female or male. Gender, then, can be thought of as encompassing the social dimensions of masculinity or femininity; sex refers to the genetic and sexual anatomy with which one is born.

To proceed a step further, **gender identity** is the psychological awareness or sense of being either a male or a female. It is generally accepted that gender identity occurs by age 3. A **gender role** refers to a set of expectations that prescribes how females and males should behave. Understanding the concept of gender roles is very important, for gender roles determine hundreds of things we do everyday. They prescribe the way we sit, the way we stand, the kinds of jobs we take, and the kinds of people we choose as mates. They also account for a host of other expectations, ranging from who washes the dishes to who stays home with the children.

A **gender-role stereotype** is a generalization that reflects our beliefs about females and males. Gender-role stereotypes reflect expected characteristics or behaviors, attributes, or actions that men and women actually possess or exhibit, or want to possess or exhibit. Gender-role stereotypes ascribe certain characteristics or behaviors to all representatives of a group whether individual members possess them or not. For example, you have surely heard people say girls are emotional and dependent and boys are aggressive and competent.

Such stereotypes abound in our society, and throughout the text we explore their impact on overall sexual and gender-specific behavior.

Theoretical Perspectives of Gender-Role Development

How do children acquire gender roles? Is gender-role learning an active or passive process? What forces shape gender-appropriate behaviors? Much like other topics we've covered in this chapter, some of lifespan development's major theories can be applied to the study of gender-role development. We review four of these theories: cognitive-developmental, behavioral, social learning, and psychoanalytic theories.

COGNITIVE-DEVELOPMENTAL THEORY Cognitive-developmental theory suggests that gender role emerges through the child's growing cognitive awareness of his or her sexual identity. Once youngsters can consistently conceive of themselves as male or female, they organize their world on the basis of gender. Put another way, heightened levels of cognition enable children to realize that specific roles, activities, and behaviors are gender appropriate. In this fashion, a young boy decides, "I am a boy. I like to do the things boys do; the chance to do these things is rewarding."

Cognitive-developmental theory emphasizes that the child is an active, rather than passive force in his or her gender-role formation. The reinforcement for imitating sex-typed behaviors originates from *within* the child, not from external socializers such as parents or siblings. Thus, rather than simply imitating behavior, the child reasons before she does so. But if gender identity is linked to the cognitive status of the youngster, cognitive-developmental theory fails to address several important issues. For example, it does not adequately explain how and why children acquire gender identity at the surprisingly early age of 3. For that matter, it does not tell us why children aged 1 to 2 years who have not acquired gender identity nonetheless display sex-typed play activities (Etaugh, Collins, & Gerson, 1975).

BEHAVIORAL THEORY Behavioral theory proposes that gender-role behaviors are conditioned by the environment through the mechanisms of reinforcement and punishment (reinforcement would serve to strengthen a desired response whereas punishment would serve to weaken an undesirable response). Children typically receive rewards and punishments from a parent for behaviors consistent with the youngster's gender role. To illustrate, a young girl rewarded (e.g., given praise or approval) for her involvement in stereotypically female activities (washing the dishes; cleaning the house) is likely to repeat such behavior in the future. A young boy who is punished, ridiculed, or scolded for engaging in feminine activities ("that's a sissy game") or being overly sensitive ("big boys don't cry") will be unlikely to repeat such behaviors in the future.

In contrast to cognitive-developmental theory, which emphasizes a person's active construction and regulation of gender development, behavioral theory views the individual as a passive participant, being shaped and molded by environmental influences. Proponents of behavioral theory maintain that children are exposed to an unending flow of environmental situations which ultimately condition behavior, be it in the home, neighborhood, school, or media. Critics point out that behavioral theory oversimplifies behavior and downplays the free

GENDER SIMILARITIES AND DIFFERENCES

How much of what you've heard about gender-role stereotypes is true? Given the fact that men and women are fairly similar in most developmental areas, why do you think gender-role stereotypes paint such a different picture? Do you think most gender-role stereotypes devalue women and place men in a more favorable light? Why is this so?

A number of forces shape the course of a child's gender-role development.

will of the child. Indeed, critics argue that gender development is more active than this theory suggests and entails considerably more cognitive involvement.

SOCIAL LEARNING THEORY The social learning theory of gender-role development, like behavioral theory, suggests that individuals are shaped by their environment. However, this approach emphasizes the way boys and girls specifically imitate the gender-typed behaviors they observe. Some of the models children use are parents, peers, teachers, and the people they see on television. Thus when a boy sees on television or in real life that men usually handle mechanical repairs around the house, he learns that tending to such chores represents an activity appropriate for him to engage in.

Social learning theorists argue that such observational learning need not involve tangible reinforcements or punishments to acquire or extinguish a behavior; rather, observation and imitation are intrinsically gratifying. In recent years, a revised social learning theory has emerged that blends internal cognitive states and social behavior. Even this new cognitive social learning theory has been criticized, however, for failing to clearly address the cognitive aspects of imitation processes.

PSYCHOANALYTIC THEORY Psychoanalytic theory proposes that a child develops gender roles by interacting closely with a parent and imitating the parent's behavior. Psychoanalytic theory holds that a boy assumes his father's gender-typed behaviors because of the Oedipus complex, or the boy's romantic attachment to his mother (see Chapter 6). The attributes of the father are perceived as being those that captured the love of the mother, and are thus emulated by the boy. For girls, the Electra complex creates a similar situation, although in this case the daughter becomes romantically attached to her father and imitates her mother's behaviors. Beyond the Oedipus and Electra complexes, Freud did offer one other perspective on identification. That is, children develop strong emotional attachment and dependence on nurturant parents. The closeness offered by such parents leads to childhood identification and emulation.

Unlike the previous frameworks, psychoanalytic theory proposes that imitation is largely an unconscious effort; that is, children are not aware of taking on the characteristics seen in others. Today, many lifespan development researchers do not feel psychoanalytic theory adequately explains the course of gender development, at least in terms of Freud's emphasis on childhood sexual attraction. However, we offer it to you as food for thought and encourage you to compare and contrast it with the book's other theoretical perspectives.

Early Gender-Role Development For many, this socialization process begins at birth, when the infant is swaddled in a pink or blue hospital blanket. As time goes on, children receive different gender-typed behaviors from their mothers and fathers. In homes having traditional gender roles, mothers are typically nurturant and affectionate and indulge in cuddling, kissing, and stroking their children. Fathers display their affection through outdoor activities, roughhousing, and sharing hobbies and sports. Many parents are concerned that their boys be "masculine" and their girls "feminine." No wonder children have established at an early age a fairly clear picture of what society thinks is appropriate gender-role behavior (Bussey & Bandura, 1992; Jacklin, 1989; Maccoby 1990; Martin & Little, 1990; Matlin, 1993).

To illustrate the traditional gender-role perceptions that adults hold, consider an investigation conducted by Denis Burnham and Mary Harris (1992). In this study, undergraduate students were shown videotapes of male and female babies, each of whom was randomly labeled with a male or female name. Infants labeled as male were perceived as significantly more masculine and stronger than those labeled as female. Analyses of actual gender showed that male babies were rated as less sensitive, more mature, more playful, and stronger than female babies. Similar results were obtained when mothers of infants evaluated the babies in the experiment.

The notion that parents have different gender expectations for the youngest of children is evident in the various paraphernalia designed for infants. Laurel Richardson (1988) observes that there are different styles and colors for male and female infants in such basics as cribs, potty seats, comforters, changing tables, diaper pins, toys, and most important, in infant clothing. For example, dresses hang on the girls' clothing racks; pants and shorts abound on the boys' racks. Even the popular and somewhat unisex romper suits are adorned with "masculine" or "feminine" motifs like baseballs or footballs and butterflies and ruffles.

Although Richardson believes some relaxation of the infant dress codes has taken place, the differences still persist. Girls are more readily dressed in boys' play clothes than the reverse. Moreover, when youngsters are "dressed up," the distinctions are more pronounced. Selecting different clothing styles not only signifies to others what sex the child is and therefore how the child is to be treated, but also facilitates or hampers the activity of the child.

A study conducted by Madeline Shakin and associates (1985) involving 24 infant girls and 24 infant boys and their parents found that although almost no parent spontaneously admitted selecting baby clothes on the basis of masculinity or femininity, most dressed their babies in colors and styles that announced the wearer's sex and surrounded them with accessories that advertised gender. Seventy-five percent of the girls in the study wore pink; 79% of the boys were dressed in blue; most of the others were dressed in either yellow or white. Blue was seldom seen on girls; red even more rarely. Even when a neutral outfit left a child's sex in question, passersby were usually tipped off by something like a

Gender roles are learned forms of behavior that children exhibit in many different ways.

THEORETICAL ISSUES

Do you think emerging gender-role behaviors reflect parental reinforcement of certain behaviors or children's emulation of adult actions? How can cognitive-developmental and psychoanalytic perspectives be applied to infant and toddler behaviors?

girl's pink pacifier or a blue carriage blanket. Despite the fact that the oldest infant in the study was only 13 months old, strangers correctly identified the babies' sex almost 90% of the time.

Reinforcement of gender differences will persist in many other ways throughout infancy and toddlerhood. Toys and games provide clues to the gender of the child, as do different sets of parental expectations for male and female youngsters. For example, parents are more likely to play vigorously with their sons and demonstrate more apprehension about physical danger to their daughters. Other cues are related to the child's general patterns of behavior. For instance, girls typically stay closer to their mothers while shopping or while playing outside. By the end of the first year, boys have usually ventured further out into their environment and attained greater degrees of social independence than girls (Brody & Steelman, 1985; Doyle, 1985; Maccoby, 1987, 1990).

Throughout all of childhood, parents must realize that gender-role development is an important facet of one's overall personality. It's in toddlerhood that parents begin to see clearly a child's first awareness of which sex he or she belongs to, the roles the identification brings with it, and some of the gender expression of that role. Toddlers of both sexes need to know that whichever sex they are, it is worthy. Moreover, both girls who are rascally and boys who are placid need to feel accepted for themselves, rather than be pushed into a stereotypical mold (Oppenheim et al., 1984; Turner & Rubinson, 1993).

■ Emotional Development

Emotions are defined as changes in arousal levels that may either interfere with or facilitate motivated behavior. Usually emotions are accompanied by a physiological response, such as an increase in blood pressure, heart rate, or muscle tension. Furthermore, there are overt emotional behaviors, such as facial expressions or body movements, as well as an individual's cognitive interpretation of his or her emotional state.

Emotions are highly complex states, not only in children but in adults as well. Consequently, a thorny issue in lifespan development is how to best classify or categorize emotions (Ekman, 1992; Izard, 1992; Panksepp, 1992; Turner & Ortony, 1992). It becomes especially hard for researchers exploring infant emotions, as there is a lack of differentiated emotional responsiveness at birth. Cultural variations in emotions also complicate classification efforts and need to be taken into account (Mesquita & Frijda, 1992; Russell, 1991).

Complicating the issue is that the infants' outward emotional expressions may not correspond to their inner state. For example, crying or weeping are behaviors that may mean, among other things, a reaction to pain, hunger, or discomfort. With time, however, it is generally acknowledged that infants' emotional behavior becomes more complex and differentiated. Moreover, their abilities to recognize emotional states in others become more sophisticated (Bloom, Beckwith, & Capatides, 1988).

Research attempts to evaluate infant emotions not by studying just the infant but by attempting to study the interaction between the infant and the environmental stimuli that are causing the emotion. More specifically, it has been theorized that infant behavior is goal directed. For example, they want to play peek-a-boo or socialize in some other way, or look at an object. If the infant changes goals while interacting with the caregiver, but the caregiver does not realize this, the interaction may become unsatisfactory to the infant, thus producing an emotional change (Tronick, 1989). For example, when mothers stare at their infants using an expressionless or "still face," 6-month-old infants decrease smiling and gazing at their mothers and grimace more during this time (Gusella, Muir, & Tronick, 1988).

The infant, then, is part of a two-way affective communication system in which the infant's goal-directed strivings are aided by the caregiver. This has been called *other-directed regulatory behaviors* because it is an attempt by infants to have some other person satisfy their goals (Gianino & Tronick, 1988). The infant, however, is not solely dependent on the caretaker, for infants have coping behaviors such as looking away or sucking the thumb during a disturbing event. Both of these actions lower the heart rate, indicating an emotional change. These coping behaviors have been labeled *self-directed regulatory behaviors,* suggesting that their function is to control and/or change the infant's emotional state (Gianino & Tronick, 1988). Let us now take a look at some emotions and emotional behaviors.

Crying   As we learned in the last unit, the infant cries with vigorous and total bodily expressions, largely as a result of hunger or other internal discomfort. Crying is also triggered by fatigue and environmental tension. The parent's ability to soothe the baby and provide continuous stimulation during these emotional outbursts is also critical to the length and the intensity of the crying.

The total amount of crying is generally reduced and the bodily expressions are milder by the end of the first year. Crying becomes less frequent over time. The reasons for crying depend on the situation, such as separation from the

INTERRELATEDNESS OF AGING PROCESSES

Think of as many different ways as you can that your emotional development—past and present— reflects biological, psychological, and social aspects of growth. How have these processes interrelated to shape the course of your emotions?

Emotions are highly complex states that become increasingly differentiated with age.

caregiver, unfamiliar and fear-invoking situations, physical pain, or frustration when goals are blocked.

Laughter and Humor   Smiling and laughter become part of a person's emotional mosaic at an early age. You will recall that smiling is usually elicited by the sound of a human voice and may eventually serve as an indicator of attachment to the caregiver. Interesting events, such as bright moving objects or the sounds of other people's voices, also produce smiling.

Simple interactions with adults may also elicit smiling and laughter. For example, the baby may smile, which prompts the mother to smile. The mother's smile may, in turn, motivate the child to smile again. In time, laughter becomes associated with other types of stimulation (e.g., tickling) or with feelings of well-being. Games, stories, and television may also develop humor at an early age. Similar to other emotions, humor becomes more fully developed as childhood progresses and cognitive skills become more mature (McGhee & Goldstein, 1983a, 1983b; Wyer & Collins, 1992).

Fear and Anxiety   A youngster's maturation level has much to do with early fears. As youngsters grow older, their social environment expands and exposes new areas of uncertainty and possible danger. However, what might have evoked fear in children at an early age may no longer do so as their cognitive skills develop. This suggests that the individual's emotional susceptibility to some fears increases with age. Supporting this is the fact that in early childhood, a youngster's fear of strangers decreases but the fear of imaginary creatures increases. As with all emotional adjustments, children unquestionably need the support, guidance, and gentle understanding of adults in overcoming their fears.

Anxiety, a state of inner apprehension toward a subjective danger, also has its beginnings in infancy. Two good examples of this emotional reaction are stranger and separation anxiety, discussed earlier in this unit. As infants and toddlers expand their social environments, they may encounter stressful situations. Parental demands such as weaning, eating on a schedule, and toilet training may contribute to their anxiety, as can traumatic situations such as abuse or hospitalization.

Anger and Aggression   Anger and aggression often result when attempts to reach a desired goal are blocked. When such an obstacle is encountered, the child will try to remove it. This reaction can be seen most readily when the child is threatened with the loss of the mother. Anger is often expressed for the first time when such a separation occurs.

As more demands are placed on the child, angry behavior becomes fairly commonplace. Temper tantrums are especially prevalent at this time (we offer some strategies on how to handle such angry outbursts in the accompanying Lifespan Development in Action box). Adjustment is particularly difficult for the infant and toddler in regard to personal care and social training. Outward-directed anger is frequently aimed at rigid demands in toilet training, dressing, eating, interruptions in desirable playtime activities, and being forced to go to

Lifespan Development in Action

CHILDREN'S TEMPER TANTRUMS: UNDERSTANDING THE EYE OF THE STORM

The scene is probably familiar to parents of young children everywhere. A youngster is interrupted during a favorite playtime activity and told to go to bed. Another picks up a new, unaffordable toy in a store and is instructed to put it down. Some youngsters may respond with a temper tantrum, an outward-directed and emotionally laden flow of anger. Temper tantrums are expressed in many ways, from crying and screaming to head banging and kicking. Yet no matter how they are channeled, tantrums seem to express the same message: anger and frustration in having to adjust to the rituals and demands of grown-up life.

Temper tantrums are a normal phase of childhood development, yet they represent the ultimate in negative expression. Although handling temper tantrums is an individual affair, most experts agree that giving in to the child's demands only reinforces this type of behavior and increases the likelihood of its future reappearance. Getting angry and upset also serves as a reinforcer because children can see their behavior is taking its toll. Most experts suggest that ignoring the tantrum until it has extinguished itself and then talking to the child at a less emotional moment is an effective technique. In social situations, some parents may prefer to remove the child in a firm manner to another location (e.g., bedroom, car) to avoid social discomfort. Whatever course of action is chosen, adults must choose an approach they are comfortable with and exercise consistency. Seeking to understand why temper tantrums develop from the child's standpoint and taking into account things such as irritability, fatigue, and adult demands on children may go a long way in dealing with this stormy stage of emotional development.

bed. Frequent irritability on the part of the child may develop from other causes, including bedwetting, fatigue, or illness.

Play Influences on the Developing Child

Play greatly influences personality and social development. In a sense, play represents children's work, a meaningful set of activities that will help them relate in a special way to their surroundings. Few activities reveal the child's character and resources for coping with the world more than everyday play does (Garvey, 1990).

A personal sense of identity is also established through play, as children realize who they are and what effects their actions may have on the people around them. In this sense, play serves important cognitive functions. Furthermore, play has individual as well as social functions. Individually, it gives children the opportunity to experience many of life's emotions and to view their position in life in relation to the rest of the world. Socially, play and games can bring children into contact with one another and enhance peer relationships. In the process, the meaning and value of cooperation, rules, order, and structure become clearer (Brownell, 1990; Howes, 1988; Howes, Unger, & Seidner, 1989; Rubin, 1990; Van Lieshout et al., 1990).

Even when toddlers are as young as 16 months, they pay attention to the behavior of others, especially slightly older children. For example, 30 toddlers aged 16 to 23 months were observed in family day-care homes. Each had access to both same-age and older peers. The toddlers preferred 2-year-olds to same-age peers and were more imitative and talkative when they were with the 2-year-olds than when they were with their peers (Rothstein-Fisch & Howes, 1988).

Exploratory and Manipulative Play   By the third or fourth month of life, infants engage in exploratory play. At this age, with their body movements becoming better controlled and organized, infants may enthusiastically examine and observe objects of interest in their surroundings (Pomerleau et al., 1992; Ruff et al., 1992). One early object of interest is their own body; delight may be expressed, for example, in placing the fingers in the mouth, inspecting the feet, or stimulating sensitive parts. Not only does this activity represent a source of amusement and pleasure, but it also enables infants to realize these body parts are their own. This realization, in turn, helps develop early self-concepts.

As infants gain control of their hands, they begin to engage in manipulative play. They become preoccupied with the feel of different items, such as a rattle, blanket, and pillow. This type of activity represents another enjoyable learning experience and allows infants to realize that objects can vary in size, shape, color, and texture. As play becomes more skilled and sophisticated, the treatment of objects becomes more diverse and sophisticated.

Interactions with the environment often lead to other types of play. As we discovered earlier, in some instances primitive games may evolve, depending on the reciprocity an adult can offer or the environmental effect a given action can cause. For example, an infant may laugh and solicit a smile from a nearby adult. This may encourage the infant to laugh again, with the hope of receiving another response. This type of exchange, with anticipated reactions from both

Early play behavior is often exploratory and manipulative.

young and old, may soon develop into a game and reflect active partnership (Fiese, 1990). However, utilizing information presented earlier in this chapter, it appears that mother-child dyads having secure attachment relationships are more adept at these active partnerships than those in insecure relationships. The former demonstrate greater capacities for synchronous, well-timed, and mutually rewarding exchanges (Isabella & Belsky, 1991).

An example of reciprocal play behaviors was evident in a research investigation involving toddlers and their mothers (Tamis-LeMonda & Bornstein, 1991). The study assessed play interactions when the toddlers were 13 and 20 months old. Between these ages, mothers and toddlers both moved toward higher levels of play, and changes in one partner's play were regularly associated with changes in the other partner's play. Thus play behaviors were increasingly characterized by mutuality and matched play interactions.

Play at this time also fuels one's sense of competence and enables children to observe the effects of their actions on their surroundings. This might occur when the infant pulls at a dangling toy, knocks toys against the sides of the crib to hear the noise they make, or drops them so as to watch them fall to the floor below. A fundamental understanding of cause-and-effect relationships has begun to develop.

Destructive Play   Another type of play taking place at this time and during the later years of childhood is *destructive play.* After building a tower in which one block is precariously balanced on another, for example, the structure may be playfully knocked down, only to be rebuilt again. Or after taking considerable time in creating a design on paper, the child may, moments later, destroy the picture by brushing wide streaks of dark paint across it.

This type of play is common and completely normal and has been given several explanations. While indulging in certain types of play, such as that just described, the child is in the process of creating. Through creating, the child

ACTIVE AND REACTIVE MODELS OF DEVELOPMENT

Do you think infant play behaviors reflect an active model of development? Or, taking a reactive position, do you think the reinforcing properties of environmental objects shape the infant's play? How do these two types of play scenarios mirror cognitive-developmental as well as behavioristic operating principles?

realizes certain objects have component parts that somehow relate to one another. Large blocks, he or she learns, will support smaller ones, and in the art example, dark colors overshadow light colors. In order to explore the endless possibilities of play toys, the child may try to change them, either by rearranging them or knocking them down. Through this process, a further understanding of causal relationships is nurtured, a cognitive development critical to the overall refinement of mental abilities.

Another explanation is that destructive play is the child's way of exhibiting control over the environment. To be sure, the creations made are the child's, and the child can do with them whatever he or she pleases. Furthermore, destructive play may serve as a means for releasing inner tensions and hostilities, particularly on nonthreatening objects. Such behavior is discussed more fully in Chapter 6, where we learn how the developing child learns to cope with life's failures and frustrations.

▬ Theories of Personality Development

Sigmund Freud's Psychosexual Theory   Sigmund Freud, as we learned in Chapter 2, was the founder of the psychoanalytic school of thought. In his psychosexual theory of personality development, Freud defined the first 18 months of life as the **oral stage** of development and suggested that the mouth is the primary source of pleasure and satisfaction to the developing child. (The mouth and other sensitive body parts, such as the anus and the genitals, are referred to in Freudian terminology as *erogenous zones.*) Freud stated that the infant is "pleasure bent on sucking," and regardless of whether or not one is an advocate of Freudian theory, any individual who observes an infant sucking nipples, thumbs, fingers, or pacifiers has little doubt that much of the infant's interaction with the environment occurs through contact with the mouth.

Freud further divided the oral stage into the oral sucking and oral biting stages. Oral sucking is a stage of dependence in which the baby can only suck, whereas the oral biting stage (commencing at 18 months) is that point at which the infant can also bite the nipple. It is possible that the latter stage occurs only in children who are frustrated when gratification is not immediate. The biting stage could thus be considered a form of aggressive behavior.

If there is satisfaction during the oral stage, a foundation will be laid for the continuation of normal personality development. However, if the infant's needs are not gratified, or if they are gratified excessively, a *fixation* is said to occur. That is, oral needs may continue throughout life and greatly influence behavior. Behavioral examples of an oral fixation include thumb sucking; cigarette, cigar, and pipe smoking; and the manipulation of the lips with the fingers or other objects such as pens or pencils. Other oral personality characteristics are overeating, greediness, and nail biting. However, research has not demonstrated any relationship between these behavioral traits and either frustration or overindulgence at the oral stage.

Erik Erikson's Psychosocial Theory   You will recall that, whereas Freud stressed psychosexual development, Erikson emphasized psychosocial stages of growth. The two psychosocial stages of importance during infancy and toddlerhood are **basic trust versus basic mistrust** and **autonomy versus**

shame and doubt. *Basic trust versus basic mistrust* occurs during the first year of life. During this time, Erikson believes the infant develops physically as well as psychologically. Furthermore, the infant learns (in an unspecified way) to deal with the environment through the emergence of trustfulness or mistrust. Trust is a feeling that some aspects of the environment are dependable. Events that may lead to such a feeling include feeding, tactile stimulation (cuddling, fondling, holding), and diaper changing.

The infant's initial relationships with the environment establish a feeling of social trust or social mistrust. Because the mother provides the child with the first social relationship, her task is to create a warm environment conducive to the nurturance of positive feelings. Trust, however, entails more than just physical reassurance:

> Let it be said that the amount of trust derived from earliest infantile experience does not seem to depend on absolute quantities of food or demonstrations of love, but rather on the quality of the maternal relationship. Mothers create a sense of trust in their children by that kind of administration which in its quality combines sensitive care of the baby's individual needs and a firm sense of personal trustworthiness. (Erikson, 1963, p. 249)

Erikson feels that trust forms the first building block of the infant's development: a sense of identity. Without the ego strength of trust, various behavior problems will arise:

> In psychopathology the absence of basic trust can best be studied in the infantile schizophrenic, while lifelong underlying weakness of such trust is apparent in adult personalities in whom withdrawal into schizoid and depressive states is habitual. The reestablishment of a state of trust has been found to be the basic requirement for therapy in these cases. (Erikson, 1963, p. 248)

We must understand that basic trust and basic mistrust are at opposite ends of a continuum. In fact, Erikson pointed out that the ego qualities at each stage have been misconstrued as discontinuous traits, with one being good and the other bad. For example, mistrust, like the other so-called negative qualities, is not to be avoided altogether, because life presents some very real dangers and pitfalls of which one should be apprehensive. Rather than viewing trust and mistrust as a dichotomy, Erikson sees them as a continuum along which it is desirable to be farther on the trust than on the mistrust side.

The adult who meets the baby's physical and psychological needs will produce a child who is happier and more content, thus reciprocating the parents' enjoyment. Parents who have happy, trusting babies are apt to spend more time with them, which in turn results in the establishment of even more trust by the infant. This phenomenon is termed the *benign cycle.* The *vicious cycle* occurs when the parent ignores the baby's needs. For example, rather than cooing and gurgling in trusting contentment, such an infant may be hungry or wet and express frustration and irritability. The infant whimpers, cries, and finally may scream as the hunger pangs or skin irritations increase. The screaming baby may become an irritant to the parent, who may become cross and handle the

EPIGENETIC PRINCIPLE

In analyzing the epigenetic blueprints established by Freud and Erikson, do you think psychological and social growth is governed by a preset plan? Do you agree the proposed stages are determined genetically and are therefore common to all human? What role, if any, does one's culture or other environmental influences play?

Basic trust provides the foundation for stable personality formation.

screaming infant roughly, which produces further annoyance in the infant. The vicious cycle eventually leads to an ego characterized by an uncomfortable and insecure relationship with the environment, resulting in a predominant sense of mistrust.

Basic trust, over time, assists in the development of a continuum of emotional responses, ranging from the very pleasant emotions to the very unpleasant. The more severe the basic mistrust is, however, the more limited the infant's repertoire of emotions will become. A child who is mistrustful of the environment may exhibit only the emotions of anger, fear, distress, or apathy. This child may never learn how to respond to positive emotions such as love and warmth. Whereas Freud emphasized in this first stage the quantity of oral pleasure that the infant feels, Erikson stressed the quality of care provided by the mother.

The second psychosocial stage of concern to us is *autonomy versus shame and doubt*. This stage occurs between the ages of 1 and 3 years. As infants become increasingly aware of their environment, they have new interactions. Their self-awareness has developed to the point that they now realize the self is an entity separate from the environment; thus their egos can develop more strengths or weaknesses. As their perceptual skills develop and their neuromuscular skills increase with maturation, their newly found self becomes aware of its autonomy but simultaneously realizes its vast limitations. Children attempt to assert themselves during this phase and frequently come into conflict with parental standards of behavior, leaving the psychological door open to feelings of shame and doubt. It is in this way that the children's developing physical abilities (walking, exploring the environment) conflict with their social interactions (parental standards) and personality dynamics (strivings for autonomy).

At this time, toddlers desire independence and want to participate in the decisions affecting their daily lives. For example, they may assert their autonomy by not eating at mealtime, by saying "no" to an adult's request, or by making demands at inappropriate times. This behavior often upsets all concerned. The child's goals of autonomy are frequently thwarted, and the parent may become angry and aggressive with the tyrant, thus producing doubt (Can I do things for myself?) and shame (Should I do things for myself?) in the child and, possibly, guilt in the parent.

This stage of psychosocial growth is all part of the socialization process, however, and strivings for autonomy are considered normal. The child's healthy autonomy will be the outcome if he or she encounters a reasonable balance between parental freedom and control. Here again, Freud's and Erikson's differences in emphasis become apparent. Whereas Freud focused on anal gratification, Erikson considered the decisive event to be the battle of wills between the parent and child.

By the second year, autonomy unfolds at higher levels (for example, a child strives for autonomy during the first year by resistance to being held), producing the conflict between independence and dependence. The child wants both, producing an ego struggle that may last months and even years until a comfortable compromise is reached. The emotions of shame and doubt may arise during this stage if the child is not allowed to develop freely. The parent who is intolerant and continually browbeats the child will raise a child who feels ashamed and doubtful and who lacks the independent spirit necessary for healthy autonomy. Adults need to be sensitive to the toddler's desire to try out new behaviors. They must realize that toddlers need to test the validity of adult standards in order to understand what will and what will not be allowed. In the midst of such strivings, overbearing adults run the risk of crushing the child's emerging self-awareness.

CHAPTER REVIEW

Unit One: Physical Development

Physical development continues to grow sequentially throughout childhood, the result of the gradual development of brain cells. This unit examined how the nervous system develops, including the central and peripheral systems. The central nervous system consists of the brain and spinal cord, and the peripheral nervous system is composed of neural tissue that connects the brain and the spinal cord with other parts of the body.

Maturation, often called readiness, is based on the development of brain parts as well as the muscle and skeletal systems. Once the organism has attained a sufficient level of maturity, environmental stimulation can speed the learning of a particular physical skill. The fact that areas of the cortex mature at different rates accounts for the emergence of thinking processes and motor reactions at varying times. Maturation and readiness are greatly affected by myelination. Myelination is the process by which a neuron develops an outside coating or sheath (myelin). Myelination allows for the rapid transmission of chemoelectrical messages.

Prehension, the ability to grasp objects, also matures as the result of sequential patterns of development, particularly those involving neuromuscular control and coordinated hand and eye movements. Children's artwork illustrates their increasing neuromuscular ability. Handedness—the preference for, and subsequent predominant use of, one hand—develops at approximately 2 years of age. There appear to be both environmental and genetic forces responsible for handedness.

Unit Two: Mental Development

Cognition refers to thinking, perceiving, and understanding. Jean Piaget's theory of cognitive development has given us insight into how mature thinking unfolds. The sensorimotor stage is characterized by six sequential substages, which lay the foundations for later cognitive functions. Important phases of development include the mastery of fundamental sensory and motor skills, the establishment of anticipatory reactions, an understanding of object permanence, and the construction of mental images that will facilitate later problem solving.

Advancements in cognitive functioning rely heavily on the establishment and refinement of concepts. A concept is a mental image that represents an object or event. Of particular importance at this time are changes in shape and size, spatial, class, and time concepts. We also explored the importance of memory to cognition and differentiated among the sensory, short-term, and long-term storage systems. The manner in which the sensory organs refine themselves during the early years was also examined.

The study of language development is known as psycholinguistics. The brain and the vocal cords enable humans to match symbolic representations with comparable meaningful vocalizations. The left hemisphere is the part of the brain most directly associated with language and its development. No one theory fully explains language development, although three theories have been proposed: the reinforcement, social learning, and innate theories. Of the three, the innate theory is considered the most influential among contemporary life-span development researchers.

Developmental patterns of language follow a fairly stable sequence. Following the cooing stage at approximately 2 months, the infant proceeds to the babbling stage at approximately 6 months. Imitation appears to pave the way for the first word, which is spoken, on the average, between 12 and 18 months. The emergence of the first word is referred to as the holophrase stage, and there is often a gap between the infant's receptive and expressive abilities. Following the emergence of the first word, vocabulary acquisition is quite rapid, and marked advancements are made in grammar during the remaining years of infancy and toddlerhood. Of particular importance in sentence development is the use of pivot and open class words, followed by telegraphic sentences.

Unit Three: Personality and Social Development

During the early years, personality and social growth are largely shaped by the family. From early interactions with the parents, children gain a better understanding of themselves and their social surroundings. This awareness of oneself and society is called social cognition and is an active field of investigation.

This unit discussed attachment, the affectionate bond between the caregiver and the infant. Four theories of attachment were considered: behavioral, cognitive-developmental, ethological, and psychoanalytic. Possible clues to the development of attachment are the selective social smile, stranger anxiety, and separation anxiety. Three categories of attachment are the securely attached, anxious-resistant, and anxious-avoidant. These three classifications underscore the individual variations that accompany attachment behaviors. Harry Harlow's research indicated that the contact/comfort motive needs to be considered when examining the topic of attachment in general.

Gender-role development begins during the years of infancy and toddlerhood, and often reflects parental gender expectations. Sex refers to a person's biological status as male or female and can be subdivided into genetic sex (determined by chromosomal makeup) and anatomical sex (physical features that distinguish females from males). Gender refers to the social meanings attached to being a female or male. Gender identity is the psychological awareness of being either a female or male, and a gender role is a set of expectations that prescribe how women and men should behave. A gender-role stereotype is a generalization that reflects our beliefs about men or women. Four prominent theories of gender-role development are the cognitive-developmental, behavioral, social learning, and psychoanalytic perspectives.

Emotions, described as changes in arousal levels, are difficult to measure because researchers are not able to record an infant's feelings. This unit examined some of the more common emotional expressions during the early years, including crying, laughter and humor, fear and anxiety, and anger and aggression. It is generally recognized that with age, emotions become more complex and differentiated.

Personality and social growth are influenced by play. During these years, play is often exploratory and manipulative. Playful interactions with the environment help foster an early sense of competence. Moreover, children will be able to observe the effects of their actions on the environment.

Freud and Erikson devised theories of personality development that cover the years of infancy and toddlerhood. Freud pointed to an oral stage of pyschosexual development, which encompasses the first 2 years of life. Two of Erikson's psychosocial stages also occur at this time: basic trust versus basic mistrust and autonomy versus shame and doubt.

TERMS YOU SHOULD KNOW

anatomical sex
anxiety
arcuate fasciculus
attachment
autonomy versus shame and
    doubt
babbling
basic trust versus mistrust
Broca's area
central nervous system
cognition
concept
consonant
cooing

deep structure
depth perception
emotion
forebrain
gender
gender identity
gender role
gender-role stereotype
genetic sex
handedness
hindbrain
holophrase
invention of new means
    through mental combinations

kernel words
language
language acquisition device
    (LAD)
lateralization
locomotion
long-term memory (LTM)
metacognition
metamemory
midbrain
morpheme
myelin
myelination
object permanence
open class word
oral stage
overregularization
perceptual constancy
peripheral nervous system
phoneme
phonology
pivot word
pragmatics
prehension
primary circular reaction

psycholinguistics
readiness principle
reflex activities
secondary circular reaction
semantics
sensorimotor stage
sensory memory
separation anxiety
serialization
sex
short-term memory (STM)
social cognition
social referencing
speech
stranger anxiety
surface structure
syntax
telegraphic sentence
tertiary circular reaction
transformation
transitional object
visual cliff
vowel
Wernicke's area

THINKING IN ACTION

• This chapter illustrates how lifespan development's major theories can be applied to a wide range of topics, including psycholinguistics, attachment, and gender-role development. Now that you've discovered their application potential, what do you regard as the strengths and weaknesses of each theoretical perspective? Record your impressions on paper, and as you read other text chapters, see if your evaluations change.

• You have just been appointed a teacher in a local infant-toddler day-care program. Building on the knowledge you gleaned from this chapter, design an environment capable of optimizing the physical, cognitive, personality, and social capacities of your children. What kinds of teaching techniques would you use to achieve your developmental objectives? How would your pedagogy differ for the infants and toddlers in your program?

• You have been asked by a group of new parents to develop a program on the importance of attachment. How do you intend to stress the significance of this early psychological and emotional bond? What kinds of parent-infant interactions will you encourage your new parents to emphasize? Conversely, what behaviors will you ask them to avoid? What advice will you have for the fathers in the audience?

• You have learned how the Eriksonian concept of basic trust represents a cornerstone of psychosocial stability, not only for infancy but later developmental stages as well. Utilizing a lifespan perspective, mentally explore the importance of basic trust in as many psychosocial situations as you can generate. For example, how might its presence (or lack of it) shape the course of peer relations? School adjustments? Intimate relationships?

• Many lifespan development researchers regard play as the "work" or "business" of childhood. If, indeed, this is the case, what do you think children are working toward? What specific developmental areas benefit from play? Moreover, what can adults do to enhance environments for playtime activities?

RECOMMENDED READINGS

1. Campbell, B. A., Hayne, H., & Richardson, R. (Eds.). (1992). *Attention and information processing in infants and adults: Perspectives from human and animal research.* Hillsdale, NJ: Erlbaum.

   Among the topics are learning and memory, sensory processing, and attentive mechanisms in information processing.

2. Fields, T. (1990). *Infancy.* Cambridge, MA: Harvard University Press.

   A noted contributor to the field supplies good coverage of this early life stage.

3. Garvey, C. (1990). *Play.* Cambridge, MA: Harvard University Press.

   Students wanting more information on children's play will find it in this well-written paperback.

4. Hulit, L. M., & Howard, M. R. (1993). *Born to talk: An introduction to speech and language development.* New York: Macmillan.

   A stage-by-stage description of how language is acquired.

5. Maxim, G. W. (1993). *The very young: Guiding children from infancy through the early years.* New York: Merrill.

   See Chapter 3 for a good overview of developmental characteristics of infants and toddlers.

Early
Childhood

What Do You Think?

Chapter Review • Terms You Should Know • Thinking in Action • Recommended Readings

• Practice makes perfect. How often children hear that expression, regarding such activities as handwriting, movement exercises, or sports. But does practice always lead to the successful execution of all motor skills? Lifespan development researchers inform us that skillful performance requires more than just practice.

• The preschooler's thinking often reflects the elements of fantasy and make-believe: Dolls and other toys have feelings, the sky has been painted blue, and the world has its own built-in sense of law and order. Preschoolers are egocentric—self-centered, often thinking the world has been created just for them. What contributes to this, and what can adults do to facilitate cognitive growth at this time?

• Boys will be boys, and girls will be girls . . . at least in traditional circles. Gender-role development begins early in childhood and exerts itself in both subtle and direct ways. How does it take place? What accounts for gender-appropriate behavior? What impact does gender-role stereotyping have on children's behavior? Are there alternatives to such traditional teachings? We seek answers to these and other questions in this chapter.

• Home sweet home. For countless children, the family unit serves as the provider of love, care, and security. Yet for a growing number of youngsters, the household has been transformed into a nightmare, filled with violent assaults, sexual molestation, verbal insults, and even death at the hands of their parents. Episodes of domestic violence have reached such huge proportions that many researchers feel the very foundation of the family structure is starting to crumble. For the abused, there's no place worse than home.

UNIT ONE: PHYSICAL DEVELOPMENT

The child's rate of physical growth begins to taper off after toddlerhood, the period when physical development is at its greatest. Yet body proportions continue to change, and motor skills continue to be refined at a relatively fast rate, enabling children to become more adept at dealing with their own needs and coping with their physical surroundings.

By the age of 5, the average child stands 43 inches tall (about 3.5 feet), which is just over double the birth length, and weighs about 43 pounds, approximately five times the weight at birth. Differences in height between the sexes are very slight, although boys weigh more than girls and tend to have more muscle and less fatty tissue.

Also during childhood, the head and brain approach their adult size. At birth, the head measures between 12 to 14 inches in circumference. By the first year it has increased 33%, and at the fourth year the head has increased approximately 48%. And by the end of the sixth year, the head has attained almost 90% of its adult size.

The brain, growing in relation to cranial growth, has attained most of its adult weight by the early years, as the billions of nerve fibers become increasingly myelinated and the dendrites in all layers of the cortex increase in both size and number. These maturation processes will enhance the connectivity and transmission of nerve impulses, which is critical to more complicated brain functions (Kalat, 1992; Levinthal, 1990). Figure 6-1 displays the growth of dendrites in the cortex.

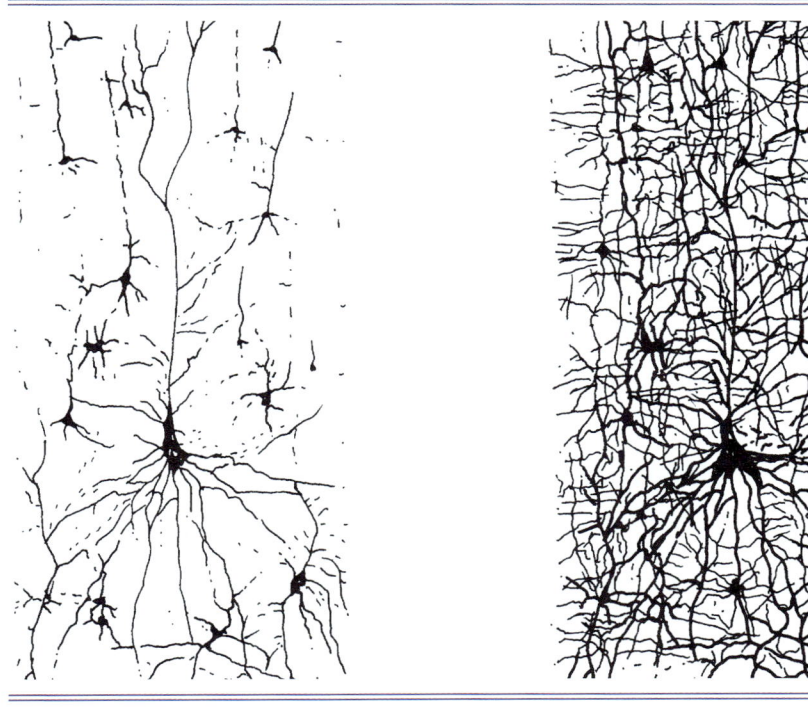

FIGURE 6-1
The Growth of Dendrites in the Cortex.

Compared to the first few months of life (left), dendrites increase in both size and number of connections (right) during the first 5 years.

Physical Changes During Early Childhood

By the time children enroll in an early childhood education setting or kindergarten, there have been noticeable physical changes in their bodies. The toddler's babylike contours, especially the round and chubby appearance, have given way to a more slender appearance. This is largely due to a growth spurt that affects height, as well as to the preschooler's participation in numerous and diverse physical activities that affect muscular growth and body build.

Changes in postural patterns also become quite evident during the early years. And changes in body dynamics contribute to the child's physical and psychological well-being, as inefficient use of the body can lead to lack of muscle tone, a lower threshold of fatigue, and less available mechanical energy (Click, 1993; Marhoefer & Vadnais, 1992; Marotz, Cross, & Rush, 1993). A number of physical and psychological factors change the child's postural patterns:

FORCE OF GRAVITY The force of gravity affects the body (the center being the trunk), whether sitting, standing, or running. Although the battle against the pull of gravity is more obvious for some children than others, each child must maintain equilibrium in order to produce good posture and balance. With age, body proportions change, and the center of gravity drops lower in the trunk. This makes it easier for the child to maintain equilibrium in the standing position.

TYPE OF BODY BUILD Posture is also affected by the child's body build. The posture of the heavier child will differ from that of the lighter or smaller one.

Correct posture is also influenced by the strength of the bones, the firmness of the muscles, and the kinesthetic sense.

COURSE OF DEVELOPMENT The stages of the child's development are another factor to consider. The early phases of locomotion, for example, influence certain parts of the body, such as the neck muscles or the lumbar curve in the lower part of the back. When walking, the weight of the body falls on the inner part of the foot, resulting in the foot's sagging in the area of the ankle.

INTERACTIONS WITH THE ENVIRONMENT Environmental factors, such as nutrition, rest, and activity, also are important to posture. The child now has incentives to excel in certain areas, such as sports, to be physically attractive, or to perfect certain motor skills. All of these may encourage a child to learn proper body balance and posture (Endres & Rockwell, 1990; Marhoefer & Vadnais, 1992).

Impact of Nutrition on Development

Good nutrition is an essential component of good health throughout the entire lifespan. By eating a well-balanced, nutritious diet, individuals can help keep their bodies healthy and promote maximum levels of growth and development. As we learned in Chapter 4, good maternal nutrition is essential to optimal fetal development, and sound nutrition and proper eating habits during the early years help set the stage for optimal functioning as one ages. Thus eating balanced, sensible meals is a cornerstone for health and well-being and is just as important during the beginnings of life as it is for later adult life (Fries, 1990; Gross, 1991; Kunkel, 1991).

Proper nutrition enables youngsters to have the energy they need as they participate in a variety of new and physically vigorous activities. On the average, the preschool child requires 1,400 to 1,800 calories per day; without the needed nutrients children will become malnourished and eventually exhibit noticeable declines in the increase of height and weight (Marotz, Cross, & Rush, 1993).

Although recommendations for balanced diets may differ somewhat in detail, it is generally recognized that children need certain fundamental nutrients. Among these are fat, proteins, carbohydrates, milk, eggs, whole grain cereals, and a variety of cooked and uncooked vegetables. Additionally, children need a supplement of citrus fruits for vitamin C, vitamin D, and foods to provide the vitamins of B complex (niacin for skin health; riboflavin for proper digestion, assimilation of food substances, and eye and skin health; and thiamine for appetite). Finally, particular attention should also be given to those proteins containing amino acids, such as milk, cottage cheese, wheat germ, and soybeans.

Motor Skill Development

Motor skills, the coordination of body movements so a particular physical task can be executed, rapidly accelerate through such activities as jumping, climbing, running, and tricycle riding. Knowing what preschoolers are physically capable of undertaking and their degree of efficiency is important not only to

Diverse physical activities affect the preschooler's muscular growth and body dynamics.

parents but also to day-care and nursery school teachers, people who will be structuring their physical activities. Adults need to structure children's motor skill activities so they will alleviate any frustration. Such frustration is usually the result of a task's being too difficult. But boredom may result if a task is too easy.

Both gross (large) and fine (small) motor skills advance during early childhood. A **gross motor skill,** requiring the coordination of large body parts, includes such activities as tumbling, skipping rope, or playing on a seesaw. A **fine motor skill** requires the coordination of small body parts, mainly the hands. Fine motor skills include such activities as turning the pages of a book, using scissors, or fitting together a jigsaw puzzle. Learning to write, which for many begins at this time with simple exercises, also gives preschoolers the opportunity to refine their fine motor skills.

A number of factors account for the preschooler's ability to engage in more diversified motor skill activities. Before early childhood, muscular development was proportionate to overall body growth. Now approximately 75% of the child's weight gains are due to muscle development. Other developments evident at this time are increases in reaction times and refinements in eye-hand coordination, manual dexterity, and general body awareness.

Stages of Motor Skill Development   Similar to other spheres of growth, the coordination of motor skills follows a sequential pattern. Although individual variations are apparent within the time frame required to perfect coordination, virtually all motor skills develop in stages, including both gross and fine motor skills.

There appear to be at least three stages of motor skill development. In the *cognitive phase*, the child seeks to understand the motor skill and what it requires. At this point, mental awareness is critical to developing certain strategies or to remembering how similar tasks were handled in the past. The *associative phase* is characterized by trial-and-error learning, in which errors in performance are recognized and corrected in the future. In this stage, the strategy changes from the previous phase's "what to do" to "how to do it." The *autonomous phase* is the last stage, in which performance is characterized by efficient responses and fewer errors. Children appear now to respond more automatically (Schmidt, 1975,1982).

This stage theory suggests that motor skills advance in a series of stages, as do the locomotion and prehension sequences of infancy and toddlerhood (see Chapter 5). Indeed, virtually every aspect of physical development seems to follow an overall order in which visible changes regularly follow one another. Thus early efforts are often prone to mistakes, whereas later attempts are characterized by skillful execution of the required task. This latter accomplishment represents mastery of the mechanics underlying motor skills: accuracy of movement, precision, and economy of performance (Malina, 1982). Table 6-1 highlights some of the major motor skill developments of preschoolers.

Rehearsal of Motor Skills   Practice makes perfect . . . or does it? We've all heard about the supposed importance of practice, be it large or small motor skills. In this context, practice is the continuous repetition of a motor skill so as to find the correct response. However, whether practice increases certain motor skill efficiency is open to question. Not everyone accepts the notion that practice leads to perfection.

Whether practice is beneficial depends on the child's maturational state. You will recall that this refers to the readiness principle discussed in Chapter 5. Unless there has been sufficient neurological maturation, certain kinds of motor skill activity are impossible, and practice will not help. Extended practice sessions or accelerated training are not necessarily linked to motor skill performances. Rather, motor skill efficiency is the product of maturation and experience.

We need to stress the role of experience in motor skill development. The youngster who has participated in a wide variety of activities and who has explored and experimented with movement is usually able to acquire a specific motor activity at an earlier age than can the child not benefiting from such experiences. Learning opportunities and adult encouragement are thus important to the development of motor skills. To this end, we supply some advice on how to guide early motor skill development in the Lifespan Development in Action box on p. 243.

Motor Skill Development and Art   While youngsters are refining their gross motor skills, their fine motor skills are also developing. As we learned in the last chapter, artwork greatly contributes to fine motor skill development. Once restricted to awkward hand movements, preschoolers are now able to use a wide variety of drawing instruments and their prehension shows marked gains. Figure 6-2 offers a rough approximation of how this phase of prehension progresses. At one year, the crayon is enveloped in the palm in a firm and primitive fashion and is wielded with full arm-banging and brushing movements. At two years, the crayon is picked up by putting the thumb at the left of the shaft and

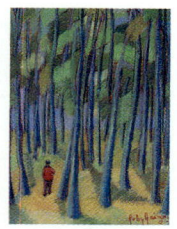

INTERACTION OF HEREDITY AND ENVIRONMENT

How would you integrate the nature-nurture issue into this discussion? How much does heredity affect the course of children's motor skill development? In what ways do you think the environment is most beneficial in assisting the skills of young children? How do you see the convergence of these two forces?

TABLE 6-1
Motor Skill Development of Preschoolers

Skill Characteristics

Motor Pattern	3-Year-Old	4-Year-Old	5-Year-Old
Walking/ running	Run is smoother; stride more even. Cannot turn or stop quickly. Can take walking and running steps on the toes.	Run improves in form and power. Greater control stopping, starting, and turning. In general, greater mobility than at age 3.	Has adult manner of running. Can use this effectively in games. Runs 35-yard dash in less than 10 seconds.
Jumping	42% rated as jumping well. Can jump down from 8-inch elevation. Leaps off floor with both feet.	72% skilled in jumping. Jumps down from 28-inch height with feet together. Standing broad jump of 8 to 10 inches.	80% have mastered the skill of jumping. Makes running broad jump of 28 to 35 inches.
Climbing	Ascends stairway unaided, alternating feet. Ascends small ladder, alternating feet.	Descends long stairway by alternating feet, if supported. Descends small ladder, alternating feet.	Descends long stairway or large ladder, alternating feet. Further increase in overall proficiency.
Throwing	Throws without losing balance. Throws approximately 3 feet; uses two-hand throw. Body remains fixed during throw.	20% are proficient throwers. Distance of throw increases. Begins to assume adult stance in throwing.	74% are proficient throwers. Introduction of weight transfer; right-foot-step-forward throw. Assumes adult posture in throwing.
Catching	Catches large ball with arms extended forward stiffly. Makes little or no adjustment of arms to receive ball.	29% are proficient in catching. Catches large ball with arms flexed at elbows.	56% are proficient in catching. Catches small ball; uses hands more than arms.

Adapted from A *Textbook of Motor Development* by C. B. Corbin, 1980, Dubuque, Iowa: W. C. Brown Co. Publishers.

the fingers at the right; most hold the butt of the crayon against the palm of the hand and extend the index finger down the shaft. At three years, the child can imitate the adult by resting the shaft at the juncture of the thumb and the index finger; the medius extends with its tip close to the point of the crayon, and the thumb opposes the index finger higher up on the shaft. At four years, the crayon is firmly gripped and moved by flexing and extending the fingers; it is held with the tip of the three radial digits near its point.

Practice with motor skills gradually produces coordination and refinement.

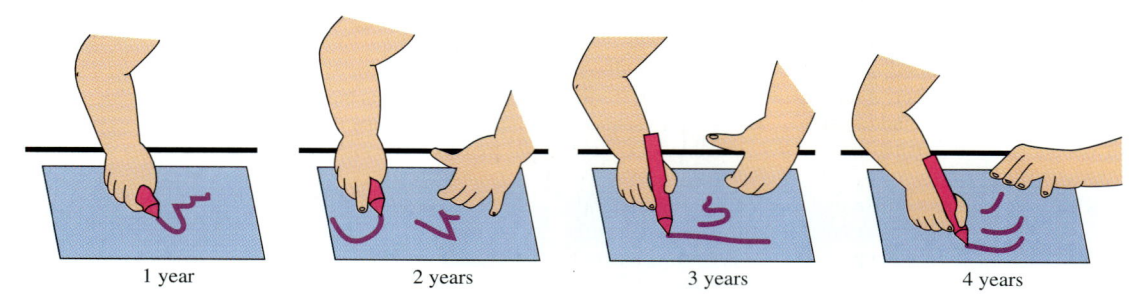

| 1 year | 2 years | 3 years | 4 years |

FIGURE 6-2
Prehension, Motor Development, and Art.

How a child grasps a crayon is an excellent clue to developing prehension abilities.

By the end of the preschool period, children can produce recognizable pictures, and such artwork provides valuable insight into their development as well as their perceptions of surroundings (Dziurawiec & Deregowski, 1992; Holmes, 1992; Klaue, 1992; Sitton & Light, 1992; Thomas & Gray, 1992). Initially, shapes are formed by concentrating scribbles on one area of the paper; a circle, for example, is the result of continual circular scribbles. The ability to draw certain shapes follows a definite pattern. Because being able to draw vertical lines seems to precede the ability to draw horizontal lines, crosses, squares, triangles, and diamonds follow a sequential order. (Try drawing a circle to see how much easier it is than drawing a triangle or a diamond. The latter require more precise movement and eye-hand coordination.) These first shapes and forms, even if they are primitive and distorted, are another satisfying accomplishment for children. Not only have they created something pleasing, but

Lifespan Development in Action

GUIDING EARLY MOTOR SKILL DEVELOPMENT

We mentioned at the outset that the years of early childhood are physically active ones. Preschoolers can now engage in playtime activities that were virtually impossible for them during infancy and toddlerhood. However, their ability to participate successfully in more demanding activities hinges not only on their overall muscular growth and coordination but also on their ability to develop a sense of self-confidence and assurance. Note the connection here between physical growth and psychological well-being, one more illustration of how developmental forces are interrelated. Adults can help nurture motor skill development by means of the following:

Provide materials and an environment in which motor skills can be exercised. Appropriate indoor and outdoor equipment, as well as space in which to run and play, helps children develop both healthy minds and bodies. When selecting toys, adults should choose those that exercise both the small and the large muscles.

Avoid comparisons. No two children develop at the same rate or exhibit the same degrees of proficiency in motor skill. Some youngsters develop rapidly, whereas others mature slowly. Likewise, some become highly skilled in an activity, and others have only little success. In this respect, comparisons accomplish little, except to produce anxious feelings about one's competencies.

Realize success in one motor skill doesn't ensure success in another. Motor skills are usually acquired individually, each requiring special training and practice. It is wrong to assume that because one skill has developed, all others will too. Proficiency will also vary from skill to skill.

Be patient with the child. Motor skills require time and effort to develop. Although encouragement is helpful, adults should avoid pushing children past their limits. Furthermore, children should be allowed to set their own pace when developing a skill, as they know best what they are capable of doing at any given time.

they also have become aware they have done it by themselves (Dileo, 1980, 1983; Francks, 1982; Isenberg & Jalongo, 1993; Mayesky, 1990).

These early attempts at shapes and forms are also characterized by isolationism, the child's tendency to create them as independent markings on the paper. Shapes and forms are not combined or interrelated, and so they have no associative values Thus children in the early stages of this period may refer to a mixture of lines on a page as being separate and distinct from a circle that appears on the same surface.

As children move into advanced stages of shape and form development (3½ to 4 years), they become more capable of using a rhythmical stroke and are more aware of the range of movements their hands can make. During this time,

CONTINUOUS AND DISCONTINUOUS HUMAN DEVELOPMENT

How do you view the development of children's art? Do you think it represents a discontinuous, age-stage progression or does it adhere more to a continuous model of development? If you lean toward the former, do you think children's art in any way reflects the epigenetic principle?

children establish associative values among shapes and forms that were lacking previously. Circles, squares, triangles, and rectangles are fused together to form numerous designs.

Between their fourth and fifth birthdays, children usually attempt to create their first pictures. Pictures do not abruptly appear but develop in a structured and orderly fashion. Early attempts are mere extensions of the shape stage; that is, children usually use a variation of one or two basic shapes to construct their early pictures. An example of this is their portrayal of the human figure, which most experts agree is the first recognizable picture to emerge. In drawing a person, children will use a large circle to represent the head and add smaller ones for the eyes, nose, mouth, and ears. Initially, longitudinal scribbles are used to represent the extension of the body, giving the human a "tadpole" appearance. Shortly afterward, however, arms and legs in the form of connected lines are added. In this way, children move from a motor exploration of marks to a symbolization of the human (Schirrmacher, 1993).

In support of artwork's unique developmental progression, researchers have examined the human figure drawings of 344 3- to 8-year-olds. Most subjects drew the head first and overestimated its size. Children who drew the trunk first portrayed relatively smaller heads. When the head was drawn first, children often left too little room for the trunk, which then had to be drawn relatively too small. However, when the trunk was drawn first, subjects always left enough space for the head, and the figures were well proportioned. The investigators contend that the typical drawing with a large head is a function of lack of planning rather than the child's misconception of the human figure (Thomas & Tsalimi, 1988). When children were asked to draw a man and a dog, or a dog and a house, young children were able to draw them to approximate size (Silk & Thomas, 1988).

UNIT REVIEW—

- ↗ Young children are becoming more physically adept at dealing with their surroundings. Rates of physical growth are slower than in previous years, but motor skills advance rapidly.

- ↗ Changes in posture become evident, caused by the force of gravity, body build, developmental forces, and interactions with the environment.

- ↗ The three motor skill development phases are the cognitive, associative, and autonomous.

- ↗ Both the child's maturation and environmental stimulation contribute to motor skill efficiency.

- ↗ Children's art is an excellent vehicle for mastering fine motor skills and many facets of expression.

UNIT TWO: MENTAL DEVELOPMENT

The progression of higher-order cognitive facilities is influenced heavily by preschool children's continuing mastery of spoken language. Using words and being able to understand what they represent give their surroundings new meaning and significance. Spoken language is the essential link in communication between meaning and sound and the means by which one person's thoughts can become another's. Because of this, language and thought are closely related developmental processes and reflect the youngster's general cognitive activity.

Cognitive advancements during early childhood enable language development to accelerate. For example, growing levels of cognitive mastery enable preschoolers to have more complex verbal exchanges with others, which in turn heightens socialization abilities. Language acquisition will also serve to stimulate the internalization of words, or thought. Additionally, language aids in the young child's internalization of action. Now rather than being purely perceptual and motor, as it was previously, action can be represented intuitively through pictures and mental experiments (Hulit & Howard, 1993; Owens, 1992).

Cognitive development also enables preschoolers to think in qualitatively different ways than infants or toddlers do. Preschoolers' thinking is more advanced, especially in regard to the refinement and elaboration of concepts. Their thinking becomes more methodical and deliberate, and they do not become discouraged as easily with cognitive challenges, so they become motivated to do the tasks at hand. Moreover, their comprehension and insight begin to take on new dimensions, such as being able to understand pretense and false beliefs (Flavell et al., 1992; Lillard & Flavell, 1992; Ruffman et al., 1993).

However, as we see shortly, there are a number of cognitive limitations at this age. For example, preschoolers' mental processes are largely dominated by perceptual processes of what seems to be, rather than what logically must be. Preschoolers have not yet mastered the logical operations that influence the thinking of older youngsters.

■■■ Piaget's Stage of Preconceptual Thought

Jean Piaget referred to the second stage of cognitive development as **preconceptual thought.** This stage occurs between the ages of 2 and 4 and is a part of the much longer **preoperational thought** stage, which encompasses ages 2 through 7. It is an important subdivision because it focuses on early childhood, a heightened period of cognitive activity.

Much like the sensorimotor development stage, preconceptual thought provides a foundation for later cognitive functions. When preschoolers have new experiences, they structure them in accordance with their existing mental schemes or place them into new mental categories. It is in this way that mental structures become more detailed and elaborate.

Several cognitive developments occur during the preconceptual thought stage, including the ability to engage in symbolic functioning. Other cognitive

Thinking during early childhood becomes more deliberate and has a quality all its own.

activities include the development of egocentrism, animism, artificialism, and immanent justice.

Symbolic Functioning   The development of symbolic functioning is an important cognitive advancement. **Symbolic functioning** is the ability to differentiate **signifiers** (words, images) from **significates** (the objects or events to which signifiers refer). In a broad sense, symbolic functioning is an act of reference whereby a mental image is created to represent what is not present. For example, a signifier such as the word *ball* can be mentally created to represent the toy when it is not present.

Symbolic functioning thus enables children's intelligence to become more flexible and elaborate (DeLoache, 1991). Earlier, their cognitive activity was restricted to immediate space and the present perceptual situation. Now, however, because of symbolic functioning and developing linguistic skills, children can generate mental images of objects not present perceptually.

Children's play behavior is one of the most clear-cut examples of symbolic functioning. When mental images are created to represent objects that are not present, children can engage in make-believe play. For example, they can select an object and imagine it to be whatever they desire. Thus a block of wood may become a car, boat, or airplane; a box may be imagined to be a fort or castle. Over time, this type of symbolic play will become more complex as pretend objects acquire various characteristics and dimensions (Goneo & Kessel, 1988; Shipley, 1993).

Egocentrism   Also emerging during this time is egocentrism. **Egocentrism** is a style of thinking that inhibits a person from seeing another person's point of view. In other words, it is a person's tendency to think that others see the world from the same perspective. As we see, egocentrism affects both social relations and problem-solving situations.

Because of their egocentrism, children may reason that everything in the world was created for them. Snow, then, as viewed by the egocentric child, is not a product of inclement weather but is something to play in; music is labeled happy because it puts them in a cheerful mood. It is also difficult for children to realize that everyone else experiences the same phenomena. Consequently, learning to share or take turns becomes a chore for many youngsters.

How preschoolers communicate with one another also reveals their egocentrism. Because of their self-orientation, each child has great difficulty "hearing" what the other is saying. Piaget called the egocentricity expressed in children's communication **collective monologue.** Because children are so involved in their own thoughts and feelings, they cannot truly listen to what others are saying, much less understand the context of the speaker's thoughts. Children talk *to* one another rather than *with* one another.

Collective monologue is similar to **parallel play,** a type of egocentricity that emerges during play sessions of two or more children. Because of children's inability to separate themselves from their own thoughts, meaningful interaction with their playmates is limited. What may appear as two children playing together may actually be two children in their own private play worlds.

Egocentrism often interferes with reasoning skills. Because real-world concepts cannot be properly understood, children relate whatever they can to their personal experience. Their interpretation of objects and events is often based exclusively on their assimilative powers; that is, children explain phenomena by consulting their existing frames of reference. As a result, many of their conceptions are illogical, either because their own imagination and personal needs are being satisfied or because their existing knowledge and understanding are extremely limited.

But not all researchers agree on the prevalence of egocentrism at this age. For example, some researchers (Black, 1981; Grusec & Arnason, 1982; Hobson, 1980) maintain that preschoolers are capable of abandoning their egocentricity to some degree and appreciating the position and feelings of others. Furthermore, research in the field of psycholinguistics (e.g., Schmidt & Paris, 1983; Warren & McCloskey, 1993) suggests that when speaking, preschoolers begin to consider the needs of listeners. Finally, research reveals that prosocial, or helping, behavior starts to develop at this time, which shows that preschoolers can think to some extent beyond themselves (Hay et al., 1991; Zahn-Waxler et al., 1992). Research such as this indicates that egocentrism may not be the driving force in all spheres of expression.

Animism   **Animism** is attributing life to inanimate objects. During early childhood, many youngsters insist that objects have lifelike properties like those of people. In an effort to understand and explain the nature of their surroundings, children often attribute thoughts and feelings to lifeless objects. Preschoolers, for example, may believe boats don't appear on lakes at night because they're "asleep"; the wind "sings" if you listen carefully; and trees "cry" when their branches are broken.

Animism is often evident in children's fairy tales. Geppetto's Pinocchio, Alice's Queen of Hearts, Dorothy's Scarecrow, and Christopher Robin's toys

INTERRELATEDNESS OF AGING PROCESSES

The manner in which egocentrism has the potential of influencing other facets of growth illuminates the fusion of developmental processes. In what specific ways do you think egocentrism affects the preschooler's personality dynamics and social relationships? How might it shape emotional behavior?

Egocentrism is apparent in the make-believe world of the young child.

were given human qualities and brought to life. With such character portrayals, is it possible that adults unwittingly contribute to the animism prevalent at this stage?

Sometimes, adults may fail to realize, or forget, that animistic qualities are attached to a child's toys. As a result, a doll with thoughts and feelings may be thrown into a toy box, or a favorite stone having animistic qualities may be maligned. For children, this type of adult behavior may be a personal blow to the world they have created.

Artificialism   Another misconception during early childhood is artificialism. **Artificialism** is the belief that everything in the world, including natural objects and events, has been created by humanity. Because they reason that everything in the world is created for human use, the child assumes that humans must be responsible for all worldly creations. The sky, then, has been painted blue by someone; rain comes from giant watering cans; and mountains are built by strong people who stacked rocks together. One 4-year-old acquaintance of ours was convinced that thunder was caused by angels bowling. Table 6-2 provides some illustrations of egocentrism, animism, and artificialism.

Immanent Justice   One final misconception obvious in early childhood thought patterns is a type of reasoning called immanent justice. **Immanent justice** is the notion that the world is equipped with a built-in code or system of law and order. Through this reasoning, children try to figure out how justice and order are maintained. Whenever there is a misfortune or wrongdoing, they try to explain why it happened. Many of the resulting interpretations are also sprinkled with egocentric overtones. For example, a child who stumbles and

TABLE 6-2
Exploring Early Childhood Thought

	Sample Questions	*Typical Answers*
Egocentrism	Why does the sun shine?	To keep me warm.
	Why is there snow?	For me to play in.
	Why is grass green?	Because that's my favorite color.
	What are TV sets for?	To watch my favorite shows and cartoons.
Animism	Why do trees have leaves?	To keep them warm.
	Why do stars twinkle?	Because they're happy and cheerful.
	Why does the sun move in the sky?	To follow children and hear what they say.
	Where do boats go at night?	They sleep like we do.
Artificialism	What causes rain?	Someone emptying a watering can.
	Why is the sky blue?	It has been painted.
	What is the wind?	A man blowing.
	What causes thunder?	A man grumbling.

falls may reason that children are not supposed to run fast. Perhaps youngsters get burned by matches because they're not supposed to handle them. In some families, children are also taught that when misfortune strikes, it is "God's way of getting even," another variation of immanent justice.

▬ Concept Development

Children's developing perceptual abilities greatly influence their concept development during early childhood. **Perception** is the cognitive activity that allows individuals to detect and interpret relevant environmental information. Although this process varies from person to person, developing perceptual awareness generally contributes to more complex and refined levels of mental operations. For instance, a youngster's growing ability to detect differences in shape, size, or space contributes to a broader understanding of the physical world. Consequently, the objects and events in their surroundings gradually acquire greater meaning and relevance (Levine & Shefner, 1991; Martindale, 1991; Reed, 1992).

Several factors distort the accurate perception of environmental information during early childhood. For one, young children tend to have limited attention and attending skills. To correct this, youngsters need to ignore irrelevant information and seek out what is applicable to the situation at hand. One's span of attention and memory skills in general also need to be upgraded. Additionally, children need to develop their understanding of how various properties are associated with categories. And, as we indicated earlier, egocentrism affects many facets of mental growth. The failure to distinguish between one's own perceptions and those of others has important implications for cognitive skills (Kail, 1990; Kalish & Gelman, 1992; Miller et al., 1991; Schulman, 1991).

Shape and Size Concepts   Accurate shape and size discrimination during childhood results from learning experiences and is affected by a number of perceptual conditions, including distance and the relation of one object to another.

Although perceptual discrimination improves during early childhood (Sera, Troyer, & Smith, 1989), the accurate perception of shape and size still remains elusive.

For instance, although children can discriminate among such shapes and sizes as big, little, or round, this does not automatically mean they have a true perception of these categories (Coley & Gelman, 1989). That is, they may not remember the existence of these objects by means of their dimensions or characteristics unless adults force them to pay close attention to such details. The fact that distance has a dramatic effect on the preschooler's perceptions supports this latter point. Because of the child's undeveloped perceptual constancies and egocentrism, objects appear to change as they move away.

In this sense, a preschooler may think a distant house becomes larger as it is approached or that a mountain changes its shape when it is viewed from a new location. Consider the following: A preschool acquaintance of ours watched his mother depart on an airplane. As the plane gradually disappeared from view, the youngster turned to us and asked, "Is Mommy getting as small as that plane?" All of these different viewing conditions tend to distort preschoolers' perception.

Spatial Concepts An accurate interpretation of the environment relies heavily on understanding spatial relationships. Similar to other perceptual challenges, advancements in understanding spatial relationships are limited during early childhood. Once again, egocentrism hampers children as they try to comprehend such spatial discriminations as near, far, down. Usually, such designations are first learned as they personally relate to the child (e.g., the toy is near me).

Egocentrism creates other problems, especially in understanding relationships in such areas as direction and distance. To make these discriminations, children must learn to coordinate their self-centered points of view with other systems of reference. To appreciate how difficult this is for young children, imagine the problems that preschoolers have in discriminating left and right. Once this has been mastered, think of the difficulty in understanding left and right from another person's perspective—especially if this person is face to face with the child. Such difficulty in perspective occurs in many situations, particularly those that require alternative points of view.

In an interesting experiment, David Uttal and Henry Wellman (1989) explored young children's representations of spatial information acquired from maps. In the first part of their investigation, the researchers found that all 6- and 7-year-old children and many 4- and 5-year-olds could learn the layout of a large playhouse composed of six adjoined rooms by memorizing a map. Children who learned the map before entering the playhouse more quickly learned a route through it than children who were not exposed to the map, and older subjects performed significantly better than younger children.

In the second part of the experiment, preschoolers learned a map of a space that contained six spatially separated small rooms within one large room. Children could therefore view the entire configuration of smaller rooms as they traveled around the larger room. The preschoolers performed significantly better in the second half of the experiment than in the first half, and the majority of them performed perfectly or almost perfectly. Taken together, these findings

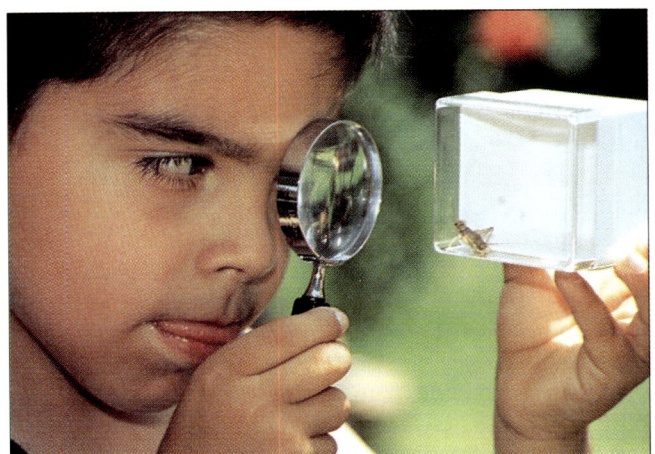

During early childhood, youngsters become more inquisitive.

suggest that preschoolers' map reading abilities and spatial understandings are more advanced than many realize.

Adults can help preschoolers acquire more accurate spatial concepts. For example, they should use precise terminology when referring to spatial relationships and provide situations that allow children to see more than one spatial orientation. Mirrors, for instance, give children the opportunity to observe different viewpoints. Activities involving maps or a globe or games requiring an analysis of spatial relations are other good learning opportunities. Adults can also encourage multiple spatial viewpoints by actively eliciting children's perceptions of their surroundings. For example, when viewing a particular situation, adults might ask, "Does it look the same for me?" or "How would that look if we moved away?" and the like. These types of activities help reduce children's egocentrism and reveal there is more than one way to view the world.

Quantity Concepts   Although preschoolers are better at discriminating quantities, they often make judgments on the basis of perception alone. Put another way, children are not yet able to discriminate quantities logically, independent of misleading perceptual cues (Charlesworth & Lind, 1990; Lind, 1991). As we have learned, this problem is often compounded by the children's lack of appropriate terminology for discriminating such quantities as more and less or few and many. Moreover, even when children have learned the correct terminology, it is no guarantee they have learned the related discrimination. For example, in one experiment, 3- and 4-year-old children were asked to sort the numbers 1 through 9 into a small, medium, or large category. Three-year-olds tended to name 1 as a small number and all others as large. Four-year-olds discriminated among 1, 2, 3, and 4, medium, and large numbers. These results suggest that readiness skills needed for early childhood mathematics education should include development of appropriate concepts of number magnitude (Murray & Mayer, 1988).

Some adults may unintentionally confuse preschoolers by using ambiguous terminology. Terms such as *some* and *many* are often confusing. Consider the problems that preschoolers may encounter when hearing sentences such as "Is

ACTIVE AND REACTIVE MODELS OF DEVELOPMENT

How do you interpret the young child's budding intellectual mastery of the world? Do you see the child self-directed and actively engaged in exploration and experimentation? Or do you see the various mental accomplishments being the result of reactive conditioning from the environment?

there *much* left?" or "We need some *more* money." Such quantitative terms are general and vague and difficult for youngsters to understand.

Numbers are an important part of quantity concepts. There is usually a significant gap between preschoolers' counting abilities and their ability to understand conceptually what is being counted (Wynn, 1992). Often, preschoolers use serial order but are unable to recognize figures. Furthermore, preschoolers poorly understand concepts of measure, simple addition, and fractional amounts. It is suggested that the development of number concepts hinges on children's ability to arrange a series of items according to their observable differences. This occurs by age 7, when the average child can arrange a series of sticks in order of their increasing lengths. Even when one stick has been omitted from the series, the proper place for it can be found.

Once again, adults can do much to help preschoolers learn number concepts. Unfortunately, counting to 10, which is so often encouraged by adults, merely represents serial and rote memory rather than conceptual understanding. Instead of this, educators (e.g., Charlesworth & Radeloff, 1991; Schultz, Colarusso, & Strawderman, 1989) suggest that children be given structured learning exercises that emphasize the quantities the numbers represent. For example, arranging groups of pencils or checkers in different patterns and having the preschooler count the items—as well as paying attention to the perceptual differences in the numbers—is one approach. Or after children have watched a "Sesame Street" episode on the number 3, adults should follow up on this learning exercise. At the dinner table, one might say, "Show me three beans or three spoons." These types of exercises emphasize the qualitative aspects of numbers and not rote memory.

Money is another facet of quantity concepts. Generally, money concepts are difficult for preschoolers to understand. However, by the end of the early childhood years, youngsters usually have some understanding of what a penny, nickel, and a dime are. The names of other coins, though, are more elusive. This age is also when children realize what the value of each coin is. By age 6, children are usually capable of using money in simple mathematical transactions.

Time Concepts   We mentioned earlier that young children refer almost exclusively to the present before they do the future or the past. Furthermore, preschoolers have difficulty distinguishing morning from afternoon and the days of the week. Usually, children's understanding of time is bound by the immediacy or recency of situations.

Similar to the difficulty with quantity concepts, children are frequently confused by adults' often vague time references. For example, such phrases as "We'll go in a *little* while," "Wait a *bit*," or "We'll do that *later*" are extremely vague and general. Although such references to time are common, adults can help preschoolers by not always speaking in such sweeping generalities.

When children have a rudimentary understanding of time, they relate events to certain hours of the day, such as the beginning of school or lunch periods. Their egocentrism is apparent when they distinguish routines in the day that relate directly to themselves. In most cases, children learn hours first, followed by half hours and then quarter hours. Children are usually able to name the days of the beginning and end of the week before they reach kindergarten, although the days in the middle of the week may remain elusive. Also elusive are the different representations for the same time designations, such as "It is now one thirty-five" or "It is now twenty-five minutes to two," or "We'll go on vacation in two weeks" or "We will go away the week after next." These different ways of referring to the same period require considerable thought and frequently confuse youngsters.

Language Development

By early childhood, youngsters have acquired the basics of the spoken language. This linguistic milestone gains significance when we consider that an 18-month-old child knows only approximately 25 words. During the next 3 years, however, this figure soars to almost 2,000 words. In addition to this dramatic vocabulary increase of approximately 600 new words per year, preschoolers also demonstrate significant gains in semantics and grammar (Bernstein, 1993; Owens, 1992).

Those adults having contact with children will agree that preschoolers are charming and entertaining conversationalists. Compared with infants and toddlers, preschoolers use language in a variety of different ways, including questions, dialogues, songs, and chants. Language also becomes a vehicle for experimentation, such as rhythm and cadence exercises (Bayless & Ramsey, 1991; Haines & Gerber, 1992; Hulit & Howard, 1993).

Influences on Language Development   Growth in language acquisition may be affected by a number of factors, most of which begin to exert their influence on the youngster's life during early childhood. These factors include socioeconomic influences, intelligence, gender, bilingualism, and the presence or absence of a twin.

SOCIOECONOMIC INFLUENCES The familial setting in which the child is reared, particularly its socioeconomic level, is believed to influence language growth. Lower-class parents often lack the vocabulary skills necessary to provide proper language instruction. They also may not verbally stimulate their children as often as middle- and upper-class parents. Upper-class parents tend to also emphasize proper word usage and correct grammar. In addition, middle- and upper-class parents tend to give more reinforcement to youngsters when they use words correctly. Middle- and upper-class homes also expose children to a greater array of educational aids. The household containing newspapers, magazines, encyclopedias, tape recorders, radios, and television offers advantages over the household that can offer the child only limited stimulation.

We need to emphasize that although there are language differences among socioeconomic classes, lower-class children are not linguistically inferior. More often than not, they have their own dialect, a language style differing from standard English (see Chapter 7). And research shows (Warren-Leubecker & Bohannon, 1989) that many children are capable of switching from their own dialect to standard English (called *code switching* by psycholinguists), such as what might occur when a child goes from a neighborhood setting to a school environment. Whatever linguistic differences surface among socioeconomic classes tend to be differences in the rules of their languages (Hoff-Ginsberg, 1991; Hulit & Howard, 1993).

A child's social relations stimulate developing language abilities, a good illustration of the interplay between developmental forces.

INTELLIGENCE The course of language development appears to be related to children's general intelligence levels, although research findings on this topic are mixed. For instance, many children with above average intelligence begin to talk at an early age, acquire words at a rapid pace, and use grammatically correct sentences. However, there is evidence (Rice, 1989) that some children with normal intellectual capacities exhibit delays in learning a language. Moreover, many developmentally disabled children are capable of understanding complex syntax as well as other facets of language acquisition (Cromer, 1988). To unravel the full impact of intelligence on language acquisition, more research is obviously needed.

GENDER Until recently, modest gender differences were found in certain aspects of language acquisition. For instance, occasional evidence pointed to the fact that females were verbally superior to males during the early school years, and that females tended to be more articulate than males in tests of word usage, grammar, and spelling. However, such findings have been challenged in recent years, and today we see a consistent pattern of minimal gender differences in verbal abilities (Matlin, 1993). This was the central finding of research (Hyde & Linn, 1988) that analyzed 165 studies dealing with gender differences in verbal ability. Although a slight edge in favor of females was apparent, the difference was so small it was practically insignificant.

But although minimal gender differences exist in language development, the manner in which females and males verbally disclose themselves contrasts. As we see throughout the text, females are more inclined to reveal themselves with friends whereas males prefer to be less disclosive. Males tend to limit their vulnerability by avoiding the discussion of feelings or personal issues. There also appear to be gender differences in listening, an important, but often overlooked, feature of language development. Females tend to be more adept at listening for the mood of the verbal exchange and picking up nonverbal cues. Males, on the other hand, are often taught to listen for facts and have trouble detecting nonverbal communication (Borisoff, 1993; Pearson & Davilla, 1993; Rawlins, 1993).

BILINGUALISM **Bilingualism** refers to the ability to speak more than one language. It is not unusual for children to be reared in a bilingual household, and contemporary researchers are exploring its impact on the course of language development (Dart, 1992; Lanza, 1992). At one time, it was maintained that attempting to learn two languages placed the youngster at a disadvantage and interfered with overall linguistic growth. Today, though, it is recognized that bilingualism often promotes cognitive flexibility and creative expression (Bialystok, 1988; Garcia, 1980; Lambert, 1981; Owens, 1992). However, a critical element in determining the effects of bilingual homes is whether adults reprimand children for using their native dialect and insist they speak standard English. Thus bilingualism is not a problem restricted to a language; rather, it may be a problem of cultural conflict. For a closer look at bilingualism, see the Focus on Diversity box on pp. 256–257.

TWINSHIP Finally, whether the child is born a singleton or a twin affects language development. Although research on this question has been limited, twins frequently have slower overall rates of language development when compared with singletons. This is particularly apparent in average lengths of responses and annual word gains. One factor contributing to the twins' lag in development may be that they grow up closely together, learning to understand each other's speech patterns at a very early age. Many twins develop what is known as **twin speech,** a type of language consisting of words known only to the two. Twins also may not have the initiative to make their verbal behavior known to others. Or twins, compared with singletons, may receive less verbal stimulation from their parents, who must divide their time between them.

Semantic Development   Semantic development is significant throughout all stages of childhood. Recall that *semantics* is the study of how words represent objects and events. Simply stated, it is the study of word meanings.

Although understanding word meaning begins with the child's first word, semantics becomes progressively harder for children as they grow older. By early childhood, the youngster is faced with having to learn the meanings and interrelationships of nearly 2,000 words. Needless to say, learning so many word meanings poses a staggering challenge to their developing cognitive skills, including memory (Gathercole et al., 1992; Pease, Gleason, & Pan, 1993; Peterson & McCabe, 1991; Waxman & Senghas, 1992).

INTERACTION OF HEREDITY AND ENVIRONMENT

As you examine these factors associated with language development, which do you think represent environmental influences? Which are dependent on genetic endowment? Which reflect an interactionist stance?

Focus on Diversity

BEYOND CONVERSATION: THE MANY SIDES TO BILINGUALISM

At first glance, studying bilingualism appears to be a research endeavor exclusively nestled within the field of psycholinguistics. However, the implications of bilingualism for other aspects of a child's life and society as a whole are both numerous and diverse (Dart, 1992). According to Kenji Hakuta and Eugene Garcia (1989), the linguistic features of bilingualism provide only a window into a complex set of social and educational processes and issues that we are now only beginning to understand and address.

From a developmental perspective, it is recognized that bilingualism affects the child in many ways. For example, we now know that bilingualism does not hamper the child's linguistic competency; indeed, research suggests the bilingual child often demonstrates considerable mental flexibility and metalinguistic awareness. But Hakuta and Garcia (1989) point out that understanding the potential benefits of bilingualism must transcend a child's knowledge and usage of two linguistic systems. Along these lines, it must be understood that bilingualism involves unique social dimensions encompassed by the languages in use. Research (e.g., Gumperz, 1982; Zentella,

1981) shows that most bilingual children are quite skilled at shifting from one language to the other depending on the conversational situation (a process known as *code-switching*), and that this behavior is not the result of the confusion of the two languages. Instead, bilingual children often do so to take advantage of the richness of the communicative situation and are likely to establish and regulate the social boundaries of two worlds. Such behavior illustrates that bilingualism is a social phenomenon which transpires between two or more parties and that questions of language use are really questions about social context, not about linguistic structure (Hakuta & Garcia, 1989).

Beyond the developmental dynamics of bilingualism are an assortment of controversial educational issues, including those involving classroom pedagogy (Lanza, 1992). According to Hakuta and Garcia (1989), the issue of how to educate children with limited ability in English typically centers on the issue of native language support in instruction. Few educators and policymakers disagree that the ultimate goal of such programming is to "mainstream" students in monolingual Eng-

Certain processes underlie semantic development during the early years. It seems that youngsters first learn simple associations or words' semantical features. Objects' perceptual features are usually learned first, such as size or shape, and the objects' functional qualities. There is no clear-cut evidence regarding which (perception or function) is learned first. We do know that the overextension of word meanings is fairly common among younger children. For example, the word *moon* may mean the spherical object in the night sky or be used to refer to such objects as cucumber slices or grapefruit halves. To help preschoolers overcome the overextension of word meanings as well as other linguistic limitations during the early years, a number of pedagogical strategies have been proposed (Machado, 1990; Sawyer & Sawyer, 1993).

Over time, children acquire more abstract word meanings that are not directly perceptible. Rather than just defining a word on the basis of its physical appearance, older children can construct word meanings on the basis of such

lish classrooms with maximal efficiency. However, disagreement typically arises on the specific instructional role of the native language: How long, how much, and how intensely should it be used? Those in favor of native language instruction recommend the aggressive development of the native language prior to the introduction of English. Opponents recommend the introduction of English from the very beginning of the child's schooling, with minimal use of the native language. Mixed findings on the effectiveness of such approaches have emerged over the last 20 years, and much of the gathered research tends to suffer from methodological flaws such as poor design and bad measurement. Moreover, the research tends to define its treatment and outcomes in strictly linguistic terms.

Another sensitive issue related to bilingualism centers on the topic of federal programming. Bilingual education legislation has provided millions of dollars to school districts in an effort to increase English language proficiency. Guidelines for student inclusion in these programs have required evidence of limited English oral ability as assessed by a standardized English measure (a similar assessment of English proficiency is required when a student leaves the program). These programs tend to focus their attention on the instructional strategies, often defined with respect to the language of instruction, that will en-

sure the development of English language proficiency. Hakuta and Garcia (1989) believe that the narrow linguistic definitions of bilingualism in such programs have created problems in accounting for whatever data are gathered. A more precise understanding of the social and cultural factors within different linguistic minority groups needs to be taken into account, as well as differences in learning styles that interact with instructional approaches.

The topic of bilingualism has captured the attention of researchers from diverse disciplines, and a considerable amount of knowledge has accumulated on the topic (Owens, 1992). However, it is obvious that certain issues beg further scientific inquiry. For instance, researchers need to learn more about how language is related to cognition and how these forces interact with variables such as attitude, self-awareness, and identity formation in bilingual individuals. A broad multidisciplinary perspective needs to be developed and applied to the increasingly important problems faced by bilinguals throughout the socialization process. And there continues to be a great need for quality research on the nature and effectiveness of educational programs that serve bilingual students. Indeed, there is more to issues confronting the bilingual individual than can be summarized by language proficiency measurements (Hakuta & Garcia, 1989).

dimensions as subjective affect. In this way semantics progresses from a concrete to an abstract level.

The fact that concrete words are learned before abstract terms may help explain why young children have trouble understanding that certain words have both physical and psychological meanings. For example, if preschoolers were asked the meanings of the words *green* or *shady,* they would most likely offer physically oriented definitions (green is a color, and shady means protected from the sun). Older children given these words, however, would most likely supply extended meanings that embody psychological connotations. Thus *green* could mean an emotional state (green with envy), and *shady* might imply unreliability (a shady character). Children's initial limited understanding of words may also explain why they literally interpret adult figures of speech or metaphors. For this reason, it is understandable that some preschoolers look skyward when someone remarks, "It's raining cats and dogs outside."

THEORETICAL ISSUES

Utilizing material from the last chapter, what theoretical perspectives (e.g., social learning, behaviorism, innate) do you think can be applied to the young child's continuing language accomplishments? Might any of the previously described cognitive-developmental processes apply to the preschooler's linguistic growth?

Certain word meanings are also more difficult to learn than others are. Especially difficult for the preschooler is mastering the correct meaning of word pairs, such as *more* and *less.* Apparently, children learn one word of the pair first and overextend its meaning to the other word. For example, if preschoolers are asked which of two trees has more or fewer apples, they frequently will be confused. Most know the meaning of more but not of fewer. As a result, the latter word is interpreted in much the same way as the former is (based on the single concept of quantity). Preschoolers have similar difficulties with such word pairs as *before* and *after, front* and *back,* and *same* and *different.*

Syntactic Development   Children's use of syntax, the use of proper grammar, is one of the best indicators of their overall cognitive development. Proper sentence structure is a key to logic and organization of thought. It also is the guiding principle in children's efforts to understand the words that are spoken to them.

Following the telegraphic sentence stage of toddlerhood, sentences have a fairly complex syntactical construction. Compound sentences, formed by joining two or more simple sentences, also begin to be formed by early childhood. Such developments indicate that youngsters are mastering the syntax of their language (Tager-Flusberg, 1993).

Most children are able to understand the concept of higher-order sentences, especially the formation of word classes and the rules for combining them. Learning the proper location of words in a sentence is a remarkable feature of language development, as is the ability to form past tenses, make words plural, and create negatives. Each of these advancements means a greater awareness of linguistic rules. As they listen to others, children are able to extract the rules for putting words together. First they master simple linguistic rules and then move on to more complex ones, such as those regulating complex syntactical structures (Bohannon & Stanowicz, 1988; Cazden, 1981; Hulit & Howard, 1993; Slobin, 1982).

Pragmatics   **Pragmatics** is how language is used in a social context, including the use of a wide range of behaviors, such as gestures, facial expressions, pauses, pointing, or turn taking. Pragmatic rules exist in every language, and adults usually begin teaching them to children at a very early age. During early verbal interactions, for example, children learn to establish eye contact and pay attention to their partners when communicating (Warren & McCloskey, 1993).

Compared with that of toddlers, a pragmatic quality of preschoolers' language is more diverse. Reciprocal turn taking and a greater range of expressions to convey messages now accompany preschoolers' speech. More complex styles of interaction between speaker and listener are also evident, such as initiating and terminating conversations. Preschoolers learn to tailor their speech, such as expanding or deleting their sentences depending on the listener's needs. Preschoolers also know that when listeners move away they have to raise their voices in order to be heard. All of this indicates that in addition to their awareness of grammatical rules (and the cognitive capacities to grasp such rules), preschoolers are better at understanding the social implications of language use (Johnson et al., 1981; Owens, 1992; Peterson & McCabe, 1991; Schmidt & Paris, 1983). This is yet another example of the interrelatedness of developmental forces.

UNIT REVIEW—

↗ Piaget's stage of preconceptual thought encompasses the early childhood years. It is a substage of the much longer preoperational thought stage, which lasts from ages 2 through 7.

↗ The key cognitive developments outlined by Piaget during preconceptual thought are symbolic functioning, egocentrism, animism, artificialism, and immanent justice.

↗ Developing perceptual awareness helps to refine overall concept development. Key advancements take place in shape and size, spatial, quantity, and time concepts.

↗ The child's language development is influenced in varying degrees by socioeconomic factors, intelligence, gender, bilingualism, and whether the youngster is a singleton or a twin.

↗ Psycholinguistic growth is evident in children's semantics, syntax, and pragmatics.

UNIT THREE: PERSONALITY AND SOCIAL DEVELOPMENT

During early childhood, children expand their social horizons and become quite independent and autonomous. Once socially restricted and dependent, preschoolers become more involved with their environment and venture into new and challenging social situations with peers and adults. Experiences in the neighborhood, school, or other socializing situations are integrated into the child's sense of being and help develop his or her personality and social awareness.

In the company of others, youngsters become individuals in their own right, gaining insight into their own personalities. Socially, children can observe what effects their behavior has on others, a developing social-cognitive power that enables them to realize the rights and privileges of others. In addition, these social interactions help children refine their self-concepts—how individuals perceive themselves.

None of these social abilities develops independently of the others. Instead, all are intertwined and related—the result of the child's growing interaction and experiences with the environment. Personality and social dynamics also blend with those cognitive and linguistic developments previously discussed.

▬ Gender-Role Development

As we learned in the last chapter, gender-role development begins early in life. As children get older and their socialization experiences become more extensive, they will learn more about gender roles from a number of different sources. Among the more influential sources are parents, play behaviors, peers, teachers and schools, children's literature, and the media. Let us examine each of these a bit more closely and discover how children broaden their knowledge of gender-role behaviors.

Parental Influences   Parents continue to exert a significant influence on a child's gender-role development. If parents hold traditional or stereotyped views of gender roles, they will teach girls to be affectionate, gentle, and quiet and they will teach boys to be aggressive, independent, and active. In time a boy will be taught that holding a job and supporting a wife and children will be his primary adult task. Girls, on the other hand, will be taught to handle most of the responsibilities associated with child rearing and maintaining a home for their husbands and children.

Today, however, many parents are attempting to ensure that both girls and boys have the same professional opportunities and that they learn to share the responsibilities of family life. However, such liberated households are still in the minority. And those parents who are not cognizant of differential treatment succeed in teaching many gender-typed standards through their own behaviors. Mothers are usually more nurturant and emotional whereas fathers are traditionally more dominant, competitive, and unemotional (Basow, 1992; Lewis, 1987; Matlin, 1993). Again, enlightened parents are exhibiting a mixture of behaviors, not necessarily gender-typed.

The way parents talk to their children when the children are interacting with peers may tend to promote particular gender-role behaviors. For example, mothers tend to provide more linguistic support for their children, tuning their language to the youngsters' needs. Fathers tend to put more demands on their children during play situations, perhaps to raise children's performance levels. Fathers also seem to be more concerned than mothers about transmitting traditional gender-role behaviors to their offspring. In support of this, research shows that many take active steps to discourage cross-sex behavior in their children (Fagot & Hagan, 1991; Richardson, 1988).

Play Behaviors   Stereotypes abound in children's play behaviors. For instance, girls are often given dolls and encouraged to play house. Boys are given guns and trucks, and are taught to play aggressive games and to avoid "sissy" play activities. Research has shown that by the preschool years, children prefer toys that are stereotypically appropriate for their gender (Lawson, 1989; O'Brien & Huston, 1985). Jill Bardwell and her colleagues (1986) found that even kindergarten children can label chores and tasks as more appropriate for either a boy or a girl.

In general, girls' play behavior is more intimate and quiet, and it often involves one other girl. Boys tend to play in groups and engage in more vigorous and independent activities (Rawlins, 1993). As we indicated, parents, usually the father, frequently support and reinforce such gender-typed play behaviors (Fagot & Hagan, 1991; Zheng & Colombo, 1989). Further pressure to engage in traditional gender-typed play emerges from the peer group, an increasingly important source of social approval and reinforcement (Berndt & Ladd, 1989; Howes, 1988; Pearson & Davilla, 1993).

In what is perhaps evidence of social learning, boys seem to be more aware of sex differences than girls and avoid playing with objects that might be

GENDER SIMILARITIES AND DIFFERENCES

Why do you suppose traditional men behave this way? Do you think they are afraid of losing their dominant role in society? Or do you think some men (and women) sincerely believe a division of labor is necessary?

Traditional gender-role behaviors are often very evident during early childhood.

labeled feminine or "sissy." Girls seem to be willing to engage in male-oriented activities. Although both sexes congregate in gender-typed play groups, boys seem to hold more rigid, stereotyped beliefs than girls (DiPietro, 1981; Fagot & Kronsberg, 1982; Richardson, 1988).

As we emphasize throughout the text, there is some evidence today that the traditional gender roles are changing. Schools are enlarging their athletic programs and encouraging females to participate more actively and more competitively. Success in sports and the accompanying social prestige no longer appear to be exclusively male. In fact, fewer activities are exclusively either female or male. It is our hope that soon any activity will be considered appropriate for either gender and that each will be equally rewarded for the same activity.

Peer Influences   As children become more socialized, they learn more about gender-role standards and behaviors from their peer group. And the child who chooses to flout these standards risks peer group rejection. The reinforcement of gender-appropriate behaviors from within the peer group also helps to explain the early gender-typed differences apparent in children's play (Hayden-Thomson, Rubin, & Hymel, 1987; Howes, 1988; Matlin, 1993).

It is during early childhood that children start to prefer same-sex peer groups and to choose same-sex best friends. This tendency persists and intensifies throughout the years of middle childhood, although it is more pronounced in boys than girls (Berndt & Ladd, 1989; Fu & Leach, 1980; Reis & Wright, 1982). Often, same-sex play groups openly torment one another, further solidifying gender boundaries. We present more information on gender-role development and peer groups later in this chapter.

School Influences   The school setting is another socialization agent responsible for shaping the gender-role behaviors of children. Teachers are significant in

THEORETICAL ISSUES

Can ecological theory be used to interpret how gender-role learning takes place in the home, school, neighborhood, and other social settings? If so, how do you see these settings relating to one another? How are these settings organized and influenced by a culture's beliefs about gender roles?

the lives of youngsters, and as a result their behaviors and attitudes are very influential. Some teachers deliberately, others unwittingly, contribute to gender-role stereotypes (Basow, 1992; Matlin, 1993). For example, some teachers may ask girls to water the plants and boys to empty the wastebaskets. Teachers may reward girls only when they are passive, well behaved, and well mannered but reinforce boys for being assertive and asking questions (Eccles & Midgley, 1990; Morrison, 1991).

As educational experiences continue, teachers and the school system exert other influences. Some teachers may perpetuate gender-role stereotypes by advising students that certain professions are appropriate for women and not for men, and vice versa. Often, a school's curriculum may stamp a course as masculine or feminine. For example, it may require girls to take a course in home economics and boys to take one in automobile mechanics. Fortunately, many U.S. schools are now recommending that all students enroll in a mixture of such courses.

It is important for teachers to deemphasize gender-role stereotyping in their classrooms. Experts (e.g., Borich, 1992; Jacobsen, Eggen, & Kauchak, 1993; Kostelnik et al., 1993) agree that children and adolescents need to receive a quality education in a professional and objective way, not filled with unfair stereotypes of men and women. To achieve this goal, educators need to examine and monitor their behaviors, and the curriculum must be objectively assessed. Moreover, school districts need to take an active role in training or retraining teachers. And because school boards are locally run and are often composed of parents, the task goes back again to the parents.

Children's Literature   Children's literature transmits early gender-role behaviors. Stereotyping is quite evident within the pages of children's books. Girls are often portrayed as passive and domestic, boys as active and adventurous. Boys also outnumber girls in many stories. Careers are often cast in exclusively masculine or feminine terms. Evelyn Pitcher and colleagues (1989) note that all too often books portray "ferocious" daddy tigers and "gentle" mommy pussycats, and that books about cars, trucks, and trains show only men at the wheel.

Today, active efforts are being made to eliminate gender stereotyping in children's books, including identifying and revising books that have sexist themes. For example, women may be portrayed as confident and independent, and they may have occupations traditionally reserved for males. Removing women from the home and placing them in business, industry, or other male-dominated areas of work helps to destroy sex stereotyping. Removing male stereotyping also helps to make books nonsexist. Instead of portraying males as cool, competent, and fearless, more books are making an effort to show that boys can be sensitive, loving, and emotional. Some stories specifically describe boys who do not fit the stereotype of the competent "superior" male but who are in charge of themselves and their emotions (Glazer, 1991; Pitcher et al., 1989; Sawyer & Comer, 1991).

There are indications that nonsexist literature can change children's stereotyped images of the sexes. However, because sexist attitudes are woven through the whole fabric of society, we can hardly expect that books alone will produce children who are unbiased and unstereotyped in their attitudes. And although nonsexist books are important, most people feel that literary quality should not be sacrificed to meet this need. Few would suggest rewriting the classics or discarding them. For example, parents and teachers can explain to children how gender roles have changed and perhaps use some of the old stories to illustrate important themes.

The Media   Gender-role stereotyping is particularly evident in television and the other media. Men are often portrayed as leaders; women are cast as passive, submissive, and defenseless characters (Condry, 1989). Also, males usually outnumber female cast members (Huston & Alvarez, 1990). Moreover, many programs lack a regular female character. The same male-female imbalances are evident in television commercials (Durkin, 1985; Wroblewski & Huston, 1987).

For example, in one study (Stewart, 1983) that examined 551 major speaking characters in 191 programs, males clearly outnumbered females in all program types. When family themes were portrayed, most men were employed in white-collar jobs; women were typically full-time homemakers. In another investigation of older persons portrayed on television (Cassata, Anderson, & Skill, 1983), males outnumbered females in professional or managerial positions by a ratio of four to one. Females accounted for 100% of homemaker, service, or clerical positions.

In recent years, television producers have made an attempt to change this picture. Today, we see more programs featuring women, including a number with women protagonists—"The Trials of Rosie O'Neill," "Murphy Brown," "The Golden Girls"—to name a few. And one study of commercials (Bretl & Cantor, 1988) revealed that men and women appeared equally often as the leading characters in prime-time commercials. Nevertheless, about 90% of all narrators of commercials were men.

Research shows (Durkin, 1984) that even very young children understand the gender-role stereotypes portrayed in television programming. In this study, 17 children aged 4½ and 9½ years were interviewed individually and asked to discuss features of a series of highly stereotyped male and female behaviors shown on television. The children were found to display considerable knowledge of gender-role conventions and could relate this to their accounts of the televised excerpts. Children could infer appropriate feelings and motives and offer plausible accounts of portrayed stereotypes by using their existent gender-role knowledge.

Contemporary Influences on Gender-Role Behaviors   Combined, these factors serve to transmit gender-role behaviors to children in a mixture of subtle and direct ways. The result is that children learn to behave in sexually appropriate fashions within the framework of their society. Furthermore, these gender-typed behaviors will become more deeply rooted as time goes on.

We'd like to spend a moment talking about androgyny and its impact on gender-role learning. **Androgyny** refers to having both female and male personality characteristics. According to this notion, both personality traits are beneficial and important to possess. Androgynous persons view themselves as human beings, not as typecast males or females. Because they do not view personality traits as compartmentalized by sex, both males and females feel free to be nurturant, assertive, sensitive, dominant, affectionate, and self-sufficient.

GENDER SIMILARITIES AND DIFFERENCES

How do you view the concept of androgyny? Do you think it is an important facet of gender-role learning for children to discover? Do you consider it important throughout the lifespan? Why or why not?

Being androgynous appears to have beneficial effects. Compared to people who exhibit traditional gender-role behaviors, androgynous individuals seem more competent and demonstrate higher levels of self-esteem. In addition, androgynous persons seem to have experienced positive parent-child relationships, have more success in maintaining good interpersonal relationships, and tend to deal more effectively with their surroundings, including situations involving stress. They also tend to be more secure with themselves, more flexible in their behavior, and less anxious (Cooper, Chassin, & Zeiss, 1985; Ganong & Coleman, 1987; Lombardo & Kemper, 1992; Payne, 1987; Solie & Fielder, 1988; Stoppard & Paisley, 1987).

On the other hand, some researchers (e.g., Baumrind, 1982; Blitchington, 1984; Downs & Langlois, 1988; Gill et al., 1987) feel the concept of androgyny is too vague, trendy, and difficult to measure. Others (e.g., Werner & LaRussa, 1985) argue that many gender-role behaviors such as male assertiveness and female nurturance have been in existence for years and will not budge to androgynous pressures.

Some critics (e.g., Sampson, 1985) maintain that androgyny is a questionable model of psychological adaptation because it suggests a person can be totally self-sufficient, completely feminine and masculine at the same time. Others (e.g., Hare-Mustin & Maracek, 1988) maintain that focusing on androgyny draws attention away from women's real needs in society, including the power imbalance between women and men. Taking a similar stance, Sandra Bem (1981) feels that rather than encourage androgyny, "human behavior and personality attributes should cease to have gender, and society should stop projecting gender into situations irrelevant to genitalia" (p. 363).

However, proponents of androgyny maintain that the removal of gender-typed behavioral constraints would allow men and women to demonstrate the best qualities of both sexes. We feel that children, especially, would benefit

Gender-role reversals during early childhood have become more evident in contemporary society.

from a more tolerant acceptance of their total selves, rather than being continually told how society expects them to behave.

Emotional Development

Emotional reactions and expressions become highly differentiated during early childhood. This is in contrast with the rather generalized responses that characterized the early years. Several factors account for this change in emotional expression. First, their increasing cognitive awareness enables children to perceive their surroundings in new and different ways. The preschoolers' imaginations, for example, are largely responsible for the imaginary fears occurring at this age. Cognitive advancements also make youngsters more alert to contextual information and enable children to detect and express a wider range of emotion and feeling (Casey, 1993; Denham, Cook, & Zoller, 1992; Denham & Zoller, 1991; Ribordy et al., 1988).

Additional factors influencing emotional expression during early childhood are expanding social horizons and new developmental challenges. An example of this is the transition from the home to an early childhood educational program or the preschooler's greater involvement with peers. Each of these experiences broadens the child's overall emotional repertoire. Clearly, emotional expression is intertwined with many developmental processes (Brown & Dunn, 1991; Hadwin & Perner, 1991; Nunner-Winkler & Sodian, 1988; Waggoner & Palermo, 1989; Wellman & Bannerjee, 1991).

Fear   Children's fears are a good illustration of how increased imaginative abilities affect emotional expression. Because they still cannot understand many objects and events, they often exaggerate them. An example is the nighttime ritual of many preschoolers. Some will not venture into a dark bedroom alone, and others will remain in the lit hallway while groping for the light switch on the bedroom wall. Others will inspect the closet before bedtime, hoping not to find an imaginary creature lurking inside. They know they will not sleep peacefully until this dreadful task is done. Still others will peer quickly under their bed, hoping the mysterious unknown will not reach out and grab them before they can jump under the covers.

In one investigation, 42 kindergartners were assigned to experimental and control conditions. The experimental group heard stories in which the characters coped positively with the dark; the control group heard neutral stories, irrelevant to the fear of the dark. Results indicated that the children in the experimental group showed a significant reduction in self-reported fear of the dark—they also increased their coping statements as compared to the control group (Klingman, 1988).

Fear of imaginary creatures and the dark are two of the more common fears expressed by preschoolers (Hawkins & Williams, 1992). Other widely reported fears are those related to death, dangerous animals, and thoughts about physical injuries, such as drowning or fire. Such an assortment of fears clearly illustrates the youngster's emotional susceptibility.

Several trends are evident in the development of fears. For instance, females appear to be more susceptible to fear than boys are. However, males tend to report a greater variety of fears. Youngsters from higher socioeconomic settings have a greater number of fears, particularly those related to personal health and safety, than do youngsters from lower-class environments. The latter tend to report more supernatural fears. Finally, television also contributes to children's fears, with its frequent attempts to scare its viewers. In the accompanying Lifespan Development in Action box, we share some thoughts on preventing children's fear.

Lifespan Development in Action

CHILDREN'S FEARS: STOPPING THE THINGS THAT GO BUMP IN THE NIGHT

Adults who understand children realize that frightening and unhappy incidents may enter a child's life any day and create special fears. Although grown-ups cannot protect the child from all fears, nor should they, they can take certain measures when the child is afraid.

Respect children's fears. Respect and understanding should always be accorded to children who are afraid of an object or event. Making fun of fears or shaming the child in front of others does not help children cope effectively with this emotion. Also, adults should never punish a child for being afraid. We point out that adults themselves take their own fears and apprehensions quite seriously.

Realize children will outgrow most fears. Because some fears may take longer than others to overcome, adults should exhibit patience. This may take the form of patiently listening to the child and exhibiting empathy and understanding. Achievements should also be praised, no matter how small.

Allow children to become accustomed to fears gradually. Adults should seek to build faith in children and their abilities. If heights are a feared situation, let the child get accustomed first to small elevations; if dogs are feared, getting the child acquainted first with a puppy may be a starting point. This gradual adjustment to a feared stimulus is called *desensitization.* Another way to help children become accustomed to fears is through imitation, or modeling. That is, fears might be overcome by watching someone else deal with the situation.

Try to understand fears in relation to the child's overall personality. Attempt to observe how fears relate to the child's daily behavioral patterns. If strange sounds, sights, and sudden movements are characteristically feared, situations causing them should be avoided as much as possible, or you can help the child to gradually develop specific means of dealing with such situations.

Familiarize yourself with the fears that children experience at different ages. A better understanding of most fears will result if adults analyze the reasons for them and their underlying dynamics. If a fear involves a major situation, such as school, adults should take the time to analyze its origin and the circumstances that caused it. Adults should also set an example by dealing rationally with their own fears.

Anger and Aggression   The expression of anger changes with age. Undirected physical angry outbursts, such as kicking and hitting, begin to decline after the second year. Temper tantrums, which started during toddlerhood, persist into the early childhood years. In addition, the use of threats and insults also increases. It can be said, then, that though the amount of anger and aggression seems to remain stable, its mode of expression changes.

There are two types of aggression. **Instrumental aggression** is directed at acquiring objects, territory, or privileges. **Hostile aggression,** on the other hand, is aimed at another person with the intention of hurting that individual. Among young children, aggression is mostly instrumental.

Outbursts of anger and aggression are influenced by certain factors. For example, males tend to display more overt anger and aggressiveness. However, the greater prevalence of this emotional expression is likely due to social influences. That is, traditional males are *expected* to be more aggressive, a finding presented in our earlier discussion of gender-role development (Basow, 1992; Maccoby, 1990; McCabe & Lipscomb, 1988).

Certain elements of the home environment are thought to be related to the expression of aggressive behavior. For instance, aggressive children are often reared by aggressive parents, the latter frequently serving as models for this type of behavior. Other models for aggressiveness can be found among peers or are portrayed on television, where frequently the program's theme is "might makes right." In regard to all of the foregoing, note the developmental interaction between socialization and emotional expression (Ridley-Johnson, Surdy, & O'Laughlin, 1991; Weiss et al., 1992).

Imitation also affects aggression, an area extensively explored by Albert Bandura in a series of research investigations. One of his studies (Bandura & Huston, 1961), you will recall, revealed that preschoolers exposed to the sight of an adult aggressively knocking down a rubber doll and then being rewarded

Outbursts of anger and aggression often punctuate children's playgroups.

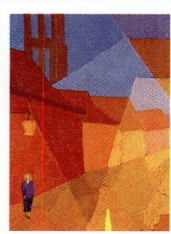

THEORETICAL ISSUES

How valuable do you think social learning theory is in explaining aggression in young children? Do you think its basic tenets can be applied to the study of aggressive behavior throughout later stages of development? Do other lifespan theories become more applicable as the child grows older?

tended to use similar types of behavior. In another study (Bandura, Ross, & Ross, 1961), the researchers sought to discover whether the sexual similarity of an aggressive adult model influenced the degree of aggressiveness that children later demonstrated. After viewing the aggressive model, the children were subjected to a mildly frustrating situation and then left to play with several toys, including the doll that had been attacked earlier by the adult model. The children's resultant behavior revealed the boys more often imitated physical aggression and identified with the actions of the same-sex models than the girls did.

Research such as this strongly suggests that modeling and reinforcement do affect children's expressions of anger and aggression. It also underscores the need for suitable adult models, not only in the home, but also on the playground and in the media. Anger and aggression may also be manipulated through the proper use of meaningful reinforcers, such as verbal approval or toys. Positive reinforcement of nonaggressive behavior often enhances the chances of that behavior being repeated. But positive reinforcement directly following aggressive behavior, such as the approval of or attention from playmates for acting tough, increases the likelihood of that behavior persisting.

Adults can do other things to reduce childhood anger and aggression. Not giving in to children's demands if they resort to aggressive behavior is vital. Firmness is also important. Grown-ups should try to comprehend why and how the child's anger originated. Observation of the events that caused the outburst is important. Lastly, youngsters should be encouraged to verbalize their feelings when the emotion of the event has subsided (Kostelnik et al., 1993).

Family Influences on the Developing Child

The family not only transmits appropriate behaviors, values, and knowledge to children, but it also provides an emotional setting in which youngsters can feel loved and accepted. Such a setting plays a critical role in shaping the child's personality and social development. A youngster's lengthy period of dependency underscores the family's overriding influence.

Certain factors related to the child's interaction with the family are particularly important during early childhood. For example, the parents' support, guidance, understanding, trust, and security are significant. Also important are the child's relations with siblings and the types of discipline employed by parents. Overall, children's personal and social growth is greatly affected by their sense of identity and belonging to the family unit, as well as the warmth and acceptance given by others (Bradley et al., 1989; Garbarino, 1992; Maccoby, 1992).

Sibling Relations   Sibling relations add an important dimension to family life and exert unique influences on the developing person. Sibling relations represent an intimate connection, one that teaches the importance of reciprocity and mutuality as well as the sharing of privileges and affection. The advantages of having siblings outweighs the disadvantages, and throughout the course of the life cycle, we can see the support and assistance that siblings bring to one another (Cicirelli, 1991; Gold, 1990; Scott, 1990).

Initially, siblings usually discover they must share possessions and compete for what the home has to offer. This has a tendency to create anxiety for many firstborns, especially if they are of the preschool age. Unsettled feelings may give rise to **sibling rivalry,** a form of competition between children of the same family for the attention of the parents. If the former only child is old enough to perceive the newcomer will be sharing the mother, there may be a considerable amount of jealousy exhibited during the early years.

Sibling rivalry is most likely to develop if the parents exercise inconsistent discipline or if household disharmony exists. Along these lines, Brenda Volling and Jay Belsky (1992) have discovered that sibling conflict and aggression are related to such factors as high levels of conflict between the mother and children, intrusive and overcontrolling parenting, and insecure infant-mother attachment. Facilitative and affectionate parenting, among fathers in particular, was associated with prosocial sibling interaction. In general, the researchers found that early relationship experiences between parents and their firstborn children had an enduring effect on the quality of later sibling relationships.

A parent's overindulgence toward a particular child may also contribute to sibling rivalry. If little time has elapsed between births, older children will still require their share of maternal attachment. If the interval is greater than 3 years, older children may develop other interests, which often serve to lessen their jealous feelings. Other factors, too, appear to lessen sibling rivalry. For example, one study (Kramer & Gottman, 1992) reveals that the transition to the sibling role for the older child is enhanced when he or she experiences positive peer relationships and demonstrates good conflict management skills.

Although jealousy toward a new arrival is a completely normal emotion for the child, parents can take definite steps to help make the adjustment period smoother. Making the child aware of the baby's arrival beforehand and attempting to tell him or her of the personal significance involved (having a new brother or sister) may prove particularly helpful. Allowing children to become involved with the infant's homecoming preparations can indicate to them that they are active and important in the family's activities. Later on, the proper attitude demonstrated by the parents can help to keep sibling rivalries at a minimum. And, as indicated, parents should avoid showing any kind of favoritism or unfairly comparing one child with another.

It is not uncommon for sibling rivalries to persist for years, however. In fact, competition between siblings may be the norm rather than the exception. Although it is recognized that the most intense sibling rivalry is between sisters, this may be because females are more willing than men to express their feelings openly. As we discovered earlier in this chapter, females are more apt to disclose their emotional side, discuss problems, and share experiences (Borisoff, 1993).

The degree and nature of sibling interaction varies greatly, not only from one set of siblings to another but within the same pair at different points in their lives. For example, some siblings become close, sometimes perceiving themselves as being more like one another than do their mothers (Graham-Bermann, 1991). As they watch out for one another, they loom as important sources of trust and support, particularly within the social arena. For example, Patricia East and Karen Rook (1992) found that support from a favorite sibling was associated with better adjustment among socially isolated children.

Other siblings detest each other and avoid contact as much as possible. Adolescence has the potential of being a particularly stormy time for sibling relations (Goodwin & Roscoe, 1990). In some instances, love and hate may exist

CONTINUOUS AND DISCONTINUOUS HUMAN DEVELOPMENT

Given the young child's escalating levels of independency and social involvement outside the family, such as within an early childhood education setting, do you see this life stage reflecting continuity, change, or a mixture of both? Also, what special adjustments do you think family development theorists would identify for families with preschoolers?

THEORETICAL ISSUES

How might behaviorists or social learning theorists explore the dynamics of sibling relationships, including sibling rivalry? Do you think the roles attached to being a sibling can be investigated with a symbolic interactionist slant? Would a social exchange perspective be worth while for exploring the ups and downs of sibling interaction?

side by side in an uneasy equilibrium. We might add, too, that *sibling abuse* is more than a remote possibility in families today. Vernon Wiehe and Teresa Herring (1991) tell us that sibling abuse is five times more prevalent than child abuse, and may include such aggressive behaviors as hitting, slapping, pushing, or the like.

Siblings appear to have the most interaction and greatest influence on one another when they are close together in age. Significant age differences alone are enough to create physical and psychological distance between siblings. If they are similar in age, siblings may experience positive patterns of interaction, such as shared activities and interests, as well as negative patterns, including intense competition and a continuous struggle for separate identities. The potential for positive patterns of interaction was evident in one study involving twin pairs during their second year of life (Zahn-Waxler, Robinson, & Emde, 1992). The twins demonstrated a steady concern for the other, such as in emotional concern and prosocial acts, with girls scoring higher than boys on these observable measures.

Research also discloses that younger siblings, more often than not, try to imitate older siblings. They are far more likely to be followers of their older siblings, the latter often assuming the role of model and initiator. In most families, the oldest sibling is usually expected to assume some degree of responsibility for younger siblings. The fact that this expectation exists may help explain why firstborns are generally more adult oriented and responsible than laterborns. Also, an older sibling serves as a potential buffer following parental divorce or separation. It has been discovered (Kempton et al., 1991) that adolescents with no older siblings from divorced families were reported by teachers as demonstrating more behavioral problems that did those with older siblings.

Although the study of sibling relations has not received as much past attention as have other aspects of family life, researchers today recognize its importance (Dunn & McGuire, 1992). Sibling relations have come to be recognized as

The attachment between siblings represents a special bond.

a unique facet of the child's life. Furthermore, the attachment between siblings often transforms itself into a special bond that endures as time goes on, even after brothers and sisters have gone their separate ways in the world (Newman, 1991).

Child Discipline   One of the more frequently discussed family interaction patterns is discipline. **Discipline** is defined as the teaching of acceptable forms of conduct or behavior. The goal of discipline is to make children responsible and to make them realize they are accountable for the consequences of their behavior.

There are several styles of parental discipline, although parents do not always fall into only one category. Rather, parents often mix approaches when dealing with their children. When **authoritarian control** is employed, parents attempt to shape and control their children's behavior by enforcing a set standard of conduct. The emphasis is on obedience and the use of punitive, forceful measures to enforce proper behavior. **Authoritative control** is characterized by attempts to direct their children's activities, but in a more rational fashion. Firm control is exerted, but verbal give-and-take is also stressed, and parents attempt to convey to the child the reasons for their discipline. Finally, **permissive control** is usually nonpunitive and parents behave in an accepting and affirmative manner toward the child. The child is consulted about policy decisions and given explanations for family rules.

As we mentioned at the outset, parents do not always fall into only one category. Rather, styles of control are often mixed. As far as overall effectiveness of each approach is concerned, the authoritarian and permissive styles appear to produce the least favorable results. Authoritarian parents generally allow little freedom of expression and dominate many aspects of the child's behavior. Frequently, this method of control breeds conformity and submissiveness. Among older children, it may breed rebellion and aggressiveness. Permissive parents, on the other hand, with their limited overall sanctions on behavior, have a tendency to nurture such child behaviors as selfishness and immaturity (Baumrind, 1991a, b; Kochanska, Kuczynski, & Radke-Yarrow, 1989; Weiss et al., 1992).

The authoritative method of control appears to produce the most favorable home climate. This democratic relationship has a tendency to foster such childhood behaviors as independence and self-confidence. Children reared in authoritative homes also have a tendency to be more cooperative and sensitive to the needs of others (Baumrind, 1991a, b). For some practical guidelines on implementing child discipline, see the Lifespan Development in Action box on pp. 272–273.

Child Maltreatment   Discipline is not always handled properly, and family life is not always harmonious and stable. Indeed, many children live in domestic disharmony and a negative emotional climate. One such family problem, growing in frightening proportions in recent years, is child maltreatment. It is estimated that as many as 1 million children are victims of maltreatment each year. Broken bones, lacerations, concussions, limb dislocations, and abrasions are commonplace. So, too, are instances of sexual and emotional abuse, neglect, and abandonment (Martin, 1992; Shengold, 1990).

What factors cause parents to maltreat their children? Pressures from work, the home, financial difficulties, a history of maltreatment in the parent's background, and low levels of self-esteem are frequently cited as reasons behind

Lifespan Development in Action

TEN STEPS TOWARD EFFECTIVE DISCIPLINE

One of the more frequently expressed concerns among parents is how to discipline children effectively. Perhaps the first step is to develop an understanding of exactly what discipline means. Discipline is the setting of limits in an effort to teach acceptable forms of conduct or behavior. Although numerous strategies exist, the ultimate goal of discipline is to produce responsibility in children (Essa, 1990; Miller, 1990). Furthermore, children must come to realize they are accountable for the consequences of their behavior. The following suggestions are recommended to assist adults confronted with the task of disciplining children:

1. **Realize there are motivations for misbehavior.** Misbehavior doesn't just happen on its own. Rather, the child may be motivated in some way to engage in disruptive behavior. Some of the more common reasons for misbehavior include boredom or a desire for attention, revenge, power, and control.

2. **Act with confidence.** Adults must believe in themselves and their abilities to promote responsible behavior. They should adopt a take-charge attitude and handle disciplinary situations with self-assuredness and confidence.

3. **Relate the discipline to the situation at hand.** Adults should focus on the central issue and not stray into unrelated problems. Also, it is important to tell children it is the misbehavior being rejected, not them as individuals. Furthermore, adults need to explain why they are upset with the misbehavior. ("You broke the vase and I'm angry because it was special to me.") This helps teach youngsters that misbehavior has implications for others.

4. **Be consistent.** Erratic discipline confuses the youngster and seems unlikely to prevent similar problems in the future. If adults are going to discipline the child for one particular type of misbehavior, the reoccurrence of this misbehavior must also be disciplined. If there is more than one child at home, discipline should also be consistent among each of them as well.

5. **Do not make discipline a public spectacle.** Discipline can be a sensitive affair, especially among older children. Talking with children alone, rather than in front of others, reduces embarrassment and other painful emotions. Also, adults should respect children's feelings after discipline has been administered. Shame and guilt are fairly common reactions. Understanding adults do not attempt to increase the child's guilt after the situation has transpired, and they are open to whatever resolution the youngster wants to make.

6. **Avoid angry emotional outbursts.** There is no evidence that yelling, screaming, or other emotional tirades promote effective discipline. In fact, it is conceivable that youngsters listen less when this sort of adult behavior occurs. Adults should avoid impulsivity and take time to carefully organize their thoughts. When this is done, speech should be deliberate and controlled, but firm. Children also seem to listen better when adults talk *with* them, not *to* them.

7. **Establish limits in a clear and precise fashion.** Children need to know what is acceptable and what is not. Spell it out so there is no question

Continued . . .

TEN STEPS TOWARD EFFECTIVE DISCIPLINE, Continued . . .

regarding what misbehavior is or what it can encompass. Also, remember that many children, naturally, are going to test limits, which is all the more reason to be clear and consistent about behavioral expectations.

8. **Make the discipline fit the misbehavior.** Adults need to carefully examine the type and degree of disciplinary measure employed in relation to the misbehavior at hand. The discipline administered should be compatible with the nature of the misconduct and not too lenient or too extreme.

9. **Discipline should be as close in time as possible to the misbehavior.** Once adults have gathered their thoughts, discipline should be quickly administered. Children have a tendency to better remember and more clearly associate those events occurring together in time and space. Misbehavior and discipline should thus be yoked together, the latter not being put off for hours or until day's end.

10. **Follow through at an appropriate time.** Discussing the disciplinary situation during a follow-up conversation often helps ensure that a lesson has been remembered. This does not mean dwelling on the misconduct nor accentuating the negative. Rather, it implies that both adult and child have the opportunity to reflect on the issue and the role that discipline plays in creating a more harmonious living arrangement.

violence (Elder, 1992; Rivera & Widom, 1990; Wolfe, 1991). And research indicates that many abusive parents were abused themselves when they were youngsters. For example, a study of transgenerational child abuse showed that mothers abused their children in much the same way they had been abused as children, and the husbands abused their wives much as they had been abused when young (Ney, 1988).

Many abusers are lonely, frequently depressed, and have never learned how to contain their aggression (Milner & Chilamkurti, 1991; Milner & Robertson, 1990; Straus & Gelles, 1988). Physical illness, untimely childbearing, and a parent's poor ability to empathize with youngsters can substantially increase the likelihood of child maltreatment (Gelles & Conte, 1990; Salzinger, 1991). This is particularly true when social stress, social isolation, and family dysfunction exist. Evidence also exists (e.g., Ammerman, 1991) that certain child characteristics such as a difficult temperament or a health problem heightens the risk for maltreatment.

Many parents also abuse their children in an effort to enforce discipline (Sabatino, 1991). Some have an overpowering need to impress other adults with a well-behaved child. Still other child abusers identify with the youngster and consider every fault and mistake of the child to be their own. Too, there are those who perceive themselves as failures in life and feel they are attaining superiority and command by exerting such forceful dominance (Ammerman, 1990; Gelles & Cornell, 1990).

A particularly bothersome feature of child abuse is the consequence of battering in later life. Many maltreated children run a risk for aggressiveness, self-destructive behaviors, school failure, and delinquency (Sternberg et al., 1993).

Physical injury is the most visible form of child abuse.

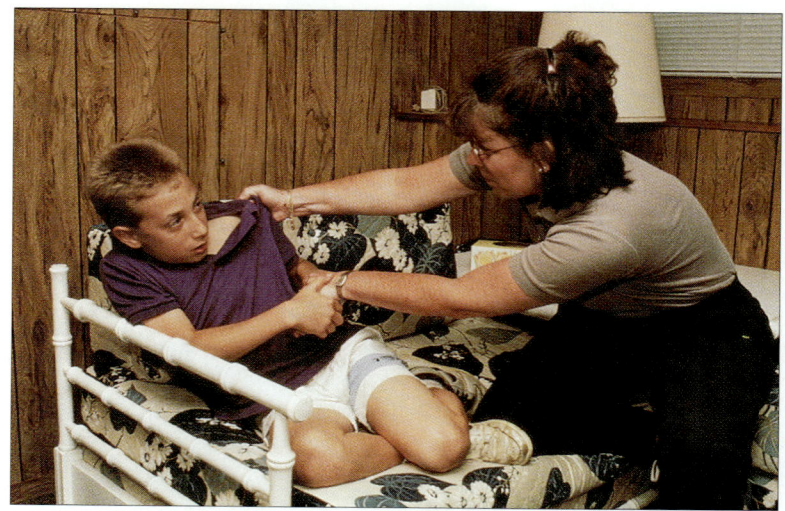

For example, research (Weiss et al., 1992) shows that early harsh discipline is associated with later aggressive behavior in kindergarteners; another study (Eckenrode, Laird, & Doris, 1993) discloses that compared to nonmaltreated public school children, maltreated youngsters had significantly more discipline referrals and suspensions. And one need not be the actual abuse victim to exhibit maladaptive behaviors. In support of this, one study (Carlson, 1990) uncovered a link between adolescent depression and aggressive behavior and witnessing parental violence. Many abused children are also insecure, are mistrusting, foster poor self-concepts, and have low overall levels of self-confidence and self-reliance (Fantuzzo, 1990; Sabatino, 1991).

Incest and Child Sexual Abuse   The maltreatment of children also includes sexual coercion, and this kind of assault can occur both within the family and outside of it. Related to the former, **incest** means sexual contact between close blood relatives. **Child sexual abuse,** on the other hand, means sexual contact between an adult and a child who are in no way related. Both usually refer to interactions between a child and adult when the youngster is being used for the sexual stimulation of that adult or another person. Let's look more closely at both incest and child sexual abuse.

INCEST Virtually every society prohibits intrafamilial sexual relationships. This prohibition is often called the *incest taboo.* In the United States, incest is a crime, and although laws in different states vary regarding the sexual relationship forbidden, close blood relatives always include father, mother, grandfather, grandmother, brother, sister, aunt, uncle, niece, nephew, and sometimes first cousins. Many states include stepparent-stepchildren, stepsibling, and in-law relationships, although these individuals are not blood related.

It is difficult to assess the prevalence of incest because it happens behind closed doors and most victims live with secrecy and isolation. However, it is estimated that as many as 20 million Americans may be incest victims, meaning about 1 in 10 have been affected. The average age of a child encountering this kind of sexual assault is 11, and the sexual activity is estimated to have begun somewhere between the ages of 5 and 8. Contrary to the belief that incest is a problem only among the poor, incestuous families are found in every socioeconomic and educational group (Patton, 1991; Weinstein & Rosen, 1988).

Ruth and Henry Kempe (1984) have provided an insightful look at incestuous child sexual abuse. Their research reveals that father-daughter and stepfather-daughter incest represent approximately three quarters of reported incest cases. Girls involved with fathers or stepfathers during preadolescence or very early adolescence are often the oldest daughters. Mother-son, mother-daughter, and brother-sister incest constitute most of the remaining one quarter of reports. Although sibling incest is rarely reported, it is probably a far more common part of the total sexual abuse picture than we know. Brother-sister incest is not unusual before or at puberty. If one sibling is near adulthood and the other a child, it is much like parent-child incest. The most prevalent sibling incest pattern is the abuse of younger sisters and brothers by an older male sibling (Pittman, 1987).

Many cases of incest are never reported or included in statistics, especially in families from upper socioeconomic brackets. Such families often seek help through other means such as private psychiatry and have not necessarily been included in statistical sources. This is particularly evident if the "victim" did not seek help until much later, as an adult. This often happens when the relationship is a more unusual one such as that between mother-in-law and son-in-law or father-in-law and daughter-in-law. Reporting of father-daughter incest is the most common because the daughter precipitates a crisis when the situation becomes intolerable to her. In the case of sibling incest, the maturing of the siblings may spontaneously change both partners and, therefore, the nature of the relationship (Ballard et al., 1990; Conte, 1990; Kempe & Kempe, 1984).

Many researchers have explored the dynamics of incest (Christiansen & Blake, 1990; Gilgun & Connor, 1990; Horton et al., 1990). One source (Stark, 1984) points out that when the incestuous activity begins, victims often believe they are holding the family together. They fear the offending parent will go to jail if the incest is discovered. Some children acquiesce because they are desperate for any type of affection. And in many situations, children believe there is no one to help them, even if they wanted help. Offenders often try to convince themselves there is nothing wrong with what they are doing. But most use either subtle coercion or direct threats to keep their children silent (Long & Jackson, 1991; Nelson, 1991; Perry & Wrightsman, 1991).

In many father-daughter incestuous relationships, the mother is aware of the circumstances. A number of mothers choose to remain uninvolved, perhaps because she was a victim of incest, or she is so insecure and frightened by her husband or significant other that she is immobilized (Strand, 1990). Given the mother's passive stance, the youngster often searches for an available and safe person with whom to communicate. However, in so doing the child runs the risk of not being believed or even being rejected (Horton et al., 1990; Weinstein & Rosen, 1988).

CHILD SEXUAL ABUSE Like incest, the sexual abuse of a young child by an adult is a punishable crime in the United States. However, the incidence of child sexual abuse is not much easier to assess than the incidence of incest. Most researchers (Faller, 1990; Gomes-Schwartz, Horowitz, & Cardarelli, 1990;

INTERRELATEDNESS OF AGING PROCESSES

How do you think child maltreatment affects the youngster's psychosocial dynamics? For example, do you think physical or sexual abuse has the potential of creating mistrust, shame, guilt, or other negative behavioral outcomes?

Watkins & Bentovim, 1992) agree the problem is occurring at a significant rate, but acknowledge that reported cases barely scratch the surface. Moreover, Gail Wyatt and Gloria Powell (1988) point out that many reports of child sex abuse are never even passed on to protective agencies. Thus there are large numbers of child victims whose abuse is never really counted. In addition, many sexual abuse cases are investigated, but do not stand up to the rigors of the court. And there are unknown numbers of youngsters who remain silent, never tell, or never seek therapeutic assistance (Priest, 1992).

Some researchers have attempted to estimate the number of children victimized by sexual abuse. As far as female victimization is concerned, Diana Russell (1983) found that 38% of the women she interviewed reported at least one instance of child sexual abuse. Judith Herman's (1981) detailed analysis of five separate surveys revealed that one fifth to one third of all the women queried said they had had some sort of childhood sexual encounter with an adult male. Other studies, most notably Briere and Runtz (1985), Finkelhor (1984), Sedney and Brooks (1984), and Bagley (1985), have estimated that 15 to 20% of the women studied experienced some type of sexual abuse during their childhood.

Research reveals that male children are abused less frequently than females. For example, a national survey in Canada (Badgley, 1984) showed that about 6% of the adult males queried had been molested under the age of 15 and almost 10% under the age of 18. Another investigation (Sorrenti-Little et al., 1984) showed that approximately 10% of the respondents experienced some type of childhood sexual abuse.

A study of African-American college students (Priest, 1992) revealed that 12% of the males queried, compared to 25% of the females, reported having been sexually abused before the age of 17. It should be noted that many researchers (Condy et al., 1987; Risen & Koss, 1987) feel that compared to females, abuse perpetrated on males is most often unreported and undisclosed. Moreover, it appears to be more prevalent today than previously assumed (Bolton et al., 1990; Faller, 1990; Finkelhor, 1990; Maletzky, 1990).

EFFECTS OF INCEST AND CHILD SEXUAL ABUSE Over the years, a rich vein of research activity has focused on the impact of incest and child sexual abuse, and numerous investigators have supplied valuable insight on the topic (Bolton et al., 1990; Faller, 1990; Gelles & Cornell, 1990; Gomes-Schwartz et al., 1990; Kendall-Tackett, Williams, & Finkelhor, 1993). One of the most comprehensive investigations of the effects of child sexual victimization was undertaken by David Finkelhor (1988). Finkelhor has developed a model of child sexual abuse suggesting the trauma of sexual victimization creates four *traumagenic dynamics* that alter a person's cognitive or emotional orientation to the world. These dynamics, which can distort the individual's self-concept, worldview, capacities, and ability to experience positive feelings for others, are traumatic sexualization, betrayal, stigmatization, and powerlessness.

TRAUMATIC SEXUALIZATION Traumatic sexualization refers to the abuse conditions in which a child's sexuality is shaped in developmentally inappropriate and interpersonally dysfunctional ways. Finkelhor believes that several processes converge to contribute to traumatic sexualization:

- Most offenders reward abused children for sexual behavior that is inappropriate to their level of development.

- Because of rewards, sexual abuse victims learn to use sexual behavior (appropriate or inappropriate) as a strategy for manipulating others to get their needs met.
- A child's sexuality can become traumatized when negative memories become associated in the youngster's mind with sexual activity.
- Children become confused and acquire inaccurate information about sexual behavior and sexual morality because of things that offenders tell them or ways offenders behave.

GENDER SIMILARITIES AND DIFFERENCES

Do you think the effects of incest or childhood sexual abuse are the same or different for boys and girls? If you agree gender differences exist, what factors do you think account for the expression of these behaviors?

The impact of traumatic sexualization may show itself in victims' later behavior in many ways, including sexual preoccupations, compulsive masturbation and sex play, and sexual knowledge and behaviors that are inappropriate to their age group (August & Forman, 1989; Corwin, 1985; Friedrich, Urquiza, & Beilke, 1986). Male children, especially, may become sexually aggressive themselves and begin to victimize peers or younger children. Others may become sexually promiscuous. Among adult symptoms related to traumatic sexualization are an aversion to sex, flashbacks during sex, and difficulty with arousal and orgasm (Briere, 1984; Langmade, 1983).

BETRAYAL When betrayal occurs, children discover that someone on whom they were vitally dependent has caused them or wishes to cause them harm. Betrayal can occur in several ways. For example, the betrayal can occur at the time of the initial abuse, as children realize a person they trusted is treating them with disregard for their well-being. In other instances, youngsters experience the betrayal belatedly and realize they were tricked into doing something bad through the use of lies or misrepresentations (Baird, 1982; Briere, 1984; Cohen, 1983; Peters, 1988).

There are other symptoms related to betrayal, many surfacing in later life. For example, abuse victims are often hostile and angry, distrustful of men or intimate relationships in general, and have a history of failed relationships or marriages. Finkelhor (1988) believes the anger and hostility may be a primitive way victims try to protect themselves from future betrayals. The distrust and difficulty in intimacy is another form of protection. The antisocial behavior may be a form of retaliation for betrayal.

STIGMATIZATION Stigmatization refers to the negative messages about the worthlessness, shamefulness, and guilt that are communicated to the child about the experience. These messages can be communicated in a variety of ways. For example, abusers say it directly when they blame and denigrate the victim, or say it indirectly through their pressures for secrecy. Much of the stigmatization, however, originates from the attitudes the victims hear or the moral judgments they infer from those around them. Victims are likely to know or discover that sexual abuse is regarded as deviant and that it's a crime (Bagley & Ramsay, 1986; Vander Mey & Neff, 1986; Weinstein & Rosen, 1988).

Related to this dynamic, child sexual abuse victims often feel isolated and turn to self-destructive behaviors. Some gravitate to stigmatized societal groups, such as drug abusers, criminals, or prostitutes. In other forms, stigmatization may manifest itself in the form of depression or suicide attempts. Victims of sexual abuse often harbor low self-esteem and feel no one else has had similar experiences. Because of the latter, many fear rejection from others if their "secret" is discovered (Kendall-Tackett, 1988; Paxton, 1991; Peters, 1988).

POWERLESSNESS Powerlessness occurs when a child's will and wishes are repeatedly overruled and frustrated, and when the child is threatened with injury. Perhaps the most basic form of powerlessness is the experience of having one's body repeatedly touched or invaded against one's wishes, whether this occurs through force or deceit. The feeling of powerlessness is intensified when children are frustrated in their efforts to terminate the sexual abuse. This can happen when a child tries unsuccessfully to fight back, to run away, or to outsmart the abuser and is frustrated in efforts to end the abuse (Gomes-Schwartz et al., 1990; Rogers & Terry, 1984).

Powerlessness appears to create three types of effects. The first includes anxiety and fear, which reflect the experience of having been unable to control a harmful and painful event. The second type of effect is the impairment of a person's coping skills. Having been frustrated in an effort to protect themselves, victims often report a low sense of personal efficacy. A third type of effect is a compensatory reaction, an unusual need to control or dominate, seen particularly in male victims. Male victims often engage in group aggressive and delinquent behavior, or become abusers or molesters themselves (Gelinas, 1983; Trainor, 1984).

INTERVENTION STRATEGIES The age and developmental status of the child sexual abuse victim usually determines the mode of therapeutic intervention. Play therapy is often regarded as the treatment of choice for the very young child. School-age youngsters often respond effectively to a mixture of activities, including therapeutic games and exercises, art therapy, and playacting (Wheeler & Berliner, 1988). Of the treatment modes available for older children and adolescents, conventional individual or group therapy (or both) are usually prescribed. Individual therapy allows privacy during the initial period of shock, and may be needed for more intensive care and closer monitoring of conditions

Child maltreatment is often kept hidden by the victim in a nightmare of secrecy.

Lifespan Development in Action

WHAT TO DO IF YOUR CHILD HAS BEEN SEXUALLY ASSAULTED

Discovering your child has been victimized can be an overwhelming experience. More than anything else, your child needs support, comfort, and love. What needs to be done immediately is to reassure your child that you:

- believe what she or he has told you
- know it is not her or his fault
- are glad she or he has told you about it
- are sorry about what happened
- will do your best to protect and support her or him

Many parents are unsure how to help a youngster. One important way is to quietly encourage your child to talk about the assault. It is important to do this gently and without pressure. If your child doesn't talk about the experience right away, you may want to provide an opportunity. ("If you don't feel like talking about this right now, I understand. But if it begins to trouble you later, or you're thinking about it a lot, it's important that we talk about it.")

While making it clear that the fault lies with the offender, parents need to remember that often he or she is someone known to the child—very often a relative, neighbor, or friend of the family. It is normal to feel angry, but angry threats about what should happen to the offender might cause your child to feel guilty about having told. Your response should place the blame and responsibility with the offender in a realistic way. ("What he did was wrong. We're going to try to get him some help so he doesn't hurt you or anyone else again.")

The decisions to be made after the sexual assault of a child are difficult ones. There are no right answers. Because sexual assault is so disruptive, most experts agree that therapeutic intervention is beneficial for both the child and you. For the parent, it is important to openly talk about the victimization in a supportive environment. Talking to a counselor trained in child sexual assault can help parents sort out their own feelings, help determine what to do next, make arrangements for follow-up medical care, and help everyone in the family (especially other children) deal with the assault. (Adapted from Los Angeles Commission on Assaults Against Women, 1983)

such as fear or severe depression or for the added support of a one-to-one relationship (Kempe & Kempe, 1984; O'Donohue & Elliott, 1992).

Group therapy, which assists victims in feeling less different and alone, has become a popular treatment approach today and is recommended by many (Mandell & Damon, 1989; Mash & Barkley, 1989; Schacht, Kerlinsky, & Carlson, 1990). Groups tend to reduce isolation and facilitate peer relationships in a manner not possible in individual therapy. The support that groups offer may also prove useful in helping to reduce the stigmatization, shame, guilt, and worthlessness, as well as other intense emotions often felt by incest and sexual abuse victims. And because anxieties, uncertainties, and sexual inhibitions may endure for years, group intervention and individual modes of therapy are often productive during the adolescent and adult years.

Intervention with parents is an important part of therapy for sexually abused children. Parents need to be educated about the effects of sexual victimization, and how to best support the youngster. They also need to know what steps to take if their child has been sexually assaulted (see the accompanying Lifespan Development in Action box). Many parents desire help with their own reactions to sexual victimization as well as other possible disruptions to their lives that may be directly or indirectly associated with the sexual abuse. Individual, family, or group therapy, or participating in support groups are therefore recognized as important adjuncts to child-focused treatment (Lipovsky, 1991; Mac-Farlane et al., 1988; Mackey, 1991; Paxton, 1991; Powell, 1988).

Another component of therapy for parents and children is education about the prevention of sexual offenses. Most researchers (e.g., Wheeler & Berliner, 1988) believe an important aspect of coping with an abuse experience is reducing the sense of vulnerability to subsequent abuse. Indeed, there is some evidence (DeYoung, 1982; Russell, 1984) that victims are at an increased risk for future victimization. Some investigators (e.g., Fromuth, 1986) feel such vulnerability represents a manifestation of the powerlessness often experienced by victims.

William Young (1988) believes that when properly executed, prevention programs reduce the numbers of children victimized by incest and sexual abuse. Such programs break the offender's pattern by furnishing children, parents, and community members with a most powerful tool: the knowledge necessary to recognize an inappropriate approach, to understand it is the offender who is responsible for deviant behavior, and to assist youngsters and those who care for them to learn how to respond when such maltreatment occurs. A pivotal feature of such prevention programming is teaching children realistic ways of saying no and being assertive (Berrick, 1991; Blumberg, 1991; Kaufman & Rudy, 1991). Other prevention efforts may include workshops geared toward teachers, day-care providers, and other professionals who work with children. Additionally, workshops for parents are often aimed at assisting them to help their youngster avoid being victimized and what to do if it should occur.

■ School Influences on the Developing Child

Early childhood education provides programs and constructive learning experiences to young children. Generally speaking, such programming seeks to stimulate all developmental spheres of the growing child through a wide variety of learning experiences. Experts in the field of early childhood education (e.g., Gordon & Browne, 1993; Kostelnik et al., 1993) stress the importance of promoting social, self-help, and self-image skills. Equally important is the role of nurturing cognitive and linguistic abilities and, in general, learning readiness skills. Many programs today place considerable emphasis on heightening the child's levels of self-sufficiency and independence. Early childhood education programs also seek to establish and maintain a healthy learning environment and provide positive guidance and discipline. Related to the former, the

TABLE 6-3
Early Childhood Education Programs: Implications for Development

Physical Development	• Meals and snacks ensure that nutritional requirements are met • Play equipment exercises gross and fine motor skills • Equipment provides for degrees of skill as well as variety • Staff monitors health and safety of child • Programming offers balance between activity and rest
Cognitive Development	• Nurturance of sensorimotor and preoperational processes • Provision of environment that encourages active exploration • Opportunities for imagination, creativity and sociodramatic play • Availability of problem-solving challenges • Stimulation of early linguistic abilities
Personality Development	• Nurturance of psychosocial traits such as trust and security • Development of independence and autonomy • Provision of positive discipline, including fair expectations and limits • Positive emotional climate fosters healthy self-concept formation • Encouragement of self-help skills (dressing, toileting, etc.)
Social Development	• Regular contact with agemates as well as staff members • Opportunities to work alone as well as in small groups • Availability of diverse play experiences • Exposure to cultural and racial diversity • Reinforcement and encouragement of prosocial behaviors

establishment of a positive emotional climate that fosters trust and security is especially important (Catron & Allen, 1993; Kostelnik, Whiren, & Soderman, 1993; Shimoni & Ferguson, 1992). Table 6-3 displays how early childhood education programs stimulate the development of the young child.

As we see throughout the course of childhood and adolescence, the teacher is in a position to nurture the individual's growth and development and to promote positive learning experiences. Within the early childhood setting, the teacher executes many functions, from guiding program activities to working cooperatively with parents (Gestwicki, 1992). How the teacher interacts with the children is especially important, particularly her or his warmth, understanding, and support of the child's strengths and weaknesses. Indeed, most recognize (e.g., Beaty, 1992; Charlesworth, 1992; Essa, 1992) that the success of early childhood education rests heavily on the teacher's commitment to youngsters, the classroom climate that is established, and the type of role model she or he represents.

The schedules and routines established by the preschool are the means through which goals and objectives are met. Although activities differ, the general thrust of programming is similar. Many schools offer a diverse mixture of free and structured play activities; creative play opportunities in art, music, and literature; and beginning subject-area exercises in cognitive skills, letter formation, language skills, and so forth. Other activities may focus on small and large muscle skills, listening abilities, recitation, or special programs, such as nutrition and safety awareness. The overall length of the early childhood education program (full- or half-day sessions) determines the extent of these activities (Hildebrand, 1991; Maxim, 1993; Taylor, 1991).

Categories of Early Childhood Education   Early childhood education programming varies in operating principles and philosophies, curriculum content, location, size, and an assortment of other details (Essa, 1992; Gordon & Browne, 1993; Morrison, 1991). To better understand their complexities, it is helpful to develop a classification system of some of the major types of early childhood programming available today. Such a classification system can serve to distinguish the basic differences in structure and operating procedure.

DAY CARE As the name implies, this program offers full-day child care coverage to parents of preschool children. Such an operation is especially appealing to dual-earner families. Although they initially had no planned educational programs, most of them have since been reorganized to meet the child's social, emotional, physical, and intellectual needs. The cost of day care varies considerably, and in some instances the centers charge fees on a sliding scale based on the family's ability to pay.

INDUSTRY-RELATED DAY CARE Industry-related day care is a response to the growing numbers of mothers in the labor force, as well as the multiple needs of dual-earner families. For employers, this kind of day care is used to attract workers and reduce turnover, as well as to decrease absenteeism and tardiness resulting from other child-care arrangements. Some of these facilities are located directly in the parents' workplace; others may be located nearby in a separate facility. Some industries absorb all programming costs, some provide partial coverage, and others just reserve a place for employees' children.

HOME DAY CARE Home day care is also attractive to working parents. It offers care and attention during the hours of the working day, but within a caregiver's residence. Similar to all early childhood facilities, a home day care must be inspected and licensed by state officials and the operator must be certified.

COMPENSATORY PROGRAMS Compensatory programs are subsidized by the federal government. The most well known of these is *Project Head Start,* which was introduced to help keep the blight of a deficient home environment from leaving a permanent impression on some of the country's children. Under the supervision of the Office of Economic Opportunity, federal grants were given to local community agencies capable of meeting basic outlined standards and implementing programs designed to improve the health of preschoolers and alleviate the prospect of school readiness deficiencies in disadvantaged children. Basically, Project Head Start consists of programs in education, medical and dental care, nutrition, social services, psychological services, parent education, and community volunteer programs.

NURSERY SCHOOL A nursery school is usually private and tends to appeal to wealthier families. Because most offer half-day sessions, this type of educational setting often does not fit the needs of dual-earner families. Nursery schools are generally more expensive than most other forms of early childhood education,

THEORETICAL ISSUES

How can you employ Bronfenbrenner's ecological theory to analyze how young children's entry into the early childhood setting is intertwined with the family, neighborhood, community, and culture? Can you see how the lives of children and the society in which they live, including school, are interdependent?

The early childhood education setting enhances many facets of growth and development.

and many place an emphasis on a learning readiness curriculum. The teacher-to-child ratio in these settings is usually small, which offers appeal to those parents desiring close individual attention for their youngster.

PARENT COOPERATIVE PROGRAM A parent cooperative program is organized by parents who employ trained teachers to plan, teach, and supervise the program. Parent cooperative programs can be found in private homes, but many programs operate in community centers, churches, or other buildings. (The more established and successful co-ops frequently have their own buildings.) Many times, parent cooperative programs are able to offer reduced tuition fees more easily than private facilities.

LABORATORY SCHOOL College or university laboratory schools were among the earliest types of nursery schools in the country. The laboratory school focuses its energies on preparental education, teacher learning, and research studies. Sometimes mobilizing the resources of an area to meet the needs of young children, the laboratory school is usually financed primarily by the academic institution.

INFANT-TODDLER PROGRAM The infant-toddler program is one of the fastest growing forms of early childhood education today. It has special appeal to dual-earner families, and offers high-quality individualized caregiving aimed at optimizing early growth and development. In addition to caregiving, programming typically focuses on babies' physical, emotional, and social needs, as well as sensory and exploratory play and peer interactions. Infant-toddler programs are expensive, particularly because individual care is required. Diapers, infant formula, and other financial considerations have the potential for further increasing center costs.

SPECIAL NEEDS PROGRAMS Some early childhood education programs employ qualified staff members who are capable of working with special needs youngsters. Many times, special needs children are mainstreamed part time or full time into a regular early childhood education setting, such as when a hearing-impaired youngster is enrolled in a group of nonhearing-impaired children. Early childhood education centers are subject to legislation designed to secure and protect the rights of special needs youngsters, including making facilities and programs accessible. To learn more about the educational considerations for special needs children, see Allen (1992) and Raver (1991). In the accompanying Focus on Diversity box, we provide a glimpse of early childhood education programming in China.

Peer Group Influences on the Developing Child

Moving from the family and being able to interact with others is an important criterion of social maturity. Peer group interaction provides opportunities for children to further understand their behavior and the effect it will have on others. Early group relationships give youngsters the opportunity to increase their independence, competence, and emotional support. Peer relations may also provide more complex and arousing sensory stimulations than those available in the home, offer new models for identification, influence self-concept development, and alter the character of children's play (Berndt & Ladd, 1989; Howes, 1988; Ladd, Price, & Hart, 1988).

As we investigate this topic, we remind you that developmental processes are not unitary, nor do they exist in a vacuum. Rather, development is multidimensional and affects the whole person. In this regard, peer and family influences are additive as well as interactive in their influence. Sometimes peer group norms reflect the influence of adults, but at other times they reflect their own.

Peer and adult influences on the child are also not always in harmony. Though there may be considerable consonance, sometimes peer and family influences produce cross pressures that can lead to conflict. How the youngster responds to such cross pressures varies. Willard Hartup (1980, 1983, 1989) maintains that sometimes the values and behaviors relative to the given situation are crucial. Other times, the attractiveness of the peer group, the extent of contact with friends, the degree to which the peer group functions as a reference, and the adequacy of family adjustment are important factors. The broader milieu of the peer group, the amount of time children spend with it, and the number of interactions they have with its members tend to intensify the group's influence.

Again, we must view development as an integrated whole rather than as a single facet of growth. For example, peer group development is affected by numerous forces, including cognitive, personality, emotional, and family influences. None of these areas of growth can be studied in a vacuum. Rather, the student of lifespan development must decide how one affects the others.

Patterns of Peer Group Interaction   Rarely do two children behave in the same way when placed in the company of others. Some may eagerly seek to join the company of others, others may scream to be taken away, and still others may become passive and watch the activity from a safe distance. When a

Focus on Diversity

EARLY CHILDHOOD EDUCATION IN CHINA

The scene is a nursery school located deep within the city of Peking, China. A middle-aged preschool teacher is reading to the 34 children in attendance, a mixture of 3- and 4-year-olds. The youngsters sit motionless and seemingly catch her every word. They do not talk, cry, or shove.

In an adjoining room, 18 toddlers are engaged in a different set of activities. Some are playing with blocks while others climb through an assortment of large makeshift cubes. When success is achieved in one physical challenge, the toddlers are given new activities to develop their growing bodies.

For years, American educators have been attracted to the early childhood education strategies employed in China. Onlookers are invariably drawn to the almost universal good behavior of Chinese children. They are quiet, eager to follow their teacher's instructions, and seldom exhibit the aggressiveness demonstrated by American children. The established learning climate also encourages a cooperative spirit among the youngsters, which, in the process, downplays individuality and encourages prosocial behavior.

Chinese parents may enroll children as young as 2 months of age, the time when the mother's maternity leave ends. Nurseries for the infants provide necessary custodial care as well as early stimulation to encourage developing cognitive skills. When the children reach their first birthday, attendants begin to toilet train them in a very structured fashion. Children are placed on enamel spittoons and kept there until they defecate.

As time progresses, more highly structured situations await the children. Lesson plans are delivered in a crisp, methodical style, and most of the teachings involve rote memory and copying tasks modeled by the adult. Children also learn at an early age the premium placed on docility. Selfishness is not tolerated by the teachers, and sharing and other forms of prosocial behavior are encouraged whenever possible.

Although methodical and organized, the teachers are warm and kind in their dealings with the children. Good behavior seldom escapes notice and children receive a steady diet of praise and encouragement. When negative behavior occurs, firm disciplinary strategies are used rather than punitive approaches. Physical punishment does not have a place in Chinese early childhood education programming, nor does harsh verbal rebuke. The dignity of the child is always acknowledged. Experts maintain that such an approach fosters an early mutual respect between young and old.

---

certain degree of group comfort has been acquired, attempts at making further social contacts are often awkward. Conflicts are common, but usually short lived, and occur as frequently among friends as nonfriends. Among friends and socially preferred agemates, though, conflicts are usually less intense, resolved more frequently with disengagement, and have a more satisfactory outcome (Clark & Bittle, 1992; Hartup, Laursen, Stewart, & Eastenson, 1988). Along these lines, research often shows (e.g., Bryant, 1992) that socially preferred children use a calm approach to resolving conflict, whereas unpopular or rejected children employ measures such as anger or retaliation.

Time and experience teach children that certain behaviors are socially acceptable and others are not. For example, hitting a playmate may release an inner impulse, but it may also cause friends and playmates to cry, strike back, or

With age, peer group interaction increases.

run away. Gradually, children realize that how they relate to their peers greatly influences the treatment they in turn receive. Because of such gains in interpersonal awareness, social competence increases during this time (Denham et al., 1991; Yeates, Schultz, & Selman, 1991).

The peer group during early childhood is quite selective, usually consisting of individuals of approximately the same age who share a common play interest. Group members tend to keep an air of exclusiveness about them, and many factors determine peer acceptance and rejection (Kemple, Speranza, & Hazen, 1992; Newcomb, Bukowski, & Pattee, 1993; Vitaro et al., 1992). For example, children's ability to gain acceptance into an established group often depends not only on their ability to comply with the members' routines, but also on the degree to which they initiate group contact and the friendliness they exhibit in the process. In support of this, one study (Ladd & Hart, 1992) found that those preschoolers who were more initiating of peer contacts displayed less anxious behavior in school and were better liked by their agemates.

Interestingly, it has been found (Kochanska, 1992) that a child's interpersonal skills with a peer group hinge considerably on the quality of interaction with one's mother. In this study of 5-year-old children, those youngsters who used abrasive strategies with their mothers tended to be aggressive and unsuccessful with their peers. Additionally, the mother's parenting style served to shape a child's social competence. Those children whose mothers employed negative control tended to be aggressive and had poor interaction skills. On the other hand, those children whose mothers used polite guidance were rarely coercive. Finally, children whose mothers tended to issue unclear commands were usually less successful with their socialization skills. Other research (Kennedy, 1992; Suess, Grossman, & Sroufe, 1992; Youngblade & Belsky, 1992) supports the notion that secure and harmonious parent-child relationships, as well as parents' interest in teaching social skills to their children, facilitates more positive peer interaction.

Peer groups also discriminate on the basis of gender (Victor, 1993). Compared with the lack of gender discrimination in play groups during toddlerhood, preschoolers prefer same-sex playmates. This trend persists and even intensifies throughout middle childhood, although it is more pronounced in males than in females (Arliss & Borisoff, 1993; Rawlins, 1993). According to Judy Pearson and Roberta Davilla (1993), it will be from these segregated play groups that gender differences begin to emerge. For instance, traditional boys will eventually learn independence and the organizational skills necessary for coordinating activities for play participants. By learning the socially approved rules of the game, boys are able to deal directly with competition from both their friends and their enemies. However, traditional girls learn cooperation, not competition. They typically play in smaller, more intimate pairs, and their identities tend to be fostered in cooperative relationships with others, rather than individual goal achievement and rule following. We have more to say about gender differences in peer groups as well as in other social spheres throughout the text.

The peer group also contains dominance hierarchies. Shortly after the group forms, internal group processes select one or a few as its leaders. Others become followers. Often, the group leaders are above average in intelligence, assertive, and well liked by the others (Weist & Ollendick, 1991). In a cross-cultural study involving Chinese and Canadian children, being accepted and well liked by one's peers was also found to be related to leadership and overall sociability (Chen, Rubin, & Sun, 1992).

Research shows (e.g., Slomkowski & Killen, 1992) that preschoolers are capable of making conceptual distinctions between friends and nonfriends in terms of judgments and justifications concerning peer group transgressions. Popular and unpopular group members also emerge over time. Popularity is usually linked to friendliness, extroversion, and the ability to get along with others. As far as unpopularity is concerned, one investigation (Cillessen et al., 1992) of peer-rejected boys found that almost one half were rated as being aggressive, impulsive, disruptive, and noncooperative. Some of the unpopular boys, though, were socially shy or perceived themselves to be negatively regarded by their peers. Another study (Tryon & Keane, 1991) noted the connection between unpopularity and aggressive behavior, including the use of demands when seeking group entry.

THEORETICAL ISSUES

According to humanistic theory, one of the requirements for a healthy personality is the fulfillment of the need for belongingness. How do you think early peer relationships sow the seeds for affiliation, acceptance, and affection? Do you perceive the child's social motivations being positive and self-directed as Maslow proclaims?

The activity of the peer group during early childhood is interesting. A cooperative attitude is more evident than during toddlerhood, and more sharing takes place. Problem-solving skills within the peer group also begin to appear, although this tends to take place more among friends than acquaintances (Caplan, Bennetto, & Weissberg, 1991). The peer group is also capable of devising more activities for all members. Goal-directed behaviors are also present. However, such developments do not imply that all signs of emotional and social immaturity have evaporated. On the contrary, selfishness, impatience, and disagreement punctuate many preschool peer groups.

Prosocial Development   An important facet of social development is being sensitive to the needs and feelings of others. Such peer sensitivity is called **prosocial behavior,** and it pertains to such areas as cooperation, comforting, sympathizing, altruism, sharing, and helping others. In a broad sense, it might be referred to as Good Samaritan behavior.

Many lifespan development researchers have supplied insight on the nature of prosocial behavior and how it is expressed during childhood. Given the prevalence of egocentrism, it may be surprising to you that certain types of prosocial behavior surface early in life. Toddlers, for example, have been observed sharing with others and even demonstrating some insight into the emotional state and needs of others (Hay et al., 1991). Carolyn Zahn-Waxler and colleagues (1992) found that prosocial behaviors in the form of sharing and the provision of comfort emerged between the first and second year. Preschoolers also perform such prosocial acts as helping, cooperating with, and comforting others. However, it is important to stress that even though the ability to demonstrate prosocial behavior appears early in life, this does not mean it is consistently expressed. Usually this does not transpire until later in childhood or adolescence (Bengtsson & Johnson, 1992; Eisenberg et al., 1991).

Several research reports support this latter contention. For example, one study (Clark & Bittle, 1992) of third, fifth, and seventh graders showed that empathic understanding steadily increased with age. Similarly, another study (Szagun, 1992) revealed how children's understanding of sympathy changed with age. Whereas younger children primarily focused on the emotion of sadness when describing sympathy, the older subjects transcended the emotional component and included other dimensions, such as helping others and being concerned about those in distress.

Susan Costin and Diane Jones (1992) demonstrated that friendship is an important factor in facilitating prosocial behavior as well as emotional responsiveness in young children. In this investigation, 4- to 6-year-old children watched puppet scenarios in which a target child was either a personal friend or an acquaintance. It was found that children in the friendship condition were more likely to report sympathetic responses to the hypothetical plight of their friend. Acquaintances, on the other hand, were more likely to be unaffected by the dilemma. Youngsters in the friendship condition also more readily proposed an intervention to alter the peer's negative state than did children in the acquaintance condition. Similar findings were obtained in a study involving Chinese children (Ma & Leung, 1992), who were more altruistic to someone they liked than to someone they disliked.

Early prosocial behavior seems to be greatly influenced by the child's exposure to positive adult role models and certain social situations. Children are apt

THEORETICAL ISSUES

How might social learning theorists and behaviorists explore the impact of imitation and reinforcement, respectively, on the expression of prosocial behavior? What mental faculties might cognitive-developmental theorists choose to examine? How might social exchange theorists examine the rewards and drawbacks of prosocial behavior?

Learning to be sensitive to the needs of others is an important feature of prosocial behavior.

to learn such behaviors as helping and cooperating by receiving adult guidance and positive reinforcement, by interacting with other children, and by observing adults and other children behaving in socially constructive ways. Youngsters exposed to altruistic adults are likely to imitate such behaviors, especially if the adult model is affectionate and nurturant. Other adult behaviors, such as handling disciplinary situations in a positive manner, have also been shown to increase children's levels of prosocial behavior (Dekovic & Janssens, 1992; Hart et al., 1992; Ladd & Hart, 1992; Volling & Belsky, 1992).

How do American children compare with children in other countries in regard to prosocial behavior? This is difficult to assess, although cross-cultural child-rearing practices have been examined. The former Soviet republics, Israel, and Mexico, for example, place a high premium on cooperation and the teaching of altruistic behavior. The same is true for Chinese children, as you'll recall from the Focus on Diversity box presented earlier. Chinese parents stress the avoidance of interpersonal conflict and, instead, encourage cooperative interaction (Xu et al., 1991). The results of such training are evident in the high levels of prosocial behavior demonstrated by children in these countries.

This doesn't imply that American children are not taught the same lessons or lack prosocial sensitivity. What it does imply is that compared with youngsters from other nations, American children are not taught altruism as consistently (Whiting & Edwards, 1988). Rather than the other countries' everyday emphasis on helping others, American children often receive sporadic instruction in prosocial development and limited structured opportunities from adults to put this behavior into practice. But given such opportunities, prosocial behavior may develop more fully (Doescher & Sugawara, 1992; Graul & Zeece, 1990; Honig & Pollack, 1990; Kostelnik et al., 1993).

■ Play Influences on the Developing Child

Throughout all of childhood, play is an important social activity, through which youngsters can better understand themselves and how they relate to others. During early childhood, play groups enhance a sensitivity for the needs of others and foster a cooperative spirit. Play groups also help youngsters relinquish their singular, self-centered frame of reference (Lewis, 1993; Shipley, 1993).

The play group during early childhood is usually small, restrictive, and short lived. That is, many groups stop playing after 10 or 15 minutes. This is due to a number of factors, including limited attending skills and impulsive desires to end activities and start others. However, one study (Howes & Matheson, 1992) notes that quality early childhood education programming has the potential of enhancing early play behaviors. In this study, those children enrolled in quality programming demonstrated more complex play forms at earlier ages and engaged in greater proportions of complex play than children enrolled in minimally adequate early childhood education centers.

The play group's temporary quality gives children the task of entering new social gatherings on a fairly regular basis. Some children are better at this than others, perhaps because they are more outgoing, gregarious, and secure in their relationships overall. The quiet, timid, or shy child may encounter more difficulty (Cillessen et al., 1992).

The play group gradually teaches youngsters that certain behaviors are expected and certain rules must be followed. Furthermore, the play setting will show children the importance of sharing and working toward group goals. Children learn these social processes as they interact with one another and with adults in situations that require grown-up supervision and guidance. The research of Gary Ladd and Craig Hart (1992) reinforces the potential positive influence that adults have in children's play. Frequent parent initiations in playtime activities of preschoolers were associated with higher levels of prosocial behavior, lower levels of nonsocial behavior, and among boys, greater peer acceptance in the preschool. Moreover, the degree to which parents involved children in the process of arranging informal play activities was positively related to the frequency with which children initiated their own peer contacts.

There has been some research on the extent to which adults should involve themselves in and structure children's playtime activities. Many maintain that adults should give children guidance, support, and a good environment for play. However, adults should not restrict the child's freedom. Frequently, adults with the best of intentions overinvolve themselves and overorganize play activities. The consequence of this is to restrict the child's spontaneity and free-play spirit. Adult intervention thus should be designed to minimize its obtrusive effects and not control all of the child's choices. There is evidence that youngsters enjoy play involving more make-believe and games that have less structure than do older children (Baumeister & Senders, 1989).

Varieties of Play   Almost all forms of play during this time give children the opportunity to develop muscular coordination, whether it be through climbing, balancing, or manipulating blocks or jigsaw puzzles. Motor skills are refined during this period, and self-confidence is increased as play materials are mastered. There is, however, considerable variation in children's performance. This is true for the physical aspects of play as well as for all motor skills. Furthermore, preschoolers often tend to perform well in one area and do poorly in others. As we mentioned earlier in this chapter, preschoolers generally have difficulty with those toys requiring fine muscle coordination.

For these reasons, certain types of play remain difficult and elusive. It is interesting that children, even at this young age, can almost sense what types of activities are overpowering challenges to their developing physical capabilities.

Of course, some activities are better suited to meet the needs of the children's developing motor abilities, so adults should learn to distinguish them. See Frost (1992), Pugmire-Stoy (1992), and Shipley (1993) for good accounts of developmentally appropriate play environments.

One important type of play during early childhood is make-believe or pretend play. This type of play encompasses imagination skills, which, as we learned earlier, are the result of developing cognitive, social, and emotional forces. Numerous studies (e.g., Doyle et al., 1992; Shapiro & Hudson, 1991) show how make-believe abilities stimulate mental faculties such as problem-solving abilities, and linguistic competencies and the complexity of social interactions as well. Often, pretend play is a reflection of the child's inner needs and desires, which in turn may originate in real-life experiences. The transformation of these inner feelings, especially during this time, can help children better understand themselves, other people, and events. Social pretend play, in particular, teaches children to negotiate play themes and roles (Black, 1992; Werebe & Baudonniere, 1991).

Research conducted by Paul Harris and Robert Kavanaugh (1993) indicates that children's understanding of adult pretense begins at remarkably early ages. Indeed, this investigation showed that between their second and third year, children were able to understand when an adult referred to a make-believe substance (e.g., tea) and could direct their pretend actions to a prop that contained the pretend tea. When they watched an adult transform the imaginary substance by "pouring" or "spilling," children produced a suitable remedial action or described what happened with appropriate nonliteral language. There is also evidence of increased symbolic representation in pretend play as children grow older. For example, children aged $4\frac{1}{2}$ were found to express more play symbols than 3-year-olds (Goneo & Kessel, 1988).

Parental interaction has been shown to enhance the development of early pretend play. Wendy Haight and Peggy Miller's (1992) investigation of toddlers and preschoolers showed that mothers were the primary play partners when children began to engage in pretend play. The mothers and their children initiated and responded to pretending, and mothers elaborated and prompted children's pretending. Pretend episodes with the mother tended to be longer than solo episodes, and children incorporated their mother's pretend talk into their own subsequent pretend play.

Imagination is also a strong indication of originality and inventiveness. For example, many children select a fantasy hero to emulate (French & Pena, 1991). Toys, too, can provide an outlet for imagination. A youngster wanting to make a toy come alive with its own individual qualities (the Piagetian concept of animism) illustrates this. In this respect, a doll may come alive with its own thoughts and feelings; a chair may become a mysterious fort or castle; and a box may be turned into a car, complete with its own noisy engine. The child's play language, too, reflects the prevalence of animism during this stage of development. Children may refer to a "sleeping" tree, the "happy" sun, or "strong" mountains.

One other form of play worthy of our consideration is sociodramatic play. **Sociodramatic play** often is the imitation and identification of adult behavioral patterns. By becoming a doctor, parent, or law officer, children act out their desire to be like adults and may benefit from a valuable learning

CONTINUOUS AND DISCONTINUOUS HUMAN DEVELOPMENT

How do you think the play behaviors of preschoolers compare with those of infants and toddlers? Are play behaviors linked to earlier stages with a thread of continuity or do they now emerge as distinct and discontinuous activities?

Play during early childhood is often sociodramatic.

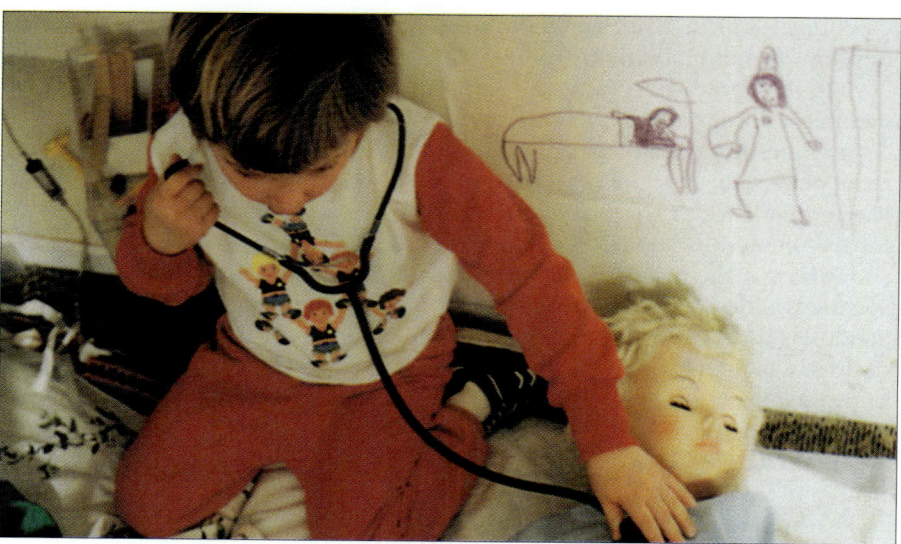

experience. Playing grown-up roles may prepare children for later life, as many of the grown-up situations acted out are characteristic of those of the adult years. In the process, children also learn a great deal about gender-role development (Isenberg & Jalongo, 1993; Pugmire-Stoy, 1992).

Sociodramatic play has many benefits. It is creative, as it encourages children to use their past experiences in the sociodramatic framework. Adjusting to the ideas of others also motivates youngsters' creativity. Sociodramatic play is also mentally stimulating because it encourages the use of cognitive powers, including linguistic ability, abstraction, concept formation, and new knowledge. Finally, children's social skills are sharpened through sociodramatic situations. Such play encourages positive give-and-take, tolerance, and consideration of others (Shipley, 1993; Van Hoorn et al., 1993).

The social benefits of pretend play were the focal point of research launched by Jennifer Connolly, Anna Doyle, and Erica Reznick (1988). The researchers observed the social interaction of preschoolers during social pretend play and nonpretend activities to determine whether positive and mature social behaviors were associated with the pretend context. Results showed that during pretend play, subjects' social interactions were more enjoyable, lasted longer, involved larger groups, and showed more play involvement and greater reciprocity. The researchers suggest that social pretend play provides a contextual framework within which mature social interaction can occur and social competencies may be acquired.

Theories of Personality Development

Sigmund Freud's Psychosexual Theory

THE ANAL STAGE OF DEVELOPMENT (AGES 2 TO 4) The preschool years are the period when children enter the **anal stage** of psychosexual development. This stage occurs when children become aware of their body's process of elimination. Pleasure is derived from both the elimination and retention of the feces. Youngsters are often fascinated by their excretions, even to the point of peering into the toilet bowl and observing or even handling the fecal matter. This also becomes a time for many children to engage in "toilet talk."

Adult reactions during this stage will determine the children's later behavior. Adults who express ideas of "dirty," "messy," or "bad" convey these feelings to the children, who may then feel this "product of the body" is "bad." Children may reason that they, in turn, must also be bad. Also, parents who force early toilet training may produce children who are obsessively clean and neat, reflecting the adults' own rigid and somewhat Victorian outlook on the body's natural functions. On the other hand, parents who neglect toilet training may produce children who will later exhibit slovenliness, indifference, and other undesirable traits.

There are other interesting aspects of Freud's anal stage. Many children of this age (the terrible twos) resent adult authority and soon learn that although they can't yell or fight back at their parents, they do have two ways to retaliate—retention of feces and violent expulsion of them at inappropriate times. According to psychoanalytic interpretation, children who are slow to be toilet trained may actually not want to be trained, as this (untrained) behavior now becomes an outlet for pent-up frustrations and hostilities.

THE PHALLIC STAGE OF DEVELOPMENT (AGES 4 TO 6) The **phallic stage** is Freud's third stage of psychosexual development and covers the latter portion of early childhood. During this stage, the child's desires for gratification shift from the anal to the genital area. Pleasure is derived from manipulating and fondling the genitals, which Freud termed childhood masturbation. Again, how parents handle children in this stage will in part determine their future psychosexual development. Maturation and phallic awareness occur simultaneously with children's social development in terms of their imitation, identification, and gender-role development.

According to Freud, boys identify with their father and imitate paternal behavior because they have developed unconscious sexual feelings toward their mother. The threat of punishment for masturbating causes boys' sexual interest to shift from their penis to their mother. The result of this is jealousy of the father. Boys' sexual feelings do not include the desire for intercourse but, rather, for hugging and affection. Their feelings are romantic, not lustful. Boys become fearful when they realize these urges place them in conflict with their father. This condition, the **Oedipus complex,** is further complicated when boys fear the reprisal of their father in the form of castration. (Boys believe that women, because they lack a penis, have already been castrated.) Castration anxiety can be resolved only by repressing these sexual desires and identifying with the father.

The less well known **Electra complex** is experienced by females during the phallic stage. Girls, according to Freud, are envious of the boys' penis (penis envy) and feel cheated. They blame this state of affairs on their mother, and their father becomes the object of their sexual attachment. Subsequently, the mother is placed in a competitive role for the father's attention.

For both the Electra and the Oedipus complexes to be resolved, the sexual attachment to the parent of the opposite sex must be discontinued. Freud considered it quite natural for a strong bond to remain between the daughter and father (he also believed girls later seek a husband like their father). For boys, however, the Oedipus complex can become a more serious problem. A fixation

THEORETICAL ISSUES

How practical do you think the theories of Freud and Erikson are in relation to some of the topics presented in this chapter? Can you take some or all psychosexual and psychosocial dynamics occurring at this time and apply them to such issues as gender-role development, patterns of family and school interaction, prosocial behavior, and peer development?

Early childhood marks a time when new facets of the personality emerge.

at this stage can produce behaviors such as being unable to reach the level of independence needed to function in society.

Erik Erikson's Psychosocial Theory

INITIATIVE VERSUS GUILT (AGES 3 TO 6) **Initiative versus guilt** is the psychosocial crisis of early childhood proposed by Erik Erikson. Having established a sense of trust and autonomy during the first few years of life, children now set out to prove they have a will of their own. Youngsters actively explore their environment and try to satisfy their curiosity. Accompanying this high energy level are rapidly developing physical skills, an increased vocabulary, and the general ability to get around and do new and different things. All of this produces an active child in pursuit of a variety of goals:

> There is in every child at every stage a new miracle of vigorous unfolding, which constitutes a new hope and a new responsibility for all. Such is the sense and the pervading quality of initiative. The criteria for all these senses and qualities are the same: a crisis, more or less beset with fumbling and fear, is resolved, in that the child suddenly seems to "grow together" both in his person and in his body. He appears "more himself," more loving, more relaxed, and brighter in his judgment, more activated and activating. He is in free possession of a surplus of energy which permits him to approach what seems desirable (even if it also seems uncertain and even dangerous) with undiminished and more accurate direction. Initiative adds to autonomy the quality of undertaking, planning, and "attacking" a task for the sake of being active and on the move, where before self-will, more often than not, inspired acts of defiance or, at any rate, protested independence. (Erikson, 1963, p. 255)

Whether or not children lean toward initiative or guilt depends largely, once again, on the quality of the children's interaction with their parents. If adults give youngsters an opportunity to exercise their physical skills, answer their questions, and encourage fantasy, initiative is likely to be the result. Conversely, if children feel their questions are annoying or a nuisance and that indulgence in fantasy is a waste of time, guilt is likely to surface.

CHAPTER REVIEW

Unit One: Physical Development

Physical growth and development during early childhood are quite rapid. By the fifth year, preschoolers have doubled their original birth length and increased their birth weight fivefold. Because of rapid muscular growth and the development of coordination abilities, preschoolers show marked gains in small and large motor skills. We discussed three phases of motor skill development: the cognitive, associative, and autonomous stages.

Unit Two: Mental Development

Piaget's stage of preconceptual thought, a substage of the larger preoperational thought stage, is characterized primarily by egocentrism, a self-centeredness that prevents children from understanding any point of view but their own. Egocentrism is evident not only in early socialization patterns, such as parallel play and collective monologues, but also in thought processes, mainly animism and artificialism.

The development of advanced cognition relies on the ability to acquire and categorize new concepts from the environment, including modifications and variations of shape, size, space, quantity, and time. Concept development is aided by perceptual advancements, although preschoolers are hindered by limited attention and attending skills.

Several factors contribute to preschoolers' overall language acquisition, including socioeconomic influences, intelligence, gender, whether they have a bilingual background, and whether they are a singleton or a twin. In contrast with their earlier telegraphic sentences, preschoolers are able to fabricate multiword sentences, complete with fairly complex syntactical constructions. They also advance in pragmatic skills during early childhood.

Unit Three: Personality and Social Development

This final unit of the chapter dealt with those factors affecting gender-role development, including parents, play behaviors, peer influences, the school environment, children's literature, and the media. In regard to emotional development, preschoolers exhibit many new fears, owing to their emotional susceptibility and because they cannot understand many objects and events. Anger is not expressed physically as often as in the past and is replaced by verbal displays of resentment.

Interaction with the family has important influences on personality and social growth. We showed how sibling relations shape the course of family life as well as the growth and development of all involved. We also examined three types of parental control: authoritarian, authoritative, and permissive. Of the three methods, the authoritative style is regarded as the most effective. Attention was also focused on the dark side of family life, namely child abuse, incest, and child sexual abuse.

Many preschoolers today are able to benefit from an early childhood education experience, and this unit explored the many varieties available. Peers enable children to develop their independence and social skills. When they are with others, children can begin to work cooperatively and develop a sympathetic attitude toward one another. Peer groups may also breed a competitive spirit among the members and encourage conformity to the group's standards of behavior. The various forms of play discussed in this chapter contribute to children's social maturity.

Finally, this chapter explored the personality theories of Freud and Erikson. Freud theorized that children pass through two psychosexual stages at this time: the anal and the phallic stages. Erikson's psychosocial crisis for this period is initiative versus guilt.

TERMS YOU SHOULD KNOW

anal stage	**bilingualism**
androgyny	**child sexual abuse**
animism	**collective monologue**
artificialism	**discipline**
authoritarian control	**egocentrism**
authoritative control	**Electra complex**

fine motor skill	phallic stage
gross motor skill	pragmatics
hostile aggression	preconceptual thought
immanent justice	preoperational thought
incest	prosocial behavior
initiative versus guilt	sibling rivalry
instrumental aggression	significates
motor skill	signifiers
Oedipus complex	sociodramatic play
parallel play	symbolic functioning
perception	twin speech
permissive control	

THINKING IN ACTION

• This first question is designed to sharpen your thinking regarding stages and patterns of growth in lifespan development. First, reflect on the material you just finished regarding early childhood. More specifically, mentally summarize the developmental status of the young child, particularly physical, mental, personality, and social considerations. Now examine these developments against those that occurred during infancy and toddlerhood. How do these patterns of growth compare and contrast? Finally, given the knowledge you now possess, what patterns of growth do you expect to see in the next chapter on middle childhood?

• Respond to this statement: "The advantages of having a sibling outweigh the disadvantages." As you give it some thought, reflect on your own experiences as a sibling and what it was like growing up in your family. Don't avoid this question if you are a single child; rather, try and envision the pros and cons that sibling relations might have brought to your life. In order to fine-tune the material presented in this chapter, make a special effort to focus on your early childhood years. Do your experiences or thoughts coincide with the cited research? What additional dimensions to sibling relations can you add?

• Incest and sexual abuse of children are often referred to as "the best kept secret." Victims tend to lead a life of concealment and isolation; only a minority ever reveal the sexual cruelty they experience. Prepare a presentation on the effects of incest and child sexual abuse. What do you think are the most difficult adjustments that abused children face? How do you perceive the long-range consequences? Finally, what do you think are the most beneficial modes of therapeutic intervention for victims of sexual abuse?

• During early childhood, youngsters expand their social horizons and venture into new and challenging social situations with family, peers, and adults. On a piece of paper, make three columns with these headings at the top of each: "family," "early childhood education program," and "peers." List as many experiences as you can under each category and how each serves to shape the preschooler's growing social maturity. How are these social experiences integrated into the child's total sense of self? Beyond the social sphere, what other developmental forces are shaped by these interactions? Finally, does your analysis reveal that one socialization category has more impact than the others? Why or why not?

• You've discovered in this chapter the merits of prosocial behavior and the importance of nurturing its development in children. Design an intervention program for young children aimed at promoting the emergence and maintenance of prosocial behavior. As you contemplate its design, think about how your program will reach the home setting, neighborhood, and school environment. What kinds of teaching strategies will you employ? How do you intend to reach and implement your goals?

RECOMMENDED READINGS

1. Asher, S. R., & Coie, J. D. (Eds.). (1990). *Peer rejection in childhood.* New York: Cambridge University Press.

   A thoughtful analysis of the behavioral and social-cognitive processes as well as the group dynamics that create and maintain rejection by the peer group.

2. Gleason, J. B. (Ed.). (1993). *The development of language* (3rd ed.). New York: Macmillan.

   Good coverage of semantics, syntax, and pragmatics, as well as the course of language development during early childhood.

3. Melhuish, E. C ., & Moss, P. (Eds.). (1991). *Day care for young children: International perspectives.* New York: Routledge.

   An emphasis is placed on day-care policies in other nations, and how they affect the type of care that young children receive.

4. Shengold, L. (1990). *Soul murder: The effects of childhood abuse and deprivation.* New Haven, CT: Yale University Press.

   The author discusses a wide range of child maltreatment and the psychological effects that often surface when adulthood is reached.

5. Thomas, G. V., & Silk, A. M. J. (1990). *An introduction to the psychology of children's drawings.* New York: New York University Press.

   The authors review psychological theories of children's drawings as well as their relation to emotional and cognitive development.

Middle Childhood

What Do You Think?

UNIT ONE: PHYSICAL DEVELOPMENT

Physical Changes During Middle Childhood
Changes in Proportion and Appearance

Muscular, Skeletal, and Organ Development
Motor Skill Development

UNIT TWO: MENTAL DEVELOPMENT

Piaget's Stages of Cognitive Development
Intuitive Thought
Concrete Operations
Concept Development
Shape and Size Concepts
Spatial Concepts
Relational Concepts
Quantity Concepts
Time Concepts
The Concept of Death
Development of Problem-Solving Abilities
Cognitive Styles

Conceptual Tempos: Impulsivity Versus Reflectivity
Learning Disabilities
Types of Learning Disabilities
Intervention for Learning Disabilities
Language Development
Vocabulary and Semantic Development
Syntactic Development
Pragmatics
Language Dialects

UNIT THREE: PERSONALITY AND SOCIAL DEVELOPMENT

Emotional Development
Fear and Anxiety
Anger and Aggression
Happiness and Humor
Love
Moral Development
Jean Piaget's Theory
Lawrence Kohlberg's Theory
A Critique of Kohlberg's Theory
Family Influences on the Developing Child
Experiencing a Favorable Home Environment
The Family and Television

School Influences on the Developing Child
The Influence of the Teacher
Methods of Classroom Control
Peer Group Influences on the Developing Child
The Development of Children's Friendships
Play Influences on the Developing Child
Play and Gender-Role Development
Team Sports
Theories of Personality Development
Sigmund Freud's Psychosexual Theory
Erik Erikson's Psychosocial Theory

Chapter Review • Terms You Should Know • Thinking in Action • Recommended Readings

WHAT
DO
YOU
THINK?

• The path to moral maturity continues throughout childhood and adolescence. The journey at best will lead to a personalized set of moral standards and a true conscience to guide behavior. But as many children will tell you, it's hard always to be good, or at least, it seems so. Indeed, life's daily testing ground for honesty and good behavior awaits the child and has the potential for triggering fibs, white lies, and crossed fingers when the truth is requested. How are such behaviors explained and overcome, if at all? How does childhood moral behavior pave the way for more advanced and sophisticated forms of expression? We spend some time in this chapter answering such questions and discuss the major theories explaining this developing morality.

• Nearly every home in the United States has a television; its presence has changed family life more than any other technological innovation of the 20th century. Today, the average television set is turned on for about 7 hours each day. We'd like you to think carefully about that statistic, mainly because it's now possible to break the activities of the modern family into three fairly equal parts: 7 hours of television viewing; 9 hours of work or school, including transportation; and 8 hours of sleep. In this chapter we examine television as part of the American lifestyle and its impact on children.

• They are inseparable during the day, call each other on the phone, fill each other in on the latest news, share jokes and gossip, and swap possessions. Having a good friend is one of life's greatest treasures. By middle childhood, youngsters' friendships become more close-knit and mutual, a marked contrast with the frequent disharmony punctuating their earlier relationships. What factors account for such changes? Are there gender differences in the establishment and maintenance of friendships? Continue reading to find the answers.

• Trevor was disappointed he didn't make the local Little League team, but he rationalized later that he now had more time to devote to his homework. Kristen broke one of her mother's favorite pieces of china but tried to blame her younger brother, who happened to be standing nearby. Such patterns of behavior in both these cases are called defense mechanisms, and they are often used when mistakes, failures, or conflicts create inner anxiety. As we'll see, by middle childhood, defense mechanisms are used with surprising frequency and become intertwined with the youngster's developing personality. When finished with this chapter, you'll better understand why many children cover up, cop out, and tattle.

UNIT ONE: PHYSICAL DEVELOPMENT

Middle childhood, also referred to as the school years, is a developmental stage embracing ages 6 through 12. On the whole, physical developments during middle childhood are slow but steady. As a result, year-to-year changes in size and proportion are less noticeable than the pronounced developments of the preschooler or toddler. This gradual physical change persists until the adolescent growth spurt.

Because bodily changes are less marked and physical size increases slowly, children gain control of and perfect motor skills they have been unable to master in the past. As a result, overall coordination, balance, and refinement in physical activities show an increase at this time. Such accomplishments affect children's physical and psychological self-concepts, not to mention their degree of acceptance into the peer culture.

▬ Physical Changes During Middle Childhood

Boys are taller than girls between the ages of 6 and 8; by age 9, differences in height are negligible; and past age 9, the average girl is taller than the average

School-age children demonstrate greater amounts of balance and agility.

boy. This trend will persist until the adolescent growth spurt, when males will catch up and then surpass females in height. On the average, children will add about 2½ inches to their height each year. By age 12, children have usually attained approximately 90% of their adult height.

Although girls weigh less than boys at birth, they are equal by age 8. By age 9, girls surpass boys in weight. As with height, however, males surpass females in weight during the adolescent growth spurt. During middle childhood, youngsters typically add approximately 5 pounds to their weight each year. By age 12, the average child weighs 80 pounds.

Remember that wide variations exist in overall rates of physical growth and development. This becomes especially apparent when we look at the wide range of height and weight differences among elementary school children. Charts, tables, and other forms of normative data describing the growth of the so-called average child must not be overused. Although normative data are useful for comparisons, each child's growth pattern is unique. This is as true during middle childhood as it is during other stages of growth. Gains in height and weight can be affected by numerous variables, including nutrition, hereditary influences, endocrine balance, health care, exercise, and socioeconomic status. The progress of individuals should be charted in relation to their own rates of growth, not purely against the mass data available in the developmental tables.

Changes in Proportion and Appearance   Despite the slow and gradual nature of physical change during middle childhood, it is a time when most youngsters lose the baby contours characterizing earlier years (see Figure 7-1). This change in physical appearance, you will recall, began during the preschool years. Generally speaking, rounded and chubby physiques give way to leaner appearances as fat layers decrease in thickness and change in overall distribution.

By age 6, the trunk is almost twice as long and twice as wide as it was at birth. As the chest broadens and flattens, the ribs shift from a horizontal position to a more oblique one. Contributing to the leaner appearance is a rapid growth spurt of the arms and legs. Throughout middle childhood, there are no marked gender differences in body proportions.

FIGURE 7-1

Changes in Body Proportions from Infancy Through Adolescence.

Note the changing physical appearance of the middle childhood youngster compared to other life stages.

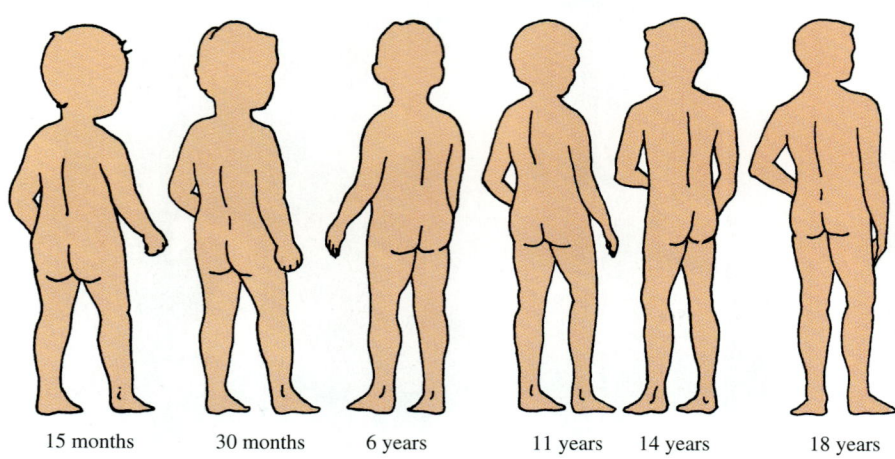

| 15 months | 30 months | 6 years | 11 years | 14 years | 18 years |

The facial structure also undergoes change during middle childhood. For example, the forehead tends to flatten and the nose grows. As permanent teeth replace baby (deciduous) teeth, the jaw lengthens, becomes more prominent, and the face enlarges. The first tooth is usually lost sometime during the sixth year, giving rise to the characteristic toothless grin of middle childhood. Girls generally lose their baby teeth earlier than boys. By age 11 or 12, the permanent teeth of both boys and girls have rooted, with the exception of the second and third molars.

Muscular, Skeletal, and Organ Development

MUSCLE GROWTH Throughout middle childhood boys have considerably more muscle tissue than girls, and girls have more fat than boys. Muscle growth tends to be extremely rapid; the muscle changes not only in composition but also becomes more firmly attached to the bones. Despite these advances, the muscles remain immature in function at times, as reflected in children's frequent awkwardness and inefficiency in movement, erratic changes in tempo, inability to sit still for long, and fatigability. Developing muscles are also more susceptible to injury from overuse (consider the large numbers of young baseball players suffering from "Little League elbow"). The fitness and development of the muscles depends not only on good physical care, rest, and activity, but also on their structure and the use made of them. Proper muscle and nerve development provides increasing steadiness of movement, speed, strength, and endurance.

SKELETAL GROWTH The skeleton continues to produce its centers of ossification (points at which ossification begins in a bone). Earlier, the child's bones were soft and spongy, consisting mostly of cartilage, but now minerals, particularly calcium and phosphorus, give hardness and rigidity to the bones (see Figure 7-2). This process of bone development continues until the individual's 20s. The growth of the skeleton is frequently more rapid than the growth of muscles and ligaments. As a result, loose-jointed and gangling postures are not uncommon in middle childhood. Growth spurts are frequently accompanied by muscle pains. For many children, these growing pains are a very real phenomenon

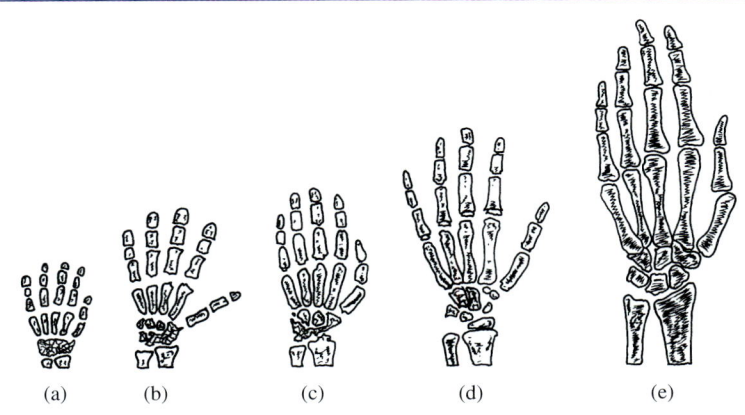

(a) (b) (c) (d) (e)

FIGURE 7-2
Development of the Skeletal System.

The skeletal system progresses through a series of changes as it approaches mature size and form. Because the skeleton takes a long time to reach full maturity, it has characteristics that provide excellent examples of growth stages. At birth, for example, the skeleton lacks carpal, or wrist, bones and epiphyses, centers of ossification at the ends of the bones. Whereas the primary centers of ossification are located in the shafts of the bones, or diaphyses, the epiphyses will produce smaller bones at the ends of the long ones. This can be seen in the skeletal structure of the hand of the youngster during early childhood (a, b) and middle childhood (c). Growth of the long bones terminates when the epiphyses and diaphyses unite. This bone fusion occurs between early and late adolescence (d, e). When we speak of an individual's skeletal maturity, then, we are referring to the progress toward union of the epiphyses and the shaft of the bone.

caused by their developing muscles' attempts to catch up with their increased skeletal size.

CIRCULATORY SYSTEM The circulatory system grows at a slow pace, although by the school years, the weight of the heart has increased to approximately five times its birth weight. The heart is now smaller in proportion to body size than at any other point in the person's life. The heart rate, relatively high during the early years, declines gradually during the middle years, and the blood pressure rises. The average pulse rate is from 85 to 100 per minute, the blood pressure 95 to 108 systolic and 62 to 67 diastolic. The heart continues to grow until the end of the teenage years.

NERVOUS SYSTEM The brain nears its mature size and weight during the years of middle childhood. Accompanying these increases in size and weight is an increase in head circumference. The average circumference grows from 20½ to 21 inches between the ages of 6 and 12. The spinal cord has quadrupled in weight by age 5 and will have increased eightfold by the end of the teenage years.

RESPIRATORY SYSTEM The respiratory system also grows and changes. The weight of the lungs has doubled by 6 months, tripled by 1 year, and increased

INTERRELATEDNESS OF AGING PROCESSES

How do you think a changing physical self creates inner confidence or security? Do you think conditions such as obesity, being shorter or taller, or physical clumsiness promote such psychological states as insecurity, shyness, or feelings of rejection? What psychological impact might chronic illness or a disability have on the child?

almost 10 times by the end of middle childhood. Rates of respiration decrease, shifting from approximately 20–25 respiratory movements per minute during early childhood to 17–22 movements per minute during middle childhood. In general, breathing becomes slower and deeper as the respiratory system works more economically and shows greater elasticity.

DIGESTIVE SYSTEM The maturation of the digestive system is reflected in fewer upset stomachs at this age and the youngster's ability to digest a wider range of foods. In general, the body's activities of secretion, digestion, absorption, and excretion become more finely regulated. The school-age child can also retain foods for longer periods of time (which means meals do not have to be served as often or as promptly), and calorie needs are not as great in relation to stomach size as they once were. Nutritional considerations are very important at this time because children need adequate protein and vitamins and not the empty calories offered in sweets, soft drinks, and starches.

Motor Skill Development   Driven by the Eriksonian desire to establish initiative and industry, the school-age child is eager to participate in a diversity of both gross and fine motor skills. The success a child experiences in motor skill activities depends on a number of factors, however, including rates of physical maturity, the cognitive skills needed to master the task, environmental opportunities to engage in physical activity, and degree of self-confidence. We must remember that children are still in the process of refining coordination abilities and mastering grace of movement. Improvement is gradual, and clumsiness and awkwardness can still be expected.

Gross motor skill achievements are numerous during middle childhood. By age 6 most children can roller skate, skip rope, and begin to ride a bicycle. By age 7, most have perfected running and jumping skills as well as the basic movements necessary for catching, throwing, and hitting a baseball.

Sports provide an excellent vehicle for the development of motor skills.

Fine motor skill coordination, although lagging behind gross motor skill development, matures at a gradual and steady pace. As children gain control of their arms, shoulders, wrists, and fingers, they become adept at a wide range of fine motor skill activities: detailed artwork, playing musical instruments, refining their handwriting, and building models. Physical activity refinement is also reflected in the everyday routines of school-age children. Youngsters are now generally capable of brushing their own teeth, combing their hair, tying their shoelaces, and dressing themselves.

Competent motor skill execution embodies the ability to refine coordination and develop overall accuracy of response toward the task at hand. This means the gradual elimination of unnecessary movements and expenditures of surplus energy to develop economy of performance. Other factors behind motor skill execution, including agility, balance, speed, and power, are depicted in Table 7-1.

One experiment that studied how the hand approaches and intercepts a moving target focused on children aged 5 to 11. Hand movement was analyzed in terms of speed and direction of the initial movement and speed and accuracy

TABLE 7-1

Components of Motor Skill Fitness and Development Patterns

Motor Fitness Component	Common Tests	Specific Aspect Measured	Synthesis of Findings
Coordination	Cable jump	Gross body coordination	Year-by-year improvement with age in gross body coordination. Boys superior from age 6 on in eye-hand and eye-foot coordination.
	Hopping for accuracy	Gross body coordination	
	Skipping	Gross body coordination	
	Ball dribble	Eye-hand coordination	
	Foot dribble	Eye-foot coordination	
Balance	Beam walk	Dynamic balance	Year-by-year improvement with age. Girls often outperform boys, especially in dynamic balance activities, until about age 8. Abilities similar thereafter.
	Stick balance	Static balance	
	One-foot stand	Static balance	
Speed	20-yard dash	Running speed	Year-by-year improvement with age. Boys and girls similar until age 6 or 7, at which time boys make more rapid improvements. Boys superior to girls at all ages.
	30-yard dash	Running speed	
Agility	Shuttle run	Running agility	Year-by-year improvement with age. Girls begin to level off after age 13. Boys continue to make improvements.
Power	Vertical jump	Leg strength and speed	Year-by-year improvement with age. Boys outperform girls at all age levels.
	Standing long jump	Leg strength and speed	
	Distance throw	Upper arm strength and speed	
	Velocity throw	Upper arm strength and speed	

From *Understanding Motor Development in Children* by David L. Gallahue. Copyright © 1982 by John Wiley & Sons, Inc. Reprinted by permission.

of the hand when near the target. It was found that the speed with which the hand initially moved was well planned based on the speed and trajectory of the moving target, but the direction in which the hand moved was not well planned. Eight-year-olds showed an increase in their ability to plan a movement, but 10-year-olds had developed the ability to control the ongoing movement (Bairstow, 1989).

As far as gender differences in motor skill development are concerned, boys are usually ahead of girls in running, jumping, and throwing. However, we must place such an edge in proper perspective (Smoll & Schutz, 1990). On the average, boys have more muscle tissue and greater levels of overall strength, which gives them an advantage in such comparisons. We must also remember that in studies in which boys are compared with girls, the outcomes become factual data. The question that remains unanswered is whether these factual differences result from genetic variance or from practice, environmental opportunities, sexism, or other social and cultural factors.

UNIT REVIEW—

↗ Physical developments during middle childhood are slow but steady. The child's physique becomes slimmer as fat decreases in thickness and changes in overall distribution.

↗ The body's bones become hard and rigid; muscle growth is rapid; the circulatory system develops at a steady but slow pace; respiration becomes more economical; the brain reaches its mature size, but still is not fully functional; and the digestive system becomes more efficient.

↗ Both gross and fine motor skills advance during the school years, although the latter proceed at slower rates.

↗ Numerous factors influence the course of motor skill attainment. Although males typically surpass females in many motor skill areas, such accomplishments must be placed into the proper perspective.

UNIT TWO: MENTAL DEVELOPMENT

Advancing mental abilities coupled with school learning experiences enable new cognitive accomplishments to take place. Words and symbols take on new meaning, and problem-solving abilities reflect greater levels of insight and deliberation. School-age children are also more adept at expressing themselves with more refined levels of linguistic proficiency (Dent & Rosenberg, 1990; Kosslyn, 1990; Lloyd, 1991).

Mental developments at this time are enhanced by the ability to deal systematically with many variables simultaneously. Speed and distance, for instance, can be successfully manipulated so that mathematical problems can be solved.

Perspective taking as well as comprehending and manipulating multiple dimensions of the environment are regarded by many as critical to advanced mental functioning (Dixon & Moore, 1990; Jacobs & Potenza, 1991; Newcombe & Huttenlocher, 1992; Taylor, Cartright, & Bowden, 1991).

School-age children do have certain cognitive limitations, however. Although they are generally more systematic and objective than younger children, they still cannot think abstractly. Abstract concepts remain completely outside the children's experience and cannot be grasped by analogy. Such cognitive accomplishments are only emerging and may not develop evenly in all content areas. Finally, there are significant differences in mental activity between younger and older school-age children (Flavell, 1992).

▬ Piaget's Stages of Cognitive Development

Intuitive Thought   Between the ages of 4 and 7, children enter the stage of cognitive development known as intuitive thought. **Intuitive thought,** similar to preconceptual thought, is also a substage of the *preoperational thought* stage, which lasts from age 2 through age 7.

Children's thinking at this time is characterized by immediate perceptions and experiences rather than mental operations. Egocentrism still exists, but it often changes because of the children's cognitive advances. As a result, these new mental structures release children from a lower form of egocentrism but trap them in a higher form, namely, an egocentric orientation to symbols and the objects they represent (Schulman, 1991).

CENTERING **Centering** means concentrating on a single outstanding feature of an object and excluding its other characteristics. Centering is a distinct limitation of cognition, as the following examples demonstrate. Suppose a child is given two identical glasses filled with marbles. Undoubtedly, the youngster would acknowledge that each contained the same amount. However, if the marbles were presented in different-sized containers, the typical child would deny they held the same amount (Figure 7-3); centering has prevented the child from attending to all facets of the problem. In other words, attending to the problem's outstanding perceptual feature (level of marbles) caused other important features to be ignored (the different sizes of the two containers). At this stage of cognitive development, limited attending skills prevent the careful exploration of one's surroundings (Ginsburg & Opper, 1988; Wadsworth, 1989).

TRANSDUCTIVE REASONING Children's thinking at this time is often characterized by **transductive reasoning,** that is, reasoning from particular to particular without seeking a generalization to connect them. Transductive reasoning is different from both **inductive reasoning** (particular to general) and **deductive reasoning** (general to particular) thought processes. Transductive reasoning may sometimes be correct, such as the statement "Mommy's got her hair up in curlers; she must be going out with Daddy tonight," but more often than not they are inaccurate.

Transductive reasoning is a good illustration of children's mental shortcomings during this time, particularly their tendency to perceive the world intuitively. Children look for some functional property to link objects or events and make statements of implication, even though there is no relationship between

FIGURE 7-3
Centering.

Centering means to focus on a single characteristic of an object while ignoring its other features. Although these two jars contain the same amount of beads, children in Piaget's intuitive thought stage will deny this fact. Rather than examining the size and shape of the containers, children are preoccupied with the different appearances of the beads.

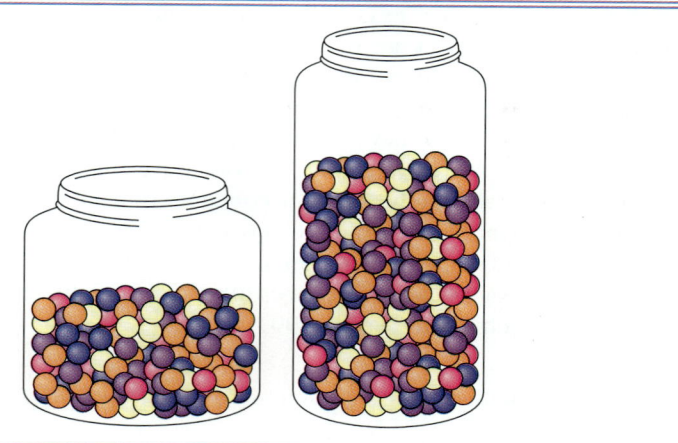

the events. Instead of seeking information systematically, children make inferences.

TRANSFORMATIONAL REASONING **Transformational reasoning** is often lacking during the intuitive thought phase. This type of reasoning means that when observing an event having a sequence of changes, a person can understand how one state is transformed into another. As an example, consider the following. You are asked to draw the sequential stages of a pencil falling from a vertical, upright position to its final horizontal position. Depicting such a sequence of change is very easy for adults to do, and we would most likely draw something resembling Figure 7-4.

Children, however, have difficulty with this task. Instead of grasping the underlying concept of total change, they tend to restrict their attention to each successive state when it occurs. Such a cognitive strategy prevents them from understanding the concept of succession. Consequently, most children during this stage can depict only the initial and final positions of the pencil. This also means their reasoning is transductive. That is, their reasoning goes from particular to particular without seeking the generalization that connects the two.

REVERSIBILITY Another significant limitation in reasoning at this time is children's inability to reverse mental operations. **Reversibility** is defined as the ability to trace one's line of thinking back to where it originated. Piaget regarded reversibility as critical to advanced thinking.

The inability of children in middle childhood to reverse mental operations can be seen most clearly with numbers. More specifically, children have difficulty comprehending that for any unit, there is an opposite operation that can cancel it. For example, the number 2 can be added to the number 3 in order to arrive at 5. However, what isn't clearly understood is that 3 can be subtracted from 5 in order to return to the original 2.

Another example of the lack of reversibility is seen when presenting a child with two identical rows of checkers (Figure 7-5). When asked if both rows contain the same number of checkers, the child in the earlier stages usually agrees. However, the youngster gives a different response when one row of checkers is

FIGURE 7-4
The Falling Pencil Problem.

Transformational reasoning enables the individual to draw the successive movements of a falling pencil in a fashion similar to this.

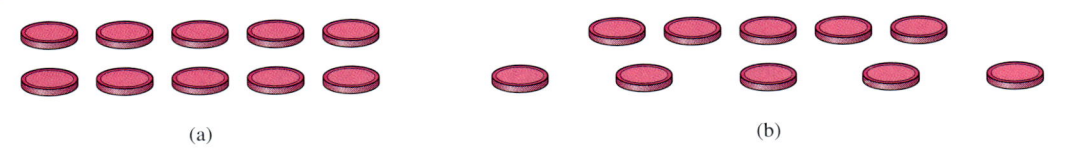

(a)   (b)

FIGURE 7-5
The Reversibility Problem.

Younger children often have trouble understanding the principle of reversibility. Although they would agree that identical rows of checkers (a) contain the same amount, they are tricked by greater spacing (b) and contend there must be more checkers in the longer arrangement.

spread out so it occupies more space. Most children reason that because the row is now longer, it must contain more checkers. Such illogical thought is due both to centering and the inability to reverse mental operations. If the child could mentally return the row of checkers to its original length, the problem would be solved.

Concrete Operations   **Concrete operations,** occurring between the ages of 7 and 11, is Piaget's third stage of cognitive development. Children can think more logically about their environment and execute mental operations that they previously had to carry out physically. More importantly, concrete operations represents a stage when children reason consistently. An especially important development is being able to plan ahead before taking a course of action (Gauvain, 1992). To be sure, there are rules of logic that still remain elusive; however, children will no longer give the impression of comprehending something only to reveal moments later that they do not understand (Sigelman & Waitzman, 1991).

Elementary school experiences do much to activate cognitive abilities. For example, mathematical exercises, such as counting, manipulating, and sorting, help develop the mental operations of reversibility, seriation, and conservation (Schulman, 1991; Tocci & Engelhard, 1991). Projects in social studies, science, and literature teach procedures for systematically obtaining facts. In this regard, a steady stream of research indicates how cognitive capacities refine themselves during middle childhood (Mitchell & Robinson, 1992; Moore et al., 1991; Sodian, Zaitchik, & Carey, 1991; Spinillo & Bryant, 1991). Social cognition also increases as school-age children learn to appreciate the ideas, feelings, and opinions of others (Dunn, 1991; Pillow, 1991).

Although children can understand concrete characteristics of objects, they still cannot understand abstractions. As the name of this stage suggests, children's thinking is restricted to the immediate and physical. Thus youngsters cannot truly analyze their own thoughts or think about problems in the future. Although they can reason about what is, they cannot visualize what may be. In other words, their thinking is bound to the here and now.

CONSERVATION Children can now understand the concept of **conservation,** something that had created considerable confusion during earlier stages, and which means the amount or quantity of matter remains the same, despite changes made in its outward physical appearance. Thus, even though the distribution of matter changes, it nonetheless conserves its properties.

Before this stage, children had trouble understanding how the same matter could take on different appearances. Think back to the problems created by the same number of marbles occupying different levels in different containers. The problem was caused not only by centering but also because the youngster did not understand that matter could be altered in one outward dimension without changing the other dimensions. Likewise, children would agree that two balls of clay are equal when they have similar shapes. But if one ball was flattened, the child would reason the flattened ball was larger because it was longer (or that the round ball had more clay because it was fatter). Although younger children can compare the like characteristics of two objects, they have difficulty accounting for physical changes.

In middle childhood, however, children can reason that matter remains the same despite changes in its outward appearance. They have thus learned to decenter as well as reverse their mental operations. That is, they understand that matter can still be restored to its original condition after changes have been made in its appearance. The ability to reverse mental operations enables youngsters to realize that the flattened ball of clay can be remolded into the original ball; a longer row of checkers can be restored to its original length; and marbles can be poured back into the first container to restore their original level. In such situations, children know that matter has been conserved despite the transformations. Moreover, children do not need to verify this by repeating the operation. The accompanying Lifespan Development in Action box describes how you can test children for their conservation abilities.

The examples just described also demonstrate that there are different types of conservation, such as the conservation of mass or volume. Also, the different types of conservation are not mastered simultaneously. In this respect, the conservation of a particular property is not an all-or-nothing phenomenon, which means children may have grasped conservation of number but not conservation of weight or volume. Table 7-2 (p. 312) displays the various types of conservation that exist and the approximate ages at which they are grasped by the child.

CLASSIFICATION Another cognitive advancement children make in middle childhood is in **classification,** the ability to understand the concepts of subclasses, classes, and class inclusion. You will recall that younger children have difficulty understanding these concepts. In particular, children are confused when they are shown four red checkers and two black checkers and asked whether there are more red or more plastic checkers. Compared with their

Lifespan Development in Action

DEMONSTRATING THE PIAGETIAN PRINCIPLE OF CONSERVATION

Piaget's research studies investigating conservation abilities are relatively easy experiments to duplicate. To observe the developmental stages through which this principle is attained, children between approximately 6 to 10 years of age should be tested.

For conservation of substance, begin by showing the child two balls of clay, asking if the two contain identical amounts. The best way to ask this is "Does this one have more?", "Does this one have more?", or "Do they both have the same?" rather than "Which one has more?" or "Are they the same?" If the child says they do contain the same amount, roll one of the balls into the shape of a sausage and then ask if they still contain the same amount. According to Piaget, children under 6 are most likely to respond that the amounts of clay now differ, reasoning that because the sausage shape occupies more space, it must therefore contain more clay. (You might employ younger subjects and record their reactions for comparison purposes.) Between ages 7 and 9, the typical response is that each still contains the same amount, an indication the law of conversation has been grasped.

Once you have tested for conservation of substance, try examining for conservation of liquid. Start with two identical glasses and pour an equal amount of liquid into both. Do they appear the same to your subjects? If so, change the size or shape of one of the containers and fill them again. Are your subjects fooled by the appearance (level) of the liquid? Have they failed to decenter? Between ages 6½ and 8½, this facet of conservation should be mastered, although individual differences must be considered.

Do your subjects follow the prescribed sequence of conservation described in this chapter? If some of your subjects mastered liquid but not substance conservation, why do you think this is so? Does coaching your younger subjects affect the outcome of your experiment? Asking yourself questions like these illustrates some of the many dimensions of conservation, not to mention why this facet of children's thinking has attracted the attention of child psychologists for years.

younger counterparts, school-age children do not perceive a class of objects as a location where all the elements must lie. Instead, they understand the same element can exist in two classes at the same time. Children now know all the checkers are plastic, and so there are more plastic checkers because there are six of them and only four red checkers. School-age youngsters thus come to recognize three classes of checkers: the red, the black, and the inclusive class of plastic checkers. This type of reasoning is an important part of mental functioning because it contributes to organization and classification abilities. In addition, it enables youngsters to move beyond a singular viewpoint and consider

TABLE 7-2

Judging the Levels of the Child's Response on Piagetian Conservation Tasks

Conservation Tasks	Approximate Age Reached	Establish Equivalence	Transform or Rearrange	Conservation Question and Justification
Conservation of number: Number is not changed despite rearrangement of objects.	6–8			Will an ant have just as far to walk or...?
Conservation of length: The length of a string is unaffected by its shape or its displacement.	6–8			Are there the same number of red & green chips or...?
Conservation of liquid amount: The amount of liquid is not changed by the shape of the container.	6½–8½			Do the glasses have the same amount of water or...?
Conservation of substance (solid amount): The amount of substance does not change by changing its shape or by subdividing it.	7–9			Do you still have the same amount of clay?
Conservation of area: The area covered by a given number of two-dimensional objects is unaffected by their arrangements.	8–10	Grass / Garden	Is there still the same amount of "room" for planting or...? / Is there still the same amount of grass to eat or...?	
Conservation of weight: A clay ball weighs the same even when its shape is elongated or flattened.	9–11			Do the balls of clay still weigh the same or...?
Conservation of displacement of volume: The volume of water that is displaced by an object depends on the volume of the object and is independent of weight, shape, or position of the immersed object.	11–14			Will the water go up as high or...?

From *The Piaget primer: Thinking, learning, teaching* by E. Labinowicz. Copyright © 1980 by Addison-Wesley.

all features of objects and events. Furthermore, researchers have found that class inclusion is consistently easier for children to understand than other concrete operational tasks (Chapman & Lindenberger, 1989).

SERIATION The ability to order objects according to size is known as **seriation**. Seriation poses problems to children who are not yet in the concrete operations stage. Most children acquire the ability to seriate by age 7 or 8.

To test seriation, children are usually given sticks of varying lengths and asked to arrange them from the smallest to the biggest. Before they reach age 7 or 8, their confusion is obvious. Children between the ages of 5 and 6, for instance, align the tops of the sticks but pay little attention to the bottom of the sticks. Their ability to grasp more than one relationship is definitely limited.

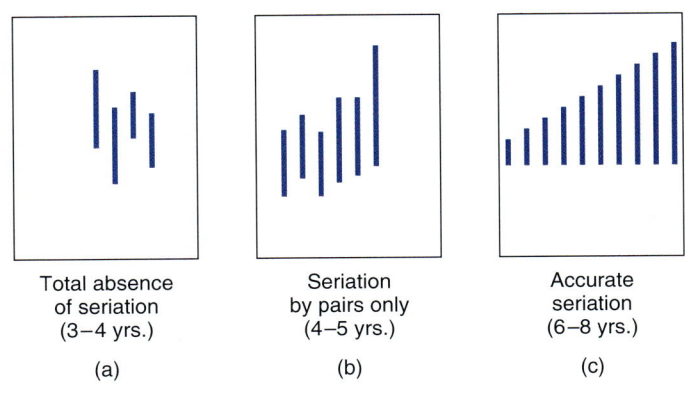

Total absence
of seriation
(3–4 yrs.)
(a)

Seriation
by pairs only
(4–5 yrs.)
(b)

Accurate
seriation
(6–8 yrs.)
(c)

FIGURE 7-6
The Development of Seriation.

The development of seriation can be seen when children are presented with sticks of varying lengths. In their efforts to seriate, preschoolers (a) exhibit no order whereas kindergartners (b) tend to create order by placing paired sticks of approximate equal length together. By middle childhood (c), youngsters are successful in ordering from shortest to longest.

SOURCE: Adapted from Wadsworth, 1989.

Younger children also try to solve this problem by using intuition and trial-and-error behavior. Older youngsters, however, order the sticks without using trial-and-error behavior. Most use methodical approaches, such as searching for the biggest stick, then the next biggest, and so on, until the task is complete. Furthermore, they understand the task before they begin and have created a subjective ordering of the series so it can be successfully constructed (Ginsburg & Opper, 1988; Wadsworth, 1989). Figure 7-6 illustrates the manner in which children attempt to seriate.

Concept Development

It is during the school years that children refine and elaborate their concepts. They also learn to mentally connect objects or events having similar properties. Consequently, their environment becomes organized and meaningful rather than confusing. Many researchers believe the organization that advanced concepts require is a major feature of developing cognition (Matlin, 1989; Reed, 1992).

Developing perceptual abilities enable concepts to mature. And maturation is enabled by children's developing attention and attending skills. Unlike younger children, youngsters in middle childhood pay more attention to environmental events. Furthermore, they are better at examining the important features of a situation and ignoring what is irrelevant. Children of this age also know their attention can be influenced by numerous variables, such as distractions and their motivation to learn (Miller & Weiss, 1981a, 1981b; Miller & Zalenski, 1982).

Children's perception also has an economical quality. Youngsters acquire more information about perceptual appearances, in the process learning to detect those properties that distinguish one object from another and those characteristics of objects that remain constant (Farrar, Raney, & Boyer, 1992; Levine & Shefner, 1991). Similar to children performing conservation tasks, youngsters demonstrating economical perception know that clay rolled into different shapes still is the same amount or that the same quantity of liquid can reach different levels depending on the container's size.

Challenging classroom environments enhance learning skills, including those related to concept formation.

Shape and Size Concepts   School-age children show a greater awareness of shape and size concepts and how they relate to the environment. In particular, youngsters have a better understanding of shape and size in relation to distance, and they can recognize forms in changed or strange surroundings. Children demonstrate growing efficiency in detecting shapes having ambiguous or hidden contours, another indication of heightened perceptual awareness (Ruffman, Olson, & Astington, 1991). Such advancements also show that children have become more selective and insightful in their overall environmental interpretations. Being able to maintain perceptual constancies also helps youngsters perceive shapes and sizes as constant.

Spatial Concepts   Older children have a fairly good understanding of how objects can occupy different spatial positions and relationships with other objects. By roughly age 7, youngsters demonstrate an understanding of perspective and of how objects may look under different viewing conditions. Before this age, children do not consider such variables as the angle or distance from which they view objects. Rather, their spatial concepts are limited to an egocentric visual perspective.

Relational Concepts   In middle childhood, children can correctly reason about relational concepts, such as left or right. Relational concepts created considerable confusion earlier, but now children can understand their own left and right perspective, as well as the perspective of those individuals opposite them. This is a noteworthy accomplishment, as it is maintained that the perception of left-right is harder to learn than other relational orientations, such as front-back and up-down. Consider the difficulty of this concept the next time you are placed in a situation requiring a relational orientation. Teaching youngsters how to tie their shoes, for example, is difficult, especially when standing opposite the child.

Quantity Concepts   Children's understanding of quantity concepts also advances in middle childhood. Numbers are gradually understood to the point that they can be manipulated and recognized as parts, wholes, and units. Most children of this age will be able to grasp the durability of numbers and not be restricted to a functional and nonverbal understanding of them (Baroody & Coslick, 1993; Heddens & Speer, 1992).

By age 8, most children can add, subtract, multiply, divide, and deal with simple fractions. These number concepts can also be applied to a wide range of measurements, such as weight, height, length, and volume. Money concepts also advance at this time. Before middle childhood, the identification of money was limited to pennies, nickels, and dimes. School-age children, though, understand the value of coins and can manipulate fairly complex money combinations.

Time Concepts   School-age children demonstrate an understanding of clock time as well as a knowledge of the days of the week, months, and seasons. Children can also reflect on what they did yesterday and anticipate what they're going to do tomorrow, another indication of developing time concepts. However, certain time concepts remain elusive, including clock time for younger children (Friedman & Laycock, 1989) and an appreciation of dates or historical chronology in general. These will not develop until the latter stages of middle childhood.

In a unique study of time orientations, 96 Canadian children between the ages of 4 and 12 were asked to speak for a doll in dialogues with an experimenter who spoke for another doll. The experimenter looked for speech acts in the dialogues that would commit the "dolls" to some future action. Each subject included at least one such speech act, but only the older subjects actually used the word *promise* to reassure the hearer of their commitment (Astington, 1988).

The Concept of Death   One of the more difficult concepts for the child to understand is death. For many children, as well as adults, death is a mysterious phenomenon. It is also a situation most youngsters are likely to encounter at some point during childhood. Rare is the child who has not experienced the death of a pet, neighbor, relative, or friend.

Children's understanding of death reflects developing cognitive awareness. During infancy and toddlerhood they show little understanding, but by the preschool years, ideas about death become more numerous and detailed, and death-related thoughts and experiences show up in songs, play, and questions. Many preschool children conceive of death as partial, reversible, and avoidable, and because of their egocentricity, many view themselves as living forever (DeSpelder & Strickland, 1992; Lazar & Torney-Purta, 1991; Leming & Dickinson, 1990).

During middle childhood, more information is acquired about death, but the new ideas are often applied illogically. For example, school-age children often reason that death happens only to the elderly. They want to know about death's physical qualities, including what happens to the body and the nature of death-related illnesses. This preoccupation with death's physical qualities appears to parallel the concrete quality evident in other cognitive spheres (Bertman, 1991; Caserta & Lund, 1992; Silverman et al., 1992).

THEORETICAL ISSUES

Think about some of the cognitive challenges awaiting school-age children, both inside and outside of the classroom. How do you think the degree to which such challenges are mastered affects the child's sense of competence? How might you connect the Eriksonian psychosocial dynamics of *industry versus inferiority* to this topic?

Children's developing awareness of death is greatly influenced by adults. How adults handle the topic is critical. Experts (e.g., Campanelli, 1990; Durlak & Riesenberg, 1991; Samarel, 1991) in the field recommend gradually introducing the youngster to the topic throughout childhood rather than initiating discussions after a death strikes close to home. Explanations should take the youngster's cognitive and emotional states into consideration.

In the final analysis, adults can do much to help children develop healthy attitudes toward death. Children need to learn that death is an expected part of the life cycle, not an unrelated occurrence. Attempting to understand death, rather than denying or repressing it, adds an important dimension to one's life (Oltjenbruns, 1991; Z. R. Wolf, 1991; Zambelli & DeRosa, 1992). We return to the topic of death and how it impacts on people of all ages in Chapter 12.

Development of Problem-Solving Abilities

The successful application of cognitive facilities to problems is one of the distinguishing features of the mature mind. With age, problem-solving abilities improve. In time, these abilities will become more systematic and reflect a distinct and orderly sequence. This methodical approach first entails the definition of the problem, particularly a clarification of its nature and the solution sought. Next a strategy, or set of strategies, must be developed in order to reach the solution. Then one must implement the decided course of action and apply whatever internal and external resources are needed. Effective problem solving requires monitoring and evaluating the progress made toward reaching the solution (Moely et al., 1992; Reed, 1992).

A number of reasons account for the child's overall improvement in problem-solving abilities. Among the obvious are the cognitive advancements described in this chapter in addition to the curriculum challenges of the elementary school. Problem-solving abilities are also enhanced by the child's work habits in general. As children grow older, most learn to develop not only persistence and concentration, but also independence when working on problems (Matlin, 1989; Reed, 1992; Schulman, 1991).

Advancements in problem-solving abilities are also a reflection of developing memory abilities. During the school years, children become more adept at organizing, searching for, and retrieving the information that has been encoded or placed in memory storage (Fivush, Kuebli, & Clubb, 1992; W. J. Friedman, 1991; Horobin & Acredolo, 1989; Kail, 1990). To illustrate, consider an experiment conducted by Michael Farrar and Gail Goodman (1992). In this study, preschool and elementary school-age children were tested for their recall of features related to a repeated event versus features that deviated from the event. When the children's recall of the various features was assessed 1 week later, younger children had more difficulty than the school-age children in distinguishing between the standard and deviation features. The school-age subjects, on the other hand, employed more refined memory skills in accurately differentiating the standard and deviation features.

Metacognition, which we learned (Chapter 5) is the application of some cognitive process to a selected cognitive task, also exhibits refinement at this time. Metacognitive skills designed to encourage remembering, known as *metamemory* skills, are particularly pronounced in their development. Examples

School-age children can apply their advanced thinking skills to many dimensions of life.

of these skills are encoding, rehearsal and elaboration, the latter being the technique of expanding verbal or visual material to increase the number of ways it may be retrieved (Cornoldi et al., 1991; Glover, Ronning, & Bruning, 1990; Hashimoto, 1991; Martindale, 1991).

Other noteworthy metacognitive advancements include the growing ability to recognize one's efforts as the primary cause of the problem's outcome and the ability to judge how accurately one is actually performing on a given problem (Kail, 1990; McGilly & Siegler, 1989; Zechmeister & Johnson, 1992). For example, to study metacognition, children in third- and fifth-grade classes were given an experimental curriculum designed to increase their awareness and use of effective reading strategies. Compared with children in the control group, who were not given the special curriculum, the experimental group made significant gains in metacognition (Cross & Paris, 1988).

Moreover, competency and proficiency in problem-solving situations are influenced by the youngster's intrinsic motivation. Intrinsic motivation means the child undertakes an activity, such as problem solving, for the rewards or pleasures derived from that particular activity. Although intrinsic motivation was limited earlier in childhood, it increases as youngsters grow older. Children learn to enjoy problems or situations that are challenging and responsive to their actions. In their quest for mastery of the environment, children develop an ever-increasing interest in what can be explored or investigated (Glover, Ronning, & Bruning, 1990; Gottfried, 1983).

Cognitive Styles   There are significant differences and variations in how children evaluate problems. The characteristic ways in which information is organized and solutions to problems are found are referred to as **cognitive style.** Put another way, cognitive style represents the general pattern of behavior that an individual applies to cognitive tasks.

Cognitive styles vary from child to child. Some children may examine the minute details of stimulus objects, establishing what is referred to as an *analytic style*. Others employ a *superordinate style* and look for shared attributes among objects. A *functional-relational style* means a group of objects or events are linked because they have some sort of interactional value. Finally, *functional-locational style* embodies a classification based on a shared location.

To examine these modes of cognitive style, children between the ages of 6 and 11 were presented with a series of pictures in a set (Figure 7-7) and were asked to determine which two figures were alike or in some way related. Older children were more likely to use superordinate or analytic styles. With the superordinate style, for example, the two shirts rather than the zebra would

FIGURE 7-7

Picture Sets Designed to Test Children's Cognitive Styles.

Subjects are asked to select two pictures in each group that are similar in some way.

SOURCE: Kagan, J., Rosman, B., Day, D., Albert, J., & Phillips, W. (1964). Information processing in the child. *Psychology Monograph 78* (1, whole no. 578).

(a)

(b)

(c)

FIGURE 7-8

Test Items Designed to Measure Impulsiveness-Reflectivity.

Subjects are asked to select from each group of six variants one that is identical to the uppermost standard figure.

SOURCE: Kagan, J. (1965). Impulsive and reflective children: Significance of conceptual tempo. In J. Krumboltz (Ed.), *Learning and the educational process.* Chicago: Rand McNally.

be paired in picture set *b;* the analytic style would mean pairing the watch and ruler in picture set *a* because both are used for measurement. Younger children, usually aged 4 to 6, have a tendency to classify the pictures with a functional-relational style. For example, pairings are made because the match lights the pipe in picture set *c* or the man wears the watch in picture set *a* (Kagan et al., 1964).

Conceptual Tempos: Impulsivity Versus Reflectivity   In addition to cognitive style, children differ in their conceptual tempos, the manner in which they evaluate and act on a problem. Should children exhibit **impulsivity,** they usually accept and hurriedly report the first idea that they can generate, giving little consideration or thought to its accuracy. Should **reflectivity** be generated, children generally devote longer periods of time considering various aspects of a hypothesis. Related to the foregoing discussion, reflective, attentive children are more apt to be analytic in their cognitive style than impulsive youngsters.

Our knowledge of impulsivity and reflectivity has been greatly enhanced by Jerome Kagan and his colleagues (Kagan, 1965, 1966; Kagan et al., 1964). In a typical test designed to measure conceptual tempo, children are shown pictures from the Matching Familiar Figures Test (Figure 7-8). In the test, children are asked to match a standard figure with one of six variants. The subjects' scores are based on the amount of time it takes them to select the appropriate figure and the number of errors they make in the process. Generally, the faster the children make their decisions, the more mistakes they are likely to make. Older children typically take longer to offer their first answer and, as a result, tend to make fewer errors. Those children exhibiting reflective behavior in this test appear to be reflective in other situations. For example, they have a tendency to wait for longer periods of time in answering questions, make fewer incorrect guesses on reading tests, and make fewer errors in reading textual material.

Other studies have generally supported Kagan's research and found other interesting dimensions of conceptual tempo. One investigation (Toner, Holstein, & Hetherington, 1977) revealed that conceptual tempos may be measured to

Lifespan Development in Action

HOW TO HELP CHILDREN BECOME BETTER THINKERS

There is much that adults can do to foster the growth and development of the youngster's problem-solving skills and thinking abilities during middle childhood. Because intrinsic motivation is an important facet of mental development, children need mental challenges so that curiosity, mastery of the environment, and a sense of competency can be nurtured. When working on problems, children also need to learn the merits of a deliberate, methodical approach. Adults should encourage the youngster to reflect on the material at hand and think about the accuracy and quality of answers before they are given.

Adults should also encourage children to develop as much independence as possible in problem-solving situations. Patience is needed on the adult's part to allow for trial-and-error learning. Jumping in and solving the problem for the child may produce the answer but frequently promotes dependency on the adult as well. Moreover, it robs the child of benefiting from a mistake or experimenting with multiple problem-solving approaches. Adult feedback, encouragement, and praise help strengthen desired problem-solving strategies, not to mention the child's motivation to succeed.

Overall thinking abilities may be groomed so that school-age children more deeply question and analyze the learning material at hand. Although children need to acquire the cognitive advancements described in this chapter, they also need to develop a capacity for genuine thought, not a mindless monologue of facts. In short, children need to learn how to think. According to James Alvino (1983), certain philosophical questions can be directed toward children to help them think and rethink ideas. When asked, these questions should convey honest interest in the child's reasoning powers, not adult smugness or arrogance. They should also serve to sow the seeds for later analytical reasoning skills. As grown-up as these questions sound, they have been implemented into the curriculum of thousands of elementary school systems. They emerged from the Institute of Philosophy for Children, a project founded by Matthew Lippman of Montclair State College. The questions and the explanation of what each query demands of the child's thought processes are as follows:

1. *"Why?"* This requests an explanation of the basis for the youngster's response.
2. *"If that is so, what follows?"* Such a question requires the child to elaborate, extrapolate, and draw a valid inference, be it hypothetical or causal.
3. *"Aren't you assuming that . . . ?"* Here the adult is asking the child to explain the premises on which the statement or argument may be based.
4. *"How do you know that?"* This calls for more information from the child, a source for the information given, or for the youngster's explanation of his or her line of reasoning.
5. *"Is the point you are making that . . . ?"* With this question, the youngster is asked to confirm the adult's comprehension of the main point.

Continued . . .

HOW TO HELP CHILDREN BECOME BETTER THINKERS, Continued . . .

6. *"Can I summarize your point as . . . ?"* This is similar to the previous question but requires the child to confirm the adult's restatement or condensation of the main point.
7. *"Is what you mean to say that . . . ?"* This rephrasing requires children to interpret their own statements and be certain of their meaning.
8. *"What is your reason for saying that?"* This is basically a request for the rationale behind making a judgment as well as the justification for it.
9. *"Doesn't what you say presuppose that . . . ?"* Here the adult is pointing out assumptions that may be hidden in the child's argument. Furthermore, this type of question requests that children explain the validity of their assumptions.
10. *"What do you mean when using that word?"* Such a question asks for the precise meanings and contextual usage of words.
11. *"Is it possible that . . . ?"* Here the adult is offering other possibilities and pointing out possible contradictions and inconsistencies in the child's argument.
12. *"Are there other ways of looking at it?"* This question calls for alternative perspectives and an examination of the child's objectivity and impartiality.
13. *"How else can we view this matter?"* Such a query places an emphasis on open-mindedness and mental flexibility. It also gives the child a chance to be creative.

some degree in children as young as 3 years of age. Another (Cohen, Schleser, & Meyers, 1981) disclosed that among younger school-age children, those classified as reflective were more apt to understand the Piagetian principle of conservation. Impulsive children were more likely to react in a preoperational fashion.

One possible cause of a child's reflective attitude is anxiety over making a mistake, although research results conflict on this topic. Some feel that if children have a strong fear of error, they may foster reflective attitudes. These children usually want to be correct and will try to avoid whatever mistakes they can. Conversely, for reasons not clearly understood, impulsive children do not appear to become upset over their mistakes and therefore respond quickly. Research has revealed that American schoolchildren become more reflective with age than do children of other cultures. This may be true because the American value system encourages children to avoid mistakes and the humiliation of being wrong, which may explain why young children become excessively cautious and inhibited (Duryea & Glover, 1982; Glover, Ronning, & Bruning, 1990; Kagan, 1966). In relation to this entire unit, the accompanying Lifespan Development in Action box supplies some tips on helping children become better thinkers.

Learning Disabilities

The cognitive developments discussed thus far in this unit, including refined concept formation, problem-solving skills, and cognitive styles, greatly influence the child's learning progress in the school setting. We need to recognize, too, that some children experience difficulty in school and face special problems. Learning disabilities represent one such problem and impact on the developing person in many ways. Broadly defined, a **learning disability** represents difficulty in processing, remembering, or expressing information.

Learning disabilities have attracted considerable attention over the past few decades, and many researchers have supplied insight as to what they are, how many youngsters are learning disabled, and how public schools should intervene (Adelman, 1992; Barsch, 1992; Bateman, 1992; Richardson, 1992). A rich vein of research activity has also focused on how learning disabilities affect the adult population, including college-age students (Brinckerhoff et al., 1992; Houck et al., 1992; Patton & Polloway, 1992; Spillane et al., 1992; Vogel & Adelman, 1992).

Thanks to the efforts of contemporary researchers, we are able to better understand the nature and scope of learning disabilities. For example, we know a learning disability is not mental retardation; indeed, those with a learning disability are usually of normal or higher intelligence. Most learning disabled individuals do not experience sensory impairment or emotional problems. Rather, processing problems are thought to originate from central nervous system dysfunctioning.

A number of different types of learning disabilities exist that create certain functional limitations, such as difficulties in oral expression, listening comprehension, or writing skills. Generally, a learning disabled person exhibits a pattern of uneven abilities. For most, a discrepancy typically exists between expected and actual performance. However, rather than originating from a poor academic background or a lack of motivation, such difficulties are presumed to be from neurological dysfunction. We must acknowledge, too, that learning disabilities do not confine themselves to academic areas. Persons may encounter difficulty, for example, in reading a map, understanding and executing a coaching strategy in sports, following directions when assembling a toy model or household product, or balancing a checkbook.

Little is known regarding the origins and causes of learning disabilities. Because of central nervous system dysfunctioning, some type of brain damage or structural differences in the brain are suspected. Such alterations are thought to be inherited because learning disabilities tend to run in families. Biochemical imbalances, a weakened immune system, malnutrition, or head injuries are other possible explanations. Also, a pregnant woman's exposure to toxins including harmful drugs may be a possible explanation (Needleman et al., 1990; Richardson, 1992; Segalowitz & Brown, 1991; C. Smith, 1991; Taylor & Shatschneider, 1992).

Types of Learning Disabilities   As we indicated, learning disabilities do not represent a homogeneous group of disorders. Different types of learning disabilities exist, which in turn create unique functional limitations. Let's turn our attention to some of the major types.

DYSLEXIA *Dyslexia* refers to a functional limitation in reading. Dyslexic individuals find it difficult to process tasks involving printed words, such as reading books, completing worksheets, or taking tests. Accurately perceiving letters, words, and symbols often creates confusion and frustration. For example, a *d* may be perceived as a *b* or *p*, or the word *rat* may appear as *tar.*

DYSGRAPHIA Dysgraphia refers to difficulty with the physical act of writing. This problem usually becomes apparent when children begin letter formation and prewriting sequences in kindergarten, and becomes more obvious as the youngster gets older. Because of poor fine motor coordination, the child's handwriting is messy, disorganized, and often illegible.

DYSCALCULIA *Discalculia* refers to difficulty with calculations. This type of learning disability may involve difficulties in written computations or those involving the processing of auditory information. The rapid processing of mathematical facts is especially troublesome.

LANGUAGE DEFICIT A *language deficit* involves difficulty in expressing oneself verbally, and may manifest itself in a number of different ways. To illustrate, a person may have difficulty articulating words or may have trouble remembering certain words to express a thought. Some may have difficulty understanding the mechanics of language, such as distinguishing or using correct verb forms or pluralizations.

AUDITORY DEFICIT An *auditory deficit* refers to difficulties in processing information through the sense of hearing. One may experience trouble hearing certain sounds over background noise, or discriminating between similar sounds. Many have difficulty remembering verbal instructions.

SPATIAL ORGANIZATION DEFICIT A *spatial organization deficit* involves difficulties in perceiving the dimensions of space. Such problems in interpreting the environment might include having trouble in distinguishing left from right, up from down, or ahead from behind. Some children with this kind of learning disability are unsure in which direction to write.

MEMORY DEFICIT A *memory deficit* refers to trouble remembering facts or what has transpired during learning episodes. For instance, a person may encounter repeated difficulty retaining facts such as multiplication tables or historical dates. Obviously, a memory deficit has significant implications for a child's success in such areas as spelling, reading, writing, and calculating.

ATTENTION-DEFICIT DISORDER An *attention-deficit disorder* (ADD) is a learning disability that refers to difficulty in concentrating for extended periods of time. Individuals tend to be easily distractible and have great difficulty organizing and finishing their work. Children, especially, usually cannot stay at their desks for long periods and consequently engage in an assortment of diversive activities (e.g., talking with others, staring out the window, continually getting up from their chair).

ATTENTION-DEFICIT HYPERACTIVE DISORDER An *attention-deficit hyperactive disorder* (ADHD), once referred to as hyperactivity, includes those characteristics from the preceding classification as well as high levels of excitability and impulsivity. Other symptoms often include behavioral unpredictability, a low tolerance for frustration, and frequent immaturity. In addition to being overly active, some youngsters are aggressive and defiant.

INTERRELATEDNESS OF AGING PROCESSES

How do you think a learning disability influences developmental forces such as personality and social dynamics? How might levels of self-esteem, confidence, or one's relationships with others be affected? How do you think the adjustment patterns of learning disabled children, adolescents, and adults compare and contrast?

SOCIAL SKILLS DEFICIT A *social skills deficit* refers to difficulty in understanding various elements of social interaction. For example, a person may have trouble interpreting body language, including facial expressions, as well as auditory cues such as voice intonation. Some are unable to determine when others are disturbed or angry, or to interpret humor and sarcasm.

The foregoing classification obviously represents a simplification of some major types of learning disabilities. For more depth on these and other categories, see Gearheart, Mullen, and Gearheart (1993), Blackhurst and Berdine (1993), and C. Smith (1991). When viewing the realm of any classification system, we must recognize that learning disabilities can manifest themselves in many academic areas. Also, as we see presently, learning disabilities such as these have differing degrees of severity, which has implications for the type of intervention needed. Also, more than one type of learning disability may be present in the same person. Finally, a learning disability is not just found in the elementary schoolchild; rather, it is a condition that persists throughout the lifespan. As such, the individual is affected in a number of different ways, including within psychological, social, and vocational spheres (Dowdy, Smith, & Nowell, 1992; Gerber et al., 1992; Polloway et al., 1992; White, 1992).

Intervention for Learning Disabilities   Individuals with learning disabilities are not intellectually incompetent, nor are they unable to compensate for difficulties posed. Research has shown that with the convergence of such factors as proper intervention, a supportive home environment, and a child's motivation to succeed, learning disabled persons are able to make satisfactory adjustments (Feagans et al., 1991; Heyman, 1990; Kershner, 1990; Morvitz & Motta, 1992; Siegel & Gaylord-Ross, 1991). Many successful and famous persons provide testimony on how learning disabilities can be managed, including General George Patton, Thomas Edison, Woodrow Wilson, Nelson Rockefeller, and Winston Churchill.

Most learning disabled students today benefit from *mainstreaming,* a form of educational intervention that places them in regular classroom settings. Special education consultants typically work with regular classroom teachers to meet the needs of the learning disabled. In some instances, the learning disabled remain in the regular classroom and the special educational consultants come to them, or students leave for part of the day and meet with the consultants in a special resource room within the school.

As we mentioned, the type of learning disability and its severity will dictate the intervention. Along these lines, what learning strategies are applied to one child may not be appropriate for another. Often, though, the needs of the learning disabled are addressed directly in a structured environment with clearly defined content and learning strategies. Information is typically presented in a step-by-step fashion and broken down into small units. Demonstrations, practice, and feedback are viewed as essential components of teacher-student interaction. Related to the latter, positive and supportive feedback is emphasized. Also, efforts are usually made to minimize distractions in the classroom or resource room, including lowering the decibel level. Finally, active efforts are made to nurture and strengthen a number of cognitive domains, including attention span, memory skills, and problem-solving abilities (Baechle & Lian, 1990; Cannon, Idol, & West, 1992; Ellett, 1993).

Language Development

Although rates of vocabulary acquisition begin to taper off after the preschool years, overall psycholinguistic development continues. By the time they are 6 years old, children know virtually all of the letters in the alphabet, recognize the printed form of a handful of words, and understand concrete terms. School-age children also increase their ability to use words as a vehicle of expression. Combined with cognitive skills and socialization experiences, language is the means by which youngsters present evidence and support their perceptions of and ideas about the world (Leaper, 1991; Winch, 1990).

Vocabulary and Semantic Development   School-age children's linguistic progress is remarkable. Consider their vocabulary acquisition. After their first year, children know only a few words. The number of words in youngsters' vocabulary by age 3, though, soars to approximately 900. About 2,600 words are known by age 6, and by the time children enter the sixth grade, they have a reading vocabulary of about 50,000 words. This large vocabulary is the result not only of growing linguistic competence, but also of cognitive growth, mainly the memory skills required to process and remember new words (Glover, Ronning, & Bruning, 1990; Kail, 1990; Martindale, 1991).

Although word acquisition rates are rapid, children's comprehension of word meaning and the relationships among words is slow to develop. The abstract qualities of many words lie beyond the cognitive capacities of school-age youngsters. Thus the physical qualities of words are restricted in much the same way that the physical aspects of the environment are limited cognitively.

With age, children learn more about word definitions, and they become more aware of abstract relationships among words. In addition, they are able to name an agent of an action. For instance, if asked "What burns?" they can supply an appropriate answer. Word pairs, such as tall-short, before-after, and big-little, are also understood. Rather than just learning the part of the meaning that was common to both words, as they once did, youngsters now grasp the part of the meaning that distinguishes the two (Glover, Ronning, & Bruning, 1990).

Syntactic Development   The use of incomplete syntactic structures declines during the school years, whereas the use of compound and complex sentences increases. At this time, the basic syntactic structure of children's sentences resembles adult grammar because they have learned the three basic rules of complex sentence formulation. First, they now recognize a sentence has a noun phrase and a verb phrase. Second, they know a noun phrase consists of an article and a noun. Finally, they know a verb phrase includes a verb and a noun phrase. Although they have yet to learn other rules, they can use these three to fabricate sentences (Miller, 1981).

Children's syntax at this time also reveals a significant increase in the number of adjectives, adverbs, and conjunctions that are used (Gropen, 1991). Their understanding of the use of proper names, pronouns, and prepositions also deepens. These advancements set the stage for the structural and functional changes in syntax that emerge during the school years. As they learn more about sentence structure, children find more ways to express different functions. One study (Silva, 1991) showed that compared to preschoolers, school-age children are more aware of the information needs of the listener and consequently use more adverbial clauses as information guideposts.

INTERRELATEDNESS OF AGING PROCESSES

How do you think children's language development and cognitive development impact on one another? Is the relationship between the two more pronounced now than it was earlier? Do you think cognitive skills always dictate language because the child must understand the rules that govern understandable speech? Why or why not?

Language skills rapidly improve during the middle years of childhood.

Understanding the concept of syntax is difficult, largely because of the complex language rules of English. In addition to comprehending the semantic features of words, children must understand sentence construction. This complex process, especially the relationship of language, memory, and thought, has always attracted considerable research attention (Howard, 1983; Hunt, 1989; Kail, 1990; Reed, 1992).

Pragmatics   In Chapter 6 we stated that children must learn the pragmatics of a language. Recall that pragmatics refers to how language is used in social contexts. As children overcome their egocentrism in solving problems, they also transcend egocentric forms of communication. When speaking, school-age children become increasingly more adept at taking their listeners into account.

Beyond the changes in pragmatics discussed earlier, such as the greater use of gestures, pauses, and facial expressions, children are now more skilled at taking turns during conversations. They also are better at adapting information to fit the listener's needs. Moreover, many can adopt the listener's point of view if the situation calls for it (Capelli, Nakagawa, & Madden, 1990).

Other advances in pragmatics include a more meaningful exchange of questions and answers. Although younger children do ask questions, they often encounter problems in listening to the answers. School-age youngsters, on the other hand, use questions to acquire desired information. Fabricating a question, asking it, and listening for the answer all are an important social exchange that improves with age.

Children sometimes learn the pragmatic qualities of language through rote memory. This appears to be especially true for expressives and declaratives. Early in life, youngsters are taught that it is polite to say "Thank you," "Please," or "I'm sorry." Such expressives place no obligations on the speaker or listener,

INTERRELATEDNESS OF AGING PROCESSES

How do advancements in pragmatics reflect a blending of linguistic, cognitive, and social dynamics? Do you think certain social forces are more influential than others in teaching pragmatics to children?

Dialectical similarities and differences reveal some of the many variations in a spoken language.

but they are usually regarded as important to harmonious social relations. Although they may or may not reflect the speaker's feelings about someone or something, they display the feeling expected by a particular society in a particular situation. As a result, expressives are often difficult to explain or justify to young children (many parents do not even attempt to). Consequently, the parents' concern may often be purely social: "Tell Grandmother how much you missed her," or "Thank your brother for his gift." It isn't until the school years and even later that children understand why such expressions are used (Clark & Clark, 1977).

Language Dialects   Not everyone in our society speaks the same language or uses the same grammatical style or slang. Instead, there are variations in language, referred to as **dialects.** Dialects have at their roots the same general language but differ in their expressions and verbal details.

Dialectical differences are caused by several factors. Among them is the profession or occupation of the person speaking. Individuals in different careers not only converse about different topics, but they also use different words to represent the same thing. For instance, the words *forecast, prognosis,* and *prediction* all have similar meanings. However, depending on the speaker's occupation, one meaning is related to the weather, another to medicine, and the last one to science (Dale, 1976).

Another factor affecting dialectical differences is age. This is especially evident in the so-called generation gap. One age group may coin new words or phrases and contrive new meanings for existing words and phrases. Among parents, especially, the failure to understand such terminology (or, worse yet, to use outdated terminology) may create a distance between young and old. The tendency of speakers to continue using the language they learned when young preserves these age differences, even though the language in general may have changed since then.

Geography is another factor influencing dialects. Certain words may be difficult to understand when listening to geographical dialect differences. Often, different words are used to refer to the same object in different geographical locations. For instance, the words *hotcake, pancake, flapjack,* and *griddle cake* are each used in different geographical regions. Likewise, *grinder* is the designation for a large sandwich in the Northeast, but elsewhere it is called a *hoagie, sub, wedge,* or *hero.*

Another factor influencing dialectical differences is social class. When a society is stratified, such as in the United States, social-class differences in language become more obvious. Often, the middle and upper classes use carefully organized and highly structured sentences, whereas the lower classes use syntactically simple and short sentences. Furthermore, although the middle and upper classes often elaborate on their meaning, the lower classes usually do not use such embellishment. Thus the former may say "Please be quiet because your father is sleeping," while the latter might simply say "Be quiet."

There is considerable interest in whether lower-class language patterns are deficient in comparison with those of the middle and upper classes. Many researchers believe persons living in lower-class environments merely have different linguistic patterns, rather than language skills deficiencies, and that they use speech adapted to their respective social class. Their language is not only fluent and functional but also complete, with its own vocabulary and rules of grammar (Hilliard & Vaughn-Scott, 1982; Hoff-Ginsberg, 1991; Schacter & Strage, 1982).

UNIT REVIEW—

➹ Piaget's stages of intuitive thought (a substage of preoperational thought) and concrete operations span the school years. This unit explored the cognitive developments of centering, transductive reasoning, transformational reasoning, reversibility, conservation, classification, and seriation.

➹ Children continue to refine their mental concepts. We studied growth in shape and size, spatial, relational, quantity, time, and death concepts.

➹ Problem-solving abilities rapidly improve at this time. The impact of cognitive styles, mainly impulsivity and reflectivity, was discussed.

➹ A learning disability, defined as difficulty in processing, remembering, or expressing information, may interfere with learning progress both inside and outside of school.

➹ Language growth is especially noticeable in vocabulary, semantics, syntax, and pragmatic development. This unit concluded with a discussion of language dialects and the variations of a spoken language.

UNIT THREE: PERSONALITY AND SOCIAL DEVELOPMENT

Middle childhood is an active period for personality and social development. At this time, the interaction between the child and society expands and becomes more complex, whether it be in peer group relations, school activities, sports, or family activities. From these social relationships, youngsters learn they must adjust their behavior to meet society's numerous expectations and demands.

Social relations enable children to gain more insight into themselves and their developing personalities. Through interactions with others and inferences from their personal experiences, they gain a sense of personal awareness. Some self-awareness was evident earlier, but it was often based on youngsters' physical qualities or possessions. Now, youngsters include other characteristics of themselves in their self-appraisals, such as how they are perceived by others and the abilities they possess.

This suggests that mental development blends once again with personality and social functions. That is, their social cognition allows children to perceive themselves and others more accurately (Dunn, 1991; Pillow, 1991; D. J. Schneider, 1991). Their developing social cognition thus paves the way for more skillful interpersonal relations. Among other social advancements, friendships acquire more depth and meaning, and youngsters come to appreciate the thoughts and sensitivities of others. Maturing social perceptions are apparent in other modes of expression, too. For example, children learn to distinguish situations requiring cooperation or competition. Youngsters also become able to detect people who are kind or unkind, selfish or unselfish, trusted or distrusted.

▄▄ Emotional Development

Greater emotional maturity accompanies middle childhood. This means there is a change from helplessness to independence and self-sufficiency. Emotional maturity also means the acquisition of emotional flexibility and greater emotional differentiation. Compared with infants and their limited forms of emotional expression, school-age children's range of emotions becomes more specific, diverse, and sophisticated. Also evident at this time is the child's growing ability to detect and understand the emotions expressed by others (Cummings, 1989; Eisenberg et al., 1992; Saarni & Harris, 1989; Wintre et al., 1990).

Gender-role stereotyping also affects the nature and quality of emotional expression. Though all youngsters need emotional outlets, gender-role stereotyping often prevents this. In our society, boys are often taught not to cry or show fear, and girls are often criticized if they are physically aggressive. Boys who do cry are often labeled sissies, and aggressive girls are called tomboys. This type of gender-role stereotyping prevents youngsters from using their whole emotional repertoire.

Fear and Anxiety   During middle childhood there is a decline in fears related to body safety (such as sickness and injury) and in the fear of dogs, noises, darkness, and storms. However, there is no significant decline in fears of supernatural forces, such as ghosts and witches. Most of the new fears emerging at this time are related to school and family, in accordance with children's expanding social boundaries. For example, test anxiety may develop in the

Frustration often rests at the foundation of anger.

school-age child. Test-anxious children also report more fears and general worries than children who do not experience test anxiety, and they also worry about negative evaluations (Beidel & Turner, 1988).

Fears of ridicule by parents, teachers, and friends also increase, as do fears of parental rejection and disapproval. Many school-age children also report fearing their parents will die (Beale & Baskin, 1983; DeSpelder & Strickland, 1992). Some researchers believe girls are more fearful than boys, that fourth and fifth graders are more fearful than sixth graders, and that rural children are more fearful than urban children (Davidson et al., 1989; King et al., 1992).

Anger and Aggression   Anger and aggression continue to be expressed physically throughout middle childhood. Such outbursts as kicking, shoving, and hitting are common. But children also learn that anger can be channeled in other ways. For instance, they can verbally express it through insults, arguing, or swearing. Anger can also be buried and expressed through passive and sullen means, such as pouting or hateful stares.

Youngsters of this age tend to express greater amounts of **hostile aggression.** Recall that hostile aggression is intended to hurt another person. Hostile aggression often is used when persons feel intentionally hurt, threatened, or unjustly accused. There is an obvious parallel here with developing cognitive abilities. Before expressing hostile aggression, youngsters must think about the intentions or motives of another. This is something younger children have difficulty doing.

The research of John Coie (1991) indicates that although aggression is often cited as a reason for peer rejection, this is not always the case. To study the role that aggression plays in peer relations, he observed play groups of 7- and 9-year-old African-American children. It was discovered that bullying and other hostile forms of aggression were related to elevated peer status among 9-year-olds but not 7-year-olds. Instrumental aggression (aggression directed at acquiring objects, territory, and the like) tended to be characteristic of highly aggressive, rejected boys at both age levels. In general, highly aggressive, rejected boys demonstrated a greater level of hostility toward their peers and a tendency to violate norms for aggressive exchange. This study tends to support the research of Richard Fabes and Nancy Eisenberg (1992), who found that socially competent and popular children coped with aggression in ways that were relatively direct and active and minimized further conflict and damage to social relationships.

Gender differences continue to be apparent with the expression of anger and aggression. Many researchers (e.g., Maccoby, 1990) have found males more aggressive than females. Moreover, males more so than females expect both less guilt and less parental disapproval for their aggressive outbursts (Perry, Perry, & Weiss, 1989). Also, aggressive boys tend to be persistent in direct confrontation and physical attacks through middle childhood and into early adolescence, whereas girls gradually show an increase in social aggression and ostracism in female-female conflicts (Cairns et al., 1989).

Happiness and Humor   A wide variety of situations elicit happiness, including feelings of acceptance, the pleasures of accomplishment, the satisfaction of curiosity, or the development of new abilities. Curiosity about and mastery of the elementary school environment also creates pleasure (Deci & Ryan, 1982; Gottfried, 1983). Being with friends and loved ones, surprises, treasured gifts and possessions, or the challenges of doing something new are other sources of joy and happiness.

Closely related to happiness is humor. Children especially enjoy jokes. Earlier, preschoolers enjoyed hearing jokes, but their understanding of them was limited. To understand jokes, youngsters need advanced cognitive facilities to appreciate such elements as subtleties, punch lines, and puns and incongruities. Only now are most of these elements appreciated. Because of their reliance on many cognitive ingredients, jokes and children's humor as a whole are regarded as an excellent reflection of their developing minds (McGhee, 1980; McGhee & Goldstein, 1983a, 1983b; Wyer & Collins, 1992).

Love   Because love has many abstract qualities, children cannot fully understand it until their cognitive facilities are mature. Usually, the physical dimensions of loving (kissing, hugging, etc.) are understood before the psychological aspects (mutuality, reciprocity, etc.) are grasped. However, youngsters learned about love early in life, particularly when they formed bonds of attachment with their parents. It is usually from these attachments that youngsters create early feelings of self-worth and acceptance. Those children who receive their parents' love usually come to accept themselves as important objects of affection to others. In addition, those who have received love and affection are capable of giving them in return (Allen, 1990; Orbuch, 1989).

The expression of love changes during childhood. Preschoolers usually express love physically, such as through kissing and hugging. This is also true of school-age children, but they have also learned that love can be expressed through other channels, such as sharing and talking. Leaving behind an egocentric point of view and developing sensitivity toward others help their expression of love gradually to mature. Children love not only their family and friends but animals as well. Once again, masculine and feminine roles often dictate how this behavior is expressed. Should it be deemed unmasculine for a male to exhibit tenderness, then tenderness may not become part of a boy's expression

GENDER SIMILARITIES AND DIFFERENCES

This discussion suggests that certain emotional behaviors are shaped by gender-role learning. Do you agree with this assessment? If so, can you supply examples beyond those given to support your views?

Expressing love and affection is an important part of learning how to relate warmly to others.

of love. Thus the gender roles that children acquire will be an important determinant of their definition and expression of love (Cox, 1984; Douglas & Atwell, 1988; Turner & Rubinson, 1993).

Moral Development

Morality is the conscious adoption of standards related to right and wrong. Although such codes of conduct differ from culture to culture, every society does adhere to certain behavioral standards. Early in childhood, these standards are established when youngsters learn that certain behaviors are labeled as good and others as bad. With age and experience, these standards of morality come to include empathy, as well as complex ideas, values, and beliefs (Bussey, 1992; Ferguson, Stegge, & Damhuis, 1991; M. L. Hoffman, 1989).

To appreciate the many dimensions of morality, including guilt, shame, lying, discipline, and religion, insight must be gained into how morality develops throughout childhood. Jean Piaget and Lawrence Kohlberg both attempted to explain the developmental aspects of morality.

Jean Piaget's Theory   Jean Piaget stated that morality is a system of rules transmitted by adults to children. Gradually, youngsters come to respect these standards of conduct. At the heart of Piaget's theory is the notion that children's understanding of right and wrong is molded by their cognitive awareness (Piaget, 1932).

To understand how morality is shaped by cognitive awareness, Piaget created pairs of stories and asked children to decide which of the two were "naughtier." In one set of stories, for example, a boy named John is called to dinner. As he opens the dining room door, it hits a tray holding 15 cups. All of the cups are broken from the door's impact. In the other story, a boy named Henry wants to get some jam from a cupboard while his mother is out of the house. He reaches for the jam while climbing on a chair, but in the process knocks over a cup and breaks it.

In the follow-up conversations, Piaget found that young children felt the first story was "naughtier," simply because of the greater number of cups broken. The fact that the youngster unintentionally broke the cups did not influence the younger subjects. They were more concerned with the property value of the mistake. The older youngsters, though, regarded the second story as worse because they had begun to judge right and wrong behavior on the basis of the actors' motives.

Piaget's conversations with children led him to devise a three-stage theory of moral development. During the **premoral stage** (before age 5), children have a limited awareness of rules and the reasons for them. Some moral judgments begin in the stage called **moral realism** (generally from ages 5 to 10). In this stage, youngsters learn rules from parents but do not yet understand the reasons for them. Instead, the rules are regarded as sacred and untouchable. Children also feel that punishment compensates for their transgressions.

During the stage of **moral relativism** (beginning after age 10), children become aware of both the meanings of rules and the reasons for them. Now rules are coming to be regarded as a product of mutual consent and respect. Rules are also understood in relation to the principles they uphold. Moreover, youngsters come to realize the seriousness of a wrongdoing if the punishment fits the act. Justice is based on an "eye for an eye, and a tooth for a tooth," so the pain felt by the transgressor must be proportional to the pain inflicted on others. Children in this stage believe punishment should put things into perspective. Thus when they hear about the boy who breaks his little brother's toy, older children suggest the boy give the brother one of his own toys (reciprocity) or pay to have it fixed (restitution). Conversely, younger children generally say the boy should be deprived of his own toys for a week. Suffice it to say, children's moral reasoning, at this time, contains a social, cooperative, logical quality.

Piaget's research has stimulated the thinking of many researchers. Over the years, his notion that morality is closely linked to cognition has gained support (see Krebs & Gillmore, 1982). Researchers have also found that younger children do judge wrongdoings on the basis of the harm done rather than on the intent or motivations of the offender (Surber, 1982). Yet to some, Piaget's research leaves many questions unanswered. Some maintain that Piaget overlooked the cultural and socioeconomic differences among children. Others criticize Piaget's notion that children's morality is formed by preadolescence. These critics argue that morality is a long and elaborate process that is not achieved until adulthood (Colby et al., 1983). Figure 7-9 shows how the stages of morality proposed by Piaget compare with those of Kohlberg.

Lawrence Kohlberg's Theory   Lawrence Kohlberg offered a more detailed explanation of the development of morality. Like Piaget, Kohlberg maintains that morality is achieved in a series of stages. Both acknowledge that children's successive stages of morality originate in the mental restructuring of their experiences. Kohlberg, however, suggests that moral development is a more complex and longer process than Piaget saw it as being. Kohlberg also sees the various stages as closely related. He believes development is characterized by

FIGURE 7-9
Piaget's and Kohlberg's Stages of Moral Development.

Both Piaget and Kohlberg proposed discontinuous age-stage models of moral development. As such, morality is described in terms of a person's sequential progression through the stages depicted.

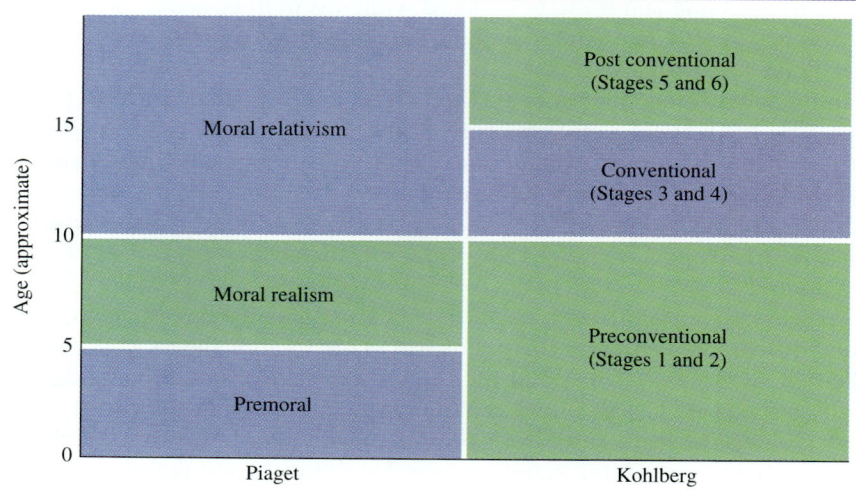

increasing differentiation and that each stage takes into account everything that transpired in the previous stages. (Table 7-3 displays how Kohlberg measured moral reasoning and proposed his chronology of stages.) Over time, the moral distinctions of which children had previously been only dimly aware are organized into a more comprehensive structure (Kohlberg, 1969, 1976, 1981a, 1981b, 1986; Kohlberg & Turiel, 1973).

Kohlberg's theory consists of six stages divided into three levels: the preconventional level (ages 0 to 9), the conventional level (ages 9 to 15), and the postconventional moral reasoning level (age 16 and onward). At the **preconventional level,** children have little awareness of socially acceptable moral behavior, but after two stages, they start to show signs of moral behavior. In stage 1, **obedience and punishment orientation,** youngsters start to follow rules in order to avoid punishment. True rule awareness has not yet been established; instead, their moral conduct is based largely on fear associated with rule violation. Kohlberg, like Piaget, also maintains that the seriousness of a violation at this time depends on the magnitude of the wrongdoing.

During the **naively egoistic orientation,** stage 2, children reason that a tangible reward usually follows their doing something right. A type of reciprocity starts to surface here; that is, youngsters will do the right thing not only to satisfy their own needs but also to satisfy the needs of others. If the latter is the case, children reason they will receive some sort of favor in return. ("You scratch my back and I'll scratch yours.")

As children approach adolescence, they reach the **conventional level.** At this level they learn the nature of authority, not only in the family, but also in society in general. During the third stage, called the **good boy-nice girl orientation,** there is a considerable degree of conformity. Children know they must obey the rules in order to win praise or approval from others. During this phase, they also usually identify with emotionally important persons. Conforming behavior eventually leads to an internal awareness of rules and behavior, which in turn leads to a sense of respect. During the fourth stage, **authority-**

TABLE 7-3
Measuring the Development of Moral Reasoning

A technique known as the Kohlberg Moral Judgment Interview is used to measure an individual's level of moral development. The technique consists of asking the person to react to several moral dilemmas. Attention is focused on the reasoning behind a person's response. The following is one of the more popular dilemmas, and this table charts typical responses according to all of Kohlberg's moral stages:

In Europe a woman was near death from cancer. One drug might save her, a form of radium that a druggist in the same town had recently discovered. The druggist was charging $2,000, ten times what the drug cost him to make. The sick woman's husband, Heinz, went to everyone he knew to borrow the money, but he could only get together about half of what it cost. He told the druggist that his wife was dying and asked him to sell the drug cheaper or let him pay later. But the druggist said "no." The husband got desperate and broke into the man's store to steal the drug for his wife. Should the husband have done that? Why?

Stages of Moral Development

Levels	Stages	Illustrative Responses to Story of Heinz Stealing the Drug
Level I: Preconventional level	Stage 1: Obedience and punishment orientation	It isn't really bad to take it— he did ask to pay for it first. He wouldn't do any other damage or take anything else and the drug he'd take is only worth $200, he's not really taking a $2,000 drug.
	Stage 2: Naively egoistic orientation	Heinz isn't really doing any harm to the druggist, and he can always pay him back. If he doesn't want to lose his wife, he should take the drug because it's the only thing that will work.
Level II: Conventional level	Stage 3: Good boy-nice girl orientation	Stealing is bad, but this is a bad situation. Heinz isn't doing wrong in trying to save his wife, he has no choice but to take the drug. He is only doing something that is natural for a good husband to do. You can't blame him for doing something out of love for his wife. You'd blame him if he didn't love his wife enough to save her.
	Stage 4: Law and order orientation	The druggist is leading a wrong kind of life if he just lets somebody like that die, so it's Heinz's duty to save her. But Heinz can't just go around breaking laws and let it go at that—he must pay the druggist back and he must take his punishment for stealing.
Level III: Postconventional moral principles	Stage 5: Contractual legalistic orientation	Before you say stealing is wrong, you've got to really think about his whole situation. Of course, the laws are quite clear about breaking into a store. And, even worse, Heinz would know there were no legal grounds for his actions. Yet, I can see why it would be reasonable for anybody in this situation to steal the drug.
	Stage 6: Conscience or principled orientation	Where the choice must be made between disobeying a law and saving a human life, the higher principle of preserving life makes it morally right—not just understandable—to steal the drug.

From "The Hierarchical Nature of Moral Judgment: The Study of Patterns of Comprehension and Preference with Moral Stages" by J. R. Rest, 1974, *Journal of Personality, 41*, pp. 92–93. Copyright © 1974 by Duke University Press.

maintaining orientation, children's identification shifts to institutions, such as church or school. Children seek to avoid the guilt and shame brought on by criticism from authoritarian figures.

The **postconventional level** is the last level of Kohlberg's theory. During this stage, individuals' morality reaches maturity. In the fifth stage, **contractual**

legalistic orientation, individuals choose the moral principles to guide their behavior, being careful not to violate the rights and wills of others. In the sixth and final stage, **universal ethical principle orientation,** the emergence of a true conscience enables individuals to uphold behavior that respects the dignity of all humans. However, this last stage is difficult to distinguish from the preceding one. Even Kohlberg himself questioned whether stages 5 and 6 can be separated. And not everyone reaches the postconventional level of morality, just as not everyone attains Piaget's stage of formal operations (Colby et al., 1983).

A Critique of Kohlberg's Theory   Lawrence Kohlberg's theory of moral development has been influential among contemporary psychologists. It has attracted the attention of researchers and has stimulated much discussion of morality and how it is acquired. Most psychologists agree with Kohlberg's contention that cognitive developments underlie the progression of morality from level to level (Fischer, 1983; Krebs & Gillmore, 1982; Page, 1981; Saltzstein, 1983; Walker, 1982, 1989).

Some feel, however, that Kohlberg's sequence hypothesis is too restrictive. Others (e.g., M. L. Hoffman, 1989; Keller, Eckensberger, & von Rosen, 1989), propose that morality may not necessarily progress in stages. There is also evidence that the stages represent alternative types of moral maturity rather than a progressive sequence. Related to this, it has been suggested that a careful examination must be made of moral judgment and moral behavior at all stages. More specifically, there may be a weak relationship between what one says and how one behaves (Blasi, 1980; Kupfersmid & Wonderly, 1980; Maccoby, 1980). Another criticism is that moral development is difficult to assess, particularly the moral dilemmas posed by Kohlberg (Rest, 1986).

In some instances, Kohlberg's theory appears to have cross-cultural application. For example, an examination of the moral responses of subjects from Taiwan and Mexico indicated that their overall development roughly parallels the maturation rate of American subjects (Kohlberg, 1969). Subjects from India and other nations also seem to follow the chronology of Kohlberg's stages (Edwards, 1982; Parikh, 1980; Snarey, 1987). However, other research (e.g., Bronstein & Paludi, 1988) maintains that Kohlberg's scheme is culture-specific and generalizations to other societies should be made with caution.

In regard to Kohlberg's theory, we should recognize that morality may be influenced by other factors, including the individual's uncertainty over how to resolve a moral conflict, the use of defense mechanisms, one's ego identity status, or informational assumptions about a moral dilemma (Hart & Chmiel, 1992; Levine, Jakubowski, & Cote, 1992; Snarey, 1992; Wainryb, 1991). Exposure to moral arguments and involvement in role-playing exercises appear to advance the individual's level of moral reasoning. And on the whole, subjects tend to prefer moral reasoning that is more sophisticated than their own. Individuals' emotions also help determine their moral judgments, an area not examined by Kohlberg. Each of these factors appears to be important to the individual's overall level of moral reasoning (Krebs & Gillmore, 1982; Rest, 1981, 1983; Shweder, 1981).

Kohlberg's theory of moral development does not appear to account for gender differences. Carol Gilligan (1982, 1990; Gilligan, Brown, & Rogers, 1990)

THEORETICAL ISSUES

Although Piaget and Kohlberg utilize a cognitive-developmental framework to explain moral reasoning, how might some of lifespan development's other theories be employed? For example, how might behavioral, social learning, and psychoanalytic theorists choose to examine morality?

maintains that females use different reasoning than males do when confronted with moral issues. More specifically, females tend to be concerned with relationships and responsibilities, whereas males typically center their responses on rights and rules. Because Kohlberg's stages of moral development are primarily structured on the basis of rules, females often fail to reach the zenith of moral functioning. Gilligan contends that the current sequence is therefore an inaccurate model by which to assess females' moral development. It should be noted that although Gilligan's research has provided fresh insights into moral development, not everyone agrees with her contention that such gender differences exist (Smetana, Killen, & Turiel, 1991; Tavris, 1992; Walker, 1989).

Family Influences on the Developing Child

The fact that children now attend school on a full-time basis, have greater interaction with their peers, and display heightened levels of independence places the family in a new perspective. Children still need and rely very much on their parents, but their boundaries with the outside world expand. As a result, their social relationships with other adults broaden considerably, including, for example, interactions with teachers, den mothers, Little League coaches, or summer camp leaders.

The negotiation of new social boundaries and the parents' reactions to the youngsters' strivings for independence earmark these years as especially challenging (Furman & Buhrmester, 1992). Fired by the Eriksonian desire of industry, most children want to spend greater amounts of time away from the family, something that threatens many parents. Parents who feel threatened need to be assured this is a completely normal phase of child development and that they will remain special and unique in the wake of these social strivings. It is interesting to note that amid these desires for social independence, many school-age children have a tendency to periodically slip back to dependency, although usually in private and on their own terms. This age also marks the time when many want to spend more time alone doing private things or being secretive about what they do, both within and away from the family.

Their greater interactions with others enable children to bring back home an abundance of social experiences, whether they be tales about school, sports exploits, or news from the neighborhood. Their increasing powers of social cognition also enable them to compare and contrast their home environment with those around them. As a result, what they see is weighed against what they are allowed to do, a comparison likely to breed a fair number of questions and possible disagreements with parents (how many parents have heard "Everyone else in the neighborhood does it, why can't I?"). Parental values and standards are also tested when children bring home ideas, language, and attitudes different from those taught at home.

Experiencing a Favorable Home Environment   Youngsters need to experience a favorable home climate throughout all of childhood, but this is especially true during the school years. Children unquestionably need the support and guidance of parents as they seek to meet the challenges of this age. This is as true for achieving personal independence as it is for other facets of growth, such as school achievement, developing a sense of morality, establishing healthy relations with siblings, learning appropriate gender roles, or building

A favorable home or family climate promotes childhood trust, security, and competency.

wholesome attitudes toward oneself (Furman & Buhrmester, 1992; Maccoby, 1992; Wentzel, Feldman, & Weinberger, 1991).

Favorable home environments are those capable of providing warmth and acceptance to children. Positive home climates usually employ consistent measures of discipline, encourage social and emotional competence, and are responsive to the child's growing needs. Healthy patterns of child development also hinge on the degree to which parents love, communicate, and seek to support the needs of their offspring (Patterson et al., 1990; Rutledge, 1990). Given these qualities, children are apt to become emotionally stable, cooperative, and happy. The unloved or rejected child, on the other hand, often becomes withdrawn, resentful, lonely, and insecure (Gray-Ray & Ray, 1990; Holcomb & Kashani, 1991).

Research conducted by Patricia East (1991) tends to support the aforementioned points. In this research design, 290 sixth graders and their parents were asked to examine the extent to which the support within the parent-child relationship and the parent-child agreement for this support differed for withdrawn, aggressive, and sociable children. Findings showed that withdrawn girls and aggressive boys perceived less support in their father-child relations than did other children, and that the mothers of withdrawn and aggressive children and the fathers of aggressive children perceived less support in the relations with their children than did other parents. Sociable children were found to be more likely to agree with their parents about the supportiveness of their relationship than were withdrawn or aggressive children.

Other research (Strassberg et al., 1992) indicates that compared to socially rejected childen, sociable children emerge from homes low in rates of adult aggression and rejection. Children experiencing physical abuse also exhibit problems with their socialization skills. For example, the research of Mary Haskett and Janet Kistner (1991) shows that when compared to nonabused youngsters, physically abused children demonstrate fewer positive interactions with peers and a higher proportion of negative behaviors. Research such as this shows the manner in which family dynamics influence a youngster's social development.

Charles Thompson and Virginia Rudolph (1992) stress the importance of nurturance and loving support in parent-child relations. They contend that among other outcomes, children from nurturing families are more likely to communicate more openly, be more honest with others, and adjust more readily to life's demands than children from nonnurturing homes. In addition, children from nurturing families know they will be listened to by their parents when they talk and that they are regarded as special individuals. Furthermore, they know their ideas will not be devalued.

A harmonious family life and a positive emotional climate are also evident in those homes sharing responsibility (Warton & Goodnow, 1991). Dolores Curran (1984) maintains that shared responsibility is a critical ingredient behind healthy family relations. By sharing responsibility, children learn to believe in their capacity to make a contribution. They also learn that each person counts in the family and makes a difference. Curran maintains that shared responsibility includes, but goes beyond, everyday chores and obligations. Responsibility also encompasses, for example, responsiveness to other family members' feelings or getting along with, and looking after, one another. Shared responsibility also has a tendency to breed other positive traits, such as affirmation, respect, and trust. In the Focus on Diversity box on pages 340–341, we provide a look at some cross-cultural experiences of Puerto Rican families.

The Family and Television The contemporary child rarely escapes the clutches of television programming because a television is available in nearly every home in America. Television has changed family life more than any other technological innovation of the 20th century. Families today often plan their schedules to accommodate television, sometimes even scheduling meals and social activities around or in front of the tube (Kubey & Csikszentmihalyi, 1990; Kunkel & Murray, 1991; Liebert & Sprafkin, 1988).

Perhaps a few statistics will illustrate how widespread television viewing is in the 1990s. For the family as a whole, the average television is turned on each day for a period of 6 to 7 hours (Greth, 1990). For children under age 6, the average viewing time per day is about 2½ hours. From age 8 until early adolescence, viewing time increases to almost 4 hours per day and then it begins to level off. By the end of high school, the average individual will have devoted about 12,000 hours to school but 15,000 hours to television. For the child born in the 1990s, more hours will be spent watching television than any other single activity besides sleep (Fabes, Wilson, & Christopher, 1989; Nielsen Media Research, 1991).

Think carefully about these statistics, particularly in relation to our analysis of the contemporary family. These figures mean the general activity of the American household can now be divided each day into three fairly equal parts: 6 to 7 hours of television viewing, 9 hours of work or school, including transportation back and forth, and 8 hours of sleep. To say that television has become part of the American lifestyle is an understatement.

One study (St. Peters et al., 1991) has shed light on some of the family dynamics attached to television viewing. In this investigation, the television viewing habits of 271 children and their families were studied over a 2-year period.

Focus on Diversity

THE FAMILY LIFE OF PUERTO RICAN CHILDREN

As we've learned throughout the text, children's family experiences differ markedly by race and ethnicity. According to Nancy Landale and Susan Hauan (1992), this is especially true for Puerto Rican households, the most disadvantaged Hispanic subgroup in the United States. In contrast to other Hispanic subgroups, such as Mexican or Cuban, Puerto Ricans have experienced serious economic setbacks during the last several decades. Of all Spanish-origin groups, Puerto Ricans have the lowest median family income, the highest percentage of families below the poverty line, the lowest labor force participation, and the highest rates of unemployment.

These trends have greatly increased the economic vulnerability of Puerto Rican children. In 1990, almost 40% of Puerto Rican families had incomes below the poverty line. Also, about two thirds of Puerto Rican families headed by a woman were living in poverty in 1990. Economic disadvantage among Puerto Ricans has also been linked to a retreat from marriage, premarital childbearing, and marital dissolution, each of which contributes to female family headship. Moreover, children who grow up in mother-only families are at an increased risk of poverty during childhood. This, in turn, heightens the risk of health problems, often delays intellectual development, and creates poor school performance. Puerto Rican children living in mother-only families are also less likely to complete high school and more likely to have low adult earnings than are children from intact families (Chadwick & Heaton, 1992; U.S. Bureau of the Census, 1992).

According to Landale and Hauan (1992), several factors help explain why Puerto Rican households experience such high rates of economic hardship. To begin with, Puerto Ricans are geo-

Programs were categorized as child informative, child entertainment, news and informative, sports, comedy, drama, action-adventure, and variety-game. The majority of child programs were viewed without parents; the majority of adult programs were watched with parents. Co-viewing patterns of adult programs were predicted from parents' individual viewing habits, but not from the child's. Co-viewing also declined with age. Another investigation (Henggeler et al., 1991a) showed that as levels of family stress increased, television viewing for both child and parent also tended to escalate.

As we learned in the last chapter, television conveys images of men and women that are influential in shaping traditional gender-role development. Usually, females appear less than males on television programming, and often the portrayal of women is exploitative. In support of this, one study (B. Carter, 1991) found that virtually all major characters on Saturday morning children's programs were male. Another investigation (Davis, 1990) revealed that female actresses on prime-time television shows were more "ornamental" than "functional." That is, they tended to be young, attractive, sexy, and with limited speaking parts. Thus television reflects gender-role stereotypes, usually reinforcing those that children have learned from other socialization experiences.

graphically concentrated in large metropolitan areas in the northeastern United States, a region that has experienced severe economic decline and industrial restructuring during the last 25 years. The shift from manufacturing to service employment has resulted in dwindling opportunities in jobs traditionally held by Puerto Ricans. Another reason Puerto Ricans have found it difficult to procure jobs in a changing economy is their relatively low level of education. The educational attainment of Puerto Ricans has been rising, but high school noncompletion remains considerably more common among Puerto Ricans than among non-Hispanic whites or any other Hispanic group, except Mexican Americans. Yet another important factor underlying Puerto Rican poverty is the earlier mentioned trend toward female-headed households.

Landale and Hauan's (1992) analysis of Puerto Rican families living in the New York City area confirms many of these trends. They found that only a small minority of Puerto Rican youngsters were born into an intact union that survived throughout childhood. Among Puerto Rican children who lived in female-headed households, the duration of time spent with a single mother was rarely brief. Indeed, approximately one half of such children remained in a one-parent family 10 years after the initial disruption. Moreover, the majority of those who experienced maternal remarriage (or a subsequent informal union) experienced the dissolution of a second union during their childhood.

Landale and Hauan (1992) also found that the one-parent families in their research fared poorly economically, and financial deprivation was connected to many of the consequences cited earlier, such as dropping out of school and low adult earnings in the workplace. Thus the trend toward female family headship exerted especially striking implications in their investigation of disadvantaged Puerto Rican children. The authors maintain that such family experiences point to a growing economic inequality among youngsters and an intensification of racial and ethnic differences in children's opportunities for socioeconomic achievement.

TELEVISED VIOLENCE Few issues related to television have aroused more concern or sparked more debate than televised violence and its effects on children. Among psychologists and educators, the study of televised violence has been a hotbed of research activity for almost 20 years. Research activity among contemporary investigators indicates that this interest will persist for years to come.

Television programming for children contains a considerable amount of violence. Cartoons are invariably the guiltiest programming culprit. Moreover, it is maintained by most (e.g., Kubey & Csikszentmihalyi, 1990) that televised violence has increased markedly over the years. For example, one investigation revealed that in the course of one program hour there is an average of nine acts of physical aggression and almost eight instances of verbal aggression (Williams, Zabrack, & Joy, 1982). It has also been found that boys pay more visual attention to high-action and high-violence animated programs than do girls, who pay more attention to low action (Alvarez et al., 1988).

What effect does viewing violence have on children's behavior? There are currently two major theories designed to answer this question. The **social learning theory of television viewing** maintains that children will imitate

THEORETICAL ISSUES

The application of social learning theory to a topic such as children's television viewing provides a good illustration of the importance of this lifespan development theory. Can you see how the theory provides a conceptual framework for research investigations? How would you evaluate its contribution to the study of children's television viewing habits?

aggressive behavior when they are exposed to it on television. The **catharsis theory of television viewing** proposes that watching aggressive behavior on television provides a vicarious outlet for the viewer's own aggressiveness. Televised aggression thus enables viewers to drain off, or discharge, their aggressive tendencies.

Of the two theories, the social learning approach is the more popular. Support for it has been steadily increasing, and many today believe there is a significant relationship between viewing televised violence and behaving aggressively (Huston, Watkins, & Kunkel, 1989; Huston et al., 1989; Liebert & Sprafkin, 1988). However, it is important to point out that many forces converge in the life of a child (or adult) to create behavioral expressions, including aggression. Although televised violence can induce aggression, it is not the single determinant.

Jerome Singer and his colleagues (Singer, Singer, & Rapaczynski, 1984) supply us with some of the details of televised violence and how it affects children's aggressiveness. The team of researchers studied 63 children over a period of 6 years. The children were 4 when the television and family environment data were first obtained and 9 when the final data were collected.

The research revealed a link between 9-year-olds' suspicious or fearful view of the world and a history of watching the most violent television programs. The data also indicated that children's later aggression can be predicted by a combination of frequent viewing of violent television programs, preschool television viewing, and a family that emphasizes physical discipline and the assertion of power. Preschool children from homes with a high level of parental cultural involvement but with long exposure to violent television programs were more aggressive in their day-care centers or nursery schools.

Televised violence has other effects on the viewer. Seeing repeated acts of violence has a tendency to slowly desensitize the viewer to aggression. Over time, even one's level of physiological arousal toward violence declines. This indicates that individuals have become hardened to violence and aggression. Rather than being emotionally sensitive to it, they are instead jaded (Geen, 1981; Thomas, 1982).

BENEFITS OF TELEVISION In spite of its potential harmful effects, television can pass along a wealth of information and positive experiences to viewers. Advancements made in educational television have proven to be beneficial. Television programming such as this can enhance a number of developmental areas, including language abilities, concept formation, reading skills, and prosocial development (Esty & Fisch, 1991; Singer et al., 1988; Tangney, 1988). In other spheres, television is a visual masterpiece that, when not overused, can be a doorway to wholesome entertainment and a source of relaxation.

With such positive potential, television looms as a powerful teacher that has the capability of enhancing the quality of life for the individual as well as society. It is the most powerful communication tool we have and without question it is here to stay. It becomes important, therefore, to continually examine the role of television in our lives. Television can be used for violence, for crass commercialism, or for instruction and for enhancing and enriching lives. The imperatives are clear. We must take charge of television and harness its potential rather than have television control our lives. In so doing, television can become an ally for all concerned, not an adversary (Honig, 1983). The Lifespan Development in Action box on page 344 supplies some thoughts on promoting healthy viewing habits.

■ School Influences on the Developing Child

Entrance into school brings children into a new and complex social environment. Most children eagerly anticipate attending elementary school and each year look forward to the classroom's developmental challenges. Not only will the cognitive domains of the child be influenced, but numerous other parameters will be influenced as well. For example, youngsters will have to adjust to many new routines and demands, task-oriented behavior, conformity to authority, and impulse control, to name but a few areas.

The Influence of the Teacher Because children are still very dependent on adults, many become attached to or are awed by their teacher. This is not only because the teacher acts in many respects as a substitute parent but also because the teacher conveys to the child the assurance that adult authority is trustworthy and that the school environment is safe, stimulating, and satisfying. In fulfilling these and other needs, teachers begin to exert strong influences on the child's behavior. In the process of instruction and the manner in which it is delivered, teachers transmit their personal attitudes and beliefs to their pupils (Armstrong, Henson, & Savage, 1993; Hessong & Weeks, 1991).

Teacher behaviors affect pupil performance. On the whole, teachers are effective when they demonstrate warmth, understanding, support, and compassion toward their students. Ineffective teachers frequently operate overly restrictive classrooms, are dependent, foster feelings of limited self-worth, and exhibit lack of self-control. Compared to effective teachers, ineffective instructors do not feel accepting of themselves and others (Borich, 1992; Jacobsen, Eggen, & Kauchak, 1993).

Successful elementary school teachers have a tendency to exhibit generosity in their appraisals of behavior and are warm, empathetic, and friendly in their social relationships (Bellon, Bellon, & Blank, 1992; Jarolimek, 1993). Conversely, unsuccessful teachers are less favorable in their expressed opinions of pupils, less satisfactory in emotional adjustment, and more critical and restrictive in their appraisals of the behavior and motives of others. Teachers who exhibit genuineness, warmth, and friendliness in their dealings with children, rather than punitive and authoritarian techniques, also encourage favorable behavior, particularly constructive attitudes, conscientious attitudes toward schoolwork, and less aggressive behavior (Borich, 1992; Kellough & Roberts, 1991).

Although the main task and responsibility is to teach academic subjects, the teacher is also responsible, to an extent, for the psychological well-being of pupils. And so it is that teacher behavior directly relates to the student's self-concept and peer acceptance. Teachers appear to be in a prime position to serve as a role model, as well as a reinforcer, of children's social interaction. The examples they set, the tone they establish for peer relations, and the feedback they give to children are important influences (Ames, 1992; Borich, 1992; McNeil & Wiles, 1990; Wynne & Ryan, 1993).

CHILDREN AND TELEVISION: PROMOTING HEALTHY VIEWING HABITS

Adults can do much to help children develop healthy television viewing habits. Most experts maintain that controlling the amount of time children watch television and the kinds of programming they watch is a step in the right direction. More specific recommendations and suggestions include the following:

Familiarize yourself with children's television. To evaluate children's television programming and provide guidance to youngsters, become familiar with the range of shows available. Sample a cross section of programs and critique each. A single Saturday morning should be an eye-opener.

Balance a child's television needs against other needs. A legitimate concern among adults is that television often detracts from other important facets of childhood. Balance television viewing against these other important activities, including play, reading, exploring, socializing, family interaction, and studying.

Decide on a schedule for television viewing. Monitor the amount of time children spend in front of the television set. Establish daily schedules specifying the hours of the morning, afternoon, or evening when television viewing is permissible. Many experts today feel that between 10 and 15 hours of television viewing per week is acceptable.

Select good television programs for children. Quality programming is available to children if one takes the time to look for it. Educational television, in particular, offers a multitude of programs for youngsters of different ages. Steer children toward suitable documentaries, music, and classic stories.

Help children distinguish between make-believe and real life. Young children, especially preschoolers, have difficulty understanding that the fantasy depicted on television cannot happen in real life. As a result, many are convinced of the extraordinary powers of their favorite superheroes, for example. Many also perceive the violence depicted in cartoons as acceptable and amusing because the victim always gets up and comes back for more. Try to help children differentiate between fantasy and fact and see the world as it really is.

Observe how children's behavior is affected by television. Too much television can overstimulate the child and cause mood shifts, including general irritability. Excessive amounts of television can also cause eyestrain and headaches. These negative reactions underscore the need to monitor television viewing time.

Share television viewing time with children. More families need to share what television brings into their lives. Adults should arrange their time so programs suitable for family viewing can be shared with the children. Moreover, adults can play instrumental roles in explaining sensitive programming topics. For example, children need understanding and support to deal with themes involving abstract dimensions, such as tragedy or loss.

Follow up on the positive qualities of television programming. Adults should seek to expand and integrate into children's lives those positive lessons reaped from television. This applies to educational instruction as well as to important life lessons portrayed in other programming endeavors.

The impact of teacher feedback on children's behavior was demonstrated in a study conducted by Karen White and Janet Kistner (1992). In this investigation, kindergarten, first-, and second-grade children viewed a videotape of a classroom scene in which a child actor exhibited behaviors characteristic of peer-rejected children. Teacher feedback varied across five conditions: neutral content, positive feedback, corrective feedback, derogatory feedback, and a combination of positive and corrective feedback. Results showed that teacher feedback had a directional and additive effect on the subjects' peer preferences and perceptions. More specifically, positive feedback resulted in higher preference and moral judgment scores and more positive descriptions. Derogatory feedback, on the other hand, produced lower social preference and more negative moral judgments and descriptions.

Methods of Classroom Control   Children are also exposed to different types of classroom control, from traditional types of leadership to more liberal approaches. In general, three types of classroom control have been identified: democratic, authoritarian, and laissez-faire. Numerous researchers have sought to focus on the effectiveness of each of these methods of classroom control. Let us uncover the major findings focusing on this topic.

Authoritarian leadership has a tendency to produce two major types of social atmospheres: aggressive or apathetic. Studies have shown that there are higher incidences of irritability and aggressiveness toward fellow group members in atmospheres created by authoritarian and laissez-faire leadership than in democratic climates. In addition, authoritarian teachers have a tendency to foster high interpersonal tension. Authoritarian classes are also often lower in task-related suggestions by the members; whenever authoritarian leaders are absent for short periods, work motivation among students has a tendency to decline.

Students taught by democratic and laissez-faire teachers often make more frequent requests for attention and approval than do students in authoritarian classrooms. Although interpersonal friendliness does not usually vary as a result of teaching styles, democratic and laissez-faire classes seem to have more of a

The elementary school classroom exposes children to new experiences, opportunities, and developmental challenges.

THEORETICAL ISSUES

Contemplate how an elementary school teacher's classroom style might complement or be in opposition to parental styles of control. How do you think this interplay between school and home shape the course of child development? Does ecological theory help you see the different contextual influences at work?

"we" feeling than their authoritarian counterparts. Finally, the absence of democratic teachers for short periods of time does not appear to affect the task-oriented efforts of the class.

Deciding which particular type of classroom climate and control to establish may be one of the most difficult chores for the beginning teacher. Certainly one's formal education and one's likes and dislikes of various approaches, to some extent, will determine the emotional climate. So, too, will the relationship between the children's temperamental characteristics and the teacher's reactions to these behaviors.

Most experts (e.g., Borich, 1992; Eby, 1992; Jacobsen, Eggen, & Kauchak, 1993; Kellough & Roberts, 1991; Lemlech, 1990) agree that no general prescription can tell teachers what choices they should make in terms of classroom control. A teacher who has a strong personality can, to some degree, persuade students to subscribe to his or her values. But such a teacher may also arouse feelings of opposition in students whose values do not concur with the teacher's. Classroom harmony usually depends on the match between the values, temperaments, and the personalities of the children and those of the teacher.

Peer Group Influences on the Developing Child

Being a member of a peer group is important to school-age children. As they spend more time with their friends, children learn more about cooperation and getting along with others. The ability to consider others, especially their needs and sensitivities, enables friendships to flourish (Berndt & Ladd, 1989; Knight & Chao, 1991; Ladd, 1988, 1990).

Williard Hartup's (1984) analysis of peer relations during middle childhood suggests that interactions intensify at this time. Preschoolers establish the communication and coordination necessary for cooperation and competition with other children, and school-age children begin new interactions. New content (such as issues related to gender roles) begins to impinge on child-child interactions, but it is integrated into normative structures that may be traced back to early childhood.

Hartup also maintained that children must begin to construct equitable interactions with others and sustain them across situations and across time. Children must also learn a wider range of accommodations to their age-mates. Learning how to deal with their peers is itself one of the greatest challenges confronting children between their 6th and 12th years. And research (e.g., Morison & Masten, 1991) shows that positive peer adjustments during the school years, most notably the development of a positive peer reputation, are important predictors for later socialization experiences.

Like those of early childhood, peer groups during the school years are very selective. Similar sex, age, social status, and race are often the criteria for acceptance. Some peer groups require physical attractiveness for membership (Finkelstein & Haskins, 1983; Schofield & Whitley, 1983; Vaughn & Langlois, 1983).

Peer groups often meet certain needs at this time, such as a desire to be away from adults or to be in the company of like-minded individuals. They also serve to promote a wide range of activities, both formal and informal. One source (Zarbatny, Hartmann, & Rankin, 1990) notes that school-age activities serve

many useful functions, such as providing a context for sociabilty, enhancing relationships, and providing children with a sense of belonging. Activities also
provide opportunities for instruction and learning, and promote concern for
achievements and integrity of the self.

School-age peer groups also select leaders and followers. Although such a division was apparent among groups of younger children, it is more consistently
expressed by school-age children (Berndt & Ladd, 1989; Schmidt, Ollendick, &
Stanowicz, 1988; Stright & French, 1988). One study (French & Stright, 1991)
reports that leadership status in cooperative school-age settings is associated
with task facilitative behavior. Prominent in the profile of the child leader are
the behaviors of organizing, soliciting opinions, and facilitating the participation of group members. Table 7-4 displays this facet of peer group interaction
along with other significant social developments.

The peer group is composed of youngsters who are popular and unpopular.
Popularity is not determined by the quantity of time youngsters spend together
but can be instead traced to other sources. Popular children, for instance, are
bright, often assertive, friendly, and cooperative (Weist & Ollendick, 1991).
They also tend to exhibit prosocial behavior (Denham, 1990) and are raised in
homes characterized by harmonious relationships (Henggeler et al., 1991b).
And, as we discovered earlier in our discussion of anger and aggression, popular children deal with anger in ways that minimize further conflict and damage
to social relationships (Fabes & Eisenberg, 1992). Thus growing emotional maturity appears to be instrumental in shaping social maturity.

On the other hand, unpopular children are often overly aggressive and display inappropriate behavior. Many unpopular children lack those social cognition skills necessary for harmonious social interaction, whereas popular
children have good group entry skills; in other words, popular children can
enter groups without disturbing the activity at hand. They also possess more of
the personality traits judged desirable by their friends (Berndt & Ladd, 1989;
Boulton & Smith, 1990; Dodge et al., 1990; French, 1990; Putallaz & Wasserman, 1989; Vitaro et al., 1992).

The consequences of peer rejection or unpopularity are worth noting. Children who are continually rejected or deemed unpopular often face negative
consequences. For some, the loneliness accompanying rejection and unpopularity persists into later developmental stages and causes such difficulties as social isolation or perceptions of social incompetence (Hymel et al., 1990). Some
may even develop more serious problems, such as neurosis or delinquent behavior (Morison & Masten, 1991; Muehlbauer & Dodder, 1983; Rubenstein &
Shaver, 1982).

The Development of Children's Friendships   Finding a friend and sharing
his or her experiences is indeed valuable. Although egocentrism hampered earlier friendships, those forming at this time are closer and more meaningful. It is
from childhood friendships that individuals learn how to create and sustain
friendships throughout life. As Sharon Brehm (1992) observes, a foundation of
friendship behaviors and attitudes needs to be established so one will always
have friends, in good times as well as bad.

One investigation (Ladd, 1990) showed that having friends and keeping
them are linked to children's early school adjustment. Studying the peer relationships of over 100 school-age children, it was discovered that children with a

THEORETICAL ISSUES

How might behaviorists and social learning theorists explore the various environmental influences at work in children's peer interactions? What thinking skills might cognitive developmentalists consider instrumental? How might symbolic interactionists explore the roles and expectations of group leaders and followers?

TABLE 7-4

Significant Social Developments During Middle Childhood

Age	Social Developments
6	Egocentrism, still present at this time, inhibits meaningful social relationships. Interactions with other children in the family are often competitive but vary according to the child's ordinal position in the family. Although friendships are sometimes erratic, 6-year-olds often establish a best friend, with whom they spend a good deal of time. Movement toward same-sex friends is most prevalent.
7	Increased sense of self and heightened sensitivity to others enhances social relationships. However, this heightened sensitivity makes the youngster acutely aware of shortcomings, failures, and criticisms. Consequently, brooding, feelings of shame, and negativism may be common. Advanced interpersonal skills allow the 7-year-old to become a better listener; growing evidence of empathy and understanding of the needs of others is present.
8	Noticeable separation between the sexes, even to the point where the opposite sex is excluded from group activities. However, the 8-year-old's attitude toward members of the opposite sex is a mixture of attraction and hostility, a pattern that will be seen again in early adolescence. At this age, most children are friendly and cooperative. Also there is social curiosity about other people, evidenced by the child's attentiveness to adult conversations and eagerness to observe at grown-up gatherings. Noticeable division of leaders and followers.
9	Heightened self-confidence and emotional security bolster social relationships. Close friendships started earlier are strengthened but a dichotomy of the sexes still exists. Much overt hostility between boys and girls. Organized games and other structured social activities begin to emerge.
10	Organized social activities continue to attract the attention of the child, and a diversity of interests emerge. Most 10-year-olds do not resent spending time with family rather than friends. A new admiration and respect for one's parents emerge. Interpersonal relationships and communication skills continue to increase.
11	A new level of maturity (the plateau between childhood and adolescence) frequently requires a redefinition of one's sense of self, as well as one's social relationships. Choices of friendships are now based on mutuality of interest and temperament rather than on proximity. Although friendships grow in number at this time, one or several intimate relationships are established. Interest in the opposite sex begins, although girls are likely to be more interested and vocal about their interest than boys.

(Adapted from Elkind, 1994)

large number of classroom friends developed favorable school perceptions. Moreover, as the school year progressed, those who maintained these relationships liked school even more. Making new friends in the classroom was associated with gains in school performance, and early peer rejection forecasted less favorable school perceptions, higher levels of school avoidance, and lower performance levels over the school year.

The influence of the peer group is unmistakable during the school years.

The fact that their egocentrism has weakened enables children to forgo some of their own personal desires and to adopt the viewpoints of others. Greater sensitivity and emotional responsiveness to others, the growing ability to engage in reciprocal exchanges, and better conflict resolution skills permit close ties among friends (Costin & Jones, 1992; de Cooke, 1992). Also, research indicates (Youngblade & Belsky, 1992) that there are parent-child antecedents of children's friendships. More specifically, positive and secure parent-child relationships tend to be associated with more positive friendships, and more negative family relationships with more negative friendships.

Robert Selman (1981) proposes four stages of friendship. The **playmate-ship stage** covers the preschool years, when friendships are greatly affected by the child's feelings at the moment, the physical presence of the other youngster, and the availability of toys or other resources. During the early school years, friendships are characterized by what Selman called the **one-way assistance stage.** At this time, a friend is someone who fills another person's need, such as providing toys or playtime companionship.

During the later school years, a stage known as **fair-weather cooperation** begins. Friendships now become more mutual and reciprocal. However, arguments and disagreements still exist and can even disrupt the relationship. By late childhood or early adolescence, friendships contain more expressions of mutuality and supportive understanding. This final stage of friendships is called **intimate and mutually shared relationships** and is supported in the literature (Borisoff, 1993; Lederman, 1993).

Youngsters usually form same-sex friendships, a pattern evident in early childhood as well. These same-sex friendships have several variations. Though both sexes focus their friendships on shared interests and activities, boys are typically more competitive and girls more cooperative. Boys tend to deemphasize the intimacy or closeness of their friendships. They are also more oriented to groups, whereas girls are drawn to one-to-one friendships. Moreover, girls are usually more expressive to one another than boys are (Borisoff, 1993; Rawlins, 1993; Rotenberg & Chase, 1992; Victor, 1993). Also, research indicates

GENDER SIMILARITIES AND DIFFERENCES

Social development, including peer group interaction and friendships, is a lifelong process. How important do you see gender-role learning during this time? How do you think it shapes later life social dynamics?

(Clark & Bittle, 1992) that girls expect and receive more kindness, loyalty, commitment, and empathic understanding from their best friendships. Finally, girls' appreciation of the emotional bond that friendships offer spills over into the adolescent years (Eaton, Mitchell, & Jolley, 1991; Lederman, 1993; Rawlins, 1993).

Play Influences on the Developing Child

Although school-age children do play alone, the company of other youngsters is usually sought for playtime activities. Neighborhood and school interactions are the most popular play groups and encourage cooperative forms of play. Play-group experiences teach children how to share with and be responsible to one another, follow the directions of a leader, nurture self-confidence in a group setting, and cope with success and failure. In short, children learn what a group is, how it operates, and their role within it (Howes & Matheson, 1992).

Play and Gender-Role Development   Although gender-typed play activities begin in early childhood, they become quite widespread during the school years. School-age children identify with those gender-typed play activities that are characteristic of their own sex. Boys, more than girls, prefer physically oriented play. Boys' toys also require more physical expressions (Jacklin, 1989; Maccoby, 1988, 1990; Martin, Wood, & Little, 1990).

The school-age child's growing cognitive awareness and expanding social horizons continue to contribute to gender-role development, not only in play but in other spheres of life. New cognitive skills enable them to understand which behaviors are appropriate to their sex; exposure to a growing number of role models in life and in the media reinforces this understanding (Basow, 1992; Carter & Levy, 1988; Martin et al., 1990). This provides another good example of the convergence of lifespan developmental forces; that is, mental dynamics and socialization experiences shape the course of gender-role expression. It also illustrates the importance of play in studying many diverse aspects of child development (Chafel, 1991).

Boys are also usually more aware of gender differences and avoid playing with objects that might be considered feminine. Girls are more willing to participate in male-oriented play activities. Though both sexes congregate into gender-typed play groups, boys tend to hold more rigid, stereotyped attitudes and beliefs (Howes, 1988; Jacklin, 1989).

Gender-typed play occurs because of other reasons. Parents, for example, sometimes encourage their children to engage in gender-typed forms of play and other activities (McHale et al., 1990; Pomerleau et al., 1990). This is more evident among fathers, who often insist on selecting gender-appropriate toys and play behaviors (Fagot & Hagan, 1991). Further pressure to engage in gender-typed play comes from the child's peer group, an increasingly important source of social approval and reinforcement (Basow, 1992; Block & Pellegrini, 1989; Howes, 1988; Martin et al., 1990).

But the traditional classification of "masculine" and "feminine" forms of play may well be eroding. The current emphasis on a more androgynous definition of the sexes has helped to reduce the separation between male and female play activities. Although girls still engage in "feminine" activities, today there are activities previously cast as "masculine" in which they enjoy competing, such as track and field events, basketball, golf, and softball.

Team sports provide school-age children with a sense of belonging and of competition.

Team Sports   Team sports are popular during the school years. Being part of a team gives children an opportunity to develop their physical and mental prowess within the framework of competitive contests. Competing as a team member also helps develop children's characters. It gives them a common goal and allows them to contribute as members (Leonard, 1993).

Team sports, however, can also bring frustration, especially if children are overeager to prove themselves on the playing field. Having to sit on the bench, striking out with the bases loaded, or experiencing defeat are difficult for children, especially if they have never dealt with such situations before. Adults need to support children in such situations.

Team sports require considerable coordination, dexterity, cooperation, and concentration. In regard to the themes of this book, organized sports can thus be said to be a fusion of the major developmental processes. That is, team sports require the successful integration of physical, cognitive, social, and personal-emotional forces. Though these processes are required in virtually all forms of play, team sports appear to require a more rigorous application and successful integration of each.

As evidence of the foregoing, let's turn to a study headed by Mia Yee and Rupert Brown (1992). The two researchers divided children into teams and asked them to make various self, interpersonal, and intergroup evaluations. As early as age 5, children showed markedly high self-evaluations, strong in-group bias in their evaluations of the two teams, and a high level of group cohesion irrespective of their own team's performance. Gender differences were also apparent in the findings. Males responded more than females to their team's performance, and females exhibited more precocious in-group favoritism than males.

Many youngsters fear failure in team sports. Sadly, many parents, coaches, and other adults dismiss these apprehensions and force children to continue playing despite these fears. Consequently, many children may become resentful, anxious, angry, or even lose their self-confidence.

Besides appreciating children's psychological needs, adults need to help children develop those skills needed for competitive play. Effective instruction usually includes mastering a skill appropriate to a specific age, not forcing youngsters to work on skills for which they are not equipped. Adults should also realize that success in one phase of the game does not automatically mean success in all other phases. Adults must recognize that the basis of training is the development of such mental skills as concentration, determination, and dedication.

Encouraging children to perform well is commendable, but children need to learn that winning is not the only goal. Winning all too often overshadows the enjoyment of just playing the game. Perhaps a solution is to emphasize developing skills, not finishing first.

■ Theories of Personality Development

Sigmund Freud's Psychosexual Theory

THE LATENCY PERIOD (AGES 6 TO 11) During middle childhood, youngsters enter the latency period of psychosexual development. Following the oral, anal, and phallic stages, the **latency period** is marked by a diminishment of the biological and sexual drives. Compared with the turbulence of the other stages, it is a relatively quiet period of transition.

Although there are no prominent instinctive urges developing within the child, Freud acknowledges that new skills do emerge at this time. Paramount among them are skills promoting ego refinement, particularly those that strengthen and protect the ego from frustration and failure. Freud called such behaviors defense, or coping, mechanisms.

FREUDIAN DEFENSE MECHANISMS **Defense** (or coping) **mechanisms** are patterns of behavior that function to relieve anxiety. We have all heard references to anxiety at one point or another: Mary has test anxiety, Stewart is anxiously awaiting the company's decision, or Phillip is always anxious and uptight. Anxiety, a most unpleasant emotion, is a reaction of inner apprehension often described as a response to a subjective, rather than an objective, danger. Put another way, it is psychological pain compared to physical pain. In many instances, anxiety originates from the conflicts in life that we face.

Defense mechanisms attempt to deal with the pain and turmoil of such threatening situations as failure, mistakes, and accidents and in some cases succeed in freeing the individual from some anxiety. By middle childhood, defense mechanisms are used with surprising frequency. With age, these mechanisms become more elaborate and intertwined with the child's overall personality. However, defense mechanisms are, at best, temporary and do not resolve underlying conflicts. In most cases, defense mechanisms produce automatic and rigid reactions that enable the individual to avoid, rather than deal with, struggles. Such patterns of behavior have a tendency to distort reality.

Although defense mechanisms are a normal behavioral expression and do have some beneficial value, they should not be used in excess. When they are used too much, such as in the case of the perpetual excuse-maker or cover-up artist, troubles begin. The very nature of their title—coping, or defense, mechanisms—indicates their temporary quality. As we are assaulted with the problems of daily life, defensive behavior yields few, if any, long-lasting solutions. Consequently, for the child or adult who persists in relying too frequently on defense mechanisms, life becomes a battle of offense versus defense, and

CONTINUOUS AND DISCONTINUOUS HUMAN DEVELOPMENT

Do you think Freud's rather tranquil portrayal of psychosexual developments during middle childhood suggests a period of continuity and stability in the life cycle? Or, reflecting on material covered in this chapter, do you see middle childhood more as a period of change and discontinuity? Might this stage reflect both continuity and discontinuity?

although we hear that "the best offense is a good defense," defense alone may win a few battles, but never the war.

It has often been said that defense mechanisms deal with the symptoms rather than the causes of problems. Just as taking two aspirins for a headache or a sleeping pill for insomnia does not explain the root of the problem, continual use of a defense mechanism does not address the need or frustration that initially caused the anxiety. Thus, although defense mechanisms are considered useful, their adjustive or maladjustive quality depends on how often the child uses them.

TYPES OF DEFENSE MECHANISMS Just as anxiety exists in all shapes and sizes, so too do defense mechanisms. It should be realized, however, that these behaviors are highly individualized and will differ from person to person and from situation to situation. In this sense, it is possible that no two people will use the same coping device in the same manner.

Rationalization is one of the most common defense mechanisms. It is the attempt to justify and provide logical reasons and explanations for one's failures or shortcomings. The youngster who is unable to make the local Little League team, for example, may attempt to rationalize this failure by claiming the games are boring and uninteresting. Or to avoid a spanking after breaking some dishes, the rationalizing child may say it never would have happened if someone else had not stacked them so high. In its simplest form, rationalization is common excuse-making.

Projection is the placing of one's difficulties or failures on someone else. In order to guard against unfavorable self-evaluations, motives that are found personally unacceptable will be attributed to others. In this sense, a child who happens to be caught copying or cheating may attempt to defend the act by saying that everyone else in the class was guilty of the same misconduct or that the teacher is to blame for not taking adequate safeguards against cheating.

Displacement is the redirection of pent-up hostile feelings to people or objects less dangerous than those that initially aroused the emotion. Displacement is observable in the case of the young girl who has been spanked by her father for committing a misdeed. Obviously, she cannot return the blow to the parent, unless she wants to deepen her predicament. Instead, she may seek other channels through which to release her internal hostile feelings, such as kicking a ball or spanking a doll. Displacement may also explain why so many adolescent bedroom doors are slammed shut following family disagreements.

Denial of reality is a defense mechanism children frequently resort to. To protect the self, children may refuse to perceive the existence of hurtful situations. For this reason, youngsters may continually deny that a beloved relative has passed away. Older children may deny to their parents that they are doing poorly in school, despite knowing they are failing four courses.

Compensation is used by many children when they seek to find a successful or rewarding activity that can be substituted for failure in another kind of activity. The unathletic boy who cannot successfully compete in sports may find satisfaction in developing a particular hobby. An unattractive girl may try to excel in all of her school subjects or seek to become the school's best dresser.

Interestingly, parents employ a type of compensation when they seek to satisfy their own ambitions through their children. A mother who experienced a

THEORETICAL ISSUES

Defense mechanisms are obviously Freudian in scope, but do you think other theories can be used to help explain their expression? For example, what cognitive developments do you think are needed to fabricate defense mechanisms? Do you think behaviorists and social learning theorists would argue that defense mechanisms are sometimes the products of reinforcement and imitation, respectively?

Defense mechanisms are often used to relieve anxiety and guilt, including situations involving stealing and cheating.

deprived childhood may go out of her way to give her children the best of everything. A father who always wanted to go to college but never had the chance may continually prod his son to pursue higher education. Although this type of compensation may satisfy the parent's needs, it is questionable whether the child's needs are met.

Regression is a retreat to earlier developmental periods to escape the anxiety of a situation. This defense mechanism is quite apparent when a new baby arrives home from the hospital and an older child regresses to infantile behavior. In an effort to regain the parental attention that has been displaced because of the new arrival, a child may regress to behavior that characterized his or her experiences as a baby, such as bed wetting, thumb sucking, or crawling. It is conceivable that in the child's mind, earlier developmental stages represented security.

Reaction formation may be used by children to prevent unwanted and perhaps objectionable desires from being expressed. In this case, the child may learn to substitute an opposing one in its place. Growing children who are becoming anxious and concerned about their passivity and dependency, for example, may exhibit a type of reaction formation by behaving in an aggressive and assertive fashion when in the company of peers.

Escape and **withdrawal** are two interrelated defense mechanisms that children can use to avoid threatening or undesirable situations. When they are employed, attempts are made to procrastinate or put off doing an unpleasant task, such as presenting an oral report in class or having to do a disliked household chore. For suggestions on how to help children understand defense mechanisms, see the accompanying Lifespan Development in Action box.

HELPING CHILDREN UNDERSTAND COPING BEHAVIORS

Everyone needs feedback on their behavior, and children are no exception as far as coping behaviors are concerned. It is important for children to be aware of their actions, especially if defensiveness is a common occurrence. The importance of objective adult feedback and meaningful guidance cannot be overstressed here. Parents, teachers, guidance counselors, and other adults are in strategic positions to observe children and help them develop a sense of personal awareness. As an effort to help youngsters understand their coping behaviors, we offer the following suggestions:

Adults should examine their own defense mechanisms. Seeking to understand their own defense mechanisms and why we use them may provide adults with meaningful insight into children's defensive behavior. Although adult defense mechanisms are more refined than children's, the fundamental design behind each is remarkably similar.

Respect the struggles, turmoils, and disappointments that are characteristic of childhood. An empathic adult is one who can appreciate the many anxious situations that confront the child throughout life. Shaming the child or making fun of coping behavior accomplishes nothing and should be avoided.

Try to teach the child that success as well as failure is part of everyone's life. Although everyone wants to succeed, only a handful are capable of succeeding on a continuous basis without failure. Accepting failure and disappointment are important dimensions of self-growth and should not be reasons for negative self-regard.

Seek to understand why defense mechanisms are used, especially those that are used excessively. This suggestion implies not only patience and gentle understanding on the adult's part but also careful observation of the events that triggered the coping device. Verbalization of the situation should be encouraged, but at a time when the anxiety of the event has diminished. It should be stated to the child that defending against and retreating from unpleasant situations are normal reactions; however, learning to deal with struggles head-on avoids reality distortion and nurtures a more accurate sense of self.

Avoid comparisons with other children. Children rarely employ defense mechanisms in exactly the same fashion nor do they accept the consequences of negative situations in similar ways. Therefore it is unfair to say such things as "You are always making excuses . . . Mary does not behave like you!" Such comparisons downplay the individuality of the child and accomplish little, except possibly to produce further anxious feelings and inferior attitudes toward one's sense of self.

Try to understand defense mechanisms as part of the child's whole personality. Defense mechanisms do not exist separately as behavioral phenomena; on the contrary, they frequently reflect significant aspects of the child's total personality. Thus, rather than attempting to understand coping behaviors and defensive episodes separately, adults might seek to explore their integration into the larger whole. This implies becoming aware of such areas as accuracy of the child's self-concept, levels of self-esteem, insecurities, and emotional sensitivities.

Erik Erikson's Psychosocial Theory

INDUSTRY VERSUS INFERIORITY (AGES 6 TO 11) The psychosocial crisis of **industry versus inferiority** occupies all of middle childhood and, as such, parallels Freud's latency period. During this crisis, children have reached the point in their cognitive development at which they can comprehend more about their surroundings. Youngsters seek to understand and build or make things that are practical to them. Play intermingles with work; play becomes productive, and the product is all-important to children's self-esteem. However, children who frequently fail to be productive may soon feel inferior and even worthless. In their search for positive self-regard and esteem, children need the support and guidance of adults.

Regardless of their culture, children need to be competent. In American society, they are expected to be competent in the classroom, whereas in simpler societies, children should be competent in the field, in tying fishnets, throwing spears, and the like. This is a time for schooling (in or out of the classroom) and continued socialization, particularly when it can lead to competence in adulthood.

Industrious youngsters take pleasure and pride in the accomplishment of new and different goals. For school-age children, these accomplishments may be excelling at a hobby or game, becoming a member of a sports team, participating in a school play, or getting A's on a report card. The attainment of each goal motivates the achievement of new ones. However, Erikson believes that for those children who lose their self-esteem because of failure, the risk is feeling inadequate and inferior. The loss of industry may cause the youngster to pull back from others and become isolated. It may also promote feelings of mediocrity and inadequacy as well as the loss of autonomy.

CHAPTER REVIEW

Unit One: Physical Development

The rates of physical growth and development are rather slow during the middle years of childhood. By age 12, children have gained about 90% of their adult height, and they weigh approximately 80 pounds. Youngsters lose their babylike contours during the school years. This chapter examined the physiological changes that occur at this time. Children also develop their motor skill abilities. By the age of 6, most children are able to participate in numerous activities that require large-muscle movement and refined coordination.

Children achieve a sense of physical self throughout childhood, through their growing awareness of bodily changes and through their improving motor skills. The degree of their achievement in motor skill abilities depends on numerous factors, including rates of physical maturity, opportunities to engage in physical activities, and level of self-confidence.

Unit Two: Mental Development

During Piaget's stage of intuitive thought, which is a substage of the much larger preoperational thought stage, children's thinking is based on immediate perceptions rather than on mental functions. Although symbolic functioning represents an important cognitive advancement, other modes of thought, particularly centering, transductive reasoning, transformational reasoning, and the inability to reverse mental operations, restrict intellectual advancement.

The stage of concrete operations is characterized primarily by the ability to comprehend conservation, a principle stating that object properties remain the same despite changes made in their shape or physical arrangement. Other advancements are made in classification and seriation. More efficient mental organization enables children to systemize and categorize concepts more finely, particularly those related to shape and size, spatial, relational, quantity, and time. Concepts about death also demonstrate advancing cognitive maturity. Advancements in problem-solving abilities also refine intellectual operations at this time. The learning progress of some children may be affected by a learning disability, defined as difficulty in processing, remembering, or expressing information.

In regard to language developments, the average child has a reading vocabulary of nearly 50,000 words by the sixth grade. Understanding abstract word meanings and the relationships among certain words usually remains elusive. The use of compound and complex sentences increases during middle childhood, largely because youngsters have grasped three important rules: A sentence consists of a noun phrase and a verb phrase; a noun phrase consists of an article and a noun; and a verb phrase consists of a verb and a noun phrase. As their knowledge of sentence structure broadens, children learn more ways to convey different functions. This chapter also explored advancements in pragmatics, or how language is used in social settings, and how dialects create variations in language usage.

Unit Three: Personality and Social Development

Gender-role development becomes more deeply rooted during the school years, largely because of growing cognitive and social maturity. The school years also are when emotions become more specific and sophisticated. This is evident in such emotions as fear and anxiety, anger and aggression, happiness and humor, and love.

Moral development also advances during the school years. Piaget emphasized the importance of cognitive development to morality and identified the premoral, moral realism, and moral relativism stages. Like Piaget, Kohlberg stressed the cognitive underpinnings of morality. He defined moral development as having preconventional, conventional, and postconventional levels.

The family and the peer group are important agents of socialization. In regard to the modern family, we explored the impact of television on children's behavior. Interactions with peer groups give youngsters the opportunity to share experiences, cooperate, and work toward group goals. Play continues to contribute to many facets of development. We concluded the chapter with an examination of Freud's latency period and Erikson's industry versus inferiority crisis.

TERMS YOU SHOULD KNOW

**authority-maintaining
   orientation**
**catharsis theory of television
   viewing**

centering
classification
cognitive style
compensation

concrete operations
conservation
contractual legalistic orientation
conventional level
deductive reasoning
defense mechanism
denial of reality
dialect
displacement
escape
fair-weather cooperation stage
good boy-nice girl orientation
hostile aggression
impulsivity
inductive reasoning
industry versus inferiority
intimate and mutually shared
    relationships
intuitive thought
latency period
learning disability
metacognition
morality
moral realism

moral relativism
naively egoistic orientation
obedience and punishment
    orientation
one-way assistance stage
playmateship stage
postconventional level
preconventional level
premoral stage
projection
rationalization
reaction formation
reflectivity
regression
reversibility
seriation
social learning theory of
    television viewing
transductive reasoning
transformational reasoning
universal ethical principle
    orientation
withdrawal

THINKING IN ACTION

• Use the moral dilemma provided in this chapter (see Table 7-3, "Measuring the Development of Moral Reasoning") or design one of your own to discover variations in moral development. Ask several male and female school-age children, adolescents, and adults to read the dilemma and provide their moral responses. Did your subjects follow the chronology of stages presented in the text? How did the responses of the younger subjects compare with those of the older subjects? Did you discover any gender differences in the responses?

• You are the spokesperson of a parents' group advocating quality programming for children's television. Your group has been asked to develop a platform summarizing its dissatisfaction with the televised violence children are exposed to, as well as its recommendations for changing the quality of television programs being broadcast today. How will you approach this assignment? What kinds of research would you use to support your views? What are your suggestions for change as well as implementation strategies?

• Teachers touch the lives of school-age children in an assortment of ways. Think of as many different influences that teachers exert on the children's development, positive as well as negative, as you can. Then, think of at least one effective and one ineffective teacher you had as a school-age child. Compare and contrast the classroom climate of the two teachers. What kinds of experiences can you remember? Think of specific ways the two educators shaped your growth and development.

• You have been asked to coach a Little League team this spring in your hometown. How might material covered in this chapter help prepare you for your coaching endeavor? What are some of the physical, cognitive, personality, and social developments of school-age children that likely intertwine with their athletic abilities? How might your understanding of developmental differences among school-age children enhance your coaching strategies for younger and older Little League ballplayers?

• For this exercise, review the chapter's material on Freudian defense mechanisms. After you've done this, think of two anxiety-provoking situations that you've experienced in your life, one where you used a defense mechanism and one where you didn't. How did the outcome of the two situations compare and contrast? Did the use of your defense mechanism mask reality and prove to be of short-term value? Now, think of at least three defense mechanisms commonly used by school-age children. Does understanding the dynamics of your own defense mechanisms help you better understand those employed by children? Do you see any similarities? How do they differ?

RECOMMENDED READINGS

1. Basow, S. A. (1992). *Gender: Stereotypes and roles* (3rd ed.). Pacific Grove, CA: Brooks/Cole.

   Basow explores what we know about gender and how it influences our behavior.

2. Damon, W. (1991). *The moral child: Nurturing children's natural moral growth.* New York: Free Press.

   An excellent exploration of the course of morality.

3. Kail, R. (1990). *The development of memory in children* (3rd ed.). New York: Freeman.

   A noted contributor to the field explores many aspects of childhood memory.

4. Kubey, R., & Csikszentmihalyi, M. (1990). *Television and the quality of life: How viewing shapes everyday experience.* Hillsdale, NJ: Erlbaum.

   A good look at how television impacts on the lives of viewers.

5. Schulman, M. (1991). *The passionate mind: Bringing up an intelligent and creative child.* New York: Free Press.

   A practical account of how to nurture intelligence, curiosity, and creativity in children.

Adolescence

What Do You Think?

UNIT ONE: PHYSICAL DEVELOPMENT

Puberty
Hormones and Puberty
Adolescent Growth Spurt
Primary and Secondary Sex Characteristics

The Psychology of Puberty
Puberty and Sexual Responsiveness
Motor Skill Development

UNIT TWO: MENTAL DEVELOPMENT

Piaget's Stages of Cognitive Development
Formal Operations

Do Other Stages of Cognition Exist?

UNIT THREE: PERSONALITY AND SOCIAL DEVELOPMENT

**Family Influences on the Developing
    Adolescent**
Styles of Parental Control
Family Disharmony
**School Influences on the Developing
    Adolescent**
**Peer Group Influences on the Developing
    Adolescent**
Patterns of Peer Group Interaction
Gender Differences in Adolescent
    Friendships
Adolescent Sexual Behavior
Patterns of Dating and Courtship

Rates of Sexual Activity
Implications of Adolescent Sexual Activity
Why Do Some Adolescents Practice
    Unsafe Sex?
Values and Adolescent Sexual
    Relationships
Sexual Value Orientations
Theories of Personality Development
Sigmund Freud's Psychosexual Theory
Erik Erikson's Psychosocial Theory
Alternative Theoretical Perspectives on
    Adolescence

UNIT FOUR: THE TROUBLED ADOLESCENT

Teenage Suicide
Eating Disorders

Drug Abuse
Juvenile Delinquency

Chapter Review • Terms You Should Know • Thinking in Action • Recommended Readings

WHAT
DO
YOU
THINK?

• Few developmental processes over the course of the life cycle have more impact than puberty. The physical changes associated with puberty affect nearly every tissue of the body and transform youngsters into sexually mature persons. Besides looking at puberty as a physiological event, this chapter examines how it affects many other developmental spheres, including psychological, social, and emotional behavior. How do teenagers react to such physical changes? Does being an early or late maturer have any bearing on the outcome of this developmental event? Read on and we'll give you some answers.

• Who am I? Where have I been in life, and where do I want to go? It is during adolescence that questions such as these begin to be asked. Some authorities, such as Erik Erikson, have supplied us with considerable information regarding identity formation during the teenage years. We share his ideas with you, as well as those of others. In the process, perhaps you'll see your own strivings for identity in a new light.

• Devin Harwood and Melissa Reynolds, both age 15, dated for 4 months before they had sexual intercourse. Both admitted their first coital experience had been unanticipated and that they were both unprepared for it. Complicating matters was that Devin felt uncomfortable discussing the topic of birth control and Melissa didn't want to "ruin the romance." Consequently, the two did not use any kind of contraception the first time they had sex. As this chapter shows, adolescent coital activity such as this is widespread in the United States, and such intimate involvement poses a number of problems: pregnancy, abortion, and sexually transmitted diseases paramount among them. How prevalent are such problems, and why do adolescents engage in unsafe sex practices? Moreover, what steps can be taken to curb sexual risk taking? We supply some answers in this chapter.

• Many teenagers are told by their elders that adolescence is the best years of their life, a time when they have everything to live for and enjoy. Yet despite such a positive portrayal, many adolescents display destructive behaviors unique to their subculture: suicide, eating disorders, drug abuse, and delinquency. Where do these problems originate? Have they been increasing during the 1990s? What can be done to correct them? The final portion of this chapter addresses these and other issues.

UNIT ONE: PHYSICAL DEVELOPMENT

Adolescence, from the Latin word *adolescere*, meaning "to grow into maturity," is the life stage between childhood and adulthood. Like other phases of the life cycle, this period is marked by great change. Among the many challenges adolescents face are the need to adjust to pronounced physical and sexual changes, the search for their own identity, and the formation of new interpersonal relationships that include, for the first time, the expression of sexual feelings.

Adolescent sexual development cannot be separated from other developmental forces. For example, how adolescents react to the physical changes that accompany sexual maturation, including whether they and others perceive these changes as attractive or unattractive, will affect how they ultimately perceive themselves. Note the connection here between physical forces and cognitive, personality, sexual, and social forces (Brooks-Gunn & Warren, 1989; Lerner, Lerner, & Tubman, 1989).

Not long ago, many writers focused on the inner turmoil and problems of adjustment faced by the typical adolescent and often borrowed the expression *Strüm und Drang* ("storm and stress") from the 18th-century movement in German literature to describe this period of life. Today the problems faced by

Adolescence is the bridge between childhood and adulthood.

many teenagers—such as sexually transmitted disease, pregnancy, and abortion—appear to a lot of adults to far exceed the difficulties they themselves confronted in adolescence. Some contemporary researchers feel, however, that most modern teenagers meet the challenges of adolescence with considerable success (Offer & Church, 1991; Offer et al., 1988; Petersen, 1988).

M. Lee Manning (1983) believes we should stop viewing adolescence as a time of disruptive and rebellious behavior because this myth distorts our perceptions of actual adolescents. Moreover, as many other researchers (e.g., Brookins, 1991; Busch-Rossnagel & Zayas, 1991; Gibbs, 1991; Spencer, 1991) have reminded us, ethnic, cultural, and class differences affect how the individual young person deals with adolescence, including the course of sexual development.

▬ Puberty

The stage of physical development during which primary and secondary sex characteristics mature and people become capable of having children is known as **puberty** (from the Latin *pubertas,* meaning "age of adulthood"). Although it is difficult to pinpoint its beginning, puberty is a gradual process that transforms the internal and external child's body into that of an adult (Brooks-Gunn, 1991; Brooks-Gunn & Reiter, 1990).

Many non-Western cultures have elaborate ceremonies at puberty to symbolize a boy or girl's transition to adulthood. Often these ceremonies require a demonstration of such skills as self-defense or hunting; in other instances they entail circumcision or other bodily alterations. In Western cultures there are few formal rites of passage marking the transition from childhood to adulthood and defining adult roles and expectations. Most of those rituals we do have are religious or social in nature, such as bar mitzvahs, confirmations, and sweet sixteen parties. But there are no special customs that accompany puberty, nor any

THEORETICAL ISSUES

Although our culture does not have a specific ritual or ceremony marking an adolescent's sexual maturity, do certain coming of age markers serve as rites of passage? Do you think high school graduation, voting age, drinking age, draft registration, and getting engaged exist as passages into adulthood? How might symbolic interactionists interpret the roles attached to each?

obvious changes in social status that follow it. Moreover, the kind of information on puberty that parents and school systems have tended until recently to provide approaches the topic from a personal hygiene perspective rather than regarding it as a maturational milestone (Dole, 1984; Greif & Ulman, 1982).

The physical changes that characterize puberty take place along a continuum, or growth sequence. Nearly every part of the muscular and skeletal system exhibits a characteristic pattern of growth. This growth sequence is the same for everyone, although the rates vary from person to person (Brooks-Gunn, 1991; Brooks-Gunn & Warren, 1989; Lerner, Lerner, & Tubman, 1989; Malina, 1991). On average, girls enter puberty about 2 years earlier than boys.

Hormones and Puberty The physiological mechanisms responsible for puberty are not fully understood, though it is known that hormones account for many of the changes which take place (Kulin, 1991; Susman & Dorn, 1991). Prior to puberty, the brain's hypothalamus stimulates the pituitary gland, which, in turn, stimulates other glands by secreting increased amounts of a growth hormone into the bloodstream. This causes a rapid increase in body development—especially in length of the limbs—signaling the onset of a growth spurt, which we discuss shortly. The growth hormone affects cell duplication of virtually all body tissue except the central nervous system. The pituitary gland also releases a hormone that stimulates the testes and ovaries. The testes and ovaries, in turn, secrete gonadotrophins, or sex hormones. The male sex hormone is *testosterone,* and the female sex hormones are *estrogen* and *progesterone.*

Testosterone directs the development of the male genitals, growth of pubic hair, and other features of sexual development. Estrogen controls, among other phases of growth, the development of the uterus, vagina, and breasts. Progesterone aids in the development of the uterine wall, particularly its preparation for implantation of the fertilized ovum and of fetal and placental development after implantation has taken place.

It is unclear how the accelerated processes triggered during puberty slow down again, although it is believed high levels of sex hormones in the bloodstream are largely responsible (Rabin & Chrousos, 1991). Once a particular phase of physical or sexual development is complete, these high levels of sex hormones signal the pituitary gland and hypothalamus to cease further production of a given hormone. Figure 8-1 displays the glands of the endocrine system.

Adolescent Growth Spurt An accelerated rate of physical growth that occurs just before puberty and continues at a lesser rate throughout adolescence is one of the most apparent physical changes of the teenage years. This adolescent growth spurt involves increases in height, weight, and skeletal growth. It generally begins about 2 years earlier in girls (10½ years) than in boys (12½ years) (Malina, 1991; Tanner, 1991).

Because girls reach physical maturity earlier than boys, they have a height superiority between the ages of 11 and 13. By the age of 15, however, boys begin a period of rapid development that enables them to surpass girls in height. During their peak years of growth, male adolescents gain from 3 to 5 inches, whereas female adolescents gain only 2 to 4 inches. Because the rate of growth is greater in the legs than in the trunk, many adolescents have a gangling appearance. By the age of 17, most young women have reached their adult height,

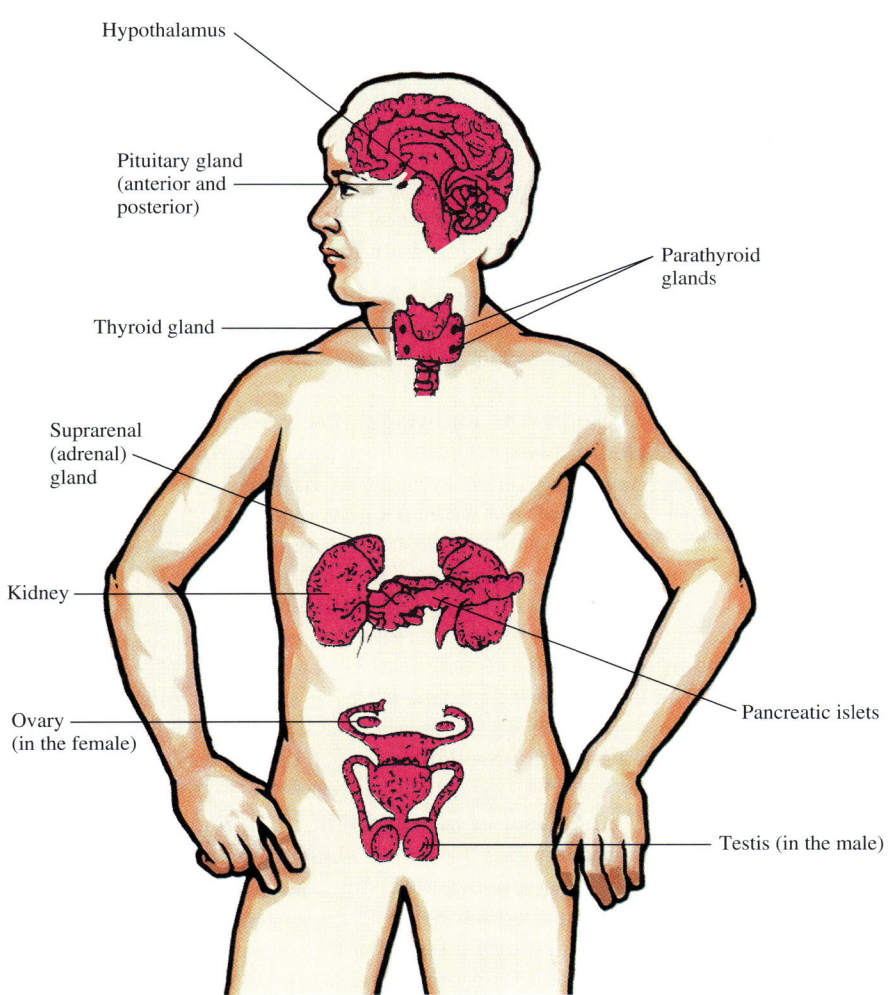

Hypothalamus

Pituitary gland
(anterior and
posterior)

Parathyroid
glands

Thyroid gland

Suprarenal
(adrenal)
gland

Kidney

Pancreatic islets

Ovary
(in the female)

Testis (in the male)

FIGURE 8-1
The Glands of the Endocrine System.

The endocrine system is a group of glands that release specific hormones into the bloodstream. During puberty, it is thought hormones are responsible for many of the physical changes that adolescents experience.

whereas for young men, this does not occur until a few years later (Chumlea, 1982; Malina, 1991; Petersen & Taylor, 1980; Tanner, 1991).

By age 11, both sexes have started to put on noticeable amounts of weight, averaging between 10 and 14 pounds a year during the peak years of development. Muscles contribute more to body weight in boys, and fat contributes more to body weight in girls.

The skeletal structure of both sexes increases in length, weight, proportion, and composition. Girls exhibit more rapid skeletal development than boys; their bone structure reaches mature size by age 17. Boys reach this mature stage of development almost 2 years later. Skeletal weight for both sexes increases throughout puberty, but appears to be more marked in boys.

CONTINUOUS AND DISCONTINUOUS HUMAN DEVELOPMENT

Do you feel the adolescent's changing physical self creates discontinuity and introduces new facets of growth and development at this time? Or are physical changes met with stability, integrated into the person the adolescent has always known? Does it become a matter of continuity *and* change?

Although height and weight gains are the most obvious changes during the adolescent growth spurt, other bodily changes are also taking place. Growth can be observed in pelvic and shoulder diameters, hand and foot length, and head circumference.

Primary and Secondary Sex Characteristics   A particularly notable development in puberty is the growth of primary and secondary sex characteristics. **Primary sex characteristics** are characteristics of the sexual and reproductive organs—the male penis and testes and the female ovaries, fallopian tubes, uterus, and vagina. **Secondary sex characteristics** are nongenital; for example, they include facial hair in boys and breast development in girls.

FEMALE SEXUAL DEVELOPMENT The female internal organs develop rapidly during puberty. The vagina increases in length and its lining becomes thicker; the uterus increases in overall weight and develops the intricate musculature it will need for pregnancy and delivery.

The ovaries also increase in size and weight. Each ovary has at birth about 400,000 primary follicles, which contain immature ova. By the time a girl reaches puberty, most of these primary follicles have degenerated and only 30,000 remain. Over the course of a woman's mature sexual life, it is estimated that only about 400 of the primary follicles will develop enough to expel ova. At puberty, this development process begins in monthly cycles.

Menstruation is the last stage of the female monthly cycle in which the uterus prepares to receive and nourish a fertilized egg, and then sloughs off the built-up lining when implantation does not take place. **Menarche,** the beginning of menstruation, is experienced by most North American girls by 13 or 14 years of age (the normal age range is 10 to 15½ years). The average age at menarche varies from 12 to 18 throughout the world (Brooks-Gunn, 1987, 1988; Hood, 1991; Paikoff, Buchanan, & Brooks-Gunn, 1991). In some societies, formal ceremonies make the onset of menstruation a happy event (see the accompanying Focus on Diversity box for some illustrations). In many Western countries, however, menarche can be confusing and frightening, usually because the female has not been adequately prepared for its occurrence.

Although menarche is the first definite sign of female sexual maturity, it does not necessarily mean attainment of reproductive capacity. Early menstrual cycles, which for some girls are more irregular than later ones, often occur without ovulation. Thus there is often a period of adolescent sterility after menarche. The average duration of this period is 12 to 18 months, but it is extremely variable (Tanner, 1981).

Breast development begins for most girls between the ages of 11 and 12, although it can start as late as age 14. The breasts develop to mature size over a span of about 3 years. During the early stages of breast development, there is elevation and enlargement, along with pigmentation of the nipple and the surrounding areola. This is followed by an increase in underlying fat surrounding the nipple and areola. Finally, there is an increase in mammary gland tissue, accounting for a larger and rounder breast.

Female pubic hair usually starts to appear after the breasts have begun to develop but before the onset of menarche. Appearing first on the outer lips of the vulva, by the end of adolescence pubic hair is dark, curly, and coarse and has

Focus on Diversity

PASSAGES TO WOMANHOOD: THE CELEBRATION OF MENARCHE

In many cultures menarche is an honored rite of passage and an occasion for special ceremony. For example, people in Ceylon have a special ritual celebrating menarche in which the young girl sits on banana leaves, eats raw egg prepared in ginger oil, and is given a milk bath. After the ceremony, her entire family joins her for a special feast in honor of her new status as a mature woman.

To the Pygmies of Central Africa, menstrual blood is a gift joyously received by the entire community. The girl who has reached this milestone enters the home of a female village elder with her closest friends, where she is taught the arts and crafts of motherhood. This is followed by a celebration lasting a month or two, during which friends come from near and far to pay their respects.

Among Native Americans, other unique rites of passage are observed. A Navajo menarche ceremony called *kinaalda* involves an elaborate 5-day-and-night celebration. During it the girl becomes Changing Woman, the Navajos' most important deity, and assumes a position of great respect in the society. Historically, *kinaalda* has been regarded as the most sacred of all Navajo religious rites.

Among the Mescalero Apaches, an annual puberty ceremony pays tribute to all the young women who began menstruating in the past year. An elaborate 4-day public ceremony, including feasting, the exchange of gifts, and other festivities, is followed by an additional 4 days of private observation. Like the Navajos, the Mescalero Apaches regard menarche as an important cultural event, and further believe that it ensures the tribe's survival. (Adapted from Taylor, 1988; Turner & Rubinson, 1993)

formed a triangular pattern over the mons. Hair under the arms usually appears about 2 years after pubic hair.

The sex hormones are also mainly responsible for the changes that transform the girl's body from its childhood shape to the contours of womanhood. Early in puberty the pelvis widens, an important change considering that childbirth usually requires the passage of a baby's head through this bony ring. At the same time, the laying down of more subcutaneous fat around the pelvic girdle exaggerates the breadth of the hips. Fat is also deposited in the shoulder girdle, back, abdomen, and legs. As the breasts develop, the apparent depth of the chest increases, enhanced by growth changes in the bony and muscular structures underlying the breasts.

MALE SEXUAL DEVELOPMENT For most boys, growth of the testes and penis begins to accelerate by approximately age 12 (Malina, 1991; Tanner, 1991). Most of the increase in the size of the testes is due to development of the seminiferous tubules. By age 18, testicular development is fairly complete. During this time the penis increases in length and circumference. In its mature state the average flaccid (unaroused) penis measures about 3 to 4 inches in length and its diameter is about 1.25 inches.

Puberty affects adolescents in many ways and represents a convergence of developmental forces.

Spontaneous erections are now experienced with increasing (and often embarrassing) frequency. The production of seminal fluid and first ejaculation, sometimes referred to as *spermarche,* occurs by about age 15. There are few viable sperm in this first ejaculate; as in girls, there is an initial period of sterility in boys undergoing puberty. When the ejaculation of seminal fluid occurs during sleep, it is known as a **nocturnal emission.** Nocturnal emissions are a normal phase of sexual development, frequently caused by sexual excitation in dreams or by a physical condition such as pressure from pajamas or a full bladder.

The development of male pubic hair begins between the ages of 13 and 14, usually starting at the base of the penis and extending upward toward the abdomen. Two years after pubic hair growth starts, hair on the limbs and the trunk begins to appear and underarm hair develops. Chest hair appears in late adolescence and continues growing throughout young adulthood. Boys often consider chest hair an important sign of virility.

Facial hair develops in a definite sequence. The downy hairs at the corners of the upper lip become noticeable and begin to extend over the entire upper lip. Slowly, the boy acquires a mustache of fine hair, which becomes coarser and more heavily pigmented with age. Later, hair appears on the upper part of the cheeks and the midline below the lower lip. Finally, it develops on the sides and border of the chin, as well as on the upper part of the face just in front of the ears.

Other secondary sex characteristics that appear in boys during puberty are increased activity of the sweat glands and marked voice changes. The deepening of the voice, due primarily to a rapid increase in the length of the vocal cords and growth of the larynx, is greater in boys than in girls. With age, there is also an increase in voice volume and tone. Table 8-1 charts the average sequence of primary and secondary sex characteristics in male and female adolescents.

The Psychology of Puberty   The pronounced physical developments that take place during puberty affect the way adolescents perceive themselves. Preoccupation with the changing sexual self is common as the primary and secondary sexual characteristics mature. The adolescent also must adjust to the changes brought on by the growth spurt. How teenagers react to this process

TABLE 8-1

The Development of Primary and Secondary Sex Characteristics

Females	Average Age of Occurrence	Males
Onset of growth spurt	10–11	
Increased activity of oil and sweat glands (acne can result from clogged glands)	11	Increased activity of oil and sweat glands (acne can result from clogged glands)
Initial breast development	11–12	Onset of growth spurt
Development of pubic hair	12	Growth of testes
Onset of menarche (age range is 10–16)	13–14	Development of pubic hair
Development of underarm hair	13–14	Growth of penis
	13–14	Deepening of the voice
Earliest normal pregnancy	14	
Completion of breast development (age range is 13–18)	15–16	Production of mature spermatozoa
	15–16	Nocturnal emissions
	15–16	Development of underarm and facial hair
Maturation of skeletal system	17–18	Maturation of skeletal system
	17–18	Development of chest hair

will greatly affect how they ultimately evaluate themselves (Adams, 1991; Koff & Riordan, 1991; Wright, 1989).

Certain aspects of the changing body may produce psychological discomfort, particularly for those who have received no advance information about what to expect. Menstruation and seminal emissions may be a source of anxiety, as may the gangling appearance and disproportionately rapid hand and foot development characteristic of the growth spurt. Considering that these developments are often accompanied by acne, physical awkwardness, and voice breaks, it is no wonder that many teenagers feel uncomfortable about their changing physical selves.

Teenagers who are late maturers may feel especially self-conscious. A **late maturer** is someone who lags behind established developmental norms; an **early maturer** is someone who spurts ahead of prescribed developmental timetables. Because physical development is an individual phenomenon, adolescents can differ dramatically in overall rates of growth.

Adolescents generally report higher levels of personal satisfaction when they mature early than when they mature late. Early maturers tend to be more independent, self-confident, and self-reliant, and are more socially adept than late maturers (Gross & Duke, 1980; Petersen, 1987; Wilen & Petersen, 1980). They also seem to be more popular and to have a greater capacity for leadership. Later maturers frequently have poorer self-concepts, are overly concerned about social acceptance, tend to be immature, and frequently resort to attention-seeking behavior.

INTERRELATEDNESS OF AGING PROCESSES

Can you think of specific ways your changing physical self during adolescence affected your psychological dynamics? What types of changes created psychological discomfort or confidence? How were your social interactions shaped by the events of puberty?

Early-maturing boys, in particular, tend to have more positive body images than their late-maturing age-mates, who often report intense dissatisfaction with their physical selves. Early-maturing boys are often given more responsibilities and privileges by their parents and have fewer conflicts with their mothers and fathers over such issues as curfews and choice of friends (Blyth, Simmons, & Zakin, 1985; Brooks-Gunn, 1984; Brooks-Gunn & Ruble, 1983; Savin-Williams & Small, 1986).

Although their overall social adjustment seems to be smoother, early maturers do encounter problems. For one thing, they have to adjust to the physical changes of puberty a lot faster than late maturers. This seems to be especially true for girls experiencing early menarche, who may be confused and anxious about the event. A few studies (Aro & Taipale, 1987; Duncan et al., 1985) have found that some early-maturing girls are somewhat less confident and popular than their late-maturing counterparts. Research on both sexes suggests that the external harmony often exhibited by the early maturer sometimes disguises internal disharmony (Livson & Peskin, 1980; Simons & Blyth, 1988). Indeed, adolescents who mature about on time tend to have the most positive self-images.

Early sexual maturation also has implications for sexual behavior. Although the early maturer is physically capable of engaging in sexual relations, a mature body is no guarantee of a mature mind. Thus many adolescents begin having sexual relations before they are psychologically ready. This is true of both sexes, but the consequences for girls are greater for the obvious reason that they can get pregnant. As we see later in this chapter, the rate of U.S. teenage pregnancy is escalating, with many mothers under age 15.

This is a good example of how development in one area (physical maturity) may affect development in other areas (sexual behavior), a point we made at the beginning of this chapter. It also underscores the need to teach teenagers what to expect from their developing bodies, which includes giving them information about the psychological and physiological risks of adolescent pregnancy. Such efforts may help reduce the exploding numbers of ill-prepared teenage parents.

Puberty and Sexual Responsiveness   The onset of sexual maturity heralds new levels of sexual understanding and responsiveness. As primary and secondary sex characteristics mature, the teenager becomes more aware of sexual feelings and desires and more interested in the social processes of dating and mate selection. When boys and girls enter adolescence, society expects them to begin the transition from childhood submissiveness, nonresponsibility, and asexuality to adult independence, responsibility, and sexuality. So there are both biological and social pressures toward full sexual development (DeLamater, 1981, 1989).

Unfortunately, society often gives teenagers confusing mixed messages regarding their sexuality. On the one hand, the media promote adolescent sexuality by using young actors and actresses and models dressed in provocative fashions. On the other hand, parents and other social agents try to discourage sexual engagement by imposing curfews and other limitations on teenagers. Adolescents have to evaluate these inconsistent messages against the background of a changing culture (Garbarino, 1985).

The sexual outcome of puberty is based on the individual's reaction to both physiological and psychological changes. Adolescents have to come to grips with the fact that they're now sexually mature, which implies coming to terms with their sexual identity. At this time of life young people consolidate their sexual preferences, think seriously about their sexual values—deciding which of their parents' values they accept and which they want to replace—and often worry about their sexual competence (Olds, 1985).

Motor Skill Development

One might expect adolescents' motor skill development to be uneven and disruptive in light of so many bodily changes. However, most adolescents exhibit steady increases in strength, reaction, and coordination abilities. Males continue to surpass females in overall motor skill development. This is largely because males have larger muscles and are able to develop more force per gram of muscle tissue.

In regard to specific motor skill activities, males are generally more proficient in such areas as accuracy in speed of response and overall body control. This proficiency may be demonstrated in running, throwing, and other motor skill tasks requiring varying degrees of physical endurance. Strength and dexterity are also more pronounced for males during the adolescent years.

We remind you, though, that such findings must be placed into the proper perspective. Much of this research was conducted before the current increase in female adolescents' athletic activities. Moreover, even though males surpass females in their overall ability to perform certain athletic tasks, this may be because of the vast amounts of time and practice they devote to developing these skills. Virtually all of the motor skill research in the past studied the typical male rather than the typical female. Physical prowess depends considerably on exercise and training, which in turn depend on personal motivation, social expectations, and practical opportunities. Males have received more encouragement in this regard, which has contributed greatly to the gap in physical ability between the sexes.

UNIT REVIEW—

- ↗ Puberty is a time of pronounced body development, including the maturation of the reproductive system and the development of secondary sex characteristics.

- ↗ The body changes associated with puberty are caused by hormones. Overall, physical developments during adolescence follow a fairly predictable timetable for both males and females.

- ↗ Whether one is an early or late maturer may influence one's psychological reactions to physical change. There are both biological and social pressures toward sexual development.

UNIT TWO: MENTAL DEVELOPMENT

■ Piaget's Stages of Cognitive Development

Formal Operations   **Formal operations** (ages 11 to 15) is the final stage of Piaget's theory. It is attained during the teenage years, and persists throughout adult life. This level of cognition heralds the abandonment of immature mental operations and signifies new ways to understand and explore the world. Such thinking abilities herald the relinquishment of childhood mental operations and the emergence of mature thought. Let us examine this stage of cognition more closely.

FORMAL OPERATIONS AND COGNITIVE MATURITY Formal operations is the crystallization and integration of all previous cognitive stages. Past developments now combine with formal operations to create a tightly organized and highly systematic mental whole. Furthermore, thinking becomes extremely rational and will continue to develop throughout adulthood as these refined mental strategies are applied to greater numbers of problem-solving situations. However, at least one source (Carey, 1988) claims that formal thought is most likely applied to areas best known by the person.

It must be understood that entry into the final stage of formal operations is gradual and sometimes unpredictable; it is not a sudden and giant leap forward. The attainment of formal operational thinking is also not an all-or-nothing situation. In this sense, individuals may reach peak levels of cognitive functioning in certain areas but not in others. And age does not guarantee automatic entry into this particular stage. On the contrary, some may achieve cognitive competence at the beginning of this age whereas others may not attain formal operational thinking until later.

It is also important to point out that some may never reach this stage of cognitive functioning (Byrnes, 1988; Orr, Brack, & Ingersoll, 1988). A critical force in promoting formal operational thinking appears to be higher education. Indeed, a growing number of researchers (e.g., Kuhn, 1989; Kuhn, Amsel, & O'Loughlin, 1988; Shute, Glaser, & Raghavan, 1989) point to the role that college courses exert on sophisticated levels of reasoning, including the enhancement of scientific thinking.

As far as specific cognitive advancements during formal operations are concerned, the individual is now capable of thinking about the past, present, and future. It is also possible to deal effectively with problems of a hypothetical nature. Moreover, when confronted with a problem, a number of possible answers can be formulated while working toward the solution (Danner, 1989). Thus, compared to earlier stages, thinking now resembles that of a scientist.

Perhaps the best word to describe the mental processes in this phase of cognitive development is *flexibility*. Cognitive maturity allows mental adaptation to whatever task is faced, thus enabling the individual to benefit and learn from those concepts and mistakes made as a growing child. Thinking is also flexible because the adolescent can now apply a diversity of logical thought processes to the problem at hand, including the use of inductive and deductive reasoning powers.

To illustrate the changing character of mature cognition as well as its overall flexibility, let us examine several key accomplishments taking place during formal operations. These accomplishments include advancements made in abstract thinking, in problem-solving strategies, and gains made in literary understanding.

ABSTRACT THINKING First of all, in early stages of cognitive development individuals are limited in their understanding of **abstractions** or relationships between abstractions. Abstractions represent subjective concepts or ideas that are apart from one's objective analysis of the tangible environment. Whereas objective reasoning skills are needed to solve concrete problems, such as those in science or math, abstract reasoning powers are needed to understand what cannot be seen.

When confronted with abstract concepts before reaching the formal operations stage, it is very likely that one is dependent on the physical or concrete properties of these concepts. The ability to move beyond the mere physical properties of the environment and understand abstractions has enormous implications for cognitive development at this time. No longer is the individual shackled to current or recent concrete experiences. Whereas earlier it was possible to reason only about what is, one can now imagine what might be (Ginsburg & Opper, 1988; Keating, 1990).

Because of abstract reasoning powers, adolescents can also think about their identity and future, including their occupational and social roles (Darmody, 1991; Nurmi, 1991). And they may experiment with these roles just as they would experiment with hypotheses about physical events. Furthermore, formal operators are able to formulate values and generate many new ideas about themselves and about life in general. Debates are now possible about a variety of moral and political issues, such as whether wars can ever be moral, whether abortions should be legal, whether there are basic inalienable rights, and what an ideal community would be like. Those in formal operations can consider these issues from a variety of perspectives and see how the issues themselves are related to a larger set of social relationships. It is in this way that cognitive

Thinking reaches a mature state during adolescence.

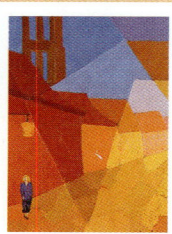

THEORETICAL ISSUES

How do you think the mental abilities of a concrete operational thinker compare and contrast with those of a formal operational thinker? How would such differing cognitive abilities affect, say, religious, moral, and political views? What would be the implications of different cognitive levels for identity formation, family relationships, school achievement, or dating relationships?

advancements fuse with numerous other aspects of development (Darmody, 1991; Hatcher, 1990; Juhasz & Palmer, 1991; Miller, 1989; Smetana, Killen, & Turiel, 1991).

PROBLEM-SOLVING STRATEGIES Approaching problems by attempting to imagine all of the possible relationships that might exist is another characteristic feature of the mature mind. The mature adult is able to accept data or propositions as purely hypothetical and tentative and then test them against whatever evidence is available. Whereas children frequently accept initial explanations to problem-solving situations as true, those in the stage of formal operations make deductions on a hypothetical basis. Unlike children, they can also make analyses of the full range of possibilities inherent in a problem before adopting one of them. James Byrnes (1988) refers to such sophisticated problem-solving strategies as "knowing how." That is, formal thinkers know the steps needed to successfully solve problems, known in some cognitive circles as procedural knowledge (Anderson, 1990).

This means that one can employ **deductive reasoning,** or reasoning from a set of premises to a conclusion. Piaget calls this **hypothetico-deductive reasoning.** One is also able to make use of **inductive reasoning.** Inductive logic means starting with specific individual experiences and proceeding to general principles.

Syllogisms provide a good example of deductive logic. For example, if given the premises that (1) Socrates is a man, and that (2) all men are mortal, those in the stage of formal operations can conclude that (3) Socrates is mortal. Deductive logic requires being able to deal with more than one aspect of a problem at a time. In this example, for instance, one must keep in mind that Socrates is a man and that all men are mortal. As time goes on, individuals are able to approach even more complex variations of syllogisms. For example, "I am a man. If Larry's son is my son's father, what relationship am I to Larry?" (To avoid frustration, the answer is that you are Larry's son.)

When approaching problems, mental strategies are methodical and efficient. The mature mind can carefully explore all features of a problem-solving situation. The hypotheses it can employ are logically more complex as well as more flexible and mobile than those of an immature mind. By testing predictions from each hypothesis, one is able to arrive with systematic deliberation at correct solutions to problems. Such problem-solving approaches will herald new levels of insight into the world, not to mention scientific inquiry in general (Danner, 1989; Keating, 1990; Kuhn, 1989; Thomas, 1992).

GAINS IN LITERARY UNDERSTANDING Finally, the formal operations stage becomes a time for heightened levels of literary understanding. Mature cognition enables adolescents to possess greater insight into literary ideas, to question what is being read, and to be generally more receptive to new facts and ideas. For example, entry into formal operations enables individuals to digest a greater range of symbols, metaphors, word meanings, and characterizations. Historical chronology can be grasped, something baffling younger persons. Certain literary techniques that had a tendency to promote earlier confusion, such as the use of irony and abstract concepts, are usually now understood. Those in formal operations are also able to respond to a wider range of humor, including riddles, cartoons, and subtle forms of expression (Couturier, Mansfield, & Gallagher, 1981; Demorest, Silberstein, & Gardner, 1981; Parr, 1982; Richardson & Sheldon, 1988).

Much of this advancement in literary understanding is due to the fact that formal operations relinquishes readers from a singular, concrete interpretation of printed or spoken words. Furthermore, the ability to engage in systematic analysis of facts and abstract reasoning opens new horizons for thought. This is as true for one's interpretation of editorial cartoons as it is for the appreciation of the moral and social significance of literary classics. Such cognitive milestones in literary insight and other spheres of thinking have important curriculum implications (Danner, 1989; Ginsburg & Opper, 1988; Katz & Chard, 1989; Mills, 1988).

ADOLESCENT EGOCENTRISM One mental development that may distort cognitive functioning at this time is adolescent egocentrism. According to David Elkind (1967, 1971, 1978, 1980, 1981, 1984, 1985; Elkind & Bowen, 1979), **adolescent egocentrism** is a form of self-centeredness characterized by teenagers' concern about what people are thinking about them. Put another way, it is the tendency to conceptualize one's own thoughts while also being preoccupied with the thoughts of others. A major consequence of adolescent egocentrism is a heightened level of self-consciousness.

According to Elkind, adolescent egocentrism promotes two unique types of thinking. The first is the construction of an **imaginary audience,** a delusion that other people are just as concerned about how they behave and look as they themselves are. Because of the imaginary audience, adolescents feel they are always the focus of attention or on center stage. This perceived existence of an imaginary audience usually intensifies during potentially threatening social situations, and may help to explain the showing off and loudness, as well as the distinctive clothing, that are characteristic of the adolescent years (Blasi & Hoeffel, 1974; Buis & Thompson, 1989; Gray & Hudson, 1984; Looft, 1972; Tice, Buder, & Baumeister, 1985).

But although adolescents are often self-critical, they also become self-admiring. During such times, the imaginary audience acquires the same affective coloration as that of the teenager. Adolescents may also construct an imaginary audience when they contemplate how others will react to their own demise. For example, a type of bittersweet pleasure might originate from anticipating the belated recognition by others of one's personal qualities, such as what might be remembered or spoken at a funeral.

It is plausible that the heightened self-consciousness brought on by the imaginary audience influences some of the problems encountered by many adolescents, such as pregnancy, sexually transmitted diseases, runaways, and juvenile delinquency. Thus many adolescents feel their peers are constantly noticing and judging their behaviors. Indeed, many adolescents allow the slightest remark or comment from the imaginary audience to inflate or deflate their esteem and self-confidence.

The **personal fable** is the second consequence of adolescent egocentrism. Personal fables are stories that adolescents fabricate and tell about themselves. Personal fables reflect the adolescent's conviction of personal uniqueness and

During formal operations, thinking often reflects heightened levels of self-consciousness.

GENDER SIMILARITIES AND DIFFERENCES

What role might traditional gender-role socialization play in the expression of adolescent egocentrism? For example, given their more interpersonal orientation, are traditional females more likely to construct imaginary audiences? Are traditional males more apt to construct personal fables because they view themselves less vulnerable to risk and harm?

may contain such mistaken beliefs that one will not die or that one leads a charmed existence. This type of thinking thus embraces the concept of perceived invulnerability; while under the spell of the personal fable, adolescents often feel as though they are protected from harm, risk, or even death.

The personal fable can be used to explain why many adolescents are willing to risk their health and well-being. It is possible that many believe they are immune to sexually transmitted diseases, becoming involved in unwanted pregnancies, or being injured on the highway when driving recklessly. Consequently, precautionary behavior may be avoided by adolescents because they don't really believe anything negative will ever happen to them.

Since the formulation of Elkind's ideas, other thoughts on the topic of adolescent egocentrism and the related constructs of the imaginary audience and personal fable have emerged. For example, the emergence of the imaginary audience and personal fable have been linked to stages of interpersonal understanding proposed by Robert Selman (1972, 1976, 1980; Selman & Byrne, 1974; Selman et al., 1986). Selman proposes that the development of interpersonal understanding is the result of increasing awareness of the self and that of other individuals in a relationship. Taking another's perspective implies the ability to shift, balance, and evaluate both perceptual and cognitive input and unfolds through a series of stages: *egocentric viewpoint* (3–6 years), *social-informational role-taking* (6–8 years), *self-reflective role-taking* (8–10 years), *mutual role-taking* (10–12 years), and *social and conventional system role-taking* (12–15 years and upward).

The presence of adolescent egocentrism and the related constructs of the imaginary audience and personal fable have been connected to the stages of *mutual role-taking* and *social and conventional system role-taking*. More specifically, these stages represent a time when adolescents develop the capacity to reflect on the self from a third-party perspective. Within relationships, individuals become aware both of the simultaneous perspective-taking of each other and the possible effects of this mutual activity. Adolescent egocentrism arises when there is an inability to engage in such perspective-taking and perceive the world from another person's point of view. Put another way, the adolescent's own perspective interferes with his or her efforts to recognize and understand the actions of others. Selman believes mutual perspective-taking is dependent on the transition from concrete to formal operational thought and feels it may be delayed for some to late adolescence or beyond (Selman, 1980).

Other efforts have been made to relate the imaginary audience and personal fable to the separation-individuation process of adolescent ego development. Dubbed the "new look" adolescent egocentrism model, Daniel Lapsley (1985, 1986, 1988, 1990, 1991; Lapsley & Murphy, 1985; Lapsley & Rice, 1988; Lapsley et al., 1989) views the imaginary audience and personal fable as adaptive ideational patterns, or defensive strategies that occur when the childhood ego separates from the egos of one's parents and becomes independent. During this time, the ego must learn to differentiate "me" from "them" by establishing an identity of its own, rather than merely reflecting the identities (egos) of parents. Prior to the separation-individuation of adolescence, the sense of self was derived from the child's identification with parents, and esteem originated from parental approval ("I am magnificent because my parents are"; "I have esteem because my parents esteem me"). Now, the psychological chore entails developing a sense of self and learning to regulate self-esteem from internal sources.

As the adolescent disengages psychologically from childhood identifications, the self becomes vulnerable and struggles with the task of identification (Blos, 1962). A poignant internal perception of the self commences, and as the spotlight of the mind's eye turns inward, elements of individuality and uniqueness are discovered. The personal fable emerges as a result of this self-scrutiny, and the adolescent, now flushed with narcissism, feels unique, invincible, and omnipotent. Additionally, adolescents must prepare themselves for connecting with others and the affective experiences that accompany interpersonal interactions. The imaginary audience unfolds in the face of such interpersonal fantasies, and the self is imagined in a wide assortment of private fantasies and imaginative interactions (Lapsley et al., 1989; Lapsley, personal communication, 1991, 1992). The imaginary audience and personal fable, then, allow the teenager to cope with self-delineation, and are thus viewed as positive features of adolescence insofar as they contribute to resilience and psychological defense.

Do Other Stages of Cognition Exist?

Do Other Stages of Cognition Exist?   Piaget maintains that formal operations is the final stage of cognitive development. Some researchers, though, feel that certain mental advancements transcend those acquired during the formal operations stage. This is the central theme of an impressive body of research by Michael Commons and his colleagues (Commons & Richards, 1982; Commons, Richards, & Armon, 1982; Commons, Richards, & Kuhn, 1982; Richards & Commons, 1982).

Commons proposed that a structural analytic stage follows formal operations. This stage includes certain qualities of cognition that are not covered by

THEORETICAL ISSUES

One of the qualities of a good theory in lifespan development (or any other discipline) is its ability to spark additional research and the discovery of new knowledge. Can you see how cognitive-developmental theory provided a conceptual framework for Elkind's visions of the imaginary audience and personal fable? Going a step further, do you understand how Elkind's ideas stimulated the thinking of Selman and Lapsley and thus encouraged further experimentation, refinement, and elaboration?

Piaget but are characteristic of the intellectually mature person. More specifically, this stage includes systematic reasoning, the capacity to use the abstract thinking originating in the formal operations stage to create complex systems of mental operations. This structural analytic aspect comes into focus when people become able to compare relationships as well as entire representational systems and models. In addition, such individuals can use metasystematic reasoning, the ability to create new mental systems. An example is Albert Einstein's general theory of relativity.

The research by Commons and his colleagues offers an interesting extension of Piaget's work and adds an exciting dimension to the overall study of cognitive development. In the next chapter, we explore other aspects of qualitative thinking that appears to unfold beyond formal operational thought.

UNIT REVIEW—

➚ Piaget's stage of formal operations encompasses the teenage years, although age does not guarantee entry into this peak level of cognitive functioning. Individuals may experience formal operational thinking in certain areas but not in others. Key cognitive advancements include the ability to think abstractly, the refinement of problem-solving abilities, and literary insight.

➚ Adolescent egocentrism, expressed in such behaviors as the imaginary audience and the personal fable, tends to distort cognitive functioning. Elkind, Selman, and Lapsley have proposed different viewpoints on the origins and expression of adolescent egocentrism.

➚ There may be other cognitive accomplishments beyond formal operations: Research by Michael Commons and associates suggests a structural analytic stage.

UNIT THREE: PERSONALITY AND SOCIAL DEVELOPMENT

Social involvement during the teenage years acquires more meaning and significance than at any previous time. Careful observers of this age group discover that personal relationships among teenagers intensify not only because it is important for adolescents to be accepted by their peers, but also because they need to share their new feelings and experiences. At this time, peer groups offer support and security to adolescents who are attempting to assert independence and autonomy from their families. In addition, peer groups provide models for teenagers seeking to establish an identity. Expressing concern over one's dress and appearance, doing extra chores around the house to earn dating money, explaining why an evening curfew was missed, bargaining for the family car, or carrying on frequent and lengthy telephone conversations are characteristic behavioral patterns that reflect adolescents' growing interest in social involvements.

Personality development and social development usually take place against the backdrop of family life.

One of the central processes of adolescence is **identity formation,** the procedure of clarifying and integrating oneself into a distinctive whole person. This is a time when adolescents cognitively reexamine old values and attitudes as they experiment with new ones, a process that requires considerable thought and deliberation. The ever-changing complexity of society and its many pressures, challenges, and options do not make the quest for identity easy for today's adolescents (Blustein & Palladino, 1991; Greene, 1990; Harper & Marshall, 1991).

Adolescent personality dynamics thus take place within the context of socialization. This means the accuracy, stability, and acceptance of the self-concept affects the nature and degree of social relationships. Conversely, the feedback and reinforcement from others influence how adolescents perceive themselves. Other developmental forces, too, blend with personality and social growth. Heightened social-cognitive skills, for example, combine with other skills to enable teenagers to examine themselves and others around them with greater understanding and awareness. Adolescents' changing physical, mental, and emotional selves together influence their heterosexual interests, sexual behavior, family life, and overall social development. Thus it can be said that personality and social changes do not operate apart from other changes. Instead, they are only some of the developmental changes affecting the whole person (Berzonsky & Sullivan, 1992; Clausen, 1991; Harper & Marshall, 1991; Masselman, Marcus, & Stunkard, 1990; Parke, 1989; Rogoff, 1989; Wertsch, 1989).

Family Influences on the Developing Adolescent

Family life is greatly affected by teenagers' desire for autonomy, including their quest for individuation. **Individuation** occurs when adolescents begin to disengage their attitudes and beliefs from those of their parents. Because of such strivings for a more independent identity, parents at this time are often forced to redefine past child-parent relations and gradually increase the teenager's responsibilities. Parents may realize for the first time that their offspring are capable of making mature decisions for themselves, and will soon be moving on and establishing their own independent lifestyle and living arrangements. How these forces blend—the adolescent's desire for an independent identity and greater autonomy, and the parents' reaction to such strivings—greatly influences the emotional climate of the home during this time (Cotterell, 1992; Paikoff & Brooks-Gunn, 1991; Richards, 1991).

At least one line of research (Bartle & Anderson, 1992) suggests that a similarity exists between adolescents' strivings for individuation and that of parents when they were younger. In this investigation, families with adolescents responded to a questionnaire assessing perceived parenting style and individuation from family of origin. Results showed that the more mothers were individuated from both parents, the more their adolescents were individuated from both parents. However, there were no significant correlations between fathers' individuation and the individuation of adolescent offspring.

Although many parents can meet the challenges of this stage, there are some who do not fare as well. Part of the problem is that they resist granting to their children even a little individuation and adult status. Rather than promoting their uniqueness and encouraging responsible behavior, such parents instead overprotect their children and encourage their dependence. Some do not let go of their teenagers because they dread the thought of the next phase of family life, the empty nest stage. Although the empty nest stage has numerous positive consequences, some parents (and adolescent offspring) have difficulty adjusting to this transition (Berman & Sperling, 1991; Gecas & Seff, 1990).

Creating effective communication between parent and adolescent is an important task at this time. So, too, is the parents' need to establish management and control of their teenagers' behavior. This latter task may have caused earlier child-rearing problems, which may now become worse. Parents naturally want to enforce their own standards and values, but these may conflict with the most effective type of authority. Society's swiftly changing values and standards may further complicate this problem.

Evidence also indicates that parents perceive their relationship with their adolescent differently than do outsiders. To show this, a study devised two tasks where mother, father, and their adolescent child had to interact. Afterward they viewed a videotape of their interaction and gave a self-rating. Self-ratings were more positive when compared with ratings from another mother-father-adolescent triad and also by a trained observer. Both sets of observers gave more negative ratings than the parents involved in the tasks (Noller & Callan, 1988).

Some parents are uncertain whether they want to (or should) be a friend or authority to their offspring. Those wanting to be a friend sometimes report their children take advantage of the friendship by trying to get out of work or obtain extra privileges. Those parents that are authority figures sometimes feel like police officers and miss an emotional bond with their offspring. But it has been suggested that being a friend does not eliminate being an authority as well. Indeed, both roles are necessary for parents at various times. Children need parents who can be trusted, who will share their problems of growing up.

THEORETICAL ISSUES

Utilizing a family development theoretical perspective, what do you think are some of the principal challenges facing the family with adolescents? What distinguishes this transition from those preceding it as well as those to follow?

They also need an authority who will teach them the social skills and work habits needed to survive in society (Knox, 1985). When successfully balanced, these two forces are likely to promote positive, close, and warm relations between young and old (Baumrind, 1991a; Josselson, 1988).

In an investigation involving sixth, ninth, and twelfth graders, it was found that the older the child, the less cohesiveness they saw in family relationships with the exception of the mother-father dyad (Feldman & Gehring, 1988). However, when there is an intimate bond between parent and child, benefits accrue. One study found that mothers share greater degrees of intimacy with their children than fathers do. On the other hand, paternal intimacy was found to be a greater predictor of positive adolescent functioning than maternal intimacy was (LeCroy, 1988).

Styles of Parental Control   The three major classifications of parental control, you will recall, are *authoritarian* (or autocratic), *authoritative* (or democratic), and *permissive*. In an authoritarian family setting, parents establish the standards of behavior to which the children must adhere. Frequently, respect for authority and work and the preservation of order and traditional structure are emphasized. Furthermore, disciplinary measures are predominantly harsh and forceful.

The authoritarian method of control often leads teenagers to rebel. Often there is a power struggle between parent and adolescent. If the parents are strict, with no room for give-and-take, this may also foster such behaviors as dependence, submissiveness, and conformity. For the parent who mixes authoritarian domination with physical punishment, other problems develop. The use of excessive physical punishment, as we learned earlier, tends to create maladjustment in many areas of personality and social development. In particular, it is likely to result in less self-reliance and confidence and more immaturity and aggressiveness (Strassberg et al., 1992; Weiss et al., 1992).

The authoritative method of parental control, in which the adolescent is consulted on family matters, given a fair share of autonomy, and disciplined primarily verbally, tends to be the most effective and rewarding. Authoritative parents are more democratic, allow ample opportunity for adolescents to make their own decisions, but retain the final authority.

In permissive households, parents offer much emotional support to their offspring but exert little control. Adolescents from these homes are frequently allowed to come and go as they please. When permitted to behave as they wish, however, these adolescents may become selfish, insecure, and immature. Sometimes adolescents interpret their parents' lack of assertion as an uncaring attitude, even though the reverse might be true.

Research indicates that authoritative parenting is more effective than either authoritarian or permissive styles. For example, Diana Baumrind (1991a) discovered that authoritative parents were more apt to instill confidence, competence, and independency in their offspring. Moreover, adolescents of authoritative parents were less likely to be rebellious. Another investigation (Lamborn et al., 1991) showed that adolescents of authoritative parents had higher levels of psychosocial competence and lower levels of dysfunctional behavior than those teenagers from authoritarian homes. Finally, a study (Steinberg, 1991) revealed that authoritative parenting tends to influence higher

Disharmony and disagreement are not uncommon between adolescents and their parents.

levels of adolescent academic achievement, more self-reliance, and less anxiety and depression than found in teenagers from permissive or authoritarian households.

How do adolescents perceive these styles of parental control? Which style do they prefer? Such questions were at the heart of research by Cay Kelly and Gail Goodwin (1983). In their study, 100 adolescents were given a questionnaire that examined a number of areas, including the style of control their parents used and their acceptance or rejection of such control.

Of the responses, 83% of the teenagers felt they had democratic parents, 11% had authoritarian parents, and 6% had permissive parents. Subjects raised in democratic homes clearly favored this form of parental control. In support of this, they responded favorably to 68% of the items on the questionnaire reflecting democratic orientations. Those from autocratic and permissive homes, by comparison, responded positively to 50% and 32% of the questions, respectively. One important area of autonomy indicated by the adolescents was the right to choose their own friends and dates. As predicted, teenagers raised under democratic parental styles tended to react more positively to parental power than did those from permissive or autocratic homes. Interestingly, even among the teenagers raised in democratic homes, some covert rebellion against parental power was manifested in their assertion of the right to choose their dates and friends.

All of this discussion shows that adolescents prefer households regulated by honesty, fairness, and mutuality. Consultations between parents and teenagers on issues of mutual concern and the provisions of opportunities to enhance the teenagers' autonomy appear to create the healthiest emotional climate. Not only are parent-adolescent relations likely to prosper with such operating principles, but the personal growth of each party is likely to flourish (Noller & Callan, 1988; Papini, 1990; Peterson & Leigh, 1990; Sroufe, 1991).

TOUGHLOVE AS A FORM OF PARENTAL CONTROL One of the more controversial methods of parental control is called **toughlove.** Developed by David and Phyllis York (York & York, 1982; York, York, & Wachtel, 1982), toughlove is designed for parents who are having extreme problems with their teenaged children. Toughlove is a self-help organization that asks parents first to admit they have a problem they can no longer handle on their own—that they cannot control their children's behavior. Parents turn to toughlove for a variety of teenage problems, including drug abuse and delinquency.

An important feature of toughlove is the view that parents often cannot be effective in a permissive, child-centered culture. Meeting regularly in parent support groups and maintaining contact between sessions with other group members, toughlove parents are encouraged to take firmer positions with their children and to set a bottom line on acceptable behavior in their household. When this standard is violated, the parents, with the support of other group members, are expected to follow through with the consequences they have established. Suppose a teenager has a drinking problem and nothing the family has done to help works. Should the teenager be arrested for drunk driving, a toughlove approach would be to let the adolescent stay in jail for 3 days. In other instances, the parents might withdraw material resources as the bottom line on unacceptable behavior.

The ultimate sanction is making the teenager move to some other living arrangement—often to the homes of other toughlove parents. These parents are called advocates, and they help the teenager and his or her parents negotiate a contract setting out the conditions for returning home. Other concerned adults in the community, such as teachers, social workers, and therapists, may also serve as part of the toughlove network (Everts, 1990).

Family Disharmony   We have stressed the importance of a favorable home environment throughout this book. During adolescence, the home environment may be affected not only by the parents' method of discipline but also by how well parents and teenagers understand each other. A lack of understanding and empathy between parents and teenagers is likely to disrupt family harmony and lead to conflicts.

The disagreements and conflicts between parents and teenagers can be numerous and diverse. Some of the common reasons cited for parent-adolescent conflicts are sexual behavior, money, dress, drugs, school performance, friendships in general, and the use of the family car. It is generally acknowledged that early adolescence is more stressful than late adolescence because parents are establishing new guidelines and parameters regarding acceptable and unacceptable behavior (Montemayor & Flannery, 1991; Steinberg, 1991).

Psychological collisions between adolescents and parents also center on values. Mary Ann Lamanna and Agnes Riedmann (1994) write that because our society increasingly requires adults to possess their own set of values, teenagers may need to reject those of their parents, at least intellectually and for the time being. Value differences become difficult to negotiate when both teenagers and parents will not compromise. What is obviously needed is good communication between the two. Parents who are available and who are willing to listen are apt to exert strong influences on their offspring, even though they may not always agree with them.

As far as gender differences are concerned, male and female adolescents tend to disagree more with their mothers than with their fathers, probably because the mother is more involved in the day-to-day operation of the household (Steinberg, 1987). One study (Holmbeck & Hill, 1991) showed that conflict engagement with parents is more frequent shortly after a female experiences

CONTINUOUS AND DISCONTINUOUS HUMAN DEVELOPMENT

Is conflict inevitable, even desirable, for the healthy development of adolescents as well as parents? Do you think domestic turmoil is a necessary by-product of adolescent strivings for individuation? Or do you think healthy development is characterized by continuing, close relationships between adolescent and parents?

menarche, particularly conflicts between mother and daughter. Withdrawal of positive affect was also found to be associated with menarcheal status; interruptions and disagreements between mother and daughter were less frequently responded to with positive affect. This is a good example of how interpersonal and intrapsychic processes occur in the family around a biological event such as puberty. Using perspectives established by conflict and family development theorists, can you see how conflict may facilitate family adaptation to pubertal change and make moderate levels of conflict normative in healthy families?

Stephen Small, Gay Eastman, and Steven Cornelius (1988) believe that gender differences also exist in parents' reactions to domestic disharmony. Fathers tend to report higher levels of stress if their offspring do not follow prescribed advice or become involved in deviant activities. For mothers, greater levels of stress are often reported when children desire more autonomy and independence.

Often contributing to domestic disharmony is the teenagers' desire for adult status and the parents' resistance. As established at the outset, many teenagers want to establish independent lifestyles in their quest for individuation. One of the more difficult challenges of the teenage years thus becomes striving for individual autonomy while maintaining harmonious family relations (Gavazzi & Sabatelli, 1990; Pardeck & Pardeck, 1990; Smetana, 1988; Whittaker & Bry, 1991).

Many teenagers try to escape adult authority in their efforts to attain autonomy. However, whether teenagers actually obtain this latter goal is open to question, especially if they seek the exclusive shelter of their peer group. Sometimes the pressure to conform to group expectations is just as great, if not greater, than the pressure to conform at home. Adolescents may also find that their desire to be with others promotes a new type of dependence.

Teenagers' very desire to be independent may produce its own conflict. Teenagers can no longer be treated as children; on the other hand, they are not yet considered adults. It is not clear when they pass from adolescent to adult status, as our culture has no rites of passage or formal initiation ceremonies that acknowledge an individual's entrance into adulthood. Complicating this issue is the fact that many adolescents have attained only token signs of independence. For example, adolescents may be given the privileges of dressing as they desire or going where they please, behaviors that on the surface seem to represent autonomy. Yet there is no guarantee that beneath the surface these same adolescents have attained psychological or emotional autonomy. Furthermore, some adolescents may have acquired privileges in exchange for their compliance with parental ideals and wishes. This type of trade-off causes many adolescents to settle for ritual signs of independence. Consequently, many forfeit true psychological growth.

TEENAGE RUNAWAYS: FLIGHT FROM THE FAMILY Family conflicts are not always resolved, and teenagers may thus decide to run away. Each year, over 1 million adolescents choose this course of action and most are between the ages of 15 and 17. There are slightly more male runaways than females (Gavazzi & Blumenkrantz, 1991; U.S. Bureau of the Census, 1992).

Most runaways are from white suburbs, although adolescent runaways come from all ethnic and social levels. Most leave home because of destructive family situations or because of a secret personal problem such as breaking the law or pregnancy. Though some travel only a short distance from home and return in less than a week, others stay away for longer periods. And some never return home.

There are several explanations of why adolescents become runaways. Some leave home to escape pressure and conflict. Others run away because of the freedom that awaits them. In relation to this, some are drawn to drugs, sex, or an escape from routines in general. Finally, some runaways are throwaways. In the face of intolerable parent-adolescent relations, including those involving abuse and neglect, many teenagers are actually encouraged, and in some cases forced, to leave home (Carlson, 1991; Hier, Koorboot, & Schweitzer, 1990; Sharlin & Mork-Barak, 1992).

David Kurtz and colleagues (1991) discovered that physical and sexual maltreatment often precipitated runaway behavior. They also found significant differences in the problems reported by physically abused and sexually abused runaways when they were compared to nonabused runaway peers. More specifically, those adolescents experiencing physical and sexual maltreatment were more vulnerable to risks and dangers faced by runaways and demonstrated poorer levels of adjustment.

In recent years, the care and treatment of runaways has increased significantly, although many runaways are never reported. Family therapy is frequently part of the overall treatment program (Gavazzi & Blumenkrantz, 1991). In cases of parental abuse or lack of parental cooperation, authorities may place the teenager in a foster home. An important step in combating this problem has been the establishment of hot lines that tell runaways the locations of temporary shelters and enable them to send messages to their parents if they desire.

School Influences on the Developing Adolescent

Today's modern world is large and confusing, technically complex, and constantly changing. In order for adolescents to acquire knowledge that will be of service to them in later life, the school remains more than ever a vital and essential institution. Through the efforts of educators, as well as continuing support from the home, adolescents are prepared and equipped to function effectively in society (Bloome, 1989; T. E. Smith, 1991; Snodgrass, 1991; Tharpe & Gallimore, 1989).

The school is important during adolescence not only because of the educational information it transmits, but for other important reasons as well. For example, beyond the sheer amount of time spent in attendance, the school will come to represent the adolescent's society. It is a social setting where individuals from the same life stage can share common experiences and interests. The school also shapes the personality and social development of the adolescent, including levels of self-esteem (Mullis, Mullis, & Normandin, 1992). It offers a testing ground for ideas and discussions, along with an opportunity to engage in decision-making strategies. As such, the school tends to improve interpersonal relationships, including sensitivity to others and communication in general (Fenzel, Blyth, & Simmons, 1991).

Although the school environment offers the adolescent the potential for valuable growth experiences, many seek to escape by dropping out. The percentage of school dropouts has diminished a great deal since the turn of the century, but the numbers are still substantial, particularly among minority

During adolescence, individuals become increasingly preoccupied with educational and career aspirations.

groups and low-income students (American Council on Education, 1991; Carrasquillo, 1991; McCall, 1991). For example, in 1989 about 28% of Hispanic high school students dropped out of school compared with 22% of the African-American students, 15% of white students, and 8% of Asians (National Center for Education Statistics, 1990).

According to William O'Hare and colleagues (1991), many dropouts later return to school or earn a high school equivalency degree, but about 10% of Americans remain "status dropouts," persons 16 to 24 years of age who have not graduated from high school and are not currently enrolled in school. In 1989, 14% of non-Hispanic African Americans remained status dropouts compared with only 9% of non-Hispanic whites. Hispanics, whose numbers include many recent immigrants, are even less likely than African Americans to complete high school. About a third of Hispanics were status dropouts in 1989.

Adolescents are more likely to drop out of school when they get poor grades, are older than their classmates, come from a single-parent family, have parents who dropped out of school, or reside in a central city rather than a suburban or nonmetropolitan area. On average, African-American adolescents fare worse than whites on almost all these, as well as other risk factors associated with dropping out of school. When these family and background differences are taken into account, however, African Americans are no more likely than whites to drop out of high school. Indeed, research (National Center for Education Statistics, 1990) shows the dropout rates for African Americans and whites living in suburban areas are about equal. For a look at the higher educational aspirations of minority adolescents, see the accompanying Focus on Diversity box.

One of the most prominent factors affecting academic performance is the teacher-student relationship. Similar to earlier school experiences, students respond most favorably to those teachers who are self-controlled, warm, and friendly in their classroom interactions. Democratic and integrative systems of classroom control tend to encourage cooperation, sensitivity toward others, and task-oriented student behaviors.

Teachers are in a prime position to enhance the many challenges that accompany the secondary school experience. More specifically, teachers can help adolescents become academically successful, earn self-respect, and heighten individuality. John Cotterell (1992) adds that for both male and female adolescents, the strength of attachment to teachers is associated with young people's positive feelings about themselves. Note the interplay here between developmental forces, notably adolescent cognitive functioning and the Eriksonian challenge of identity formation.

It is especially important for teachers to help teenagers achieve a sense of identity because the educational process tends to manufacture high levels of conformity. This may explain why so many adolescents are without any commitment to self, morally parochial, and compliant. It may also explain, in part, why identity foreclosure is so common at this age.

A possible solution to this may be the development of a curriculum that is suited to each individual's capacity to absorb, rather than follow prearranged outlines. Treating the adolescent in a mature fashion and teaching the importance of responsibility are also important. The school needs to represent an environment where the adolescent can develop each day. All too often, teachers forget how many times the adolescent can be regarded as an adult, treating them instead with childish protectiveness and circumventing them with restrictions. Often, adolescents react to such measures with predictable behaviors: apathy, passive resignation, and rebellion.

The most favorable attitudes and greatest learning readiness evolve when students perceive that their teachers are interested in them as well as the subject material being taught. In an ideal setting, the two can discuss not only academics, but also the student's career ambitions, interests, and goals. Should this result, the teacher looms as an instrumental force in shaping the adolescent's mental awareness and nurturing the development of dignity and self-respect.

Peer Group Influences on the Developing Adolescent

As the need to be recognized and accepted magnifies during adolescence, the peer group becomes a critical agent of socialization. With the teenagers' dependence on the family lessened, replacement security is found among peers who share similar feelings and attitudes. Adolescence thus becomes a critical time for developing friendships and becoming a member of a meaningful peer group. Such social networks supply important psychological benefits to adolescents, including feelings of trust, acceptance, and companionship (Cotterell, 1992; Romig & Bakken, 1992; Wintre et al., 1988).

Teenagers' interactions with peers continue to be heavily influenced by their developing social cognition abilities. More specifically, their advanced mental abilities enhance their interpersonal awareness. For instance, adolescence is the time when individuals can share, empathize, and understand the perspectives of others (Buhrmester, Goldfarb, & Cantrell, 1992). As a result, teenagers become more sensitive to the needs of others. Adolescents are also able to develop expectations about friendships and make psychological inferences about

THEORETICAL ISSUES

Employing an ecological perspective, how do you think teenagers and their families are influenced by interactions involving the mesosystem and exosystem? Do you think minority adolescents encounter different interactions involving these two systems? How do you think the macrosystem impacts on the lives of adolescents, such as in educational values, goals, and resources?

Focus on Diversity

COLLEGE-BOUND MINORITY ADOLESCENTS

What role does higher education play in the lives of African-American and Hispanic adolescents? Today, the percentage of African Americans attending college is around 20%; the percentage of Hispanics enrolled in institutions of higher education is about 16%. These figures compare with just over about 30% of whites enrolled in college, and represent a decrease in enrollment figures from the previous decade. This decline in college attendance may be linked to cuts in student aid for minorities and the rapidly increasing costs of college tuition.

African-American women in the 1990s are more likely to attend college than African-American men. During the previous decade, the percentage of African-American women going on to college continued a modest increase; the percentage of African-American men in college declined. Among whites, the percentages in college also are slightly higher for women; however, the gap between the sexes is much smaller.

White students are twice as likely as African Americans to graduate from college. About 20% of whites ultimately earn a degree, compared

people, cognitive capacities that eluded them earlier (Buhrmester, 1990; Clark & Ayers, 1988; Kelly & deArmas, 1989; Youniss & Haynie, 1992).

Adolescents typically do not want to be perceived as being different from one another. As a result, they tend to conform closely to established peer group norms. Eager to attain social acceptance, adolescents pay close attention to current fads, such as length of hair, style of dress, and popular activities. They are also acutely aware of the types of behavior that will earn peer approval (Berndt & Perry, 1990; Urberg, 1992).

Susan O'Brien and Karen Bierman (1988) have supplied insight into how the peer group influences adolescent behavior. In their study, 72 fifth, eighth, and eleventh graders were interviewed to investigate developmental changes in perceptions of peer groups and group influence. Younger subjects defined groups on the basis of common activities and social behavior and considered group influence to be greatest in these domains. Older adolescents were more likely to describe peer group influence as global and far-reaching, affecting one's appearance, attitudes, and values. Older adolescents, more so than the younger subjects, felt that peer group acceptance or rejection influenced self-evaluation.

Patterns of Peer Group Interaction   Observe any adolescent social setting, whether it be a high school rock concert, a weekend sporting event, or any number of after-school activities, and you're likely to witness several socialization processes: the development of close-knit friendships, cliques, and crowds. Such gatherings represent elite and exclusive socialization processes. Membership is frequently determined on the basis of similarity in such areas as social class, interest areas (such as style of dress), use of slang, athletics, and intellectual abilities.

A **friendship** is the smallest type of peer group and is the pairing off of two individuals who are likely to have similar personalities and temperaments.

with just over 10% of African Americans. Between 1977 and 1987, the number of African Americans completing a bachelor's degree declined by 3% while the number of college-age African Americans increased by 31%. The racial differences were considerably greater for the more advanced master's or doctoral degrees. Such developments do not bode well for the entrance of more African Americans into the higher paying, higher status occupations.

One positive indicator of black educational progress should be noted: The number of African Americans earning professional degrees in medicine and law increased by 35% between 1977 and 1987. The total number of professional degrees awarded to African Americans remains fairly small, however. In 1987, nearly 3,500 profes- sional degrees were awarded to African Americans, 883 more than in 1977. The share of all these degrees going to African Americans changed little, from 4 to 5%, even though the dominance of whites fell from 92 to 89%. Other minorities—Hispanics, Asians, and American Indians—have succeeded in gaining an even larger share of these high-status degrees over the past decade. This reflects, at least in part, the rapid growth of other minority groups during the last decade, but it also signals a slowdown in the educational advancement of African Americans. (Adapted from O'Hare et al., 1991)

Usually, early teenage friendships are based on shared interests and activities. This is also true of older adolescents' friendships, but they are also accompanied by a strong emotional bond and psychological commitment between the partners. Females are more drawn to emotional and intimate aspects of a friendship. For this reason, female friendships are said to be "face to face," and male friendships are "side to side" (Eaton, Mitchell, & Jolley, 1991; Parker & Gottman, 1989; Rawlins, 1993).

Similar to the friendship, but larger in size, is the **clique.** Cliques usually consist of three or more persons who have common interests and a strong emotional attachment to one another. The clique is highly exclusive, usually consisting of adolescents of the same socioeconomic background who hold similar interests, attitudes, and beliefs. Usually, members of a clique come into contact daily, such as in school or neighborhood cliques.

Finally, we come to the **crowd.** Although the crowd is more impersonal and lacks the strong bonds of attachment that cliques offer, it maintains rather rigid membership requirements. Being a member of a clique is often a prerequisite for crowd membership. The distinguishing features of crowds are heterosexual interaction, and emphasis is often on social events, such as athletic contests, concerts, and dances. However, crowds often have no planned activities. Many crowds congregate in a meeting place popular with all members, such as a parking lot, street corner, or neighborhood park.

Gender Differences in Adolescent Friendships   From the adolescent years on, the behavioral dimensions of female and male friendships acquire unique characteristics. Let us first examine the importance of intimacy, an ingredient of friendships that increases during this time. A number of researchers (e.g., Berndt & Perry, 1990; Buhrmester, 1990; Shaughnessy & Shakesby, 1992) write that intimacy becomes a cornerstone for meaningful relationships, not only during adolescence but throughout the course of adult life.

The peer group is an indispensable source of approval, support, and security.

Females tend to have more intimate and exclusive friendships than males do. Moreover, the closer the female's friendships are, the more revealing her self-disclosure will be. This is often true regardless of whether females are interacting with the same or the opposite sex. Males, on the other hand, tend to downplay intimate self-disclosure and the emotional closeness of a relationship. Their emphasis is, rather, on such things as interest in the same activities (Borisoff, 1993; Lederman, 1993; Rawlins, 1993; Victor, 1993).

The notion that there are gender differences in the intimacy of self-disclosure has received considerable research attention. In one study (Grigsby & Weatherley, 1983), female and male adolescents were involved in a deception that led them to believe they were sharing self-disclosures with a stranger of the same sex whom they would later meet. The recorded comments revealed clear-cut gender differences in the tendency to self-disclose. Clearly, females were more likely to disclose revealing information about themselves during the acquaintanceship process.

There are other differences in regard to female and male friendships. For example, Deborah Tannen (1990) believes that females, more than males, expect to share thoughts and feelings with their partners. Along these lines, females' communication style centers around affiliation and reassurance whereas that of males centers around dominance and competition. Such themes tend to create gender differences in listening behavior. Males are often taught to listen for facts, and females are taught to listen for the mood of the communication. Males thus often have trouble listening for nonverbal cues, whereas females, who are listening for the mood of the communication, pick them up much more readily (Booth-Butterfield, 1984; Matlin, 1993; Tannen, 1990).

Other researchers (e.g., Santilli & Hudson, 1992) have found that females are more adept at social perspective-taking; females also tend to learn how to communicate with close friends sooner (Rawlins, 1993). Carol Gilligan (1982) adds that females are also likely to be more selective and exclusive in their friendships. This may be because once they have found a friend, females are more apt to invest their resources emotionally and offer a strong psychological commitment to their partner. The commitment from males is often not as great and is more objective and rational. Thus females tend to reside in the emotional plane whereas males inhabit the realm of ideas and facts rather than feelings (Borisoff, 1993; Pearson & Davilla, 1993).

In regard to these gender differences in friendships, we should acknowledge the viewpoints of Sharon Brehm (1992). She finds that both males and females need the same qualities in their interactions in order to avoid loneliness. Males usually desire emotional intimacy just as much as females do. But unfortunately, it is often difficult for them to express this and to achieve interpersonal comfort and acceptance with their partners.

GENDER SIMILARITIES AND DIFFERENCES

How important do you think gender-role learning is during adolescence? Do you think the peer group is more influential in shaping gender-role learning now than during earlier life stages? During later life stages?

Adolescent Sexual Behavior

Few topics about the development of adolescents arouse more curiosity than their sexual behavior. The most consistent research finding is that teenagers' attitudes toward sex have become more relaxed and tolerant in recent decades. As American society has moved from an antisex to a prosex orientation, that change has become quite obvious in teenage dating patterns. In this chapter, we explore some of these patterns as they exist in heterosexual relationships. In the next chapter, coverage is extended to some of the dynamics apparent in gay and lesbian relationships.

Dating generally begins during the teenage years. It is especially popular in the United States, and American teenagers begin dating earlier than teenagers in other countries. Over the years, the complexion of dating has changed for both adolescents and adults. In the past, dating was a structured and formal affair, profoundly affected by traditional gender-role stereotyping. The male usually took the initiative to ask the female out, provided transportation, and absorbed all of the expenses. Although traditional behaviors still exist, dating is more casual today, especially among the teenage population, and many couples share expenses and the transportation involved. Some females even take the initiative to ask the male out (Arliss, 1993; Cate & Lloyd, 1992; Dickinson & Leming, 1990; Lauer & Lauer, 1991; Zinn & Eitzen, 1990).

Patterns of Dating and Courtship   In general, females start dating earlier than males. They also tend to have different attitudes about dating. Although anxious about dating during the early stages of adolescence, females tend to exhibit deep understanding, sensitivity, and emotional involvement toward their partners by late adolescence. Males, meanwhile, often deemphasize the emotional and intimate features of the relationship. Thus gender differences in adolescent intimate involvement tend to reflect the patterns we described earlier

Dating helps teach adolescents the importance of reciprocity, mutuality, and sensitivity toward others.

(Arliss & Borisoff, 1993; Berndt & Perry, 1990; Parker & Gottman, 1989; Tannen, 1990).

Adolescents look for certain qualities in a date. Physical attractiveness is equally important for both males and females, as are personality and compatibility. How prestigious a date is appears to be more important for females. This latter consideration might be linked to the fact that females, more than males, view dating as a way to increase their popularity and status in the peer group. Finally, both males and females value honesty and the degree to which a partner can bring companionship and enjoyment to a relationship (Cate & Lloyd, 1992; Duck, 1991; Lerner & Lerner, 1989).

Laurie Arliss (1993) writes that given the traditional gender-role behaviors that abound during this stage of life, adolescents typically develop different expectations and impressions of romantic interaction. Traditional females tend to emphasize getting noticed by males, often by one special male. Many begin to fantasize about true, lasting love. A good deal of the time, female adolescents are devoted to the refinement of appearance through hairstyles, makeup, clothes, and the like. *Who* one dates may well be the most important determinant of status. In line with stereotypic myths, athletes, social leaders, and those with material possessions are believed to be good catches.

According to Arliss (1993), traditional males are also concerned with their appearances, although some do not primp publicly. Many males choose to emphasize overt signs of maturity, strength, and athleticism as evaluated by their male peers. Often, talk of athletic achievements dominates their conversations, but adolescent males, similar to females, also confide in friends about the opposite sex. Lasting love is seldom a theme in the conversations of traditional adolescent males. Instead, males choose to emphasize sexual activity in their discussions. When they do discuss females, males tend to focus on the topic of sexual activity. In this sense, *who* you date may be significant for males as well as females, but *how you did* on the date is more apt to be the most important factor in gaining status for males.

More serious dating may lead to going steady (also simply called "seeing" or "going with" someone). Although the meaning of this type of relationship varies from couple to couple, going steady generally implies a rather permanent relationship in which both parties refrain from dating others. In general, going steady is more common today than in the past and it also begins earlier in the lives of teenagers. Many teenagers go steady as early as age 14 or 15.

Compared to random, casual dating, going steady has its share of advantages. One of the more practical benefits is that dates are assured, which promotes a sense of security for many adolescents. Going steady also encourages independence and practice with interpersonal communication skills. In this sense, going steady teaches adolescents the importance of openness, feedback, and conflict resolution skills, all important prerequisites to marriage.

There are disadvantages to going steady, too. Exclusive dating arrangements reduce the adolescent's heterosexual experiences and many times remove the teenager from same-sex peers, which may restrict the adolescent's overall social development. Going steady also promotes the escalation of physical intimacy, which often leads to sexual intercourse before the partners are ready for it. This in turn increases the risk of teenage pregnancy and premature marriage.

Rates of Sexual Activity   Rates of sexual activity among adolescents in the United States have dramatically increased over the past three decades. Most adolescents in the United States have become sexually active by age 19, although rates of coital activity are usually higher for men, especially among African Americans (Brooks-Gunn & Furstenberg, 1989; Centers for Disease Control, 1992b; London, Masher, Pratt, & Williams, 1989; Mott & Haurin, 1988; National Research Council, 1987; Walsh, 1989). One study (Moore & Peterson, 1989) estimates that 80% of both white and African-American women have engaged in coital activity by this age. Another investigation (Sonenstein, Pleck, & Ku, 1989) shows that among men, 85% of white, 96% of African-American, and 82% of Hispanic 19-year-olds were sexually active.

It is important to point out that most of the increase in female sexual activity in the past decade was among white adolescents and those in higher income families, narrowing the previous racial, ethnic, and income differences (London et al., 1989; Moore & Peterson, 1989). One source (Voydanoff & Donnelly, 1990) points out that the percentages of sexually active female adolescents tended to peak for African-American women in the 1970s, although they continue to increase for white females. Thus although rates are consistently higher for African-American adolescent women, over the past 10 years a leveling off or even a decrease has become apparent.

Other studies, although not reporting as high percentages as those just cited, nonetheless illustrate how widespread adolescent coital activity is. For example, in one survey (Mott & Haurin, 1988) 68% of females and 78% of males reported having premarital intercourse by age 19. An investigation (Pratt et al., 1984) of adolescent females between the ages of 15 and 19 revealed that by their 19th birthday, over one half of the respondents reported having sexual intercourse. In this study, the proportion engaging in intercourse rose steadily with age, from 18% at age 15, to 29% at age 16, to 40% at age 17, to 54% at age 18, and to 66% at age 19. The proportions engaging in regular sexual relations were lower, but nonetheless substantial. About 25% of those aged 15 to 17 engaged in regular sexual intercourse, but this figure escalated to 49% among those aged 18 and 19. Another survey (Coles & Stokes, 1985) of over 1,000 adolescent males and females unveiled that rates of premarital intercourse were about equal between the sexes: 53% of the females and 46% of the males reported having had intercourse by age 18.

In a more recent investigation (Centers for Disease Control, 1992b) of adolescent males and females between the ages of 15 and 18, over 50% of the respondents reported ever having had sexual intercourse. Almost 40% reported having had sexual intercourse during the 3 months preceding the survey. Males were significantly more likely than females to ever have had sexual intercourse (60% and 48%, respectively) and to have had sexual intercourse during the 3 months preceding the survey (42% and 36%, respectively). The percentage of adolescents ever having had sexual intercourse and having experienced coitus during the 3 months preceding the survey increased significantly with age.

Many teenagers have their first coital experience at early ages. Research gathered by the Alan Guttmacher Institute (1991) shows that in 1982, 19% of unmarried women aged 15 had experienced intercourse; in 1988, this figure had increased to 27%. Another investigation (Pratt, 1990) disclosed that by age 15, about one quarter of the females surveyed had coital experience, but by age 19 the statistic jumped to about four out of five. In another study involving male and female adolescents (mean age of 13.9 years), 28% reported having sexual intercourse at least once (Scott-Jones & White, 1990).

One investigation (Zelnick et al., 1981) examined the sexual behavior of adolescent females between the ages of 15 and 19 and found that the time of first intercourse was about age 16. Partners tended to be about 3 years older than the females, and about 80% of those females who had been sexually active for 4 or more years had more than one partner. Intercourse took place about three times per month. Another study (Zelnick & Shah, 1983) revealed that the average female adolescent had her first coital experience at 16.2 years of age; the corresponding male figure was 15.7 years.

There are many motives for sexual intimacy among adolescents.

It is important to point out that those adolescents who engage in coital activity at early ages are less likely than those who have intercourse at later ages to use effective contraception (Brooks-Gunn & Furstenberg, 1989; Faulkenberry et al., 1987; Moore & Peterson, 1989). For example, one study (Sonenstein, Pleck, & Ku, 1989) found that rates of condom use were lower and rates of ineffective or no method use were higher for adolescents initiating coital activity before age 15 as compared with those initiating between the ages of 15 and 19. As the accompanying Lifespan Development in Action box shows, consistently and correctly using latex condoms and spermicides are important safer sex guidelines that reduce the risk of infection from sexually transmitted diseases.

Finally, it should be pointed out that few adolescents experience coital activity only once. Research shows (Miller & Moore, 1990; Moore & Peterson, 1989; Sonenstein, Pleck, & Ku, 1989) that over two thirds of adolescents experience sex again within 6 months of first intercourse. One investigation (Alan Guttmacher Institute, 1991) discloses that about 6 in 10 sexually active adolescent females between the ages of 15 and 19 reported having had two or more sexual partners. An investigation (National Center for Health Statistics, 1991) reports that among those adolescent females who initiated sexual intercourse before age 18, 75% reported having two or more partners and 45% reported having had four or more partners. Also, a study of 15- to 18-year-old adolescents (Anderson et al., 1990) reveals that among those having had sexual intercourse, 40% reported four or more partners. Finally, research (Cates, 1991) tells us that one quarter of females who began sexual activity by age 15 had 10 or more lifetime sex partners, compared to less than 6% of those beginning coitus at age 20.

Implications of Adolescent Sexual Activity   The research just cited illustrates how widespread coital activity is among today's adolescents. These studies also bring to light three areas of concern regarding the sexually active adolescent: pregnancy, abortion, and the risk of contracting a sexually transmitted disease. Let's examine each of these areas more closely.

ADOLESCENT PREGNANCY There are more than 1 million pregnancies a year among adolescent females in the United States today, and about 500,000 give birth to their babies. Although the overall birthrate among teenage mothers tended to stabilize during the last decade, the birthrate among 15- to 17-year-old adolescents now is on the increase. Today, approximately 1 out of every 10 teenagers will become a mother by her 19th birthday. Many adolescents become pregnant in their early or middle teens, about 30,000 of them each year under age 15. If present trends continue, it is estimated that 40% of today's 14-year-old females will be pregnant at least once before the age of 20. Currently, adolescents in the United States have one of the highest pregnancy rates in the Western world—twice as high as in England and Wales, France, and Canada; three times as high as in Sweden; and seven times as high as in the Netherlands (Alan Guttmacher Institute, 1989, 1991; Henshaw & Van Vort, 1989; Rickel, 1989; Roosa, 1991).

Pregnancy rates are higher for African-American than white adolescent females (Dash, 1989; Franklin, 1988). Particularly disturbing is the fact that approximately one half of all African-American adolescent females are estimated to become pregnant at least once before turning 20 (Forrest, 1986; Hayes,

THEORETICAL ISSUES

If an adolescent is engaging in coitus to bolster an ego or to feel wanted and loved, how can principles of behaviorism be applied? Can social learning theory be used to study those sexually active adolescents influenced by the media or peers? If teenagers maintain that the rewards of coitus outweigh the risks involved, might exchange theory be used as a potential theoretical framework?

Lifespan Development in Action

RESPONSIBLE SEX: HOW TO PROTECT YOURSELF FROM STD INFECTION

Prevention is the best way to minimize the risks associated with STDs. *At the cornerstone of sexual health and well-being is individual responsibility and intelligent and informed decision making.* By intelligent and informed decision making, we mean building a foundation of knowledge and applying that information on a regular basis. (The most current information regarding STDs is available from the National STD Information Hot Line, 1-800-227-8922.)

A recurrent theme in the literature today is "safer sex" and the prevention of STDs (Bingham, 1989; Fogel, 1990; Fogel, Forker, & Welch, 1990; Smith, Lauver, & Gray, 1990; Whipple & Ogden, 1989). Sexual freedom has become a way of life in modern society, and we have seen how casual sexual relationships have resulted in an increased number of illnesses and infections. Thus learning how to protect oneself and one's partner from STDs is vitally important. To this end, we recommend the following safer sex guidelines to reduce the risks of contracting an STD:

- Two uninfected, mutually monogamous partners run the least risk of anyone for STDs, but even they can contract infections through such avenues as drug use, poor personal hygiene, or blood transfusions. In any case, it is advisable for each partner to be tested for asymptomatic infection at the beginning of the relationship.
- Unless you and your partner are in a long-term, mutually monogamous relationship and uninfected to the best of your knowledge, always use a latex condom for intercourse—either a condom prelubricated with spermicide or a condom in conjunction with spermicidal cream, jelly, or foam.
- Talk with—and examine—any new or nonmonogamous partner for oral or genital warts, blisters, ulcers, rashes, or discharges. This isn't the most romantic thing in the world to do, but it may help you avoid becoming infected. If you discover any signs of possible infection, avoid sexual intimacy until a clinician has examined and treated the person if necessary. Get into the habit of asking (and disclosing) information about previous partners and infections once it is clear a new relationship might become sexual.
- Avoid oral-anal and finger-anal contact. If finger-anal or instrument-anal contact occurs, wash the contaminated hand(s) or object(s) with soap and water before having any other oral or genital contact.
- The following sexual activities are low risk—that is, reasonably safe if no lesions are visible: hugging, massage, body contact, dry kissing, and masturbation in another's presence. But remember, only total abstinence with no body-to-body contact is 100% risk free.
- The following activities are possibly safe if no lesions are visible: vaginal or anal intercourse with a latex condom, fellatio with a latex condom, cunnilingus with a rubber barrier, hand- or finger-to-genital contact (mutual masturbation) with a rubber glove, and kissing with an open mouth.

Continued . . .

> **RESPONSIBLE SEX: HOW TO PROTECT YOURSELF FROM STD INFECTION,**
> Continued . . .
>
> - The following activity is considered risky: hand- or finger-to-genital contact without a glove.
> - The following sexual activities are definitely high risk for STD transmission unless you are absolutely certain that neither you nor your partner has any infections: vaginal intercourse without a condom, fellatio, cunnilingus, a partner's semen or urine touching a mucous membrane (vagina, rectum, urethra, mouth, or eye), oral-anal contact, blood contact (including menstrual blood or blood transferred by sharing IV needles), and sharing sex toys that have had contact with body fluids without washing them. The highest risk of all is receptive anal intercourse without a latex condom. (Adapted from Hatcher et al., 1990; Turner & Rubinson, 1993)

1987; O'Hare et al., 1991). One source (Henshaw & Van Vort, 1989) discloses that in 1985, the pregnancy rate of 18.6% for African-American adolescent females between the ages of 15 to 19 was twice that of the 9.3% rate for whites. Racial differences are greatest for adolescents under age 15, 5.1% for African Americans and 0.9% for white women. Adolescent pregnancy rates are also disturbingly high among Hispanics (Lopez, 1987).

There are many health risks for the children of adolescent mothers (see the accompanying Focus on Diversity box for a cross-cultural look at these risks). For example, the younger the mother is, the greater the chances of infant death. Adolescent mothers are more apt to have premature births than older mothers and are more likely to experience labor and delivery complications, including toxemia and anemia. The babies themselves often have low birth weights and frequently suffer from neurological problems and birth defects. Children of adolescent mothers also tend to have lower IQs and perform more poorly in school than children of older mothers (Franklin, 1988; Furstenberg, Brooks-Gunn, & Chase-Lansdale, 1989; Giblin et al., 1989).

Children also introduce drastic changes and disruptions into the lives of adolescents, their offspring, their parents, and the society as a whole. Many adolescent parents lack a supportive family as well as parenting skills (Davis, 1989; Jones & Battle, 1990; Thomas et al., 1990). Adolescent mothers also cost the taxpayers huge sums of money each year and, in addition, they often face social disapproval and financial hardships. Moreover, those adolescents who marry have an exceptionally high divorce rate (Furstenberg, Brooks-Gunn, & Chase-Lansdale, 1989; Lockhart & Wodarski, 1990; Miller & Moore, 1990; Teti & Lamb, 1989).

ABORTION Of the approximately 1 million adolescents who become pregnant annually, about 45% have abortions. Adolescents have about one quarter of all abortions performed in the United States, and this overall rate more than doubles that of any other nation. Abortion rates are higher for black female adolescents than white female adolescents between the ages of 15 to 19. The ratio of abortions to live births, however, is generally similar among black and white female adolescents. The higher rates of abortion among African-American

Focus on Diversity

CHILDREN HAVING CHILDREN: THE RISKS OF TEENAGE PREGNANCY

In cultures all around the world, the consequences of adolescent pregnancy and child rearing are dramatic. The most obvious set of risks are health related. Mothers under age 20, as a group, suffer more pregnancy and delivery complications than women who bear children at age 20 or later. Problems reported from diverse parts of the world include higher than average levels of toxemia, anemia, bleeding, cervical trauma, disproportion between the size of the infant's head and the mother's pelvis, prolonged and difficult labor, and death. The risk of a teenage mother developing such problems, though, are greater in developing than in developed nations, and greater among those from lower socioeconomic brackets within countries.

Worldwide, pregnancy-related deaths are the primary cause of death among females between the ages of 15 and 19. In Sierra Leone, Africa, the 15 to 28 age group accounts for almost 40% of pregnancy-related complications. Poor living conditions in that country, as well as inadequate nutrition, prenatal care, and health education, aggravate the risks compared to developed nations. In most Latin American and Caribbean countries, childbearing and abortion are ranked in the top five causes of death for 15- to 19-year-old women, with the phenomenon most common in Jamaica. In Bangladesh, birth-related complications, including those developing from abortion, are the leading cause of death among teenage women.

Furthermore, pregnancy-related mortality rates are higher for teenagers than for older women in developed countries. In Canada, as an illustration, they are twice as high. Maternal mortality rates for females under 16 in England are four times the overall rate for older women. Additionally, many women are attributable to higher pregnancy rates rather than to a greater likelihood of ending a pregnancy through abortion (Children's Defense Fund, 1988; Hayes, 1987; Henshaw & Van Vort, 1989; Voydanoff & Donnelly, 1990).

Researchers have been able to establish a profile of the adolescent female choosing abortion. For example, she is likely to be enrolled in school and doing well, and is usually from a middle- or upper-socioeconomic bracket. The adolescent female who uses illicit drugs is also more apt to obtain an abortion. Conversely, the adolescent female who chooses not to abort is usually poor, has friends or relatives who had children as teenagers, and emerges from a very religious family (Henshaw & Silverman, 1988; Leibowitz, Eisen, & Chow, 1986; Yamaguchi & Kandell, 1987).

The overall rise in teenage abortion rates is due to many factors, including legalization of abortion and its overall accessibility (Korenbrot, Brindis, & Priddy, 1990; Nathanson & Kim, 1989). Unmarried adolescents who marry during pregnancy are less likely to seek an abortion whereas teenagers receiving support for abortion from their boyfriends are more likely to elect abortion. Significant others beyond one's partner are also influential in the decision to abort. For instance, support for abortion from family members, especially the adolescent's own mother and sister, and from close friends, are important influences (Brazzell & Acock, 1988; Miller & Moore, 1990).

children born to teenage mothers suffer from reduced mental capability and psychological consequences. For example, many European babies born to teenage mothers suffer from slightly lower IQs, compared to children born to older mothers, and many are also at a greater risk for abuse and health hazards.

We must recognize, however, that many of the consequences just described are not related directly to age but rather to inadequate prenatal care and nutrition. For example, European adolescents having first births and who participate in special prenatal programs tend to have no greater obstetrical risks than adult women. Among Swedish teenage mothers, complications are no more frequent than with older mothers if they experience proper prenatal attention. The same holds true for teenage mothers in Kenya.

However, one of the most dramatic and long-term consequences of teenage pregnancy is the curtailment of a woman's education and vocational aspirations. In the United States, just over 60% of teenage mothers have not completed high school at the time of their child's birth. This does not mean all of these young women are high school dropouts. Many eventually receive a high school diploma. But women who bear children in their teens are less likely to go on to (or complete) college than those who delay childbearing, and they are more likely to suffer long-term economic consequences because of their lower skill levels.

Finally, developing as well as developed nations report lowered occupational status and reduced income as a direct result of curtailed education. In the United States and many European nations, women who are teenage mothers earn about 50% of the income of those who first gave birth in their 20s. Moreover, the cycle of poverty is influenced by this fertility pattern. That is, the children of teenage parents are more likely to become teenage parents themselves than those who were born when their parents were older (Ahlburg & DeVita, 1992; Ajayi, 1991; Boohene, 1991; Freedman, 1990; Harris, 1991; McCullough & Scherman, 1991; McKenry, Kotch, & Browne, 1991; Senderowitz & Paxman, 1985).

SEXUALLY TRANSMITTED DISEASES The association between early age of coital activity and greater numbers of both recent and lifetime sex partners represents a connection to a higher incidence rate of sexually transmitted diseases (STDs). Over 85% of all STDs occur among persons aged 15 to 29 years (Centers for Disease Control, 1990). Males and females who have multiple partners over a specified period (e.g., several months) are at an increased risk for gonorrhea, syphilis, chlamydia, and chancroid. Increased numbers of sex partners over a lifetime is also associated with a greater cumulative risk for acquiring viral infections such as hepatitis B, genital herpes, and the human immunodeficiency virus (HIV) (Aral & Holmes, 1990; Cates & Stone, 1992; Centers for Disease Control, 1992a; National Center for Health Statistics, 1991; Vail-Smith & White, 1992).

A few statistics can be used to illustrate the foregoing. For instance, the prevalence of gonorrhea, syphilis, and chlamydia among sexually active females shows that the highest rates of infection are among adolescents between 14 and 19 years of age (Centers for Disease Control, 1990). Genital warts, caused by the human papilloma virus (HPV) and one of the fastest growing STDs in the United States today, is particularly prevalent among sexually active adolescent females (Amschler, 1991). All of this runs contrary to the impression that STDs are a problem endemic to the adult population. Moreover, epidemiologic data

Adolescent pregnancy has a variety of implications for both mother and child.

indicate that the rate of STDs declines exponentially past the age of 19 years (DiClemente, 1990).

Minority adolescents have higher rates for STDs with rates for gonorrhea, pelvic inflammatory disease (PID), and syphilis substantially higher among African-American adolescents as compared to their white counterparts (Aral & Holmes, 1990; Cates, 1991). The average age-adjusted gonorrhea rate in African-American males age 15 to 19 years is approximately 15 times greater than that of white males, and that of African-American females in the same age group is approximately tenfold that of white females. The ratio of primary and secondary syphilis among African-American females is more than threefold greater than for white females, and the relative risk of death attributable to syphilis is more than three times greater for African-American than for white females. Rates for chlamydia are also substantially higher among African-American females as compared to white females (Aral & Holmes, 1990; Cates, 1990, 1991; Centers for Disease Control, 1990; DiClemente, 1990).

Infections caused by HIV are obviously the sexually transmitted diseases of greatest importance. Although relatively few persons develop AIDS as adolescents, this is a misleading picture. Approximately 20% of all AIDS cases have been diagnosed in the 20- to 29-year-old age group. Because the time between infection with HIV and the onset of AIDS symptoms is a median of 8 to 10 years, a large proportion of those aged 20 to 29 years diagnosed with AIDS were most likely infected with HIV as adolescents (Bingham, 1989; Boyer & Hein, 1991; Cates, 1991; DiClemente, 1990; Freudenberg, 1992; Friedman, 1992; Gayle et al., 1990; Hein, 1989a, 1989b; Rotheram-Borus & Koopman, 1991; Schinke, Holden, & Moncher, 1989).

Particularly disturbing is the fact that during 1991, the number of new cases of AIDS among 13- to 19-year-olds in the United States increased by 12%, compared to an 8% increase for adults of all ages. Rates of infection are highest among street and homeless teenagers who exchange sex for money or drugs (Freudenberg, 1992). As with other STDs, Hispanic and African-American teenagers are highly overrepresented among persons with AIDS. More specifically, they comprise more than one half of all adolescents and three quarters of all younger children (babies of infected parents) known to have the disease (Dryfoos, 1990).

Why Do Some Adolescents Practice Unsafe Sex?   Given the high rates of pregnancy, abortion, and STDs in their age group, why do so many young people engage in unsafe sex practices? Most sexually active adolescents do not consistently use any type of contraception, and many are misinformed about available birth control methods (Hayes, 1987; Hofferth & Hayes, 1987). Most adolescents of both sexes say they believe in responsible use of contraceptives, but few put this belief into practice (Chilman, 1988). This is especially true of male teenagers. Most of them are unwilling to assume any responsibility for contraception, although in recent years there has been some increase in condom use (Sonenstein, Pleck, & Ku, 1989). The younger they are, the more likely male adolescents are to view birth control as their partner's "problem." Moreover, many adolescents have a firm prejudice against condoms, even though condoms are a good method of preventing both pregnancy and STDs, especially HIV infection (Hofferth & Hayes, 1987; Jones et al., 1986; Kegeles, Adler, & Irwin, 1988; Pleck, 1989; Strunin & Hingston, 1987).

Contraceptive use varies according to age and other characteristics. One study (Morrison, 1985) that focused on contraceptive behavior among adolescents and young adults discovered that one third to two thirds of adolescents used no contraception at first intercourse. However, use increased with age and overall rates tended to be higher among young women. The reasons given for not using contraception ranged from erroneous beliefs about fertility, problems getting contraceptive devices, and the feeling that pregnancy wouldn't be such a negative event. Condoms and withdrawal were the most commonly used methods at first intercourse, but with experience, many adolescents shifted to oral contraceptives. Several researchers (Harlap, Kost, & Forrest, 1991; Hayes, 1987; Jones & Forrest, 1989) note the popularity of the pill among sexually active adolescents. However, we should note that oral contraceptives provide no protection against STDs.

One study (Sonenstein, Pleck, & Ku, 1989) of 15- to 19-year-old male adolescents found that 55% of them used a condom at first intercourse, 7% used an effective female method without a condom, and 38% used an ineffective method or no contraception at all. African-American male adolescents were less likely to use a condom and more likely to use an ineffective method or none at all at first intercourse than whites or Hispanic Americans. Rates of condom use were lower and rates of ineffective methods or no method were higher for adolescents who started coital activity before the age of 15 than for those who began between 15 and 19.

Utilizing material we covered earlier in this chapter, many adolescents seem to cling to the personal fable and believe they are invulnerable to the risks of pregnancy and of contracting a sexually transmitted disease. Others have difficulty understanding such issues as shared responsibility for contraception, birth control alternatives, and the consequences of unsafe sexual practices. Finally, some are simply too immature to envision the possibility of pregnancy. Debra Gordon's (1990) review of the literature indicates that the same kind of

THEORETICAL ISSUES

Think about how Elkind's concepts of the imaginary audience and the personal fable can be applied to the sexual behavior of adolescents, including sexual risk taking. For example, do you think the imaginary audience can help explain why many males insist on "one-upmanship" whenever exploits are shared and compared? Do you think the personal fable explains why they often perceive themselves as being invulnerable to STDs, including HIV infection?

immature thinking which prevents a lot of teenagers from understanding the needs of their sexual partners makes it impossible for them to grasp elementary probability theory. The fact that once a month, month after month, a woman continues to have the same probability of conceiving a child if she has sexual intercourse fails to get through to them. They think if they escaped pregnancy one month, they will be that lucky again and again. The inability to think maturely also prevents these teenagers from realistically weighing the alternatives when they do get pregnant (e.g., adoption, abortion, raising the child with the support of their family, establishing an independent household, marriage).

We believe adolescent sexuality education programs should take account of these common limitations in thinking skills. Educators need to recognize that although adolescents can usually grasp certain elements of sexuality education, others are more elusive. It is fairly easy, for example, for teenagers to understand the anatomy and physiology of the reproductive systems and facts about STDs. But personal and shared responsibility for safer sex practices and the psychological, reproductive, and social consequences of having intercourse at an early age are more abstract and not so easily understood.

For these reasons, sexuality education should seek to foster more sophisticated thinking and reasoning in adolescents. (As we pointed out earlier, though, not all individuals reach peak levels of cognitive maturity, which may make pedagogy such as this elusive. Should advanced mental faculties be only partially present, an important goal would be to enhance how they are employed.) Rather than tell teenagers *what* to think, we need to teach them *how* to think. To this end, programs should not only teach adolescents to systematically explore and evaluate alternatives, such as the range of contraceptive choices available, but also to analyze why safer sex practices are important. They should show teenagers how to overcome their tendencies to impulsiveness. Research (e.g., Victor, Halverson, & Montague, 1985) reveals that the ability to use reflective cognitive strategies promotes more deliberate and cautious behavior.

Sexuality educators should also focus on overcoming the teenage myth of invulnerability. As we've noted, many adolescents cling to the personal fable and do not perceive a personal risk in their dangerous behaviors. To take one example, AIDS will not be eliminated merely by providing young people with concrete facts about how the disease is passed on. As Debra Haffner (1989) aptly shows, adolescents tend to take risks even when they are well informed about the theoretical consequences of their behavior. It is better, therefore, to emphasize concrete strategies to alter the motivations and attitudes behind so much adolescent risk taking. Areas that should be covered are chance and probability (e.g., helping adolescents to understand the real chances of becoming pregnant and of getting an STD when they engage in unprotected intercourse), sexual decision making (e.g., assertiveness training and learning how to say no), sexual alternatives (e.g., noncoital expressions of sexual intimacy), and negotiation strategies (e.g., how to bring up and effectively discuss safer sex practices with partners).

Adolescents also benefit from learning cognitive skills aimed at relationship building, including the ability to communicate. Effective contraceptive use is often linked to good communication between partners (Cvetkovich & Grote, 1983; Herold & McNamee, 1982; Milan & Kilman, 1987). Cognitive enrichment techniques also help adolescents understand such important abstract qualities

Among other functions, adolescent sexuality education seeks to prevent problems such as sexually transmitted diseases and unwanted pregnancies.

of a sexual relationship as reciprocity, mutuality, sensitivity, and empathy. As Catherine Chilman (1990) points out, the typical adolescent finds it hard to form a close, value-compatible egalitarian relationship because these relational qualities require the kind of advanced thinking they have not yet learned. Learning about such relational qualities provides numerous rewards (Weinstein & Rosen, 1991). For example, maturing adolescents are able to see sexual activity as an expression of closeness, respect, and sensuality, as well as to take responsibility both for themselves and for their partner. This view enriches their intimate relationships.

Advanced cognitive skills make shared contraceptive responsibility possible because they move the adolescent away from an egocentric style of thinking. Interestingly, research (e.g., MacCorquodale, 1984; Rosen & Ager, 1981) shows that nontraditional gender roles are associated with more consistent contraceptive use. Sexuality education should combat the idea that contraception is solely a female responsibility by using role-reversal or perspective-taking exercises. The common male notion that condoms are outmoded or inhibit sexual pleasure should be challenged through concrete reasoning. Both sexes need to be shown that condoms offer excellent protection against both unwanted pregnancies and STDs (Conant et al., 1986; DiClemente, 1990; Goedert, 1987; Kegeles, Adler, & Irwin, 1988; Reitmeijer et al., 1988).

Sexuality education programs that emphasize abstinence-based prevention (Christopher & Roosa, 1990; Moyse-Steinberg, 1990; Roosa & Christopher, 1990; Shornack & Ahmed, 1989) can also benefit from a cognitive enrichment format in such areas as how and why to defer sexual activity, values clarification (including asserting one's beliefs and learning to say no), and problem solving and decision making.

Finally, a cognitive enrichment format is useful in intervention efforts for pregnant teenagers and teenage parents. It has been shown (Baranowski, Schilmoeller, & Higgins, 1990; Cervera, 1991; Hanson, 1990; Rubenstein, Panzarine, & Lanning, 1990; Thomas, Rickel, & Butler, 1990) that adolescents benefit from a sophisticated cognitive approach to pregnancy resolution and the development of parenting skills. Pregnant adolescents are taught how to use reflective thinking skills to explore such issues as abortion and adoption. For those adolescents who decide to keep their babies, the cognitive approach emphasizes problem-solving skills (geared to the problems posed by infants and children), perspective-taking capacities (geared to reducing egocentrism and learning how to take the child's point of view), and decision-making abilities (geared to envisioning parenting alternatives).

Values and Adolescent Sexual Relationships   As we bring this unit to a close, we examine the impact of values on the sexual relationships of adolescents. Values are an important integrating force of men's and women's sexuality and influential in shaping the course of close relationships. A *value* is a conceptual structure of a prescriptive nature, representing a person's beliefs about what is appropriate or inappropriate, desirable or undesirable. Important determinants of one's values are moral values, ethical standards of right and wrong that guide decision making and overall standards of conduct. Related to sexual relationships, values combine to produce a value system, a framework that enables people to appraise, explain, and integrate sex-related situations. In a broad sense, a sexual value system is a set of assumptions that shapes a person's sexual life.

We feel that developing mature and responsible sexual values is important during adolescence, particularly in light of the escalating rates of premarital intercourse and assortment of risks just presented. The selection of values to guide one's sexual life is a multifaceted process, one that follows a sequential pattern. Initially a person may be confronted with an issue that stimulates her to form an opinion of what is good and bad, right and wrong. Some such issues are the acceptability of premarital intercourse, the practice of safer sex guidelines, the notion of shared contraceptive responsibility, the "fairness" of traditional gender-role behaviors, and the desirability of same-sex relationships. When a person confronts such an issue, she usually recognizes the need to establish some type of sexual value. Beyond consulting one's existing sexual value system (which consists, at this point, of values that one has been taught), one may solicit input from family, friends, teachers, or other sources of socialization. The values gathered are then compared and contrasted, and one is ultimately chosen. The choice reflects the most suitable standard for that person for the time being, and usually reflects the following dimensions or characteristics (Fogel, 1990):

- The value has been chosen from the available alternatives.
- The value has been selected with knowledge of the consequences involved.
- The value has been chosen freely, without coercion.
- The value is prized and cherished by the person.
- The value will be publicly affirmed when appropriate.
- The value will be acted upon and become a consistent behavior pattern.

Our discussion has implied that values may be extrinsic or intrinsic. *Extrinsic values* are derived from society's standards of right or wrong and are usually grounded in intellectual conviction. Because extrinsic values typically are a conception of the ideal, they are sometimes limited in their practical application. *Intrinsic values,* on the other hand, derive from personal experience and are the beliefs that govern a person's everyday behavior. Because there may be a gap between people's extrinsic and intrinsic values, it is important to examine both what a person says and how that person actually behaves. The husband who extols agape love outside of the family but batters his wife, and the woman who promotes the value of self-disclosure but always keeps her problems to herself, reflect discrepancies between their conceived and their operative values.

Sexual Value Orientations   Every society has sought to regulate and control human sexuality. According to John DeLamater (1989), the social controls of sexual expression are intertwined with the basic institutions of society, such as religion and the family. Religion offers a set of shared values and rituals that reinforce social solidarity; the family fills society's need to regulate sexual behavior and reproduction and ensure that young children are cared for and socialized properly. To these two ancient institutions we can add the more modern educational institution, which is charged with socializing young people with regard to sexuality, and the medical institution, which evaluates sexual behavior on a healthy-unhealthy dimension. Finally, more informal socialization agents, such as peers and the media, are also instrumental in shaping people's sexual values.

It is from socialization frameworks such as these that sexual value orientations or ideologies emerge: sets of assumptions about the purpose(s) of sexual activity and its place in human life. Such orientations represent the basis for norms that specify what types of activity are appropriate and inappropriate, and what types of persons are appropriate partners for sexual activity (DeLamater, 1989; Walsh, 1989). The following are some of the more common sexual value orientations or ideologies that may offer guidelines for people making decisions about their sexuality.

ASCETIC ORIENTATION The roots of the **ascetic orientation** in the West can be traced back to early Christianity. Essentially, the ascetic orientation, also known as celibacy, advocates sexual self-denial, the avoidance of all sexual activity, and the implementation of spiritual self-discipline. Rather than sexual involvement, emphasis is placed on developing the romantic and spiritual facets of a relationship.

PROCREATIONAL ORIENTATION The **procreational orientation,** another Christian ideology, emphasizes that coital activity is acceptable only within marriage for the purpose of having children. This orientation also views any behavior other than vaginal intercourse as undesirable. Most religions in the United States espouse a procreational, somewhat ascetic, sexual value orientation.

RELATIONAL ORIENTATION The **relational orientation,** also called "person-centered" sexuality or "permissiveness with affection," views sexual activity as a natural extension of intimate relationships. Although coital activity within casual relationships is considered wrong, sexual intercourse is acceptable if accompanied by love and emotional attachment between partners. Indeed, sexual intimacy within a committed relationship is perceived as enhancing emotional attachment.

SITUATIONAL ORIENTATION The **situational orientation,** made popular by humanist Joseph Fletcher in his book *Situation Ethics* (1966), suggests that sexual decision making should take place in the context of the particular situation and people involved. Rather than making decisions about sexual matters solely

INTERRELATEDNESS OF AGING PROCESSES

What cognitive faculties do you think are needed to create and maintain meaningful values? Do you think those teenagers who successfully resolve the Eriksonian psychosocial stages of identity versus role confusion are likely to become aware of the personal significance of the values they hold (as opposed to their absolute meaning)? Is it more likely that sound values help guide a person in the quest for self-actualization?

The ability to talk honestly and openly, including about sexual matters, is critical to an intimate relationship.

on the basis of rules, this case-by-case orientation carefully examines motivations and consequences. Thus the acceptability or unacceptability of a sexual act depends on what it is intended to accomplish and its foreseeable consequences.

HEDONISTIC ORIENTATION The **hedonistic orientation,** sometimes called the recreational sexual standard, emphasizes the importance of sexual pleasure and satisfaction rather than moral constraint (you may recognize elements of ludic styles of loving within this standard). Sexual desire is seen as a legitimate and appropriate appetite to be satisfied with maximum gratification and enjoyment. Unlike the relational standard, which views coital activity as acceptable provided there is attachment between partners, the hedonistic orientation views sexual gratification in intercourse as an end in itself. Although the hedonistic orientation received considerable attention in the 1960s, probably only a small number of men and women cling to this standard today. Fear of contracting HIV-AIDS and other STDs has created a shift toward more conservative sexual value orientations.

Obviously, then, our complex and changing society offers divergent sexual value orientations, from celibacy to casual sex. Because people are usually exposed to several different orientations throughout the course of their lives, making value choices is difficult. We should point out, though, that these orientations are not entirely separate; rather, many people incorporate portions of all these sexual ideologies into their sexual value systems. In the accompanying Lifespan Development in Action box, we suggest some ways to explore your own sexual values.

Theories of Personality Development

Sigmund Freud's Psychosexual Theory

THE GENITAL STAGE (PUBERTY ONWARD) The onset of the final psychosexual developmental stage, the **genital stage,** commences a turbulent time period for the adolescent male or female. The biochemical upheaval associated

Lifespan Development in Action

EXPLORING YOUR OWN SEXUAL VALUES

The task of selecting suitable sexual values involves examining extrinsic values, such as those just discussed, and adopting those values that have intrinsic worth and validity. As we've indicated, this is no easy chore because people must strike some kind of balance between the values they have been taught while growing up and those that have become personally meaningful. Although it is not our purpose to promote any one sexual value or orientation, we do endorse the concept of responsible sexual decision making. To this end, we offer the following thoughts on developing an adequate and sound value system.

First, keep in mind that you do not arrive at a sound value system overnight; on the contrary, it is a process that takes time, dedication, and considerable deliberation (Breckler & Wiggins, 1989; Feather, 1984). You should avoid making snap judgments or gravitating toward values just because they are popular or trendy. Once you have examined and weighed different sexual values, you should have faith and confidence in the ones you choose as your own. The overall system selected should be consistent with your personality and everyday behavior; there should not be a gap between what you say and what you do.

Those with sound value systems also hold accurate assumptions about reality. Thus they tend to be fully informed and up-to-date in their knowledge about human sexuality. Those with healthy value systems often recheck their values, testing them against their feelings and life experiences. Moreover, they are tolerant of the value systems of others. They are usually able to accept other people's sexual orientations and activities without feeling personally threatened and without moralizing or judging. Sound and healthy values are also flexible ones, open to new ideas and fluid enough to allow for adjustment or correction. Finally, people with healthy systems derive satisfaction from living by their chosen values—these values provide meaning to their sexuality and a sense of purpose to their overall life (Darling & Mabe, 1989; Fogel, 1990; Reiss & Reiss, 1990; Turner & Rubinson, 1993).

with the growth and development of primary and secondary sex characteristics makes youths acutely aware of the erotic zones of their bodies. Following the relatively calm and tranquil latent years, the sensual pleasures associated with the genital zone become apparent.

Unlike the early pregenital stages in which each period marked the onset of a new conflict, the genital stage revives old conflicts, particularly the Oedipus complex. Thus Freudians view adolescence as a recapitulation of infantile sexuality. Even though Freud saw adolescence as a distinct era in psychosexual growth, he continued to emphasize the all-important role of experiences during the first few years of life. The only new feature of the genital stage is the sublimation of Oedipal feelings through the expression of libido, by falling in love with an opposite-sex person other than one's parent.

Erik Erikson's Psychosocial Theory

IDENTITY VERSUS ROLE DIFFUSION Erik Erikson's fifth crisis, **identity versus role diffusion,** often referred to as the *search for identity,* is possibly the most famous of his eight crises of psychosocial development. Upon the onset of puberty and genital maturity, youths realize their childhood has disappeared and adulthood is approaching. Because of this, their egos must reevaluate reality and, in so doing, teenagers become conscious of the ideas and opinions of others and pay particular attention to any discrepancies between their self-perception and the perception of others. Adolescents also become increasingly concerned with their skills and self-perceptions, especially when fitting these into society's occupational prototypes. During this stage all previous stages should blend into an integrated ego:

> The integration now taking place in the form of ego identity is, as pointed out, more than the sum of the childhood identifications. It is the accrued experience of the ego's ability to integrate all identifications with the vicissitudes of the libido, with the aptitudes developed out of endowment, and with the opportunities offered in social roles. The sense of ego identity, then, is the accrued confidence that the inner sameness and continuity prepared in the past are matched by the sameness and continuity of one's meaning for others, as evidenced in the tangible promise of a career. (1963, p. 261)

Some form of role diffusion results when this integration fails to occur. The eternal adolescent questions of "Who am I?" and "What is my purpose in life?" indicate ego confusion, especially in attempts to integrate various roles and experiences. The teenager's dilemma is to choose a possible role with which to identify—to be rugged and masculine like a cousin, jolly and humorous like a sibling, warm and affectionate like a parent, perceptive and intellectual like a grandparent, or athletic and worldly like some other relative. Meanwhile, adolescents often develop subcultures with which they may also identify. Thus they become clannish and accept very little deviance in dress, thought, or behavior. This intolerance of others is a temporary defense against role diffusion until the ego can develop a sense of identity. Ego identity is evidently enhanced when adolescents are in a caring family; they are more likely to explore ego identity when there is a good parent-adolescent relationship (Papini, Sebby, & Clark, 1989).

James Marcia (1980, 1987, 1991) proposes that an individual possesses one of four identity statuses. These four statuses are determined by the extent of the teenager's commitment and crisis. According to Marcia, a commitment means the level of investment in life planning. A crisis is the period of choosing meaningful life alternatives. His theory has been challenged, however, because some feel it lacks adequate integration of Erikson's theory (Cote & Levine, 1988).

Identity achievement, the first identity status, means a person has appraised his or her values and choices in life and has made a commitment to some goal or occupation. An **identity moratorium** is the time when an individual is rethinking his or her values and goals and is in the midst of an identity crisis. No commitment has yet been made to any goals or values. **Identity**

EPIGENETIC PRINCIPLE

Following adolescence, the epigenetic schemes proposed by Freud and Erikson sharply contrast: Psychosexual development completes itself during the teenage years; psychosocial development continues throughout adulthood. How do you regard such differences? Do you think Freud failed to recognize any postadolescent psychosexual stages? If so, what Freudian dynamics might additional stages embrace?

Developing a sense of identity is an important psychosocial task during adolescence.

diffusion occurs when the person has not even begun to examine his or her goals or values. Finally, **identity foreclosure** is said to result when an individual's goals have been established by others, usually the parents, and the individual chooses not to question or even examine them. These four identity possibilities add another dimension to Erikson's theory and show that the concept of identity is multifaceted, rather than being a singular psychological concept.

The growth in other developmental areas can also affect identity formation. For example, the attainment of Piaget's stage of formal thought facilitates identity formation during adolescence. However, this does not mean an adolescent in the stage of formal thought automatically achieves identity status. That is, there is no guarantee that arrival in one stage ensures achievement in another. However, certain cognitive capacities in operation at this time, namely, the ability to think abstractly, enable teenagers to differentiate better among and integrate identities and new role behaviors into the self-system (Bernstein, 1980; Leadbeater & Dionne, 1981).

Alternative Theoretical Perspectives on Adolescence   Besides the theoretical perspectives of adolescence developed by Erik Erikson and Sigmund

Freud, there are other conceptualizations of the teenage years. Among the more prominent theories are those of Kurt Lewin, G. Stanley Hall, Anna Freud, and Margaret Mead. The following is a brief description of each perspective.

KURT LEWIN'S THEORY Kurt Lewin (1935) viewed adolescence as a turbulent time marked by pronounced growth and change. These changes affect teenagers' *life space,* that is, all of the personal and mental characteristics that affect their behavior. Lewin viewed the life space as a network of interrelated and interdependent characteristics. When one aspect of the life space is affected, all others are too. Thus pronounced physical growth at this time affects all other domains: self-image, confidence, social comfort, and the like. Should adolescence produce negative reactions in one sphere, negative behaviors may result in other areas as well.

Lewin also emphasized that adolescence offers a marked contrast with earlier developmental stages. The childhood years brought stability to the individual's life space. Adolescence, though, often begins change, unreliability, and uncertainty. New and demanding social expectations, such as relinquishing childish behavior and acting in mature and responsible ways, require the negotiation and restructuring of new behaviors. Teenagers' expanding life space requires increasing refinement and differentiation.

G. STANLEY HALL'S THEORY G. Stanley Hall was a notable early contributor to the discipline of human development, particularly his investigations of adolescence. Indeed, his book on adolescence (1904) was the first systematic attempt to explore this life stage. Like Lewin, Hall viewed adolescence as a disruptive life stage. He labeled the conflicts and uncertainties at this time *Stürm und Drang,* or storm and stress.

Hall and Lewin differed, though, in regard to the origins of this turbulence. Whereas Lewin emphasized the concept of the life space, Hall focuses on evolutionary possibilities. More specifically, Hall viewed adolescence as an important transitional period, a time of awakened impulse and change. Adolescence is an evolutionary passage from earlier immature, childish behaviors to new levels of functioning. This is true for all developmental spheres, including a temporary dominance of sexual impulses. All of this, Hall maintained, brings the adolescent to higher levels of differentiation, but not without extremes in temperament, attitudes, and behavior.

ANNA FREUD'S THEORY Anna Freud (1958) emphasized that a "second awakening" of libidinal urges affects the teenager's personality functioning. You will recall that earlier in childhood, during the phallic stage, youngsters had romantic desires for the opposite-sex parent (the Oedipus or Electra complex). Anna Freud maintained that renewed—and more intense—desires now appear along with other forces, the result being inner turmoil and conflict. Should these feelings not be adequately resolved, maladaptive behavior at this time and even into adulthood could result.

How do adolescents confront these rekindled feelings? How do they cope with the disharmony among the id, ego, and superego? To resolve romantic attachments to their parents, adolescents typically engage in retreat behaviors, such as staying away from their parents or ignoring them. Being secretive and private and maintaining a distant psychological posture from the parents are examples. All of this represents the teenager's way of dealing with these uncomfortable sexual feelings.

Other ways of coping with these and other sexual feelings is to adopt new ego defense mechanisms. *Intellectualization,* for example—the use of elaborate logic and reason—and *asceticism*—the effort to avoid any type of physical pleasure or excitement—may be used to shroud inner sexual feelings. Adolescent asceticism may take the form of maintaining strict sexual rules of conduct on dates or dressing in a conservative fashion so as to downplay one's sexuality.

MARGARET MEAD'S THEORY Finally, let us acknowledge the contributions of Margaret Mead (1928). Mead was a cultural anthropologist who observed the adolescent experience in several non-Western societies, including those of Samoa and New Guinea. Unlike those theorists who painted a stormy and disruptive picture of adolescence, Mead observed that adolescence in these societies was a smooth and tranquil period. For most, it was a time for happiness, self-indulgence, and a relatively carefree—and conflict-free—lifestyle.

Such observations prompted Mead to discount the notion that a difficult adolescence was a universal experience, that it was always a period of conflict and turmoil. Rather, she maintained the experience of adolescence varies according to cultural influences. Because of the role of culture, it is incorrect to assume that all adolescents share the same experiences.

CONTINUOUS AND DISCONTINUOUS HUMAN DEVELOPMENT

Once you've had a chance to review all of the theories in this section, think about the continuity and discontinuity issue. Which theories appear to emphasize a subtle flow of personality dynamics rather than distinct changes? Does such an analysis enable you to see the concepts of stability and change in lifespan development with greater clarity?

UNIT REVIEW—

↗ The teenager's desire for individuation affects numerous social spheres, including family life. We explored the importance of harmonious family relations and the authoritarian, authoritative, and permissive styles of parental control.

↗ Family disharmony may originate from many sources, including the adolescent's strivings for individuation and autonomy, the parents' resistance to such strivings, and disagreements over values. In the wake of family discontent, some teenagers choose to run away from home.

↗ Involvement in the peer group intensifies during adolescence, in friendships, cliques, and/or crowds. Similar to earlier ages, gender differences are apparent in male and female friendships.

↗ Dating usually begins during the teenage years, and many adolescents are sexually active at young ages. A number of risks are attached to adolescent coital activity, including pregnancy, abortion, and sexually transmitted diseases. Sexual value orientations include the ascetic, procreational, relational, situational, and hedonistic.

↗ Freud's genital stage encompasses the teenage years, as does Erikson's stage of identity versus role diffusion. Other theories, by Lewin, Hall, Anna Freud, and Mead, were also described briefly.

UNIT FOUR: THE TROUBLED ADOLESCENT

At the outset of this chapter, we noted that not all teenagers successfully accomplish the developmental tasks of adolescence. When faced with the complexities and pressures of modern society, some may exhibit a generalized feeling of futility or hopelessness. Many are simply not capable of dealing with life's demands and, as a result, react to this developmental stage with a mixture of self-defeating behaviors.

In recent years, a number of adolescent maladjustment problems have received attention from psychologists. All have grown alarmingly and have generated a great deal of public concern. These areas are teenage suicide, eating disorders, drug abuse, and juvenile delinquency.

■■■ Teenage Suicide

At an age when they should have everything to live for, about 5,000 American teenagers and young adults, or about 13 a day, commit suicide each year. After accidents, the leading cause of death among young people is suicide. Perhaps the most shocking statistic is that since 1960, the suicide rate among adolescents has increased by *300%*. Overall, suicide accounts for about 12% of the mortality in the teenage and young adult age brackets (Brent, 1989; Gaines, 1991).

But the number of teenage suicides may be even greater than the statistics indicate, because many attempts fail and many medical examiners routinely list questionable deaths—especially for teenagers—as accidents. The actual suicide attempts are believed to be well over 100,000 each year. The use of firearms, shooting, and poison are the most common suicide methods (Gaines, 1991; Maltsberger, 1988; U.S. Bureau of the Census, 1992).

Suicide victims range from the happy-go-lucky types, who give no clear clues before acting, to the classic loners, who scream silently for help. Victims come from many different backgrounds, but statistics reveal a significant increase of suicides among minority youths. Males outnumber females in the number of suicidal deaths reported each year. In regard to attempted suicides, females clearly outnumber males; however, there has been an increase of completed suicides among females in recent years (Brent, 1989; Males, 1991; U.S. Bureau of the Census, 1992).

There are a number of reasons why adolescents commit suicide. One persistent theme is depression; many teens have a pervasive feeling of worthlessness, apprehension, and hopelessness. Alcohol abuse and dependence is another contributing factor. Other probable reasons are feelings of being overwhelmed, being in the midst of a crisis, or experiencing the loss of a loved object. Many suicide victims are rejected youths who receive little affection or attention. Most are alienated persons who feel socially isolated from the rest of the world (Adcock, Nagy, & Simpson, 1991; Connell & Meyer, 1991; de Jong, 1992; Hutchinson et al., 1992; Simonds, McMahon, & Armstrong, 1991).

Unfortunately, it is difficult to intervene and offer preventive measures to suicidal youths because of the difficulty of recognizing the symptoms. Few lay-people (parents, teachers, etc.) have the knowledge to recognize the symptoms. Therapists and counselors, on the other hand, are best able to

Depression is often a cause of adolescent suicide.

identify the characteristics of adolescent depression and offer therapeutic intervention. Because of their efforts, new strategies of intervention have emerged for treating adolescent depression and suicidal behavior (Garrison, 1991; Gibbs & Moskowitz-Sweet, 1991; Grove, 1991; G. L. White, 1990).

The increase of teenage suicide in recent years has prompted many segments of society to take preventive measures. The detection and identification of conflict and stress are vital and require the collaboration of parents, teachers, counselors, and other concerned adults. Crisis intervention programs are important to prevention and follow-up, the latter helping the victim cope with reality. Improving the conditions that may increase suicidal tendencies, such as human relations or educational and employment atmospheres, is important too. The establishment of community resources, such as halfway houses, shelters, hot lines, and adolescent clinics, is a necessary step in prevention (Blumenthal & Kupfer, 1988; Cole, 1991; Gaines, 1991; Neiga & Hopkins, 1988; Simonds et al., 1991).

▬ Eating Disorders

A second problem related to adolescence falls under the category of *eating disorders* (American Psychiatric Association, 1993). One type of eating disorder is **anorexia nervosa,** a type of self-imposed starvation that affects growing numbers of teenagers each year. It is often referred to as a teenager's disorder because it affects adolescents, usually junior high school and high school females, more than it does any other age group. Each year about 1 out of every 200 female adolescents is diagnosed as having anorexia nervosa (Howatt & Saxton, 1988; Hsu, 1990; Schlundt & Johnson, 1990).

At the root of anorexia nervosa is a relentless desire to be thin. The desire to lose weight becomes an obsession, and the anorectic becomes terrified of becoming fat. As this drastic type of dieting continues, many anorectics fail to eat at all; some resort daily to laxatives; and virtually all deny their eventual emaciated appearances. Anorexia nervosa is a condition severe enough to cause serious dehydration, malnutrition, complications of metabolic and endocrine functions, the cessation of menstruation in females, and death (Brumberg, 1988; Fisher & Brone, 1991; Hsu, 1990).

Anorexia nervosa usually is found among members of the upper and middle classes, perhaps because of these families' emphasis on fitness and leanness. It also afflicts individuals with above-average intelligence. Shame and guilt in relation to eating also seems to play a role (Frank, 1991). Additionally, it appears that the families of many anorectics are characterized by overprotectiveness, which can result in a poor sense of identity (Russell, Halasz, & Beumont, 1990). These children, often compliant and dependent during childhood, misuse eating as an attempt to assert their independence (Brone & Fisher, 1988). Thus anorectics tend to be perfectionists who feel they are in complete control of themselves, even while they are starving. The typical patient has a distorted view of reality, a sense of inadequacy, sexual conflicts, and, perhaps, severe depression bordering on the suicidal level (Litt, 1991; Nagel & Jones, 1992; Price, 1990).

As anorectics begin to starve themselves, they frequently induce vomiting and suffer from constipation. Their skin becomes dry, cracked, and rough. Their nails become brittle, and their hair thins. In addition to the cessation of menstruation, the development of secondary sex characteristics is curtailed in adolescent girls. In addition, there is usually no ovulation, and the vagina becomes vulnerable to infection. Males' sexual interest diminishes, and in some cases, impotence ensues. Both sexes have extremely high activity levels (Fisher & Brone, 1991; Hsu, 1990; Schlundt & Johnson, 1990).

The treatment of anorexia nervosa is usually a long and tedious process. Behavior modification has proved to be somewhat effective; other techniques are individual psychotherapy, nutritional counseling, and the use of insulin to induce weight gain. Sometimes intravenous or tube feeding is necessary when individuals are too weak to eat or refuse to eat. Treatment includes family therapy as well as helping anorectics to eat at regular intervals and to establish some self-sufficiency. Psychotherapy is often aimed at helping patients develop more effective problem-solving strategies, more self-esteem, and more accurate body images (Casper, 1989; Hertzler & Grun, 1990; Hsu, 1990; Wilson, 1989).

Anorexia nervosa is not the same as **bulimia nervosa,** another type of eating disorder particularly common among college females. (Note that other variations of eating disorders exist, often including symptoms of both anorexia nervosa and bulimia nervosa. For example, an eating disorder might consist of binge eating, vomiting, and self-starvation.) Bulimia nervosa is gorging oneself with excessive amounts of food and then inducing vomiting and/or using large amounts of laxatives. Bulimia (from the Greek word meaning "ox hunger") nervosa is often called the binge-purge disease. In addition to these two serious disorders, there are adolescents who are compulsive overeaters. This latter group does not appear to have poorer health (mental or physical) than nonovereaters do, but they often perceive themselves and the quality of their relationships with others as less positive (Leon, 1991; Marston et al., 1988; Stein & Reichert, 1990).

Thanks to the efforts of concerned researchers and organizations such as the Anorexia Nervosa Aid Society and the American Anorexia/Bulimia Association, our understanding of these disorders has increased markedly over the past decade. Knowledge and treatment of anorexia nervosa and bulimia nervosa seem likely to increase in the future (Halmi, 1983; Herzog et al., 1991; Hsu, 1990; Irving et al., 1990; Neuman & Halvorson, 1983).

Drug Abuse

Historically, drugs have been used to alter moods or produce intoxication. Today, drugs serve a wide range of purposes, both medical and recreational. Many drugs serve as protective armor—chemical shelters to combat and ward off the stresses and insecurities of modern life. Although many teenagers drink alcohol, smoke marijuana, or take hallucinogens, equally as many adults take medicines that may be harmful, such as barbiturates, amphetamines, and painkillers. Many do not realize, do not care, or will not admit they have become dependent on drugs (Wodarski, 1990).

ALCOHOL Alcohol consumption is widespread among both teenagers and adults. The consumption of alcohol is accepted in most societies and, as a result, it is often not regarded as a drug. However, it is a drug because it affects the central nervous system. Acting as a depressant, alcohol numbs the higher brain centers. As the concentration of blood alcohol increases, a progressive impairment of or a reduction in normal brain functions results. Gradually, the individual's awareness of and response to stimuli from the outside are diminished (Carrol, 1989; Steele & Josephs, 1990).

When alcohol is consumed in large quantities, behavior often becomes impulsive, unstable, and unpredictable (Meyer, 1988). Indeed, drunkenness is one of the most common reasons that juveniles break the law (Beatty, 1991). Regular users of alcohol also run the risk of becoming alcoholics. In the United States, approximately 8 to 10% of males and 2 to 4% of females can be described as alcoholics at some point in their lives. Among teenage drinkers, heavy alcohol consumption is much more common among males (Bettes, 1990; Johnston, O'Malley, & Bachman, 1988, 1990; Oetting & Beauvais, 1990).

Adolescents are attracted to alcohol and other drugs for numerous reasons. Conformity to peer pressure and the desire to appear more grown-up are popular explanations. Because drinking is associated with adult role behavior, it may symbolize the attainment of adult status. It may also reduce anxiety or serve as a way to overcome loneliness. It is known that adolescent drinking patterns are influenced by those of others in the community. Thus examples set by parents and other adults need to be examined when seeking to understand teenagers' drinking behavior (Brinson, 1991; Downs & Rose, 1991; Friedman & Granick, 1990; Kafka & London, 1991; Page & Cole, 1991; Searight, 1991).

As far as parents are concerned, the home environment has been shown to influence teenagers' problem drinking and substance use (Brook et al., 1992; Novacek, Raskin, & Hogan, 1991; Toray et al., 1991). For example, one study

(Chassin, Rogosch & Barrera, 1991) uncovered a link between father alcoholism and adolescent drug abuse. Diane McDermott (1984) found that adolescents who used drugs were more likely to have one or both parents who did the same. Along similar lines, Glenn Johnson and his colleagues (1984) observed that relationships between the parents' use of drugs and teenagers' use of the same drugs were moderate and roughly equivalent across drugs.

MARIJUANA Next to alcohol, the most frequent and widely used nonmedical drug is **marijuana.** Marijuana is classified as a hallucinogen because it is capable of producing a hallucination. Although the results of surveys vary from region to region, it has been estimated that the number of Americans who have tried marijuana at least once in their lives may be as many as 62 million (Insel & Roth, 1991). Among adolescents, marijuana use is also extensive. In one investigation, it was estimated that about 50% of the respondents had tried it at some point in their lives, most during the previous year (Johnston, O'Malley, & Bachman, 1990).

The behavioral effect of marijuana is mostly determined by the dosage and the user's personality. The average person generally experiences a sense of relaxed well-being or exhilaration and an increased sensitivity to sounds and sights. Time, distance, vision, hearing, hand-leg reactions, and body balance may be slowed or distorted. Some people may feel drowsy and also have a feeling of greater physical and mental capacities than they actually possess. Marijuana also moderately increases the heart rate but does not seem to affect the respiratory rate, blood sugar, or pupil size. It also has a tendency to cause bloodshot and itchy eyes, a dry mouth, and increased appetite. When severely abused, marijuana produces lethargy and passivity, and excessive use may create high blood pressure and even lung cancer (Fligiel et al., 1988; Gieringer, 1988; Goode, 1989).

LSD AND OTHER HALLUCINOGENS Marijuana is considered a mild hallucinogen. There are other drugs that are much stronger. For example, psychedelic drugs such as **LSD** and mescaline are capable of changing perceptions and the normal ways of looking at the world and at oneself. Affecting cells, tissues, and organs, and changing the transmission of neural impulses in the lower brain centers, LSD produces profound physiological and psychological reactions. Its effects, like those of other drugs, depend on its potency, the user's personality, and the social and psychological context in which it is taken (Baker, 1988; Goode, 1989).

LSD reached its peak of popularity during the mid-1960s. Since then, its use among adolescents and young adults has steadily declined, largely because of the increased awareness and apprehension of "bad trips," the recurrence of frightening "flashbacks," and the fear of brain damage or chromosomal defects.

AMPHETAMINES Adolescents may also turn to **amphetamines,** which act on the central nervous system. Examples of amphetamines are cocaine, benzedrine, and dexedrine. Amphetamines are known to produce many reactions, including constriction of peripheral blood vessels; increased blood pressure and heart rate; relaxation of the smooth muscles of the stomach, intestines, and bladder; and suppressed appetite.

Drug abuse among adolescents is an acute social problem.

Overdoses of amphetamines produce high blood pressure, enlarged pupils, unclear and rapid speech, and confusion. For some, the racing world created may be "out of control" and lead to temporary psychosis, characterized by panic, delusions, and hallucinations. When the drug wears off, individuals frequently "crash," by sleeping for long periods. Afterward, they are highly irritable, belligerent, and impulsive (Carroll, 1989; Goode, 1989).

Cocaine has increased in popularity in recent years; an estimated 15% of all adolescents have experimented to some degree with it. Cocaine is processed from the leaves of the coca bush. It produces effects similar to those of amphetamines and in mild doses creates heightened levels of energy and alertness. Cocaine initially produces a sense of euphoria and well-being. Users tend to feel smarter, more competent, and more masterful than others. However, these effects are temporary and tolerance sets in rapidly; and, as a result, increased dosages are needed to obtain the initial effect. Heavier doses and prolonged use, though, can induce hostility, withdrawal, and paranoid feelings. Collapse and death from cocaine are not uncommon (Cheung, Erikson, & Landau, 1991; Goode, 1989; R. Siegel, 1990).

There are a number of ways to self-administer cocaine. One way is to snort it, that is, take the powder into the nose. Cocaine can also be injected and smoked. Freebasing is a preparation method that uses flammable chemicals to produce "base," the smokable cocaine product. A cheaper and easier method produces "crack," or "rock," another variation of smokable cocaine. Crack has opened whole new drug markets because of its low price, and many deaths from its use have been reported.

BARBITURATES Known by many as "downers," **barbiturates** were designed primarily to induce sleep and relaxation. Barbiturates exist in a variety of forms:

INTERACTION OF HEREDITY AND ENVIRONMENT

To what extent do you see such environmental forces as lack of parental attachment/affection, broken homes, negative peer influences, or economic deprivation contributing to such maladaptive behavior? Utilizing a nativist perspective, do you think one's genetic endowment, such as a possible predisposition to alcoholism or a mood disorder, influences the course of adolescent maladaptive behavior? How do you think the two forces interact?

Nembutal, Seconal, and Librium are but a few. Barbiturates are physiologically addictive and are frequently used to commit suicide. Tolerance of the effects of barbiturates as well as withdrawal symptoms have been reported among heavy users.

Teenagers who are hard-core drug users often take barbiturates as supplements to other drugs. Barbiturates are addictive and are especially dangerous when taken in conjunction with alcohol. Barbiturates are also frequently used to moderate the stimulating actions of amphetamines or to accentuate the actions of heroin. Their habitual use produces drowsiness, mental confusion, and the loss of muscular coordination. In addition, the withdrawal symptoms of barbiturates may become particularly severe, often resulting in delusions, hallucinations, and even coma (Goode, 1989).

ADDICTING NARCOTICS Of all the **addicting narcotics,** heroin is the favorite drug of virtually all addicts because of its potency and ability to produce euphoric effects. Heroin is almost five times as powerful as morphine. After alcohol, heroin is the most physically addictive and accounts for the most drug-related deaths.

Heroin initially produces a feeling of relief and euphoria that lasts for a few minutes. The next several hours are characterized by a "high." The individual is usually in a state of well-being but is lethargic and withdrawn during this time. Following the euphoric and lethargic stages is a negative phase that produces a strong desire for more of the drug. When deprived of the drug, heavy users begin to experience withdrawal symptoms, the severity of which increase without the reintroduction of the drug. Restlessness, excessive sweating, nausea, severe abdominal cramps, vomiting, and delirium are a few of these withdrawal symptoms (Carroll, 1989; Goode, 1989; R. Siegel, 1990).

Juvenile Delinquency

Juvenile delinquency is behavior by youths 18 years of age and younger that society deems unacceptable. The rates of juvenile delinquency have increased significantly in recent years. In support of this, consider the following: In the 1960s the majority of people arrested in this country were *over* 25 years of age. During the last two decades, over half of those arrested were 25 or *younger* (U.S. Bureau of Census, 1992).

Rates of delinquency are highest for teenagers between the ages of 15 and 16. By age 18, delinquent behavior is likely to decline. In many instances, it is the young adolescent who commits the less serious forms of delinquency, such as vandalism or running away from home, whereas the older adolescent is more likely to commit such offenses as drug abuse or truancy. More violent crimes, such as aggravated assault or forcible rape, are more apt to be committed by individuals between the ages of 18 and 24 or older (Federal Bureau of Investigation, 1992; U.S. Bureau of the Census, 1992).

It is also known that the percentages of juvenile offenses are greater among African Americans than whites and among males than females. Males heavily outnumber females in the number of offenses, sometimes by as much as four to one. As far as violent offenses are concerned, males outnumber females by approximately seven to one (Federal Bureau of Investigation, 1992; Gold, 1987; Hindelang, 1981; U.S. Bureau of the Census, 1992).

FACTORS AFFECTING JUVENILE DELINQUENCY Researchers have been able to uncover a number of factors related to delinquent behavior:

1. Broken homes. Households divided by divorce, death, desertion, or a lack of affection, attention, and understanding can produce great stress in the child, not only before and during the time of separation but also during subsequent social development (Henggeler, 1989; Kennedy, 1991).

2. Lack of parental affection. In homes in which children are exposed to warm and affectionate relationships, delinquency is rare. Conversely, when there is persistent parental conflict, or little affection and attachment directed to children, there is a strong likelihood that rebellious or delinquent behavior will result. Thus a parent's psychological absence from the home can contribute to delinquency just as much as his or her physical absence can (Gartland & Day, 1992; Gray-Ray & Ray, 1990; Holcomb & Kashani, 1991).

3. Abusive discipline. Rates of delinquency are higher when parents employ abusive and hostile measures of discipline. Adolescent attitudes of rebelliousness and defiance are likely to be created when whippings, beatings, and other types of physical punishment are used as methods of control. Hostile behavior by adolescents also may persist throughout adult life. This appears to be especially true when individuals start their own families. Those who were abused themselves have a strong tendency to employ similar violent techniques with their children (Gelles & Cornell, 1990; Muster, 1992; Peters, McMahon, & Quinsey, 1992; Steinberg, 1991).

4. Unstable parental behavior. Delinquent youths are more apt to be brought up by one or both parents exhibiting maladjustment problems. These problems include emotional disorders, alcoholism or other drug dependencies, antisocial attitudes, and sociopathic tendencies. When these problems are combined with patterns of rejection and hostility, delinquent behavior may be the result (Cavan & Ferdinand, 1981; Rosenbaum, 1989; Stott, 1982).

5. Economic deprivation. Economic deprivation is also related to juvenile delinquency. When economic deprivation is joined by such factors as low educational level, high unemployment, and overcrowding, rates of juvenile delinquency escalate. But although rates of delinquency are higher among lower, urban socioeconomic classes, it is incorrect to assume the rural middle and upper socioeconomic classes are free of this problem. Especially the notion that juvenile crime is restricted to inner-city youth is erroneous. Delinquency is fairly commonplace in rural, affluent neighborhoods. In fact, some of the biggest annual crime increases among juveniles are in rural communities with populations of less than 25,000 (Chesney-Lind, 1989; Conger et al., 1992; Henggeler, 1989; Simons & Gray, 1989; Skinner, Elder, & Conger, 1992; U.S. Bureau of the Census, 1992).

CHARACTERISTICS OF DELINQUENTS Certain patterns of behavior appear to be common among juvenile delinquents. For instance, many delinquents feel deprived, insecure, and defiant; that is, most juvenile delinquents deliberately set out to break the law. Many researchers (e.g., Cervantes, 1992; Elliot,

Many juvenile delinquents follow a pattern of defiant and impulsive behavior.

Huizinga, & Menard, 1989; Van Kammen et al., 1991; Watts & Wright, 1990) believe that illicit drug use and dropping out of school increase the probability of juvenile delinquency.

Many juvenile delinquents are also excitable and impulsive. Many have low levels of moral development and deviant values. Consistent in the literature (Rosenbaum, 1989; Simonian et al., 1991) is the finding that delinquents harbor poor self-concepts and poor social skills. Such behaviors seem to originate from past failures in family, school, or other social situations. These inadequacies frequently produce behavior that is defensive, including ambivalence toward authority, hostility, and destructiveness (Armistead et al., 1992; Holcomb & Kashani, 1991; Kupersmidt & Coie, 1990).

Research suggests that some delinquents have lower levels of intelligence than nondelinquents, indicating they may be unable to foresee the consequences of their actions. School failure, whether because of low intelligence, learning disability, or a lack of motivation, also appears to be a contributor of delinquency (Grande, 1988). Delinquents also appear to have other cognitive detriments. For example, in a study involving 150 18-year-old delinquent and nondelinquent males, it was discovered that delinquents displayed significantly more immature modes of role-taking, logical thinking, and moral reasoning than nondelinquents (Lee & Prentice, 1988).

It has also been found that delinquents experience other school-related difficulties, often as early as kindergarten. Lynn Meltzer (1984), for example, found that by the second grade, 45% of a group of delinquents were already delayed in reading and 36% in handwriting, compared with only 14% of a control group. Higher percentages in other skill areas were also found among delinquents. Thus early learning difficulties may be an indication of risk for later delinquency.

Finally, researchers (e. g., Peters, McMahon, & Quinsey, 1992) have explored the dynamics of aggression, violence, and destructive behavior of delinquents. For instance, in an effort to identify differences in aggression, delinquents incarcerated for antisocial aggression were compared with high school students with high aggression, and another group with low aggression. The antisocial aggressive individuals were most likely to solve social problems by adopting hostile goals, seeking few additional facts, generating few alternative solutions to problems, and anticipating few consequences for their aggression. They were also more likely to have a belief system in support of aggression, including the idea that aggression is a legitimate response and that it increases self-esteem (Slaby & Guerra, 1988).

A study of public school vandalism involved 1,171 students in the seventh through twelfth grades. The highest rate of vandalism was found in seventh graders and decreased progressively with each increase in grade level. The strongest predictor of school vandalism was being from classes in the lowest academic track. High school vandals were generally those students who had a junior high school record of vandalism. Other factors included high rates of absenteeism and coming from higher status homes (Tygart, 1988).

CHAPTER REVIEW

Unit One: Physical Development

Pronounced bodily changes take place during the teenage years. Puberty, a time when sexual maturity is attained, is accompanied by a growth spurt. Height and weight gains are especially great during this time, as are skeletal changes and the further development of the internal organs. The maturation of the primary and secondary sex characteristics is also evident, triggered by the pituitary gland and directed by hormones of the endocrine system. The physical changes associated with puberty may produce psychological discomfort. We also explored the concepts of early and late maturation. Motor skill development and coordination, in addition to strength and the speed of reaction time, steadily increase. Although males continue to surpass females in those motor skills that have been tested, it can be rightfully argued this is because of the time and practice they devote to developing these skills.

Unit Two: Mental Development

By the time Piaget's stage of formal operations is reached, individuals are able to deal with concrete as well as hypothetical and abstract problems. However, as we pointed out, not everyone reaches this stage. Formal operations is the last stage of the Piagetian design for intellectual growth, and it represents a period in which all past learning experiences are crystallized and contribute to higher-level thought processes. An outstanding feature of abstract thinking is the ability to use inductive and deductive reasoning. Other key cognitive advancements that have been studied are refined problem-solving abilities and insight into literary materials. A limitation in reasoning at this time is adolescent egocentrism, best seen in the fabrication of the imaginary audience and the personal fable. Explanations of adolescent egocentrism have been proposed by Elkind, Selman, and Lapsley.

Unit Three: Personality and Social Development

Social involvement reaches new heights during adolescence. One of the more important developmental tasks associated with socialization is establishing harmonious family relationships. We identified three styles of parental control in this chapter: authoritarian, authoritative, and permissive. Of the three, adolescents tend to favor the authoritative, or democratic, style. We also discussed family disharmony and the problems of teenage runaways. Each year, over 1 million adolescents decide to flee from their homes. Interactions with the school setting affect many areas of growth and development.

The peer group continues to be an important agent of socialization. During this time, adolescents may join a number of different social groups, ranging from friendships to cliques and crowds. There are gender differences in adolescent friendships, the main one being that females are more emotionally intimate with their partners. Dating typically begins during adolescence, and we explored the nature of teenagers' sexual interactions. Three areas of growing concern related to adolescent coital activity are pregnancy, abortion, and sexually transmitted diseases. The risks posed by such problems heighten the need for effective sexuality education programming. Adolescents also need to formulate mature and responsible sexual values to guide their behavior.

Freud and Erikson both proposed stages of adolescent personality functioning. For Freud, this is the genital stage, and for Erikson, it is the psychosocial stage known as identity versus role diffusion. We also examined other theories regarding the adolescent experience. In particular, we discussed the works of Kurt Lewin, G. Stanley Hall, Anna Freud, and Margaret Mead.

Unit Four: The Troubled Adolescent

This portion of the chapter dealt with four problems affecting the teenager: adolescent suicide, eating disorders, drug abuse, and juvenile delinquency. After accidents, suicide is the leading cause of death among young people. There are a number of reasons why adolescents commit suicide, but a persistent theme is depression. Anorexia nervosa is a type of self-imposed starvation that usually leads to physiological decline and psychological complications. Bulimia nervosa is gorging oneself with excessive amounts of food and then inducing vomiting and/or using large amounts of laxatives.

Drug abuse among teenagers was also explored in this unit. Alcohol and marijuana tend to be the most popular drugs, but we also examined the use of other hallucinogens, amphetamines, barbiturates, and the addicting narcotics. Finally we discussed juvenile delinquency, defined as the behavior by youths ages 18 and younger that society deems unacceptable. Many factors contribute to delinquency, including broken homes, lack of parental affection, abusive discipline, unstable parental behavior, and economic deprivation. Many delinquents are insecure, defiant, and impulsive.

TERMS YOU SHOULD KNOW

abstraction
addicting narcotic
adolescent egocentrism
amphetamine
anorexia nervosa
ascetic orientation
barbiturate
bulimia nervosa
clique
cocaine
crowd
deductive reasoning
early maturer
formal operations
friendship
genital stage
hedonistic orientation
hypothetico-deductive
   reasoning
identity achievement
identity diffusion

identity foreclosure
identity formation
identity moratorium
identity versus role diffusion
imaginary audience
individuation
inductive reasoning
juvenile delinquency
late maturer
LSD
marijuana
menarche
nocturnal emission
personal fable
primary sex characteristics
procreational orientation
puberty
relational orientation
secondary sex characteristics
situational orientation
toughlove

THINKING IN ACTION

• You are asked by an editor to write a chapter for a forthcoming book on adolescent development. The proposed chapter, "Puberty: A Psychological and Social Perspective," is designed to help students, teachers, and parents better understand the multifaceted nature of this important life transition. How would you approach this chapter? To prepare yourself, develop an outline suggesting how sexual maturity triggers psychological and social functioning, and vice versa. At the end of your chapter, make sure you include a section detailing what adults can do to better understand and help the maturing adolescent.

• After reading the section exploring Erik Erikson's psychosocial crisis of identity versus role diffusion, you are interested in updating the noted scholar's work. More specifically, you maintain that the establishment of one's identity in the 1990s is different than it was 25 years ago. What contemporary social and cultural forces do you think affect the outcome of this psychosocial crisis today? Do you think establishing a sense of identity is more difficult or easier for today's teenagers? Would the widespread nature of adolescent problems such as runaways, suicide, drug abuse, and the like, indicate growing levels of role diffusion? Be able to defend your thinking.

• You will need a partner or two for this thinking exercise. Together, reflect on the nature of your family relationships during the early stages of your adolescent years. What were your family relationships like? Did they change when you entered this stage of life? If so, develop a list describing changes that you experienced, and then do the same for perceived parental changes. How do your lists compare and contrast? Do the lists reflect an increase in bickering? Did attitudes toward family activities (e.g., picnics, vacations) change? When you are finished with this, brainstorm as to how both adolescent and parent can successfully meet the challenges of this family transition.

• Sexual values are important dimensions of cognitive and personality dynamics and are instrumental in shaping the course of sexual intimacy with another person. Select one of your own sexual values, perhaps one relating to gender roles, commitment, promiscuity, or responsibility. How was this value developed and nurtured? How has it shaped your sexual life? Do you see it changing in the future?

• You are employed by a local youth services bureau and have been asked by your supervisor to develop some programming for at-risk adolescents. More specifically, your bureau is interested in upgrading the lives of at-risk youth by providing them with communitywide intervention. After reading the last unit of this chapter, did you discover any common themes shared by troubled teenagers, particularly those related to their home lives? How would your programming enhance the well-being of at-risk adolescents in your community and help them to become responsible and productive adults? How do you intend to involve parents? What kinds of assistance would you need to implement your ideas?

RECOMMENDED READINGS

1. Esman, A. H. (1991). *Adolescence and culture*. New York: Columbia University Press.

   A fascinating exploration of the adolescent culture, both yesteryear and today.

2. Feldman, S. S., & Elliott, G. R. (1990). *At the threshold: The developing adolescent*. Cambridge, MA: Harvard University Press.

   An in-depth analysis of the biological, social, and psychological changes of adolescence.

3. Gaines, D. (1991). *Teenage wasteland: Suburbia's dead end kids*. New York: Pantheon.

   The author supplies a comprehensive, but disturbing, look at the many causes of adolescent suicide.

4. Gullotta, T. P. (Ed.). (1992). *Adolescent sexuality.* Newbury Park, CA: Sage.

   Among the topics are the promotion of sexual responsibility, sexually transmitted diseases, and adolescent pregnancy and parenting.

5. Montemayor, R. (Ed.). (1990). *Advances in adolescent research.* Greenwich, CT: JAI Press.

   A good assortment of articles on many aspects of adolescent growth and development.

Young Adulthood

What Do You Think?

UNIT ONE: PHYSICAL AND MENTAL DEVELOPMENT

Physical Development
Exercise and Physical Well-Being
Nutrition and Physical Well-Being

Mental Development
Qualitative Mental Dimensions
Quantitative Mental Dimensions

UNIT TWO: PERSONALITY AND SOCIAL DEVELOPMENT

Adult Maturity
Allport's Seven Dimensions of Maturity
Theories of Personality Development
Erik Erikson's Theory
Daniel Levinson's Theory
Roger Gould's Theory

Development of Adult Intimate Relationships
Dating and Intimate Relationships
Gender Roles and Intimate Relationships
Love and Intimate Relationships

UNIT THREE: LIFESTYLE CHOICES AND OPTIONS

Marriage
The Postponement of Marriage
Motivations for Marriage
Adjusting to Married Life
Divorce and Separation
Adjusting to Divorce
Children and Divorce
Remarriage
Single-Parent Households

Cohabitation
Singlehood
Gay and Lesbian Relationships
Parenthood
Fertility Patterns in the United States
Childless Marriages
Parenting Adjustments and Adaptations
Parental Roles

UNIT FOUR: CAREER DEVELOPMENT

Selecting a Career
Theories of Vocational Development
The Search for Job Satisfaction

Chapter Review • Terms You Should Know • Thinking in Action • Recommended Readings

• Over 30 million Americans are overweight, and far too many don't bother to exercise. Leading sedentary lives, most people don't realize they're programming themselves for cardiovascular illness and other assorted ailments at early ages. What prompts such attitudes and behaviors, and what steps can adults take to launch a regimen of exercise and proper nutrition? This chapter examines the benefits of adopting such a healthy lifestyle, pointing out the merits of eating right and working up a sweat during adult life.

• How do I love thee? Let me count the ways. Indeed you must, when seeking to understand this complex psychological state. We've all thought about love at one time or another, and we are constantly reminded of its presence—or lack of it—in adult intimate relationships. It's difficult to escape the numerous portrayals of love in popular songs, soap operas, and pulp novels. But what exactly is love, and are there different ways to express it? We try to supply some answers.

• "I do." The decision to marry is something about 93 percent of us will do at some point in our lives. What reasons account for its popularity, and what are some of the motivations behind going to the altar? We also focus on some alternatives to traditional marriage, such as cohabitation and singlehood. How popular are these lifestyles and why do they appeal to some adults?

• Having children is always something Regina and Michael wanted. When they were engaged, they always talked about how they really wanted to be parents someday. They both enjoy being around children and often envision what it would be like to have their own. When Regina and Michael become parents, what kinds of adaptations and transitions will they encounter? How will their lives change as they adjust to their new roles of mother and father? In this chapter, we explore such issues and carefully examine the impact that children have on couples.

UNIT ONE: PHYSICAL AND MENTAL DEVELOPMENT

Young adulthood is the dawning of a new stage of life. Individuals have traveled beyond the throes of adolescence and youth and now seek to attain the psychological maturity to face the challenges of adult life. The challenges to be met are perhaps more complex and diverse than any they have previously faced, but the rewards to be reaped in terms of successfully meeting these challenges are boundless.

Young adulthood marks a time when individuals can embark on a chosen life course and find their niches in the outside world. Earlier, individuals could only chart their plans, thinking about what they would like to do with their lives. But now, having launched themselves from the family and completed formal schooling, at least for the most part, plans can be put into action. In the process, individuals will gain more confidence in their abilities, and their thinking will become more systematic and analytical. To actively shape a dream is no longer a remote thought, but a reality of everyday life. Adulthood has begun.

■ Physical Development

During late adolescence and early adulthood, almost all physical growth and maturation has been completed. Very young adults (20 to 30 years of age) generally give the appearance of youth and vitality, especially if they take care of themselves. Some, of course, gain excessive weight or display some premature gray hairs, but most people in early adulthood have developed pleasant body proportions, having outgrown the more gangly appearance of oversized limbs and adolescent facial characteristics that often mark the teenage years. Thus, for most, early adulthood is characterized by vim, vigor, freshness, and the general physical attractiveness of youth.

By young adulthood, muscle growth is complete, but the potential for increases in strength remains until about age 30. Even though peak strength is reached, however (few actually realize their potential), it must be remembered that in any phase of life, the maximal is not maintained for very long. Thus, for a few, gradual physical deterioration begins in young adulthood. For those who lead a sedentary life, it may begin as early as adolescence. For those who choose to pursue excellence in physical activities (professionals or serious amateurs), early adulthood represents less a time of preparing for the future than the peak of their careers.

The body reaches its maximum physical potential during young adulthood, at least as far as the muscles and internal organs are concerned. In relation to the circulatory system, the heart and its network of blood vessels are fully mature. For the average adult male, the heart weighs about 10 ounces and for females about 8 ounces. In its mature state, it is approximately the size of a closed fist and will beat about 72 times each minute of one's life. The average blood pressure is between 100 and 120 systolic and 60 to 80 diastolic. Systolic and diastolic are terms used to designate specific amounts of blood pressure. Systolic is the greatest force caused by the heart's contractions. Systolic pressure is compared to diastolic, or the relaxation phase that exists between heartbeats.

The *nervous system* has been gradually developing and maturing since the organism was an embryo. Many people mistakenly believe a young child is neurologically mature. This is not so, since the brain will continue to grow into adolescence or young adulthood. Brain size and weight, for example, will reach a maximum during young adulthood, and then decline during middle and late adulthood (for a review of structural changes in the brain during adulthood, see Haug, 1991; Itil, Sloane, & Itil, 1990; Scheibel, 1992). If we were to examine the electroencephalograph (EEG) waves of adults, mature patterns of brain wave activity do not appear until about 20 years of age, and for some, the period of maturation continues to age 30. It is important to note that with advancing age, electroencephalograph evaluations, especially those indicating brain impairments, are considered significant predictors of longevity.

An examination of the *respiratory system* reveals that compared to earlier years breathing during adulthood has become slower and deeper. The average adult has a breathing rate of about 12 to 20 times a minute and this will accelerate to about 40 breaths per minute during vigorous exercise. However, there are variations attached to these figures: Larger people usually have slower breathing rates; smaller people have faster rates. Since birth the lungs have increased in weight 20 times.

The *sense modalities* exhibit little change in young adult life. A slight difference in hearing ability exists between the two sexes, in that men are less likely than women to detect high tones. The lens of the eye loses some of its elasticity and becomes less able to change shape and to focus on near objects. This represents a continuation of a hardening process that probably began at age 10 and is an example of aging beginning early in life. By age 30, however, the changes are seldom sufficient to cause a significant effect on the function of the eyes. Any slight loss of functional efficiency in the sensory mechanisms of young adults is more than compensated for by the fact that they learn to make fuller use of their senses than they did as children or adolescents. For a detailed description of the sensory changes that occur throughout the course of adulthood, see Schieber (1992).

As far as other changes in the body are concerned, the accordionlike vertebrae and spinal disks begin to settle, causing a slight decrease in height. This represents the start of a slow imperceptible bodily change. For some, an increase in weight begins; even for those who maintain a consistent weight, there is an increase in fatty tissue with a corresponding decrease in muscle tissue. There is a slight loss in muscle strength between early and middle adulthood, although wide individual differences exist.

In sports such as boxing, baseball, and skiing, the speed, strength, and quick reactions of young adulthood are needed if one is to be competitive. Sports such as golf or bowling or even tennis can be played fairly well through the use of concentration and planning and can, therefore, be played throughout the lifespan, especially by those who do not become obese, smoke, or drink heavily. Given good health, a person can participate in such sports as swimming, skiing, tennis, or bowling for decades.

Exercise and Physical Well-Being   In countries all over the world today, there is an ever-increasing emphasis placed on physical fitness and well-being. More than ever before, adults are aware of the benefits of regular exercise and a healthy lifestyle. As a result, many adults of all ages pursue a diversity of physical activities, including competitive sports (Ericsson, 1990; Herman, 1990; D. Menard, 1991; O'Brien & Conger, 1991). Jogging, swimming, joining a bowling or softball league, working out at the local Y or Nautilus center, playing golf or tennis, or skiing on weekends have come to characterize the adult wishing to stay in shape.

Regular exercise and proper nutrition undoubtedly help to keep the individual healthy and fit. Regular physical activity promotes healthy aging processes, as well as heightened levels of psychological well-being. Warren Boskin and associates (1990) note that regular exercise can help reduce anxiety, relieve depression, and improve self-esteem. It is also recommended by many (Edelson, 1991; Gross, 1991; Karasek & Theorell, 1990) as a way to relieve the body and mind of stress and help combat stress-related illnesses (for more information on this topic see Chapter 10).

Regular exercise is extremely important at all ages. Among adults, though, regular exercise reduces the risk of an early death from a heart attack. The person who exercises on a regular basis can improve the strength and circulatory capacity of cardiac muscles and reduce the severity of arteriosclerotic lesions. Exercise also keeps the body's blood vessels open (a process known as *capillarization*) and helps overall circulation. In addition, it helps improve the coordination of the heart's fibers (Beychok, 1991; Lawton, 1991; Reed, 1991).

In addition to its cardiac benefit, regular exercise increases muscle strength and joint flexibility, as well as lung efficiency. Regular exercise also helps fight fat buildups, perhaps the most visible result of physical inactivity. Exercise can also enhance one's immune response, helping the body to fight off infection. Because of all of these benefits, exercise coupled with a healthy lifestyle greatly determines longevity (Austin, 1991; Fries, 1990; Gadow, 1991; Lawton, 1991; Poehlman, Melby, & Badylak, 1991; Rowe, 1991).

INTERRELATEDNESS OF AGING PROCESSES

Can you see the convergence of biological and psychological forces when the topics of physical fitness and proper nutrition are discussed? Do you agree that health and wellness are connected to psychological processes enhancing a person's well-being?

Health, well-being, and physical endurance during adult life affect many facets of development, including biological, psychological, and social spheres.

Nutrition and Physical Well-Being   Proper nutrition in the form of balanced diets, like regular exercise, is important throughout the entire life cycle (Benfante, Reed, & Frank, 1991; Jacyk, 1991; Liptzin, 1991; Sytkowski, Kannel, & D'Agostino, 1990). However, eating right is especially important during adult life. As Paul Insel and Walton Roth (1991) point out, most individuals arrive at young adulthood with the advantage of having a "normal" body weight—that is, neither too fat nor too lean. In fact, some young adults get away with poor eating and exercise habits and do not develop a weight problem. However, as the rapid growth period of adolescence slows and the steady state of growth maintenance takes over in adult life, choosing a healthy lifestyle is necessary to maintain normal weight without undue effort. As family and career obligations increase, as well as the potential to adopt a sedentary lifestyle, eating right and exercising regularly become increasingly important. In relation to the problems posed by being overweight, consider the following:

- It is estimated that 34 million American adults are overweight.
- Overweight persons are found at all ages, although the proportion of overweight adults increases with age.
- During young and middle adulthood, the typical body both adds fat and loses muscle. The fat content of a man's body usually doubles; a woman's increases by half.
- About 25 to 45% of adult American men and women are overweight.
- The rate of dieting reaches 60% or more during the college years.
- About 25% of all American children are overweight.
- About 75% of people who lose weight regain it within a year. (Boskin, Graf, & Kreisworth, 1990; Gamon & O'Brien, 1991; Horwath, 1991; Johnson, 1990; Morley & Glick, 1990)

What nutritional factors account for being overweight? Excess fat and cholesterol build up when people ingest more calories than they use. Thus, when individuals consume more calories than they expend throughout the day, they will gain weight. It is therefore important for adults to limit daily calorie intake, particularly in relation to fats and sugars, and to realize that the recommended daily caloric intake declines with age. In support of the latter, young adult males need about 2,700 calories a day; young adult females require approximately 2,000. Middle-aged males require 2,400 calories a day, and the corresponding figure for females is 1,800. For males in late adulthood, 2,050 calories per day are needed; females require 1,600 (Food and Nutrition Board, National Research Council, 1989).

With excess weight usually come medical complications, including poor digestion and susceptibility to stress-linked illnesses (Delafuente, 1990; Ebersole & Hess, 1990; Glick, 1990; Rolfes & DeBruyne, 1990). Six of the top 10 causes of death in the United States are associated with diet—heart disease, some types of cancer (e.g., colon, breast, uterus), stroke, non-insulin-dependent diabetes mellitus, atherosclerosis, and chronic liver disease (Anspaugh, Hamrick, & Rosato, 1991). Often linked to such disorders is a disproportionate consumption of foods high in fats, often at the expense of foods high in complex carbohydrates and fiber. Given such dietary excess and imbalance, it is easy to see why proper nutrition is important during the adult years (Antonini & Vannucci, 1990; Bidlack, 1990; Cesario & Hollander, 1991; Lewis & Bell, 1990).

Mental Development

By the time young adulthood is reached, the ability to acquire and utilize knowledge nears maximum capacity. This becomes a time for systematic and sophisticated problem-solving abilities, in addition to new levels of creative thought. The mental advancements evident during young adulthood are both qualitative and quantitative in nature. *Qualitatively,* we are able to see that over time, developing cognitive abilities have brought mental flexibility and adaptation. *Quantitatively,* we discover that mental abilities have become greatly differentiated and reached new levels of proficiency. Thus both the kinds and amounts of knowledge possessed by young adults have changed from earlier years.

Qualitative Mental Dimensions   Several researchers have attempted to unravel the qualitative operations of adults and have explored the mental processes of the adult mind. Differences between adolescent and adult thought have been discovered, prompting some to believe that mental dynamics continue to develop beyond formal operations. One example of postformal reasoning is *dialectical thought,* thinking involving the recognition and acceptance of contradictions and the attempt to synthesize. Dialectical thought embraces the notion that every idea has its opposite and that such opposing viewpoints can be considered simultaneously.

Perhaps an example would illustrate the quality of thinking transcending formal operations. Consider a longitudinal investigation examining the mental dynamics of university students (Perry, 1968). In this study, an effort was made to discover how students "made sense" of their personal and classroom experiences. They were interviewed at the end of each of their four years, especially on the conflicting viewpoints to which they were exposed. It was found they progressed from interpreting their world in authoritarian dualistic ways (e.g., good and bad, right and wrong) partly because they had expected their professors to give them the answers. In other words, they assumed there was only one correct answer to every problem or moral dilemma they encountered.

Soon, these students began to realize the inherent subjectivity of experience, and they believed everything was relative and nonabsolute. These students were overwhelmed by the uncertainty of it all. As they experienced differing viewpoints, they were eventually able to accept and respect a diversity of opinion and the rights of others—a relativistic perspective. Thus students were seen as moving from a basic dualism to a tolerance for competing points of view—conceptual relativism. They were able to construct this information into a meaningful body of knowledge. Notice how this type of mental operation differs from that transpiring during formal operations, such as what might be applied to solving a chemistry or physics problem.

Other theorists believe the practicality of everyday life pushes adults away from, or beyond, the logic of formal operations into other cognitive styles. For example, Gisela Labouvie-Vief (1982, 1986, 1990) suggests that formal operations may not be the pinnacle of thought Piaget believed. Formal operations is excellent in adolescence and young adulthood when we use logical possibilities to explore our options and develop an identity. However, in adulthood, we begin to turn away from the purely logical, analytic approach as we move toward a deeper form of understanding that deals more with myth and metaphor and paradox than with certainty.

Quantitative Mental Dimensions   The quantitative changes that take place with age can be revealed through standardized intelligence tests. Researchers have also found that these changes are best measured by employing a longitudinal study, which, as we know, is a research design used to collect data from the same individuals at different points in their lives. This interpretation of intelligence appears to be the most widely accepted today.

The longitudinal research design tends to produce more accurate intellectual data than findings uncovered in cross-sectional methods. As we stated in Chapter 1, the cross-sectional technique is based on comparisons of different age groups at a given time. Such a research technique was used in the early 1930s and 1940s and indicated that intelligence declines with age. It is maintained, however, that the decline measured was due to differences in the age groups other than age—such as educational background or socioeconomic status.

DOES INTELLIGENCE CHANGE WITH AGE? Whether intelligence remains continuous throughout adult life or demonstrates age-related fluctuations reflects the issue of stability versus change that we discussed in the last chapter. Paul Baltes and K. Warner Schaie are among the growing number of researchers seeking to explore this important issue and have shed considerable light on the topic (Baltes & Baltes, 1990; Baltes & Schaie, 1974; Schaie, 1982, 1983, 1990; Willis & Baltes, 1980). In one representative longitudinal study (Baltes & Schaie, 1974), they were interested in discovering whether four types of intellectual functioning change with age. The first type of mental operation, called **crystallized intelligence,** includes those skills acquired through education and acculturation, such as verbal comprehension, numerical skills, and inductive

THEORETICAL ISSUES

Do you think a level of thinking exists beyond Piaget's stage of formal operations? If so, can you think of ways the cognitive capacities during this stage differ from mental faculties exhibited by adolescents?

reasoning. **Cognitive flexibility** encompasses the individual's ability to shift from one way of thinking to another, within the context of familiar intellectual operations, as when one must provide either an antonym or synonym for a word, depending on whether the word appears in capital or lowercase letters. **Visuomotor flexibility** is the capacity to shift from familiar to unfamiliar patterns in tasks dictating coordination between visual and motor abilities. Finally, **visualization** consists of the ability to organize and process visual materials, and involves such tasks as finding a simple figure contained in a complex one or identifying a picture that is incomplete.

The researchers compared test performances on these four dimensions in 1956 and then again in 1963. Although no strong age-related change appeared in cognitive flexibility, crystallized intelligence and visualization test scores improved. For these two dimensions of intelligence, scores increased even into the retirement years. Only visuomotor flexibility demonstrated a significant decrease with age.

Such findings apparently help to dispel the myth of intellectual decline during the twilight years. As such, we can say that intellectual functioning is characterized more by stability than change and discontinuity in adult life. In fact, such studies as this support the notion that adults with above-average intelligence can improve—or at the very least maintain—their abilities until later adulthood, whereas those of average intelligence may experience a decline in some mental capacities. Whatever declines do exist appear to be in the realm of visuomotor tasks. Because of the time limits imposed on them, the structure of standardized IQ tests, particularly those emphasizing visuomotor flexibility, therefore, favor the young (Cunningham, 1988, 1989; Tomer, 1989).

It is important to realize that observations and conclusions concerning intelligence are somewhat biased and based on inferences. Inferences, at best, are

Much like other stages of the lifespan, young adulthood presents individuals with unique developmental challenges.

only guesses grounded in probability and, by definition, inferences are subject to error. How one behaves or what a person does may in no way accurately reflect mental abilities or intelligence. Take, for example, the adult who enrolls in college and receives an F at the end of the semester. The inference might be that the person is lacking in intelligence. The adult who receives the failing grade could, however, conceivably possess little or no motivation in regard to earning grades, and furthermore may feel no need to demonstrate to others that the subject matter has been mastered. Thus a cut-and-dried grade may tell us nothing about the individual. Similar circumstances might also apply to the unmotivated adult who reluctantly agrees to participate in intelligence testing (Charness, 1985; McKenzie, 1980; Schaie, 1990; Willis & Baltes, 1980).

EVALUATING METHODS OF EVALUATION Certain factors must be taken into account when evaluating adult learning performances on standardized tests. For example, a person may be anxious, rigid, or bored in testing situations. Also, younger and older persons differ in their reactions to standardized testing situations. Older persons are more likely to be anxious, see less value in the testing, and less prone to guess, even when the latter would be a good strategy. Young subjects often make many more errors of commission than omission, but the reverse is true for elderly people. It is conceivable that elderly individuals are more cautious because they have been discouraged more for doing the wrong thing. In this respect, caution may make elderly people appear less competent than they actually are (Baltes, 1990; Hertzog, 1989; Kausler, 1982; Schaie, 1983).

All of this suggests we need to rethink the nature of standardized test situations. As indicated, most standardized tests are biased in favor of young persons for reasons other than age. To illustrate, persons in their 60s or 70s may score lower on an intelligence test than those in their 20s not because they are older but because they have less experience taking standardized tests or less education. Thus differences that appear may originate from generational differences, not intellectual ability (Cockburn & Smith, 1990).

From this discussion you should now realize that adults as they grow older do not experience a decline in all facets of intelligence. For abilities where speed is not of primary importance, there is little change in intellectual functioning throughout adulthood. Should a decline in intellectual capacity occur during late adulthood, it is more likely due to the previously described reasons or because of physical factors, such as fatigue, sensory impairment, or declining health (Cunningham & Haman, 1992; Elias et al., 1990; Hayslip, Kennelly, & Maloy, 1990; Perlmutter & Nyquist, 1990). This is another good illustration of how development forces, namely physical and intellectual capacities, converge to affect behavior.

Additionally, Gary Evans and Megan Lewis (1990) remind us that other factors need to be acknowledged when examining the concept of intellectual functioning. For instance, differences in resources among the rich and poor, as well as the urban and rural, are likely to shape the course of intellectual capacities. Differences in norms and practices among cultures also shape what intelligent behavior is, as do cohort differences between cultures. Also, it can be argued that cognition and behaviors which help older adults function competently and meet everyday demands are manifestations of intelligence.

ACTIVE AND REACTIVE MODELS OF DEVELOPMENT
How do you think college or other educational settings are responsible for changing the way adolescents and young adults express their intelligence? Do you view students as being active or reactive in their relationships with such learning environments? In what way(s)?

In relation to this last point, Walter Cunningham and Kirsten Haman (1992) feel that new intelligence tests for elderly people need to be developed. Existing tests may be too narrowly focused on academic topics and not reflective of intellectual demands in the real world. What seem to be needed are comprehensive and creative tests that seek to identify new factors of intellectual ability germane to late adulthood. Cynthia Berg (1990) concurs with this and feels that future research needs to analyze how intelligence interacts with the elderly's daily living skills, including problem-solving abilities, conflict resolution capacities, and stress management techniques.

In summary, adulthood marks a time when individuals can sustain or even increase their qualitative and quantitative mental capacities. This is especially true for those living in varied rather than static environments. Adulthood also represents a period in which individuals can excel in a wide range of learning activities. Furthermore, the efficiency of adults, especially that of older generations, can be enhanced when their special interests are taken into account and the tasks are satisfying. Along these lines, some researchers (e.g., Dittmann-Kohli et al., 1991; Hill, Storandt, & Simeone, 1990; Ressler, 1991) feel that certain mental abilities can be trained, most notably those related to crystallized intelligence and recall ability.

Finally, let us close by saying that with advancing age, adults have typically acquired practical insight into life and considerable real-world learning. Chances are that older adults have also acquired good judgment, discretion, and wisdom. These are important mental vitamins that transcend book learning and have taken many years to acquire. They are sought-after dimensions of mature thought, not evidence of intellectual decline (Baltes, 1990; Kliegl, Smith, & Baltes, 1989; Meier-Ruge, 1990).

UNIT REVIEW—

↗ Physical maturation has been virtually completed by young adulthood. The body reaches its maximum physical potential during this time, at least as far as the muscles and internal organs are concerned.

↗ Regular exercise, proper nutrition, and a healthy lifestyle are important throughout all stages of adulthood.

↗ Mental development nears its maximum capacity during young adulthood. The mental advancements evident at this time are both qualitative and quantitative in nature.

↗ Of the four main types of intellectual operations presented, only visuomotor flexibility decreases with age.

↗ Observations and conclusions regarding adult intelligence are often based on inferences and are subject to error. We must move beyond the realm of IQ test scores to evaluate adult learning performances effectively.

UNIT TWO: PERSONALITY AND SOCIAL DEVELOPMENT

Young adulthood provides a diverse landscape for learning about oneself and others, and embarking on new and challenging life paths. Many dreams are shaped during this time, and although putting one's aspirations into effect is difficult, such lifework can be both exhilarating and rewarding. Indeed, such a quest enables young adults to realize their potential in life. In the midst of self-discovery, decision-making skills are learned, important values are nurtured, and responsibility blossoms.

During young adulthood, many developments take place within the spheres of personality and social functioning. Whether it be launching a career, embarking on an independent lifestyle, sharing an intimate friendship, marrying, or becoming a parent, this represents a time when individuals can inquire, experiment, and explore. In the midst of self-discovery, a foothold in the world of grown-ups can be established.

▬ Adult Maturity

Adequately meeting the challenges of adulthood requires a considerable degree of **maturity.** Generally speaking, maturity refers to a state that promotes physical and psychological well-being. In most instances, the mature person possesses a well developed value system, an accurate self-concept, stable emotional behavior, satisfying social relationships, and intellectual insight. Coping with the demands of adulthood, a mature individual is realistic in the assessment of future goals and ideals. Maturity implies the ability to cope more successfully with life's problems, increasing the effectiveness of our planning strategies, deepening our appreciation of the surroundings, and expanding our resources for happiness.

Maturity is not a unitary concept or an all-or-nothing phenomenon. Rather, there are many facets of maturity that need to be carefully examined. For example, some people may have attained moral maturity, but are not emotionally mature. Furthermore, age is no guarantee of maturity. The fact that one has reached adult status does not mean maturity is automatic. As we shall see, maturity requires considerable conscious effort that depends on the individual and not on a preset age.

Attaining adult maturity is a difficult task. In the process, individuals must re-examine old values and attitudes as they experiment with new ones, a process that may be anxiety-producing for many young people. Yet although anxiety is essential for growth, many Western cultures frequently regard this emotional reaction negatively. Consequently, some members of the older generation may become poor guides for younger generations, being unable to teach them to tolerate growing pains in their quest for maturity.

Unfortunately, there are many who do not attain a sense of maturity and as a result fall short of accurate identity achievement. Instead, a type of personality foreclosure results, in which young people identify with the values and goals of their parents without questioning whether they are right for them. Thus there are those who abandon the painful task of self-growth and the quest for adult maturity for the easier alternative of letting themselves be socialized by others. If this is the chosen path, the price to be paid for social maturity may be lifelong psychological immaturity.

Now that we have touched on the general concept of maturity, we turn our attention to some of the more specific aspects of maturity. Gordon Allport (1961) has provided one of the more in-depth investigations of the subject. Although an older piece of research, Allport's work has withstood the test of time, and his observations have been widely referred to and acclaimed.

Allport's Seven Dimensions of Maturity Gordon Allport (1961) postulates that maturity is an ongoing process best characterized by a series of attainments on the part of the individual. Each period of life has its share of obstacles that must be overcome—roadblocks that require the development of goal-formulation and decision-making abilities. Methods for dealing with life's failures and frustrations—as well as accepting its triumphs and victories—have to be devised, if maturity is to be nurtured.

Allport has identified seven specific dimensions or criteria of maturity that manifest themselves during adulthood. These seven dimensions include extension of the self, relating warmly to others, emotional security, realistic perception, possession of skills and competencies, knowledge of the self, and establishing a unifying philosophy of life.

EXTENSION OF THE SELF The first criterion of maturity, *self-extension,* requires that individuals gradually extend their comprehension to encompass multiple facets of their environment. The sphere of the young child is primarily limited to the family, but over time the child becomes involved in various peer groups, in school activities, and in clubs. Eventually, strong bonds develop with members of the opposite sex, and interest toward vocational, moral, and civic responsibilities is generated. Each outlet provides the young adult with the opportunity to become involved in more meaningful personal relationships and to fulfill the need of sharing new feelings and experiences with others.

RELATING WARMLY TO OTHERS Allport's second criterion of maturity is the ability to relate the self warmly to others. By this Allport means the capacity to be intimate with, as well as compassionate toward, others. Intimacy is defined by Allport as understanding, acceptance, and empathy toward others. Despite the wide differences that exist between people, intimacy implies the ability to overcome whatever interpersonal boundaries exist. The fully mature person places a high premium on platonic love and a sense of oneness with others. Intimacy also involves a tolerance of the weaknesses and shortcomings of others.

EMOTIONAL SECURITY Although numerous dimensions of maturity can be grouped under emotional security, Allport maintains that four qualities in particular are important: self-acceptance, emotional acceptance, frustration tolerance, and confidence in self-expression. Self-acceptance is the ability to acknowledge one's self fully, particularly in terms of one's imperfections. By mature emotional acceptance, people accept emotions as being part of the normal self. Frustration tolerance is the capacity to continue functioning even during times of stress. As far as confidence in self-expression is concerned, a mature person is aware of one's own emotions, is not afraid of them, and has control over their expression.

REALISTIC PERCEPTION Quite simply, maturity in this sense means being able to keep in touch with reality, without distorting the environment to meet

Extension of the self, including the development of compassion for others is an important element of adult maturity.

individual needs and purposes. Sometimes the complexities of events and situations, combined with the ego defenses of the individual, may produce an inaccurate interpretation of the environment. The mature mind is able to perceive the surroundings accurately.

POSSESSION OF SKILLS AND COMPETENCIES Possessing some type of skill or competence represents Allport's fifth dimension of maturity. Unless one possesses some basic skill, it is virtually impossible to nurture the kind of security necessary for maturity to develop. While the immature adolescent may argue, "I'm no good at anything," mature adults strive to develop whatever skills they feel they possess. Furthermore, skilled individuals are driven by a need to express their competence through some type of activity.

KNOWLEDGE OF THE SELF Knowledge of the self, or *self-objectification,* is criterion number six. Most mature people possess a great deal of self-insight, of which many immature individuals have little. According to Allport, knowledge of the self involves three capacities: knowing what one *can* do, knowing what one *cannot* do, and knowing what one *ought* to do.

ESTABLISHING A UNIFYING PHILOSOPHY OF LIFE The final criterion or dimension of maturity outlined by Allport is the development of a unifying philosophy of life that embodies the concepts of a guiding purpose, ideals, needs, goals, and values. Because the mature human being is a goal-seeking person, such a synthesis enables him or her to develop an intelligent theory of life and to work toward implementing it. Mature people tend to view goals from a balanced perspective and are able to cope with failure if these goals are not met.

THEORETICAL ISSUES

Do you think any Piagetian developments during formal operations (or beyond) contribute to adult maturity? How might Freudian defense mechanisms distort perceptions of oneself and others? Do you think a connection exists between Maslow's concept of self-actualization and the attainment of a unifying philosophy of life?

To summarize, the seven dimensions proposed by Allport are important factors in the development of maturity. Because of Allport's emphasis on individual uniqueness, it should be mentioned that these dimensions can be expressed differently by different people. The dimensions may not be possessed by everyone. On the contrary, unfavorable conditions may hinder personality growth and prevent the attainment of maturity. Some people may remain immature because they are trapped in a conflict between cultural expectations and personal requirements. Others may be prevented at the very beginning of life, by forces outside their control, from ever reaching personal fulfillment.

Theories of Personality Development

The developmental challenges of adult life, as we mentioned earlier, tend to shape and mold the personality of the individual. Three personality theorists have helped us better understand the changes that take place at this time: Erik Erikson, Daniel Levinson, and Roger Gould.

Erik Erikson's Theory

INTIMACY VERSUS ISOLATION During early adulthood, mature psychosocial development is measured by the successful resolution of the crisis known as **intimacy versus isolation.** Before early adulthood, recall that the individual was in the midst of an identity crisis, a struggle that reached its peak during adolescence. Erikson now stresses that as a young adult, the individual is motivated to fuse the newly established identity with that of others.

Only after a person has established an identity can a truly intimate relationship be established with another. Intimacy results from the ability to fuse your identity with someone else's. It comes from the ability to love one another. An intimate relationship is built on mutual trust and love and from this the young adult develops a sense of interdependence, a sense of *we*. People who have not developed their identity tend to shy away from interpersonal relationships that lead to intimacy, and a feeling of isolation may result.

Although most young adults seek to gratify the need for intimacy through marriage, it is important to stress that intimate relationships other than sexual ones are possible. Individuals may develop strong bonds of intimacy in friendships that offer, among other features, mutuality, empathy, and reciprocity (Blieszner & Adams, 1992; Hendrick & Hendrick, 1992; Roscoe, Kennedy, & Pope, 1987; White et al., 1986). Intimate relationships may easily develop out of a capacity to share with and understand others. The socially mature adult is capable of effectively communicating with others, being sensitive to another person's needs, and, in general, exhibiting tolerance toward humankind. The growth of friendship, love, and devotion is much more prominent among mature people than among the more immature (Blieszner & Adams, 1992; Duck, 1991).

Daniel Levinson's Theory

Recall from Chapter 2 that Daniel Levinson (1977, 1980, 1981, 1984, 1986, 1990, in press; Levinson & Gooden, 1985; Levinson et al., 1978) sought to trace the course of male adult development. Although he limited his study to 40 males, he has succeeded in supplying unique insights into the nature of the adult personality. It is conceivable that women pass through similar stages.

EPIGENETIC PRINCIPLE

One of the criticisms leveled at Erikson's theory is that compared to earlier stages, his psychosocial crises of adulthood tend to lack substance and depth. What are your impressions of Erikson's epigenetic scheme? Do you think this criticism is warranted? Why or why not?

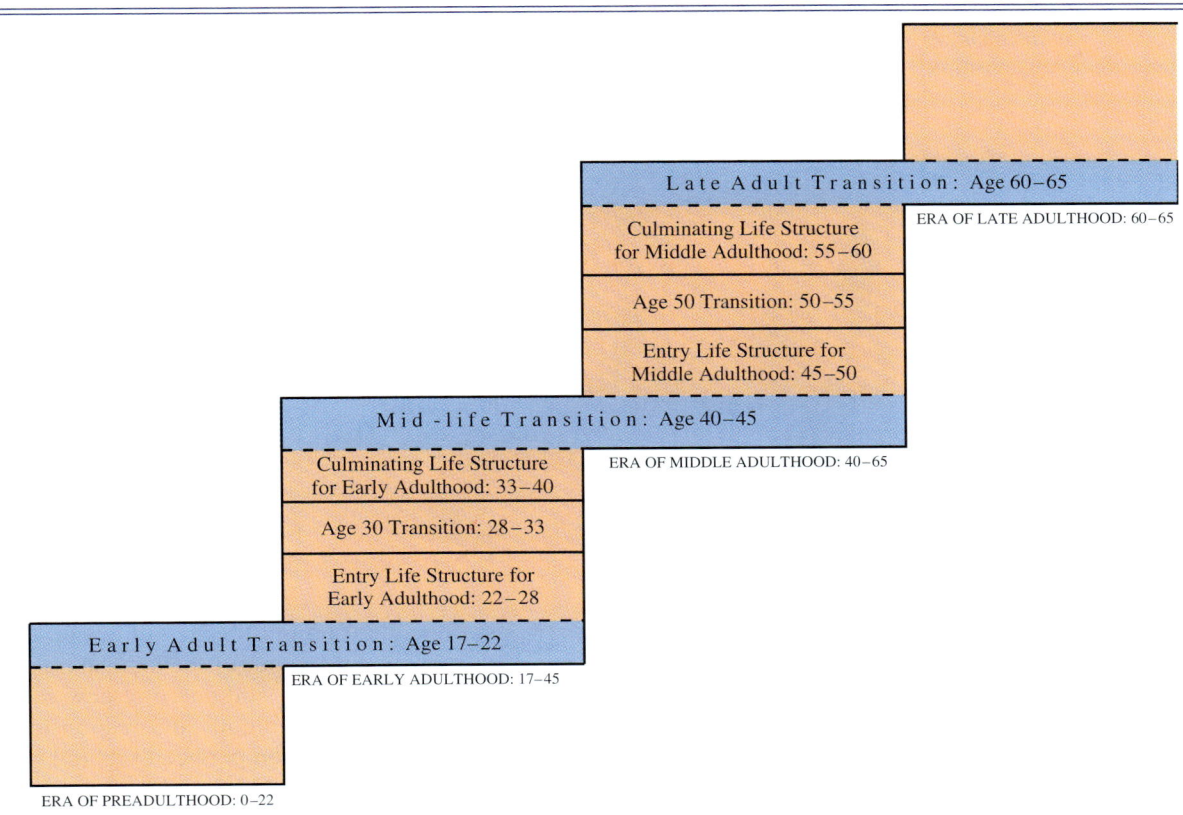

ERA OF LATE ADULTHOOD: 60–65

Late Adult Transition: Age 60–65

Culminating Life Structure
for Middle Adulthood: 55–60

Age 50 Transition: 50–55

Entry Life Structure for
Middle Adulthood: 45–50

Mid-life Transition: Age 40–45

ERA OF MIDDLE ADULTHOOD: 40–65

Culminating Life Structure
for Early Adulthood: 33–40

Age 30 Transition: 28–33

Entry Life Structure for
Early Adulthood: 22–28

Early Adult Transition: Age 17–22

ERA OF EARLY ADULTHOOD: 17–45

ERA OF PREADULTHOOD: 0–22

FIGURE 9-1

Developmental Periods
in the Eras of Early
and Middle Adulthood.

According to Daniel
Levinson and his
colleagues, unique
personality eras
characterize the years
of young and middle
adulthood. As you can
see, each era is
differentiated by
developmental periods.
These stages confront the
individual with an
assortment of adjustment
challenges.

Levinson suggests that our lives are divided into *eras* of approximately 25 years each, and each era consists of developmental periods, marked by a distinct "biopsychosocial character" (Levinson, 1986). Between each era a major transition occurs (there are also transitions within eras).

Individuals make adjustments when entering an era during what Levinson calls the novice phase. A reassessment of the developing life structure occurs during the middle of each era—the transition phase. Finally, one enters the culminating phase of the era where the life structure is reassessed and fine-tuned.

Prior to early adulthood is the *era of preadulthood* (ages 0–22), followed by the *era of early adulthood* (ages 17–25). The years of overlap between these two eras are termed the *early adult transition* (17–22). The periods within the early adulthood era include the *entry life structure for early adulthood* (22–28), the *age 30 transition* (28–33), and the *culminating life structure for early adulthood* (33–40). This is followed by the *mid-life transition* (40–45), which marks the entry into middle age or what Levinson calles the *era of middle adulthood* (40–45). Figure 9-1 illustrates the developmental periods of early adulthood proposed by Levinson, in addition to his developmental scheme for adult life.

The *early adult transition* presents two major tasks. The first is to terminate the adolescent life structure and leave the preadult world. Separation from the

Maturity involves initiating and maintaining meaningful relationships.

preadult world means becoming less dependent on one's family of origin. Decreased dependency can be external, such as moving out of the familial home, becoming less financially dependent on one's parents, and entering new roles and living arrangements in which one is more autonomous and responsible. Separation can also be internal: increasing differentiation between self and parents, greater psychological distance from the family, and lessened emotional dependency on parental support.

The second task of the early adult transition is to form a basis for living in the adult world before fully becoming a part of it. A young man's knowledge, aspirations, and values for a particular kind of adult life are frequently ambiguous and colored by parental fantasies. The task here is to obtain further training to learn more about oneself and the world in general. During this time, more clearly defined options for adult living must be made, specific life goals must be planned, and a higher measure of self-definition as an adult must be gained. Thus, whereas the first task of this stage was one of termination, this second task can best be characterized as one of initiation.

The second developmental period proposed by Levinson is the *entry life structure for early adulthood* (22–28). At this time young adults have to fashion and test out initial life structures that provide a viable link between their valued selves and the adult society. As Levinson observes, young men are at a point where they should explore available options and possibilities in the world to arrive at a crystallized (though by no means final) definition of themselves as adults, and to make and live with their initial choices regarding occupation, love relationships, lifestyle, and values.

The *age 30 transition* (28–33) is Levinson's third stage of young adulthood. This period provides the individual with the opportunity to work on flaws in the life structure formed in the previous period and to create a basis for a more satisfactory structure that will typically be created in the ensuing period. At this time, the provisional, exploratory quality of the 20s is ending and the individual experiences a sense of great urgency. Life is becoming more serious, more restrictive, and more realistic.

The *culminating life structure for early adulthood* (33–40) represents the last developmental period for the young adult years. Two tasks in particular need to be resolved during the settling-down stage. The first is to establish one's niche in society or, as Levinson describes it, to dig in, build a nest, and pursue one's interest within a defined pattern. Successful resolution of such a task requires some type of deliberation, order, and stabilization.

The second task is to work at advancement and strive to succeed onward and upward. Whereas the first task contributes to the stability of a defined structure, Levinson stresses that the second task implies progression within the structure. Advancement in this sense may mean building a better life, improving and using one's skills, becoming more creative, or in general contributing to society. Becoming strongly connected to a segment of society, being responsive to its demands, and seeking the affirmation and rewards that it offers are the developmental tasks of becoming one's own man.

Roger Gould's Theory   The underpinnings of Roger Gould's (1978, 1980) theory of adult personality development rests on the notion that adults must strive to eliminate irrational childhood ideas which have a tendency to restrict their lives. These false assumptions frequently embody the concept of parental dependency, as Levinson proposed. Ideally, as life experience builds, adults must abandon these unwarranted expectations, rigid rules, and inflexible roles, which hinder individual autonomy. If this is accomplished, in time adults will come to be true owners of their selves with a more mature level of consciousness.

Gould maintains that young adulthood is a critical period of development, since it is at this point that individuals realize how they can begin to take control of their lives. In particular, it is understood that four major false assumptions acquired in childhood need to be questioned: Adults will always live with their parents; one's parents will always be there to help when things go wrong or not exactly as one wants; parents can always offer a simplified version (and solution) to complicated inner realities; and no evil or death exists in the world.

Gould believes that by the time young adulthood is reached, individuals know intellectually that these assumptions are factually incorrect, but emotionally they retain hidden control of adult life until significant events unveil them as emotional as well as intellectual fantasies. The gradual shedding of these false assumptions, a process that lasts throughout adulthood, signifies an individual's shift from childhood consciousness to more mature levels of adult reasoning.

Although these are the major false assumptions intertwined throughout all of adulthood, Gould suggests that additional irrational ideas can be found within specific stages of adult life. Young adulthood contains three stages—*leaving our parents' world* (ages 16–22); *I'm nobody's baby now* (ages 22–28); and *opening up to what's inside* (ages 28–34)—each with accompanying false assumptions about adult life. The major false assumption to be challenged in the stage called *leaving our parents' world* is that individuals will always belong to their parents and believe in their world. The thrust here is that parental influence is at times domineering, and young adults are in the midst of striving for independence and autonomy. Interwoven with this major theme are other component false assumptions, such as "If I get any more independent, it

THEORETICAL ISSUES

The adult personality theories of Levinson and Gould are relative newcomers to the field of lifespan development. How do their theories compare and contrast with some of the older, more established ones you've read about? Do Levinson and Gould clearly present the conceptual framework of their theories?

Western culture dictates that adults must learn to take control of their lives and establish self-sufficiency.

will be a disaster"; "I can view the world only through my parents' eyes"; "Only my parents can guarantee my safety"; and "My parents are my only family." Notice how each embodies the concept of parental dependency and the lack of individual freedom. The young adult will soon learn, however, that such life events as establishing independence away from the home, embarking on a career, expanding social horizons, or developing personal convictions about life in general will go a long way toward establishing adult independence.

The stage of *I'm nobody's baby now* provides young adults with the opportunity to challenge another false assumption. The illogical thought here is that adults feel they have to do things their parents' way. Furthermore, if individuals become too frustrated, confused, or tired, parents will step in and show them the right way.

This false assumption is similar to that of the previous stage; that is, young adults frequently adhere to the concept of absolute safety offered by omnipotent parents. Gould emphasizes, however, that as the architects of their own existence, young adults must learn to accept full responsibility for their life course and not depend on parental intervention. This means certain life skills must be developed. Thinking and planning must become critical, analytical, sequential, and goal-oriented. Young adults must also learn to value such attributes as perseverance, willpower, and common sense. Equally important is the ability to learn how to tolerate being wrong in order to learn how to be right.

For those willing to accept the challenges of this stage, a solid base of confidence built on true competence will be nurtured. As young adults meet each novel experience or tackle each larger task, their sense of accomplishment grows. As Gould declares, fantasy powers are replaced by real powers. A feeling of movement or growth replaces the fear that we will always be small and appendages of our parents. As our confidence, our competence, and our sense of being adult increase, the mocking voices within us grow silent.

TABLE 9-1
Levinson's and Gould's Stages of Young Adulthood

	Levinson	Gould
Stages and Ages	Early Adult Transition (17–22)	Leaving Our Parent's World (16–22)
	Entry Life Structure for Early Adulthood (22–28)	I'm Nobody's Baby Now (22–28)
	Age 30 Transition (28–30)	Opening Up to What's Inside (28–34)
	Culminating Life Structure for Early Adulthood (33–40)	

Opening up to what's inside is the third stage of young adulthood proposed by Gould. By this time in life, most adults have had 8 to 10 years of experience living outside their parents' homes, or as Gould describes it, outside the world of absolute safety. The basic ingredients of independent life have been established, and most adults have become prideful and self-reliant. Now, however, individuals have the opportunity to challenge the major false assumption that dominates this age period: Life is simple and controllable.

This age period provides adults with the opportunity to turn inward and reexamine themselves for something other than the narrow limits of independence and competence that loomed so critical a few years earlier. Should they decide to turn their energies inward, coexisting contradictory forces themselves are usually discovered. A new region of adult consciousness that is intensely private and personal is found. This region of consciousness may consist of desires, tendencies, wishes, talents, and strengths that adults have shut out of their lives during their early 20s, because they did not fit or caused too much conflict. These feelings now have a tendency to surface, and adults find themselves in a position to open up to what is experienced inside. The end result of this growth stage is that many adults discover a new way of perceiving the world.

The process of opening up in the 30s obviously requires an in-depth analysis of oneself. Consistent with Gould's overall theory, certain illogical ideas about life, especially its perceived simplicity and controllability, have to be examined. Close inspection will reveal that life is not as simple or as well ordered as one would imagine. Adults must learn to shape their future on the basis of a realistic interpretation of what exists inside them as well as what surrounds them in their environment. For a comparison of Levinson's and Gould's theories, see Table 9-1.

INTERRELATEDNESS OF AGING PROCESSES

How do you think Gould's false psychological assumptions blend with social dynamics? For example, are they "convenient fictions" that help keep youngsters secure in the world? How would the psychological and social lives of children and adolescents be affected if they didn't cling to such assumptions?

Development of Adult Intimate Relationships

As we learned in the last chapter, dating begins at an early age. This is largely due to our encouragement of early heterosexual interactions in the school system or at social functions, or through the individual's contact with the mass media. Dating provides an opportunity to meet a number of men and women and serves as a vehicle for recreation, companionship, and socialization. As far as the latter is concerned, dating provides people with opportunities to learn about roles, values, and norms (Cate & Lloyd, 1992).

Beyond the functions just mentioned, dating has other purposes. Nijole Benokraitis (1993) believes dating provides an opportunity for participants to gain insight into their identities. That is, being in the company of a partner enables individuals to confirm their identities as well as any self-doubts that exist. Finally, dating brings status achievement. Dating is generally regarded as a positively evaluated activity, and the more one dates, the more likely status is to rise in one's social group.

According to Maxine Zinn and Stanley Eitzen (1990), the courtship process can be conceptualized as a continuum beginning with casual dating with many partners to those of a more serious, steady nature. Gradually, there will be a narrowing of choices for a partner with increasing levels of emotional involvement and seriousness of commitment. Through continuous interaction during the courtship process, a couple's deeper understanding of one another usually emerges. These are pivotal features of intimate relationships and often determine whether two people are compatible (Cate & Lloyd, 1992).

Dating becomes a conscious, deliberate process of mate selection by young adulthood. Because of heightened levels of maturity, dating now tends to be characterized by greater levels of mutuality and reciprocity. Young adults have typically declared their identity and have reached a point where they can share themselves intimately with others (Davidson & Moore, 1992; Edwards & Demo, 1991).

Dating and Intimate Relationships   For some, dating will always be a casual and lighthearted form of interaction. For others, though, dating brings about the establishment of a serious, intimate relationship. Most adults will be involved in one or more of these relationships over the course of their lives, and we now explore some of the dynamics of such arrangements.

Some important terminology needs to be clarified before proceeding, particularly the word **intimacy.** Intimacy originates from the Latin *intimus,* meaning "inner." In its broadest sense, intimacy means becoming close with another person. An **intimate relationship** represents a process in which we come to know the innermost, subjective aspects of another person—and we are known in a like manner. Put another way, an intimate relationship involves the mutual exchange of experiences in such a way that a further understanding of oneself and one's partner is achieved. For this to occur, intimate relationships require such important ingredients as knowledge of one's partner, trust, commitment, and caring (Chelune, Robison & Kommor, 1984; Hendrick & Hendrick, 1992; Rook, 1987).

Also important to intimate relationships is **self-disclosure,** the process by which individuals let themselves be known by others. Self-disclosure involves decisions about whether to reveal one's thoughts, feelings, or past experiences to another person; at what level of intimacy to reveal personal information; and the appropriate time, place, and target person for disclosure. As a relationship progresses to more intimate levels, partners generally disclose more information about themselves and at a more personal level (Derlega, 1984; Lauer & Lauer, 1991).

Individuals can disclose themselves through a number of different channels. Verbal self-disclosure uses words to let others know about you. Self-disclosure can also take place through body language or by one's tone of voice. The manner in which one gestures or chooses to emphasize words also says something about the person. Finally, people disclose themselves through their actions (Corey, 1990; Lamanna & Riedmann, 1994).

Gender Roles and Intimate Relationships   The impact of gender roles on the dynamics of intimate relationships is an important area of investigation. Letitia Peplau's (1983) observations of traditional relationships suggest that gender differences exist in the following areas: language and nonverbal communication; self-disclosure; falling in love; performance of daily tasks; decision-making strategies; conflict and aggression; personal attitudes and values; and reactions to the ending of a relationship.

LANGUAGE AND NONVERBAL COMMUNICATION Men, in a dominant-style role, tend to do more verbal interrupting, to claim greater personal space when communicating with a woman, and to initiate more touching. They are poorer at decoding nonverbal communications than are women (Drass, 1986; Jose & McCarthy, 1988). Women, on the other hand, appear better at initiating and maintaining conversations (Kohn, 1988). Women also seem to be more supportive of men than men are of women. Women also seem to be better than men—at least among husbands and wives—at delivering nonverbal messages. Women apparently make more eye contact, particularly when they are sitting close to a partner, than men (Kahn, 1984). Men tend to make eye contact only when their partners are farther away.

Sandra Metts and William Cupach (1989) add that differences in the meanings men and women attach to sexual behavior are also reflected in the manner in which partners communicate sexual interest. Men usually do less kissing, holding, or touching, and women often prefer more conversation, playfulness, and slower courting in bed. Men are often reluctant to verbalize appreciation of a spouse, to talk about their fantasies during love play, or to talk about their feelings after coitus (Brown & Auerback, 1981).

SELF-DISCLOSURE Women tend to disclose close personal information more easily in friendships than do men. In dating relationships and marriage, we need to distinguish preferences for disclosure from what actually occurs. In an actual relationship, the amount of reciprocal self-disclosure generally represents a compromise between the preferences of both partners. When one partner discloses more than the other, however, it is usually the woman (Snell, Miller, & Belk, 1988). However, even when men and women disclose in equal amounts, there are often differences in the *content* of their self-disclosures. For instance, men are more likely than women to reveal their strengths and conceal their weaknesses. For traditional men, this often means hiding feelings (Arliss & Borisoff, 1993; Tannen, 1990).

FALLING IN LOVE Does it surprise you to read that men are more likely than women to endorse "romantic beliefs," such as love comes but once, love lasts

THEORETICAL ISSUES

In what ways do you think self-disclosure is influenced by such personality dynamics as maturity, authenticity, and comfort with one's identity? Related to humanism, do you think the security offered by intimate relationships helps to fulfill such basic needs as belongingness, self-esteem, and strivings for self-actualization?

forever, love conquers barriers of social class or custom? And men tend to fall in love more quickly than women. Women are more likely to be pragmatists, saying they can love many individuals, that some disillusionment often accompanies long-term relationships, and that economic security is as important as passion in relationships (Rubin, Peplau, & Hill, 1981).

Both men and women seem to love their partners equally, but women are more apt to report emotional signs of love (Cancian, 1985). The latter include such things as feeling euphoric or having trouble concentrating on work and other activities because one can think only of the loved person.

TASK PERFORMANCE The evidence indicates that husbands and wives perform different types and amounts of family tasks. It's been traditional, at least in American marriages, for women and men to divide up the labor generally according to how much physical strength it may require or whether it is performed inside or outside the home (Brehm, 1992; Matlin, 1993). For example, for years women have done the cooking and cleaning and baby tending, whereas men have washed the family car, done the yard work, and carried out the garbage (see, for example, Lewin & Tragos, 1987; Werner & LaRussa, 1985).

DECISION MAKING AND INFLUENCE STRATEGIES Women and men in a close relationship tend to specialize in different areas of decision making. To illustrate, Judith Howard and her associates (1986) found that the traditional woman is less likely to influence and more apt to be influenced by the traditional man. Traditional husbands are likely to make major financial decisions for the family, whereas traditional wives are likely to make domestic decisions, such as those related to meals or home decorating.

Men and women often use somewhat different tactics to try to influence each other. For example, men are more likely than women to use direct means of influencing their wives, as for example by logical arguments. In contrast,

Mutual trust and sharing are important dimensions of intimate relationships.

women are more likely to report using indirect strategies, such as withholding speech or affection (Fitzpatrick, 1988; Howard, Blumstein, & Schwartz, 1986).

CONFLICT AND AGGRESSION Women and men react differently to conflict situations. Men are often motivated to resolve conflict and restore harmony whereas women are often rejecting, cold, or use appeals to fairness and guilt (Peplau, 1983). Studies of couples (e.g., Pearson, 1985) have found that both men and women expect women to react to conflict by crying, sulking, and criticizing their partner's insensitivity. Often both sexes expect men to show anger, reject the woman's tears, call for a logical approach to the problem, or sometimes try to delay the discussion. Men are more likely to use physical force to resolve conflicts, and women are more apt to be the victims of physical abuse (Gelles & Cornell, 1990; Gelles & Straus, 1988; Gubrium, 1992; Retzinger, 1991).

PERSONAL ATTITUDES AND VALUES Most men and women express a desire for a permanent relationship with someone. Both sexes value companionship and affection and give relatively less importance to social status in a relationship. In actual relationships, similarity is usually further enhanced by the selection of a partner whose attitudes are compatible with one's own and who has a similar background and values. Not surprisingly, marital discord may be at its greatest when a husband is more traditional and a wife more modern in gender-role orientation (Bowen, 1987).

Men and women also seem to value somewhat different qualities in an ideal love partner, although findings are mixed on this topic. For example, women often value such dimensions as intelligence and occupational achievement in their partners, whereas men value such characteristics as youth and sexual attractiveness (Peplau, 1983). However, other research (Daniel et al., 1985) suggests that men and women value similar qualities in a partner: intelligence, sensitivity, physical attractiveness, a sense of humor, and ambition. And one study (Buss & Barnes, 1986) showed that qualities valued in a potential partner differed for married and unmarried subjects. Among married persons, the desired qualities included good companionship, consideration, honesty, affection, and dependability. Unmarried people looked for kindness, an exciting personality, intelligence, physical attractiveness, and good health.

REACTIONS TO RELATIONSHIP DISSOLUTION The evidence suggests that men tend to react more negatively to relationship breakups than do women (Peplau, 1983). Moreover, the association between marital disruption and a variety of illnesses and disorders is stronger for men than for women. And, contrary to what many people might suppose, there is also some evidence (Beck, 1988; Peplau, 1983) that men react more severely than women to the end of a dating relationship. This may be partly because, as the research suggests, men are less sensitive to problems in their dating relationships and less likely either to foresee or to initiate a breakup.

Love and Intimate Relationships   Love is a complex and multifaceted human emotion and rests at the heart of the intimate relationship. Love can be expressed and received in many different ways. Love and love relationships are often the central theme of movies, plays, and popular songs. Descriptions, accounts, and narratives of it can be found in virtually all forms of the media, from

GENDER SIMILARITIES AND DIFFERENCES

How do you think gender-related differences in communication and other facets of intimate relationships create the potential for misunderstanding? What steps can individuals take to be more sensitive to the gender-role behaviors of their partners?

The intimate and tender nature of love is expressed and received in many ways.

movies and television to paperback books and supermarket tabloids. The study of love has also produced a wide variety of thoughts and opinions (see, for example, Douglas & Atwell, 1988; Feeney & Noller, 1990; Hendrick & Hendrick, 1992; Sarnoff & Sarnoff, 1989).

From childhood on, most of us learn the romantic ideal attached to love. From many different agents of socialization, we are taught to expect to "fall" in love at some point in our lives. Moreover, we are taught that love is the eventual outcome of dating and the appropriate basis for establishing marriage and having children. Because of this programming, we come to expect the experience of love (Henslin, 1992).

CONCEPTUAL MODELS OF LOVE Just as there are many different ways to experience and express love, so too are there a plethora of models to describe it. One such model, called the *wheel theory,* was developed by Ira Reiss (1960, 1980). He suggested that love consists of four components: rapport (feeling at ease with each other); self-revelation (disclosing personal details about each other's lives); mutual dependency (developing a reliance on one another and establishing interdependence); and personality and need fulfillment (satisfying each other's emotional needs). Figure 9-2 illustrates the wheel theory proposed by Reiss.

In a serious, long-lasting intimate relationship, the wheel will turn indefinitely; it may turn only a few times in a short-lived romance. Also, the weight of each component will cause the wheel to move forward or backward. To illustrate how the wheel can reverse itself, consider that the self-revelation component has been reduced because of some type of relationship disharmony. This

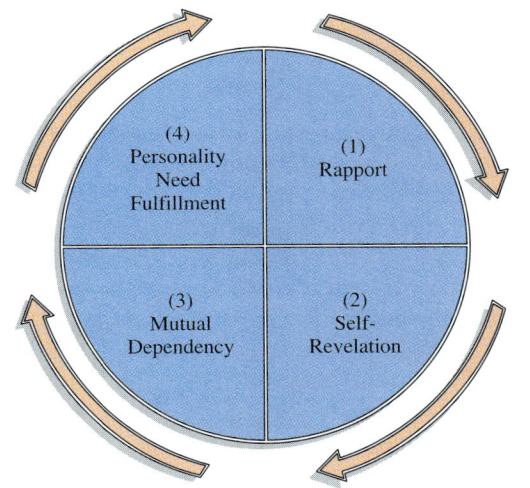

FIGURE 9-2
The Wheel Model of Love.

Ira Reiss maintains that love is a circular process that consists of four interrelated components. In serious, long-lasting relationships, the wheel will turn indefinitely. Conversely, passing romances may turn the wheel only a few times.

reduction would affect the dependency and personality need fulfillment processes, which would in turn weaken rapport, which would in turn lower the revelation level even further.

Another conceptual model of love was developed by John Lee (1973, 1976, 1988). Lee developed a unique typology of love that consisted of three primary types—eros, ludus, and storge love—and three secondary types—mania, agape, and pragma love. Lee likened these six styles of loving to a color wheel: Just as all colors are derived from the three primary colors (red, yellow, and blue), so do all styles of loving evolve from the three primary ones.

- **Eros love** is characterized by the desire for sexual intimacy and a preoccupation with the physical aspects of the relationship. Erotic lovers usually report powerful attraction toward one another, as well as intense feelings of excitement and anticipation.

- **Ludus love** is a playful type of love often self-centered in its expression. Ludus lovers are often flirtatious and do not want long-range attachments from their partners. Most also do not want their partners to be dependent on them. Ludus, or playful, lovers often regard love as a game.

- **Storge love** (pronounced "stor-gay") is a Greek term in origin and means calm, affectionate love. It is characterized by quiet commitment and companionship. Storge lovers enjoy doing things together, but intense emotional involvement is usually deemphasized.

- **Manic love** is intense and obsessive. Many manic lovers are overwhelmed by thoughts of their partners, so much so that they are always in a state of anxiety. They need continual affection and attention from their partners, as well as constant reassurance about the other's sincerity and commitment.

- **Agape love** is also a Greek term in origin and means altruistic love. Agape lovers care deeply about their partners and seek to satisfy their well-being in a warm and kind fashion. This gentle style of loving also asks nothing in return.

- **Pragma love** is from the Greek word *pragmatikos,* meaning practical and realistic. This type of love is characterized by sensibleness and logic. Pragma lovers are realistic when they approach a potential partner, seeking to match themselves with someone whose background is compatible with their own.

Lee believes many combinations of love are possible. For example, by mixing the primary and secondary styles one may have storgic-ludus love, ludic-eros love, or storgic-eros love. Although in one person a particular style usually dominates, we are all capable of experiencing each type. Different relationships, for example, may elicit different styles.

Research suggests that women tend to be more pragmatic, manic, and storgic with their styles of loving, whereas men often demonstrate erotic and ludic styles (Dion, 1985). It has also been suggested that individuals in love demonstrate higher levels of erotic and agape love than those not in love (Hendrick & Hendrick, 1988).

Another thought-provoking model of love was developed by Robert Sternberg (1986, 1988). Sternberg maintains that love is based on three components: passion (an intense physical attraction and desire for someone); intimacy (feelings of closeness and concern for a partner's well-being); and decision/commitment (recognition of the fact one is in love and a willingness to maintain the relationship). Sternberg conceptualizes these components as a triangle (see Figure 9-3).

Like Lee's model, Sternberg's love triangle enables us to see how the three components can exist in different patterns and different degrees. Based on different combinations of passion, intimacy, and decision/commitment, Sternberg identifies seven forms of love:

FIGURE 9-3
The Triangular Model of Love.

According to Robert Sternberg, the foundation of love consists of three parts: intimacy, passion, and decision/commitment. The combination of these three components helps to explain the different positive emotions people can have for others.

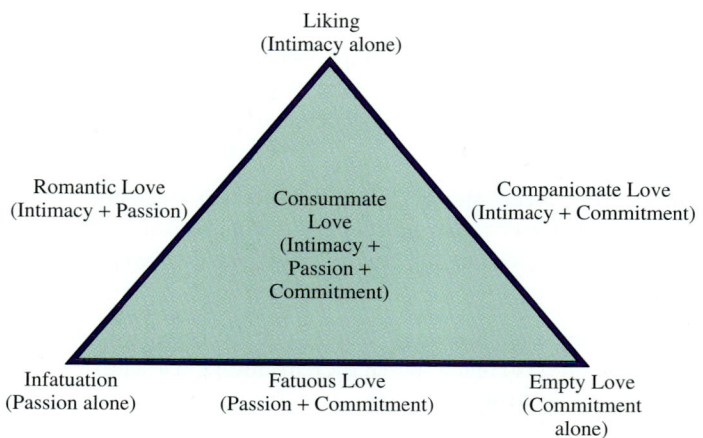

- *Liking:* Intimacy, but no commitment or passion.
- *Infatuation:* Passion without commitment or intimacy.
- *Empty Love:* Commitment without passion or intimacy.
- *Romantic Love:* Intimacy and passion, but no commitment.
- *Fatuous Love:* Commitment and passion but no intimacy.
- *Companionate Love:* Commitment and intimacy, but no passion.
- *Consummate Love:* Commitment, intimacy, and passion.

Sternberg maintains that the combinations of love just described can help explain different interpersonal relationships. Liking, for example, is characteristic of friendships, and companionate love is common in long-term relationships. Empty love can probably be applied to those relationships that have become devoid of meaning. Sternberg feels that consummate love represents an ideal, complete form of love. It is the most rewarding of all love experiences and embraces all three components.

PUTTING MODELS OF LOVE INTO PERSPECTIVE These conceptualizations of love are useful in understanding the different experiences of love, including its many complexities. For example, Reiss's wheel theory sheds light on how a love relationship can be conceptualized as an ongoing cycle. The typologies offered by Lee and Sternberg illustrate how love can reflect different feelings, thoughts, and actions. Better yet, they show how in real life, a loving relationship rarely consists of a unitary style. Instead, love relationships are often characterized by the *interaction* of several styles. Taking such conceptual models into consideration and intertwining this unit's focus on maturity and intimacy may help you gain a better understanding of your own friendships and love relationships, including the styles inherent in each.

THEORETICAL ISSUES

Beyond these models, how might other theoretical perspectives be used to explain how love is expressed and received? For instance, how might social learning theorists explore the impact of imitation on these behaviors? Do you think reinforcement plays a role? Are certain thinking skills necessary to give and receive love?

UNIT REVIEW—

↗ Adult maturity promotes physical and psychological well-being. Allport's theory of maturity consists of seven psychological dimensions.

↗ Adult personality theories have been proposed by Erikson, Levinson, and Gould.

↗ An intimate relationship involves the mutual exchange of experiences, thus requiring considerable self-disclosure. The formation, maintenance, and dissolution of intimate relationships usually reflect gender differences.

↗ Love is a complex emotion and an important facet of intimate relationships. Several conceptual models of love exist, including theories proposed by Reiss, Lee, and Sternberg.

UNIT THREE: LIFESTYLE CHOICES AND OPTIONS

A number of lifestyle choices and options exist in the United States, the most traditional being marriage and parenthood. As we see, marriage is more popular today than it was at the turn of the century, and having children remains an ideal, although family size has been shrinking in the United States, and more couples are delaying parenthood than ever before. But although getting married and having children are the chosen paths for most, not everyone makes such traditional lifestyle choices. On the contrary, growing numbers of adults are choosing to adopt such lifestyles as cohabitation and singlehood, and many couples are opting for childless marriages.

■ Marriage

Marriage in the United States is more popular today than it was at the turn of the century. If current trends continue, about 93% of the population will exchange marriage vows at one time or another in their lifetime. However, there have been some notable shifts in marriage trends among young Americans. In 1970, about 45% of males and 64% of females in their 20s had already married. By 1990, though, corresponding figures had dipped to 30% and 50%. Thus, while demographic trends indicate that most people marry, among modern Americans the decision is being postponed (National Center for Health Statistics, 1992b; U.S. Bureau of the Census, 1992).

In 1992, total number of marriages in the United States was over 2.4 million. Such large numbers existed even in the presence of a declining **marriage rate,** the number of marriages each year per 1,000 members of the population. This is because the maturing of the large post–World War II baby boom generation increased the number of people in the most common marriage ages (National Center for Health Statistics, 1992b; U.S. Bureau of the Census, 1992).

Marriage rates peaked in the United States in 1946 in the surge of marriages that occurred following World War II. During that time, the marriage rate was 16.4 per 1,000 people. Marriage rates remained relatively high throughout the 1950s and then started to show a decline in the 1960s and 1970s. Today, the marriage rate per 1,000 persons is about 9.5 (National Center for Health Statistics, 1991, 1992b; U.S. Bureau of the Census, 1992).

The Postponement of Marriage The timing of marriage in the 1990s has changed from past eras. Because of the growing numbers who are postponing marriage, the median age at first marriage has increased (median age means that one half of the people marrying for the first time in a given year get married before the given age, and one half after).

The following statistics help show how the median age at first marriage has changed over the years. In 1890, the median age was 26.1 for men and 22 for women. In 1976, it was 23.8 and 21.3 for men and women, respectively. In 1983, it was 24.4 for grooms and 22.5 for brides. In 1991, the median age increased once more: 25.9 for men and 23.6 for women. This represents the highest median age ever recorded for American women, and the highest for men since the median age of 25.9 in 1900 (National Center for Health Statistics, 1991, 1992b; U.S. Bureau of the Census, 1992).

Marriage represents a unique transition in the lifespan.

A number of reasons account for the postponement of marriage. A strictly demographic factor during the last two decades has been the "marriage squeeze." Given that women are usually two or three years younger than men at marriage, the marriage squeeze developed as a consequence of the upward trend of births during the baby boom. Because of this, a female born in 1947, when the birthrate had risen, was likely to marry a male born in 1944 or 1945, when the birthrate was still low. Consequently, about 20 years later, there was an excess of women in the primary ages for marriage, and this phenomenon continued for the length of time that the baby boom lasted. Therefore, by 1970, the number of men 20 to 26 years of age was only 93% of the number of women 18 to 24. The corresponding figure for African-American males was 82% (Glick, 1984, 1988).

This meant that by 1970, there was a shortage of men in the primary marriageable ages for women. This was true for young adults regardless of race. By 1980, this percentage had escalated somewhat, to 98% for all races. By 1995, the figure is expected to reach 108%, as the declining birthrates of the 1960s and early 1970s create a reversal of the marriage squeeze phenomenon.

There are other reasons for marriage postponement in the 1990s. More persons, especially women, are enrolling in college, graduate school, and professional schools. There are also expanding employment and career opportunities for women, and many men and women are placing their careers ahead of marriage plans. Finally, the high divorce rate in this country has prompted some to seriously question the traditional appeal of marriage and family life.

Motivations for Marriage   Why do people marry? Although the motives for entering married life are numerous and diverse, it is possible to identify some of the more popular reasons. The following represents some of these motives.

GENDER SIMILARITIES AND DIFFERENCES

Critically evaluate these motivations for marriage. Which of these represents your strongest motive? Do you think there are any gender differences or similarities in these motivations? In what area(s)?

LOVE The love and commitment shared by partners is often the primary reason for getting married. Couples desire to share themselves in an enduring and intimate relationship, one they feel is best represented within the institution of marriage.

COMPANIONSHIP The chance to spend one's life with someone in a permanent and visible institution is another important motive. The prospect of a regular companion also tends to generate emotional and psychological well-being, which in turn breeds feelings of security and comfort. Along similar lines, companionship provides couples with the opportunity to share, be it the routines attached to domestic life or leisurely activities.

CONFORMITY For many couples, marriage represents the "thing to do" or the "natural progression" of relationship building. After courting and the engagement period, getting married is seen as the final stage of the mate selection process. Contributing to this motive are the social pressures, both subtle and direct, from family, friends, and others prompting the couple to marry.

LEGITIMIZATION OF SEX Married status still provides social approval for many with respect to sexual behavior, even though a large proportion of men and women today engage in nonmarital intercourse. Also, many of today's Americans have adopted a more tolerant attitude toward premarital sexual relationships.

LEGITIMIZATION OF CHILDREN Children born into a marital relationship have a legitimate identity. Some segments of society strongly feel that a child born out of wedlock is immoral. We should acknowledge, also, that many couples would never consider getting married unless they wanted to have a child.

SENSE OF READINESS Many couples report that a decision to marry occurred when they felt "ready." The couple had done the things they wanted to accomplish before marrying. This might have included finishing an education, launching a career, or tending to personal or family matters.

LEGAL BENEFITS This may not be one of the strongest motives for marriage but it deserves to be acknowledged. Married status does have its share of tax advantages and for couples concerned with the economic welfare of their relationship, this motive may receive more than cursory notice.

We might add that there are motives for *not* getting married. For example, some may feel that many of the goals just outlined are possible through cohabitation, particularly the attainment of love, companionship, and sharing. Other motives against marriage might include a perceived reduction of freedom and a loss of independence.

There are also numerous questionable reasons for getting married. That is, some people may choose to marry for selfish reasons—for instance, to acquire a sexual partner or to obtain economic or emotional security. Some marry to escape the loneliness of a solitary existence or because they want to get away from an unhappy home situation. Some couples are also pressured into marrying by family and friends.

Adjusting to Married Life   In the minds of many there is an idealistic image attached to the early phases of marriage. Some tend to picture the young couple

Newly married couples learn that they must focus on the many adjustments that characterize day-to-day married life.

as always engulfed in romantic bliss, perfectly tuned to each other's needs and responding favorably to every marital challenge. We have a tendency to look at young married couples and think "and they lived happily ever after"—further emphasis on the idealistic dream.

Although the attainment of marital happiness is an admirable goal, the quest for a perfectly adjusted relationship is at best unrealistic. Sooner or later, most couples discover that the romance and happiness attached to the wedding and honeymoon do not last forever. Indeed, reality asserts itself and they see the world is less than ideal. Ups and downs will begin to punctuate the relationship. The first misunderstanding or fight leads the couple to realize that each partner is only a human being, complete with weaknesses and differences. On a larger scale, they come to realize that their marriage does not fit into the "perfect" mold.

Of course, there are some couples, young and old, who will deny that problems exist in their marriage. Tim Heaton and Stan Albrecht (1991) maintain that many individuals may remain in unsatisfactory marriages if barriers are strong or alternatives are lacking. In this respect, some may bury their problems in a shroud of silence because they are afraid the underlying issues are too threatening or disruptive to bring up. Many feel they are better off living with their problems because any discussion of them will "rock the boat." Still others view the threat of divorce as a worse evil than existing difficulties. Notice how such reasoning—analyzing the costs and benefits of remaining in a current marriage—reflects social exchange theory (Chapter 2). As a result of such thinking, many couples live in empty-shell marriages, the basic foundation of which is general unhappiness.

What factors promote marital happiness and satisfaction? Marital happiness and harmony are determined by the amount of effective interaction between the two partners. In this respect, stability is how two individual personalities blend and successfully meet one another's expectations for married life. Going a step further, marriages usually succeed when partners are trusting, share similar interests, demonstrate reciprocity, and perceive the presence of equity and agreement on important relationship issues. And almost invariably, the successful marriage is one in which there is good communication. Effective communication encompassing the clear and consistent expression of ideas, feelings, and wishes is the cornerstone for a healthy and satisfying relationship (Kelley & Burgoon, 1991; Lauer, Lauer, & Kerr, 1990; Peterson, 1990; Prosky, 1991).

Divorce and Separation

The dissolution of a family by divorce or separation can occur at any stage of adulthood and can be a major crisis for all its members. The United States has the rather dubious distinction of having a higher divorce rate than any other Western nation. Divorce rates hit an all-time peak in 1946 and then steadily declined until the late 1950s. Since then, however, the proportion of first marriages ending in divorce has sharply risen. The approximately 1 million divorces granted in 1974 marked the first time in American history that more marriages ended in divorce than through death. Between 1970 and 1980, the number of divorces in this country increased almost 70%. In 1992, over 1.17 million divorces were granted, and this total involved about 1 million children (Coleman & Ganong, 1990; National Center for Health Statistics, 1992b; U.S. Bureau of the Census, 1992).

It is often reported that almost 50% of all marriages end in divorce. This is a very misleading statement to make, and such a statistical analysis must be placed into a proper perspective. This percentage was arrived at by comparing all divorces granted in one year with the marriages performed in that same year. In 1991, for example, there were about 50.5 divorces for all new marriages (National Center for Health Statistics, 1992b). This is quite different from the crude divorce rate and tends to be somewhat misleading. This is because divorces granted in any year are the result of marriages performed in earlier years. Also, divorce does not affect all social groups equally. The poor and the poorly educated, members of the working class, and those who marry young have higher divorce rates than better educated and middle-class professionals (National Center for Health Statistics, 1992b; U.S. Bureau of the Census, 1992; L. K. White, 1990).

Adjusting to Divorce Divorce involves a number of adjustments and adaptations for all concerned. It is not uncommon to experience many psychological states, including a sense of failure, loneliness, sadness, and fear. Of course, amid the disruption that often characterizes the rebulding process, many people feel relieved to be starting over.

Paul Bohannon (1970, 1985a, 1985b) proposes that six components, or processes, of divorce exist. These components are not sequential and can overlap. Bohannon feels it is important to understand these processes in order to find order and direction in the emotional chaos that frequently accompanies divorce.

EMOTIONAL DIVORCE This component typically begins long before the actual break. It is centered around the deteriorating marriage and the initial motivations for considering a divorce. A wide range of negative feelings and behaviors characterize this component, including betrayals, accusations, and lack of affection and support. Partners usually feel misunderstood, rejected, and disillusioned. In many instances, one or both partners have psychologically departed long before the actual physical separation.

LEGAL DIVORCE Here, couples go to court to sever the civil ties of marriage. The legal grounds for obtaining a divorce vary from state to state, so many couples find themselves lost in the shuffle of courtroom proceedings. Many partners never envisioned the many complexities of divorce proceedings or the amount of psychological energy needed. Although couples typically experience relief once the legal separation is final, many exhibit varying levels of emotional sensitivity throughout this entire period.

ECONOMIC DIVORCE Couples also have to decide how they are going to divide their money and property. This is no simple task because complications arise due to tax laws. Legal assistance is usually needed, and couples frequently feel resentment, anger, and hostility concerning the redistribution of money and property. Bohannon also acknowledges that the economic divorce can be difficult for two reasons: First, there is never enough money or property to go around; second, people get attached to certain objects and may need them to support their image of themselves. As a result of these interacting forces, psychological turbulence is to be expected during this divorce component.

COPARENTAL DIVORCE The focus of this component is on the issue of child custody. The parental responsibility for child rearing and custody is determined by the court on the basis of the children's well-being. Visitation rights for the parent not getting custody must be determined. Worry and concern about the effects of the divorce on the children is frequently expressed during this stage. Bohannon points out that the issue of custody, along with economic settlement, represent the two greatest difficulties divorcing couples face. Also, more divorces fail in the coparental aspect than in any other way. We return to the topic of child custody and the effects that divorce has on children a bit later.

COMMUNITY DIVORCE The community divorce implies that a divorced person's status in the surrounding neighborhood changes in certain ways. Divorce is viewed differently by people, and separated individuals must learn to adapt to these varying perceptions. Sometimes relationships with friends are altered. Many divorced persons report feelings of isolation and loneliness; some also feel degrees of social disapproval. To ease such feelings, the social support of friends and family members is often stressed (McKenry & Price, 1991). Some divorced persons regret that divorcing one's spouse involves "divorce" from one's in-laws. Conversely, in-laws may become "outlaws." However, many divorced persons keep in touch with those they now call "the children's relatives."

DIVORCE FROM DEPENDENCY The focus here is on the importance of divorced parties regaining psychological autonomy. The shift from being in a couple-oriented situation to being a single person requires role realignment and considerable psychological adjustment. Expectedly, those couples who maintained high levels of independence in their marriages are likely to regain autonomy more rapidly than those marriage partners who were dependent on one another.

CONTINUOUS AND DISCONTINUOUS HUMAN DEVELOPMENT

What impact do you think divorce has on the issue of continuity and discontinuity in lifespan development? Do you think postdivorce life is qualitatively different from that life before? Might stability *and* change capture the lives of divorced individuals?

Bohannon's theory enables us to see the many complexities of divorce as well as the interacting forces that operate before, during, and after marital dissolution. However, none of the identified processes exist in a vacuum, nor are they independent or mutually exclusive of one another. Also, because reactions to divorce are highly individualized, variations of the identified components are more than likely. They should not be taken as precise and rigid blueprints that everyone follows. Nonetheless, Bohannon's ideas are useful in helping us understand the changes that people face when negotiating this painful process. They also succeed in capturing how divorce represents a complex and multifaceted experience.

Children and Divorce   Each year, nearly 1 million children will see their parents' marriage collapse. Should current rates hold, one of every three white children and two of three black children born within marriage will experience a parental marital dissolution by age 16. Most children of divorced parents live with their mother, and the majority will experience living in a fatherless home for at least 5 years. Moreover, the divorce experience is not necessarily over when the mother remarries. About one third of white and one half of African-American children whose mothers remarry will experience a second parental marital dissolution before they reach adulthood (Ahlburg & DeVita, 1992; Chadwick & Heaton, 1992; National Center for Health Statistics, 1992b; U.S. Bureau of the Census, 1992).

Divorce has the potential of creating numerous problems for children. Some children feel personally responsible for the divorce. Many are persuaded by their parents to take sides. Others may bear the brunt of displaced parental aggression. Coping with the divorce may also spill over to other aspects of the child's life and create additional problems, such as in schoolwork (see, for example, Mulholland, 1991; Shaw, 1991). And children may exhibit a wide range of emotional reactions: fear of abandonment, disturbed sleep patterns, anger, rejection, and sadness, to name but a few (Tschann, 1990; Wallerstein, 1991). Interestingly, at least one source (Elliot & Richards, 1991) points out that some of the problems which have been attributed to divorce may, in fact, be present prior to the parental separation. Nonetheless, given the potential for such turbulence, experts agree that children of divorce need love, understanding, and support to help them adjust (Furstenberg & Cherlin, 1991; Gander, 1991; Garvin, Leber, & Kalter, 1991; Gately & Schwebel, 1991; Hall, Beougher, & Wasinger, 1991; Portes, Haas, & Brown, 1991). We supply more specific ideas on this topic in the accompanying Lifespan Development in Action box.

Some children of divorce show remarkable resilience in the face of multiple life stressors. E. Mavis Hetherington (1990) points out that despite a period of initial distress, some youngsters may even be enhanced by coping with domestic instability. Her investigation of 124 divorced children showed that individual characteristics, such as having an easy temperament, and familial factors, such as parental patience and affection, play an important role in buffering children from negative consequences associated with their parents' separation. Also important to the child is the presence of a meaningful support system, such as the presence and reassurance of other family members, friends, and teachers.

Referring back to our earlier discussion, custodial arrangements greatly influence a child's adjustment to divorce. Unfortunately, conclusive answers about

Lifespan Development in Action

HELPING CHILDREN COPE WITH DIVORCE

No matter how hard it is to face children and talk about an impending divorce, it is a job that must be done. It also is a chore that cannot be done in the form of a simple announcement. The dialogue between parent and child is the beginning of a process where youngsters can express feelings, get reassurance, and gradually integrate this important change into their lives. The following suggestions may prove helpful:

Your most important task is telling children clearly and directly what divorce means. Explain to them in an understandable way what problems and issues have led you to the decision. Be prepared to repeat this information several times before the younger children really acknowledge what has happened.

Encourage children to ask questions. Do not let their thoughts and feelings about the divorce get psychologically buried. This includes not just at the beginning, but throughout the long process of adjustment. In your own words, let them know you are listening by reiterating the concerns they express to you.

Do not assess blame. State that each parent has been hurt in his or her own way and that each has felt pain. If you are angry, acknowledge it, but do not express your rage and blame to the kids.

Emphasize that the children in no way caused the divorce, nor are they responsible for their parents' problems. Explain you are divorcing each other, not your kids. It is equally important to let children know that nothing they do can bring about a reconciliation. Young children often harbor fantasies of mending your broken marriage.

If possible, describe any changes the children can expect in their day-to-day experiences. Give specific detail and reassurance about issues directly related to their lives (e.g., living arrangements, school, finances), and tell children that all decisions will be immediately and openly discussed with them.

Make sure you stress both parents will continue to love and care for the children. Be specific. Share your tentative decisions about visitation or shared custody.

Assure children they will always remain free to love both parents. No pressure will be brought to reject one parent in order to continue getting nurtured by the other. (Adapted from McKay et al., 1984)

the best arrangements remain elusive (D'Errico & Elmore, 1991). Judicial decisions over time regarding child custody reflect the uncertainty that has plagued this issue. For example, until the middle of the 19th century, children automatically went to their fathers. But as economic conditions changed, the laws were modified to award custody to mothers as the natural nurturers of children during their "tender years." Now judges make custody decisions on the basis of the child's best interests. Mothers still obtain custody in about 9 out of 10 cases; but

As one might expect, children of divorce face numerous adjustments.

fathers are more often seeking custody. Grandparents can also go to court to obtain the right to visit with their grandchildren (Sorensen & Goldman, 1990; Thompson, 1991; Thornton & Freedman, 1983; Trombetta, 1991).

An alternative that brings flexibility to the courts is **joint custody.** Joint custody embodies the mutual sharing of parental rights and responsibilities after the divorce. Joint custody actually has two meanings. One is that both parents retain the rights they always have had as parents: for instance, the right to participate in decisions about schooling or health/medical considerations. The other meaning of joint custody is that every week, month, or year parents will alternate in providing the child's shelter. This is called *joint residential custody* (Seltzer, 1991; Weiss, 1984).

There are advantages and disadvantages to joint custodial arrangements. On the positive side, such arrangements may reduce the bitterness often resulting from sole-custody decisions, particularly among fathers who pay child support but have only limited access to their children. Joint custody may also reduce the loss a noncustodial parent often experiences following a traditional sole-custody decision. However, negative dimensions of joint custody often arise when children are faced with two sets of house rules, two neighborhoods, and sometimes different friends and schools. Additionally, joint custody does not ensure that each parent is capable of handling the responsibilities of child rearing. Research suggests that children might be best served if their parents have joint custody in the legal sense, but are not required to alternate residences. At the same time, children should have easy access to the parent with whom they do not live (Folberg, 1991; Gardner, 1982; Kalter, 1990; Weiss, 1984).

Remarriage   The United States has the highest remarriage rate in the world. Statistics tell us that over 40% of marriages are remarriages for one or both partners. Each year, about 1.5 million people will remarry. This means that in the United States today, divorce tends to be a transitional rather than a terminal event for those committed to marriage. However, it is important to point out that the pathways to remarriage are varied. For example, partners can be single, divorced, or widowed with no children, divorced or widowed with custody of children, divorced or widowed without custody of children, or divorced or widowed with custody of some children but not others (Coleman & Ganong, 1990; Furstenberg & Spanier, 1987; Glick, 1989; National Center for Health Statistics, 1992b; U.S. Bureau of the Census, 1992).

Those who choose to remarry do so within relatively short periods of time. The average interval between divorce and remarriage is approximately 3 years. Widowed men and women who do remarry tend to take longer to remarry than divorced individuals, even when age is considered. A divorced person at any given age has a greater chance of marrying a second time than a never-married person has of marrying a first time (Coleman & Ganong, 1990; Furstenberg, 1988; Furstenberg & Spanier, 1987; Glick, 1988, 1989).

Additionally, remarriage rates for women of all ages have diminished over the last 20 years. White women are more likely than African-American women to remarry, and for the most part, they remarry more quickly. Younger women are far more likely to remarry quickly following a divorce, especially when their first marriages were relatively brief. Rapid remarriage is also more likely among females who were married when they were young and who had less than a college education. Also men and women in remarriages tend to differ in age by a greater margin than do men and women in first marriages. In both first marriages and remarriages, the man is the same age or older than the woman in approximately four in five marriages. However, the magnitude of the difference is significantly greater in remarriages than in first marriages (Furstenberg & Spanier, 1987; Glick, 1989; Levitan, Belous, & Gallo, 1988).

There is also evidence (Bumpass, Sweet, & Martin, 1990) that rates of remarriage among African Americans are only one quarter those of white non-Hispanics and that remarriage rates have been declining disproportionately among African Americans over the last two decades. Because of lower marriage rates and higher rates for divorce and illegitimacy, the low rate for African-American remarriage reinforces a pattern in which a much smaller proportion of the life course is spent in conventional two-parent families among African-Americans than among whites—with many more years spent in female-headed households both in childhood and for women as adults.

A large number of remarriages involve children. Today, there are over 11 million remarried families in the United States, including 4.3 million stepfamilies. About one out of five of all married-couple families are remarried families, and about 8% of all married-couple families are stepfamilies. Approximately 10 million children under age 18 are in remarried families, about 9 million are in stepfamilies, and almost 7 million are stepchildren. The reason for the differences in the numbers is that some children are born to remarried parents whereas others are brought into the remarriage. The numbers mean that of all youngsters in the United States under the age of 18, nearly 1 in 6 lives in a remarried family, and about 1 out of 10 is a stepchild (Demo & Adcock, 1988; Glick, 1989; Lauer & Lauer, 1991).

Paul Glick (1990) adds that the approximately 6 million stepchildren at the present time constitute one of every seven children under 18 years of age who are living in a home with two parents. Furthermore, some children who are not now stepchildren will become stepchildren before age 18, and some children who were formerly stepchildren have seen their parent and stepparent divorce.

INTERRELATEDNESS OF AGING PROCESSES

What factors do you think create the most satisfactory postdivorce adjustment for adults, adolescents, and children? What physical, personality, and social forces are likely to promote harmony and stability? Conversely, what forces have the potential for creating tension and friction?

It is thus reasonable to expect that one third of the children now under 18 have already experienced being a stepchild in a two-parent family or will do so before they reach 18.

Finally, divorce rates among the remarried are high. One source (Bumpass & Martin, 1989) points out that the divorce rate for remarriages is about 25% higher than it is for first marriages. However, Lynn White and Allan Booth (1985) point out that the divorce rate varies by the type of remarriage. Their research indicates that when only one of the partners is remarried and the other is single, chances for divorce are no greater than they are for marriages in which both partners are in a first marriage. However, the chances for divorce escalate about 50% if both partners were previously married and have no children. The chances for divorce rise another 50% if both partners were previously married and one or both of them brought children into the remarriage.

Single-Parent Households

The single-parent household is the fastest growing family form in the United States today. The proportion of single-parent households almost tripled from 9% in 1960 to almost 25% in 1991. Nearly one in eight families was headed by a single parent in 1991, with women five times more likely than men to be raising a family alone (Ahlburg & DeVita, 1992; Chadwick & Heaton, 1992; U.S. Bureau of the Census, 1992).

Although the single-parent household often consists of a divorced mother and her children, divorce does not represent the only reason for this domestic arrangement. Rather, single parents may also be widowed, separated, or never-married men or women. Others may have had their children naturally, through adoption, or through artificial means.

African Americans are almost three times more likely than whites to be single parents. Single-parent families represent 1 in 5 white families with children, 1 in 3 Hispanic families with children, and 6 in 10 African-American families with children. It is projected that a significant majority of all African-American children will experience a single-parent household and will spend a majority of their childhood in such a living arrangement (Ahlburg & DeVita, 1992; O'Hare et al., 1991; U.S. Bureau of the Census, 1992).

Single parents face numerous problems; paramount among them is financial hardship. Many single-parent families are poor, especially if a female is head of the household. Such economic difficulty reflects the problems associated with conflicts between employment and home responsibilities, job discrimination against women, and a reluctance by ex-husbands to assist the female head of household. Related to the latter, court-ordered child support is not large and is frequently not paid. Moreover, it is time consuming and expensive for mothers to collect unpaid child support from their former husbands, and few are successful (Belle, 1990; Olson & Banyard, 1993).

The supervision and care of the children becomes an additional financial problem, not to mention the quest for reliable and affordable day care. As we discover later in this chapter, this is difficult for couples and magnified even more for single parents, particularly if one considers the absorption costs, transportation, teacher conferences, and the like. Role alignment, loneliness, and stigmatization are other commonly reported adjustment problems. Furthermore, both parent and child have to adapt to a changed family structure (Korritko, 1991; D. G. Stewart, 1991).

Post-divorce adjustment often entails a new orientation to daily chores and responsibility.

Today, we have a better understanding of the needs of single parents and their children. Most experts stress the importance of minimizing guilt and ambivalence toward single parenthood and generating positive acceptance about this new social role. Many emphasize the positive features of rearing children this way, from the establishment of a single and consistent standard of discipline within the home to the encouragement of more self-reliance within one's offspring. Although single parenting is a draining and often thankless task, it is not without its reward (Olson & Banyard, 1993; Kissman & Allen, 1992; Quinn & Allen, 1989; Knight, 1986).

Cohabitation

Cohabitation is defined as the living together of an unmarried man and an unmarried woman. Cohabitation is extremely popular in the 1990s. Indeed, since 1970 the number of unmarried couples living together has increased by at least 495%. Moreover, it is projected that during the 1990s, about 7% of all U.S. households will consist of unmarried couples living together (Glick, 1988; National Center for Health Statistics, 1991, 1992b; U.S. Bureau of the Census, 1992).

There are many reasons behind a couple's decision to cohabit. As we witnessed in the last chapter, sexual values are changing—for example, the gradual weakening of the double standard and the widespread acceptance of the permissiveness with affection moral standard. Additionally, the availability of contraceptives and the relative ease of obtaining an abortion have reduced the risk of pregnancy among sexually active cohabitants. Peer support for cohabitation represents an additional reason, and many cohabitants are today less concerned about the status of marriage. Adults who have witnessed their parents' marriage break down may also have less faith in formal marriage as an institution that can provide security and happiness (Oliver, 1982).

Today, most cohabitants are under age 35. One source (Macklin, 1988) reveals that cohabiting couples tend to be about 6 years older than the average couple at first marriage. Often, one of the partners is likely to have been separated or divorced. Cohabitation is also popular among college students, due largely to the availability of off-campus housing, coed dormitories, and liberal student attitudes. In recent years, there has been an increase in the number of older cohabitants as well. It is estimated there are approximately 350,000 persons over age 55 living together (Glick, 1988; Glick & Spanier, 1980; U.S. Bureau of the Census, 1992).

There are many types of cohabitation arrangements. Some couples live together for purely economic reasons. Some cohabit without any desire to become involved in a personal intimate relationship. For others, the opposite is true: Cohabitation offers the opportunity to establish a close relationship. The largest number of cohabitants, however, are those who believe marriage is on the horizon. In this sense, cohabitation is a precursor to marriage, not an alternative (Bumpass, 1989; Bumpass, Sweet, & Cherlin, 1991; Cherlin & Furstenberg, 1983; Macklin, 1988). In support of this, one study (Bumpass & Sweet, 1988) found that more than one half of recently married couples had cohabited first.

Age differences need to be taken into account when we analyze cohabitation. Older male and female singles tend to perceive living together as a transitory experience rather than a preliminary to wedlock. Young men and women, especially students, consider living together a trial marriage. The younger partners are, the more likely they are to view cohabitation this way. Besides age, few important characteristics differentiate the different groups. To a certain degree, college-educated persons are more likely to judge living together as a permanent relationship than those who attended high school only. Professionals are less prone to live together than white- and blue-collar singles. These differences, however, are not profound. What is profound is the fact that for the younger and hence statistically never-married single, cohabitation is thought to be part of the marriage process, whereas older and hence statistically more frequently divorced singles see it as an escape from marriage (Simenauer & Carroll, 1982).

Although cohabitation has positive features, it is not without its share of problems. Potential legal problems are an important consideration, such as when "rights" regarding property and earnings surface. Some partners report guilt over their living arrangements, and even more are fearful of their parents' reaction. Because of the latter, many refuse to disclose their living arrangements to their parents. Another problem is that many couples feel closed in and stunted by their lifestyle. Pregnancy often poses complications for those choosing cohabitation over marriage (Macklin, 1988). For example, when cohabitants do have children, separating can be as difficult and distressing as any legal divorce.

Singlehood

Singlehood is a lifestyle in which persons choose not to marry. There are currently over 20 million never-married single adults 18 years of age and older. Moreover, this figure has been steadily rising. Since 1960, the numbers of singles living apart from relatives has increased over 100% (U.S. Bureau of the Census, 1992).

These statistics do not include the numbers of divorced and widowed persons, also single populations that are increasing as well. One out of every three married persons will be single within the next 5 years, and the figure will inflate to about one in every two by the end of the 1990s. They will join the ranks of the 67 million single adults in America, a group comprised of divorced and widowed individuals as well as those who have chosen to postpone marriage or never marry at all (Simenauer & Carroll, 1982; U.S. Bureau of the Census, 1992).

There are many reasons why singlehood is so popular in the 1990s. One important reason is the fact that there are growing career and education opportunities for women. Pursuing a career or a degree rather than marrying at an early age is today attractive to many. Both single men and women are able to devote more time and energy to their careers. Another reason for the increase in singlehood is that there are more women than men of marriageable age, thus creating a surplus of singles. Yet another reason is that more individuals desire freedom and autonomy. Many who choose this lifestyle are also aware of today's gloomy divorce statistics.

Singlehood is a lifestyle that offers considerable potential for happiness, productivity, and self-actualization. Among the positive features of single life are its unfettered opportunities for development and change. The years following high school and college are typically a time for men and women to clarify career goals, lifestyle preferences, and political and sexual identities; by remaining single, an individual enjoys that much more freedom to reflect, experiment, and make significant changes in beliefs and values should he or she so desire. The single person has an enormous opportunity to construct new identities—or, of course, perhaps to be confused by finding too many new identities. Yet the friends and other support networks that singles can develop may help to redress some of those conflicts (Stein, 1981, 1989; Stein & Fingrutd, 1985).

Singlehood has had various images and misconceptions attached to its lifestyle. For some, singlehood was viewed with suspicion. Singles were regarded by many as being different or lonely losers. Other societal images paint the swinging single picture: a jet-set lifestyle characterized by fast-paced excitement and exclusive forms of entertainment and recreation. These types of myths and stereotypes are not representative of the singlehood lifestyle. The latter, for example, is characteristic of only a select few, contrary to the images generated in the media.

Finally, the literature indicates that singles are not as lonely as society paints them to be (see, for example, Stein, 1989; Cargan & Melko, 1982, 1985). Robert and Jeanette Lauer (1991) point out that to be single does not necessarily mean to be alone. This is particularly true in regard to living arrangements. For example, many single adults live with their parents, share apartments with friends, or cohabit.

Single people usually want to meet other people to date and for companionship. Where do single people meet? Singles bars were very popular in the 1980s, but seem to have lost their appeal in the 1990s. Women, especially, do not like the "meat market" feeling, and some men do not appreciate having to take on the role of the "aggressor." Presently, fitness clubs, ads in newspapers

People have various reasons for remaining single.

INTERRELATEDNESS OF AGING PROCESSES

What personality and social dynamics do you think are affected by one's lifestyle choice? Do you believe a couple's paired relationship creates a strong sense of identity—not only as a couple but individually as well? Do you think singles construct their identity primarily on their own?

and magazines, and dating services have become popular among single adults. Introductions by friends to other available people, and engaging in sports or hobbies are other ways to meet people.

▬ Gay and Lesbian Relationships

Some people are attracted to members of the other sex, some are attracted to members of their own sex, and some are attracted to members of both sexes. The direction of our preferences for partners, including sexual as well as affectional attraction, is known as sexual orientation. Whereas **heterosexuality** involves attraction to members of the other sex, **homosexuality** refers to sexual attraction and emotional attachment to persons of the same gender. Today, there is movement away from using the term *homosexual* because of the tendency to think of it in sexually exclusive ways. Although sexual interaction is shared by many partners, it is not the primary focus of all relationships. The terms **gay** and **lesbian** are preferred because they seek to take into account nonsexual aspects of a person's life. The word *gay* is a term sometimes applied to both men and women; *lesbian* is applied exclusively to women. Finally, **bisexuality** refers to sexual attraction and emotional attachment to both women and men.

Gays have long been viewed with mistrust and suspicion, and the object of considerable fear, dread, and hostility (Mihalik, 1991; Whitman, 1991). However, beginning during the late 19th century and persisting today, the medical and academic professions sought to better understand them, and a diverse body of literature began to accumulate on the topic. In 1973, the trustees of the American Psychiatric Association removed homosexuality from its classification of mental disorders. Coupled with society's liberalization of sexual attitudes, the general public's perceptions of gays began to slowly change. Gays and lesbians banded together to assert their human rights and demanded the respect and equality that had been denied. Many openly declared their sexual orientation, and phrases such as "gay pride" were heard more and more. Meanwhile, researchers began launching scientific inquiry into the many complexities of same-sex preferences. Homosexuality began to be better understood not just as sexual preferences, but also as identities, lifestyles, and subcultures (Turner & Rubinson, 1993).

Thus, contrary to what was once thought, homosexuality is not a form of abnormal behavior or mental illness. Indeed, most gays are well adjusted and emotionally stable. Although some may exhibit anxiety or depression, so too do some heterosexuals. When maladaptive behavior does occur in gays, some clinicians propose it is often attributable to the social stigma attached to homosexuality instead of to something pathological in the nature of homosexuality itself (Ross, Paulsen, & Stalstrom, 1988; Sarason & Sarason, 1989; Stein, 1988)

And, contrary to popular notion, gays and lesbians are not confused about their gender identity (the psychological awareness of being either male or female). Lesbians are not different from heterosexual women in their sureness of being female, nor do gays differ from heterosexual men on this dimension. Related to behavior, most gays are not effeminate in dress or manner, nor are lesbians usually "masculine" in their behavior (Peplau & Gordon, 1983; Silberman & Hawkins, 1988).

Exploring the dynamics of gay relationships is a relatively recent research pursuit.

Also, gay men and lesbian women often want the type of relationship heterosexual couples have, and they hold many of the same values. They are likely, however, to reject traditional roles in favor of an egalitarian relationship. Given the fact that most lesbians, gays, and heterosexual couples are more alike than dissimilar in terms of coupling, we do not have to use a different language to describe relationship dynamics. We can use the same terms as we would in describing a relationship between two heterosexuals. In our intimate relationships, we are all much more similar than we are different (Brehm, 1992).

Aging experiences from a gay standpoint have only recently been explored (see, for example, Adelman, 1990; Bennett & Thompson, 1990; Deevey, 1990; Friend, 1990; Galassi, 1991; Lee, 1990; Steinman, 1990). One source (Berger, 1982) maintains that although gays adjust well to aging processes, they are often doubly constrained. That is, they are often shunned by a society that is predominantly heterosexual and continues to put a premium on youth. Also, older gays have also been neglected by younger gays.

However, it might be argued (Almvig, 1982) that the battle gays and lesbians fight against alienation may have beneficial effects with age. That is, one's struggle for identity may result in an enhanced sense of self. One investigation (Harry, 1982) discovered that gays, over time, have devised varying solutions to their problems of alienation. Some of these solutions turn out to be quite advantageous during adulthood for educational and career advancement. For instance, through their alienation from conventional male-gender culture, they have been freed to originate modified gender roles, which draw on varying components of masculine and feminine culture that are closer to their individual needs.

Parenthood

The transition from a dyad to a triad relationship is one of the most complex and dramatic changes that most people will ever make in their lives. As Anne-Marie Ambert (1992) sees it, parenthood signifies full entrance into an important adult transition, a time when new roles have to be negotiated and values reoriented. Family development experts (e.g., Cowan & Cowan, 1992; Cowan & Hetherington, 1991; Rossi & Rossi, 1990) agree that becoming a parent thrusts couples into a continual state of transition and exposes them to numerous challenges and rewards over the course of the family life cycle.

There are many reasons for wanting children. For many, children represent an extension of the self. They are also a source of personal fulfillment and represent an enhancement of a couple's identity. Some adults want children because they look forward to the companionship they will bring. Others maintain that children will provide security to them when they are old. Finally many want children because of social expectations. In other words it is the thing to do when you are an adult.

Of course, just as with marriage, there are many questionable reasons for having children. Having a baby because one's parents want grandchildren should not be the only motivation. Furthermore, a baby is not the cure for a marriage void of meaning. Some couples use the exclusive measure of a financial goal before they have children, but financial security by itself is not a sound motive for having children. Neither is the singular motive that a baby will give a totally bored couple something to do. Although a child will certainly be a source of activity, couples with this underlying motive often become just as bored with child-care chores.

Fertility Patterns in the United States Although large families were once the norm in the United States, this is not the case today. The average number of children in a family reached an all-time low of 1.74 children in 1976, and it has remained relatively low ever since. As we go to press, the average number of children in a family had edged up to a 2.1 child average. This decline in fertility can be explained by a number of factors, including the postponement of marriage and the widespread use of contraception and abortion. Despite the fact that few American women believe childless or one-child families are ideal, many women have delayed marriage and childbearing so long that they will have only one child or no children at all.

According to Joseph McFalls (1991), although the overall fertility rate in the United States has remained fairly stable over the last 20 years, there is considerable variation among individual couples. Among all women of reproductive age (roughly ages 15 to 44), only 23% conform to the two-child average. Forty-two percent have not yet had any children, and 2% have had five or more children. What accounts for these differences? According to McFalls (1991), the most predictable and obvious explanation of fertility differentials is age, but income, race, religion, and many other social, economic, and cultural factors influence childbearing. Let's examine each more closely.

AGE Women are able to conceive a pregnancy beginning in their early teens and ending in their late 40s. Over this roughly 30-year span, birthrates vary substantially by age. Over the last 20 years, U.S. women ages 25 to 29 have had the highest birthrates, slightly higher than women ages 20 to 24, the previous leaders. Also, childbearing among women age 30 to 44 reversed its steep decline and increased over the course of the last 15 years. Many of these older mothers began to have the children they had postponed earlier in life.

The birthrates by the age of mother follow the same general pattern in most societies—rates are low in the teens, peak in the 20s, and decline thereafter.

But comparisons of the age-specific rates in different countries reveal significant variations. For example, in Japan, where the average number of children in a family is 1.7, there is a remarkable concentration of childbearing among women 25 to 29 years of age. These women produce nearly one half of all Japanese births. In the United States, birthrates also are highest for women 25 to 29 years of age, but they account for just under 30% of all births. In the West African country of Ghana, where the average number of children in a family is 6.4, birthrates rise very gradually from the teens to a peak in the late 20s and then decline slowly into the 40s. At every age, Ghanaian women have higher birthrates than American and Japanese women.

RACE AND ETHNICITY In many countries, racial and ethnic minorities have higher fertility than majority groups. Often these differences arise from religious beliefs and cultural traditions, but they also are linked to the lower economic status of minority groups and the number of years they have lived in their adopted country. As immigrant groups assimilate socially and economically they tend to adopt the fertility patterns of the majority. In the United States, for example, fertility differences among white ethnic groups (e.g., Irish, German, or Italian Americans) are becoming less distinguishable over time. Groups that have not fully "assimilated" may maintain their distinctive fertility patterns. In the United States, Hispanics, African Americans, and Native Americans have higher fertility than the white non-Hispanic majority. The average number of children in a family is about 1.8 for white women and 2.4 for African-American women. The average number of children in a family for Hispanic women is about 2.6. Asian Americans tend to have rates close to non-Hispanic whites.

SOCIOECONOMIC STATUS In nearly every contemporary society, the poor have more children than the rich. This is also true for the United States within all major racial and ethnic groups. In general, fertility goes down as the income and educational attainment of women increase. For example, today's women between the ages of 35 and 44 with 5 or more years of college average 1.6 births compared with 2.3 births for women who complete high school only, and nearly 3 births for non-high school graduates.

OTHER DIFFERENTIALS Numerous other social, religious, and cultural factors are associated with fertility differences. Most of these can be explained by the age, income, or education differences among these groups. For example, in just about every culture, women who work outside the home have fewer children than those who do not, and rural women have more children than urbanites. People who actively practice a religion tend to have higher fertility than nonreligious people. There are long-standing differences between major religious groups in many countries, but these often are intertwined with ethnic and socioeconomic differences (McFalls, 1991). For a glimpse at fertility patterns in the People's Republic of China, see the accompanying Focus on Diversity box.

Childless Marriages   As we mentioned at the outset, growing numbers of married couples today are choosing not to have children. Unlike couples wanting a family voluntarily, childless couples do not regard parenthood as a necessary ingredient for marital happiness or satisfaction. Although the numbers of childless marriages have increased in recent years, they are a minority. The

Focus on Diversity

WHERE ARE CHINA'S FEMALE CHILDREN?

No discussion of fertility differentials is complete without some reference to the People's Republic of China. Here, family planning is not a voluntary decision made by couples. Rather, it is the government that dictates family planning. In an effort to reduce overpopulation, which is expected to reach over 1.5 billion by the turn of the century, couples in this nation are allowed to have only one child. China is thus the first nation to ever restrict a couple's right to procreate. It has also raised the minimum age for marriage to 20 for women and 22 for men. Even later marriages are encouraged to reduce the couple's risk of having more than one child.

The government imposes the one-child limit through incentives, peer pressure, and attempts to persuade newly married couples that their rational fertility decisions will mean a better future for their own families, their communities, and their nation. If the one-child limit is successful, it is estimated the population will stabilize by the turn of the century. If unsuccessful and the population continues to grow, China's ability to feed its people is in jeopardy, among other consequences. China occupies only 7% of the globe's arable land but supports 22% of its population.

If Chinese couples follow government legislation, they are entitled to numerous benefits, including increased living space, pensions, free education, lower-cost health care, and better medical intervention. Eventually, the only child receives preferential treatment in the school system as well as in the labor force. Should couples give birth to a second child, the family forfeits all of these benefits.

Chinese families have traditionally preferred male children. Should a firstborn be female, couples may try to conceive again in an effort to bring a male into the world. This places couples at odds with the government, not to mention the consequences. Indeed, in several Chinese provinces, couples expecting a second child will have their wages docked if the woman decides not to have an abortion.

number of childless couples is estimated to be between 5 and 7% of all married couples (Chadwick & Heaton, 1992; U.S. Bureau of the Census, 1992).

Child-free marriages present an interesting contrast to the high premium placed on having children during early historical periods. For example, in the Old Testament, God's directive to Noah was "Be fruitful and multiply." Often, parents faced certain consequences if they did not bear children and produce large families. In the classical age of Greece, barrenness was sufficient grounds for a man to divorce his wife. And in colonial America, single men were viewed with suspicion and penalized with special taxes for not doing their share to increase the population. This is a far cry from the sentiment expressed in certain countries, such as China, where family size is restricted to one child.

Those couples choosing voluntary childlessness tend to be well educated, financially well off, and involved in their careers, although there are exceptions to these patterns. Often, the decision to remain childless is a difficult one. An organization called the National Alliance for Optional Parenthood helps couples in their decision making, its central theme being that parenthood is a life option for couples, not a duty. The organization seeks to promote the idea that it is perfectly acceptable not to have children.

In 1993, worldwide attention became riveted on China when its Family Planning Commission revealed figures on female-to-male birth ratios. These figures showed that for every 100 female infants born in China, 111.3 male infants were also born. According to demographic experts, these figures represent a highly unlikely ratio because the average global ratio is 106 males to 100 females. Interestingly, China matched that ratio before the government launched its one-child policy in 1979.

The mystery of what happened to China's female infants has become one of the deepest enigmas of a nation determined to curb its runaway population plight. If government figures are correct, about 750,000 female infants born in China are unaccounted for. What has happened to them? Demographic experts believe that one half to three quarters of them are simply not reported by parents, who hide them or send them to relatives in remote areas. In so doing, a woman can become pregnant a second time, hopefully with a male, without incurring any of the earlier-mentioned loss of privileges or fines.

The remainder of the missing girls, officials say, are aborted. About 14 million abortions are performed annually in China, and even rural towns now have ultrasound machines to determine the sex of the fetus. Although doctors are legally barred from revealing the sex of a fetus, many can be bribed to do so. In backward areas of China, infanticide is performed by a midwife should a female baby be born. Although many Western demographers support China's efforts to reduce its birthrate, they are concerned by such side effects of the one-child system.

China's one-child policy ran into trouble in 1991 when officials realized from birth registries that the policy was being increasingly flouted by peasants who either bribed local officials or had saved enough money to pay the fine for a second or third child. Chinese officials reported that 1 million "unauthorized" babies were born that year, thus creating serious consequences for the nation's family planning movement. A crackdown on offenders was implemented in 1991, and since then, the birthrate has declined and the use of contraceptives has increased to 83% of married couples. In 1993, China introduced its version of the controversial French abortion pill RU-486. When taken over a 3-day period, it induces a miscarriage. (Schmetzer, 1993)

Parenting Adjustments and Adaptations   The arrival of an infant changes parents' lives considerably. For example, mothers and fathers must learn to adjust to loss of sleep and frequent physical fatigue. Many express increased worry over financial matters, and soon discover that the costs of rearing a child quickly escalate. Food, clothing, furniture, toys, and the like make parenthood an expensive venture. Most new parents also experience uneasiness about the unknown aspects of parenthood, particularly unfamiliar child-care routines and demands. Unsuredness often elevates parental anxiety and confusion, and many adults experience added pressure in the wake of mounting child-care chores (Ambert, 1992; Cowan & Cowan, 1992; Ferree, 1991; Palkovitz & Sussman, 1988).

In the midst of such adjustments, new parents often discover it is difficult to enjoy each other's exclusive company. With the baby's arrival, patterns of intimacy and affection are changed and need to be redefined. Additionally, interactions and visits with friends become restricted. Parenthood may also mean the child's needs compete with those of the spouse. Because of the latter, it is not uncommon for parents during stressful times to feel angry, jealous, and resentful.

THEORETICAL ISSUES

How do you think voluntary childlessness affects Erikson's epigenetic scheme, particularly the concepts of generativity or one's instinct to nurture? In what alternative way(s) might these psychosocial needs be satisfied?

There are many young mothers, though, who do report being overwhelmed by the constant flow of infant-oriented tasks to be carried out. Feeding and bathing of the baby and laundering clothing, added to the regular household routines of cleaning, cooking, and shopping, is a full day's work. Countless other chores can be added to this list. A few representative studies illustrate how the foregoing challenges and demands create the potential for domestic turmoil. For instance, Jacqueline Ventura (1987) explored the adjustment concerns of over 100 mothers and fathers of infants 3 to 5 months of age. She found that about one third of the mothers and two thirds of the fathers experienced stresses originating from the multiple demands of child care, work, and marriage. Many had difficulty adapting to unfamiliar child-care demands, such as infant soothing techniques, and marital conflict was common.

As far as the multiple demands of parent, spouse, and worker were concerned, mothers portrayed juggling parenting responsibilities with work and home schedules as "working full-time, doing housecleaning and laundry and taking care of husband and baby," and "having only small segments of time to accomplish personal things." Fathers' responses dealt primarily with career and work demands involving "being responsible for several technical areas," "doing everyone else's job," "supervising employees," "ambiguous, multiple deadlines," "travel as a job requirement," and "problems with boss or employment situation." A small number of fathers also described the struggle to finish take-home work or household tasks and help with child care.

Diane Ruble and a team of researchers (1988) investigated the increased workload of 670 mothers after the birth of a first child and the "violated expectations" of the father with respect to the sharing of child-care responsibilities. It was found that the mothers did much more of the housework and child care than they had expected, and the women reported less positive feelings about their husbands during the postpartum period than during pregnancy. Moreover, violated expectations concerning division of labor were related to negative feelings postpartum concerning the overall marital relationship. Similar findings were uncovered by Debra Kalmus and colleagues (1992), who added that postpartum adjustment is more difficult when mothers' expectations exceeded experiences in support and assistance from extended family.

We certainly do not want to give the impression that parenthood is a totally negative experience. Indeed, not all experts contend that parenthood looms as a turbulent and unstable period. Although it has its share of demands and strains, most parents are able to weather its difficulties. And even though some researchers find that the addition of children reduces marital happiness (e.g., Belsky & Rovine, 1990; Belsky, Spanier, & Rovine, 1983; Harriman, 1986), most parents express overall satisfaction with their children and the parenting role in general. Indeed, a number of researchers have explored the positive features that children bring to couples (e.g., Goetting, 1986; Goldberg, Michaels, & Lamb, 1986; Harriman, 1986). Such research acknowledges the demands attached to parenthood, but also emphasizes the bright side to raising children.

It is our contention that right from the very beginning, parents need to reject the idealistic myth of having the perfect family. Just like marriage, parenthood has its share of triumphs, but also its share of ups and downs, heartaches, and headaches. Too many new parents strive for perfection, and in the process program themselves for failure. It is important for new parents to be flexible

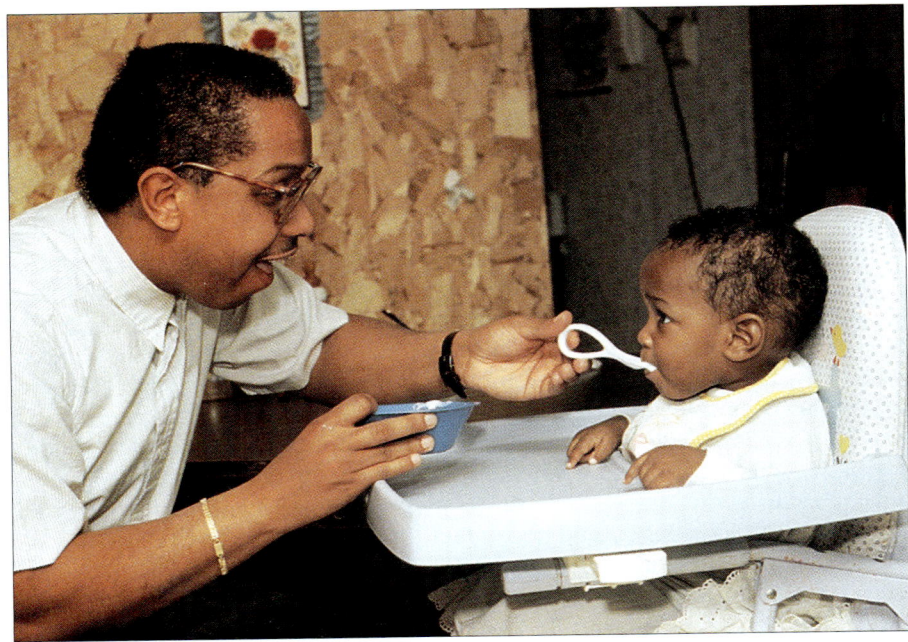

The numerous life adjustments of parenthood include child care routines and financial considerations.

with their expectations, and learn to take pride in their daily accomplishments. Fears and anxieties about child care tend to fade when parents learn they do not have to do everything by the book. As a result of the experiences gained and lessons learned firsthand, parenthood begins to acquire a less tense and more realistic relaxed quality.

A critical component of effective parenting adjustment is the support partners give to one other, physical as well as psychological. For new parents, especially, openly discussing concerns and problems and working together as a team are instrumental in creating a favorable family climate. And research clearly shows that both informal and formal support beyond that offered by one another eases the transition to parenthood (Affleck et al., 1989; Telleen, Herzog, & Kilbane, 1989; Ventura, 1987). Parents also need to get away from the baby periodically and enjoy their own private space. This is said even though it seems that too much work and effort are required for a night out on the town. In the long run, it is worth it. Husband and wife need to maintain a loving, harmonious relationship so they can better fill the roles of mother and father (Ambert, 1992; Lamanna & Riedmann, 1994). For a look at how racial, ethnic, and class differences shape parenting, see the accompanying Focus on Diversity box.

Parental Roles   For first-time mothers and fathers, the parenting role needs to be defined, assigned, perceived, performed, and integrated with other role demands. In stable families, the foregoing is usually done with some degree of competency. Conversely, in unstable homes, role confusion often results and disorganization occurs. Whereas minor roles can be performed indifferently without creating much disruption, the parenting role requires constant and at least adequate role performance (LeMasters & DeFrain, 1989).

THEORETICAL ISSUES

Establish several alternative theoretical perspectives for viewing the assortment of adjustments facing new parents. For example, is the costs and rewards concept suggested by exchange theorists or the inevitable friction and turbulence proposed by conflict theorists worthy of consideration? Would a family development perspective help you better analyze how the addition of an infant forces a major reorganization of the marital system?

Focus on Diversity

AND BABY MAKES THREE: A MOSAIC OF PARENTING EXPERIENCES

All racial, ethnic, and class groups may not have the same needs and value orientations, nor share the same experiences related to parenthood. Moreover, the circumstances of a family's existence and background, to a large extent, shape patterns and processes of overall functioning during the parenting transition (Locke, 1992; McAdoo, 1993). An awareness of racial, ethnic, and class variations enables us to develop tolerance and sensitivity toward differences and distinctions.

Unfortunately, limited information exists on parenting among different racial, ethnic, and class groups. However, interest is growing, as evidenced by the research attention given to Jewish, Irish-American, Italian-American, African-American, Hispanic, and other families (see, for example, Boyd-Franklin, 1989; McGoldrick, 1982; Vega, 1990). Such research is a welcome contribution to the literature because it moves us away from making generalizations about racial, ethnic, or class contexts. Racial, ethnic, and class images all too often contain stereotypes or simplified pictures of a culture.

Consider Harriette McAdoo's (1983) research focusing on African-American family life. To begin with, McAdoo believes that African-American families share many of the same characteristics and problems as white families. For example, they experience the developmental changes in children and parents as they grow older as well as the problems attached to single parenthood. However, a racist environment often intensifies and changes the impact and meaning of life events. African-American families often do not have the same opportunities and experiences as white families, thus creating unique stressors and patterns of coping (Burlew et al., 1992; Jackson, 1991; McAdoo, 1993).

In regard to class differences, we must not make generalizations regarding socioeconomic status, nor should we automatically link culture and social class together. In relation to the latter, Charles Willie (1986) observes that when an ethnic group is disproportionately poor (or wealthy), parenting differences due to ethnicity become confused with those originating from socioeconomic status. To illustrate, because African Americans have been disproportionately poor, many tend to think of the African-American family as one in which poverty-level mothers are invariably teenagers and fathers take little

THE ROLE OF THE MOTHER Many first-time mothers often feel inadequate to the task, mainly because they have had limited contact with children prior to their own. However, some type of formal or informal support system during the early weeks is usually of great value. Should a supportive relative or friend assist with child care and domestic chores, the new mother is usually able to adjust to infant demands and develop confidence and competency in her new role.

Often, the mother discovers that an infant is more work than she ever imagined. Unfortunately, society tends to paint an unrealistic image of motherhood, in some instances idealizing it beyond recognition. The truth of the matter is that mothers find their lives significantly altered with an ever-increasing workload. Many feel overwhelmed in the face of physical demands, not only those responsibility for their children. However, as rising numbers of African Americans move into the working class and middle class, it becomes increasingly apparent that to say "an African-American family is an African-American family is an African-American family" is inappropriate.

Going a step further, John McAdoo (1986, 1988) writes that African-American parents' hopes, attitudes, and behaviors for their children are more alike than dissimilar to those of other parents in their social class. As an illustration, consider the trend of greater father participation in child care. McAdoo (1988) maintains that "when economic sufficiency rises within Black families, an increase in the active participation of the Black father in the socialization of his children is observed" (p. 266). In other research focusing on middle-income families (McAdoo, 1986), African-American fathers exhibited similarities to other middle-income fathers, including patterns of nurturance and love with their children. The notion that minority parents resemble other parents in their social class is supported in the parenting literature (Connor, 1986; Ho, 1992; Jackson, 1991; M. F. Peters, 1988).

It is generally acknowledged that social class limits or expands parents' decisions and options in a variety of ways. To illustrate, birthrates tend to increase as socioeconomic status declines, and divorce rates are more common among families of lower class status (Fergusson, Horwood, & Shannon, 1984; Kitson & Raschke, 1981; O'Hare et al., 1991). Working-class parents also tend to maintain a more rigid division of household responsibilities, whereas middle-class parents tend to be more egalitarian (Bott, 1971). Socioeconomic status also impacts on parent-child relations. A body of research (e. g., Locksley, 1982; Moss, Abramowitz, & Racusin, 1985; Rumberger, 1983) tends to indicate that lower- and working-class parent-child relationships are oriented more toward obedience, perhaps to assure family respectability. Middle-class parent-child relationships, on the other hand, tend to focus on internalized standards of conduct, leading to independent achievement and self-satisfaction.

Finally, besides fulfilling the health needs of their children and having access to quality medical care, upper-class parents typically create environments that nurture the talents and abilities of their youngsters. Indeed, upper-class homes have the material and educational resources to develop the budding potential of their children. On the other hand, raising children in lower socioeconomic settings is qualitatively different. Health-care considerations, including access to quality medical care, are acute concerns. Moreover, access to child-oriented resources and educational support systems is elusive for most lower socioeconomic families (Burlew et al., 1992; McLanahan, Wedemeyer, & Adelberg, 1981; O'Hare et al., 1991; Slesinger, 1980; M. N. Wilson, 1989).

attached to caregiving, but also those related to the father's needs. It may well be that one of the major problems facing the contemporary U.S. mother is overcommitment. She has more responsibilities than most can meet, and she is putting in more hours than her grandmother did running the household.

Not too long ago, mothers were expected to remain at home and care for their children, particularly during their offspring's early years of development. Many felt this was the only way a mother could love and properly rear her children during this important life stage. To venture away from the family in search of a paycheck was viewed as uncaring and unwise. Today, however, increasing numbers of women are breaking this traditional stereotype of mothering and working outside of the home. Moreover, there is growing acceptance that a woman can handle the multiple roles of breadwinner and mother. A few statistics shed light on the large numbers of working women in the United States today, as well as how the labor force is changing:

• In 1991, the proportion quitting their jobs during first pregnancies dropped to 28%, compared to 63% in 1965.

• Unlike earlier times, when mothers took years away from the labor force for childbearing, modern women return to the labor force rather quickly. In 1992, one half were back on the job within 1 year, and one in four returns within 3 months.

• In 1991, the percentage of all of the nation's working-age women in the labor force was about 57%, compared to 76% of working-age men.

• The proportion of families in which men are the sole breadwinner declined from 42% in 1960 to 15% in 1991.

• In 1992, 65% of women in their first pregnancies worked at least 6 months while pregnant, compared to 44% in 1965.

Finding quality child care is an important concern for many working parents.

- More than 55% of married women with a child under 6, and 75% with children ages 6 to 17 are working. By 1995, it is anticipated that two thirds of all mothers with preschoolers will be employed outside the home (Ahlburg & DeVita, 1992; Chadwick & Heaton, 1992; U.S. Bureau of the Census, 1992; U.S. Bureau of Labor Statistics, 1991, 1992).

Although the dual-earner family reaps its share of benefits and personal satisfaction (see, for example, Gilbert, 1993; Hanson & Ooms, 1991; Kelly, 1991; Markus, 1990), certain sacrifices are common in homes with younger children. The responsibility of child rearing and tending to domestic chores appears to be the biggest obstacle for women to hurdle in pursuing careers. In most instances, the woman still carries the brunt of the household tasks, which intensify when employment outside of the home occurs. Consequently, the problem is that a two-career marriage is really a three-career marriage, with the woman typically holding down two careers (Blair & Johnson, 1992; Blair & Lichter, 1991; Hawkins & Roberts, 1992).

Often, a mother's employment status has minimal effect on what the husband does. Thus, although many husbands may say they prefer an equitable domestic arrangement, in actual practice this is the exception rather than the rule (Benin & Agostinelli, 1988; Kamo, 1988). And, should fathers offer child-care assistance, it is often qualitatively different from that provided by mothers. Often, paternal involvement falls under the category of "play," whereas mothers involve themselves in custodial activities such as feeding, diapering, and bathing (Brayfield, 1992; Darling-Fisher & Tiedje, 1990; Lamb, 1987; LaRossa, 1988; Ninio & Rinott, 1988).

There are other difficulties among working mothers. Many report some anxiety about their child's well-being and wonder if they have made the right choice. Many who are full-time mothers, however, often want to go back into the labor force. Thus a type of Catch-22 situation exists. In other instances, working mothers are happy and satisfied with their chosen profession, but feel inadequate in the mothering role. In this respect, many working mothers feel role conflict.

THE CHILD-CARE DILEMMA The issue of who is going to care for the children of working parents is an important one today. Whereas the Industrial Revolution virtually dictated that mothers would remain at home to care for their young, today's dual-earner couples must turn to the outside for child-care assistance. The relinquishment of the youngster to child-care facilities offers a new twist to child-rearing practices, and may place contemporary parents at odds with *their* parents. Many older generations cling to the notion that a woman's place is in the home. The modern woman's removal of these chains sometimes produces ambivalence on the older generation's part, and in some cases, hostility. There is, however, a growing acceptance of women entering the employment world, and we are certain to see increasing approval of child-care assistance.

Child-care facilities for the children of working parents are often too expensive or insufficient in number. The demand for affordable child care is especially apparent among single parents, particularly when we consider that one half of the households headed by single mothers aged 25 to 44 are poor (Culkin, Morris, & Helburn, 1991; Parton, 1991). Those able to take advantage

THEORETICAL ISSUES

Using Bronfenbrenner's ecological perspective, how do you think parents and their youngsters are influenced by the child-care environment, and vice versa? How do you think the macrosystem has changed over the years regarding working mothers and child-care arrangements?

of a day-care center or nursery school are usually well educated, work full time, and have a comfortable family income. Lower-income couples often find female relatives to care for their young, with grandparents an especially popular choice.

Among the child-care facilities that do exist, the day-care facility is the most convenient for working parents. It offers full child-care sessions, often beginning at 7 a.m. and lasting until 6 p.m. Some specialize in infant and toddler care and offer meals and learning sessions. For those offering a curriculum component, activities that encourage and facilitate learning are directed toward physical, cognitive, linguistic, personality, and social capacities. A good review of day-care programming as well as those offered in other child-care arrangements can be found in Morrison (1991).

However, day-care centers have aroused considerable controversy among child psychologists, educators, family studies experts, and parents (see, for example, Hewlett, 1991; Lamb et al., 1992; Waite, Leibowitz, & Witsberger, 1991; Zigler & Lang, 1991). Though such facilities offer protective care to children and enable mothers to work, concern is frequently voiced about the effects of day care on youngsters. Maternal separation and the disruption of attachment bonds to the caregiver are central issues for many (see, for example, Belsky, 1988; Clark-Stewart, 1989). Some maintain that a full-time day-care center cannot provide this essential early social relationship, except under ideal conditions. Usually a child must share with other youngsters the attention of a day-care worker, and in the typical 10-hour center day, work shifts change at least once. Add to this vacations and job turnovers, and a child may well have no one special person to be close to. Sometimes the mother compounds the problem of an unhappy child by blaming the center and switching the child to another. Finally, it has been noted (Donowitz, 1991) that children in day care face considerable risk in the transmission of such diseases as respiratory and gastrointestinal illnesses.

Not everyone agrees on such potential negative effects of day care (Jaeger & Weinraub, 1990; Weinraub & Jaeger, 1990). Many feel that children are capable of adjusting well to day-care situations at an early age, and many also believe these institutions offer rewarding learning experiences. Among proponents of day care, it is maintained that such arrangements promote socialization and stimulate important cognitive and linguistic competencies. Some feel the developmental stimulation provided by effective day-care programming transcends levels available at home (Sonenstein & Wolf, 1991; Zaslow, 1991).

Obviously, then, it becomes a matter of searching for a quality day-care center and not settling for a mediocre one. This can be a tedious chore, but one well worth the effort. Parents need to look for centers with such positive features as low adult-to-child ratios, good nutrition programs, excellent sanitation conditions, and adequate staff training (the accompanying Lifespan Development in Action box provides more detail on selecting a quality child-care program). A successful day-care experience goes beyond the center's qualifications, though. The parental warmth, acceptance, and care the child receives in the home may greatly influence his or her response to the overall day-care experience (McBride, 1990; Weinraub & Jaeger, 1990).

In relation to this last point, it is maintained by most child-care and family studies experts that the critical variables in a youngster's adjustment are the parents' satisfaction with their lives and the quality, rather than quantity, of parent-child interactions. Sandra Scarr and colleagues (1990) echo this sentiment by saying that paternal and maternal employment per se are not the major issue in either a child's adjustment to child care or for that matter, smooth marital relations. Rather, the circumstances and stability of the family, the climate of togetherness it offers, the attitudes and expectations held by the parents, and the distribution of the time available for meaningful interaction shape the course of domestic harmony and happiness for all concerned.

THE ROLE OF THE FATHER Until recently the role and impact of the father in child care had been overlooked. Although the importance of the father in the household is generally recognized, part of the problem is that American society has been "mother-centered" in its philosophy of child care. With more dual-earner households, the father's influence on various aspects of child growth and development is now being increasingly recognized. Many researchers have actively explored the father's role and have provided the field of family studies with a wealth of information (see, for example, Ahmeduzzaman & Roopnarine, 1992; Bozett & Hanson, 1991; Kraemer, 1991; Nugent, 1991; Volling and Belsky, 1991).

Ralph LaRossa (1986) believes that considerable attention today has focused on the "new father." In many ways, the new father wants to avoid the mistakes he feels his father made. He also does not want to be so absorbed with his vocation and friends that he neglects his children. Thus the new father makes a conscious effort to spend more time with his children, perhaps in an effort to be the father he never had. The new father also does not wait until his children are older before he gets to know them; he starts early. And, as much as he might not like it, he devotes more time to child-care responsibilities. But, as pointed out earlier, the involvement of the new father still lags behind that of the mother. Research consistently shows that when it comes to child care, women still shoulder most of the responsibility (Brayfield, 1992; Darling-Fisher & Tiedje, 1990).

Adjusting to fatherhood may prove difficult for some men. Brent McBride (1989) observes that many fathers are simply unprepared to assume an active parental role. This lack of preparation for fatherhood is often seen in such areas as developmentally appropriate parenting skills, knowledge of normal child development, and sensitivity to their youngster's needs. According to one researcher (Palkovitz, 1984), poor preparation usually originates from limited contact with paternal role models, restricted institutional support for the paternal role, and few opportunities to prepare for parenthood. However, uncertainty and confusion about parenting is normal for *both* fathers and mothers throughout the course of the family life cycle (Ambert, 1992; Cowan & Cowan, 1992; Cowan & Hetherington, 1991; Pillemer & McCartney, 1991; Rossi & Rossi, 1990).

According to one source (Lamb, 1986), the key element for new fathers is development of confidence—skills can usually be acquired later. Many fathers do not realize that most first-time mothers are just as incompetent and terrified as they are. It is conceivable that the difference, from a symbolic interactionist point of view, is that women are expected to know "how" to parent and cannot just withdraw from the challenges involved. Along these lines, the role of

Over the years, the scope of fatherhood has changed considerably.

Lifespan Development in Action

SELECTING A QUALITY CHILD-CARE PROGRAM

Specialists working in early childhood education and child development have identified several indicators of quality care for preschoolers. These are important to identify because quality care can benefit a child, her or his family, and one's community. A youngster's educational, physical, personal, and social development will be nurtured in a well-executed program. The following represents some of the important areas of concern:

STAFFING CONSIDERATIONS

- The adults should enjoy and understand how young children learn and grow. Do adult expectations vary appropriately for children of differing ages and interests?
- The staff should view themselves positively and therefore continually foster children's emotional and social development. Are the adults consistent but flexible in their guidance of children?
- There should be enough adults to work with a group and to care for the individual needs of the children. Is there at least one teacher and an assistant with every group of children?
- All staff members should work together cooperatively. Also, the staff should observe and record each child's progress and development.

PROGRAM AND ACTIVITY CONSIDERATIONS

- The environment should foster the development of young children working and playing together. Does the center have realistic goals for children?
- A good center should provide appropriate and sufficient equipment and play materials and make them readily available. Is there large climbing equipment as well as toys for small motor skill development?
- Children should be helped to increase their language skills and expand their understanding of the world. Are the children encouraged to solve their own problems, to think independently, and to respond to open-ended questions?

STAFF, FAMILY, AND COMMUNITY CONSIDERATIONS

- A good program should consider and support the needs of the entire family. Are parents welcome to observe, discuss policies, make suggestions, and participate in the work of the center?
- A good center should be aware of and contribute to community resources. Does the staff share information about community recreational and learning opportunities with families?

Continued . . .

SELECTING A QUALITY CHILD-CARE PROGRAM, Continued . . .

HEALTH AND SAFETY CONSIDERATIONS

- The health of children, staff, and parents should be protected and promoted. Are current medical records and emergency information maintained for each child and staff member?
- The facility should be safe for children and adults. Are the building and grounds well lighted and free of hazards?
- The environment should be spacious enough to accommodate a variety of activities and equipment. (Adapted from the National Association for the Education of Young Children, 1983)

mother embraces specific knowledge, ability, and motivation. Mothers who are uninformed often have to pretend they know what they are doing, and thus must learn the necessary child-care skills as soon as they can. One study (Stevens, 1988) disclosed that if a father has difficulty in dealing with an infant, he invariably turns to his wife for help. If the mother needs assistance, she is more likely to seek help from a relative, friend, or pediatrician.

Certain research (e.g., Baruch & Barnett, 1986; Dickie & Gerber, 1980; Russell, 1982) indicates that paternal involvement is linked to a father's perceptions of competence as a parent. In other words, the father's appraisal of his parenting skills determines the level of his interaction. If this is true, a system of social exchange may be in operation. By this, perceptions of competency may prove quite rewarding and push the father toward heightened levels of involvement. Perceived incompetency, on the other hand, may prove discouraging and herald reduced involvement.

Whether or not the father's influence becomes positive is an important issue. This hinges on a number of forces, including involvement in child-care and family activities, his upbringing, the quality of his other relationships, personality characteristics (e.g., self-esteem and sensitivity) and the characteristics of his offspring (Adams, 1984; Clay, 1987; Coverman & Sheley, 1986; Volling & Belsky, 1991). Michael Lamb (1986) adds that fathers influence their children by the way they behave toward their offspring and the manner in which they interact with their wives. Related to the latter, research shows (e.g., Ahmeduzzaman & Roopnarine, 1992; Belsky, 1984; Easterbrooks & Emde, 1988) that satisfying marital relationships as well as social support enhance both fathers' and mothers' sensitivity and responsivity to the needs of their children.

And it must be noted that greater paternal involvement does not always create domestic harmony. Certain research (e.g., Crouter et al., 1987; Stanley, Hunt, & Hunt, 1986) indicates that paternal involvement in child care in dual-earner families is related to heightened marital conflict and lowered levels of marital satisfaction. Similar findings were revealed in an investigation conducted by Brent McBride (1989). He found that when mothers were employed outside the home, fathers tended to perceive their roles as being more restricted, experienced more depression in their parental role, and saw their children as being more moody and demanding. McBride notes that many mothers

THEORETICAL ISSUES

How might symbolic interactionists explore the father role, particularly the meanings attached to his involvement or retreat from child care? How might exchange theorists examine the benefits and drawbacks attached to paternal involvement?

have been subject to the stresses associated with the multiple role demands of being a parent and working outside the home. Most fathers, on the other hand, have not, and may experience stress as they attempt to meet the changing expectations for paternal involvement in response to maternal employment.

UNIT REVIEW—

↗ Most people in the United States will marry. The reasons for marriage are diverse, from companionship to legitimization of sex and children.

↗ The early years of marriage represent a time for adaptation and adjustment. In general, happy marriages are determined by the amount of constructive interaction between the two partners and the use of good communication skills.

↗ Divorce is a crisis that affects the whole family. Bohannon's emotional, legal, economic, coparental, community, and psychic divorce processes help us see the multifaceted nature of divorce.

↗ Cohabitation and singlehood have become popular lifestyles in recent years. As far as homosexuality is concerned, the relationship dynamics of gays, lesbians, and heterosexuals are more alike than dissimilar.

↗ People decide to have children for many reasons, and the arrival of an infant heralds an assortment of domestic adjustments. Transitions to parenthood can be identified, as well as racial, ethnic, and class variations in parenting interactions.

↗ The parental roles of the mother and father have changed from those of earlier times. Increasing numbers of mothers in the labor force and the increased participation of fathers in child-care duties are but two examples of these changing roles.

UNIT FOUR: CAREER DEVELOPMENT

Career development blends with many other facets of the lifespan. Obviously, one's work serves a financial purpose, but it also represents an important part of one's identity. In relation to the latter, when asked "Who are you?", it is likely that employed adults will answer in terms of their occupation. One's vocation also contributes to feelings of self-worth, dignity, and ego fulfillment. In addition, work provides an activity through which creativity and originality can be channeled. In this respect, work is a form of self-expression. Finally, work represents status and a source of pride as well as satisfaction (Henze, 1992; Laureau, 1992; Zunker, 1990).

Young adults discover that work and its consequent lifestyle are bound up tightly with one's ego and self-image. They discover that "what a person does" greatly affects one's perceptions of people, sometimes at the expense of overlooking someone's total identity. In the world of work, young adults learn new skills and change some behaviors to fit new roles. The implications extend far beyond the workplace, as individuals discover new involvements and new ways of perceiving themselves (Michelozzi, 1992).

Selecting a Career

By young adulthood individuals are expected to have made a vocational choice. The complexity, however, of today's vocational world and the pressures imposed by society make the career-selection process a most difficult one. Many younger adults remain confused and bewildered over the mere thought of choosing and then entering a profession. The pressure may seem especially unreasonable for those of college age, who have not yet learned enough about themselves or about possible occupations to be able to make a satisfying choice the first time (Asher, 1992; Laureau, 1992; Lloyd, 1992).

Because of the foregoing, attention has been directed toward the career planning needs of young adults. High schools and colleges have implemented courses designed to orient students to the world of work and assist them in the career-selection process. A number of books, too, have been written with the young adult's career needs in mind (see, for example, Basta, 1991; Beatty, 1992; Bloom, 1991; Bolles, 1992; Kennedy & Laramore, 1993; Morrisey, 1992; Shingleton, 1992). In the Lifespan Development in Action box on page 487, we offer some thoughts on how to narrow down career possibilities.

Today there are thousands of different jobs to choose from, compared to only several hundred at the turn of the century. Finding one's vocational niche in the face of such overwhelming numbers can be, to say the least, a bit unsettling. Complicating matters is that new jobs are constantly evolving within the vocational arena while some are being phased out. This heightens the need to choose jobs that offer stimulation, some promise of stability, and an outlet for creative talents (Bloom, 1991; Lowstuter & Robertson, 1992).

Unfortunately, many young adults are unable to engage in efficient career-planning strategies. For instance, many hold romantic stereotypes of jobs that distort reality. Some approach a career decision with fear and anxiety, lest they make a mistake. Others shortchange themselves because they choose from among a very narrow group of occupations. Still others avoid the process altogether, certain it will nail them down to a lifelong commitment they can never change. And there are those who feel that even if they conducted a thorough career search, it would turn up absolutely nothing (Henze, 1992; McLaughlin, 1992; Michelozzi, 1992).

Career decisions are often postponed for so long by students in the United States—as opposed to what occurs in Japan and Europe—that many individuals never really make one. For better or worse, young adults enter the work world when schooling is completed, and many react to it as though they were college freshmen who still had plenty of time to select a major, to say nothing of a career. Years may go by, apparently without their being aware of it, and without their having settled on a career direction. All that many have concluded over the years is "I want to be a success" (Blotnick, 1984).

Amid the complexities and problems of choosing a career, though, are some very rewarding moments. A career search can be a time when people orient themselves to a new facet of their lives. It can be a time when individuals can

Leaving the educational arena and launching a career is an important developmental task during young adulthood.

critically examine themselves, look at where they have been in life, and where they are going. As Betty Michelozzi (1992) puts it, picking a career can lead you to question how you intend to spend your life for a time, or your time for the rest of your life.

▬ Theories of Vocational Development

What compels a person to undertake a career in business administration or medical technology? What prompts a college graduate to pursue a postgraduate degree in marine biology, or a 25-year-old high school dropout to return to a trade school to undertake a career in automotive mechanics? Numerous theories have been proposed to explain the mechanisms behind the career-selection process. In order to understand why young adults choose the type of work they do, it is important to recognize what may have predisposed them to certain fields. Although these are older theories, they have withstood the test of time and are widely referred to in the existing literature.

Eli Ginzberg (1951) maintains that career choice is a process encompassing three fairly distinct phases: fanciful (6–11 years), tentative (12–17 years), and realistic (18 years onward). The realistic phase, of particular relevance to this text, can be divided into three substages. In the *exploration phase,* a person attempts to acquire the experience needed to make his or her occupational selection. The *crystallization phase* enables individuals to evaluate critically all the factors involved in the selection process and eventually to commit themselves to the selected field. Finally, the *specification phase* allows the individual to review the alternative positions within a given field carefully and to arrive at some type of specialization.

Anne Roe (1956) believes that basic human needs and early family experiences affect subsequent career choices. She has proposed a theory that emphasizes the importance of the child's early experiences with parents, the relationship between parental attitudes and beliefs and need satisfaction, and the manner in which the child is reared. Each of these factors nurtures within the individual a general, broad vocational orientation. For example, a warm, loving household with close interpersonal relations may foster an individual's interest in socially oriented occupations. The cold, rejecting household may

Lifespan Development in Action

NARROWING DOWN THE FIELD OF CAREER POSSIBILITIES

By the time a person reaches young adulthood, it is expected that some type of career commitment will have been made. In this sense, these years mark a time when individuals orient and organize their lives. But how do adults get started selecting a line of work? Although precise answers are elusive, Robert Lock (1992) proposes that the career decision-making process tends to consist of eight basic parts:

1. **Awareness and commitment.** During this initial phase, individuals become conscious that they are undecided about their career future and are willing to dedicate themselves to a program of action toward resolving this problem.

2. **Generating alternatives.** Here, several goals, plans, or courses of action are devised. In this part of the process, alternatives for different potential occupations become clearer.

3. **Information gathering.** Now the person collects and studies accurate information about occupational prospects. An important part of this phase is whether one's personality characteristics are compatible with the vocational prospects.

4. **Investigating the environment.** At this point, it is important to examine the surrounding social, economic, political, and geographic setting in order to weigh the environmental factors influencing a career choice.

5. **Self-study.** It is important to make an honest assessment of oneself so that interests, achievements, abilities, and values can be clearly recognized. Accurate self-knowledge is critical in making judgments about occupational prospects.

6. **Decision making.** Here, a career goal is determined from judgments persons make about themselves and the characteristics of their occupational prospects. It is important to recognize that career decisions are subject to change as new prospects and information become available.

7. **Implementing the decision.** The career decision is now put into action as individuals develop their own job search campaign. The campaign might encompass education and training, getting work experience, or following up on job leads.

8. **Obtaining feedback.** In this final phase, a person evaluates how well the career decision process is working. If there is too much negative feedback, the process starts over again.

motivate an individual to reject close interpersonal relationships and pursue careers that are not related to people. Depending on which of the domestic situations is experienced, attitudes, interests, and capacities are formed, which will be given expression in the general pattern of the adult's life. They will appear in personal relations, emotional reactions, activities, and in vocational choice.

Donald Super (1951) suggests that occupational choice is an implementation of one's self-concept. When individuals express a vocational preference, Super

CONTINUOUS AND DISCONTINUOUS HUMAN DEVELOPMENT

Do you think Ginzberg's theory reflects a discontinuous, developmental model? Can you draw any parallels between Roe's theory and psychoanalytic dynamics? Does Super's theory embody any aspects of humanism? Do these vocational choice theories compare or contrast with any other lifespan development frameworks?

believes, they put into occupational terminology the kind of person they perceive themselves to be. A selected job allows for the implementation of the self-concept (the occupation makes possible the play of a role appropriate to the self-concept) and enables one to achieve self-actualization.

John Holland's (1966) theory of vocational development operates on the assumption that the occupational structure can be categorized into specific personal types or themes: namely, realistic, intellectual, social, conventional, enterprising, and artistic. Holland has devised empirical goals, role preferences, activities, and self-concepts for each of these types for both men and women. For example, realistic individuals prefer physical and technical activities, hold conventional economic values, and accord social and aesthetic values little importance. Most perceive themselves to be practical, conventional, submissive, and uncreative. Such a classification theory, Holland believes, will assist the individual to consider the complex personality dimensions of occupations in a systematic and realistic fashion.

In sum, these vocational theories are useful in helping us better understand the dynamics of career choice. However, they are not without their share of drawbacks. To illustrate, vocational development theories tend to downplay the career dynamics of minorities and women. They also tend to dwell on the work lives of young people rather than addressing issues over the course of the entire vocational life cycle. Finally, even though the bedrock of these theories has withstood the test of time, they have been criticized for omitting the economic and social circumstances of modern society (Brooks, 1990).

■ The Search for Job Satisfaction

Many adults today are concerned with *job satisfaction,* the desire to find work that is meaningful, rewarding, and challenging. As evidence of the desire among adults to find rewarding work, consider the large numbers of workers switching jobs. Although some workers are forced to change jobs, such as aging athletes or dancers, others change vocations because they discover their job no longer serves personal goals and needs. It is estimated that in the course of one's vocational life, six or seven major changes in work patterns will occur (Calhoun & Acocella, 1990).

In addition to meaningful and challenging work, what other factors constitute job satisfaction? If we had to rank the factors, the ability to make meaningful contributions, the ability to express oneself and have others listen, and pay would head the list. Other equally important factors, though, would be job security, the chances for advancement, quality of working conditions, and the status or prestige of the job (Bloom, 1991; Bolles, 1992; James & James, 1992; Zunker, 1990).

Career changes and the drive toward job satisfaction are more common among young adults than older adults, and greater among those having a college education. Although meaningful and challenging work is desired by high school graduates, they realistically do not expect to acquire such jobs, because of their limited education. It is conceivable that young adults have stronger desires for job satisfaction because they have just launched themselves into the work force and are at the bottom of the career ladder. The jobs they hold often offer limited satisfaction (Carney & Wells, 1991; McLaughlin, 1992; Zunker, 1990).

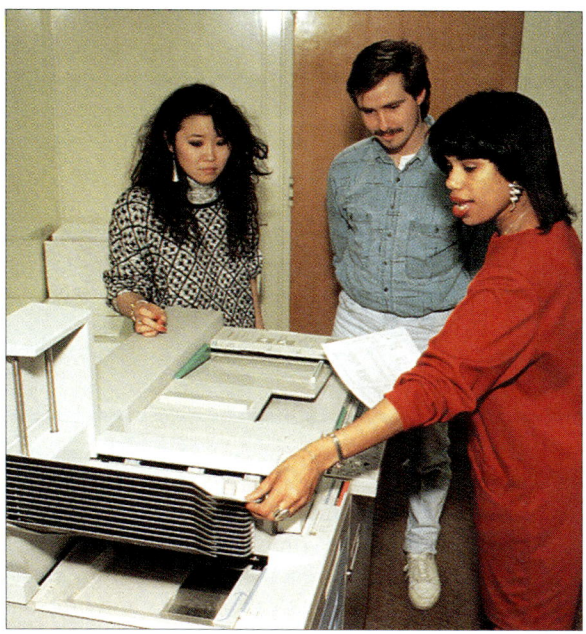

Establishing a rewarding and meaningful work environment is important during the greater part of adulthood.

Seeking to obtain career satisfaction is an admirable goal, especially because it helps create pride in vocational contributions and a commitment to one's employer. Furthermore, job satisfaction helps promote sound mental and physical health as well as family stability (Campbell & Moen, 1992; Hughes, Galinsky, & Morris, 1992; Michaels & McCarty, 1992). When workers are happy and satisfied, they tend to have a brighter outlook about themselves, feel more secure in their jobs, get along better with their co-workers. Moreover, satisfied workers tend to report less job-related stress and work-related illness (Allen, 1990; Carroll & Miller, 1990; Hales, 1992; Insel & Roth, 1991). Notice how the benefits of rewarding work cut across psychological, social, and physical borders. This provides further testimony to a major theme in this text: Development in one sphere affects development in other domains.

Because of the premium being placed on job satisfaction, a new set of work values is emerging. Many question the traditional work ethic and feel there is more to a job than punching a time clock and receiving a paycheck. Although pay is important, the challenge of meaningful work is becoming equal, if not greater, in significance. Daniel Yankelovich (1981) believes the quest for career satisfaction is an excellent reflection of a much larger theme: searching for personal fulfillment in a bustling society often turned upside down. He sees more young adults than ever before striving for personal satisfaction. For example, he sees today's young people as less fearful of economic insecurity than in the past. They want interesting and challenging work, but often assume their employers cannot—or will not—provide it. They are not as automatically loyal to the organization as older generations are, and they are tuned in to their own needs and rights. Nor are they as awed by organizational and hierarchical authority. They are less fearful of "discipline" and the threat of losing their jobs. As a result, they feel free to express their discontent. Young people want more freedom and will bargain hard to keep their options open.

We might note that in the face of growing levels of career dissatisfaction, many industries and companies are designing more stimulating work environments. More flexible schedules, the encouragement of employee input, and the implementation of job incentives are examples of this trend. Workplace wellness programs run by companies also reflect a desire to make the vocational environment healthier and more productive. All of these changes represent steps to enhance job satisfaction, encourage healthy behaviors among employees, and open new doors for creativity and learning. Moreover, such environments instill in workers the feeling that they are an important and worthwhile investment to the company (Brannon & Feist, 1992; Cranny, Smith, & Stone, 1992; Sharf, 1992; Smith, 1992).

CHAPTER REVIEW

Unit One: Physical and Mental Development

By young adulthood, physical growth and development have been virtually completed. The body reaches its maximum physical potential during young adulthood, at least as far as the muscles and internal organs are concerned. Regular exercise and proper nutrition are important health considerations throughout all of adulthood. Regular exercise increases muscle strength, joint flexibility, lung efficiency; and it helps rid the body of stress and stress-related illnesses. A healthy diet is important so the body receives the nutrients it needs for maintenance and repair.

The mental advancements evident during young adulthood are both qualitative and quantitative. From a qualitative perspective, mental abilities may extend beyond formal operations, including dialectical thought patterns. Quantitative dimensions of intelligence are best measured by longitudinal studies. Three aspects of intelligence appear to remain constant over the adult years: crystallized intelligence, cognitive flexibility, and visualization. Visuomotor flexibility, on the other hand, seems to decrease with age. This unit stressed how we must move beyond the realm of IQ test scores to evaluate adult learning performances effectively.

Unit Two: Personality and Social Development

Young adulthood is a time for important decision making and careful life planning. Meeting the numerous developmental tasks that this time period encompasses requires considerable maturity, which we defined in this unit as a state that promotes physical and psychological well-being. The concept of maturity as proposed by Gordon Allport was presented. Allport's research is not recent, but nonetheless still relevant today. Allport contends that maturity consists of seven important dimensions: (1) extension of the self; (2) relating warmly to others; (3) emotional security; (4) realistic perception; (5) possession of skills and competencies; (6) knowledge of the self; and (7) establishing a unifying philosophy of life.

Three noteworthy theories of personality development were discussed in this unit. Erik Erikson proposes that young adulthood is the time to resolve the psychosocial crisis known as intimacy versus isolation. Daniel Levinson suggests that male development at this time begins with the stage of early adult transition, followed by the entry life structure for early adulthood, the age 30 transition, and the culminating life structure for early adulthood. Roger Gould, stressing the notion that adults must learn to overcome irrational childhood notions and parental dependencies, proposes three stages: leaving our parents' world; I'm nobody's baby now; and opening up to what's inside.

An intimate relationship involves the mutual exchange of experiences in such a way that a further understanding of oneself and one's partner is achieved. Intimacy embodies self-disclosure, the process by which individuals let themselves be known by others. Numerous forms of self-disclosure exist, such as through verbal means, body language, tone of voice, or by one's actions. Gender differences exist in relationship formation, maintenance, and dissolution. Love is a complex emotion and rests at the foundation of intimate relationships. Several conceptual models of love exist, including theories proposed by Reiss, Lee, and Sternberg.

Unit Three: Lifestyle Choices and Options

It has been estimated that approximately 93% of U.S. citizens will marry at some point in their lives. This statistic places the United States among the world leaders in marriage rates. However, today many are choosing to postpone marriage. The primary motives for marriage are love, companionship, conformity, legitimization of sex, legitimization of children, sense of readiness, and legal benefits.

The early years of marriage represent a time for adaptation and adjustment. In general, happy marriages are characterized by the mutual provision of psychological, sexual, and material needs. Most experts agree that marital happiness is determined by the amount of constructive interaction between the two partners and the use of good communication skills.

Divorce is a crisis that affects the whole family. We spent some time examining Paul Bohannon's theory of divorce, particularly the emotional, legal, economic, coparental, community, and divorce from dependency processes. Because divorce has the potential of creating numerous problems for children, they need love, understanding, and support from parents and concerned adults. Adjustments and adaptations are also required among remarrieds as well as those single parents who head households.

Not all people choose traditional forms of marriage, and we explored alternative lifestyle choices and options. Cohabitation, although it did not come into prominence until the 1960s, is a very popular lifestyle, as is singlehood. Homosexuality refers to sexual attraction and emotional attachment to persons of the same gender. Confusion has long abounded in relation to the lifestyle, sexuality, and gender roles chosen by gays and lesbians. As far as intimate relationship dynamics are concerned, gays, lesbians, and heterosexuals are more alike than dissimilar.

People decide to have children for many reasons. Among the motives given in this unit were extension of the self, personal fulfillment, enhancement of a couple's identity, companionship, the security they will bring when the parents are old, and social conformity. There is considerable variation in the fertility rate among individual couples. Among the reasons for such variation are age, income, race, religion, and an assortment of social, economic, and cultural factors. For growing numbers of couples, a conscious decision has been made not to have children. Adjusting to the role of mother or father presents adults with numerous challenges, and this unit explored the many adjustments and adaptations of new parents.

Unit Four: Career Development

By the time they are young adults, most individuals are expected to have arrived at a vocational choice. It is fairly well accepted, however, that the pressures imposed by society and the complexity of today's vocational world make the career-selection process a most difficult one. With thousands of different jobs to choose from, young adults need to deliberate in their career planning. Vocational choice theories developed by Ginzberg, Roe, Super, and Holland help us to better understand why we choose the work we do.

This unit also covered the early career adjustments adults have to make, including the developmental tasks that must be learned. Essentially, workers must learn both written and unwritten rules attached to a new job and perform their tasks with efficiency, reliability, and responsibility. Also important is making the transition from school to workplace successfully. An important goal among workers of all ages is the attainment of job satisfaction. Employees appear to be happiest when they have challenging work, can make meaningful contributions, and can express themselves.

TERMS YOU SHOULD KNOW

agape love	joint custody
bisexuality	lesbian
cognitive flexibility	ludus love
cohabitation	manic love
crystallized intelligence	marriage rate
eros love	maturity
gay	pragma love
heterosexuality	self-disclosure
homosexuality	singlehood
intimacy	storge love
intimacy versus isolation	visualization
intimate relationship	visuomotor flexibility

THINKING IN ACTION

• Think about how negative attitudes and behaviors can undermine health and well-being during all phases of adulthood. Have you had firsthand experience with any of these? How can negative attitudes and behaviors be removed and replaced with positive and healthier lifestyle dimensions? After you have thought about these issues, devise 10 lifestyle changes that can bring more physical activity and proper nutrition into your world. Include how you are going to implement and maintain these changes during your young, middle, and late adulthood years.

• Maturity is a state that promotes physical and psychological well-being. Using Allport's criteria for maturity, evaluate yourself, a close friend, and someone you dislike on all seven dimensions. After you have completed this, look back and judge if your thoughts and feelings influenced your evaluation of self and others. In other words, did you evaluate them fairly or did your positive and/or negative feelings get in the way of objectivity? Based on these self-findings, you may wish to reevaluate yourself.

• You are thinking of cohabiting with your partner in the near future but after reading this chapter, you have become more aware of its complexities, including the possibility of legal and financial problems should separation occur. Make a list of the pros and cons of cohabitation, as well as how both of you can protect your interests should things not work out. As you reflect on this, you might want to talk with several cohabiting couples to learn of their experiences.

• You are a parent of a preschooler and will be returning to full-time work in 2 months. As such, you are investigating the extent and quality of child-care facilities available in your community. What do you consider quality child care for your youngster? How will you evaluate the various types of programming available? Make a list of potential questions for directors, teachers, and parents of preschoolers in the programs you are visiting. Then, decide how you are going to compare and contrast the adequacies or inadequacies of the child-care centers.

• Think back to your years of formal schooling and evaluate the vocational awareness programs and vocational counseling you received. Do you consider it comprehensive in scope, informative, and applied? Ask your friends these questions. What were the strengths of these programs? Weaknesses? What would you suggest school systems do to improve their vocational guidance programs? In what grade should a guidance program start? How would it progress from year to year?

RECOMMENDED READINGS

1. Ambert, A. M. (1992). *The effects of children on parents.* New York: Haworth.

   An excellent account of how children shape the lives of those who raise them.

2. Blieszner, R., & Adams, R. (1992). *Adult friendship.* Newbury Park, CA: Sage.

   A good review of friendship research as well as processes and phases of friendship.

3. Furstenberg, F. F., Jr., & Cherlin, A. J. (1991). *Divided families: What happens to children when parents part.* Cambridge, MA: Harvard University Press.

   A clear and thoughtful account on the effects of marital breakup on children.

4. Michelozzi, B. N. (1992). *Coming alive from nine to five* (4th ed.). Palo Alto, CA: Mayfield.

   Coupled with much information on the career world are a number of self-awareness and self-assessment exercises and tests.

5. Salthouse, T. A. (1991). *Theoretical perspectives on cognitive aging.* Hillsdale, NJ: Erlbaum.

   The author analyzes age-related differences in cognitive functioning.

Middle Adulthood

What Do You Think?

Chapter Review • Terms You Should Know • Thinking in Action • Recommended Readings

WHAT
DO
YOU
THINK?

• Receding hairline . . . a bulging waistline . . . the need for reading glasses. Sooner or later, the various aging signs of middle adulthood are noticed. This may be a time when adults pause and reflect on their lives, taking a psychological inventory of their past and what lies ahead. For many, middle adulthood is a period to readjust and reassess, to take stock of triumphs and failures, and perhaps to reshape dreams. Does this happen to everyone at this time? Is it a negative event, as captured by the expression *midlife crisis?* What gender similarities or differences are apparent? We seek answers to these questions when we examine the psychological crossroads of midlife.

• The 35th reunion of Ridgewood High School was a delightful affair, a nostalgic waltz down memory lane that gave everyone a chance to get reacquainted and caught up on each other's lives. Good old Andy Wallace hadn't changed a bit, still free-spirited and able to bring the house down with his great sense of humor. Class president Jill Conway had changed, though, much to the surprise of her old classmates. Once well known for her radical political stances and liberal outlooks, she had become quite subdued and remarkably conventional over the years. And, although coach Taylor still seemed grouchy and callous, many remarked later that he had mellowed out and did not seem to be taking himself quite so seriously anymore. How might such personality dynamics be explained? Why do some people's personalities remain consistent over time while other people's change? And why do some personalities reflect a mixture of both endurance and alteration? As we'll see, many questions swirl around the issue of personality stability and change, and this chapter supplies you with some answers.

• Stress. The mere mention of this word conjures up images of clenched fists, worry lines, sleepless nights, and the like. Stress comes in all shapes and sizes during adult life and can originate from a variety of sources, from economic worries and marital spats to employment blues. Stress is part of life, and learning to deal with it is of primary importance. What do you know about stress? Do you always give it a negative connotation? Can stress be positive or even desirable? Can one person's pleasure be another person's poison? Stress research in the 1990s has supplied us with some answers.

UNIT ONE: PHYSICAL AND MENTAL DEVELOPMENT

Middle adulthood, the longest portion of the adult life cycle, is a stage filled with an assortment of developmental issues and challenges. As such, it has the potential of sparking many different reactions, feelings, and emotions. For example, it can loom as a time of turbulence, a time of quiescence; a time of success, a time of failure; a time of joy, and a time of sadness.

There seem to be two almost diametrically opposed interpretations of the nature of middle age. To some it is a crisis, a period of self-evaluation (frequently with negative conclusions), unhappiness, and even depression. Evidently, to many, reaching age 40 (or thereabouts) means "over the hill." Consequently, jokes about the "middle-aged" individual proliferate: for example, the running gag by the great comedian Jack Benny, who spent nearly half his life stating his age as "39."

The brighter side of middle age has been touted in such books as *Life Begins at 40,* writings that stress the "now you are free" and "do your own thing" themes. This viewpoint also emphasizes that middle age is a developmental period when individuals come into their own, are more accepting of themselves, and mature into more nearly perfect harmony with the universe as they develop a broader perspective. Thus, in many respects, middle age is what each person makes of it.

Following the years of early adulthood, middle age has a tendency to creep up on many people, seemingly without warning. At this time, adults begin to tune into various psychological, social, and biological aging cues. For instance, Barbara Shapiro and colleagues (1991) note that many adults now become acutely aware of the conflicting pressures of caring for aging parents at the same time they are trying to satisfy the demands of work and caring for their children. Some may begin to notice signs of physical aging for the first time, such as graying hair, a receding hairline, or the need for reading glasses. Others may experience the death of a friend or a parent, which sparks thoughts of one's own mortality.

Whatever the cues or clues, middle age is a time when people often pause and ponder. In the journey of adulthood, this stage of life represents a cross-roads, a point where individuals can look ahead and look back (M. A. Wolf, 1991). In so doing, it often becomes a time for reflection, a period of evaluation and assessment. Adults usually discover that their lives have changed, subtly but significantly. As we shall see, whether people understand their adult lives any better than they ever have, or whether they ever will, many at least begin to try from now on.

Physical Development

We established in the last chapter that during late adolescence and early adulthood, physical growth and maturation is completed. Some individuals are able to improve on or sustain muscle strength during middle adulthood, but most experience a slight loss due to a decrease in the number of the body's muscle fibers. This is usually accompanied by a gradual loss of lean body mass, along with a gradual increase in the amount of subcutaneous fat. It is also during middle adulthood that a slight decrease in stature begins to occur. This decrease is caused by the compression of the spinal column, which results from progressive narrowing of the intervertebral discs and loss of height of individual vertebrae. The disc changes begin during this time; the loss of height of individual vertebrae occurs during later adulthood (see Chapter 11).

We stress, again, the importance of physical fitness, proper nutrition, and a healthy lifestyle when meeting the challenges of biological aging (Gadow, 1991; Lawton, 1991; Reed, 1991). Keeping fit and exercising on a regular basis slows aging processes, thus retarding declines in muscle strength, increasing bone mass and joint flexibility, improving balance and agility, and reducing fatigue (Beychok, 1991; Herman, 1990; Menard, 1991). For the middle-aged adult wishing to stay in shape, exercises such as jogging, hiking, bicycling, or swimming help to reduce fat buildups and improve circulatory and respiratory efficiency. In addition to these exercises, many middle-aged adults staying in shape enjoy such sports as racquetball, tennis, golf, or bowling.

Many persons arrive at middle adulthood realizing for the first time that they need to make a serious commitment to some type of exercise regimen. Years of inactivity and eating the wrong foods end up taking their toll, and many recognize at midlife that modifications and improvements must be made. If this is the case, individuals should plan a program of physical fitness that establishes the

Regular exercise is an important feature of a healthy lifestyle.

specific goals desired (e.g., losing weight, lowering pulse rate, improving respiratory functioning). Before beginning to participate in any active physical fitness program, a thorough medical examination and clearance from a physician should be sought. This is particularly important if one suffers from a chronic illness, physical disability, or a sensitive condition (e.g., recovering from an illness or accident). One should also receive professional guidance when undergoing fitness tests or upon commencing an aerobics program. Additionally, persons should upgrade their knowledge on sports injuries as well as on exercising in both hot and cold weather (Carroll & Miller, 1990; Smith & Smith, 1990).

External Aging   As we established in Chapter 2, biological aging represents processes that are little understood. We think, however, that at least part of these processes are influenced by heredity and part by environment. Because each of us is genetically different, we tend to age at different rates. For some the process is very gradual and barely noticeable on a year-to-year basis whereas others appear to age rapidly before our very eyes.

We also know that no part of the body escapes aging processes. This is as true for those changes that are outwardly visible known as **external aging,** as well as those occurring within the body referred to as **internal aging.** As time

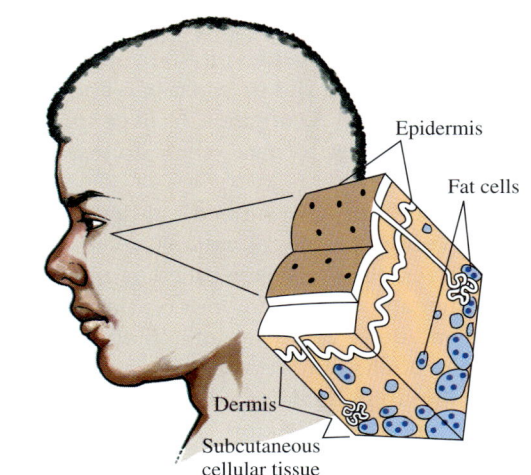

Epidermis

Fat cells

Dermis

Subcutaneous
cellular tissue

FIGURE 10-1

*Age-Related Changes
in the Skin.*

With age, the skin is more
prone to injury and
slower to heal. Wrinkled
skin also becomes an
inevitable part of aging
processes. Usually by
middle adulthood, a
thickening of the
epidermis becomes
evident, as well as a
thinning of the dermal
layer. A gradual decrease
in collagen also occurs,
which results in reduced
skin elasticity and the
onset of wrinkling.

SOURCE: Adapted from Pesmen,
C. (1984). *How a Man Ages.* New
York: Ballantine.

goes on both forms of aging will register their effects in both subtle and direct
ways. As you read the changes accompanying external and internal aging, it
might be useful to refer back to Chapter 2 and make connections to the cellular,
immunity, and wear-and-tear theories. Let us look first at changes in the skin
and hair.

THE SKIN By middle adulthood the skin is no longer able to stretch so tightly
over the muscles. The sun's ultraviolet rays as well as normal aging processes
are responsible for such a change. The epidermis, or outer layer of the skin,
thins with age and becomes flattened, although there may be some thickening
in sun-exposed areas. Thinning occurs because the underlying ground substance in the dermis has become more fibrous or stringy and less gel-like. When
the collagen and elastin fibers in the ground substance break down and lose
their elasticity, the skin loses its firmness and begins to wrinkle and sag. The
subcutaneous layer of fat beneath the skin begins to decrease, also contributing
to wrinkling. Individuals begin to discover at midlife that the skin is more prone
to injury and slower to heal.

Among middle-agers, the facial area exhibits the most change. Wrinkles
make their appearance at the corners of the eyes, referred to by many as crow's
feet or laugh lines (see Figure 10-1). Other wrinkles become evident around the
mouth, forehead, and neck area. Sagging typically appears in the jowls, and dark
circles begin to make their way under the eyes.

Additionally, the sebaceous oil glands and sweat glands in the skin exhibit
change with age. The sebaceous glands exhibit little atrophy, but diminish in
their ability to produce sebum secretions. During earlier life stages these glands
were more active and served to lubricate the skin, keeping it smooth and sup-
ple. Less moisture is now produced and consequently the skin dries out and begins to crack. This decrease is more pronounced among women, particularly
after menopause. The sweat glands begin to decrease in size, number, and function, which by late adulthood may affect a person's ability to maintain an even
body temperature.

INTERACTION OF HEREDITY AND ENVIRONMENT

How does the interaction of heredity and environment shape external signs of aging? For example, can you see the interaction when a person is born with the potential to retain youthful-looking skin (nature) but over the years experiences extensive exposure to the sun without protection (nurture)? Can you think of other examples?

Other skin changes may begin at midlife and become more pronounced with advancing age. Because the skin is thinner and less elastic and because the circulation of the blood is becoming less efficient, the complexion becomes more sallow. It also may become splotchy and irregular in color, due primarily to the fluctuating supply of pigmentation. Lentigines, or liver spots, caused primarily by exposure to the sun, may start to make their appearance on the face or backs of the hands.

The blood vessels close to the skin's surface can develop bulges due to vascular problems that can cause blue discolorations called *venous lakes* on the lips and dilated red blood vessels on the face called *telangiectases*. Blue-red discolorations on the scrotum and cherry-red ones on the trunk are called *senile angiomas*. These skin conditions, as well as an itching disorder known as *pruritus*, typically afflict older adults but are not uncommon among middle-agers. Pruritus occurs because the thin dried-out skin becomes sensitive to extremes of temperature, especially in dry winter air.

Exposure to sunlight is the most significant factor in age-related skin changes, including skin cancer. **Basal-cell carcinoma** is the most common form of cancer seen in the United States (American Cancer Society, 1992). It is a malignant epithelial tumor that rarely metastasizes, and seldom occurs prior to middle adulthood. Although it occurs in all races, it is uncommon in dark-skinned persons such as African Americans or East Indians. It is also more common in men than women.

Basal-cell carcinomas usually occur on the head and neck, and contrary to popular thought, they can also appear on relatively sun-protected areas such as the scalp and behind the ears. The most common variety consists of a smooth-surfaced nodule with the border often raised and pearly. If not removed, it will progressively enlarge and can result in considerable tissue destruction (American Cancer Society, 1992; Lin & Carter, 1986).

What can adults do to help protect and care for aging skin? Avoiding excessive exposure to strong sunlight is a recommendation that cannot be overemphasized. Although a suntan may appear to be healthy looking, it increases the risk of skin cancer and over time creates leathery and prematurely aged skin (Angier, 1990; Sweet, 1989). At particular risk are those with fair complexions, blond or red hair, a family history of melanoma, and a history of blistering sunburns during adolescence. Should exposure to the sun be unavoidable, medical experts recommend that protective clothing be worn and a proper sunscreen applied on a regular basis (Abel, 1991; Bamboa, 1990; Gross, 1991).

Proper skin care always includes regular cleansing and, with the exception of those who have oily skin, the use of a moisturizer. Remember that the body is losing its ability to produce natural oils and water, therefore a moisturizer serves a practical replacement function. A moisturizer cannot prevent wrinkling, but it can make wrinkles less apparent. Also, middle-aged adults should avoid the use of excessive soaps and detergents because they tend to remove natural oil from the skin.

Finally, a word or two about exercise and skin tone. As we know, exercise tones the muscles and increases the body's circulation. However, exercise does not remove wrinkles, even though the skin typically flushes and seems healthier. The same holds true for facials, steam baths, and saunas. Whatever improvements observed are at best temporary.

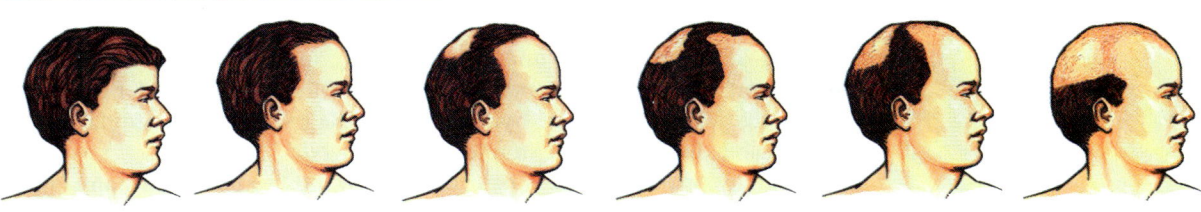

Typical Progression →

FIGURE 10-2
Male Pattern Baldness.

In a typical progression of male pattern baldness, hair loss begins with a receding hairline at the temples, followed by thinning at the crown or "monk's spot." Eventually, these two areas meet, leaving the head bald except for a horseshoe-shaped pattern of hair. This pattern will usually last for the rest of the lifespan.

THE HAIR Most adults have gray hair by age 50. This color change is due to the progressive loss of melanin from the hair bulb. Scalp hair is believed to gray more rapidly than any other body hair because its growth-to-resting phase ratio is considerably greater than that of other body hair.

The hair of both men and women also begins to thin during middle adulthood. This is due to several reasons. Hair growth slows and the hairs are therefore replaced more slowly. Also, the hair resting and growing cycle undergoes change. Earlier in life, each hair has a growing cycle of 3 to 5 years, during which time it grows about ½ inch a month. The hair then enters a resting cycle, at which it ceases growth for 2 to 4 months. Approximately 10 to 15% of the hair is in this resting cycle at any time. During middle adulthood, however, the hair resting cycle becomes longer (Donohugh, 1981; Rossman, 1986).

Hair loss becomes a consequence of this longer resting cycle, for both men and women. However, among men it is much more pronounced. Interestingly, both sexes have been losing about 50 to 100 hairs each day with normal brushing, but in earlier years new hair had been growing in at roughly the same amount. Now, the longer resting cycle leads to an increased shedding of resting hairs. When this happens, the hair becomes thinner and miniaturized. Fine nonpigmented hairs end up replacing coarse pigmented ones, or in extreme cases, the replacement procedure does not happen at all (Matteson, 1988).

For men, hair loss due to heredity is called *male pattern baldness.* Such hair loss usually begins with a receding hairline, sometimes as early as young adulthood. An area on the back of the head, sometimes called the "monk's spot," is usually next. In extensive baldness, the monk's spot often enlarges and eventually meets the receding hairline. Figure 10-2 illustrates the typical progression of male pattern baldness.

Women experience hair loss at much later ages, and the loss itself is less pronounced than it is in men. Thinning usually occurs at the vertex and frontal regions. The hair may also become finer and less dense over time. Some women also experience significant hair loss after menopause. However, most women who develop this condition have a hereditary predisposition to hair loss.

As women and men experience varying degrees of hair loss, they may be developing hair in unwanted areas. Coarse pigmented hairs may develop on the chin and upper lip of women; similar hair structures appear on the ears, nose, and eyebrows of men. Many men also experience hair growth on the back. For both sexes, axillary (underarm) and pubic hair usually becomes finer and not as thick as it once was (Matteson, 1988).

Numerous suggestions exist on the topic of proper hair care and aging processes. To help slow down hair loss, persons should brush gently, avoid excess heat from blow drying, and rinse with a conditioner after shampooing. Chemical treatments such as permanents and bleaching should be avoided. Hair breakage can be reduced by keeping the hair short. And, similar to skin care, excessive direct sunlight should be minimized.

Although a cure for baldness has yet to be found, a number of hair replacement options exist. Although hairpieces offer the fewest complications, many persons today turn to other approaches to the problem. One such procedure is surgical hair transplantation. Small cylindrical grafts of hair are taken from hair-bearing regions of the scalp (usually from the back of the head) and transplanted to the desired area. Sometimes, an entire strip of hair grafts is used to create a more natural hairline. Another approach is scalp reduction. Here, an incision is made and a small section of scalp is removed to reduce the area of baldness needing to be filled in by transplant grafts.

Finally, a drug called minoxidil (Rogaine) has been shown to be a hair growth stimulant for many men and women. Originally prescribed as antihypertensive medication, minoxidil has the side effect of increasing hair growth. It is applied topically to the scalp and creates new hair growth in 25 to 30% of those using it. However, minoxidil is a treatment, not a cure, and new hair will shed within a few months if the drug is not continually administered. Minoxidil is also an expensive venture: In 1994, a year's supply cost approximately $600.

Internal Aging   Unlike the visible signs of external aging, internal aging cannot be seen. We become aware of such aging processes only indirectly, when we notice a difference in the way we feel or act, or when they are brought to our attention by a physician. In this section, we discuss those internal changes associated with the cardiovascular, nervous, and respiratory systems.

THE CARDIOVASCULAR SYSTEM With age, there is a stiffening and decreased elasticity of the heart's tissues and a decrease in cardiac output and blood volume. Assuming the heart functions at 100% capacity for a 30-year-old, its efficiency drops down to 80% by age 50. By age 80, it will decrease to 70%. However, loss of cardiovascular function may be more related to lack of conditioning than to aging processes, thus underscoring the need for regular physical exercise (Beychok, 1991; Lawton, 1991). Many middle-aged adults experience a moderate increase in blood pressure, especially systolic blood pressure. Also, **arteriosclerosis,** or hardening of the arteries, may begin at this time. We supply more information on this topic a bit later in the chapter.

THE NERVOUS SYSTEM The speed at which a nerve impulse travels from the brain to a muscle fiber in the body decreases only by approximately 10% throughout the life cycle. Approximately one half of that figure is reached by one's 50th birthday. Structural changes in the brain at midlife are negligible, although there is thought to be a gradual loss of neurons in the brain and spinal cord. Such neural loss is most pronounced in the cortex, particularly in the frontal areas (see Figure 10-3). Neuronal losses do not necessarily affect brain function, but over time cause a reduction in overall brain weight (Kalat, 1992; Purves, 1988; Scheibel, 1992). As we discover in Chapter 11, disorders of the nervous system are primarily responsible for the conditions of delirium and dementia.

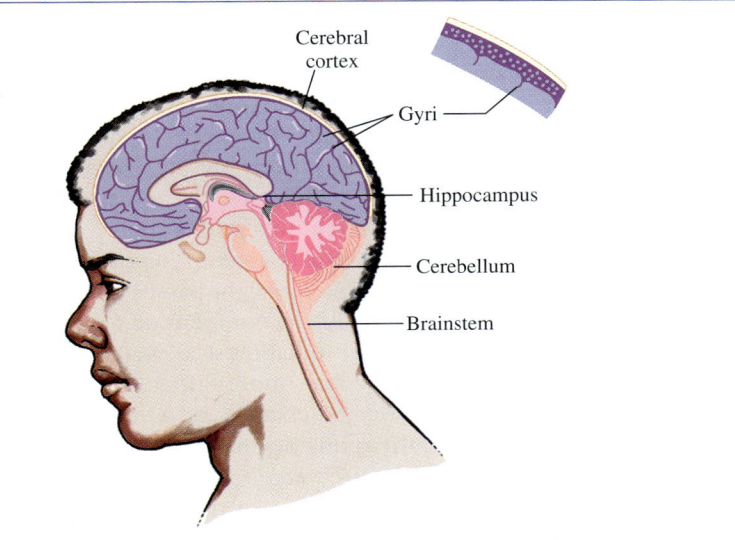

Cerebral cortex

Gyri

Hippocampus

Cerebellum

Brainstem

FIGURE 10-3
Age-Related Changes in the Brain.

Aging processes create certain changes in the brain. For instance, the brain decreases in size as a function of age and by midlife is smaller and lighter than it once was. The shrinkage of brain size results in a greater separation from the cortical mantle. There is also a decrease in the cortical area due to the narrowing and flattening of the gyri (brain folds). With aging, there will also be a steady loss of neurons in the brain and the spinal cord. Note, however, that none of these age-related changes in the healthy brain have an effect on thinking and cognition.
SOURCE: Adapted from Pesmen, 1984.

THE RESPIRATORY SYSTEM At midlife, breathing capacity is down to 75% (compared to 100% at age 30). A slow loss of lung elasticity also begins at this time, and the thorax begins to become shorter. Also, the chest cage becomes stiffer and the muscles that move the chest during inhalation and exhalation have a tendency to become weaker. In time, usually by late adulthood, such stiffness and diminished muscular strength reduces the efficiency of breathing. As with the cardiovascular system, the respiratory system is adversely affected by inactivity, and its efficiency can be enhanced with regular exercise (Morey, 1991; Schilke, 1991).

Changes in Sensory Capacities   Although sensory changes were slight during the early adulthood years, more significant alterations characterize middle adulthood. Sensory contact with the physical environment is an extremely important aspect of overall aging processes. What a person is capable of perceiving or sensing may well influence overall behavior and personality, thus illustrating again the convergence of developmental forces presented in Chapter 2. The self-concept can easily be damaged when a sense defect hinders an individual from coping with numerous and diverse amounts of incoming perceptual information. Changes in sensory capacities are something we will all experience to a certain degree. Provided there are no serious impairments, most adjust effectively to these changes (Botwinick, 1981, 1984).

Vision, the sense we most depend on, changes noticeably during the middle years, especially after age 40. This is the age when many people begin holding newspapers and books farther in front of them, and bifocals make their appearance to compensate for **presbyopia,** a condition of farsightedness. Presbyopia is the result of a change in the lens of the eye. The lens continues to grow throughout life, but because its cells are not shed, like those of the skin, it slowly compacts from childhood on. This ultimately affects accommodation, the manner in which the lens adapts to near and far vision.

Accommodation is achieved by the contraction and relaxation of the muscles of the lens, flattening the lens or allowing it to become rounder by its own elasticity. By the fifth decade of life, the loss of accommodation becomes so great that most persons require optical correction to read within arm's length. Some adults may be able to get by and compensate by holding objects farther away or by increasing illumination. Ultimately, though, reading glasses are a necessity of life (Orr, 1991). Figure 10-4 illustrates the visual condition of presbyopia and the way reading glasses correct this problem.

Other changes occur with the visual system. For example, the pupil becomes smaller with age and, as a result, less light passes through it. Middle-aged adults generally need more illumination to compensate for this. They also may need longer periods of time to adapt to darkness as well as to glare. This latter fact explains why night driving becomes more difficult with age (Barr & Eberhard, 1991). As far as other age-related changes are concerned, the lens of the eye becomes less transparent, the retina begins to lose rods and cones, and the number of fibers composing the optic nerve tends to decline (Schieber, 1992).

A change in visual abilities is often one of the earlier signs of middle age. Again, we find that psychologically most people are able to laugh and kid one another about their farsightedness and needing longer arms to read the newspaper; these people wear their new glasses and accept their condition. Others, however, try to hide their visual liabilities by memorizing menus at favorite eating places, or by asking waiters what they recommend, rather than show the world they have to wear glasses.

Hearing is another sense that may start declining by age 40, and although most of us do not seem embarrassed to wear eyeglasses as vision declines, we are apt to remain "tuned out" rather than wear a hearing aid (Olinger, Dancer, & Patterson, 1991). The ability to hear low-pitched sounds seems to remain constant in adulthood, but men, especially, lose auditory acuity for the higher

FIGURE 10-4

The Correction of Presbyopia.

Presbyopia, or far-sightedness, is caused by an inability to focus images on the fovea, which is located on the retina. This results in blurred vision at reading distance. Presbyopia can be corrected with reading glasses, which serve to sharpen images and restore visual acuity.

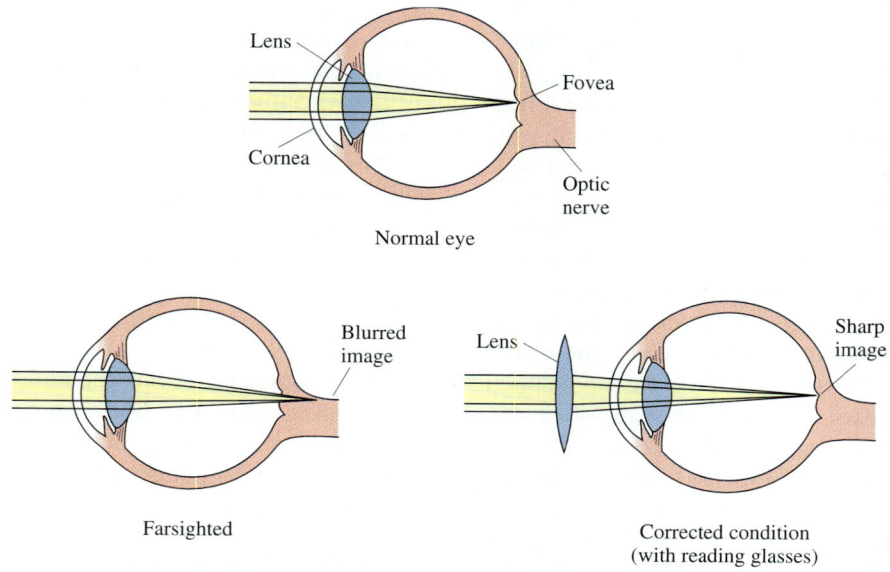

pitches (Hudson, 1990). This loss may begin as early as young adulthood. Hearing problems with age-related causes occur when the ear is unable to pick up and transmit sound to its inner parts. This may be caused by the loss of hair cells along the cochlea, or other degenerative changes of the auditory system (Palumbo, 1990; Schieber, 1992).

Auditory differences between the sexes may be caused, at least in part, by men's greater exposure to noise in association with certain traditionally male occupations: truck driving, mining, auto assembly-line work, and the like. But whereas people know their vision is worsening, they are generally not aware of the gradual loss of hearing. Thus, unless one is noticeably hard of hearing, this unawareness may have little psychological implication in one's development.

The senses of *taste, smell,* and *touch* in adulthood have not been investigated nearly as extensively as vision and hearing. These senses seemingly decline at least somewhat, over the years, but because they are difficult to study in the first place, the evidence is at best general. The ability to distinguish tastes and odors, as well as to perceive cutaneous sensitivity, remains constant during middle adulthood, but may exhibit change during the retirement years (see Chapter 11).

Health Disorders   We indicated earlier that middle adulthood usually represents the prime of one's life. This is as true for physical capacities as it is for other developmental spheres. However, similar to other life stages, middle adulthood brings along its own unique set of health concerns.

OBESITY Of all the preventable disorders in middle age, obesity looms as the most threatening. It is important to note that obesity and being overweight are not the same thing. **Obesity** refers to an excessive accumulation of body fat, usually 10 to 20% or more above one's suggested normal weight. **Overweight,** on the other hand, refers to body heaviness; that is, a person's body weight is greater than what is recommended for one's size. A person can be overweight—because of heavy muscle and bone—without being fat. On the other hand, an obese person is fat (Boskin, Graf, & Kreisworth, 1990).

Middle-aged obesity can originate from many different sources, and health experts (e.g., Anspaugh, Hamrick, & Rosato, 1991; Brannon & Feist, 1992; Hales, 1992) have shed light on some of the possible causes. For example, the tendency for obesity may be inherited, or the number of fat cells in the body may predispose an individual to obesity. In relation to the latter, the greater the number of fat cells, the greater the capacity to store more energy in the form of fat. Another possible explanation is the set point theory, which proposes the body has an internal control mechanism that helps it to maintain a certain level of body fat. Using this explanation, weight thus returns to a certain level after a person either gains weight or loses pounds.

Other explanations originate from a mixture of biological, behavioral, psychological, and environmental factors. The lack of regular exercise and poor eating habits usually rest at the foundation of obesity. As far as eating habits are concerned, food is often the focus of obese individuals. Sometimes food is used as a coping mechanism to relieve anxiety or stress. Obese persons tend to select foods of borderline nutritional value, consume them in unbalanced quantities, and eat them at the wrong time of the day. Consequently, fat molecules build up and the heart, lungs, and other organs must work harder.

INTERRELATEDNESS OF AGING PROCESSES

Do you agree that physical aging has more to do with the way people *look* than with the way they *feel?* How do you think middle-aged adults can develop positive attitudes about their changing bodies? What role do psychological dynamics and cultural prescriptions play in accepting one's changing physical self?

Obesity is associated with a number of health disorders, including coronary artery disease.

The link between obesity and chronic diseases such as heart disease, some types of cancer, and stroke is well established. Additionally, the older individuals are, the greater their chances of dying because of obesity (Edelson, 1991). Dianne Hales (1992) puts the risks attached to obesity and aging into the following perspective: In a group of 100 people of normal weight, 90 can expect to live to age 60, 50 will survive to age 70, and 30 will live into their 80s. However, only 60 of every 100 obese persons will survive to age 60, one half of these will live another decade, and no more than 10 will survive to age 80.

In addition to the medical hazards, obese individuals often suffer from social discrimination and hold poor body images and lowered self-concepts. Obese individuals usually pay higher premiums for health insurance or are denied coverage, are often ridiculed by others, and armed forces personnel are forced out of the military if they gain weight beyond an acceptable level. Given such negative scenarios, it is fortunate that obesity is reversible, and so too are the many risks associated with it (Anspaugh, Hamrick, & Rosato, 1991).

HYPERTENSION **Hypertension,** usually referred to as high blood pressure, is a common circulatory disorder. It is estimated that as many as 58 million U.S. citizens have high blood pressure that requires monitoring or treatment, mostly middle-aged men and women. Among younger adults, more men than women have high blood pressure, but after age 55 the problem becomes more acute for females. As the accompanying Focus on Diversity box discloses, African Americans and those from lower socioeconomic settings are also more vulnerable to hypertension (Centers for Disease Control, 1990; Simpson et al., 1991).

Hypertension is often called the silent killer because it usually presents no observable symptoms. If left untreated, it can wear down vital organs and lead to heart disease, stroke, or kidney failure. To understand the danger this disorder presents, we must first develop an appreciation of what **blood pressure** is: the pressure exerted by the blood on the artery walls. A blood pressure reading, measured by a device called a sphygmomanometer, is expressed as a larger number (systolic) over a smaller number (diastolic). As an example, consider the blood pressure reading of 120 over 80. When the heart contracts to pump out blood to the arteries (systole), the resulting reading on the pressure meter is 120 millimeters. When the heart relaxes between beats and is filling with blood (diastole), the blood pressure reading falls to 80 millimeters.

As we pointed out earlier in this chapter, a moderate increase in blood pressure occurs during middle adulthood, especially systolic blood pressure. This is the result of the body's small arteries decreasing in diameter and elasticity. To illustrate the nature of age-related blood pressure changes, a reading of 120/80 is considered normal for persons under age 18. Between ages 18 and 50, however, a normal blood pressure reading extends to 140/85. Should the latter set of numbers continue to increase, though, a medical consultation is usually needed. As a footnote, there is no medical support that your blood pressure should be 100 plus your age.

Certain risk factors make persons more vulnerable to hypertension. For example, high blood pressure is thought to run in families, suggesting a genetic link to this disorder. Too much sodium (salt) in one's diet tends to create fluid retention, which is thought to promote hypertension. Obesity, prolonged exposure to stress, and excessive amounts of alcohol also tend to aggravate blood pressure (Julius, 1990).

Although hypertension cannot be cured, a proper diet and a healthy lifestyle usually controls it. To accomplish this, physicians often recommend a weight loss program, regular exercise, relaxation techniques, restricted salt and cholesterol consumption, and moderate alcohol consumption. Some physicians also recommend increasing levels of potassium and magnesium intake.

Should medication be needed to control hypertension, **diuretics** are often prescribed. Such drugs cause excess fluid and sodium to leave the body, which reduces the volume of blood and, in turn, lowers blood pressure. If the condition does not improve with diuretics, other drugs designed to relax and open up the body's blood vessels (called adrenergic-inhibiting agents) may be prescribed. Other drug possibilities include beta blockers, which block the action of epinephrine (adrenaline) and norepinephrine, thus decreasing the heartbeat rate and the vigor of each contraction. Finally, calcium channel blockers prevent calcium from entering the artery muscles and causing them to constrict, thus raising blood pressure.

ATHEROSCLEROSIS **Atherosclerosis** is the most common form of arteriosclerosis, or hardening of the arteries. It is a type of cardiovascular disease in which plaque (fatty material) becomes attached to the inner walls of arteries. Beyond making the arteries thick and hard, plaque will also clog and even block the flow of blood.

Plaque consists of such fats as cholesterol. **Cholesterol** is a lipid (fat) that is produced naturally in the body. It is found in many locations, including in the blood, and is present in such foods as eggs, meat, and shellfish. Cholesterol is not soluble and is transported through the bloodstream via *lipoproteins* (fatty proteins). When this takes place and movement occurs, the excess cholesterol

GENDER SIMILARITIES AND DIFFERENCES

In looking at the health problems often afflicting middle-aged adults, men are more likely than women to die from diseases such as heart disease or stroke. Why do you think such gender differences exist? What gender differences in lifestyle might be cited as possible explanations?

Focus on Diversity

ENDANGERED LIVES: HEALTH PROBLEMS OF AFRICAN AMERICANS

African Americans are more likely to suffer from chronic health problems than whites or other Americans. Such problems are often caused by the degenerative diseases that claim most American lives—such as heart disease and stroke—and they exact a high economic price for the families of individuals disabled by these ailments. Low-income persons suffer the greatest economic costs because they are least likely to have good insurance or pension plans. Blacks' low socioeconomic status, in fact, accounts for their higher incidence of long-term disability (O'Hare et al., 1991).

African Americans have higher chronic health problems than whites for a number of reasons. When seeking to understand such reasons among any racial or ethnic segment of the population, it is important to take into account biological, psychological, and social factors. Health experts (e. g., Brannon & Feist, 1992; Kaplan, Sallis, & Patterson, 1993) refer to such considerations as *biopsychosocial* factors, and emphasize how these elements converge to create illness or dis-

ease. Notice how this interpretation of health parallels the interrelatedness of developmental forces, one of the major themes of this book.

Utilizing this biopsychosocial approach to health, the biological emphasis might embrace how certain diseases are caused by microorganisms, deficiencies in the immune system, or problems with specific organ systems. Or, an Afrocentric bioevolutionary perspective might be established so that kidney functioning, salt retention, and blood pressure are viewed as related to aspects of biological developmental human heritage, not as being African American in terms of carrier social identification.

Psychological features of the biopsychosocial model include behaviors, thoughts, and feelings; social factors encompass the influence of others as well as the impact of one's surroundings on health. Psychological and social forces help to explain a person's lifestyle choices, including health-care use. As this chapter reveals, specific lifestyle traits have been linked to the prevalence of certain health disorders. To illustrate, smoking

is deposited along artery walls and begins to create circulation problems. Thus cholesterol in itself is not bad. On the contrary, the body needs cholesterol to assist in digestion and hormonal production, among other functions. It is excessive cholesterol intake that creates problems, particularly cardiovascular difficulties.

The measurement of the amount of cholesterol carried in the serum (the liquid cell-free part of the blood) is typically expressed in milligrams of total cholesterol per deciliter of blood (mg/dl). This measurement is a ratio, but it is generally abbreviated in the cholesterol count. Thus a cholesterol reading of 210 means 210 mgs of cholesterol per 100 dl of blood serum. However, *total* serum cholesterol may not be the best predictor of cardiovascular disease because not all lipoproteins are equally implicated in atherosclerosis. *High-density lipoproteins* (HDLs) are considered good cholesterol, since they remove other cholesterol from the walls of the arteries. *Low-density lipoproteins* (LDLs), on the other hand, are considered bad types of cholesterol because they allow the cholesterol to circulate in the bloodstream. Thus high LDL levels has been connected to lung cancer and heart disease; obesity is associated with circulatory disease, diabetes, and hypertension (high blood pressure); hypertension, in turn, with strokes and heart disease. African Americans fare worse than whites on all of these factors. A higher percentage of black than white men smoke, are more likely to be obese (especially at older ages), and to suffer from hypertension. African Americans are also less likely than whites to visit a doctor (O'Hare et al., 1991).

The social component of the biopsychosocial model is helpful in understanding how socioeconomic influences impact on the health of African Americans. Information about the importance of regular medical checkups and early diagnosis and treatment of disease is not as likely to reach poorly educated individuals. Even when such information arrives, the poor often have limited access to quality medical care. In support of this is the lack of health-care coverage—by private insurance, Medicare, or Medicaid. About 16% of all Americans under age 65 have no health insurance; the figure is 22% for African Americans under age 65 and 34% for black adults age 18 to 24 (O'Hare et al., 1991).

One study (Simpson et al., 1991) noted that African Americans who suffer heart attacks often jeopardize their lives by not going to the hospital soon enough. In a study involving 83 men and women (17 African Americans and 66 white persons) who experienced a heart attack, African Americans waited, on average, 23 hours before going to a hospital; the corresponding time for whites was an average of 8 hours. At least part of the reason for this delay, related to points just covered, is that African Americans had less education about the classic symptoms of a heart attack. And a similar delay was noted among African Americans experiencing strokes. This delay was responsible for greater early impairment at admission among African Americans; they needed more help in such everyday activities as walking, eating, and bathing; and they improved more slowly than whites.

Such racial differences prompt the need for education and prevention efforts within the African-American community, and for health-care workers to be sensitive and alert to such differences. It also means developing comprehensive biopsychosocial services for the elderly as a whole, intervention which recognizes that health is determined by many complex and interacting forces.

pose a cardiovascular risk, but the same holds true for low HDL levels. Some doctors believe it is more important to raise HDL levels than to lower LDL levels.

Carefully monitoring cholesterol levels is an important health guideline. In an effort to make people more aware of the importance of cholesterol levels, diet considerations, and treatment intervention, the federal government established the National Cholesterol Education Program. The program recommends the following:

- Total cholesterol should be below 200 mg of total cholesterol per deciliter of blood (mg/dl).
- A reading of 201–239 mg/dl is considered borderline and presents a moderate-to-high risk for cardiovascular disease.
- Levels of 240 or more mg/dl are dangerously high.
- LDL levels should be less than 130 mg/dl; a level of 160 mg/dl or more is considered high.

FIGURE 10-5

Atherosclerosis.

When atherosclerosis occurs, plaque begins to form on the lining of arteries. Eventually, blockage of the artery results.

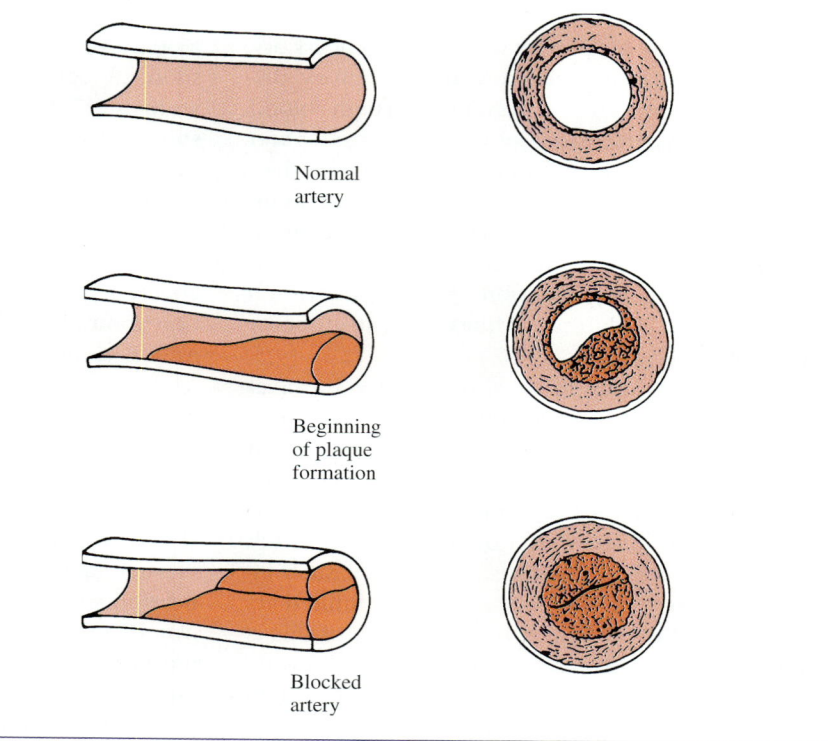

Normal artery

Beginning of plaque formation

Blocked artery

- HDL levels should be at least 35 mg/dl. (National Cholesterol Education Program, 1991)

Blockage due to fat buildups can lead to serious complications when the arteries involved service vital organs. For example, if blockage or clogging occurs in a vessel leading to the brain, a stroke can occur. Should a coronary artery be partially blocked, *angina* (chest pain) is usually experienced. Total coronary artery blockage leads to a heart attack.

Atherosclerosis is thought to develop early in life, slowly blocking the body's network of arteries. Such changes usually go undetected for years because this disease presents no visible symptoms. Indeed, it is usually not until middle adulthood that any problems begin. By this time, artery walls may have become significantly reduced in size by fatty deposits, preventing blood from delivering life-sustaining oxygen to body parts. Figure 10-5 illustrates how atherosclerosis affects the lining of an artery.

Although the exact causes of atherosclerosis remain elusive, several factors that increase its progress have been identified. For example, the tendency to manufacture large amounts of cholesterol is thought to have a genetic basis. Hypertension, cigarette smoking, lack of exercise, and stress represent other risk factors. Diabetes has also been cited, since blood sugar abnormalities appear to promote the production of cholesterol.

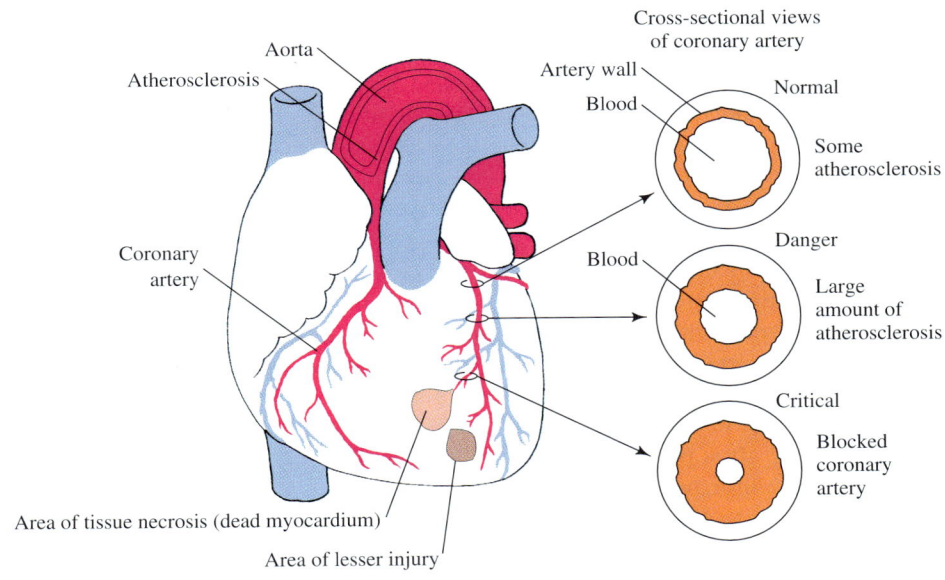

Aorta
Atherosclerosis
Coronary artery
Area of tissue necrosis (dead myocardium)
Area of lesser injury

Cross-sectional views of coronary artery
Artery wall
Blood
Normal
Some atherosclerosis
Danger
Blood
Large amount of atherosclerosis
Critical
Blocked coronary artery

FIGURE 10-6
How a Heart Attack Occurs.

The treatment of atherosclerosis typically involves changes in lifestyle and eating habits. Among the recommendations are a reduction in cholesterol intake, including a low-fat diet (Cooper, 1990; Piscatella, 1990). Other suggestions include the elimination of cigarette smoking, and the implementation of sensible exercise and weight loss programs. Should medication be needed, **anticoagulants** are often prescribed to thin the blood and prevent clotting. Surgical procedures to remove plaque from blocked arteries may also be necessary. However, such procedures are usually performed on relatively large vessels, such as those entering the heart, kidneys, or brain. Surgery typically cannot remove plaque deposits in the small blood vessels of these organs (Hellerstein & Perry, 1990; Ornish, 1990).

CORONARY ARTERY DISEASE **Coronary artery disease (CAD)** is the presence of atherosclerosis in the coronary arteries. When this happens, the coronary arteries are narrowed so that less blood flows to the heart muscle. Coronary artery disease is serious and can cause heart attacks. Indeed CAD remains the most common cause of cardiac disease in adults and the leading cause of death in the United States (National Center for Health Statistics, 1992a).

What specifically happens when a heart attack is experienced? Although there are variations, most heart attacks occur when a poor blood supply causes a portion of the heart muscle (myocardium) to die (see Figure 10-6). The destruction of myocardiac tissue is known as a **myocardial infarction** and the infected tissue is called an **infarct.** Atherosclerosis can cause this to happen in one of three ways:

Myocardial infarction results when the central area around the blocked artery actually dies (necrosis). Atherosclerotic deposits have blocked the coronary arteries (see right-side views), preventing the heart muscles from getting enough oxygen. The result is a heart attack (Sorochan, 1981, p. 311).

- Atherosclerosis can completely block a coronary artery.
- The rough surface of the atherosclerosis can provide a location for a blood clot (**thrombus**) to form. If the clot gets big enough, it has the potential of closing off an artery. This kind of a heart attack is called a *coronary thrombosis*.
- Coronary arteries narrowed by atherosclerosis, but not completely blocked, may be unable to give the heart muscle enough blood. This may occur when there is extreme physical exertion or emotional excitement. If there is not enough oxygen-rich blood, the heart may stop beating rhythmically.

If damage from the heart attack creates a small infarct, the heart will continue to function and scar tissue will form over the dead area. New blood vessels will develop to compensate for blocked or damaged ones. This is the heart's adaptive approach to the attack, a process known as *collateral circulation*. If damage to the heart tissue is massive and the coronary blood supply is not immediately restored, death results.

It is possible for someone to experience a heart attack without realizing it. Minor heart attacks are characterized by shortness of breath, sweating, blueness of the fingertips and lips, fatigue, pale complexion, possible dizziness, and an irregular heartbeat. Often these symptoms subside and return. Usually, a minor heart attack is an indication that a major one is forthcoming. The symptoms of a major heart attack are more obvious and are described in the accompanying Lifespan Development in Action box.

The chances of recovery from a heart attack today are better than ever before. A variety of medications are used to treat heart attack patients, such as anticoagulants, diuretics, beta blockers, digitalis (which establishes a steady heartbeat); antiarhythmics (which inhibit irregularities in the heartbeat); and sedatives (which relax the body).

Treatment is also directed at changes in lifestyle and eating habits, including some of the earlier mentioned recommendations. For example, a healthier cardiovascular system can be promoted by quitting cigarette smoking, beginning a regular exercise program, reducing the amounts of stress in one's life, lowering fat intake, eating a diet high in fresh fruits and vegetables and low in refined sugars, cutting salt intake, and reducing intake of alcoholic beverages.

CANCER **Cancer** is a large group of diseases characterized by the uncontrolled growth and spread of abnormal cells. If the spread of cancer is not controlled or checked, it can result in death. However, many cancers can be cured if detected and treated promptly.

Cancer is the second most common cause of death in the United States (second only to heart disease), killing over 500,000 Americans annually. In certain age groups, such as among women aged 30 to 54, cancer is the leading cause of death. In 1992, more than 1 million people were diagnosed as having this disease. It is estimated that one person in three will develop cancer in her or his lifetime, although about one half of those will survive the disease (American Cancer Society, 1992).

THE NATURE OF CANCER Throughout the body, cells normally reproduce themselves in an orderly manner so that worn out tissues are replaced, injuries are repaired, and growth of the body proceeds. Occasionally, certain cells undergo an abnormal change and begin a process of uncontrolled growth and

Lifespan Development in Action

WHAT TO DO IN CASE OF A HEART ATTACK

When it comes to a heart attack, delay spells danger. Minutes make a difference, so it's important to know what to do. The following are some guidelines to keep in mind:

KNOW THE SIGNALS OF A HEART ATTACK

- Uncomfortable pressure, fullness, squeezing, or pain in the center of the chest lasting 2 minutes or more.
- Pain may spread to shoulders, neck, or arms.
- Severe pain, dizziness, fainting, sweating, nausea, or shortness of breath may also occur. Sharp, stabbing twinges of pain are usually not signals of a heart attack.

KNOW WHAT EMERGENCY ACTION TO TAKE

- If you are having typical chest discomfort that lasts for 2 minutes or more, call the local emergency rescue service immediately.
- If you can get to a hospital faster by car, have someone drive you. Find out ahead of time which hospitals have 24-hour emergency cardiac care and discuss with your doctor the possible choices. Plan in advance the route that's best from where you live and work.
- Keep a list of emergency rescue service numbers next to your telephone and in a prominent place in your pocket, wallet, or purse.

KNOW HOW TO HELP

- If you are with someone who is having the signals of a heart attack, take action even if the person denies there is something wrong.
- Call the emergency rescue service, or
- Get to the nearest hospital emergency room that offers 24-hour emergency cardiac care, and
- Give mouth-to-mouth breathing and chest compression (CPR) if it is necessary and if you are properly trained. (Insel & Roth, 1991)

---

spread. These abnormal cells grow into masses of tissue called **tumors** (or neoplasms). Tumors can impinge on vital organs and block blood vessels, in the process robbing normal cells of needed nutrients.

Tumors can be either benign or malignant. A **benign tumor** typically is harmless and does not invade normal tissue. If it does, the invasion is limited. A **malignant tumor** is cancerous and invades surrounding tissues. It also can spread cancer throughout the body, known as *metastasis*. This can be accomplished by the direct extension of the original growth, or by it becoming detached and carried through the lymph or blood systems to other body parts.

INTERACTION OF HEREDITY AND ENVIRONMENT

Does anyone in your family have a history of any of the health problems presented in this unit? How does your lifestyle compare with those who do have health disorders? Can you establish any kind of perspective on the nature-nurture issue as you contemplate these questions?

Four types of cancer have been identified. *Carcinomas* arise from epithelial cells (skin, mucous membranes, etc.) and tend to be solid tumors. *Sarcomas* develop from muscle, bone, fat, and other connective tissues. *Lymphomas* originate in lymphoid tissues. Finally, *leukemias* are those cancers developing in the hematological system.

No one knows for sure how a normal cell becomes a cancer cell. However, it is generally acknowledged that cancer has some hereditary component. Also, cancer can be contracted through repeated or long-term contact with one or more cancer-causing agents called *carcinogens.* Carcinogens cause body cells to change their structures and grow out of control. Examples of carcinogens are tobacco, excessive exposure to sunlight, and radiation.

Cancer specialists have also identified seven warning signs associated with cancer: a sore that does not heal; unusual bleeding or discharge; a change in bowel or bladder habits; nagging cough or hoarseness; indigestion or difficulty in swallowing; thickening or lump in the breast or elsewhere; and an obvious change in a mole or wart.

Cancer can occur at any point in the life cycle, although more than one half of all cancer deaths occur in persons over age 65. From age 20 through 40 cancer is more common in women than in men, but between ages 60 and 80 more cancers occur in men. Overall, more men than women die of cancer. In women, the principal fatal cancers are in the breast, colon and rectum, lung, and uterus. In men, the leading sites are the prostate, lung, colon and rectum, and bladder.

Menopause and the Climacteric   **Menopause** is a normal developmental event in a woman's life. The term comes from two Greek words meaning "to cease" and "month." Today, menopause is defined simply as the cessation of menstruation. This is a straightforward medical definition, though, making absolutely no reference to the physiological changes that occur in all women, or to the many psychological changes that occur in some women.

The culture in which a woman lives is influential in shaping reactions to menopause. In many Western societies, menopause tends to be accompanied by negative stereotypes. For example, menopause is often viewed as a time when women become depressed, irritable, or irrational. It may well be that perceptions of menopause are closely linked to how a given society perceives women in general. For example, negative perceptions of menopause such as those evident in many Western societies tend to be absent in China, where women (especially older females) are highly regarded and respected. This prompts some (e.g., Adler, 1991) to speculate that negative perceptions of menopause in many Western societies are linked to at least some of the problems that women face, including devalued behaviors and personality characteristics.

Menopause generally occurs during the late 40s or early 50s, though some women have been known to experience it as early as the mid-30s. The period from the onset of irregularity of the menses to total cessation (menopause) is called the **climacteric.** The female climacteric may last only a few months or may extend over several years. During the climacteric, ovulation, menstruation, and reproductive capacity gradually cease.

What causes menopause? After 30 to 40 years of menstrual cycles, a woman has released almost all her ova (eggs). Although the male continues to produce new sperm throughout adulthood, the human female is born with a fixed number of ovarian follicles (immature ova and their cases). The number of follicles present at birth is estimated to be 1 or 2 million. By the time puberty is reached, however, the number has reduced itself to about 300,000. Of this number only 300 to 500 will mature. The rest will deteriorate. By age 45, a woman's supply of follicles is nearly depleted, and only a few remain (Tyler & Woodall, 1982). As the number of follicles decreases, there is an accompanying decline in production of the female sex hormone **estrogen.** One result of this is that menstrual periods become irregular and often unpredictable. When estrogen production continues to lessen, the climacteric culminates in the complete cessation of cyclic ovarian activity—the menopause. Because of the rapid decrease in secretion of the hormones estrogen and progesterone, mammary glands atrophy, as do the uterus and vagina in varying degrees. Contrary to myth, menopause does not signal the end of a woman's sexual desires (Siegal, 1990).

Estrogen production does not stop after menopause, a commonly held misconception. Rather, it continues to be produced in areas other than the ovaries. The adrenal glands, the fatty tissue in the body, and the brain all begin to increase their levels of estrogen production. Even though some estrogen is produced, however, it is not enough to continue the ovulatory cycle (Millette & Hawkins, 1983).

We indicated at the outset that female reactions to menopause are multiple and diverse. It is possible, however, to isolate two general periods when women experience the psychological effects of long-term hormonal changes. One occurs during the climacteric, the other occurs upon reaching menopause.

During the climacteric, a woman must readjust her life from one that has been physiologically stimulated by the production of estrogen and progesterone to one devoid of these feminizing hormones. Loss of these hormones may cause such symptoms as hot flashes (moments of feeling warm and uncomfortable, often accompanied by perspiration), irritability, insomnia, including frequent mood changes and even depression, fatigue and anxiety, and, often, sensations of dyspnea (labored or difficult breathing). It has been estimated that between 50 and 85% of all women experience some of these symptoms. It is not known, however, whether these conditions result solely from hormonal changes or are, in part, a reflection of societal beliefs such as those that affect menstrual mood swings (Bachmann, Leiblum, & Grill, 1989; Lark, 1990; Leiblum & Segraves, 1989; Turner & Rubinson, 1993; Wells, 1990).

Millions of women in the United States take estrogen in an effort to deal with menopausal symptoms. In 1990, 31 million estrogen prescriptions were filled, mostly for postmenopausal women, compared to only 14 million in 1980 (Elias, 1990). Estrogen replacement is used to counteract such physiological symptoms as hot flashes, hair loss, atrophy of the breasts and vagina, and loss of skin elasticity. Estrogen replacement also helps protect older women from osteoporosis and the risk of stroke and cardiovascular disease (Schover & Jensen, 1988).

Estrogen replacement therapy (ERT) unfortunately has some negative side effects. For example, the long-term use of high-dose estrogen has been associated with uterine cancer. Some studies (e.g., Bergkrist, 1989) have uncovered a possible link between long-term estrogen therapy and increases in the

INTERRELATEDNESS OF AGING PROCESSES

What kinds of psychological issues do you see weaving themselves around menopause? For example, do you think some women associate menopause with a loss of youth and sexual attractiveness? Or is menopause welcomed as a period of increased personal freedom, including not having to worry about pregnancy or menstruation?

Menopause is a normal phenomenon in a woman's life. Knowledge of this developmental event helps people to deal successfully with its biological and psychological components.

incidence of breast cancer. Other negative side effects sometimes associated with estrogen are high blood pressure, vaginal infections, and breast discomfort. Because of such problems, many physicians are less than enthusiastic about prescribing estrogen to menopausal women unless their symptoms are severe—and even then, the lowest possible dose is usually given for the shortest period of time (Elias, 1990; Schover & Jensen, 1988; Utian, 1990).

Most menopausal women benefit from a meaningful support system that can offer understanding and sensitivity as this life transition is faced (Lark, 1990). In addition, Brenda Millette and Joellen Hawkins (1983) feel a woman's adjustment to menopause depends, in part, on the experiences of her mother, her peers, and other significant women in her life. A woman also needs factual information about what to expect during this important developmental event. A fully prepared woman usually sees menopause as a milestone, not a millstone, in her life.

Mental Development

Intellectual Functioning at Midlife   Earlier, we stated that for the most part, intelligence remains fairly constant throughout adult life. Although tasks involving visuomotor flexibility may pose some problems, few young adults concern themselves with this issue. To many older adults either approaching middle age or already there, however, it becomes something to think about. The possibility of a decline in certain aspects of memory with age may also arouse some anxiety.

Intelligence (whether in the middle-aged, older, or younger adult) is difficult not only to measure but even to define. Historically, the IQ test was designed to predict academic achievement, which it does rather well especially for those who are very like the white middle-class children on whom the test was standardized. Intelligence tests for adults, however, pose certain problems. If the principal purpose of the IQ test is to predict academic achievement, the test loses value when applied to grown-ups because it may not be a true indicator of adult intelligence. This fact should be kept in mind when declines in test scores appear. Very limited data exist telling what test decline means in the daily routines of adulthood (LaBouvie-Vief, 1990; Sinnott & Cavanaugh, 1991).

What is known about the mental functioning of the middle-aged population? As we discussed earlier in this chapter, structural changes in the brain at midlife are negligible, such as a gradual neuronal loss, and these changes do not necessarily affect brain function (Kalat, 1992; Scheibel, 1992). In fact, Walter Cunningham and Kirsten Haman (1992) report that intellectual stability is the rule for most middle-aged adults on most abilities. However, reaction times decrease as an individual ages, which tends to affect the outcome of speed-of-response measures. Such reductions in reaction time are slight and do not generally affect the lives of middle-aged adults, except in those situations requiring split-second decisions.

Middle-aged people may be slower in grasping and solving a problem. This is probably due to such variables as anxiety, rigidity, cautiousness, and general deliberation. The degree of motivation a person has related to the intelligence test at hand is another important consideration. The middle-aged adult's wider life experiences usually prompts the recognition of more variables in a given situation, which in turn consumes more test-taking time (Evans & Lewis, 1990).

Two types of intelligence are noteworthy. Drawing on life experiences and learned abilities is referred to as **crystallized intelligence. Fluid intelligence,** on the other hand, is defined as mental functioning based on the organization or reorganization of information to be directed toward problem solving. In general, it is maintained that whereas fluid intelligence decreases with age, crystallized intelligence increases over time. In problem-solving situations, such as those employed in standardized intelligence tests, young adults typically possess higher levels of fluid intelligence and confine themselves directly to the problem at hand. Confronting the same problems, older subjects employ higher degrees of crystallized intelligence and may deliberate longer

Intelligence expresses itself in many ways and remains fairly constant throughout adult life.

before a response is made. Thus, in a psychometric sense, speeded tests are unfair and inappropriate when testing older subjects (Botwinick, 1984; Jensen & Goldstein, 1991; Madden, 1990; McKenzie, 1980).

To briefly summarize: Although some decline on standardized tests is evident in areas involving speed of response, this in no way implies that intellectual capacities are diminishing at this time. Most contemporary researchers believe intellectual stability rather than decline during midlife is the case. Aside from psychomotor responses and the limitations imposed by timed tests, there is little or no decrement in the use of information and the skills one has already achieved (Berg, 1990; France, 1990; Kasworm & Medina, 1990)

Changes in Memory How memory changes throughout the course of adult development is a popular area among contemporary researchers (see, for example, Byrd, 1991; G. Cohen, 1990; Gerard, 1991; Hess & Flannagan, 1992; Norman, 1991). You will recall (Chapter 5) that the information processing model identifies three types of memory: sensory memory, short-term memory, and long-term memory. *Sensory memory* refers to the information stored in a sense organ. Information in sensory memory lasts for a fraction of a second. *Short-term memory* is a temporary bank for very small amounts of information, and its storage capacity lasts for about 20 seconds. *Long-term memory* refers to the storage of information for relatively long periods of time, even a lifetime. Once stored, memory can be retrieved, either through *recall* or *recognition.*

Generally, researchers have found that sensory memory changes little with age whereas short-term memory exhibits a slight decline, particularly when new memories are processed and stored for short periods of time. More pronounced declines are evident in long-term memory, presumably because encoding and retrieval processes become less efficient with age (Erber, Rothberg, & Szuchman, 1991; Hultsch, Masson, & Small, 1991; Loewen, Shaw, & Craik, 1990; Stine & Wingfield, 1990; Sugar & McDowd, 1992). Some researchers (e.g., Manning et al., 1990) propose that deficiencies in the neurotransmitters that flow through the brain are at least partly responsible for memory decline.

A word of caution about making generalizations related to memory changes and aging processes. Although some individuals may exhibit a memory deficit with age, others may not. Generalizations fail to take into account individual differences, particularly within the realm of intellectual capacities (Rosen, 1990; Ryan, 1992; Sugar & McDowd, 1992) Throughout this book we have tried to stress the uniqueness of each person's aging experiences. Although there are general developmental patterns, aging follows no exact, predictable timetable. This holds true for trends in memory abilities, as well as for aspects of biological aging and personality dynamics, to name but a few areas.

It is important to stress, too, that even though some middle-aged people experience memory changes, measures can be taken to help individuals improve this mental capacity. Moreover, such measures are applicable to young and old alike (Camp & McKitrick, 1989; Finkel & Yesavage, 1989; Ressler, 1991). For example, such techniques as giving adults instructions regarding organizational skills and attending skills, as well as the provision of meaningful processing techniques, have been shown to be helpful (Backman, 1989; Leirer, 1990). In the accompanying Lifespan Development in Action box, we provide some ideas on memory enhancement.

Lifespan Development in Action

STRATEGIES TO IMPROVE MEMORY ABILITIES

Contrary to what you might think, adults of all ages can improve their memory skills. What is needed is a commitment to sharpen this mental ability, perhaps shifting away from old habits. The following are some tips you might keep in mind:

Strive for mental organization. One prominent explanation why adults have memory problems is that they don't organize the information they want to remember. For example, instead of trying to remember 10 grocery items at random, place the list into a meaningful organization. Try grouping or clustering the vegetables and fruits together, then the paper products, followed by items from the dairy counter.

Use practice and reinforcement. Adults of all ages need to get into the practice of remembering. Memory is a mental skill that needs to be cultivated, and its repeated use can make all the difference. Look for activities to exercise memory skills and get into the habit of reinforcing yourself for information that can be successfully recalled.

Don't give yourself the chance to forget. Do things as you think of them, rather than procrastinate about the tasks at hand. You might also want to jot ideas down when you think of them. Along these lines, make use of such aids as calendars, appointment books, and notepads whenever possible.

Use imagery. Imagery refers to the creation of mental images or pictures. The creation of such images often helps persons remember the desired information, and sometimes the more bizarre the better. For instance, if you need to go to the grocery store for eggplant and ice cream and then need to stop at the shoe repair, you might create an image of a large purple eggplant bulging out of a sugar cone stuck in your shoe.

Devise prompts to help you remember. Prompts are hints that can be either physical or mental. For instance, if you have trouble remembering someone's name, try to recall where you met this person. Did you meet him at a party, work, or in the neighborhood? Often providing a context will trigger your memory for the name. A prompt can be more tangible, too. For instance, if you're going to a family reunion and haven't seen relatives for years, do some homework before you go. Look at old photographs (perhaps with another family member) and familiarize yourself with names and faces.

Avoid fatigue. Similar to other forms of learning, fatigue is an enemy of memory. Memory skills quickly evaporate when you are overworked and tired. Always begin memorization tasks when you're fully rested and at your best.

Exercise. Here is a good example of how the physical sphere affects the cognitive domain. Regular exercise can improve your memory, as well as other mental operations. Similar to good nutrition, exercise improves the functioning of the cardiovascular system, thus enabling more oxygen and blood to reach the brain. Additionally, exercise helps alleviate depression, often a cause of memory difficulties. (Averyt, 1987)

UNIT REVIEW—

↗ Physical aging during middle adulthood is both external and internal. Keeping fit, exercising on a regular basis, and being mindful of proper nutrition continue to be important when meeting the challenges of biological aging.

↗ Of the sensory changes at this time, vision and hearing are the most apparent. Many middle-aged adults develop presbyopia, or farsightedness, and males especially may lose auditory acuity for higher pitches.

↗ Coronary artery disease and cancer are the leading causes of death during middle adulthood. Hypertension is also widespread among middle-aged adults.

↗ Menopause, the cessation of menstruation, is a normal developmental event in a woman's life. Menopause has biological, psychological, and social implications, thus reflecting the intertwining nature of developmental forces.

↗ Intellectual stability is the rule for most middle-aged adults on most mental abilities, although reaction times tend to decrease as an individual ages. Whereas sensory memory and short-term memory change little during this life stage, long-term memory demonstrates some decline.

UNIT TWO: PERSONALITY AND SOCIAL DEVELOPMENT

Although middle adulthood represents the longest stage of the life cycle, it is not the most widely researched. In fact, it has been only in recent years that researchers have concentrated their efforts and sought to better understand this life stage. The result of their labor is that we are getting a clearer picture of the special challenges facing middle-aged adults, the developmental forces in operation, and how such forces interact and affect the whole person (Shapiro et al., 1991; M. A. Wolf, 1991).

The study of personality during middle adulthood provides an excellent illustration of how developmental processes blend together. For example, how people react to the physical changes at midlife, including the perceived attractions or unattractiveness of the aging process, as well as the nature of treatment accorded by others, usually affects the manner in which middle-agers ultimately perceive themselves. Note the connection here between physical, cognitive, personality, and social forces. Along similar lines, career triumphs and reactions to failures have important implications for personality stability and the flavoring of social relationships, not to mention the body's stress levels. Clearly, developmental forces are fused together.

With this understanding in mind, how might we best describe personality development at midlife? Is the adult personality characterized by continuity from previous stages or is this a period of change? As we discover a little later in the chapter, we think it is a bit of both. We explore how some personality features have a thread of continuity about them and remain unaltered throughout adult life. Other facets of the personality change as contact is made with new experiences and challenges at midlife. Supportive of the latter is the fact that many people report changes in their outlook on life after experiencing such events as the empty nest stage, a midlife career switch, or becoming a grandparent.

Affecting whatever personality dynamics exist during middle adulthood is the realization that one has reached an in-between stage of life, the middle of one's existence. One can look back and ahead, perhaps more so than at any other age. For many, examining the past and anticipating the future often leads to an assessment of one's life: Where have I been, where am I now, and where do I want to go? Seeking to honestly answer these questions, as we shall soon see, has important implications for personality growth.

The Midlife Transition

Crisis or Transition? Some prefer to view the middle years as a chaotic and often crisis-oriented period filled with numerous conflicts. They emphasize the many changes that take place at this time, such as the permanent departure of children from the home, vocational adjustments, and the necessity of coping with the physiological and psychological consequences of aging. To be sure, as in previous stages of life, certain developmental tasks must be addressed. Proponents of this interpretation of middle age, however, emphasize the disruption that such challenges bring.

Others regard middle adulthood as just another stage of life, having its equal and expected share of developmental challenges and responsibilities. These tasks are no more complex or intense than those at any other age. In fact, some go so far as to label middle adulthood as a euphoric stage of life. Emphasis is often placed on enthusiasm for one's career, the financial stability one is likely to now have, as well as the freedom from the responsibilities of parenthood (O'Connor & Wolfe, 1991).

Thus, depending on the interpretation taken, we are likely to read about the negative or positive aspects of midlife. We are also likely to run into some reference to the "inevitability" of a midlife "crisis" and the profound impact it has on the adult. According to some, heavy is the heart and overworked is the mind struggling with the midlife crisis and the problems of this age.

Personally, we take exception to such portrayals of the midlife crisis. To begin with, it is not inevitable: There are many adults who go through life without any such experiences. Also, we think the word *crisis* has a negative and disruptive ring to it. Our objection is that many midlife challenges and personal assessments are positive, productive, and rewarding. Although there are some serious moments, it is not a time characterized by continual conflict.

Because of this, we much prefer to label this time of life as a *transition,* not a crisis. It is a time when there are new dimensions to one's family life, career,

People respond in diverse ways to the midlife transition.

intimate relationships, community, and inner life. The midlife transition is characterized by a change in the way individuals see themselves and others around them. As persons move toward these new dimensions and experience changed perceptions, they may encounter uncertainty or strangeness. This is only natural, however, as one moves from one stable state to another.

During the transition, people often reflect on their life successes and failures. For some, this may be anxiety producing and even painful. There are some who just cannot bear to look at their inadequacies or shortcomings. As a result, they rob themselves of total growth and self-understanding. In its most productive form, the midlife transition enables individuals to examine their total selves, carefully exploring strengths as well as weaknesses.

The midlife transition acquires negative dimensions when anxiety, depression, and a sense of futility enter into the picture. Some become preoccupied with signs of aging and premature doom. (Incidentally, it is very normal at this age to read the obituary column regularly.) Others dwell totally on the negative side of their lives and regard themselves as failures. Some report gloom and despair as they recall youthful dreams, current accomplishments, and the gap that exists between the two.

This last point is an important one because the successful resolution of issues raised depends on one's ability to reassess and readjust. The optimism and dreams of early adulthood need to be put into perspective by the realities of midlife. It is possible that certain goals in life will not be met, and this requires acceptance and adaptation. This may be a painful procedure for many, but it is important to renounce some dreams while critically evaluating modes of life that are possible and available. This type of reassessment may well lead to greater self-fulfillment in later adult life.

Gender Differences in the Midlife Transition Although the points made thus far can apply to both men and women, there appear to be gender differences in the midlife transition. These differences become clearer particularly when traditional family roles are taken into account. Consider the situation of the traditional male. His transition often places more emphasis on career assessment than on family issues. This is not to mean that his family is unimportant; indeed research (Barnett, Marshall, & Pleck, 1992; Keith & Schafer, 1991) indicates that both job and family roles affect men's psychological well-being. It emphasizes, though, that in our competitive society, making it in the career world is a critical issue for males (Basow, 1992; Sharf, 1992; Zunker, 1990). Connected to our earlier discussions of gender-role learning (see Chapters 5 and 6), traditional males are taught to be successful and competitive.

Women appear to confront the same issues and tasks at midlife as men, and they too create visions of future accomplishments. However, a noticeable difference between the sexes is that women's dreams tend to include both career *and* marriage. And for large numbers of women, even among those working outside the home, the family is often the focus (Kelly, 1991; Moen, 1991). A traditional woman's midlife transition is apt to revolve around her husband, the growing independence of her children, and ultimately their departure from the home. When her children do leave, she may feel no longer needed and perceive that a chapter in her life has ended. Also, along traditional lines, a woman spends years standing by her husband's side, often offering unfailing support as he gropes for his occupational niche in the world.

Many traditional women also define their life cycle in terms of their children's and husband's ages, or better yet, family stages. Whereas midlife may mean, for men, taking on new career challenges, such as becoming a mentor for younger workers, for women it may herald the beginnings of a career commitment. Once the major obligations of motherhood are met, many cease defining themselves exclusively in terms of mother or wife and instead see the vocational or career sides to their identity (Basow, 1992; Gergen, 1990; Lieberman & Peskin, 1992). Research (Helson & Wink, 1992) also tells us that women at midlife become more self-confident, independent, decisive, and dominant. Interestingly, when launching career or educational plans at midlife, many women encounter some of the tasks, challenges, and problems faced by their husbands when they were younger.

Of course, there are variations on all of these traditional patterns, particularly when the mother has worked for most of her adult life (Michaels & McCarty, 1992). As we discover later in this chapter, a growing number of women now do so, and the manner in which vocational and family life converge begs further scientific inquiry. Future research needs to explore such dynamics and discover how the abandonment of traditional domestic roles impacts on all facets of adult life, not just during the midlife transition. Along these lines, tomorrow's lifespan development researchers need to continue their explorations of the quality of marriage in two-paycheck households, the division of household labor when both parents work, perceptions of family stages among working women, the impact of employed mothers on children of all ages, and

GENDER SIMILARITIES AND DIFFERENCES

Do you feel that people react differently when a woman grows older than when a man ages? Do you think this double standard attached to aging encourages many women to keep their age a secret? In light of society's growing sexual equality, do you think attitudes toward older women will change? Why or why not?

the manner in which employment affects the formation and dissolution of marriage, to name but a few areas.

Beyond career and family life, other gender differences appear to exist in the midlife transition. For instance, the way aging processes are perceived deserves mention. Accepting one's changing physical self is an important facet of overall psychological adjustment. Often, though, there is a double standard attached to growing old that frequently places women on the losing end. Just consider how the same aging processes for men and women are often perceived differently. Older men get silver hair, women turn gray. Men get more distinguished looking with age; women just grow old. Character lines crease men's faces; women own a collection of wrinkles. Unfortunately, many segments of society will not allow women to grow old gracefully. Why is this so? Perhaps the biggest reason is that too much of what is valued about women is connected to their physical appearance. On the other hand, men at midlife appear to be perceived and measured more by what they have accomplished in life than by how they appear to others. Therefore, physical signs of aging are often perceived as part of the male's achievement of worldly success.

■ Personality at Midlife: Stability, Change, or Both?

As we see in the pages that follow, some researchers feel that personality dynamics remain relatively unaltered throughout adulthood, connected to earlier years by a thread of continuity. Others argue that the adult personality undergoes change as contact is made with new experiences and challenges. Still others contend that both continuity and change characterize the adult personality. Let's examine some representative research that supports each of these positions.

A Case for Stability   Perhaps the most compelling evidence for personality stability and continuity has emerged from the interdisciplinary longitudinal research of Paul Costa and Robert McCrae (1976, 1977, 1978, 1980a, 1980b, 1982, 1984, 1986, 1988, 1989). Costa and McCrae were interested in studying personality traits and whether or not they changed over time. To do this, they studied the personalities of approximately 2,000 men ranging in age from 20 to 80. Every 6 years, the subjects were given a personality test that consisted of five independent dimensions of personality: neuroticism, extroversion, openness to experience, agreeableness, and conscientiousness. Each of these five dimensions reflected six traits, displayed in Table 10-1. Essentially, the test asked subjects to agree or disagree with statements such as "Often I get angry with people too quickly." As they gathered their data at the prescribed intervals, Costa and McCrae were able to discover systematically if the traits remained stable or fluctuated with age.

As it turned out, the subjects' trait ratings remained highly stable and reflected considerable consistency from study to study (e.g., Costa & McCrae, 1980a, 1980b, 1988). Indeed, in one investigation (Costa, McCrae, & Arenberg, 1980), the correlations between personality trait scores on two occasions 12 years apart ranged from approximately .65 to .85. This prompted Costa and McCrae (1982) to remark, "For the great majority of people, the self-concept at age 30 is a good guide to personality at age 80." And it was discovered that personality ratings by spouses of each other exhibited little change over a 6-year period (Costa & McCrae, 1988).

TABLE 10-1

Costa and McCrae's (1989) Personality Traits

Dimensions of Personality	Personality Traits
Neuroticism	Calm–Worrying Even-tempered–Temperamental Self-satisfied–Self-pitying Comfortable–Self-conscious Unemotional–Emotional Hardy–Vulnerable
Extraversion	Reserved–Affectionate Loner–Joiner Quiet–Talkative Passive–Active Sober–Fun-loving Unfeeling–Passionate
Openness	Down-to-earth–Imaginative Uncreative–Creative Conventional–Original Prefer routine–Prefer variety Uncurious–Curious Conservative–Liberal
Agreeableness	Ruthless–Soft-hearted Suspicious–Trusting Stingy–Generous Antagonistic–Acquiescent Critical–Lenient Irritable–Good-natured
Conscientiousness	Negligent–Conscientious Lazy–Hard-working Disorganized–Well-organized Late–Punctual Aimless–Ambitious Quitting–Persevering

From: Costa, P. T., Jr., and McCrae, R. R. (1989). Personality continuity and the changes of adult life. In M. Storandt and G. R. VandenBos (Eds.), *The Adult Years: Continuity and Change*, p. 52. Washington, DC: American Psychological Association.

Research such as this offers strong support for the notion that personality is marked by stability and continuity, not change and discontinuity. Costa and Mc-Crae (1989) suggest that humans are less a product of their environment than many social scientists have imagined (an interesting thought in relation to the theories we presented at the outset). They contend that people are not passive victims of life events, historical movements, or changing social roles. Rather, they maintain their distinctive characteristics in the face of all these forces.

CONTINUOUS AND DISCONTINUOUS HUMAN DEVELOPMENT

Reflect on the issue of stability and change in regard to your own personality. Do you feel your personality is characterized more by continuity or discontinuity, or a combination of both? Do you think family members would agree with your assessment? Why or why not?

Given such a life perspective, these researchers see stability having important implications for the person:

> Enduring dispositions provide one of the foundations for a sense of identity and a basis for conducting our lives. Planning for a career, marriage, or retirement should be based on realistic projections of our needs, abilities, and styles, and the continuity of personality allows us to use the current self as a reliable indicator of the future self. Knowledge that social and emotional characteristics remain intact with age should be comforting to individuals who fear old age as a period of isolation and depression. (Costa & McCrae, 1989, p. 68)

As one final piece of evidence for personality stability, we draw reference to a fairly recent study conducted by McCrae and Costa (1990). Over 350 30- to 60-year-old men were given a Midlife Crisis Scale assessing job and family dissatisfaction, degrees of meaninglessness and mortality, and inner turmoil and confusion. The researchers uncovered no evidence that such concerns peaked during middle adulthood, shattering the myth that many adults experience a midlife crisis. On the contrary, the findings reflected remarkable continuity. In another part of the study, McCrae and Costa gave their scale to a new group of 300 men, and a measure of stability to nearly 10,000 men and women. The results reflected a similar pattern: not the slightest evidence that emotional disharmony peaked anywhere in the midlife age range.

A Case for Change   Those researchers viewing the adult personality as changing, rather than remaining stable, tend to see age-linked shifts in behavior. In other words, personality is seen as a sequence of stages or transitions, each of which reveals qualitatively different characteristics. In this section, we briefly review some representative age-stage theories of personality, including those of Erik Erikson, Robert Peck, Daniel Levinson, and Roger Gould. Table 10-2 displays each of these theories.

ERIK ERIKSON'S THEORY Erik Erikson (1950, 1958, 1959, 1963, 1968a, 1968b, 1969, 1978, 1982) considers the essence of personality development during middle adulthood to be the resolution of the psychosocial crisis known as **generativity versus self-absorption.** For many, this is a time of productive work and caring. Much attention is directed toward one's children and their well-being and happiness. Children need and depend on their parents, but Erikson emphasizes that this is a reciprocal arrangement. Parents, too, depend on their children. Children add a dimension to life that is beyond description. For many, it is hard to find the words to share the joy and happiness a parent feels as he or she watches a son or daughter grow from infancy to maturity.

By generativity, Erikson means that one seeks to attain a sense of sharing, giving, or productivity. Caring about the well-being of future generations and the world in which they will live embodies the concept of generativity. So, too, does making use of one's abilities, penchants, and talents. The fully functioning person will seek to channel his or her efforts into the most productive means possible to reap satisfaction. Life fulfillment may well be measured by knowing one has made a contribution to the growth and betterment of others through personal, social, and vocational commitments.

TABLE 10-2
Comparison of Midlife Personality Development Theories

Erikson	Peck	Levinson	Gould
Psychosocial Crisis	Adjustment Tasks	Stages of Midlife Development	Irrational Assumptions
Generativity vs. self-absorption	1. Valuing wisdom vs. valuing physical powers 2. Socializing vs. sexualizing in human relationships 3. Cathectic flexibility vs. cathectic impoverishment 4. Mental flexibility vs. mental rigidity	1. Midlife transition (40–45) 2. Entry life structure for middle adulthood (45–50) 3. Age 50 transition (50–55) 4. Culminating life structure for middle adulthood (55–60)	1. The illusion of safety can last forever 2. Death cannot happen to me or my loved ones 3. It is impossible to live without a partner in the world 4. No life or change exists beyond the family 5. I am innocent

The force countering generativity is self-absorption, which may take the form of egocentrism or self-indulgence. Compared to the people-oriented quality of generativity, self-absorption implies caring exclusively about oneself. Erikson prefers to label this type of attitude as personal impoverishment. A sense of emptiness characterizes the person's life, and abilities are not used to their fullest. The chronic complainer, critic, or grumbler may epitomize the life of stagnation. Life is dull and dreary and many individuals feel trapped or confined in their life situations. Typically, whatever gains are made in life are measured in terms of personal relevancy, reinforcing the concept of egocentrism.

ROBERT PECK'S THEORY Robert Peck (1968) has added an interesting dimension to Erikson's work. Believing that Erikson placed too much emphasis on the psychosocial crises of childhood and adolescence and not enough on the last 40 or 50 years of life, Peck suggests it might be useful to divide middle age into several phases of psychological adjustment. Four such adjustments include **valuing wisdom versus valuing physical powers, socializing versus sexualizing in human relationships, cathectic flexibility versus cathectic impoverishment,** and **mental flexibility versus mental rigidity.**

Valuing Wisdom Versus Valuing Physical Powers. After the late 20s, one of the inescapable consequences of aging is a decrease in physical strength, stamina, and attractiveness (if "attractive" is defined as "young looking"). Yet the sheer experience acquired through living longer may enable the middle-aged adult to accomplish considerably more than a younger counterpart. The term *wisdom* sums up this increment in judgmental powers that living longer brings. Wisdom is not the same as intellectual capacity. It is perhaps best defined as the

THEORETICAL ISSUES

Erikson's epigenetic scheme stimulated Peck's ideas and illustrates how theoretical positions can be modified and expanded. How do Erikson's and Peck's stages compare and contrast? Do Peck's stages add more depth to what goes on intrapersonally during the years of middle adulthood?

ability to make the most effective choices among the alternatives that intellectual perception and imagination present for one's decision. Such choice making is affected by several factors, including emotional stability, unconflicted or conflicted motivation set, and mental ability. Individuals who age most successfully are those who "invert" their previous hierarchy of values, giving mental ability a higher position than physical prowess, both as their standard for self-evaluation and as their primary means of problem solving.

Socializing Versus Sexualizing in Human Relationships. This adjustment focuses on the sexual climacteric, which coincides with general physical decline, but is partially separate from it. The climacteric may motivate men and women to value one another as individual personalities rather than primarily as sex objects. The sexual element may become decreasingly significant as interpersonal living takes on new dimensions of empathy, understanding, and emotional compassion.

Cathectic Flexibility Versus Cathectic Impoverishment. Psychological development in the sense of *cathectic flexibility* means the ability to be emotionally flexible—to be able to shift emotional investments from one person or activity to another. Emotional flexibility is crucial in middle age because of psychologically critical developments such as the loss of parents, the departure of children from the home, and the death of friends and relatives of similar age. Unfortunately, some people experience an increasingly impoverished emotional life because, as their cathexis objects disappear, they are unable to reinvest their emotions in other people or pursuits. Adapting positively by finding new objects of emotional focus is required to overcome this crisis.

Mental Flexibility Versus Mental Rigidity. It is important for middle-aged people to remain flexible in their opinions and actions and to be receptive to new ideas. Elderly people are often said to be "set in their ways," but "hardening of the mental arteries" is likely to appear at midlife—a point when people may have achieved peak status and have devised a set of "answers" to life, tempting them to forgo the mental effort of envisioning novel solutions to problems. Some people become dominated by their experiences and use them as the basis for fixed rules that almost automatically govern their subsequent behavior. The flexible individual will strive to master life's experiences, to achieve some degree of detached perspective on them, and to use them as provisional guides to the solution of new problems.

DANIEL LEVINSON'S THEORY Daniel Levinson (1977, 1980, 1981, 1984, 1986, 1990, in press; Levinson et al., 1978; Levinson & Gooden, 1985) suggests that a period of time called the *midlife transition* provides a bridge from early to middle adulthood. This stage, which exists approximately between the ages of 40 and 45, brings a new set of developmental tasks to be met. In particular, it is a time for a man to assess his success or failure in meeting the goals he established for himself in the previous developmental period, the *culminating life structure for early adulthood.* Success is typically measured by whether a person feels he had been affirmed within the personal, social, and occupational world. Life satisfaction emerges from assessing all aspects of one's life and feeling comfortable toward what is inwardly discovered.

In his research, Levinson found that some individuals do very limited searching or questioning during the midlife transition. The majority of men in Levinson's

Middle adulthood usually brings an assortment of new life experiences and opportunities, including those related to personality and social functioning.

study, however, find this stage to be a period of significant struggle within the self and with the external world. As such, the midlife transition looms as a crisis period. Some men question nearly every aspect of their lives and feel as though they cannot proceed in life as they once had. They feel they need more time to form a new life path or to modify the existing one.

Three developmental tasks must be dealt with during middle adulthood. The first is to reappraise the past. The need to reconsider the past develops in part from a heightened awareness of one's own mortality and a desire to use the remaining time wisely. Assessing the past also helps reduce illusions, which are hopes, dreams, assumptions, and beliefs about the self and world that are not true.

The second task of middle adulthood is to take steps toward initiating this new period of life. Although the person is not yet ready to start constructing such a new life structure, choices must be made that will modify the negative elements of one's existing structure and provide the central elements for a new one. As a commitment to these choices is made and the individual embarks on a new plan of existence, the midlife transition draws to a close, and a new stage in adult life, the *entry life structure for middle adulthood,* begins between the ages of 45 and 50.

Although the amount of change made at this time will be highly individualized, the changes can be characterized as being *external* or *internal.* External changes may be drastic, such as a divorce or a major shift in occupation, or subtle, such as modifications in the character of one's work. Internal changes may include changes in one's social outlook, personal values, or inner convictions. Inner changes may be highly conscious and openly expressed, or subtle and hidden.

The third task of middle adulthood is to experience what Levinson calls *individuation.* Individuation refers to a person's relationship to himself and to the external world. Specifically, the goal of individuation at this time is to deal with the polarities that sometimes become sources of deep division in a person's life. Levinson suggests that adults must confront and integrate those tendencies or states that are usually experienced as opposites, almost as if the person must be one or the other and cannot be both. Such paired tendencies, however, are not mutually exclusive, and both sides coexist within virtually everyone. To illustrate, a *young/old* polarity means a person feels young in many respects, yet a sense of growing old is prevalent. Middle-aged men alternately feel young, old, and "in between." The developmental task is to come to grips with this condition of "in between" young and old. Other examples of polarities are masculine/feminine and attachment/separateness. As time wanes during middle adulthood, such polarities should ideally be overcome and integrated into one's life structure.

The process of individuation encompasses all developmental transitions, including what Levinson labels the *age 50 transition* (ages 50–55). Typically, adults can work further on the tasks described as well as the life structure formed in the mid-40s. Levinson reports that the age 50 transition may have its share of stresses and turmoils for those who changed too little in the midlife transition and hence constructed an unsatisfactory life structure.

Between 55 and 60, adults reach a stage referred to as the *culminating life structure for middle adulthood*. This stage provides a vehicle for completing middle adulthood. For those who were able to rejuvenate themselves and enrich their lives, the decade of the 50s can be a period of great fulfillment. In overall scope, this stage is analogous to the *culminating life structure for early adulthood*. Progress in one's overall aspirations will bring its share of affirmation and rewards but also the responsibilities that accompany greater attainments in adult life.

ROGER GOULD'S THEORY Roger Gould (1978, 1980) designates ages 35 to 45 as the *midlife decade* of adult life. During one's early 30s, there is a tendency to act tentatively in regard to making life changes. Uncertainty is frequently expressed when inner dissatisfaction or restlessness surfaces. The thrust of the midlife decade is a strong impetus for adults to act on their new visions of themselves and the world. The stability and continuity characterizing earlier years is now being replaced with a relentless inner demand for action. Quite simply, the sense of timelessness that embodied the 30s gives way to an awareness of the pressure of time of the 40s. Gould maintains that perceptions of life change, and the adult feels whatever is to be done must be done at this point.

Consistent with earlier discussions of Gould's theory, growth during adulthood is in part measured by one's ability to overcome irrational notions that restrict the emergence of mature adult consciousness. Gould proposes five irrational assumptions characteristic of the midlife decade.

The first is the illusion that *safety can last forever.* In one way or another, middle-agers are losing the vestiges of parental protection. As Gould notes, even if both parents are alive, vigorous, and independent, a role reversal takes place. Gradually, middle-aged adults end up standing in their parents' place. Many middle-aged adults now find themselves in commanding positions at work and feel powerful in the world while their parents may have lost power through retirement or semiretirement.

The second false assumption of middle age is that *death cannot happen to me or my loved ones.* The reality of middle age, though, is that the illness or death of a parent and a complex set of signals about one's own mortality are part of the life cycle. Losing one's parents is the realization of a fear that most individuals have carried with them for most of their lives. Many adults have continually denied the possibility of such an event, but when it does happen the limitation of one's own powers and the limited quantity of time that life offers become a stark reality.

The third false assumption is that it is *impossible to live without a partner in the world.* The fact that one's mortality is acknowledged under the previous assumption frequently traumatizes people for long periods of time. Women, though, realizing their own mortality, feel an increased mandate to act on their own behalf. Whatever fears have interfered with the female achieving independence up to this point must now be confronted and mastered. Traditional women, more so than men, are especially vulnerable to the notion that life cannot go on without some type of protector. Once women shed this protector myth, they are free to experience a broader range of social contacts and expand their own personalities, whether through career, family, or leisure pursuits.

The fourth false assumption that many adults subscribe to is that *no life or change exists beyond the family.* This notion means that one's family life is compartmentalized and paralyzed, especially if the husband and wife refuse to work on the continual growth and maturity of their relationship. Many couples avoid working on improvement because they fear dialogue and conflict may endanger the stability of the old marriage structure. However, those seeking to improve their relationship often discover that realignment brings new levels of satisfaction and fulfillment. Still others discover through the process of renegotiation, experimentation, and self-renewal that change and a new life can exist outside the family, if that is desired.

The final irrational assumption that characterizes midlife is the notion that *I am innocent.* As Gould points out, this is not always the case. Many adults have acknowledged in the past that such character traits as greed, envy, jealousy, and competition always exist in other people. Now they can see that they, too, have degrees of these or similar traits. As a result, some adults come to realize they are not as innocent as they once believed. In short, a realization of one's strengths as well as weaknesses becomes more apparent. The task here is not only to realize that the potential for such character traits exists, but also to learn how to best contain their expression. Gould proposes that if individuals work long enough on such traits, they can learn not only to diffuse their power but harness it as well.

In summation of the tasks of the midlife experience, Gould is advocating that the fundamental goal is one of personal growth and self-renewal. Midlife is not a sedentary period. On the contrary, midlife for many looms every bit as turbulent as adolescence. The primary difference is that now adults can utilize their past experiences and striving for self-renewal to blend a healthier, happier life. Unlike many adolescents, middle-agers can know and accept who they are.

A Case for Stability and Change   Thus far, we have explored two bodies of research, one supporting the concept of personality stability and the other espousing personality change through age-stage sequences. At this point, we

ACTIVE AND REACTIVE MODELS OF DEVELOPMENT

How do you view adult personality dynamics in terms of active and reactive models of development? Do you think the environment is largely responsible for shaping any changes evident at this time? Or do you see adults largely responsible for whatever dynamics that unfold?

introduce a third body of research, one that champions both personality stability *and* change. For example, in the Fels Longitudinal Research Project (Kagan & Moss, 1962; Moss & Kagan, 1964), researchers sought to chart the course of personality development from birth through early adulthood. To do this, the personality variables of 71 subjects were assessed during five age periods: 0–3, 3–6, 6–10, 10–14, and 19–29. These assessments were based on interviews, observations, and behavioral ratings.

The most striking discovery in this study was the emergence of a general pattern of personality stability by middle childhood. Moreover, many of the behaviors exhibited by children aged 6 to 10 were reasonably good predictors of similar behaviors during adulthood. Dependency on family, ease of anger arousal, passive withdrawal from stressful situations, patterns of sexual behavior, gender-role identification, involvement in intellectual mastery, and social interaction in adulthood reflected similar personality dynamics during the childhood years. Such findings, according to Kagan and Moss (1962), offer strong support to the popular notion that aspects of the adult personality begin to take form during childhood.

However, the degree of stability exhibited in these behaviors from childhood to adulthood was linked to cultural expectations for appropriate gender-role behavior during the historical period (related to the theoretical issues presented earlier, this reflects an interesting variation of the contextual model). If a pattern of childhood behavior was consistent with gender-role expectations, it was more apt to remain stable over time. For example, passivity was acceptable for females but not for males (thus passivity was stable from childhood to adulthood for females but changed for males). Conversely, achievement was an acceptable behavior for both females and males, and remained stable for both genders over the course of the study. Thus, although this investigation demonstrated personality stability over time, it also revealed that personality can change on the basis of gender-role expectations.

Other longitudinal studies have discovered a mixture of stability and change with respect to personality dynamics. Consider, for example, research undertaken at the Institute of Human Development in Berkeley beginning in the early 1930s. In all, three longitudinal studies were launched: the Berkeley Guidance Study, the Berkeley Growth Study, and the Oakland Growth Study. In addition to assessing children over time, the parents of the youngsters were studied, once when they were about 30 years of age and again when they were about 70 years old (Maas, 1985; Maas & Kuypers, 1974; Mussen, 1985).

Emerging from one of these studies (Maas & Kuypers, 1974) was the identification of ten lifestyle components, six for the mothers ("husband-centered," "uncentered," "socializing," "work-centered," "disabled-disengaging," and "group-centered") and four for the fathers ("family-centered," "hobbyist," "remotely sociable," and "unwell-disengaged"). In general, it was found that the lifestyle one leads shows consistency over time, although this was more true for fathers than mothers. For example, fathers characterized as "family-centered" demonstrated this focus throughout their adult lives, beginning at age 30. Whereas "husband-centered" mothers exhibited few changes in their lifestyle throughout the study, other lifestyles did show change. For example, "work-centered" mothers exhibited the most movement, shifting from marital dissatisfaction and economic frustration in their 30s to fulfilling employment and new

Middle adulthood often heralds new perceptions of the self and one's surroundings.

friendships by middle age. Other types, such as "group-centered" and "uncentered," also exhibited lifestyle changes.

Maas and Kuypers (1974) also identified seven personality clusters, four for mothers and three for fathers. Again, there was consistency over time in terms of these clusters, but change was also apparent. Unlike the lifestyle clusters, continuity was more apparent for the mothers than fathers. For the fathers who did change, the most prominent modifications were among those who were shy, withdrawn, conflicted, and experiencing marital turbulence in their 30s. By age 70, these fathers had become controlling, conventional, and even more distant. Also, fathers who were explosive, irritable, tense, and nervous in their 30s became capable, charming, and conforming during late adulthood. The researchers thus discovered both continuity and change in their research on personality and lifestyles, as well as some interesting gender differences. One unmistakable finding was that the majority of lives studied ran contrary to the popular myth of inescapable decline during late adulthood.

Another study emerging from the Berkeley data (Block, 1971) assessed patterns of personality development from early adolescence to adulthood. Data were gathered from the subjects when they were in junior and senior high school, as well as when they were in their mid-30s. From this data, five personality types for males and six personality types for females were established. In general, these personality types remained stable over time for both genders. However, when new data on the same subjects at middle age were examined focusing on personality traits instead of types, patterns of stability as well as change began to surface (Haan, 1976, 1981, 1985; Haan et al., 1986). More specifically, characteristics such as "interpersonal relations" and "information processing" tended to change, whereas elements such as "socialization" and "self-presentation" tended to remain consistent. Moreover, it was pointed out (Haan et al., 1986) that transformations in personality probably originate from life experiences that may force a person to change. Connecting this to a point made in the first part of our presentation, this shows the influence of life events in shaping the adult personality.

Finally, research conducted by Bernice Neugarten (1964, 1968) also reveals a combination of personality stability and change. Neugarten and a team of researchers studied healthy adults between the ages of 40 and 80 over a 10-year span in Kansas City. Among the assessment devices employed were in-depth interviews, the Thematic Apperception Test (a projective personality test), and an assessment of general personality structure. It was discovered that adaptational processes such as life satisfaction, goal-related behaviors, and coping styles remained stable over time. However, marked age differences were found in the individual's style of coping with the inner world of experience, particularly among the men in the sample. More precisely, a change from "active mastery" to "passive mastery" became apparent. Whereas 40-year-olds felt in charge of their environment, energetic, and positive about risk taking, 60-year-olds saw the environment as threatening and harmful and themselves as more passive.

Interestingly, this shift from active to passive mastery is apparent in other cultures (Gutmann, 1964, 1978; Neugarten & Datan, 1973). Finally, with increasing age there is a tendency to become more preoccupied with inner feelings. Older persons also tend to withdraw emotional investments and become less assertive (Rosen & Neugarten, 1964). Thus, even though continuity of personality is evident in the Kansas City studies, change is also apparent, particularly the person's style of coping with the inner world of experience.

PUTTING PERSONALITY AT MIDLIFE INTO PERSPECTIVE As we draw this portion of the chapter to a close, we are left with the question, "Does personality reflect stability, change, or a mixture of the two?" Social scientists have long struggled with this question, and the goal of our presentation was to sort out some representative research. Given one's theoretical perspective, as well as one's needs and purposes, an argument can certainly be made for each position. For example, the five-factor model of Paul Costa and Robert McCrae provides strong support for the notion that trait ratings remain relatively stable over long periods of time. However, other research, such as the Berkeley or Kansas City studies, provides evidence for both personality stability and change. Discontinuous models emphasizing change, exemplified in the research of Erikson, Peck, Levinson, and Gould, present plausible sequences of personality development.

We think both stability *and* change characterize the adult personality. We see adults maintaining their underlying personality dispositions over time, and in this sense continuity is quite evident. However, we also see the potential for personality fluctuations due to changes in such areas as historical time periods, culture, religion, family, work, and play. During adult life, especially, many life events may impact on the person and affect change. As examples, parenthood requires adults to face an assortment of routines and expectations; a recently acquired job heralds new demands and responsibilities; purchasing a new home requires budgetary flexibility; or the death of a loved one creates loss and sadness.

Although we are skeptical of efforts to describe stability and change as a series of neatly packaged stages (as a discontinuous theorist would argue), we do see merit in acknowledging the contextual influences (see Chapter 1) that create a constant interplay between stability and change, continuity and discontinuity. Appreciating contextual influences enables us to see the person existing in multiple levels of embeddedness in his or her environment, such as at the historical, individual psychological, family, and community levels (Hetherington & Baltes, 1988). By exploring such sociocultural and historical contexts that are simultaneously part of one's past, present, and future, we think a better position can be established to understand how the issue of stability and change shapes the course of adult life. This is as true for the study of personality as it is for other features of growth and development throughout the lifespan.

The Self-Actualizing Personality

Throughout the course of adulthood many people strive to reach a psychological ideal, a harmonious integration of their personality. Attaining self-actualization requires considerable ego strength and the ability to make use of all potentialities and capabilities. In those who reach self-actualization, we can expect to find a highly refined dimension of growth that is characterized by autonomy, individuation, and authenticity. Of course, not everyone reaches self-actualization, and the criteria for self-actualization may vary.

The Concept of Self-Actualization An extensive description of self-actualization has been provided by Abraham Maslow, who defined the need for **self-actualization** as the desire to become more and more what one is, to become everything that one is capable of becoming. He argues that human behavior is motivated by far more than hedonistic pleasure seeking and pain avoidance or mere striving to reduce internal tension. Maslow does acknowledge that many motives are generated by the tension in the organism and that higher forms of behavior are possible only after the tension level has been reduced (Maslow, 1968, 1970).

Maslow suggests that several preconditions must be satisfied before self-actualization can be attained. Individuals must be relatively free of mundane worries, especially those related to survival. They should be comfortable in their vocation and should feel accepted in their social contacts, whether these be with family members or associates at work. Furthermore, individuals should genuinely respect themselves.

It may very well be that self-actualization is not attained until the middle years of adulthood. In the years prior to middle age, energy is frequently dissipated in diverse directions, including sexual relationships, educational advancement, career alignment, marriage, and parenthood. The need to achieve financial stability during these young adult years consumes considerable psychic energy. By middle age, though, many people have managed to fulfill most of these needs and can spare the energy to strive toward ego maturity.

Characteristics of Self-Actualizers In order to study the self-actualizing personality, Maslow selected 48 individuals who appeared to be making full use of their talents and were at the height of humanness. His subjects were students and personal acquaintances, as well as historical figures. In the final analysis, he described 12 "probable," 10 "partial," and 26 "potential or possible" self-actualizers. His analysis of these individuals revealed 15 traits he felt were characteristic of the self-actualizing personality.

THEORETICAL ISSUES

Is there anyone in your life who you would classify as a self-actualizing person? What is the basis for your evaluation and selection of this individual? Does this person share any of the character traits identified by Maslow?

1. *More efficient perception of reality.* Many self-actualizing persons are able to perceive people and events realistically. That is to say, their own wishes, feelings, or desires do not distort reality. They are objective in their analysis of the environment, and are able to detect what is dishonest or false.

2. *Acceptance of self and others.* People with self-actualizing personalities lack such negative characteristics as guilt, shame, doubt, and anxiety—characteristics that sometimes interfere with the perception of reality. Individuals with healthy personalities are capable of accepting themselves for what they are and know their strengths and weaknesses without being guilty or defensive.

3. *Spontaneity.* Self-actualizing people are relatively spontaneous in their overt behavior as well as in their inner thoughts and impulses. Although many conform to societal standards, there are those who are unconcerned about the roles society expects them to play. Self-actualizing people develop their own values and do not accept everything just because others do.

4. *Problem centering.* Unlike the ego-centered personality, who spends much time in such activities as introspection or self-evaluation, problem-centered individuals direct their energies toward tasks or problems. Problem-centered persons are also likely to consider their goals important.

5. *Detachment.* Maslow discovered that his subjects needed more solitude than the average person. The average person frequently needs to be with others and soon seeks the presence of other people when left alone. (This reflects the need for belongingness and esteem derived from others.) Self-actualizers, on the other hand, enjoy privacy and do not mind being alone.

6. *Autonomy.* As can be inferred from nearly all the other characteristics of the self-actualizing personality, such people have a certain independence of spirit. Individuals are propelled by growth motivation more than by deficiency motivation and are self-contained personalities.

7. *Continued freshness of appreciation.* Self-actualizing people have the capacity to continually appreciate all of nature and life. There is a naiveté, a pleasure, even an ecstasy about experiences that have become stale to others. For some, these feelings are inspired by nature, for others the stimulus may be music, for still others, it may be children. But, regardless of the source, these occasional ecstatic feelings are very much a part of the self-actualizing personality.

8. *The mystic experience.* Self-actualizers are not religious in the sense of attendance at formal worship, but they do have periodic peaks of experience. Self-actualizers describe such experiences with feelings of great ecstasy and wonder, and say that such events have strengthened their lives.

9. *Gemeinschaftsgefühl.* This German word, first coined by Alfred Adler, is used by Maslow to describe the feelings toward humankind that self-actualizing persons experience. This emotion, which might be loosely described as "the love of an older sibling," is an expression of affection, sympathy, and identification.

10. *Unique interpersonal relations.* Self-actualizers have fewer "friends" than others, but they have profound relationships with those friends they do have. Outside of these friendships they tend to be kind to and patient with everyone they meet.

Self-actualizing people make full use of their abilities and talents.

11. *Democratic character structure.* Maslow found that without exception, the self-actualizing people he studied were democratic, being tolerant of others with suitable character regardless of their social class, race, education, religion, or political belief.

12. *Discrimination between means and ends.* Unlike the average person, who may make decisions on expedient grounds, self-actualizing people have a highly developed ethical sense. Even though they cannot always verbalize their moral positions, their actions frequently take the "higher road." Self-actualizers will not pursue even a highly desirable end by means that are not morally correct.

13. *Philosophical, unhostile sense of humor.* Self-actualizers do not enjoy certain types of humor, such as that directed toward hurting others or poking fun at someone else's inferiority. Their humor is more closely allied to philosophy than to anything else. They may enjoy humor directed at themselves, but this is not done in any masochistic or clownlike way.

14. *Creativeness.* Without exception, every self-actualizing person that Maslow studied was creative in some way. This creativity is not to be equated with the genius of a Mozart or an Einstein because the dynamics of that type of creativity are still not understood. Maslow links creativity to being spontaneous and less inhibited than others on a daily basis, and a freshness of thought, ideas, and actions.

15. *Resistance to enculturation.* Self-actualizers accept their culture in most ways, but they still, in a profound sense, resist becoming enculturated. Many desire social change

INTERRELATEDNESS OF AGING PROCESSES

In reflecting back on the personality theories described in this unit, do you think certain personality dynamics shape one's strivings toward self-actualization? What cognitive, social, and vocational domains do you think are influential?

but are not rebellious in the adolescent sense. Rather, they are generally independent of their culture and manage to exhibit tolerant acceptance of the behavior expected of their society.

The subjects studied by Maslow were for the most part highly intelligent and possessed several or even many of the characteristics so far presented. This does not mean, however, that they were perfect. In fact, Maslow noted a number of human failings associated with self-actualizing people. Some can be boring, stubborn, or vain, have thoughtless habits, be wasteful or falsely proud. They may have emotions of guilt, anxiety, or inner strife and conflicts. They are also "occasionally capable of an extraordinary and unexpected ruthlessness." This ruthlessness may be seen when they feel they have been deceived by a friend or if someone has been dishonest with them. They might, with a surgical coldness, cut the person verbally or abruptly sever the relationship.

Stress During Adulthood

Theories of personality have a tendency to center around the idea that successful adjustment involves mastering tasks, challenges, and stresses that confront individuals at various points in their lives. For example, during young adulthood, developmental tasks include establishing an intimate relationship with a mate, rearing children, and finding a suitable career. These are all life changes that bring their respective share of stress.

For many, the stresses and strains of adult life persist into middle and late adulthood. During midlife, coping with the departure of children during the empty nest stage, caring for one's aging parents, or adjusting to aging processes are but a few of the many potentially stressful life situations. Job-related stress is especially prominent among adults today (Arsenault et al., 1991; Evans & Carrere, 1991; Ganster & Schaubroeck, 1991; Ironson, 1992; Ragatt, 1991; Rice, 1992).

Stress is a busy research topic among today's psychologists, and at the heart of this activity is the notion that changes in life are part of everyone's existence, and necessary adjustments have to be made both physically and psychologically. Although certain levels of stress accompanying life changes are minimal and can be easily handled, other levels are not so easily managed. Learning how to avoid crisis situations and taking charge of one's life is an important feature of the well-adjusted and smoothly functioning personality. Not handling stress effectively, on the other hand, brings the potential for an assortment of problems. In support of this, consider how stress takes its toll in the United States:

- Cardiovascular disease has increased 500% in the last 50 years.
- One in four Americans has some form of cardiovascular disease. Over 1.25 million Americans have a heart attack each year.
- About 58 million Americans have high blood pressure that requires monitoring or treatment.
- One in three Americans regularly use some form of tobacco. About 1,000 die of tobacco-related causes every day.
- Over 10 million adults have some symptoms of alcohol dependence.
- One out of every seven adults takes some form of tranquilizer regularly.
- Fifty to 80% of all diseases are stress related.

Distress often brings psychological turbulence.

- The direct and indirect costs to U.S. business and industry because of stress are approximately $150 billion. (Adapted from Brannon & Feist, 1992; Hales, 1992; Rice, 1992)

Defining Stress and Stressors   **Stress** can be defined as the common non-specific response of the body to any demand made upon it, be it psychological or physiological. **Stressors** are external events or conditions that affect the equilibrium of the organism. Put another way, stressors are those situations placing the person in a stressful state. For some, stress is self-imposed; that is, some persons worry about what never happens. Some common stressors include fatigue, disease, physical injury, and emotional conflict. The latter might include tension and frustration. Day-to-day stressors might include financial worries, relationship tensions, pollution, pressures at work, and so on. Obviously, stressors become very individualized, and a number of them may be working together at the same time. One person's stressor may be viewed with indifference by someone else. In this sense, one person's poison may be another's pleasure (Karasek & Theorell, 1990; Noshpitz & Coddington, 1990).

Most stress experts (e.g., Insel & Roth, 1991; Smith & Smith, 1990; S. E. Taylor, 1991) maintain that different categories of stressors can be established. For example, **social stressors** reflect our interactions with others and might include such conditions as crowding, noise, or social pressures to conform. **Psychological stressors** create mental stress and encompass, among others, frustration, conflict, and anxiety. **Physical stressors** create physiological demands on the body and might include hunger, thirst, heat, cold, injury, pollutants, toxicants, or poor nutrition. Finally, **endemic stressors** are those situations that produce "passive stress" because they can't be controlled, such as inflation or the destructive presence of nuclear arms.

INTERRELATEDNESS OF AGING PROCESSES

Conduct a mental inventory of the stressors you think confront individuals during adult life. Do your stressors capture a convergence of biological, psychological, and social forces? How do these stressors compare quantitatively and qualitatively with those you might have experienced during childhood and adolescence?

Stressors should thus be viewed as conditions producing bodily turbulence or some type of reactive change that triggers bodily reactions. But we must acknowledge, too, that both good and bad can interfere with the body's equilibrium and create stress. **Eustress,** or positive stress, occurs when the body's reactive change is put to productive use. For example, athletes often use the anxiety and tension in their bodies before a game as a method of psyching themselves up for the competition. Some researchers, such as Charles Carroll and Dean Miller (1990), feel that eustress provides interest, comfort, and excitement to life. It helps us concentrate better, focus our efforts, and reach our peak of efficiency. In fact, too little stress actually contributes to a somewhat boring and joyless existence.

Distress, however, is harmful and unpleasant stress. It occurs when the body and mind are worn down from repeated exposure to an unpleasant situation. In this respect, stress can affect the body's overall immunity, nervous system, hormone levels, and metabolic rates. When one's emotional state leads to real physical illnesses, the disease is called *psychosomatic* (psycho = mind, soma = body). Such disorders include hypertension, headache, arthritis, rheumatism, peptic ulcers, obesity, backache, skin disorders, impotence, menstrual irregularities, and possibly even some types of heart ailments (Rice, 1992; S. E. Taylor, 1991).

Stress and Behavior Patterns   Some individuals are more susceptible to stress than others. Indeed, there is growing evidence that the study of individual personality differences is just as important as the external forces creating stress (Friedman, 1990). In an effort to analyze individual differences, researchers have identified certain behavior patterns and how they relate to stress.

The **Type A behavior pattern (TABP)** is characterized by extreme competitiveness, aggressiveness, and impatience. Usually, Type A individuals strive to accomplish more than is feasible, and they have difficulty controlling their anger. Their hostility usually persists beneath the surface and is expressed in the form of fist clenching, facial grimaces and nervous tics, and tensing of the muscles. Also, Type A behaviors often include irritation toward hassles, hurried speech, and feelings of guilt during periods of relaxation (Chesney & Rosenman, 1980a, 1980b; Rosenman & Chesney, 1980, 1982; Strube, 1990).

The **Type B behavior pattern (TBBP)** is characterized by a generally relaxed attitude toward life, no hostility, and competitiveness only when the situation demands it. Individuals with such a behavior pattern have no sense of urgency about them and do not have free-floating hostility. They tend to accomplish things slowly and methodically, are less concerned with the quantity than with the quality of their output, and are content with doing a few things really well. Unlike those with Type A behaviors, Type B individuals have the ability to relax without guilt (Anspaugh, Hamrick, & Rosato, 1991; Insel & Roth, 1991).

At one time, researchers thought (e.g., Friedman & Rosenman, 1974) that people exhibiting Type A behavior patterns were more likely than those associated with Type B to develop cardiovascular disease. However, contemporary researchers (e.g., Brannon & Feist, 1992; Hales, 1992; Rice, 1992) point out that only a certain facet of the Type A behavior pattern is likely to lead to cardiovascular disease. More specifically, *hostility* is seen as the toxic element of the

Type A behavior pattern. One type of hostility known as *cynical hostility,* which is characterized by anger, distrust in others, and antagonism, appears to be especially detrimental to one's health (Barefoot et al., 1989).

Interestingly, one investigation (Ragland & Brand, 1988) discovered that individuals with Type A behavior patterns were more susceptible to heart attacks than Type B's. However, Type A's were more likely than Type B's to recover from the heart attack. It seems their hard-driving behavior patterns enabled them to rebound and take charge of their treatment regimen, including the implementation of needed diet and lifestyle changes.

The study of Type A and B behavior patterns adds an interesting dimension to the study of stress. It certainly gives us something to think about in regard to our day-to-day living patterns. Such research serves to uncover risks associated with Type A behaviors, in addition to acting as a springboard for other researchers to develop their own ideas on the subject (see, for example, Edwards & Baglioni, 1991; Jamal & Baba, 1991; Malcolm & Janisse, 1991; Rhodewalt et al., 1992).

Stress and the General Adaptation Syndrome   Hans Selye (1976, 1980a, 1980b, 1982), a Canadian scientist, coined the phrase **general adaptation syndrome (GAS)** to help explain the physiological changes that occur when a person remains under prolonged physical or emotional stress. There are three successive stages in GAS: the alarm reaction, the stage of resistance, and the stage of exhaustion.

During the first stage, or *alarm reaction,* the body's defenses prepare for the stressful situation. Hormones that arouse—for example, epinephrine (adrenaline)—are produced, and the person switches from the parasympathetic nervous system (the system that controls internal organs on a day-to-day basis) to the sympathetic nervous system (the system that is a "backup" or "reserve" and emergency system). For short spurts of energy, the backup nervous and hormonal (endocrine) systems are quite remarkable.

If, however, one continues to remain under stress, the stage of *resistance* is encountered. In this stage, the body continues to produce huge amounts of energy. People may remain in this second stage for hours, days, months, or years. With the body in high metabolic gear during this stage, the wear and tear on the organism can be phenomenal. Selye proposes, however, that each of us goes through these two stages regularly with no significant impact on our health and well-being. This is because most stressors are placed before us and removed with regularity.

The final stage of GAS is *exhaustion.* Exhaustion occurs when a counter reaction of the nervous system occurs, and the body's functions slow down to abnormal levels. Continued stress during this stage may lead to depression or even death. Whether one reaches the stage of exhaustion depends on a number of factors, including the intensity of the stressor and the amount of time spent in resistance. The exhaustion stage often produces stress-related diseases, the most common being high blood pressure, heart attacks, and nervous disturbances.

These three stages must be regarded as a cycle of adaptation. If used repeatedly, Selye (1982) also cautions that the human machine runs the risk of wear and tear. Our reserves of adaptation energy can be compared to an inherited

THEORETICAL ISSUES

How can the wear-and-tear theory of biological aging illustrate the effects of prolonged exposure to stress? Do you agree that every biological activity, including the body's efforts to defend itself against stress, produces wear and tear? Does such activity leave some irreversible chemical scar that ultimately contributes to aging processes?

bank account from which we can make withdrawals, but cannot make deposits. Following exhaustion from stressful activity, sleep can restore resistance and overall adaptation almost to previous levels, but total restoration is probably impossible.

Handling the Stresses of Adult Life   We established at the outset that the key to harmonious living is the ability to handle physically and psychologically the stresses of everyday life. Martin Seligman (1991) feels that such healthy adjustment is characterized by *optimism*. Those who look at the brighter side of life rather than dwelling on its negative features tend to be healthier, experience fewer physical symptoms when ill, and recover faster from certain maladies. Compared to pessimistic types, optimistic individuals also tend to live longer.

Those who effectively handle stress are able to cope with it *without* being in distress. They deal directly with stress and do not become a defensive participant. This concept of control embodies the notion of strengthening the body's overall reserves. As the GAS activates itself to meet daily challenges, precious energy sources are depleted. This means that individuals must work to restore the body's reserves or run the risk of reaching a state of exhaustion. Consequently, sufficient sleep, proper nutrition, and regular exercise are needed (Gadow, 1991; Masoro, 1990; Poehlman, Melby, & Badylak, 1991).

Other effective coping strategies are self-relaxation techniques, including deep breathing exercises, progressive relaxation exercises, and meditation. Deep breathing exercises help individuals restore their breathing to normal, if it becomes too fast or shallow during stressful times. Properly done, deep breathing exercises can increase the amount of oxygen in the blood and cleanse the system of carbon dioxide and other waste chemicals. Progressive muscle relaxation, in which persons tense and then release specific muscles or groups of muscles, is particularly effective in discharging stress from the body. Although many meditation techniques exist, most are based on bringing the mind to stillness and relieving it of anxious thoughts (Smith & Smith, 1990).

Developing *time management skills* is also helpful for handling stress. Time tends to loom as a stressor, and its effective management can help restore stability and harmony to our lives. Procrastination, in particular, can undermine school work, personal relationships, and work efforts. Carefully planning and managing time, then, is instrumental in making the most of the time available each day (Anspaugh, Hamrick, & Rosato, 1991; Bruess & Richardson, 1989).

Biofeedback is another technique of stress management. With biofeedback, a person's skin temperature, muscle contractions, and electrical conductance are monitored by sensors attached to the body. A person in a stressful state can perceive this condition through feedback, and with guidance, hopefully, can learn to control behavior. Although the effectiveness of biofeedback varies, particular success has been reported among those with certain stress-related conditions, including muscle tension and migraine headaches (Carroll & Miller, 1990).

Finally, let us acknowledge the importance of having a meaningful support system when going through stressful times. Talking out one's problems with supportive friends or family members is an important prescription for stress reduction (Pennebaker, 1990). Not having the emotional support of others often intensifies the effects of stressors. As we discover in Chapter 11, having a support system is especially important for elderly persons when they are confronted with the stresses of growing old. Indeed, a meaningful support system enhances both physical and psychological well-being during late adulthood (Antonucci, 1990; Armstrong, 1991; Trippet, 1991).

UNIT REVIEW—

➤ The midlife transition is a time of reassessment, a psychological inventory of one's life. It can have positive as well as negative dimensions, and is a highly individual experience. There appear to be gender differences in the midlife transition.

➤ The study of personality at midlife raises the lifespan development issue of continuity and discontinuity. Costa and McCrae, among others, argue that personality dynamics remain relatively unaltered throughout adulthood; Erikson, Peck, Levinson, and Gould propose discontinuous theories. Other research investigations, including the Berkeley studies, highlight the importance of both continuity and change.

➤ Self-actualization is a highly refined dimension of growth characterized by autonomy, individuation, and authenticity. Maslow's research supplies insight into the concept of self-actualization, including character traits of those who reach this level of functioning.

➤ Stress is a normal part of development, and learning to deal with it is an important task. Research into the many sides of stress, such as Type A and B behavior patterns, the general adaptation syndrome, and stress reduction techniques, have given us much insight and understanding.

UNIT THREE: THE FAMILY

Many marriages begin in early adulthood, with children being added to the primary family unit shortly thereafter. By the time these children are teenagers or young adults, and their numbers have stabilized, many of their parents have reached middle age. During this time, middle-aged parents find they must face a number of developmental tasks. For example, many middle-aged parents discover they represent the "squeeze," or "sandwich," generation. That is, they have their children on one end of the generational cycle, their aging parents on the other, and themselves in the middle. As a result of this squeeze, middle-aged persons frequently face growing pressures as they cope with the needs of their offspring and parents simultaneously (Gibson & Gibson, 1991; Rossi & Rossi, 1990).

▬ Parent-Adolescent Interaction

As we learned in Chapter 2, family development researchers have helped us to better understand the complexities of family life as it unfolds in a series of stages. Thanks to their efforts, we have a clearer understanding of the dynamics that occur in families with adolescents, including the tasks facing both parents and offspring (Cowan & Hetherington, 1991; Pillemer & McCartney, 1991; White, 1991). For example, adjusting to the adolescent's desire to be independent, redefining past child-parent relations, and gradually increasing responsibility usually occur at this time. This also becomes a time when many parents first realize that their offspring will soon be moving on, establishing their own independent lifestyle and living arrangements. This latter point, adjusting to the empty nest stage of life, is a developmental challenge in itself.

The creation of effective communication patterns between parent and adolescent is especially important, including effective conflict resolution skills (Paikoff & Brooks-Gunn, 1991). Parent-adolescent communication must, of course, work two ways. Teenagers as well as parents are responsible for developing meaningful communication skills, and this can be the most difficult of all the developmental challenges that face both parties. Stephen Small and Gay Eastman (1991) maintain that effective communication rests at the foundation of healthy family functioning. Indeed, communication is the primary vehicle through which family members express warmth and affection, indicate their respect for one another, set limits, and make decisions. Effective communication also enables parents to convey their values and beliefs about the issues that are important to them, such as issues of safety and health, and to learn more about their adolescent's interests, values, and worries.

Whether or not a **generation gap** exists between parents and teenagers may also be an issue at this time. A generation gap refers to differences in values, attitudes, and behavior between two generational groups. For example, teenagers often have a knack of telling parents about the distance that separates the two age groups. Some may remark that their parents are "over the hill" and that their ideas are "outdated" or "out of step" with the times. Language use, especially slang and catch phrases, has a tendency to differ between young and old. Adults are often told that certain words and expressions just are not used anymore and are a sure giveaway to a person's age. The same may hold true for everything from hairstyles and clothing to preferences in music.

Does a generation gap always exist between young and old? Is it an inevitable part of family life, or is it more of a myth? To answer these questions, we must realize that the stresses, values, attitudes, and beliefs of teenagers in the 1990s are different from those of adolescents 10 or 20 years ago (Colten & Gore, 1991). As they seek to nurture accurate self-concepts, teenagers have to discover what they believe in, which may include perceptions of what is right or wrong, moral or immoral, and important or unimportant to them (Esman, 1991). To do this, they must look around and examine the views of their own generation and compare their beliefs with numerous societal agents. As young adults, they will learn that numerous environmental factors—including parents, peers, schools, and the communication media—can influence their value system.

Since childhood, youths have incorporated their parents' values into many of their own, but teenagers are quick to realize that times have changed since

Living harmoniously with adolescents is a challenge for middle-aged parents.

their parents' youth. Although there are those who adopt parental viewpoints without question, there are many who do not. The desire to be independent, plus newly discovered cognitive skills that enable the adolescent to analyze the world more fully, may promote a more questioning attitude than ever before. Mary Ann Lamanna and Agnes Riedmann (1994) add that because many Western cultures increasingly require an adult to display a distinctly personal set of values, adolescents may feel the need to reject their parents' values, at least intellectually and for the time being, to gain adult status.

Do age differences contribute to the creation of contrasting points of view? Is a generation gap almost certain to develop between young and old? Not necessarily. In fact, we regard the generation gap as largely a myth. More often than not, differences that exist between parent and adolescent are ideological, not generational. That is, conflict results between new and old, not young and old. Moreover, adolescents and parents are likely to agree on more issues than one might expect. Although teenagers may overtly differ from parents in such areas as dress or mannerisms, both groups are surprisingly similar in such areas as attitudes and fundamental values.

Before leaving this discussion of parent-adolescent interaction, let us acknowledge the importance of maintaining satisfactory methods of parental control during the teenage years. A compelling body of research (e.g., Esman, 1991; Feldman & Elliott, 1990; Gecas & Seff, 1990; Johnson, Shulman, & Collins, 1991; Masselman, Marcus, & Stunkard, 1990; Steinberg, 1991) states that adolescents, given a choice, want a democratic relationship with their parents. They prefer households that are regulated on the basis of honesty, fairness, and mutuality. Consultations between parents and teenagers on issues of mutual concern and the provisions of opportunities to enhance teenage autonomy appear to foster the healthiest emotional climate. Not only are the parent-adolescent relations likely to prosper with such operating principles, but the personal growth of each party is likely to flourish.

INTERRELATEDNESS OF AGING PROCESSES

Might any of the adolescent psychological and social developments covered in Chapter 8 be used to explain the potential for household conflict? Relatedly, might any of the midlife personality and social developments covered in this chapter be applied to the topic?

▬ Postparental Adjustments

The Empty Nest   Postparental life is characterized by the **empty nest** stage, that point in the family circle where children have grown and departed from the home. For the middle-aged couple, this means a time when they are alone and living in a house filled with memories of their children. For some parents, this becomes a period of reflection, restlessness, and even dissatisfaction (Kalish, 1989). For others, the empty nest stage brings new levels of marital satisfaction and fulfillment.

Let us examine why the empty nest stage might be viewed as a crisis period. Many parents, more often the mother, have focused a considerable amount of time and attention on their children. Those mothers who totally wrap themselves up in their offspring discover that when they reach the empty nest stage of life, adjustment difficulties may begin (Grambs, 1989; Lewis, Volk, & Duncan, 1989; Mercer, Nichols, & Doyle, 1989). As Marcia & Thomas Lasswell (1991) see it, this becomes a period of important self-evaluation and reflection. Some become severely depressed and lonely. The key issue appears to be "Now what do I do?" There is new freedom to fulfill some of one's own needs for a change, but some mothers are uncertain about what they want to do. Such patterns will vary among those women who have been at home for years compared to those who have held a job outside of the home during the stages of parenthood.

The opposing view of the empty nest stage maintains it is a positive stage of growth. Although a period of adjustment is typical for parents, once children have left the home, positive feelings accompany the postparental phase of life. Kenneth Davidson and Nelwyn Moore (1992) note that this often becomes a time for high degrees of marital happiness, shared activities, and open communication. It may also create freedom from financial worries, freedom from extra housework, and freedom to travel. Furthermore, many postparental adults look back at their child-rearing years and report a high degree of pleasure, reward, and inner satisfaction in their roles as parents. Although some sadness is experienced, this emotion is outweighed by the joys and pleasures of past parenting.

It appears that the parents who best weather the empty nest stage are those who do not try to foster dependency on the part of their children, but rather encourage autonomy and independence. Parents who believe their children are mature enough for the work world, college, or marriage are more apt to let go than parents who still perceive their young adults as immature. Ideally, parents recognize their children as separate individuals in their own right and strive to show genuine care and concern, but not to the extent of overinvolvement. Ross Eshleman (1991) adds that such parents are not affected negatively when their children leave home. Indeed, a greater stressor may be the unexpected *return* of a young adult to the home.

Some parents may adjust to the empty nest stage on a gradual basis. For instance, college, military service, or extended trips away from home may separate young adults from their parents for relatively short periods of time. This allows the parents to experience a household with one less child—or no children—without the feeling they will never see the child again. Thus, even though the nest is semi-empty, the experience is at least softened by the expectation that the child will return. Gradual adjustments to the empty nest stage may also give parents time to evaluate themselves and their goals.

The empty-nest stage brings new meaning to middle-aged marriages.

Once children have left the home, the husband and wife may discover they have drifted apart over the years. With time together now, they may even be surprised at changes in one another that had gone unnoticed for some time. A popular anecdote involving a middle-aged couple says it all: The two are sitting at the breakfast table, sipping coffee and earnestly reading the morning newspaper. The husband, out of the blue, lowers his paper, and with a puzzled expression on his face says, "When did you get reading glasses?" The wife looks at him and replies, "About 5 years ago. By the way," she adds, "when did you go bald?"

If couples find themselves dissatisfied with their marriage and discover they no longer really "know" each other, it is difficult for them to offer mutual support and understanding during the critical middle years. Some couples, assuming a pessimistic attitude, believe their functions and responsibilities as parents are finished and thus view their lives as practically over. Some feel there is little left to do with a life that has become devoid of meaning. In this sense, the parental role has eclipsed the marital role (Keith & Schafer, 1991). One source (Lamanna & Riedmann, 1994) maintains that the outcome of this stage is more positive when parents have other meaningful roles, such as work, school, or community involvement. The prospects for those seeking to revitalize or reconstruct a sagging marriage are considered favorable because the older couple now typically has more time, energy, and financial resources to invest into the relationship.

For many couples, the postparental stage is the most rewarding and happiest period of their life. When the children are gone from the home, mothers as well as fathers report an improvement in marital relations. Some feel these years rival the happiness and satisfaction felt when the couple first met. Some even go so far as to label these years as a second honeymoon. Couples feeling this way usually have experienced much mutual understanding and support over the years. They are also likely to be optimistic about the future and have confidence in themselves and their abilities as a couple. They are also likely to have good communication skills, a strong sense of intimacy, and feelings of mutuality and reciprocity.

The Full Nest   By middle age, parents usually experience the empty nest stage of family life. Their offspring will have grown up, set their sights on the future, and physically left the home. However, for a growing segment of the young adult population, moving out of the home right away is not the chosen lifestyle. Indeed, the family of the 1990s reflects a relatively new trend in household living: the **full nest.** Today, about 20 million adults aged 18 to 34 are living in their parents' homes. For adults between the ages of 18 and 24, this breaks down to about 58% of all men and 47% of all women. Moreover, all indications are that this number will swell in years to come (U.S. Bureau of the Census, 1992).

The full nest represents an interesting demographic trend, and some of the reasons given for remaining at home reflect modern times. Financial explanations invariably find their way to the top of the list: Young people often have trouble affording an independent lifestyle. Some remain in the roost to combat loneliness. There are also those who are still going to school, those who are postponing marriage, and those who have divorced (with or without children). Also, grown children may be using the home as a haven or retreat during times they are out of work.

The full nest often brings its share of domestic happiness and satisfaction. However, it can also herald pressures and problems. For example, there is an attitude among some outsiders that effective parenthood includes launching children out of the home and into the mainstream of society. Other internal problems include conflicts over possessions and noise as well as disagreements about household space or territory. Finally, grown children may be disruptive to everyday household activity and thus create stress on the parental marriage bond (Schnaiberg & Goldenberg, 1989).

Grandparenthood   Another family development in the lives of many middle-aged adults is grandparenthood. The grandchild typically establishes a bond of common interest between the grandparents and the younger couple. Becoming a grandparent also adds a new dimension to the lives of middle-aged and older adults, and, in most instances, this dimension is a positive one. Grandparents can serve as sources of knowledge, wisdom, love, and understanding and can greatly affect the lives of their grandchildren. Among grandparents, many idealize their roles and importance (Brubaker, 1990a; Elkind, 1990; McMillan, 1990; Miller & Cavanaugh, 1990; Strom & Strom, 1990; Thomas, 1990b; L. B. White, 1990).

But becoming a grandparent does not always have positive features. For some, it represents a visible sign of aging. There may be disagreements between grandparents and adult offspring regarding child rearing. Many resist the stereotyped qualities and expectations attached to grandparenthood, such as the time, care, and services grandparents are supposed to render to their grandchildren. Along these lines, some feel exploited for baby-sitting services. Certain research (e.g., Burton & Dilworth-Anderson, 1991) notes that not all grandparents are willing to involve themselves in the perceived expectations of grandparenthood, most notably child care. Future research needs to explore the costs as well as the benefits of elders' family roles, especially in terms of the liabilities of the roles for aged grandparents (Langer, 1990).

Like so many other topics covered in this text, gender differences are apparent in grandparenting. For example, the role of grandparent seems to have special significance for the grandmother. Grandparenthood may even be viewed as a maternal experience, largely because of the traditional woman's dominant role in child rearing. Although most men enjoy grandparenthood, traditional grandmothers assume a more active role right from the very beginning. Grandmothers frequently care for the new mother, her baby, and her family during the immediate postnatal period. She, therefore, often becomes the person who first diapers, bathes, and otherwise cares for the baby, except for the brief intervals while the mother does so. After she returns to her own home, she is usually expected to continue a grandmotherly concern for the mother's well-being and the grandchild's care (Gee, 1991; Leslie, 1982; Wasserman, 1990).

Grandfathers appear to become more involved with their grandchildren after retirement. Without jobs to claim most of their energy, many are able to identify with their grandchildren, and some want to spend more time with them. They begin to visit with them more, take them for walks, buy them gifts, and participate in their overall care (Leslie, 1982). Vira Kivett's (1991) study of African-American and white grandfathers shows similarities in ranked importance to the grandfather role as well as the amount of assistance provided by grandchildren. However, the grandfather role was more central to African-American men than to whites. For other differences in grandparenting between whites and African Americans, see the Focus on Diversity box on pages 552–553.

We might point out, though, that the roles attached to grandparenthood have changed over the years. For example, the grandmother today is apt to be a working woman, and the daily routines of raising her own children are likely to be over (Hagestad, 1991). How her greater involvement in the labor force impacts on the grandparenting experience is an important area for future research. So too is how more flexible gender roles for men and women affect the

GENDER SIMILARITIES AND DIFFERENCES

How do you think the gender differences apparent in grandparenthood affect the gender-role socialization of grandchildren? Do you think an androgynous orientation to grandparenthood would affect grandchildren differently? How?

Grandparenthood offers a unique bond between young and old.

course of grandparenthood. And, as noted earlier, the fact that many grandparents are middle-aged means the rocking chair image of grandparenthood needs revision. Additionally, Linda Burton and Peggy Dilworth-Anderson (1991) note that the upswing in single-parent households has thrust grandparenthood into an increasingly important role.

In light of all of these changes, Robert and Shirley Strom (1990) suggest that adults need to define and better understand this important family role. Among other chores, grandparents need to make themselves aware of familial expectations, as well as the principles that parents are employing to guide the upbringing of their grandchildren. Jeanne Thomas (1990b) found that a lack of understanding about child-rearing principles, as well as the violation of them, poses distinct threats to family harmony. Clear communication and consistent expectations make it easier for grandparents to support and reinforce parents and act as partners with them.

Caring for Aging Parents

Today, about 1 million adults provide direct physical and medical care to their parents every day, and many more tend to daily living needs, including financial support, household chores, shopping, and transportation. All indications are that such involvement will increase in years to come (Gubrium, 1991; Malone-Beach & Zarit, 1991; Suitor & Pillemer, 1990).

As we've pointed out, most elderly people in the United States are neither feeble nor sickly. On the contrary, today's elderly are living longer than ever before, and most are enjoying healthy and rewarding lives. Indeed, the majority are capable of carrying out daily routines and activities on their own (Chappell, 1991; Sterneck, 1990). However, advancing age often brings the need for assistance in day-to-day living. Moreover, incidences of chronic illness and disability steadily increase with age, further necessitating the need for a more active caregiving role for adult children, or more formal intervention (Baldwin, 1990; Montgomery & Datwyler, 1990). The need for assistance in essential personal care and home management activities shows corresponding increases in the upper age ranges. In relation to this, Beverly Sanborn and Sally Bould (1991) point out that those elderly 85 years of age and older have the highest potential for functional disability and, thus, the greatest need for caregiver support.

But this does not mean that elderly people needing care and attention are nursing home candidates or residents. This is a myth that needs to be debunked. The fact of the matter is that only about 5% of the entire elderly population 65 years of age or older can be found within institutional settings. Most of today's aged reside instead in family settings: About 75% of men and 40% of women live with a spouse; 8% of men and 18% of women live with relatives. The remaining numbers live alone or with nonrelatives (U.S. Bureau of the Census, 1992).

Patterns of Care and Assistance   When elderly people need care and assistance, it is more likely to originate from adult offspring, since four out of five elderly persons have children. Many daughters and sons tend to live within close proximity of their parents, a factor making them more available for assistance when it is needed. However, visitation and care tends to be more frequent along the female line (Aronson, 1992; Cicirelli, 1992; Green, 1991;

Walker & Allen, 1991; Walter, 1991). Husbands are more likely to be in touch with the wives' parents than their own, unless the wife mediates contact with the husband's parents. Thus there appears to be some truth to the maxim that "a son's a son 'til he gets a wife, and a daughter's a daughter all her life" (Glezer, 1991; Kart, 1990; Stone, 1991).

Most younger generations want to provide care and support to aging family members, and not because they are obliged to do so. Adult children wanting to offer caregiving assistance cite various reasons for pitching in, but one desire looms dominant: to return the kind of support and security that was once received. Most feel it is the right and proper thing for a child to do, an unwritten expectation that is an integral part of the family life cycle. For some cross-cultural variations on this theme, see the Focus on Diversity box on pages 552-553.

Although women carry the brunt of caregiving responsibilities, it is likely that we will see more male caregivers in the future (Gregory, Peters, & Cameron, 1990; Kaye & Applegate, 1990). This is already occurring for spouses, but we may even see more sons begin to help caregiving daughters and daughters-in-law in the care of elderly parents. Also, the gender differences in caregiving for others, which have been pronounced in the child-raising years because of occupational and family structures, do not seem as prevalent in the later years with retirement (Chang & White-Means, 1991). There are not large differences between male and female caregivers in the later years. Whether the number of younger male caregivers will increase and whether younger male and female caregivers will adapt similarly to their caregiving is unclear (Fitting & Rabins, 1985).

In analyzing patterns of female intergenerational care, it appears that certain demographic and social trends will affect the quantity and quality of services rendered. For example, it is believed that changing gender roles, coupled with increased labor force participation among middle-aged women, may place an additional burden on already strained family resources. Additionally, an important question to ask is whether assistance to the aged will decline as more women enter the workplace. Women traditionally have spent many hours in support of the aged in their families and in their communities. With escalating proportions of females in the labor force, assistance may not be as readily available in the future. A squeeze on the time and resources of women in the middle generation is already evident. These women are being called on to offer financial and emotional support to their adult children as well as their aging parents (Ory et al., 1992; Walter, 1991).

All of the foregoing means that a new wrinkle in caregiving patterns will become evident: the old helping the old. Indeed, in years to come we'll see the existence of more four- and five-generation families (Himes, 1992). This means that older impaired parents needing assistance will be getting it from their offspring, who are themselves aging. Thus, in the not too distant future, it will become increasingly common for 90-year-old parents to be cared for by their 65-year-old children.

However, at least one source (Morrison, 1990) points out that a growing number of elderly Americans may have no one to care for them. As longevity has increased, new patterns of home life have reduced the capacity of families to care for their aged parents. Low fertility in the last two decades and the rise in female employment compound the difficulty of caring for elderly people. In

THEORETICAL ISSUES

How do you think family development theorists can utilize the concept of the family life cycle to better understand the interactions of aging parents and adult children? How might conflict theorists address the potential for disharmony and stress that caregiving brings? How would symbolic interactionists analyze adjusting to the caregiving role?

Focus on Diversity

WHO'S GOING TO CARE FOR MOM AND DAD?

In the past, limited attention has been directed toward the topics of ethnic variations in caregiving, although we are seeing more interest today. Generally, elderly people of different ethnic and racial backgrounds in the United States are not isolated from their kinship networks and are the recipients of considerable intergenerational care and assistance. Caregivers typically live within visiting distance, interact by choice, and are connected to one another by means of mutual aid and social activities. Thus patterns of care and assistance tend to be more alike than dissimilar to the earlier described trends (Taylor, 1985).

However, having family members nearby does not guarantee that sufficient help will be available to minority elders. For example, certain research (e.g., Weeks & Cuellar, 1981) indicates that some Hispanic elderly are less likely to turn to family members in times of need despite the fact that those who live alone have an average of four times more extended kin in the area than nonminority elders. Other research (Torres-Gil & Negm, 1980) reveals that some Mexican-American elders do not have full access to the necessary and culturally preferred caregiver patterns and social interactions.

Shirley Lockery (1985) observes that contrary to common belief, the minority family, with elderly people as a key component, represents a strong social force. Traditionally, the minority family has had to assume the role of caregiver. Minority families often rely on their own resources

for the provision of social, economic, and physical needs of the aged. For example, both African Americans and Hispanics have large and cohesive family systems that provide a great deal of help and emotional support to their kin. Rather than serving as an alternative support system, the role of the minority family is that of providing supplementary assistance to elderly members in need (Burton & Dilworth-Anderson, 1991; Cox & Monk, 1990; Johnson & Barer, 1990).

In one study of ethnic differences (Cantor, 1979a), it was discovered that frequent face-to-face and telephone contact with children was experienced by a majority of elderly respondents. Most of the respondents had an informal support network, and only a handful (8%) appeared to be without any type of supportive network. Hispanic elderly had consistently higher levels of interaction and a greater potential for support from children than either white or African-American elderly, despite controls for gender, social class, income, and level of functional ability. African-American and white respondents were comparable with reference to interaction with children and social support received from children, but both African-American and Hispanic elderly tended to give a greater amount of help than did white elderly. Similar findings have been reported in other investigations (Barresi & Menon, 1990; Bengston, Rosenthal, & Burton, 1990; Mutran, 1985; Sakauye, 1989).

Another study (Shanas, 1979) studied support

the past, adult daughters were traditionally the ones who provided elderly parents with home care. Today's smaller families, however, eventually will disrupt this custom. Baby boomers, having produced so few offspring, will have few adult children to fill the caregiver role when they grow old next century. Moreover, these prospective caregivers—women now in their 20s—typically hold jobs already, leaving little time for those traditional home responsibilities. Trends strongly suggest that at least four fifths of women now in their 20s will

relations between elderly and their children, grandchildren, and great-grandchildren. It was discovered that white elderly (72%) were more likely to be the providers of assistance to their children than were African-American elderly (51%). Interestingly, among African-American elderly there was a greater tendency to receive help (63%) from their children, whereas among white elderly a lower percentage received help (68%) than gave it. A regular money allowance, occasional gifts of money, and payment of medical costs/bills were the three types of support provided to elderly people. Of these three, occasional gifts of money was the most prevalent form of aid, with 24% of African-American and 13% of white elderly reporting they received this type of support.

Robert Taylor's (1985) research indicates that African-American elderly are active participants in family networks. Elderly respondents reported significant levels of interaction with family, relatively close residential proximity to immediate family, extensive familial affective bonds, and a high degree of satisfaction derived from family life. With reference to support from family, over one half of the respondents indicated receiving assistance from family members. Collectively, these results are consistent with existing literature on the kinship interaction patterns and support networks of older African Americans and the general African-American population (Hatch, 1991; Shanas, 1979; Taylor & Chatters, 1991).

Other research (e.g., Bengston, 1979; Cantor, 1979b; Dowd & Bengston, 1978) revealed no consistent differences in family support between minorities and whites. For example, it had often been thought that minority elderly possessed a larger and more active instrumental social support system than did whites due to extended family structure and cultural values. However, these studies discovered that socioeconomic status was a better predictor of the structure and nature of the social support system. Indeed, Cantor (1979b) found that aging parents from low socioeconomic backgrounds had a greater likelihood than those from high socioeconomic levels to have more contact with their children. This is because working-class people are more likely to live near their relatives whereas middle- and upper-middle-class persons have a greater tendency to move to another town or part of the country. Thus socioeconomic status was the most stable and overriding predictor of the informal support networks of elderly people.

An investigation of elderly Korean Americans (Koh & Bell, 1987) showed that aging parents maintained frequent contact with their adult children. Over 70% of the parents wanted to live independently, and most relied on their children for assistance. However, reciprocal patterns of assistance were also noted. A study involving Mexican, Puerto Rican, and Cuban elderly families living in the United States revealed similar support systems (Bastida, 1987). And in an investigation of Asian-American caregivers (Goodman, 1990), the family network, both immediate and extended, was the major means of assistance and reflected considerable reciprocity.

be in the labor force when their parents reach old age. It may be that few will be inclined to quit a paying job to become an unpaid caregiver to an elderly parent if any other alternatives exist.

Complexities and Costs of Caregiving   The care of aging parents brings many adjustment challenges and demands. Today, the typical caregiver is middle-aged and often caught in the earlier mentioned squeeze generation. Couples

INTERRELATEDNESS OF AGING PROCESSES

Do you think the caregiving transition is handled better by some cultures than others? Why? How do you see cultural prescriptions affecting the extent to which adult children expect to assist their parents in later life?

at midlife are also typically confronted with competing role responsibilities and time demands. The rigors of providing regular care while maintaining one's own household is physically and psychologically exhausting. The loss of personal freedom, the lack of time for social and recreational activities, and other restrictions are often part of the sacrifices to be made. Also, research indicates (e.g., Adamson, 1992) that the caregiving burden directly affects the caregiver's marital happiness.

Unrelenting friction and turbulence between adult child and dependent parent has been known to produce a dark side to caregiving patterns: abuse of elderly people. Abusers of the aged are not maladaptive personality types such as those portrayed in the media. Rather, the abuser is more likely to be a parent's middle-aged caregiver, often the daughter. In most instances, abusers are typically normal persons who are tending to multiple responsibilities and encountering escalating stress levels (Anetzberger, 1990; Blakely, 1991; Foelker, 1990; Janz, 1990; Johns, Hydle, & Aschjem, 1991).

For middle-aged female caregivers, such stress may accompany their traditional nurturing role. Connecting this to our earlier discussion of the empty nest, women most likely start caring for an elderly parent at the time when their own children are beginning to leave home. Being placed back into a nurturing role, just when it is expected that this responsibility is finished, may prove overwhelming (Gelles & Cornell, 1990; Long, 1991; Payne, 1990; Stephens, Ogrocki, & Kinney, 1991). The caregiver's age, the quality of the relationship between the caregiver and the elderly person, as well as the amount of assistance provided by other family members are important factors to consider when examining the caregiver's burden (Jutras & Veilleux, 1991; Killeen, 1990; Malone-Beach & Zarit, 1991; Pearlin, 1990; Rankin, 1990; Stephens, 1990).

A number of publications have emerged on the topic of caregiving and its conflicting pressures (Horne, 1991; Kenny & Oettinger, 1991; Rob & Reynolds, 1991; Shapiro, Konover, & Shapiro, 1991). Also, support groups have been established to help adult children better handle the pressures of caring for aging parents, including abusive tendencies (Hamlet & Read, 1990). One such group is Children of Aging Parents, based in Pennsylvania but branching out recently to other states. Other organizations, recognizing the need for providing support services, offer a wide range of guidance and assistance (Barusch, 1991; C. C. Goodman, 1991; Lidoff, 1990; Tosseland, 1990; Wenger, 1990). In the accompanying Lifespan Development in Action box, we offer some hints on how to ease caregiving stress.

Finally, whether sharing a residence or tending to the needs of elderly people on a visitation basis, caregivers must reckon with the financial burden. The material support of an aging parent is an expensive venture, be it the amount of time given or actual dollars expended. Medical costs at hospitals and nursing homes have increased dramatically, resulting in depletion of Medicare and Medicaid funds. If there is no one at home to care for the elderly parent, services must be paid for from someone's pocket. Obviously, the continuing care for a loved one represents a most expensive venture (Armstrong, 1990; Moskowitz & Moskowitz, 1991; Somers, 1985; Sterneck, 1990).

All of this means that adult children need to seriously address the issue of who is going to care for Mom and Dad. Obviously, planning in advance is the key. When an aged parent is stricken with an illness or faces acute financial

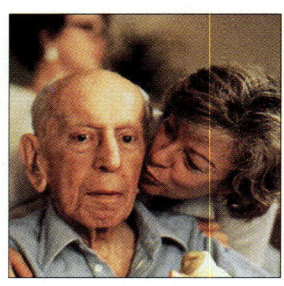

Caring for aging parents presents numerous rewards as well as complexities.

Lifespan Development in Action

EASING THE BURDEN OF CAREGIVING

Caregiving can be a most stressful situation, and those providing the assistance must take steps to safeguard their health and well-being. Along these lines, David Solomon and associates (1992) offer the following advice:

Identify people who can provide you with respite. The daily care a parent needs will not be covered either by Medicare or private insurance, so you and a parent may decide to employ a family member, friend, or aide to assist. Training on how to provide safe personal care is available; check with geriatric centers at local hospitals, or contact a home health agency or visiting nurse association for assistance.

Be realistic about what you can do each day. This means getting into the habit of setting priorities. You will not always be a caregiver, so put off the less important tasks for the future, when you will have more time.

Find a local support group. Meet regularly with other caregivers or children of aging parents to help each other with anger, frustration, guilt, grief, and other feelings. You can also share valuable tips on solving problems, take turns caring for each other's loved ones for short periods, and offer respite in emergencies.

Maintain your own health. Eat a balanced diet, get regular exercise, and take care of your own medical problems promptly. You may have to leave another caregiver in charge of your parent or spouse so you can take care of your own health.

Prepare yourself for the day you can no longer be the caregiver. Turning the responsibility over to someone else—admitting you no longer have the energy, strength, skills, or resources to provide what your parent or spouse needs—can be an act of love. Give yourself credit for all you have done.

Be creative about finances. Perhaps you can offer a service to a friend, neighbor, or member of your church in exchange for keeping your parent company. Many service agencies loan equipment free or at a reduced price to people suffering from illness. Check your local senior newspaper classified ads for used sickroom equipment.

hardship, it is often too late to do the most effective planning. The time to work out financial and legal considerations possibly lurking ahead is *before* they occur, when parents are optimally healthy and content with their lives. Nothing has to be decided definitively after the first conversation because most strategies and decisions need to evolve. Family discussions and advance planning need not be restricted to finances either. Frank, open discussions are needed about all aspects of family life. When this is done in productive and healthy ways, an assortment of parents' plans and wishes usually unfolds. Better yet, difficult situations in later years can be eased, since a well-informed adult child is in the best position to ensure that parents' best interests are protected (Averyt, 1987; Bayless, 1985; Levin, 1990; Levy, 1991; R. Robinson, 1990).

UNIT REVIEW—

↗ Living harmoniously with adolescent offspring and supporting them in their overall adjustment are key elements of family life at this time.

↗ The empty nest, which occurs when grown children physically leave the home, can cause both negative and positive emotions. Fairly recently, there has been an increase in the full nest, households where young adults choose to continue living with their parents for extended periods of time.

↗ Grandchildren add a new dimension to the lives of many middle-aged couples, and similar to most behaviors explored in the text, grandparenthood mirrors gender differences.

↗ Millions of middle-aged persons care for their aging parents, a task bringing its share of rewards as well as demands. Caregiving heralds an assortment of challenges for middle-agers, including competing role responsibilities, time constraints, and financial considerations.

UNIT FOUR: VOCATIONAL DEVELOPMENT

Traditionally, Western cultures have encouraged people to adhere to the work ethic, a value that emphasizes hard work and dedication to one's chosen profession. If the work ethic is adopted, it is expected that people will be able to focus their vocational aspirations and direct their energies accordingly. Moreover, they will realize in the process that work represents its own reward; that is, one's job is a source of satisfaction, fulfillment, and incentive.

For many middle-aged workers, work is characterized by stability and maintenance. Although there may be frustrations and difficulties, careers represent a plateau in the overall scheme of vocational development. As such, middle-agers report that they enjoy their work and are happy with their chosen professions. For others, though, the midlife experience is one of reestablishment rather than of maintenance. As we'll see, the processes of change in our culture contribute to a search by many for a new sense of establishment in life and work. People feel disestablished and look for certainty and confirmation, for ways to realign themselves comfortably and meaningfully within the same occupational milieu, if not the same job.

▬ Careers at Midlife

As we have learned, midlife often brings a reassessment of goals, aspirations, and life ambitions. For some it heralds a full-scale reorientation of major values, including those associated with one's work. The person who has spent a major portion of life searching for power or responsibility may now want inner meaning. Such an inner quest may produce tranquillity or, in some cases, turbulence. As far as the latter is concerned, an internal reassessment may raise havoc not only with one's work but also with one's lifestyle, interpersonal relationships, and family life.

Careers at midlife provide an interesting comparison to those launched during the young adult years. For those involved in an assessment of their lives, it is likely that some appraisal will be made of time, or better yet, the amount of time left. Many perceive that time is short in relation to the world of work. Unlike young adulthood, where idealistic assumptions are often made about career goals, many middle-agers assume it is too late to launch new career plans or engage in another trial stage of work. Moreover, many adults at midlife feel that life is not as flexible as it once was. As we see presently, however, middle adulthood is a stage of life filled with numerous options and possibilities, especially in regard to the career world (Bolles, 1992; Lowstuter & Robertson, 1992).

Douglas Kimmel (1990) suggests that the issue of time and the midlife career assessment embodies a concept known as the **career clock.** The career clock represents a person's subjective sense of being "on time" or "behind time" in relation to career development or accomplishments. Middle-aged individuals are often acutely aware of the number of years left before retirement and of the speed with which they are reaching their goals. If individuals are "behind time" or if their goals are unrealistic, reassessment and readjustment are necessary.

If the concept of the career clock holds true, then we would expect the young adult years to be a time for the development and implementation of a career path. If this is not done, it usually becomes evident later and may even accentuate the stresses of midlife. Of course, the process of career assessment and planning can still be done at midlife, but the realization that it was not accomplished earlier is often painful.

Also, let us not forget that the vocational involvement converges with other developmental spheres. One's work performance does not exist in a vacuum; rather, it intertwines with the other forces shaping adult life. Along these lines, for example, career reassessment impacts on marital relations as well as the quality of family life. It is important to recognize how individual, family, and vocational roles are linked and need to be balanced (Cooney & Uhlenberg, 1991; Googins, 1990; Hughes, Galinsky, & Morris, 1992; Michaels & McCarty, 1992; Orthner, Bowen, & Beare, 1990; Young, 1990).

One needs to weigh the satisfactions and dissatisfactions of all of these roles, discover which impinge on others too much, and decide what priorities in life need to be established. Men, for example, may discover that their occupational roles have dominated their lives, but having proven they can be successful, they can change their priorities (Barnett, Marshall, & Pleck, 1992). Women may discover that they have put their occupational roles on the back burner for too long, and now is the time to give priority to these needs (Grambs, 1989; Moen, 1991). Of course, any change in role priorities for both men and women will affect other life roles. In this respect, an important task is to determine the allocation and balance of one's resources and energies (Okun, 1984; Spitze & Logan, 1990).

THEORETICAL ISSUES

In what ways do you think vocational issues contribute to the midlife transition? What kinds of application do the theories of Erikson, Levinson, Peck, and Gould have to the vocational arena? How would ecological theory seek to explain the impact of vocational issues on the family unit?

An assessment of one's vocation is usually part of the midlife transition.

▬ Changing Careers at Midlife

From the foregoing discussion, it should be evident that many middle-agers critically evaluate their past career accomplishments as well as their hopes and aspirations for the future. In a growing number of cases, especially among white-collar professionals, such an assessment may trigger a midlife career change. Such changes are not restricted to males, either. Both males and females are part of a throng of workers switching careers in an effort to seek new horizons and greater levels of personal fulfillment.

The quest for fulfillment in the workplace represents a motive virtually unheard of among our forebears. For that matter, the entire notion of changing careers at any point in the life cycle was practically nonexistent among our grandparents and previous generations. People were expected to stay at one job for the entire course of their work lives and not question whether they were happy or not, let alone make a job change. Job satisfaction was secondary to job subservience. In modern times, though, a new value has permeated many facets of society, including the workplace: the need to be satisfied and fulfilled in one's life. This value has prompted both young and old alike to question themselves and the work they do each day. Taking this value into account may help explain why so many workers today are vocationally packing it in and embarking on new and different career paths.

Career changes can be minor or major in scope. Some may choose to shift emphasis within the same general career area—for example, a public health nurse may decide to switch to pediatric nursing. This is known technically as movement within a career cluster. Other career changes are more dramatic and involve a complete vocational switch, for example, an accountant becoming a sociologist. Such changes are more disruptive and require more adaptation than those within a career cluster.

Reasons for Changing Careers The motives for changing careers vary widely, from boredom to burnout. Some workers are dissatisfied because their jobs are tedious and offer little or no challenge. Others switch jobs in search of better pay and advancement. Some object to the excessive use of authority in the workplace; others are restless after sticking with the same grinding routine for too long. There are those who are bothered by the lower status accorded to their work, and many have been burdened by excessive employer demands and expectations. Others have encountered vocational inequality or sexual harassment. Any of these situations may prompt a person to change vocation with the hope of discovering a job more important, satisfying, and enjoyable (Brammer, 1990; Steers & Porter, 1991).

Dissatisfied employees contemplating a career change often fail to achieve a sense of accomplishment from their work contributions. Along these lines, many workers report unhappiness because of poor employer-employee relations, or because their ideas are constantly being sidetracked, devalued, or ignored. Related to this, research (e.g., Repetti & Cosmas, 1991) usually shows that the quality of supervisor relations is a critical determinant of job satisfaction. Also, many unhappy workers recognize that a gap exists between their perceived abilities and the utilization of these abilities on the job. Many report a lack of conformity between their own personal goals and the company's goals and policies (Zunker, 1990).

We might add, too, that career success does not guarantee vocational satisfaction. Many men and women achieve long-sought career goals only to ask, "Was it worth it?" Some may have moved up into administration and now find themselves in prestigious positions they do not enjoy. Sometimes such jobs involve long hours, frequent moving, and trips away from home. The results are often alienation from the family and a loss of nurturing that can be critical, especially during the midlife transition (Michelozzi, 1992).

As indicated, **burnout** may be another reason for changing vocations. Burnout is a concept associated with our earlier discussion of stress and refers to the depletion of physical, emotional, and mental resources due to repeated pressure. A number of studies (e.g., Appels & Schouten, 1991; Cherniss, 1992; Elloy & Anderson, 1991; Firth-Cozens, 1992; Ganster & Schaubroeck, 1991) have shed light on the negative implications of burnout. For example, we know that burnout is particularly common in the helping professions, such as nursing or social work, in which women and men who have dedicated themselves to others may realize they have nothing left in themselves to give (Hales, 1992). Although burnout can happen at earlier ages, growing numbers of middle-aged workers are reporting this condition. Robert Lock (1992) points out that burnout can leave a person feeling drained, emotionally exhausted, and inadequate. In addition to the depletion of physical, mental, and emotional resources, those suffering from burnout often discover that vocational idealism has been replaced by indifference and cynicism.

Burnout also strikes a fairly predictable segment of the population. Those most susceptible are dynamic, goal-oriented men and women who are determined idealists. They want their career accomplishments to sparkle, their marriages to be the best, and their children to shine. Although these are commendable life goals, the burnout victim makes the mistake of striving for

GENDER SIMILARITIES AND DIFFERENCES

Do you think negative aspects of the vocational arena affect women and men the same or differently? What gender similarities or differences do you think are apparent in physical, psychological, and family dynamics?

perfection. They are also *over*committed and *over*dedicated to their life ambitions (Freudenberger & Richelson, 1980).

There are other motives or reasons for switching careers. Some workers do so for family-related reasons, such as a divorce or the death of one's spouse. The departure of the last child from the home often prompts middle-aged women to consider a career change, many times to a position that can reaffirm a sense of self-worth and usefulness (Wingrove & Slevin, 1991). For many women at midlife, a career change means moving from part-time to full-time employment.

Finally, some workers change jobs involuntarily. For instance, unemployment forces many into entirely new lines of work. The threat of unemployment may do the same thing. That is, employees may change vocations because they know their company is failing and being laid off lies on the not-too-distant horizon (Lock, 1992; Morrisey, 1992). Others switch career fields because they know their jobs are soon going to be phased out by automation. Given such scenarios, it is likely that blue-collar workers experience more involuntary mid-career changes whereas those of white-collar workers are more voluntary.

Women in the Labor Force

We discussed earlier that increasingly large numbers of women, single and married, are active in the nation's labor force. Perhaps a few statistics will illustrate how widespread female labor force participation is. Currently, women constitute about 45% of the total labor force. By the year 2050, the 67 million women projected to be working will constitute about 47% of the entire labor force, up from 40% in 1976 and 45% in 1988. Over 60% of all adult females will participate in the labor force by the year 2050. For every two men who enter the workplace today, three women join (U. S. Department of Labor, 1992).

What factors account for such increases in female labor force involvement? Obviously, economic necessity is one reason. A single income is no longer enough for many couples. Also, growing numbers of women are heading single-parent families. Higher divorce or separation rates require more women to live on their own incomes. Another motive is the need for achievement beyond the home and family, particularly among college-educated women (Lock, 1992).

Although there are still problems facing the working woman, which we examine momentarily, there are more career options available today than ever before. Women now represent more than one half the work force in nearly a dozen industries, including the fast-growing health services, banking, legal services, insurance, and retail trade. Women also hold jobs previously held down only by men: firefighters, pilots and navigators, professional athletes, auto mechanics, and electricians, to name but a few. Many women have also moved into managerial and professional specialty occupations (Michelozzi, 1992).

Sex Discrimination   Legal efforts have focused on the attempt to eliminate **sex discrimination,** the unfair and unequal treatment of a person on the basis of gender. In 1964 Title VII of the Civil Rights Act prohibited discrimination in private employment on the basis of sex as well as race, color, religion, and national origin. And in 1971 the Supreme Court ruled that unequal treatment based on sex violated the Fourteenth Amendment to the U.S. Constitution, which mandates equal protection of all citizens.

Unfortunately, the most comprehensive statement of the equality of the sexes before the law, the Equal Rights Amendment (ERA), is still far from becoming a part of the U.S. Constitution. First introduced into Congress in 1923, this amendment was finally passed by both the Senate and the House of Representatives in 1972 and, with a 7-year deadline for ratification attached to it, was sent to the states for their action. As 1979 approached, an insufficient number of states had ratified the amendment, and an extension of time was granted in response to the lobbying efforts of women's groups. However, by the extended deadline of June 1982, only 35 of the required 38 states (three quarters of all states must ratify a constitutional amendment) had ratified the ERA.

Thus we are back at square one. The ERA has been reintroduced into every session of Congress since 1982, but by 1993 no body of Congress had passed it for a second time. When both the Senate and the House have again voted in favor of the amendment, each by the required two-thirds majority, it will again go to the states for ratification. To date the ERA has been mired in the legislative process for more than 70 years.

Let's examine sex inequality and discrimination in the work force a bit more closely. A century and a half ago women were excluded from all paying occupations of any significance. They couldn't vote or hold public office, and married women couldn't make contracts or hold property. Despite the fact that growing numbers of women are entering the labor force today, many are still confined to low-status occupations. Women continue to be a minority in professional and skilled careers, especially managerial positions. The majority of women who work in office settings today handle secretarial and clerical chores; the more prestigious and better-paying executive positions are held mostly by men. This unequal treatment extends even to such areas as access to credit and obtaining insurance at reasonable rates (Andersen, 1988; Mason, 1991; Matlin, 1993; Rothenberg, 1988; Tittle, 1988; Vianello & Siemienska, 1990).

Today's women have entered new positions of employment, but they still face career discrimination and financial inequality.

GENDER SIMILARITIES AND DIFFERENCES

What are your perceptions regarding women in the workplace? Do you hold gender-role stereotypes that reflect negative attitudes toward working women? How and where did you acquire these stereotypes? Did they originate from the sources described in Chapter 6?

Consider some occupational groupings. Most physicians, dentists, and lawyers are men, whereas most secretaries, nurses, schoolteachers, and librarians are women. Few women work in construction or engineering, although their representation in such nontraditional jobs has been increasing from the negligible levels of a decade ago. The number of women holding political office has also gone up in recent years, but remains disappointingly small. As of 1992, just 2 of the nation's 100 senators and only 28 of the 435 representatives were women. At the state level, women have done a little better: About 18% of state legislators are women. In 10 states, women hold 25% or more of the seats (Diamond, 1988; Gutek, 1988; U.S. Bureau of the Census, 1992). Results were slightly more encouraging in 1994 elections.

Worse, even when they occupy the same jobs as men, women receive substantially lower salaries. The clustering of women in low-paying jobs is the largest factor accounting for this pay discrepancy, but even women with college degrees tend to earn less than men who have only high school diplomas. This is true no matter which ethnic group is examined (Matlin, 1993). The accompanying Focus on Diversity box shows that female vocational discrimination is also a worldwide trend.

To illustrate the pay differential between men and women, a college-educated woman between the ages of 18 and 24 earns an average of 92 cents for every dollar earned by a man of the same age and education. Her earnings drop steadily and by the time she is between ages 55 and 64, the average female worker is making about 54 cents for every dollar earned by a man. Retirement benefits are also far lower for women. In 1991 retired female workers averaged 76 cents for every dollar paid to retired male workers (Andersen, 1988; Gutek, Stromberg, & Larwood, 1988; Helson, Elliot, & Leigh, 1989; Rose & Larwood, 1988; U.S. Bureau of the Census, 1992; U.S. Department of Labor, 1992).

Vocational inequalities exist in other ways. For example, a study of the career development of social work managers (Zunz, 1991) showed that females were promoted at a significantly lower rate than were men. Another investigation (Cox & Harquail, 1991) revealed that although women in managerial careers did not differ from men on total promotions and career satisfaction, they did experience lower salary increases and fewer management promotions when compared with men of similar education, age, experience, performance, and career paths.

As we indicated earlier, Title VII of the Civil Rights Act of 1964 prohibits sex discrimination in the workplace. This is the principal law that protects workers from sexual inequality because it prohibits discrimination in recruitment, testing, referrals, hiring, wages, promotion, and fringe benefits. The Equal Employment Opportunity Commission (EEOC), which has the primary responsibility for enforcing Title VII, has published guidelines on sex discrimination making it a violation of Title VII to refuse to hire any individual on the basis of stereotyped characteristics of the sexes. It is also a violation to base employment decisions on the preferences of co-workers, the employer, clients, or customers. An employer cannot label a job a "man's job" or a "woman's job" or indicate a preference or limitation based on sex in a help wanted advertisement—unless sex is a bona fide occupational qualification for the job (which it rarely is).

Focus on Diversity

WOMEN, WORK, AND VOCATIONAL DISCRIMINATION

Around the world, women comprise more than one third of the total paid labor force, with 47% of all women aged 15 to 64 working. However, this percentage varies depending on the nation being studied. For instance, about 71% of women in the former Soviet Union are employed whereas in Latin America, only 30% of females are in the paid labor force. Arab countries have the lowest percentage of women employed—8% in Algeria and 10% in Egypt.

There is no mistaking the fact that women all around the globe earn less than men. In support of this, a recent study by the International Labor Organization (1992) revealed that the differences between pay for men and women widened in both developing and industrialized countries. Women work more hours a week, including housework, than men in every part of the world except North America and Australia. They work the hardest in Africa: It is estimated that African women work 67 hours a week compared to 53 for men. In Asia, women work 62 hours; men average 48 hours a week.

In North America and Australia men work 49 hours a week; women work 47.5. In Western Europe, women average 48 hours, men 43; Japan's women work 56 hours and men 54; in Latin America, women work 60 hours to 54 for men. Australian women are at the top of the pay equality scale, with salaries nearly 88% of men's. Other nations at the top of the pay equality scale include Denmark and France, 82%; Britain, 76%; Belgium, 75%; and West Germany, 74%.

Unequal pay is also usually accompanied by other negative employment conditions. Compared to men, women are trapped in lower paying unskilled types of occupations. Additionally, their chances for advancements in all vocational areas are fewer around the globe, and they are usually the first ones fired during recessions. Thus inequality and discrimination are problems that plague most females workers, not just those from the United States. (Cancellier & Crews, 1986; Dale & Glover, 1990; Hewlett, 1986; International Labor Organization, 1992)

Times are changing. According to James Calhoun and Joan Acocella (1990) one reason so many women are confined to low-status jobs is that many were educated during the years when it was generally assumed women neither needed nor could handle high-status jobs. As a result, they received shorter and poorer educations; they also had lesser ambitions and expectations. It shouldn't be a revelation, then, that few of them entered high-status occupations. But women's vocational opportunities will improve as women's education improves. And it is improving: Over half of all college students are now women, and every year more and more women enter medical school, law school, and business school. As more women become doctors, lawyers, and business executives, they will serve as important role models for the next generation of females, who will thus feel more free in their choice of careers. Moreover, the success of these women will lessen the prejudice of many Western cultures (women included) against women in responsible positions, so that when the next generation comes through, there will be less job discrimination. All this is happening, but it takes time.

CHAPTER REVIEW

Unit One: Physical and Mental Development

Aging during middle adulthood is external as well as internal. Skin and hair changes are the most obvious external aging processes. As far as internal aging is concerned, the amount of blood pumped by the heart decreases and one's blood pressure tends to rise. Degrees of arteriosclerosis, hardening of the arteries, and atherosclerosis, narrowing of the arteries due to fatty deposits, may also occur at this time. Structural changes in the brain at midlife are negligible. In the respiratory system, a slow loss of lung elasticity begins at this time, and overall breathing capacity is down 25%. The most pronounced sensory changes are vision and hearing.

Of the preventable health problems associated with middle age, obesity looms as the most threatening. The link between obesity and chronic diseases such as heart disease, some types of cancer, and stroke is well established. Coronary artery disease and cancer are the leading causes of death during middle adulthood. Menopause, generally occurring during the late 40s or early 50s, is defined as the cessation of menstruation. The period from the onset of irregularity of the menses to total cessation, or menopause itself, is called the climacteric.

Intellectual stability is the rule for most middle-aged adults on most abilities, although reaction times tend to decrease as an individual ages. In a practical sense, the older one gets, the better one can draw on previous experience—a perspective that can be termed wisdom. Although sensory storage and short-term memory change little with age, long-term memory exhibits some decline, presumably because encoding and retrieval processes become less efficient.

Unit Two: Personality and Social Development

The midlife transition, which reflects gender differences, often results in a reassessment of the self and a realignment of life goals, if needed. Some researchers, most notably Paul Costa and Robert McCrae, feel that personality dynamics remain relatively unaltered throughout adulthood, connected to earlier years by a thread of continuity. Others, such as Erik Erikson, Robert Peck, Daniel Levinson, and Roger Gould, argue that the adult personality undergoes change as contact is made with new experiences and challenges. Yet another perspective, reflected in data gathered in the Berkeley Guidance Study, the Berkeley Growth Study, and the Oakland Growth Study, contend that both continuity and change characterize the adult personality. According to Abraham Maslow, adulthood represents a time when many individuals strive for self-actualization, a highly refined dimension of growth that is characterized by autonomy, individuation, and authenticity.

Stress is defined as the common nonspecific response of the body to any demand made on it, be it psychological or physiological. Stress can have both positive (eustress) or negative (distress) dimensions. Stress is a response to stimuli called stressors, which may range from fear and fatigue to physical injury and emotional conflict. There can be a variety of stressors working together at any one time. Stressors can be social, psychological, physical, and endemic in scope. Hostility, often found in Type A behavior patterns, can lead to cardiovascular disease. Selye's notion of the general adaptation syndrome, consisting of the alarm, resistance, and exhaustion stages, enable us to better see the progression of stress events. The unit concluded with some thoughts on coping with stress, including the importance of rest, proper nutrition, regular exercise, the implementation of stress reduction techniques, and the maintenance of a social support system.

Unit Three: The Family

The middle-aged couple is faced with a number of important challenges during this stage of the family life cycle. Among the more important are adjusting to the adolescent's striving for independence, and assisting them in becoming responsible, independent, and well-adjusted young adults. The empty nest occurs when grown children physically leave the home, and this family transition can have both negative and positive emotions. Those who gracefully weather the empty nest period are usually the parents who have encouraged their children to be independent. In recent years we have seen an increase in the full nest, households where young adults choose to continue living with their parents for extended periods of time. A number of reasons can be given to explain the popularity of the full nest: financial reasons, loneliness, postponement of marriage, and career changes. Many middle-aged adults become grandparents, and this unit explored some of the more common rewards, drawbacks, expectations, and gender differences attached to this family transition.

Caring for aging parents is another important task for middle-aged persons. Caregiving brings its share of rewards as well as demands. Related to the latter, many middle-aged adults face competing role responsibilities and time constraints. This unit explored the many complexities of caregiving arrangements, including the social, psychological, and financial implications. The pressures of caregiving are especially evident among daughters, who traditionally shoulder most of the work.

Unit Four: Vocational Development

Reassessing one's career life is often an important part of the midlife transition. For many, it is likely that a career reappraisal will be taken, particularly of the amount of time left in the workplace before retirement. Douglas Kimmel's concept of the career clock reflects how persons can be behind time, on time, or ahead of time in regard to career accomplishments.

In the quest for vocational satisfaction, middle-aged adults may make a career change. Many reasons are given for making a career change: lack of fulfillment at one's present job, a limited sense of accomplishment, boredom, involuntary reasons such as unemployment, and burnout. Women are joining the labor force in increasing numbers. But although there are more vocational options for women today than ever before, female workers encounter considerable job segregation and salary discrimination.

TERMS YOU SHOULD KNOW

anticoagulant	**basal-cell carcinoma**
arteriosclerosis	**benign tumor**
atherosclerosis	**blood pressure**

burnout
cancer
career clock
cathectic flexibility versus
   cathectic impoverishment
cholesterol
climacteric
coronary artery disease (CAD)
crystallized intelligence
distress
diuretic
empty nest
endemic stressor
estrogen
eustress
external aging
fluid intelligence
full nest
general adaptation syndrome
   (GAS)
generation gap
generativity versus self-
   absorption
hypertension
infarct

internal aging
malignant tumor
menopause
mental flexibility versus mental
   rigidity
myocardial infarction
obesity
overweight
physical stressor
presbyopia
psychological stressor
self-actualization
sex discrimination
socializing versus sexualizing in
   human relationships
social stressor
stress
stressor
thrombus
tumor
Type A behavior pattern (TABP)
Type B behavior pattern (TBBP)
valuing wisdom versus valuing
   physical powers

THINKING IN ACTION

• You have been asked by a national fitness council to give a speech entitled "Wellness: Living the Healthy Way." To prepare yourself, you have decided to develop an outline listing approximately five key suggestions on the do's and don'ts of establishing a healthier life. What would your key points be and why? You then decide to expand your speech and turn your attention to the pros and cons of stress. For this part of your outline, develop at least five guidelines on how to avoid distress and seek eustress for a healthier and more productive life.

• While sitting at your desk pondering the very essence of thought, a Muse descends from Mount Olympus and offers to grant you a wish. "Which," she asks, "would you rather enjoy—a high degree of crystallized intelligence, or a wellspring of fluid intelligence?" What advantages would each form of mental faculty bring to your life? Can you think of any potential shortcomings attached to each? Think carefully before the die is cast.

• Take out a piece of paper and label it "The Fully Functioning Personality at Midlife." Under this heading, list as many personality and character traits as you can that capture this theme. As you go to work, think about the various positive personality dimensions established by Erikson, Peck, Levinson, and Gould. Are any of these dimensions worthy of inclusion in your list? Additionally, give consideration to components of the self-actualizing personality as well as personality dimensions that best handle stress. Would your list remain constant for all of adulthood or change for the stages of young and late adulthood? What insights might this provide you with on the issue of personality continuity and discontinuity?

• Caring for aging parents is an important issue for family members today, and one that is often not addressed until the need arises. Assume for the moment that your parents do *not* need caregiving assistance. Given the focus of this chapter on planning ahead, what kinds of things can you begin to think about now, either alone or with the help of siblings? What financial and legal issues are likely to arise? Should caregiving obstacles and hurdles be envisioned, what stress reduction techniques would you want to remember from this chapter?

• You are the president of a large manufacturing plant and wish to nurture the most productive and fulfilling work environment for your employees. Utilizing material you've gleaned from this chapter, how would you seek to maximize vocational satisfaction from your labor force? To upgrade morale, would you implement a system emphasizing rewards and incentives? How would you deal with those workers reporting dissatisfaction and disillusionment? Finally, what steps would you take to discourage sex discrimination in your manufacturing plant and encourage fair and equal treatment of your male and female employees?

RECOMMENDED READINGS

1. Birren, J. E., Sloane, R. B., & Cohen, G. D. (Eds.). (1992). *Handbook of mental health and aging* (2nd ed.). San Diego, CA: Academic Press.

   Chapters 11 and 12 offer good discussions of memory and intelligence over the course of adult life.

2. Greenberg, E. M., Bergquist, W. H., & Klaum, G. A. (1993). *In our fifties: Voices of men and women reinventing their lives.* San Francisco: Jossey-Bass.

   Interviews with men and women at midlife shed light on the psychological dynamics of this life stage.

3. Koch, T. (1990). *Mirrored lives: Aging children and elderly parents.* New York: Praeger.

   An intriguing look at how adult children and aging parents face the many challenges and complexities of aging.

4. Matlin, M. W. (1993). *The psychology of women* (2nd ed.). Fort Worth, TX: Harcourt Brace Jovanovich.

   Chapter 6 provides an excellent analysis of women in the workplace, including the issues of discrimination and the impact of work on family life.

5. Sheehy, G. (1992). *Silent passage: Menopause.* New York: Random House.

   A highly readable book about menopause and the positive and negative effects that may accompany it.

Late Adulthood

What Do You Think?

UNIT ONE: PHYSICAL AND MENTAL DEVELOPMENT

Aging and Ageism
Physical Development
External Aging
Internal Aging
Changes in Sensory Capacities
Health Disorders

Physical Well-Being During Late
  Adulthood
Mental Development
Trends in Intellectual Functioning
Changes in Memory

UNIT TWO: PERSONALITY AND SOCIAL DEVELOPMENT

Theories of Personality Development
The Continuity Perspective
The Discontinuity Perspective
Patterns of Successful Aging
The Disengagement Theory
The Activity Theory

Personality Makeup and Successful Aging
The Life Review and Reminiscence
Psychological Maladjustment
Prevalency and Trends
Functional Disorders
Organic Brain Syndrome

UNIT THREE: THE FAMILY

Marital Relations
Living Arrangements
Institutional Care
Types of Institutional Care

Adjustment to Institutionalization
Kin Relations
Patterns of Care and Interaction

UNIT FOUR: RETIREMENT

Dimensions of Retirement
Adjusting to Retirement
Psychological Adjustments
Financial Adjustments
Marital Adjustments
Other Social Adjustments
The Process of Retirement
Preretirement Phase

Honeymoon Phase
Disenchantment Phase
Reorientation Phase
Stability Phase
Termination Phase

Chapter Review • Terms You Should Know • Thinking in Action • Recommended Readings

WHAT
DO
YOU
THINK?

• They're often seen as being lonely, sick, frail, grouchy, and a burden to all. These negative stereotypes regarding elderly people have existed for years but are scarcely representative of the truth. Also bothersome are the often gloomy and depressing connotations given to the life stage of late adulthood. Where do such attitudes and appraisals originate, and why do some people choose to cling to them? What are your perceptions of this final stage of the life cycle? What have researchers done to dispel myths about aging and to replace them with accurate portrayals of growing old?

• It has been labeled by medical experts as one of the most puzzling diseases of the 1990s. Alzheimer's disease claims between 100,000 to 120,000 victims each year and carries a prognosis of 50% reduction in remaining life expectancy. It is characterized by progressive neurological degeneration that reduces victims to an immobile, speechless, and vegetative state. To date, there is no known cure. What do we know about this devastating disease? How does the disease progress, and just how much can be accomplished with medical intervention?

• The company retirement party for Bob Prescott had all of the usual touches: sit-down luncheon, speeches, gold watch, and other farewell gifts. Bob had been a good employee for years, and had even been asked to remain with the company because of his outstanding career accomplishments. He politely declined, though, admitting that 44 years on the job was "enough for anyone." Besides, Bob had been planning on his retirement for a long time and was eagerly looking forward to traveling and spending time with his family. What do you think Bob's retirement will be like? What are the special adjustments that he and millions like him face during this important life transition? This chapter studies what it's like to leave the labor force, including the many adaptations required of retired men and women.

UNIT ONE: PHYSICAL AND MENTAL DEVELOPMENT

Late adulthood represents the last developmental stage of the lifespan. It is a time of life that presents the potential for considerable happiness, satisfaction, and fulfillment. Unfortunately, societal images of elderly people capture elderly people in an opposite light: unhappy, feeble, crippled, and sick. As with all stages of the life cycle, late adulthood has its share of difficulties, and numerous challenges require unique adjustment in terms of flexibility and adaptability. Such adjustments need not undermine satisfaction, though, and most elderly persons demonstrate that late adulthood can be an emotionally fulfilling time of life, with a minimum of physical and mental impairment (Birkel & Freitag, 1991; Minkler, 1990; Ory, Abeles, & Lipman, 1992; Victor, 1991).

Perhaps we need to pay greater attention to the perceptions and treatment accorded to elderly persons in other countries. In Eastern cultures, such as Japan and China, elderly persons are revered. Older persons are respected for the wisdom they possess, and they are not ignored or rejected by their younger counterparts. In such cultures, late adulthood is recognized as a graceful and triumphant period of life, not a period of degeneration and deterioration. From where we sit, there is a critical need to reconceptualize the roles of older persons in many Western cultures and change popular stereotypes of the retirement years. Rather than rejecting or isolating older persons, we need to appreciate them as important individuals who still have much to contribute to the good of society (Dean, 1992; Gross, 1991; Kiefer, 1990).

The study of the aged as well as aging processes is known as **gerontology,** a term that originates from the Greek word *geras,* meaning old age and *logos,* meaning the study of something. Gerontology is a very broad and active investigatory discipline within the field of developmental psychology. Closely allied with it is the subfield known as **social gerontology.** Social gerontologists seek to meet the needs of elderly people by providing them with special services, programs, and policies. They are most concerned with the quality of life for elderly persons. **Geriatrics,** a related field but differing in its emphasis, is the branch of medicine that provides elderly individuals with health care and health-related services. Each year, these allied fields of study have supplied fresh insights into the needs of the aged population, including interventions designed to upgrade the quality of life for older adults. Moreover, the combined efforts of these disciplines have helped us better understand the dynamics of growing old, including the multifaceted and complex nature of physical, intellectual, psychological, and social processes of aging (Levi, 1992; Rosenstock, 1990; Siegler, 1992).

Aging and Ageism

Ageism, in its broadest sense, refers to discrimination and prejudice leveled against individuals on the basis of their age. Unfair and demeaning stereotypes are often attached to the person being viewed. Elderly persons are usually vulnerable to ageist attitudes because they are frequently seen as being sick, senile, or useless (Bodily, 1991; Fraboni et al., 1990; Gerike, 1990; Minkler & Robertson, 1991; Paludi, 1990; Rubinstein, 1990).

Yet although elderly people are usually the victims of ageist attitudes, it is possible that some ageism is leveled at all life stages. Consider some of the unfair, yet nonetheless frequently exercised generalities about certain age groups: Children do not respect their elders and are spoiled; teenagers are lazy and flighty; college students are irresponsible and liberal; young adults have just too many idealistic plans; and the middle-aged are too busy to do anything except work on their midlife crises. Humorous as these clichés sound, it is surprising how many people have come to accept them. A person who has reached a certain age is assumed to have acquired generalized qualities. In other words, it is guilt by age association.

Lifespan development researchers actively seek to combat ageism and societal misconceptions about aging processes, especially among elderly persons. These investigators, trying to paint a realistic picture about growing old, have supplied accurate and detailed explanations in the recent past. Although this topic is explored later in the text, some coverage is needed here. Terrie Wetle (1991) summarizes some of the ageist stereotypes persisting in our culture:

- Elderly persons are senile or depressed.
- Elderly individuals are all sick and live sedentary lives.
- The elderly are asexual.
- Elderly persons have exhausted their financial resources.
- All old people live alone and are therefore lonely.
- Old people all die in institutions.

GENDER SIMILARITIES AND DIFFERENCES

As you read this discussion about ageism, think of gender differences that exist in society's perceptions of elderly persons. Are elderly men and women perceived the same way? Do you hold any stereotyped images of aged men and women?

Where do such ageist attitudes originate? Apparently many have deep historical roots, at least in the United States. Starting with the colonial period, a proportion of elderly people were categorized as superannuated, unnecessary, and a burden to others. With the growth of cities and the Industrial Revolution of the 19th century, these attitudes became applicable to greater numbers of the aged. By the early 20th century, aged persons were already recognized as a wide-ranging social problem. Old age had become characterized as a time of dependence and disease (Covey, 1991; Featherstone & Hepworth, 1990; Haber, 1983; Palmore, 1990; Vinovskis, 1989).

Ageist attitudes, like other attitudes, are a product of the socialization process. As such, they can be transmitted by a number of social agents: parents, siblings, school, peers, books, and other forms of the media. In many instances elderly people are portrayed by the media in such a way that the aforementioned stereotypes are reinforced. At other times, they are practically invisible to the general public; that is, the media prefer to capture the image of the younger adult.

Joetta Vernon's (1990) research captured this last point. She analyzed the content of television programming to discover how elderly persons, particularly elderly women, are presented. She discovered that compared to other age groups, elderly individuals were significantly underrepresented. Comparisons of aged men and women revealed regular patterns of ageist images, although television's portrayal of elderly people had improved. Also, television seemed to be more accepting and open to the portrayal of older middle-aged men than women in the same category. Other research focusing on the portrayal of elderly persons in the media (e.g., Hiemstra, 1983; Kuansnicka, Beymer, & Perloff, 1982) has uncovered similar ageist images.

More exposure to elderly people and increasing the younger public's knowledge of elderly individuals are needed to break ageist stereotyping. This will also enhance our knowledge of the aging process. Too many young people regard aging as a distant and remote event, something that cannot happen to

For most people, late adulthood represents a satisfying and rewarding stage of the lifespan.

them. It may also help to remove the overall negative qualities attached to the aging process itself, another belief held by many young people (Couper, Sheehan, & Thomas, 1991; Dooley & Frankel, 1990; Rosenthal, 1990; Shimp, 1990; Simons, 1990; M. W. F. Smith, 1991).

Michael Featherstone and Michael Hepworth (1990) maintain that more positive images of elderly persons and aging in general are spreading today because of four developments linked with major socioeconomic change. First, there has been progress in medical science that has made people more aware of aging processes and the effects of the passage of time. Second, there has been an increase in life expectancy, which means that in general people live into their 60s and 70s and are more likely to die from diseases associated with late adulthood, thus leading to an upsurge in demand for medical treatment that will cure or control these diseases. Third, increased consumerism has created a way of promoting mass-produced goods, which succeeds in enhancing the lifestyles of adults of all ages. Finally, the expansion of the mass media allows information related to aging to occur at a faster pace, thus reaching a wider audience than ever before.

Physical Development

As we've stressed throughout this book, aging processes are lifelong. We readily accept these processes up through young adulthood because they signal our physical readiness to enter the adult world (something most of us have dreamed of doing since early childhood). We soon discover, however, that being a grown-up entails a bit more responsibility than we were initially prepared to assume. By the time reality catches up with our earlier fantasies about what it means to be labeled an adult, most of us are rapidly approaching middle age. Suddenly, we become acutely, if not painfully, aware of our own aging processes. Many individuals caught up in the later stages of these processes may begin to experience a good deal of anxiety over physical changes. This is perhaps out of fear of losing their membership in one of the most exclusive clubs in the world: youth.

During these years, people experience the highest incidence of physical disorders and are the largest users of medication. Why aging leaves people more susceptible to physical illness is not completely understood; what must be accepted is that certain biological changes take place in the course of normal aging. These changes bring about an inevitable decline in the function of specific organs and in the body as a whole, and are comparatively independent of other factors such as stress, trauma, and disease. In addition to the many normal biological and physiological changes elderly persons undergo, there is also a progressive rise in the incidence of chronic disease (Ben-Sira, 1991; Gadow, 1991; Hickey & Stilwell, 1991; Kiyak & Borson, 1992; Oriol, 1991; Rose, 1991).

A review of the literature by Cynthia Thomas and Howard Kelman (1990) shows that gender differences exist in the health problems of aged persons. For example, men experience higher rates of potentially fatal diseases. Women, on the other hand, have more nonfatal illnesses and chronic health problems. Also, women make more ambulatory health-care visits than men only because they are sicker. Men are hospitalized more often than women, and women visit physicians more frequently than men.

External Aging As we know, external aging refers to the superficial symptoms of growing old. The more observable changes are those associated with the skin, hair, teeth, and general posture. Let us examine each more closely.

THE SKIN The most pronounced change in skin is wrinkling, a process begun during the middle years. Wrinkling is influenced by consistency of expression, loss of subcutaneous fat tissue, and loss of skin elasticity. Recall from Chapter 2 that changes in collagen are largely responsible for such processes. One source (Matteson, 1988) notes that collagen fibers appear to rearrange into thicker bundles, and there is an alteration in their cross-linkage configuration. Subcutaneous fat insulates the body; therefore diminished tissue results in the loss of body heat. The loss of subcutaneous fat also accounts for the characteristically emaciated look of old age (Kart, 1990).

Normal skin cells in an average 70-year-old live only 46 days, compared to about 100 days for a 30-year-old. Skin cells are replaced more slowly among the aged. Also, the number of nerve cells enervating the skin declines, so the tactile sense is less sensitive. Furthermore, with age, the skin loses its ability to retain fluids and consequently becomes dry and less flexible. Spots of darker pigmentation accompany the physical aging process, and wounds tend to heal less quickly than before because thinning cells and vessels have a slower rate of repair (Kermis, 1984). One source (Schieber, 1992) does not find an age-related change in the ability to detect the warming or cooling of the skin. Evidence regarding age-related differences in cutaneous pain sensitivity remains inconclusive.

THE HAIR With advancing age, the hair continues to gray and lose its luster. Graying becomes more extensive at the temples of the head and extends to the vertex of the scalp. Compared to the darker and thicker hair of earlier years, the hair of aged adults is lighter and thinner. Hair loss on the arms and legs is not uncommon at this time for both sexes. Frontal recession of the hairline occurs in almost all older males and about 80% of females. Men also usually experience the growth of coarse longer hair on the eyebrows as well as in the ears and nostrils. In women more so than men, hair loss is experienced on the trunk, and women also often experience the emergence of facial hair on the upper lip and chin.

THE TEETH Most problems associated with the teeth are due to pathological processes and not to normal aging. Older persons today retain more of their natural dentition, mainly because of increased awareness of and compliance with the idea of prevention of disease and maintenance of good dental health. As far as normal aging changes are concerned, the teeth often darken and acquire a flattened surface. There may also be a decrease in dentine production, shrinkage of the root pulp, gingival retraction, and a loss of some bone density (Matteson & McConnell, 1988).

GENERAL POSTURE Among elderly people, shrinkage of disks in the spinal column leads to a slight loss of physical stature. This process, you may recall, began gradually during young adulthood, but only now becomes evident to the eye (Lord, Clark, & Webster, 1991). Loss of collagen between the spinal vertebrae also causes the spine to bow. This, coupled with the tendency of elderly people to stoop, often gives them an even shorter appearance. Postural changes may be especially evident in older women, who often develop a widow's or dowager's "hump" at the back of the neck. As we discuss later, this hump is the result of *osteoporosis,* a disorder common among older women, which results in a gradual loss of bone mass.

Related to general posture changes are changes in the gait patterns of older adults (Ferrandez, Pailhous, & Durup, 1990). With age, elderly individuals tend to experience loss of muscle power along with diminished bone and muscle mass, changes that may cause stiffness, unsteadiness, and falls (Lord, Clark, & Webster, 1991; Teasdale, Stelmach, & Breunig, 1991; Vandervoort, 1992; Walker & Howland, 1991; Williams, Haywood, & VanSant, 1991). One researcher (Chen, 1991) focused on changes in physical mobility by asking 24 healthy young and 24 healthy older adults to approach and step over obstacles of 0, 25, 51, or 152 millimeters in height and also engage in obstacle-free walking. When stepping over obstacles, older subjects exhibited a significantly more conservative strategy, using slower crossing speed, a shorter step length, and shorter obstacle-to-heel strike distance. Although all subjects successfully avoided the riskiest form of obstacle contact, tripping, 4 of the 24 older adults stepped on an obstacle, showing increased risk for obstacle contact with age.

Jill Rhymes (1990) maintains that it is important for caregivers to realize walking becomes more laborious with age. Gait problems—whether from disease, disuse, drug side effects, or physiological deterioration—can lead to decreased mobility, inactivity, dependence, and falls. Effectively managing the underlying cause of a gait disorder is an important first step for caregivers. Identifying patterns of gait abnormalities and selecting specific interventions, such as gait retraining, mechanical aids, strength training, or surgery, can enhance an older person's independence. A number of studies (e.g., Frontera & Meredith, 1989; Martinez, 1990; O'Brien & Vertinsky, 1990) have shown that creative treatment options have enabled elderly persons to maintain a range of independent daily living activities (e.g., personal hygiene routines, shopping, cooking) rather than just walking or sitting.

Internal Aging Internal aging refers to the invisible degenerative changes that occur within the body. We examine some of the changes within the nervous, cardiovascular, respiratory, gastrointestinal, musculoskeletal, urinary, and immune systems. Although these systems decline in old age, there is a reserve capacity for individuals to maintain adequate levels of daily functioning although they may take longer to do something and longer to recover after activity.

THE NERVOUS SYSTEM As we indicated in Chapter 3, the brain decreases in size and weight as a function of age. Such changes, though, are by no means uniform. For example, the cerebral cortex atrophies more than the brain stem. Also, certain neurons demonstrate greater age-dependent changes than others. The brain also continues to gradually pull away from its sheath, the cortical mantle. It is calculated that the amount of space between the brain and skull approximately doubles between the ages of 20 and 70. A reduction of cerebral blood flow, as well as a decline in oxygen and glucose consumption, also occurs at this time (Scheibel, 1992).

THE CARDIOVASCULAR SYSTEM The heart has a tendency to maintain its size with age, although heart tissue may atrophy. The aorta, the large artery responsible for receiving blood pumped from the heart and whose branches ultimately carry blood to all body parts, loses elasticity. Also, the hardening and shrinking of the arteries makes it hard for blood to flow freely in the body. As a

THEORETICAL ISSUES

How would you account for the bodily changes that occur during late adulthood? Which biological theory of aging do you think best explains the external and internal aging processes discussed in this section? What role do proper nutrition and regular exercise play in such aging processes?

result, the heart has to work harder to accomplish less. In addition, there is a loss of cardiac muscle strength, reduced cardiac-muscle cell size, and reduced **cardiac output** among the aged. The cardiac output, at best, for an average 75-year-old is about 70% of that of an average 30-year-old (Kart, 1990).

THE RESPIRATORY SYSTEM With age, there is a measurable reduction in the efficiency of the respiratory system. There are decreases in the maximum breathing capacity, residual lung volume, total capacity, and basal oxygen consumption. All of these bring about a diminished metabolic rate. There is also decreased flexibility and elasticity of the lungs, the result of collagen change in the lung tissue and the walls of blood vessels (Weg, 1983). Additionally, the muscles of respiration, the diaphragm, intercostal muscles, and accessory muscles, like other muscles in the body, weaken with age. Also, osteoporosis of the ribs and vertebrae and calcification of cartilage may contribute to chest wall stiffness (Harrell, 1988). We discuss osteoporosis later in this chapter.

THE GASTROINTESTINAL SYSTEM The gastrointestinal system changes with age, producing, most notably, a decreased production of digestive juices and a reduction in peristalsis. Peristaltic action, waves of contractions that serve to push the contents of the digestive system downward, is involved in metabolism and the excretion of food. It therefore is very important to overall health. Constipation, which occurs frequently among the aged, is indicative of how the digestive system changes (Kermis, 1984).

THE MUSCULOSKELETAL SYSTEM During this time, there is a progressive decrease in stature, particularly among older women. Recall that this decrease is mainly attributed to the compression of the spinal column, which results from progressive narrowing of the discs as well as a loss of height of individual vertebrae (see Figure 11-1). Height diminishes by about 1.2 cm per 20 years, which appears to be universal among all races and both sexes (Matteson & McConnell, 1988). The bones tend to become more brittle, and muscle mass as well as strength tend to decline. However, as far as the latter are concerned, such decrements may be due more to nonuse than degenerative processes. Research has shown that those who exercise regularly show less of a decline in muscle mass and strength than those who lead sedentary lives (Blumenthal, 1991; Morey, 1991; Reed, 1991).

THE URINARY SYSTEM The kidneys, bladder, and ureters constitute the urinary system. In general, the efficiency of the urinary system decreases with age. The desire to urinate is often delayed among elderly people. The number of cells in the kidneys decrease, causing diminished excretion of toxins and wastes from the body. In addition, the bladder becomes less elastic. The bladder of an aged person has a capacity of less than one half that of a young adult. A common urinary problem of older males is frequent urination, caused by the enlargement of the prostate gland (Kart, 1990; Kermis, 1984).

THE IMMUNE SYSTEM Immune capacity appears to be less responsive and efficient with age. The body is just not as effective in eliminating foreign substances from its system as it once was. The immune system loses its efficiency partially because of a breakdown in the body's feedback system. As we learned

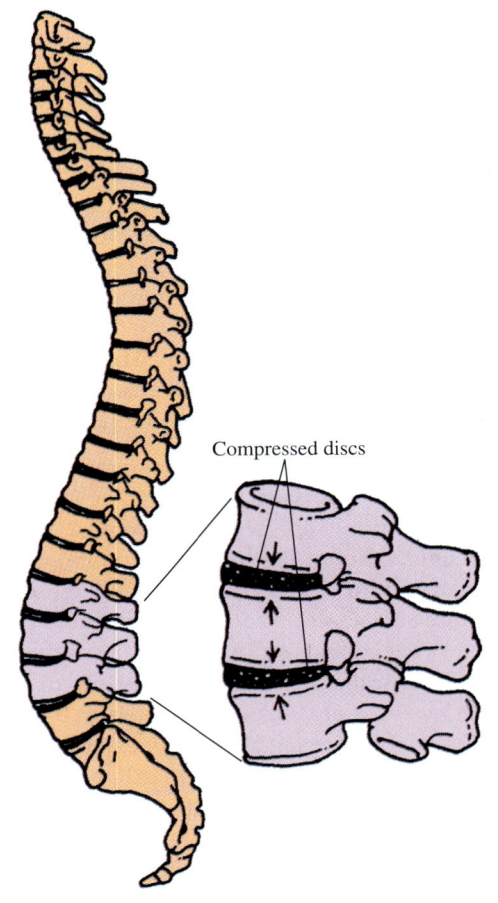

Compressed discs

FIGURE 11-1
Age-Related Changes in the Spinal Column.

Over time, there is a compression of the spinal column, which results in a progressive decrease in stature. This occurs because of a narrowing and compression of the discs between the bones of the spine. By late adulthood, an inch or two of height will be lost. The arms and legs do not decrease in length and therefore appear longer in relation to the shortened torso.

SOURCE: Adapted from Pesmen, 1984.

in Chapter 2, the immune system tends to turn against the body in an autoimmune response, as increasing numbers of cells become faulty. The body's failing immune system is most evident in health statistics for elderly people. For example, the mortality rate among the aged for pneumonia is six to seven times the rate for young adults, and they have higher incidence rates of cancer and tuberculosis (Kermis, 1984; Nandy, 1983; Verbrugge, 1990; Weg, 1983).

PUTTING LATER LIFE PHYSICAL CHANGES INTO PERSPECTIVE In light of the many physical changes that take place during late adulthood, many people feel this life stage is nothing more than a downward slide, a total degenerative series of bodily changes that leave elderly people in physical disrepair. However, as we pointed out at the beginning of this chapter, the notion that all elderly are invalid or feeble is incorrect. Although it is obvious that systematic decrement does occur, this does not mean late adulthood is characterized by disease, disability, or frailty. For most aged persons, there are more than enough reserve and systematic capacities to meet the demands of everyday life with a sense of control and competence (Birkel & Freitag, 1991; Mount, 1991; Rakowski, 1992; Rodin & Timko, 1992; Stofo, Behrens, & Rosemont, 1990).

Changes in Sensory Capacities Advancing age brings changes in sensory abilities. In general, there is a gradual diminishment. Older individuals usually do not react as quickly to sensory stimuli, and they often no longer receive adequate perceptive information about their environment. These physiological changes have psychological consequences. It is through the senses of vision, hearing, taste, touch, and smell that the individual is linked to the outside world (Kart, 1990). By this, the senses orient a person to the world and interpret it. Certain research (e.g., Claussen & Patil, 1990; LaForge, Spector, & Sternberg, 1992) indicates that sensory impairment, most notably vision and hearing, tends to promote dependency in daily living and represents significant risk factors for functional decline. Finally, the world's perception of elderly people may be influenced by the sensory changes they have experienced. For example, the older person with impaired vision or hearing may be viewed as being stubborn, senile, or eccentric. Because we covered changes in the skin senses earlier in this chapter, we focus our energies now on vision, hearing, taste, and smell.

THE VISUAL SENSE As we pointed out in the last chapter, there are several age-related structural changes in the visual system. For example, there is a reduction in the diameter of the pupil, an increased irregularity of the surface of the cornea, and a decreasing ability of the lens to accommodate, and hence, focus on near objects. The lens of the eye also becomes less transparent with age, the number of fibers composing the optic nerve diminishes, and color vision may become less efficient. This is because of a loss of sensitivity in the eyes' photoreceptors and their transmission of visual impulses to the nervous system (B. A. Cooper, 1991; Owsley & Sloane, 1990; Schieber, 1992).

Such visual changes accompanying aging processes have practical, everyday implications. The elderly generally need brighter light for tasks like reading or cooking. The decreasing ability to adapt to glare makes night driving especially difficult (Barr & Eberhard, 1991; Kline, 1992). Eye strain may also reduce the amount of time a person can spend concentrating on activities. However, eyeglasses can correct many of these visual difficulties. For those with more severe impairments, books and other reading material in large print or a magnifying glass may be necessary. (Akutsu, 1991; Burack-Weiss, 1991; Cherry, Keller, & Dudley, 1991; Orr, 1991).

EYE DISEASES AMONG THE ELDERLY Beyond the changes in the eye that often accompany normal aging processes is the risk of eye disease (Crews, 1991; Horowitz, Teresi, & Cassels, 1991; Hudson, 1990; Ringgold, 1991). Two visual conditions, in particular, are more common among older adults: cataracts and glaucoma.

Cataracts are opaque areas on the lens that interfere with the passage of light to the retina, producing blurred vision. Cataracts usually develop gradually and without pain, redness, or tearing, typically in both eyes. Some will remain small and do not affect vision. If they become larger or denser, though, visual problems usually result.

Besides blurred vision, persons with cataracts often experience glare in bright light because the clouded lens scatters rather than focuses incoming light. This visual limitation is especially pronounced when focusing on distant objects. As the condition progresses, the lens becomes milky white, causing further visual degeneration. Left untreated, cataracts can cause blindness.

Although they face systematic degeneration of bodily functions, most elderly people can successfully meet the challenges of everyday life.

However, cataracts can be surgically removed in a relatively safe and highly successful procedure. After the operation, vision is restored by using special eyeglasses or contact lenses or by an intraocular lens implant (a plastic lens implanted in the eye surgically).

Glaucoma is pressure within the eyeball caused by a buildup of aqueous humor, a fluid that circulates in the eye's anterior chamber. This buildup of fluid disturbs the normal drainage ability of the eye, creating internal pressure as well as damage to the eye's structure and nerve endings. Like cataracts, glaucoma can cause blindness if left untreated.

Glaucoma often begins without any noticeable symptoms. In this respect, visual deterioration is gradual and painless. However, its progression usually brings impairment of peripheral vision, blurring, difficulty in adjusting to brightness and darkness, and pain in or around the eye. In most instances, glaucoma also causes individuals to perceive a halo effect surrounding lights (Farber, 1990; Weinstock & Zucker, 1990).

The effective treatment of glaucoma relies on its early detection. Among the measures taken are special eyedrops (to promote fluid drainage) and oral medications (to decrease production of eye fluid). Should either approach prove unsuccessful, surgery may be needed to restore the eye's draining ability.

THE AUDITORY SENSE Changes in hearing can be noted by examining developments in the outer, middle, and inner ear. Many elderly persons experience an increased secretion of ear wax, which results in excessive accumulation that blocks the auditory canal. In the middle ear, the joints of the ossicular bone chain often become calcified and less elastic. In the inner ear, the cochlear membranes may lose flexibility and responsiveness, and there may be a diminished cochlear blood flow (Schieber, 1992).

Hearing impairments are much more common in elderly people than in middle-aged adults. It has been estimated that approximately 30% of adults aged 65 through 74 and about 50% of those aged 75 through 79 suffer some degree of hearing loss. In the United States, more than 10 million older adults are hearing impaired (Hudson, 1990; Palumbo, 1990; Ross, Echevarria, & Robinson, 1991).

Presbycusis is the most common hearing impairment among elderly people. Changes in the workings of the inner ear lead to difficulties in understanding speech, sometimes an intolerance for loud sounds, but rarely total deafness. This hearing loss, you will recall, begins first in the higher sound frequencies. Remember, too, that men have more trouble hearing higher sound frequencies than women.

Conductive deafness is another form of hearing loss sometimes experienced by elderly people. This type of deafness typically involves blockage or impairment of the outer or middle ear so that sound waves are not able to travel properly. Such a condition can be caused by packed ear wax, excessive fluid, abnormal bone growth in the ear, or infection. Individuals suffering from conductive deafness usually find that sounds have a muffled quality, but their own voices sound louder than normal. Consequently, they often speak softly.

One other form of hearing loss among elderly people, although less common than those already mentioned, is **sensorineural deafness.** Sensorineural deafness is a hearing loss caused by damage to the inner ear, to the auditory nerve carrying sound messages to the brain, or to the hearing center of the brain itself. This type of deafness has many possible causes, including extended bacterial and viral infections, head injuries, and prolonged exposure to loud noises.

The nature of the hearing loss as well as its extent will determine the treatment. In some instances, flushing the ear canal to remove packed ear wax may restore some or all hearing ability, or surgery may be needed. A hearing aid may also provide restoration. It is estimated that more than three quarters of older people with permanent hearing loss can benefit from the use of a hearing aid. However, only one in five hearing-impaired older adults use them. Why is this so? Anxiety, vanity, and a lack of understanding are the major reasons (Olinger, Dancer, & Patterson, 1991; Patterson, Dancer, & Clark, 1990). Of course, there are those who cannot be helped by hearing aids, as well as those who totally refuse help (Weinstein, 1991).

A hearing impairment can lead to a diminished social life, leaving a person lonely and sometimes even with a paranoid sense of abandonment. Some, thinking their verbal responses are inappropriate, may shun social interactions. The convergence of biological, social, and psychological forces will again be obvious to the alert student. All of this underscores the need to be aware of those factors that can enhance communication with the hearing impaired. To this end, we offer the following suggestions:

- Speak to the person at a distance of 3 to 6 feet. Make sure that you position yourself near adequate lighting so your lip movements, facial expressions, and gestures may be seen clearly.

INTERRELATEDNESS OF AGING PROCESSES

Can you think of examples illustrating how a hearing loss or other type of sensory impairment affects other developmental parameters? For example, consider self-esteem or feelings of loneliness.

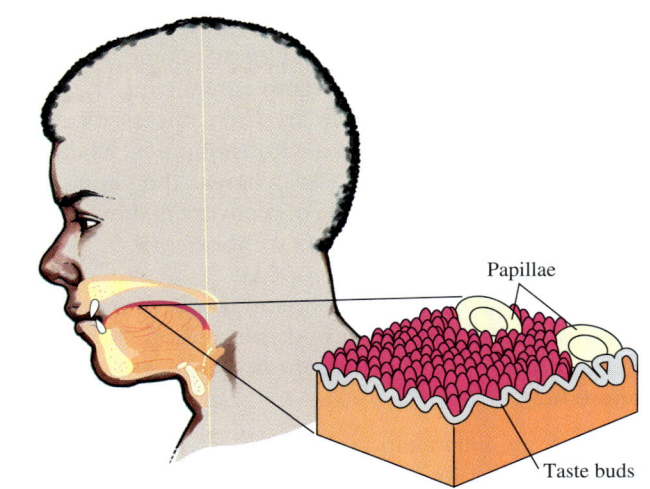

Papillae

Taste buds

FIGURE 11-2
Age-Related Changes in Tasting Ability.

The structural mechanisms responsible for taste are affected by aging processes. By late adulthood, there is a gradual diminishment in the number of taste buds, which are located in the papillae on the tongue's upper surface. The taste buds also begin to atrophy during this time. However, because of mixed research findings, we are unsure how these structural changes affect the tasting abilities of older adults. Decrements in tasting sensitivity are not believed to be as significant as once thought.

SOURCE: Adapted from Pesmen, 1984.

• Don't begin speaking until you are visible to the person. Do not cover your mouth when speaking, and avoid chewing and eating.

• Speak slightly louder than normal. Realize, though, that shouting will not make the message any clearer. In fact, it might distort it.

• Speak at your normal rate, but not too rapidly. Also, do not overarticulate because this distorts the sounds of speech and makes the use of visual clues more difficult.

• If what you say is not understood, rephrase the idea in short, simple sentences.

• Never speak directly into the person's ear. This prevents the listener from making use of visual clues.

• Arrange rooms so everyone will be clearly visible and not more than 6 feet apart.

• Always treat the hearing impaired with respect. Include the person in all discussions that deal with him or her. This will help to reduce the feelings of isolation that many hearing impaired experience.

THE SENSES OF TASTE AND SMELL The four basic tastes—sweet, bitter, sour, and salty—often diminish in sensitivity. This is largely because there has been a gradual diminution in the number of taste buds, beginning in females at 40 to 50 years and in males at 50 to 60 years (see Figure 11-2). But these changes do not affect sensitivity to the four taste qualities until after age 60, and for some, this sensory reduction does not occur at all (Matteson & McConnell, 1988; Myslinski, 1990).

One's taste of food is affected by the sense of smell. With age, there appears to be a generalized atrophy of the olfactory bulbs with a moderate loss of neurons. However, to date there is little conclusive evidence showing that such changes create smell decreases with age. Certain factors play a role in both smell and taste, such as one's general health (Doty, 1989; Myslinski, 1990; Schieber, 1992; Weiffenbach, Tylenda, & Baum, 1990).

Health Disorders As indicated, elderly people are not always sick or unhealthy. Although some need care, most do not. Late adulthood is not synonymous with poor health. The health status of elderly people need not be viewed apart from younger adults either. In preventive medicine, the surgical procedures and drugs used on elderly people are the same as those used on the young. For example, pneumonia is treated with antibiotics, whether the person is 18 or 88 years old. The difference is that whereas the young have a natural tendency to rebound from illness, the rate of recovery is slower for the aged, or the condition will deteriorate even further (Abbey, 1991; Goodwin, 1991; Kaplan, 1992; Rogers, Rogers, & Belanger, 1992).

The aged population is vulnerable to certain disorders and diseases though. Among the more prevalent are arthritis, hypertension, heart disease, cerebrovascular accident, cancer, and osteoporosis. Let us examine the nature of each of these more fully.

ARTHRITIS **Arthritis,** an inflammation of a joint, is a disorder common among older adults. Few cures exist for this condition, which can last for years and intensify with the aging process. Of the nearly 100 types of arthritis, two are most common: osteoarthritis and rheumatoid arthritis.

Osteoarthritis is also called degenerative arthritis, and is the most common form of arthritis. It affects over 40 million persons living in the United States, and is characterized by the gradual wearing away of cartilage in the joints. In its most common form, osteoarthritis involves large weight-bearing joints such as the knees and hip area. Usually, pain and swelling result from the cartilage degeneration, and joints stiffen. Joint stiffness can be brief, is often relieved by activity, but can recur upon rest.

Rheumatoid arthritis affects all of the connective tissues in the body. It typically develops slowly, and most often has its onset before later adulthood. Rheumatoid arthritis is much more common in women than men. In its most severe form, this arthritic condition inflames the membranes lining and lubricating the joints. Pain and swelling are common reactions to this inflammation, as well as fatigue and fever. Eventually, the cartilage will be destroyed. As scar tissue gradually replaces the damaged cartilage, the joint becomes rigid and misshapen. One review of the literature (Gibson, 1991) indicates that elderly African Americans have higher rates of rheumatoid arthritis until age 64, but whites have higher rates in the 65 and older age group.

Treatment for both forms of arthritis is geared to relieving stiffness and pain, halting joint degeneration, and maintaining mobility. Aspirin and anti-inflammatory drugs are typically prescribed to treat arthritis, as well as carefully designed exercise programs. Contrary to popular thought, rest is not always the best medicine for arthritis. Although rest can reduce joint inflammation, too much of it tends to create stiffness. Therefore, physicians are likely to recommend daily exercise programs such as walking or swimming. Finally, for those with severely damaged joints, surgery often helps relieve pain and restore mobility (Verbrugge, Lepkowski, & Konkol, 1991).

HYPERTENSION Recall from earlier discussions (Chapter 10) that *hypertension* refers to high blood pressure. It is a disorder characterized by persistently elevated pressure of blood within and against the walls of the arteries, which carry blood from the heart through the body. This excessive force being exerted on the artery walls often causes damage to the arteries themselves and thereby to such body organs as the heart, brain, and kidneys.

Although many middle-aged persons have hypertension, the chances of contracting this disorder steadily increase with age (Messerli, 1990). In support of this, about 40% of whites and over 50% of African Americans 65 years of age and older have significant elevations of blood pressure. Such elevations are thought to be part of the aging processes because there is a gradual loss of elasticity and decreasing diameter of the small arteries throughout the body (American Heart Association, 1992).

Similar to earlier stages of adulthood, hypertension presents few, if any, reliable symptoms during the retirement years. Although palpitations, excessive headaches, and anxiety are thought to be cues, high blood pressure may exist for years without being detected. For this reason, elderly people need to have their blood pressure taken at least once a year. Left untreated, hypertension can lead to heart and brain disease, among other complications. It is also a condition that can be aggravated by such factors as smoking, poor dietary habits, and lack of exercise.

Although high blood pressure can usually be controlled by drugs and changes in daily habits, misconceptions about prescribed medicines exist. For example, some feel that once blood pressure is brought down to acceptable levels, medication is no longer needed. Antihypertensive drugs are typically prescribed with long-term use in mind, although reductions in amount are possible over time.

HEART DISEASE As we know, a heart attack is a life threatening disease. Indeed, it is the largest single cause of death in the United States. Approximately one sixth of white men and women between the ages of 45 and 65 are affected with heart disease, whereas over one third of African-American men and women have this condition. For older age groups, these percentages increase significantly. Heart disease also leads all other diseases in visits to the doctor, hospitalization required, and days spent recuperating in bed (American Heart Association, 1992; National Center for Health Statistics, 1992; Young, 1991). For a review of the causes of heart disease, see Chapter 10.

CEREBROVASCULAR ACCIDENT A **cerebrovascular accident (CVA),** or *stroke,* is any interruption of the brain's arterial flow that results in a loss of body functions. When such an interruption occurs, the brain is deprived of its supply of oxygen and nutrients. Depending on the side of the brain that is affected (damage to cells on the right side of the brain, for example, will impair function on the left side of the body), strokes have the potential for creating numerous impairments. Among these include loss of vision, paralysis, speech difficulties, memory loss, and comas. Should the brain's vital centers be destroyed, such as those controlling circulation or breathing, death can result (Biller, 1991; Foley & Pizer, 1990). Figure 11-3 illustrates how a stroke blocks the flow of blood and nerve impulses to the affected side of the body.

About 80% of stroke victims are 65 years of age and older. Each year in the United States, about 450,000 persons suffer from stroke, and approximately 150,000 die immediately or shortly after the stroke's onset. Of every 100 who survive the accident, about 10 will be able to return to work virtually without impairment, 40 will be slightly disabled, 40 will be more seriously disabled and

INTERRELATEDNESS OF AGING PROCESSES

How does one's health status—good or bad—affect other facets of a person's life? Given the fusion of developmental forces, what social and psychological considerations should be given to the person experiencing physical impairment or disease?

FIGURE 11-3
How a Stroke Occurs.

When a person suffers a stroke, the flow of blood as well as the nerve impulses to the affected side of the body are blocked. (Adapted from Nelson et al., 1986)

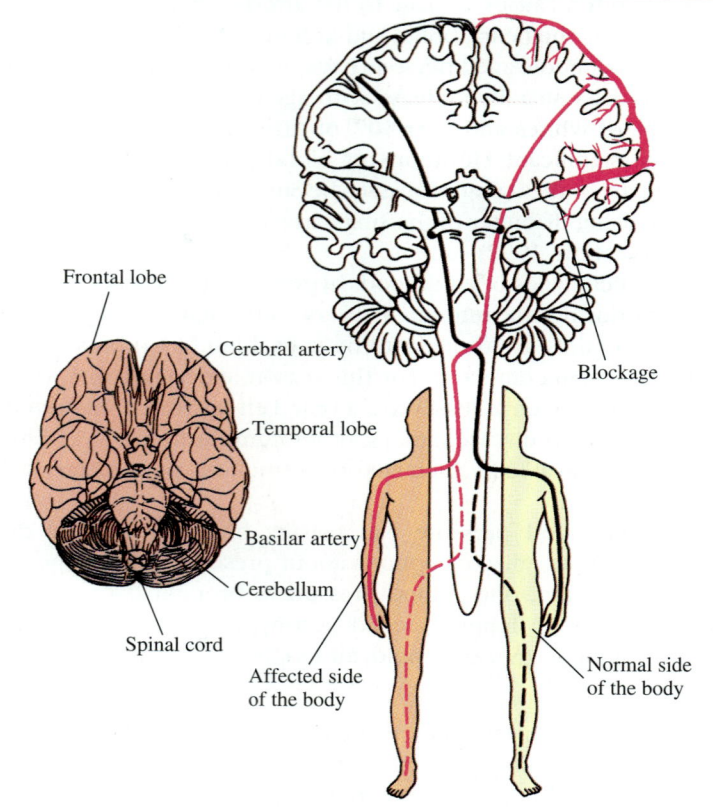

Frontal lobe

Cerebral artery

Temporal lobe

Basilar artery

Cerebellum

Spinal cord

Affected side of the body

Blockage

Normal side of the body

require special services, and 10 will need institutional care. Only about 16% of the 1.8 million people today who have survived a stroke are completely independent (National Center for Health Statistics, 1992; Zamula, 1986).

Cerebrovascular accidents can be caused in several different ways. Most are caused by the narrowing of a brain artery and/or by a blood clot. Another possibility is that a blood clot formed in another part of the body finds its way to an artery leading to or within the brain. Strokes may also result from hemorrhage, or bleeding, into the brain after damage to a blood vessel.

Certain conditions increase the risk of a cerebrovascular accident. Unchecked hypertension is an especially dangerous risk because this disease promotes weakened and damaged arteries, not to mention hemorrhaging. A personal history of heart attack or other forms of heart disease also increases the risk of cerebrovascular accident. Also at risk are those with a family history of strokes. Smoking, heavy alcohol consumption, high cholesterol intake, and diabetes also increase the risk of contracting this disease. As far as gender differences are concerned, strokes are more frequent in males until the age of 75. After this point, the incidence is about the same for both males and females. Finally, African-American persons are more vulnerable to cerebrovascular accidents because hypertension is much more common in African Americans than it is among whites.

Some of the more common symptoms of a stroke include sudden weakness or numbness in the leg, arm, or face on one side of the body, slurring of speech, difficulty in understanding others speak, and physical unsteadiness. In some instances, a minor stroke may be experienced, called a **transient ischemic attack (TIA).** Although such strokes cause an abrupt loss of body function, the symptoms usually clear up within 24 hours. However, a TIA often precedes the appearance of a larger, and much more serious, cerebrovascular accident.

The prevention of strokes rests heavily on the control of high blood pressure and the careful monitoring of the risk conditions just described. For persons experiencing stroke warning signs or a TIA, an arteriography is usually performed to locate obstructions of the arteries. If needed, arteries can then be surgically cleaned out or treated with **anticoagulants** (agents that inhibit the normal clotting of the blood). For those suffering from severe strokes, blood pressure must be normalized and drug therapy administered to halt further damage to the brain. Once the crisis period is over, physical, speech, and occupational therapy are aimed at restoring as much of the patient's lost functions as possible.

CANCER Although cancers can occur at any point in the life cycle, the risk of contracting this disease steadily increases with age (American Cancer Society, 1992; Silverberg, Boring, & Squires, 1990; Worcester, 1991). As we learned in the last chapter, more than one half of all cancer deaths occur in persons over age 65, and the disease is more common in men during late adulthood. Of course, understanding the causes of cancer can help adults of all ages to lessen the risks. And the early diagnosis of cancer is critical so a malignancy can be detected before it has the opportunity to spread.

OSTEOPOROSIS **Osteoporosis** is a disorder characterized by a decrease in the calcium content of bone tissue. The word *osteoporosis* means literally "holes in the bones," and the condition has the potential of leading to fragility of bones and increased porosity. Also called brittle bone disease or "widow's hump," osteoporosis can cause bone deformity, crippling, and even a reduction in height.

An estimated 15 million U.S. citizens suffer from osteoporosis, but it is eight times more common in women. It afflicts one in four women over the age of 60, and fair-skinned white females are affected most often. Also, thin women with small frames are more susceptible to osteoporosis than larger, heavier females.

It is believed that osteoporosis is triggered by menopause and natural aging processes, although conclusive explanations remain elusive. Menopause is frequently cited because of the dramatic decrease in **estrogen** production, a hormone that affects the calcium content of bones. However, other reasons for its onset are also cited, including inactivity, inadequate exposure to sunlight (which helps the body manufacture vitamin D, essential for normal calcium absorption and use), and not enough calcium and protein in the diet (Gennari & Montagnani, 1990; Roberto & Johnston, 1991).

Certain conditions also seem to accentuate the possibility of contracting osteoporosis. Females with a family history of osteoporosis and those who have had their ovaries removed at an earlier age run a greater risk of developing this condition. Medical conditions such as chronic arthritis, alcoholism, thyroid problems, and liver disease also increase the likelihood of osteoporosis (Gold, 1991; Isaia, 1990).

In its early stages, osteoporosis often goes unnoticed. For many, it presents no observable symptoms and little, if any, pain. Often, the only warning sign occurs when a minor fall or mishap results in a broken bone. Or some may realize that the spine has become slightly curved. These are all indications that the disease has advanced.

Over time and left untreated, osteoporosis becomes a crippling disease. Simple exertion creates muscle spasms and pain, and the progressive loss of bone can lead to complicated fractures of the spine and limbs. The teeth can also fall out as the jawbone decays. Furthermore, the spinal column becomes progressively curved and the shoulders rounded. Victims can actually lose several inches in height because of a reduction in the length of the spinal column.

The prevention of osteoporosis is relatively simple. Women need to ensure that their bodies are receiving an adequate supply of calcium and vitamin D. This is true for all women, not just those nearing menopause or afflicted with osteoporosis. Although the current recommended dietary allowance for calcium is 800 mg per day, most medical experts believe women past the age of 40 need 1,000 to 1,500 mg daily. Keep in mind, too, that calcium supplements exceeding this daily requirement do not ensure added prevention. On the contrary, too much can create a toxic reaction, and individuals should always check with a physician before increasing dosage levels. Along similar lines, excessive intake of proteins does not ensure the prevention of osteoporosis. Rather, this tends to create bone loss rather than strengthen the skeletal framework.

One study of women with postmenopausal osteoporosis (Campagnoli, 1990) showed that an equilibrated diet with food rich in calcium, especially milk and milk products, helped to promote bone mass formation. Some dietary habits, conversely, contributed to a negative calcium balance. These included diets too rich in proteins, sodium chloride, fiber, and caffeine. Another negative factor was the excessive use of alcohol. Finally, physical exercise was shown to repress the loss of bone tissue even in elderly women who previously led sedentary lives.

Regular medical examinations are important for preventing osteoporosis. As we have indicated, feeling physically fit offers no guarantee whatsoever that osteoporosis is absent from the system. A number of methods are available for diagnosing osteoporosis, including X-rays and devices that assess bone loss. Such diagnostic approaches are often part of annual checkups for any woman over the age of 25.

For patients afflicted with osteoporosis, doctors usually prescribe high dosages of calcium and vitamin D tablets. This usually retards the rate of bone loss but will not cause new bone to form. For females, estrogen slows the rate of bone loss and might be prescribed. However, as we cautioned earlier, estrogen may cause adverse side effects and each patient needs to be carefully monitored. For men with osteoporosis, the male hormone testosterone might be administered because it stimulates the growth of body tissues. For both females and males, physicians usually urge that nutritionally sound diets be followed, as well as an exercise program that will strengthen the muscles supporting weakened bones.

Physical Well-Being During Late Adulthood   Throughout this book we have stressed the importance of proper nutrition and staying physically fit through regular exercise. These considerations are important to physical well-being throughout all of adulthood, especially old age. Indeed, it is generally acknowledged that eating well-balanced meals and engaging in regular exercise help retard aging processes and extend a person's longevity (Arking, 1991; Beychok, 1991; Cesario & Hollander, 1991; Fries, 1990).

The nutritional needs of elderly people do not differ significantly from those of younger adults. The primary bodily changes are in the speed and completeness of digestion and absorption; glucose tolerance; utilization of protein, fat, calcium, and thiamine; and decreased appetite. The elderly person's lowered metabolism and general levels of diminished activity decrease the overall calorie need (Fries, 1990; Krause, 1984; Kunkel, 1991).

One study (Johnson, 1992) examined the dietary patterns of white and African-American elderly persons, including centenarians. Compared to the younger cohorts, centenarians consumed breakfast more regularly, avoided weight loss diets and large fluctuations in body weight, consumed more vegetables, and relied on their doctor and family more than on the news media for nutritional information. However, centenarians were less likely to consume diets low in fat and to comply with nutritional guidelines designed to reduce the risk of chronic disease. Elderly male African Americans were significantly less likely than white persons to use vitamin or mineral supplements or to eat breakfast every day. Elderly male African Americans also consumed diets higher in sweets and fat than those of female African Americans, white men, and white women. High nutrition risks, particularly in African Americans, were associated with lower physical and mental health and impaired activities of daily living.

The foregoing suggests that elderly people represent a segment of the population at considerable nutritional risk. In the United States, it has been estimated that over half of the aged population suffers from inadequate nutrient intake and that, surprisingly, malnutrition is not confined to any one socioeconomic group. Elderly people who are most at risk live alone, have disabilities that restrict their mobility, are mentally confused, and are very old (Manson & Shea, 1991).

There are several reasons why proper nutrition is often ignored among elderly people. If people live alone, they may feel little or no motivation to prepare and eat well-balanced meals. Cooking may not seem worth the effort, and snack foods may be eaten instead. Decreases in smell and taste sensitivity may also precipitate negative changes in eating habits. Other reasons for poor nutrition include the fact that some elderly may not be able to afford the food they should be eating (Ponza & Wray, 1990). Others may be so socially isolated that they cannot get to the grocery store. Some, having low educational levels, do not recognize the value of proper nutrition in their lives (Horwath, 1991; McKenzie, 1980). Finally, a body of research (Ardigo, 1990; Manson & Shea, 1991; Mowe & Bohmer, 1991; Thompson & Morris, 1991) notes that poor nutrition is often linked with the outcome of medical and surgical treatment, including prolonged hospitalization. One study (Finn, 1990) discovered that 52 to 85% of long-term care elderly patients exhibited some degree of malnutrition.

Marie Krause (1984) writes that poor diets can lead to malnutrition on the one hand or an overweight condition on the other. Rigidity of eating habits, such as limited dietary intake and non-nutritionally balanced meals, is probably the primary reason for malnutrition among elderly people. Poor appetite, impaired digestion and/or absorption, lowered gastric acidity and/or inadequate food intake, as well as poor choice of foods, are some of the factors that may

The health benefits of exercise are lifelong and have special importance to aged people.

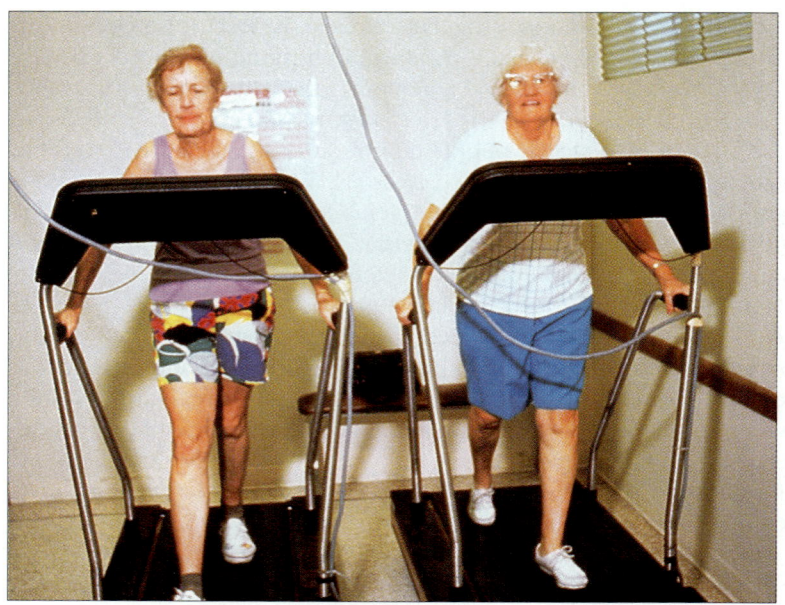

contribute toward being underweight. According to Susan Finn (1990), other contributing reasons include the use of medications that impact on nutrition and reduced sense of taste. However, increasing caloric intake with concentrated nutritive foods, prepared and served to suit individual taste, usually corrects this condition.

As mentioned, staying physically fit is essential for healthy living during all stages of adulthood, but especially so for the retirement years. Regardless of chronological age, physical activity helps slow the aging process. Regular exercise among elderly people also helps maintain good health, improves respiration and circulation, promotes body flexibility, and induces better sleeping patterns. People who exercise also reduce the risk of heart attack. Moreover, should one occur, the fact that they have exercised on a regular basis increases their chances of survival (Barrow & Smith, 1983; Birkel & Freitag, 1991; Schilke, 1991).

Another benefit attached to physical activity is that it improves blood cholesterol levels and blood pressure. Regular exercise also increases muscle strength and offers protection against ligament injuries (W. B. Carter, 1991; Reed, 1991). One study (Blumenthal, 1991) found that exercise training among older adults was associated with significant increases in bone density, although this was more true for males than for females. Additionally, there is even evidence that with regular exercise a person can substantially postpone the age-related decline in the brain's oxidative capacity, in the process improving the information processing that occurs (Birren, Vercruyssen, & Fisher, 1990; Schilke, 1991). Finally, evidence exists (e.g., Blumenthal, 1991; Cowper, 1991; Hansell & Mechanic, 1991; McAuley, Courneya, & Lettunich, 1991; O'Brien & Conger, 1991) that exercise enhances perceived efficacy and psychological well-being among adults, including improvement in psychiatric disturbances such as mood disorders.

The consequences of not exercising and adopting a sedentary lifestyle during the retirement years are numerous. In general, disuse of the body results in decline, including the skeletal system, heart, lungs, and muscles. One becomes weak, has low levels of energy, and has a drooped posture from not exercising. Also, muscle tissue gradually is replaced by fat tissue. Ultimately, all unused tissues and functions atrophy (Antonini & Vannucci, 1990; Barrow & Smith, 1983). As Darrell Menard (1991) puts it, the greatest threat to the continued health of the aged person is not aging processes, but rather the inactivity associated with a sedentary lifestyle. Indeed, there is less risk in activity than there is for continuous inactivity.

▬ Mental Development

Many of us regard elderly people as forgetful, unable to think clearly, repetitive in their storytelling, and even senile. As we explained earlier, many of our impressions of old age originate from inaccurate knowledge or social stereotypes. Although it is true that sensory and motor abilities decline with age, judgment and accumulated knowledge can compensate for these losses. A majority of older people are capable of functioning satisfactorily, the most practical criterion of adaptive ability. Thus it is unfair to say that all elderly persons experience a decline in all phases of mental ability (Aiken 1982; Labouvie-Vief, 1990; Park & Smith, 1991; Sinnott & Cavanaugh, 1991).

Trends in Intellectual Functioning   How do elderly people perform on IQ tests? For this information to be at all meaningful, we must first understand what it is the standard intelligence test is measuring. Research findings indicate a general decline in the capacity to successfully complete tasks requiring physical performance (for example, arranging blocks) and speed (when the score is based on this). Thus lower scores on IQ tests may be due not to a decline in intellectual functions, but, in part, to slower reaction times. Indeed, as we have repeatedly emphasized, many individuals can improve, or at the very least maintain, certain intellectual abilities well into old age (Botwinick, 1984; Schaie, 1980, 1990; Schaie & Willis, 1991).

Some decline may be evident on tests requiring a response within a fixed interval of time, but general knowledge does not appear to decline with age. Also, it should be noted that scores on verbal subtests (for example, vocabulary) occasionally decline slightly with age, but generally remain constant. For more intelligent individuals, it is not uncommon to find an actual increase in certain verbal abilities. Thus, among elderly people, we often find reduced abilities for complex decision making, diminished speed of performance, and a decline in some forms of perception, such as attentional selectivity (Allen, 1991; Jensen & Goldstein, 1991; Madden, 1990; Ng, Giles, & Moody, 1991; Salthouse, 1991).

A study conducted by Robert Kerr and Martha Teaffe (1991) illustrates the foregoing. In their investigation, the manner in which responses to changes in a tracking task were assessed in young and old adult subjects. The researchers found that older subjects had slower reactions and movement times, and the differences became greater as the information processing demands of the task increased. However, elderly people appeared to be just as capable as their younger counterparts in correcting unanticipated movement errors.

Elderly people can maintain
and even improve certain
types of intellectual
functioning.

In areas such as verbal comprehension, social awareness, or the application of experience, elderly people exhibit few losses (Stuart-Hamilton, 1991). For instance, consider a study exploring the academic abilities of elderly college students in Great Britain (Clennel, 1986). Because many of Great Britain's more than 70,000 students in its Open University are aged, administrators set out to determine whether special provisions or accommodations were needed. The results indicated that none were. Indeed, the academic performance of the majority of older students was as good as that of all students above the age of 21. Moreover, the 60 to 64 age group proved to be among the most successful in this unconventional university. Overall, older students reported fewer problems than younger ones. Although 47% expected to have problems with memory, only 26% experienced any. And, where 47% worried about examinations, only 27% had difficulty in practice.

Elderly learners were also more apt to attend special tutorial/counseling sessions organized by the university at local study centers. Additionally, older students were quite amenable to using new technology, such as telephone conference calls, computer terminals, microcomputers, computer-marked assignments, and home experiment kits that included a wide range of specialized equipment. Although arts and social science courses proved most popular with the older student body, a substantial number chose mathematics and science and technology courses, all of which required them to become familiar with new techniques and technology.

Such studies debunk the myth of intellectual deterioration during late adulthood. Additionally, they emphasize how we must place all forms of mental testing into perspective. We need to look carefully at tests and other forms of assessment and examine what they are trying to measure. We cannot generalize about mental abilities; each facet of intelligence needs to be scrutinized. Moreover, when we give elderly persons everyday learning tasks, we should take into consideration what has been revealed in clinical settings. The elderly work best when they are unpressured and can set their own pace. Allowing them to proceed at their own speed enhances learning performances (Pezdek & Miceli, 1982; Rabitt & Backman, 1990).

Another factor to consider regarding intellectual functioning and old age is general state of health (Morris & McManus, 1991; Sinnott & Cavanaugh, 1991; Yesavage, 1990). Healthy aged people generally show little or no loss of intellectual abilities, whereas those approaching death or combating disease may exhibit a marked decline in intellectual function. Such deterioration of intellectual functioning prior to death is referred to by psychologists as the **terminal decline,** or *terminal drop.* In addition to the terminal drop, thinking processes may be altered by a decrease in the blood supply to the brain, extensive hardening of the arteries, significantly high blood pressure, and other cardiovascular problems (Johansson & Berg, 1989; Riegel & Riegel, 1972; Siegler, McCarty, & Logue, 1982).

Let us also acknowledge the continuing creative potential of the older adult. Similar to the myth of intellectual decline, many believe that aging processes rob the person of creative talents. On the contrary, older persons continually succeed in proving that later adulthood can be a productive period of growth and development in terms of intellectual and creative output. In addition, Jon Eisenson (1991) believes the use of creative insights and personal strategies often compensates for declines that otherwise might take place. Indeed, elderly people are often able to improve on their ability to engage in original and spontaneous thinking. Lesa Lorenzen-Huber (1991) adds that creativity can help older adults find satisfaction and meaning in life. In support of the creative potential that looms during late adulthood, consider the following:

CONTINUOUS AND DISCONTINUOUS HUMAN DEVELOPMENT

How do you see the issue of continuity and discontinuity in relation to intelligence during late adulthood? Do you see intelligence remaining continuous or exhibiting decrements during late adulthood? Do you think people get wiser as they get older?

- Johann von Goethe finished the masterpiece *Faust* at age 82.
- Sophocles wrote *Oedipus Rex* when he was 70 and *Electra* when he was 90.
- St. Augustine continued his theological doctrines well beyond his 70th birthday.
- Giuseppe Verdi composed the opera *Otello* at 72 and *Falstaff* at 77.
- Laura Ingalls Wilder wrote some of her best children's stories when she was in her 70s. In fact, her very first book was not published until she was 65.
- Mohandas (Mahatma) Gandhi led India's moral opposition to British rule when he was 77.
- Albert Schweitzer was awarded the Nobel Prize in recognition of his efforts toward world peace when he was 77.
- At 73, Konrad Adenauer became chancellor of West Germany. He served in that capacity for 14 years.
- Jomo Kenyatta became Kenya's first president when he was 70.
- Douglas MacArthur was appointed commander of U.N. forces in Korea when he was 70.
- Cecil B. DeMille remade *The Ten Commandments* when he was 75.
- Ronald Reagan celebrated his 70th birthday during his first year in office as president of the United States.

Such examples of intellectual and creative ability have undoubtedly etched themselves forever in the annals of time. One need not, however, soar to such lofty heights to disprove the myth of mental decline during the retirement years. Intellectual and creative mastery of the world exists in many shapes and forms and may manifest itself in the everyday exploits of older individuals.

INTERRELATEDNESS OF AGING PROCESSES

Can you think of any biological, psychological, or social forces that affect memory dynamics during late adulthood? For instance, do good physical health and stimulating mental environments enhance memory? Drawing from your acquaintances of all ages, can you give examples to support your views?

Thus, although earlier periods of adulthood provide a rich terrain for the accumulation of life experiences and accomplishments, many are now realizing the retirement years offer an equally fruitful and productive span of the life cycle (Butler, 1990; Lorenzen-Huber, 1991; Morris & McManus, 1991; Rabitt & Backman, 1990; Simonton, 1990; Sinnott & Cavanaugh, 1991).

Changes in Memory   In Chapter 10, we discussed the importance of individual variations in mental processes. Although aging processes may bring decreased efficiency in memory abilities for some, this in no way implies that similar changes will occur for all. Whereas sensory and short-term memory do not change much with age, long-term memory exhibits some decline. The problem appears to be less efficient encoding and retrieval processes, although it is recognized that more research is needed on how aging processes affect memory dynamics (Light, 1991).

For example, when considering the changes just described, the character of long-term memory needs to be critically examined before making any definitive conclusions. It may well be that practical long-term memories—for example, those that are frequently recalled—can be readily retrieved compared to those memories that go unrehearsed. Additionally, similar to circumstances in intelligence testing, meaningless and unfamiliar memory tasks testing long-term storage often place elderly people at a disadvantage. And, in virtually every instance, physically healthy, well-educated, and mentally active people do not exhibit the same memory decline as those not sharing similar characteristics (Hendricks & Hendricks, 1981; Sinnott & Cavanaugh, 1991; Stine & Wingfield, 1990).

Also, any discussion of memory changes accompanying aging needs to take into account two of its unique dimensions, namely recall and recognition memory. **Recall memory,** which seems to decrease with age, is searching for and retrieving information in storage (Byrd, 1991; Gerard, 1991; Kausler & Wiley, 1990; Maylor, 1991; Mungas, Ehlers, & Blunden, 1991). **Recognition memory,** which does not appear to decline with age, does not involve retrieval, but rather selecting a correct response from incoming information. For example, in a test situation designed to test recall memory, a subject might be asked, "Who was the third president of the United States?" The correct answer requires a search of one's memory storage system and retrieval of the answer: Thomas Jefferson. To test recognition memory, the subject would be asked, "Among these five names, which one is the third president of the United States?" Here, a match is required. Retrieval is not thought of as part of the mental process (Birren, Woods, & Williams, 1980; Botwinick, 1984; Maylor, 1990; Smith, 1980).

Finally, we remind you that adults of all ages can improve on their memory skills. Among younger and older adults, improvement has been shown using techniques such as practice, reinforcement, and imagery. In fact, one study (Fozard, 1980) shows that older persons are extremely efficient in retrieving information from long-term storage, particularly when they are not anxious or when they receive some type of cognitive support. Indeed, Lars Backman and colleagues (1990) note that adult age-related differences in memory decrease or even disappear when the environment guides the older learner in initiating appropriate operations of remembering.

Along these lines, a study conducted by Lawrence Ressler (1991) illustrates how a bimodal presentation enhances an older person's retention abilities. In this investigation, subjects between the ages of 61 and 89 were studied. One group was presented with oral information about hospital discharge planning; a second group was given identical information but with both oral information and visual aids. Subjects from both groups were interviewed the next day to discover how much of the information they had retained. The results showed that the bimodal presentation increased the amount of information recalled by the subjects. However, it was noted that even a bimodal presentation does not ensure older persons will be able to recall all information. Rather, other aids, such as writing the information down, may be necessary.

UNIT REVIEW—

- ↗ Gerontology and allied disciplines such as social gerontology and geriatrics are extremely active fields of study in lifespan development today.

- ↗ Physical aging processes during late adulthood continue to be both external and internal. There is also a gradual decrease in sensory capacities, most notably vision and hearing.

- ↗ Late adulthood is not synonymous with poor health. However, certain health disorders are more prevalent at this time, including arthritis, hypertension, heart disease, cerebrovascular accident, cancer, and osteoporosis.

- ↗ Although elderly people may exhibit declines in certain mental functions, such as reaction times, intelligence for most is characterized more by continuity than discontinuity and change. If memory storage systems are affected by aging processes, it is more likely to be the long-term bank.

UNIT TWO: PERSONALITY AND SOCIAL DEVELOPMENT

The retirement years, much like any other stage of the life cycle, pose their unique share of developmental tasks and challenges. In many respects the tasks posed at this time—such as changes in physical health, financial status, or social adjustments—are more of a challenge than those faced during any other stage of adulthood. Late adulthood is also a critical period of self-assessment, a time to reevaluate one's successes and failures. And, while evaluating the past and attempting to deal with the present, the older person is faced with preparing for the future. As we see throughout this chapter, successfully adjusting to later life challenges requires considerable flexibility and adaptation (Hildebrand, 1990; Seedsman, 1990; Stuart-Hamilton, 1991).

▬ Theories of Personality Development

A number of noteworthy theories have been proposed to explain the dynamics of personality growth in later life. Once again, we encounter the issue of long-term continuity or change in the adult personality (see Chapter 10 for a detailed discussion of this issue). Let's explore each perspective.

The Continuity Perspective   As we have learned, some investigators maintain the adult personality remains relatively unaltered from earlier years. Support for this perspective emerges from longitudinal studies, most notably the research of Paul Costa and Robert McCrae (1976, 1977, 1978, 1980a, 1980b, 1982, 1984, 1986, 1988, 1989). To review, Costa and McCrae measured the personality dimensions of 2,000 men between the ages of 20 to 80 every 6 years. Results showed that these personality dimensions remained highly stable over time, prompting the researchers to observe that early personality functioning is a good guide to that unfolding during the retirement years.

Other research demonstrates evidence for stability of personality in late adulthood (Hagberg, 1991). For example, the research of Dorothy Field and Roger Millsap (1991) centers on the Berkeley Older Generation Study, a longitudinal investigation of adults launched in 1928. This investigation of elderly adults found evidence of personality continuity throughout all of adult life. More specifically, repeated measures on five personality traits reflected considerable stability: agreeableness, satisfaction, intellect, extraversion, and energetic. Satisfaction remained particularly continuous and stable throughout adult life. But, some change was also apparent. For instance, an upswing in agreeableness and a decline in extraversion became apparent with advancing years in late adulthood. Studies measuring psychological well-being over the course of adulthood (e. g., Markides & Lee, 1990) also provide evidence of stability and continuity.

But although there is growing evidence that enduring personality traits exist, certain dispositions can and do change over the course of the adult years. For

The convergence of psychological and social forces is evident throughout the entire life course.

example, interests and attitudes appear to fluctuate over time, as do levels of self-assurance and patterns of role-taking behaviors (Bengston, Reedy, & Gordon, 1985). Yet, despite the fact that some personality traits are less consistent over time, the notion of personality consistency has important implications for the study of the aging adult. Indeed, enduring traits help shed light on the abilities and needs of aging persons as they face such developmental challenges as retirement or widowhood. Also, the stability of personality traits figures prominently into the overall concept of successful aging, which we discuss later on in this chapter.

The Discontinuity Perspective   Unlike the continuous perspective, the discontinuous theories of Erik Erikson, Robert Peck, and Daniel Levinson propose that personality during late adulthood is characterized by change. Recall that these theories have woven their way throughout all of adulthood (see Chapters 9 and 10). Let's examine each of these theories in more detail.

ERIK ERIKSON'S THEORY Erik Erikson (1950, 1958, 1959, 1963, 1968a, 1968b, 1969, 1978, 1980, 1982) suggests that the key to harmonious personality development in the later years of life is the ability to resolve the psychosocial crisis known as **integrity versus despair.** Ego *integrity* implies a full unification of the personality. The manner in which this crisis is met depends on a number of other factors, including the relevance of social roles, the lifestyle, and physical health.

Ego integration enables individuals to view their lives with satisfaction and contentment. Having had satisfying social relationships and a productive life promotes a feeling of well-being and a sense of purpose. The lack of this accrued ego integration is frequently signaled by a fear of death and the feeling that life is too short. Individuals experiencing *despair* feel time is running out and it is too late to start another life or try out alternate roads to integrity. Consequently, they view their lives with regret and disappointment. Many wish they had made fuller use of their potential to attain goals established earlier in life. Thus the stage of integrity versus despair has psychological as well as social relevance to development in the retirement years.

EPIGENETIC PRINCIPLE

How do you view this final stage of Erikson's epigenetic design? In your estimation, does it bring lifelong psychosocial dynamics to a satisfactory conclusion? Why or why not?

ROBERT PECK'S THEORY Robert Peck (1968) maintains that psychological growth during the retirement years is characterized by three primary psychological adjustments: **ego differentiation versus work-role preoccupation, body transcendence versus body preoccupation,** and **ego transcendence versus ego preoccupation.**

Ego Differentiation Versus Work-Role Preoccupation. The central issue here is the impact of vocational retirement. This represents a crucial shift in individual value systems. Personal worth must be reappraised and redefined, so the retiree can take satisfaction in activities extending beyond his or her long-time specific work role. Peck believes ego differentiation is a centrally important issue at the time of retirement. A sense of self-worth derived from activities beyond one's career is apparently crucial to establishing a continued, vital interest in living instead of a despairing loss of meaning in life. Consequently, establishing a variety of valued self-attributes so any one of several alternatives can be pursued with satisfaction may be a critical prerequisite for successful aging.

Body Transcendence Versus Body Preoccupation. The retirement years bring most people a marked decline in resistance to illness, a decline in recuperative powers, and an increase in bodily aches and pains. For those who equate comfort and pleasure with physical well-being, this decline in health may represent the gravest of insults. There are other older people, however, who experience declining health, yet enjoy life greatly. This has led some to believe that the elderly person's bodily concerns are not related to age per se, but rather reflect special life circumstances. Some people may have learned to define "happiness" and "comfort" in terms of satisfying human relationships or creative mental activities, with which only sheer physical destruction could seriously interfere. In their value system, social and mental pleasures and self-respect may go beyond physical comfort alone. This kind of value system may well have to be developed by early adulthood, if it is to be achieved at all, and the retirement years may bring the most critical test of whether such a value system has indeed been internalized.

Ego Transcendence Versus Ego Preoccupation. One of the crucial tasks of elderly people is coming to the realization they will die. In earlier years, death often comes unexpectedly, but in old age its inevitability is recognized. Accepting its inevitability is not a stage of passive resignation or ego denial. On the contrary, it requires a deep, active effort to make life more secure and meaningful, or happier, for those who will go on living after one dies. In so doing, elderly people are experiencing a vital, gratifying absorption in the future, and they are doing all they can to make it a good world for their familial or cultural descendants. This might be interpreted as vicarious satisfaction, but it actually represents an active and significant involvement with daily life as long as one lives. It might also be viewed as the most complete kind of ego realization, even as it is focused on people and issues that go far beyond immediate self-gratification in the narrow sense.

DANIEL LEVINSON'S THEORY Daniel Levinson (1977, 1980, 1981, 1984, 1986, 1990, in press; Levinson et al., 1978; Levinson & Gooden, 1985) theorizes that late adulthood, like early and middle adulthood, is initially characterized by a transition period. The *late adult transition* occurs between the ages of 60 and 65. He stresses that a person does not suddenly become "old" at this time, but changing mental and physical capacities intensify one's awareness of aging and sense of mortality.

Like Robert Peck, Levinson pays attention to the relationship between physical changes of the body and one's personality. He suggests that at this time there is an increasing frequency of death and serious illness among a person's loved ones and friends. There may also be reminders of decreasing capacities, such as aches and pains. Although there are always wide individual variations in health, there is a strong likelihood that a person will experience at least one major illness or impairment—whether it be heart disease, cancer, defective vision or hearing, or depression. Such physical changes may be hard to accept, especially for a person accustomed to good health in previous years.

The late adult transition is also marked by the individual's awareness that there is a culturally defined change of generation in the 60s. A person who found the term *middle age* vague and frightening may find it even more difficult to accept society's terminology and imagery for the subsequent years of life. Such terms as *elderly, golden age,* and *senior citizen* have a tendency to acquire negative connotations, reflecting personal and cultural anxiety about aging. As Levinson says, to a person in his 20s it appears as though passing 30 is getting "over the hill." When 30, turning 40 is a powerful threat. At each point in life, it seems the passing of the next age threshold is anticipated as a total loss of youth, vitality, and life itself.

In late adulthood, people come to the realization that they can no longer occupy center stage in their world. They are called upon, and increasingly call upon themselves, to reduce middle adulthood's heavy responsibilities and to live in a changed relationship with society and themselves. Moving out of center stage can be a traumatic affair because people receive less recognition and have less power and authority. Their generation is no longer the dominant one. As part of the "grandparent" generation within the family, individuals still can be helpful to their grown offspring and serve as a source of wisdom, guidance, and support.

Retiring with dignity and security is another important developmental challenge. Whatever the age of retirement happens to be, this event should reflect a person's needs, capabilities, and life circumstances. If this is the case, then after retirement the individual can engage in valued work. Now, however, it should stem from creative energies, rather than from external pressure and financial need. Having paid one's dues to society, an individual has earned the right to be and do what is personally rewarding and pleasing.

At the end of the life cycle, people come to grips with the process of dying and prepare for their own death. Whereas at the end of the previous stages they looked forward to the start of a new era and a new basis for living, now they know death is imminent. Although death may come in a few months or 20 years, individuals live in its shadow and at its call.

At this time, people are, above all else, reaching ultimate involvement with themselves. What matters most now is their final sense of what life is about, what Levinson describes as "one's view from the bridge" at the end of the life cycle. Such an analysis offers a unique parallel to the Eriksonian sense of integrity described earlier. The ultimate task is finally coming to terms with the self, particularly knowing it and loving it reasonably well, and being ready to give it up.

▬ Patterns of Successful Aging

Successful aging is difficult to explain, and frequently the description merely reflects the values of the person doing the defining. However, Linda George and Elizabeth Clipp (1991) maintain that successful aging and subjective well-being have become synonymous with life satisfaction and related concepts, such as happiness and morale. Their review of the literature indicates that three major findings on the topic of successful aging have surfaced. First, strong evidence exists that most older people have successfully aged and are generally satisfied with their lives. Second, levels of life satisfaction tend to be stable over time. Third, life satisfaction and successful aging are related strongly to objective life conditions, including socioeconomic status, health, and relationships with family and friends.

A number of studies have supplied insight into the concept of successful aging, and have emphasized such components as self-esteem, role adaptation, resiliency, and personal control over one's life (Baltes & Baltes, 1990; Brandstadter

& Baltes-Gotz, 1990; Carlsen, 1991; Eisenson, 1991; Krause & Alexander, 1990). One of the more interesting research ventures was a longitudinal study of individuals tracked since 1940 (Vaillant, 1990). It was discovered that mental health between the ages of 30 and 50 proved to be the best predictor of later life outcomes. The absence of psychiatric vulnerability in young adulthood, along with the absence of the use of psychiatrists or tranquilizers in the same period, appeared to be the most important variables in predicting later adjustment. Other, more obvious negative causal variables, such as shortened familial longevity, maladaptive childhoods, and alcoholism, appeared to be associated more frequently with physical decline. Other outcomes were more surprising. For example, extensive exercise in college predicted psychosocial adjustment at age 65 better than it did good health. And a warm and nurturant childhood environment predicted good physical health in later adulthood better than it did happiness and vigor.

Other research centers on successful aging and the relative degree of involvement with one's surroundings. For example, is successful aging characterized by an active lifestyle and heightened involvement with others, or are elderly persons more satisfied when their life space shrinks and their responsibilities and roles lessen? Two of the older, yet noteworthy efforts to find answers to such questions are the disengagement and activity theories. Although each offers unique insight into the topic of successful aging, and certain support for each theoretical position can be found, it is important to note that neither perspective fully explains the phenomenon of successful adjustment.

The Disengagement Theory   **Disengagement theory** views aging as a mutual withdrawal process between aging persons and the social system to which they belong. Contrary to popular impression, such a gradual withdrawal from society is not a negative experience for elderly people. The aged frequently view disengagement in a positive light because this is an age of increased reflection, preoccupation with the self, and decreased emotional investment in people and events. Thus disengagement is viewed as a natural rather than an imposed process.

The disengagement theory was the result of a 5-year investigation of a sample of 275 elderly persons aged between 50 and 90. The study was conducted in Kansas City, Missouri, and headed by Elaine Cumming and William Henry (1961). The researchers noted that disengagement was generally initiated by the individuals themselves or by the social system. Retirement, for example, is an event that releases older people from specific social roles and enables them to become disengaged to some extent. Loss of a spouse serves as another example. In time, when disengagement is complete, the balance that existed between the individual and society in the middle years has shifted to an equilibrium characterized by greater psychological distance, altered types of relationships, and decreased social interaction.

Seven years after this study, a follow-up was launched by Robert Havighurst, Bernice Neugarten, and Sheldon Tobin (1968). Because of such factors as deaths and geographical moves, the follow-up sample contained only 55% of the people in the original study. This second study showed that although increasing age is accompanied by increasing disengagement from common social roles, some elderly people who remained active and engaged reported relatively

Patterns of living vary widely among elderly people. While some prefer to withdraw gradually from others and pursue individual activities, others are happiest when they remain socially active.

high degrees of contentment. On the whole, those who were most active were happiest.

This latter point represents the biggest criticism of the disengagement theory, which in general has aroused considerable controversy among gerontologists. That is, many feel (e.g., Holahan, 1988) that those who disengage least are happier than those who have chosen to withdraw more fully. Furthermore, many of the past societal conditions forcing adults into restricted environments have changed. Improved health care, early retirement, increased Social Security benefits, and higher education levels have created new areas of pursuit for elderly people. Because of these social factors, disengagement may be discouraged and more active lifestyles encouraged. The current view among gerontologists is that disengagement represents only one of many possible patterns of aging. It has no blanket application to all old people (Kermis, 1984).

The Activity Theory   The **activity theory** of successful aging, developed by George Maddox (1964) and his colleagues at Duke University, suggests that retired individuals prefer to remain productive and active. In contrast to the theory of disengagement, this viewpoint maintains that the aged prefer to resist preoccupation with the self and psychological distance from society. Happiness and satisfaction originate from involvement and the older person's ability to adjust to changing life events.

How valid is the activity theory of aging? Once again, just as we pointed out in the theory of disengagement, the activity viewpoint looms as only one possible aging pattern. It cannot be applied to all because not all activities influence the self-concept and life satisfaction in general. As Russell Ward (1984) points out, one's activity can decline without affecting morale. Indeed, a more leisurely lifestyle is often regarded as one of the rewards of old age. Some research, such as that conducted by Charles Longino and Cary Kart (1982), actually reveals a negative association between formal social activities and overall life satisfaction.

Such findings lead many to believe the activity theory has oversimplified the issues involved. It may hardly be appropriate to substitute pastimes, geared to what is believed to be older persons' interests and abilities, for those roles they

ACTIVE AND REACTIVE MODELS OF DEVELOPMENT

How might active and reactive models of development be applied to the study of successful aging? Do you think the environment is largely responsible for shaping the adjustments of older adults, or do you feel active involvement regulates successful aging? Have your views of active and reactive models changed from earlier developmental stages?

relinquished as they moved beyond middle age. Occupying oneself with enterprises that are meaningless in terms of dominant cultural values, presumably still subscribed to by older people, may not in itself contribute to adjustment. Nevertheless, it may be that there is an association between morale, personality adjustment, and activity levels (Hendricks & Hendricks, 1981).

Personality Makeup and Successful Aging   Because some individuals are satisfied with disengagement and others prefer to maintain a high level of social engagement, it is evident that a broader perspective is needed to provide gerontologists with a useful theory of successful aging. Many agree a theory of the relationship of personality to successful aging is needed.

One such theory was developed by Suzanne Reichard, Florine Livson, and Paul Peterson (1962). In an analysis of 87 men ranging in age from 55 to 84, these researchers identified five personality types: mature (constructive); rocking chair type (dependent); armored (defensive); angry (hostile); and self-haters. *Mature* people seem to be ideally adjusted. They accept themselves (strengths as well as weaknesses) and their past lives. Most are relatively free of neurotic conflicts and maintain close personal relationships. The *rocking chair* type also has a high level of self-acceptance, although this acceptance is frequently passive. Individuals in this category are dependent on others and perceive old age as freedom from responsibility. The *armored* rely considerably on defense mechanisms to cope with whatever negative emotions arise. Typically well adjusted, the armored are fairly rigid individuals who have active lifestyles, presumably as a means of demonstrating their independent character. The *angry* are not well adjusted and make a habit of expressing their bitterness, often in an aggressive manner. They openly blame others for their troubles and are easily frustrated. The *self-haters* are similar to the angry, but blame themselves for their difficulties and failures. They are characteristically depressed and view old age as a demoralizing stage of life. The mature, the rocking chair type, and the armored in the study were successful at aging. The angry and the self-haters were less adaptive.

A similar classification of personality types and their implication for successful aging is apparent in another study (Neugarten, Havighurst, & Tobin, 1968). Investigating elderly subjects between the ages of 70 and 79, these researchers viewed personality and role activity as critical determinants of life satisfaction. They identified personality types similar to those devised by Reichard and her associates (1962), namely, integrated, armored-defended, passive-dependent, and unintegrated. Unlike the Reichard group, however, Neugarten and her associates categorized specific types of role activities within these major types.

The *integrated* type of personality includes the reorganizers, the focused, and the successfully disengaged. The reorganizers are involved in a wide range of activities and as the title suggests, they reorganize their lives to substitute new activities for lost ones. The focused engage in moderate levels of activity. They are more selective about their activities than the reorganizers, and they tend to devote their energy to one or two role areas. The disengaged have low activity levels and high life satisfaction (thus supporting the disengagement theory of successful aging). With age they have voluntarily moved away from role commitments.

The *armored-defended* category includes holding-on and constricted personality patterns. Holding-on individuals attempt to cling as long as possible to activities of middle age. As long as they succeed in doing this, they attain high levels of life satisfaction. The constricted reduce their role activities and involvements with other people, presumably as a defense against aging. They differ from the focused group in that they have less integrated personalities.

The *passive-dependent* personality category consists of two types: succorance seeking and apathetic. The succorance seekers are dependent on others and frequently seek emotional support. They maintain a medium level of role activity and life satisfaction. Apathetic individuals are characteristically passive and have little or no interest in their surroundings.

The last category consists of *disorganized* persons. Many have poor control over their emotions and have deteriorated thought processes. They barely maintain themselves in the community and have low or at best medium levels of life satisfaction.

These two studies indicate that personality is the pivotal factor in determining whether an individual will age successfully, and that the activity and disengagement theories, alone, are inadequate to explain successful aging. Successful aging is greatly influenced by many factors, including health, socioeconomic status, level of self-esteem, and self-concept. The relationships between levels of activities and life satisfaction are influenced by all facets of one's personality makeup, and particularly by the extent to which the individual remains able to integrate emotional and rational elements of the personality (Sherman, 1981).

It is also apparent that no one pattern of aging guarantees satisfaction in the later years. Satisfaction, morale, and adaptation in later life generally appear to be closely related to a person's lifelong personality style and general way of dealing with stress and change. In this sense, the past is prologue to the future. Although the personality changes somewhat in response to various life events and changes, it generally remains stable throughout all of adult life (Reedy, 1983). In the Lifespan Development in Action box on pages 602–603, we offer some of the factors we feel are important in regard to successful aging.

The Life Review and Reminiscence Among older adults, it is fairly common to reminisce about the past with advancing years. Gerontologist Robert Butler (1968; Butler & Lewis, 1981) refers to this psychological process as the **life review** and describes it as a looking-back process set in motion by the prospect of one's mortality. Such a mental process allows the individual to relive past experiences and perhaps deal with persisting conflicts. It may culminate in wisdom, serenity, and peace, or it may produce depression, guilt, or anger.

Reviewing one's past life is especially important for the aged. Faced with isolation, the loss of loved ones, and the nearness of death, elderly people frequently seek to escape into the past. Reminiscing may produce nostalgia, happiness, and satisfaction, but in other instances it can trigger mild regret or even despair. Reminiscing may first consist of stray and seemingly insignificant thoughts about one's self and one's life history. These thoughts may persist in brief intermittent spurts or may become continuous. Some thought patterns

Lifespan Development in Action

GROWING OLD GRACEFULLY: INGREDIENTS TO SUCCESS

The retirement years can be just as positive, satisfying, and rewarding as any other period in the life cycle. Testimony to this are the millions of older adults in the United States who are leading active, happy, and useful lives. What is it about their lifestyle or personality dynamics that promote fulfillment? Can any factors be identified that promote successful aging? Although answers to such questions are complex, certain factors associated with successful aging have nonetheless been identified:

A high degree of life satisfaction. Those who feel their life has been rewarding typically face their later years with few regrets and considerable personal satisfaction. Persons with considerable life satisfaction also have a positive attitude about the past and the future. Consequently, life remains stimulating and interesting. Moreover, those who have met most of their personal, career, and financial goals will be able to relax during retirement and even go on to set new goals.

Harmonious integration of one's personality. This dimension of adjustment is connected to Maslow's concept of self-actualization (see Chapter 10). Individuals demonstrating satisfaction, individuation, and authenticity during late adulthood are likely those who have developed ego strength and maturity over the years. Their personalities are marked by integration and unity, and they continue to make use of their potentialities and capabilities during this life stage. Moreover, they possess accurate self-concepts as well as stable and meaningful value systems.

Maintenance of a meaningful social support system. We are all social creatures, and the need for human contact is lifelong. All adults need a stimulating, caring network of family and friends to keep involved and interested in life. One's social network fills the need for affection, attachment, belonging, and a positive sense of well-being. All of these needs are psychological vitamins that better prepare individuals for the retirement experience.

Good physical and mental health. The status of body and mind is critical to one's overall sense of well-being. Proper nutrition, exercise, and preventive health care are the ingredients to good health and to feeling positive about oneself. Developing healthy lifestyle habits will keep the body fit, improve mental attitudes, help relieve anxiety and depression, and stimulate mental functioning.

Establishment of financial security. Not having enough money to meet the demands of day-to-day living can cause concerns throughout all of adulthood, not just the retirement years. However, the lack of financial security can intensify many of the problems associated with growing old. This underscores the need for careful financial planning, including investment protection and adequate health-care coverage. Also, older adults need to familiarize themselves with community programs, such as senior discounts,

GROWING OLD GRACEFULLY, Continued . . .

prescription subsidies, and fuel or telephone assistance. Steps taken to safe-guard financial stability will help promote inner security and well-being.

Personal control over one's life. Everyone needs to feel independent and autonomous, especially so during late adulthood. Personal control plays an important role in successful aging because adults need to be in charge of their personal fate. Even the well-intentioned intervention of family and friends can rob an older adult not only of control, but sometimes of the will to continue living. Independence is vital to the maintenance of a positive self-concept, sense of dignity, and self-worth. (Adapted from Averyt, 1987)

may undergo continual reorganization and reintegration at various levels of awareness.

The existence of the life review and reminiscing is also evident in dreams and thoughts. The elderly frequently report dreams and nightmares that focus on the past and even on death. Furthermore, images of past events appear frequently in waking life as well, indicating that reminiscing is a highly visual process. Those who can think clearly and have good memory skills can bring clear and accurate episodes of their past to the conscious level.

The life review and reminiscing in general serve as a major step in overall personality functioning at this time. Such reflection provides continuity to one's life and renews an awareness of the present. By recalling the past, the older adult is able to survey, observe, and reflect on years gone by, and thus new insight into life's experience is often achieved. Additionally, elderly people can establish new insights by being good listeners, even though they have heard the story or the exchange of other information before.

In recent years, a rich vein of research has focused on the importance of reminiscence (Beaton, 1991; Habegger & Blieszner, 1990; Haight, 1991b; Hewett, 1991; Taft & Nehrke, 1990; Watt & Wong, 1991; Weiss et al., 1991). Edmund Sherman (1991), for instance, feels that no other private mental activity appears to encourage to such a degree an inclination toward sharing and mutuality in human discourse. It looms as a powerful force in enhancing mental health and socializing older adults. David Unruh (1989) feels reminiscence is an important psychological process influenced by social setting and situations. Emotional states and outcomes are important features of recalling past experiences. Indeed, the moods and sentiments that lead people into a state of reminiscence are as important as the emotional outcome of the process. In one study of widowed men (David, 1990), elaboration of memories and life reviewing were associated with life satisfaction and positive adaptation. Another investigation (Giltinan, 1990) focusing on perceived quality of life among elderly women in a group setting found that reminiscing fostered positive self-regard and a sense of belongingness among group members.

Finally, in addition to its psychological benefits, Howard Thorsheim and Bruce Roberts (1990) feel that reminiscing enhances memory abilities. By this, reflecting on the past activates memories consisting of thoughts, feelings, and

Reminiscing about the past enables elderly people to relive past experiences and remember special moments.

experiences within each person. One way to aid memory is the use of mnemonic devices, which may consist of mental pictures, sounds, aromas, or sensations of touch associated with particular things an individual wants to remember. One effective aid in recalling experiences is to use photographs. Many photographs contain details that evoke people, scenes, events, or specific objects experienced in the past. Another aid to reminiscence is to recall the titles, words, and music of old songs. These songs may bring to mind the people, places, and activities associated with them in the past (Kartman, 1991). Reminiscence is even used as a therapeutic tool to increase the functioning level of demented patients.

Psychological Maladjustment

The retirement years, or for that matter any stage of the life cycle, are not always characterized by successful adjustments. On the contrary, the stresses associated with aging may cause some individuals to become maladjusted. Such maladjustment can be principally psychological, in which case we say the individual has a **functional disorder.** Examples of functional disorders include anxiety disorders (e.g., phobias, panic attacks), mood disorders (e.g., major depression, bipolar disorder), or somatoform disorders (e.g., hypochondria, conversion disorders). The elderly may also suffer from **organic brain syndrome,** cognitive and behavioral maladjustment due to brain dysfunction. Examples of organic brain syndrom include the dementias, which, as we see shortly, can be reversible or irreversible.

Prevalency and Trends   About 15 to 25% of adults over age 65 in the United States exhibit some symptoms of mental illness. The incidence rate is higher for those in poor physical health, advanced in age, or unmarried as a result of divorce, separation, or widowhood. Older adults also represent about 20% of all first admissions to psychiatric hospitals (Haight, 1991a; Stephens, 1990). One source (Harper, 1990) estimates that more than one half of the residents in long-term care facilities demonstrate some type of mental illness. Given such widespread proportions, researchers agree we need to learn more about maladjustment among elderly people, particularly its causes and the most effective avenues of treatment (Cohen, 1991; Faulkner, 1991; Harper, 1991; Hinrichsen, 1990; Hogstel, 1990).

It is recognized that elderly people make little use of mental health services (Fogel, Gottlieb, & Furino, 1990; Lundervold et al., 1990). Several reasons account for this. For one, older persons are often reluctant to seek help. Many turn to their inner resources for help, such as family and friends. Also, a certain amount of mental illness may be more expected and tolerated in the aged. Another reason is that some therapists may be reluctant to treat elderly people because they mistakenly think the aged cannot benefit from counseling. Finally therapists may not have the training or background to deal with the psychological problems of elderly people. Thus although the need of mental health services of this age group is as great if not greater than that of any other adult age group, limited numbers secure such help (Cutrona, 1991; Gurland & Toner, 1991; Kamholz & Gottlieb, 1990; Reedy, 1983) .

The financial problems often besetting elderly people affect the nature and quality of mental health care received. Many simply cannot afford care, and those who can may receive less than adequate treatment. The medical profession is sometimes guilty of misdiagnosing symptoms or misprescribing medication among the aged (Richelson, 1990; Snow, 1990; Taft & Barkin, 1990). Some aren't knowledgeable about the side effects of certain drugs; others may prescribe medication when it is not needed or go to the extreme of prescribing excessive amounts (Ghose, 1991; Tully & Tallis, 1991). Drug-taking patterns among elderly people, too, may pose problems. For example, in one study (Enlund, 1990) of noninstitutionalized men between the ages of 64 to 84 using prescription drugs, 41% had deviated from instructions to some extent. Noncompliance was more common among those with complex medication regimens and poor memory. Other studies (Jankel, 1991; Kottke, 1990; Palmieri, 1991) report similar difficulties among elderly people in taking prescribed medication, particularly adhering to the actual dosage and properly reading medication labels.

At least part of the problem appears to be the limited numbers of mental health professionals specializing in geriatric psychiatry (Adelman, Greene, & Charon, 1991; Lunardini, Cunningham, & Warren, 1991). Some physicians regard old age as irreversible; illness (particularly mental illness) occurring in later life is viewed as beyond therapeutic intervention. In the past, excessive reliance on physical and chemical restraints often became treatment practices, with scarcely any concern for finding reversible causes, effecting a remission, or bringing about optimal rehabilitation. More and more, the goal of optimal psychopharmacological technique in the treatment of elderly people is the production of remission in the shortest time possible, avoiding as many side effects as possible (Buckwalter, 1991; Feinberg, 1990; Heath, 1991; Levenson & Beller, 1983; Maletta, Mattox, & Dysken, 1991).

INTERACTION OF HEREDITY AND ENVIRONMENT

Do you think the interaction of heredity and environment can help explain later life psychological stability or instability? Do you think elderly people face unique stressors that create vulnerability to psychological maladjustment? If so, how might the environment be shaped to reduce the risk of mental illness?

Functional Disorders   Functional disorders in old age are related to psychological causes and interpersonal factors that may persist from youth into the later years or may appear for the first time in the aged person. The following represents a brief overview of some of the more common functional disorders during late adulthood.

ANXIETY DISORDERS People suffering from **anxiety disorders** may have tension, trembling, rapid heartbeat, or accelerated breathing. Anxiety disorders are less common among the aged than among younger adults. Among the more frequent sources of anxiety during old age is perceived helplessness or loss (Alexopoulos, 1991; Birkett, 1991; Bowman, 1992; Gurian & Miner, 1991). One source (Blazer, George, & Hughes, 1991) indicates that anxiety disorders such as phobic disorders, panic disorders, and obsessive-compulsive disorders are less common during later life than during earlier adult years. People suffering from anxiety disorders do not grossly distort reality or exhibit profound personality disorganization.

SCHIZOPHRENIC DISORDERS With **schizophrenic disorders,** the disorganization of the personality is extensive, and there is failure to evaluate reality correctly. Memory distortion as well as deficiencies in language and perception are characteristic symptoms. Paranoid disorders have a tendency to increase among the aged, including feelings of persecution and suspicion. Whereas in young people paranoia often reflects severe psychiatric disturbance, among elderly people, there are fewer psychiatric implications. Along these lines, degrees of paranoia and suspiciousness often exist among those who have sensory deficiencies, particularly in hearing (Birkett, 1991; C. Cohen, 1990; Reedy, 1983; Riley, 1990; Yassa, Uhr, & Jeste, 1991).

AFFECTIVE DISORDERS **Affective disorders,** broadly defined, are mood disturbances. These can include a *manic disorder,* in which the person feels unusually elated; **depression,** characterized by sadness and a sense of hopelessness; and a *bipolar disorder,* marked by fluctuations of both mania and

For some, late adulthood brings psychological maladjustment.

depression. Of these, depression is most common during late adulthood (Cadieux & Adams, 1990; Molinari, 1991; Schooler, 1991). The elderly are vulnerable because they usually experience multiple losses during these years, including declining health (Freedland, 1991; Grossberg, 1990). One study of elderly African Americans (Husaini, 1991) showed that low feelings of self-regard and reduced contact with family and friends also triggered depression, although the latter was more true for women than men. Depression in severe form is characterized by intense sadness, hopelessness, pessimism, and poor self-regard. Depressed individuals usually experience a weight loss, sleeplessness, fatigue, and poor concentration abilities. Many exhibit decreased purposeful activity (Buckwalter, 1990; Dhingra & Rabins, 1991; George, 1992; J. Stewart, 1991).

It is not uncommon for severe depression to be accompanied by suicidal thoughts (Koenig, 1991; Newmann, Engel, & Jensen, 1991). The suicide rate for men increases steadily with age. Nancy Osgood (1991) informs us that the suicide rate for those 65 years of age and older is 50% higher than for those who are 15 to 24, and higher than the nation as a whole. For women, the suicide rate reaches a peak in middle age and always remains lower than it is for men. Organic brain syndromes, substance abuse, terminal illness, and mood disorders increase the risk of suicide among the aged. Compared to younger people, elderly people are also more likely to be successful in the actual suicide attempt (Blazer, 1991; Reedy, 1983; Strasburger & Welpton, 1991).

PERSONALITY DISORDERS **Personality disorders** reflect maladaptive patterns of thinking or behaving. Those with a *narcissistic personality disorder* exhibit a grandiose sense of self-importance; the *antisocial personality disorder* is characterized by the absence of any internal discomfort. The prevalency of both types is considered low among elderly people compared to rates for younger adults (George, 1990; Rosowsky & Gurian, 1991).

SUBSTANCE-USE DISORDERS **Substance-use disorders** include the physical and psychological dependence on alcohol and drugs. Among elderly people, alcohol abuse is considered widespread (Avogaro, 1990; Dunlop, Manghelli, & Tolson, 1990; Jacyk, 1991; Liptzin, 1991; Merrill, 1990). One source (Green & Bridgham, 1991) estimates that over 3 million people aged 65 and over have alcohol-related problems. Furthermore, many nursing homes for elderly people report that as many as one half of their patients have lost the ability to live independently because of alcohol abuse. Lawrence Schonfeld and Lawrence Dupree (1990) identify two types of older problem drinkers: the "early onset" and "late-life" alcohol abusers. The "early onset" elderly drinker has demonstrated significant alcohol-related problems for many years, having begun drinking by his or her 30s or 40s. In contrast, the "late-life" elderly drinker usually begins abusing alcohol in his or her 50s or 60s and is often viewed as a reactive drinker, that is, one whose problem begins after the occurrence of such events as the death of a spouse, retirement, or impaired health.

Organic Brain Syndrome Individuals with organic brain syndrome constitute the largest group of institutionalized elderly mental patients. Organic brain syndrome disorders afflict 5 to 10% of people between the ages of 65 and 75 and a steadily rising proportion in older age groups. Among individuals between the ages of 90 and 100, the figure climbs to 20%. For reasons unknown, organic brain syndrome is more common among women than men. Organic brain syndromes are primarily the result of massive loss of brain cells in the cerebral cortex. They produce such symptoms as disorientation, delusions, paranoia, verbal irritability, wandering, frequent nighttime awakenings, loss of memory for both recent and distant events, and the inability to perform routine tasks (Ballard, 1991; Chithiramohan, 1991; Cohen, 1989; Gottfries, 1990; Knopman & Sawyer-DeMaris, 1990; Reedy, 1983).

THE DEMENTIAS The family of disorders caused by brain impairment are known technically as the dementias. **Dementia** refers to generalized cognitive and behavioral deterioration due to brain dysfunction. At one time, age was used as a classification for dementia, with clinicians using nomenclature such as "presenile" and "senile" to describe its onset. However, contemporary researchers (e.g., Brock, 1990; Mace, 1991; Reisberg, 1990) prefer to move away from such classifications, largely because age makes little difference in the varieties of neurological changes experienced. Reference is instead made to *reversible* dementia and *irreversible* degenerative dementia. Reversible dementia is known as **delirium.** The causes of delirium are varied, including the toxic effects of medications, malnutrition, poor oxygenation, heart disease, seizures, and infection. Some of the symptoms are restlessness, disorientation, delusions, disturbances in sleep patterns, and memory deficits (Berg, 1991; Folstein, 1991; Harper, 1991).

David Solomon and colleagues (1992) point out that once the underlying cause of the delirium is corrected, the disorder will usually subside spontaneously, albeit sometimes slowly. It is usually helpful to have a quiet, well-lit environment to help reduce the stimulation that may aggravate delirium. Having a family member or friend nearby may also help. Sometimes, medications are needed to control the individual's restlessness and agitation. However bad the symptoms of delirium may seem, the condition is usually temporary and reversible.

Irreversible degenerative dementias include multi-infarct dementia, Pick's disease, and Alzheimer's disease. In **multi-infarct dementia** (sometimes called vascular dementia) changes in the brain's blood vessels result in widespread death of brain tissue. This interferes with the exchange of essential substances between the bloodstream and the brain tissue. When the loss of brain tissue becomes widespread, the brain is deprived of oxygen and nutrients. Such damage may result in a variety of psychological and physical problems, including mental confusion, dizziness, headaches, and unsteadiness in gait. A succession of small strokes is possible, resulting in cumulative brain damage. Rupture of a large vessel causes a major stroke, which as we earlier learned is called a cerebrovascular accident. Here, the person may experience paralysis, loss of vision, memory loss, or a coma. The causes of multi-infarct dementia include poor diet, smoking, lack of exercise, or genetic factors (Biller, 1991; Foley & Pizer, 1990; Nelson, 1990).

Pick's disease is considered a rare form of dementia and is more common in women than in men. Those afflicted with this disorder experience disorientation, impaired judgment, fatigability, and impaired physical and intellectual functions. Atrophy of the frontal and prefrontal lobes of the brain is common. The prognosis of this disorder is unfavorable. Most deaths occur within 5 years after the disease first occurs (Hogstel, 1990; Somerfield, 1991).

Alzheimer's disease was a relatively obscure disease 20 years ago and received little study. Today, it is recognized as the most common form of degenerative dementia, and it has emerged as the fourth leading killer of adults, after heart disease, cancer, and strokes. Alzheimer's disease has claimed the lives of over 2.5 million persons in the United States and claims 100,000 to 120,000 lives each year. It carries a prognosis of 50% reduction in remaining life expectancy (Coons, 1991; Dippel & Hutton, 1991; Evans, 1990; Nelson, 1990; Reisberg, 1990).

According to the National Institute on Aging (1992), the prevalence of Alzheimer's disease increases dramatically with age. Persons age 65 to age 74 have a 1 in 25 chance of contracting the disease. For those 85 years of age and older, the likelihood rises to a staggering nearly 1 in 2 chance. As we learned earlier in this chapter, the 75 years of age and older group is the most rapidly growing sector of the U.S. population, thus portending a dramatic increase in the overall number of Alzheimer's disease cases in the coming century. The Focus on Diversity box on pages 610–611 also reveals the prevalence of Alzheimer's disease and other dementias around the globe.

This disorder is marked by progressive, irreversible neurological degeneration. The natural course of the degeneration is not known at this time. Some individuals decline rapidly, others more slowly. Some cope successfully with their disabilities and progressive losses; others do not (Burns, Jacoby, & Levy, 1991; Cummings & Miller, 1990; Reisberg, 1990).

The earliest symptom of Alzheimer's disease is forgetfulness. Later on, individuals no longer function well in demanding jobs or social situations. A sense of confusion and helplessness often sets in. As the disease continues, deficiencies develop in all cognitive and functional areas. Persons with Alzheimer's disease often become unsteady in their movements and ultimately lose psychomotor abilities to such an extent that they can no longer ambulate. Many are overtly agitated, talk to themselves, cry, and eventually become very passive. In the latter stages of the disease, all ability to speak is lost. Most can only stare blankly and make grunting, guttural sounds (Cooper, Mungas, & Weiler, 1990; Gilley, 1991; Lee, 1991; Martin, 1990; Venable & Mitchell, 1991).

The exact cause of Alzheimer's disease is not known, but the following possible explanations exist:

1. It has been suggested that in Alzheimer's disease there is a deficit or imbalance of neurochemicals—particularly the enzyme choline acetyltransferase. The latter is a catalyst responsible for the synthesis of acetylcholine, an essential neurotransmitter involved in learning and memory.
2. Excessive accumulations of toxins in the brain may trigger this disease. Research has focused on the effects of repeated exposure to such elements as aluminum and certain salt compounds, although a definite association for any of these elements has yet to be made.
3. It is possible that the brain has somehow lost its capacity for synthesizing proteins.
4. There might be a genetic connection to Alzheimer's disease, suggesting that family members are at risk for inheriting it.
5. Alzheimer's disease might be the result of a unique viral infection—one that does not feature the standard symptoms of infection such as a fever or an elevated white blood-cell count.

INTERACTION OF HEREDITY AND ENVIRONMENT

How do you view the possible explanations of Alzheimer's disease? Can you group these explanations according to environmental and hereditary causes? Do some explanations reflect a mixture of both environment and heredity?

Focus on Diversity

TREATING THE PUZZLE OF DEMENTIAS

The widespread nature of dementias does not restrict itself to the United States. Around the world, it is estimated that 5 to 8% of persons aged 65 and over suffer from severe dementia. About half of the dementias occurring in the older population have Alzheimer's disease, and another 20 to 30% suffer from multi-infarct dementia. It is projected we will see a 100% or more increase in dementias in less developed nations before the year 2000, and a 50% increase in developed countries.

Even though most dementia patients live in the community, those suffering from this illness constitute the majority of elderly people found in long-term care facilities. In Japan, for instance, about one half of elderly people in psychiatric hospitals suffer from dementia, as do about one quarter of those in special nursing homes. In the Netherlands, an overall prevalence rate of about 25% has been found. Almost 50% of all of the institutionalized psychiatric elderly patients in France are also dementia patients. In relation to all of these statistics, it must be pointed out that family members usually seek institutional care as a last resort. Therefore, many institutionalized dementia victims are in the latter stages of the disease.

Learning how to provide optimal care to dementia patients is an active pursuit in many nations. Many countries are experimenting with variations of day care and day hospitals, other forms of respite care, home health services, and family support groups. In Stockholm, Sweden,

---

6. A final explanation is the blood-flow theory. This theory suggests that Alzheimer's disease is caused by a marked decrease in blood flow to the brain, as well as a reduction in the amount of oxygen and glucose present in the blood. (Abraham & Neundorfer, 1990; Becker & Giacobini, 1990; Cummings, 1990; Edwards, 1991; Joiner, 1990; Khachaturian, Radebaugh, & Monjan, 1990; Nalbantoglu, Lacoste-Royal, & Gauvreau, 1990)

Of these explanations, genetic possibilities have attracted the attention of researchers in recent years. The National Institute on Aging (1992) reports that in up to 20% of cases, Alzheimer's disease occurs in a familial form, in which many members of a family are affected by the disease. It is believed that a defect involving the substitution of amino acid, located on the 21st pair of chromosomes, is responsible for the genetic transmission of the disease. The ability of the defect to be inherited has been demonstrated by the presence of the same mutation in members of two generations affected by Alzheimer's disease.

The primary areas of the brain affected by Alzheimer's disease are several regions of the cerebral cortex that form the outer layer of the brain and are thought to be responsible for cognitive functions such as language. The hippocampus, part of the cortex located deep within the brain and involved in memory functions, is also frequently affected. As the disease progresses, a thinning process seems to occur in these regions, particularly in dendritic areas. Also becoming evident are tangled bundles of fibers within the nerve cells (known as neurofibrillary tangles, or NFTs), and deposits or plaques of an unidentified substance over the cortex and external to the cells (Bayles, 1991; Galasko, Corey-Bloom, & Thal, 1991; Reisberg, 1990).

special day-care programs affiliated with nursing homes tend to delay institutionalization for many dementia patients. In Great Britain, doctors often alternate periods of inpatient care with periods of care at home in an effort to buttress families who are caring for loved ones with dementia. Such respite care is also growing in Japan, where medical programs have been established to provide accommodations for dementia patients whose families face emergency situations. In Israel, respite care services are available to families caring for relatives with dementia, and in Germany, a hot line for family caregivers was made available in 1990 and expanded in 1993.

The care and treatment of dementia patients within the institutional framework presents special problems and concerns. Increasing numbers of dementia victims are being cared for in nursing homes and other long-term care facilities that are poorly equipped and insufficiently funded to meet the special needs of this population. As an illustration, many nursing homes do not have the staff to patient ratios or specially trained staff needed to meet the special needs of dementia patients.

To overcome these problems, many nations are implementing model institutional-care programs. In Japan, the Ministry of Health designated existing nursing homes in each of its prefectures as a specialized facility for treating dementia victims. In Australia, an innovative program focuses on those who are ambulant but suffering from dementia. The program includes thorough assessment, special environmental design features, recreational and other forms of therapy, and research. And in Spain, the first homes for dementia victims were recently built in Orense, an area with a high proportion of elderly persons. (M. J. Gibson, 1984; Heeren, 1991; Kashiwase & Watanabe, 1991; Pritchard, 1990)

The family of an Alzheimer's disease patient endure years of emotional and physical distress. In addition, they frequently bear the frustration which results from knowing that no matter how much effort goes into caring for the patient, there is no hope for recovery. Because of such a tremendous psychological burden, family members need formalized clinical and community services to help guide them (Fortinsky & Hathaway, 1990; Gonyea, 1990; Hamby, 1990; Lawton, Brody, & Saperstein, 1991). One organization offering support to family caregivers is the Alzheimer's Disease and Related Disorders Association (ADRDA). Families must also learn to cope with their own feelings and maintain their health throughout this ordeal, as well as after the actual caregiving (refer back to the guidance we gave in Chapter 10). Also, an important task for the family is to try to restore dignity to the patient in the wake of progressive deterioration (Anifantakis, 1991; Dixon, 1991; Farren, 1991; Mace & Rabins, 1991; Meddaugh, O'Bryant, & Straw, 1991; Pynoos & Ohta, 1991).

Especially hard for families is placing an Alzheimer's disease patient in a nursing home, which usually happens when home care is no longer possible. Of course, the decision ought to be based on what is best, both for the patient and for the family. If the patient is disabled, needs continual assistance at night, wanders and gets lost, makes dangerous mistakes in judgment and behavior, or no longer recognizes others as individuals, then institutionalized care is probably best (Cairl, 1990; J. K. Cooper, 1991; Fish, 1990; Gwyther, 1990; Pruchno, Michaels, & Potashnik, 1990; Rader & Hoeffer, 1991; Reed, 1990).

The financial complexities created by Alzheimer's disease are overwhelming. The total annual cost to the United States for the care of Alzheimer's disease patients is estimated at $90 billion, including medical and nursing home care, social services, lost productivity, and early death. Related to our earlier points, the toll of caring for Alzheimer's disease patients must also be calculated in terms of the burden on families and caregivers. The average duration of Alzheimer's disease is 8 years, with more than 70% of patients with less severe disease cared for at home at an annual cost of $12,000 each. The cost of nursing home care is more than double this figure, and most patients eventually spend some time in nursing homes. Furthermore, patients may be repeatedly hospitalized during the course of their illness, at greatly increased cost (National Institute on Aging, 1992).

In summary, researchers of the 1990s are trying to fit together the pieces of this puzzling disorder. We need to fully identify the causes and mechanisms of its development, determine who is at risk and why, devise methods of early and accurate diagnosis, and apply the knowledge through well-trained and organized caregivers. The provision of adequate social support to family caregivers is especially important (Bottomley, 1990; Dippel & Hutton, 1991; Gonyea & Silverstein, 1991; Gottlieb, 1990; Robbert, 1991; U.S. Department of Health & Human Services, 1991).

UNIT REVIEW—

↗ The important lifespan issue of continuity and change resurfaces when late life personality dynamics are examined. Those favoring the continuity or stability perspective maintain that the adult personality remains relatively unaltered from earlier years. Discontinuous personality theories have been developed by Erik Erikson, Robert Peck, and Daniel Levinson.

↗ A number of ingredients appear to be associated with successful aging, including subjective well-being, good self-esteem, positive role adaptation, resiliency, and personal control over one's life. Two of the older, yet nonetheless noteworthy theories of successful aging are the disengagement and activity theories.

↗ Psychological maladjustment at this time may be functional in scope, such as in anxiety, schizophrenic, affective, personality, and substance-use disorders. Other types of maladaptive behavior fall under the category of organic brain syndrome, including reversible and irreversible dementias. Delirium is an example of a reversible dementia; irreversible types include multi-infarct dementia, Pick's disease, and Alzheimer's disease.

↗ Of all the forms of maladaptive behavior among elderly people, Alzheimer's disease is receiving the most attention in the 1990s. It is the fourth leading killer of adults, after heart disease, cancer, and strokes, and to date, there is no cure.

UNIT THREE: THE FAMILY

By the time most married couples approach the age of retirement, their children have already matured, married, and established independent households. As a result, the typical older family in society today is comprised of simply the husband and wife, most of whom maintain their own household (U.S. Bureau of the Census, 1992). As we've learned throughout this book, the family life cycle is filled with numerous developmental chores, and late adulthood is no exception. Paramount among the adjustment tasks facing elderly couples are lifestyle changes brought about by retirement, physical living arrangements, and kin relations. Let's explore each in more detail.

▬ Marital Relations

Generally speaking, most marriages are characterized by satisfaction and not disenchantment during the retirement years. Indeed, the event of retirement may be responsible for bringing elderly couples closer together. For many, the relationship becomes the focal point of everyday life and interests become increasingly directed toward one another. Shared interests typically provide a reflection of satisfaction, caring, mutuality, and reciprocity (Peterson, 1990; R. J. Siegel, 1990). These important relationship ingredients are particularly evident when partners care for one another in times of illness or disability (Johansson, 1991; Opie, 1991; Schrauben, 1991).

In later life, most marriages are characterized by happiness and satisfaction.

The notion that later life marriages are characterized by satisfaction and happiness was evident in a research study conducted by Barbara Vinick and David Ekerdt (1991). In this investigation, 92 couples from urban, suburban, and rural communities were studied. Overall, it was found that retirement did not constitute a crisis in the lives of couples. Although this family life stage engenders some strain, it rarely represented a period of upheaval. The majority of husbands and wives in the sample were satisfied with their married lives. While some strains surfaced during the first year of retirement, most proved to be mild, fleeting, or caused by conditions unrelated to retirement itself. These findings were especially true for husbands and wives with adequate incomes and a history of marital compatibility.

For those relationships characterized by unhappiness, it is plausible that the event of retirement heralded disruption and disharmony. For example, there are many wives who resent the intrusion of the husband into the household on a full-time daily basis. Some, such as Judith Treas (1983), feel that incorporating a newly idle husband into the daily household routine is a stressful and turbulent experience for a wife. The new intimacy brought on by retirement may produce a strain on the marriage. By this, more regular daily contact may represent a domestic intrusion for one or both and breed tension rather than marital intimacy (Ekerdt & Vinick, 1991; Jerome, 1990). We return to the topic of marital relations toward the end of this chapter.

▬ Living Arrangements

Of the approximately 91 million households in the United States, about 21% are headed by persons 65 years of age or older. The number of elderly persons living with a spouse varies greatly between men and women. About 75% of men aged 65 or over live with their spouse, compared to only about 40% of women. Such gender differences become even more pronounced for those 75 years of age and older: About 67% of men live with their spouse, compared to less than 24% of women. These figures reflect the fact that men tend to marry women younger than themselves and therefore are more likely to die first, and because men are more likely to remarry (U.S. Bureau of the Census, 1992).

Today, approximately a quarter of elderly people live in rural areas, a third live in inner cities, and another 40% reside in older working-class neighborhoods on the fringes of central cities. Overall, about 75% of all aged persons own their home. The median amount spent on housing by elderly householders with a mortgage is about 28% of income, and without a mortgage, approximately 18%. Because most elderly persons live in older houses, frequent and more expensive repairs are commonplace (Rickman, 1991). Failing health and physical ability, coupled with reduced and fixed income, often makes home ownership an expensive venture for elderly people (Carp, 1991; Moore & Arthur, 1991; Porcino, 1991; Redfoot & Gaberlavage, 1991).

Given these concerns, the maintenance of suitable living arrangements represents an important consideration for elderly people. Whether existing residences or new locations, housing accommodations are important to aged persons because they spend so much time at home. Furthermore, suitable living arrangements and neighborhood belongingness have significant influences on one's morale and sense of well-being (Crown & Longino, 1991; Longino, 1991; Reitzes et al., 1991; Sheehan, 1992).

Judging from the statistics, retired couples prefer to remain in the same geographical location. The U.S. Bureau of the Census (1992) tells us that compared to all other segments of the population, elderly people change residency the least. Only about 15% of the aged tend to move during any given year, and 80% of those who choose to relocate remain in the same state. Moving is disruptive at any age, but apparently more so for elderly people because of such factors as financial difficulties, physical frailty, or illness. Those aged persons who do change residency are usually the affluent and healthy (Crown & Longino, 1991; U.S. Bureau of the Census, 1992).

Institutional Care

When older people are disabled or can no longer take care of themselves, institutional care may be required. Although only 5% of elderly people 65 years of age and older are institutionalized at any one time, the population of nursing homes is disproportionately old, in many cases over age 80. To illustrate, whereas only 17% of persons aged 65 to 74 reside in a nursing home, 36% of persons aged 75 to 84 live in a nursing facility, and about 60% of persons 85 years and older are institutionalized. Gender differences in life expectancy also create variations in institutionalization. For example, more women than men will enter nursing homes (52% versus 33%), and among them, more women than men will have resided in a nursing home for 5 years or more (25% versus 13%) (Kemper & Murtaugh, 1991).

Types of Institutional Care It is incorrect to think that all institutional-care facilities for elderly people are the same. On the contrary, several different categories of care exist, depending on the functional status and needs of the elderly person. These include the skilled-nursing, intermediate-care, residential-care, and adult day-care facilities.

SKILLED-NURSING FACILITY (SNF) In the **skilled-nursing facility,** medical care is available to residents on a full-time basis. Because of this, the skilled-nursing facility is suited for aged persons with chronic illnesses such as stroke, heart disease, or rheumatism. Aged persons who are bedridden or require frequent medications, catheterizations, or orthopedic care also tend to be skilled-nursing facility residents.

INTERMEDIATE-CARE FACILITY (ICF) The emphasis of the **intermediate-care facility** is more on personal care and less on medical assistance. The typical resident does not have a serious illness nor is bedridden. Rather, she or he often needs assistance in daily routines and activities, such as eating, dressing, or walking. The intermediate-care and skilled-nursing facilities constitute most of the institutional-care arrangements in the United States.

RESIDENTIAL-CARE FACILITY (RCF) The **residential-care facility** is designed for independent elderly persons who require a safe and sheltered environment in which to live. The focus of this facility tends to be on professional services, such as housekeeping and laundering, as well as any other aspect of domestic life warranting intervention and assistance.

ADULT DAY-CARE FACILITY (ADCF) In the **adult day-care facility,** elderly persons maintain their own residences but receive medical support and assistance in a specially designated center. Beyond medical care, the adult day-care facility offers a wide range of programming, including meals, traveling, exercise, and social activities (Gelfand, Bechill, & Chester, 1991; Krout, 1991; Ralston, 1991). Some of the centers offer day-care supervision to children as well, creating a unique blend of young and old. Many spokespersons, such as Roseanne Kocarnik and James Ponzetti (1991), feel such a mixture of ages is a positive arrangement that enables the young to better understand the old, and vice versa.

Adjustment to Institutionalization   For many elderly residents, adjusting to institutional care may pose problems. Let us make it clear at the outset that there are many who adjust well; many, however, do not. For example, many view nursing homes in a very negative light. Such perceptions originate partly from a desire to remain in familiar surroundings and near relatives and friends. Most negative feelings toward institutionalization, however, are because of a perceived loss of independence and because of a belief that placement in a nursing home represents formal proof that death is near. Many of the aged also have a fear that once placed in a nursing home, they will be rejected and forgotten by their children (Applebaum & Phillips, 1990; Atchley, 1991). Older people have often never heard a good word about nursing homes—no wonder they don't want to go to one. But there are many good nursing homes and many benefits of nursing home care such as immediate health care in times of crisis, companionship, more regular nutritious meals, organized activities, and so forth.

A study by Paula Biedenharn and Janice Normoyle (1991) sheds light on the elderly person's concerns and expectations of one day entering a nursing

Institutional care may be needed for those elderly persons unable to care for themselves.

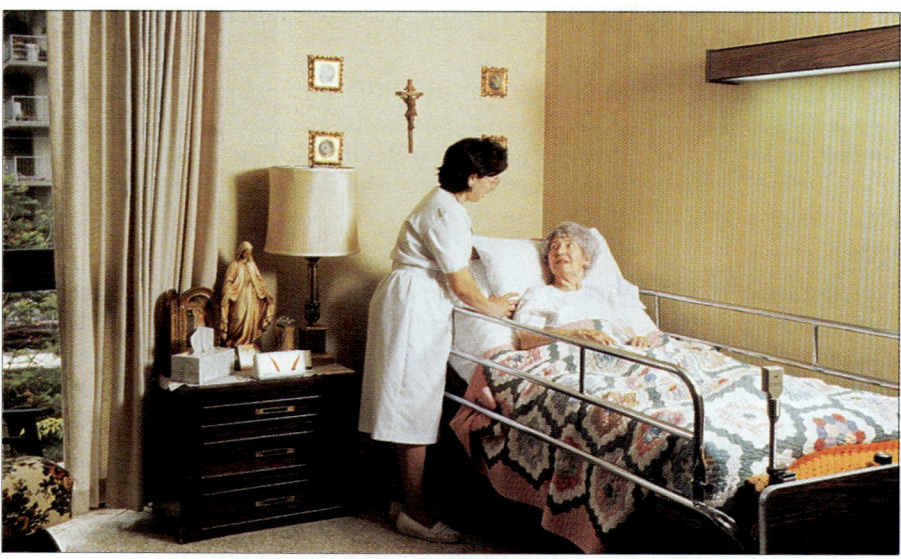

home. Surveying over 250 older adults, the researchers found that beliefs regarding care-related issues were more important determinants of reactions to nursing homes than were the risks posed by individual health care situations. Indeed, the subjects' fears and expectations of one day entering a nursing home tended to be the products of beliefs they held. Of particular prominence were concerns regarding the quality of care within the institution, the costs of care, and the family's role once institutionalization took place.

Many elderly residents react negatively to the frequent impersonalization of nursing homes. Many are uncomfortable with the loss of privacy, and others resent the limited individual treatment accorded by staff members. Research (e.g., Davidson & O'Connor, 1990) also shows that perceived loss of control is an important concern among many elderly residents. According to Sandra Foy and Marlys Mitchell (1990) the loss of perceived control promotes declines in physical and psychological status. For many, a sense of learned helplessness unfolds, a condition creating cognitive, affective, and functional deficits. There is also the risk of excess disability and possibly premature death.

In the midst of such impersonalization and uncertainty, many elderly residents develop what Robert Butler and Myrna Lewis (1981) call **institutionalism.** Essentially, this is a psychological state brought about by a depersonalized environment. Persons afflicted with institutionalism often develop automatic behaviors, expressionless faces, and general apathy. They become disinterested in their personal appearance and suffer from a deterioration of morale. Social relationships for many become nonexistent. In those nursing homes where the identity, interests, and strengths of the resident are not assessed and developed, degrees of institutionalism are likely to surface.

Depersonalized nursing home environments have created a fair amount of criticism in recent years, and many thoughts on upgrading the quality of life exist (Skipwith, 1991; Spector & Takada, 1991). Other criticism is leveled at programming in general, including limited intellectual stimulation of the residents. In short, many feel elderly people simply have nothing to do in many institutions. There are also many nursing homes in the nation that are substandard, in some instances failing to provide minimal conditions for humane treatment (Bushy, 1991; Harrington, 1991; Kosloski, Montgomery, & Borgatta, 1990). The Lifespan Development in Action box appearing on page 618 provides features of quality institutional care.

Numerous recommendations have been made to upgrade institutional care facilities, particularly the improvement of the psychological and social climate. Attempts have to be made to promote the growth of new relationships to take the place of those lost in the process of growing old or sick. Social integration of long-term care residents is very important, particularly if social isolation and detachment are to be avoided. Residents should participate as much as possible in establishing the ground rules for their living situations. Achieving a sense of mastery and control is crucial to preserving a resident's self-concept and identity. Physical structuring of space should offer freedom and safety as well as privacy. Finally, regular interpersonal contacts with the residents are critical as the transition to the nursing home is made. This conveys to residents that they are not alone and isolated, not discarded, and still valued (Glass, 1991; Hawes, 1991; Kermis, 1984).

Other recommendations are aimed at improving the professionalism of the institution's personnel, including doctors. In the past, as well as the present, doctors have had little contact with nursing home patients. This is due to several reasons, including the low reimbursement from Medicaid and Medicare and because many physicians regard elderly institutionalized patients as depressing. **Medicaid** is a government-sponsored medical care plan for welfare clients, regardless of age. **Medicare** is a government-sponsored insurance program that partially finances the health-care costs of persons 65 years of age and older. Increasing all areas of medical coverage, including psychiatric and dental care, is a consistent theme in the literature. So, too, is implementing more in-service training on all facets of geriatric health care (Garrard, 1991; George & Maddox, 1990; Heiselman & Noelker, 1991; Karuza & Katz, 1991; Tipton, 1990).

Raised standards of accreditation and certification have upgraded many institutions and closed down those deemed inadequate in meeting the needs of their residents. Continued investigation and reform are needed to ensure that the best possible care and treatment are available in these facilities. At the very least, institutional care needs to be made more accountable (Abdellah, 1991; Branch, 1991; Johnson, 1991; Meyer, 1991).

INTERRELATEDNESS OF AGING PROCESSES

What kinds of care and services do you think are essential for nursing home residents? How do you think tending to a resident's physical needs affects such psychological dynamics as integrity, self-worth, and security? How is social well-being affected by the institutional environment?

Kin Relations

The elderly usually keep in touch with whatever kin they have. For some, this means considerable contact with aging brothers and sisters, but for most, the focus of kin relations is on children and grandchildren. Upward of 80% of the aged have living children, and interaction with them is considerable (Cicirelli, 1991; High, 1991; Taylor & Chatters, 1991; U.S. Bureau of the Census, 1992).

Patterns of Care and Interaction   Some aged couples live with their children, especially when independent living in a separate location is no longer feasible. More elderly people are likely to live with an unmarried child than with a

Lifespan Development in Action

GUIDELINES FOR CHOOSING A QUALITY NURSING HOME

Selecting a good institutional-care facility for elderly people is not easy. Programming designs are not universal, they differ in methods of care and treatment, and costs fluctuate from institution to institution. In an effort to narrow down the choices and find the best possible facility, consider the following:

- Discover which type of facility the elderly person needs. Does the person have adequate financial resources? Does he or she qualify for government-funded nursing home care? Some nursing homes will not accept nonprivate patients or those who will become so in the near future.

- Investigate the credentials of the medical staff. One problem for nursing homes is a serious shortage of physicians qualified to serve this population. Only about 700 doctors in this country have completed training in geriatric medicine or geriatric psychiatry, yet people over 65 account for 36% of physicians' working time, and about 40% of all acute hospital days. Also, find out if the staff-to-patient ratio is adequate. How many staff members are licensed professionals (RNs and LPNs)? Does the facility have a licensed physical therapist or a registered dietitian on staff? Also, ask if aides receive training from the professional staff (aides have the most direct contact with patients).

- Make several visits—some unannounced—to each facility. Does the facility seem neat and comfortable? Are meeting rooms cheerful? Check the bulletin boards, dayrooms, and other areas for evidence of programs and activities. Is there an activities director?

- Is the staff sincere, warm, and friendly? Are they willing to answer your questions fully?

- Look to see if the residents are clean and neat. Are those residents who are able to sit up dressed in street clothes by 10 a.m.?

- Make sure the food is of good quality and that daily nutritional needs are met. If possible, order a tray while visiting and try it yourself.

- Discover if the facility works with the families of its residents. Does it provide educational programs or support groups for the resident's family?

- What do others say about the facility? Do doctors, nurses, and the families of residents recommend it? Nursing homes often are required to show the results of licensing inspections. Don't be hesitant to ask for them, but be aware that many inspections concentrate only on small violations. (Deane, 1985; Forrest et al., 1990; Sharp, 1990)

married one, and more with a daughter than with a son. However, at least one study (Coward & Cutler, 1991) notes that in two-generational households, more elders live with sons than daughters. The proportion of elderly living with their offspring is also higher for the widowed, divorced, and separated than for married persons (Kart, 1990; U.S. Bureau of the Census, 1992).

In general, elderly individuals live near their children, although this is more true in urban environments than in rural settings. Females maintain closer relationships with other family members than do males. Couples tend to live nearer to the wife's parents and are likely to visit them more often. Also, working-class families are likely to have close family ties, and these ties are maintained by living near one another. Middle- and upper-class families have strong ties, too, but members are often geographically scattered because of career obligations (Barrow & Smith, 1983; Kauffman & Ames, 1983; Kosberg, 1992; U.S. Bureau of the Census, 1992).

A study of extended family networks among elderly African-American adults (Taylor & Chatters, 1991) provides evidence of the close family interaction that takes place during the retirement years. Overall, this investigation uncovered high levels of interaction and strong emotional bonds between aging adults and extended family members. Although the oldest respondents in this sample were less likely to reside near immediate family and other relatives, there were no age differences in levels of contact and emotional closeness. Having an adult child and relatives nearby tended to facilitate the emotional and social integration of older African Americans in family networks. For more detail on intergenerational dynamics in African-American families, see the Focus on Diversity box on pages 620–621.

An investigation of elderly Native Americans (John, 1991) shows that strong, enduring sibling ties are important, but apparently more so between brothers than between sisters. Also, the presence of a spouse tends to insulate elders rather than invigorating contact within the overall family support network. Finally, marital dissolution, whether through widowhood, divorce, or separation, does not isolate aged family members from their children or siblings.

For both older and younger generations, the family represents an important source of love, support, and trust.

Focus on Diversity

THE TIES THAT BIND: INTERGENERATIONAL RELATIONS OF AFRICAN AMERICANS

Georgette Miller is a 78-year-old African American who lives independently in an efficiency apartment in a quiet suburban area. She has lived in roughly the same geographical location all of her life and has a number of family members living close by, including her oldest daughter. She is the proud mother of three children, and often boasts of her seven grandchildren and two great-grandchildren. Georgette is in excellent health, and although she fractured her hip when she was in her early 60s, her family rallied to give her the attention and support she needed during her recovery period. Today, Georgette has little or no difficulty tending to daily living chores, usually cooking her own meals and always seeing to it that her apartment is tidy and clean. She loves to visit on a regular basis with relatives and friends, entertaining both young and old with richly descriptive stories about her past and present experiences.

This brief snapshot of Georgette Miller and her family mirrors many of the intergenerational relations characteristic of African Americans. As we noted in the last chapter, young and old African-American family members are noted for their emotional connectedness as well as for the provision of many different types of assistance and support. For example, Robert Taylor (1990) and colleagues observe that elderly adults are more likely to receive support from their children in

THEORETICAL ISSUES

How might symbolic interactionism be used as a theoretical base to explore the shifting roles and expectations of old and young family members? In light of such changes, what recommendations do you think symbolic interactionists would give to ensure family solidarity and cohesion?

Such patterns of closeness debunk the myth that elderly people are alienated from their children or rejected by their families. However, most research (e.g., Glezer, 1991; Schultz, 1990; Sprey, 1991) points out that elderly people often worry about their families no longer wanting or needing them. Further, when old people have no children, a principle of family substitution seems to operate, and brothers, sisters, nephews, and nieces often fill the roles and assume the obligations of children. The truly isolated old person, despite his or her prominence in the media, is a rarity in the United States. Although retirees live apart from their children, they remain psychologically close. Another myth to be rejected is the notion that because of the existence of large human service bureaucracies, families are no longer important as caretakers for elderly persons. The family of the 1990s looms as an extremely important source of care and support, more so now, perhaps, than ever before. Moreover, research reveals (P. Brown, 1990; Hirshorn, 1991; Kahana & Kinney, 1991; Levy, 1991; Sussman, 1991) that individuals are concerned about the welfare of their elderly parents and want to be an integral part of the care and support they receive.

The emotional support given to aged parents is more critical to their psychological well-being than financial support. Furthermore, a large percentage of retired persons refuse to accept financial assistance from their children, largely because they want to be financially independent. This notion of independence goes beyond financial matters, and for many aged persons, a certain degree of ambivalence surrounds it. The aged generally do not wish to impose or to be dependent, but neither do they wish to be neglected or ignored (Stone, 1991; Sussman, 1991; Ward, 1984).

times of need than from formal support networks. Adult daughters, in particular, are typically selected as the person to provide help when sickness or disability strikes. Childless black elderly, on the other hand, are more apt to rely on brothers, sisters, and friends. It is important to point out that the parent-child bond is important across the entire life cycle of African Americans. Younger adults tend to rely heavily on their parents, elderly adults are apt to rely on their adult children, and middle-aged African Americans tend to depend on both their parents and children.

Taylor's (1990) review of the literature also indicates that compared to whites, African-American grandparents take a more active role in grandparenting. This greater involvement may be traced to several reasons. For one, the greater probability of African Americans residing with grandchildren and in three-generational households offers increased opportunities for contact and involvement. Another possible reason is that a higher incidence of divorce, unemployment, and mortality among African Americans has important consequences for both household arrangements and family child-care responsibilities. A third possible reason is that rather explicit cultural norms in support of extended family relations are in operation among African Americans.

It might be added that mothers of African-American teenage parents play a prominent role in the lives of their children and grandchildren. The support and assistance that teenage mothers receive from their extended family, particularly from their mothers, exerts many positive influences. Among other benefits, such intergenerational support assists adolescent mothers with their educational and economic achievements, parenting skills, and their children's development. (Taylor et al., 1990)

Aging parents need to establish generational roles as they become the family system's elderly members. They pass the "baton of power" on to the middle generation, in the process attempting to retain as much independence and involvement as the family system allows. Through a great portion of the life cycle, help flows mainly from parents to children. This flow gradually reverses itself as parents get old and need help from their offspring. As a result, the adult offspring become the caretakers and the elderly parents the receivers. For some elderly couples, this can be distressing, particularly if the children do not perceive this need and desire of the parents to lead more independent lives. Often, ambivalence is reflected in over- or underattachment. Consequently, it is important to assess the realities of everyone's perceptions of need (Morgan, Schuster, & Butler, 1991; Okun, 1984).

According to Frank Pittman (1987), friction may also develop as the child grapples with the task of becoming "parent to the parent." Either party can become offended. Either may also overplay the role—the child may be autocratic or the aged parent may collapse dependently and demandingly. Compounding the problem is that children may have to coax the parent to draft a will, or make decisions about funeral arrangements and division of property. Such dreaded subjects may detonate psychological explosions and consequently may have to be negotiated by an outside objective professional.

Problems can also arise when the aged have frequent interaction with their children. Often the family relations between young and old are characterized by regular contact, affection, and an obligation to assist in time of need. When, however, obligation to help becomes the dominant element in the family relationship, trouble usually begins. Problems may even arise when actual aid enters into the relationship, because it can weaken the affectional and enjoyable aspects of that relationship. Conceivably, the shifting of the help patterns from the old to the young creates the basis for problems, because it represents something neither party is used to (Bell, 1983). And, as we learned in Chapter 10, there are multiple stresses attached to caring for an ill or disabled parent, forces that further serve to create intergenerational tension and friction (Sanborn & Bould, 1991; Scharlach, Sobel, & Roberts, 1991).

UNIT REVIEW—

↗ Most marriages during late adulthood are characterized by happiness and satisfaction, not disenchantment. Many relationships reflect a mixture of satisfaction, caring, mutuality, and reciprocity.

↗ Most retired couples do not want to change their residence, with declining health and limited income often representing anchoring variables.

↗ When aged persons are afflicted with a disability or can no longer care for themselves, institutional care may be required. Types of institutional care include skilled-nursing facilities, intermediate-care facilities, residential-care facilities, and adult day-care facilities.

↗ Satisfying kin relations are important throughout the entire life cycle, and the notion that elderly persons are alienated from their families is a myth.

UNIT FOUR: RETIREMENT

From a definitive point of view, **retirement** means the end of formal work and the beginning of a new role in life, one that involves behavioral expectations and a redefinition of self. It involves moving from an economically productive role, which is clearly defined, to an economically unproductive role, which is often vague and ambiguous (Ransom, Sutch, & Williamson, 1991; Schuller, 1989). This ambiguity in the retirement role is because of its relatively new and different social position, for which there is no precedent. In the past, people worked for nearly their entire lives. But today, people retire and live out their remaining years doing other things (Laczko, 1989; McPherson, 1990; Ruhm, 1990; Sterns, Matheson, & Schwartz, 1990; Veninga, 1991).

Retirement is recognized as a normative transition, an experience that originates from a predictable developmental change over the life cycle. Numerous researchers (e.g., Bond, Briggs, & Coleman, 1990; Hagestad, 1990; McNaught, Barth, & Henderson, 1991; Munnell, 1991) inform us that although we are learning more about such later life transitions, many issues require more in-depth investigation. For example, very little empirical work has investigated the interrelationships between retirement and the other transitions that exist during late adulthood. Also, limited amounts of research have focused on the female retirement experience. More women than ever before are retiring from the labor force, and we need to better understand what prompts their decision to leave, as well as how they adapt to the retirement role (Day, 1991; Dietz, 1991; Gustafson & Magnusson, 1991; Logue, 1991; Wingrove & Slevin, 1991).

■■■ Dimensions of Retirement

Retirement is a phenomenon of modern industrial society. In the United States, there are more than 27 million persons over the age of 65 who are classified as retired. Furthermore, the proportion of retirees in the general population will steadily increase. If present trends continue, it is estimated there will be 33 million retirees in the year 2000. The retirement period for most people is also growing longer. On the average, the man who retires at age 65 will live for another 14.8 years. A woman who retires at age 65 will live for another 18.6 years. By the turn of the century, it is expected that, on the average, a person will live another 25 years after retirement (Bond & Coleman, 1990; Fries, 1991; Laczko & Phillipson, 1991; National Center for Health Statistics, 1992; U.S. Bureau of the Census, 1992).

One source (Kutscher & Fullerton, 1990) notes that labor force activity rates have changed significantly since 1950. Women's participation has increased while the participation rate of men, particularly men who are 55 and older, has dropped. The authors of this investigation analyzed in detail the trends projected for the 1990s for various subgroups among those 55 and older. The labor force participation of white men age 55 and older is projected to drop by 6.1 percentage points; the rate for African-American men of the same age group will drop by 7.6 points and for Hispanic men by 6.6 points. For older women, on the other hand, the participation rates for white women are projected to drop by only 0.7 percentage points, reflecting an anticipated rise in participation of women aged 55 to 59. The projected participation rate for African-American women in the 1990s drops by 1.2 points but remains 2 points higher than the overall participation rate for white women. The participation rate for Hispanic women is projected to remain the same.

Retirement policies in the United States reflect a unique history. In 1935, the Social Security Act institutionalized retirement and formally defined "old age" by establishing pension eligibility at age 65. The choice of age 65 as the age for retirement appears to have been influenced by the Old Age and Survivor's Pension Act that Otto Von Bismarck enacted as the first chancellor of the German empire in 1889. Although the Social Security Act of 1935 was not involved in establishing a compulsory retirement age, the choice of age 65 appears to have carried over from Social Security to mandatory retirement policies.

In 1967, Congress passed the Age Discrimination Employment Act and amended it in 1974, 1978, and 1986. Essentially, this legislation protects most workers in the United States from mandatory retirement policies. The federal law forbids discrimination in the hiring or discharging of a person on the basis of age, as well as discrimination in pay and other privileges and conditions of employment. The 1986 legislation in particular protects virtually all employees in the United States aged 40 or older. Exceptions include law enforcement officers, firefighters, and tenured faculty at institutions of higher learning, who until December 31, 1993, could be discharged on the basis of age at age 70 or older (Achenbaum, 1991; Bessey & Ananda, 1991; Borgatta, 1991).

Older workers are a vital part of the U.S. labor force.

In the 1990s, many workers opt for early retirement. Unlike our historical counterparts, growing numbers of today's employees look forward to the time when they won't have to work. However, early retirement poses a unique set of adjustment challenges, and considerable role ambiguity surrounds it, perhaps even more so than regular retirement. Statistics show that workers are retiring earlier than ever before; the average retirement age in the United States is edging closer to age 60. To illustrate, one study (Soldo & Agree, 1988) revealed over the past four decades, labor force participation rates for men ages 55 through 64 had dropped from 87% in 1950 to 68% in 1987. Among those 65 years of age and older, the rate had dropped by more than 50%, from 45.8% in 1950 to 16.3% in 1987.

Many of these early retirees are military personnel and civil servants, but this vocational trend is spreading among workers in a diversity of employment settings (Bond & Coleman, 1990; Cliff, 1991; Day & Jackson, 1991; Ransom, Sutch, & Williamson, 1991). Early retirement is often associated with a favorable financial outlook and a suitable standard of living for the retiree. Likewise, many retire early because pension plans are financially attractive. Some early retirees want a lighter workload; others may be in declining health. Some opt for early retirement because they are having difficulty keeping up with their work. Some are drawn to the status and positive image that early retirement often generates. Finally, we can add to this list that many retire early because of the support they receive from others. Family and friends, as well as fellow workers, may endorse early retirement (Phillipson, 1990; Sheppard, 1990; Stanford, 1991).

Adjusting to Retirement

Today's retired persons, particularly those who decide to retire early, are healthier than retirees of past generations. Nevertheless, when retirement takes

The retirement adjustments of elderly people occupy a busy area of investigation among developmental psychologists. Del Webb, a former carpenter (shown on the right), developed the concept of active retirement and opened the community of Sun City, Arizona, in 1960. Sun City consists mainly of retirement housing and recreation facilities for elderly people who wish to maintain an active lifestyle.

place, functions must be reintegrated if life is to continue fruitfully and harmoniously. Because retirement as a stage of life is such a new developmental phenomenon, however, our culture has yet to prescribe suitable behavior for this period. Consequently, each of us may react differently (Henretta, Chan, & O'Rand, 1992; Richardson & Kilty, 1991).

Psychological Adjustments   Leaving the world of work and relinquishing a significant part of one's identity is a difficult psychological adjustment. For many, such a transition brings about a major loss of self-esteem. The ability to deal with this stage of life depends to a considerable extent on past adjustment patterns. Those who adjust well to retirement are typically able to develop a lifestyle that provides continuity with the past and meets their long-term needs. Successful adjustment is also characterized by the harmonious resolution of demands and tasks throughout the course of one's life (Featherman, Smith, & Peterson, 1990; Marsh, 1991).

In general, most are able to adjust effectively to the retirement role (Coberly, 1991). Should the experience be negative, it is usually because the retirement event was perceived as being stressful or because of health and/or financial trouble (Iams & McCoy, 1991). Some are unhappy because of inappropriate expectations for retirement or because they were overcommitted to the work role. Related to the latter, Helen Neuhs (1990) found that women involved in preretirement planning, compared to those who were uninvolved, were more apt to adjust effectively to the retirement role. They tended to develop more realistic expectations about retirement and were more optimistic and open-minded about life options away from the workplace.

Raymond Bosse (1991) discovered that retirement tends to be a stressful event for those whom retirement, has negative implications. By this we mean those women and men who are forced to retire involuntarily or unexpectedly

THEORETICAL ISSUES

In what ways might retirement experiences fuel the Eriksonian psychosocial crisis of *integrity versus despair,* or Peck's adjustment task of *ego differentiation versus work-role preoccupation?* How might the theories of *activity* and *disengagement* be applied to adjustments during the retirement transition?

for reasons of health or company layoffs, or who experience financial or health declines after retirement, tend to experience greater retirement stress than those whose retirement is voluntary, on schedule, and not financially burdensome. Such research underscores the need to examine all facets of preretirement life and prior strains when seeking to assess psychological adjustment to the retirement role (Cook, 1991; Hughes, 1990; O'Brien, 1990).

Financial Adjustments   Financial hardships, in particular, are common during retirement. Indeed, it is not uncommon for personal income to drop by one third to one half with retirement. This kind of financial reduction means that many persons encounter poverty for the first time in their lives. And, as we learned in the last chapter, the chances of improving one's economic status during late adulthood are extremely limited (Crystal & Shea, 1990; Grad, 1990; Hellman & Hellman, 1991; Staebler, 1991; Tracey & Pampel, 1991).

Perhaps a few statistics will bear out the financial burden affecting retired persons. In 1991, 3.5 million elderly people, or about 1 in 8 (12.4%) had incomes below the poverty level. Less than 1 in 10 younger adults were similarly impoverished. In that same year, the median income of families with heads of household 65 or over was $14,923 compared with $31,260 for households headed by younger adults. At the extremes of poverty are those who suffer the cumulative effects of being old, female, and a member of a minority group— about 60% of African-American women 65 years of age and older, not living in families, were below the poverty level in 1990 (B. L. Friedman, 1991; McCarthy, 1991; Petras & Petras, 1991; Stuart & Ruhlman, 1991; U.S. Bureau of the Census, 1992).

A few studies illustrate how minorities and female elderly are especially vulnerable to poverty. One source (Andrews, 1989) estimates that 1 million elderly Hispanic people now live in the continental United States, and this figure is expected to increase to 4 million by the year 2020. Although some Hispanics have shared in the prosperity of this country, a great number face a daily struggle living on limited incomes and are trying to cope with financial hardship and poor health. Some of these problems, such as ineligibility for Social Security and Medicare, are related to the immigration patterns and work histories of this generation and may improve for future generations. Furthermore, as younger cohorts of Hispanic people grow older, language and educational barriers that elderly Hispanics face now may diminish. Nevertheless, for others, including new groups of immigrants, these patterns may reemerge.

Rose Gibson (1987, 1991) observes that African Americans have experienced vocational disadvantages across the life course: They are likely to have worked in low-status jobs characterized by sporadic work patterns and low earnings. Over a lifetime these handicapping work patterns have had negative effects on the economic well-being of African Americans as they reach old age. Employment in old age, in the same low-status jobs, therefore becomes a necessity for many. The level and source of income for African Americans during the retirement years have also been affected by their lifetime work experiences. A restriction to jobs characterized by low earnings, few benefits, and instability is directly related to low levels of retirement pensions and Social Security benefits. Consequently, the income packages of older African Americans, compared to other groups, contain a greater proportion of money from their own work and nonretirement sources.

As far as females are concerned, Judith Martindale and Mary Moses (1991) observe that the average age at which a woman is widowed is 56, and 70% of older poor people are women. Many women fear poverty in their old age, but we feel that paying careful attention to finance, health, and networking will help diminish that threat. Planning for retirement is particularly important for women for several reasons: (1) women often earn less than men, so the total assets available to them for retirement often are less; (2) they tend to work for smaller organizations that often do not provide private pension plans; (3) women often take time off from work for child care and accumulate fewer total years to contribute to retirement plans, and this diminishes the benefits they get on retirement. Another investigation (Scott, 1991) showed that aged women represent a large portion of the aged poor, not only because of their weak earnings histories, but also because of their inability to establish entitlement to Social Security benefits through marriage.

Poverty and unequal Social Security benefits are problems not unique to women in the United States. Irene Hoskins (1992) informs us that even in the Netherlands, where the elderly population benefits from a relatively generous level of income protection, single elderly women constitute 57% of the lowest income households. The reasons for the persistence of poverty among older women is related not only to their longer life expectancy but also to lower Social Security benefits. Average survivors' benefits as a proportion of average earnings range from 55% in Belgium to 30% in France and 17% in the United Kingdom. In the United States, retired women workers average 76 cents from Social Security for every dollar paid to retired male workers. Women's average private pension income is about 60% of that of men.

According to Virginia Richardson (1990), gender differences also exist in retirement planning. She studied over 3,000 retirees from a major state retirement system, 69% of whom were female. Significant gender differences were found in amount of personal financial planning, perceived adequacy of planning, and attendance at retirement workshops, with women planning less than men. The factors influencing retirement planning levels among women included the following: (1) retirement planning was more difficult for women, who tended to have fewer financial resources than men and lower levels of income; (2) workers highly committed to their work avoided planning for retirement and women were increasingly more committed to work; (3) women who delayed entry into the labor force were less likely to plan for retirement; (4) many older women were not socialized to become actively involved in financial matters; and (5) some women avoided thinking about retirement, associating it with old age.

Marital Adjustments Most retired couples share a relationship that has endured, and their experiences during this family transition can be intimately shared with a marital partner. In the retirement years, marriage "for better or worse" has meaning because partners experience positive, enjoyable experiences as well as negative, trying times. During this period, those who have vital, rewarding relationships will most generally experience continued positive interactions within the marriage, whereas partners with difficult, unsatisfying

GENDER SIMILARITIES AND DIFFERENCES

Why do you think research on female retirement is scant compared to male retirement experiences? Is it solely because women (until recently) were less likely than men to be employed outside the home? Do you think certain segments of society perceive and react differently to men's and women's retirement?

relationships will most likely face continued negative marital interactions (Brubaker, 1990b).

It appears that marital harmony during retirement, as well as during earlier family transitions, arises from the level of regard and esteem that partners hold for one another. A number of researchers (Anderson, Russell, & Schumm, 1983; Johnson et al., 1986; Schumm & Bugaighis, 1986) report that marital satisfaction tends to increase during the retirement years. Indeed, Rosalie Gilford (1984) goes so far as to label the retirement years a "honeymoon" transition because the couple now has greater opportunities for involvement with one another. For those who share marital intimacy and pursue mutual interests, retirement can mean years of relaxation and the enjoyment of one another's company (Jerome, 1990). However, many sources (e.g., Lee & Shehan, 1989; Mann, 1991; Peterson, 1990; R. J. Siegel, 1990) emphasize that the degree of marital harmony experienced hinges on the support each spouse is able to give to the other after the retirement event occurs, as well as the importance of relationship durability and adaptation. Also, coping and eventual adaptation by the older couple is often facilitated when partners view the retirement transition as a challenge or an opportunity for growth. In this respect, attitudes toward retirement often determine patterns of adjustment (Coleman, 1990; Hughes, 1990).

One investigation (Lauer, Lauer, & Kerr, 1990) explored the importance of support to marital harmony among retired couples. Data were gathered from 100 couples who were recruited from retirement communities in California, New York, Florida, Pennsylvania, Arizona, Illinois, Oregon, and Nebraska. The couples had been married from 45 to 65 years, with a median length of 54.5 years. All were ambulatory, and 97% had some kind of religious affiliation. The couples were mainly upper-middle class, with 74% having at least some college education and 84% reporting annual incomes over $20,000. The variables identified as important to their marriages were being married to someone they liked as a person and enjoyed being with; commitment and support to the spouse and to the marriage; a sense of humor; and consensus on various matters such as aims and goals in life, friends, and decision making.

Certain elements appear to characterize unsatisfactory marriages during the retirement years. For example, in traditional retirement patterns, wives may resent the intrusion of the husband into the household on a full-time, daily basis. This may be stressful and turbulent for the wife. In this respect, the husband's daily absence from the home except on weekends, because of work, was an acceptable pattern of life for the couple. The closer interpersonal contact now experienced is not. Another research investigation (Lee & Shehan, 1989) tells us that who retires first creates unique stress to this family transition. For example, an employed wife with a retired husband often encounters lower marital satisfaction than a wife in a dual-retired domestic arrangement or in a relationship where she retired first.

In relation to the latter, a retired man with a working wife may belatedly learn domestic skills, take over at home, and be useful, occupied, and appreciated. For many, such arrangements are satisfactory and fulfilling. However, if the husband is dependent, unable to take care of himself, or just doesn't like the prospects of being alone, he may push his wife to retire also (and take on the full-time task of his care and feeding and entertainment). Things may get

Companionship and sharing acquire special significance for couples during later life.

more complicated if the wife is younger than he and is just reaching the zenith of her career. Indeed, she may resent his pressure so much that she may, understandably, choose her career over her marriage (Pittman, 1987).

It is also important for the retired couple to adjust to new household routines during the final stage of the marriage cycle (J. P. Robinson, 1991). When the husband retires and spends most of his time in the household he frequently becomes aware of new responsibilities and expectations (as indicated earlier, this is especially true if the wife continues working). For example, husband and wife often become co-equals in domestic authority. However, this may not always be the case. The changing roles and relationships in retirement marriages may alter the relative power of some husbands and wives. It is possible that a husband's power declines when he loses the leverage provided by the breadwinner role. It seems the same would hold true for women who are wage earners, although current literature on the topic is scant.

The sharing of certain domestic chores and tasks is evident among many retired couples, thus giving the relationship an egalitarian flavor. Certain research (e.g., Brubaker & Ade-Ridder, 1986; Keith et al., 1981; Rexroat & Shehan, 1987) reports increased involvement in domestic chores among retired husbands. However, for traditional marriages, a continuation of division-of-labor patterns is apparent (Ade-Ridder & Brubaker, 1988; Brubaker & Hennon, 1982; Brubaker & Kinsel, 1985; Keating & Cole, 1980). This prompts Timothy Brubaker (1990b) to observe that for the most part, retired couples adhere to domestic responsibilities established earlier in their marriages, even though many expect to share more after retirement.

Changes in the health status of married couples may affect patterns of dyadic adjustment, including levels of satisfaction and happiness. When one partner needs assistance because of health reasons, the other is likely to become the caregiver (Johnson, 1983; Martens & Davies, 1990; Stone, Cafferata, & Sangl, 1987; Wenger, 1990; Zarit, Birkel, & Malone-Beach, 1989). However, gender differences arise when caregiving situations develop. A steady stream of literature indicates that caregiving wives tend to experience more stress and feelings of burden than husbands, and husbands are more likely to receive help from other relatives when caring for their spouses (Fitting, Rabins, Lucas, & Eastham, 1986; Johnson, 1985; Zarit, Birkel, & Malone-Beach, 1989).

Such gender differences in spousal caregiving were apparent in an interesting study involving two samples totaling 431 older married couples (Vinokur & Vinokur-Kaplan, 1990). In the first sample, data were collected from husbands and their wives, half of whom were long-term breast cancer survivors and half who constituted an asymptomatic matched control group. The second sample included data from husbands and their wives who had recently been diagnosed with breast cancer. Wives reported giving more social support to their husbands than they felt they received from them; and they reported giving more support than their husbands reported giving to them. Similarly, husbands reported receiving more social support from their wives than their wives reported receiving from them, except for the group with recently diagnosed breast cancer. Advanced age was correlated with husbands' reports of receiving more social support, and in the two breast cancer groups, of also giving more social support and engaging in less social undermining. The researchers found that among the women in the asymptomatic control group, those who were more physically impaired reported both giving and receiving less social support, and this was corroborated by husbands' reports.

As we learned in Chapter 10, a change in health status or the need for daily assistance may also cause older retired couples to rely on their adult children for help (Gubrium, 1991; Malone-Beach & Zarit, 1991; Mancini & Blieszner, 1989; Suitor & Pillemer, 1990). This is another force that could affect patterns of marital adjustment. Fortunately, a plethora of resource materials are available for those desiring more information on the topic of intergenerational caregiving (Armstrong, 1990; Deane, 1989; Lustbader, 1991; Qureshi & Walker, 1989; R. Robinson, 1990; Silverstone & Hyman, 1989; Sterneck, 1990).

Other Social Adjustments Retirement signifies the loss of job-related social contacts, although many compensate for this by establishing new friendships and involvements. The retiree must adjust to the fact that a work-related reference group is now gone. That feedback from employer and co-workers no longer exists has important implications for one's sense of identity. For many, this becomes a time to search elsewhere for a meaningful reference group and realign and reassess one's self-image (Crose, 1990; Krause & Alexander, 1990; Waters, 1990).

It appears that those who effectively adjust are the ones who manage to develop new interests and resist the shrinkage of one's social world (Bury & Holme, 1990; Francis, 1990; Ishii-Kuntz, 1990; Jacobs, 1990). According to Toni Antonucci and Hiroko Akiyama (1991), maintaining a support network of friends is important when meeting the challenges of retirement and other life cycle transitions. These authors feel that men and women have qualitatively and sometimes quantitatively different social networks. Both men and women have more women than men in their networks. Women usually report providing more support to more types of people than do men. Older people who have a lifetime of positive social relations believe that because of their interactions with others, they are able to cope with the experiences of life and will be able to age well. Social relations influence how individuals experience their lives and how they feel about their experiences, thus determining whether they will age well. At the same time, as older people experience specific crises, supportive people often provide them with help (Antonucci, 1990; Armstrong & Goldsteen, 1990; Auslander & Litwin, 1990; Bear, 1990; Jacobs, 1990).

An interesting investigation (Connidis & Davies, 1990) explored the nature of confidants and companions in the social support networks of older adults. The researchers gathered responses from a sample of 400 older persons to determine the relative importance of various family members (spouse, children, siblings, other relatives) and friends in the confidant and companion networks of later life. Significant differences were found among older persons (based on gender, marital status, and availability of children) in the salience of these ties as confidants and companions. There were also major differences in the configuration of the confidant versus companion networks. For example, children were more likely to be specialists as confidants; spouses and friends predominated as companions. Given the same range of accessibility, the researchers also discovered a greater dominance of a spouse in the companion rather than the confidant network among the married; a greater dominance of children in the confidant rather than the companion network among those with children; a greater dominance of friends in the companion rather than the confidant network for all groups; and a greater dominance of siblings and other relatives in the confidant rather than the companion network for all groups.

The development of a number of organizations in recent years has provided retirees with other types of of social support, either by facilitating existing social ties or creating new ones. Examples include senior centers, clubs, or social organizations. Also, various agencies provide opportunities for retirees to help others. Among the more common are Foster Grandparents, Senior Companions, the Retired Senior Volunteer Program, and the Service Corps of Retired Executives.

Related to the latter, it should be acknowledged that volunteer work offers a unique form of social support for retired adults. In addition to filling the gap left by work, Mary Kouri (1990) observes that many retirees volunteer because they want to do something that is useful to others. She estimates that about 40% of all U.S. citizens age 65 to 74, and about 29% of those over 75, are volunteers. Regula Herzog and James House (1991) add that volunteerism enables retirees to make several contributions: Through both paid and unpaid work, they produce valuable goods and services (the estimated financial value of volunteer services is about $150 billion a year); volunteers avoid reliance on hired help and public assistance; and, to the extent that activities increase their health and well-being, retirees benefit themselves as well as society as a whole.

A unique twist to the adjustments made during the retirement years are the increasing numbers of elderly involving themselves in educational pursuits. For example, the Elderhostel, started in 1975, has become especially attractive to

CONTINUOUS AND DISCONTINUOUS HUMAN DEVELOPMENT

Can you apply the issue of continuity and discontinuity to the retirement transition? Do you think retirees' adjustments and behaviors unfold in a smooth fashion with new dynamics gradually being added? Or do you see retirement adjustments developing at different rates, sometimes alternating between tranquil periods and times of abrupt, rapid change?

older individuals. The Elderhostel invites persons over 55 to reside for short periods on college campuses at low cost and attend a wide variety of classes, seminars, and workshops. In addition to Elderhostel, specialized educational programs for elderly persons are offered by government and industry as well as voluntary and religious organizations. Such programming, according to Sandra Pearce (1991), will increase in years to come. Because of this, it is incumbent on adult educators, as both researchers and practitioners, to discover more about adult learners and the best ways to meet their needs (Chene, 1991; Cox, 1991; DeCosta, 1991; Kuznar, 1991; McNeely, 1991; Weinrich & Boyd, 1992).

The Process of Retirement

To better understand the adjustments faced by retired couples, it is helpful to develop an awareness of the various phases through which the retirement role is acquired. Social gerontologist Robert Atchley (1982a, 1982b, 1991; Atchley & Robinson, 1982) believes role adjustments occur through a series of six phases. Because the retirement period is an individual phenomenon that varies in duration, relating these six phases to chronological ages is impossible. Also, individuals may not experience all the phases or encounter them in the order given here.

Before we examine these six phases, we need to make sure we understand the total significance and ramifications of retirement. Atchley (1982b) maintains that the process of retirement begins with attitudes toward retirement, retirement policies, and factors in the decision to retire. The retirement transition has varying effects, depending on how one arrives at retirement. Those who retire voluntarily usually have little or no difficulty adjusting. Those who are forced out by mandatory retirement policies tend to be dissatisfied at first, but eventually adjust. Those who retire because of poor health are understandably the most dissatisfied, although retirement improves health for many of them. Retirement itself has no predictable negative effect on physical health, self-esteem, or life satisfaction. It does tend to reduce activity level. A good adjustment in the retirement years depends on having a secure income, good health, meaningful activities, and high marital satisfaction.

Preretirement Phase   The **preretirement phase** can be divided into two substages, remote and near. In the remote phase, retirement is perceived as an event in the reasonably distant future. Anticipatory socialization and adjustment for retirement in this period are usually informal and unsystematic. The near phase emerges when workers become aware they will soon be retiring and that adjustments are necessary for a successful transition. Some workers may develop negative attitudes during the near phase because the realities of retirement are much clearer and financial prerequisites for the retirement role may not have been met. However, preretirement programs appear to be successful in reducing anxiety about retirement and reducing some of the ambiguity surrounding this new social role.

Honeymoon Phase   The **honeymoon phase** immediately following the actual retirement event is frequently characterized by a sense of euphoria that is partly the result of one's newfound freedom. It is often a busy period for many retirees, filled with such activities as visiting family members, traveling, and hobbies. The honeymoon period may be short or long, depending on the resources available and people's imaginativeness in using them.

Disenchantment Phase   After the honeymoon phase is over and life begins to slow down, some retirees become disenchanted and feel let down or even depressed. The depth of the emotional letdown in this **disenchantment phase** is related to a variety of factors, such as declining health, limited finances, or being unaccustomed to an independent lifestyle. In some cases, eagerly anticipated postretirement activities (for example, extensive traveling) may have lost their original appeal. Unrealistic preretirement fantasies, as well as inadequate anticipatory socialization for retirement, may also promote disenchantment.

Reorientation Phase   For those whose retirements either never got off the ground or landed with a loud crash, a **reorientation phase** of adjustment is necessary. At this time one's experience as a retired person is used to develop a more realistic view of life alternatives. Reorientation often embodies seeking social support and may also involve exploring new avenues of involvement.

Stability Phase   In the **stability phase,** the individual has mastered the retirement role. Stability does not refer to the absence of change, but rather to the routinization of criteria for dealing with change. People who reach this stage have established a well-developed set of criteria for making choices, which allows them to deal with life in a fairly comfortable and orderly fashion. They know what is expected of them and know what they have to work with, strengths as well as weaknesses.

Termination Phase   The **termination phase** occurs when the retirement role is cancelled out by the illness and disability that sometimes accompany late adulthood. When people are no longer capable of housework or self-care, they are transferred from the retirement role to the sick and disabled role. This role transfer is based on the loss of able-bodied status and autonomy, both of which are instrumental in carrying out the retirement role. Retired status is also lost, of course, if a full-time job is taken.

CHAPTER REVIEW

Unit One: Physical and Mental Development

The technical name for the study of aging and the aged population is gerontology. Social gerontologists seek to meet the needs of elderly persons by providing them with special services, programs, and policies. Geriatrics is the branch of medicine that provides aged persons with health care and health-related services. These and related disciplines succeed each year in providing the public with increasing amounts of knowledge concerning the aged population.

Physical aging represents complex degenerative physiological processes, characterized by many external and internal changes. Externally, the skin wrinkles and loses its elasticity, the hair grays and becomes sparse, and many elderly lose their teeth. Internally, the heart and lungs no longer operate at full potential, and in the brain there is a reduction of cerebral blood flow as well as a decline in oxygen and glucose consumption. A gradual decrease in sensory capacities also occurs, most notably vision and hearing.

Elderly people suffer from the same diseases as younger adults, but younger persons have a natural tendency to recover, whereas elderly persons have a tendency toward further deterioration. Among the more prevalent disorders and diseases among the aged are arthritis, hypertension, heart disease, cerebrovascular accident, cancer, and osteoporosis. To safeguard their health, elderly people need to take special care of themselves. Balanced diets and regular physical activity are considered essential in the overall maintenance of one's health.

Intellectual functions do change during late adulthood, but not to the extent our cultural myths would have us believe. Very few actually lose intellectual abilities. Although many aged individuals exhibit a decline in reaction times, general knowledge and vocabulary tend to remain constant over time and, for some people, verbal abilities may even increase. Some, however, may experience what is known as a terminal drop, a deterioration of intellectual functioning prior to death. Sensory and short-term memory storage systems appear to change little with age but long-term storage exhibits some decline. The elderly may also demonstrate losses in recall memory, compared to little or no change in recognition memory.

Unit Two: Personality and Social Development

Most experts agree that late adulthood is also a time to reevaluate past successes and failures. When studying personality dynamics during late adulthood, we again face the issue of long-term continuity or change. Those favoring the continuity or stability perspective maintain that the adult personality remains relatively unaltered from earlier years. Discontinuous personality theories, captured in the writings of Erik Erikson, Robert Peck, and Daniel Levinson, choose to characterize late adulthood as a period of change.

Successful aging is difficult to define, although it appears that satisfactory adjustment has an inner or psychological aspect and an outer, socially oriented aspect. Depending on the researcher consulted, we find a number of important dimensions attached to successful aging: subjective well-being, good self-esteem, positive role adaptation, resiliency, and personal control over one's life. Two of the older, yet nonetheless noteworthy theories of successful aging are the disengagement and activity theories. Personality dynamics are also important to study when investigating successful aging. We also noted that with age, it is not uncommon to engage in a life review, or reminiscing about the past. Reflecting on one's life has numerous positive benefits, including reliving past experiences and perhaps dealing with persisting conflicts.

Not all retired persons age successfully. Some may react negatively to the pressures of later life. Rates of psychiatric disturbances are higher for those in poor health, advanced in age, or who are unmarried because of divorce, separation, or widowhood. One category of maladaptive behavior is functional, and includes anxiety, schizophrenic, affective, personality, and substance-use disorders. Other types of maladaptive behavior fall under the category of organic brain syndrome. This category of brain impairment includes the dementias, which, as we learned, includes both reversible and irreversible categories. Delirium is an example of a reversible dementia. Irreversible and degenerative dementia includes multi-infarct dementia, Pick's disease, and Alzheimer's disease.

Unit Three: The Family

Most retired couples report considerable satisfaction with their marriages. For many, interests become increasingly directed toward one another, reflecting a mixture of satisfaction, caring, mutuality, and reciprocity. However, for those relationships characterized by unhappiness, it is plausible that the event of retirement heralds disruption and disharmony.

Most retired couples do not want to change their residence, primarily because they do not wish to face adjustment difficulties associated with moving. Declining health and limited income are other anchoring variables. When elderly people are afflicted with a disability or can no longer care for themselves, institutional care may be required. Four types of institutions for elderly persons were discussed in this unit: skilled-nursing facilities, intermediate-care facilities, residential-care facilities, and adult day-care facilities. All types of institutional-care facilities have recently fallen under the scrutiny of concerned officials, and efforts have been made to improve the quality and standards of living for the residents.

Kin relations for most retired couples focus on their children and grandchildren. Many aged people live near their children and interact rather frequently, although this is more true in urban environments than in rural settings. As far as family relationships are concerned, the emotional support given by adult children to aged parents is especially important during this stage of life.

Unit Four: Retirement

Retirement entails the transition from an economically productive role that is clearly defined to an economically nonproductive role that is often vague and ambiguous. The ambiguity stems from the relative newness of the retirement role in history. This particular unit stressed the importance of more fully defining the retirement role, for men as well as women.

Adjusting to retirement has psychological, financial, and social dimensions. Psychologically, retirees must relinquish a significant part of their lives and reassess their identities. Too often, people wrap their total identity around what they do. Financial adjustments usually represent the biggest chore for retirees. For many, Social Security benefits represent the only source of income, which may mean economic hardship. In addition to marital adjustments, retirement also brings about the loss of work-related social contacts and an important reference group.

The retirement transition has varying effects. Robert Atchley views retirement not only as a process but also as a social role that unfolds through a series of six phases: preretirement phase, honeymoon phase, disenchantment phase, reorientation phase, stability phase, and termination phase.

TERMS YOU SHOULD KNOW

activity theory
adult day-care facility
affective disorder
ageism
Alzheimer's disease
anticoagulant

anxiety disorder
arthritis
body transcendence versus body
    preoccupation
cardiac output
cataract

cerebrovascular accident (CVA)
conductive deafness
delirium
dementia
depression
disenchantment phase
disengagement theory
ego differentiation versus work-
    role preoccupation
ego transcendence versus ego
    preoccupation
estrogen
functional disorder
geriatrics
gerontology
glaucoma
honeymoon phase
institutionalism
integrity versus despair
intermediate-care facility
life review
Medicaid
Medicare

multi-infarct dementia
organic brain syndrome
osteoarthritis
osteoporosis
personality disorder
Pick's disease
preretirement phase
presbycusis
recall memory
recognition memory
reorientation phase
residential-care facility
retirement
rheumatoid arthritis
schizophrenic disorder
sensorineural deafness
skilled-nursing facility
social genontology
stability phase
substance-use disorder
terminal decline
termination phase
transient ischemic attack (TIA)

THINKING IN ACTION

• Good physical health is important at any age but for elderly persons it can make the difference between being an invalid or being very mobile. If you were chairing a physical fitness committee, what kind of a physical exercise regimen would you design for the younger elderly; for the older elderly? How would it differ, if at all, from programs geared toward younger adults? What kinds of nutritional recommendations would you make? Finally, as chair of this committee, describe how both physical fitness and proper nutrition influence other spheres of development, such as social interactions, self-worth, and stress management.

• Find a partner to approach this next exercise. On separate pieces of paper, define what you regard to be successful aging and growing old gracefully. Next, list and briefly describe 10 characteristics of people who age successfully. When you have finished, swap papers. Are your definitions similar or dissimilar? Do you agree on the ingredients of successful aging? For an added dimension, consider doing the same exercise with an older and younger adult.

• Assume you have been asked to serve on the Housing Commission for Elderly People and you are part of a group looking for a site to establish a one- and two-bedroom apartment complex. What facilities would you include within the complex itself? In what type of neighborhood would you build? Would the residents have easy access to grocery stores, entertainment, a library, and so on? What safety factors both inside and outside of your complex are important to include? Develop a plan that would be a credit to your community.

• Your elderly father can no longer care for himself, and you are faced with the institutional-care decision. Keeping in mind the material covered in this chapter, what kinds of options do you have with care facilities? How will you determine if a facility offers quality care? Finally, how can you help your father adjust to institutional care? What kinds of things can you and your family do to ease the transition?

• You are the president of a large corporation and would like to design a preretirement program for your older employees. More specifically, you want to make sure your workers receive guidance on important financial, psychological, and social matters. Think about how you would design such a program, particularly the topics it might include, when it should begin, how it should be taught, and how you follow up on its success or failure.

RECOMMENDED READINGS

1. Baltes, P. B., & Baltes, M. M. (Eds.). (1990). *Successful aging: Perspectives from the behavioral sciences.* New York: Cambridge University Press.

   A multifaceted approach to the study of successful aging.

2. Harel, Z., McKinney, D. A., & Williams, M. (Eds.). (1990). *Black aged: Understanding diversity and service needs.* Newbury Park, CA: Sage.

   The diversity of African-American family caregiving as well as family economics are among the topics included.

3. Laczko, F., & Phillipson, C. (1991). *Changing work and retirement: Social policy and the older worker.* Philadelphia: Open University Press.

   Many topics related to the experience of retirement are available in this text.

4. Pfeifer, S. K., & Sussman, M. B. (Eds.). (1991). *Families: Intergenerational and generational connections.* Binghamton, NY: Haworth Press.

   This text offers good coverage of intergenerational dynamics, including factors that promote family cohesion and solidarity.

5. Schaie, K. W., Blazer, D., & House, J. S. (Eds.). (1992). *Aging, health behaviors, and health outcomes.* Hillsdale, NJ: Erlbaum.

   Depression in elderly persons is one of the many topics available.

Death and Bereavement

What Do You Think?

DEATH AND DYING IN MODERN SOCIETY

Dimensions of Death

THEORIES OF PSYCHOLOGICAL DYING PROCESSES

Elisabeth Kübler-Ross's Theory
Denial Stage
Anger Stage
Bargaining Stage
Depression Stage
Acceptance Stage

Edwin Shneidman's Theory
E. Mansell Pattison's Theory
The Acute Phase
The Chronic Living-Dying Interval
The Terminal Phase

DYING WITH DIGNITY

The Hospice Program

The Right to Die

AT THE MOMENT OF DEATH

DEFINITIONS AND COMPONENTS OF DEATH

Functional Death
Cellular Death

Brain Death

IS THERE LIFE AFTER DEATH?

BEREAVEMENT AND GRIEF

Coping with Loss
Expressions of Grief
Physical Expressions
Cognitive Expressions
Affective Expressions
Behavioral Expressions
Stages of Grief
The Impact Stage
The Recoil Stage

The Accommodation Stage
Dysfunctional and Functional Methods of Coping
Avoidance
Obliteration
Idolization
Patterns of Functional Coping
Endings and New Beginnings

Chapter Review • Terms You Should Know • Thinking in Action • Recommended Readings

WHAT
DO
YOU
THINK?

• Eastern cultures regard death as part of life. Life and death are said to complement each other. Hinduism, for example, teaches that the body passes through the life stages and that at death, the soul assumes another body. Western culture, though, tends to view death apart from life, and many people have difficulty accepting it. Why is this so? What makes us uneasy and anxious about death? Why is death a taboo subject of conversation?

• How do dying persons come to terms with their fate? What kinds of psychological processes do they experience? Why are some better able to cope with death than others? As we discover in this chapter, many forces interact and influence how individuals will react to death. Some researchers, such as Elisabeth Kübler-Ross, maintain that individuals will pass through fairly predictable stages when informed of impending death. Other researchers have identified a complex interplay of emotional reactions as death draws near, and still others maintain it is the course of the illness itself that triggers a person's psychological reaction. Obviously, responses to death vary greatly, and this chapter is designed to shed light on some of the psychological experiences of dying.

• How can the many needs of the dying person best be met? Is there a way to humanize death and avoid the impersonalization often found in sterile hospitalized environments? Today, many favor hospice programs, humane care to terminally ill patients in a homelike environment and freedom from physical and psychological suffering. In so doing, proponents of hospice feel the indignities often associated with dying in conventional medical settings are removed. We provide coverage of hospice in this chapter, including its program design and goals.

• Today a number of complex issues surround euthanasia, also known as mercy killing. For example, is euthanasia moral? What ethics are involved in life and death situations? Who makes the decision to end a life? In the recent past, a number of important cases have underscored the controversy regarding euthanasia, whether it be the now famous Karen Ann Quinlan and Nancy Cruzan Supreme Court rulings or the assisted suicides performed by Michigan physician Jack Kevorkian. As we see in this chapter, euthanasia sparks a flurry of medical, legal, religious, and moral questions. How do you feel about euthanasia? Do you think most people are in favor of it? Are we likely to see more right-to-die legislation in the future?

DEATH AND DYING IN MODERN SOCIETY

For everyone, to live means to eventually die. Death is the end of life, and no one escapes having to face and cope with it. This inevitable consequence attached to life looms as the final developmental task. It is a chore formidable in scope, and people react to death in different fashions. Indeed, emotional reactions are especially diverse, from fear and sorrow to resignation or defiance. Following death, mourning the loss of a loved one knows equally wide variation (Burns, 1991; Detmer & Lamberti, 1991; Horacek, 1991; O'Brien et al., 1991).

Cultural beliefs greatly influence the way people perceive and react to dying and death. As such, attitudes toward the end of life are usually consistent with the way people live. For example, Hindus and Buddhists celebrate death because it symbolizes a new beginning or rebirth. They place a great premium on cultivating a disciplined mind and body, largely because these forces will be used to conquer and transcend death. In Tibet, individuals are taught that accepting death and dealing with their own impending mortality are important life skills. Being able to die with contentment and satisfaction, rather than with grief or shame, is viewed as a skillful art. Tibetans maintain that contented dying persons are able to see their whole lives reflected before them during final moments.

In Western culture, the subject of death seems to be taboo. It is for most a sensitive topic, and one that is avoided and frequently repressed. Some people try to deny it; others live in fear of it. Most of us have difficulty believing we're going to die. Further, when many discuss death, true feelings are masked in favor of such euphemisms as "kicked the bucket," "knocked off," or "bit the dust." Even medical specialists are frequently uncomfortable with the subject of death and do not like to be present when their patients die (R. Brown, 1990; Feinstein & Mayo, 1990; Samarel, 1991).

To many, death is not a real part of the human experience. Yet paradoxically, the thoughts of death that are denied by the culture reemerge in perverse forms, as seen in the large segments of the population who are preoccupied with violence, killing, and war. John Stephenson (1985) goes so far as to say that the subject of death is sometimes obscene and pornographic. Multitudes are drawn to newspaper and television accounts of death and react with a mixture of fascination, curiosity, and excitement. Others are attracted to violent movies and paperback novels that depict death in countless ways. We deny death, but we are also obsessed by it.

In many instances the dying are kept hidden or isolated from all but close relatives, doctors, and nurses. We frequently give hospitals the responsibility of caring for the dying, yet many are ill equipped to deal with the task. It goes without saying that death is disturbing to virtually everyone, but the facility with which it can be hidden makes it possible to deny its presence. Frequently it is treated as a closely guarded secret, even when it is obvious and everyone talks about it (Charmaz, 1980; Seale, 1990; Z. R. Wolf, 1991).

Partly because of this isolation and denial, death, like other disturbing events, arouses awe and dread. Death has been made more difficult to comprehend and accept. Younger people frequently have little direct experience with death and the sense of humility it can bring. This distancing of death from the living also offers a striking contrast to past societal customs. Death before the turn of the century usually meant that people died in their own homes, with the remaining family present. Dealing with the dead body was an ordinary part of domestic life. Today, people die away from the home and the tasks of preparing the dead for burial are handled by others who are paid to perform these services. Our participation today in the rituals surrounding the dead is minimal (DeSpelder & Strickland, 1992).

Because the dying are kept isolated and hidden from us, death has become secretive and elusive. Children, adolescents, and adults alike often fail to come to grips with death because they don't have the chance to confront it. Most experts (e.g., Bertman, 1991; Samarel, 1991) agree that such denial results in limited self-growth. Seeking to comprehend it, on the other hand, may add a new and healthy dimension to our existence (Caserta & Lund, 1992; Durlak & Riesenberg, 1991; Oltjenbruns, 1991). Death always has been and always will be with us. It is a part of everyone's existence and needs to be recognized as a natural component of the life cycle. It is our task to learn to view death, not as an unexpected event, but rather as a certainty. If this can be accomplished, we will undoubtedly learn to live our lives with more meaning and nurture a greater

INTERRELATEDNESS OF AGING PROCESSES

How have your psychological reactions to dying and death been shaped by your social experiences? Have any family experiences or social customs caused you to deny and avoid the topic of death? Do you think seeking to understand death will help you focus on life and set priorities in living?

For all humanity, to live means eventually to die.

appreciation of the amount of time we have on earth (R. Brown, 1990; Campanelli, 1990).

In recent years, there has been growing interest in the field of death and dying, an area known technically as **thanatology.** *Thanatologists,* specialists within the field of death and dying, have succeeded in educating increasingly larger segments of the population. Books, journals, classes, and research centers devoted to the exploration of this topic have emerged. Articles in popular magazines, television talk shows, and documentaries attest to the fact that the shroud which once engulfed this topic is being lifted.

▬ Dimensions of Death

Understanding death becomes especially difficult when people think about the ending of their own particular lives. This is especially true among younger people, who have a tendency to cling to personal invulnerability and immortality. For example, many adolescents perceive themselves as being invulnerable to the risks of contracting HIV (Dryfoos, 1990; Gray & Saracino, 1991; Hansen, Hahn, and Wolkenstein, 1990). We often avoid the mention of death when it has a personal connotation. It is impossible for us to picture an ending to our own lives, and such an end is usually attributed to a malicious intervention from the outside by another party. To put it another way, in our unconscious, we can only be killed; we cannot die of old age or a natural cause (Leming & Dickinson, 1990; Marshall, 1980).

It is difficult to conceive of one's own death, and many don't want to contemplate its prospects. But think of it or not, we all know that death lies in wait for us. Not knowing when our deaths will arrive gives urgency to the question of what we should do with our lives. To answer this question, though, means to consider another: We have to decide whether death is the end or whether it is a doorway to another life. The ultimate meaning we attach to death, our personal death, can fill us with satisfaction or pain and fear (Rowe, 1982).

Although death can—and does—occur at any age, elderly people are more aware of its imminence. And even though death preoccupies them more than it does younger people, elderly people seem less afraid of it. In support of this, one investigation (Gesser, Wong, & Reker, 1988) showed that death anxiety tends to peak during middle adulthood and then decline during the years of late adulthood. However, the fact that elderly people have lower levels of death anxiety should not be interpreted as a resignation to or desire for death. Rather, it may mean they are more philosophical about death than younger adults, as well as more realistic and accepting of their own mortality.

One study (Henderson, 1990) involving older adults with living wills sought to discover if more control over one's dying would decrease anxiety about death. Subjects assigned to an experimental group received intervention in the form of counseling and filling out a questionnaire regarding specific treatments (e.g., CPR, feeding tubes), proxy decision making, and other related questions. Results show that the mean death anxiety score for the experimental group decreased, whereas the control group's mean score did not change significantly. The experimental group's score was further reduced by the presentation of and replies to an addendum to the living will, specifying the person's wishes about his or her own death. We have more to say about the living will a bit later in this chapter.

As we've indicated, the dying person is sometimes trapped in a conspiracy of silence by relatives or medical staff members. Frequently, the situation is discussed, but the patient is excluded. Some relatives and friends may avoid any discussion whatsoever, because they are too uncomfortable with the topic. When dying people ask questions about their fate, their inquiries are often avoided. Usually, questions are turned aside and any means are employed to deny the central issues (Seale, 1990; Weisman, 1984).

David Hendin (1984) refers to this as the "say nothing" philosophy, indicating that it is just as common among family members as it is for physicians. Studies repeatedly show that a majority of physicians favor a conspiracy of silence regarding their fatally ill patients. There are at least three reasons for this. One, there is a real fear among physicians that patients, when given such information, may give up or attempt to commit suicide. Two, a physician simply may have no way of telling how long a person has to live. Furthermore, the possibility of spontaneous remission of a disease always exists. Three, there is always a chance a cure will be found.

When told about impending death, most dying people are thankful to have learned the truth and to have been able to discuss it. Being honest with patients about their fate is believed to be instrumental in helping them reach an acceptance of their impending death. We must keep in mind, however, the previously mentioned variations among people about the topic of death. *When* and *how* such news is to be shared are delicate issues, and the best interests of the patient have to be served. Factors of personality, emotional constitution, and one's ability to function under stress must be considered on an individual basis (DeSpelder & Strickland, 1992; Lynn, 1991; Samarel, 1991).

Accepting the reality of death looms as life's final developmental task.

THEORETICAL ISSUES

How can you apply the Eriksonian stage of integrity versus despair to one's attitudes about dying and death? Do you think developing a sense of integrity promotes one's acceptance, rather than denial, of one's mortality? Why or why not?

THEORIES OF PSYCHOLOGICAL DYING PROCESSES

How do individuals come to terms with the prospect of their own death? What are some of the psychological reactions and adaptations when facing death? In an effort to address such questions, we can examine a number of theories that explore what happens when death draws closer. Among the more prominent explanations are theories proposed by Elisabeth Kübler-Ross, Edwin Shneidman, and E. Mansell Pattison.

■■■ Elisabeth Kübler-Ross's Theory

Described by herself as a "country doctor," Kübler-Ross is a psychiatrist who joined the faculty at the University of Chicago in 1965. Shortly afterward, she served as an adviser to a group of theology graduate students who were investigating various aspects of death. To gather more complete information and to increase her own knowledge of death, Kübler-Ross began interviewing dying patients. It was from these interviews, hundreds in number, as well as from her seminars, workshops, and lectures, that her thoughts on the topic of death emerged (Kübler-Ross, 1969, 1974, 1975, 1981, 1982, 1983).

At the heart of Kübler-Ross's research is the concept of the dying process as consisting of five interrelated stages. Individuals will pass through these stages as death draws nearer, although individual differences can exist. For example, some people may skip a stage whereas others may not go through all five stages in the order proposed. It is also not uncommon for individuals to get stuck in a particular stage, or to vacillate from one stage to another. Finally, the five stages may overlap. The underlying emotion in all of these stages is hope. Hope springs eternal.

Denial Stage   The first phase of the dying process is called the **denial stage.** When informed of impending death, most people react with shock and the general feeling of, "No, not me, it can't be true." Because in our unconscious minds we are all immortal, it is inconceivable for us to acknowledge that we have to face death. When first told they are going to die, some patients may demand more tests, or change doctors with the hope of receiving a more favorable prognosis. In essence, the stark reality of the situation is denied.

One terminally ill patient described by Kübler-Ross was convinced her X-rays were "mixed up" by the hospital and could not possibly be back so soon. When none of this could be confirmed, she asked to leave the hospital and began to search for other physicians to get a more satisfactory explanation for her symptoms. Whether these doctors confirmed the original diagnosis or not, she reacted in a similar fashion each time; she requested examination and reexamination, partially aware that the original diagnosis was accurate, but also wanting additional opinions in the hope the first conclusion was an error. At the same time, she wanted to stay in contact with these doctors so she could have their help "at all times."

Denial, or at least partial denial, is employed by virtually all patients and is believed to be a relatively healthy way of initially dealing with this uncomfortable situation. Denial can serve as a buffer after unexpected shocking news. It enables patients to collect their thoughts and, with time, to utilize other, less radical defenses. The use of these other defenses, however, will depend on several factors, including how patients are told the news and how much time they have to acknowledge the inevitable event gradually.

David Carroll's (1985) research reveals that three forms of denial exist. *Absolute denial* is a flat refusal to believe what one has been told. According to his research, some patients refuse to accept the diagnosis and others block it out. Thus people who otherwise seem stable can exhibit a sudden pathological response to news of terminal illness. Such people can, for instance, wipe out the memory of weeks, even months spent in the hospital, staring blankly at anyone who mentions the event. At times it may even seem the person is losing his or her mind, but the truth is we all have our own tolerance for bad news and our own method of digesting it.

Fluctuating denial is another form. Individuals under a sentence of death often change their capacity to deal with the truth. Sometimes this capacity may be puzzlingly inconstant, emerging and vanishing from hour to hour like the sun through the clouds. A dying patient may carry on long discussions with the night nurse or even the janitor, making it quite clear that he or she is aware of the seriousness of the disease. Then, in front of family members or friends, the patient does a complete about-face, chatting away, quite sincerely, about personal plans that extend far into the future.

In many respects, the ego is a wise and kindly governor. It knows its own limitations; it knows when to shut down. If a moment arrives when it can no longer endure bad news, it mercifully sets up a dividing wall between itself and the world and protects its integrity. The amount of avoidance a dying person employs is exactly the amount he or she needs in order to function.

Finally, there is *modified denial,* in which a person may acknowledge part of the truth, but a truth tailored to suit his or her particular needs. A patient may, for instance, admit to being very sick but not to being terminally sick. The patient may twist medical opinion, considering a physician's statement that "We'll do everything we possibly can" as a promise of cure. The patient may inform friends, "They're not giving me radiation treatment. I think that must mean I don't have cancer." This type of avoidance behavior allows a person to acknowledge that something is wrong, perhaps seriously amiss, but not amiss enough to constitute a crisis.

Anger Stage   The second phase of the dying process is the **anger stage.** When denial is no longer successful, the patient typically experiences feelings of anger, rage, envy, and resentment. Whereas the patient's reaction to catastrophic news in stage 1 is "No, it's not true, there must be some mistake," the patient may say in stage 2, "Why me? Why not someone else?"

Compared to the period of denial, this stage is difficult for the family and medical staff to handle, largely because the patient's anger is projected and displaced at random. Kübler-Ross illustrates how patients may displace anger. They may complain that

> . . . the doctors are just no good, they don't know what tests to require and what diet to prescribe. They keep the patients too long in the hospital or don't respect their wishes in regard to special privileges. They allow a miserably sick roommate to be brought into their room when they pay so much money for some privacy and rest, etc. The nurses are even more often a target of their anger. Whatever

they touch is not right. The moment they have left the room the bell rings. The light is on the very minute they start their report for the next shift of nurses. When they do shake the pillows and straighten out the bed, they are blamed for never leaving the patients alone. When they do leave the patients alone, the light goes on with the request to have the bed arranged more comfortably. The visiting family is received with little cheerfulness and anticipation, which makes the encounter a painful event. They then either respond with grief and tears, guilt or shame, or avoid future visits, which only increases the patient's discomfort and anger. (1969, pp. 50–51)

It is important for family members and hospital personnel to empathize with the dying patient and realize why and how anger originates. To be sure, wherever patients look at this stage they will find grievances. Yet patients who are understood and given some time and attention will soon lower their voices and reduce their angry demands. In time, they will come to realize they are valuable human beings who are cared for and permitted to function at the highest possible level as long as they can.

Bargaining Stage   The third component of the dying process is termed the **bargaining stage.** Patients who were unable to face the truth in the first stage and were generally angry in the second now hope that death can be postponed or delayed in some way. Some may entertain thoughts of entering into some type of agreement with their creator: "If God has decided to take me from this earth and He did not respond to my angry pleas, He may be more favorable if I ask nicely."

The terminally ill patient may know from past experience (usually from childhood) that good behavior results in a reward, sometimes the granting of a wish for special privileges. Now the patient usually wishes for an extension of life, or for a few days without pain or physical discomfort. Kübler-Ross supplies an example of bargaining with a patient who was

> . . . in utmost pain and discomfort, unable to go home because of her dependence on injections for pain relief. She had a son who proceeded with his plans to get married, as the patient had wished. She was very sad to think that she would be unable to attend this big day, for he was her oldest and favorite child. With combined efforts, we were able to teach her self-hypnosis which enabled her to be quite comfortable for several hours. She had made all sorts of promises if she could only live long enough to attend the marriage. The day preceding the wedding she left the hospital as an elegant lady. Nobody would have believed her real condition. She was "the happiest person in the whole world" and looked radiant. I wondered what her reaction would be when the time was up for which she had bargained. I will never forget the moment when she returned to the hospital. She looked tired and somewhat exhausted, and before I could say hello said, "Now don't forget I have another son!" (Kübler-Ross, 1969, p. 83)

Thus, in essence, bargaining is an attempt to postpone. Among its most important features, bargaining includes a prize offered "for good behavior," a self-imposed "deadline" (for example, the son's wedding), and an implicit promise that the patient will not request more, if this one delay is granted. (In regard to the last, however, few if any patients keep their promises.) Interestingly, Kübler-Ross reports that a large number of patients promise "a life dedicated to God" or "a life in the service of the church" in exchange for some additional time. Many also promise to donate parts of their body to science, if, in return, the doctors will use their knowledge of science to extend their lives.

Interestingly, a person's will to live appears to postpone death, at least for a while. This was the central finding of several studies headed by David Phillips (1992; Phillips & Smith, 1990). He discovered that the death rates of elderly Chinese women decreased before and during those holidays in which they played a pivotal role. After the celebration, the death rate increased. Also, deaths of Jewish persons dipped 31% before the holiday of Passover and peaked by the same amount just afterward. Finally, women are slightly more likely to die of natural causes in the week after their birthdays than any other week of the year. In contrast, men are more likely to die in the weeks before a birthday than during the rest of the year.

In analyzing these findings, Phillips proposes that some dying patients are able to prolong life briefly until they have reached a positive symbolic occasion. Thus his research supports anecdotal evidence of people clinging to life to survive milestones such as a birthday, wedding, anniversary, or holiday. Such events may consciously or unconsciously be an opportunity to say good-bye, a way to bring closure to one's life, or to celebrate life with relatives one might not otherwise see. Regarding the gender differences that surfaced with birthdays, Phillips speculates that men are more likely than women to dread birthdays. They are less likely to place importance on relationships with family and friends, which are celebrated on such occasions. He adds that men often use birthdays for taking stock of their lives and noting failure to achieve unrealistic career goals.

CONTINUOUS AND DISCONTINUOUS HUMAN DEVELOPMENT

Is Kübler-Ross's stage theory truly discontinuous such as those proposed by, say, Piaget or Erikson? Since she, herself, admits her stages are subject to individual variation and may not be sequential, is the use of the word *stages* misleading? Do you think dying processes can be reduced to such a stagelike chronology?

Depression Stage   The **depression stage** is the fourth part of the dying process. When the terminally ill cannot deny their illnesses any longer, when additional surgery or hospitalization is required, when more symptoms develop, they become engulfed by a sense of great loss. To be sure, the terminally ill patient must endure numerous hardships in addition to physical problems, including financial burdens and the loss of employment, because of many absences or an inability to function. Instead of reacting with anger or rage at this point, as they might have earlier, patients are likely to experience depression.

Two kinds of depression can be identified. The first, called **reactive depression,** results from a loss that has already occurred. The cause of the depression can usually be elicited by an understanding person, and some of the unrealistic guilt or shame that often accompanies this depression can be alleviated. The woman who has had breast surgery and is worried about no longer being a woman can be complimented for some especially feminine feature. In some way she can hopefully be reassured she is still as much a woman as she was before the operation.

The second type of depression, called **preparatory depression,** occurs in response to impending loss. Whereas encouragement and reassurance are useful in helping people suffering from reactive depression, they are not effective in helping those experiencing preparatory depression. Here, depression is a preparation for the impending loss of love objects, a means by which the state of acceptance can be facilitated. For this reason, it would be contradictory for us to tell the patient to look at the sunny side of things and not to be sad, especially because everyone is terribly sad when a loved one is lost.

A better approach would be to allow depressed patients who are terminally ill to express their sorrow so a final acceptance of their condition will be easier. Such patients frequently express gratitude toward those who can sit nearby during this period of depression and not constantly remind the patient that sadness is to be avoided. Unlike reactive depression, preparatory depression is frequently a silent response. Many times there is little or no need for words:

> It is much more a feeling that can be mutually expressed and is often done better with a touch of a hand, a stroking of the hair, or just a silent sitting together. This is the time when the patient may just ask for a prayer, when he begins to occupy himself with things ahead rather than behind. It is a time when too much interference from visitors who try to cheer him up hinders his emotional preparation rather than enhances it. (Kübler-Ross, 1969, pp. 87–88)

Acceptance Stage   The fifth and final phase of the dying process is called the **acceptance stage.** If patients have had enough time, that is, if the death is not sudden or unexpected, and if they have been given some assistance in working through the four previous stages, they will reach a stage where they are neither depressed nor angry about their "fate."

In most instances patients in the acceptance stage have had the opportunity to express their feelings: their envy of the healthy and living and their anger and resentment toward those who do not have to face death so soon. The need to mourn the impending loss of meaningful people and places has usually been met, and patients typically contemplate their approaching death with a certain degree of quiet expectation. Acceptance is a period almost devoid of feeling. For this reason, families usually need more help and support during this time than patients themselves.

Patients prefer to be left alone much of the time, and their interests generally diminish. They also need frequent brief intervals of sleep. Because patients in the acceptance stage are seldom talkative, communication is generally more nonverbal than verbal. It is as if the pain has disappeared and the struggle is over. It becomes a time for the final rest before the long journey.

A few patients may struggle right to the very end, fighting to keep alive whatever hopes they can. For these individuals, it is impossible to reach the stage of acceptance. In other words, the harder one fights to avoid the inevitable death and the more one denies it, the more difficult it is to die with peace and dignity. In the accompanying Lifespan Development in Action box, we supply some thoughts on how to communicate with a terminally ill person throughout the course of these stages. Figure 12–1 illustrates the five stages of dying proposed by Kübler-Ross.

Edwin Shneidman's Theory

Edwin Shneidman (1978, 1980, 1984), although acknowledging the existence of such feelings as denial, anger, bargaining, depression, and acceptance, does not believe these states represent stages in the dying process. He suggests that

Lifespan Development in Action

PROVIDING SUPPORT TO A TERMINALLY ILL PERSON

Learning how to relate to a dying individual requires special sensitivity and understanding. Many of us are uncomfortable with the topic of dying, let alone finding the right things to say to a terminally ill person. In an effort to improve the interactions that take place between the living and dying, the following suggestions are offered:

Take steps to understand your own feelings about dying and death. You need to work on accepting your own eventual death, and viewing death as a normal part of life. If this cannot be done, chances are you will be uncomfortable talking with someone who is terminally ill. You may also not be able to discuss the dying person's concerns in an understanding fashion.

Show you are willing to talk about the person's concerns. This can be done verbally as well as with body language, including touching or hugging. Also respect the person's right *not* to talk about certain concerns. Seek to show you are emotionally supportive, caring, and available to listen.

If you have trouble talking about certain topics, tell the person. Do not be afraid to inform the patient about your limitations or sensitivities. This takes the guesswork out of the relationship. Honesty, openness, and mutual respect are important ingredients in this kind of relationship.

Answer questions as accurately as you can. If you do not know an answer, such as to a medical concern, seek out someone who can provide the requested information. Being evasive or ambiguous often heightens a dying person's concerns. If there is a chance for recovery, this could be mentioned. Indeed, even a small margin of hope can be a comfort to dying persons. However, chances for recovery should never be exaggerated.

Allow the dying person to accept the reality of the situation at his or her own pace. Do not try and force acceptance. The psychological acceptance of one's fate is an extremely important facet of the dying process. To this end, relevant information should never be withheld. Remember, the dying have rights too, including access to all of the facts.

Respect the religious or philosophical viewpoints of the dying person. Do not prejudge or condemn a person's views because they are inconsistent with yours. Also, do not impose your own personal views. When listening, try instead to be open-minded, accepting, and supportive.

Help family and friends accept the reality of a dying person's death. If those close to the patient accept the inevitable, it often helps the dying person to do the same. Keep in mind, too, that they may have a number of concerns they want to share. Make it known that you are available to provide assistance, if needed. (Adapted from Zastrow & Kirst-Ashman, 1987)

FIGURE 12-1
Kübler-Ross's Model of the Dying Process.

This diagram shows five stages of dying, as proposed by Kübler-Ross.

SOURCE: From E. Kübler-Ross, *Death: The Final Stage of Growth*. Englewood Cliffs, NJ: Prentice-Hall, 1975. Reprinted by permission of Simon & Schuster, Inc.

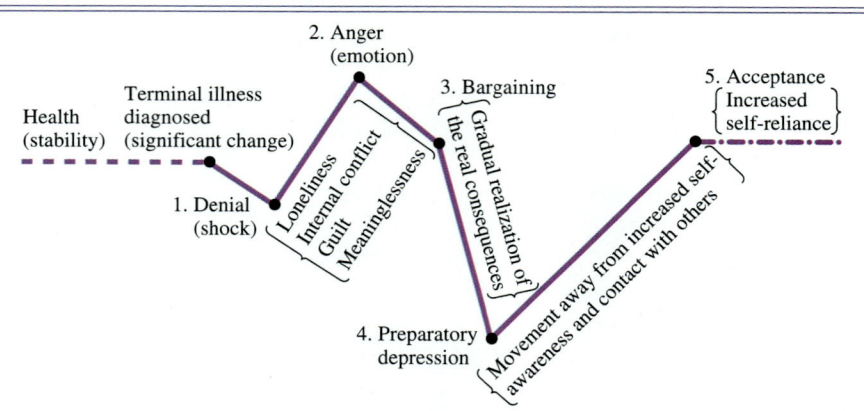

people experience a clustering of intellectual and affective states. Such states may be fleeting, lasting for a day or a week, and are set, not unexpectedly, against the backdrop of one's total personality and philosophy of life. Rather than progressing through a series of five stages, people instead experience a variety of emotional states in which there is a constant coming and going. Shneidman believes the emotional states include a constant interplay between disbelief and hope. There is a waxing and waning of anguish, terror, acquiescence and surrender, rage and envy, disinterest and ennui, pretense, taunting and daring, and even yearning for death. All of these emotions are in the context of bewilderment and pain.

▬ E. Mansell Pattison's Theory

E. Mansell Pattison (1977), like Shneidman, believes each patient is an individual and will react differently to the experience of dying. Pattison has proposed a model of the dying process that suggests three possible *processes,* rather than stages. He emphasizes that individual differences can be expected, as well as a wide range of emotional responses. The three processes or phases are the acute phase, the chronic living-dying interval, and the terminal phase.

The Acute Phase   The **acute phase** begins when an individual comes to the realization that death due to a terminal illness is imminent. The knowledge of impending death produces a crisis event and creates considerable anxiety. The anxiety may be accompanied by other emotions, such as anger, fear, or resentment.

The Chronic Living-Dying Interval   The **chronic living-dying interval** is characterized initially by a reduction in anxiety, but is soon replaced by numerous and diverse emotional states not previously experienced. The following represent some of the more common feelings of the dying patient at this time:

• *Fear of the unknown.* As death draws nearer, dying patients may be afraid because they do not know what lies ahead. They wonder: What is my fate in the hereafter? What will happen to my body after death? How will my family and friends respond to my dying? What will happen to my survivors? Some of these questions can be answered rather quickly, but others will take longer. Some will remain unanswered.

• *Loneliness.* With sickness, there appears to be a sense of isolation from oneself and from others. For the dying person, this feeling becomes even more evident and produces a fear of loneliness—in many cases, right from the very beginning. Withdrawal from work or recreational activities, increasing physical debilitation and bed confinement, and perhaps not knowing what to say when friends do visit, may contribute to this fear.

• *Sorrow.* The dying face many losses, including loved ones, their jobs, and future plans, to mention but a few. Accepting these losses and learning to tolerate the painful experience of sorrow that accompanies each may produce a state of fear or anxiety.

• *Loss of body.* Because our bodies represent part of our self-concept, illnesses affect us both physically and psychologically. Patients may react to debilitating conditions with shame and feelings of disgrace, inadequacy, and lowered self-esteem.

• *Loss of self-control.* As debilitating diseases progress, we become less capable of self-control. Generally speaking, there is less energy, vitality, and responsiveness. Most people think less quickly and accurately, and may fear this loss of mental function.

• *Suffering and pain.* The dread of suffering and pain is not just a physical fear, but rather a fear of the unknown and the unmanageable. Although senseless pain is intolerable to most people, pain may be accepted and dealt with if it does not involve punishment, being ignored, or not being cared for.

• *Loss of identity.* The loss of human contact, family and friends, body structure and function, self-control, and total consciousness all threaten one's sense of identity. Human contacts affirm who we are, family contacts affirm what we have shared, and contact with our body and mind affirms our own self-being. The dying process, to be sure, threatens many facets of one's self-identity.

The Terminal Phase   The **terminal phase** is the third process of dying. This is a time when the patient begins to withdraw from people and events. The emotional states described in the previous phase may still be evident, but withdrawal seems to dominate. Figure 12-2 depicts the phases of dying outlined by Pattison.

To fully appreciate these three phases of dying, an understanding is needed of what is referred to as a **dying trajectory.** A dying trajectory is the duration and form the dying process will take. There are four possible trajectories. First, a person may face a certain death in that he or she is told the end of life is near (one is given 6 months to live). Second, certain death may also be faced, but the exact time be unknown (one is told death can strike any time, from 6 months to a year). Third, the possibility of an uncertain death means it is unclear whether a patient will die. The question, though, will be answered in time (if surgery is successful, a person may recover). Fourth, death may also be uncertain if it is not known whether a person will die, and the question remains unanswered (the patient may have a chronic heart problem). These four dying trajectories have obvious implications for the three phases of dying just described (Glasser & Strauss, 1968; Strauss & Glasser, 1970).

PUTTING THEORIES OF DYING INTO PERSPECTIVE Theories such as those proposed by Kübler-Ross, Shneidman, and Pattison have helped us better understand the psychological processes involved in death or loss. Comprehending such complex dynamics is useful in helping people talk with and assist

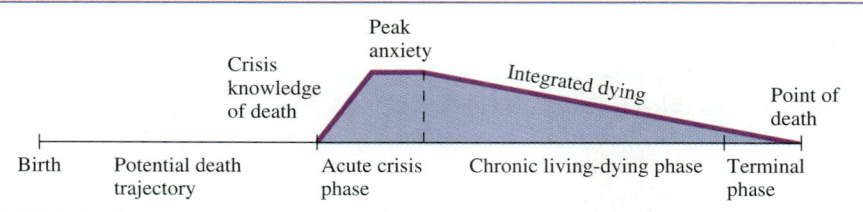

FIGURE 12-2
Pattison's Model of the Dying Process.

This diagram illustrates the phases of dying proposed by Pattison.

SOURCE: Pattison, E. M. (1977). The experience of dying. In E. M. Pattison (Ed.), *The experience of dying.* Englewood Cliffs, NJ: Prentice-Hall.

those who are dying. Kübler-Ross's theory enables us to see the progression of psychological states that people experience as they await impending death. Shneidman's theory emphasizes the fluctuations of behavioral states that dying persons experience. Pattison suggests that death is not the primary issue for caregivers; rather it is how the patient faces death and goes about the process of dying. All of these theoretical positions have merit and suggest ways we can be more alert to the needs of those facing death. However, we remind you that the experience of dying is highly variable. A multitude of situations and factors influence how individuals accept death, thus making it impossible to predict behavior.

DYING WITH DIGNITY

Whatever the specific illness or situation, the quality of life of the terminally ill should reflect peace and tranquillity. Psychologically this means that dying patients need to maintain their dignity, self-respect, and honor. Retaining control over the remaining portion of their life is especially important. Dying persons also need to know they are valued, and efforts should be made to help relieve their anxiety, depression, and fears. The ultimate sting of death, though, may well be the loneliness and solitude it brings. Placing a person in familiar surroundings with loved ones is an important step in overcoming such feelings (Benoliel, 1991; Crabtree & Caron-Parker, 1991; Lawton, Moss, & Glicksman, 1990).

Attention obviously needs to be directed toward the physical comfort of the patient. Even when a cure to a disease is unavailable, it is important for the dying to be free from pain, as well as alert and aware. Most patients need only adequate local pain relief and effective analgesics and thus can be kept quite awake (Lynn, 1991). Unfortunately, although most unpleasant symptoms accompanying terminal illness can be controlled by skilled medical care, many medical personnel have never learned how to do so. The physical symptoms accompanying terminal illness are sometimes inadequately treated, prompting many (e.g., Doyle, 1991) to underscore the importance of palliative care education.

Of particular importance among the dying is the need to share emotional pain. Emotional pain can be just as overwhelming as physical pain, and health-care professionals need a great deal of sympathy and understanding in dealing with its complexities. Emotional pain is often expressed in body language and physical symptoms because it is too agonizing and too difficult to express in words; but it can be eased, if the underlying fear and anxiety are elicited and

THEORETICAL ISSUES

Do you think any psychosocial dynamics (e.g., the need for trust or experiencing integrity) can be applied to the concept of "dying with dignity"? How might the quality of a person's final months, days, or even hours shape Butler's concept of the "life review"?

shared. In terminal illness, the slow, relentless destruction of the body seems to threaten the destruction of the social and emotional life of the individual and the family, but when the deteriorating body is loved and cared for, the emotional pain is often relieved, and the family reintegrated and enabled to support one another (Earnshaw-Smith, 1982; Seale, 1990).

An individualized and flexible care system greatly enhances the quality of life before death (Samarel, 1991). However, all too often a hospital's bureaucratic organization hinders such efforts. Many patients experience loneliness and a loss of identity, as they often become part of impersonal routines and daily rituals. Often, the patient's concerns and values are not known, including those of a spiritual nature (Missinne, 1990; Wald & Bailey, 1990). Many are hooked up to mechanical life-sustaining equipment that transforms them into a set of repetitious life signs to be measured and monitored. The constantly changing shifts of all hospital personnel, coupled with everyone's heavy workloads, often prevent the patient from striking up an intimate relationship, one where sensitivities and fears can be brought out into the open and shared (Binstock & Post, 1991).

Finally, we need to recognize that family and friends are also affected by the quality of life as death draws near. Joanne Lynn (1991) points out that the care system needs to be sensitive to the needs of this circle of concerned others. Sometimes the care options are shaped in important ways by the preferences and concerns of the family and friends. Providing the patient does not object, it is reasonable to shape the care plan so it serves the needs of the survivors as well as the patient. Because they are persons directly affected by the impending loss of life, family and friends have needs that could be met by professional caregivers and the health-care delivery system.

■ The Hospice Program

Hospice programs seek to provide terminally ill patients with humane, individual care. The word *hospice* extends back to the Middle Ages and at that time referred to a place where travelers could rest and receive hospitality before they continued on with their journeys. It has since come to mean care for the terminally ill, based on a homelike environment and freedom from physical or psychological pain.

Hospice embraces a humanistic approach to terminal illness. The major theme running through it is comforting rather than curative care. Emphasis is placed on the control of pain, and no heroic measures are taken to prolong life unnecessarily. Hospice thus embodies moving away from the indignities of dying often associated with conventional medical settings. The hospice program may include a separate facility, a hospice ward in a general hospital with special routines and staff, or hospice care in a dying patient's home.

Whether in a hospice facility or a home-care situation, the hospice staff works closely with both patient and family. Patients are active in decisions concerning themselves as long as it is possible and in their best interests. As such, they are key members of the treatment team composed of doctors, nurses, clergy, and, as already mentioned, the patient's family. Also, there are no restrictions on visiting hours at a hospice facility. In fact, the family of the terminal patient is encouraged to visit as often as possible, as well as participate in the

Hospice programs offer a wide range of supportive services and care for terminally ill persons.

INTERRELATEDNESS OF AGING PROCESSES

Can you think of specific ways that developmental forces converge in the care and treatment of the terminally ill? For example, what kinds of social support such as from family and friends do you think ease a patient's psychological pain? How can humane medical treatment help to reduce a patient's feelings of fear and anxiety?

treatment program. By participating, relatives and loved ones outside the family have the opportunity not only to work through their relationship with the patient but also to perform practical services for the dying, such as preparing special meals. Finally, the staff's involvement with relatives and friends does not end with the patient's death. Relatives and friends are encouraged to consult with the hospital staff, should support be needed during bereavement (Austin & Melbourne, 1990; Gochman & Bonham, 1990; Levy, 1989; McCracken & Gerdsen, 1991; Neigh, 1990).

▬ The Right to Die

Euthanasia is an extremely controversial subject. Essentially, it concerns itself with whether we should prolong useless life or painful dying with the use of modern medical technology. It is an issue that affects the conscience, not only of the dying and their relatives but also that of the physician. The moral balance between preserving life and preventing suffering needs to be determined. Large numbers of people today are concerned about the quality of lives being saved by modern technology (DeSpelder & Strickland, 1992; Fenigsen, 1990; Singer & Siegler, 1990).

The term *euthanasia* is derived from the Greek *eu* meaning "well," and *thanatas* meaning "death." Combined, they mean "a good or peaceful death." Its original meaning, however, has become both expanded and somewhat obscured. Known popularly as "mercy killing," it has come to mean assisting the dying in hastening their death. Two types of euthanasia can be identified.

Positive, or *active,* **euthanasia** means steps are taken to hasten another's death for reasons of mercy. **Negative,** or *passive,* **euthanasia** means death is not actively prevented through any type of intervention.

As we said at the outset, the concept of euthanasia is a controversial one. Many are opposed to the very thought of taking another's life, regardless of the circumstances. They view life as sacred and see mercy killing as morally wrong. Moreover, *who* exercises control over life and death raises important issues, such as abuses of power. Others, though, emphasize it is the *quality* of life, not its quantity, that represents the key issue. When dying is painful and prolonged, proponents of this position usually stress the importance of death with dignity. When a person has no hope for recovery, it is argued that extreme suffering is immoral, dehumanizing, and degrading.

The euthanasia movement first started in England in 1935, in an effort to advance legislation to "make the act of dying more gentle." In the United States the euthanasia movement was begun in 1938 to educate the medical profession and public alike on the ultimate realities of death. Emphasis was placed on examining medical procedures and attitudes toward terminal illness and on seeking ways to humanize death. Today, the *Euthanasia Society* and the *Euthanasia Educational Council* are organizations promoting the concept of death with dignity. The *living will,* developed by the Euthanasia Educational Council, supports the individual's right to die. It seeks to give dying individuals some choice or control over their ultimate fate. Most states today recognize the living will as legally binding. Figure 12-3 displays a copy of the living will.

Over the years, the moral and medical dilemmas involved in sustaining life in patients with no chances for recovery have become apparent. For example, before the widely publicized Karen Ann Quinlan case of 1976 there were no legally sanctioned procedures for stopping treatment of any kind. Karen Ann Quinlan lapsed into a coma in 1975 and remained in it for over a year before the New Jersey Supreme Court gave Quinlan's parents permission to have her life-supporting respirator removed. The unexpected happened, however. Despite the removal of the respirator, which doctors felt would cause death, Quinlan lived until 1985.

In 1990, the parents of 32-year-old Nancy Cruzan went to the Supreme Court for permission to halt the artificial feeding that had kept her alive in a persistent vegetative state for 7 years. The parents argued that Nancy said she would not want to be kept alive if she could not lead a normal life. However, this wish had not been documented by either a living will or a durable power of attorney. The Supreme Court denied the family's wishes and cited the absence of "clear and convincing evidence of a person's expressed decision while competent to have hydration and nutrition withdrawn in such a way as to cause death." Within months of the ruling, the family went back to a lower court, this time with friends also testifying that Nancy would not want to be kept alive. The court gave permission for her artificial feeding to stop and Nancy Cruzan died.

In 1991, the medical community made an effort to address dilemmas such as these with the *Patient Self-Determination Act.* This act stipulates that any health-care facility receiving Medicare or Medicaid must advise patients of their rights to sign advance directives for health-care decisions, such as being kept alive by artificial means. In so doing, medical personnel become knowledgeable about a patient's wishes and can follow an appropriate course of action.

My Living Will
To My Family, My Physician, My Lawyer and All Others Whom It May Concern

Death is as much a reality as birth, growth, maturity and old age,—it is the one certainty of life. If the time comes when I can no longer take part in decisions for my own future, let this statement stand as an expression of my wishes and directions, while I am still of sound mind.

If at such a time the situation should arise in which there is no reasonable expectation of my recovery from extreme physical or mental disability, I direct that I be allowed to die and not be kept alive by medications, artificial means or "heroic measures". I do, however, ask that medication be mercifully administered to me to alleviate suffering even though this may shorten my remaining life.

This statement is made after careful consideration and is in accordance with my strong convictions and beliefs. I want the wishes and directions here expressed carried out to the extent permitted by law. Insofar as they are not legally enforceable, I hope that those to whom this Will is addressed will regard themselves as morally bound by these provisions.

Optional specific provisions to be made in this space

DURABLE POWER OF ATTORNEY (optional)

I hereby designate _____ to serve as my attorney-in-fact for the purpose of making medical treatment decisions. This power of attorney shall remain effective in the event that I become incompetent or otherwise unable to make such decisions for myself.

Optional Notarization:

"Sworn and subscribed to

before me this _____ day

of _____, 19_____."

_____
Notary Public
(seal)

Signed _____

Date _____

Witness _____

_____
Address

Witness _____

_____
Address

Copies of this request have been given to _____

_____   _____

(Optional) My Living Will is registered with Concern for Dying (No. _____)

FIGURE 12-3
The Living Will.

The living will is a document supporting a person's right to die. It directs physicians and family to refrain from any heroic and life-sustaining measures when no hope of recovery exists.

More active steps to end another person's suffering have also taken place in recent years. In 1990, a Michigan physician named Jack Kevorkian used a suicide machine he had devised to end the life of 54-year-old Janet Adkins, who had been diagnosed with Alzheimer's disease. The machine, activated by pushing a button, releases anesthesia and then a heart-stopping drug. Criminal charges were filed against Kevorkian, but later dismissed because at that time Michigan had no law banning assisted suicides. Since that time, Kevorkian, dubbed "Dr. Death," has assisted in 19 other suicides involving sick and elderly persons. Kevorkian was charged with murder in the first three assisted suicides, but charges were dropped because Michigan had no law against the practice. In 1993, however, Michigan declared such assisted suicides a felony punishable by up to 4 years in jail and a $2,000 fine. This new law did not stop Kevorkian, who assisted a 54-year-old cancer-stricken man to kill himself shortly after the bill was passed. Kevorkian was arrested and released into his attorney's custody, but as we go to press his case is still pending because the new law is being constitutionally challenged. In the meantime, Kevorkian continues to believe in assisted suicide. For a stark contrast to the Kevorkian case, see the Focus on Diversity box on page 658.

Finally, many persons choose to take their own lives, adding yet another dimension to the right-to-die issue. Large percentages of those who commit suicide are terminally ill persons as well as those afflicted with other health problems. In the midst of prolonged pain and suffering, it might be reasoned that suicide promotes an easier and swifter alternative to hopelessness and lessens the burden placed on others. One study (Conwell, Rotenberg, & Caine, 1990) revealed that with age, physical illness and loss became the most common definable precipitants to suicide, whereas job, financial, and family relationship problems became less frequent. Other researchers (e.g., Kinsella, 1990; Meehan, Saltzman, & Sattin, 1991; Moore & Tanney, 1991; Runwell, 1991; Weisman, 1991) confirm the association between suicide attempts and deteriorating physical capacities, despondency, and hopelessness in later life. We might note that the general public's interest in this dimension of the right to life surfaced in 1991 with the publication of Derek Humphry's best-selling book, *Final Exit.* In this book, Humphry, a right-to-die proponent, provides guidelines on how to take one's life.

Needless to say, the right to die is a controversial topic, one that poses numerous policy implications and ethical dilemmas. As Barry Robinson (1990) observes, it doesn't really matter if the practice being discussed is referred to as mercy killing or assisted suicide, pulling the plug or euthanasia, or even suicide. In the final analysis, the most important issue is one of control over how a particular life ends and who has the power to make that decision and implement it. The medical profession continues to grapple with the problem of futile resuscitation in which incurably ill patients are revived, sometimes against their will, through the use of modern emergency procedures (Montalvo, 1991; Teno & Lynn, 1991). Pressure is rising for physicians and policymakers to find ways to respect the right and wishes of patients who want to be kept alive regardless of the state of their health and of those who prefer to die after they reach a certain stage of deterioration (Glick, 1991; Hanson & Danis, 1991; Rosenblum & Forsythe, 1990; Scharer, 1991; Thomasma & Graber, 1990). Relatedly, the medical profession is faced with ethical dilemmas of caring for older patients who

Focus on Diversity

LIFE AND DEATH DECISIONS IN THE NETHERLANDS

Debates focusing on euthanasia grow more complex when we examine some rather radical medical practices in the Netherlands. Here, physicians can give a lethal injection to a terminally ill patient who has requested death and not be punished for it. Such medically assisted suicide is called the "gentle death" and is performed on about 7,500 people each year. The usual Dutch method is to induce sleep with a barbiturate, followed by a lethal injection of the drug curare.

Medically assisted suicides in the Netherlands represent an informal and basically unofficial approach. Although providing assistance in committing suicide is officially illegal and punishable by a prison term of up to 12 years, it has been understood at virtually all levels of Dutch society for nearly 20 years that doctors will not be prosecuted if they adhere to strict criteria (Robinson, 1991). To illustrate, two doctors must conclude the patient is terminally ill; there must be physical or mental suffering the patient finds unbearable; the decision to die must be the voluntary decision of an informed patient, who makes his or her request in writing; and the next of kin are informed beforehand so as not to cause avoidable misery.

Dutch physicians are known for their psychologically supportive medical care. Paramount in patient care is the establishment of empathy rather than paternalism between doctor and patient. It is recognized that how the doctor informs the patient and his or her family about the course of the illness affects how the information will be accepted. Dutch doctors feel that if patients are informed gradually, according to their own needs and initiative, they will be in a better position to accept death.

It is also felt that telling family members about a terminal illness before telling the patient can do much harm. Often, this leads to disturbances in the relationships between the patient and the family. Finally, it has been observed that Dutch patients who learn of their condition as soon as they are capable of processing the information are more likely to die at home rather than in a hospital or nursing home. (Gomez, 1991; Nussberg, 1984; Robinson, 1991)

are decisionally incapacitated (Coni, 1991; Crabtree & Caron-Parker, 1991; High, 1990). There are no easy solutions to these complex and controversial issues; indeed, there well may not even be any final answers.

AT THE MOMENT OF DEATH

Contrary to what one might have learned, most terminally ill patients die peacefully (Lichter & Hunt, 1990). Symptom management is addressed by consistent and competent medical care so that pain is not endured and the patient is kept comfortable to the end. This was the case in one study (Somerville, 1991) that examined the final days of elderly men and women. Over one half of the subjects died peacefully in their sleep with loved ones nearby, and over 60% were pain free on the day they died. Other researchers (e.g., Gray, 1984) have supplied insight into what happens as death draws near:

- *The patient's sensation and power of motion as well as reflexes are lost in the legs first and then gradually in the arms.* Pressure on the extremities seems to bother the patient, such as when bedsheets are too tight. Careful positioning and turning of the body seems to help reduce the discomfort.

- *As peripheral circulation fails, there is frequently a drenching sweat, and the body surface cools, regardless of room temperature.* Sweating tends to be most profuse on the upper parts of the body and on the extensor surfaces rather than on the flexor surfaces. Many dying patients are never conscious of being cold, though, regardless of how cold their body surface becomes. Their restlessness is often caused by the sensation of heat.

- *Dying persons characteristically turn their heads toward the light.* As sight and hearing fail, the patient can see only what is near and hear only what is distinctly spoken. Because of this, adequate lighting should be provided, visitors should sit at the head of the patient's bedside, and whispering should be avoided.

- *The dying patient's touch sensation is diminished, yet one's sense of pressure remains.* When touch sensation fails, patients may not realize, for example, that a hand is being held. Slight pressure may increase the person's awareness of a visitor's intention to initiate physical contact.

- *Dying patients may be in less pain than onlookers think.* As we've indicated, most dying patients need only local pain relief and effective analgesics. Patients also frequently reach a point where they feel as though they have said all that needs to be said, a state of mind that brings internal serenity to many. Frequently, only minimal pain medication is needed as death nears.

- *The dying patient is often conscious to the very end.* A comatose state or period of unconsciousness does not always precede death. The fact that many patients remain conscious before death strikes emphasizes the need for total care to the very end.

- *Spiritual needs often arise strongly at night.* If dying patients have led a strong spiritual life, they are apt to want to talk about their experiences with those near them. Many want to talk specifically with their minister, rabbi, or priest. This need has been known to intensify during the night.

- *There seems to be an interval of peace before death.* Those patients who are conscious to the very last minute answer, almost invariably, that they are not suffering. In fact, many report a feeling of tranquillity and peace, as if a long journey is finally over. As William Hunter, the noted anatomist, whispered just before he died, "If I had the strength to hold a pen, I would write how easy and pleasant a thing it is to die."

DEFINITIONS AND COMPONENTS OF DEATH

Death is a process as well as an event, and although there are numerous signs that serve to signal the termination of life, each manifestation, in itself, does not prove irreversible extinction has taken place. Complicating matters is that we now have artificial means to keep people alive when, in similar circumstances just a few decades ago, they would have been dead. The following definitions illustrate how death is subjected to different biological perspectives.

The lifespan culminates at the moment of death.

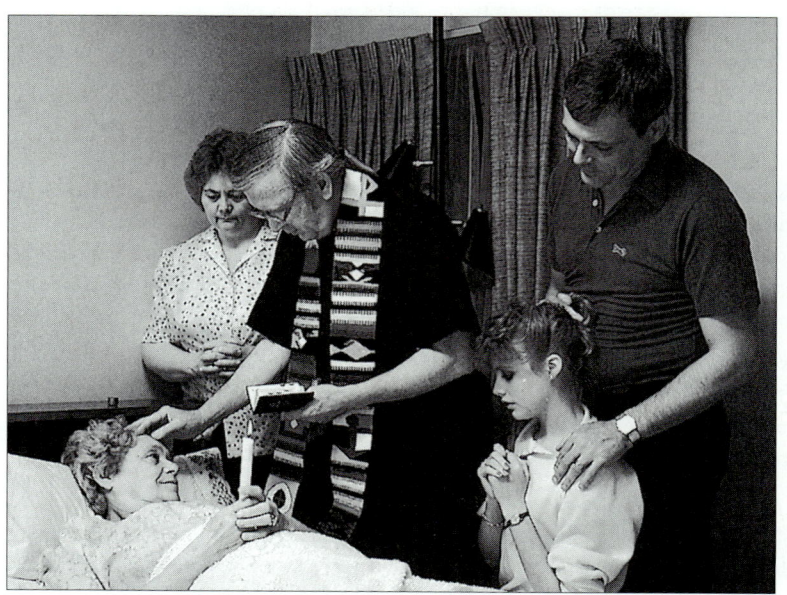

Functional Death

Functional death occurs when there is an absence of heartbeat and respiration. When considering this definition, note that both cardiac and pulmonary functioning can be resuscitated, and the brain continues to function for a short time (5 to 8 minutes) after the heart stops beating. Consequently, the brain and not the heart is viewed as the criterion for determining the termination of life.

Cellular Death

Cellular death is a gradual process that occurs after the vital organs cease to function. The hair, for example, continues to grow for several hours; the liver converts glycogen to glucose; and the muscles contract (this is referred to as *rigor mortis*). Rigor mortis generally begins 2 hours after death, the muscles remaining contracted for approximately 30 hours.

Brain Death

Brain death refers to a flat tracing recorded by an electroencephalogram. As indicated, this definition of death is perhaps the most widely accepted today. The brain is the only system that cannot be directly supported by machines, and the cessation of its activity results in the absence of respiration and heartbeat, the lack of reflexes, the clouding of the cornea, and the absence of bodily movement.

Most states today declare a person legally dead when brain death has occurred. However, not everyone agrees on a legal definition of death. Sometimes, the definition of death is primarily determined by hospital policy. This becomes a delicate and frequently controversial issue, if one hospital defines death as the cessation of heartbeat and respiration, whereas another uses brain death as the defining criterion. It may be possible, then, that the same person could be pronounced dead in one hospital and not dead in another. Such inconsistent criteria impact on a number of areas, including eventual treatment of the body, organ transplantation, criminal prosecution, and inheritance, to name but a few.

IS THERE LIFE AFTER DEATH?

I had heart failure and clinically died . . . I remember everything perfectly vividly. . . . Suddenly I felt numb. Sounds began sounding a little distant . . . All this time I was perfectly conscious of everything that was going on. I heard the heart monitor go off. I saw the nurse come into the room and dial the telephone, and the doctors, nurses, and attendants came in.

As things began to fade there was a sound I can't describe; it was like the beat of a snare drum, very rapid, a rushing sound, like a stream rushing through a gorge. And I rose up and I was a few feet up looking down on my body. There I was, with people working on me. I had no fear. No pain. Just peace. After just probably a second or two, I seemed to turn over and go up. It was dark—you could call it a hole or a tunnel—and there was the bright light. It got brighter and brighter. And I seemed to go through it.

All of a sudden I was just somewhere else. There was a gold-looking light, everywhere. Beautiful. I couldn't find a source anywhere. It was just all around, coming from everywhere. There was music. And I seemed to be in a countryside with streams, grass, and trees, mountains. But when I looked around—if you want to put it that way—there were not trees and things like we know them to be. The strangest thing to me about it was that there were people there. Not in any kind of form or body as we know it; they were just there.

There was a sense of perfect peace and contentment, love. It was like I was part of it. That experience could have lasted the whole night or just a second . . . I don't know. (Moody, 1977, pp. 138–139)

This description is from a middle-aged woman who suffered severe cardiac arrest. Although pronounced functionally dead, she was resuscitated and brought back to life. That she is able to relate such a unique series of events is remarkable in itself. What is even more fascinating, however, is that hundreds of other persons who have had near-death experiences give similar reports.

A number of researchers (Moody, 1975, 1977; Morse, 1990; Morse & Perry, 1992; Ring, 1980; Sabom, 1982; R. Siegel, 1980; Vicchio, 1981a, 1981b) have launched research into what is now called the **near-death experience (NDE).** Many have collected scores of interviews with persons pronounced functionally dead, and although individual differences exist, the stories bear a striking resemblance to one another. The following are some of the more common features of the near-death experience:

1. Awareness of loud noises (some people report buzzing, vibrations, or loud clicking sounds).

2. A feeling of being drawn through a dark tunnel, funnel, or cave. At the end of the passage is a bright light.
3. Recognizing the presence of dead relatives who were reportedly there to help the person make the transition from life to death.
4. Being asked by a distant voice in the presence of a brilliant light to provide a review of one's life. The light is described by many as "a being of love." Questions ranged from "Are you satisfied with your life?" to "What do you want to share with me?"
5. Seeing a panoramic view of one's life. Many report watching their entire lives pass before them in color, three dimensions, and third persons.
6. Being given full acceptance by the "being of love," even though some persons felt their past actions and behaviors were cause for rejection or embarrassment.

Also, many persons reporting such experiences are not afraid of death anymore and have a more positive attitude toward life. Many report a greater compassion for, and appreciation of, those around them. However, although the data gathered are certainly thought provoking, one should not automatically assume that an afterlife exists. Remember that this research was conducted with persons experiencing functional death, which is not the same as brain death. Whether one experiences such events after brain death has occurred is a question defying a scientific answer. Indeed, some people have had negative near-death experiences and are afraid to die.

BEREAVEMENT AND GRIEF

No one is ever fully prepared for the loss of a loved one. Rather, death invariably has a sudden and profound impact, even in those cases where it was anticipated. The reality of loss is very hard for most of us to accept, and the expression of our grief is usually painful and disturbing. It varies in intensity and may take months or years. Regardless of its duration, grieving is a way of healing. When survivors allow themselves to express their innermost feelings, a loss is usually more clearly understood (Kinderknecht & Hodges, 1990; Wortman & Silver, 1990).

But death is a fact of life and as we learned in the last chapter, accepting its inevitability is everyone's chore. The psychological pain that survivors face—including such feelings as loneliness, despair, and fear—are normal reactions in the face of loss. Learning how to free oneself emotionally from the deceased, readjusting to a life of missing the dead person, and forming new relationships with other individuals are important tasks for the mourner (R. Brown, 1990; Lieberman & Peskin, 1992).

Before we proceed, we need to first clarify some terminology. **Bereavement** is defined as the loss of a loved one by death. It is a statement of fact and does not embody one's reactions to a loss. **Grief** refers to the deep and poignant distress caused by such a loss. It represents one's emotional reaction to another's death. **Grief work** means coming to terms with the physical and emotional demands brought on by another's death. Rather than denying or suppressing feelings, grief work acknowledges the importance of facing the loss, dealing with the emotions that accompany it, and moving to resolution.

Coping With Loss

There are many stress points across the life cycle, but few (if any) parallel the loss of a loved one. For example, it is generally acknowledged among researchers (e.g., Gallagher & Thompson, 1989; Williams, 1989; Wortman & Silver, 1990) that the loss of a spouse looms as one of the most serious threats to the health, well-being, and productivity of the surviving partner during later adulthood. But although death has the potential of emerging as a catastrophic event, John Crosby and Nancy Jose (1983) feel that the *degree* of stress and grief experienced is dependent on several interacting variables. The first variable is how death occurs. Unexpected death often creates extreme stress because survivors are totally unprepared for it. Other forms of death produce different levels of stress, such as the emotional depletion that often accompanies anticipated, but prolonged death.

Whether the survivor is encountering other stressful crises is another variable to consider. The death of a loved one usually increases the level of stress to an almost intolerable level. That is, personal and interpersonal resources may be depleted by the other stressors, leaving little in reserve to cope with the death. The accumulation of many stressors acting upon the survivor may lead to or compound the crisis, taxing the person's resources and coping ability to such a point that coping becomes increasingly dysfunctional.

Other important variables contributing to the survivor's stress are the numerous "arrangements" that require attention following the death. Consider this in relation to surviving spouses: Initially, the spouse must deal with the funeral and burial. This includes contacts with morticians, cemeteries, and well-meaning sympathizers. Moreover, the survivor is inundated by a myriad of professionals involved in settling the estate (lawyers, employers, insurance company, and government employees). Combined, each of these factors will affect the stress level of loss. Moreover, they will interact and influence the nature and duration of grieving.

In the pages that follow, we explore the grief after the death of a parent, a child, and a spouse. The loss of a parent enables the concept of death to edge in. Many individuals perceive one's parent as a buffer between themselves and death. With the loss of a parent, the force of the finality of death becomes apparent in a way that the loss of, say, a grandparent can not compare. And the realization that "I, too, am mortal" is now apparent. Sibling rivalries often resurface, sometimes triggered by inheritance (Doka, 1992). A different view of life and death may affect interpersonal relationships and relationships with one's spouse during the grieving period. And when the ultimate point is reached that both parents have died, the realization occurs that one is an orphan for life (Bass & Bowman, 1990; Bass, Bowman, & Noelker, 1991; Pratt, Walker, & Wood, 1992; Robbins, 1990).

The loss of a child is also traumatic. The usual expectation is that the offspring will outlive the parent. Lynne DeSpelder and Albert Strickland (1992) write that it is almost expected the child will carry something of the parent into the future, even after the parent's death. In this sense, the child's very existence grants a kind of immortality to the parent, and this is taken away if the child dies before the parent's own life has ended. The parent's plans for the child are suddenly of no consequence.

Parental bereavement spans the marriage and family life cycle. It is just as intense for 30-year-old parents as it is for 60-year-olds. Their dreams, fantasies, and plans may be as strong for an infant as they are for a teenaged or adult offspring. Pregnancy loss, too, triggers intense grief among parents (Smart, 1992; Stinson, 1992). The death of a child often brings chaos into the lives of parents. Many times, loss of a direction is felt, which is part of a pervasive sense that parents have been robbed of a past and a future. And because each parent may have separate grieving styles, they may be left feeling unsupported and isolated by the only person who understands the magnitude of the loss (DeSpelder & Strickland, 1992; Hoekstra-Weebers, 1991).

The loss of a spouse is a serious crisis at any time, but especially so during late adulthood. Restructuring one's existence after a loved one has died represents one of the most difficult of all life challenges. With a major source of love and caring taken from one's life, a surviving spouse must come to grips with loss and to progress with hope to a changed world. For many older survivors, accompanying grief takes a severe toll on health and well-being. Momentarily, we will take a look at some of the adjustments and adaptations facing surviving spouses.

▬ Expressions of Grief

Grief is a complex and multifaceted form of expression. Richard Kalish (1987) believes, though, that grief can be categorized physically, cognitively, affectively, and behaviorally. He also maintains that certain distinctions can be made concerning how older and younger persons express grief.

Physical Expressions   Grieving persons report many different physical symptoms, including a tight feeling in the throat and chest, hollow feeling in the stomach, oversensitivity to noise, sense of numbness and depersonalization (nothing seems physically real), dry mouth, breathlessness, muscular weakness, and a lack of energy. Although it is unlikely that the first four symptoms are age related, the last four are typically reported more by elderly persons.

Cognitive Expressions   Among the cognitive reactions to loss are confusion, disbelief, preoccupation with thoughts about the deceased, and attempting to make sense of the event. Attempting to relate cognitive expressions to age is problematic. However, we do know that when the age of the mourner is concerned, people react differently to cognitive expressions of grief. For example, when the grieving person is not elderly, expressions of confusion, disbelief, and preoccupation are likely to be attributed to the loss and are usually assumed to be temporary. Among aged persons, though, especially those who have already displayed some forgetfulness, these same cognitive expressions might be interpreted as deterioration rather than the reversible results of situational stress and loss.

Affective Expressions   The affective expressions that typically accompany loss are well known. Among the more common are sorrow, sadness, guilt, anger, relief, denial, and depression. Although depression tends to be the most familiar expression, particularly among the aged, it must be understood that these affective states usually mix together. Consequently, for both young and old, affective expressions often create a snowball effect. For example, consider

INTERRELATEDNESS OF AGING PROCESSES

How do expressions of grief mirror the interrelatedness of developmental processes? Do you agree that these converging forces often differ between young and old? Why do you think this occurs?

There are numerous and diverse facets to grief and bereavement.

the loss of a spouse. The survivor has experienced the severance of an important attachment, with all of its emotional implications, as well as an alteration of many life circumstances. These developments in turn may create a multitude of additional affective expressions, such as fear, anxiety, or withdrawal.

Behavioral Expressions   Invariably, grief leads to changes in behavior. However, each variety of behavior can also be viewed as the outcome of a physical, cognitive, or affective change as well. For instance, the affective responses of sadness coupled with the physical symptoms of lack of energy may lead to slow movement or longer reaction time. Research also suggests that a few of these behavioral expressions are unique to young and old. For example, bereaved elderly persons tend to cry more often and to experience insomnia more than younger bereaved individuals.

▬ Stages of Grief

People react to loss in different ways. For instance, it may be perceived as a tragedy, a blessing, a mystery, a transition, or a release. Grieving behaviors also know wide variation, from sorrow and anguish to loneliness and depression. Some report a general feeling of numbness and only vague awareness of the events taking place around them. For others, life may not seem worth living anymore, and some may even look forward to their own early demise. Recognizing individual grieving patterns is especially important for those providing support to family members. Because each person may be at a different stage of appraising and dealing with death, the kind of support needed often differs (Stern, 1990; Vail, 1982; Williams, 1989).

According to Phyllis Silverman (1986), the process of grieving and the psychological healing process follow a chronology of three stages: impact, recoil, and accommodation. She developed these stages while observing the behaviors

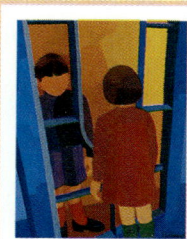

GENDER SIMILARITIES AND DIFFERENCES

Although Silverman's research was confined to females, do you think males experience similar behaviors? Or do you feel bereavement is marked more by gender differences?

of 233 widows over a 6-year period. The following discussion is based on Silverman's research.

The Impact Stage   During the **impact stage,** widows report that numbness envelops them when they are told of their husbands' death. Many experience a sense of disbelief, and their behavior becomes still and robotlike. The woman's new legal status as a widow has no social and emotional meaning to her. Automatically, she thinks and acts as her husband's wife, still tailoring her behavior as she probably did while he was alive, and doing those things that would please him. Continuing to play the role of wife, she knows how to behave and what is expected of her. Her numbness helps her perform her role reflexively.

The intensity and duration of a widow's numbness during this stage will vary depending on whether her husband died suddenly or after a long illness. When death follows a long illness, the widow inevitably has a certain sense of relief, and the shock is not as profound as when death comes as a surprise. This observation by Silverman is compatible with our earlier discussion of stress and the variations that can exist at the moment of death.

Psychological numbness often becomes a valuable asset in averting a state of collapse. In this sense, it may help the survivor handle emotionally taxing chores, such as arranging the funeral. However, this protection against acute anguish is only temporary, and widows need the support and assistance of loved ones.

Along these lines, most widows are grateful that someone else is willing to help, and even think for them at this time. Relatives and friends usually help to arrange the funeral, help with shopping and housekeeping chores, or chauffeur the children to visit friends. At a time when she is least able, the widow must begin dealing with a complex set of financial issues; others may be able to help with these matters as well. Among other tasks, the widow has to find out about their insurance, collect back pay, determine what money she has for current expenses, apply for Social Security and veterans' benefits, and, if there is an estate, deal with the lawyer. Some things only she can handle. Eventually she will have to go to bed in the empty bedroom, see her husband's belongings around her, eat alone, and cope, by herself, with household routines.

It is important to emphasize that the impact stage has no predictable duration. Nor is it a purely numb period without any breakthrough of feelings. The widow does have many concrete chores that involve her in necessary and important activities, and these keep her engaged in the real world. However, the meaning of what has happened also begins to enter her consciousness. The people who are available to help at this time may be deceived by her outward reactions. They may think she is doing well, and they are pleased about how well she is holding up. They are unaware, and she also may not recognize, that this is but the first stage in a long and painful process.

The Recoil Stage   During the **recoil stage,** numbness will begin to lessen, yet most widows fight its departure. This is because the return of feelings brings the full realization of the loss. Many have avoided the meaning of the loss, and may continue to do so as their new reality intermittently breaks through.

At this time, many widows report that a part of them is missing. Also common is a loss of appetite, sleeplessness, or, conversely, a desire to eat or sleep all of the time. A widow may find herself impatient and restless, not wanting to be with people but not wanting to be alone either. She may begin to feel increasingly misunderstood, that friends and relatives are becoming impatient and uncomfortable with her continuing grief. Some women feel if they can simply keep themselves so busy that they grow too tired to do anything except fall into bed they will be able to keep their feelings at bay. This way they can avoid thinking about either the past or the future.

Many widows want to review the circumstances of their spouses' deaths over and over again wondering whether anything could have been done. Feelings of anger and remorse are not unusual. The widow may feel angry her husband did not take better care of himself. She may also feel remorseful that she did not do enough.

Ann Stearns (1984) points out that although survivors may genuinely *feel* blameworthy, usually their self-blaming thoughts are unrealistic; in other words, they are overly harsh on themselves. They stretch their imaginations to believe they are responsible for anticipating or preventing events that ordinary mortals could not possibly have prevented. Or twisting human-sized mistakes into criminal proportions, they feel as guilty as if they had intentionally brought themselves or others harm, which is rarely the case. The following are examples of unrealistic guilt: "Maybe if I weren't so selfish and caught up in my work our marriage could have lasted"; "If I had stayed home that night, the accident would never have happened"; and "I never had the chance to tell her how much she really meant to me."

It is normal to feel that one could have loved a departed spouse better. However, we all feel guilty during a time of loss. What survivors need is a support system to help them sort out these feelings, one that can minimize unrealistic guilt. For example, a comforting friend can help to separate realistic from unrealistic guilt by asking questions: Why are you the only one to blame? How could you have known that? Are you expecting yourself to have known things that could not have been known with certainty? Are you tormenting yourself with thoughts of self-blame, as if no other reason or explanation could account for the events that happened?

During the recoil stage, many widows are not prepared for the negative feelings that are experienced. They have to discover there is no easy way around their misery, given the nature and meaning of their loss. If they know their suffering is normal and inevitable, they may find it easier to endure. Of course, this underscores the need for a reassuring and trusting support network.

Toward the end of this stage, loved ones may be misled by how well the widow is doing. Many may assume the worst of grief and mourning is over. Friends and relatives also have their own lives to lead, becoming impatient with any continuing need the widow may express. When family and friends do remain available and supportive, therefore, their attention may not be helpful. They will often try to help by distracting the widow from her grief, but the grief is what she needs to experience at this stage. Only when the widow can at last acknowledge her pain, doubts, and fears can she begin to make the necessary changes toward the last stage of grief.

The Accommodation Stage   During the **accommodation stage,** the survivor discovers new ways of looking at the world. Entering this final stage does

INTERRELATEDNESS OF AGING PROCESSES

How might the interplay of physical, psychological, and social forces affect bereaved persons? For example, what physical symptoms often accompany tragedy and loss? What kinds of social support do you think are most beneficial to a bereaved person's psychological well-being and stability?

not mean the end of depressed feelings or an end to the pain of her loss. These feelings do become less intense and pervasive, however, creating a different perspective on her experience.

The survivor learns, for instance, that she can laugh and she has things worth living for; she can enjoy people and look forward to getting up in the morning. She can look upon her husband and her past without despairing of her present or her future. Remembering that past, she can cry without becoming frightened or uncomfortable about it, without worrying about other people's reactions. Survivors within this stage accept the fact that part of them will always be sad when they think about the past; most consider this natural and right.

It is important for the widow to *remember* during this stage. Her ways of remembering are her ways of honoring her dead husband and of building continuity between her past and her future. Some widows set up memorial funds, some donate flowers annually on their husbands' birthdays, some become active in a project or area that was important to him. Others make scrapbooks, or carefully store those personal possessions that their children will use when they are older.

Becoming involved in work and leisure, as well as discovering new friends, are ways of building new identity roles for herself. She may also begin to change the old habits of daily living that framed her life, developing new ones appropriate to her current situation. She finds ways of taking charge of her own life and, in the process, achieves a new sense of competence. Additional suggestions for dealing with loss are contained in the accompanying Lifespan Development in Action box.

Dysfunctional and Functional Methods of Coping

Sorting through complex feelings and confronting the many demands and pressures of bereavement can produce a wide range of behaviors. Some of these will be healthy and productive; others will not. John Crosby and Nancy Jose (1983) expound on the diversity of behaviors by referring to dysfunctional and functional modes of coping. The following represents three examples of dysfunctional coping observed by these researchers; and later, we offer some patterns for functional coping.

Avoidance   Known as the "keep busy" strategy, many feel that *avoidance* is therapeutic and functional. However, when used over extended time, it more often than not is a dysfunctional ploy that may encourage the denial of a loved one's death. By keeping busy we defend ourselves against the anxiety that arises when we "are doing nothing." Keeping busy enables survivors to put their mental/emotional energy into the task at hand, thus diverting thoughts and feelings away from death. Keeping busy is, in itself, not wrong. It turns into a dysfunctional strategy, though, when it becomes the primary method of coping.

Some survivors employ a variation of this by utilizing a "getting away" or "taking a trip" strategy. Grief resolution requires coming to grips with loss, loneliness, personal effects, routines, and all manner of behaviors of the deceased. When the bereaved takes a trip (visits relatives, vacations, tours) soon after the death of a loved one, the grief work is partially postponed. The

Lifespan Development in Action

EASING THE PSYCHOLOGICAL PAIN OF LOSS

Losing a loved one is devastating at any point in the life cycle and poses an assortment of adjustments for survivors. Although no perfect answers exist as to how one should adapt and rebound from loss, numerous suggestions have been proposed. Among the major recommendations are the following:

Be patient with yourself. There is no predictable timetable that indicates how long or short grieving processes should be. Each particular case is unique and the overall duration of recovery knows wide variations.

Do not be afraid or ashamed to express your emotions. Grieving processes include a wide range of affective states, including sadness, remorse, anger, depression, and anxiety. Releasing these emotions, rather than suppressing them, is both normal and healthy.

Realize that emotional reactions to loss vary widely. There will be days when the sorrow of loss will be more evident than others. Sensitivity usually heightens, for example, around holiday times, birthdays, or other special days shared with the deceased. Be prepared for good and bad days as you reorganize your life, especially during the early stages of recovery.

Seek to accentuate the positive memories you have of the deceased. Survivors tend to dwell on the things they did not do for the deceased, or think of the parts of a relationship that could have been improved. Although it is normal to feel guilty, remember that guilt is self-imposed and needs to be put into a proper perspective. This means not ignoring the positive dimensions of your relationship with the deceased.

Share your feelings with others. It is important to talk about your loss, be it with friends, relatives, or skilled helpers. Along these lines, a support group may be an excellent source of guidance, security, and trust. Working through your grief with others also helps combat the loneliness that is prevalent following the loss of a loved one.

Take steps to maintain your physical and psychological well-being. Losing a loved one is a stressful life event that has the potential of creating inner turmoil and disruption. It is important to safeguard your health by getting adequate rest, nutrition, and exercise. Your susceptibility to illness may also be greater than it was before the loss; and many bereaved persons suffer from insomnia, loss of appetite, migraine headaches, and excessive anxiety. Should any of these conditions persist, do not hesitate to see a physician, psychologist, or licensed mental health professional.

portion that is postponed is precisely what needs to be confronted first. A person only needs to fantasize coming back home after such a trip (that is, walking into the empty house, the empty bedroom, and so on) in order to appreciate that the first level of grief work needs to be dealt with in the context of the deceased person's position, role, and immediate family environment prior to death.

THEORETICAL ISSUES

Do you think these dysfunctional methods of coping parallel any of the psychoanalytic defense mechanisms presented in Chapter 7? Can you think of any additional defense mechanisms that might explain dysfunctional behaviors?

Obliteration   **Obliteration** represents an effort by survivors to erase the former existence of the deceased. This goes beyond denial and avoidance. Obliteration involves the attempt of total erasure of the deceased person's prior existence. This may involve disposal of all personal effects, belongings, collections, hobbies, pictures, and other possessions. In short, obliteration means wiping away all memories of the deceased.

Idolization   **Idolization** is just the opposite of obliteration. Here, the survivor makes the deceased greater in death than he or she was in life. The deceased is endowed with a quality of perfection that is suprahuman. It is to restore life by holding fast to the belief that the deceased is really present. Personal effects are left intact. Possessions, mementos, pictures, and hobbies are endowed with an importance they previously lacked. No survivor can ever hope to measure up; and shame, self-doubt, guilt, and inferiority are prescribed feelings for those who must live in the wake of such splendor.

Patterns of Functional Coping   Constructive grief work relies on the support network being permissive of feelings. Additionally, the network needs to be positively accepting and supportive. This implies the ability to engage in honest and frank types of communication and that energies need to be directed at the actual loss as experienced collectively and individually. In order to accomplish this freedom of mutual acceptance, there needs to be an absence of scapegoating, blaming, excessive caretaking, and computerlike rationale that substitutes reason and logic for feelings and emotion. Commitment to the process of communication creates an atmosphere or context wherein the individuals may feel secure in their grief. With this, survivors are free to self-disclose. They are free to feel *whatever* they feel; but they are also free to challenge their own beliefs and the beliefs of others, knowing that feelings are often the result of internalized beliefs which are often irrational or illogical.

Unlimited possibilities for grief reduction are created when open communication is established. If feelings are shared (even if not in identical ways), there is an open stage for talk and reliving of past episodes. At this time, beliefs and values may need to be questioned openly, that is, challenged and confronted. Moreover, the open confrontation of beliefs may help survivors see the sometimes irrational assumptions they make regarding their personal role and responsibility in events that, in actuality, are far beyond their control. As we have learned, those who are in mourning and grief sometimes have an enormous overestimation of their own power: They reason that if they had done something differently, the death would never have happened. Thus the stage is set for prolonged grieving due to the fact grievers take on themselves responsibility for things far beyond their own control. This accounts for much of the guilt that becomes mixed up with grief.

▬ Endings and New Beginnings

As we have seen, adjusted widowed persons have developed ways to cope with the day-to-day problems of living alone, and they receive emotional support from various individuals. Their support networks include various relatives, especially children and siblings, and former or new friends. Although there are still feelings of loneliness and a sense of loss, successfully adjusted widowed persons have developed ways to cope with these problems. These survivors have established a new identity with the help of their support network (Brubaker, 1985).

One investigation of older widows (O'Bryant & Morgan, 1990) showed that most adjusted quite successfully with respect to independence and self-sufficiency. Although there were initial difficulties, most widows in good health managed to rebound from their loss and make necessary psychological and social adjustments. Those who were independent and undertook a range of tasks and activities prior to their husband's death continued to do so afterward.

Along similar lines, Mark Stern (1990) reports that dependency issues play a major role in how well widowed patients are able to develop emotionally. He feels that when recovery has been successful, widowhood does little to damage an individual's self-regard. The widowed, like other bereaved people, move from the sadness of loss to a gradual sense of incorporating the loss and detaching from the deceased spouse. Some researchers, such as Morton Lieberman (1992), feel that for many bereaved persons, such psychological processes promote new patterns of positive behavior and/or ways of thinking. Some who lose spouses, however, seem unable ever to fully resolve the pain of their loss. Ambivalence, guilt, and helplessness characterize many of those who seek psychotherapeutic help. Michael Caserta and Dale Lund (1992) add that those seeking professional help often report poorer perceived health, lower self-esteem, and reduced coping abilities.

Sidney Zisook and Stephen Schuchter (1991) have provided insight into recovery processes by evaluating bereaved persons at 2 months and 7 months following the loss of their partners. Overall, they found no consistent progression of grief resolution. At 7 months, grief-specific feeling states remained similar to

Overcoming the loss of a loved one is difficult and presents many adjustment chores, including overcoming loneliness. Some survivors decide to remarry, and others choose to live alone and construct a new lifestyle.

GENDER SIMILARITIES AND DIFFERENCES

What is your reaction to the observed gender differences that exist in bereavement and grief? What factors do you think account for these differences? Can you draw any parallels to these gender differences and those expressed at other points in the lifespan?

what they were at 2 months. Anxiety levels remained high and changed little from 2 to 7 months. When changes did occur, they were not unidirectional. For example, subjects were about as likely to increase as to decrease their drinking or smoking. Furthermore, depression scores at the second month correlated well with depression and anxiety scores at the seventh month. Over 50% of the subjects were depressed at some time during the study period, but this depression could initially manifest itself at any time during this period. Despite the presence of psychological distress in some, most bereaved individuals reported good health, satisfactory work performance, and good adjustment to widowhood.

When examining recovery from bereavement, one discovers that interesting gender differences exist. More specifically, it seems that men more so than women face difficulty in adjusting to their new roles as widowers. Researchers such as John Stephenson (1985) acknowledge that men are less apt to express grief and tend to be more socially isolated than widows. Also hampering the recovery process is the fact that ties with the extended family are typically maintained by the woman. Often, the man lacks the skills for maintaining or reestablishing such relationships. Men also report difficulty taking care of themselves during the recovery process, having previously left household responsibilities to their wives.

Many male and female survivors today turn to support groups and other service programs for assistance. Research (e.g., O'Bryant & Morgan, 1990) indicates that widows' support groups provide a safe, nurturant, and mutually supportive environment that can facilitate a healthy grieving process. Perhaps the most widely known is the *Widow-to-Widow Program*. Volunteers who have been widowed maintain phone hot lines and make home visits to newly widowed persons. The phone hot lines serve to provide listeners to the lonely, to help widowed persons make new friends, and to provide some specific piece of information. The primary aim of the entire program is to help the widowed person progress through the developmental stages involved in the transition from married life to widowed life. Aides provide support and serve as role models of what it is to be widowed. In addition to the hot line and home visits, another program providing social gatherings and community seminars has also been developed (Balkwell, 1981).

The path to recovery from bereavement may include remarriage. Many widowed adults choose to do so, although remarriage is more true for widowers than it is for widows (Cherlin, 1990; Steitz & Welker, 1990). According to some (e.g., Lauer & Lauer, 1991), widowed older adults who remarry often have higher morale and a better self-image than those choosing not to remarry. This was the finding of a study undertaken by Judith Stryckman (1981), who studied the lives of 400 widowed persons 55 years of age and older. Most of the remarried said they would make the same choice again if given the opportunity. What remarriers liked most about remarriage was "someone to love and who loves me" and the fact that they had "someone to keep me company." Most said they were more content, and one half of the men said they ate better and took better care of themselves. Although the remarried were relatively poorer financially than their widowed peers, they suffered less from anxiety and feelings of insecurity.

This entire discussion illustrates that successfully adjusted widowed persons have found new outlets for their energies. Moreover, they have sorted out their feelings surrounding the loss, enabling them to reflect on the past and recall both the pleasure and pain of a departed loved one. The successfully adjusted have come to terms with themselves and their future, which serves to create a renewal and reestablishment of their normal lifestyle. For many, this means the establishment of new intimate relationships. It may well be that experiencing widowhood promotes a stronger faith and more compassionate care and appreciation of the living. Those who have felt the pain of loss often learn to live their lives with more meaning—with appreciation of their finiteness and of the limits of their time here (Kinderknecht & Hodges, 1990; Miles & Crandall, 1983; Schneider, 1984; Stern, 1990; Weizman & Kamm, 1984).

CHAPTER REVIEW

One of life's most formidable tasks is learning to understand and accept death. For many people death is a sensitive topic that is avoided in conversations and often repressed. Because the dying are kept isolated and hidden from us, death has become secretive and elusive. Elderly people are more aware of death's imminence, and tend to exhibit less anxiety toward it.

Contrary to the popular tradition, dying patients usually want to talk openly about their impending death. Unfortunately, well-meaning family members or medical personnel may trap the terminally ill in a shroud of silence and avoid any discussion of the topic whatsoever. Most experts agree that being honest with patients is instrumental in helping them reach an acceptance of their impending death.

The psychological processes experienced by dying persons have fallen under the scrutiny of many researchers. Elisabeth Kübler-Ross has proposed a five-stage theory consisting of the denial, anger, bargaining, depression, and acceptance stages. Edwin Shneidman theorizes that the terminal patient experiences a variety of different emotions against a constant interplay of disbelief and hope. E. Mansell Pattison maintains that death is approached through three phases: the acute phase, the chronic living-dying interval, and the terminal period.

The quality of life before death is important for critically ill persons and their loved ones. In addition to adequate symptom management, dying patients need to retain control over their lives while maintaining their dignity, self-respect, and honor. The hospice approach seeks to improve every aspect of the quality of life for the terminally ill. Hospice embraces a humanistic approach to terminal illness and emphasizes comforting rather than curative care. The hospice philosophy also embodies the notion that families can share in the care of the terminally ill.

The right to die is a most controversial topic in the field of dying and death today. Passive euthanasia means that death is not actively prevented through any type of intervention; active euthanasia implies that steps are taken to cause death. The numerous medical and ethical dilemmas sparked by the Quinlan and Cruzan cases as well as by physician-assisted suicides heighten the need for policy intervention. It is likely this topic will grow in importance as medical technology improves and attitudes toward life and death change.

Several definitions of death exist. Functional death occurs when there is an absence of heartbeat and respiration. Cellular death is a gradual process that occurs after the vital organs cease to function. Brain death refers to a flat tracing recorded by an electroencephalogram. Brain death is perhaps the most widely accepted, and most states today declare a person legally dead when it has occurred. Many contemporary researchers have focused their attention on near-death experiences, those experiences of persons who are functionally dead but who are later resuscitated.

This chapter also examined the nature of bereavement and grief. Bereavement is the loss of a loved one by death; grief refers to the deep distress caused by such a loss. Grief work means coming to terms with the physical and emotional demands brought on by another's death. The loss of a loved one is stressful at any time in the life cycle, and survivors face many adjustment tasks. Expressions of grief can be placed into physical, cognitive, affective, and behavioral categories.

Phyllis Silverman has proposed three fairly distinct periods of grief: the impact, recoil, and accommodation stages. There are dysfunctional and functional coping strategies. The former includes such behaviors as avoidance, obliteration, and idolization. Patterns of functional coping are most often characterized by the sharing of feelings, the absence of scapegoating and blaming, and the substitution of reason and logic for feelings.

Over time, successfully adjusted bereaved persons have developed ways to cope with the day-to-day problems of living alone and receive emotional support from various persons. Most survivors rebound from their loss and make necessary psychological and social adjustments. Dependency issues appear to play a major role in how well widowed patients are able to develop emotionally. Those who remain independent and have managed to sort out their feelings surrounding the loss are likely to return to a normal lifestyle and live their lives with more meaning.

TERMS YOU SHOULD KNOW

acceptance stage
accommodation stage
acute phase
anger stage
bargaining stage
bereavement
brain death
cellular death
chronic living-dying interval
denial stage
depression stage
dying trajectory
euthanasia
functional death

grief
grief work
hospice
idolization
impact stage
near-death experience (NDE)
negative euthanasia
obliteration
positive euthanasia
preparatory depression
reactive depression
recoil stage
terminal phase
thanatology

THINKING IN ACTION

• Think about the information you learned in this chapter as you reflect on your own personal losses over the years. How has death affected your life, including the attitudes you now hold about living and dying? What have you learned about yourself in the face of personal loss?

• A close relative of yours is terminally ill and is not expected to live more than 3 months. You will be seeing him within a few days and are concerned about the quality of interaction that will take place. How might you prepare for the visit? What kinds of things can you do to support him as well as other close family members? While reflecting on the major points covered in this chapter, mentally rehearse how you intend to supply comfort and assistance during this time.

• Part of this chapter was designed to enhance your knowledge of euthanasia, including the many thorny issues surrounding it. Utilizing the information you acquired, think about euthanasia as it relates to your own personal life. Do your opinions on euthanasia change when you personalize the issue? If you were terminally ill and in pain, would you want to be kept alive by life support machines or allowed to die naturally? Do others know your wishes before your death? Why or why not?

• You have been asked to develop a workshop for widows and widowers on the topic of "New Beginnings: Coping with the Challenges of Spousal Loss." Design a program that explores such topics as recognizing and combating loneliness and depression, improving physical and emotional health, finding a meaningful support network, and developing independent living skills. To involve your participants, use your creative energies to design several different self-awareness and self-growth exercises.

RECOMMENDED READINGS

1. Bertman, S. L. (1991). *Facing death: Images, insights, and interventions.* Bristol, PA: Hemisphere.

   A handbook for those working with the terminally ill and their caregivers.

2. DeSpelder, L., & Strickland, A. L. (1992). *The last dance: Encountering death and dying* (3rd ed.). Palo Alto, CA: Mayfield.

   A comprehensive examination of all facets of dying, death, grief, and bereavement.

3. Morse, M. L., & Perry, P. (1992). *Transformed by the light.* New York: Villard.

   A captivating account of near-death experiences.

4. Samarel, N. (1991). *Caring for life and death.* Bristol, PA: Hemisphere.

   An insightful look at the pressures faced by the caregivers of the terminally ill.

5. Thomasma, D. C., & Graber, G. C. (1990). *Euthanasia: Toward an ethical social policy.* New York: Continuum.

   A penetrating investigation of the moral proprieties of euthanasia.

Glossary

abstraction Subjective concept or idea apart from one's objective analysis of the tangible environment.

acceptance stage According to Kübler-Ross, the fifth psychological stage of dying. The person is no longer angry or depressed but desires to be left alone or with just a few loved ones.

accommodation According to Piaget, the restructuring of mental organizations so that new information or previously rejected information may be processed.

accommodation stage Third stage of grief and mourning identified by Silverman. During this time, survivors reorganize their lives and view the deceased in a healthy perspective.

acquired immune deficiency syndrome (AIDS) Disorder characterized by a specific defect in the body's natural immunity against disease.

active model of development Model of lifespan development stating that individuals are capable of actively governing and regulating their own development. An example is cognitive-developmental theory.

activity theory Theory that active and productive people are happiest, even in old age.

acute phase According to Pattison, the first of three phases of dying.

addicting narcotic Narcotic such as opium and heroin that produces pronounced physical and psychological addiction.

adolescent egocentrism Ability to conceptualize one's own thoughts in addition to being preoccupied with the thoughts of those in one's surroundings. Two types of adolescent egocentrism are the imaginary audience and the personal fable.

adult day-care facility Facility that offers daily nursing, nutritional, and medical monitoring to the elderly, who, however, maintain their own residences.

affective disorders Functional disorders characterized by mood disturbances. These can include *manic disorder*, in which the person feels unusually elated; *depression*, characterized by sadness and a sense of hopelessness; and *bipolar disorder*, marked by fluctuations of both mania and depression.

agape love Type of love characterized by altruistic and caring behavior.

ageism Discrimination against or unkind stereotyping of a person on the basis of his or her age. Ageism is most prevalent against the elderly.

agenesis Failure of embryonic tissue to develop.

allele Any of several alternative genes at a given chromosomal locus.

Alzheimer's disease Category of dementia characterized by progressive mental deterioration.

amino acid Basic unit of structure for protein.

amniocentesis Removal of fluid from the amniotic sac so chromosomes of the fetus may be analyzed.

amniotic fluid Liquid that holds the embryo or fetus in suspension and protects it against jarring and from any pressure exerted by the mother's internal organs.

amniotic sac Transparent membrane completely enveloping the embryo or fetus, except where the umbilical cord passes through the placenta.

amphetamine Drug that serves as a stimulant and acts on the central nervous system. Examples of amphetamines are cocaine, benzedrine, dexedrine, and methedrine.

anal stage Freud's second stage of psychosexual development. During this period, children's erotic feelings center on the anus and on elimination.

anatomical sex Physical characteristics and features that distinguish females from males.

androgyny Having both masculine and feminine personality traits.

anger stage According to Kübler-Ross, the second psychological stage of dying. The person accepts the fact of his or her impending death but is angry about its seeming unfairness: "Why does it have to be me?"

animism According to Piaget, the tendency of children to give life to inanimate objects. Animism is most prevalent between the ages of 2 and 4.

anorexia nervosa Severe diminishment of appetite, particularly among teenagers. This disorder is more common in females than in males and is believed to have psychogenic origins.

anticoagulant Drug that thins the blood and prevents clotting.

anxiety State of inner apprehension most frequently characterized as a generalized fear of a subjective danger.

anxiety disorder Functional disorder frequently characterized by subjective distress. Symptoms may take the form of tension, trembling, rapid heartbeat, and accelerated breathing.

Apgar test Evaluation of the newborn's basic life processes, administered approximately 1 minute after birth and again 5 minutes later. The life signs tested are heart rate, respiratory regularity, muscle tone, reflex irritability, and coloration.

arcuate fasciculus Area of the brain that plays a significant role in producing meaningful speech.

arteriosclerosis Abnormal hardening or thickening of the arterial walls, making a person more prone to conditions like heart attacks and strokes.

arthritis Inflammation, pain, and swelling of the joints.

artificial insemination Procedure in which sperm (fresh or frozen) are artificially injected into a woman's vagina, either on or near the cervix, at the time of ovulation.

artificialism Childhood notion that everything in the world, including natural objects and events, is designed by human beings.

ascetic orientation Sexual value orientation advocating sexual self-denial, the avoidance of all sexual activity, and the implementation of spiritual self-discipline. Also known as celibacy.

assimilation Perceiving and interpreting new information in terms of existing knowledge and understanding.

atherosclerosis Condition that results when fatty deposits narrow the arteries and reduce or block the flow of blood through them.

attachment Affectionate bond between infant and caregiver.

authoritarian control Attempt to control behavior by enforcing a set standard of conduct. Emphasis is placed on obedience and punitive discipline.

authoritative control Attempt to control behavior by establishing democratic, meaningful, and realistic expectations.

authority-maintaining orientation Kohlberg's fourth stage of moral development.

autonomy versus shame and doubt Erikson's second psychosocial crisis, occurring between the ages of 1 and 3, in which the child must achieve independence and self-control.

autosomes Chromosomes other than the sex chromosomes.

babbling Stage of early language development, beginning by approximately the sixth month. Babbling first emerges a syllable at a time and includes both vowels and consonants.

baby biography Day-to-day account of the development of an infant or child.

barbiturate Depressant drug that induces sleep and provides relaxation. Examples are Nembutal, Seconal, and Librium.

bargaining stage According to Kübler-Ross, the third psychological stage of dying. The dying person bargains with God, doctors, or anyone else he or she believes can stave off death.

basal-cell carcinoma Form of skin cancer that usually appears on the head and neck. It is a malignant tumor that rarely metastasizes.

basic trust versus mistrust Erikson's first psychosocial crisis, occurring in the first year of life, in which the child must learn not only to trust others but to trust oneself.

behavioral genetics Study of inherited behavior.

behavioral predisposition Term implying that one has an inborn (inherited) tendency toward certain behavioral characteristics, given certain environmental conditions.

behaviorism School of thought emphasizing that an organism's behavior is a product of conditioning and learning experiences. Emphasis is on the organism's observable behaviors.

benign tumor Tumor that is typically harmless and does not invade normal tissue.

bereavement Loss of a loved one through death.

bilingualism Ability to speak more than one language.

biological aging One of the three main types of aging processes. Biological aging refers to physiological functioning over time.

biological theories of lifespan development One of the three major categories of lifespan development theories. These theories focus on the complex physiological processes that occur over the course of the life cycle. Examples include the wear-and-tear, cellular, and immunity theories.

birthing room For the parents of newborns, a room offering a homelike and relaxed atmosphere within the hospital's general delivery unit.

bisexuality Sexual attraction and emotional attachment to both women and men.

blastocyst Technical name given to the mass of cells that results after several days of zygotic cell division.

blending action Type of biochemical activity in which no one gene dominates the other; rather, the two proteins manufactured by the ribosome mix together.

blood pressure Pressure exerted by the blood on the artery walls.

body transcendence versus body preoccupation According to Peck, a psychological adjustment to be made during the later years of adulthood.

brain death Most widely accepted definition of death. Brain death is characterized by a flat electroencephalogram; an electroencephalogram measures the degree of brain wave activity in the neocortex and the brain stem.

breech presentation Delivery of a baby's buttocks or feet first.

Broca's area Portion of the brain that is located adjacent to the motor cortex and controls the muscles involved in speech. Damage to this area produces motor aphasia and causes speech to be slow and labored.

bulimia nervosa Eating disorder characterized by gorging oneself with excessive amounts of food and then inducing vomiting and/or using large amounts of laxatives.

burnout Depleting of physical and mental resources because of stress.

cancer Large group of diseases characterized by uncontrolled growth and the spread of abnormal cells.

cardiac output Amount of blood released each minute by the heart's ventricles.

career clock According to Kimmel, a person's subjective sense of being on time or behind time in regard to career development.

case study Research technique that focuses on a single person rather than a group of people.

cataract Visual problem characterized by opacity in the lens of the eye.

catharsis theory of television viewing Theory proposing that watching aggressive behavior on television provides a vicarious outlet for the viewer's own aggressiveness.

cathectic flexibility versus cathectic impoverishment According to Peck, a psychological adjustment to be made during middle adulthood.

cell Living unit of organized material that contains a nucleus and is enclosed in a membrane.

cellular death Gradual process that occurs after the vital organs cease to function. Examples of cellular death include hair growth, the liver's conversion of glycogen to glucose, and muscle contractions.

cellular theory Theory of biological aging that emphasizes the role errors in cell division play in aging processes.

centering Tendency to concentrate on the outstanding characteristics of an object while excluding its other features.

central nervous system Part of the nervous system that consists of the brain and the spinal cord.

cephalocaudal development Physical growth that takes place from the head downward.

cerebrovascular accident (CVA) Rupture or blockage of a large cerebral blood vessel, usually leading to a stroke.

cesarean delivery Delivery of the baby through a surgical incision made in the mother's abdominal and uterine walls.

chain Term used in behaviorism to refer to a number of stimulus-response units placed in a series.

child sexual abuse Sexual contact between a child and an unrelated adult in which the child is used for the sexual stimulation and pleasure of the adult.

cholesterol Lipid (fat) produced naturally in the body.

chorionic villus sampling Method for diagnosing defects in the developing fetus. Procedure involves the insertion of a thin catheter into the uterus where some of the chorion are removed and analyzed.

chromosomes Thin rodlike structures in a cell that contain the essential mechanisms for directions of the cell's activity.

chronic living-dying interval According to Pattison, the second of three phases of dying.

circumcision Surgical procedure in which all or part of the foreskin of the penis is removed.

classification In Piagetian logic, the ability to understand the concepts of subclasses, classes, and class inclusion.

climacteric Period of life from the onset of irregularity of the menses to total cessation.

clique Small peer group characterized by social exclusiveness and a strong emotional bond among its members.

cocaine Amphetamine that exists as a bitter crystalline alkaloid.

cognition An individual's intellectual activity. The mental process involving all aspects of thought and perception.

cognitive-developmental theory Theory of development that proposes specific stages leading to mature thinking.

cognitive flexibility Ability to shift from one way of thinking to another.

cognitive social learning theory Theory that integrates what is known about learning processes to explain social behavior.

cognitive style Manner in which an individual organizes information and discovers solutions to problems.

cognitive theories Category of theories embracing such elements as how individuals perceive, think, and understand. Examples include cognitive-developmental and information processing theories.

cohabitation Man and woman living together who are not married.

cohort Group of persons born approximately at the same time.

cohort analysis Analysis of the experiences common to a particular age group.

cohort sequential design Complex research design involving two or more longitudinal studies of people of the same age but of different cohorts.

collective monologue Type of egocentric communication characterized by inability to listen effectively to what others are saying.

compensation Finding a successful or rewarding activity that can be substituted for failure in another kind of activity.

concept Mental image formed to represent an object or event.

concrete operations Fourth stage of Piaget's theory of cognitive development, occurring approximately from ages 7 to 11. The stage marks a time when cognition is used consistently and the child can reason logically in new and challenging situations.

conductive deafness Deafness involving blockage or impairment of the outer or middle ear so that sound waves are not able to travel properly.

conflict theory Sociological theory of lifespan development suggesting that disequilibrium, disharmony, and conflict are inevitable features of aging experiences.

confounded data Data (such as age and cohort) in a research study that cannot be assessed separately.

conjoined twins Twins that result when a single fertilized egg does not completely split after conception. Also called Siamese twins.

conscious In psychoanalytic theory, thoughts and experiences of which the individual is aware of at any given moment.

conservation Recognition that the amount or quantity of matter remains the same despite changes in its outward physical appearance.

consonant Speech sound characterized by constriction or closure at one or more points in the breath channel.

contextual influences Those influences that arise from the interrelationships between the changing person and the changing world. Examples are culture, history, and life events.

continuity-discontinuity issue Lifespan development issue focusing on whether development is gradual and continuous or adhering to age-prescribed stages.

continuous model of development Model of develop-ment not adhering to age-prescribed stages. Rather, it sees change as gradual and continuous.

contractual legalistic orientation Kohlberg's fifth of six moral development stages. This stage is grouped under the major division or level known as postconventional morality.

control group Group of subjects in a research study who receive the same treatment as does the group being experimented upon, except they do not receive the stimulus (independent variable) under observation.

controlled experiments An experimental situation in which the subject is placed in a structured and perhaps unnatural environment that can be manipulated by the experimenter.

conventional level Kohlberg's second of six moral development stages, covering ages 9 through 15.

cooing Type of vocalization taking place during the second month of infancy.

coronary artery disease (CAD) Disease characterized by the presence of atherosclerosis in the coronary arteries.

correlational method Research method that seeks to explore whatever relationship exists between variables. Correlations may be *positive* (one variable tends to increase as the other increases) or *negative* (one variable tends to decrease while the other increases). When no relationship exists between variables, they are said to be *uncorrelated.*

cri-du-chat syndrome Genetic disorder caused by a partial loss of a chromosome on the fifth position. Characteristics include severe mental retardation, microcephaly, growth retardation, low birth weight, limited eye control, and a peculiar catlike cry.

critical period Point in an organism's early life stages at which strong bonds of attachment are established with the mother or other caregiver.

cross-sectional design Research design comparing developmental trends among groups who differ in age at a given time.

cross-sequential design Complex research design in which individuals of different ages are measured at different intervals. It involves a series of longitudinal studies with a cross-sectional twist.

crowd Group of people larger than a clique but more impersonal and lacking strong bonds of attachment but having rather rigid membership requirements.

crowning During childbirth, the encirclement of the largest diameter of the baby's head by the vulva.

crystallized intelligence Dimension of intelligence that includes verbal comprehension, numerical skills, and inductive reasoning.

cytoplasm Protoplasm found inside the cell but outside the nucleus.

daughter cell New cell created in cell division.

deductive reasoning Reasoning from a set of premises to a conclusion. Piaget called this hypothetico-deductive reasoning.

deep structure Conceptual framework or meaning of a particular sentence.

defense mechanism Behavioral response enabling one to escape from anxiety. Also called coping mechanism.

delirium Reversible dementia caused by such factors as the toxic effects of medications, malnutrition, and infection. Symptoms often include disorientation, delusions, disturbances in sleep patterns, and memory deficits.

dementia Generalized cognitive and behavioral deterioration due to brain dysfunction.

denial of reality Defense mechanism characterized by the individual's refusal to perceive the existence of hurtful situations.

denial stage According to Kübler-Ross, the first psychological stage of dying. During this stage, the person is unable to accept that he or she is going to die.

deoxyribonucleic acid (DNA) Chemical substance constituting chromosomes and genes.

dependent variable The change, if any, brought about by the independent variables in experimental studies. Changes appear in the experimental group, especially when contrasted with the control group.

depression Emotional state characterized by feelings of sadness, lack of energy, and feelings of hopelessness and despair.

depression stage According to Kübler-Ross, the fourth stage of dying. When the patient can no longer deny the illness, he or she becomes engulfed with a sense of great loss.

depth perception Visual ability enabling persons to judge distance and descent.

developmental excess Term given to the overgrowth of the whole organism or any of its parts.

developmental psychology General term encompassing the psychology of childhood, adolescence, and all the remaining years of the human lifespan. Also called lifespan development or human development.

dialect Regional variation of a language.

diploid state Cell that has its full quota of chromosomes.

discipline Teaching of acceptable forms of conduct or behavior.

discontinuous model of development Model of development emphasizing distinct spurts in growth and development. Also called an age-stage model or theory.

disenchantment phase Third of six retirement stages proposed by Atchley. Here, retirees typically become disillusioned over the retirement role.

disengagement theory Theory that it is natural and indeed desirable to withdraw gradually from society as one grows old.

displacement Releasing of pent-up hostile feelings onto objects less dangerous than those that initially aroused the emotion.

distress Harmful and unpleasant stress. Distress occurs when the body and mind are worn down from repeated exposure to an unpleasant situation.

diuretic Drug that causes excess fluid and sodium to leave the body.

dominant gene Gene that always expresses its hereditary characteristic.

Down syndrome Also referred to as trisomy 21, a chromosomal abnormality in which there is an extra chromosome on the 21st position. Children afflicted with this disorder have, among other characteristics, epicanthic eye folds, round heads, and are almost always mentally retarded.

dying trajectory Duration and form of the dying process.

early maturer Person who matures physically before the prescribed timetables.

ecological theory Theory focusing on the importance of culture or context in shaping the course of development.

ectopic pregnancy Pregnancy that results when the fertilized egg becomes lodged in the wall of the fallopian tube.

ego In psychoanalytic theory, the part of the personality that serves as a rational agent and the mediator between the id and the superego.

egocentrism Style of thinking that causes children difficulty in seeing any point of view other than their own; self-centeredness.

ego differentiation versus work-role preoccupation According to Peck, a psychological adjustment to be made during the later years of adulthood.

ego transcendence versus ego preoccupation According to Peck, a psychological adjustment to be made during the later years of adulthood.

Electra complex According to Freud, a girl's romantic feelings for her father and aggressive feelings for her mother. The Electra complex is prevalent during the phallic stage of psychosexual development.

embryo Organism between the second and eighth weeks of prenatal development.

embryonic period Period of prenatal development beginning when the ovum is implanted in the uterine wall and the cells begin to exhibit marked differentiation.

embryo transfer Reproductive technology that involves impregnating another woman with the father's sperm. After several days, the fertilized ovum is removed from her uterus and placed within the wife's uterus, which has been hormonally prepared to accept it.

emotion Variation or change in one's arousal level that may either interfere with or facilitate motivated behavior.

empty nest Period of life when the children have left home and the couple is now alone.

endemic stressor Stressor that is long term and often cannot be eliminated.

environmentalist Person who asserts the environment is the major contributor to an individual's behavior and development.

epigenetic principle Theory stating that all development is genetically programmed.

equilibration According to Piaget, the balance between assimilation and accommodation.

eros love Type of love characterized by the desire for sexual intimacy and a preoccupation with the physical aspects of the relationship.

escape Defense mechanism characterized by retreat or withdrawal behaviors.

estrogen Female sex hormone.

ethological theory Theory centering on the study of human and animal behavior in natural settings, including the role of instincts and biologically inherited responses in growth and development.

eustress Type of positive stress that occurs when the body's reactive change is put to productive use.

euthanasia Act of ending a life to alleviate suffering.

experimental group Group of subjects in an experimental study that receives a special stimulus or treatment, the effect of which is under observation.

experimental method Series of steps by which the researcher tries to determine relationships among differing phenomena either to discover principles underlying behavior or to find cause-and-effect relationships. The method is characterized by control and repetition.

external aging Physical aspects of aging that are visible to the eye.

fair-weather cooperation stage According to Selman, friendships made during the later school years.

family development theory Sociological theory of life-span development suggesting that family life represents a series of stages, orderly transitions that present members with an assortment of life course events and challenges.

fetal alcohol syndrome Condition among newborns caused by excessive alcohol consumption by the mother. Affected infants are often born undersized, mentally deficient, and with assorted physical deformities.

fetal distress Condition characterized by a slow irregular fetal heart, or a change in fetal activity.

fetal period Period between 8 weeks of prenatal development and birth.

fetoscopy Technique that photographs the fetus and samples fetal tissue and blood.

fetus Human organism in the womb from approximately the third prenatal month until birth.

fine motor skills Motor skills requiring the use of small body parts, particularly the hands. Examples are writing and sewing.

fixation Preoccupation with one particular aspect of psychosexual development (e.g., thumb sucking) that may interfere with or be manifested in subsequent psychosexual stages.

fluid intelligence General cognitive ability that reflects relational thinking and the capability of thinking independently of culturally based content. Fluid intelligence is believed to peak during young adulthood.

forebrain Frontal and upper portion of the brain. The forebrain consists of the cerebrum, cerebral cortex, corpus callosum, thalamus, and hypothalamus.

formal operations Final stage of Piaget's theory of cognitive development, occurring between the ages of 11 and 15. The stage is characterized by systematic reasoning abilities and the successful integration of all past cognitive operations.

fraternal twins Twins conceived when two ova are released simultaneously by the female and both are penetrated by male sperm cells. Also referred to as dizygotic twins.

free association Cathartic process used in psychoanalysis. When patients use free association, they verbalize whatever comes into their minds.

friendship The pairing off of, usually, two individuals who are likely to be similar in temperament and personality and share common interests.

full nest Reference to the period of life when a couple's children have reached adult status, but residency within the home continues.

functional death Definition of death characterized by an absence of heartbeat and respiration.

functional disorder Disorder characterized by psychological causes. Examples of functional disorders include anxiety disorders (e.g., phobias, panic attacks), mood disorders (e.g., major depression, bipolar disorder), or somatoform disorders (e.g., hypochondria, conversion disorders).

gamete Reproductive cell, either the female ovum or the male sperm.

gay Males whose sexual orientation and affectional attraction are to other men. The word *gay* is sometimes applied to both men and women.

gender Social meanings attached to being a female or male.

gender identity Psychological awareness or sense of being either a male or a female.

gender role Set of expectations that prescribes how females and males should behave.

gender-role stereotype Generalization that reflects our beliefs about females and males.

general adaptation syndrome (GAS) Selye's model of

stress reaction. The three stages are alarm, resistance, and exhaustion.

generation gap   Term applied to the differences in values, attitudes, and behavior between two generational groups.

generativity versus self-absorption   According to Erikson, the psychosocial crisis that typically takes place during middle adulthood. Important at this time is caring for younger generations and adopting responsible adult roles in the community.

genes   Biological units contained in the chromosomes, the transmitters of hereditary characteristics.

genetics   Science of heredity.

genetic sex   Person's chromosomal makeup.

genital stage   According to Freud, the stage of psychosexual development at which normal and mature sexual behavior is attained.

genotype   Actual genetic makeup (gene pair) of an organism.

geriatrics   Branch of medicine that pertains to the health problems of the elderly.

germ cells   Cells frequently referred to as sex cells, or gametes.

gerontology   Branch of developmental psychology that investigates the aged and aging processes.

glaucoma   Eye disease that results from increased pressure within the eyeball. Glaucoma causes a gradual loss of vision and damage to the optic disk.

gonads   Reproductive organs: the ovaries in the female and the testes in the male.

good boy-nice girl orientation   Kohlberg's third of six stages of moral development. This stage is grouped under the major division or level known as conventional morality.

grief   Deep distress caused by the loss of a loved one.

grief work   Coming to terms with the physical and emotional demands brought by another's death.

gross motor skills   Motor skills requiring the coordination of large body parts. Examples are running, tumbling, and climbing a ladder.

growth   Physical changes in the body or any of its parts because of an increase in cell number.

handedness   An individual's hand preference.

haploid state   Biological condition in which a cell contains only half the number of chromosomes that are natural for its species.

hedonistic orientation   Sexual value orientation that emphasizes the importance of sexual pleasure and satisfaction rather than moral constraint. Sometimes called the recreational sexual standard.

hedonistic principle   Motivation to seek out what is pleasurable and to avoid what creates discomfort.

heredity   Characteristics genetically transmitted to offspring by their parents.

heterosexuality   Sexual attraction and emotional attachment to members of the opposite sex.

heterozygous   Genetic condition in which both gene pairs in an organism differ for a given trait (one dominant, one recessive).

hindbrain   Lower portion of the brain responsible for those bodily functions necessary for survival. The hindbrain consists of the medulla, cerebellum, pons, and part of the reticular activating system.

holophrase   One-word stage of language development that occurs between 12 and 18 months.

home birth   Delivery of a baby in the parents' home rather than in a hospital. The delivery is often conducted by a licensed nurse-midwife.

homosexuality   Sexual attraction and emotional attachment to persons of the same sex.

homozygous   Genetic condition in which both genes are identical for a given trait (two dominant or two recessive).

honeymoon phase   Second of six retirement stages proposed by Atchley. Here, a state of euphoria over newfound freedom from the workplace is experienced.

hospice   Facility for terminally ill patients that focuses not only on providing humane medical care but also on fulfilling the patients' emotional needs.

hostile aggression   Type of aggression directed at another person with the intention of hurting that person.

humanistic theory   One of lifespan development's major schools of thought. Humanists such as Maslow and Rogers stress the importance of helping people maximize their uniqueness and potential in life.

hypertension   High blood pressure.

hypothesis   Predicted solution of a problem.

hypothetico-deductive reasoning   See deductive reasoning.

id   According to psychoanalytic theory, the instinctual part of the personality, which is concerned with the immediate gratification of motives.

identical twins   Twins that occur as the result of the zygote splitting into two separate but genetically identical cells. Also referred to as monozygotic twins.

identity achievement   According to Marcia, an appraisal of values and choices in life and a commitment to some goal.

identity diffusion   According to Marcia, the failure to examine any goals or values.

identity foreclosure   According to Marcia, the idea of having life goals established by others.

identity formation   Establishment of an integrated ego, usually during adolescence.

identity moratorium   According to Marcia, the notion of rethinking values and goals, which often leads to an identity crisis.

identity versus role diffusion   Fifth of Erikson's eight psychosocial crises. Identity versus role diffusion occupies the teenage years and presents adolescents with the chore of establishing a sense of identity and understanding life roles.

idolization Among widows and widowers, the effort to make the deceased greater in death than he or she was in life. This is a type of dysfunctional coping.

imaginary audience Consequence of adolescent egocentrism. Teenagers imagine they are always the focus of attention.

immanent justice Childhood assumption that the world has a built-in system of law and order.

immunity theory Theory of biological aging suggesting that the body's immune system degenerates with age.

impact stage First stage of grief and mourning proposed by Silverman. It is characterized by shock, psychological numbness, and the need for help from family and friends.

imprinting Organism's rapid attachment to an object (generally its caregiver), usually shortly after birth.

impulsivity Conceptual tempo characterized by a hurried response and little, if any, consideration of the response's accuracy.

incest Sexual intercourse or sexual relations between persons so closely related they are forbidden by law to marry.

incomplete development Failure of genes to complete the development or growth already commenced.

independent variable Stimulus administered to the experimental group of subjects but not to the control group.

individuation Process of disengaging or separating one's attitudes and beliefs from those of one's parents.

inductive reasoning Reasoning from specific individual experiences and proceeding to general principles.

industry versus inferiority Fourth of Erikson's eight psychosocial crises. Industry versus inferiority occupies all of middle childhood and presents the challenges of achieving adequacy, competence, and self-worth.

infarct Infected tissue of a myocardial infarction.

infertility Inability to achieve a pregnancy after at least 1 year of regular unprotected intercourse.

information processing theory Cognitive theory explaining how individuals acquire, store, and retrieve information.

initiative versus guilt Third of Erikson's eight psychosocial crises. Initiative versus guilt occurs between the ages of 3 and 6 and its central challenge is achieving greater levels of environmental mastery and a sense of purpose.

institutionalism Psychological state of apathy and deterioration, brought about by a depersonalized, institutionalized environment.

instrumental aggression Type of aggression aimed at acquiring objects, territory, or privileges.

integrity versus despair Eighth psychosocial crisis proposed by Erikson. At this time (late adulthood), individuals seek to nurture a sense of accomplishment about one's life rather than negative attitudes.

interactionist Individual who believes development is shaped by the interaction of heredity and environment.

intermediate-care facility Nursing facility that places less emphasis on intensive care nursing and more on personal care service.

internal aging Physical aspects of aging that cannot be seen.

intimacy Becoming close with another person through the process of self-disclosure.

intimacy versus isolation Sixth of eight psychosocial crises postulated by Erik Erikson. It occurs during young adulthood and presents individuals with the challenge of forming close, meaningful relationships with others.

intimate and mutually shared relationships According to Selman, friendships during late childhood and early adolescence.

intimate relationship Process in which a person comes to know the innermost, subjective aspects of another individual.

intrauterine fetal surgery Microsurgery on the unborn child to correct problems diagnosed during the mother's pregnancy.

intuitive thought Substage of preoperational thought that occurs approximately between the ages of 4 and 7. The child's thought patterns are bound by immediate perceptions and experiences rather than by flexible mental functions.

invention of new means through mental combinations Last of Piaget's six substages of sensorimotor development. This substage occurs between 18 and 24 months.

in-vitro fertilization Form of reproductive technology in which one or more ova are surgically removed from the mother, combined with the father's sperm, and placed into the uterus.

joint custody Mutual sharing of parental rights and responsibilities after a divorce has taken place.

juvenile delinquency Behavior by youths 18 and under that society deems unacceptable.

kernel words Words that can be strung together to make a statement that is usually declarative.

Klinefelter's syndrome Chromosomal abnormality in which males have two normal X chromosomes plus the Y (XXY). Those afflicted have small external male sex organs but the general contour of a female and are sterile.

labor Process of giving birth, including uterine contractions, actual delivery of the baby, and expulsion of the placenta.

Lamaze method Natural childbirth approach emphasizing a conditioned learning technique in which the mother replaces one set of learned responses (fear, pain) with another (relaxation, muscle control).

language System of grammatical rules and semantics that makes speech meaningful.

language acquisition device According to Chomsky, a system of linguistic programming dependent on mature cells in the cerebral cortex.

lanugo Fine downy growth of hair appearing on the entire body of the fetus and newborn.

late maturer Person who matures physically after the prescribed timetables.

latency period Fourth stage of Freud's psychosexual theory in which the individual's sexual feelings are submerged. The emergence and refinement of defense mechanisms also occurs at this time.

lateralization Specialization of the left and right cerebral hemispheres.

learning Relatively permanent change in behavior as the result of experience.

learning disability Learning problem characterized by difficulty in processing, remembering, or expressing information.

learning theories Category of theories focusing on how behavior is shaped by interaction with the environment. An example is behaviorism.

Leboyer method Proposed by French obstetrician Frederic Leboyer, this technique emphasizes a gentle delivery of the baby as well as the establishment of a peaceful and soothing delivery room environment.

lesbian Female whose sexual orientation and affectional attraction are to other women.

libido According to Freud, energy, which is basically sexual, that serves the basic human instincts.

life review According to Butler, a form of reminiscing that occurs with advancing age. Such a mental process allows individuals to relive past experiences and perhaps deal with persisting conflicts as they approach death.

lightening Uterine descent into the pelvis during early stages of labor.

locomotion Organism's ability to move from place to place; to walk.

longitudinal design Research design in which the researcher repeatedly collects data on the same group of individuals over a long period of time.

long-term memory (LTM) Storage system that enables individuals to retain information for relatively long periods of time.

LSD Lysergic acid diethylamide, a hallucinogenic compound produced from ergot.

ludus love Playful, self-centered form of love.

malignant tumor Tumor that is cancerous and invades surrounding tissues.

manic love Intense and obsessive love.

marijuana Hallucinogenic drug obtained from a mixture of the tops, leaves, seeds, and stems of female hemp or cannabis plants. The strongest grade of marijuana is known as hashish.

marriage rate Number of marriages each year per 1,000 members of a population.

maturation Development of body cells to full maturity, at which time they are fully utilized by the organism.

maturity State that promotes physical and psychological well-being.

Medicaid Government-sponsored medical care plan for welfare clients, regardless of age.

Medicare Government-sponsored insurance program that partially finances the health-care costs of persons 65 years and older.

meiosis Process of germ cell division.

menarche First menstrual period.

menopause Cessation of menstruation, generally in the mid-to-late 40s or early 50s.

mental flexibility versus mental rigidity According to Peck, a psychological adjustment to be made during middle adulthood.

messenger RNA Type of RNA that carries the DNA message to the ribosomes so that protein can be synthesized.

metacognition Person's awareness of how a cognitive process can be applied to a selected mental task.

metamemory Person's awareness of how a memory strategy can be employed to prevent forgetting the material at hand.

midbrain Connecting link between the forebrain and the hindbrain.

miscarriage Natural termination of a pregnancy before the embryo or fetus has the opportunity to fully develop.

mitosis Process of somatic cell division.

morality Conscious adoption of standards related to right and wrong.

moral realism According to Piaget, a stage of morality during which children between the ages of 5 and 10 perceive rules but do not understand why they exist.

moral relativism According to Piaget, a stage of morality in which children 10 years of age and older view rules in relation to the principles they uphold.

morpheme Smallest unit of a language that has recognizable meaning. The word *boys,* for example, has two morphemes, *boy* and *s.*

motor skill Ability to coordinate the bodily movements that enable an individual to execute a particular physical task.

multi-infarct dementia Type of organic brain disorder characterized by the widespread death of brain tissue, which interferes with the exchange of essential substances between the bloodstream and the brain tissue. Sometimes called vascular dementia.

mutation Gene error or dysfunction that produces a change in the characteristic the gene determines. Mutations may be positive, negative, or neutral.

myelin White fatty substance that covers many nerve fibers of the body. Nerves that are covered with myelin transmit their electrochemical messages at a more rapid rate than nonmyelinated nerves.

myelination Process by which the neuron develops an outer sheath.

myocardial infarction Destruction of myocardial tissue.

naively egoistic orientation Kohlberg's second of six moral development stages. This stage is grouped under the major division or level known as preconventional morality.

nativist Researcher who believes much behavior is dependent on genetic endowment. Also called hereditarian.

naturalistic observation Examination of behavior under unstructured or natural conditions.

nature-nurture issue Issue that focuses on the relative importance of the genetic endowment and the nurturing environment.

near-death experience (NDE) Experience of persons who are pronounced clinically dead but who are later resuscitated.

negative euthanasia Type of euthanasia in which death is not actively prevented through any type of intervention. Also referred to as *passive euthanasia.*

negative reinforcement In instrumental conditioning, an unpleasant stimulus is taken away from a subject following a desired response. This is done in order to strengthen that particular response.

neonate Term for the newborn infant during the first few weeks of life.

nocturnal emission Ejaculation of semen during sleep.

nonnormative influences Biological and environmental forces that are unpredictable and do not affect everyone, for example, sudden unemployment, sudden onset of disease.

normative age-graded influences Those behaviors (e.g., walking, talking) that have a biological basis and influence all humans at approximately the same age.

normative history-graded influences Those cultural events that influence people of the same age, such as war or economic depression.

nucleoplasm Protoplasm found inside the nuclear membrane.

nucleus Control center for the cell's activity, located in or near the center of the cell.

nurse-midwife Trained delivery specialist who provides qualified medical care to expectant mothers. Usually the midwife has earned a bachelor's degree in nurse midwifery and works on a medical team including a gynecologist and an obstetrician.

obedience and punishment orientation Kohlberg's first of six stages of moral development. This stage is grouped under the major division or level known as preconventional morality.

obesity An excessive accumulation of body fat, usually 10 to 20% or more than one's suggested normal weight.

object permanence Mental ability that enables one to realize objects exist even if they are out of one's field of vision.

obliteration Among widows and widowers, an attempt to totally erase the former existence of the deceased. Obliteration is a form of dysfunctional coping.

observational learning Learning by watching others and observing the consequences of their actions.

Oedipus complex According to Freud, the romantic feelings a boy has for his mother and the fear of the father's retaliation. The Oedipus complex is prevalent during the phallic stage of psychosexual development.

one-way assistance stage According to Selman, friendships made during the early school years.

open class word Word in early sentence structure that is connected to pivot words. Pivot words rarely exist as single-word utterances and are usually in the first position of early two-word sentences.

operants According to Skinner, instrumentally conditioned responses.

oral stage According to Freud, the initial phase of psychosexual development. During this period infants seek gratification from stimulation of the mouth.

organic brain syndrome Cognitive and behavioral maladjustment due to brain dysfunction.

organogenesis Period marking the beginning of organ development, from the third week of pregnancy through the second or third month.

osteoarthritis Inflammation of the joints, usually caused by changes in bone and cartilage.

osteoporosis Gradual loss of bone density.

overregularization Extension of a grammatical rule to situations to which it does not apply—for example, *goed* instead of *went.*

overweight General term referring to body heaviness; that is, a person's body weight is greater than that recommended for one's size.

ovum Female egg or germ cell (plural: ova).

parallel play Variation of egocentrism expressed in young children's playtime activities. Because children between 2 and 4 are fundamentally self-centered and unable to separate themselves from their thoughts, playmate interaction is restricted.

parent cell Original cell in cell division.

participant observation Form of observation in which the researcher is a participant in the interaction being studied.

perception Process of being aware of and interpreting stimuli in the environment.

perceptual constancy Tendency of an object to remain the same under different viewing conditions.

peripheral nervous system Network of neural tissue that connects the brain and the spinal cord with other parts of the body.

permissive control Style of parental control characterized by a nonpunitive orientation and relaxed rules and regulations.

personal fable Consequence of adolescent egocentrism. Teenagers are convinced of their personal uniqueness and construct stories about themselves that are not true.

personality disorder Functional disorder reflecting maladaptive patterns of thinking or behaving. Examples include a *narcissistic personality disorder,* marked by a grandiose sense of self-importance, and the *antisocial personality disorder,* characterized by the absence of any internal discomfort.

phallic stage According to Freud, the period characterized by genital manipulation and attraction for the parent of the other sex.

phenotype Visible or easily measurable appearance of an organism.

phoneme Most fundamental element of a language. The sound of *b* in *big* or *th* in *thick* is a phoneme.

phonology The study of phonemes and other sounds made in speech.

physical stressor Stressor creating a physiological demand on the body, such as hunger, thirst, heat, cold, injury, pollutants, toxicants, or poor nutrition.

Pick's disease Type of organic brain disorder often characterized by atrophy of the frontal and prefrontal lobes of the brain. Symptoms include disorientation and impaired physical and intellectual functions.

pilot study Experiment or other research method with a very small sample in order to ascertain, among other things, that the equipment is operable, the researcher feels confident with the experimental procedures, or the subjects understand the directions.

pivot word Word that is usually small in size and connected to open class words. Pivot words are usually used in the second position or early two-word sentences.

placenta Organ that allows nourishment to pass from the mother to the embryo and fetus and waste products to be channeled from the embryo and fetus to the mother.

playmateship stage According to Selman, friendships made during the preschool years.

polygenes Number of genes that work together with additive and/or complementary effects.

positive euthanasia Type of euthanasia in which definite steps are taken to cause the death of another person. Also called *active euthanasia.*

positive reinforcement In instrumental conditioning, a pleasant stimulus given to a subject following a desired response, so as to strengthen that response.

postconventional level Kohlberg's third major division or level of moral development, occurring from age 16 onward. Stages within this level include the contractual legalistic orientation and the universal ethical principle orientation.

pragma love Love that is practical and sensible.

pragmatics Manner in which language is used in a social context.

preconceptual thought Substage of Piaget's preoperational thought stage. It occurs between the ages of 2 and 4 and is characterized by egocentric forms of thinking and perceiving.

preconscious In psychoanalytic theory, region of the mind that is the storehouse of an individual's experiences. Preconscious material can usually be brought to the conscious mind with relative ease.

preconventional level According to Kohlberg, the initial phase of moral development occurring during the early childhood years. Substages within this period include obedience and punishment orientation and naively egoistic orientation.

prehension Ability to grasp objects between the fingers and opposable thumb.

prematurity Term applying to infants weighing less than 2,500 grams and who have spent less than 36 weeks in utero.

premoral stage According to Piaget, a stage of morality in which children 5 and under have little, if any, awareness of rules.

preoperational thought Second stage of cognitive development proposed by Piaget. It embraces the years 2 to 7, and includes the substages of preconceptual thought (2–4) and intuitive thought (4–7).

preparatory depression According to Kübler-Ross, an emotional reaction to an expected loss in the future.

preretirement phase First of six retirement stages proposed by Atchley. Emphasis here is placed on preparing for the adjustments that impending retirement will bring.

presbycusis Impaired hearing caused by the aging process.

presbyopia Farsighted condition that occurs when the lens of the eye loses its elasticity.

primary circular reactions Second of six substages comprising Piaget's sensorimotor stage of cognitive development. This substage occurs between 1 and 4 months of age.

primary reinforcement Satisfying stimulus related to

primary, unlearned drives. Food and drink are primary reinforcers related to the hunger and thirst drives.

primary sex characteristics Sex characteristics that relate directly to the sex organs—the penis and testes in the male, and the ovaries, clitoris, and vagina in the female.

procreational orientation Sexual value orientation emphasizing that coital activity is acceptable only within marriage for the purpose of having children.

projection Defense mechanism of blaming one's difficulties or failures on someone else.

prosocial behavior Being sensitive to the needs and feelings of others.

protoplasm Entire living substance that constitutes a cell.

prototheory Theory in the midst of being developed; an explanation that is incomplete or not fully consistent.

proximodistal development Growth from the center of the body outward.

psychoanalytic theory School of thought proposed by Sigmund Freud.

psychodynamic theories Psychological theories that emphasize the dynamics of the unconscious mind and one's past experiences as being the major determinants of future behavior. An example is psychoanalysis.

psycholinguistics Study of developing communication processes from early stages of crying and babbling to spoken words and meaningful sentences. Psycholinguistics includes the closely related areas of language, mental imagery, cognitive development, and symbolization.

psychological aging One of the three main types of aging processes. Psychological aging refers to one's self-awareness and ability to adapt to progressive aging.

psychological stressor Stressor such as worry or anxiety.

psychological theories of lifespan development One of the three major categories of lifespan development theories. These theories focus on behavioral characteristics and include such dimensions as personality, cognition, self-esteem, motivation, and feelings. Examples include psychoanalysis, cognitive-developmental, behaviorism, social learning, ethological, humanism, and ecological theories.

psychosexual stages of development Stages supporting the Freudian notion that early sexual experiences are important to personality development. The individual must successfully pass through a series of five sequential stages to reach psychosexual maturity.

psychosocial stages of development Stages supporting the Eriksonian idea that social interactions are critical to personality development. The person must successfully resolve eight sequential crises to attain psychosocial maturity.

puberty Point in the lifespan when sexual maturity is attained.

quickening Fetal movements that can be felt by the mother. Quickening usually begins between 16 and 18 weeks.

rationalization Attempt to justify and provide logical reasons and explanations for particular patterns of behavior.

reaction formation Defense mechanism of substituting an opposing attitude for an unwanted and perhaps objectionable desire.

reactive depression According to Kübler-Ross, an emotional reaction to a loss that has already occurred.

reactive model of development Model emphasizing the importance of the environment as a critical determinant in shaping the course of growth and development.

readiness principle State of maturation that enables a child to perform a task.

reality principle The ego's selection of attainable goals before discharging tension or energy.

recall memory Search for and retrieval of information in storage.

recessive gene Gene whose hereditary characteristics are present only when paired with another recessive gene.

recognition memory Selection of a correct response from incoming information.

recoil stage Second stage of grief and mourning proposed by Silverman. Survivors at this time must come to grips with the full realization of loss as well as coping with the many emotional complexities that accompany widowhood.

reflectivity Conceptual tempo characterized by a careful and deliberate approach to problem solving.

reflex activities First of six substages constituting Piaget's sensorimotor stage of cognitive development. This substage occurs during approximately the first month of life.

regression Defense mechanism characterized by the individual's reverting to behavioral responses characteristic of earlier developmental levels.

reinforcer Anything that strengthens the probability of a response.

relational orientation Sexual value orientation that views sexual activity as a natural extension of intimate relationships. Also called "person-centered" sexuality or "permissiveness with affection."

reorientation phase Fourth of six retirement stages proposed by Atchley. Here, individuals make necessary lifestyle adjustments in order to adapt to the retirement role.

repression Defense mechanism characterized by the pushing away of anxiety-producing thoughts to an unconscious level.

residential-care facility Home for aged persons who are functionally independent but who desire a safe, hygienic, and sheltered environment in which to live.

retirement   Withdrawal from one's professional occupation or from an active working life.

reversibility   Ability to trace one's line of reasoning back to where it originated.

Rh factor   Substance found in red blood cells. An Rh incompatibility between mother and father can create serious difficulties in their newborn baby.

rheumatoid arthritis   Type of arthritis that inflames the membranes lining and lubricating the joints.

ribonucleic acid (RNA)   Substance formed by DNA that carries genetic messages to the ribosomes for the manufacturing of specific proteins.

ribosomes   Small particles in the cytoplasm that manufacture proteins under the direction of DNA.

rooming-in hospital facility   Facility allowing the parents to care for their baby in the mother's hospital room.

schemata   Organized patterns of thought. Sensory stimuli, objects, and events are examples of schematic organizations.

schizophrenic disorder   Type of functional disorder characterized by extensive disorganization of the personality and the failure to correctly perceive reality. Memory distortion as well as deficiencies in language and perception are characteristic symptoms.

scientific method   Testing of hypotheses concerning natural events and relationships.

secondary circular reactions   Third of six substages constituting Piaget's sensorimotor stage of cognitive development. This substage occurs between 4 and 8 months.

secondary reinforcement   Stimulus that was previously neutral but when paired frequently over successive trials with a primary reinforcer gains reinforcing qualities.

secondary sex characteristics   Sex characteristics that are not related directly to the sex organs but distinguish a mature male from a mature female. Examples include breasts in the female and the beard in males.

self-actualization   According to Maslow, the fullest development of one's potentials, capacities, and talents.

self-disclosure   Process by which individuals let themselves be known by others.

semantics   Study of meaning in a language.

sensitive period   According to ethologists, a highly significant time frame early in a person's life that affects the course of developmental dynamics.

sensorimotor stage   Piaget's first stage of cognitive development (0 through 2 years). Learning activities at this point are directed toward the coordination of simple sensorimotor skills.

sensorineural deafness   Hearing loss caused by damage to the inner ear, to the auditory nerve carrying sound messages to the brain, or to the hearing center of the brain itself.

sensory memory   All of the sensory stimuli to which the individual is exposed. Many of these impressions can be held for only a few seconds and are subject to decay.

separation anxiety   Distress reaction expressed by infants upon separation from the caregiver. Separation anxiety occurs approximately by 1 year.

sequential designs   Research designs combining various aspects of longitudinal and cross-sectional methodologies. Examples are time-lag, time-sequence, cohort, and cross-sequential designs.

serialization   Ordering subjects on a perceptual basis.

seriation   Ordering objects according to size.

sex   Person's biological status of being a male or female.

sex discrimination   Unfair and unequal treatment of a person on the basis of his or her sex.

sex-limited genes   Genes that are normally expressed in only one sex, although they are carried by both sexes.

sex-linked characteristics   Inherited characteristics carried by the genes of the X and Y chromosomes.

shaping behavior   In operant conditioning, a procedure in which part of a behavior is reinforced, ultimately leading to the whole behavior that is desired.

short-term longitudinal method   Research design in which data are gathered over a short period of time and fewer behavioral phenomena are studied.

short-term memory (STM)   Temporary retention of information (usually up to 20 seconds). Unlike long-term memory, short-term memory is affected considerably by interference and interruption.

sibling rivalry   Form of competition between siblings.

sickle-cell anemia   Disease of the red blood cells, common among blacks of African background.

significates   Objects or events that signifiers are used to represent.

signifiers   Words or images.

singlehood   Lifestyle marked by a person's desire not to get married.

situational orientation   Sexual value orientation suggesting that sexual decision making should take place in the context of the particular situation and people involved.

skilled-nursing facility   Nursing facility that provides full-time nursing for persons with a chronic illness or who are convalescing.

social aging   One of the three main types of aging processes. Social aging refers to one's perceptions of the aging process as it relates to a given society.

social cognition   Awareness of how individuals perceive themselves and others, including other persons' thoughts and feelings.

social exchange theory   Sociological theory of lifespan development suggesting that individuals desire the maximum positive outcomes or rewards in relationships along with the least amount of costs or trade-offs.

social gerontology   Branch of gerontology that seeks to meet the diverse social needs of the aged population by providing them with special services, programs, and policies.

socializing versus sexualizing in human relationships According to Peck, a psychological adjustment to be made during middle adulthood.

social learning theory One of lifespan development's major schools of thought. This theory proposes that behavior is influenced by observing and copying others.

social learning theory of television viewing Theory proposing that persons will imitate aggressive behavior when they are exposed to it on television.

social referencing Type of behavioral regulation in which infants watch facial or emotional expressions of others to clarify uncertain situations.

social stressor Stressor reflecting interactions with others, including such conditions as crowding, noise, or social pressures to conform.

sociodramatic play Imaginative or make-believe play shared with a partner.

sociological theories of lifespan development One of the three major categories of lifespan development theories. These theories focus on how growth and development occurs against the backdrop of society. Examples include symbolic interactionism, social exchange, family development, and conflict theories.

somatic cells Cells in the human body, with the exception of the sex cells.

speech Concrete physical act that consists of forming and sequencing the sounds of oral language.

sperm Reproductive cells produced in the testes.

stability phase Fifth of six retirement stages proposed by Atchley. Here, retirees have made the necessary adjustments and adaptations required of the retirement role.

storge love Type of love characterized by affection and companionship.

stranger anxiety Distress reaction expressed by infants when unfamiliar people are introduced. Infants show stranger anxiety after the sixth month of life.

stress The body's common nonspecific response to any demand made upon it, be it psychological or physiological.

stressor External event or condition that affects an organism's equilibrium.

structured observation Extension of naturalistic observation that enables the researchers to administer simple tests.

substance-use disorders Functional disorder characterized by the physical and psychological dependence on alcohol and drugs.

superego According to Freud, the moral component of one's personality that represents societal expectations and demands.

surface structure Sentence structure that is dictated by the rules of grammar.

surrogate motherhood Alternative childbearing technique in which a chosen surrogate mother is artificially inseminated with the husband's sperm. The surrogate mother carries and bears the child, which is then given back to the couple.

survey Technique of gathering information from people. Surveys usually take the form of questionnaires or interviews.

symbolic functioning Act of reference in which a mental image is created to stand for something that is not present.

symbolic interactionism Sociological theory of lifespan development emphasizing the association between symbols (i.e., shared meanings) and interactions (i.e., verbal and nonverbal actions and communications). Essentially, this approach seeks to understand how humans create symbolic worlds and how these worlds, in turn, shape human behavior.

syntax Rules for combining words into sentences.

telegraphic sentence Type of sentence used by children at approximately 2 years. Telegraphic sentences include only the words necessary to give meaning. Connecting words are usually omitted.

teratogenic agent Any substance that causes a change in the genetic code, which in turn may produce an abnormality, anomaly, or malformation.

terminal decline Drop in intelligence and personality functioning in the months preceding death.

terminal phase According to Pattison, the third of three dying processes.

termination phase Final stage of retirement proposed by Atchley. This phase is characterized by the end of retirement due to illness or disability.

tertiary circular reactions Fifth of six substages constituting Piaget's sensorimotor stage of cognitive development. This substage occurs between 12 and 18 months.

testis-determining factor Gene responsible for the sequence of events that leads to male sexual development.

thanatology Study of dying and death.

theory Formulation of apparent relationships that have some degree of verification and supportive evidence.

thrombus Blood clot.

time-lag design Research methodology whereby researchers can compare people of similar ages but different cohorts.

time sequential design Research design in which parallel cross-sectional studies are staggered over time.

toughlove Style of discipline used by parents to control teenagers' extreme, problematical behaviors.

toxemia Presence of a toxic substance in the blood.

transductive reasoning Reasoning from particular to

particular without generalization.

transformation Understanding the relationship between the deep and surface structures of a sentence.

transformational reasoning Ability to appreciate how one state transforms itself into another when an event has a sequence of change.

transient ischemic attack (TIA) Minor stroke causing an abrupt loss of body function but usually subsiding within 24 hours. Often this type of stroke precedes a larger and more serious cerebrovascular accident.

transitional object Soft object such as a security blanket or huggable stuffed doll or animal that offers comfort to children.

trimester One of the three 3-month segments of pregnancy.

triple X syndrome Female chromosomal abnormality that produces mental retardation, menstrual irregularity, and premature menopause.

trisomy 21 See Down syndrome.

trophoblast Outer layer of cells covering the blastocyst. The trophoblast helps the blastocyst implant itself in the uterine wall and eventually gives rise to the placenta.

tumor Mass of tissues created by the uncontrolled growth and spread of cells. Also called neoplasms, tumors can be either benign or malignant.

Turner's syndrome Female chromosomal abnormality (only one sex chromosome) distinguished by a webbed neck, short fingers, and short stature. No secondary sex characteristics appear at the time of puberty (XO).

twin speech Style of language used by twins, usually consisting of private and unique forms of communication.

Type A behavior pattern A behavior pattern characterized by extreme competitiveness, aggressiveness, and impatience.

Type B behavior pattern Behavior pattern characterized by a generally relaxed attitude toward life, no hostility, and competitiveness only when the situation demands it.

ultrasonography Use of sound waves to examine internal body structures. Often used to determine a fetus's size and position.

umbilical cord "Body stalk" containing three blood vessels: a vein carrying oxygenated blood from the placenta to the infant and two arteries carrying blood and waste products from the infant to the placenta.

unconscious In psychoanalytic theory, a vast region of an individual's mental life that contains biological motives and repressed anxiety-producing material that cannot readily be brought to the conscious level.

universal ethical principle orientation Kohlberg's sixth stage of moral development. This stage is grouped under the major division or level known as postconventional morality.

valuing wisdom versus valuing physical powers According to Peck, a psychological adjustment to be made during middle adulthood.

variations Term used in genetics when offspring, whether plant or animal, show differences from their parents.

vernix caseosa Waxy substance covering the fetus during prenatal development.

visual cliff Testing apparatus designed to measure depth perception in infants and animals.

visualization Mental operation requiring the ability to organize and process visual materials.

visuomotor flexibility Capacity to shift from familiar to unfamiliar patterns in tasks dictating coordination between visual and motor abilities.

vowel The one most prominent sound in a syllable where no friction is audible.

wear-and-tear theory Theory of biological aging which asserts that organisms wear out, much like machines, over their life cycle.

Wernicke's area Portion of the brain, located in the temporal lobe; it is responsible for the comprehension of speech.

withdrawal Ego defense mechanism characterized by the avoidance of, or movement away from, undesirable or hurtful situations.

XYY syndrome Also called the aggressive syndrome, this chromosomal abnormality evidently has the potential to increase aggressive behavior, especially when the recipient of this condition is raised in an environment conducive to aggressiveness.

zygote Cell formed by the union of the male sperm and the female ovum; the fertilized egg.

References

Abbey, J. C. (1991). Physiological illness in aging. In E. M. Baines (Ed.), *Perspectives on gerontological nursing*. Newbury Park, CA: Sage.

Abbott, J. T. (1989). Vaginal bleeding: Matching the cause and the cure. *Emergency Medicine, 21* (5), 84–96.

Abdellah, F. G. (1991). Public policy impacting on nursing care of older adults. In E. M. Baines (Ed.), *Perspectives on gerontological nursing*. Newbury Park, CA: Sage.

Abel, E. (1991, June). Reversing the melanoma surge. *Patient Care*, pp. 12–17.

Abel, E. L. (1990). *New literature on fetal alcohol exposure and effects*. Westport, CT: Greenwood Press.

Abraham, I. L., & Neundorfer, M. M. (1990). Alzheimer's: A decade of progress, a future of nursing challenges. *Geriatric Nursing, 11* (3), 116–119.

Achenbaum, W. A. (1991). Putting ADEA into historical context. *Research on Aging, 13* (4), 463–469.

Achermann, J., Dinneen, E., & Stevenson-Hinde, J. (1991). Clearing up at 2.5 years. *British Journal of Developmental Psychology, 9* (3), 365–376.

Adams, G. R. (1991). Physical attractiveness and adolescent development. In R. M. Lerner, A. C. Petersen, & J. Brooks-Gunn (Eds.), *The encyclopedia of adolescence*. New York: Garland.

Adams, G. R., & Schvaneveldt, J. D. (1985). *Understanding research methods*. New York: Longman.

Adams, P. L. (1984). Fathers absent and present. *Canadian Journal of Psychiatry, 29* (3), 228–233.

Adams, R. (1989). Newborns' discrimination among mid- and long-wave-length stimuli. *Journal of Experimental Child Psychology, 47* (1), 130–141.

Adams, R., Maurer, D., & Davis, M. (1986). Newborns' discrimination of chromatic from achromatic stimuli. *Journal of Experimental Child Psychology, 41*, 267–281.

Adamson, D. (1992). Factors affecting marital happiness of caregivers of the elderly in multigenerational families. *American Journal of Family Therapy, 20* (1), 62–70.

Adamson, L. B. (1992). Variations in the early use of language. In J. Valsiner & L. T. Winegar (Eds.), *Children's development within social context*. Hillsdale, NJ: Erlbaum.

Adcock, A. G., Nagy, S., & Simpson, J. A. (1991). Selected risk factors in adolescent suicide attempts. *Adolescence, 26* (104), 817–828.

Adelman, H. S. (1992). Learning disabilities: The next 25 years. *Journal of Learning Disabilities, 25* (1), 17–22.

Adelman, M. (1990). Stigma, gay lifestyles, and adjustment to aging: A study of later-life gay men and lesbians. In J. A. Lee (Ed.), *Gay midlife and maturity*. Binghamton, NY: Haworth Press.

Adelman, R. D., Greene, M. G., & Charon, R. (1991). Issues in physician-elderly patient interaction. *Ageing and Society, 11* (2), 127–148.

Ade-Ridder, L., & Brubaker, T. H. (1988). Expected and reported division of responsibility of household tasks among older wives in two residential settings. *Journal of Consumer Studies and Home Economics, 12*, 59–70.

Adler, T. (1991, July). Women's expectations are menopause villains. *APA Monitor*, p. 14.

Affleck, G., Tennen, H., Rowe, J., & Roscher, B. (1989). Effects of formal support on mothers' adaptation to the hospital-to-home transition of high-risk infants: The benefits and costs of helping. *Child Development, 60* (2), 488–501.

Ahlburg, D. A., & DeVita, C. J. (1992). *New realities of the American family*. Washington, DC: Population Reference Bureau.

Ahmed, B., & Smith, S. K. (1992). How changes in components of growth affect the population aging of states. *Journal of Gerontology: Social Sciences, 47* (1), S27–S37.

Ahmeduzzaman, M., & Roopnarine, J. L. (1992). Sociodemographic factors, functioning style, social support, and fathers' involvement with preschoolers in African American families. *Journal of Marriage and the Family, 54*, 699–707.

Aiken, L. R. (1982). *Later life* (2nd ed.). New York: Holt, Rinehart and Winston.

Ainsworth, M. D. (1967). *Infancy in Uganda*. Baltimore: Johns Hopkins Press.

Ajayi, A. (1991). Adolescent sexuality and fertility in Kenya: A survey of knowledge, perceptions, and practice. *Studies in Family Planning, 22* (4), 205–216.

Akutsu, H. (1991). Psychophysics of reading: X. Effects of age-related changes in vision. *Journal of Gerontology: Psychological Sciences, 46* (6), P325–P331.

Alan Guttmacher Institute. (1989). *Teenage pregnancy: The problem that hasn't gone away*. New York: Author.

Alan Guttmacher Institute. (1991). *Teenage sexual and reproductive behavior in the United States*. New York: Author.

Aldous, J. (1977). *Family careers: Developmental change in families*. New York: Wiley.

Alexopoulos, G. S. (1991). Anxiety and depression in the elderly. In C. Salzman & B. D. Lebowitz (Eds.), *Anxiety in the elderly: Treatment and research*. New York: Springer.

Allen, B. (1990). *Personality, social, and biological perspectives on personal adjustment*. Pacific Grove, CA: Brooks/Cole.

Allen, K. E. (1992). *The exceptional child: Mainstreaming in early childhood education* (2nd ed.). Albany, NY: Delmar.

Allen, P. A. (1991). On age differences in processing variability and scanning speed. *Journal of Gerontology: Psychological Sciences, 46* (5), P191–P201.

Allport, G. (1961). *Pattern and growth in personality*. New York: Holt, Rinehart and Winston.

Almvig, C. (1982). *The invisible minority: Aging and lesbianism*. Syracuse, NY: Utica College Press.

Alvarez, M. M., Huston, A. C., Wright, J. C., & Kerkman, D. D. (1988). Gender differences in visual attention to television form and content. *Journal of Applied Developmental Psychology, 9*, 459–475.

Alvino, J. (1983, December). Philosophical questions help children think and rethink ideas. *Gifted Children Newsletter*, pp. 1–6.

Ambert, A. (1992). *The effects of children on parents*. New York: Haworth.

American Academy of Pediatrics, Committee on Fetus and Newborn. (1989). Report of the Ad Hoc Task Force on Circumcision. *Pediatrics, 83*, 388–397.

American Cancer Society. (1992). *Cancer facts and figures, 1992*. New York: Author.

American Council on Education. (1991). *Graduation rates for ethnic minority students*. Washington, DC: Author.

American Heart Association. (1992). *Heart and stroke facts*. Dallas, TX: Author.

American Psychiatric Association. (1993). *Diagnostic and statistical manual of mental disorders* (4th ed.). Washington, DC: Author.

American Psychological Association. (1979, 1981, 1990, 1992). *Ethical principles of psychologists*. Washington, DC: Author.

Ames, C. (1992). Classrooms: Goals, structures, and student motivation. *Journal of Educational Psychology, 84* (3), 261–271.

Ammerman, R. T. (1990). Etiological models of child maltreatment: A behavioral perspective. *Behavior Modification, 14* (3), 230–254.

Ammerman, R. T. (1991). The role of the child in physical abuse: A reappraisal. *Violence and Victims, 6* (2), 87–102.

Amschler, D. H. (1991). The rising incidence of HIV infection and its implications for reproductive health. *Journal of Sex Education and Therapy, 17*, 244–250.

Andersen, M. (1988). *Thinking about women*. New York: Macmillan.

Anderson, J. E., Kann, L., Hotlzman, D., Arday, S., Truman, B., & Kolbe, L. J. (1990). HIV/AIDS knowledge and sexual behavior among high school students. *Family Planning Perspectives, 22*, 252–255.

Anderson, J. R. (1990). *Cognitive psychology and its implications* (3rd ed.). New York: Freeman.

Anderson, M. (1989). *Basic maternal nursing*. New York: Delmar.

Anderson, S. A., Russell, C. S., & Schumm, W. R. (1983). Perceived quality and family life-cycle categories: A further analysis. *Journal of Marriage and the Family, 45*, 127–139.

Andrews, J. (1989). *Poverty and poor health among elderly Hispanic Americans*. Baltimore: Commonwealth Fund Commission on Elderly People Living Alone.

Anetzberger, G. J. (1990). Abuse, neglect, and self-neglect: Issues of vulnerability. In Z. Harel, P. Ehrlich, & R. Hubbard (Eds.), *The vulnerable aged: People, services, and policies*. New York: Springer.

Angier, N. (1990, June). Scientists struggle to undo tanning's deadly damage. *New York Times*, p. 10.

Anifantakis, H. (1991). *The diminished mind: One family's extraordinary battle with Alzheimer's*. Blue Ridge Summit, PA: Tab Books.

Anspaugh, D. J., Hamrick, M. H., & Rosato, F. D. (1991). *Wellness: Concepts and applications*. St. Louis: Mosby.

Antonini, F. M., & Vannucci, A. (1990). Exercise and nutrition in the elderly. In F. Fabrizio, L. Pernigotti, & E. Ferrario (Eds.), *Sedentary life and nutrition*. New York: Raven Press.

Antonucci, T. C. (1990). Social supports and social relationships. In R. H. Binstock & L. K. George (Eds.), *Handbook of aging and the social sciences*. San Diego: Academic Press.

Antonucci, T. C., & Akiyama, H. (1991). Social relationships and aging well. *Generations, 15* (1), 39–44.

Appels, A., & Schouten, E. (1991). Burnout as a risk factor for coronary heart disease. *Behavioral Medicine, 17* (2), S3–S9.

Applebaum, R., & Phillips, P. (1990). Assuring the quality of in-home care: The "other" challenge for long-term care. *Gerontologist, 30* (4), 444–450.

Aral, S. O., & Holmes, K. K. (1990). Epidemiology of sexual behavior and sexually transmitted diseases. In K. K. Holmes, P. A. Mardh, & F. P. Sparling (Eds.), *Sexually transmitted diseases*. New York: McGraw-Hill.

Archer, D. F. (1989). Effects of clomiphene citrate on episodic luteinizing hormone secretion throughout the menstrual cycle. *American Journal of Obstetrics and Gynecology, 161* (3), 581–593.

Ardigo, A. (1990). Sedentary life and nutrition: A sociologist's point of view. In F. Fabris, L. Pernigotti, & E. Ferrario (Eds.), *Sedentary life and nutrition*. New York: Raven Press.

Arking, R. (1991). Modifying the aging process. In R. F. Young & E. A. Olson (Eds.), *Health, illness, and disability in later life: Practice issues and interventions*. Newbury Park, CA: Sage.

Arliss, L. P. (1993). When myths endure and realities change: Communication in romantic relationships. In L. P. Arliss & D. J. Borisoff (Eds.), *Women and men communicating*. Fort Worth, TX: Harcourt Brace Jovanovich.

Arliss, L. P., & Borisoff, D. J. (1993). *Women and men communicating*. Fort Worth, TX: Harcourt Brace Jovanovich.

Armistead, L., Wierson, M., Forehand, R., & Frame, C. (1992). Psychopathology in incarcerated juvenile delinquents: Does it extend beyond externalizing problems? *Adolescence, 27* (106), 309–314.

Armstrong, D. G., Henson, K. T., & Savage, T. V. (1993). *Education: An introduction*. New York: Macmillan.

Armstrong, M. J. (1991). Friends as a source of informal support for older women with physical disabilities. *Journal of Women and Aging, 3* (2), 63–83.

Armstrong, M. J., & Goldsteen, K. S. (1990). Friendship support patterns of older American women. *Journal of Aging Studies, 4* (4), 391–404.

Armstrong, M. J. (1990). *Caregiving for your loved ones*. Elgin, IL: David C. Cook.

Aro, H., & Taipale, V. (1987). The impact of timing of puberty on psychosomatic symptoms among fourteen- to sixteen-year-old Finnish girls. *Child Development, 58*, 261–268.

Aronson, J. (1992). Women's sense of responsibility for the care of old people: "But who else is going to do it?" *Gender and Society, 6* (1), 8–29.

Arsenault, A., Dolan, S. L., & Van Ameringen, M. R. (1991). Stress and mental strain in hospital work: Exploring the relationship beyond personality. *Journal of Organizational Behavior, 12* (6) 483–493.

Asher, D. (1992). *From college to career*. Berkeley, CA: Ten Speed Press.

Astington, J. W. (1988). Children's production of commissive speech acts. *Journal of Child Language, 15*, 411–423.

Atchley, R. C. (1982a). Retirement as a social institution. In R. Turner & J. Short (Eds.), *Annual review of sociology*. Palo Alto, CA: Annual Reviews.

Atchley, R. C. (1982b). Retirement: Leaving the world of work. *Annals of the American Academy of Political and Social Science, 464*, 120–131.

Atchley, R. C. (1991). *Social forces and aging: An introduction to social gerontology* (6th ed.). Belmont, CA: Wadsworth.

Atchley, R. C., & Robinson, J. L. (1982). Attitudes toward retirement and distance from the event. *Research on Aging, 4* (3), 288–313.

August, R. L., & Forman, B. D. (1989). A comparison of sexually abused and non-sexually abused children's behavior responses to anatomically correct dolls. *Child Psychiatry and Human Development, 20*, 39–47.

Auslander, G. K., & Litwin, H. (1990). Social support networks and formal help seeking: Differences between applicants to social services and a nonapplicant sample. *Journal of Gerontology, 45* (3), S112–S119.

Austin, B., & Melbourne, P. (1990). Hospice services for the terminal Alzheimer's patient. *Caring, 9* (11), 60–62.

Austin, C. D. (1991). Aging well: What are the odds? *Generations, 15* (1), 73–75.

Averyt, A. C. (1987). *Successful aging*. New York: Ballantine.

Avogaro, P. (1990). Alcohol: A risk or protective factor in aging. In F. Fabris, L. Pernigotti, & E. Ferrario (Eds.), *Sedentary life and nutrition*. New York: Raven Press.

Bachmann, G., Leiblum, S., & Grill, J. (1989). Brief sexual inquiry in gynecologic practice. *Obstetrics and Gynecology, 73* (3), 425–427.

Backman, L. (1989). Varieties of memory compensation by older adults in episodic remembering. In L. W. Poon, D. C. Rubin, & B. A. Wilson (Eds.), *Everyday cognition in adulthood and late life*. New York: Cambridge University Press.

Backman, L., Mantyla, R., & Herlitz, A. (1990). The optimization of episodic remembering in old age. In P. B. Baltes & M. M. Baltes (Eds.), *Successful aging: Perspectives from the behavioral sciences*. New York: Cambridge University Press.

Badgley, R. (1984). *Sexual offenses against children: Report of the Committee on Sexual Offenses Against Children and Youths*. Ottawa: Government of Canada.

Baechle, C., & Lian, M. J. (1990). The effects of direct feedback and practice on metaphor performance in children with learning disabilities. *Journal of Learning Disabilities, 23* (7), 451–455.

Bagley, C. (1985). Child sexual abuse: A child welfare perspective. In K. Levitt & B. Wharf (Eds.), *The challenge of child welfare*. Vancouver: University of British Columbia Press.

Bagley, C., & Ramsay, R. (1986). Disrupted childhood and vulnerability to sexual assault: Long-term sequels with implications for counseling. *Social Work and Human Sexuality, 4*, 33–48.

Bailey, N., & Pillard, R. (1991, December 17). Are some people born gay? *New York Times*, p. 13.

Baillargeon, R., & DeVos, J. (1991). Object permanence in young infants: Further evidence. *Child Development, 62* (6), 1227–1246.

Baillargeon, R., & Graber, M. (1988). Evidence of location memory in 8-month-old infants in a nonsearch AB task. *Developmental Psychology*, *24*, 502–511.

Baird, P. A. (1982). Children of incest. *Journal of Pediatrics*, *101*, 854–857.

Bairstow, P. J. (1989). Development of planning and control of hand movement to moving targets. *Journal of Developmental Psychology*, *7*, 29–42.

Baker, T. B. (1988). Models of addiction. *Journal of Abnormal Psychology*, *97*, 115–117.

Baldwin, B. A. (1990). Family care giving: Trends and forecasts. *Geriatric Nursing*, *11* (4), 172–174.

Balkwell, C. (1981). Transition to widowhood: A review of the literature. *Family Relations*, *12* (1), 117–127.

Ballard, C. G. (1991). Paranoid features in the elderly with dementia. *International Journal of Geriatric Psychiatry*, *6* (3), 155–157.

Ballard, D. T., Blair, G. D., Devereaux, L. K., Valentine, A. L., Horton, B., & Johnson, L. (1990). A comparative profile of the incest perpetrator: Background characteristics, abuse history, and use of social skills. In A. L. Horton, B. Johnson, L. M. Roundy, & D. Williams (Eds.), *The incest perpetrator: A family member no one wants to treat*. Newbury Park, CA: Sage.

Baltes, P. B. (1979). Life-span developmental psychology: Some converging observations on history and theory. In P. B. Baltes & O. G. Brim, Jr. (Eds.), *Life-span development and behavior* (Vol. 2). New York: Academic Press.

Baltes, P. B. (1987). Theoretical propositions of life-span developmental psychology: On the dynamics between growth and decline. *Developmental Psychology*, *23*, 611–626.

Baltes, P. B. (1990). Wisdom: One facet of successful aging? In M. Perlmutter (Ed.), *Late life potential*. The Presidential Symposium Series. Washington, DC: Gerontological Society of America.

Baltes, P. B., & Baltes, M. M. (1990). Psychological perspectives on successful aging: The model of selective optimization with compensation. In P. B. Baltes & M. M. Baltes (Eds.), *Successful aging: Perspectives from the behavioral sciences*. New York: Cambridge University Press.

Baltes, P. B., Cornelius, S. W., & Nesselroade, J. R. (1979). Cohort effects in developmental psychology. In J. R. Nesselroade & P. B. Baltes (Eds.), *Longitudinal research in the behavioral sciences: Design and analysis*. New York: Academic Press.

Baltes, P. B., & Reese, H. W. (1984). The life-span perspective. In M. H. Bornstein & M. E. Lambe (Eds.), *Developmental psychology: An advanced textbook*. Hillsdale, NJ: Erlbaum.

Baltes, P. B., & Schaie, K. W. (1974). Aging and the IQ: The myth of the twilight years. *Psychology Today*, *7*, 35–40.

Bamboa, M. (1990, July). Rx for avoiding sun damage. *NIH Healthline*, pp. 7–8.

Bandura, A. (1962). Social learning through imitation. In J. Suls (Ed.), *Nebraska Symposium on Motivation* (pp. 211–269). Lincoln: University of Nebraska Press.

Bandura, A. (1977). *Social learning theory*. New York: General Learning Press.

Bandura, A. (1986). *Social foundations of thought and action: A social cognitive theory*. Englewood Cliffs, NJ: Prentice Hall.

Bandura, A. (1989). Social cognitive theory. In R. Vasta (Ed.), *Six theories of child development*. Greenwich, CT: JAI Press.

Bandura, A. (1991). Social cognitive theory of moral thought and action. In W. M. Kurtines & J. Gewirtz (Eds.), *Moral behavior and development: Advances in theory, research, and application*. Hillsdale, NJ: Erlbaum.

Bandura, A., & Huston, A. (1961). Identification as a process of incidental learning. *Journal of Abnormal Social Psychology*, *63*, 311–318.

Bandura, A., Ross, D., & Ross, S. (1961). Transmission of aggression through imitation of aggressive models. *Journal of Abnormal Social Psychology*, *63*, 575–582.

Bandura, A., & Walters, R. (1963). *Social learning and personality development*. New York: Holt, Rinehart and Winston.

Banks, W. P., & Krajicek, D. (1991). Perception. *Annual Review of Psychology*, *42*, 305–331.

Baranowski, M. D., Schilmoeller, G. L., & Higgins, B. S. (1990). Parenting attitudes of adolescent and older mothers. *Adolescence*, *25*, 781–790.

Bardwell, J. R., Cochran, S. W., & Walkers, S. (1986). Relationship of parental education, race, and gender to sex-role stereotyping in five-year-old kindergartners. *Sex Roles*, *15*, 275–281.

Barefoot, J. C., Dodge, K. A., Peterson, B. L., Dahlstrom, W. G., & Williams, R. B. (1989). The Cook-Medley hostility scale: Item content and ability to predict survival. *Psychosomatic Medicine*, *51*, 46–57.

Barnett, R. C., Marshall, N. L., & Pleck, J. H. (1992). Men's multiple roles and their relationship to men's psychological distress. *Journal of Marriage and the Family*, *54*, 358–367.

Baroody, A. J., & Coslick, T. T. (1993). *Problem solving, reasoning, and communicating: Helping children to think mathematically*. New York: Macmillan.

Barr, R. A., & Eberhard, J. W. (1991). Safety and mobility of elderly drivers. *Human Factors*, *33* (5), 497–603.

Barresi, C. M., & Menon, G. (1990). Diversity in black family care giving. In Z. Harel, E. A. McKinney, & M. Williams (Eds.), *Black aged: Understanding diversity and service*. Newbury Park, CA: Sage.

Barrow, G. M., & Smith, P. A. (1983). *Aging, the individual, and society* (2nd ed.). St. Paul, MN: West.

Barsch, R. H. (1992). Perspectives on learning disabilities: The vectors of a new convergence. *Journal of Learning Disabilities*, *25* (1), 6–16.

Bar-Tal, D., Raviv, A., & Shavit, N. (1981). Motives for helping behavior: Kibbutz and city children in kindergarten and school. *Developmental Psychology*, *17*, 766–772.

Bartle, S. E., & Anderson, S. A. (1992). Similarity between parents' and adolescents' levels of individuation. *Family Therapy*, *19* (1), 73–84.

Baruch, G. K., & Barnett, R. C. (1986). Fathers' participation in family work and children's sex-role attitudes. *Child Development*, *57* (5), 1210–1223.

Barusch, A. S. (1991). *Elder care: Family training and support*. Sage Source Books for the Human Services Series. Newbury Park, CA: Sage.

Basow, S. A. (1992). *Gender: Stereotypes and roles* (3rd ed.). Pacific Grove, CA: Brooks/Cole.

Bass, D., & Bowman, K. (1990). The impact of an aged relative's death on the family. In K. F. Ferraro (Ed.), *Gerontology: Perspectives and issues*. New York: Springer.

Bass, D., Bowman, K., & Noelker, L. (1991). The influence of caregiving and bereavement support on adjusting to an older relative's death. *Gerontologist*, *31*, 32–42.

Basta, N. (1991). *Major options*. New York: HarperCollins.

Bastida, E. (1987). Sex-typed age norms among older Hispanics. *Gerontologist*, *27*, 59–63.

Bateman, B. (1992). Learning disabilities: The changing landscape. *Journal of Learning Disabilities*, *25* (1), 29–36.

Batterman, R. (1985, Winter). A comprehensive approach to treating infertility. *Health and Social Work*, *12*, 46–54.

Baumeister, R. F., & Senders, P. S. (1989). Identity development and the role structure of children's games. *Journal of Genetic Psychology*, *150*, 19–37.

Baumrind, D. (1982). Are androgynous individuals more effective persons and parents? *Child Development*, *53* (1), 44–75.

Baumrind, D. (1991a). Parenting styles and adolescent development. In R. M. Lerner, A. C. Petersen, & J. Brooks-Gunn (Eds.), *The encyclopedia of adolescence*. New York: Garland.

Baumrind, D. (1991b). The influence of parenting style on adolescent competence and substance use. *Journal of Early Adolescence*, *11*, 56–95.

Bayles, K. A. (1991). Alzheimer's disease symptoms: Prevalence and order of appearance. *Journal of Applied Gerontology*, *10* (4), 419–430.

Bayless, K. M., & Ramsey, M. E. (1991). *Music: A way of life for young children* (4th ed.). New York: Macmillan.

Bayless, P. J. (1985). *Caring for dependent parents*. New York: Research Institute of America.

Beale, C. J., & Baskin, D. (1983). Children's fears: Who's afraid of the big bad wolf? *Child Psychiatry Quarterly*, *16* (2), 68–75.

Bear, M. (1990). Social network characteristics and the duration of primary relationships after entry into long-term care. *Journal of Gerontology*, *45* (4), S156–S162.

Beaton, S. R. (1991). Styles of reminiscence and ego development of older women residing in long-term care settings. *International Journal of Aging and Human Development*, *32* (1), 53–63.

Beatty, P. (1991). Foreword. *The Journal of Drug Issues*, *21*, 1–7.

Beatty, R. (1992). *The new complete job search*. New York: Wiley.

Beaty, J. J. (1992). *Skills for preschool teachers* (4th ed.). New York: Macmillan.

Beck, A. (1988). *Love is never enough*. New York: HarperCollins.

Becker, R. E., & Giacobini, E. (1990). *Alzheimer's disease: Current research in early diagnosis*. New York: Taylor and Francis.

Behrman, R. E., & Vaughn, V. C. (1987). *Nelson textbook of pediatrics*. Philadelphia: Saunders.

Beidel, D. C., & Turner, S. M. (1988). Comorbidity of test anxiety and other anxiety disorders in children. *Journal of Abnormal Child Development*, *16*, 275–287.

Beilin, H. (1989). Piagetian theory. In R. Vasta (Ed.), *Six theories of child development: Revised formulations and current issues*. Greenwich, CT: JAI Press.

Bell, R. R. (1983). *Marriage and family interaction* (6th ed.). Homewood, IL: Dorsey Press.

Belle, D. (1990). Poverty and women's mental health. *American Psychologist, 45,* 385–389.

Bellon, J. J., Bellon, E. C., & Blank, M. A. (1992). *Teaching from a research knowledge base: A development and renewal process.* New York: Macmillan.

Belsky, J. (1984). The determinants of parenting: A process model. *Child Development, 55,* 83–96.

Belsky, J. (1988). The effects of infant day care reconsidered. *Early Childhood Research Quarterly, 3,* 235–272.

Belsky, J., & Rovine, M. (1990). Patterns of marital change across the transition to parenthood: Pregnancy to three years postpartum. *Journal of Marriage and the Family, 52,* 5–19.

Belsky, J., Spanier, G. B., & Rovine, M. (1983). Stability and change in marriage across the transition to parenthood. *Journal of Marriage and the Family, 45,* 567–577.

Bem, S. L. (1981). Gender schema theory: A cognitive account of sex typing. *Psychological Review, 88,* 354–364.

Benfante, R., Reed, D., & Frank, J. (1991). Does cigarette smoking have an independent effect on coronary heart disease incidence in the elderly? *American Journal of Public Health, 81* (7), 897–899.

Bengston, V. L. (1979). Ethnicity and aging: Problems and issues in current social science inquiry. In D. E. Gelfand & A. J. Kutzik (Eds.), *Ethnicity and aging: Theory, research, and policy.* New York: Springer.

Bengston, V. L., Reedy, M. N., & Gordon, C. (1985). Aging and self-conceptions: Personality processes and social contexts. In J. E. Birren & K. W. Schaie (Eds.), *Handbook of the psychology of aging* (2nd ed.). New York: Van Nostrand Reinhold.

Bengston, V. L., Rosenthal, C., & Burton, L. (1990). Families and aging: Diversity and heterogeneity. In R. H. Binstock & L. George (Eds.), *Handbook of aging and the social sciences* (3rd ed.). New York: Academic Press.

Bengtsson, H., & Johnson, L. (1992). Perspective taking, empathy, and prosocial behavior in late childhood. *Child Study Journal, 22* (1), 11–22.

Benin, M. H., & Agostinelli, J. (1988). Husbands' and wives' satisfaction with the division of labor. *Journal of Marriage and the Family, 50,* 349–361.

Bennett, K. C., & Thompson, N. L. (1990). Accelerated aging and male homosexuality: Australian evidence in a continuing debate. In J. A. Lee (Ed.), *Gay mid-life and maturity.* Binghamton, NY: Haworth Press.

Benokraitis, N. V. (1993). *Marriage and families.* Englewood Cliffs, NJ: Prentice Hall.

Benoliel, J. Q. (1991). Multiple meanings of death for older adults. In E. M. Baines (Ed.), *Perspectives on gerontological nursing.* Newbury Park, CA: Sage.

Ben-Sira, Z. (1991). *Regression, stress, and readjustment in aging: A structured bio-psychological perspective on coping and professional support.* New York: Praeger.

Bentzen, W. R. (1993). *Seeing young children: A guide to observing and recording behavior* (2nd ed.). New York: Delmar.

Berg, C. A. (1990). What is intellectual efficacy over the life course? Using adults' conceptions to address the question. In J. Rodin, C. Schooler, & K. W. Schaie (Eds.), *Self-Directedness: Cause and effects throughout the life course.* Hillsdale, NJ: Erlbaum.

Berg, L. (1991). Special care units for persons with dementia. *Journal of the American Geriatrics Society, 39* (12), 1229–1236.

Berger, R. M. (1982). *Gay and gray: The older homosexual man.* Champaign: University of Illinois Press.

Bergkrist, L. (1989). The risk of breast cancer after estrogen and estrogen-progestin replacement. *New England Journal of Medicine, 8* (3), 113–126.

Berman, W. H., & Sperling, M. B. (1991). Parental attachment and emotional distress in the transition to college. *Journal of Youth and Adolescence, 20* (4), 427–440.

Berndt, T. J., & Ladd, G. W. (1989). *Peer relationships in child development.* New York: Wiley.

Berndt, T. J., & Perry, T. B. (1990). Distinctive features and effects of early adolescent friendships. In R. Montemayor (Ed.), *Advances in adolescent research.* Greenwich, CT: JAI Press.

Bernstein, D. K. (1993). Language development: The preschool years. In D. K. Bernstein, E. Tiegerman, & C. Radziewicz (Eds.), *Language and communication disorders in children* (3rd ed.). New York: Macmillan.

Bernstein, I. L. (1990). Salt preference and development. *Developmental Psychology, 26* (4), 552–554.

Bernstein, R. M. (1980). The development of the self-system during adolescence. *Journal of Genetic Psychology, 136* (2), 231–245.

Berrick, J. D. (1991). Sexual abuse prevention training for preschoolers: Implications for moral development. *Children and Youth Services Review, 13* (1/2), 61–75.

Bertman, S. L. (1991). *Facing death: Images, insights, and interventions.* Bristol, PA: Hemisphere.

Berzonsky, M., & Sullivan, C. (1992). Social-cognitive aspects of identity style: Need for cognition, experiential openness, and introspection. *Journal of Adolescent Research, 7* (2), 140–155.

Bessey, B. L., & Ananda, S. M. (1991). Age discrimination in employment: An interdisciplinary review of the ADEA. *Research on Aging, 13* (4), 413–457.

Bettes, B. A. (1990). Ethnicity and psychosocial factors in alcohol and tobacco use in adolescence. *Child Development, 61* (2), 557–565.

Beychok, I. A. (1991). *Better bodies after 35: A commonsense approach to healthful living.* Bedford, MA: Mills and Sanderson.

Bialystok, E. (1988). Levels of bilingualism and levels of linguistic awareness. *Developmental Psychology, 24,* 560–567.

Bidlack, W. R. (1990). Nutritional requirements of the elderly. In J. E. Morley, Z. Glick, & L. Z. Rubenstein (Eds.), *Geriatric nutrition: A comprehensive review.* New York: Raven Press.

Biedenharn, P. J., & Normoyle, J. B. (1991). Elderly community residents' reactions to the nursing home: An analysis of nursing home-related beliefs. *Gerontologist, 31* (1), 107–115.

Biller, J. (1991). *Cerebrovascular disorders in the 1990s.* Philadelphia: Saunders.

Bingham, C. R. (1989). AIDS and adolescents: Threat of infection and approaches for prevention. *Journal of Early Adolescence, 9,* 50–66.

Binstock, R. H., & Post, S. G. (1991). *Too old for health care? Controversies in medicine, law, economics, and ethics.* Baltimore: Johns Hopkins University Press.

Birkel, D. A. G., & Freitag, S. B. (1991). *Forever fit: A step-by-step guide for older adults.* New York: Insight Books.

Birkett, D. P. (1991). *Psychiatry in the nursing home: Assessment, evaluation, and intervention.* Binghamton, NY: Haworth Press.

Birren, J. E., Vercruyssen, M., & Fisher, L. M. (1990). Aging and speed of behavior: Its scientific and practical significance. In M. M. E. Bergener & H. B. Stahelin, (Eds.), *Challenges in aging.* San Diego: Academic Press.

Birren, J. E., Woods, A. M., & Williams, M. V. (1980). Behavioral slowing with age: Causes, organization, and consequences. In L. W. Poon (Ed.), *Aging in the 1980s.* Washington, DC: American Psychological Association.

Birsner, P. (1991). *Mid-career job hunting.* New York: Simon & Schuster.

Bisping, R., Steingrueber, H. J., Oltmann, M., & Wenk, C. (1990). Adults' tolerance of cries: An experimental investigation of acoustic features. *Child Development, 61* (4), 1218–1229.

Black, B. (1992). Negotiating social pretend play: Communication differences related to social status and sex. *Merrill-Palmer Quarterly, 38* (2), 212–232.

Black, J. K. (1981). Are young children really egocentric? *Young Children, 36* (6), 16–22.

Black, R. B., & Weiss, J. D. (1989). Genetic support groups in the delivery of comprehensive genetic services. *American Journal of Human Genetics, 45,* 647–654.

Blackhurst, A. E., and Berdine, W. H. (Eds.). (1993). *An Introduction to Special Education* (3rd Ed.). New York: HarperCollins.

Blair, S. L., & Johnson, M. P. (1992). Wives' perceptions of the fairness of the division of household labor: The intersection of household and ideology. *Journal of Marriage and the Family, 54,* 570–581.

Blair, S. L., & Lichter, D. T. (1991). Measuring the division of household labor: Gender segregation of household among American couples. *Journal of Family Issues, 12,* 91–113.

Blake, J., & Boysson-Bardies, B. (1992). Patterns in babbling: A cross-linguistic study. *Journal of Child Language, 19* (1), 51–74.

Blakely, B. E. (1991). The relative contributions of occupation groups in the discovery and treatment of elder abuse and neglect. *Journal of Gerontological Social Work, 17* (1/2), 183–199.

Blasi, A. (1980). Bridging moral cognition and moral action: A critical review of the literature. *Psychological Bulletin, 88,* 1–45.

Blasi, A., & Hoeffel, E. (1974). Adolescence and formal operations. *Human Development, 17,* 344–454.

Blass, E. M. (1990). Suckling: Determinants, changes, mechanisms, and lasting impressions. *Developmental Psychology, 26* (4), 520–533.

Blazer, D. (1991). Suicide risk factors in the elderly: An epidemiological study. *Journal of Geriatric Psychiatry, 24* (2), 175–190.

Blazer, D., George, L. K., & Hughes, D. (1991). The epidemiology of anxiety disorders: An age comparison. In C. Salzman & B. D. Lebowitz (Eds.), *Anxiety in the elderly: Treatment and research.* New York: Springer.

Blieszner, R., & Adams, R. (1992). *Adult friendship.* Newbury Park, CA: Sage.

Blitchington, W. P. (1984). Traditional sex-roles result in healthier sexual relationships and healthier, more stable family life. In H. Feldman & A. Parrot (Eds.), *Human sexuality: Contemporary controversies.* Beverly Hills, CA: Sage.

Block, J. (1971). *Lives through time.* Berkeley, CA: Bancroft.

Block, M. N., & Pellegrini, A. D. (1989). *The ecological context of children's play.* Norwood, NJ: Ablex.

Bloom, B. (1991). *Fast track to the best job.* Scarsdale, NY: Blazer.

Bloom, F. E., & Lazerson, A. (1988). *Brain, mind, and behavior* (2nd ed.). New York: Freeman.

Bloom, L., Beckwith, R., & Capatides, J. B. (1988). Developments in the expression of affect. *Infant Behavior and Development, 11* (2), 169–186.

Bloomberg, S. (1980). Influence of maternal distress during pregnancy on complications in labor and delivery. *Acta Psychiat. Scand., 62* (5), 339–404.

Bloome, D. (1989). *Classrooms and literacy.* Norwood, NJ: Ablex.

Blos, P. (1962). *On adolescence.* New York: Free Press.

Blotnick, S. (1984). *The corporate steeplechase.* New York: Facts on File.

Blumberg, E. J. (1991). The touch discrimination component of sexual abuse prevention training: Unanticipated positive consequences. *Journal of Interpersonal Violence, 6* (1), 12–28.

Blumenthal, J. A. (1991). Effects of exercise training on bone density in older men and women. *Journal of the American Geriatrics Society, 39* (11), 1065–1070.

Blumenthal, S. J., & Kupfer, D. J. (1988). Overview of early detection and treatment strategies for suicidal behavior in young people. *Journal of Youth and Adolescence, 17,* 1–14.

Blustein, D. L., & Palladino, D. E. (1991). Self and identity in late adolescence: A theoretical and empirical integration. *Journal of Adolescent Research, 6* (4), 437–453.

Blyth, D. A., Simmons, R. G., & Zakin, D. F. (1985). Satisfaction with body image for early adolescent females. *Journal of Youth and Adolescence, 14,* 207–225.

Bodily, C. L. (1991). "I have no opinions. I'm 73 years old!" Rethinking ageism. *Journal of Aging Studies, 5* (3), 245–264.

Bohannon, J. N., & Stanowicz, L. B. (1988). The issue of negative evidence: Adult responses to children's language errors. *Developmental Psychology, 24,* 684–689.

Bohannon, P. (1970). *Divorce before and after.* New York: Doubleday.

Bohannon, P. (1985a). *All the happy families: Exploring the varieties of family life.* New York: McGraw-Hill.

Bohannon, P. (1985b). The six stations of divorce. In L. Cargan (Ed.), *Marriage and family: Coping with change.* Belmont, CA: Wadsworth.

Bohlen, C. (1990, January 15). AIDS epidemic among Romanian babies. *New London (CT) Day,* p. 14.

Boller, K., Rovee-Collier, C., Borovsky, D., & O'-Connor, J. (1990). Developmental changes in the time-dependent nature of memory retrieval. *Developmental Psychology, 26* (5), 770–779.

Bolles, R. (1992). *The 1992 what color is your parachute?* Berkeley, CA: Ten Speed Press.

Bolton, F. G., Jr., Morris, L. A., & MacEachron, A. E. (1990). *Males at risk: The other side of child sexual abuse.* Beverly Hills, CA: Sage.

Bond, J., Briggs, R., & Coleman, P. (1990). The study of aging. In J. Bond & P. Colemen (Eds.), *Aging in society: An introduction to social gerontology.* Newbury Park, CA: Sage.

Bond, J., & Coleman, P. (1990). Aging into the twenty-first century. In J. Bond & P. Colemen (Eds.), *Aging in society: An introduction to social gerontology.* Newbury Park, CA: Sage.

Boohene, E. (1991). Fertility and contraceptive use among young adults in Harare, Zimbabwe. *Studies in Family Planning, 22* (4), 264–271.

Booth-Butterfield, M. (1984). She hears . . . he hears: What they hear and why. *Personnel Journal, 63,* 36–41.

Borgatta, E. F. (1991). Age discrimination issues. *Research on Aging, 13* (4), 476–484.

Borgotta, L., Piening, S. L., & Cohen, W. R. (1989). Association of episiotomy and delivery position with deep perineal laceration during spontaneous delivery in nulliparous women. *American Journal of Obstetrical Gynecology, 160,* 1294–1298.

Borich, G. D. (1992). *Effective teaching methods* (2nd ed.). New York: Macmillan.

Borisoff, D. (1993). The effect of gender on establishing and maintaining intimate relationships. In L. P. Arliss & D. J. Borisoff (Eds.), *Women and men communicating.* Fort Worth, TX: Harcourt Brace Jovanovich.

Bornstein, M. H., (Ed.). (1987). *Sensitive periods in development.* Hillsdale, NJ: Erlbaum.

Bornstein, M. H., & Krasnegor, N. A. (1989). *Stability and continuity in mental development.* Hillsdale, NJ: Erlbaum.

Boskin, W., Graf, G., & Kreisworth, V. (1990). *Health dynamics: Attitudes and behaviors.* St. Paul, MN: West.

Bosse, R. (1991). How stressful is retirement? Findings from the Normative Aging Study. *Journal of Gerontology: Psychological Sciences, 46* (1), P9–P14.

Bott, E. (1971). *Family and social network.* New York: Free Press.

Bottomley, J. M. (1990). Rehabilitation. In J. L. Cummings & B. L. Miller (Eds.), *Alzheimer's disease: Treatment and long-term management. Neurological disease and therapy.* New York: Marcel Dekker.

Botwinick, J. (1981). *We are aging.* New York: Springer.

Botwinick, J. (1984). *Aging and behavior* (3rd ed.). New York: Springer.

Bouchard, T. J. (1984). Twins reared together and apart: What they tell us about human diversity. In S. W. Fox (Ed.), *Individuality and determinism.* New York: Plenum.

Boulton, M. J., & Smith, P. K. (1990). Affective bias in children's perceptions of dominance relationships. *Child Development, 61,* 221–229.

Bowen, G. L. (1987). Changing gender-role preferences and marital adjustment: Implications for clinical practice. *Family Therapy, 14,* 17–29.

Bowlby, J. (1989). *Secure attachment.* New York: Basic Books.

Bowles, L. T. (1981). Wear and tear: Common biological changes of aging. *Geriatrics, 36* (4), 77–86.

Bowman, A. M. (1992). The relationship of anxiety to development of postoperative delirium. *Journal of Gerontological Nursing, 18* (1), 24–30.

Boyd-Franklin, N. (1989). *Black families in therapy: A multisystems approach.* New York: Guilford.

Boyer, C. B., & Hein, K. (1991). AIDS and HIV infection in adolescents: The role of education and antibody testing. In R. M. Lerner, A. C. Petersen, & J. Brooks-Gunn (Eds.), *The encyclopedia of adolescence.* New York: Garland.

Bozett, F., & Hanson, S. (Eds.). (1991). *Fatherhood and families in cultural context.* New York: Springer.

Bradley, R. H., Caldwell, B. M., Rock, S. L., & Ramey, C. T. (1989). Home environment and cognitive development in the first 3 years of life: A collaborative study involving six sites and three ethnic groups in North America. *Developmental Psychology, 25,* 217–235.

Brammer, L. M. (1990). *How to cope with life transitions: The challenge of personal change.* Bristol, PA: Hemisphere.

Branch, L. G. (1991). The future of long-term care. In J. C. Rorneis & R. M. Coe (Eds.), *Quality and cost containment in care of the elderly: Health services research perspectives.* New York: Springer.

Brandstadter, J., & Baltes-Gotz, B. B. (1990). Personal control over development and quality of life perspectives in adulthood. In P. B. Baltes & M. M. Baltes (Eds.), *Successful aging: Perspectives from the behavioral sciences.* New York: Cambridge University Press.

Brannon, L., & Feist, J. (1992). *Health psychology: An introduction to behavior and health.* Belmont, CA: Wadsworth.

Brayfield, A. A. (1992). Employment resources and housework in Canada. *Journal of Marriage and the Family, 54* (1), 19–30.

Brazzell, J. F., & Acock, A. C. (1988). Influence of attitudes, significant others, and aspirations on how adolescents intend to resolve a premarital pregnancy. *Journal of Marriage and the Family, 50,* 413–425.

Breckler, S. J., & Wiggins, E. C. (1989). On defining attitudes and attitude theory: Once more with feeling. In A. R. Pratkanis, S. J. Breckler, & A. C. Greenwald (Eds.), *Attitude structure and function.* Hillsdale, NJ: Erlbaum.

Brehm, S. S. (1992). *Intimate relationships* (2nd ed.). New York: McGraw-Hill.

Brendt, R. L., & Beckman, D. A. (1990). Teratology. In R. D. Eden, F. H. Boehm, & M. Haire (Eds.), *Assessment and care of the fetus: Physiological, clinical, and medicolegal principles.* Norwalk, CT: Appleton and Lange.

Brent, D. A. (1989). Suicide and suicidal behavior in children and adolescents. *Pediatrics in Review, 10,* 269–275.

Bretl, D., & Cantor, J. (1988). The portrayal of men and women in United States television commercials: A recent content analysis and trends over fifteen years. *Sex Roles, 18,* 595–609.

Briere, J. (1984, April). *The effects of childhood sexual abuse on later psychological functioning: Defining a post-sexual abuse syndrome.* Paper presented at the annual meeting of the American Psychological Association, Los Angeles.

Briere, J., & Runtz, M. (1985, June). *Symptomatology associated with prior sexual abuse in a nonclinical sample.* Paper presented at the Third National Conference on Sexual Victimization of Children, Washington, DC.

Briggs, R. (1990). Biological aging. In J. Bond & P. Coleman (Eds.), *Aging in society: An introduction to social gerontology.* Newbury Park, CA: Sage.

Brinckerhoff, L. C., Shaw, S. F., & McGuire, J. M. (1992). Promoting access, accommodations, and independence for college students with learning disabilities. *Journal of Learning Disabilities, 25* (7), 417–429.

Brinson, J. A. (1991). A comparison of the family environments of black male and female adolescent alcohol users. *Adolescence, 26* (104), 877–884.

Brock, M. A. (1991). Chronobiology and aging. *Journal of the American Geriatrics Society, 39* (1), 74–91.

Brody, C. H., & Steelman, L. C. (1985). Sibling structure and parental sex-typing of children's household tasks. *Journal of Marriage and the Family, 47,* 265–273.

Brone, R. J., & Fisher, C. B. (1988). Determinants of adolescent obesity: A comparison with anorexia nervosa. *Adolescence, 23,* 155–169.

Bronfenbrenner, U. (1979). Contexts of child rearing: Problems and prospects. *American Psychologist, 34,* 844–850.

Bronfenbrenner, U. (1986) Ecology of the family as a context for human development: Research perspectives. *Developmental Psychology, 22,* 723–742.

Bronfenbrenner, U. (1989). Ecological systems theory. In R. Vasta (Ed.), *Annals of child development* (Vol. 6). Greenwich, CT: JAI Press.

Bronstein, P., & Paludi, M. (1988). The introductory course from a broader human perspective. In P. A. Bronstein & K. Quina (Eds.), *Teaching a psychology of people.* Washington, DC: American Psychological Association.

Brook, J. S., Whiteman, M., Cohen, P., & Tanaka, J. S. (1992). Childhood precursors of adolescent drug use: A longitudinal analysis. *Genetic, Social, and General Psychology Monographs, 118* (2), 195–213.

Brookins, G. B. (1991). Socialization of African-American adolescents. In R. M. Lerner, A. C. Petersen, & J. Brooks-Gunn (Eds.), *The encyclopedia of adolescence.* New York: Garland.

Brooks, L. (1990). Recent developments in theory building. In D. Brown & L. Brooks (Eds.), *Career choice and development* (2nd ed.). San Francisco: Jossey-Bass.

Brooks-Gunn, J. (1984). The psychological significance of different pubertal events to young girls. *Journal of Early Adolescence, 4,* 315–327.

Brooks-Gunn, J. (1987). Pubertal processes: Their relevance to developmental research. In V. B. Van Hasselt & M. Hersen (Eds.), *Handbook of adolescent psychology.* New York: Pergamon.

Brooks-Gunn, J. (1988). Antecedents and consequences of variations in girls' maturational timing. In M. D. Levine & E. R. McAnarney (Eds.), *Early adolescent transitions.* Lexington, MA: Lexington Books.

Brooks-Gunn, J. (1991). Antecedents of maturational timing variation in adolescent girls. In R. M. Lerner, A. C. Petersen, & J. Brooks-Gunn (Eds.), *The encyclopedia of adolescence.* New York: Garland.

Brooks-Gunn, J., & Furstenberg, F. F., Jr. (1989). Adolescent sexual behavior. *American Psychologist, 44,* 249–257.

Brooks-Gunn, J., & Reiter, E. O. (1990). The role of pubertal processes. In S. S. Feldman & G. R. Elliott (Eds.), *At the threshold: The developing adolescent.* Cambridge, MA: Harvard University Press.

Brooks-Gunn, J., & Ruble, D. N. (1983). The experience of menarche from a developmental perspective. In J. Brooks-Gunn & A. C. Petersen (Eds.), *Girls at puberty.* New York: Plenum.

Brooks-Gunn, J., & Warren, M. P. (1989, April). *How important are pubertal and social events for different problem behaviors and contexts?* Paper presented at the biennial meeting of the Society for Research in Child Development, Kansas City.

Brown, J. R., & Dunn, J. (1991). "You can cry, mum": The social and developmental implications of talk about internal states. *British Journal of Developmental Psychology, 9* (2), 237–256.

Brown, M., & Auerback, A. (1981). Communication patterns in initiation of marital sex. *Medical Aspects of Human Sexuality, 15,* 107–117.

Brown, P. (1990). Family caregivers: Experiences and consequences associated with caring for family members with dementia. *Australian Journal of Ageing, 9* (2), 44–48.

Brown, R. (1973). *First language: The early stages.* Cambridge, MA: Harvard University Press.

Brown, R. (1990). Death and dying: A societal process. *Australian Journal on Ageing, 9* (4), 8–12.

Brownell, C. A. (1990). Peer social skills in toddlers: Competencies and constraints illustrated by same-age and mixed-age interaction. *Child Development, 61* (3), 838–848.

Brubaker, T. H. (1985). *Later-life families.* Beverly Hills, CA: Sage.

Brubaker, T. H. (1990a). Continuity and change in later life families: Grandparenthood, couple relationships and family care giving. *Gerontology Review, 3* (1), 24–40.

Brubaker, T. H. (1990b). Families in later life: A burgeoning research area. *Journal of Marriage and the Family, 52,* 959–981.

Brubaker, T. H., & Ade-Ridder, L. (1986). Husbands' responsibility for household tasks in older marriages: Does living situation make a difference? In R. A. Lewis & R. E. Salt (Eds.), *Men in families.* Beverly Hills, CA: Sage.

Brubaker, T. H., & Hennon, C. B. (1982). Responsibility for household tasks: Comparing dual-earner and dual-retired marriages. In M. E. Szinovacz (Ed.), *Women's retirement: Policy implications of recent research.* Beverly Hills, CA: Sage.

Brubaker, T. H., & Kinsel, B. I. (1985). Who is responsible for household tasks in long term marriages of 'young-old' elderly. *Lifestyles: A Journal of Changing Patterns, 7,* 238–247.

Bruess, C. E., & Richardson, G. E. (1989). *Decisions for health* (2nd ed.). Dubuque, IA: Wm. C. Brown.

Brumberg, J. J. (1988). *Fasting girls.* Cambridge, MA: Harvard University Press.

Bryant, B. K. (1992). Conflict resolution strategies in relation to children's peer relations. *Journal of Applied Developmental Psychology, 13* (1), 35–50.

Buckwalter, K. C. (1990). How to unmask depression. *Geriatric Nursing, 11* (4), 179–181.

Buckwalter, K. C. (1991a). Mental health services of the rural elderly outreach program. *Gerontologist, 31* (3), 408–412.

Buckwalter, K. C. (1991b). The chronically mentally ill elderly in rural environments. In E. Light & B. D. Lebowitz (Eds.), *The elderly with chronic mental illness.* New York: Springer.

Buhrmester, D. (1990). Intimacy of friendship, interpersonal competence, and adjustment during preadolescence and adolescence. *Child Development, 61* (4), 1101–1111.

Buhrmester, D., Goldfarb, J., & Cantrell, D. (1992). Self-presentation when sharing with friends and nonfriends. *Journal of Early Adolescence, 12* (1), 61–79.

Buis, J. M., & Thompson, D. N. (1989). Imaginary audience and personal fable: A brief review. *Adolescence, 24,* 773–781.

Bumpass, L. L. (1989, March). Panel discussion of the results of a 1987 cohabitation survey by Larry L. Bumpass, James A. Sweet, and Andrew Cherlin. Annual meeting of the Population Association of America, San Francisco.

Bumpass, L. L., & Martin, T. C. (1989). Recent trends in marital disruption. *Demography, 2,* 26–41.

Bumpass, L. L., & Sweet, J. A. (1988, June 14). University of Wisconsin survey on cohabitation. *Wall Street Journal,* p. 37.

Bumpass, L. L., Sweet, J. A., & Cherlin, A. (1991). The role of cohabitation in declining rates of marriage. *Journal of Marriage and the Family, 53* (4), 913–927.

Bumpass, L. L., Sweet, J. A., & Martin, T. C. (1990). Changing patterns of remarriage. *Journal of Marriage and the Family, 52,* 747–756.

Burack-Weiss, A. (1991). In their own words: Elders' reactions to vision loss. *Journal of Gerontological Social Work, 17* (3/4), 15–23.

Burlew, A. K., McAdoo, H. P., & Azibo, D. A. (1992). *African American psychology: Theory, research, and practice.* Newbury Park, CA: Sage.

Burnham, D. K., & Harris, M. B. (1992). Effects of real gender and labeled gender on adults' perceptions of infants. *Journal of Genetic Psychology, 153* (2), 165–183.

Burns, A., Jacoby, R., & Levy, R. (1991). Progression of cognitive impairment in Alzheimer's disease. *Journal of the American Geriatrics Society, 39* (1), 39–45.

Burns, S. (1991). The spirituality of dying. *Health Progress, 72* (7), 48–52.

Burris, B. H. (1991). Employed mothers: The impact of class and marital status on the prioritizing of family and work. *Social Sciences Quarterly, 72,* 50–65.

Burton, L. M., & Dilworth-Anderson, P. (1991). The intergenerational family roles of aged black Americans. In S. K. Pfeifer & M. B. Sussman (Eds.), *Families: Intergenerational and generational connections.* Binghamton, New York: Haworth Press.

Bury, M., & Holme, A. (1990). Quality of life and social support in the very old. *Journal of Aging Studies, 4* (4), 345–357.

Busch-Rossnagel, N. A., & Zayas, L. H. (1991). Hispanic adolescents. In R. M. Lerner, A. C. Petersen, & J. Brooks-Gunn (Eds.), *The encyclopedia of adolescence.* New York: Garland.

Bushnell, I. W., Sai, F., & Mullin, J. T. (1989). Neonatal recognition of the mother's face. *British Journal of Developmental Psychology, 7,* 3–15.

Bushy, A. (1991). Quality assurance: considerations for rural health care institutions. In A. Bushy (Ed.), *Rural nursing* (Vol. 2). Newbury Park, CA: Sage.

Buss, D. M., & Barnes, M. (1986). Preferences in human mate selection. *Journal of Personality and Social Psychology, 50,* 559–570.

Bussey, K. (1992). Lying and truthfulness: Children's definitions, standards, and evaluative reactions. *Child Development, 63* (1), 129–137.

Bussey, K., & Bandura, A. (1992). Self-regulatory mechanisms governing gender development. *Child Development, 63* (5), 1236–1250.

Butler, R. N. (1968). The life review: An interpretation of reminiscence in the aged. In B. Neugarten (Ed.), *Middle age and aging*. Chicago: University of Chicago Press.

Butler, R. N. (1990). The contributions of late-life creativity to society. *Gerontology and Geriatrics Education, 11*, 45–51.

Butler, R. N., & Lewis, M. (1981). *Aging and mental health*. St. Louis: Mosby.

Butterworth, G., & Hopkins, B. (1988). Hand-mouth coordination in the newborn baby. *British Journal of Developmental Psychology, 6*, 303–314.

Butterworth, G., & Jarrett, N. (1991). What minds have in common is space: Spatial mechanisms serving joint visual attention in infancy. *British Journal of Developmental Psychology, 9* (1), 55–72.

Byrd, M. (1991). Adult age differences in the ability to read and remember metaphor. *Educational Gerontology, 17* (4), 297–313.

Byrnes, J. P. (1988). Formal operations: A systematic reformulation. *Developmental Review, 8*, 66–87.

Cadieux, R. J., & Adams, D. G. (1990). Recognizing and treating depression. *Senior Patient, 2* (8), 24–29.

Cairl, R. (1990). *Special care for Alzheimer's disease patients: An exploratory study of dementia specific care units*. Tampa, FL: National Resource Center on Alzheimer's Disease.

Cairns, R. B., Cairns, B. D., Neckerman, H. J., & Ferguson, L. L. (1989). Growth and aggression: I. Childhood to early adolescence. *Developmental Psychology, 25*, 320–330.

Calhoun, J. F., & Acocella, J. R. (1990). *Psychology of adjustment and human relationships* (3rd ed.). New York: McGraw-Hill.

Camp, C. J., & McKitrick, L. A. (1989). Memory interventions in old age. *Southwestern: The Journal of Aging for the Southwest, 5* (1), 62–73.

Campagnoli, C. (1990). Prevention and therapy of postmenopausal osteoporosis. In F. Fabris, L. Pernigotti, & E. Ferrario (Eds.), *Sedentary life and nutrition*. New York: Raven Press.

Campanelli, L. C. (1990). Working with the dying older patient. In C. B. Lewis (Ed.), *Aging: The health care challenge* (2nd ed.). Philadelphia: F. A. Davis.

Campbell, M. L., & Moen, P. (1992). Job-family role strain among employed single mothers of preschoolers. *Family Relations, 41* (2), 205–211.

Campos, J. J., Bertenthal, B. I., & Caplovitz, K. (1982). The interrelationship of affect and cognition in the visual cliff situation. In C. Izard, J. Kagan, & R. Zajonc (Eds.), *Emotion and cognition*. New York: Plenum.

Campos, J. J., Haitt, S., Rampsay, D., Henderson, C., & Svejda, M. (1978). The emergence of fear on the visual cliff. In M. Lewis & L. Rosenblum (Eds.), *The origins of affect*. New York: Wiley.

Camras, L. A., & Sachs, V. B. (1991). Social referencing and caretaker expressive behavior in a day care setting. *Infant Behavior and Development, 14* (1), 27–36.

Cancellier, P. H., & Crews, K. A. (1986). *Women in the world: The women's decade and beyond*. Washington, DC: Population Reference Bureau.

Cancian, F. M. (1985). Gender politics: Love and power in the private and public sphere. In A. Rossi (Ed.), *Gender and the life course*. New York: Aldine.

Cannon, G. S., Idol, L., & West, J. F. (1992). Educating students with mild handicaps in general classrooms: Essential teaching practices for general and special educators. *Journal of Learning Disabilities, 25* (5), 300–317.

Cantor, M. H. (1979a). The informal support system of New York's inner city elderly: Is ethnicity a factor? In D. E. Gelfand & A. J. Kutzik (Eds.), *Ethnicity and aging: Theory, research, and policy*. New York: Springer.

Cantor, M. H. (1979b). Neighbors and friends: An overlooked resource in the informal support system. *Research on Aging, 1*, 434–463.

Capelli, C. A., Nakagawa, N., & Madden, C. M. (1990). How children understand sarcasm: The role of context and intonation. *Child Development, 61*, 1824–1841.

Caplan, M., Bennetto, L., & Weissberg, R. P. (1991). The role of interpersonal context in the assessment of social problem-solving skills. *Journal of Applied Developmental Psychology, 12* (1), 103–114.

Carey, S. (1988). Are children fundamentally different kinds of thinkers and learners than adults? In K. Richardson & S. Sheldon (Eds.), *Cognitive development to adolescence*. Hillsdale, NJ: Erlbaum.

Cargan, L., & Melko, M. (1982). *Singles: Myths and realities*. Beverly Hills, CA: Sage.

Cargan, L., & Melko, M. (1985). Being single on Noah's art. In L. Cargan (Ed.), *Marriage and family: Coping with change*. Belmont, CA: Wadsworth.

Carlsen, M. (1991). *Creative aging: A meaning-making perspective*. New York: Norton.

Carlson, B. E. (1990). Adolescent observers of marital violence. *Journal of Family Violence, 5*, 285–299.

Carlson, B. E. (1991). Outcomes of physical abuse and observation of marital violence among adolescents in placement. *Journal of Interpersonal Violence, 5* (4), 526–534.

Carney, C. G., & Wells, C. F. (1991). *Discover the career within you* (3rd ed.). Pacific Grove, CA: Brooks/Cole.

Carp, F. M. (1991). Living environments of older adults. In E. M. Baines (Ed.), *Perspectives on gerontological nursing*. Newbury Park, CA: Sage.

Carrasquillo, A. L. (1991). *Hispanic children and youth in the United States*. New York: Garland.

Carrol, C. R. (1989). *Drugs in modern society* (2nd ed.). Dubuque, IA: Wm. C. Brown.

Carroll, C., & Miller, D. (1990). *Health: The science of human adaptation*. Dubuque, IA: Wm. C. Brown.

Carroll, D. (1985). *Living with dying*. New York: McGraw-Hill.

Carter, B. (1991, May 1). Children's TV: Where boys are king. *New York Times*, pp. A1, C18.

Carter, D. B., & Levy, G. D. (1988). Cognitive aspects of early sex-role development: The influence of gender schemas on preschoolers' memories and preferences for sex-typed toys and activities. *Child Development, 59*, 782–792.

Carter, W. B. (1991). Participation of older adults in health programs and research: A critical review of the literature. *Gerontologist, 31* (5), 584–592.

Case, R. (1991a). Advantages and disadvantages of the neo-Piagetian position. In R. Case (Ed.), *The mind's staircase*. Hillsdale, NJ: Erlbaum.

Case, R. (1991b). Stages in the development of the young child's first sense of self. *Developmental Review, 11* (3), 210–230.

Case, R., Kurland, D. M., & Goldberg, J. (1982). Operational efficiency and the growth of short-term memory span. *Journal of Experimental Child Psychology, 33*, 386–404.

Caserta, M. S., & Lund, D. A. (1992). Bereaved older adults who seek early professional help. *Death Studies, 16* (1), 17–30.

Casey, R. J. (1993). Children's emotional experience: Relations among expression, self-report, and understanding. *Developmental Psychology, 29* (1), 119–129.

Casper, R. C. (1989). Psychodynamic psychotherapy in acute anorexia nervosa and acute bulimic nervosa. In A. H. Esman (Ed.), *International Annals of Adolescent Psychiatry*. Chicago: University of Chicago Press.

Caspi, A. (1987). Personality in the life course. *Journal of Personality and Social Psychology, 53*, 1203–1213.

Caspi, A., Bem, D. J., & Elder, G. H., Jr. (1989). Continuities and consequences of interactional styles across the life course. *Journal of Personality, 57*, 375–406.

Cassata, M., Anderson, P. A., & Skill, T. (1983). Images of old age on daytime television. In M. Cassata & T. Skill (Eds.), *Life on daytime television*. Norwood, NJ: Ablex.

Cate, R. M., & Lloyd, S. A. (1992). *Courtship*. Newbury Park, CA: Sage.

Cates, W., Jr. (1990). The epidemiology and control of sexually transmitted diseases in adolescents. In M. Schydlower & M. A. Shafer (Eds.), *AIDS and the other sexually transmitted diseases*. Philadelphia: Hanley and Belfus.

Cates, W., Jr. (1991). Teenagers and sexual risk-taking: The best of times and the worst of times. *Journal of Adolescent Health, 12*, 84–94.

Cates, W., Jr., & Stone, K. M. (1992). Family planning, sexually transmitted diseases, and contraceptive choice: A literature update. *Family Planning Perspectives, 24*, 75–84.

Catron, C. E., & Allen, J. (1993). *Early childhood curriculum*. New York: Macmillan.

Cavan, R. S., & Ferdinand, T. N. (1981). *Juvenile delinquency* (4th ed.). New York: Harper & Row.

Cazden, C. B. (1981). *Language in early childhood education* (rev. ed.). Washington, DC: National Association for the Education of Young Children.

Centers for Disease Control. (1990). 1990 sexually transmitted diseases treatment guidelines. *Morbidity and Mortality Weekly Report, 39*, J-3.

Centers for Disease Control. (1990, October). Progress toward achieving the 1990 high blood pressure objectives. *Journal of the American Medical Association*, 113–116.

Centers for Disease Control. (1992a). The second 100,000 cases of acquired immunodeficiency syndrome. *Morbidity and Mortality Report, 40*, 63–77.

Centers for Disease Control. (1992b). Sexual behavior among high school students, United States, 1990. *Morbidity and Mortality Weekly Report, 40*, 85–88.

Centers for Disease Control. (1993). Projections of the number of persons diagnosed with AIDS and of immunosuppressed HIV-infected persons, 1992–1994. *Morbidity and Mortality Weekly Report, 41*, 92–996.

Cervantes, R. C. (Ed.). (1992). *Substance abuse and gang violence.* Newbury Park, CA: Sage.

Cervera, N. (1991). Unwed teenage pregnancy: Family relationships with the father of the baby. *Families in Society: The Journal of Contemporary Human Services, 72* (1), 29–37.

Cesario, T. C., & Hollander, D. (1991). Life span extension by means other than control of disease. In F. C. Ludwig (Ed.), *Life span extension consequences and open questions.* New York: Springer.

Chadwick, B. A., & Heaton, T. B. (1992). *Statistical handbook on the American family.* Phoenix: Oryx Press.

Chafel, J. A. (1991). The play of children: Developmental processes and policy implications. *Child and Youth Care Forum, 20* (2), 115–132.

Chalmers, B. (1982). Psychological aspects of pregnancy: Some thoughts for the 80's. *Social Science and Medicine, 16* (3), 323–331.

Chandra, P. S. (1991). Marital life among infertile spouses: The wife's perspective and its implications in therapy. *Family Therapy, 18* (2), 145–154.

Chang, C. F., & White-Means, S. I. (1991). The men who care: An analysis of male primary caregivers who care for frail elderly at home. *Journal of Applied Gerontology, 10* (3), 343–358.

Chapman, M., & Lindenberger, U. (1989). Concrete operations and attentional capacity. *Journal of Experimental Child Psychology, 47,* 236–258.

Chappell, N. L. (1991). Living arrangements and sources of caregiving. *Journal of Gerontology, 46* (1), S1–S8.

Charlesworth, R. (1992). *Understanding child development: For adults who work with young children* (3rd ed.). Albany, NY: Delmar.

Charlesworth, R., & Lind, K. R. (1990). *Math and science for young children.* Albany, NY: Delmar.

Charlesworth, R., & Radeloff, D. J. (1991). *Experiences in math for young children* (2nd ed.). Albany, NY: Delmar.

Charmaz, K. (1980). *The social reality of death.* Reading, MA: Addison-Wesley.

Charness, N. (1985). Aging and problem-solving performance. In N. Charness (Ed.), *Aging and human performance.* London: Wiley.

Chassin, L., Rogosch, F., & Barrera, M. (1991). Substance use and symptomatology among adolescent children of alcoholics. *Journal of Abnormal Psychology, 4,* 449–463.

Chelune, G. J., Robison, J. T., & Kommor, M. J. (1984). A cognitive interactional model of intimate relationships. In V. J. Derlega (Ed.), *Communication, intimacy, and close relationships.* New York: Academic Press.

Chen, H. (1991). Stepping over obstacles: Gait patterns of healthy young and old adults. *Journal of Gerontology: Medical Sciences, 46* (6), M196–M203.

Chen, X., Rubin, K. H., & Sun, Y. (1992). Social reputation and peer relationships in Chinese and Canadian children: A cross-cultural study. *Child Development, 63* (6), 1336–1343.

Chene, A. (1991). Self-esteem of the elderly and education. *Education Gerontology, 17* (4), 343–353.

Cherlin, A. (1990). Recent changes in American fertility, marriage, and divorce. *Annals of the American Association of Political and Social Science, 510,* 145–154.

Cherlin, A., & Furstenberg, F. (1983). The American family in the year 2000. *The Futurist, 17,* 7–14.

Cherniss, C. (1992). Long-term consequences of burnout: An exploratory study. *Journal of Organizational Behavior, 13* (1), 1–11.

Cherry, K. E. M., Keller, J., & Dudley, W. M. (1991). A needs assessment of persons with visual impairments: Implications for older adults and service providers. *Journal of Gerontological Social Work, 17* (3/4), 99–123.

Chesney, M. A., & Rosenman, R. H. (1980a). Strategies for modifying type A behavior. *Consultant, 20,* 216–222.

Chesney, M. A., & Rosenman, R. H. (1980b). Type A behavior in the work setting. In C. Cooper & R. Payne (Eds.), *Current issues in occupational stress.* New York: Wiley.

Chesney-Lind, M. (1989). Girl's crime and woman's place: Toward a feminist model of female delinquency. *Crime and Delinquency, 35,* 5–30.

Cheung, Y. W., Erikson, P. G., & Landau, T. C. (1991). Experience of crack use: Findings from a community-based sample in Toronto. *Journal of Drug Issues, 21,* 121–140.

Chez, R. A., & Chervenak, J. L. (1990). Nutrition in pregnancy. In R. D. Eden, F. H. Boehm, & M. Haire (Eds.), *Assessment and care of the fetus: Physiological, clinical, and medicolegal principles.* Norwalk, CT: Appleton and Lange.

Chhaya, M. (1987, July 16). Amniocentesis leads to abortion of female fetuses in India. *New London (CT) Day,* p. C–12.

Children's Defense Fund. (1988). *Teenage pregnancy: An advocate's guide to the numbers.* Washington, DC: Author.

Chilman, C. S. (1988). Single adolescent parents. In C. Chilman, E. Nunnally, & F. Cox (Eds.), *Families in trouble.* Newbury Park, CA: Sage.

Chilman, C. S. (1990). Promoting healthy adolescent sexuality. *Family Relations, 39,* 123–131.

Chithiramohan, R. N. (1991). Paranoid features in the elderly with dementia. *International Journal of Geriatric Psychiatry, 6* (3), 155–157.

Chomsky, N. (1968). *Language and mind.* New York: Harcourt Brace Jovanovich.

Chomsky, N. (1980). *Rules and representation.* New York: Columbia University Press.

Christiansen, J. R., & Blake, R. H. (1990). The grooming process in father-daughter incest. In A. L. Horton, B. Johnson, L. M. Roundy, & D. Williams (Eds.), *The incest perpetrator: A family member no one wants to treat.* Newbury Park, CA: Sage.

Christopher, F. S., & Roosa, M. W. (1990). An evaluation of an adolescent pregnancy prevention program: Is "just say no" enough? *Family Relations, 39,* 68–72.

Chumlea, W. C. (1982). Physical growth in adolescence. In B. B. Wolman (Ed.), *Handbook of developmental psychology.* Englewood Cliffs, NJ: Prentice Hall.

Cicirelli, V. G. (1991). Sibling relationships in adulthood. In S. K. Pfeifer & M. B. Sussman (Eds.), *Families: Intergenerational and generational connections.* Binghamton, NY: Haworth Press.

Cicirelli, V. G. (1992). *Family caregiving: Autonomous and paternalistic decision making.* Newbury Park, CA: Sage.

Cillessen, A. H., Van Ijzendoorn, M. H., Hendrik, W., Van Lieshout, C. F., & Hartup, W. W. (1992). Heterogeneity among peer-rejected boys: Subtypes and stabilities. *Child Development, 63* (4), 893–905.

Clark, H. H., & Clark, E. V. (1977). *Psychology and language: An introduction to psycholinguistics.* New York: Harcourt Brace Jovanovich.

Clark, M. L., & Ayers, M. (1988). The role of reciprocity and proximity in junior high school friendships. *Journal of Youth and Adolescence, 17,* 403–407.

Clark, M. L., & Bittle, M. L. (1992). Friendship expectations and the evaluation of present friendship in middle childhood and early adolescence. *Child Study Journal, 22* (2), 115–135.

Clark, N., & Bennetts, A. (1982). Vital statistics and nonhospital births: A mortality study of infants born out of hospital in Oregon. *Research issues in the assessment of birth settings.* Washington, DC: National Academy Press.

Clarke-Stewart, K. A. (1989). Infant day care: Maligned or malignant? *American Psychologist, 44,* 266–273.

Clausen, J. S. (1991). Adolescent competence and the shaping of the life course. *American Journal of Sociology, 96* (4), 805–842.

Claussen, C. F., & Patil, N. P. (1990). Sensory changes in later life. In M. Bergener & S. I. Finkel (Eds.), *Clinical and scientific psychogeriatrics.* New York: Springer.

Clay, James W. (1987). Involving fathers in day care. *Nurturing Today, 9* (3), 23–29.

Clennel, S. (1986, Fall). Technology and open-university older students. *Ageing International,* pp. 4–5.

Click, P. (1993). *Caring for school age children.* Albany, NY: Delmar.

Cliff, D. (1991). Negotiating a flexible retirement: Further paid work and the quality of life in early retirement. *Ageing and Society, 11* (3), 319–340.

Clifton, R. K., Perris, E. E., & Bullinger, A. (1991). Infants' perception of auditory space. *Developmental Psychology, 27* (2), 187–197.

Coberly, S. (1991). Older workers and the Older Americans Act. *Generations, 15* (3), 27–30.

Cockburn, J., & Smith, P. T. (1990). The relative influence of intelligence and age on everyday memory. *Journal of Gerontology, 45,* P31–P36.

Cohen, C. (1990). Outcome of schizophrenia into later life: An overview. *Gerontologist, 30* (6), 790–797.

Cohen, C. I. (1991). The chronic mentally ill elderly: Service research issues. In E. Light & B. D. Lebowitz (Eds.), *The elderly with chronic mental illness.* New York: Springer.

Cohen, G. (1990). Recognition and retrieval of proper names: Age differences in the fan effect. *European Journal of Cognitive Psychology, 2* (3), 193–204.

Cohen, G. D. (1989). Psychodynamic perspectives in the clinical approach to brain disease in the elderly. In D. K. Conn, A. Grek, & J. Sadavoy (Eds.), *Psychiatric consequences of brain disease in the elderly.* New York: Plenum.

Cohen, N. W., & Estner, L. J. (1983). *Silent knife: Cesarean prevention and vaginal birth after cesarean.* South Hadley, MA: Bergin and Garvey.

Cohen, P. T., Sande, M. A., & Volberding, P. A. (Eds.). (1990). *The AIDS knowledge base.* Waltham, MA: Medical Publishing Group.

Cohen, R. L. (1982). A comparison study of women choosing two different childbirth alternatives. *Birth, 9,* 13–19.

Cohen, R., Schleser, R., & Meyers, A. (1981). Self-instructions: Effect of cognitive level and active rehearsal. *Journal of Experimental Child Psychology, 32,* 65–76.

Cohen, T. (1983). The incestuous family revisited. *Social Casework, 64,* 154–161.

Coie, J. D. (1991). The role of aggression in peer relations: An analysis of aggression episodes in boys' play groups. *Child Development, 62* (4), 812–826.

Colby, A., Kohlberg, L., Gibbs, J., & Lieberman, M. (1983). A longitudinal study of moral judgment. *Monographs of the Society for Research in Child Development* (1, Serial No. 200).

Cole, D. A. (1991). Adolescent suicide. In R. M. Lerner, A. C. Petersen, & J. Brooks-Gunn (Eds.), *The encyclopedia of adolescence.* New York: Garland.

Coleman, M., & Ganong, L. H. (1990). Remarriage and stepfamily research in the 1980's: Increased interest in an old family form. *Journal of Marriage and the Family, 52* (4), 925–940.

Coleman, P. (1990). Adjustment in later life. In J. Bond & P. Coleman (Eds.), *Aging in society: An introduction to social gerontology.* Newbury Park, CA: Sage.

Coles, R., & Stokes, G. (1985). *Sex and the American teenager.* New York: Harper & Row.

Coley, J. D., & Gelman, S. A. (1989). The effects of object orientation and object type on children's interpretation of the word *big. Child Development, 60,* 372–380.

Colombo, J., Mitchell, D. W., Coldren, J. T., & Freeseman, L. J. (1991). Individual differences in infant visual attention: Are short lookers faster processors or feature processors? *Child Development, 62* (6), 1247–1257.

Colten, M. E., & Gore, S. (Eds.). (1991). *Adolescent stress: Causes and consequences.* New York: Aldine de Gruyter.

Commons, M. L., & Richards, F. A. (1982). A general model of stage theory. In M. L. Commons, F. A. Richards, & C. Armon (Eds.), *Beyond formal operations: Late adolescent and adult cognitive development.* New York: Praeger.

Commons, M. L., Richards, F. A., & Armon, C. (1982). *Beyond formal operations: Late adolescent and adult cognitive development.* New York: Praeger.

Commons, M. L., Richards, F. A., & Kuhn, D. (1982). Systematic and metasystematic reasoning: A case for levels of reasoning beyond Piaget's stage of formal operations. *Child Development, 53,* 1058–1069.

Conant, M., Hardy, D., Sernatinger, J., Spicer, D., & Levy, J. A. (1986). Condoms prevent transmission of AIDS-associated retrovirus. *Journal of the American Medical Association, 255,* 1706.

Condry, J. C. (1989). *The psychology of television.* Hillsdale, NJ: Erlbaum.

Condy, S. R., Templer, D. I., Brown, R., & Veaco, L. (1987). Parameters of sexual contacts of boys with women. *Archives of Sexual Behavior, 16,* 379–393.

Conger, R. D., Conger, K. J., Elder, G. H., & Lorenz, C. (1992). A family process model of economic hardship and adjustment of early adolescent boys. *Child Development, 63* (3), 526–541.

Coni, N. K. (1991). Ethical dilemmas faced in dealing with the aged sick. In F. C. Ludwig (Ed.), *Life span extension: Consequences and open questions.* New York: Springer.

Conkling, W. (1991). From infertility to fatherhood: New techniques can increase the odds for conception. *American Health, 10* (1), 10–13.

Conley, J. J. (1984). Longitudinal consistency of adult personality: Self-reported psychological characteristics across 45 years. *Journal of Personality and Social Psychology, 47,* 1325–1333.

Conley, J. J. (1985a). A personality theory of adulthood and aging. In R. Hogan & W. H. Jones (Eds.), *Perspectives in personality.* Greenwich, CT: JAI Press.

Conley, J. J. (1985b). Longitudinal stability of personality traits: A multitrait-multimethod-multioccasion analysis. *Journal of Personality and Social Psychology, 49,* 1266–1282.

Connell, D. K., & Meyer, R. G. (1991). Adolescent suicidal behavior and popular self-report instruments of depression, social desirability, and anxiety. *Adolescence, 26* (101), 113–120.

Connidis, I. A., & Davies, L. (1990). Confidants and companions in later life: The place of family and friends. *Journal of Gerontology, 45* (4), S141–S149.

Connolly, J. A., Doyle, A. B., & Reznick, E. (1988). Social pretend play and social interaction in preschoolers. *Journal of Applied Development, 9* (3), 301–313.

Connor, M. E. (1986). Some parenting attitudes of young black fathers. In R. A. Lewis & R. E. Salt (Eds.), *Men in families.* Beverly Hills, CA: Sage.

Conte, J. R. (1990). The incest offender: An overview and introduction. In A. L. Horton, B. Johnson, L. M. Roundy, & D. Williams (Eds.), *The incest perpetrator: A family member no one wants to treat.* Newbury Park, CA: Sage.

Conwell, Y., Rotenberg, M., & Caine, E. D. (1990). Completed suicide at age 50 and over. *Journal of the American Geriatrics Society, 38* (6), 640–644.

Cook, A. S. (1991). A comparison of leisure patterns and morale between retired professional and nonprofessional women. *Journal of Women and Aging, 3* (3) 59–68.

Cooney, T. M., & Uhlenberg, P. (1991). Changes in work-family connections among highly educated men and women: 1970 to 1980. *Journal of Family Issues, 12* (1), 69–90.

Coons, D. H. (1991). *Specialized dementia care units. Johns Hopkins Series in Contemporary Medicine and Public Health.* Baltimore: Johns Hopkins University Press.

Cooper, B. A. (1991). The use of the Lanthony New Color Test in determining the effects of aging on color vision. *Journal of Gerontology: Psychological Sciences, 46* (6), P320–P324.

Cooper, J. K. (1991). Alzheimer's disease. Answering questions commonly asked by patients' families. *Geriatrics, 46* (3), 38–40.

Cooper, J. K., Mungas, D., & Weiler, P. G. (1990). Relation of cognitive status and abnormal behaviors in Alzheimer's disease. *Journal of the American Geriatrics Society, 38* (8), 867–870.

Cooper, K. (1990). *Controlling cholesterol.* New York: Basic Books.

Cooper, K., Chassin, L., & Zeiss, A. (1985). The relation of sex role self-concept and sex-role attitudes to the marital satisfaction and personal adjustment of dual-worker couples with preschool children. *Sex Roles, 12,* 227–241.

Corey, G. (1990). *I never knew I had a choice* (4th ed.). Monterey, CA: Brooks/Cole.

Cornoldi, C., Gobbo, C., & Mazzoni, G. (1991). On metamemory-memory relationship: Strategy availability and training. *International Journal of Behavioral Development, 14* (1), 101–121.

Corwin, D. (1985, September). *Sexually abused child's disorder.* Paper presented at the National Summit Conference on Diagnosing Child Sexual Abuse, Los Angeles.

Costa, P. T., Jr., & McCrae, R. R. (1976). Age differences in personality structure: A cluster analytic approach. *Journal of Gerontology, 31,* 564–570.

Costa, P. T., Jr., & McCrae, R. R. (1977). Age differences in personality structure revisited: Studies in validity, stability and change. *International Journal of Aging and Human Development, 8,* 261–275.

Costa, P. T., Jr., & McCrae, R. R. (1978). Objective personality assessment. In M. Storandt, I. C. Siegler, & M. F. Elias (Eds.), *The clinical psychology of aging.* New York: Plenum.

Costa, P. T., Jr., & McCrae, R. R. (1980a). Influence of extraversion and neuroticism on subjective well-being: Happy and unhappy people. *Journal of Personality and Social Psychology, 38,* 668–678.

Costa, P. T., Jr., & McCrae, R. R. (1980b). Still stable after all these years: Personality as a key to some issues in adulthood and old age. In P. B. Baltes & O. C. Brim, Jr. (Eds.), *Life span development and behavior.* New York: Academic Press.

Costa, P. T., Jr., & McCrae, R. R. (1982). An approach to the attribution of age, period, and cohort effects. *Psychological Bulletin, 92,* 238–250.

Costa, P. T., Jr., & McCrae, R. R. (1984). Personality as a lifelong determinant of well-being. In C. Malatesta & C. Izard (Eds.), *Affective processes in adult development and aging.* Beverly Hills, CA: Sage.

Costa, P. T., Jr., & McCrae, R. R. (1986). Personality stability and its implications for clinical psychology. *Clinical Psychology Review, 6,* 407–423.

Costa, P. T., Jr., & McCrae, R. R. (1988). Personality in adulthood: A six-year longitudinal study of self-report and spouse ratings on the NEO Personality Inventory. *Journal of Personality and Social Psychology, 54,* 853–863.

Costa, P. T., Jr., & McCrae, R. R. (1989). Personality continuity and the changes of adult life. In M. Storandt & G. R. VandenBos (Eds.), *The adult years: Continuity and change.* Washington, DC: American Psychological Association.

Costa, P. T., Jr., McCrae, R. R., & Arenberg, D. (1980). Enduring dispositions in adult males. *Journal of Personality and Social Psychology, 38,* 793–800.

Costin, S. E., & Jones, D. C. (1992). Friendship as a facilitator of emotional responsiveness and prosocial interventions among young children. *Developmental Psychology, 28* (5), 941–947.

Cote, J. E., & Levine, C. (1988). A critical examination of the ego identity status paradigm. *Developmental Review, 8,* 147–184.

Cotterell, J. L. (1992). The relation of attachments and supports to adolescent well-being and school adjustment. *Journal of Adolescent Research, 7* (1), 28–42.

Couper, D. P., Sheehan, N. W., & Thomas, E. L. (1991). Attitudes toward old people: The impact of an intergenerational program. *Educational Gerontology, 17* (1), 41–53.

Coustan, D. R. (1990). Diabetes mellitus. In R. D. Eden, F. H. Boehm, & M. Haire (Eds.), *Assessment and care of the fetus: Physiological, clinical, and medicolegal principles.* Norwalk, CT: Appleton and Lange.

Couturier, L. C., Mansfield, R. S., & Gallagher, J. M. (1981). Relationships between humor, formal operational ability, and creativity in eighth graders. *Journal of Genetic Psychology, 139* (2), 221–226.

Coverman, S., & Sheley, J. F. (1986). Change in men's housework and child-care time, 1965–1975. *Journal of Marriage and the Family, 48,* 413–422.

Covey, H. C. (1991). *Images of older people in Western art and society.* New York: Praeger.

Cowan, C. P., & Cowan, P. A. (1992). *When partners become parents: The big life change for couples.* New York: Basic Books.

Cowan, C. P., Cowan, P. A., Heming, G., Garett, E., Coysh, W. S., Curtis-Boles, H., & Boles, A. J. (1985). Transitions to parenthood: His, hers, and theirs. *Journal of Family Issues, 6,* 451–481.

Cowan, N., Saults, J. S., Winterowd, C., & Sherk, M. (1991). Enhancement of 4-year-old children's memory span for phonologically similar and dissimilar word lists. *Journal of Experimental Child Psychology, 51* (1), 30–52.

Cowan, P. A., & Hetherington, E. M. (1991). *Family transitions.* Hillsdale, NJ: Erlbaum.

Cowan, W. M. (1986). The development of the brain. In R. Thompson (Ed.), *Progress in neuroscience.* New York: Freeman.

Coward, R. T., & Cutler, S. J. (1991). The composition of multi-generational households that include elders. *Research on Aging, 13* (1), 55–73.

Cowper, P. A. (1991). The impact of supervised exercise on the psychological well-being and health status of older veterans. *Journal of Applied Gerontology, 10* (4), 469–485.

Cox, C. (1991). Why older adults leave the university: A comparison of continuing and noncontinuing students. *Educational Gerontology, 17* (1), 1–10.

Cox, C., & Monk, A. (1990). Minority caregivers of dementia victims: A comparison of black and Hispanic families. *Journal of Applied Gerontology, 9* (3), 340–354.

Cox, F. D. (1984). *Human intimacy: Marriage, the family, and its meaning.* St. Paul, MN: West.

Cox, M. J., Owen, M. T., Henderson, V. K., & Margand, N. A. (1992). Prediction of infant-father and infant-mother attachment. *Developmental Psychology, 28* (3), 474–483.

Cox, T. H., & Harquail, C. V. (1991). Career paths and career success in the early career stages of male and female MBA's. *Journal of Vocational Behavior, 39* (1), 54–75.

Crabtree, J. L., & Caron-Parker, L. M. (1991). Long-term care of the aged: Ethical dilemmas and solutions. *American Journal of Occupational Therapy, 45* (7), 607–612.

Crain, W. C. (1985). *Theories of development: Concepts and applications.* Englewood Cliffs, NJ: Prentice Hall.

Cranny, C. J., Smith, P. C., & Stone, E. F. (Eds.). (1992). *Job satisfaction.* New York: Lexington Books.

Crews, J. E. (1991). Measuring rehabilitation outcomes and the public polices on aging and blindness. *Journal of Gerontological Social Work, 17* (3/4), 137–151.

Crnic, K. A. (1983). Social interaction and developmental competence of preterm and full-term infants during the first year of life. *Child Development, 54* (5), 1199–1210.

Cromer, R. F. (1988). The cognition hypothesis revisited. In F. S. Kessel (Ed.), *The development of language and language researchers.* Hillsdale, NJ: Erlbaum.

Crosby, J. F., & Jose, N. L. (1983). Death: Family adjustment to loss. In C. R. Figley & H. I. McCubbin (Eds.), *Stress and the family.* New York: Brunner/Mazel.

Crose, R. (1990). Reviewing the past in the here and now. *Journal of Mental Health Counseling, 12* (3), 279–287.

Cross, D. R., & Paris, S. G. (1988). Development and instructional analyses of children's metacognition and reading comprehension. *Journal of Educational Psychology, 80,* 131–142.

Crouter, A. C., Perry-Jenkins, M., Huston, T. L., & McHale, S. M. (1987). Processes underlying father involvement in dual-earner and single-earner families. *Developmental Psychology, 23,* 431–440.

Crown, W. H., & Longino, C. F., Jr. (1991). State and regional policy implications of elderly migration. *Journal of Aging and Social Policy, 3* (1/2), 185–207.

Cruikshank, D. P. (1990). Cardiovascular, pulmonary, renal, and hematologic diseases in pregnancy. In J. R. Scott (Ed.), *Danforth's obstetrics and gynecology* (6th ed.). Philadelphia: Lippincott.

Crystal, S., & Shea, D. (1990). Cumulative advantage, cumulative disadvantage, and inequality among elderly people. *Gerontologist, 30* (4), 437–443.

Culkin, M., Morris, J. R., & Helburn, S. W. (1991). Quality and the true cost of child care. *Journal of Social Issues, 47* (2), 71–86.

Cumming, E., & Henry, W. E. (1961). *Growing old.* New York: Basic Books.

Cummings, E. M. (1989). Children's responses to different forms of expression of anger between adults. *Child Development, 60* (6), 1392–1404.

Cummings, J. L. (1990). Clinical diagnosis of Alzheimer's disease. In J. L. Cummings & B. L. Miller (Eds.), *Alzheimer's disease: Treatment and long-term management.* New York: Marcel Dekker.

Cummings, J. L., & Miller, B. L. (Eds.). (1990). *Alzheimer's disease: Treatment and long-term management.* New York: Marcel Dekker.

Cuneo, K. M., & Welsh, M. C. (1992). Perception in young children: Developmental and neuropsychological perspectives. *Child Study Journal, 22* (2), 73–92.

Cunningham, F. G., MacDonald, P. C., & Gant, N. F. (1989). *Williams obstetrics* (18th ed.). Norwalk, CT: Appleton and Lange.

Cunningham, W. R. (1988, August). *Perspectives on aging and abilities.* Paper presented at the American Psychological Association, Atlanta, GA.

Cunningham, W. R. (1989). Intellectual abilities and age. In V. L. Bengston & K. W. Schaie (Eds.), *The course of later life: Research and reflections.* New York: Springer.

Cunningham, W. R., & Haman, K. (1992). Intellectual functioning in relation to mental health. In J. E. Birren, R. B. Sloane, & G. D. Cohen (Eds.), *Handbook of mental health and aging* (2nd ed.). San Diego: Harcourt Brace Jovanovich.

Curran, D. (1984). *Traits of a healthy family.* Minneapolis: Winston Press.

Cutrona, C. E. (1991). Social support and chronic mental illness among the elderly. In E. Light & B. D. Lebowitz (Eds.), *The elderly with chronic mental illness.* New York: Springer.

Cvetkovitch, G., & Grote, B. (1983). Adolescent development and teenage fertility. In D. Byrne & W. A. Fisher (Eds.), *Adolescents, sex, and contraception.* New York: McGraw-Hill.

Dale, A., & Glover, J. (1990). *An analysis of women's employment patterns in the UK, France, and the USA: The value of survey based comparisons.* London: Employment Department.

Dale, P. (1976). *Language development: Structure and function* (2nd ed.). New York: Holt, Rinehart and Winston.

Daniel, B. M., & Lee, D. N. (1990). Development of looking with head and eyes. *Journal of Experimental Child Psychology, 50* (2), 200–216.

Daniel, H., O'Brien, K. F., McCabe, R. B., & Quinter, V. E. (1985). Values in mate selection: A 1984 campus survey. *College Student Journal, 19,* 44–50.

Danner, F. (1989). Cognitive development in adolescence. In J. Worrell & F. Danner (Eds.), *The adolescent as decision-maker.* New York: Academic Press.

Danziger, S. K., & Wertz, D. C. (1989). Sociological and social psychological aspects of reproduction. In K. McKinney & S. Sprecher (Eds.), *Human sexuality: The societal and interpersonal context.* Norwood, NJ: Ablex.

Darling, C. A., & Mabe, A. R. (1989). Analyzing ethical issues in sexual relationships. *Journal of Sex Education and Therapy, 15,* 126–144.

Darling-Fisher, C. S., & Tiedje, L. B. (1990). The impact of maternal employment characteristics on fathers' participation in child care. *Family Relations, 39,* 20–26.

Darmody, J. P. (1991). The adolescent personality, formal reasoning, and values. *Adolescence, 26* (103), 731–742.

Dart, S. N. (1992). Narrative style in the two languages of a bilingual child. *Journal of Child Language, 19* (2), 367–387.

Dash, L. (1989). *When children want children: The urban crisis of teenage childbearing.* New York: William Morrow.

David, D. (1989). Reminiscence, adaptation, and social context in old age. *International Journal of Aging and Human Development, 30* (3), 175–188.

Davidson, H. A., & O'Connor, B. P. (1990). Perceived control and acceptance of the decision to enter a nursing home as predictors of adjustment. *International Journal of Aging and Human Development, 31* (4), 307–318.

Davidson, J. K., & Moore, N. B. (1992). *Marriage and family.* Dubuque, IA: Wm. C. Brown.

Davidson, P. M., White, P. N., Smith, D. J., & Poppen, W. A. (1989). Content and intensity of fears in middle childhood among rural and urban boys and girls. *Journal of Genetic Psychology, 150,* 51–58.

Davis, D. M. (1990). Portrayals of women in prime-time network television: Some demographic characteristics. *Sex Roles, 23,* 325–332.

Davis, L. K., & Rosen, S. L. (1986). Cesarean section. In B. P. Sacks & D. Acker (Eds.), *Clinical obstetrics: A public health perspective.* Littleton, MA: PSG.

Davis, R. A. (1989). Teenage pregnancy: A theoretical analysis of a social problem. *Adolescence, 24,* 19–28.

Day, A. T. (1991). *Remarkable survivors: Insights into successful aging among women.* Lanham, MD: Urban Institute Press.

Day, F., & Jackson, C. (1991). How to reach military retirees. *American Demographics, 13* (4), 40–44.

Dean, A. (1992). The influence of living alone on depression in elderly persons. *Journal of Aging and Health, 4* (1), 3–18.

Deane, B. (1985, April). When your parents need help. *Ladies Home Journal,* pp. 74–82.

Deane, B. (1989). *Caring for your aging parents: When love is not enough.* Colorado Springs, CO: Navpress.

DeBell, C. S., & Harless, D. K. (1992). B. F. Skinner: Myth and misperception. *Teaching of Psychology, 19,* 68–73.

Deci, E. L., & Ryan, R. M. (1982). Curiosity and self-directed learning: The role of motivation in education. In L. G. Katz (Ed.), *Current topics in early childhood education.* Norwood, NJ: Ablex.

de Cooke, P. A. (1992). Children's understanding of indebtedness as a feature of reciprocal help exchanges between peers. *Developmental Psychology, 28* (5), 948–954.

DeCosta, S. B. (1991). Head start-late start: Retrieving education and identity. *Educational Gerontology, 17* (2), 123–139.

Deevey, S. (1990). Older lesbian women: An invisible minority. *Journal of Gerontological Nursing, 16* (5), 35–39.

deJong, M. L. (1992). Attachment, individuation, and risk of suicide in late adolescence. *Journal of Youth and Adolescence, 21,* 357–373.

Dekovic, M., & Janssens, J. M. (1992). Parents' child-rearing style and child's sociometric status. *Developmental Psychology, 28* (5), 925–932.

Delafuente, J. C. (1990). Senescence of the immune system: Nutritional and pharmacologic modulation. *Journal of Geriatric Drug Therapy, 4* (3), 7–27.

DeLamater, J. (1981). The social control of sexuality. *Annual Review of Sociology, 7,* 76–89.

DeLamater, J. (1989). The social control of human sexuality. In K. McKinney & S. Sprecher (Eds.), *Human sexuality: The societal and interpersonal context.* Norwood, NJ: Ablex.

DeLeo, D., & Diekstra, R. F. (1990). *Depression and suicide in late life.* Lewiston, NY: Hogrefe and Huber.

DeLoache, J. S. (1991). Symbolic functioning in very young children: Understanding of pictures and models. *Child Development, 62* (4), 736–752.

Demo, D. H., & Adcock, A. C. (1988). The impact of divorce on children. *Journal of Marriage and the Family, 50,* 619–648.

Demorest, A., Silberstein, L., & Gardner, H. (1981, April). *From understatement to hyperbole: Recognizing nonliteral language and its intent.* Paper presented at the meetings of the Society for Research in Child Development, Boston.

Denham, S. A. (1990). Emotional and behavioral predictors of preschool peer ratings. *Child Development, 61* (4), 1145–1152.

Denham, S. A., Cook, M., & Zoller, D. (1992). "Baby looks *very* sad": Implications of conversations about feelings between mother and preschooler. *British Journal of Developmental Psychology, 10* (3), 301–315.

Denham, S. A., Zahn-Waxler, C., Cummings, E. M., & Iannotti, R. J. (1991). Social competence in young children's peer relations: Patterns of development and change. *Child Psychiatry and Human Development, 22* (1), 29–44.

Denham, S. A., & Zoller, D. (1991). "When my hamster died, I cried": Preschoolers' attributions of the causes of emotions. *Journal of Genetic Psychology, 152* (3), 371–373.

Dent, C., & Rosenberg, L. (1990). Visual and verbal metaphors: Developmental interactions. *Child Development, 61* (4), 983–994.

Derlega, V. J. (1984). Self-disclosure and intimate relationships. In V. J. Derlega (Ed.), *Community, intimacy, and close relationships.* New York: Academic Press.

D'Errico, M. G., & Elmore, A. (1991). Are self-determined divorce and child custody agreements really better? *Family and Conciliation Courts Review, 29* (2), 104–113.

DeSpelder, L., & Strickland, A. L. (1992). *The last dance: Encountering death and dying* (3rd ed.). Palo Alto, CA: Mayfield.

Detmer, C. M., & Lamberti, J. W. (1991). Family grief. *Death Studies, 15* (4), 363–374.

deVries, H. A. (1983). Physiology of exercise and aging. In D. S. Woodruff & J. E. Birren (Eds.), *Aging: Scientific perspectives and social issues* (2nd ed.). Monterey, CA: Brooks/Cole.

Devroey, P. (1989). Zygote intrafallopian transfer as a successful treatment for unexplained infertility. *Fertility and Sterility, 52* (2), 246–256.

DeYoung, M. (1982). *The sexual victimization of children.* Jefferson, NC: McFarland.

Dhingra, U., & Rabins, P. V. (1991). Mania in the elderly: A 5–7 year follow-up. *Journal of the American Geriatrics Society, 39* (6), 581–583.

Diamond, E. E. (1988). Women's occupational plans and decisions: An introduction. In B. A. Gutek (Ed.), *Applied psychology: An international review.* Beverly Hills, CA: Sage.

Dickie, J. R., & Gerber, S. C. (1980). Training in social competence: The effects on mothers, fathers, and infants. *Child Development, 51* (3), 1248–1251.

Dickinson, G. E., & Leming, M. R. (1990). *Understanding families: Diversity, continuity, and change.* Boston: Allyn & Bacon.

DiClemente, R. J. (1990). The emergence of adolescents as a risk group for human immunodeficiency virus infection. *Journal of Adolescent Research, 5,* 7–17.

Dietz, M. (1991). Stressors and coping mechanisms of older rural women. In A. Bushy (Ed.), *Rural nursing* (Vol. 1). Newbury Park, CA: Sage.

Dileo, J. H. (1980). Graphic activity of young children: Development and creativity. In L. Lasky & R. Mukerji (Eds.), *Art: Basic for young children.* Washington, DC: National Association for the Education of Young Children.

Dileo, J. H. (1983). *Interpreting children's drawings.* New York: Brunner/Mazel.

Dion, K. K. (1985). Personality, gender, and the phenomenology of romantic love. In P. Shaver (Ed.), *Self, situations, and social behavior.* Beverly Hills, CA: Sage.

DiPietro, J. (1981). Rough and tumble play: A function of gender. *Developmental Psychology, 17,* 50–58.

Dippel, R. L., & Hutton, J. H. (1991). *Caring for the Alzheimer patient: A practical guide* (2nd ed.). Buffalo, NY: Prometheus Books.

Dittmann-Kohli, F., Lachman, M. E., Kliefl, R., & Baltes, P. B. (1991). Effects of cognitive training and testing on intellectual efficacy beliefs in elderly adults. *Journal of Gerontology, 46,* P162–P165.

Dixon, J. A., & Moore, C. F. (1990). The development of perspective taking: Understanding differences in information and weighting. *Child Development, 61* (5), 1502–1513.

Dixon, M. A. (1991). Alzheimer's disease: The victim and the family. In M. S. Harper (Ed.), *Management and care of the elderly: Psychosocial perspectives.* Newbury Park, CA: Sage.

Dodge, K. A., Cole, J. D., Pettit, G. S., & Price, J. M. (1990). Peer status and aggression in boys' groups: Developmental and contextual analyses. *Child Development, 61,* 1289–1309.

Doescher, S. M., & Sugawara, A. I. (1992). Impact of prosocial home and school-based interventions on preschool children's cooperative behavior. *Family Relations, 41,* 200–204.

Doka, K. J. (1992). The monkey's paw: The role of inheritance in the resolution of grief. *Death Studies, 16,* 45–58.

Dole, P. (1984). Sex development in adolescence. In J. M. Swanson & K. A. Forrest (Eds.), *Men's reproductive health.* New York: Springer.

Donohugh, D. (1981). *The middle years.* Philadelphia: Saunders.

Donowitz, L. G. (Ed.). (1991). *Infection control in the child care center and preschool.* Baltimore: Williams and Wilkins.

Dooley, S., & Frankel, B. G. (1990). Improving attitudes toward elderly people: Evaluation of an intervention program for adolescents. *Canadian Journal on Aging, 9* (4), 400–409.

Doty, R. L. (1989). The influence of age and age-related diseases on olfactory function. In C. Murphy, W. S. Cain, & D. M. Hegsted (Eds.), *Nutrition and the chemical senses in aging: Recent advances and current research needs.* New York: Annals of the New York Academy of Sciences.

Douglas, J. D., & Atwell, F. C. (1988). *Love, intimacy, and sex.* Beverly Hills, CA: Sage.

Dowd, J. J., & Bengston, V. L. (1978). Aging in minority populations: An examination of the double jeopardy hypothesis. *Journal of Gerontology, 33,* 427–436.

Dowdy, C. A., Smith, T. E., & Nowell, C. H. (1992). Learning disabilities and vocational rehabilitation. *Journal of Learning Disabilities, 25* (7), 442–447.

Downs, A. C., & Langlois, J. H. (1988). Sex typing: Construct and measurement issues. *Sex Roles, 18*, 87–100.

Downs, W. R., & Rose, S. R. (1991). The relationship of adolescent peer groups to the incidence of psychosocial problems. *Adolescence, 26* (102), 473–492.

Doyle, A., Doehring, P., Tessier, O., & de Lorimier, S. (1992). Transitions in children's play: A sequential analysis of states preceding and following social pretense. *Developmental Psychology, 28* (1), 137–144.

Doyle, D. (1991). Palliative care education and training in the United Kingdom: A review. *Death Studies, 15*, 95–103.

Doyle, J. (1985). *Sex and gender.* Dubuque, IA: Wm. C. Brown.

Drass, K. (1986). The effect of gender identity on conversation. *Social Psychology Quarterly, 49*, 294–301.

Dryfoos, J. G. (1990). *Adolescents at risk: Prevalence and prevention.* New York: Oxford University Press.

Duck, S. (1991). *Human relationships.* Newbury Park, CA: Sage.

Duncan, P., Ritter, P. L., Dornbusch, S. M., Gross, R. T., & Carlsmith, J. M. (1985). The effects of pubertal timing on body image, school behavior and deviance. *Journal of Youth and Adolescence, 14*, 227–235.

Dunlop, J., Manghelli, D., & Tolson, R. (1990). Older problem drinkers: A community treatment continuum. *Aging, 361*, 33–37.

Dunn, J. (1991). Young children's understanding of other people's feelings and beliefs: Individual differences and their antecedents. *Child Development, 62* (6), 1352–1366.

Dunn, J., & McGuire, S. (1992). Sibling and peer relationships in childhood. *Journal of Child Psychology and Psychiatry and Allied Disciplines, 33* (1), 67–105.

Dunn, J., & Shatz, M. (1989). Becoming a conversationalist despite (or because of) having an older sibling. *Child Development, 60*, 399–410.

Dunn, L. J. (1990). Cesarean section and other obstetric operations. In J. R. Scott (Ed.), *Danforth's obstetrics and gynecology* (6th ed.). Philadelphia: Lippincott.

Dunn, P. C., Ryan, I. J., & O'Brien, K. (1988). College students' level of acceptability of the new medical science of conception and problems of infertility. *Journal of Sex Research, 24*, 282–287.

Durkin, K. (1984). Children's account of sex-role stereotypes in television. *Communication Research, 11*, 341–362.

Durkin, K. (1985). Television and sex-role acquisition. *British Journal of Social Psychology, 24*, 101–113.

Durlak, J. A., & Riesenberg, L. A. (1991). The impact of death education. *Death Studies, 15* (1), 39–58.

Durrett, M. E., Otaki, M., & Richards, P. (1984). Attachment and the mother's perception of help from the father. *International Journal of Behavioral Development, 7*, 167–176.

Duryea, E. J., & Glover, J. A. (1982). A review of the research on reflection and impulsivity in children. *Genetic Psychology Monographs, 106* (2), 217–237.

Dziurawiec, S., & Deregowski, J. B. (1992). "Twisted perspective" in young children's drawings. *British Journal of Developmental Psychology, 10* (1), 35–49.

Earnshaw-Smith, E. (1982). Emotional pain in dying patients and their families. *Nursing Times, 78* (44), 1865–1867.

East, P. L. (1991). The parent-child relationships of withdrawn, aggressive, and sociable children: Child and parent perspectives. *Merrill-Palmer Quarterly, 37* (3), 425–444.

East, P. L., & Rook, K. S. (1992). Compensatory patterns of support among children's peer relationships: A test using school friends, nonschool friends, and siblings. *Developmental Psychology, 28* (1), 163–172.

Easterbrooks, M. A., & Emde, R. N. (1988). Marital and parent-child relationships: The role of affect in the family system. In R. A. Hinde & J. Stevenson-Hinde (Eds.), *Relationships within families: Mutual influences.* New York: Oxford University Press.

Eaton, Y. M., Mitchell, M. L., & Jolley, J. A. (1991). Gender differences in the development of relationships during late adolescence. *Adolescence, 26* (103), 565–568.

Ebeling, K. S., & Gelman, S. A. (1988). Coordination of size standards by young children. *Child Development, 59*, 888–896.

Ebersole, P., & Hess, P. (1990). *Toward healthy aging: Human needs and nursing response* (3rd ed.) St. Louis: Mosby.

Eby, J. W. (1992). *Reflective planning, teaching, and evaluation for the elementary school.* New York: Macmillan.

Eccles, J. S., & Midgley, C. (1990). Changes in academic motivation and self-perception during early adolescence. In R. Montemayor, G. R. Adams, & T. P. Gullotta (Eds.), *From childhood to adolescence: A transitional period?* Newbury Park, CA: Sage.

Eckenrode, J., Laird, M., & Doris, J. (1993). School performance and disciplinary problems among abused and neglected children. *Developmental Psychology, 29* (1), 53–62.

Edelson, E. (1991). *Aging: The encyclopedia of health.* New York: Chelsea House.

Edwards, C. P. (1982). Moral development in comparative cultural perspective. In D. A. Wagner & H. W. Stevenson (Eds.), *Cultural perspectives on child development.* San Francisco: Freeman.

Edwards, J. K. (1991). Are there clinical and epidemiological differences between familial and non-familial Alzheimer's disease? *Journal of the American Geriatrics Society, 39* (5) 477–483.

Edwards, J. N., & Demo, D. H. (Eds.). (1991). *Marriage and family in transition.* Boston: Allyn & Bacon.

Edwards, J. R., & Baglioni, A. J.(1991). Relationship between Type A behavior pattern and mental and physical symptoms: A comparison of global and component measures. *Journal of Applied Psychology, 76* (5), 643–653.

Egeland, B. (1989, January 12). *Secure attachment in infancy and competence in the third grade.* Paper presented at the meeting of the American Association for the Advancement of Science, San Francisco.

Eisenberg, A., Murkoff, H. E., & Hathaway, S. E. (1991). *What to expect when you're expecting* (rev. ed.). New York: Workman.

Eisenberg, N., Fabes, R. A., Carlo, G., & Troyer, D. (1992). The relations of maternal practices and characteristics to children's vicarious emotional responsiveness. *Child Development, 63* (3), 583–602.

Eisenberg, N., Hertz-Lazarowitz, R., & Fuchs, I. (1990). Prosocial moral judgment in Israeli kibbutz and city children: A longitudinal study. *Merrill-Palmer Quarterly, 36* (2), 273–285.

Eisenberg, N., Miller, P. A., Shell, R., & McNalley, S. (1991). Prosocial development in adolescence: A longitudinal study. *Developmental Psychology, 27* (5), 849–857.

Eisenson, J. (1991). *Growing up while growing older.* Palo Alto, CA: Pacific Books.

Ekerdt, D. J., & Vinick, B. H. (1991). Marital complaints in husband-working and husband-retired couples. *Research on Aging, 13* (3), 364–382.

Ekman, P. (1992). Are there basic emotions? *Psychological Review, 99* (3), 550–553.

Elder, G. H., Jr. (1977). Family history and the life course. *Journal of Family History, 2*, 279–304.

Elder, G. H., Jr. (1991). Making the best of life: Perspectives on lives, times, and aging. *Generations, 15* (1), 12–17.

Elder, G. H., Jr. (1992). Families under economic pressure. *Journal of Family Issues, 13* (1), 3–37.

Elias, M. (1990, March 12). Women weighing the benefits and risks of estrogen therapy. *Norwich Bulletin*, p. C5.

Elias, M. F., Robbins, M. A., Schultz, N. R., & Pierce, T. W. (1990). Is blood pressure an important variable in research on aging and neuropsychological test performance? *Journal of Gerontology, 45*, P128–P135.

Elkind, D. (1967). Egocentrism in adolescence. *Child Development, 38*, 1025–1034.

Elkind, D. (1971). *A sympathetic understanding of the child: Six to sixteen.* Boston: Allyn & Bacon.

Elkind, D. (1978). Understanding the young adolescent. *Adolescence, 13*, 127–134.

Elkind, D. (1980). Strategic interactions in early adolescence. In J. Adelson (Ed.), *Handbook of adolescent psychology.* New York: Wiley.

Elkind, D. (1981). *Children and adolescents: Interpretative essays on Jean Piaget* (3rd ed.). New York: Oxford University Press.

Elkind, D. (1984). *All grown up and no place to go: Teenagers in crisis.* Reading, MA: Addison-Wesley.

Elkind, D. (1985). Egocentrism redux. *Developmental Review, 5*, 218–226.

Elkind, D. (1990). *Grandparenting: Understanding today's children.* Glenview, IL: Scott, Foresman.

Elkind, D., & Bowen, R. (1979). Imaginary audience behavior in children and adolescents. *Developmental Psychology, 15*, 38–44.

Ellett, L. (1993). Instructional practices in mainstreamed secondary classrooms. *Journal of Learning Disabilities, 2* (1), 57–64.

Elliot, B. J., & Richards, M. P. (1991). Children and divorce: Educational performance and behavior before and after parental separation. *International Journal of Law and the Family, 5* (3), 258–276.

Elliot, D. S., Huizinga, D., & Menard, S. (1989). *Multiple problem youth: Delinquency, substance abuse, and mental health problems.* New York: Springer-Verlag.

Elloy, D., & Anderson, K. S. (1991). An exploratory analysis of burnout across dual-income and single-income families. *Journal of Health and Human Resources Administration, 13* (4), 457–469.

Emde, R. N., Biringen, Z., Clyman, R. B., & Oppenheim, D. (1991). The moral self of infancy: Affective core and procedural knowledge. *Developmental Review, 11* (3), 251–270.

Endres, J. B., & Rockwell, R. E. (1990). *Food, nutrition, and the young child* (3rd ed.). New York: Macmillan.

Enlund, H. (1990). Problems with drug use among elderly men. *Journal of Geriatric Drug Therapy, 4* (4), 81–94.

Erber, J. T., Rothberg, S. T., & Szuchman, L. T. (1991). Appraisal of everyday memory failures by middle-aged adults. *Educational Gerontology, 17* (1), 63–72.

Ericsson, K. A. (1990). Peak performance and age: An examination of peak performance in sports. In P. B. Baltes & M. M. Baltes (Eds.), *Successful aging: Perspectives from the behavioral sciences.* New York: Cambridge University Press.

Erikson, E. H. (1950). *Childhood and society.* New York: Norton.

Erikson, E. H. (1958). *Young man Luther.* New York: Norton.

Erikson, E. H. (1959). Identity and the life cycle. *Psychological Issues Monograph, 1.*

Erikson, E. H. (1963). *Childhood and society.* New York: Norton.

Erikson, E. H. (1968a). *Life cycle.* In *International Encyclopedia of the Social Sciences* (Vol. 9), 286–292. New York: Free Press.

Erikson, E. H. (1968b). *Identity, youth and crisis.* New York: Norton.

Erikson, E. H. (1969). *Gandhi's truth.* New York: Norton.

Erikson, E. H. (Ed.). (1978). *Adulthood.* New York: Norton.

Erikson, E. H. (1980). *Identity and the life cycle.* New York: Norton.

Erikson, E. H. (1982). *The life cycle completed: A review.* New York: Norton.

Erikson, E., Erikson, J. M., & Kivnick, H. Q. (1986). *Vital involvement in old age: The experience of old age in our time.* New York: Norton.

Eshleman, J. R. (1991). *The family: An introduction* (6th ed.). Boston: Allyn & Bacon.

Esman, A. H. (1991). *Adolescence and culture.* New York: Columbia University Press.

Essa, E. (1990). *Practical guide to solving preschool behavior problems* (2nd ed.). Albany, NY: Delmar.

Essa, E. (1992). *Introduction to early childhood education.* Albany, NY: Delmar.

Esty, E. T., & Fisch, S. M. (1991, April). *SQUARE ONE TV: Using television to enhance children's problem solving.* Paper presented at the biennial meeting of the Society for Research in Child Development, Seattle.

Etaugh, C., Collins, G., & Gerson, A. (1975). Reinforcement of sex-typed behaviors of two-year-old children in a nursery school setting. *Developmental Psychology, 11,* 255–278.

Evans, D. A. (1990). Estimated prevalence of Alzheimer's disease in the United States. *Milbank Quarterly, 68* (2), 267–289.

Evans, G., & Carrere, S. (1991). Traffic congestion, perceived control, and psychophysiological stress among urban bus drivers. *Journal of Applied Psychology, 76* (5), 658–663.

Evans, G. W., & Lewis, M. A. (1990). The role of adaptive processes in intellectual functioning among older adults. In J. Rodin, C. Schooler, & K. W. Schaie, (Eds.), *Self-directedness: Cause and effects throughout the life course.* Hillsdale, NJ: Erlbaum.

Everts, J. F. (1990). Critical issues in the development of Toughlove as a self-help program in Australia: An empirical investigation. *Australian Journal of Marriage and Family, 11* (3), 158–164.

Eyre, D. R. (1980). Collagen: Molecular diversity in the body's protein scaffold. *Science, 20,* 1315–1322.

Fabes, R. A., & Eisenberg, N. (1992). Young children's coping with interpersonal anger. *Child Development, 63* (1), 116–128.

Fabes, R. A., Wilson, P., & Christopher, F. S. (1989). A time to reexamine the role of television in family life. *Family Relations, 38,* 337–341.

Fagot, B. I., & Hagan, R. (1991). Observations of parent reaction to sex-stereotyped behaviors: Age and sex effects. *Child Development, 62* (3), 617–628.

Fagot, B. I., & Kavanaugh, K. (1990). The prediction of antisocial behavior from avoidant attachment classification. *Child Development, 61* (3), 864–873.

Fagot, B. I., & Kronsberg, S. J. (1982). Sex differences: Biological and social factors influencing the behavior of young boys and girls. In S. G. Moore & S. G. Cooper (Eds.), *The young child: Reviews of research* (Vol. 3). Washington, DC: National Association for the Education of Young Children.

Faller, K. C. (1990). *Understanding child sexual maltreatment.* Newbury Park, CA: Sage.

Fantuzzo, J. W. (1990). Behavioral treatment of the victims of child abuse and neglect. *Behavior Modification, 14* (3), 316–339.

Farber, M. E. (1990). When floaters signal an eye emergency: How to tell. *Senior Patient, 2* (11), 50–53.

Farrar, M. J., & Goodman, G. S. (1992). Developmental changes in event memory. *Child Development, 63* (1), 173–187.

Farrar, M. J., Raney, G. E., & Boyer, M. E. (1992). Knowledge, concepts, and inferences in childhood. *Child Development, 63* (3), 673–691.

Farren, C. J. (1991). Finding meaning: An alternative paradigm for Alzheimer's disease family caregivers. *Gerontologist, 31* (4), 483–489.

Faulkenberry, J. R., Murray, V., Arnold, J., & Johnson, W. (1987). Coital behaviors, attitudes, and knowledge of students who experience early coitus. *Adolescence, 22,* 321–332.

Faulkner, A. O. (1991). Culture, chronic mental illness, and the aged: Research issues and directions. In E. Light & B. D. Lebowitz (Eds.), *The elderly with chronic mental illness.* New York: Springer.

Fawcett, J. T. (1988). The value of children and the transition to parenthood. In R. Palkovitz & M. B. Sussman (Eds.), *Transitions to parenthood.* New York: Haworth Press.

Feagans, L. V., Merriwether, A. M., & Haldane, D. (1991). Goodness of fit in the home: Its relationship to school behavior and achievement in children with learning disabilities. *Journal of Learning Disabilities, 24* (7), 413–420.

Feather, N. T. (1984). Masculinity, femininity, psychological androgyny, and the structure of values. *Journal of Personality and Social Psychology, 47,* 604–620.

Featherman, D. L., Smith, J., & Peterson, J. G. (1990). Successful aging in a post-retired society. In P. B. Baltes & M. M. Baltes (Eds.), *Successful aging: Perspectives from the behavioral sciences.* New York: Cambridge University Press.

Featherstone, M., & Hepworth, M. (1990). Images of aging. In J. Bond & P. Coleman (Eds.), *Aging in society: An introduction to social gerontology.* Newbury Park, CA: Sage.

Federal Bureau of Investigation. (1992). *Uniform crime reports for the United States, 1991.* Washington, DC: U.S. Government Printing Office.

Feeney, J. A., & Noller, P. (1990). Attachment style as a predictor of adult romantic relationships. *Journal of Personality and Social Psychology, 58,* 281–291.

Feinberg, J. L. (1990). Nonpharmacologic alternatives to chemical restraints. *Consultant Pharmacist, 5* (7), 370–371.

Feinbloom, R. I. (1993). *Pregnancy, birth, and the early months* (2nd ed.). Reading, MA: Addison-Wesley.

Feinbloom, R. I., & Forman, B. Y. (1987). *Pregnancy, birth, and the early months.* Reading, MA: Addison-Wesley.

Feinstein, D., & Mayo, P. E. (1990). *Rituals for living and dying: From life's wounds to spiritual awakening.* San Francisco: HarperCollins.

Feldman, S. S., & Elliott, G.R. (1990). *At the threshold: The developing adolescent.* Cambridge, MA: Harvard University Press.

Feldman, S. S., & Gehring, T. M. (1988). Changing perceptions of family cohesion and power across adolescence. *Child Development, 59,* 1034–1045.

Felsenfeld, G. (1985). DNA. *Scientific American, 253* (4), 58–68.

Fenigsen, R. (1990). Euthanasia: A breach of trust. *Senior Patient, 2* (7), 52–54.

Fenzel, L. M., Blyth, D. A., & Simmons, R. G. (1991). Secondary school transitions. In R. M. Lerner, A. C. Petersen, & J. Brooks-Gunn (Eds.), *The encyclopedia of adolescence.* New York: Garland.

Ferguson, T. J., Stegge, H., & Damhuis, I. (1991). Children's understanding of guilt and shame. *Child Development, 62* (4), 827–839.

Fergusson, D. M., Horwood, L. J., & Shannon, F. T. (1984). A proportional hazards model of family breakdown. *Journal of Marriage and the Family, 46,* 539–549.

Ferrandez, A. M., Pailhous, J., & Durup, M. (1990). Slowness in elderly gait. *Experimental Aging Research, 16* (2), 78–89.

Ferree, M. M. (1991). The gender division of labor in two-earner marriages: Dimensions of variability and change. *Journal of Family Issues, 12* (2), 158–180.

Field, D., & Millsap, R. E. (1991). Personality in advanced old age: Continuity or change? *Journal of Gerontology: Psychological Sciences, 46* (6), P299–P308.

Fiese, B. H. (1990). Playful relationships: A contextual analysis of mother-toddler interaction and symbolic play. *Child Development, 61* (5), 1648–1656.

Finkel, S. I., & Yesavage, J. A. (1989). Learning mnemonics: A preliminary evaluation of a computer-aided instruction package for the elderly. *Experimental Aging Research, 15* (4), 199–201.

Finkelhor, D. (1984). *Child sexual abuse: New theory and research.* New York: Free Press.

Finkelhor, D. (1988). The trauma of child sexual abuse. In G. E. Wyatt & G. J. Powell (Eds.), *Lasting effects of child sexual abuse.* Beverly Hills, CA: Sage.

Finkelhor, D. (1990). Sexual abuse in a national survey of adult men and women: Prevalence, characteristics, and risk factors. *Child Abuse and Neglect, 14,* 19–28.

Finkelstein, N., & Haskins, R. (1983). Kindergarten children prefer same-color peers. *Child Development, 54* (2), 502–508.

Finn, S. C. (1990). Nutrition in home care. *Caring, 9* (10), 4–6.

Finn, S. E. (1986). Stability of personality self-ratings over 30 years: Evidence for an age/cohort interaction. *Journal of Personality and Social Psychology, 50,* 813–818.

Firth-Cozens, J. (1992). Why me? A case study of the process of perceived occupational stress. *Human Relations, 45* (2), 131–141.

Fischer, K. W. (1983). Illuminating the processes of moral development. *Monographs of the Society for Research in Child Development,* 48(1–2, Serial No. 200), 97–107.

Fish, S. (1990). *Alzheimer's: Caring for your loved one, caring for yourself.* Batavia, IL: Lion.

Fisher, C. B., & Brone, R. J. (1991). Adolescent eating disorders. In R. M. Lerner, A. C. Petersen, & J. Brooks-Gunn (Eds.), *The encyclopedia of adolescence.* New York: Garland.

Fitting, M., & Rabins, P. (1985). Men and women as caregivers. *Generations, 10* (1), 23–26.

Fitting, M., Rabins, P., Lucas, M. J., & Eastham, J. (1986). Caregivers for demented patients: A comparison of husbands and wives. *Gerontologist, 26,* 248–252.

Fitzpatrick, M. (1988). *Between husbands and wives: Communication in marriage.* Newbury Park, CA: Sage.

Fivush, R., Kuebli, J., & Clubb, P. A. (1992). The structure of events and event representations: A developmental analysis. *Child Development, 63* (1), 188–201.

Flavell, J. H. (1992). Cognitive development: Past, present, and future. *Developmental Psychology, 28* (6), 998–1005.

Flavell, J. H., Lindberg, N. A., Green, F. L., & Flavell, E. R. (1992). The development of children's understanding of the appearance-reality distinction between how people look and what they are really like. *Merrill-Palmer Quarterly, 38* (4), 513–524.

Fletcher, J. (1966). *Situation ethics: The new morality.* Philadelphia: Westminister.

Fligiel, S. E., Venkat, H., Gong, H., & Tashkin, D. P. (1988). Bronchial pathology in chronic marijuana smokers: A light and electron microscope study. *Journal of Psychoactive Drugs, 20,* 33–42.

Foelker, G. A. (1990). A community response to elder abuse. *Gerontologist 30* (4), 560–562.

Fogel, B. S., Gottlieb, G. L., & Furino, A. (1990). Minds at risk. In B. S. Fogel, A. Furino, & G. L. Gottlieb (Eds.), *Mental health policy for older Americans: Protecting minds at risk.* Washington, DC: American Psychiatric Press.

Fogel, C. I. (1990). Sexual health promotion. In C. I. Fogel & D. Lauver (Eds.), *Sexual health promotion.* Philadelphia: Saunders.

Fogel, C. I., Forker, J., & Welch, M. B. (1990). Sexual health care. In C. I. Fogel & D. Lauver (Eds.), *Sexual health promotion.* Philadelphia: Saunders.

Fogel, C. I., & Lauver, D. (Eds.). (1990). *Sexual health promotion.* Philadelphia: Saunders.

Folberg, J. (Ed.). (1991). *Joint custody and shared parenting* (2nd ed.). New York: Guilford Press.

Foley, C., & Pizer, H. F. (1990). *The stroke fact book* (rev. ed.). Golden Valley, MN: Courage Press.

Folstein, M. R. (1991). Dementia: Case ascertainment in a community survey. *Journal of Gerontology: Medical Sciences, 46* (4), M132–M138.

Food and Nutrition Board, National Research Council. (1989). *Recommended daily dietary allowances.* Washington, DC: National Academy Press.

Forrest, J. (1986). *Women ever pregnant before age twenty.* New York: Alan Guttmacher Institute.

Forrest, M. B., Forrest, C. B., & Forrest, R. (1990). *Nursing homes: The complete guide.* New York: Facts on File.

Fortinsky, R. H., & Hathaway, T. J. (1990). Information and service needs among active and former family caregivers of persons with Alzheimer's disease. *Gerontologist, 30* (5), 604–609.

Foster, P. (1983). *Activities and the well elderly.* New York: Haworth.

Fox, N. A., Kimmerly, N. L., & Schafer, W. D. (1991). Attachment to mother/attachment to father: A meta-analysis. *Child Development, 62* (1), 210–225.

Fox, N. A., Sutton, B., Aaron, N., & Luebering, A. (1989, April 26). *Infant temperament and attachment: A new look at an old issue.* Paper presented at the Society for Research in Child Development meeting, Kansas City.

Fox, S. W. (Ed.). (1984). *Individuality and determinism.* New York: Plenum.

Foy, S. S., & Mitchell, M. M. (1990). Factors contributing to learned helplessness in the institutionalized aged: A literature review. *Physical and Occupational Therapy in Geriatrics, 9* (2), 1–23.

Fozard, J. L. (1980). The time for remembering. In L. W. Poon (Ed.), *Aging in the 1980s: Psychological issues.* Washington, DC: American Psychological Association.

Fraboni, M., Saltstone, R., & Hughes, S. (1990). The Fraboni Scale of Ageism (FSA): An attempt at a more precise measure of ageism. *Canadian Journal on Aging, 9* (1), 56–66.

France, A. C. (1990). Psychology of aging: Stability and change in intelligence and personality. In K. F. Ferraro (Ed.), *Gerontology: Perspectives and issues.* New York: Springer.

Francis, D. (1990). The significance of work friends in late life. *Journal of Aging Studies, 4* (4), 405–424.

Francks, O. R. (1982). Scribbles? Yes, they are art. In J. F. Brown (Ed.), *Curriculum planning for young children.* Washington, DC: National Association for the Education of Young Children.

Frank, D. I. (1984). Counseling the infertile couple. *Journal of Psychosocial Nursing, 22,* 17–23.

Frank, E. S. (1991). Shame and guilt in eating disorders. *American Journal of Orthopsychiatry, 61* (2), 303–306.

Frankel, K. A., & Bates, J. E. (1990). Mother toddler problem solving: Antecedents in attachment, home behavior, and temperament. *Child Development, 61* (3), 810–819.

Franklin, D. (1988). Race, class, and adolescent pregnancy. *American Journal of Orthopsychiatry, 58,* 339–354.

Freedland, K. E. (1991). Depression in elderly parents with congestive heart failure. *Journal of Geriatric Psychiatry, 24* (1), 59–71.

Freedman, R. (1990). Family planning programs in the third world. *Annals of the American Association of Political and Social Science, 510,* 33–43.

Freeman, R. K. (1990, April). *Can we lower the cesarean birth rate?* Paper presented at the Tenth International Symposium on Perinatal Medicine and Obstetrical Ultrasound, Las Vegas, NV.

French, D. C. (1990). Heterogeneity of peer-rejected girls. *Child Development, 61,* 2028–2031.

French, D. C., & Stright, A. L. (1991). Emergent leadership in children's small groups. *Small Group Research, 22* (2), 187–199.

French, J., & Pena, S. (1991). Children's hero play of the 20th century: Changes resulting from television's influence. *Child Study Journal, 21* (2), 79–94.

Freud, A. (1958). Adolescence. *Psychoanalytic Study of the Child, 13,* 255–278.

Freud, S. (1905). *Three essays on the theory of sexuality.* London: Hogarth Press.

Freudenberg, N. (1992). AIDS and adolescents: Preparing for the second decade. *Family Life Educator, 11,* 16–18.

Freudenberger, H. J., & Richelson, G. (1980). *Burnout: The high cost of high achievement.* New York: Bantam.

Freund, L. S., Baker, L., & Sonnenschein, S. (1990). Developmental changes in strategic approaches to classification. *Journal of Experimental Child Psychology, 49* (3), 343–362.

Friedman, A. S., & Granick, S. (Eds.). (1990). *Family therapy for adolescent drug abuse.* Lexington, MA: Lexington Books.

Friedman, B. L. (1991). Social protection for retirees: The diminishing role of employers. *Journal of Aging and Social Policy, 3* (1/2), 21–39.

Friedman, H. A. (Ed.). (1990). *Personality and disease.* New York: Wiley.

Friedman, H. L. (1992). Changing patterns of adolescent sexual behavior: Consequences for health and development. *Journal of Adolescent Health, 13,* 345–350.

Friedman, M., & Rosenman, R. H. (1974). *Type A behavior and your heart.* New York: Knopf.

Friedman, W. J. (1991). The development of children's memory for the time of past events. *Child Development, 62* (1), 139–155.

Friedman, W. J., & Laycock, F. (1989). Children's analog and digital clock knowledge. *Child Development, 60,* 340–356.

Friedrich, W. N., Urquiza, A. J., & Beilke, R. (1986). Behavioral problems in sexually abused young children. *Journal of Pediatric Psychology, 11,* 47–57.

Friend, R. A. (1990). Older lesbian and homosexual people: A theory of successful aging. In J. A. Lee (Ed.), *Gay mid-life and maturity.* Binghamton, NY: Haworth Press.

Fries, J. F. (1990). Medical perspectives on successful aging. In P. B. Baltes & M. M. Baltes (Eds.), *Successful aging: Perspectives from the behavioral sciences.* New York: Cambridge University Press.

Fries, J. F. (1991). The workspan and the compression of morbidity. In A. H. Munnell (Ed.), *Retirement and public policy.* Proceedings of the Second Conference of the National Academy of Social Insurance. Dubuque, IA: Kendall/Hunt.

Fromuth, M. E. (1986). The relationship of childhood sexual abuse with later psychological and sexual adjustment in a sample of college women. *Child Abuse and Neglect, 10,* 5–15.

Frontera, W., & Meredith, C. N. (1989). Strength training in the elderly. In R. Harris & S. Harris (Eds.), *Physical activity, aging, and sports.* Albany, NY: Center for the Study of Aging.

Frost, J. (1992). *Play and playscapes*. Albany, NY: Delmar.

Fu, V., & Leach, D. J. (1980). Sex-role preferences among elementary school children in rural America. *Psychological Reports, 46*, 555–560.

Furman, W., & Buhrmester, D. (1992). Age and sex differences in perceptions of networks of personal relationships. *Child Development, 63* (1), 103–115.

Furstenberg, F. F., Jr. (1988). Child care after divorce and remarriage. In E. M. Hetherington & J. D. Arasteh (Eds.), *Impact of divorce, single-parenting, and stepparenting on children*. Hillsdale, NJ: Erlbaum.

Furstenberg, F. F., Jr., Brooks-Gunn, J., & Chase-Lansdale, L. (1989). Teenage pregnancy and childbearing. *American Psychologist, 44*, 313–320.

Furstenberg, F. F., Jr., & Cherlin, A. J. (1991). *Divided families: What happens to children when parents part*. Cambridge, MA: Harvard University Press.

Furstenberg, F. F., Jr., & Spanier, G. B. (1987). *Recycling the family: Remarriage after divorce* (updated ed.). Newbury Park, CA: Sage.

Gadow, S. (1991). Recovering the body in aging. In N. S. Jecker (Ed.), *Aging and ethics: Philosophical problems in gerontology. Contemporary issues in biomedicine, ethics, and society*. Clifton, NJ: Humana Press.

Gaines, D. (1991). *Teenage wasteland: Suburbia's dead end kids*. New York: Pantheon.

Galasko, D., Corey-Bloom, J., & Thal, L. J. (1991). Monitoring progress in Alzheimer's disease. *Journal of the American Geriatrics Society, 39* (9), 932–941.

Galassi, F. S. (1991). A life-review workshop for gay and lesbian elders. *Journal of Gerontological Social Work, 16* (1/2), 75–86.

Gallagher, D., & Thompson, L. W. (1989). Bereavement and adjustment disorders. In E. W. Busse & D. G. Blazer (Eds.), *Geriatric psychiatry*. Washington, DC: American Psychiatric Press.

Gamon, D., & O'Brien, K. (1991). *Your personal fitness survey: A guide to your current state of health*. North Hollywood, CA: Newcastle.

Gander, A. M. (1991). After the divorce: Familial factors that predict well-being for older and younger persons. *Journal of Divorce and Remarriage, 15* (1/2), 175–192.

Ganong, L. H., & Coleman, M. (1987). Do mutual children cement bonds in stepfamilies? *Journal of Marriage and the Family, 50*, 687–698.

Ganster, D. C., & Schaubroeck, J. (1991). Work stress and employee health. *Journal of Management, 17* (2), 235–271.

Garbarino, J. (1985). *Adolescent development: An ecological perspective*. Columbus, OH: Merrill.

Garbarino, J. (Ed.). (1992). *Children and families in the social environment*. New York: Aldine.

Garcia, E. E. (1980). Bilingualism in early childhood. *Young Children, 35* (4), 4–11.

Garcia-Coll, C. T., Halpern, L. F., Vohr, B. R., & Seifer, R. (1992). Stability and correlates of change of early temperament in preterm and full-term infants. *Infant Behavior and Development, 15* (2), 137–153.

Gardner, R. A. (1982). Joint custody is not for everyone. *Family Advocate, 5* (2), 7–9.

Garrard, J. (1991). The impact of nurse practitioners on the care of nursing home residents. In P. R. Katz, R. L. Kane, & M. D. Mezey (Eds.), *Advances in long term care*. New York: Springer.

Garrison, C. Z. (1991). The assessment of suicidal behavior in adolescents. *Suicide and Life-Threatening Behavior, 21* (3), 217–230.

Gartland, H. J., & Day, H. D. (1992). Parental conflict and male adolescent problem behavior. *Journal of Genetic Psychology, 153* (2), 201–209.

Garvey, C. (1990). *Play*. Cambridge, MA: Harvard University Press.

Garvin, V., Leber, D., & Kalter, N. (1991). Children of divorce: Predictors of change following preventative intervention. *American Journal of Orthopsychiatry, 61* (3), 438–447.

Gately, D. W., & Schwebel, A. I. (1991). The challenge model of children's adjustment to parental divorce: Explaining favorable postdivorce outcomes in children. *Journal of Family Psychology, 5* (1), 60–81.

Gathercole, S. E., Willis, C. S., Emslie, H., & Baddeley, A. D. (1992). Phonological memory and vocabulary development during the early school years: A longitudinal study. *Developmental Psychology, 28* (5), 887–898.

Gauvain, M. (1992). Social influences on the development of planning in advance and during action. *International Journal of Behavioral Development, 15* (3), 377–398.

Gavazzi, S. M., & Blumenkrantz, D. G. (1991). Teenage runaways: Treatment in the context of the family and beyond. *Journal of Family Psychotherapy, 2* (2), 15–30.

Gavazzi, S. M., & Sabatelli, R. M. (1990). Family system dynamics, the individuation process, and psychosocial development. *Journal of Adolescent Research, 5*, 500–519.

Gayle, H.D., Keeling, R. P., Garcia-Tunon, M., Kilbourne, B. W., Narkunas, J. P., Ingram, F. R., Rogers, M. F., & Curran, J. W. (1990). Prevalence of the human immunodeficiency virus among university students. *New England Journal of Medicine, 323* (22), 1538–1541.

Gearheart, B., Mullen, R. C., and Gearheart, C. J. (1993). *Exceptional individuals*. Pacific Grove, CA: Brooks/Cole.

Geary, D. D., Klosterman, I. H., & Adrales, K. (1990). Metamemory and academic achievement: Testing the validity of a group-administered metamemory battery. *Journal of Genetic Psychology, 151* (4), 439–450.

Geber, M., & Dean, R. F. (1957). The state of development of newborn African children. *Lancet, 272*, 1216–1219.

Gecas, V., & Seff, M. A. (1990). Families and adolescents: A review of the 1980s. *Journal of Marriage and the Family, 52* (4), 941–958.

Gee, E. M. (1991). The transition to grandmotherhood: A quantitative study. *Canadian Journal on Aging, 10* (3), 254–270.

Geen, R. G. (1981). Behavioral and physiological reactions to observed violence: Effects of prior exposure to aggressive stimuli. *Journal of Personality and Social Psychology, 40*, 868–875.

Gelfand, D. E., Bechill, W., & Chester, R. L. (1991). Core programs and services at senior centers. *Journal of Gerontological Social Work, 17* (1), 145–161.

Gelinas, D. J. (1983). The persisting effects of incest. *Psychiatry, 46*, 312–332.

Gelles, R. J., & Conte, J. R. (1990). Domestic violence and sexual abuse of children: A review of research in the eighties. *Journal of Marriage and the Family, 52* (4), 1045–1058.

Gelles, R. J., & Cornell, C. P. (1990). *Intimate violence in families*. Newbury Park, CA: Sage.

Gelles, R. J., & Straus, M. A. (1988). *Intimate violence*. New York: Simon & Schuster.

Gelman, R. (1991). Epigenetic foundations of knowledge structures: Initial and transcendent constructions. In S. Carey & R. Gelman (Eds.), *The epigenesis of the mind: Essays on biology and cognition*. Hillsdale, NJ: Erlbaum.

Gelman, S. A., & O'Reilly, A. W. (1988). Children's inductive influences within superordinate categories: The role of language and category structure. *Child Development, 59*, 876–887.

Gennari, C., & Montagnani, M. (1990). Role of nutrition in the pathogenesis of osteoporosis. In F. Fabris, L. Pernigotti, & E. Ferrario (Eds.), *Sedentary life and nutrition*. New York: Raven Press.

George, L. K. (1989). Stress, social support, and depression over the life course. In K. Markides & C. Cooper (Eds.), *Aging, stress, and health*. London: Wiley.

George, L. K. (1990). Gender, age, and psychiatric disorders. *Generations, 14* (3), 22–24.

George, L. K. (1992). Social factors and the onset and outcome of depression. In K. W. Schaie, D. Blazer, & J. S. House (Eds.), *Aging, health behaviors, and health outcomes*. Hillsdale, NJ: Erlbaum.

George, L. K., & Clipp, E. C. (1991). Subjective components of aging well. *Generations, 15* (1), 57–60.

George, L. K., & Maddox, G. L. (1990). Social and behavioral aspects of institutional care. In M. G. Ory & K. Bond (Eds.), *Aging and health care: Social science and policy perspectives*. New York and London: Routledge.

Gerard, L. (1991). Age deficits in retrieval: The fan effect. *Journal of Gerontology: Psychological Sciences, 46* (4), P131–P136.

Gerber, P. J., Ginsberg, R., and Reiff, H. B. (1992). Identifying alterable patterns in employment success for highly successful adults with learning disabilities. *Journal of Learning Disabilities, 25* (8), 475–487.

Gergen, M. (1990). Finished at 40: Women's development within the patriarchy. *Psychology of Women Quarterly, 14* (4), 471–493.

Gerike, A. E. (1990). On gray hair and oppressed brains. *Journal of Women and Aging, 2* (2), 35–46.

Gerritsen, J. C., Wolffensperger, E. W., & Van Den Heuve, W. J. (1990). Rural-urban differences in the utilization of care by the elderly. *Journal of Cross-Cultural Gerontology, 5* (2), 131–147.

Geschwind, N., & Bahan, P. (1982). Left-handedness: Association with immune disease, migraine, and developmental learning disorder. *Proceedings of the National Academy of Science USA, 79*, 5097–5100.

Gesser, G., Wong, P. T., & Reker, G. T. (1988). Death attitudes across the life-span: The development and validation of the Death Attitude Profile (DAP). *Omega: Journal of Death and Dying, 18*, 113–128.

Gestwicki, C. (1992). *Home, school, and community relations: A guide to working with parents* (2nd ed.). Albany, NY: Delmar.

Ghose, K. (1991). The need for a review journal of drug use and the elderly. *Drugs and Aging, 1* (1), 2–5.

Gianino, A., & Tronick, E. Z. (1988). The mutual regulation model: The infant's self and interactive regulation coping and defense. In T. Field, P. McCabe, & N. Schneiderman (Eds.), *Stress and coping*. Hillsdale, NJ: Erlbaum.

Gibbs, J. T. (1991). Black adolescents at risk: Approaches to prevention. In R. M. Lerner, A. C. Petersen, & J. Brocks-Gunn (Eds.), *The encyclopedia of adolescence*. New York: Garland.

Gibbs, J. T., & Moskowitz-Sweet, G. (1991). Clinical and cultural issues in the treatment of biracial and bicultural adolescents. *Families in Society, 72* (10), 579–592.

Giblin, P. T., Poland, M. L., Waller, J. B., Jr., & Ager, J. W. (1989). Correlates of neonatal morbidity: Maternal characteristics and family resources. *Journal of Genetic Psychology, 149*, 527–533.

Gibson, D., & Gibson, R. (1991). *The sandwich years: When your kids need friends and your parents need parenting*. Grand Rapids, MI: Baker Book House.

Gibson, M. J. (1984). Some societal responses to dementia in developed countries. *Ageing International, 11* (5), 11–16.

Gibson, R. C. (1987). Reconceptualizing retirement for black Americans. *Gerontologist, 27* (6), 691–698.

Gibson, R. C. (1991). Age-by-race differences in the health and functioning of elderly persons. *Journal of Aging and Health, 3* (3), 335–351.

Gieringer, D. H. (1988). Marijuana, driving, and accident safety. *Journal of Psychoactive Drugs, 20*, 93–102.

Gilbert, L. A. (1993). *Two careers/one family*. Newbury Park, CA: Sage.

Gilford, R. (1984). Contrasts in marital satisfaction throughout old age: An exchange theory analysis. *Journal of Gerontology, 39*, 325–333.

Gilgoff, A. (1988). *Home birth: An invitation and guide*. Westport, CT: Greenwood Press.

Gilgun, J. F., & Connor, T. M. (1990). Isolation and the adult male perpetrator of child sexual abuse: Clinical concerns. In A. L. Horton, B. Johnson, L. M. Roundy, & D. Williams (Eds.), *The incest perpetrator: A family member no one wants to treat*. Newbury Park, CA: Sage.

Gill, S., Stockard, J., Johnson, M., & Williams, S. (1987). Measuring gender differences: The expressive dimension and critique of the androgyny scales. *Sex Roles, 17*, 375–400.

Gilley, D. W. (1991). Predictors of behavioral disturbance in Alzheimer's disease. *Journal of Gerontology: Psychological Sciences, 46* (6), P362–P371.

Gilligan, C. (1982). *In a different voice*. Cambridge, MA: Harvard University Press.

Gilligan, C. (1990). Teaching Shakespeare's sister. In C. Gilligan, N. Lyons, & T. Hanmer (Eds.), *Making connections: The relational worlds of adolescent girls at Emma Willard School*. Cambridge, MA: Harvard University Press.

Gilligan, C., Brown, L. M., & Rogers, A. G. (1990). Psyche embedded: A place for body, relationships, and culture in personality theory. In A. I. Rabin, R. A. Zucker, R. A. Emmons, & S. Frannk (Eds.), *Studying persons and lives*. New York: Springer.

Giltinan, J. M. (1990). Using life review to facilitate self-actualization in elderly women. *Gerontology and Geriatrics Education, 10* (4), 75–83.

Ginsburg, H., & Opper, S. (1988). *Piaget's theory of intellectual development* (3rd ed.). Englewood Cliffs, NJ: Prentice Hall.

Ginzberg, E. (1951). *Occupational choice: An approach to general theory*. New York: Columbia University Press.

Glass, A. P. (1991). Nursing home quality: A framework for analysis. *Journal of Applied Gerontology, 10* (1), 5–18.

Glasser, B. G., & Strauss, A. (1968). *Time for dying*. New York: Macmillan.

Glazer, J. I. (1991). *Literature for young children* (3rd ed.). New York: Macmillan.

Gleason, J. B. (1993). *The development of language* (3rd ed.). New York: Macmillan.

Glezer, H. (1991). Cycles of care: Support and care between generations. *Family Matters, 30*, 44–46.

Glick, H. R. (1991). The right-to-die: State policy making and the elderly. *Journal of Aging Studies, 5* (3), 283–307.

Glick, P. C. (1984). How American families are changing. *American Demographics, 6*, 21–25.

Glick, P. C. (1988). Fifty years of family demography: A record of social change. *Journal of Marriage and the Family, 50*, 861–873.

Glick, P. C. (1989). Remarried families, stepfamilies, and stepchildren: A brief demographic profile. *Family Relations, 38*, 24–27.

Glick, P. C. (1990). American families: As they are and were. *Sociology and Social Research, 74*, 139–145.

Glick, P. C., & Spanier, G. (1980). Married and unmarried cohabitation in the United States. *Journal of Marriage and the Family, 42*, 19–30.

Glover, J., Ronning, R., & Bruning, R. (1990). *Cognitive psychology for teachers*. New York: Macmillan.

Gochman, D. S., & Bonham, G. S. (1990). The social structure of the hospice decision. *Hospice Journal, 6* (1), 15–36.

Goedert, J. (1987). What is safe sex? Suggested standards linked to testing for HIV. *New England Journal of Medicine, 316*, 1339–1341.

Goetting, A. (1986). Parental satisfaction: A review of research. *Journal of Family Issues, 7*, 83–109.

Gold, D. T. (1990, December). Late-life sibling relationships: Does race affect typological distribution? *Gerontologist, 30* (6), 741–747.

Gold, D. T. (1991). Osteoporosis in late life: Does health locus of control affect psychosocial adaptation? *Journal of the American Geriatrics Society, 39* (7), 670–675.

Gold, M. (1987). Social ecology. In H. C. Quay (Ed.), *Handbook of juvenile delinquency*. New York: Wiley.

Goldberg, W. A., Michaels, G. Y., & Lamb, M. E. (1986). Husbands' and wives' adjustment to pregnancy and first parenthood. *Journal of Family Issues, 16*, 483–503.

Goldsmith, J. P. (1990). Neonatal morbidity. In R. D. Eden, F. H. Boehm, & M. Haire (Eds.), *Assessment and care of the fetus: Physiological, clinical, and medicolegal principles*. Norwalk, CT: Appleton and Lange.

Goldsmith, M. F. (1992). 'Critical moment' at hand in HIV/AIDS pandemic, new global strategy to arrest its spread proposed. *Journal of the American Medical Association, 268*, 445–446.

Gomes-Schwartz, B., Horowitz, J. M., & Cardarelli, A. P. (1990). *Child sexual abuse: The initial effects*. Beverly Hills, CA: Sage.

Gomez, C. F. (1991). *Regulating death: Euthanasia and the case of the Netherlands*. New York: Free Press.

Goneo, A., & Kessel, F. (1988). Preschoolers' collaborative construction in planning and maintaining imaginative play. *International*

Journal of Behavioral Development, 11, 327–344.

Gonyea, J. G. (1990). Alzheimer's disease support group participation and caregiver well-being. *Clinical Gerontologist, 10* (2), 17–34.

Gonyea, J. G., & Silverstein, N. M. (1991). The role of Alzheimer's disease support groups in families' utilization of community services. *Journal of Gerontological Social Work, 16* (3/4), 43–55.

Goode, E. (1989). *Drugs in American society* (3rd ed.). New York: Knopf.

Goodman, C. C. (1990). The caregiving roles of Asian American women. *Journal of Women and Aging, 2* (1), 109–120.

Goodman, C. C. (1991). Perceived social support for caregiving: Measuring the benefit of self-help/support group participation. *Journal of Gerontological Social Work, 16* (3/4): 163–175.

Goodwin, J. S. (1991). Geriatric ideology: The myth of the myth of senility. *Journal of the American Geriatrics Society, 39* (6), 627–631.

Goodwin, M. P., & Roscoe, B. (1990). Sibling violence and agonistic interactions among middle adolescents. *Adolescence, 25*, 451–468.

Googins, B. K. (1990). *Work/family conflicts: Private lives-public responses*. Westport, CT: Auburn House.

Gordon, A., & Browne, K. (1993). *Beginnings and beyond: Foundations in early childhood education* (3rd ed.). Albany, NY: Delmar.

Gordon, D. E. (1990). Formal operational thinking: The role of cognitive-developmental processes in adolescent decision-making about pregnancy and contraception. *American Journal of Orthopsychiatry, 60* (3), 346–356.

Gorga, D., Stern, F. M., Ross, G., & Nagler, W. (1991). The neuromotor behavior of preterm and full-term children by three years of age: Quality of movement and variability. *Journal of Developmental and Behavioral Pediatrics, 12* (2), 102–107.

Gottesman, I. I., & Shields, J. (1982). *The schizophrenic puzzle*. New York: Cambridge University Press.

Gottfried, A. E. (1983). Intrinsic motivation in young children. *Young Children, 39* (1), 64–73.

Gottfries, C. G. (1990). Biological markers in dementia disorders. In M. Bergener, M. Ermini, & H. B. Stahelin (Eds.), *Challenges in aging*. San Diego: Academic Press.

Gottlieb, G. L. (1990). Rehabilitation and dementia of the Alzheimer's type. In S. J. Brody & L. G. Pawlson (Eds.), *Aging and rehabilitation: The state of the practice*. New York: Springer.

Gould, R. L. (1978). *Transformations: Growth and change in adult life*. New York: Simon & Schuster.

Gould, R. L. (1980). Transformations during early and middle adult years. In N. Smelser & E. Erikson (Eds.), *Themes of work and love in adulthood*. Cambridge, MA: Harvard University Press.

Grad, S. (1990). Income of the population 55 or older, 1986. *SSA Publication, No. 13–11871*. Washington, DC: U.S. Government Printing Office.

Graham-Bermann, S. A. (1991). Siblings in dyads: Relationship among perceptions and behavior. *Journal of Genetic Psychology, 152* (2), 207–216.

Grambs, J. D. (1989). *Women over forty: Visions and realities* (rev. ed.). New York: Springer.

Grande, C. G. (1988). Delinquency: The learning disabled student's reaction to academic school failure. *Adolescence, 23*, 209–219.

Graul, S. K., & Zeece, P. D. (1990). Effects of play training of adults on the cognitive and play behavior of preschool children. *Early Child Development and Care, 57*, 15–22.

Gray, L. A., & Saracino, M. (1991). College students' attitudes, beliefs, and behaviors about AIDS: Implications for family life educators. *Family Relations, 40*, 258–263.

Gray, V. R. (1984). The psychological response of the dying patient. In P. S. Chaney (Ed.), *Dealing with death and dying* (2nd ed.). Springhouse, PA: International Communications/Nursing Skillbooks.

Gray, W. M., & Hudson, L. M. (1984). Formal operations and the imaginary audience. *Developmental Psychology, 20*, 619–627.

Gray-Ray, P., & Ray, M. C. (1990). Juvenile delinquency in the black community. *Youth and Society, 22* (1), 67–84.

Green, C. P. (1991). Clinical considerations: Midlife daughters and their aging parents. *Journal of Gerontological Nursing, 17* (11), 6–12.

Green, N. M., & Bridgham, J. D. (1991). The older alcoholic client. In R. F. Young & E. A. Olson (Eds.), *Health, illness, and disability in later life: Practice issues and interventions*. Newbury Park, CA: Sage.

Greene, A. L. (1990). Great expectations: Constructions of the life course during adolescence. *Journal of Youth and Adolescence, 19* (4), 289–306.

Greenfeld, D., Diamond, M., Breslin, R., & DeCherney, A. (1986). Infertility and the new reproductive technology. *Social Work in Health Care, 12*, 71–81.

Gregory, D. M., Peters, N., & Cameron, C. F. (1990). Elderly male spouses as caregivers: Toward an understanding of their experience. *Journal of Gerontological Nursing, 16* (3), 20–24.

Greif, E. B., & Ulman, K. (1982). The psychological impact of menarche on early adolescent females: A review. *Child Development, 53*, 1413–1430.

Greil, A. L. (1991). *Not yet pregnant: Infertile couples in contemporary America*. New Brunswick, NJ: Rutgers University Press.

Greth, C. V. (1990, February 4). TV free: Tubeless families turn prime time into quality time. *Austin American Statesman*, pp. E1, E15.

Grigsby, J. P., & Weatherley, D. (1983). Gender and sex role differences in intimacy of self-disclosure. *Psychological Reports, 53* (1), 891–897.

Gropen, J. (1991). Syntax and semantics in the acquisition of locative verbs. *Journal of Child Language, 18* (1), 115–151.

Gross, P. A. (1991). *Managing your health: Strategies for lifelong good health*. Yonkers, NY: Consumer Reports Books.

Gross, R. T., & Duke, P. M. (1980). The effect of early vs. late maturation on adolescent behavior. *Pediatric Clinics of North America, 27*, 71–77.

Grossberg, G. T. (1990). Psychiatric problems in the nursing home: St. Louis University geriatric grand rounds. *Journal of the American Geriatrics Society, 38* (8), 907–917.

Grossman, M. (1988). Children with AIDS. In I. C. Corless & M. Pittman-Lindeman (Eds.), *AIDS: Principles, practices, and politics*. New York: Hemisphere.

Grove, K. J. (1991). Identity development in interracial, Asian/white late adolescents: Must it be so problematic? *Journal of Youth and Adolescence, 20* (6), 617–628.

Grusec, J. E., & Arnason, L. (1982). Consideration for others: Approaches to enhancing altruism. In S. G. Moore & C. R. Cooper (Eds.), *The young child: Reviews of research* (Vol. 3). Washington, DC: National Association for the Education of Young Children.

Gubrium, J. (1991). *The mosaic of care: Frail elderly and their families in the real world*. New York: Springer.

Gubrium, J. (1992). *Out of control: Family therapy and domestic disorder*. Newbury Park, CA: Sage.

Gumperz, J. (1982). *Discourse strategies*. New York: Cambridge University Press.

Gunter, L. M. (1991). Cultural diversity among older Americans. In E. M. Baines (Ed.), *Perspectives on gerontological nursing*. Newbury Park, CA: Sage.

Gurian, B. S., & Miner, J. H. (1991). Clinical presentation of anxiety in the elderly. In C. Salzman & B. D. Lebowitz (Eds.), *Anxiety in the elderly: Treatment and research*. New York: Springer.

Gurland, B., & Toner, J. A. (1991). The chronically mentally ill elderly: Epidemiological perspectives on the nature of the population. In E. Light & B. D. Lebowitz (Eds.), *The elderly with chronic mental illness*. New York: Springer.

Gusella, J. L., Muir, D., & Tronick, E. A. (1988). The effect of manipulating maternal behavior during an interaction on three- and six-month-olds' affect and attention. *Child Development, 59*, 1111–1124.

Gustafson, G. E., & Green, J. A. (1991). Developmental coordination of cry sounds with visual regard and gestures. *Infant Behavior and Development, 14* (1), 51–57.

Gustafson, S. B., & Magnusson, D. (1991). *Female life careers: A pattern approach*. Hillsdale, NJ: Erlbaum.

Gutek, B. A. (1988). Sex segregation and women at work: A selective review. In B. A. Gutek (Ed.), *Applied psychology: An international review*. Beverly Hills, CA: Sage.

Gutek, B. A., Stromberg, A. H., & Larwood, L. (Eds.). (1988). *Women and work*. Newbury Park, CA: Sage.

Gutmann, D. (1978). *Personal transformation in the post-parental period: A cross-cultural view*. Washington, DC: American Association for the Advancement of Science.

Gutmann, D. L. (1964). An exploration of ego configurations in middle and later life. In B. L. Neugarten (Ed.), *Personality in middle and late life*. New York: Atherton Press.

Guyton, A. C. (1981). *Textbook of medical physiology* (6th ed.). Philadelphia: Saunders.

Gwyther, L. P. (1990). Letting go: Separation-individuation in a wife of an Alzheimer's patient. *Gerontologist, 30* (5), 698–702.

Haan, N. (1976). Personality organization of well-functioning younger people and older adults. *International Journal of Aging and Human Development, 7*, 117–127.

Haan, N. (1981). Common dimensions of personality. Early adolescence to middle life. In D. H. Eichorn, N. Haan, J. Clausen, M. Honzik, & P. Mussen (Eds.), *Present and past in middle life*. New York: Basic Books.

Haan, N. (1985). Common personality dimensions or common organization across the life span? In J. M. Munnichs, P. Mussen, E. Olbrich, & P. G. Coleman (Eds.), *Lifespan and change in gerontological perspective*. New York: Academic Press.

Haan, N., Millsap, R., & Hartka, E. (1986). As time goes by: Change and stability in personality over fifty years. *Psychology and Aging, 1*, 220–232.

Habegger, C. E., & Blieszner, R. (1990). Personal and social aspects of reminiscence: An exploratory study of neglected dimensions. *Activities, Adaptation and Aging, 14* (4), 21–38.

Haber, C. (1983). *Beyond sixty-five: The dilemma of old age in America's past*. Cambridge, England: Cambridge University Press.

Hadwin, J., & Perner, J. (1991). Pleased and surprised: Children's cognitive theory of emotion. *British Journal of Developmental Psychology, 9* (2), 215–234.

Haffner, D. W. (1989). The AIDS epidemic and sexuality education. In C. Cassell & P. M. Wilson (Eds.), *Sexuality education: A resource book*. New York: Garland.

Hagberg, B. (1991). Stability and change of personality in old age and its relation to survival. *Journal of Gerontology: Psychological Sciences, 46* (6), P285–P292.

Hagestad, G. O. (1990). Social perspectives on the life course. In R. H. Binstock & L. K. George (Eds.), *Handbook of aging and the social sciences*. San Diego: Academic Press.

Hagestad, G. O. (1991). The aging society as a context for family life. In N. S. Jecker (Ed.), *Aging and ethics: Philosophical problems in gerontology. Contemporary issues in biomedicine, ethics, and society*. Clifton, NJ: Humana Press.

Haight, B. K. (1991a). Psychological illness in aging. In E. M. Baines (Ed.), *Perspectives on gerontological nursing*. Newbury Park, CA: Sage.

Haight, B. K. (1991b). Reminiscing: The state of the art as a basis for practice. *International Journal of Aging and Human Development, 33* (1), 1–32.

Haight, W., & Miller, P. J. (1992). The development of everyday pretend play: A longitudinal study of mothers' participation. *Merrill-Palmer Quarterly, 38* (3), 331–349.

Haines, B. J., & Gerber, L. L. (1992). *Leading young children to music: A resource book for teachers* (4th ed.). New York: Macmillan.

Hakuta, K., & Garcia, E. E. (1989). Bilingualism and education. *American Psychologist, 44* (2), 374–379.

Halamandaris, V. J. (1991). The power of caring: Management by values. *Caring, 10*, 4–6.

Hales, D. (1989). *Pregnancy and birth*. New York: Chelsea House.

Hales, D. (1992). *An invitation to health: Taking charge of your life*. Menlo Park, CA: Benjamin/Cummings.

Hales, D., & Creasy, R. K. (1982). *New hope for problem pregnancies*. New York: Harper & Row.

Hall, C., Beougher, K., & Wasinger, K. (1991). Divorce: Implications for services. *Psychology in the Schools, 28* (3), 267–275.

Hall, D. G. (1991). Acquiring proper nouns for familiar and unfamiliar animate objects: Two-year-olds' word-learning biases. *Child Development, 62* (5), 1142–1154.

Hall, G. S. (1904). *On adolescence*. New York Appleton.

Halmi, K. A. (1983). Psychosomatic illness review: Anorexia nervosa and bulimia. *Psychosomatics, 24*, 111–132.

Hamby, R. C. (1990). *Alzheimer's disease: A handbook for caregivers*. St. Louis: Mosby.

Hamlet, E., & Read, S. (1990). Caregiver education and support group: A hospital-based group experience. *Journal of Gerontological Social Work, 15* (1/2), 75–88.

Hans, S. (1989, April). *Infant behavioral effects of prenatal exposure to methadone*. Paper presented at the biennial meeting of the Society for Research in Child Development, Kansas City.

Hansell, S., & Mechanic, D. (1991). Body awareness and self-assessed health among older adults. *Journal of Aging and Health, 3* (4), 473–492.

Hansen, W. B., Hahn, G. L., & Wolkenstein, B. H. (1990). Perceived personal immunity: Beliefs about susceptibility to AIDS. *Journal of Sex Research, 27,* 622–628.

Hanson, L. C., & Danis, M. (1991). Use of life-sustaining care for the elderly. *Journal of the American Geriatrics Society, 39* (8), 772–777.

Hanson, R. A. (1990). Initial parenting attitudes of pregnant adolescents and a comparison with the decision about adoption. *Adolescence, 25,* 629–643.

Hanson, S. L., & Ooms, T. (1991). The economic costs and rewards of two-earner, two-parent families. *Journal of Marriage and the Family, 53* (3), 622–634.

Hare-Mustin, R., & Maracek, J. (1988). The meaning of difference: Gender theory, postmodernism, and psychology. *American Psychologist, 43,* 455–464.

Harlap, S., Kost, K., & Forrest, J. D. (1991). *Preventing pregnancy, protecting health: A new look at birth control choices in the United States*. New York: Alan Guttmacher Institute.

Harlow, H. F. (1958). The nature of love. *American Psychologist, 13,* 637–685.

Harlow, H. F. (1962). The heterosexual affectional system in monkeys. *American Psychologist, 16,* 1–9.

Harlow, H. F. (1971). *Learning to love*. San Francisco: Albion.

Harlow, H. F., & Zimmerman, R. R. (1959). Affectual responses in the infant monkey. *Science, 130,* 421–432.

Harper, J. F., & Marshall, E. (1991). Adolescents' problems and their relationship to self-esteem. *Adolescence, 26* (104), 799–808.

Harper, M. S. (1990). Mental health and older adults. In M. O. Hogstel (Ed.), *Geropsychiatric nursing*. St. Louis: Mosby.

Harper, M. S. (1991). An overview: Mental disorders of the elderly. In M. S. Harper (Ed.), *Management and care of the elderly: Psychosocial perspectives*. Newbury Park, CA: Sage.

Harrell, J. S. (1988). Age-related changes in the respiratory system. In M. A. Matteson & E. S. McConnell (Eds.), *Gerontological nursing: Concepts and practice*. Philadelphia: Saunders.

Harriman, L. C. (1986). Marital adjustment as related to personal and marital changes accompanying parenthood. *Family Relations, 35,* 233–239.

Harrington, C. (1991). Developing public information on nursing home quality. *Journal of Aging and Social Policy, 3* (1/2), 127–148.

Harris, G., Thomas, A., & Booth, D. A. (1990). Development of salt taste in infancy. *Developmental Psychology, 26* (4), 534–538.

Harris, K. M. (1991). Teenage mothers and welfare dependency: Working off welfare. *Journal of Family Issues, 12* (4), 492–518.

Harris, P. L., & Kavanaugh, R. D. (1993). Young children's understanding of pretense. *Monographs of the Society for Research in Child Development, 58* (1), 231.

Harrison, C. A. (1991). Older women in our society: America's silent, invisible majority. *Educational Gerontology, 17* (2), 121.

Harry, J. (1982). *Gay children grown up: Gender culture and gender deviance*. New York: Praeger.

Hart, C. H., DeWolf, D. M., Wozniak, P., & Burts, D. C. (1992). Maternal and paternal disciplinary styles: Relations with preschoolers' playground behavioral orientations and peer status. *Child Development, 63* (4), 879–892.

Hart, D., & Chmiel, S. (1992). Influence of defense mechanisms on moral judgment development: A longitudinal study. *Developmental Psychology, 28* (4), 722–730.

Hartup, W. W. (1980). Peer relations and family relations: Two social worlds. In M. Rutter (Ed.), *Scientific foundations of developmental psychiatry*. London: Heinemann Medical Books.

Hartup, W. W. (1983). Peer relations. In P. H. Mussen (Ed.), *Handbook of child psychology* (4th ed.). New York: Wiley.

Hartup, W. W. (1984). The peer context in middle childhood. In W. A. Collins (Ed.), *Development during middle childhood: The years from six to twelve*. Washington, DC: National Academy Press.

Hartup, W. W. (1989). Social relationships and their developmental significance. *American Psychologist, 44,* 120–126.

Hartup, W. W., Laursen, B., Stewart, M. I., & Eastenson, A. (1988). Conflict and the friendship relations of young children. *Child Development, 59,* 1590–1603.

Hashimoto, N. (1991). Memory development in early childhood: Encoding process in a spatial task. *Journal of Genetic Psychology, 152* (1), 101–117.

Haskett, M. E., & Kistner, J. A. (1991). Social interactions and peer perceptions of young physically abused children. *Child Development, 62* (5), 979–990.

Hatch, L. R. (1991). Informal support patterns of older African-American and white women: Examining effects of family, paid work, and religious participation. *Research on Aging, 13* (2), 144–170.

Hatcher, R., (1990). Psychological mindedness and abstract reasoning in late childhood and adolescence: An exploration using new instruments. *Journal of Youth and Adolescence, 19* (4), 307–326.

Hatcher, R. A., Stewart, F., Trussell, J., Kowal, D., Guest, F., Stewart, G. K., & Cates, W. (1990). *Contraceptive technology, 1990–1992* (15th ed.). New York: Irvington.

Haug, H. (1991). Aging of the brain. In F. C. Ludwig (Ed.), *Life span extension: Consequences and open questions*. New York: Springer.

Havighurst, R. J. (1972). *Developmental tasks and education* (3rd ed.). New York: David McKay.

Havighurst, R. J. (1980). More thoughts on developmental tasks. *Personnel and Guidance Journal, 58,* 330–335.

Havighurst, R. J. (1987). Adolescent culture and subculture. In V. B. Van Hasselt & M. Hersen (Eds.), *Handbook of adolescent psychology*. New York: Pergamon.

Havighurst, R. J., Neugarten, B. L., & Tobin, S. S.

(1968). Disengagement and patterns of aging. In B. L. Neugarten (Ed.), *Middle age and aging*. Chicago: University of Chicago Press.

Hawes, C. (1991). The Institute of Medicine study: Improving the quality of nursing home care. In P. R. Katz, R. L. Kane, & M. D. Mezey (Eds.), *Advances in long-term care* (Vol. 1). New York: Springer.

Hawkins, A. J., & Roberts, T. A. (1992). Designing a primary intervention to help dual-earner couples share housework and child care. *Family Relations, 41* (2), 169–177.

Hawkins, C., & Williams, T. I. (1992). Nightmares, life events and behaviour problems in preschool children. *Child: Care, Health and Development, 18* (2), 117–128.

Hay, D. A. (1985). *Essentials of behaviour genetics*. Melbourne: Blackwells.

Hay, D. F., Caplan, M., Castle, J., & Stimson, C. A. (1991). Does sharing become increasingly "rational" in the second year of life? *Developmental Psychology, 27* (6), 987–993.

Hayden-Thomson, L., Rubin, K. H., & Hymel, S. (1987). Sex preferences in sociometric choices. *Developmental Psychology, 23,* 558–562.

Hayes, C. D. (1987). Introduction. In S. L. Hofferth & C. D. Hayes (Eds.), *Risking the future: Adolescent sexuality, pregnancy, and childbearing*. Washington, DC: National Academy Press.

Hayslip, B., Jr., Kennelly, K. J., & Maloy, R. M. (1990). Fatigue, depression, and cognitive performance among aged persons. *Experimental Aging Research, 16* (3), 111–115.

Heath, J. M. (1991). Outpatient geriatric assessment: Associations between referral sources and assessment findings. *Journal of the American Geriatrics Society, 39* (3), 267–272.

Heaton, T. B., & Albrecht, S. L. (1991). Stable unhappy marriages. *Journal of Marriage and the Family, 53* (3), 747–758.

Heddens, J. W., & Speer, W. R. (1992). *Today's mathematics* (7th ed.). New York: Macmillan.

Heeren, T. J. (1991). Prevalence of dementia in the "oldest old" of a Dutch community. *Journal of the American Geriatrics Society, 39* (8), 755–759.

Heery, K. (1991). Eldercare: The challenge of the '90s. *Caring, 10,* 62–66.

Hein, K. (1989a). Commentary on adolescent acquired immunodeficiency syndrome: The next wave of immunodeficiency virus epidemic. *Journal of Pediatrics, 114,* 144–149.

Hein, K. (1989b). AIDS in adolescence. *Journal of Adolescent Health Care, 10,* 105–135.

Heiselman, T., & Noelker, L. S. (1991). Enhancing mutual respect among nursing assistants, residents, and residents' families. *Gerontologist, 31* (4), 552–555.

Hellerstein, H., & Perry, P. (1990). *Healing your heart*. New York: Simon & Schuster.

Hellman, S., & Hellman, L. H. (1991). *Medicare and medigaps: A guide to retirement health insurance*. Newbury Park, CA: Sage.

Helson, R., Elliot, T., & Leigh, J. (1989). Adolescent antecedents of women's work patterns. In D. Stern & D. Eichorn (Eds.), *Adolescence and work*. Hillsdale, NJ: Erlbaum.

Helson, R., & Moane, G. (1987). Personality change in women from college to midlife. *Journal of Personality and Social Psychology, 53,* 176–186.

Helson, R., & Wink, P. (1992). Personality change in women from the early 40's to the early 50's. *Psychology and Aging, 7,* 46–55.

Henderson, M. (1990). Beyond the living will. *Gerontologist, 30* (4), 480–485.

Henderson, N. D. (1982). Human behavior genetics. *Annual Review of Psychology, 33,* 403–440.

Hendin, D. (1984). *Death as a fact of life.* New York: Norton.

Hendrick, C., & Hendrick, S. S. (1988). Lovers wear rose colored glasses. *Journal of Social and Personal Relationships, 5,* 161–183.

Hendrick, S., & Hendrick, C. (1992). *Liking, loving, and relating* (2nd ed.). Belmont, CA: Wadsworth.

Hendricks, J., & Hendricks, C. D. (1981). *Aging in mass society: Myths and realities* (2nd ed.). Cambridge, MA: Winthrop.

Henggeler, S. W. (1989). *Delinquency in adolescence.* Beverly Hills, CA: Sage.

Henggeler, S. W., Cohen, R., Edwards, J. J., & Summerville, M. B. (1991a). Family stress as a link in the association between television viewing and achievement. *Child Study Journal, 21* (1), 1–10.

Henggeler, S. W., Edwards, J. J., Cohen, R., & Summerville, M. B. (1991b). Predicting changes in children's popularity: The role of family relations. *Journal of Applied Developmental Psychology, 12* (2), 205–218.

Henretta, J. C., Chan, C. G., & O'Rand, A. M. (1992). Retirement reason versus retirement process: Examining the reasons for retirement typology. *Journal of Gerontology: Social Sciences, 47* (1), S1 –S7.

Henry, A. K., & Feldhausen, J. (1989). *Drugs, vitamins, and minerals during pregnancy.* Tucson, AZ: Fisher Books.

Henry, L. A., & Millar, S. (1991). Memory span increase with age: A test of two hypotheses. *Journal of Experimental Child Psychology, 51* (3), 459–484.

Henshaw, S. K., & Silverman, J. (1988). The characteristics and prior contraceptive use of U.S. abortion patients. *Family Planning Perspectives, 20,* 158–168.

Henshaw, S. K., & Van Vort, J. (1989). Teenage abortion, birth, and pregnancy statistics: An update. *Family Planning Perspectives, 21,* 85–88.

Henslin, J. M. (Ed.). (1992). *Marriage and family in a changing society* (4th ed.). New York: Free Press.

Henze, G. (1992). *Winning career moves.* Homewood, IL: Business One Irwin.

Herman, J. (1981). *Father-daughter incest.* Cambridge, MA: Harvard University Press.

Herman, J. B. (1990). An overview of physical ability with age: The potential for health in later life. *Gerontology and Geriatrics Education, 11,* 11–25.

Herold, E. S., McNamee, J. E. (1982). An exploratory model of contraceptive use among young single women. *Journal of Sex Research, 18,* 289–304.

Hertzler, A. A., & Grun, I. (1990). Potential nutrition message in magazines ready by college students. *Adolescence, 25,* 717–724.

Hertzog, C. (1989). The influence of cognitive slowing on age difference in intelligence. *Developmental Psychology, 25,* 636–651.

Herzog, A. R., & House, J. S. (1991). Productive activities and aging well. *Generations, 15* (1), 49–54.

Herzog, D. B., Keller, M. B., Lavori, P. W., & Bradburn, I. S. (1991). Bulimia nervosa in adolescence. *Journal of Developmental and Behavioral Pediatrics, 12* (3), 191–195.

Hess, T. M., & Flannagan, D. A. (1992). Schema-based retrieval processes in young and older adults. *Journal of Gerontology: Psychological Sciences, 47* (1), P52–P58.

Hessler, R. M. (1992). *Social research methods.* St. Paul, MN: West.

Hessong, R. F., & Weeks, T. H. (1991). *Introduction to the foundations of education* (2nd ed.). New York: Macmillan.

Hetherington, E. M. (1990). Coping with family transitions: Winners, losers, and survivors. In S. Chess & M. E. Hertzig (Eds.), *Annual progress in child psychiatry and child development.* New York: Brunner/Mazel.

Hetherington, E. M., & Baltes, P. B. (1988). Child psychology and life-span development. In E. M. Hetherington, R. M. Lerner, & M. Perlmutter (Eds.), *Child development in life-span perspective.* Hillsdale, NJ: Erlbaum.

Hewett, L. J. (1991). Group reminiscence with nursing home residents. *Clinical Gerontologist, 10* (4), 69–72.

Hewlett, S. (1986). *A lesser life: The myth of women's liberation in America.* New York: William Morrow.

Hewlett, S. (1991). *When the bough breaks: The costs of neglecting our children.* New York: Basic Books.

Heyman, W. B. (1990). The self-perception of a learning disability and its relationship to academic self-concept and self-esteem. *Journal of Learning Disabilities, 23* (8), 472–475.

Hickey, T., & Stilwell, D. L. (1991). Health promotion for older people: All is not well. *Gerontologist, 31* (6), 822–829.

Hiemstra, R. (1983). How older persons are portrayed in television advertising: Implications for educators. *Educational Gerontology, 9,* 111–122.

Hier, S. J., Koorboot, P. J., & Schweitzer, R. D. (1990). Social adjustment and symptomatology in two types of homeless adolescents: Runaways and throwaways. *Adolescence, 25* (100), 761–771.

Higgins, B. S. (1990). Couple infertility: From the perspective of the close-relationship model. *Family Relations, 39,* 81–86.

High, D. M. (1990). Who will make health care decisions for me when I can't? *Journal of Aging and Health, 2* (3), 291–309.

High, D. M. (1991). A new myth about families of older people? *Gerontologist, 31* (5), 611–618.

Hildebrand, H. P. (1990). Toward a psychodynamic understanding of later life. In M. Bergener & S. L. Finkel (Eds.), *Clinical and scientific psychogeriatrics.* New York: Springer.

Hildebrand, V. (1991). *Introduction to early childhood education* (5th ed.). New York: Macmillan.

Hill, R. (1964). Methodological problems with the developmental approach to family study. *Family Process, 3,* 186–206.

Hill, R. D., Storandt, M., & Simeone, C. (1990). The effects of memory skills training and incentives on free recall in older learners. *Journal of Gerontology, 45,* P227–P232.

Hillard, P. A., & Panter, G. G. (1985). *Pregnancy and childbirth.* New York: Ballantine.

Hilliard, A. G., & Vaughn-Scott, M. (1982). The quest for the "minority" child. In S. G. Moore & C. R. Cooper (Eds.), *The young child: Reviews of research* (Vol 3). Washington, D.C.:

National Association for the Education of Young Children.

Hilts, P. (1991, November 21). Fetus to fetus transplant blocks deadly genetic defect. *New York Times,* p. B14.

Himes, C. L. (1992). Future caregivers: Projected family structures of older persons. *Journal of Gerontology: Social Sciences, 47* (1), S17–S26.

Hinde, R. A. (1983). Ethology and child development. In P. H. Mussen (Ed.), *Handbook of child psychology* (4th ed.). New York: Wiley.

Hinde, R. A. (1989). Ethological and relationship approaches. In R. Vasta (Ed.), *Six theories of child development: Revised formulations and current issues.* Greenwich, CT: JAI Press.

Hindelang, M. J. (1981). Variations in sex-race-age-specific incidence rates of offending. *American Sociological Review, 46,* 461–474.

Hindley, C. B., Filliozat, A. M., Klakenberg, G., Nocolet-Meister, D., & Sand, E. A. (1966). Differences in age of walking in five European longitudinal samples. *Human Biology, 38,* 364–379.

Hinrichsen, G. A. (1990). *Mental health problems and older adults: Choices and challenges.* Santa Barbara, CA: ABC-CL10.

Hirshberg, L. M. (1990). When infants look to their parents: II. Twelve-month-olds' response to conflicting parental emotional signals. *Child Development, 61* (4), 1187–1191.

Hirshberg, L. M., & Svejda, M. (1990). When infants look to their parents: I. Infants' social referencing of mothers compared to fathers. *Child Development, 61* (4), 1175–1186.

Hirshorn, B. (1991). Family caregiving as an intergenerational transfer. In R. F. Young & E. A. Olson (Eds.), *Health, illness, and disability in later life: Practice issues and interventions.* Newbury Park, CA: Sage.

Ho, M. K. (1992). *Minority children and adolescents in therapy.* Newbury Park, CA: Sage.

Hobbs, M., & Bacharach, V. R. (1990). Children's understanding of big buildings and big cars. *Child Study Journal, 20* (1), 1–18.

Hobson, R. P. (1980). The question of egocentrism: The young child's competence in the coordination of perspectives. *Journal of Child Psychology and Psychiatry, 21,* 325–331.

Hoekstra-Weebers, J. E. (1991). A comparison of parental coping styles following the death of adolescent and preadolescent children. *Death Studies, 15* (6), 565–575.

Hofferth, S. L., & Hayes, C. D. (Eds.). (1987). *Risking the future: Adolescent sexuality, pregnancy, and childbearing.* Washington, DC: National Academy Press.

Hoff-Ginsberg, E. (1991). Mother-child conversation in different social classes and communicative settings. *Child Development, 62* (4), 782–796.

Hoffman, L. W. (1989). Effects of maternal employment in the two-parent family. *American Psychologist, 44,* 283–292.

Hoffman, M. L. (1989). Empathy, social cognition and moral action. In W. Kurtines & J. Gewirtz (Eds.), *Moral behavior and development: Advances in theory, research and application.* Hillsdale, NJ: Erlbaum.

Hogge, W., Schonberg, S., & Golbus, M. (1986). Chorionic villus sampling: Experience of the first 1,000 cases. *American Journal of Obstetrics and Gynecology, 154,* 1249–1252.

Hogstel, M. O. (1990). Mental illness in the nursing home. In M. O. Hogstel (Ed.), *Geropsychiatric nursing.* St. Louis: Mosby.

Holahan, C. K. (1988). Relation of life goals at age 70 to activity participation and health and psychological well-being among Terman's gifted men and women. *Psychology and Aging, 3,* 286–291.

Holcomb, W. R., & Kashani, J. H. (1991). Personality characteristics of a community sample of adolescents with conduct disorders. *Adolescence, 26* (103), 579–586.

Holland, J. L. (1966). *The psychology of vocational choice.* Waltham, MA: Blaisdell.

Holmbeck, G. N., & Hill, J. P. (1991). Conflictive engagement, positive affect, and menarche in families with seventh-grade girls. *Child Development, 62* (5), 1030–1048.

Holmes, R. M. (1992). Children's artwork and nonverbal communication. *Child Study Journal, 22* (3), 157–166.

Honig, A. (1983). Research in review: Television and young children. *Young Children, 38* (4), 63–76.

Honig, A., & Pollack, B. (1990). Effects of a brief intervention program to promote prosocial behaviors in young children. *Early Education and Development, 1,* 438–444.

Hood, K. E. (1991). Menstrual cycle. In R. M. Lerner, A. C. Petersen, & J. Brooks-Gunn (Eds.), *The encyclopedia of adolescence.* New York: Garland.

Hook, E. (1981). Rates of chromosome abnormalities at different maternal ages. *Obstetrics and Gynecology, 114,* 282–284.

Horacek, B. J. (1991). Toward a more viable model of grieving and consequences for older persons. *Death Studies, 15* (5), 459–472.

Horne, J. (1991). *A survival guide for family caregivers: Strength, support, and sources of help for all those caring for the aged or impaired family members.* Minneapolis: CompCare.

Horobin, K., & Acredolo, C. (1989). The impact of probability judgments on reasoning about multiple possibilities. *Child Development, 60,* 183–200.

Horowitz, A., Teresi, J. A., & Cassels, L. A. (1991). Development of a vision screening questionnaire for older people. *Journal of Gerontological Social Work, 17* (3/4), 37–56.

Horowitz, G. P., & Dudek, B. C. (1983). Behavioral pharmacogenetics. In J. L. Fuller & E. C. Simmel (Eds.), *Behavior genetics.* Hillsdale, NJ: Erlbaum.

Horton, A. L., Johnson, B. L., Roundy, L. M., & Williams, D. (Eds.). (1990). *The incest perpetrator: A family member no one wants to treat.* Newbury Park, CA: Sage.

Horwath, C. C. (1991). Nutrition goals for older adults: A review. *Gerontologist, 31* (6), 811–821.

Hoskins, I. (1992). Social security protection of women: Prospects for the 1990's. *Ageing International, 19,* 27–32.

Hotchner, T. (1990). *Pregnancy and childbirth* (rev. ed.). New York: Avon.

Houck, C. K., Asselin, S. B., Troutman, G. C., & Arrington, J. M. (1992). Students with learning disabilities in the university environment: A study of faculty and student perceptions. *Journal of Learning Disabilities, 25* (10), 678–684.

Howard, D. V. (1983). *Cognitive psychology: Memory, language, and thought.* New York: Macmillan.

Howard, J. A., Blumstein, P., & Schwartz, P. (1986). Sex, power, and influence tactics in intimate relationships. *Journal of Personality and Social Psychology, 51,* 102–109.

Howatt, P. M., & Saxton, A. M. (1988). The incidence of bulimic behavior in a secondary and university school population. *Journal of Youth and Adolescence, 17,* 221–231.

Howe, M. L., & Rabinowitz, F. M. (1991). Gist another panacea? Or just the illusion of inclusion. *Developmental Review, 11* (4), 305–316.

Howes, C. (1988). Peer interaction of young children. *Monographs of the Society for Research in Child Development, 53,* 94–104.

Howes, C., & Hamilton, C. E. (1992). Children's relationships with caregivers: Mothers and child care teachers. *Child Development, 63* (4), 859–866.

Howes, C., & Matheson, C. C. (1992). Sequences in the development of competent play with peers: Social and social pretend play. *Developmental Psychology, 28* (5), 961–974.

Howes, C., Unger, D., & Seidner, L. B. (1989). Social pretend play in toddlers: Parallels with social play and with solitary pretend. *Child Development, 60,* 77–84.

Hsu, L. K. (1990). *Eating disorders.* New York: Guilford Press.

Hudson, M. J. (1990). Hearing and vision loss in an aging population: Myths and realities. *Educational Gerontology, 16* (1), 87–96.

Hughes, B. (1990). Quality of life. In S. M. Peace (Ed.), *Researching social gerontology: Concepts, methods, and issues.* Newbury Park, CA: Sage.

Hughes, D., Galinsky, E., & Morris, A. (1992). The effects of job characteristics on marital quality: Specifying linking mechanisms. *Journal of Marriage and the Family, 54* (1), 31–42.

Hulit, L. M., & Howard, M. R. (1993). *Born to talk: An introduction to speech and language development.* New York: Macmillan.

Hultsch, D. F., Masson, M. E. J., & Small, B. J. (1991). Adult age differences in direct and indirect tests of memory. *Journal of Gerontology: Psychological Sciences, 46* (1), P22–P30.

Humphry, D. (1991). *Final exit: The practicalities of self-deliverance and assisted suicide for the dying.* Eugene, OR: The Hemlock Society.

Hunt, E. (1989). Cognitive science: Definition, status, and questions. *Annual Review of Psychology, 40,* 603–629.

Husaini, B. A. (1991). Social density, stressors, and depression: Gender differences among the black elderly. *Journal of Gerontology: Psychological Sciences, 46* (5), P236–P242.

Huston, A. C., & Alvarez, M. (1990). The socialization context of gender role development in early adolescence. In R. Montemayor, G. R. Adams, & T. P. Gulotta (Eds.), *From childhood to adolescence: A transitional period?* Newbury Park, CA: Sage.

Huston, A. C., Watkins, B. A., & Kunkel, D. (1989). Public policy and children's television. *American Psychologist, 44,* 424–433.

Hutchinson, R. L., Tess, D. E., Gleckman, A. D., & Spence, W. G. (1992). Psychosocial characteristics of institutionalized adolescents: Resilient or at risk? *Adolescence, 27* (106), 339–356.

Hyde, J. S., & Linn, M. C. (1988). Gender differences in verbal ability: A meta-analysis. *Psychological Bulletin, 104,* 53–69.

Hymel, S., Rubin, K. H., Rowden, L., & LeMare, L. (1990). Children's peer relationships:

Longitudinal prediction of internalizing and externalizing problems from middle to late childhood. *Child Development, 61* (6), 2004–2021.

Iams, H. M., & McCoy, J. L. (1991). Predictors of mortality among newly retired workers. *Social Security Bulletin, 54* (3), 2–10.

Iams, J. D., & Zuspan, F. P. (1990). *Zuspan and Quilligan's manual of obstetrics and gynecology.* St. Louis: Mosby.

Insel, P. M., & Roth, W. T. (1991). *Core concepts in health* (6th ed.). Mountain View, CA: Mayfield.

International Labor Organization. (1992). *Worldwide trends in household and vocational gender inequality.* New York: Author.

Ironson, G. (1992). Job stress and health. In C. J. Cranny, P. C. Smith, & E. F. Stone (Eds.), *Job satisfaction.* New York: Lexington Books.

Irving, L. M., McClusky-Fawcett, K., & Thissen, D. (1990). Sexual attitudes and behavior of bulimic women: A preliminary investigation. *Journal of Youth and Adolescence, 19* (4). 395–412.

Isabella, R. A., & Belsky, J. (1991). Interactional synchrony and the origins of infant-mother attachment: A replication study. *Child Development, 62* (2), 373–384.

Isaia, G. C. (1990). Role of sedentary life in the pathogenesis of osteoporosis. In F. Fabris, L. Pernigotti, & E. Ferrario (Eds.), *Sedentary life and nutrition.* New York: Raven Press.

Isenberg, J. P., & Jalongo, M. R. (1993). *Creative expression and play in the early childhood curriculum.* New York: Macmillan.

Ishii-Kuntz, M. (1990). Formal activities for elderly women: Determinants of participation in voluntary and senior center activities. *Journal of Women and Aging, 2* (1), 79–97.

Issacs, S. (1986, January). High-tech pregnancies. *Working Mother,* pp. 18–26.

Issacs, S., & Holt, R. J. (1987). Redefining procreation: Facing the issues. *Population Bulletin, 42,* 1–37.

Itil, T. M., Sloane, H. L., & Itil, K. Z. (1990). Brain function evaluation in normal and pathological aging and during its treatment. In M. Bergener & S. I. Finkel, (Eds.), *Clinical and scientific psychogeriatrics.* New York: Springer.

Izard, C. E. (1992). Basic emotions, relations among emotions, and emotion-cognition relations. *Psychological Review, 99* (3), 561–565.

Izard, C. E., Haynes, O. M., Chisholm, G., & Baak, K. (1991). Emotional determinants of infant-mother attachment. *Child Development, 62* (5), 906–917.

Jacklin, C. N. (1989). Female and male: Issues of gender. *American Psychologist, 44,* 27–133.

Jackson, J. S. (1991). *Life in black America.* Newbury Park, CA: Sage.

Jackson, J. S., Chatters, L. M., & Taylor, R. J. (Eds.). (1992). *Aging in black America.* Newbury Park, CA: Sage.

Jacobs, J. E., & Potenza, M. (1991). The use of judgment heuristics to make social and object decisions: A developmental perspective. *Child Development, 62,* 166–178.

Jacobs, R. H. (1990). Friendships among old women. *Journal of Women and Aging, 2* (2), 19–32.

Jacobsen, D. A., Eggen, P. D., & Kauchak, D. P. (1993). *Methods for teaching: A skills approach* (4th ed.). New York: Macmillan.

Jacobson, S. W., & Frye, K. F. (1991). Effect of maternal social support on attachment: Experimental evidence. *Child Development, 62* (3), 572–582.

Jacobson, S. W., Jacobson, J. L., O'Neill, J. M., & Padgett, R. J. (1992). Visual expectation and dimensions of infant information processing. *Child Development, 63* (3), 711–724.

Jacyk, W. R. (1991). Chemical dependency in the elderly: Identification phase. *Canadian Journal on Aging, 10* (1), 10–17.

Jaeger, E., & Weinraub, M. (1990). Early nonmaternal care and infant attachment: In search of process. In K. McCartney (Ed.), *Child care and maternal employment: A social ecology approach.* San Francisco: Jossey-Bass.

Jamal, M., & Baba, V. (1991). Type A behavior, its prevalence and consequences among women nurses: An empirical examination. *Human Relations, 44* (11), 1213–1228.

James, C. R., & James, L. (1992). Psychological climate and affect. In C. J. Cranny, P. C. Smith, & E. F. Stone (Eds.), *Job satisfaction.* New York: Lexington Books.

Jankel, C. A. (1991). Evaluating drugs for use in the elderly. *Journal of Geriatric Drug Therapy, 6* (1), 5–12.

Janz, M. (1990). Clues to elder abuse. *Geriatrics Nursing, 11* (5), 220–222.

Jarolimek, J. (1993). *Teaching and learning in the elementary school* (5th ed.). New York: Macmillan.

Jenike, M. A. (1989). *Geriatric psychiatry and psychopharmacology: A clinical approach.* St. Louis: Mosby.

Jensen, G. D., & Goldstein, L. (1991). A microcomputerized task assessment of cognitive change in normal elderly and young adults. *Experimental Aging Research, 17* (2), 119–121.

Jerome, D. (1990). Intimate relationships. In J. Bond & P. Coleman (Eds.), *Aging in society: An introduction to social gerontology.* Newbury Park, CA: Sage.

Johansson, B., & Berg, S. (1989). The robustness of the terminal decline phenomenon: Longitudinal data from the digit-span memory test. *Journal of Gerontology, 44,* P184–P186.

Johansson, L. (1991). Informal care of the dependent elderly at home: Some Swedish experiences. *Ageing and Society, 11* (1), 41–58.

John, R. (1991). Family support networks among elders in a Native American community: Contact with children and siblings among the Prairie Band Potawatomi. *Journal of Aging Studies, 5* (1), 45–59.

Johns, S., Hydle, I., & Aschjem, O. (1991). The act of abuse: A two-headed monster of injury and offense. *Journal of Elder Abuse and Neglect, 3* (1), 53–64.

Johnson, B. M., Shulman, S., & Collins, W. A. (1991). Systematic patterns of parenting as reported by adolescents: Developmental differences and implications for psychosocial outcomes. *Journal of Adolescent Research, 6* (2), 235–252.

Johnson, C. (1985). The impact of illness on late-life families. *Journal of Marriage and the Family, 47,* 165–172.

Johnson, C. A. (1990). Perceived barriers to exercise and weight control practices in community women. *Women and Health, 16,* 177–199.

Johnson, C. J., Pick, H. L., Jr., Siegel, G. M., Cicciarelli, A. W., & Garber, S. R. (1981). Effects of interpersonal distance on children's vocal intensity. *Child Development, 52,* 721–723.

Johnson C. L. (1983). Dyadic family relationships and family supports: An analysis of the family caregiver. *Gerontologist, 23,* 377–383.

Johnson, C. L., & Barer, B. M. (1990). Families and networks among older inner-city blacks. *Gerontologist, 30* (6), 726–733.

Johnson, D., & Fein, E. (1991). The concept of attachment: Applications to adoption. *Children and Youth Services Review, 13* (5/6), 397–412.

Johnson, D. R., White, L. K., Edwards, J. N., & Booth, A. (1986). Dimensions of marital quality: Toward methodological and conceptual refinement. *Journal of Family Issues, 7,* 31–49.

Johnson, G. M., Shontz, F. C., & Locke, T. P. (1984). Relationship between adolescent drug use and parental drug behaviors. *Adolescence, 19,* 295–299.

Johnson, M. A. (1992). Nutritional patterns of centenarians. *International Journal of Aging and Human Development, 34* (1), 57–76.

Johnson, S. H. (1991). Nursing home restraints: The legal issues. *Health Progress, 72* (7), 18–19.

Johnston, L. D., O'Malley, P. M., & Bachman, J. G. (1988). *Illicit drug use, smoking, and drinking by America's high school students, college students, and young adults, 1975–1987.* Washington, DC: National Institute of Drug Abuse.

Johnston, L. D., O'Malley, P. M., & Bachman, J. G. (1990, February). Drug use continues to decline [News release]. Ann Arbor, MI: Institute for Social Research.

Joiner, J. (1990). Alzheimer's disease: A study of assessment and stages. *American Journal of Alzheimer's Care and Related Disorders and Research, 5* (2), 28–36.

Jones, D. J., & Battle, S. F. (1990). *Teenage pregnancy: Developing strategies for change in the twenty-first century.* New Brunswick, NJ: Transaction.

Jones, E. F., & Forrest, J. (1989). Contraceptive failure in the United States: Revised estimates from the 1982 National Survey of Family Growth. *Family Planning Perspectives, 17,* 53–63.

Jones, E. F., Forrest, J., Goldman, N., Henshaw, S., Lincoln, R., Rossoff, J., Westoff, C., & Wulf, D. (1986). *Teenage pregnancy in industrialized counties.* New Haven, CT: Yale University Press.

Jones, S. S., Smith, L. B., & Landau, B. (1991). Object properties and knowledge in early lexical learning. *Child Development, 62* (3), 499–516.

Jose, P. E., & McCarthy, W. J. (1988). Perceived agentic and communal behavior in mixed-sex group interactions. *Personality and Social Psychology Bulletin, 14,* 57–67.

Josselson, R. (1988). The embedded self: I and thou revisited. In D. K. Lapsley & F. C. Powers (Eds.), *Self, ego, and identity: Integrative approaches.* New York: Springer-Verlag.

Juhasz, A. M., & Palmer, L. L. (1991). Adolescent perspectives of ways of thinking and believing that promote peace. *Adolescence, 26* (104), 849–855.

Julius, S. (1990, July 18). The association of borderline hypertension with target organ change and higher coronary risk. *Journal of the American Medical Association,* pp. 24–27.

Jutras, S., & Veilleux, F. (1991). Informal caregiving: Correlates of perceived burden. *Canadian Journal of Aging, 10* (1), 40–55.

Kaffman, M. (1989). Divorce in the kibbutz: Determinants of emotional adjustment. *Contemporary Family Therapy, 11* (3), 189–211.

Kafka, R. R., & London, P. (1991). Communication in relationships and adolescent substance use: The influence of parents and friends. *Adolescence, 26* (103), 587–598.

Kagan, J. (1965). Impulsive and reflective children: Significance of conceptual tempo. In J. Krumboltz (Ed.), *Learning and the educational process.* Chicago: Rand McNally.

Kagan, J. (1966). Reflection-impulsivity: The generality and dynamics of conceptual tempo. *Journal of Abnormal Psychology, 71,* 17–24.

Kagan, J. (1991). The theoretical utility of constructs for self. *Developmental Review, 11* (3), 244–250.

Kagan, J., & Moss, H. A. (1962). *Birth to maturity: A study in psychological development.* New York: Wiley.

Kagan, J., Reznick, J. S., Snidman, N., & Gibbons, J. (1988). Childhood derivatives of inhibition and lack of inhibition to the unfamiliar. *Child Development, 59,* 1580–1589.

Kagan, J., Rosman, B., Day, D., Albert, J., & Phillips, W. (1964). Information processing in the child. *Psychology Monograph, 78* (1, Whole No. 578).

Kahana, E., & Kinney, J. (1991). Understanding caregiving interventions in the context of the stress model. In R. F. Young & E. A. Olson (Eds.), *Health, illness, and disability in later life: Practice issues and interventions.* Newbury Park, CA: Sage.

Kahn, A. (1984). *Social psychology.* Dubuque, IA: Wm. C. Brown.

Kail, R. (1990). *The development of memory in children* (3rd ed.). New York: Freeman.

Kalat, J. W. (1992). *Biological psychology* (4th ed.). Belmont, CA: Wadsworth.

Kalish, C. W., & Gelman, S. A. (1992). On wooden pillows: Multiple classification and children's category-based inductions. *Child Development, 63* (6), 1536–1557.

Kalish, R. A. (1987). Older people and grief. *Generations, 21* (3), 33–38.

Kalish, R. A. (1989). *Midlife loss: Coping strategies.* Newbury Park, CA: Sage.

Kalmus, D., Davidson, A., & Cushman, L. (1992). Parenting expectations, experiences, and adjustment to parenthood: A test of the violated expectations framework. *Journal of Marriage and the Family, 54,* 516–526.

Kalter, N. (1990). *Growing up with divorce: Helping your child avoid immediate and later emotional problems.* New York: Free Press.

Kamholz, B., & Gottlieb, G. L. (1990). The nature and efficacy of interventions for depression and dementia. In B. S. Fogel, A. Furino, & G. L. Gottlieb (Eds.), *Mental health policy for older Americans: Protecting minds at risk.* Washington, DC: American Psychiatric Press.

Kamo, Y. (1988). Determinants of household division of labor. *Journal of Family Issues, 9,* 177–200.

Kaplan, G. A. (1992). Health and aging in the Alameda County study. In K. W. Schaie, D. Blazer, & J. S. House (Eds.), *Aging, health behaviors, and health outcomes.* Hillsdale, NJ: Erlbaum.

Kaplan, P. S., Scheuneman, D., Jenkins, L., & Hilliard, S. (1988). Sensitization of infant visual attention: Role of pattern contrast. *Infant Behavior and Development, 11* (3), 265–276.

Kaplan, R. M., Sallis, J. F., Jr, & Patterson, T. L. (1993). *Health and human behavior*. New York: McGraw-Hill.

Karasek, R., & Theorell, T. (1990). *Healthy work: Stress, productivity, and the reconstruction of the working life*. New York: Basic Books.

Kart, C. S. (1990). *The realities of aging* (3rd ed.). Boston: Allyn & Bacon.

Kartman, L. L. (1991). Life review: One aspect of making meaningful music for the elderly. *Activities, Adaptations, and Aging, 15*, 42–45.

Karuza, J., & Katz, P. R. (1991). Psychosocial interventions in long-term care: A critical overview. In P. R. Katz, R. L. Kane, & M. D. Mezey (Eds.), *Advances in long-term care*. New York: Springer.

Kashiwase, H., & Watanabe, M. (1991). Geriatric psychiatry in Japan. *Journal of Geriatric Psychiatry, 24* (1), 47–57.

Kasworm, C. E., & Medina, R. A. (1990). Adult competence in everyday tasks: A cross-sectional secondary analysis. *Educational Gerontology, 16* (1), 27–48.

Katz, L., & Chard, S. C. (1989). *Engaging children's minds: The project approach*. Norwood, NJ: Ablex.

Kauffman, J. F., & Ames, B. D. (1983). Care of aging family members. *Journal of Home Economics, 75* (1), 45–46.

Kaufman, K. L., & Rudy, L. (1991). Future directions in the treatment of physical child abuse. *Criminal Justice and Behavior, 18* (1), 82–97.

Kausler, D. H. (1982). *Experimental psychology and human aging*. New York: Wiley.

Kausler, D. H., & Wiley, J. G. (1990). Effects of prior retrieval on adult age differences in long-term recall of activities. *Experimental Aging Research, 16* (4), 185–189.

Kaye, L. W., & Applegate, J. S. (1990). Men as elder caregivers: Building a research agenda for the 1990's. *Journal of Aging Studies, 4* (3), 289–298.

Keating, D. P. (1990). Adolescent thinking. In S. S. Feldman & G. R. Elliott (Eds.), *At the threshold: The developing adolescent*. Cambridge, MA: Harvard University Press.

Keating, N., & Cole, P. (1980). What do I do with him 24 hours a day? *Gerontologist, 20*, 84–89.

Kegeles, S., Adler, N., & Irwin, C. (1988). Sexually active adolescents and condoms. *American Journal of Public Health, 78*, 460–466.

Keith, P. M., Dobson, C. D., Goudy, W. J., & Powers, E. A. (1981). Older men: Occupation, employment status, household involvement, and well-being. *Journal of Family Issues, 2*, 336–349.

Keith, P. M., & Schafer, R. B. (1991). *Relationships and well-being over the life stages*. New York: Praeger.

Keller, M., Eckensberger, L. H., & von Rosen, K. (1989). A critical note on the conception of preconventional morality: The case of stage 2 in Kohlberg's theory. *International Journal of Behavioral Development, 12*, 57–69.

Kelley, D. L., & Burgoon, J. K. (1991). Understanding marital satisfaction and couple type as functions of relational expectations. *Human Communication Research, 18* (1), 40–69.

Kellough, R. D., & Roberts, P. L. (1991). *A resource guide for elementary school teaching: Planning for competence* (2nd ed.). New York: Macmillan.

Kelly, C., & Goodwin, G. C. (1983). Adolescents' perception of three styles of parental control. *Adolescence, 18*, 567–571.

Kelly, J. A., & deArmas, A. (1989). Social relationships in adolescence: Skill development and training. In J. Worell & F. Danner (Eds.), *The adolescent as decision-maker*. San Diego: Academic Press.

Kelly, R. M. (1991). *The gendered economy: Work, careers, and success*. Newbury Park, CA: Sage.

Kempe, R. S., & Kempe, C. H. (1984). *The common secret: Sexual abuse of children and adolescents*. New York: Freeman.

Kemper, P., & Murtaugh, C. M. (1991). Lifetime use of nursing home care. *New England Journal of Medicine, 324* (9), 595–600.

Kemple, K., Speranza, H., & Hazen, N. (1992). Cohesive discourse and peer acceptance: Longitudinal relations in the preschool years. *Merrill-Palmer Quarterly, 28* (3), 364–381.

Kempton, T., Armistead, L., Wierson, M., & Forehand, R. (1991). Presence of a sibling as a potential buffer following parental divorce: An examination of young adolescents. *Journal of Clinical Child Psychology, 20* (4), 434–438.

Kendall-Tackett, K. A. (1988). Molestation and the onset of puberty: Data from 363 adults molested as children. *Child Abuse and Neglect, 12*, 73–81.

Kendall-Tackett, K. A., Williams, L. M., & Finkelhor, D. (1993). Impact of sexual abuse on children: A review and synthesis of recent empirical studies. *Psychological Bulletin, 113* (1), 164–180.

Kennedy, J., & Laramore, D. (1993). *Joyce Lain Kennedy's career book*. Lincolnwood, IL: NTC.

Kennedy, J. H. (1992). Relationship of maternal beliefs and childrearing strategies to social competence in pre-school children. *Child Study Journal, 22* (1), 39–60.

Kennedy, R. E. (1991). Delinquency. In R. M. Lerner, A. C. Petersen, & J. Brooks-Gunn (Eds.), *The encyclopedia of adolescence*. New York: Garland.

Kenny, D. E., & Oettinger, N. (Eds.). (1991). *The family carebook: A comprehensive guide for families of older adults*. Seattle: Care Source Program Development.

Kermis, M. D. (1984). *The psychology of aging: Theory, research, and practice*. Boston: Allyn & Bacon.

Kerr, R., & Teaffe, M. S. (1991). Aging and the response to changes in task difficulty. *Canadian Journal on Aging, 10* (1), 18–28.

Kershner, J. R. (1990). Self-concept and IQ as predictors of remedial success in children with learning disabilities. *Journal of Learning Disabilities, 23* (6), 368–374.

Kessen, W. (1965). *The child*. New York: Wiley.

Khachaturian, Z. S., Radebaugh, T. S., & Monjan, A. A. (1990). Alzheimer's disease: Causes, controls, and cures. In J. L. Cummings & R. L. Miller (Eds.), *Alzheimer's disease: Treatment and long-term management*. New York: Marcel Dekker.

Khourg, M. J., Gomez-Farias, M., & Mulinare, J. (1989). Does maternal cigarette smoking during pregnancy cause cleft lip and palate in offspring? *American Journal of Diseases of Children, 143*, 333–338.

Kiefer, C. (1990). Aging and the elderly in Japan. In R. L. Rubinstein (Ed.), *Anthropology and aging: Comprehensive reviews*. Boston: Kluwer Academic Publishers.

Killeen, M. (1990). The influence of stress and coping on family caregivers' perceptions of health. *International Journal of Aging and Human Development, 30* (3), 197–211.

Kilner, J. F. *Who lives? Who dies? Ethical criteria in patient selection*. New Haven, CT: Yale University Press.

Kimmel, D. C. (1990). *Adulthood and aging: An interdisciplinary view* (3rd ed.). New York: Wiley.

Kinderknecht, C. H., & Hodges, L. (1990). Facilitating productive bereavement of widows: An overview of the efficacy of widows' support groups. *Journal of Women and Aging, 2* (4), 39–54.

King, N. J., Gullone, E., & Ollendick, T. H. (1992). Manifest anxiety and fearfulness in children and adolescents. *Journal of Genetic Psychology, 153* (1), 63–73.

King, P. A., Caddy, G. M., & Cohen, S. H. (1989). Circumcision: Maternal attitudes. *Pediatric Surgical Intervention, 4*, 222–238.

Kinsella, K. (1990). Suicide at older ages: An international enigma. *Ageing International, 17* (2), 36–37.

Kissman, K., & Allen, J. (1992). *Single-parent families*. Newbury Park, CA: Sage.

Kitson, G. C., & Raschke, H. J. (1981). Divorce research: What we know; what we need to know. *Journal of Divorce, 4*, 1–37.

Kivett, V. (1991). The grandparent-grandchild connection. In S. K. Pfeifer & M. B. Sussman (Eds.), *Families: Intergenerational and generational connections*. Binghamton, NY: Haworth Press.

Kiyak, H. A., & Borson, S. (1992). Coping with chronic illness and disability. In M. G. Ory, R. P. Abeles, & P. D. Lipman (Eds.), *Aging, health, and behavior*. Newbury Park, CA: Sage.

Klahr, D. (1989). Information processing approaches. In R. Vasta (Ed.), *Six theories of child development: Revised formulations and current issues*. Greenwich, CT: JAI Press.

Klaue, K. (1992). The development of depth representation in children's drawings: Effects of graphic surface and visibility of the model. *British Journal of Developmental Psychology, 10* (1), 71–83.

Klein, J. M. (1989, November 15). The fate of the frozen embryos. *New London (CT) Day*, p. C-7.

Kliegl, R., Smith, J., & Baltes, P. B. (1989). Testing the limits and the study of age differences in cognitive plasticity of a mnemonic skill. *Developmental Psychology, 25*, 247–256.

Kline, D. W. (1992). Vision, aging, and driving: The problems of older drivers. *Journal of Gerontology: Psychological Sciences, 47* (1), P27–P34.

Klingman, A. (1988). Biblioguidance with kindergartners: Evaluation of a primary prevention program to reduce fear of the dark. *Clinical Child Psychology, 17*, 237–241.

Knight, B. (1983). Assessing a mobile outreach team. In M. A. Smyer & M. Gatz (Eds.), *Mental health and aging: Programs and evaluations*. Beverly Hills, CA: Sage.

Knight, B. M. (1986). *Enjoying single parenthood*. New York: Van Nostrand Reinhold.

Knight, G. P., & Chao, C. C. (1991). Cooperative, competitive, and individualistic social values among 8- to 12-year old siblings, friends, and acquaintances. *Personality and Social Psychology Bulletin, 17* (2), 201–211.

Knopman, D. S., & Sawyer-DeMaris, S. (1990). Practical approach to managing behavioral problems in dementia patients. *Geriatrics, 45* (4), 27–30.

Knox, D. (1985). *Choices in relationships.* St. Paul, MN: West.

Kocarnik, R. A., & Ponzetti, J. J., Jr. (1991). The advantages and challenges of intergenerational programs in long-term care facilities. *Journal of Gerontological Social Work, 16* (1/2), 97–107.

Kochanska, G. (1992). Children's interpersonal influence with mothers and peers. *Developmental Psychology, 28* (3), 491–499.

Kochanska, G., Kuczynski, L., & Radke-Yarrow, M. (1989). Correspondence between mother's self-reported and observed child-rearing practices. *Child Development, 60,* 56–63.

Koenig, H. G. (1991). Major depressive disorder in hospitalized medically ill patients: An examination of young and elderly male veterans. *Journal of the American Geriatrics Society, 89* (9), 881–890.

Koff, E., & Riordan, J. (1991). Menarche and body image. In R. M. Lerner, A. C. Petersen, & J. Brooks-Gunn (Eds.), *The encyclopedia of adolescence.* New York: Garland.

Kogan, N. (1990). Personality and aging. In J. E. Birren & K. W. Schaie (Eds.), *Handbook of the psychology of aging* (3rd ed.). San Diego: Academic Press.

Koh, J. Y., & Bell, W. G. (1987). Korean elderly in the United States: International relations and living arrangements. *Gerontologist, 27,* 66–71.

Kohlberg, L. (1969). *Stages in the development of moral thought and action.* New York: Holt, Rinehart and Winston.

Kohlberg, L. (1976). Moral stages and moralization. In T. Lickona (Ed.), *Moral development and behavior.* New York: Holt, Rinehart and Winston.

Kohlberg, L. (1981a). Moral education in the schools: A developmental view. In M. Kaplan-Sanoff & R. Yablans-Magid (Eds.), *Exploring early childhood: Readings in theory and practice.* New York: Macmillan.

Kohlberg, L. (1981b). *Philosophy of moral development.* New York: Harper & Row.

Kohlberg, L. (1986). A current statement on some theoretical issues. In S. Modgil & C. Modgil (Eds.), *Lawrence Kohlberg.* Philadelphia: Farmer Press.

Kohlberg, L., & Turiel, E. (1973). Continuities in childhood and adult moral development revisited. In P. B. Baltes & K. W. Schaie (Eds.), *Life span developmental psychology: Personality and socialization.* New York: Aca-demic Press.

Kohn, A. (1988, February). Girl talk, guy talk. *Psychology Today,* pp. 65–66.

Kolb, B., & Wishaw, I. (1988). *Fundamentals of human neuropsychology.* New York: Freeman.

Konner, M. J. (1976). Infant behavior and development among the !Kung. In R. B. Lee & I. DeVore (Eds.), *Kalahari hunter-gatherers.* Cambridge, MA: Harvard University Press.

Korenbrot, C. C., Brindis, C., & Priddy, F. (1990). Trends in rates of live births and abortions following state restrictions on public funding of abortion. *Public Health Reports, 105* (6), 555–562.

Korones, S. B. (1986). *High risk newborn infants.* St. Louis: Mosby.

Korritko, A. (1991). Family therapy with one-parent families. *Contemporary Family Therapy, 13,* 625–640.

Kosberg, J. I. (Ed.). (1992). *Family care of the elderly: Social and cultural changes.* Newbury Park, CA: Sage.

Kosloski, K. D., Montgomery, R. J. V., & Borgatta, E. F. (1990). Predicting nursing home utilization: Is this the best we can do? In S. M. Stahl (Ed.), *The legacy of longevity: Health and health care in later life.* Newbury Park, CA: Sage.

Kosslyn, S. (1990). Age differences in imagery abilities. *Child Development, 61* (4), 995–1010.

Kostelnik, M. J., Stein, L., Whiren, A. P., & Soderman, A. K. (1993). *Guiding children's social development* (2nd ed.). Albany, NY: Delmar.

Kostelnik, M. J., Whiren, A. P., & Soderman, A. K. (1993). *Developmentally appropriate programs in early childhood education.* New York: Macmillan.

Kottke, M. K. (1990). Problems encountered by the elderly in the use of conventional dosage forms. *Journal of Geriatric Drug Therapy, 5* (2), 77–92.

Kouri, M. A. (1990).Volunteerism and older adults. *Choices and challenges: An older adult reference series.* Santa Barbara, CA: ABC-CLIO.

Kraemer, S. (1991). The origins of fatherhood: An ancient family process. *Family Process, 30* (4), 377–392.

Kramer, L., & Gottman, J. M. (1992). Becoming a sibling: "With a little help from my friends." *Developmental Psychology, 28* (4), 685–699.

Krause, M. V. (1984). *Food, nutrition and diet therapy* (7th ed.). Philadelphia: Saunders.

Krause, N. (1990). Stress and isolation from close ties in later life. *Journal of Gerontology: Social Sciences, 46* (4), S183–S194.

Krause, N., & Alexander, G. (1990). Self-esteem and psychological distress in later life. *Journal of Aging and Health, 2* (4), 419–438.

Krebs, D., & Gillmore, J. (1982). The relationships among the first stages of cognitive development, role-taking abilities, and moral development. *Child Development, 53,* 877–886.

Krout, J. A. (1991). Senior center participation: Findings from a multidimensional analysis. *Journal of Applied Gerontology, 10* (3), 244–257.

Kuansnicka, E., Beymer, B., & Perloff, R. M. (1982). Portrayals of the elderly in magazine advertisements. *Journalism Quarterly, 59* (4), 656–658.

Kubey, R., & Csikszentmihalyi, M. (1990). *Television and the quality of life: How viewing shapes everyday experience.* Hillsdale, NJ: Erlbaum.

Kübler-Ross, E. (1969). *On death and dying.* New York: Macmillan.

Kübler-Ross, E. (1974). *Questions and answers on death and dying.* New York: Macmillan.

Kübler-Ross, E. (1975). *Death: The final stage of growth.* Englewood Cliffs, NJ: Prentice Hall.

Kübler-Ross, E. (1981). *Living with death and dying.* New York: Macmillan.

Kübler-Ross, E. (1982). *Working it through.* New York: Macmillan.

Kübler-Ross, E. (1983). *On children and death.* New York: Macmillan.

Kübler-Ross, E., & Magno, J. B. (1983). *Hospice: A handbook for families and others facing terminal illness.* Sante Fe, NM: Bear.

Kuhn, D. (1989). Children and adults as intuitive scientists. *Psychological Review, 96,* 674–689.

Kuhn, D., Amsel, E., & O'Loughlin, M. (1988). *The development of scientific thinking skills.* Orlando, FL: Academic Press.

Kulin, H. E. (1991). Hypothalamic-pituitary changes of puberty. In R. M. Lerner, A. C. Petersen, & J. Brooks-Gunn (Eds.), *The encyclopedia of adolescence.* New York: Garland.

Kunitz, S., & Levy, J. E. (1991). *Navajo aging: The transition from family to institutional support.* Tucson: University of Arizona Press.

Kunkel, D. & Murray, J. (1991). Television, children, and social policy: Issues and resources for child advocates. *Journal of Clinical Child Psychology, 20* (1), 88–95.

Kunkel, M. E. (1991). Nutrition and aging. In E. M. Baines (Ed.), *Perspectives on gerontological nursing.* Newbury Park, CA: Sage.

Kupersmidt, J. B., & Coie, J. D. (1990). Preadolescent peer status, aggression, and school adjustment as predictors of externalizing problems in adolescence. *Child Development, 61,* 1350–1362.

Kupfersmid, J. H., & Wonderly, D. M. (1980). Moral maturity and behavior: Failure to find a link. *Journal of Youth and Adolescence, 9,* 249–262.

Kupke, K. G., & Muller, U. (1989). Parental origin of the extra chromosome in trisomy 18. *American Journal of Human Genetics, 45,* 599–605.

Kurtz, P. D., Kurtz, G. L., & Jarvis, S. V. (1991). Problems of maltreated runaway youth. *Adolescence, 26* (103), 543–555.

Kutscher, R. E., & Fullerton, H. N. (1990). The aging labor force. In I. Bluestone, R. Irving, J. V. Montgomery, & J. D. Owen (Eds.), *The aging of the American work force.* Detroit: Wayne State University Press.

Kuznar, E. (1991). Learning style preferences: A comparison of younger and older adult females. *Journal of Nutrition for the Elderly, 10* (3), 21–33.

Labouvie-Vief, G. (1982). Dynamic development and mature autonomy: A theoretical prologue. *Human Development, 25,* 161–191.

Labouvie-Vief, G. (1986, August). *Modes of knowing and life-span cognition.* Paper presented at the American Psychological Association, Washington, DC.

Labouvie-Vief, G. (1990). Models of cognitive functioning in the older adult: Research needs in educational gerontology. In R. H. Sherron & D. B. Lumsden (Eds.), *Introduction to education gerontology* (3rd ed.). New York: Hemisphere.

Lacoste-Utamsing, D., & Holloway, R. (1982). Sexual dimorphism in the human corpus callosum. *Science, 216,* 1431–1432.

Laczko, F. (1989). Between work and retirement: Becoming old in the 1980's. In B. Bytheway, T. Keil, P. Allat, & A. Bryan (Eds.), *Becoming and being old: Social approaches to later life.* Newbury Park, CA: Sage.

Laczko, F., & Phillipson, C. (1991). *Changing work and retirement: Social policy and the older worker.* Philadelphia: Open University Press.

Ladd, G. W. (1988). Friendship patterns and peer status during early and middle childhood. *Journal of Developmental and Behavioral Pediatrics, 9,* 229–238.

Ladd, G. W. (1990). Having friends, keeping friends, making friends, and being liked by peers in the classroom: Predictors of children's early school adjustment? *Child Development, 61,* 1081–1100.

Ladd, G. W., & Hart, C. H. (1992). Creating informal play opportunities: Are parents' and preschoolers' initiations related to children's competence with peers? *Developmental Psychology, 28* (6), 1179–1137.

Ladd, G. W., Price, J. M., & Hart, C. H. (1988). Predicting preschoolers' peer status from their playground behaviors. *Child Development, 59,* 986–992.

LaForge, R. G., Spector, W. D., & Sternberg, J. (1992). The relationship of vision and hearing impairment to one-year mortality and functional decline. *Journal of Aging and Health, 4* (1), 126–148.

Lamanna, M. A., & Riedmann, A. (1994) *Marriages and families: Making choices and facing change* (5th ed.). Belmont, CA: Wadsworth.

Lamb, M. E. (1986). The changing role of fathers. In M. E. Lamb (Ed.), *The father's role: Applied perspectives.* New York: Wiley.

Lamb, M. E.(1987). The emergent American father. In M. E. Lamb (Ed.), *The father's role: Cross-cultural perspectives.* Hillsdale, NJ: Erlbaum.

Lamb, M. E., Steinberg, K. J., Hwang, C. P., & Broberg, A. G. (1992). *Child care in context.* Hillsdale, NJ: Erlbaum.

Lambert, W. E. (1981). *Faces and facets of bilingualism.* Washington, DC: Center for Applied Linguistics.

Lamborn, S. D. (1991). Patterns of competence and adjustment among adolescents from authoritative, authoritarian, indulgent, and neglectful families. *Child Development, 62* (5), 1605–1616.

Landale, N. S., & Hauan, S. M. (1992). The family life course of Puerto Rican children. *Journal of Marriage and the Family, 54,* 912–924.

Landers, D. V., & Sweet. R. L. (1990). Perinatal infections. In J. R. Scott (Ed.), *Danforth's obstetrics and gynecology.* Philadelphia: Lippincott.

Landry, S., Chapieski, L., Richardson, M. A., Palmer, J., & Hall, S. (1990). The social competence of children born prematurely: Effects of medical complications and parent behaviors. *Child Development, 61,* 1049–1065.

Langer, N. (1990). Grandparents and adult grandchildren: What do they do for one another? *International Journal of Aging and Human Development, 31* (2), 101–110.

Langmade, C. J. (1983). The impact of pre- and postpubertal onset of incest experiences in adult women as measured by anxiety, sex guilt, sexual satisfaction, and sexual behavior. *Dissertation Abstracts International, 44,* 917B.

Lanza, E. (1992). Can bilingual two-year-olds code-switch? *Journal of Child Language, 19* (3), 633–658.

Lapsley, D. K. (1985). Elkind on egocentrism. *Developmental Review, 5,* 227–236.

Lapsley, D. K. (1986). Adolescent egocentrism and formal operations: Tests of a theoretical assumption. *Developmental Psychology, 22,* 800–807.

Lapsley, D. K. (1990). Continuity and discontinuity in adolescent social cognitive development. In R. Montemayor, G. Adams, & T. Gullota (Eds.), *From childhood to adolescence: Advances in adolescent development* (Vol. 2). Newbury Park, CA: Sage.

Lapsley, D. K. (1991). The adolescent egocentrism theory and the "new look" at the imaginary audience and personal fable. In R. M. Lerner, A. C. Petersen, & J. Brooks-Gunn (Eds.), *The encyclopedia of adolescence.* New York: Garland.

Lapsley, D. K., Fitzgerald, D. P., Rice, K. G., & Jackson, S. (1989). Separation-individuation and the "new look" at the imaginary audience and personal fable: A test of an integrative model. *Journal of Adolescent Research, 4,* 483–505.

Lapsley, D. K., & Murphy, M. N. (1985). Another look at the theoretical assumptions of adolescent egocentrism. *Developmental Review, 5,* 201–217.

Lapsley, D. K., & Rice, K. G. (1988). The "new look" at the imaginary audience and personal fable: Toward a general model of adolescent ego development. In D. K. Lapsley & F. C. Power (Eds.), *Self, ego, and identity: Integrative approaches.* New York: Springer.

Lark, S. M. (1990). *The menopause self-help book: A woman's guide to feeling wonderful for the second half of her life.* Berkeley, CA: Celestial Arts.

LaRossa, R. (1986). *Becoming a parent.* Beverly Hills, CA: Sage.

LaRossa, R. (1988). Fatherhood and social change. *Family Relations, 37,* 451–457.

LaRossa, R., & Reitzes, D. C. (in press). Symbolic interactionism and family studies. In P. Boss, W. Doherty, R. LaRossa, W. Schumm, & S. Steinmetz (Eds.), *Sourcebook of family theories and methods: A contextual approach.* New York: Plenum.

Lasker, J. N., & Borg, S. (1987). *In search of parenthood: Coping with infertility.* Boston: Beacon Press.

Lasswell, M., & Lasswell, T. (1991). *Marriage and the family* (3rd ed.). Belmont, CA: Wadsworth.

Lauer, R. H., & Lauer, J. C. (1991). *Marriage and family: The quest for intimacy.* Dubuque, IA: Wm. C. Brown.

Lauer, R. H., Lauer, J. C., & Kerr, S. T. (1990). The long-term marriage: Perceptions of stability and satisfaction. *International Journal of Aging and Human Development, 31* (3), 189–195.

Lauersen, N. (1983). *Childbirth with love.* New York: Berkley.

Lauersen, N. H., & Bouchez, C. (1991). *Getting pregnant: What couples need to know right now.* New York: Fawcett.

Laureau, W. (1992). *Where am I now? Where am I going?* Clinton, NJ: New Line Publishers.

Lawson, C. (1989, June 15). Toys: Boys fight wars, girls still apply makeup. *New York Times,* p. C-1.

Lawton, M. P. (1991). Functional status and aging well. *Generations, 15* (1), 31–34.

Lawton, M. P., Brody, E. M., & Saperstein, A. R. (1991). *Respite for caregivers of Alzheimer patients: Research and practice.* New York: Springer.

Lawton, M. P., Moss, M., & Glicksman, A. (1990). The quality of the last year of life of older persons. *Milbank Quarterly, 68* (1), 1–28.

Lazar, S., & Torney-Purta, J. (1991). The development of the subconcepts of death in young children: A short-term longitudinal study. *Child Development, 62* (6), 1321–1333.

Leadbeater, B. J., & Dionne, J. P. (1981). The adolescent's use of formal operational thinking in resolving problems related to identity resolution. *Adolescence, 16* (61), 111–121.

Leaper, C. (1991). Influence and involvement in children's discourse: Age, gender, and partner effects. *Child Development, 62* (4), 797–811.

LeCroy, C. W. (1988). Parent-adolescent intimacy: Impact on adolescent functioning. *Adolescence, 23,* 137–147.

Lederman, L. C. (1993). Gender and the self. In L. P. Arliss & D. J. Borisoff (Eds.), *Women and men communicating.* Fort Worth, TX: Harcourt Brace Jovanovich.

Lederman, S. (1992). Estimating infant mortality from human immunodeficiency virus and other causes in breast-feeding and bottle-feeding populations. *Pediatrics, 89,* 290–296.

Lee, G. R., & Shehan, C. L. (1989). Retirement and marital satisfaction. *Journal of Gerontology, 44,* S226–S230.

Lee, J. A. (1973, October). The styles of loving. *Psychology Today,* pp. 43–52.

Lee, J. A. (1976). *The colors of love.* Englewood Cliffs, NJ: Prentice Hall.

Lee, J. A. (1988). Love styles. In R. J. Sternberg & M. L. Barnes (Eds.), *The psychology of love.* New Haven, CT: Yale University Press.

Lee, J. A. (1990). Can we talk? Can we really talk? Communication as a key factor in the maturing homosexual couple. In J. A. Lee (Ed.), *Gay mid-life and maturity.* Binghamton, New York: Haworth Press.

Lee, M., & Prentice, N. M. (1988). Interrelations of empathy, cognition and moral reasoning with dimensions of juvenile delinquency. *Journal of Abnormal Child Psychology, 16,* 127–139.

Lee, V. K. (1991). Language changes and Alzheimer's disease: A literature review. *Journal of Gerontological Nursing, 17* (1), 16–20.

Leiblum, S. R., & Segraves, R. T. (1989). Sex therapy with aging adults. In S. R. Leiblum & R. C. Rosen (Eds.), *Principles and practices of sex therapy* (2nd ed.). New York: Guilford Press.

Leibowitz, A., Eisen, M., & Chow, W. K. (1986). An economic model of teenage pregnancy decision-making. *Demography, 23,* 67–77.

Leirer, V. O. (1990). Memory skills elders want to improve. *Experimental Aging Research, 16* (3), 155–158.

LeMasters, E. E., & DeFrain, J. (1989). *Parents in contemporary America* (5th ed.). Belmont, CA: Wadsworth.

Leming, M. R., & Dickinson, G. E. (1990). *Understanding death, dying, and bereavement* (2nd ed.). Ft. Worth, TX: Holt, Rinehart and Winston.

Lemlech, J. K. (1990). *Curriculum and instruction methods for the elementary school* (2nd ed.). New York: Macmillan.

Lenneberg, E. H. (1962). Understanding language without the ability to speak. *Journal of Abnormal Social Psychology, 65,* 419–425.

Lenneberg, E. H. (1967). *Biological foundations of language.* New York: Wiley.

Leon, G. R. (1991). Bulimia nervosa. In R. M. Lerner, A. C. Petersen, & J. Brooks-Gunn (Eds.), *The encyclopedia of adolescence.* New York: Garland.

Leonard, W. M. (1993). *A sociological perspective of sport* (4th ed.). New York: Macmillan.

Lerner, R. M., Lerner, J. V., & Tubman, J. (1989). Organismic and contextual bases of development in adolescence: A developmental contextual view. In G. R. Adams, R. Montemayor, & T. P. Gullota (Eds.), *Biology of adolescent behavior and development.* Beverly Hills, CA: Sage.

Leslie, G. R. (1982). *The family in social context* (5th ed.). New York: Oxford University Press.

Lester, B. M., Corwin, M. J., Sepkoski, C., & Seifer, R. (1991). Neurobehavioral syndromes in cocaine-exposed newborn infants. *Child Development, 62* (4), 694–705.

LeVay, S. (1991). A difference in hypothalamic structure between heterosexual and homosexual men. *Science, 253,* 1034.

Levenson, A. J., & Beller, S. A. (1983). Psychotropic drug use in the elderly: Optimal technique. *Urban Health, 12* (2), 32–35.

Levi, L. (1992). Intervening in social systems to promote health. In M. G. Ory, R. P. Abeles, & P. D. Lipman (Eds.), *Aging, health, and behavior.* Newbury Park, CA: Sage.

Levin, N. J. (1990). *How to care for your parents: A handbook for adult children.* Washington, DC: Storm King Press.

Levine, C., Jakubowski, L., & Cote, J. (1992). Linking ego and moral development: The value consistency thesis. *Human Development, 35* (5), 286–301.

Levine, M. W., & Shefner, J. M. (1991). *Fundamentals of sensation and perception* (2nd ed.). Pacific Grove, CA: Brooks/Cole.

Levinson, A. (1984). Home birth: Joy or jeopardy? In O. Pocs (Ed.), *Human sexuality, 1984/85.* Guilford, CT: Dushkin.

Levinson, D. J. (1977). The mid-life transition. *Psychiatry, 40,* 99–112.

Levinson, D. J. (1980). Toward a conception of the adult life course. In N. J. Smelser & E. H. Erikson (Eds.), *Themes of love and work in adulthood.* Cambridge, MA: Harvard University Press.

Levinson, D. J. (1981). Explorations in biography. In A. L. Rabin, J. Aronoff, A. M. Barclay, & R. A. Zucker (Eds.), *Further explorations in personality.* New York: Wiley.

Levinson, D. J. (1984). The career is in the life structure, the life structure is in the career: An adult development perspective. In M. B. Arthur, L. Bailyn, D. J. Levinson, & H. Shepard (Eds.), *Working with careers.* New York: Columbia University, School of Business.

Levinson, D. J. (1986). A conception of adult development. *American Psychologist, 41,* 3–13.

Levinson, D. J. (1990). A theory of life structure in adulthood. In C. N. Alexander & E. J. Langer (Eds.). *Higher stages of human development: Perspectives on adult growth.* New York: Oxford University Press.

Levinson, D. J. (in press). *The seasons of a woman's life.* New York: Knopf.

Levinson, D. J., Darrow, C. N., Klein, E. B., Levinson, M. H., & McKee, B. (1978). *The seasons of a man's life.* New York: Knopf.

Levinson, D. J., & Gooden, W. E. (1985). The life cycle. In H. I. Kaplan & B. J. Sadock (Eds.), *Comprehensive textbook of psychiatry* (4th ed.). Baltimore: Williams and Wilkins.

Levinthal, C. F. (1990). *Introduction to physiological psychology* (3rd ed.). Englewood Cliffs, NJ: Prentice Hall.

Levitan, S. A., Belous, R. S., & Gallo, F. (1988). *What's happening to the American family: Tensions, hopes, and realities* (rev. ed.). Baltimore: Johns Hopkins University Press.

Levitt, A. G., & Utman, J. G. A. (1992). From babbling towards the sound systems of English and French: A longitudinal two-case study. *Journal of Child Language, 19* (1), 19–49.

Levy, J. A. (1989). The hospice in the context of an aging society. *Journal of Aging Studies, 3* (4), 385–399.

Levy, M. T. (1991). *Parenting Mom and Dad: A guide for the grown-up children of aging parents.* Englewood Cliffs, NJ: Prentice Hall.

Levy-Shiff, R. (1983). Adaptation and competence in early childhood: Communally raised kibbutz children versus family raised children in the city. *Child Development, 54,* (6), 1606–1614.

Levy-Shiff, R., Hoffman, M. A., Mogilner, S., Levinger, S., & Mogilner, M. B. (1990). Fathers' hospital visits to their preterm infants as a predictor of father-infant relationship and infant development. *Pediatrics, 86* (2), 289–293.

Lewin, K. (1935). *Dynamic theory of personality.* New York: McGraw-Hill.

Lewin, M., & Tragos, L. M. (1987). Has the feminist movement influenced adolescent sex role attitudes? A reassessment after a quarter century. *Sex Roles, 16,* 125–135.

Lewis, E. J., & Bell, S. J. (1990). Nutritional assessment of the elderly. In J. E. Morley, Z. Glick, & L. Z. Rubenstein (Eds.), *Geriatric nutrition: A comprehensive review.* New York: Raven Press.

Lewis, J. M. (1993). Childhood play in normality, pathology, and therapy. *American Journal of Orthopsychiatry, 63* (1), 6–15.

Lewis, M. (1987). Early sex-role behavior and school age adjustment. In J. M. Reinisch, L. A. Rosenblum, & S. A. Sanders (Eds.), *Masculinity/feminity: Basic perspectives.* New York: Oxford University Press.

Lewis, M. (1991). Ways of knowing: Objective self-awareness or consciousness? *Developmental Review, 11* (3), 231–243.

Lewis, R. A., Volk, R. J., & Duncan, S. F. (1989). Stress on fathers and family relationships related to rural youth leaving and returning home. *Family Relations, 38,* 174–181.

Lichter, I., & Hunt, E. (1990). The last 48 hours of life. *Journal of Palliative Care, 6* (4), 7–15.

Lidoff, L. (1990). *Caregiver support groups in America.* Washington, DC: National Council on the Aging.

Lieberman, A. F., Weston, D. R., & Pawl, J. H. (1991). Preventive intervention and outcome with anxiously attached dyads. *Child Development, 62* (1), 199–209.

Lieberman, M. A. (1992). A re-examination of adult life crises: Spousal loss in mid and late life. In G. H. Pollock (Ed.), *The course of life.* New York: International Universities Press.

Lieberman, M. A., & Peskin, H. (1992). Adult life crises. In J. E. Birren, R. B. Sloane, & G. D. Cohen (Eds.), *Handbook of mental health and aging* (2nd ed.). San Diego: Harcourt Brace Jovanovich.

Liebert, R. M., & Sprafkin, J. (1988). *The early window: Effects of television on children and youth* (3rd ed.). New York: Pergamon Press.

Lieven, E. V., Pine, J. M., & Barnes, H. D. (1992). Individual differences in early vocabulary development: Redefining the referential-expressive distinction. *Journal of Child Language, 19* (2), 287–310.

Light, E., & Lebowitz, B. D. (Eds.). (1991). *The elderly with chronic mental illness.* New York: Springer.

Light, L. L. (1991). Memory and aging: Four hypotheses in search of data. *Annual Review of Psychology, 42,* 333–376.

Lillard, A. S., & Flavell, J. H. (1992). Young children's understanding of different mental states. *Developmental Psychology, 28* (4), 626–634.

Lin, A. N., & Carter, D. M. (1986). Skin cancer in the elderly. In B. A. Gilchrest (Ed.), *The aging skin.* Philadelphia: Saunders.

Lind, K. K. (1991). *Exploring science in early childhood: A developmental approach.* Albany, NY: Delmar.

Lipovsky, J. A. (1991). Disclosure of father-child sexual abuse: Dilemmas for families and therapists. *Contemporary Family Therapy, 13* (2), 85–101.

Lips, H. (1991). *Women, men, and power.* Mountain View, CA: Mayfield.

Lipsitt, L. P. (1989). Fetal development in the drug age. *Brown University Child Behavior and Development Newsletter, 1,* 1–3.

Liptzin, B. (1991). Masked anxiety—alcohol and drug use. In C. Salzman & B. D. Lebowitz (Eds.), *Anxiety in the elderly: Treatment and research.* New York: Springer.

Litt, I. F. (1991). Medical complications of eating disorders. In R. M. Lerner, A. C. Petersen, & J. Brooks-Gunn (Eds.), *The encyclopedia of adolescence.* New York: Garland.

Livson, N., & Peskin, H. (1980). Perspectives on adolescence from longitudinal research. In J. Adelson (Ed.), *Handbook of adolescent psychology.* New York: Wiley.

Lloyd, J. (1992). *The career decision-maker.* Linwood, IL: NTC.

Lloyd, P. (1991). Strategies used to communicate route directions by telephone: A comparison of the performance of 7-year olds, 10-year olds, and adults. *Journal of Child Language, 18* (1), 171–189.

Lock, R. D. (1992). *Taking charge of your career direction* (2nd ed.). Pacific Grove, CA: Brooks/Cole.

Locke, D. C. (1992). *Multicultural understanding: A comprehensive understanding.* Newbury Park, CA: Sage.

Lockery, S. A. (1985). Care in the minority family. *Generations, 10* (1), 27–29.

Lockhart, L. L., & Wodarski, J. S. (1990). Teenage pregnancy: Implications for social work practice. *Family Therapy, 17* (1), 29–47.

Locksley, A. (1982). Social class and marital attitudes and behavior. *Journal of Marriage and the Family, 44*, 427–440.

Loehlin, J. C., Willerman, L., & Horn, J. M. (1988). Human behavior genetics. *Annual Review of Psychology, 38*, 101–133.

Loevinger, J. (1966). The meaning and measure of ego development. *American Psychologist, 21*, 195–206.

Loevinger, J. (1976). *Ego development: Conceptions and theories*. San Francisco: Jossey-Bass.

Loevinger, J. (1979). Construct validity of the Sentence Completion Test of Ego Development. *Applied Psychological Measures, 3*, 281–311.

Loevinger, J., Cohn, L., Redmore, C., Bonneville, L., Streich, D., & Sargent, M. (1985). Ego development in college. *Journal of Personality and Social Psychology, 48*, 947–962.

Loevinger, J., Wessler, R., & Redmore, C. (1970a). *Measuring ego development: Construction and use of a sentence completion test*. San Francisco: Jossey-Bass.

Loevinger, J., Wessler, R., & Redmore, C. (1970b). *Measuring ego development: Scoring manual for women and girls*. San Francisco: Jossey-Bass.

Loewen, E. R., Shaw, R. J., & Craik, F. I. M. (1990). Age differences in components of metamemory. *Experimental Aging Research, 16* (1), 43–48.

Logue, B. J. (1991). Women at risk: Predictors of financial stress for retired women workers. *Gerontologist, 31* (5), 657–665.

Lombardo, J. P., & Kemper, T. R. (1992). Sex role and parental behaviors. *Journal of Genetic Psychology, 153* (1), 103–113.

London, K., Masher, W., Pratt, W., & Williams, L. (1989, April). *Preliminary findings from the NSFG, Cycle IV*. Paper presented at the annual meeting of the Population Association of America, Baltimore.

Long, C. M. (1991). Family care of the elderly: Stress, appraisal, and coping. *Journal of Applied Gerontology, 10* (3), 345–358.

Long, P. J., & Jackson, J. L. (1991). Children sexually abused by multiple perpetrators: Familial risk factors and abuse characteristics. *Journal of Interpersonal Violence, 6* (2), 147–159.

Longino, C. F. (1991). The second move: Health and geographic mobility. *Journal of Gerontology: Social Sciences, 46* (4), S218–S224.

Longino, C. F., & Kart, C. (1982). Explicating activity theory: A formal replication. *Journal of Gerontology, 37*, 713–722.

Looft, W. R. (1972). Egocentrism and social interaction across the lifespan. *Psychological Bulletin, 78*, 73–92.

Lookabaugh, S. L., & Fu, V. R. (1992). Children's use of inanimate transitional objects in coping with hassles. *Journal of Genetic Psychology, 153* (1), 37–46.

Lopez, N. (1987). *Hispanic teenage pregnancy*. Washington, DC: National Council of La Raza.

Lord, S. R., Clark, R. D., & Webster, I. W. (1991). Physiological factors associated with falls in an elderly population. *Journal of the American Geriatrics Society, 39* (12), 1194–1200.

Lorenz, K. (1965). *Evolution and the modification of behavior*. Chicago: University of Chicago Press.

Lorenzen-Huber, L. (1991). Self-perceived creativity in the later years: Case studies of older Nebraskans. *Educational Gerontology, 17* (4), 379–390.

Los Angeles Commission on Assaults Against Women. (1983). *Surviving sexual assault*. New York: Congdon and Weed.

Lowstuter, C., & Robertson, D. (1992). *In search of the perfect job*. New York: McGraw-Hill.

Lunardini, S., Cunningham, T., & Warren, D. (1991). Geriatric mental health comes of age. *Aging, 362*, 14–21.

Lund, M. M. (1990). Perspectives on newborn male circumcision. *Neonatal Network, 9* (3), 7–15.

Lundervold, D., Lewin, L. M., & Bourland, G. (1990). Older adults' acceptability of treatments for behavior problems. *Clinical Gerontologist, 10* (1), 17–28.

Lustbader, W. (1991). *Counting on kindness: The dilemmas of dependency*. New York: Free Press.

Lynch, M., & McKeon, V. A. (1990). Cocaine use during pregnancy. *Journal of Gynecological Nursing, 19*, 285–293.

Lynn, J. (1991). Dying well. *Generations, 15* (1), 69–72.

Lyons-Ruth, K., Connell, D. B., Grunebaum, H. U., & Botein, S. (1990). Infants at social risk: Maternal depression and family support services as mediators of infant development and security of attachment. *Child Development, 61*, 85–98.

Ma, H. K., & Leung, M. C. (1992). Effects of age, sex, and social relationships on the altruistic behavior of Chinese children. *Journal of Genetic Psychology, 153* (3), 293–303.

Maas, H. S. (1985). The development of adult development: Recollections and reflections. In M. A. Munnichs, P. Mussen, E. Olbrich, & P. G. Coleman (Eds.), *Life-span and change in a gerontological perspective*. New York: Academic Press.

Maas, H. S., & Kuypers, J. A. (1974). *From thirty to seventy*. San Francisco: Jossey-Bass.

Maccoby, E. E. (1987). The varied meanings of "masculine" and "feminine." In J. M. Reinisch, L. A. Rosenblum, & S. A. Sanders (Eds.), *Masculinity/femininity: Basic perspectives*. New York: Oxford University Press.

Maccoby, E. E. (1988). Gender as a social category. *Developmental Psychology, 24*, 755–765.

Maccoby, E. E. (1990). Gender and relationships: A developmental account. *American Psychologist, 45*, 513–520.

Maccoby, E. E. (1992). The role of parents in the socialization of children: An historical overview. *Developmental Psychology, 28* (6), 1006–1017.

MacCorquodale, P. (1984). Gender roles and premarital contraception. *Journal of Marriage and the Family, 46*, 57–63.

Mace, N. L. (1991). *Dementia care: Patient, family, and community*. Baltimore: Johns Hopkins University Press.

Mace, N. L., & Rabins, P. V. (1991). *The 36-hour day: A family guide to caring for persons with Alzheimer's disease, related dementing illnesses, and memory loss in later life* (rev. ed.). Baltimore: Johns Hopkins University Press.

MacFarlane, K., Waterman, J., Conerly, S., Damon, L., Durfee M., & Long, S. (1988). *Sexual abuse of young children: Evaluation and treatment*. New York: Guilford.

Machado, J. M. (1990). *Early childhood experiences in language arts: Emerging literacy* (4th ed.). Albany, NY: Delmar.

Mack, S. A., & Berman, L. C. (1988). A group for parents of children with fatal genetic illnesses. *American Journal of Orthopsychiatry, 58*, 397–404.

Mackey, T. F. (1991). Comparative effects of sexual assault on sexual functioning of child sexual abuse survivors. *Issues in Mental Health Nursing, 12* (1), 89–112.

Macklin, E. (1988). Heterosexual couples who cohabit non-maritally: Some common problems and issues. In C. S. Chilman, E. W. Nunnally, & F. M. Cox (Eds.), *Variant family forms*. Newbury Park, CA: Sage.

Madden, D. J. (1990). Adult age differences in attention selectivity and capacity. *European Journal of Cognitive Psychology, 2* (3), 229–252.

Maddox, G. L. (1964). Disengagement theory: A critical evaluation. *The Gerontologist, 4*, 80–82, 103.

Maddox, G. L. (1992). Discussion of socioeconomic status, health behaviors, and health status among blacks. In K. W. Schaie, D. Blazer, & J. S. House (Eds.), *Aging, health behaviors, and health outcomes: Trial structure and aging*. Hillsdale, NJ: Erlbaum.

Mahlstedt, P. P. (1987). The crisis of infertility: An opportunity for growth. In G. R. Weeks & L. Hof (Eds.), *Integrating sex and marital therapy: A clinical guide*. New York: Brunner/Mazel.

Malcolm, A., & Janisse, M. (1991). Additional evidence for the relationship between Type A behavior and social support in men. *Behavioral Medicine, 17* (3), 131–134.

Males, M. (1991). Teen suicide and changing cause-of-death certification, 1953–1987. *Suicide and Life-Threatening Behavior, 21* (3), 245–259.

Maletta, G., Mattox, K. M., & Dysken, M. (1991). Guidelines for prescribing psychoactive drugs in the elderly. *Geriatrics, 46* (9), 40–47.

Maletzky, B. M. (1990). *Treating the sexual offender*. Newbury Park, CA: Sage.

Malina, R. M. (1991). Adolescent growth spurt. In R. M. Lerner, A. C. Petersen, & J. Brooks-Gunn (Eds.), *The encyclopedia of adolescence*. New York: Garland.

Malina, R. M. (1982). Motor development in the early years. In S. G. Moore & C. R. Cooper (Eds.), *The young child: Reviews of research* (Vol. 3). Washington, DC: National Association for the Education of Young Children.

Malone-Beach, E., & Zarit, S. (1991). Current research issues in caregiving to the elderly. *International Journal of Aging and Human Development, 32* (2), 103–114.

Maltsberger, J. T. (1988). *Suicide risk*. New York: Human Sciences Press.

Mancini, J. A., & Blieszner, R. (1989). Aging parents and adult children: Research themes in intergenerational relations. *Journal of Marriage and the Family, 51*, 275–290.

Mandell, J. G., & Damon, L. (1989). *Group treatment of sexually abused children*. New York: Guilford.

Mangelsdorf, S. C. (1992). Developmental changes in infant-stranger interaction. *Infant Behavior and Development, 15* (2), 191–208.

Mann, J. (1991). Retirement: What happens to husband-wife relationships? *Journal of Geriatric Psychiatry, 24* (1), 41–46.

Mann, J. (1992). AIDS: The second decade: A global perspective. *Journal of Infectious Diseases, 165*, 245–250.

Manning, C. A., Hall, J. L., & Gold, P. E. (1990). Glucose effects on memory and other neuropsychological tests in elderly humans. *Psychological Science, 1,* 307–311.

Manning, M. L. (1983). Three myths concerning adolescence. *Adolescence, 18,* 823–829.

Manson, A., & Shea, S. (1991). Malnutrition in elderly ambulatory medical patients. *American Journal of Public Health, 81* (9), 1195–1197.

Marcia, J. (1980). Identity in adolescence. In J. A. Adelson (Ed.), *Handbook of adolescent psychology.* New York: Wiley.

Marcia, J. (1987). The identity status approach to the study of ego identity development. In T. Honess & K. Yardley (Eds.), *Self and identity perspectives across the lifespan.* London: Routledge and Kegan Paul.

Marcia, J. E. (1991). Identity and self-development. In R. M. Lerner, A. C. Petersen, & J. Brooks-Gunn (Eds.), *The encyclopedia of adolescence.* New York: Garland.

Marcos, H., & Kornhaberle, C. M. (1992). Learning how to insist and clarify in the second year: Reformulation of requests in different contexts. *International Journal of Behavioral Development, 15* (3), 359–376.

Marcus, G. F., Pinker, S., Ullman, M., & Hollander, M. (1992). Overregulation in language acquisition. *Monographs of the Society for Research in Child Development, 57* (4), 1–182.

Marean, G. C., Werner, L. A., & Kuhl, P. K. (1992). Vowel categorization by very young infants. *Developmental Psychology, 28* (3), 396–405.

Marhoefer, P., & Vadnais, L. (1992). *Caring for the developing child.* Albany, NY: Delmar.

Markides, K. S., & Lee, D. J. (1990). Predictors of well-being and functioning in older Mexican Americans and Anglos: An eight-year follow-up. *Journal of Gerontology, 45,* S69–S73.

Markus, E. J. (1990). Does it pay for a woman to work outside her home? *Journal of Comparative Family Studies, 21* (3), 397–412.

Marotz, L. R., Cross, M. Z., & Rush, J. M. (1993). *Health, safety, and nutrition for the young child* (3rd ed.). Albany, NY: Delmar.

Marsh, D. L. (1991). *Retirement careers: Combining the best of work and leisure.* Charlotte, VT: Williamson.

Marshall, C. (1992). *The expectant father.* Rockland, CA: Prima.

Marshall, V. W. (1980). *Last chapters: A sociology of aging and death.* Belmont, CA: Wadsworth.

Marston, A. R., Jacobs, D. F., Singer, R. D., & Wideman, K. F. (1988). Characteristics of adolescents at risk for compulsive overeating on a brief screening test. *Adolescence, 23,* 59–65.

Martens, N., & Davies, B. (1990). The work of patients and spouses in managing advanced cancer at home. *Hospice Journal, 6* (2), 55–73.

Martin, A. (1990). Neuropsychology of Alzheimer's disease: The case for subgroups. In M. F. Schwartz (Ed.), *Modular deficits in Alzheimer-type dementia: Issues in the biology of language and cognition.* Cambridge, MA: MIT Press.

Martin, C. L., & Little, J. K. (1990). The relation of gender understanding to children's sex-typed preferences and gender stereotypes. *Child Development, 61* (5), 1427–1439.

Martin, C. L., Wood, C. H., & Little, J. K. (1990). The development of gender stereotype components. *Child Development, 61* (6), 1891–1904.

Martin, H. P. (1992). Child abuse and neglect. In R. A. Hoekleman, S. B. Friedman, N. M. Nelson, & H. M. Seidel (Eds.), *Primary pediatric care* (2nd ed.). St. Louis: Mosby.

Martindale, C. (1991). *Cognitive psychology: A neural-network approach.* Pacific Grove, CA: Brooks/Cole.

Martindale, J. A., & Moses, M. J. (1991). *Creating your own future: A woman's guide to retirement planning.* Naperville, IL: Sourcebooks Trade.

Martinez, S. F. (1990). Is it safe for your patients to exercise? *Senior Patient, 2* (11), 38–42.

Masataka, N. (1992). Early ontogeny of vocal behavior of Japanese infants in response to maternal speech. *Child Development, 63* (5), 1177–1185.

Mash, E. J., & Barkley, R. A. (1989). *Treatment of childhood disorders.* New York: Guilford.

Maslow, A. H. (1968). *Toward a psychology of being* (2nd ed.). Princeton, NJ: Van Nostrand Reinhold.

Maslow, A. H. (1970). *Motivation and personality* (2nd ed.). New York: Harper & Row.

Mason, M. A. (1991). Equal rights fails American mothers: The limitations of an equal rights strategy in family law and the workplace. *International Journal of Law and the Family, 5* (3), 211–240.

Masoro, E. J. (1990). Nutrition and longevity. In J. E. Morley, Z. Glick, & L. Z. Rubenstein (Eds.), *Geriatric nutrition: A comprehensive review.* New York: Raven Press.

Masselman, V. S., Marcus, R. F., & Stunkard, C. L. (1990). Parent-adolescent communication, family functioning, and school performance. *Adolescence, 25* (99), 725–737.

Masters, W. H., Johnson, V. E., & Kolodny, R. C. (1992). *Human sexuality* (4th ed.). New York: HarperCollins.

Mathew, A., & Cook, M. L. (1990). The control of reaching movements by young infants. *Child Development, 61* (4), 1238–1257.

Matlin, M. W. (1989). *Cognition* (2nd ed.). Fort Worth, TX: Harcourt Brace Jovanovich.

Matlin, M. W. (1993). *The psychology of women* (2nd ed.). Fort Worth, TX: Harcourt Brace Jovanovich.

Mattesich, P., & Hill, R. (1987). Life cycle and family development. In M. B. Sussman & S. K. Steinmetz (Eds.), *Handbook of marriage and the family.* New York: Plenum.

Matteson, M. A. (1988). Age-related changes in the integument. In M. A. Matteson & E. S. McConnell (Eds.), *Gerontological nursing: Concepts and practice.* Philadelphia: Saunders.

Matteson, M. A., & McConnell, E. S. (Eds.). (1988). *Gerontological nursing: Concepts and practice.* Philadelphia: Saunders.

Maxim, G. W. (1993). *The very young: Guiding children from infancy through the early years.* New York: Macmillan.

Mayesky, M. E. (1990). *Creative activities for young children* (4th ed.). Albany, NY: Delmar.

Maylor, E. A. (1991). Recognizing and naming tunes: Memory impairment in the elderly. *Journal of Gerontology: Psychological Sciences, 46* (5), P207–P217.

Mazer, B., Piper, M. C., & Ramsay, M. (1988). Developmental outcome in very low birth weight infants six months to 36 months old. *Journal of Developmental and Behavioral Pediatrics, 9* (5), 293–297.

Maziade, M., Boudreault, M., Copte, R., & Thivierge, J. (1986). Influence of gentle birth delivery procedures and other perinatal circumstances on infant temperament: Developmental and social implications. *Journal of Pediatrics, 108,* 134–136.

McAdoo, H. P. (1983). Societal stress: The black family. In C. R. Figley & H. I. McCubbin (Eds.), *Stress and the family.* New York: Brunner/Mazel.

McAdoo, H. P. (1993). *Family ethnicity: Strength in diversity.* Newbury Park, CA: Sage.

McAdoo, J. L. (1986). Black fathers' relationships with their children and the children's development of ethnic identity. In R. A. Lewis & R. E. Salt (Eds.), *Men in families.* Beverly Hills, CA: Sage.

McAdoo, J. L. (1988). The role of black fathers in socialization of black children. In H. P. McAdoo (Ed.), *Black families* (2nd ed.). Newbury Park, CA: Sage.

McAuley, E., Courneya, K. S., & Lettunich, J. (1991). Effects of acute and long-term exercise on self-efficacy responses in sedentary, middle-aged males and females. *Gerontologist, 31* (4), 534–542.

McBride, B. A. (1989). Interaction, accessibility, and responsibility: A view of father involvement and how to encourage it. *Young Children, 44* (5), 13–19.

McBride, S. (1990). Maternal modulators of child care: The role of maternal separation anxiety. In K. McCartney (Ed.), *New directions for child development: No. 49. Child care and maternal employment: A social ecology approach.* San Francisco: Jossey-Bass.

McCabe, A., & Lipscomb, T. J. (1988). Sex differences in children's verbal aggression. *Merrill-Palmer Quarterly, 34,* 389–401.

McCall, R. B. (1991). Underachievers and dropouts. In R. M. Lerner, A. C. Petersen, & J. Brooks-Gunn (Eds.), *The encyclopedia of adolescence.* New York: Garland.

McCarthy, J. T. (1991). *Financial planning for a secure retirement.* Brookfield, WI: International Foundation of Employee Benefit Plans.

McCracken, A. L., & Gerdsen, L. (1991). Sharing the legacy: Hospice care principles for terminally ill elders. *Journal of Gerontological Nursing, 17* (12), 4–8.

McCrae, R. R., & Costa, P. T., Jr. (1987). Validation of the five-factor model of personality across instruments and observers. *Journal of Personality and Social Psychology, 52,* 81–90.

McCrae, R. R., & Costa, P. T., Jr. (1990). *Personality in adulthood.* New York: Guilford.

McCulloch, B. J. (1991). Health and health maintenance profiles of older rural women, 1976–1986. In A. Bushy (Ed.), *Rural nursing* (Vol. 1). Newbury Park, CA: Sage.

McDermott, D. (1984). The relationship of parental drug use and parents' attitude concerning adolescent drug use. *Adolescence, 19,* 89–97.

McFalls, J. A., Jr. (1991). *Population: A lively introduction.* Washington, DC: Population Reference Bureau.

McGhee, P. E. (1980). Development of the sense of humour in childhood: A longitudinal study. In P. E. McGhee & A. J. Chapman (Eds.), *Children's humour.* New York: Wiley.

McGhee, P. E., & Goldstein, J. H. (Eds.). (1983a). *Handbook of humor research, Vol 1: Basic issues.* New York: Springer-Verlag.

McGhee, P. E., & Goldstein, J. H. (Eds.). (1983b). *Handbook of humor research, Vol. 2: Applied studies.* New York: Springer-Verlag.

McGilly, K., & Siegler, R. S. (1989). How children choose among serial recall strategies. *Child Development, 60,* 172–182.

McGoldrick, M. (1982). Normal families: An ethnic perspective. In F. Walsh (Ed.), *Normal family processes*. New York: Guilford.

McGoldrick, M., & Carter, E. A. (1982). The stages of the family life cycle. In F. Walsh (Ed.), *Normal family processes*. New York: Guilford.

McHale, S. M., Bartko, W. T., Crouter, A. C., & Perry-Jenkins, M. (1990). Children's housework and psychosocial functioning: The mediating effects of parents' sex-role behaviors and attitudes. *Child Development, 61,* 1413–1426.

McHale, S. M., & Huston, T. L. (1985). The effect of the transition to parenthood on the marriage relationship. *Journal of Family Issues, 6* (4), 409–433.

McKay, M., Rogers, P. D., Blades, J., & Goose, R. (1984). *The divorce book*. Oakland, CA: New Harbinger.

McKenry, P., Kotch, J. B., & Browne, D. H. (1991). Correlates of dysfunctional parenting attitudes among low-income adolescent mothers. *Journal of Adolescent Research, 6* (2), 212–234.

McKenry, P. C., & Price, S. J. (1991). Alternatives for support: Life after divorce—a literature review. *Journal of Divorce and Remarriage, 15* (3/4), 1–19.

McKenzie, S. C. (1980). *Aging and old age*. Glenview, IL: Scott, Foresman.

McLanahan, S. S., Wedemeyer, N. V., & Adelberg, J. (1981). Network structure, social support, and psychological well-being in the single-parent family. *Journal of Marriage and the Family, 43,* 601–611.

McLaughlin, M. (1992). *The complete career handbook*. Saratoga, CA: R and E Publishers.

McMillan, L. (1990). Grandchildren, chocolate and flowers. *Australian Journal on Ageing, 9* (4), 13–17.

McNaught, W., Barth, M. C., & Henderson, P. H. (1991). Older Americans: Willing and able to work. In A. H. Munnell (Ed.), *Retirement and public policy. Proceedings of the second conference of the National Academy of Social Insurance*. Dubuque, IA: Kendall/Hunt.

McNeely, E. (1991). Computer-assisted instruction and the older-adult learner. *Educational Gerontology, 17* (3), 229–237.

McNeil, J. D., & Wiles, J. (1990). *The essentials of teaching: Decisions, plans, and methods*. New York: Macmillan.

McPherson, B. D. (1990). *Aging as a social process: An introduction to individual and population aging*. Toronto: Butterworths.

Mead, M. (1928). *Coming of age in Samoa*. New York: Mentor Books.

Meddaugh, D., O'Bryant, S. L., & Straw, L. B. (1991). After-effects of Alzheimer's care giving on widows' health and financial well-being. *Journal of Women and Aging, 3* (2), 45–62.

Meehan, P. J., Saltzman, L. E., & Sattin, R. W. (1991). Suicides among older United States residents: Epidemiologic characteristics and trends. *American Journal of Public Health, 81* (9), 1198–1200.

Meier-Ruge, W. (1990). Aging and well-being in business life. In M. Bergener & S. I. Finkel (Eds.), *Clinical and scientific psychogeriatrics*. New York: Springer.

Meltzer, L. (1984). An analysis of the learning styles of adolescent delinquents. *Journal of Learning Disabilities, 17* (10), 600–608.

Menard, D. (1991). The aging athlete. *Topics in Geriatric Rehabilitation, 6* (4), 1–16.

Menard, S. (1991). *Longitudinal research*. Newbury Park, CA: Sage.

Mercer, R. T., Nichols, E. G., & Doyle, G. C. (1989). *Transitions in a woman's life: Major life events in developmental context*. New York: Springer.

Merrill, M. (1990). *Chemically dependent older adults: How do we treat them?* Center City, MN: Hazelden.

Mervis, C. B., & Mervis, C. A. (1988). Role of adult input in young children's category evolution: An observational study. *Journal of Child Language, 15,* 257–272.

Mesquita, B., & Frijda, N. H. (1992). Cultural variations in emotions: A review. *Psychological Bulletin, 112* (2), 179–204.

Messerli, F. H. (1990). Hypertension in the elderly: How innocent a bystander? In M. Bergener, M. Ermini, & H. B. Stahelin (Eds.), *Challenges in aging. Sandoz lectures in gerontology*. San Diego: Academic Press.

Metts, S., & Cupach, W. R. (1989). The role of communication in human sexuality. In K. McKinney & S. Sprecher (Eds.), *Human sexuality: The societal and interpersonal context*. Norwood, NJ: Ablex.

Meyer, J. E. (1988). The personality characteristics of adolescents who use and misuse alcohol. *Adolescence, 23,* 385–404.

Meyer, M. H. (1991). Assuring quality of care: Nursing home resident councils. *Journal of Applied Gerontology, 10* (1), 103–116.

Michaels, B., & McCarty, E. (1992). *Solving the work/family puzzle*. Homewood, IL: Business One Irwin.

Michelozzi, B. N. (1992). *Coming alive from nine to five* (4th ed.). Palo Alto, CA: Mayfield.

Mihalik, G. J. (1991). Homosexuality, stigma, and biocultural evolution. *Journal of Gay and Lesbian Psychotherapy, 1* (4), 15–29.

Milan, R. J., & Kilman, P. R. (1987). Interpersonal factors in premarital contraception. *Journal of Sex Research, 23,* 289–321.

Miles, M. S., & Crandall, E. K. (1983). The search for meaning and its potential for affecting growth in bereaved parents. *Health Values: Achieving High Level Wellness, 7* (1), 19–23.

Miller, B. C. (1986). *Family research methods*. Beverly Hills, CA: Sage.

Miller, B. C., & Moore, K. A. (1990). Adolescent sexual behavior, pregnancy, and parenting: Research through the 1980's. *Journal of Marriage and the Family, 52,* 1025–1044.

Miller, D. F. (1990). *Positive child guidance*. Albany, NY: Delmar.

Miller, G. A. (1981). *Language and speech*. San Francisco: Freeman.

Miller, N. E., & Dollard, J. (1941). *Social learning and imitation*. New Haven, CT: Yale University Press.

Miller, P. H. (1993). *Theories of developmental psychology* (3rd ed.). New York: Freeman.

Miller, P. H., Seier, W. L., Probert, J. S., & Aloise, P. A. (1991). Age differences in the capacity demands of a strategy among spontaneously strategic children. *Journal of Experimental Child Psychology, 52* (2), 149–165.

Miller, P. H., & Weiss, M. G. (1981a). Children's and adults' knowledge about what variables affect selective attention. *Child Development, 53,* 543–549.

Miller, P. H., & Weiss, M. G. (1981b). Children's

attention location, understanding attention, and performance on the incidental learning task. *Child Development, 52,* 1183–1190.

Miller, P. H., & Zalenski, R. (1982). Preschoolers' knowledge about attention. *Developmental Psychology, 18* (6), 871–875.

Miller, S. S., & Cavanaugh, J. C. (1990). The meaning of grandparenthood and its relationship to demographic relationship, and social participation variables. *Journal of Gerontology: Psychological Sciences, 45* (6), P244–P246.

Millette, B., & Hawkins, J. (1983). *The passage through menopause: Women's lives in transition*. Reston, VA: Reston.

Milligan, S. E. (1990). Understanding diversity of the urban black aged: Historical perspectives. In Z. Harel, E. A. McKinney, & M. Williams (Eds.), *Black aged: Understanding diversity and service needs*. Newbury Park, CA: Sage.

Mills, R. K. (1988). Using Tom and Huck to develop moral reasoning in adolescents: A strategy for the classroom. *Adolescence, 23,* 325–329.

Milner, J. S., & Chilamkurti, C. (1991). Physical child abuse perpetrator characteristics: A review of the literature. *Journal of Interpersonal Violence, 6* (3), 345–366.

Milner, J. S., & Robertson, K. R. (1990). Comparison of physical child abusers, intrafamilial sexual child abusers, and child neglecters. *Journal of Interpersonal Violence, 5* (1), 37–48.

Minkler, M. (1990). Aging and disability: Behind and beyond the stereotypes. *Journal of Aging Studies, 4* (3), 245–260.

Minkler, M., & Robertson, A. (1991). The ideology of "age/race wars": Deconstructing a social problem. *Aging and Society, 11* (1), 1–22.

Mischel, W. (1987). *Personality* (4th ed.). New York: Holt, Rinehart and Winston.

Mischel, W., & Mischel, H. N. (1977). *Essentials of psychology*. New York: Random House.

Missinne, L. E. (1990). Death and spiritual concerns of older adults. *Generations, 14* (4), 45–47.

Mitchell, P., & Robinson, E. J. (1992). Children's understanding of the evidential connotation of "know" in relation to overestimation of their own knowledge. *Journal of Child Language, 19* (1), 167–182.

Moely, B. E., Hart, S. S., Leal, L., & Santulli, K. A. (1992). The teacher's role in facilitating memory and study strategy development in the elementary school classroom. *Child Development, 63* (3), 653–672.

Moen, P. (1991). Transitions in mid-life: Women's work and family roles in the 1970s. *Journal of Marriage and the Family, 53* (1), 135–150.

Moghissi, K. (1989). The technology of AID and surrogacy. In L. Whiteford & M. Polan (Eds.), *Approaches to human reproduction*. Boulder, CO: Westview.

Molinari, V. A. (1991). Mental health issues in the elderly. *Physical and Occupational Therapy in Geriatrics, 9* (3/4), 23–30.

Montalvo, B. (1991). The patient chose to die: Why? *Gerontologist, 31* (5), 700–703.

Montemayor, R., & Flannery, D. J. (1991). Parent-adolescent relations in middle and late adolescence. In R. M. Lerner, A. C. Petersen, & J. Brooks-Gunn (Eds.), *The encyclopedia of adolescence*. New York: Garland.

Montgomery, R. J., & Datwyler, M. M. (1990). Women and men in the care giving role. *Generations, 14* (3), 34–38.

Moody, R. A. (1975). *Life after life.* New York: Bantam.

Moody, R. A. (1977). Cities of light. In R. Fulton (Ed.), *Death and dying: Challenge and change.* Reading, MA: Addison-Wesley.

Moore, C. F., Dixon, J. A., & Haines, B. A. (1991). Components of understanding in proportional reasoning: A fuzzy set representation of developmental progressions. *Child Development, 62* (3), 441–459.

Moore, K., & Peterson, J. (1989). *The consequences of teenage pregnancy: Final report.* Washington, DC: Child Trends.

Moore, K. L. (1988). *The developing human* (4th ed.). Philadelphia: Saunders.

Moore, S. L., & Tanney, B. L. (1991). *Suicide in older adults: Selected readings.* Calgary, Alberta: Suicide Information and Education Centre.

Moore, S. T., & Arthur, H. F. (1991). The critical role of social work in developing alternative housing options for elders: Foster family care, home sharing, and shared housing. *Adult Residential Care Journal, 5* (3), 199–209.

Morey, M. C. (1991). Two-year trends in physical performance following supervised exercise among community-dwelling older veterans. *Journal of the American Geriatrics Society, 39* (10), 986–992.

Morford, M., & Goldin-Meadow, S. (1992). Comprehension and production of gesture in combination with speech in one-word speakers. *Journal of Child Language, 19* (3), 559–580.

Morgan, D. L., Schuster, T. L., & Butler, E. W. (1991). Role reversals in the exchange of social support. *Journal of Gerontology: Social Sciences, 46* (5), S278–S287.

Morison, P., & Masten, A. S. (1991). Peer reputation in middle childhood as a predictor of adaptation in adolescence: A seven-year follow-up. *Child Development, 62* (5), 991–1007.

Morley, J. E., & Glick, Z. (1990). Obesity. In J. E. Morley, Z. Glick, & L. Z. Rubenstein (Eds.), *Geriatric nutrition: A comprehensive review.* New York: Raven Press.

Morris, J. C., & McManus, D. O. (1991). The neurology of aging: Normal versus pathologic change. *Geriatrics, 46* (8), 47–48.

Morrisey, G. (1992). *Creating your future.* San Francisco: Berrett-Koehler.

Morrison, D. M. (1985). Adolescent contraceptive behavior: A review. *Psychological Bulletin, 98,* 538–568.

Morrison, G. (1991). *Early childhood education today* (5th ed.). New York: Macmillan.

Morrison, P. A. (1991, June). Demographic factors reshaping ties to family and place. *The RAND Corporation,* p. P-7650.

Morrongiello, B. A., Hewitt, K. L., & Gotowiec, A. (1991). Infants' discrimination of relative distance in the auditory modality: Approaching versus receding sound sources. *Infant Behavior and Development, 14* (2), 187–208.

Morrongiello, B. A., & Rocca, P. T. (1990). Infants' localization of sounds within hemifields: Estimates of minimum audible angle. *Child Development, 61* (4), 1258–1270.

Morse, M. L. (1990). *Closer to the light.* New York: Villard.

Morse, M. L., & Perry, P. (1992). *Transformed by the light.* New York: Villard.

Mortensen, K. V. (1991). *Form and content in children's human figure drawings: Development, sex differences, and body experience.* New York and London: New York University Press.

Morvitz, E., & Motta, R. W. (1992). Predictors of self-esteem: The roles of parent-child perceptions, achievement, and class placement. *Journal of Learning Disabilities, 25* (1), 72–80.

Moskowitz, F., & Moskowitz, R. (1991). *Parenting your aging parents.* Woodland Hills, CA: Key.

Moss, H. A., & Kagan, J. (1964). Report on personality consistency and change from the Fels longitudinal study. *Vita Humana, 7,* 127–138.

Moss, N. E., Abramowitz, S. I., & Racusin, G. R. (1985). Parental heritage: Progress and prospect. In L. L'Abate (Ed.), *The handbook of family psychology and therapy.* Homewood, IL: Dorsey Press.

Mott, F. L., & Haurin, R. J. (1988). Linkages between sexual activity and alcohol and drug use among American adolescents. *Family Planning Perspectives, 20,* 129–136.

Mount, J. (1991). Evaluation of a health promotion program provided at senior centers by physical therapy students. *Physical and Occupational Therapy in Geriatrics, 10* (1), 15–25.

Mowe, M., & Bohmer, T. (1991). The prevalence of undiagnosed protein-calorie undernutrition in a population of hospitalized elderly patients. *Journal of the American Geriatrics Society, 39* (11), 1089–1092.

Moyse-Steinberg, D. (1991). A model for adolescent pregnancy prevention through the use of small groups. *Social Work with Groups, 13* (2), 57–64.

Muasher, S. J. (1987). Infertility. In Z. Rosenwaks, F. Benjamin, & M. Stone (Eds.), *Gynecology: Principles and practice.* New York: Macmillan.

Muehlbauer, G., & Dodder, L. (1983). *The losers: Gang delinquency in an American suburb.* New York: Praeger.

Mulholland, D. J. (1991). Academic performance in children of divorce: Psychological resilience and vulnerability. *Psychiatry, 54* (3), 268–280.

Mullis, A. K., Mullis, R. L., & Normandin, D. (1992). Cross-sectional and longitudinal comparisons of adolescent self-esteem. *Adolescence, 27* (105), 51–61.

Mungas, D., Ehlers, C. L., & Blunden, D. (1991). Age differences in recall and information processing in verbal and spatial learning. *Canadian Journal on Aging, 10* (4), 320–332.

Munnell, A. H. (1991). Retirement and public policy. *Proceedings of the second conference of the National Academy of Social Insurance, Washington, DC.* Dubuque, IA: Kendall/Hunt.

Murray, P. L., & Mayer, R. E. (1988). Preschool children's judgements of number magnitude. *Journal of Educational Psychology, 80,* 206–209.

Mussen, P. (1985). Early adult antecedents of life satisfaction at age 70. In J. M. A. Munnichs, P. Mussen, E. Olbrich, & P. C. Coleman (Eds.), *Lifespan and change in a gerontological perspective.* New York: Academic Press.

Muster, N. J. (1992). Treating the adolescent victim-turned-offender. *Adolescence, 27* (106), 441–450.

Mutran, E. (1985). International family support among blacks and whites: A response to culture or to socioeconomic difference? *Journal of Gerontology, 40,* 382–389.

Myers, B. J., Jarvis, P. A., Creasey, G. L., & Kerkering, K. W. (1992). Prematurity and respiratory illness: Brazelton scale performance of preterm infants with bronchopulmonary dysplasia, respiratory distress, or no respiratory illness. *Infant Behavior and Development, 15* (1), 27–41.

Myers, D. A. (1991). Work after cessation of a career job. *Journal of Gerontology, 46* (2), S93–S102.

Myslinski, N. R. (1990). The effects of aging on the sensory systems of the nose and mouth. *Topics in Geriatric Rehabilitation, 5* (4), 21–30.

Nagel, K. L., & Jones, K. H. (1992). Predisposition factors in anorexia nervosa. *Adolescence, 27* (106), 381–386.

Nalbantoglu, J., Lacoste-Royal, G., & Gauvreau, D. (1990). Genetic factors in Alzheimer's disease. *Journal of the American Geriatrics Society, 38* (5), 564–568.

Nandy, K. (1983). Immunologic factors. In B. Reisberg (Ed.), *Alzheimer's disease: The standard reference.* New York: Free Press.

Nathanson, C. A., & Kim, Y. J. (1989). Components of change in adolescent fertility, 1971–1979. *Demography, 26,* 85–98.

National Association for the Education of Young Children. (1983, November). How to choose a good early childhood program. Author, pp. 28–32.

National Center for Education Statistics. (1990). *Dropout rates in the United States: 1989.* Washington, DC: U.S. Government Printing Office.

National Center for Health Statistics. (1991, January). Premarital sexual experience among adolescent women. *Morbidity and Mortality Weekly Report, 39* (51/52), 929–932.

National Center for Health Statistics. (1991). *Vital statistics of the United States.* Washington, D.C: U.S. Government Printing Office.

National Center for Health Statistics. (1992a). *Health, United States, 1991.* Public Health Service. Washington, DC: U.S. Government Printing Office.

National Center for Health Statistics. (1992b). *Vital statistics of the United States.* Washington, DC: U.S. Government Printing Office.

National Cholesterol Education Program. (1991). *Cholesterol level guidelines for adults.* Bethesda, MD: National Heart, Lung, and Blood Institute.

National Institute on Aging. (1992). *Progress report on Alzheimer's disease, 1992.* Washington, DC: U.S. Department of Health and Human Services.

National Research Council. (1987). *Risking the future: Adolescent sexuality, pregnancy, and childbearing.* Washington, DC: National Academy Press.

Needleman, H. L., Schell, A., Bellinger, D., & Leviton, A. (1990). The long-term effects of exposure to low doses of lead in childhood: An 11-year follow-up report. *New England Journal of Medicine, 322* (2), 83–88.

Neiga, B. L., & Hopkins, R. W. (1988). Adolescent suicide: Character traits of high-risk teenagers. *Adolescence, 23,* 467–475.

Neigh, J. E. (1990). Hospice: An essential and growing part of the continuum of care. *Caring, 9* (11), 4–5.

Neisser, U. (1991). Two perceptually given aspects of the self and their development. *Developmental Review, 11* (3), 197–209.

Nelson, M. (1991). Empowerment of incest survivors: Speaking out. *Families in Society, 72* (10), 618–624.

Nelson, M. K. (1990). Organic mental disorders. In M. O. Hogstel (Ed.), *Geropsychiatric nursing.* St. Louis: Mosby.

Nelson, N. M., Murray, W. E., Saroi, S., Bennet, K. J., Milner, R., & Sackett, D. L. (1980). A randomized clinical trial of the Leboyer approach to childbirth. *New England Journal of Medicine, 303,* 655–660.

Neugarten, B. L. (1964). *Personality in middle and late life.* New York: Atherton Press.

Neugarten, B. L. (1968). *Middle age and aging.* Chicago: University of Chicago Press.

Neugarten, B. L., & Datan, N. (1973). Sociological perspectives on the life cycle. In P. B. Baltes & K. W. Schaie (Eds.), *Life-span developmental psychology: Personality and socialization.* New York: Academic Press.

Neugarten, B. L., Havighurst, R. J., & Tobin, S. S. (1968). Personality and patterns of aging. In B. L. Neugarten (Ed.), *Middle age and aging.* Chicago: University of Chicago Press.

Neuhs, H. P. (1990). Predictors of adjustment in retirement of women. In C. L. Hayes & J. M. Deren (Eds.), *Pre-retirement planning for women: Program design and research.* New York: Springer.

Neuman, P. A., & Halvorson, P. A. (1983). *Anorexia nervosa and bulimia: A handbook for counselors and therapists.* New York: Van Nostrand Reinhold.

Neuspiel, D. R., & Hamel, S. C. (1991). Cocaine and infant behavior. *Journal of Developmental and Behavioral Pediatrics, 12* (1), 55–64.

Newcomb, A. F., Bukowski, W. M., & Pattee, L. (1993). Child's peer relations: A meta analytic review of popular, rejected, neglected, controversial, and average sociometric status. *Psychological Bulletin, 113* (1), 99–128.

Newcombe, N., & Huttenlocher, J. (1992). Children's early ability to solve perspective-taking problems. *Developmental Psychology, 28* (4), 635–643.

Newell, K. M. (1991). Motor skill acquisition. *Annual Review of Psychology, 42,* 213–237.

Newman, J. (1991). College students' relationships with siblings. *Journal of Youth and Adolescence, 20* (6), 629–644.

Newmann, J. P., Engel, R. J., & Jensen, J. E. (1991). Age differences in depressive symptom experiences. *Journal of Gerontology: Psychological Sciences, 46* (5), P224–P235.

Ney, P. G. (1988). Transgenerational child abuse. *Child Psychiatry and Human Development, 18,* 151–168.

Ng, S. H., Giles, H., & Moody, J. (1991). Information-seeking triggered by age. *International Journal of Aging and Human Development, 33* (4), 269–277.

Nichollas, A. L., & Kennedy, J. M. (1992). Drawing development: From similarity of features to direction. *Child Development, 63* (1), 227–241.

Nielsen Media Research. (1991). 1990 Nielsen Report on TV. In S. A. Hewlett (Ed.), *When the bough breaks: The cost of neglecting our children.* New York: Basic Books.

Ninio, A., & Rinott, N. (1988). Fathers' involvement in the care of their infants and their attributions of cognitive competence in infants. *Child Development, 59,* 652–663.

Nisan, M. (1984). Distributive justice and social norms. *Child Development, 55,* 1020–1029.

Noller, P., & Callan, V. J. (1988). Understanding parent-adolescent interactions: Perceptions of family members and outsiders. *Developmental Psychology, 24,* 707–714.

Norman, S. (1991). Syntactic complexity and adults' running memory span. *Journal of Gerontology: Psychological Sciences, 46* (6), P346–P351.

Noshpitz, J., & Coddington, R. D. (1990). *Stressors and the adjustment disorders.* New York: Wiley.

Nottebohm, F., & Arnold, A. P. (1976). Sexual dimorphism in vocal control areas of the songbird brain. *Science, 194,* 211–213.

Novacek, J., Raskin, R., & Hogan, R. (1991). Why do adolescents use drugs? Age, sex, and user differences. *Journal of Youth and Adolescence, 20* (5), 475–492.

Nugent, J. K. (1991). Cultural and psychological influences on the father's role in infant development. *Journal of Marriage and the Family, 53,* 475–486.

Nunner-Winkler, G., & Sodian, B. (1988). Children's understanding of moral emotions. *Child Development, 59,* 1323–1328.

Nurmi, J. (1991). How do adolescents see their future? A review of the development of future orientation and planning. *Developmental Review, 11* (1), 1–59.

Nussberg, C. (1984). Acceptance of death facilitated by supportive Dutch physicians. *Ageing International, 11* (2), 2–3.

Obler, L. K. (1993). Language beyond childhood. In J. B. Gleason (Ed.), *The development of language* (3rd ed.). New York: Macmillan.

O'Brien, J. M., Goodenow, C., & Espin, O. (1991). Adolescents' reactions to the death of a peer. *Adolescence, 26* (102), 431–440.

O'Brien, M., & Huston, A. C. (1985). The development of sex-typed play behavior in toddlers. *Developmental Psychology, 21,* 866–871.

O'Brien, M. E. (1990). Elders and stress: Controlling a medical hazard. *Senior Patient, 2* (7), 31–34.

O'Brien, S. F., & Bierman, K. L. (1988). Conceptions and perceived influence of peer groups: Interviews with preadolescents and adolescents. *Child Development, 59,* 1360–1365.

O'Brien, S. J., & Conger, P. R. (1991). No time to look back: Approaching the finish line of life's course. *International Journal of Aging and Human Development, 33* (1), 75–87.

O'Brien, S. J., & Vertinsky, P. A. (1990). Unfit survivors: Exercise as a resource for aging women. *Gerontologist, 31,* 347–357.

O'Bryant, S. L., & Morgan, L. A. (1990). Recent widows' kin support and orientations to self-sufficiency. *Gerontologist, 30,* 391–398.

O'Connor, D., & Wolfe, D. M. (1991). From crisis to growth at midlife: Changes in personal paradigm. *Journal of Organizational Behavior, 12* (4), 323–340.

O'Donohue, W. T., & Elliott, A. N. (1992). Treatment of the sexually abused child: A review. *Journal of Clinical Child Psychology, 21* (3), 218–228.

Oetting, E. R., & Beauvais, F. (1990). Adolescent drug use: Findings of national and local surveys. *Journal of Consulting and Clinical Psychology, 58* (4), 385–394.

Offer, D., & Church, R. B. (1991). Turmoil in adolescence. In R. M. Lerner, A. C. Petersen, & J. Brooks-Gunn (Eds.), *The encyclopedia of adolescence.* New York: Garland.

Offer, D., Ostrov, E., Howard, K. I., & Atkinson, R. (1988). *The teenage world: Adolescents' self-image in ten countries.* New York: Plenum.

O'Grady-LeShane, R. (1990). Older women and poverty. *Social Work, 35* (5), 422–424.

O'Hare, W. P., Pollard, K. M., Mann, T. L., & Kent, M. M. (1991). *African Americans in the 1990's.* Washington, DC: Population Reference Bureau.

Okun, B. F. (1984). *Working with adults: Individual, family, and career development.* Monterey, CA: Brooks/Cole.

Olds, S. B., London, M. L., & Ladewig, P. W. (1992). *Maternal-newborn nursing* (4th ed.). Redwood Park, CA: Addison-Wesley Nursing.

Olds, S. W. (1985). *The eternal garden: Seasons of our sexuality.* New York: Times Books.

Olinger, B., Dancer, J., & Patterson, K. (1991). Misconceptions of health professionals regarding hearing loss in the elderly. *Educational Gerontology, 17* (1), 33–40.

Oliver, D. (1982). Why do people live together? *Journal of Social Welfare, 7,* 209–222.

Oller, D. K., & Eilers, R. E. (1982). Similarity of babbling in Spanish- and English-learning babies. *Journal of Child Language, 9* (3), 565–577.

Olson, S. L., & Banyard, V. (1993). Stop the world so I can get off for a while: Sources of daily stress in the lives of low-income single mothers of young children. *Family Relations, 42,* 50–56.

Oltjenbruns, K. A. (1991). Positive outcomes of adolescents' experience with grief. *Journal of Adolescent Research, 6* (1), 43–53.

Opie, A. (1991). The informal caregivers of the confused elderly and the concept of partnership: a New Zealand report. *Pride Institute of Long Term Home Health Care, 10* (2), 34–40.

Oppenheim, J., Boegehold, B., & Breener, B. (1984). *Raising a confident child.* New York: Pantheon Books.

Orbuch, T. L. (1989). Human sexuality education. In K. McKinney & S. Sprecher (Eds.), *Human sexuality: The societal and interpersonal context.* Norwood, NJ: Ablex.

Oriol, W. (1991). Chronic pain. *Perspectives on Aging, 20* (6), 6–13.

Ornish, D. (1990). *Dr. Dean Ornish's program for reversing heart disease.* New York: Random House.

Orr, A. L. (1991). The psychosocial aspects of aging and vision loss. *Journal of Gerontological Social Work, 17* (3/4), 1–14.

Orr, D. P., Brack, C. J., & Ingersoll, G. (1988). Pubertal maturation and cognitive maturity in adolescence. *Journal of Adolescent Health Care, 9,* 273–279.

Orthner, D. K., Bowen, G. L., & Beare, V. G. (1990). The organization family: A question of work and family boundaries. *Marriage and Family Review, 15* (3/4), 15–36.

Ory, M. G. (1985). The burden of care. *Generations, 10,* 14–18.

Ory, M. G., Abeles, R. P., & Lipman, P. D. (1992). An overview of research on aging, health, and behavior. In M. G. Ory, R. P. Abeles, & P. D. Lipman (Eds.), *Aging, health, and behavior.* Newbury Park, CA: Sage.

Osgood, N. J. (1991). Prevention of suicide in the elderly. *Journal of Geriatric Psychiatry, 24* (2), 293–306.

Owens, R. E., Jr. (1992). *Language development: An introduction* (3rd ed.). New York: Macmillan.

Owsley, C., & Sloane, M. E. (1990). Vision and aging. In F. Boller & J. Grafman (Eds.), *Handbook of neuropsychology.* Amsterdam: Elsevier.

Page, D. C., Mosher, R., Simpson, E. M., Fisher, E. M. C., Mardon, G., Pollack, J., & Brown, L. G. (1987). The sex-determining region of the human Y chromosome encodes a finger protein. *Cell, 51*, 1091–1104.

Page, R. A. (1981). Longitudinal evidence for the sequentiality of Kohlberg's stages of moral judgment in adolescent males. *Journal of Genetic Psychology, 139* (1), 3–9.

Page, R. M., & Cole, G. E. (1991). Loneliness and alcoholism risk in late adolescence: A comparative study of adults and adolescents. *Adolescence, 26* (104), 925–930.

Paikoff, R. F., & Brooks-Gunn, J. (1991). Do parent-child relationships change during puberty? *Psychological Bulletin, 110* (1), 47–66.

Paikoff, R. L., Buchanan, C. M., & Brooks-Gunn, J. (1991). Methodological links in the study of hormone-behavior links at puberty. In R. M. Lerner, A. C. Petersen, & J. Brooks-Gunn (Eds.), *The encyclopedia of adolescence*. New York: Garland.

Palkovitz, R. (1984). Parental attitudes and fathers' interactions with their five-month-old infants. *Developmental Psychology, 20*, 1054–1060.

Palkovitz, R., & Sussman, M. B. (Eds.). (1988). *Transitions to parenthood*. New York: Haworth Press.

Palmieri, D. T. (1991). Clearing up the confusion: Adverse effects of medications in the elderly. *Journal of Gerontological Nursing, 17* (10), 32–35.

Palmore, E. (1990). *Ageism: Negative and positive*. New York: Springer.

Paludi, M. A. (1990). Mentoring and being mentored: Issues of sex, power, and politics for older women. *Journal of Women and Aging, 2* (3), 81–92.

Palumbo, M. V. (1990). Hearing Access 2000: Increasing awareness of the hearing impaired. *Journal of Gerontological Nursing, 16* (9), 26–31.

Pang, K. C. (1991). *Immigrant communities and ethnic minorities in the United States and Canada*. New York: AMS Press.

Panksepp, J. (1992). A critical role for "affective neuroscience" in resolving what is basic about basic emotions. *Psychological Review, 99* (3), 554–560.

Papini, D. R. (1990). Early adolescent age and gender differences in patterns of emotional self-disclosure to parents and friends. *Adolescence, 25* (100), 959–976.

Papini, D. R., Sebby, R. A., & Clark, S. (1989). Affective quality of family relations and adolescent identity exploration. *Adolescence, 24*, 457–466.

Pardeck, J. A., & Pardeck, J. L. (1990). Family factors related to adolescent autonomy. *Adolescence, 25*, 311–319.

Parer, J. T. (1989). Fetal heart rate. In R. K. Creasy & R. Resnik (Eds.), *Maternal-fetal medicine: Principles and practice*. Philadelphia: Saunders.

Parer, J. T., & Livingston, E. G. (1991). What is fetal distress? *American Journal of Obstetrics and Gynecology, 162*, 1421–1433.

Parikh, B. (1980). Development of moral judgment and its relation to family environmental factors in Indian and American families. *Child Development, 51*, 1030–1039.

Park, D. C., & Smith, A. D. (1991). Importance of basic and applied research from the viewpoints of investigators in the psychology of aging. *Experimental Aging Research, 17* (2), 79–102.

Parke, R. D. (1989). The role of the family in the development of peer relations. In K. Kreppner & R. M. Lerner (Eds.), *Family systems and lifespan development*. Hillsdale, NJ: Erlbaum.

Parker, J. G., & Gottman, J. M. (1989). Social and emotional development in a relational context: Friendship interaction from early childhood to adolescence. In T. J. Berndt & G. W. Ladd (Eds.), *Peer relationships in child development*. New York: Wiley.

Parr, S. R. (1982). *The moral of the story: Literature, values, and American education*. New York: Columbia Teachers College Press.

Parton, N. (1991). *Governing the family: Child care, child protection and the state*. New York: St. Martin's Press.

Passuth, P., & Bengston, V. (1992). Sociological theories of aging: Current perspectives and future directions. In J. Birren & V. Bengston (Eds.), *Emerging theories of aging*. New York: Springer.

Patterson, K., Dancer, J., & Clark, D. (1990). Myth perceptions of hearing loss, hearing aids, and aging. *Educational Gerontology, 16* (3), 289–296.

Patterson, R. L. (1982). *Overcoming deficits of aging: A behavioral approach*. New York: Plenum.

Pattison, E. M. (1977). The experience of dying. In E. M. Pattison (Ed.), *The experience of dying*. Englewood Cliffs, NJ: Prentice Hall.

Patton, J. R., & Polloway, E. A. (1992). Learning disabilities: The challenges of adulthood. *Journal of Learning Disabilities, 25* (7), 410–415.

Patton, M. Q. (Ed.). (1991). *Family sexual abuse: Frontline research and evaluation*. Newbury Park, CA: Sage.

Paxton, C. (1991). A bridge to healing: Responding to disclosures of childhood sexual abuse. *Health Values, 15* (5), 49–56.

Payne, F. D. (1987). "Masculinity," "femininity," and the complex construct of adjustment. *Sex Roles, 17*, 359–372.

Payne, M. (1990). Elder abuse: An unspeakable shame. *Ohio's Heritage, 22* (3), 10–13.

Pearce, S. D. (1991). Toward understanding the participation of older adults in continuing education. *Educational Gerontology, 17* (5), 451–464.

Pearlin, L. I. (1990). Caregiving and the stress process: An overview of concepts and their measures. *Gerontologist, 30* (5), 583–594.

Pearse, W. H. (1987). Parturition: Place and priorities. *American Journal of Public Health, 77*, 923–924.

Pearson, D., & Shaw, S. (1982). *Life extension: A practical scientific approach*. New York: Warner.

Pearson, J. C. (1985). *Gender and communication*. Dubuque, IA: Wm. C. Brown.

Pearson, J. C., & Davilla, R. A. (1993). The gender construct. In L. P. Arliss & D. J. Borisoff (Eds.), *Women and men communicating*. Fort Worth, TX: Harcourt Brace Jovanovich.

Pease, D., Gleason, J. B., & Pan, B. A. (1993). Semantic development. In J. B. Gleason (Ed.), *The development of language* (3rd ed.). New York: Macmillan.

Peck, R. C. (1968). Psychological developments in the second half of life. In B. L. Neugarten (Ed.), *Middle age and aging*. Chicago: University of Chicago Press.

Pederson, D. R., Moran, G., Sitko, C., Campbell, K., Ghesquire, K., & Acton, H. (1989, April). *Maternal sensitivity and the security of infant-mother attachment*. Paper presented at the biennial meeting of the Society for Research in Child Development, Kansas City.

Pennebaker, J. W. (1990). *Opening up: The healing power of confiding in others*. New York: Morrow.

Pepe, M., & Byrne, T. J. (1991). Women's perceptions of immediate and long-term effects of failed infertility treatment on marital and sexual satisfaction. *Family Relations, 40* (3), 303–309.

Peplau, L. A. (1983). Roles and gender. In H. H. Kelley (Ed.), *Close relationships*. New York: Freeman.

Peplau, L. A., & Gordon, S. L. (1983). The intimate relationships of lesbians and gay men. In E. R. Allgeier & N. B. McCormick (Eds.), *Changing boundaries: Gender roles and sexual behavior*. Palo Alto, CA: Mayfield.

Perlmutter, M., & Nyquist, L. (1990). Relationships between self-reported physical and mental health and intelligence performance across adulthood. *Journal of Gerontology, 45*, P145–P155.

Perry, D. G., Perry, L. C., & Weiss, R. J. (1989). Sex differences in the consequences that children anticipate for aggression. *Developmental Psychology, 25*, 312–319.

Perry, N. W., & Wrightsman, L. S. (1991). *The child witness: Legal issues and dilemmas*. Newbury Park, CA: Sage.

Perry, W. B. (1968). *Forms of intellectual development in the college years: A scheme*. New York: Holt, Rinehart and Winston.

Peters, M. F. (1988). Parenting in black families with young children. In H. P. McAdoo (Ed.), *Black families* (2nd ed.). Newbury Park, CA: Sage.

Peters, R. D., McMahon, R. L., & Quinsey, V. L. (Eds.). (1992). *Aggression and violence throughout the lifespan*. Newbury Park, CA: Sage.

Peters, S. D. (1988). Child sexual abuse and later psychological problems. In G. E. Wyatt & G. J. Powell (Eds.), *The lasting effects of child sexual abuse*. Newbury Park, CA: Sage.

Petersen, A. C. (1987, June). Those gangly years. *Psychology Today*, p. 28–34.

Petersen, A. C. (1988). Pubertal change and psychosocial development. In D. L. Baltes, R. M. Featherman, & R. M. Lerner (Eds.), *Lifespan development and behavior* (Vol. 9). New York: Academic Press.

Petersen, A. C., & Taylor, B. (1980). The biological approach to adolescence: Biological change and psychological adaptation. In J. Adelson (Ed.), *Handbook of adolescent psychology*. New York: Wiley.

Peterson, C., & McCabe, A. (1991). On the threshold of the story realm: Semantic versus pragmatic use of connectives in narratives. *Merrill-Palmer Quarterly, 37* (3), 445–464.

Peterson, C. C. (1990). Husbands' and wives' perceptions of marital fairness across the family life cycle. *International Journal of Aging and Human Development, 31* (3), 179–188.

Peterson, G. W., & Leigh, G. K. (1990). The family and social competence in adolescence. In T. P. Gullotta, G. R. Adams, & R. Montemayor (Eds.), *Developing social competency in adolescence*. Newbury Park, CA: Sage.

Petras, K., & Petras, R. (1991). *The only retirement guide you'll ever need.* New York: Poseidon Press.

Pezdek, K., & Miceli, L. (1982). Life-span differences in memory integration as a function of processing time. *Developmental Psychology, 18* (3), 485–490.

Phair, J. P., & Chadwick, E. G. (1992). Human immunodeficiency virus infection and AIDS. In S. T. Shulman, J. P. Phair, & H. M. Sommers (Eds.), *The biological and clinical basis of infectious diseases* (4th ed.). Philadelphia: Saunders.

Phelps, S., & Mason, M. (1991). When women lose their jobs. *Personnel Journal, 70* (8), 64–69.

Phillips, D. (1992, September 26). Death postponement and birthday celebrations. *Psychosomatic Medicine,* pp. 12–18.

Phillips, D., & Smith, D. (1990, April 11). Postponement of death until symbolically meaningful occasions. *Journal of the American Medical Association,* pp. 27–38.

Phillipson, C. (1990). The sociology of retirement. In J. Bond & P. Coleman (Eds.), *Aging in society: An introduction to social gerontology.* Newbury Park, CA: Sage.

Piaget, J. (1926). *The language and thought of the child* (M. Worden, Trans.). New York: Harcourt Brace Jovanovich.

Piaget, J. (1928). *Judgement and reasoning in the child* (M. Worden, Trans.). London: Routledge and Kegan Paul.

Piaget, J. (1929). *The child's conception of the world* (J. and A. Tomlinson, Trans.). New York: Harcourt Brace Jovanovich.

Piaget, J. (1932). *The moral judgment of the child* (M. Worden, Trans.). New York: Harcourt Brace Jovanovich.

Piaget, J. (1952). *The origins of intelligence in children* (M. Cook, Trans.). New York: International Universities Press.

Piaget, J. (1954). *The construction of reality in the child* (M. Cook, Trans.). New York: Basic Books.

Piaget, J. (1962). *Play, dreams, and imitation in childhood* (C. Gattegno and F. M. Hodgson, Trans.). New York: Norton.

Piaget, J. (1965). *The child's conception of number* (C. Gattegno and F. M. Hodgson, Trans.). New York: Norton.

Piaget, J. (1969). *The child's conception of time* (A. J. Pomerans, Trans.). London: Routledge and Kegan Paul.

Piaget, J. (1972). Intellectual evolution from adolescence into adulthood. *Human Development, 15,* 1–12.

Pillemer, K., & McCartney, K. (Eds.). (1991). *Parent-child relations throughout life.* Hillsdale, NJ: Erlbaum.

Pillow, B. H. (1991). Children's understanding of biased social cognition. *Developmental Psychology, 27* (4), 539–551.

Pipp, S., Easterbrooks, M. A., & Harmon, R. J. (1992). The relation between attachment and knowledge of self and mother in one-to-three-year-old infants. *Child Development, 63* (3), 738–750.

Piscatella, J. (1990). *The don't eat your heart out cookbook.* New York: Workman.

Pitcher, E. G., Feinberg, S. G., & Alexander, D. (1989). *Helping young children learn* (5th ed.). Columbus, OH: Merrill.

Pittman, F. S. (1987). *Turning points: Treating families in transition and crisis.* New York: Norton.

Pleck, J. (1989). Correlates of black adolescent males' condom use. *Journal of Adolescent Research, 4,* 247–253.

Plomin, R. (1986). *Development, genetics, and psychology.* Hillsdale, NJ: Erlbaum.

Plomin, R. (1988). The nature and nurture of cognitive abilities. In R. J. Sternberg (Ed.), *Advances in the psychology of human intelligence.* Hillsdale, NJ: Erlbaum.

Plomin, R. (1989). Environment and genes: Determinants of behavior. *American Psychologist, 44* (2), 105–111.

Plomin, R. (1990). *Nature and nurture: An introduction to human behavioral genetics.* Pacific Grove, CA: Brooks/Cole.

Plomin, R., DeFries, J. C., & McClearn, G. E. (1989). *Behavioral genetics: A primer* (2nd ed.). San Francisco: Freeman.

Plomin, R., McClearn, G. E., Pederson, N. L., & Nesselroade, J. R. (1988). Genetic influence on childhood family environment perceived retrospectively from the last half of the life span. *Developmental Psychology, 24,* 738–745.

Plomin, R., & Rende, R. (1991). Human behavioral genetics. *Annual Review of Psychology, 42,* 161–190.

Plomin, R., & Thompson, L. (1988). Life-span developmental behavioral genetics. In P. B. Baltes, D. L. Featherman, & R. M. Lerner (Eds.), *Lifespan development and behavior.* Hillsdale, NJ: Erlbaum.

Poehlman, E. T., Melby, C. L., & Badylak, S. F. (1991). Relation of age and physical exercise status on metabolic rate in younger and older healthy men. *Journal of Gerontology: Biological Sciences, 46* (2), B54–B58.

Polloway, E. A., Schewel, R., & Patton, J. R. (1992). Learning disabilities in adulthood: Personal perspectives. *Journal of Learning Disabilities, 25* (8), 520–522.

Pomerleau, A., Bolduc, D., Malcuit, G., & Cossette, L. (1990). Pink or blue: Environmental stereotypes in the first two years of life. *Sex Roles, 22,* 359–367.

Pomerleau, A., Malcuit, G., & Seguin, R. (1992). Five-month-old girls' and boys' exploratory behaviors in the presence of familiar and unfamiliar toys. *Journal of Genetic Psychology, 153* (1), 47–61.

Ponza, M., & Wray, L. (1990). *Evaluation of the food assistance needs of the low-income elderly and their participation in USDA programs: Final results of the elderly programs study.* Princeton, NJ: Mathematical Policy Research.

Porcino, J. (1991). *Living longer, living better: Adventures in community housing for those in the second half of life.* New York: Continuum.

Portes, P., Haas, R. C., & Brown, J. (1991). Identifying family factors that predict children's adjustment to divorce: An analytic synthesis. *Journal of Divorce and Remarriage, 15* (3/4), 87–103.

Powell, G. J. (1988). Child sexual abuse research: The implications for clinical practice. In G. E. Wyatt & G. J. Powell (Eds.), *The lasting effects of child sexual abuse.* Newbury Park, CA: Sage.

Pratt, C. C., Walker, A. J., & Wood, B. L. (1992). Bereavement among former caregivers to elderly mothers. *Family Relations, 41,* 278–283.

Pratt, W. (1990, April). *Premarital sexual behavior, multiple sexual partners, and marital experience.* Paper presented at the annual meeting of the Population Association of America, Toronto.

Pratt, W., Mosher, W., Bachrach, C., & Horn, M. (1984). Understanding U.S. fertility: Findings from the National Survey of Family Growth, Cycle III. *Population Bulletin, 39,* 1–42.

Price, D. W., & Goodman, G. S. (1990). Visiting the wizard: Children's memory for a recurring event. *Child Development, 61* (3), 664–680.

Price, J. A. (1990). School counselors' knowledge of eating disorders. *Adolescence, 25* (100), 945–958.

Priest, R. (1992). Child sexual abuse histories among African-American college students: A preliminary study. *American Journal of Orthopsychiatry, 62* (3), 475–476.

Pritchard, R. J. (1990). A "better way" to care for dementia sufferers. *Ageing International, 16* (1), 44–46.

Prosky, P. (1991). Marital life. *Family Therapy, 18* (2), 129–144.

Prothrow-Stith, D. (1989). Excerpts from address to the Massachusetts Department of Public Health *Journal of Adolescent Health Care, 10,* 5–7.

Pruchno, R. A., Michaels, J. I., & Potashnik, S. L. (1990). Predictors of institutionalization among Alzheimer's disease victims with caregiving spouses. *Journal of Gerontology: Social Sciences, 45* (6), S259–S266.

Pugmire-Stoy, M. C. (1992). *Spontaneous play in early childhood.* Albany, NY: Delmar.

Purves, D. (1988). *Body and brain.* Cambridge, MA: Harvard University Press.

Putallaz, M., & Wasserman, A. (1989). Children's naturalistic entry behavior and sociometric status: A developmental perspective. *Developmental Psychology, 25,* 297–305.

Pynoos, J., & Ohta, R. J. (1991). In-home interventions for persons with Alzheimer's disease and their caregivers. *Physical and Occupational Therapy in Geriatrics, 9* (3/4), 83–92.

Quadagno, J. S., & Hardy, M. (1991). Regulating retirement through the Age Discrimination in Employment Act. *Research on Aging, 13,* 470–475.

Quinn, P., & Allen, K. R. (1989). Facing challenges and making compromises: How single mothers endure. *Family Relations, 38,* 390–395.

Qureshi, H., & Walker, A. (1989). *The caring relationship: Elderly people and their families.* Philadelphia: Temple University Press.

Rabin, D. S., & Chrousos, G. P. (1991). Gonadal androgens. In R. M. Lerner, A. C. Petersen, & J. Brooks-Gunn (Eds.), *The encyclopedia of adolescence.* New York: Garland.

Rabitt, P., & Backman, L. (1990). Cognitive gerontology: A special issue. *European Journal of Cognitive Psychology, 2* (3), 193–304.

Rader, J., & Hoeffer, B. (1991). Caring for persons with Alzheimer's disease in long-term care facilities. In M. S. Harper (Ed.), *Management and care of the elderly: Psychosocial perspectives.* Newbury Park CA: Sage.

Ragatt, P. T. (1991). Work stress among long-distance coach drivers: A survey and correlational study. *Journal of Organizational Behavior, 12* (7), 565–579.

Ragland, D. R., & Brand, R. J. (1988). Type A behavior and mortality from coronary heart disease. *New England Journal of Medicine, 318,* 65–69.

Rakowski, W. (1992). Disease prevention and health promotion with older adults. In M. G. Ory, R. P. Abeles, & P. D. Lipman (Eds.), *Aging, health, and behavior.* Newbury Park, CA: Sage.

Ralston, P. A. (1991). Determinants of senior center attendance and participation. *Journal of Applied Gerontology, 10* (3), 258–273.

Rancourt, A. M. (1991). Programming quality services for older adults in long-term care facilities. *Adaptation and Aging, 15,* 1–11.

Rankin, E. D. (1990). Caregiver stress and the elderly: A familial perspective. *Journal of Gerontological Social Work, 15* (1/2), 57–73.

Ransom, R. L., Sutch, R., & Williamson, S. H. (1991). Retirement: Past and present. In A. H. Munnell (Ed.), *Retirement and public policy. Proceedings of the second conference of the National Academy of Social Insurance.* Dubuque, IA: Kendall/Hunt.

Raver, S. (1991). *Strategies for teaching at-risk and handicapped infants and toddlers: A transdisciplinary approach.* New York: Macmillan.

Rawlins, W. K. (1993). Communicating in cross-sex friendships. In L. P. Arliss & D. J. Borisoff (Eds.), *Women and men communicating.* Fort Worth, TX: Harcourt Brace Jovanovich.

Rayman, P., & Allshouse, K. (1990). *Resiliency amidst inequity: Older women workers in an aging United States. Project on women and population aging.* Southport, CT: Southport Institute for Policy Analysis.

Redfoot, D., & Gaberlavage, G. (1991). Housing for older Americans: Sustaining the dream. *Generations, 15* (3), 35–38.

Reed, A. T. (1990). Alzheimer's disease and the need for supervision. *American Journal of Alzheimer's Care and Related Disorders and Research, 5* (5), 29–34.

Reed, R. L. (1991). The interrelationship between physical exercise, muscle strength and body adiposity in a healthy elderly population. *Journal of the American Geriatrics Society, 39* (12), 1189–1193.

Reed, S. K. (1992). *Cognition: Theory and applications* (3rd ed.). Pacific Grove, CA: Brooks/Cole.

Reedy, M. N. (1983). Personality and aging. In D. S. Woodruff & J. E. Birren (Eds.), *Aging: Scientific perspectives and social issues* (2nd ed.). Monterey, CA: Brooks/Cole.

Reichard, S., Livson, F., & Peterson, P. G. (1962). *Aging and personality.* New York: Wiley.

Reis, H. T., & Wright, S. (1982). Knowledge of sex-role stereotypes in children aged 3–5. *Sex Roles, 8,* 10–49.

Reisberg, B. (1990). Some observations on the diagnosis of dementia of the Alzheimer type. In M. Bergener & S. I. Finkel (Eds.), *Clinical and scientific psychogeriatrics.* New York: Springer.

Reiss, I. L. (1960). Toward a sociology of the heterosexual love relationship. *Marriage and Family Living, 26,* 139–145.

Reiss, I. L. (1980). *Family systems in America* (3rd ed.). New York: Holt, Rinehart and Winston.

Reiss, I. L., & Reiss, H. M. (1990). *An end to shame: Shaping our next sexual revolution.* New York: Prometheus.

Reite, M., Kaemingk, K., & Boccia, M. L. (1989). Maternal separation in bonnet monkey infants: Altered attachment and social support. *Child Development, 60,* 473–480.

Reitmeijer, C., Krebs, J., Feorino, P., & Judson, F. (1988). Condoms as physical and chemical barriers against human immunodeficiency virus. *Journal of the American Medical Association, 259,* 1851–1853.

Reitzes, D. C., Mutran, E., & Pope, H. (1991). Location and well-being among retired men. *Journal of Gerontology: Social Sciences, 46* (4), S195–S203.

Repetti, R. L., & Cosmas, K. A. (1991). The quality of the social environment at work and

job satisfaction. *Journal of Applied Social Psychology, 21* (10), 840–854.

Ressler, L. E. (1991). Improving elderly recall with bimodal presentation: A natural experiment of discharge planning. *Gerontologist, 31* (3), 364–370.

Rest, J. R. (1981, April). *The impact of higher education on moral judgment development.* Paper presented at the convention of the American Educational Research Association, Los Angeles.

Rest, J. R. (1983). Morality. In P. H. Mussen (Ed.), *Handbook of child psychology.* New York: Wiley.

Rest, J. R. (1986). *Moral development: Advances in theory and research.* New York: Praeger.

Retzinger, S. M. (1991). *Violent emotions: Shame and rage in marital quarrels.* Newbury Park, CA: Sage.

Rexroat, C., & Shehan, C. (1987). The family life cycle and spouses' time in housework. *Journal of Marriage and the Family, 49,* 737–750.

Reyna, V. F. (1991). Class inclusion, the conjunction fallacy, and other cognitive illusions. *Developmental Review, 11* (4), 317–336.

Reznick, S. J., & Goldfield, B. A. (1992). Rapid change in lexical development in comprehension and production. *Developmental Psychology, 28* (3), 406–413.

Rhodewalt, F., Sansone, C., Hill, A., & Chemers, M. (1992). Stress and distress as a function of Jenkins Activity Survey-defined Type A behavior and control over the work environment. *Basic and Applied Social Psychology, 12* (2), 211–226.

Rhymes, J. A. (1990). Can you correct your patient's gait disorder? *Senior Patient, 2* (12), 36–40.

Ribordy, S. C., Camras, L. A., Stefani, R., & Spaccarelli, S. (1988). Vignettes for emotional recognition research and affective therapy with children. *Journal of Clinical Child Psychology, 17* (4), 322–325.

Rice, M. L. (1989). Children's language acquisition. *American Psychologist, 44,* 149–156.

Rice, P. L. (1992). *Stress and health: Principles and practice for coping and wellness* (2nd ed.). Pacific Grove, CA: Brooks/Cole.

Richards, F. A., & Commons, M. L. (1982). Systematic, metasystematic, and crossparadigmatic reasoning: A case for stages of reasoning beyond formal operations. In M. L. Commons, F. A. Richards, & S. Armon (Eds.), *Beyond formal operations: Late adolescent and adult cognitive development.* New York: Praeger.

Richards, M. (1991). Adolescent personality in girls and boys: The role of mothers and fathers. *Psychology of Women Quarterly (UK), 15* (1), 65–81.

Richardson, K., & Sheldon, S. (Eds.). (1988). *Cognitive development to adolescence.* Hillsdale, NJ: Erlbaum.

Richardson, L. (1988). *The dynamics of sex and gender* (3rd ed.). New York: Harper & Row.

Richardson, S. O. (1992). Historical perspectives on dyslexia. *Journal of Learning Disabilities, 25* (1), 40–47.

Richardson, V. (1990). Gender differences in retirement planning among educators: Implications for practice with older women. *Journal of Women and Aging, 2* (3), 27–40.

Richardson, V., & Kilty, K. M. (1991). Adjustment to retirement: Continuity vs. discontinuity. *International Journal of Aging and Human Development, 33* (2), 151–169.

Richelson, E. (1990). Psychopharmacology, technology, and aging. *International Journal of Technology and Aging, 3* (1), 19–28.

Rickel, A. U. (1989). *Teen pregnancy and parenting.* New York: Hemisphere.

Rickman, L. M. (1991). *A comprehensive approach to retrofitting homes for a lifetime.* Washington, DC: National Association of Home Builders.

Ridley-Johnson, R., Surdy, T., & O'Laughlin, E. (1991). Parent survey on television violence viewing: Fear, aggression, and sex differences. *Journal of Applied Developmental Psychology, 12* (1), 63–71.

Riegel, K. F., & Riegel, R. M. (1972). Development, drop, and death. *Developmental Psychology, 6* (2), 306–319.

Riley, B. (1990). Schizophrenia, paranoid disorders, anxiety disorders, and somatoform disorders. In M. O. Hogstel (Ed.), *Geropsychiatric nursing.* St Louis: Mosby.

Ring, K. (1980). *Life at death: A scientific investigation of the near death experience.* New York: Coward, McCann, and Geoghegan.

Ringgold, N. P. (1991). *Out of the corner of my eye: Living with vision loss in later life.* New York: American Foundation for the Blind.

Risen, L. I., & Koss, M. P. (1987). The sexual abuse of boys: Prevalence and descriptive characteristics of childhood victimizations. *Journal of Interpersonal Violence, 2,* 309–323.

Rivera, B., & Widom, C. S. (1990). Childhood victimization and violent offending. *Violence and Victims, 5* (1), 19–36.

Rob, C., & Reynolds, J. (1991). *The caregiver's guide: Helping elderly relatives cope with health and safety problems.* Boston: Houghton Mifflin.

Robbert, R. (1991). The emergence of Alzheimer's disease: Issues and concerns. In R. F. Young & E. A. Olson (Eds.), *Health, illness, and disability in later life: Practice issues and interventions.* Newbury Park, CA: Sage.

Robbins, M. A. (1990). *Midlife women and death of mother: A study of psychohistorical and spiritual transformation.* New York: Peter Lang.

Roberto, K. A., & Johnston, M. M. (1991). The impact of osteoporosis on the quality of informal relationships. *Journal of Gerontological Social Work, 16* (1/2), 179–193.

Robinson, B. (1990). Death, dying, and debate: Questions of life and death. *Ageing International, 17* (2), 27–35.

Robinson, B. (1991). Contemplating suicide: New questions, no answers. *Ageing International, 18* (2), 24–31.

Robinson, J. P. (1991). Quitting time. *American Demographics, 13* (5), 34–36.

Robinson, R. (1990). *When your parents need you: A caregiver's guide.* Santa Monica, CA: IBS Press.

Rockner, G., Wahlberg, V., & Olund, A. (1989). Episiotomy and perineal trauma during childbirth. *Journal of Advanced Nursing, 14,* 264–279.

Rodin, J. (1987). Personal control through the life course. In R. P. Abeles (Ed.), *Life-span perspectives and social psychology.* Hillsdale, NJ: Erlbaum.

Rodin, J., & Timko, C. (1992). Sense of control, aging, and health. In M. G. Ory, R. P. Abeles, & P. D. Lipman (Eds.), *Aging, health, and behavior.* Newbury Park, CA: Sage.

Roe, A. (1956). *The psychology of occupations.* New York: Wiley.

Rogers, C., & Terry, T. (1984). Clinical intervention with boy victims of sexual abuse. In I. Stewart & J. Greer (Eds.), *Victims of sexual aggression*. New York: Van Nostrand Reinhold.

Rogers, C. R. (1961). *On becoming a person*. Boston: Houghton Mifflin.

Rogers, C. R. (1974). In retrospect: Forty-six years. *American Psychologist, 29*, 115–123.

Rogers, C. R. (1980). *A way of being*. Boston: Houghton Mifflin.

Rogers, R. G., Rogers, A., & Belanger, A. (1992). Disability-free life among the elderly in the United States: Sociodemographic correlates of functional health. *Journal of Aging and Health, 4* (1), 19–42.

Rogoff, B. (1989). *Apprenticeship in thinking: Cognitive development in a social context*. New York: Oxford University Press.

Rolfes, S. R., & DeBruyne, L. K. (1990). *Lifespan nutrition: Conception through life*. St. Paul, MN: West.

Romig, C., & Bakken, L. (1992). Intimacy development in middle adolescence: Its relationship to gender and family cohesion and adaptability. *Journal of Youth and Adolescence, 21* (3), 325–338.

Rook, K. S. (1987). Reciprocity of social exchange and social satisfaction among older women. *Journal of Personality and Social Psychology, 52*, 145–154.

Roosa, M. W. (1991). Adolescent pregnancy programs collection: An introduction. *Family Relations, 40*, 370–372.

Roosa, M. W., & Christopher, S. F. (1990). Evaluation of an abstinence only adolescent pregnancy prevention program: A replication. *Family Relations, 39*, 363–367.

Roscoe, B., Kennedy, D., & Pope, T. (1987). Adolescents' views of intimacy: Distinguishing intimate from nonintimate relationships. *Adolescence, 22*, 511–516.

Rose, J. H. (1991). A life course perspective on health threats in aging. *Journal of Gerontological Social Work, 17* (3/4), 85–97.

Rose, S., & Larwood, L. (Eds.). (1988). *Women's careers: Pathways and pitfalls*. Westport, CT: Greenwood Press.

Rose, S. A. (1983). Differential rates of visual information processing in full-term and preterm infants. *Child Development, 54*, 1189–1198.

Rose, S. A. (1988). Shape recognition in infancy: Visual integration of sequential information. *Child Development, 59*, 1161–1176.

Rose, S. A., & Orlian, E. K. (1991). Asymmetries in infant cross-modal transfer. *Child Development, 62* (4), 706–718.

Rosen, J. L., & Neugarten, B. L. (1964). Ego functions in the middle and later years: A thematic apperception study. In B. L. Neugarten (Ed.), *Personality in middle and late life*. New York: Atherton Press.

Rosen, R., & Ager, J. W. (1981). Self-concept and contraception: Preconception decision-making. *Population and Environment, 4*, 11–23.

Rosen, T. J. (1990). Age-associated memory impairment: A critique. *European Journal of Cognitive Psychology, 2* (3), 275–287.

Rosen, W. D., Adamson, L. B., & Bakeman, R. (1992). An experimental investigation of infant social referencing: Mothers' messages and gender differences. *Developmental Psychology, 28*, (6), 1172–1178.

Rosenbaum, J. L. (1989). Family dysfunction and female delinquency. *Crime and Delinquency, 35*, 31–44.

Rosenblum, V. G., & Forsythe, C. D. (1990). The right to assisted suicide: Protection of autonomy or an open door to social killing? *Issues in Law and Medicine, 6* (1), 3–31.

Rosenman, R. H., & Chesney, M. A. (1980). The relationship of Type A behavior pattern to coronary heart disease. *Activitas Nervosa Superior, 22*, 1–45.

Rosenman, R. H., & Chesney, M. A. (1982). Stress, type A behavior, and coronary disease. In L. Goldberger & S. Breznitz (Eds.), *Handbook of stress*. New York: Free Press.

Rosenstein, D., & Oster, H. (1988). Differential facial response to four basic tastes in newborns. *Child Development, 59*, 1555–1568.

Rosenstock, I. M. (1990). Personal responsibility and public policy in health promotion. In S. A. Shumaker (Ed.), *The handbook of health behavior change*. New York: Springer.

Rosenthal, E. R. (Ed.). (1990). *Women, aging, and ageism*. New York: Harrington Park Press.

Rosenthal, M. K. (1991). Daily experiences of toddlers in three child care settings in Israel. *Child and Youth Care Forum, 20* (1), 37–58.

Rosowsky, E., & Gurian, B. (1991). Borderline personality disorder in late life. *International Psychogeriatrics, 3* (1), 39–52.

Ross, M. W., Paulsen, J. A., & Stalstrom, O. W. (1988). Homosexuality and mental health: A cross-cultural review. In M. W. Ross (Ed.), *The treatment of homosexuals with mental health disorders*. New York: Harrington Park Press.

Ross, V., Echevarria, K. H., & Robinson, B. (1991). Geriatric tinnitus: Causes, clinical treatment, and prevention. *Journal of Gerontological Nursing, 17* (10), 6–11.

Rossi, A., & Rossi, P. (1990). *Of human bonding: Parent-child relations across the life course*. New York: Aldine.

Rossman, I. (1986). The anatomy of aging. In I. Rossman (Ed.), *Clinical geriatrics* (3rd ed.). Philadelphia: Lippincott.

Rothenberg, K. J., & Chase, N. (1992). Development of the reciprocity of self-disclosure. *Journal of Genetic Psychology, 153* (1), 75–86.

Rothenberg, E. P. S. (1988). *Racism and sexism: An integrated study*. New York: St. Martin's Press.

Rotheram-Borus, M. J., & Koopman, C. (1991). AIDS and adolescents. In R. M. Lerner, A. C. Petersen, & J. Brooks-Gunn (Eds.), *The encyclopedia of adolescence*. New York: Garland.

Rothstein-Fisch, C., & Howes, C. (1988). Toddler peer interaction in mixed-age groups. *Journal of Applied Developmental Psychology, 9*, 211–218.

Roug, L., Landberg, I., & Lundberg, L. J. (1989). Phonetic development in early infancy: A study of four Swedish children during the first eighteen months of life. *Journal of Child Language, 16*, 19–40.

Rovet, J., & Netley, C. (1983). The triple X chromosome syndrome in childhood: Recent empirical findings. *Child Development, 54*, 831–845.

Rowe, D. (1982). *The construction of life and death*. New York: Wiley.

Rowe, G. P. (1981). The developmental conceptual framework to the study of the family. In F. I. Nye & F. Berardo (Eds.), *Emerging conceptual frameworks in family analysis*. New York: Macmillan.

Rowe, J. W. (1991). Reducing the risk of usual aging. *Generations, 15* (1), 25–28.

Rubenstein, C., & Shaver, P. (1982). *In search of intimacy*. New York: Delacorte Press.

Rubenstein, E., Panzarine, S., & Lanning, P. (1990). Peer counseling with adolescent mothers: A pilot program. *Families in Society, 71* (3), 136–141.

Rubin, K. H. (1990). Peer relationships and social skills in childhood: An international perspective. *Human Development, 33* (4–5), 221–224.

Rubin, R., Reinisch, J., & Haskett, R. (1981). Postnatal gonadal steroid effects on human behavior. *Science, 211*, 1318–1324.

Rubin, Z., Peplau, A., & Hill, C. T. (1981). Loving and leaving: Sex differences in romantic attachments. *Sex Roles, 7*, 821–834.

Rubinson, L., & Neutens, J. (1987). *Research techniques in the health sciences*. New York: Macmillan.

Rubinstein, R. L. (1990). Nature, culture, gender, age: A critical review. In R. L. Rubinstein (Ed.), *Anthropology and aging: Comprehensive reviews*. Boston: Kluwer Academic.

Ruble, D. N., Fleming, A. S., Hackel, L. S., & Stangor, C. (1988). Changes in the marital relationship during the transition to first time motherhood: Effects of violated expectations concerning division of household labor. *Journal of Personality and Social Psychology, 55*, 78–87.

Ruchlin, H. S., & Morris, J. N. (1992). Deteriorating health and the cessation of employment among older workers. *Journal of Aging and Health, 4*, 43–57.

Ruff, H. A., Saltarelli, L. M., Capozzoli, M., & Dubiner, K. (1992). The differentiation of activity in infants' exploration of objects. *Developmental Psychology, 28* (5), 851–861.

Ruffman, T., Olson, D. R., Ash, T., & Keenan, T. (1993). The ABCs of deception: Do young children understand deception in the same way as adults? *Developmental Psychology, 29* (1), 74–87.

Ruffman, T., Olson, D. R., & Astington, J. W. (1991). Children's understanding of visual ambiguity. *British Journal of Developmental Psychology, 9* (1), 89–102.

Ruhm, C. J. (1990). Determinants of the timing of retirement. In P. B. Doeringer (Ed.), *Bridges to retirement: Older workers in a changing labor market*. Ithaca, NY: ILR Press.

Rumberger, R. (1983). The influence of family background on education, earnings, and wealth. *Social Forces, 61*, 755–773.

Runwell, Y. (1991). Suicide in later life: Psychological autopsy findings. *International Psychogeriatrics, 3* (1), 59–66.

Russell, D. E. H. (1983). The incidence and prevalence of intrafamilial and extrafamilial sexual abuse of female children. *Child Abuse and Neglect, 7*, 133–146.

Russell, D. E. H. (1984). *Sexual exploitation: Rape, child sexual abuse, and sexual harassment*. Beverly Hills, CA: Sage.

Russell, G. (1982). Highly participant Australian fathers: Some preliminary findings. *Merrill-Palmer Quarterly, 28* (1), 137–156.

Russell, J., Halasz, G., & Beumont, P. J. (1990). Death related themes in anorexia nervosa: A practical exploration. *Journal of Adolescence, 13,* 311–326.

Russell, J. A. (1991). Culture and the categorization of emotions. *Psychological Bulletin, 110* (3), 426–450.

Rutledge, E. M. (1990). Black parent-child relations: Some correlates. *Journal of Comparative Family Studies (Canada), 21* (3), 369–378.

Rutter, M. (1990). Adult outcome of institution-reared children: Males and females compared. In L. Robins & M. Rutter (Eds.), *Straight and devious pathways from childhood to adulthood.* Cambridge: Cambridge University Press.

Ryan, E. B. (1992). Beliefs about memory changes across the adult life span. *Journal of Gerontology: Psychological Sciences, 47* (1), P41–P46.

Saarni, C., & Harris, P. L. (1989). *Children's understanding of emotion.* New York and London: Cambridge University Press.

Sabatelli, R. M. (1988). Exploring relationship satisfaction: A social exchange perspective on the interdependence between theory, research, and practice. *Family Relations, 37,* 217–222.

Sabatelli, R. M., & Shehan, C. L. (in press). Exchange and resource theories. In P. Boss, W. Doherty, R. LaRossa, W. Schuum, & S. Steinmetz (Eds.), *Sourcebook of family theories and methods: A contextual approach.* New York: Plenum.

Sabatino, D. A. (1991). *A fine line: When discipline becomes child abuse.* Blue Ridge Summit, PA: TAB Books.

Sabom, M. B. (1982). *Recollections of death: A medical investigation.* New York: Harper & Row.

Sachs, J. (1993). Communication development in infancy. In J. B. Gleason (Ed.), *The development of language* (3rd ed.). New York: Macmillan.

Sagi, A. (1981). Mothers' and non-mothers' identification of infant cries. *Infant Behavior and Development, 4* (1), 37–40.

Sakauye, K. M. (1989). Ethnic variations in family support of the frail elderly. In M. Z. Goldstein (Ed.), *Family involvement in treatment of the frail elderly.* Washington, DC: American Psychiatric Press.

Salthouse, T. A. (1991). *Theoretical perspectives on cognitive aging.* Hillsdale, NJ: Erlbaum.

Saltzstein, H. D. (1983). Critical issues in Kohlberg's theory of moral reasoning. *Monographs of the Society for Research in Child Development, 48* (1–2, Serial No. 200), 108–119.

Salzinger, S. (1991). Risk for physical child abuse and the personal consequences for its victims. *Criminal Justice and Behavior, 18* (1), 64–81.

Salzman, C., & Lebowitz, B. D. (Eds.). (1991). *Anxiety in the elderly: Treatment and research.* New York: Springer.

Samarel, N. (1991). *Caring for life and death.* Bristol, PA: Hemisphere.

Sampson, E. E. (1985). The decentralization of identity: Toward a revised concept of personal and social order. *American Psychologist, 40,* 1203–1211.

Samuels, J., Vlaho, D., Anthony, J., & Chaisson, R. (1992). Measurement of HIV risk behaviors among intravenous drug users. *British Journal of Addiction, 87,* 417–428.

Sanborn, B., & Bould, S. (1991). Intergenerational caregivers of the oldest old. In S. K. Pfeifer & M. B. Sussman (Eds.), *Families: Intergenerational and generational connections.* Binghamton, NY: Haworth.

Santilli, N. R., & Hudson, L. M. (1992). Enhancing moral growth: Is communication the key? *Adolescence, 27* (105), 145–160.

Sarason, B. R., Sarason, I. G., & Pierce, G. R. (Eds.). (1990). *Social support: An interactional view.* New York: Wiley.

Sarason, I. G., & Sarason, B. R. (1989). *Abnormal psychology* (6th ed.). Englewood Cliffs, NJ: Prentice Hall.

Sarnoff, I., & Sarnoff, S. (1989). *Love-centered marriage in a self-centered world.* New York: Hemisphere.

Savin-Williams, R. C., & Small, S. A. (1986). The timing of puberty and its relationship to adolescent and parent perceptions of family interactions. *Developmental Psychology, 32,* 342–347.

Sawyer, W., & Comer, D. E. (1991). *Growing up with literature.* Albany, NY: Delmar.

Sawyer, W. E., & Sawyer, J. C. (1993). *Integrated language arts for emerging literacy.* Albany, NY: Delmar.

Scarr, S., & Kidd, K. K. (1983). Developmental behavior genetics. In P. H. Mussen (Ed.), *Handbook of child psychology* (14th ed.). New York: Wiley.

Scarr, S., Phillips, D., & McCartney, K. (1990). Working mothers and their families. In S. Chess & M. E. Hertzig (Eds.), *Annual progress in child psychiatry and child development.* New York: Brunner/Mazel.

Schacht, A. J., Kerlinsky, D., & Carlson, C. (1990). Group therapy with sexually abused boys: Leadership, projective identification, and countertransference issues. *International Journal of Group Psychotherapy, 40* (4), 401–417.

Schacter, F. F., & Strage, A. A. (1982). Adult's talk and children's language development. In S. G. Moore & C. R. Cooper (Eds.), *The young child: Reviews of research* (Vol. 3). Washington, DC: National Association for the Education of Young Children.

Schaie, K. W. (1980). Intelligence and problem solving. In J. Birren & R. B. Sloane (Eds.), *Handbook of mental health and aging.* Englewood Cliffs, NJ: Prentice Hall.

Schaie, K. W. (1982). The Seattle longitudinal study: A twenty-one year exploration of psychometric intelligence in adulthood. In K. W. Schaie (Ed.), *Longitudinal studies of adult psychological development.* New York: Guilford.

Schaie, K. W. (1983). Age changes in adult intelligence. In D. S. Woodruff & J. E. Birren (Eds.), *Aging: Scientific perspectives and social issues* (2nd ed.). Monterey, CA: Brooks/Cole.

Schaie, K. W. (1990). The optimization of cognitive functioning in old age: Predictions based on cohort-sequential and longitudinal data. In P. B. Baltes & M. M. Baltes (Eds.), *Successful aging: Perspectives from the behavioral sciences.* New York: Cambridge University Press.

Schaie, K. W., & Willis, S. L. (1991). Adult personality and psychomotor performance: Cross-sectional and longitudinal analyses. *Journal of Gerontology: Psychological Sciences, 46* (6), P275–P234.

Scharer, L. K. (1991). Ethical issues in long-term care: Whose ethics is it anyway? *Pride Institute Journal of Long Term Home Health Care, 10* (1), 2–39.

Scharlach, A. E., Sobel, E. L., & Roberts, R. (1991). Employment and caregiver strain: An integrative model. *Gerontologist, 31* (6), 778–787.

Scharli, A. F. (1989). Circumcision: An everlasting discussion. *Pediatric Surgical Intervention, 4,* 219–221.

Scheibel, A. B. (1992). Structural changes in the aging brain. In J. E. Birren, R. B. Sloane, & G. D. Cohen (Eds.), *Handbook of mental health and aging* (2nd ed.). San Diego: Harcourt Brace Jovanovich.

Scheinfeld, A. (1950). *The new you and heredity.* Philadelphia: Lippincott.

Schieber, F. (1992). Aging and the senses. In J. E. Birren, R. B. Sloane, & G. D. Cohen (Eds.), *Handbook of mental health and aging* (2nd ed.). San Diego: Harcourt Brace Jovanovich.

Schilke, J. M. (1991). Slowing the aging process with physical activity. *Journal of Gerontological Nursing, 17* (6), 4–8.

Schinke, S. P., Holden, G. W., & Moncher, M. S. (1989). Preventing HIV infection among black and Hispanic adolescents. *Journal of Social Work and Human Sexuality, 8,* 63–73.

Schinzel, A. (1984). *Catalogue of unbalanced chromosome aberrations in men.* Berlin: Walter de Gruyter.

Schirrmacher, R. (1993). *Art and creative development for young children* (2nd ed.). Albany, NY: Delmar.

Schlundt, D. G., & Johnson, W. G. (1990). *Assessment and treatment of anorexia nervosa and bulimia nervosa.* Needham Heights, MA: Allyn & Bacon.

Schmetzer, U. (1993, May 15). What's happened to China's female children? *New London (CT) Day,* pp. 7–8.

Schmidt, C. R., Ollendick, T. H., & Stanowicz, L. B. (1988). Developmental changes in the influence of assigned goals on cooperation and competition. *Developmental Psychology, 24,* 574–579.

Schmidt, C. R., & Paris, S. G. (1983). The development of children's communication skills. In H. Reese & L. Lipsitt (Eds.), *Advances in child development and behavior.* New York: Academic Press.

Schmidt, R. (1975). *Motor skills.* New York: Harper & Row.

Schmidt, R. (1982). *Motor control and learning: A behavioral emphasis.* Champaign, IL: Human Kinetics.

Schnaiberg, A., & Goldenberg, S. (1989). From empty nest to crowded nest: The dynamics of incompletely-launched young adults. *Social Problems, 36,* 251–269.

Schneider, D. J. (1991). Social cognition. *Annual Review of Psychology, 42,* 527–561.

Schneider, J. (1984). *Stress, loss, and grief: Understanding their origins and growth potential.* University Park, MD: University Park Press.

Schneider, L. E. (1991). Attachment theory and research: Review of the literature. *Clinical Social Work Journal, 19* (3), 251–266.

Schneider, W., & Sodian, B. (1991). A longitudinal study of young children's memory behavior and performance in a sort-recall task. *Journal of Experimental Child Psychology, 51* (1), 14–29.

Schofield, J. W., & Whitley, B. E., Jr. (1983). Peer nomination vs. rating scale measurement of children's peer preferences. *Journal of Personality and Social Psychology, 46,* 242–251.

Schonfeld, L., & Dupree, L. W. (1990). Older problem drinkers: Long-term and late-life onset abusers. What triggers their drinking? *Aging, 361,* 5–11.

Schooler, C. (1991). Statistical and causal interaction in the diagnosis and outcome of depression. In K. W. Schaie, D. Blazer, & J. S. House (Eds.), *Aging, health behaviors, and health outcomes.* Hillsdale, NJ: Erlbaum.

Schover, L. R., & Jensen, S. B. (1988). *Sexuality and chronic illness.* New York: Guilford.

Schrauben, L. (1991). Intervention strategies: Support services for family caregivers. In R. F. Young & E. A. Olson (Eds.), *Health, illness, and disability in later life: Practice issues and interventions.* Newbury Park, CA: Sage.

Schuller, T. (1989). Workending, employment, and ambiguity in later life. In B. Bytheway, T. Keil, P. Allat, & A. Bryan (Eds.), *Becoming and being old: Social approaches to later life.* Newbury Park, CA: Sage.

Schulman, M. (1991). *The passionate mind: Bringing up an intelligent and creative child.* New York: Free Press.

Schultz, C. L. (1990). Aging, care giving, and support systems: An overview. *Australian Journal on Ageing, 9* (2), 56–59.

Schultz, K., Colarusso, R., & Strawderman, V. (1989). *Mathematics for every child.* New York: Macmillan.

Schumm, W. R., & Bugaighis, M. A. (1986). Marital quality over the marital career: Alternative explanations. *Journal of Marriage and the Family, 48,* 165–168.

Scott, C. G. (1991). Aged SSI recipients: Income, work history, and Social Security benefits. *Social Security Bulletin, 54* (8), 2–11.

Scott, J. P. (1990). Sibling interaction in later life. In T. Brubaker (Ed.), *Family relationships in later life.* Newbury Park, CA: Sage.

Scott-Jones, D., & White, A. B. (1990). Correlates of sexual activity in early adolescence. *Journal of Early Adolescence, 10,* 221–238.

Seale, C. (1990). Caring for people who die: The experience of family and friends. *Aging and Society, 10* (4), 413–428.

Searight, R. H. (1991). The families of origin of adolescent drug abusers: Perceived autonomy and intimacy. *Contemporary Family Therapy, 13* (1), 71–81.

Secundy, M. G. (1992). *Trials, tribulations, and celebrations: African-American perspectives on health, illness, aging, and loss.* Yarmouth, ME: Intercultural Press.

Sedney, M. A., & Brooks, B. (1984). Factors associated with a history of childhood sexual experiences in a nonclinical female population. *Journal of the American Academy of Child Psychiatry, 23,* 215–218.

Seedsman, T. A. (1990). Skill acquisition for a productive old age. *Australian Journal on Ageing, 9* (4), 3–7.

Segalowitz, S. J., & Brown, D. (1991). Mild head injury as a source of developmental disabilities. *Journal of Learning Disabilities, 24* (9), 551–559.

Seibel, M. M. (1990). *Infertility: A comprehensive text.* Norwalk, CT: Appleton and Lange.

Seligman, M. (1991). *Learned optimism: The skill to conquer life's obstacles, large and small.* New York: Knopf.

Selman, R. (1976). Toward a structural analysis of developing interpersonal relations concepts: Research with normal and disturbed preadolescent boys. In A. D. Pick (Ed.), *Minnesota Symposia on Child Psychology, 10,* 156–200. Minneapolis: University of Minnesota Press.

Selman, R. (1980). *The growth of interpersonal understanding.* New York: Academic Press.

Selman, R. (1981). The child as friendship philosopher. In J. M. Gottman (Ed.), *The development of children's friendships.* Cambridge, England: Cambridge University Press.

Selman, R. L. (1972). Taking another's perspective: Role-taking development in early childhood. *Child Development, 42,* 1721–1734.

Selman, R. L., & Byrne, D. F. (1974). A structural-developmental analysis of levels of role-taking in middle childhood. *Child Development, 45,* 803–806.

Selman, R., Beardslee, W., Schultz, L., Krupa, M., & Podo-refsky, D. (1986). Assessing adolescent interpersonal negotiation strategies: Toward the integration of structural and functional models. *Developmental Psychology, 22,* 450–459.

Seltzer, J. A. (1991). Legal custody arrangements and children's economic welfare. *American Journal of Sociology, 96* (4), 895–929.

Selye, H. (1976, October). Stress. *The Rotarian,* pp. 12–18.

Selye, H. (Ed.). (1980a). *Selye's guide to stress research.* New York: Van Nostrand.

Selye, H. (1980b). The stress concept today. In I. L. Kutash & L. B. Schlesinger (Eds.), *Handbook of stress and anxiety.* San Francisco: Jossey-Bass.

Selye, H. (1982). History and present status of the stress concept. In L. Goldberger & S. Breznitz (Eds.), *Handbook of stress.* New York: Free Press.

Sena, R., & Smith, L. B. (1990). New evidence on the development of the word *big. Child Development, 61* (4), 1034–1052.

Senderowitz, J., & Paxman, J. M. (1985). Adolescent fertility: Worldwide concerns. *Population Bulletin, 40* (2), 2–36.

Sera, M. D., Troyer, D., & Smith, L. B. (1989). What do two-year-olds know about the sizes of things? *Child Development, 59,* 1497–1503.

Shakin, M., Sternglanz, S. H., & Shakin, D. (1985). Infant clothing: Sex labeling for strangers. *Sex Roles, 5,* 28–37.

Shanas, E. (1979). *National survey of the elderly: Report to the administration on aging.* Washington, DC: U.S. Department of Health and Human Services.

Shapiro, A. H. (1982). Test anxiety: Urban/kibbutz differences. *Journal of Genetic Psychology, 141,* 287–288.

Shapiro, B. A., Konover, V., & Shapiro, A. (1991). *The big squeeze: Balancing the needs of aging parents, dependent children, and you.* Bedford, MA: Mills and Sanderson.

Shapiro, H. L. (1983). *The pregnancy book for today's woman.* New York: Harper & Row.

Shapiro, L. R., & Hudson, J. A. (1991). Tell me a make-believe story: Coherence and cohesion in young children's picture-elicited narratives. *Developmental Psychology, 27* (6), 960–974.

Sharf, R. S. (1992). *Applying career development theory to counseling.* Pacific Grove: Brooks/Cole.

Sharlin, S. A., & Mork-Barak, M. (1992). Runaway girls in distress: Motivation, background, and personality. *Adolescence, 27* (106), 387–405.

Sharp, A. (1990). *The nursing home connection: A handbook for visitors.* San Diego: Anne Sharp.

Shaughnessy, M. F., & Shakesby, P. (1992). Adolescent sexual and emotional intimacy. *Adolescence, 27,* 475–480.

Shaw, D. S. (1991). The effects of divorce on children's adjustment: Review and implications. *Behavior Modification, 15* (4), 456–485.

Sheehan, N. W. (1992). *Successful administration of senior housing: Working with elderly residents.* Newbury Park, CA: Sage.

Shengold, L. (1990). *Soul murder: The effects of childhood abuse and deprivation.* New Haven, CT: Yale University Press.

Sheppard, H. L. (1990). The "new" early retirement: Europe and the United States. In I. Bluestone, J. V. Montgomery, & J. D. Owen (Eds.), *The aging of the American work force.* Detroit: Wayne State University Press.

Sheridan, M. K., & Radlinski, S. (1988). Brief report: A case study of an adolescent male with XXY Klinefelter's syndrome. *Journal of Autism and Developmental Disorders, 18,* 449–456.

Sherman, E. (1981). *Counseling the aged: An integrative approach.* New York: Free Press.

Sherman, E. (1991). *Reminiscence and the self in old age.* New York: Springer.

Shimoni, R., & Ferguson, B. (1992). Rethinking parent involvement in child care programs. *Child and Youth Care Forum, 21* (2), 105–118.

Shimp, S. (1990). Debunking the myths of aging. In D. Gibson (Ed.), *Evaluation and treatment of the psychogeriatric patient.* Binghamton, NY: Haworth Press.

Shingleton, J. (1992). *Successful interviewing for college students.* Lincolnwood, IL: NTC.

Shipley, D. (1993). *Empowering children: Play based curriculum for lifelong learning.* Albany, NY: Delmar.

Shneidman, E. S. (1978). Death work and the stages of dying. In R. Fulton (Ed.), *Death and dying.* Reading, MA: Addison-Wesley.

Shneidman, E. S. (1980). *Voices of death.* New York: Harper & Row.

Shneidman, E. S. (Ed.). (1984). *Death: Current perspectives* (3rd ed.). Palo Alto, CA: Mayfield.

Shornack, L. L., & Ahmed, F. (1989). Adolescent religiousness and pregnancy prevention. *Journal of Marriage and the Family, 51,* 1083–1089.

Shute, V., Glaser, R., & Raghavan, K. (1989). Discovery and inference in an exploratory laboratory. In P. Ackerman, R. Sternberg, & R. Glaser (Eds.), *Learning and individual differences.* San Francisco: Freeman.

Shweder, R. A. (1981). What's there to negotiate? Some questions for Youniss. *Merrill-Palmer Quarterly, 27,* 405–412.

Siegal, D. L. (1990). Women's reproductive changes: A marker, not a turning point. *Generations, 14* (3), 31–32.

Siegel, L. (1990). *Intoxication.* New York: Pocket Books.

Siegel, R. J. (1990). Love and work after 60: An integration of personal and professional growth within a long-term marriage. *Journal of Women and Aging, 2* (2), 69–79.

Siegel, R. K. (1980). The psychology of life after death. *American Psychologist, 35*, 911–931.

Siegel, S., & Gaylord-Ross, R. (1991). Factors associated with employment success among youths with learning disabilities. *Journal of Learning Disabilities, 24* (1), 40–47.

Siegler, I. C. (1992). Aging and the public health: Reflections on Kaplan's report of health and aging in the Alameda County Study. In K. W. Schaie, D. Blazer, & J. S. House (Eds.), *Aging, health behaviors, and health outcomes*. Hillsdale, NJ: Erlbaum.

Siegler, I. C., McCarty, S. M., & Logue, P. E. (1982). Wechsler memory scale scores, selective attention, and distance from death. *Journal of Gerontology, 37*, 176–181.

Sigelman, C. K., & Waitzman, K. A. (1991). The development of distribution justice orientations: Contextual influences on children's resource allocations. *Child Development, 62* (6), 1367–1378.

Sigman, M., Neumann, Carter, E., & Cattle, D. (1988). Home interactions and the development of Embu toddlers in Kenya. *Child Development, 59*, 1251–1261.

Silberman, B. O., & Hawkins, R. O. (1988). Lesbian women and gay men: Issues for counseling. In E. Weinstein & E. Rosen (Eds.), *Sexuality counseling: Issues and implications*. Monterey, CA: Brooks/Cole.

Silk, A. M., & Thomas, G. V. (1988). The development of size scaling in children's figure drawings. *British Journal of Developmental Psychology, 6*, 285–299.

Silva, M. N. (1991). Simultaneity in children's narratives: The case of *when, while* and *as*. *Journal of Child Language, 18* (3), 641–662.

Silverberg, E., Boring, C. C., & Squires, T. S. (1990). Cancer statistics, 1990. *CA: A Cancer Journal for Clinicians, 40* (1), 9–26.

Silverman, P. R. (1986). *Widow to widow*. New York: Springer.

Silverman, P. R., Nickman, S., & Worden, J. W. (1992). Detachment revisited: The child's reconstruction of a dead parent. *American Journal of Orthopsychiatry, 62* (4), 494–503.

Silverstone, B., & Hyman, H. K. (1989). *You and your aging parent: The modern family's guide to emotional, physical, and financial problems* (2nd ed.). New York: Pantheon Books.

Simenauer, J., & Carroll, D. (1982). *Singles: The new Americans*. New York: Simon & Schuster.

Simkins, L. (1984). Consequences of teenage pregnancy and motherhood. *Adolescence, 19*, 39–54.

Simonds, J. F., McMahon, T., & Armstrong, D. (1991). Young suicide attempters compared with a control group: Psychological, affective, and attitudinal variables. *Suicide and Life-Threatening Behavior, 21* (2), 134–151.

Simonian, S. J., Tarnowski, K. J., & Gibbs, J. C. (1991). Social skills and antisocial conduct of delinquents. *Child Psychiatry and Human Development, 22* (1), 17–27.

Simons, H. C. (1990). Countering cultural metaphors of aging. *Journal of Religious Gerontology, 7*, 153–165.

Simons, R. G., & Blyth, D. A. (1988). *Moving into adolescence: The impact of pubertal change and school context*. New York: Aldine.

Simons, R. L., & Gray, P. A. (1989). Perceived blocked opportunity as an explanation of delinquency among lower-class black males:

A research note. *Journal of Research in Crime and Delinquency, 26*, 90–101.

Simonton, D. K. (1990). Does creativity decline in later years? Definition, data, and theory. In M. Perlmutter (Ed.), *Late life potential. The presidential symposium series*. Washington, DC: Gerontological Society of America.

Simpson, J. L. (1990). Genetic causes of spontaneous abortion. *Contemporary Obstetrics and Gynecology, 35*, 25–34.

Simpson, R., Kelly, S. F., Flood, R., Atkinson, H. P., Turner, M., Greiser, K., & Zhao, D. (1991). Racial and ethnic differences in heart attacks and strokes. *Circulation, 84* (4), 334, no. 1330.

Singer, J. L., Singer, D. G., Desmond, R., & Hirsch, B. (1988). Family mediation and children's cognition, aggression, and comprehension of television: a longitudinal study. *Journal of Applied Developmental Psychology, 9*, 329–347.

Singer, J. L., Singer, D. G., & Rapaczynski, W. (1984). Family patterns and television viewing as predictions of children's belief and aggression. *Journal of Communication, 34* (2), 73–89.

Singer, P. A., & Siegler, M. (1990). Euthanasia: A critique. *New England Journal of Medicine, 322* (26), 1881–1883.

Sinnott, J. D., & Cavanaugh, J. C. (1991). *Bridging paradigms: Positive development in adulthood and cognitive aging*. New York: Praeger.

Sitton, R., & Light, P. (1992). Drawing to differentiate: Flexibility in young children's human figure drawings. *British Journal of Developmental Psychology, 10* (1), 25–33.

Skinner, B. F. (1951). How to teach animals. *Scientific American, 185*, 26–29.

Skinner, B. F. (1953). *Science and human behavior*. New York: Macmillan.

Skinner, B. F. (1957). *Verbal behavior*. New York: Appleton.

Skinner, B. F. (1961). *Cumulative record*. New York: Appleton.

Skinner, M. L., Elder, G. H., & Conger, R. D. (1992). Linking economic hardship to adolescent aggression. *Journal of Youth and Adolescence, 21* (3), 259–276.

Skipwith, D. H. (1991). Nursing care in acute and long-term care settings. In M. S. Harper (Ed.), *Management and care of the elderly: Psychosocial perspectives*. Newbury Park, CA: Sage.

Skouteris, H., McKenzie, B. E., & Day, R. H. (1992). Integration of sequential information for shape perception by infants: A developmental study. *Child Development, 63* (5), 1164–1176.

Slaby, R. G., & Guerra, N. G. (1988). Cognitive mediators of aggression in adolescent offenders: I. Assessment. *Developmental Psychology, 24*, 580–588.

Slater, A., Mattock, A., Brown, E., & Bremner, J. G. (1991). Form perception at birth: Cohen and Younger (1984) revisited. *Journal of Experimental Child Psychology, 51* (3), 395–406.

Slesinger, D. P. (1980). Rapid changes in household composition among low income mothers. *Family Relations, 29*, 221–228.

Slobin, D. (1970). Universals of grammatical development in children. In G. B. Flores d'Arcais & W. J. M. Levelt (Eds.), *Advancements in psycholinguistics*. Amsterdam: North Holland.

Slobin, D. (Ed.). (1982). *The cross-cultural study of language acquisition*. Hillsdale, NJ: Erlbaum.

Slomkowski, C. L., & Killen, M. (1992). Young children's conceptions of transgressions with friends and nonfriends. *International Journal of Behavioral Development, 15* (2), 247–258.

Small, S. A., & Eastman, G. (1991). Rearing adolescents in contemporary society: A conceptual framework for understanding the responsibilities and needs of parents. *Family Relations, 40*, 455–462.

Small, S., Eastman, G., & Cornelius, S. (1988). Adolescent autonomy and parental stress. *Journal of Youth and Adolescence, 17* (5), 377–391.

Smart, L. S. (1992). The marital helping relationship following pregnancy loss and infant death. *Journal of Family Issues, 13* (1), 81–98.

Smetana, J. G., (1988). Concepts of self and social convention: Adolescents' and parents' reasoning about hypothetical and actual family conflicts. In M. R. Gunnar & W. A. Collins (Eds.), *The Minnesota symposia* (Vol. 21). Hillsdale, NJ: Erlbaum.

Smetana, J. G., Killen, M., & Turiel, E. (1991). Children's reasoning about interpersonal and moral conflicts. *Child Development, 62*, 629–644.

Smith, A. (1980). Age differences in encoding, storage and retrieval. In L. W. Poon, J. L. Fozard, L. S. Cermak, D. Arenberg, & L. Thompson (Eds.), *New directions in memory and aging*. Hillsdale, NJ: Erlbaum.

Smith, C. (1991). *Learning Disabilities*. Boston: Allyn & Bacon.

Smith, L. S., Lauver, D., & Gray, P. A., Jr. (1990). Sexually transmitted diseases. In C. I. Fogel & D. Lauver (Eds.), *Sexual health promotion*. Philadelphia: Saunders.

Smith, M. W. F. (1991). The role of age and ageism in the "80% barrier." *ASHA, 33* (12), 36–38.

Smith, P. B., & Pederson, D. R. (1988). Maternal sensitivity and patterns of infant-mother attachment. *Child Development, 59*, 1097–1101.

Smith, P. C. (1992). In pursuit of happiness. In C. J. Cranny, P. C. Smith, & E. F. Stone (Eds.), *Job satisfaction*. New York: Lexington Books.

Smith, P. K., Eaton, L., & Hindmarch, A. (1982). How one-year-olds respond to strangers: A two-person situation. *Journal of Genetic Psychology, 140* (1), 147–148.

Smith, R. M. (1991). Self-other orientation and sex-role orientation of men and women who remarry. *Journal of Divorce and Remarriage, 14* (3/4), 3–32.

Smith, R. T. (1965). A comparison of socio-environmental factors in monozygotic and dizygotic twins: Testing an assumption. In S. G. Vandenberg (Ed.), *Methods and goals in human behavior genetics*. New York: Academic Press.

Smith, S. F., & Smith, C. M. (1990). *Personal health choices*. Boston: Jones and Bartlett.

Smith, T. E. (1991). Agreement of adolescent educational expectations with perceived maternal and paternal educational goals. *Youth and Society, 23* (2), 155–174.

Smoll, F. L., & Schutz, R. W. (1990). Quantifying gender differences in physical performance: A developmental perspective. *Developmental Psychology, 26*, 360–369.

Snarey, J. (1987, June). A question of morality. *Psychology Today*, pp. 6–8.

Snarey, J. (1992). "Linking ego moral development: The value consistency thesis": Commentary. *Human Development*, 35 (5), 302–305.

Snarey, J., & Lydens, L. (1990). Worker equality and adult development: The kibbutz as a developmental model. *Psychology and Aging*, 5 (1), 86–93.

Snell, W. E., Jr., Miller, R. S., & Belk, S. S. (1988). Development of the emotional self-disclosure scale. *Sex Roles*, 18, 59–73.

Snodgrass, D. M. (1991). The parent connection. *Adolescence*, 26 (101), 83–88.

Snow, W. G. (1990). Avoiding misdiagnosis of Alzheimer's disease: The role of neuropsychological testing. *Clinical Gerontologist*, 10 (1), 64–67.

Sodian, B., Zaitchik, D., & Carey, S. (1991). Young children's differentiation of hypothetical beliefs from evidence. *Child Development*, 62 (4), 753–766.

Soldo, B. J., & Agree, E. M. (1988). *America's elderly*. Washington, DC: Population Reference Bureau.

Solie, L. J., & Fielder, L. J. (1988). The relationship between sex role identity and a widow's adjustment to the loss of a spouse. *Omega*, 18, 33–40.

Solomon, D. H., Salend, E., Rahman, A. N., Liston, M. B., & Reuben, D. B. (1992). *A consumer's guide to aging*. Baltimore: Johns Hopkins University Press.

Somerfield, M. R. (1991). Physician practices in the diagnosis of dementing disorders. *Journal of the American Geriatrics Society*, 39 (2), 172–175.

Somers, T. (1985). Caregiving: A woman's issue. *Generations*, 10 (1), 9–15.

Somerville, J. (1991, January 7). The final days. *American Medical News*, pp. 12–19.

Sonenstein, F. L., Pleck, J. H., & Ku, L. C. (1989). Sexual activity, condom use, and AIDS awareness in a national sample of adolescent males. *Family Planning Perspectives*, 21, 152–158.

Sonenstein, F. L., & Wolf, D. A. (1991). Satisfaction with child care: Perspectives of welfare mothers. *Journal of Social Issues*, 47 (2), 15–31.

Sorce, J. F., Emde, R. N., Campos, J. J., & Klinnert, M. D. (1985). Maternal emotional signaling: Its effect on the visual cliff behavior of one-year-olds. *Developmental Psychology*, 21, 195–200.

Sorensen, E. D., & Goldman, J. (1990). Custody determinants and child development: A review of the current literature. *Journal of Divorce*, 13 (4), 53–67.

Sorochan, W. D. (1981). *Promoting Your Health*. New York: Wiley.

Sorrenti-Little, L., Bagley, C., & Robertson, S. (1984). An operational definition of the long-term harmfulness of sexual relations with peers and adults by young children. *Canadian Children: Journal of the Canadian Association for Young Children*, 9, 26–33.

Soules, M. R. (1985). The in-vitro fertilization pregnancy rate: Let's be honest with one another. *Fertility and Sterility*, 43 (4), 512–521.

Spar, J. E., & Asenath, L. (1990). *Concise guide to geriatric psychiatric*. American psychiatric press

concise guides. Washington, DC: American Psychiatric Press.

Spector, W. D., & Takada, H. A. (1991). Characteristics of nursing homes that affect resident outcomes. *Journal of Aging and Health*, 3 (4), 427–454.

Spelke, E. S. (1991). Physical knowledge in infancy: Reflections on Piaget's theory. In S. Carey & R. Gelman (Eds.), *The epigenesis of the mind: Essays on biology and cognition*. Hillsdale, NJ: Erlbaum.

Spencer, M. B. (1991). Identity development and minority adolescents. In R. M. Lerner, A. C. Petersen, & J. Brooks-Gunn (Eds.), *The encyclopedia of adolescence*. New York: Garland.

Speroff, L., Glass, R., & Kase, N. (1989). *Clinical gynecologic endocrinology and infertility* (4th ed.). Baltimore: Williams and Wilkins.

Spetner, N., & Olsho, L. W. (1990). Auditory frequency resolution in human infancy. *Child Development*, 61 (3), 632–652.

Spillane, S. A., McGuire, J. M., & Norlander, K. A. (1992). Undergraduate admission policies, practices, and procedures for applicants with learning disabilities. *Journal of Learning Disabilities*, 25 (10), 665–670.

Spinillo, A. G., & Bryant, P. (1991). Children's proportional judgments: The importance of "half." *Child Development*, 62 (3), 427–440.

Spitze, G. (1988). Work and family. *Journal of Marriage and the Family*, 50, 37–48.

Spitze, G., & Logan, J. (1990). More evidence on women (and men) in the middle. *Research on Aging*, 12 (2), 182–198.

Sprey, J. (1975). Family power and process: Toward a conceptual integration. In R. E. Cromwell & D. H. Olson (Eds.), *Power and families*. New York: Wiley.

Sprey, J. (1979). Conflict theory and the study of marriage and the family. In W. Burr, R. Hill, F. I. Nye, & I. L. Reiss (Eds.), *Contemporary theories about the family*. New York: Free Press.

Sprey, J. (1991). Studying adult children and their parents. In S. K. Pfeifer & M. B. Sussman (Eds.), *Families: Intergenerational and generational connections*. Binghamton, NY: Haworth Press.

Sroufe, J. W. (1991). Assessment of parent-adolescent relationships: Implications for adolescent development. *Journal of Family Psychology*, 5 (1), 21–45.

Staebler, R. (1991). Medicaid: Providing health care to (some of) America's poor. *Caring*, 10 (6), 4–6.

Stanford, E. P. (1991). Early retirement and functional impairment from a multi-ethnic perspective. *Research on Aging*, 13 (1), 5–38.

Stanford, E. P., Lockery, S. A., & Schoenrock, S. A. (1990). *Ethnicity and aging: Mental health issues*. San Diego: University Center on Aging, College of Health and Human Services, San Diego State University.

Stanley, S. C., Hunt, J. G., & Hunt, L. L. (1986). The relative deprivation of husbands in dual-earner households. *Journal of Family Issues*, 7, 3–20.

Stark, E. (1984, May). The unspeakable family secret. *Psychology Today*, pp. 38–46.

Stearns, A. K. (1984). *Living through crises*. New York: Ballantine.

Steele, C. M., & Josephs, R. A. (1990). Alcohol myopia: Its prized and dangerous effects. *American Psychologist*, 45, 921–933.

Steers, R. M., & Porter, L. W. (1991). *Motivation and work behavior* (5th ed.). New York: McGraw-Hill.

Stein, D. M., & Reichert, P. (1990). Extreme dieting behaviors in early adolescence. *Journal of Early Adolescence*, 10, 108–121.

Stein, P. J. (Ed.). (1981). *Single life: Unmarried adults in social context*. New York: St. Martin's Press.

Stein, P. J. (1989). The diverse world of the single adult. In J. M. Henslin (Ed.), *Marriage and family in a changing society* (3rd ed.). New York: Free Press.

Stein, P. J., & Fingrutd, M. (1985). The single life has more potential for happiness than marriage and parenthood for both men and women. In H. Feldman & M. Feldman (Eds.), *Current controversies in marriage and family*. Beverly Hills, CA: Sage.

Stein, T. S. (1988). Theoretical considerations in psychotherapy with gay men and lesbian women. In M. W. Ross (Ed.), *The treatment of homosexuals with mental health disorders*. New York: Harrington Park Press.

Steinberg, L. (1987). Recent research on the family at adolescence. *Journal of Youth and Adolescence*, 16, 191–197.

Steinberg, L. (1991). Parent-adolescent relations. In R. M. Lerner, A. C. Petersen, & J. Brooks-Gunn (Eds.), *The encyclopedia of adolescence*. New York: Garland.

Steinman, R. (1990). Social exchanges between older and younger gay male partners. In J. A. Lee (Ed.), *Gay midlife and maturity*. Binghamton, NY: Haworth Press.

Steitz, J. A., & Welker, K. G. (1990). Remarriage in later life: A critique and review of the literature. *Journal of Women and Aging*, 2 (4), 81–90.

Stephens, M. A. (1990). Social relationships as coping resources in later-life families. In M. A. P. Stephens (Ed.), *Stress and coping in later life families*. New York: Hemisphere.

Stephens, M. A. P., Ogrocki, P. K., & Kinney, J. F. (1991). Sources of stress for family caregivers of institutionalized dementia patients. *Journal of Applied Gerontology*, 10 (3), 328–342.

Stephenson, J. S. (1985). *Death, grief, and mourning*. New York: Free Press.

Stern, E. M. (1990). *Psychotherapy and the widowed patient*. Binghamton, NY: Haworth.

Sternberg, K. J., Lamb, M. E., Greenbaum, C., & Cicchetti, D. (1993). Effects of domestic violence on children's behavior problems and depression. *Developmental Psychology*, 29 (1), 44–52.

Sternberg, R. J. (1986). A triangular theory of love. *Psychological Review*, 93, 119–135.

Sternberg, R. J. (1987). Liking versus loving: A comparative evaluation of theories. *Psychological Bulletin*, 102, 331–345.

Sternberg, R. J. (1988). Triangulating love. In R. J. Sternberg & M. L. Barnes (Eds.), *The psychology of love*. New Haven, CT: Yale University Press.

Sterneck, J. G. (1990). Family caregiving: What price love? *Journal of Long-Term Care Administration*, 18 (2), 16–21.

Sterns, H. L., Matheson, N. K., & Schwartz, L. S. (1990). Work and retirement. In K. F. Ferraro (Ed.), *Gerontology: Perspectives and issues*. New York: Springer.

Stevens, D. P., & Truss, C. V. (1985). Stability and change in adult personality over 12 and 20 years. *Developmental Psychology, 21*, 568–584.

Stevens, J. C. (1992). Aging and spatial acuity of touch. *Journal of Gerontology: Psychological Sciences, 47* (1), P35–P40.

Stevens, J. H. (1988). Shared knowledge about infants among fathers and mothers. *Journal of Genetic Psychology, 149*, 515–525.

Stewart, D. E. (1983). *The television family: A content analysis of the portrayal of family life in prime time television.* Melbourne: Institute of Family Studies.

Stewart, D. G. (1991). Single custodial females and their families: Housing and coping strategies after divorce. *International Journal of Law and the Family, 5* (3), 296–317.

Stewart, J. (1991). Diagnosing and treating depression in the hospitalized elderly. *Geriatrics, 46* (1), 64–66.

Stine, E. A. L., & Wingfield, A. (1990). How much do working memory deficits contribute to age differences in discourse memory? *European Journal of Cognitive Psychology, 2* (3), 289–304.

Stine, G. J. (1993). *Acquired immune deficiency syndrome: Biological, medical, social and legal issues.* Englewood Cliffs, NJ: Prentice Hall.

Stinson, K. M. (1992). Parent's grief following pregnancy loss: A comparison of mothers and fathers. *Family Relations, 41* (2), 218–223.

St. James-Roberts, I., & Halil, T. (1991). Infant crying patterns in the first year: Normal community and clinical findings. *Journal of Child Psychology and Psychiatry and Allied Disciplines, 32* (6), 951–968.

Stockman, I. J., & Vaughn-Cooke, F. (1992). Lexical elaboration in children's locative action expressions. *Child Development, 63* (5), 1104–1125.

Stofo, M. A., Behrens, R., & Rosemont, C. (1990). *Healthy people 2000: Citizens chart the course.* Washington, DC: National Academy Press.

Stone, R. (1991). Familial obligation: Issues for the nineties. *Generations, 15* (3), 47–50.

Stone, R., Cafferata, G. L., & Sangl, J. (1987). Caregivers of the frail elderly: A national profile. *Gerontologist, 27*, 616–626.

Stoppard, J. M., & Paisley, K. J. (1987). Masculinity, femininity, life stress, and depression. *Sex Roles, 16*, 489–496.

Storandt, M., & VandenBos, G. R. (Eds.). (1989). *The adult years: Continuity and change.* Washington, DC: American Psychological Association.

Stott, D. (1982). *Delinquents, parents, and maladjustment.* New York: SP Medical and Scientific Books.

St. Peters, M., Fitch, M., Huston, A. C., & Wright, J. C. (1991). Television and families: What do young children watch with their parents? *Child Development, 62* (6), 1409–1423.

Strand, V. (1990). Treatment of the mother in the incest family: The beginning phase. *Clinical Social Work Journal, 18* (4), 353–366.

Strasburger, L. H., & Welpton, S. S. (1991). Elderly suicide: Minimizing risk for patient and professional. *Journal of Geriatric Psychiatry, 24* (2), 235–259.

Strassberg, Z., Dodge, K. A., Bates, J., & Pettit, G. S. (1992). The longitudinal relation between parental conflict strategies and children's sociometric standing in kindergarten. *Merrill-Palmer Quarterly, 38* (4), 477–493.

Straus, M. A., & Gelles, R. J. (1988). Violence in American families: How much is there and why does it occur? In E. W. Nunnally, C. S. Chilman, & F. M. Cox (Eds.), *Troubled relationships.* Beverly Hills, CA: Sage.

Strauss, A., & Glasser, B. G. (1970). *Anguish: A case study of a dying trajectory.* Mill Valley, CA: Sociology Press.

Strawbridge, W. J., & Wallhagen, M. I. (1991). Impact of family conflict on adult child caregivers. *Gerontologist, 31*, 770–777.

Streissguth, A. P., Barr, H. M., & Martin, D. C. (1983). Maternal alcohol use and neonatal habituation assessed with the Braezelton Scale. *Child Development, 54*, 1109–1118.

Streissguth, A. P., Barr, H. M., Sampson, P. D., & Darby, B. (1989). IQ at age four in relation to maternal alcohol use and smoking during pregnancy. *Developmental Psychology, 25*, 3–11.

Stright, A., & French, D. C. (1988). Leadership in mixed-age children's groups. *International Journal of Behavioral Development, 11* (4), 507–516.

Strom, R., & Strom, S. (1990). Raising expectations for grandparents: A three generational study. *International Journal of Aging and Human Development, 31* (3), 161–167.

Strube, M. J. (Ed.). (1990). *Type A behavior.* Corte Madera, CA: Select Press.

Strunin, L., & Hingston, R. (1987). Acquired immunodeficiency syndrome and adolescents: Knowledge, beliefs and attitudes, and behaviors. *Pediatrics, 79*, 825–828.

Stryckman, J. (1981, November). *The decision to remarry: The choice and its outcome.* Paper presented at the joint meetings of the Gerontological Society of America and the Canadian Association on Gerontology, Toronto.

Stuart, L. H., & Ruhlman, M. E. (1991). *Planning for retirement in the 21st century.* Topeka, KS: Lone Tree.

Stuart-Hamilton, I. (1991). *The psychology of aging: An introduction.* London: Jessica Kingsley.

Suess, F. J., Grossman, K. E., & Sroufe, L. A. (1992). Effects of infant attachment to mother and father on quality of adaptation in preschool: From dyadic to individual organization of self. *International Journal of Behavioral Development, 15* (1), 43–65.

Sugar, J. A., & McDowd, J. M. (1992). Memory, learning, and attention. In J. E. Birren, R. B. Sloane, & G. D. Cohen (Eds.), *Handbook of mental health and aging* (2nd ed.). San Diego: Harcourt Brace Jovanovich.

Sugarman, L. (1986). *Life-span development: Concepts, theories, and interventions.* New York: Routledge.

Suitor, J., & Pillemer, K. (1990). Transition to the status of family caregiver: A new framework for studying social support and well-being. In S. Stahl (Ed.), *The legacy of longevity: Health and health care in later life.* Newbury Park, CA: Sage.

Sullivan, D. A., & Weitz, R. (1988). *Labor pains: Modern midwives and home birth.* New Haven CT: Yale University Press.

Sullivan, S. A., & Birch, L. L. (1990). Pass the sugar, pass the salt: Experience dictates preference. *Developmental Psychology, 26* (4), 552–554.

Suomi, S. J., & Harlow, H. F. (1971). Abnormal social behavior in young monkeys. In J. Helmuth (Ed.), *Exceptional infant: Studies in abnormalities* (Vol. 2). New York: Brunner/Mazel.

Super, C. M. (1981). Cross-cultural research on infancy. In H. C. Triandis & A. Heron (Eds.), *Handbook of cross-cultural psychology.* Boston: Allyn & Bacon.

Super, D. E. (1951). Vocational adjustment: Implementing a self-concept. *Occupations, 30*, 88–92.

Surber, C. F. (1982). Separable effects of motives, consequences, and presentation order on children's moral judgments. *Developmental Psychology, 18*, 257–266.

Surgeon General's Report on HIV Infection and AIDS. (1993). Washington, DC: Author.

Susman, E. J., & Dorn, L. D. (1991). Hormones and behavior in adolescence. In R. M. Lerner, A. C. Petersen, & J. Brooks-Gunn (Eds.), *The encyclopedia of adolescence.* New York: Garland.

Sussman, M. B. (1988). Another perspective on the trials and triumphs in the transition to parenthood. In R. Palkovitz & M. B. Sussman (Eds.), *Transitions to parenthood.* New York: Haworth Press.

Sussman, M. B. (1991). Reflections on intergenerational and kin connections. In S. K. Sussman & M. B. Sussman (Eds.), *Families: Intergenerational and generational connections.* Binghamton, NY: Haworth Press.

Sutton, H. E. (1980). *An introduction to human genetics* (3rd ed.). Philadelphia: Saunders.

Sweet, C. A. (1989). Health tan—A fast-fading myth. *FDA Consumer, 23*, 11–13.

Sytkowski, P. A., Kannel, W. B., & D'Agostino, R. B. (1990). Changes in risk factors and the decline in mortality from cardiovascular disease: The Framingham Heart Study. *New England Journal of Medicine, 322* (23), 1635–1641.

Szagun, G. (1992). Children's understanding of the feeling experience and causes of sympathy. *Journal of Child Psychology and Psychiatry and Allied Disciplines, 33* (7), 1183–1191.

Taft, L. B., & Nehrke, M. F. (1990). Reminiscence, life review, and ego integrity in nursing home residents. *International Journal of Aging and Human Development, 30* (3) 189–196.

Taft, L. P., & Barkin, R. L. (1990). Drug abuse? Use and misuse of psychotropic drugs in Alzheimer's care. *Journal of Gerontological Nursing, 16* (8), 4–10.

Tager-Flusberg, H. (1993). Morphology and syntax in the preschool years. In J. B. Gleason (Ed.), *The development of language* (3rd ed.). New York: Macmillan.

Tamis-LeMonda, C. S., & Bornstein, M. H. (1991). Individual variation, correspondence, stability, and change in mother and toddler play. *Infant Behavior and Development, 14* (2), 143–162.

Tangney, J. P. (1988). Aspects of the family and children's viewing content preferences. *Child Development, 59*, 166–182.

Tannen, D. (1990). *You just don't understand: Women and men in conversation.* New York: William Morrow.

Tanner, J. M. (1981). Growth and maturation during adolescence. *Nutrition Review, 39*, 43–55.

Tanner, J. M. (1991). Adolescent growth spurt. In R. M. Lerner, A. C. Petersen, & J. Brooks-Gunn (Eds.), *The encyclopedia of adolescence.* New York: Garland.

Tavris, C. (1992). *The mismeasure of women.* New York: Simon & Schuster.

Taylor, B. J. (1991). *A child goes forth: A curriculum guide for preschool children* (7th ed.). New York: Macmillan.

Taylor, D. (1988). *Redflower: Rethinking menstruation.* Freedom, CA: Crossing Press.

Taylor, H. G., & Shatschneider, C. (1992). Academic achievement following childhood brain disease: Implications for the concept of learning disabilities. *Journal of Learning Disabilities, 25* (10), 630–638.

Taylor, M., Cartright, B. S. & Bowden, T. (1991). Perspective taking and theory of mind: Do children predict interpretive diversity as a function of differences in observers' knowledge? *Child Development, 62,* (6), 1334–1351.

Taylor, R. J. (1985). The extended family as a source of support for elderly blacks. *Gerontologist, 25* (5), 488–495.

Taylor, R. J., & Chatters, L. M. (1991). Extended family networks of older black adults. *Journal of Gerontology: Social Sciences, 46* (5), S250–S258.

Taylor, R. J., Chatters, L. M., Tucker, M. B., & Lewis, E. (1990). Developments in research on black families. *Journal of Marriage and Family, 52,* 993–1014.

Taylor, S. E. (1991). *Health psychology* (2nd ed.). New York: Random House.

Teasdale, N., Stelmach, G. E., & Breunig, A. (1991). Postural sway characteristics of the elderly under normal and altered visual and support surface conditions. *Journal of Gerontology: Biological Sciences, 46* (6), B233–B244.

Telleen, S., Herzog, A., & Kilbane, T. L. (1989). Impact of a family support program on mothers' social support and parenting stress. *American Journal of Orthopsychiatry, 59* (3), 410–419.

Tellegen, A., Lykken, D. T., Bouchard, T. J., & Wilcox, K. J. (1988). Personality similarity in twins reared apart and together. *Journal of Personality and Social Psychology, 54,* 1031–1039.

Teno, J., & Lynn, J. (1991). Voluntary active euthanasia: The individual case and public policy. *Journal of the American Geriatrics Society, 39* (8), 827–830.

Teti, D. M., & Lamb, M. E. (1989). Socioeconomic and marital outcomes of adolescent marriage, adolescent childbirth, and their co-occurrence. *Journal of Marriage and the Family, 51,* 203–212.

Teusink, J. P., & Shamolan, C. A. (1983). Understanding the body: Aging, illness, and medications. *Generations, 8,* 6–9.

Thane, R. R. (1992). *Women and aging.* New York: Haworth Press.

Tharpe, R. G., & Gallimore, R. G. (1989). *Rousing minds to life.* New York: Cambridge University Press.

Thomas, C., & Kelman, H. R. (1990). Gender and the use of health services among elderly persons. In M. G. Ory & H. G. Warner (Eds.), *Gender, health, and longevity: Multidisciplinary perspectives.* New York: Springer.

Thomas, E., Rickel, A. U., & Butler, C. (1990). Adolescent pregnancy and parenting. *Journal of Primary Prevention, 10* (3), 195–206.

Thomas, G. V., & Gray, R. (1992). Children's drawings of topics differing in emotional significance: Effects on placement relative to a self-drawing: A research note. *Journal of Child Psychology and Psychiatry and Allied Disciplines, 33* (6), 1097–1104.

Thomas, G. V., & Tsalimi, A. (1988). Effects of order of drawing head and trunk on their relative sizes in children's human figure drawings. *British Journal of Developmental Psychology, 6,* 191–203.

Thomas, J. L. (1990a). Grandparenthood and mental health: Implications for the practitioner. *Journal of Applied Gerontology, 9* (4), 464–479.

Thomas, J. L. (1990b). The grandparent role: A double bind. *International Journal of Aging and Human Development, 31* (3), 169–177.

Thomas, M. H. (1982). Physiological arousal, exposure to a relatively lengthy aggressive film, and aggressive behavior. *Journal of Research in Personality, 16,* 72–81.

Thomas, R. M. (1992). *Comparing theories of child development* (3rd ed.). Belmont, CA: Wadsworth.

Thomasma, D. C., & Graber, G. C. (1990). *Euthanasia: Toward an ethical social policy.* New York: Continuum.

Thompson, C. L., & Rudolph, V. B. (1992). *Counseling children* (3rd ed.). Pacific Grove, CA: Brooks/Cole.

Thompson, M. P., & Morris, L. K. (1991). Unexplained weight loss in the ambulatory elderly. *Journal of the American Geriatrics Society, 39* (5), 497–500.

Thompson, R. A. (1991). Grandparent visitation rights: A psychological analysis. *Family and Conciliation Courts Review, 29* (1), 9–25.

Thompson, R. A., Connell, J. P., & Bridges, L. J. (1988). Temperament, emotion, and social interactive behavior in the strange situation: A component process analysis of attachment system functioning. *Child Development, 59,* 1102–1110.

Thornton, A., & Freedman, D. (1983). The changing American family. *Population Bulletin, 38* (4), 7–17.

Thorp, J. M., & Bowes, W. A. (1989). Episiotomy: Can its routine use be defended? *American Journal of Obstetrical Gynecology, 160,* 1027–1033.

Thorsheim, H. I., & Roberts, B. B. (1990). *Reminiscing together: Ways to help us keep mentally fit as we grow older.* Minneapolis: CompCare.

Tice, D. M., Buder, J., & Baumeister, R. F. (1985). Development of self-consciousness: At what age does audience pressure disrupt performance? *Adolescence, 20,* 301–305.

Tiegerman, E. (1993). Early language development. In D. K. Bernstein, E. Tiegerman, & C. Radziewicz (Eds.), *Language and communication disorders in children.* New York: Macmillan.

Tipton, C. A. (1990). *Practical guide for the director of staff development in long-term care.* Springfield, IL: Charles C Thomas.

Tittle, C. K. (1988). Validity, gender research, and studies of the effects of career development interventions. In B. A. Gutek (Ed.), *Applied psychology: An international review.* Beverly Hills, CA: Sage.

Tocci, C. M., & Engelhard, G., Jr. (1991). Achievements, parental support, and gender differences in attitudes toward mathematics. *Journal of Educational Research, 84* (5), 280–286.

Tomer, A. (1989). Slowing with age as an explanation of age changes in fluid intelligence. Unpublished doctoral dissertation, University of Florida.

Toner, I. J., Holstein, R. B., & Hetherington, E. M. (1977). Reflection-impulsivity and self-control in preschool children. *Child Development, 48,* 39–245.

Toray, T., Coughlin, C., Vuchinich, S., & Patricelli, P. (1991). Gender differences associated with adolescent substance abuse: Comparisons and implications for treatment. *Family Relations, 40,* 338–344.

Torres-Gil, F., & Negm, M. (1980). Policy issues concerning the Hispanic elderly. *Aging, 12,* 305–318.

Toseland, R. W. (1990). Comparative effectiveness of individual and group interventions to support family caregivers. *Social Work, 35* (3), 209–217.

Tracey, M. B., & Pampel, F. C. (1991). *International handbook on old age insurance.* New York: Greenwood Press.

Trainor, C. (1984, August). *Sexual maltreatment in the United States: A five-year perspective.* Paper presented at the International Congress on Child Abuse and Neglect, Montreal.

Treas, J. (1983). Aging and the family. In D. S. Woodruff & J. E. Birren (Eds.), *Aging: Scientific perspectives and social issues* (2nd ed.). Monterey, CA: Brooks/Cole.

Trehub, S. E., Scheider, B. A., Thorpe, L. A., & Judge, P. (1991). Observational measures of auditory sensitivity in early infancy. *Developmental Psychology, 27* (1), 40–49.

Trippet, S. E. (1991). Being aware: The relationship between health and social support among older women. *Journal of Women and Aging, 3* (3), 69–80.

Trombetta, D. A. (1991). Custody evaluations: A realistic view. *Family and Conciliation Courts Review, 29* (1), 45–55.

Tronick, E. Z. (1989). Emotions and emotional communication in infants. *American Psychologist, 44,* 112–119.

Tryon, A. S., & Keane, S. P. (1991). Popular and aggressive boys' initial social interaction patterns in cooperative and competitive settings. *Journal of Abnormal Child Psychology, 19* (4), 395–406.

Tschann, J. M. (1990). Conflict, loss, change, and parent-child relationships: Predicting children's adjustment during divorce. *Journal of Divorce, 13* (4), 1–22.

Tully, M. P., & Tallis, R. (1991). Inappropriate prescribing and adverse drug reactions in patients admitted to an elderly care unit. *Journal of Geriatric Drug Therapy, 6* (1), 63–74.

Turner, J. S., & Rubinson, L. (1993). *Contemporary human sexuality.* Englewood Cliffs, NJ: Prentice Hall.

Turner, P. J. (1991). Relations between attachment, gender, and behavior with peers in preschool. *Child Development, 62* (6), 1475–1488.

Turner, T. J., & Ortony, A. (1992). Basic emotions: Can conflicting criteria converge? *Psychological Review, 99* (3), 566–571.

Tygart, C. (1988). Public school vandalism: Toward a synthesis of theories and transition to paradigm analysis. *Adolescence, 23,* 171–185.

Tyler, S., & Woodall, G. (1982). *Female health and gynecology across the life-span*. Bowie, MD: Robert J. Brady.

U.S. Bureau of the Census. (1992). *Statistical abstract of the United States: 1992* (112th ed.). Washington, DC: U.S. Government Printing Office.

U.S. Bureau of Labor Statistics. (1991, December). *Monthly labor review*. Washington, DC: U.S. Department of Labor.

U.S. Bureau of Labor Statistics. (1992, July). *Monthly labor review*. Washington, DC: U.S. Department of Labor.

U.S. Department of Health and Human Services. (1991). *Advisory panel on Alzheimer's disease. Second report of the advisory panel on Alzheimer's disease*. Washington, DC: Government Printing Office.

U.S. Department of Labor. (1992). *Occupational outlook handbook*. Washington, DC: U.S. Government Printing Office.

Ungerer, J. A., & Sigman, M. (1983). Developmental lags in preterm infants from one to three years of age. *Child Development, 54*, 1217–1228.

Unruh, D. (1989). Toward a social psychology of reminiscence. In D. Unruh & G. S. Livings (Eds.), *Current perspectives on aging and the life cycle: A research annual*. Greenwich, CT: JAI Press.

Urberg, K. A. (1992). Locus of peer influence: Social crowd and best friend. *Journal of Youth and Adolescence, 21*, 439–450.

Utian, W. (1990). Current thoughts on the postmenopausal patient [Special issue]. *Clinical Practice in Sexuality, 10*, 22–24.

Uttal, D. H., & Wellman, H. M. (1989). Young children's representation of spatial information acquired from maps. *Developmental Psychology, 25*, 128–138.

Vail, E. (1982). *A personal guide to living with loss*. New York: Wiley.

Vaillant, G. E. (1990). Avoiding negative life outcomes: Evidence from a forty-five year study. In P. B. Baltes & M. M. Baltes (Eds.), *Successful aging: Perspectives from the behavioral sciences*. New York: Cambridge University Press.

Vail-Smith, K., & White, D. M. (1992). Risk level, knowledge, and preventive behavior for human papilloma-viruses among sexually active college women. *Journal of American College Health, 40*, 227–230.

Valdez-Menchaca, M. C., & Whitehurst, G. J. (1992). Accelerating language development through picture book reading: A systematic extension to Mexican day care. *Developmental Psychology, 28* (6), 1106–1114.

Vander Mey, B. J., & Neff, R. L. (1986). *Incest as child abuse: Research and applications*. New York: Praeger.

Vandervoort, A. A. (1992). Age and sex effects on mobility of the human ankle. *Journal of Gerontology: Medical Sciences, 47* (1), M17–M21.

Van Hoorn, J. V., Nourot, P. M., Scales, B. J., & Alward, K. R. (1993). *Play at the center of the curriculum*. New York: Macmillan.

Van Ijzendoorn, M. H., Goldberg, S., Kroonenberg, P. M., & Frenkel, O. J. (1992). The relative effects of maternal and child problems on the quality of attachment: A meta-analysis of attachment in clinical samples. *Child Development, 63* (4), 840–858.

Van Kammen, W. B., Loeber, R., & Stouthamer-Loeber, M. (1991). Substance use and its relationship to conduct problems and delinquency in young boys. *Journal of Youth and Adolescence, 20* (4), 399–413.

Van Lieshout, C. F., Van Aken, M. A., & Van Seyen, E. T. (1990). Perspectives on peer relations from mothers, teachers, friends, and self. *Human Development, 33* (4–5), 225–237.

Vaughn, B. E., & Langlois, J. H. (1983). Physical attractiveness as a correlate of peer status and social competence in preschool children. *Developmental Psychology, 19*, 561–567.

Vaughn, B. E., Stevenson-Hinde, J., Waters, E., & Kotsaftis, A. (1992). Attachment security and temperament in infancy and early childhood: Some conceptual clarifications. *Developmental Psychology, 28* (3), 463–473.

Vega, W. A. (1990). Hispanic families in the 1980's: A decade of research. *Journal of Marriage and the Family, 52*, 1015–1024.

Venable, S. D., & Mitchell, M. M. (1991). Temporal adaptation and performance of daily living activities in persons with Alzheimer's disease. *Physical and Occupational Therapy in Geriatrics, 9* (3/4), 31–51.

Veninga, R. L. (1991). *Your renaissance years: Making retirement the best years of your life*. Boston: Little, Brown.

Ventura, J. N. (1987). The stresses of parenthood reexamined. *Family Relations, 36*, 26–29.

Verbrugge, L. M. (1990). The iceberg of disability. In S. M. Stahl (Ed.), *The legacy of longevity: Health and health care in later life*. Newbury Park, CA: Sage.

Verbrugge, L. M., Lepkowski, J. M., & Konkol, L. L. (1991). Levels of disability among U.S. adults with arthritis. *Journal of Gerontology: Social Sciences, 46* (2), S71–S83.

Vernon, J. A. (1990). Media stereotyping: A comparison of the way elderly women and men are portrayed on prime-time television. *Journal of Women and Aging, 2* (4), 55–68.

Vianello, M., & Siemienska, R. (1990). *Gender inequality: A comparative study of discrimination and participation*. Newbury Park, CA: Sage.

Vicchio, S. J. (1981a). Near death experiences: Some logical problems and questions for further study. *Anabiosis: The Journal of the International Association for Near Death Studies, 1*, 66–87.

Vicchio, S. J. (1981b). Near death experiences: A critical review of the literature and some questions for further study. *Essence: Issues in the Study of Aging, Death, and Dying, 5* (1), 77–89.

Victor, C. R. (1991). Continuity or change: Inequalities in health in later life. *Ageing and Society, 11* (1), 23–39.

Victor, D. A. (1993). A cross-cultural perspective on gender. In L. P. Arliss & D. J. Borisoff (Eds.), *Women and men communicating*. Fort Worth, TX: Harcourt Brace Jovanovich.

Victor, J. B., Halverson, C. F., & Montague, R. B. (1985). Relations between reflection-impulsivity and behavioral impulsivity. *Developmental Psychology, 21*, 141–148.

Vinick, B. H., & Ekerdt, D. J. (1991). Retirement: What happens to husband-wife relationships? *Journal of Geriatric Psychiatry, 24* (1), 23–40.

Vinokur, A. D., & Vinokur-Kaplan, D. (1990). In sickness and in health: Patterns of social support and undermining in older married

couples. *Journal of Aging and Health, 2* (2), 215–241.

Vinovskis, M. A. (1989). Stepping down in former times: The view from colonial and 19th century America. In D. I. Kertzer & K. W. Schaie (Eds.), *Age structuring in comparative perspective*. Hillsdale, NJ: Erlbaum.

Vitaro, F., Tremblay, R. E., Gagnon, C., & Boivin, M. (1992). Peer rejection from kindergarten to grade 2: Outcomes, correlates, and prediction. *Merrill-Palmer Quarterly, 38* (3), 382–400.

Vogel, C. H., & Mercier, J. (1991). The effect of institutionalization on nursing home populations. *Journal of Gerontological Nursing, 17*, 30–34.

Vogel, S. A., & Adelman, P. B. (1992). The success of college students with learning disabilities: Factors related to educational attainment. *Journal of Learning Disabilities, 25* (7), 430–441.

Volling, B. L., & Belsky, J. (1991). Multiple determinants of father involvement during infancy in dual-earner and single-earner families. *Journal of Marriage and the Family, 53*, 461–474.

Volling, B. L., & Belsky, J. (1992). The contribution of mother-child and father-child relationships to the quality of sibling interaction: A longitudinal study. *Child Development, 63* (5), 1209–1222.

von Knorring, A. (1991). Children and alcoholics. *Journal of Child Psychology and Psychiatry and Allied Disciplines, 62* (3), 411–421.

Vorhees, C. V., & Mollnow, E. (1987). Behavioral terato-genesis: Long-term influences in behavior from early exposure to environmental agents. In J. D. Osofsky (Ed.), *Handbook of infant development*. New York: Wiley.

Voydanoff, P., & Donnelly, B. W. (1990). *Adolescent sexuality and pregnancy*. Newbury Park, CA: Sage.

Wadsworth, B. (1989). *Piaget's theory of cognitive and affective development* (4th ed.). New York: Longman.

Waggoner, J. E., & Palermo, D. S. (1989). Betty is a bouncing bubble: Children's comprehension of emotion descriptive metaphors. *Developmental Psychology, 25*, 152–163.

Wainryb, C. (1991). Understanding differences in moral judgments: The role of informational assumptions. *Child Development, 62* (4), 840–851.

Waite, L. J., Leibowitz, A., & Witsberger, C. (1991). What parents pay for: Child care characteristics, quality, and costs. *Journal of Social Issues, 47* (2), 33–48.

Wald, F. S., & Bailey, S. S. (1990). Nurturing the spiritual component in care for the terminally ill. *Caring, 9* (11), 64–68.

Walford, R. L. (1983). *Maximum life-span*. New York: Avon.

Walker, A. J., & Allen, K. R. (1991). Relationships between care giving daughters and their elderly mothers. *Gerontologist, 31* (3), 389–396.

Walker, J. E., & Howland, J. (1991). Falls and fear of falling among elderly persons living in the community: Occupational therapy interventions. *American Journal of Occupational Therapy, 45* (2), 119–122.

Walker, L. J. (1982). The sequentiality of Kohlberg's stages of moral development. *Child Development, 53*, 1330–1336.

Walker, L. J. (1989). A longitudinal study of moral reasoning. *Child Development, 60,* 157–166.

Walker-Andrews, A., & Lennon, E. (1991). Infants' discrimination of vocal expressions: Contributions of auditory and visual information. *Infant Behavior and Development, 14* (2), 131–142.

Wallach, H. (1985). Perceiving a stable environment. *Scientific American, 252* (5), 118–124.

Wallerstein, J. S. (1991). Tailoring the intervention to the child in the separating and divorced family. *Family and Conciliation Courts Review, 29* (4), 448–459.

Walsh, R. H. (1989). Premarital sex among teenagers and young adults. In K. McKinney & S. Sprecher (Eds.), *Human sexuality: The societal and interpersonal context.* Norwood, NJ: Ablex.

Walter, C. A. (1991). Adult daughters' and mothers' stress in the care giving relationship. *Journal of Women and Aging, 3* (3), 39–58.

Walton, G. E., Bower, N. J., & Bower, T. G. (1992). Recognition of familiar faces by newborns. *Infant Behavior and Development, 15* (2), 265–269.

Ward, R. A. (1984). *The aging experience: An introduction to social gerontology* (2nd ed.). New York: Harper & Row.

Warren, A., & McCloskey, L. (1993). Pragmatics. In J. B. Gleason (Ed.), *The development of language* (3rd ed.). New York: Macmillan.

Warren-Leubecker, A., & Bohannon, J. N. (1989). Pragmatics: Language in social contexts. In J. B. Gleason (Ed.), *The development of language* (2nd ed.). New York: Macmillan.

Warton, P. M., & Goodnow, J. J. (1991). The nature of responsibility: Children's understanding of "your job." *Child Development, 62* (1), 156–165.

Wasserman, S. (1990). *The long distance grandmother: How to stay close to distant grandchildren* (rev. ed.). Point Roberts, WA: Hartley & Marks.

Waters, E. B. (1990). The life review: Strategies for working with individuals and groups. *Journal of Mental Health Counseling, 12* (3), 270–278.

Watkins, P. L., Eisler, R. M., Carpenter, L., & Schechtman, K. B. (1991). Psychosocial and physiological correlates of male gender role stress among employed adults. *Behavioral Medicine, 17* (2), 86–90.

Watkins, W. G., & Bentovim, A. (1992). The sexual abuse of male children and adolescents: A review of current research. *Journal of Child Psychology and Psychiatry and Allied Disciplines, 33* (1), 197–248.

Watt, L. M., & Wong, P. T. (1991). A taxonomy of reminiscence and therapeutic implications. *Journal of Gerontological Social Work, 16,* 37–57.

Watts, W. D., & Wright, L. S. (1990). The relationship of alcohol, tobacco, marijuana, and other illegal drug use to delinquency among Mexican-American, black, and white adolescent males. *Adolescence, 25,* 171–181.

Waxman, S. R., & Senghas, A. (1992). Relations among word meanings in early lexical development. *Developmental Psychology, 28* (5), 862–873.

Weeks, J. R., & Cuellar, J. B. (1981). The role of family members in the helping networks of older people. *Gerontologist, 21,* 388–394.

Weg, R. B. (1983). Changing physiology of aging: Normal and pathological. In D. S. Woodruff & J. E. Birren (Eds.), *Aging: Scientific perspectives and social issues.* Monterey, CA: Brooks/Cole.

Weiffenbach, J. M., Tylenda, C. A., & Baum, B. J. (1990). Oral sensory changes in aging. *Journal of Gerontology: Medical Sciences, 45* (4), M121–M125.

Weinraub, M., & Jaeger, E. (1990). The timing of mothers' return to the workplace: Effects on the developing mother-infant relationship. In J. S. Hyde & M. J. Essex (Eds.), *Parental leave and child care: Setting a research and policy agenda.* Philadelphia: Temple University Press.

Weinrich, S. P., & Boyd, M. (1992). Education in the elderly: Adapting and evaluating teaching tools. *Journal of Gerontological Nursing, 18 (1),* 15–20.

Weinstein, B. E. (1991). Hearing aids at my age: Why bother? *ASHA, 33* (12), 36–40.

Weinstein, E., & Rosen, E. (1988). Intrafamily sexual intimacy. In E. Weinstein & E. Rosen (Eds.), *Sexuality counseling: Issues and implications.* Monterey, CA: Brooks/Cole.

Weinstein, E., & Rosen, E. (1991). The development of adolescent sexual intimacy: Implications for counseling. *Adolescence, 26,* 331–339.

Weinstock, F. J., & Zucker, J. L. (1990). Is your patient at risk for glaucoma? *Senior Patient, 2* (12), 13–16.

Weisman, A. (1984). Common fallacies about dying patients. In E. S. Shneidman (Ed.), *Death: Current perspectives.* Palo Alto, CA: Mayfield.

Weisman, A. D. (1991). Vulnerability and suicidality in the aged. *Journal of Geriatric Psychiatry, 24* (2), 191–201.

Weiss, B., Dodge, K. A., Bates, J. E., & Pettit, G. S. (1992). Some consequences of early harsh discipline: Child aggression and a maladaptive social information processing style. *Child Development, 63* (6), 1321–1335.

Weiss, C. R., Blake, D., & Koscianski, V. (1991). Enhancing family council members' ability to relate to and reminisce with older disoriented residents: Replication and extension. *Topics in Geriatric Rehabilitation, 7* (2), 45–59.

Weiss, R. S. (1984). The issue of custody. *Remarriage, 1* (2), 5–8.

Weist, M. D., & Ollendick, T. H. (1991). Toward empirically valid target selection: The case of assertiveness in children. *Behavior Modification, 15* (2), 213–227.

Weizman, S. G., & Kamm, P. (1984). *About mourning: Support and advice for the bereaved.* New York: Human Sciences Press.

Wellman, H. M., & Banerjee, M. (1991). Mind and emotion: Children's understanding of the emotional consequences of beliefs and desires. *British Journal of Developmental Psychology, 9* (2), 191–214.

Wells, R. G. (1990). The hot flash: Answering patients' pleas for help. *Senior Patient, 2* (6), 24–27.

Wenger, G. C. (1990). Elderly carers: The need for appropriate intervention. *Aging and Society, 10* (2), 197–219.

Wentzel, K. R., Feldman, S. S., & Weinberger, D. A. (1991). Parental child rearing and academic achievement in boys: The mediational role of social-emotional adjustment. *Journal of Early Adolescence, 11* (3), 321–339.

Werebe, M. G., & Baudonniere, P. (1991). Social pretend play among friends and familiar preschoolers. *International Journal of Behavioral Development, 14* (4), 411–428.

Werner, P. D., & LaRussa, G. W. (1985). Persistence and change in sex-role stereotypes. *Sex Roles, 12* (9), 1089–1100.

Wertsch, J. V. (1989). A sociocultural approach to the mind. In W. Damon (Ed.), *Child development: Today and tomorrow.* San Francisco: Jossey-Bass.

Wertz, R. W., & Wertz, D. C. (1989). *Lying-in: A history of childbirth in America.* New Haven, CT: Yale University Press.

Wetle, T. (1991). Successful aging: New hope for optimizing mental and physical well-being. *Journal of Geriatric Psychiatry, 24* (1), 3–12.

Whaley, L., & Wong, D. L. (1989). *Essentials of pediatric nursing* (3rd ed.). St. Louis: Mosby.

Wheeler, R. J., & Berliner, L. (1988). Treating the effects of sexual abuse on children. In G. E. Wyatt & G. J. Powell (Eds.), *The lasting effects of child sexual abuse.* Newbury Park, CA: Sage.

Whipple, B., & Ogden, G. (1989). *Safe encounters: How women can say yes to pleasure and no to unsafe sex.* New York: McGraw-Hill.

White, G. L., Jr. (1990). Development of a tool to assess suicide risk factors in urban adolescents. *Adolescence, 25* (99), 655–666.

White, J. M. (1991). *Dynamics of family development: A theoretical perspective.* New York: Guilford Press.

White, K., & Kistner, J. (1992). The influence of teacher feedback on young children's peer preferences and perceptions. *Developmental Psychology, 28* (5), 933–940.

White, L. B. (1990). *The grandparent book.* San Francisco: Gateway Books.

White, L. K. (1990). Determinants of divorce: A review of research in the eighties. *Journal of Marriage and the Family, 52* (4), 904–912.

White, L. K., & Booth, A. (1985). Stepchildren in remarriages. *American Sociological Review, 50,* 689–698.

White, P., Mascalo, A., Thomas, S., & Shoun, S. (1986). Husbands' and wives' perceptions of marital intimacy and wives' stresses in dual-career marriages. *Family Perspectives, 20,* 27–35.

White, W. J. (1992). The postschool adjustment of persons with learning disabilities: Current status and future projections. *Journal of Learning Disabilities, 25* (7), 448–456.

Whiting, B. B., & Edwards, C. P. (1988). *Children of different worlds: The formation of social behavior.* Cambridge, MA: Harvard University Press.

Whitman, F. L. (1991). Homophobia and heterosexism in sociology. *Journal of Gay and Lesbian Psychotherapy, 1* (4), 31–34.

Whittaker, S., & Bry, B. H. (1991). Overt and covert parental conflict and adolescent problems: Observed marital interaction in clinic and non-clinic families. *Adolescence, 26* (104), 865–876.

Wiehe, V. R., & Herring, T. (1991). *Perilous rivalry: When siblings become abusive.* Lexington, MA: D.C. Heath.

Wilen, J. B., & Petersen, A. C. (1980, June). *Young adolescents' responses to the timing of pubertal changes.* Paper presented at the Psychology of Adolescence Conference, Chicago.

Wilkinson, A. C. (1981). Growth functions for rapid remembering. *Journal of Experimental Child Psychology, 32*, 354–371.

Williams, F. R. (1989). Bereavement and the elderly: The role of the psychotherapist. *Journal of Psychotherapy and the Family, 5* (1/2), 225–241.

Williams, K., Haywood. K., & VanSant, A. (1991). Throwing patterns of older adults: A follow-up investigation. *International Journal of Aging and Human Development, 33* (4), 279–294.

Williams, T. M., Zabrack, M. L, & Joy, L. A. (1982). The portrayal of aggression on North American television. *Journal of Applied Social Psychology, 12*, 360–380.

Willie, C. V. (1986). The black family and social class. In R. Staples (Ed.), *The black family: Essays and studies*. Belmont, CA: Wadsworth.

Willis, S. L., & Baltes, P. B. (1980). Intelligence in adulthood and aging: Contemporary issues. In L. W. Poon (Ed.), *Aging in the 1980s*. Washing-ton, DC: American Psychological Association.

Wilson, G. T. (1989). The treatment of bulimia nervosa: A cognitive-social learning analysis. In A. J. Stunkard & A. Baum (Eds.), *Perspectives in behavioral medicine: Eating, sleeping, and sex*. Hillsdale, NJ: Erlbaum.

Wilson, M. N. (1989). Child development in the context of the black extended family. *American Psychologist, 44*, 380–385.

Wilson, V. (1990). The consequences of elderly wives caring for disabled husbands: Implications for practice. *Social Work, 35*, 417–421.

Winch, C. (1990). *Language, ability, and educational achievement*. New York and London: Routledge.

Winchester, A. M. (1975). *Human genetics* (2nd ed.). Columbus, OH: Merrill.

Wingrove, C. R., & Slevin, K. F. (1991). A sample of professional and managerial women: Success in work and retirement. *Journal of Women and Aging, 3* (2), 95–117.

Wintre, M. G., Hicks, R., McVey, G., & Fox, J. (1988). Age and sex differences in choice of consultant for various types of problems. *Child Development, 59*, 1046–1055.

Wintre, M. G., Polivy, J., & Murray, M. A. (1990). Self-predictions of emotional response patterns: Age, sex, and situational determinants. *Child Development, 61* (4), 1124–1133.

Witkin, H., Mednick, S., Schulsinger, F., Bakkestrom, E., Christiansen, K., Goodenough, D., Hirschorn, K., Lundsteen, C., Owen, D., Philip, J., Rubin, D., & Stoking, M. (1976). Criminality in XYY and XXY men. *Science, 193*, 147–155.

Wodarski, J. S. (1990). Adolescent substance abuse: Practical implications. *Adolescence, 25* (99), 667–688.

Wolf, M. A. (1991). The discovery of middle age: An educational task in training gerontologists. *Educational Gerontology, 17* (6), 559–571.

Wolf, Z. R. (1991). Care of dying patients and patients after death: Patterns of care in nursing history. *Death Studies, 15* (1), 81–93.

Wolfe, D. A. (1991). *Preventing physical and emotional abuse of children*. New York: Guilford Press.

Wolfson, C. (1986). Midwives and home birth: Social, medical, and legal perspectives. *Hastings Law Journal, 37*, 909–967.

Worcester, M. (1991). Cancer symptom management in the elderly. *Home Health Care Services Quarterly, 12* (2), 53–169.

World Health Organization. (1991, April). Update: AIDS cases reported to surveillance, forecasting, and impact assessment unit. *Global Program on AIDS*, Geneva.

Wortman, C. B., & Silver, R. C. (1990). Successful mastery of bereavement and widowhood: A life-course perspective. In P. B. Baltes & M. M. Baltes (Eds.), *Successful aging: Perspectives from the behavioral sciences*. New York: Cambridge University Press.

Wray, L. A. (1991). Public policy implications of an ethnically diverse elderly population. *Journal of Cross-Cultural Gerontology, 6* (2), 243–257.

Wright, M. R. (1989). Body image satisfaction in adolescent girls and boys. *Journal of Youth and Adolescence, 18*, 71–84.

Wroblewski, R., & Huston, A. C. (1987). Televised occupational stereotypes and their effects on early adolescents: Are they changing? *Journal of Early Adolescence, 7*, 283–297.

Wyatt, G. E., & Powell, G. J. (Eds.). (1988). *The lasting effects of child sexual abuse*. Newbury Park, CA: Sage.

Wyer, R. S., & Collins, J. E. (1992). A theory of humor elicitation. *Psychological Review, 99* (4), 663–688.

Wynn, K. (1992). Children's acquisition of the number words and the counting system. *Cognitive Psychology, 24* (2), 220–251.

Wynne, E. A., & Ryan, K. (1993). *Reclaiming our schools: A handbook on teaching character, academics, and discipline*. New York: Macmillan.

Xu, Z., Wan, C. W., Mussen, P. H., & Shen, J. (1991). Family socialization and children's behavior and personality development in China. *Journal of Genetic Psychology, 152* (2), 239–253.

Yamaguchi, K., & Kandell, D. (1987). Drug use and other determinants of premarital pregnancy and its outcome: A dynamic analysis of competing life events. *Journal of Marriage and the Family, 49*, 257–270.

Yankelovich, D. (1981). *New rules in American life: Searching for self-fulfillment in a world turned upside down*. New York: Random House.

Yassa, R., Uhr, S., & Jeste, D. V. (1991). Gender differences in chronic schizophrenia: Need for further research. In E. Light & B. D. Lebowitz (Eds.), *The elderly with chronic mental illness*. New York: Springer.

Yeates, K. O., Schultz, L. H., & Selman, R. L. (1991). The development of interpersonal negotiation strategies in thought and action: A social-cognitive link to behavioral adjustment and social status. *Merrill-Palmer Quarterly, 37* (3), 369–405.

Yee, M. D., & Brown, R. (1992). Self-evaluations and intergroup attitudes in children aged three to nine. *Child Development, 63* (3), 619–629.

Yesavage, J. A. (1990). Age-associated memory impairment: Conceptual background and treatment approaches. In M. Bergener, M. Ermini, & H. B. Stahelin (Eds.), *Challenges in aging*. San Diego: Academic Press.

York, P., & York, D. (1982). Toughlove. *Family Therapy Networker, 6* (5), 35–37.

York, P., York, D., & Wachtel, T. (1982). *Toughlove*. New York: Bantam.

Young, C. (1990). *Balancing families and work: A demographic study of women's labor force participation*. Canberra, Australia: Australian Government Publishing Service.

Young, R. F. (1991). Family implications of heart disease among the elderly. In R. F. Young & E. A. Olson (Eds.), *Health, illness, and disability in later life: Practice issues and interventions*. Newbury Park, CA: Sage.

Young, W. C. (1961). Hormones and mating behavior. In W. C. Young (Ed.), *Sex and internal secretions*. Baltimore: Williams and Wilkins.

Young, W. M. (1988). Structuring a response to child sexual abuse. In A. Salter (Ed.), *Treating child sex offenders and victims*. Newbury Park, CA: Sage.

Youngblade, L. M., & Belsky, J. (1992). Parent-child antecedents of 5-year-olds' close friendships: A longitudinal analysis. *Developmental Psychology, 28* (4), 700–713.

Youniss, J., & Haynie, D. L. (1992). Friendship in adolescence. *Journal of Developmental and Behavioral Pediatrics, 13*, 59–66.

Zahn-Waxler, C., Radke-Yarrow, M., Wagner, E., & Chapman, M. (1992). Development of concern for others. *Developmental Psychology, 28* (1), 126–136.

Zahn-Waxler, C., Robinson, J. L., & Emde, R. (1992). The development of empathy in twins. *Developmental Psychology, 28* (6), 1038–1047.

Zambelli, G. C., & DeRosa, A. P. (1992). Bereavement support groups for school-age children: Theory, intervention, and case example. *American Journal of Orthopsychiatry, 62* (4), 484–493.

Zamula, E. (1986). Stroke: Fighting back against America's number three killer. *The consumer*. Washington, DC: U.S. Government Printing Office.

Zarbatny, L., Hartmann, D. P., & Rankin, D. B. (1990). The psychological functions of preadolescent activities. *Child Development, 61* (4), 1067–1080.

Zarit, S. H., Birkel, R. C., & Malone-Beach, E. (1989). Spouses as caregivers: Stresses and interventions. In M. Z. Goldstein (Ed.), *Family involvement in the treatment of the frail elderly*. Washington, DC: American Psychiatric Press.

Zaslow, M. J. (1991). Variation in child care quality and its implications for children. *Journal of Social Issues, 47* (2), 125–138.

Zastrow, C., & Kirst-Ashman, K. (1987). *Understanding human behavior and the social environment*. Chicago: Nelson-Hall.

Zechmeister, E. B., & Johnson, J. E. (1992). *Critical thinking: A functional approach*. Pacific Grove, CA: Brooks/Cole.

Zelnick, M., Kantner, J. F., & Ford, K. (1981). *Sex and pregnancy in adolescence*. Beverly Hills, CA: Sage.

Zelnick, M., & Shah, T. (1983). First intercourse among young Americans. *Family Planning Perspectives, 15*, 64–70.

Zentella, A. C. (1981). Language variety among Puerto Ricans. In C. A. Ferguson & S. B. Heath (Eds.), *Language in the USA*. New York: Cambridge University Press.

Zeskind, P. S., Klein, L., & Marshall, T. R. (1992). Adults' perceptions of experimental modifications of durations of pauses and expiratory sounds in infant crying. *Developmental Psychology, 28* (6), 1153–1162.

Zheng, S., & Colombo, J. (1989). Sibling configuration and gender differences in preschool social participation. *Journal of Genetic Psychology, 150,* 45–50.

Zigler, E. F., & Lang, M. E. (1991). *Child care choices: Balancing the needs of children, families, and society.* New York: Free Press.

Zinn, M. B., & Eitzen, D. S. (1990). *Diversity in Families* (2nd ed.). New York: Harper & Row.

Zisook, S., & Schuchter, S. (1991). Early psychological reaction to the stress of widowhood. *Psychiatry, 54* (4), 320–333.

Zunker, V. G. (1990). *Career counseling: Applied concepts of life planning* (3rd ed.). Pacific Grove, CA: Brooks/Cole.

Zunz, S. J. (1991). Gender-related issues in the career development of social work managers. *Affilia, 6* (4), 39–52.

Text Acknowledgments

Table 3.4, p. 111
Gottesman, I. I. "Schizophrenia: Concordance in Recent Twin Studies." From Schizophrenia, 2. Copyright ©
1976. Reprinted by permission of the author.

Table 7.2, p. 312
Labinowicz, E. "Judging the Levels of the Child's Response on Piagetian Conservation Tasks." From *The Piaget
Primer: Thinking, Leaning, Teaching* by E. Labinowicz. Reprinted by permission of the author.

Figure 7.7, p. 318
Kagan, Rosman, Day, Albert, & Phillips. "Information Processing in the Child." From *Psychology Monograph,* 78.
Copyright © 1964. Reprinted by permission of the authors.

Figure 7.8, p. 319
Kagan, J. "Impulsive and Reflective Children: Significance of Conceptual Tempo." From *Learning and the
Educational Process,* John D. Krumboltz, Editor. Copyright © 1965. Reprinted by permission of John D.
Krumboltz.

Table 7.3, p. 335
Rest, James R. "The Hierarchical Nature of Moral Judgment: A Study of Patterns of Comprehension and
Preference of Moral Stages." *Journal of Personality,* 41:1. Copyright Duke University Press, 1973. Reprinted
with permission.

Figure 9.1, p. 441
Levinson, Daniel J. "Developmental Periods in the Eras of Early and Middle Adulthood." From THE SEASONS OF
A MAN'S LIFE by Daniel J. Levinson, et al. Copyright © 1978 by Daniel J. Levinson. Reprinted by permission of
Alfred A. Knopf, Inc.

Figure 9.2, p. 451
Reiss, Ira L. Figure from FAMILY SYSTEMS IN AMERICA, Third Edition by Ira L. Reiss, copyright © 1980 by Holt,
Rinehart and Winston, Inc., reproduced by permission of the publisher.

Figure 9.3, p. 452
Sternberg, Robert J. "A Triangular Theory of Love." From *Psychological Review,* 93. Copyright © 1986.
Reprinted by permission of the author.

Table 10.1, p. 525
Costa, Jr., Paul T., & R. McCrae. "Personality Continuity and the Changes of Adult Life." From *The Adult Years:
Continuity and Change* by M. Storandt and G. Vandenbos, Eds., Copyright © 1989. Reprinted by permission
of the authors.

Figure 12.3, p. 656
Choice in Dying, Inc. "Living Will." Reprinted by permission of Choice in Dying (formerly Concern for
Dying/Society for the Right to Die) 200 Varick Street, 10th Floor, New York, NY 10014-4810.

Photo Acknowledgments

Name Index

Subject Index